W9-BMR-045

Introduction to Accounting

An Integrated Approach

Sixth Edition

Penne Ainsworth
University of Wyoming

Dan Deines
Kansas State University

The McGraw·Hill Companies

McGraw-Hill Irwin

INTRODUCTION TO ACCOUNTING: AN INTEGRATED APPROACH, SIXTH EDITION

Published by McGraw-Hill, a business unit of The McGraw-Hill Companies, Inc., 1221 Avenue of the Americas, New York, NY 10020.

Some ancillaries, including electronic and print components, may not be available to customers outside the United States.

This book is printed on recycled, acid-free paper containing 10% postconsumer waste.

1 2 3 4 5 6 7 8 9 0 WDQ/WDQ 1 0 9 8 7 6 5 4 3 2 1 0

ISBN 978-0-07-813660-3
MHID 0-07-813660-1

Vice President & Editor-in-Chief: *Brent Gordon*
VP EDP / Central Publishing Services: *Kimberly Meriwether David*
Editorial Director: *Stewart Mattson*
Publisher: *Tim Vertovec*
Executive Editor: *Richard T. Hercher, Jr.*
Marketing Manager: *Michelle Heaster*
Editorial Coordinator: *Rebecca Mann*
Project Manager: *Robin A. Reed*
Design Coordinator: *Brenda A. Rolwes*
Cover Designer: *Studio Montage, St. Louis, Missouri*
Cover Image Credit: *Jack Hollingsworth/Getty Images*
Production Supervisor: *Laura Fuller*
Media Project Manager: *Balaji Sundararaman*
Composition: *Glyph International*
Typeface: *10/12 Times New Roman*
Printer: *World Color Press, Inc.*

All credits appearing on page or at the end of the book are considered to be an extension of the copyright page.

Library of Congress Cataloging-in-Publication Data

Ainsworth, Penne.
Introduction to accounting : an integrated approach / Penne Ainsworth,
Dan Deines.— 6th ed.
p. cm.
Summary: "The Sixth Edition of Introduction to Accounting: An Integrated Approach revolves around three major themes: The overriding theme of the text is that accounting is an information system that serves many stakeholders, some internal and some external to the organization. The second theme is business processes. The final theme is the balanced scorecard"—Provided by publisher.

ISBN 978-0-07-813660-3 (alk. paper)
1. Accounting. I. Deines, Dan S. II. Title.
HF5636.A35 2010
657—dc22

2009039037

www.mhhe.com

First and foremost, we dedicate this text to our families, without whose love and support we never could have completed this project. To our spouses, Scott Ainsworth and Linda Deines, to our children and their spouses, and to our precious grandchildren, Jackson, Jakob, Julia, and Jaime, we love you and we thank you. Second, we would like to thank Dick Hercher, Robin Reed, Rebecca Mann, and the production and marketing departments at McGraw-Hill/Irwin.

Penne Ainsworth
Dan Deines

To the Instructor

WHY INTEGRATE?

The primary reason to integrate financial and managerial accounting is that it mirrors the way businesses operate. In addition, having as many as 85 percent non-accounting majors in a first accounting course is not unusual. These students need to understand that accounting is an information system that serves a wide variety of stakeholders, both internal and external to the organization. Rather than separating financial accounting from managerial accounting, we emphasize the business processes, and how to plan and evaluate the related activities from both a financial (external reporting) and a managerial (internal reporting) perspective.

UNDERSTANDING THE INTEGRATED APPROACH

The Sixth Edition of *Introduction to Accounting: An Integrated Approach* revolves around three major themes:

- The overriding theme of the text is that accounting is **an information system** that serves many stakeholders, some internal and some external to the organization. Traditionally, *Introduction to Accounting* has been taught as two separate and distinct segments: financial accounting and managerial accounting. Consequently, many of our non-accounting students never gain an understanding of accounting as a process of providing information about business to both internal and external stakeholders. An understanding of why and how accounting information is used by internal and external stakeholders is vital, regardless of a student's major.
- The second theme is **business processes.** We introduce the four major business processes in the second chapter and use these processes to divide content between the first and second halves of the text (courses). The four business processes are (1) business organization and strategy, (2) operating, (3) capital resources, and (4) performance measurement and management. We describe how the business organization and strategy process provide a long-term direction for the company and how the performance measurement and management process provides the evaluation of the company. Then we divide content into operating processes (first half) and capital resources processes (second half). This mirrors the operating, investing, and financing activities on the statement of cash flows.

  We chose to cover operating processes first for two reasons: First, these activities are more intuitive to students—they have been customers and employees, now we must get them to think like businesspeople. Second, investing and financing activities require the time-value-of-money, a somewhat complex topic. Our classroom experience shows that investing and financing activities are more easily understood after learning about operating activities.
- The final theme is the **balanced scorecard.** The balanced scorecard is a holistic approach to planning and evaluating that translates a company's strategy (from the business organization and strategy process) into measurable objectives (for the operating and capital resources processes) organized into four perspectives: (1) financial, (2) internal, (3) customer, and (4) learning and growth. That is, the balanced scorecard approach plans and evaluates business success using financial *and other measures* of success. The balanced scorecard approach provides a number of measures of success that, in turn, managers use to evaluate performance and plan for the future. This is important because these other measures impact the financial performance of the company in future periods. Thus, the

balanced scorecard approach is a forward-looking planning and evaluating tool, in that we begin by planning the activities in the operating and capital resources processes, then we record and evaluate the results to provide feedback to the next planning phase. Therefore, in each half of the text, we examine planning activities followed by recording and evaluating activities.

By concentrating on these three themes, students learn why and how activities are planned and evaluated by different stakeholders. In addition, students gain a greater understanding of business, which will certainly help them in whatever careers they may choose.

WHAT ARE THE MAIN OBJECTIVES OF THIS UNIQUE APPROACH?

Introduction to Accounting: An Integrated Approach is designed to benefit everyone, regardless of major. We consciously integrated life skills into the content along with business skills. In designing the text, we incorporated three objectives:

1. **To focus on accounting as an information system used in each business process to provide information to holistically plan and evaluate activities.** As outlined above we believe that students must understand that accounting is the information infrastructure of business, that it serves a wide variety of stakeholders, and that it is used for both planning and evaluating business activities. We believe that content organized around business processes provides students with linkages often missing when financial accounting is separated from managerial accounting. Finally, we believe that planning, recording, and evaluating activities involve more than financial information.
2. **To stimulate interest in the field of accounting.** Classroom experience has shown that *Introduction to Accounting: An Integrated Approach* serves as a way to increase interest in the discipline of accounting. As students gain an understanding and appreciation of the broader role of accounting in the business world, they are more likely to express interest in accounting as a major field of study. In addition, we have seen the drop-out rates in our introductory accounting courses decline from almost 50 percent to less than 20 percent.
3. **To promote active and cooperative learning.** Various pedagogical devices in this book stimulate active and cooperative learning for the students. Most obvious are the Enhance Your Understanding questions posed throughout the text. These questions serve as checkpoints for students as well as stimulate their critical thinking. Additionally, the Cases, Computer Applications, Critical Thinking, and Ethical Challenge materials provide opportunities for teamwork. The Instructor's Resource Manual provides additional cooperative learning experiences for students. We have found that active and cooperative learning promotes retention of the material and deeper learning.

CHANGES IN THE SIXTH EDITION

Based on extensive feedback from instructors using the first five editions as well as our combined 50+ years of teaching experience, the Sixth Edition focuses on improving the text's readability and real-world examples. In particular, the following changes have been made:

- Updates for IFRS developments.
- Updates for XBRL developments.
- Updates for FASB Codification.
- More numerical examples have been added.
- End-of-chapter materials, particularly Ethical Challenges have been updated.

Integrate Sixth Edition Features into Your Course

ENHANCE YOUR UNDERSTANDING

These boxed features get students thinking about key chapter concepts. A question is posed and its suggested solution is listed below so that students can immediately compare their resolution to that of the authors.

Enhance Your Understanding

What is the relationship between lead time and customer response time discussed in Chapter 2?

Answer: Customer response time and lead time are the same concepts from different viewpoints. Both measure the time that elapses from when the buyer places an order until that order is received.

FAST FACT

These features tie chapter content to business events or product trivia. These interesting real-world scenarios show students how course topics are related to events outside of the classroom.

FAST FACT

It pays to pay attention to quality in your manufacturing processes. In 1903, 21-year-old William S. Harley and 20-year-old Arthur Davidson produced the first Harley-Davidson motorcycle. Their factory was a 10 × 15 foot wooden shed with the words "Harley-Davidson Motor Company" written on the door. By 1920, Harley-Davidson (HD) was the largest motorcycle manufacturer in the world. In 1969, HD merged with American Machine & Foundry Company (AMF) and quality began to suffer. Throughout the 1970s, HD had the dubious reputation of poor quality resulting in motorcycles prone to breaking down on the highway. In 1981, 13 senior executives sought to buy back the company from AMF and return HD to its former glory. By 1986 the buy-back was complete and HD renewed its commitment to quality manufacturing. In 2001, *Forbes* magazine named Harley-Davidson its company of the year. In 2008, more than 250,000 people came to Milwaukee to celebrate the 105th anniversary of Harley, some riding more than 5,000 miles to be there.

Source: www.harleydavidson.com.

OF INTEREST

These features, which were well-received in the previous editions, supplement the chapter with additional information. Professors can use Of Interest features to get students talking about the current issues in accounting.

OF INTEREST Using Excel for Sensitivity Analysis

Using Excel (or another spreadsheet package) is a fast and easy way to perform sensitivity analyses. You simply set up cells for each variable in the cost-volume-profit formula and then write a formula to have Excel calculate the number of units. For example, the spreadsheet shown represents the CVP information in the chapter. In cell A6 we enter the following formula: ((E3/(1−D3))+C3)/(A3−B3) and the result is the number of units required to have a profit of $150 after taxes.

Now to perform sensitivity analysis, we copy this information to cells A8 through E13 and change a cell representing the variable of interest. For example, assume the selling price is reduced to $2.50, we simply change cell A10 to $2.50 and the results tell us that we must sell 629 units to have a profit of $150 after taxes with a selling price of $2.50 per unit.

	A	B	C	D	E
1	Selling	Variable	Fixed	Tax	Target
2	Price	Costs	Costs	Rate	Profit
3	3	1.1	703	0.15	150
4					
5	Cost-volume-profit analysis				
6	462.897				
7					
8	Selling	Variable	Fixed	Tax	Target
9	Price	Costs	Costs	Rate	Profit
10	2.5	1.1	703	0.15	150
11					
12	Cost-volume-profit analysis				
13	628.193				

KEY CONCEPTS

These features highlight important concepts in each chapter.

Discounts and premiums
Think of discounts as being "less than" as in the "proceeds are less than the face value of the note." Likewise, think of premiums as being "more than" as in the "proceeds are more than the face value of the note."

Market Rate Less Than Face Rate

When the market rate of interest is *less* than the face rate of interest on the note, the proceeds of the note will be *greater* than the face value of the note. This means that the note is issued at a *premium* to make the note yield the market rate of interest, which is less than the face rate of interest. A **premium,** then, is the amount that the present value (cash proceeds) of a note exceeds its face value because the market rate of interest is less than the face rate of interest.

To illustrate, assume that PCs to Go takes the same $500,000 note to Citicorp when the market rate of interest is 7 percent. In this case, PCs to Go will not incur 8 percent because the market rate of interest is 7 percent. To determine the proceeds of this note, the lender finds the present value of the two promised cash flows using the 7 percent market rate; that is, the promise to pay $20,000 every six months and the promise to pay $500,000 in four years. We know:

$$FV = \$500{,}000;\ ANN = 20{,}000;\ c = 2;\ n = 8;\ r = 7;\ \text{therefore: } PV = 517{,}184.89$$

LEARNING OBJECTIVES

After being presented at the beginning of the chapter, learning objectives are linked to end-of-chapter material. Icons next to questions or problems indicate the learning objectives to which they are related.

END-OF-CHAPTER MATERIAL

Much of the end-of-chapter material can and should be used to enhance students' written and oral communication skills.

- For easy reference, each end-of-chapter section begins with a list of **Key Terms** and definitions.
- **Questions, Exercises,** and **Problems** follow to test how much of the chapter's content students recall.
- **Cases, Computer Applications, Critical Thinking,** and **Ethical Challenge** sections give students the opportunity to apply their accounting knowledge in a broader business setting. These problems almost always require learning and exploring outside of the text.
- An additional problem set for each chapter is available on the book's Online Learning Center at **www.mhhe.com/ainsworth6e.**

EXCEL SPREADSHEET ASSIGNMENTS

These are tied to the Computer Application problems and are located on the text Online Learning Center at **www.mhhe.com/ainsworth6e.** Excel icons appear next to problems that have corresponding spreadsheet assignments.

Supplements to Help Implement the Integrated Approach

FOR THE STUDENT: ONLINE LEARNING CENTER www.mhhe.com/ainsworth6e

The Student Center on the text's Web site provides several features to enhance course content:

- PowerPoint presentations created by Penne Ainsworth are on the Web site to highlight and elaborate key chapter concepts.
- Excel template exercises prepared by Jack Terry are referenced in the text and posted on the Student Center on the Web site.
- The site also features additional review material by chapter such as flash card exercises, online quizzes, and a practice case.
- Links to text-referenced and other useful Web sites.
- Additional end-of-chapter problem set for each chapter.

FOR THE INSTRUCTOR: INSTRUCTOR'S RESOURCE MANUAL

Printed on demand; contact your McGraw-Hill sales rep.

Designed by Penne Ainsworth, the Instructor's Resource Manual provides information to ease your transition to *Introduction to Accounting: An Integrated Approach.* Based on user comments and interviews conducted by Penne Ainsworth as she worked with teachers on their classroom issues, this manual contains these learning aids for each chapter: Discussion Outline—to promote active learning; Test/Retest Quizzes—to promote cooperative learning (two per chapter); In-Class Cases—to promote cooperative learning (at least two per chapter); Start-to-Finish, a comprehensive problem set—to promote active learning.

TEST BANK (ON THE INSTRUCTOR CENTER OF THE TEXT WEBSITE)

Prepared by Dan Deines, the test bank consists of virtually all new multiple choice, matching, problem, and essay exercises to accompany every chapter of the text.

ONLINE LEARNING CENTER www.mhhe.com/ainsworth6e

The Instructor Center on the book's Web site offers downloadable files of the Instructor's Resource Manual, Solutions Manual, Test Bank, PowerPoint slides, Excel templates and solutions, Web-based problems and solutions, and links to professional resources—all in a password-protected environment.

TEGRITY CAMPUS: LECTURES 24/7

Tegrity Campus is a service that makes class time available 24/7 by automatically capturing lectures in a searchable format for students to review when they study and complete assignments. With a simple one-click start-and-stop process, you capture all computer screens and corresponding audio. Students can replay any part of any class with easy-to-use browser-based viewing on a PC or Mac.

To learn more about Tegrity, watch a two-minute Flash demo at **http://tegrity campus.mhhe.com.**

Acknowledgments

The Sixth Edition of *Introduction to Accounting: An Integrated Approach* has been tremendously aided by feedback given in text reviews, surveys, and focus groups. We would like to thank the following colleagues for their helpful comments and suggestions:

Don Kent
SUNY–Brockport

Kathy Otero
University of Texas–El Paso

Mary Stevens
University of Texas–El Paso

Jayne Maas
Loyola College in Maryland

E. Thomas Robinson
University of Alaska

David Dibblee
Benedictine University

Stacy Kovar
Kansas State University

Joyce Griffin
Kansas City, Kansas, Community College

Fred Richardson
Virginia Polytechnic Institute and State University

Lamont Steedle
Towson University

Carol Springer
Georgia State University

Carol Keller
Coastal Carolina University

Marilyn Collins
John Carroll University

Karen Walton
John Carroll University

Angela Letourneau
Winthrop University

Gregory Della Franco
Lee University

Henry Elrod
University of the Incarnate Word

Dan Hubbard
University of Mary Washington

Leon Korte
University of South Dakota

Ken Machande
University of Mary Washington

Wanda DeLeo
Winthrop University

Gail Hoover
Rockhurst University

Mohamed Gaber
Plattsburgh State University of New York

Lori Zulauf
Slippery Rock University

Richard Helleloid
University of Wisconsin–Eau Claire

Richard Newmark
Old Dominion University

Jane Campbell
Keenesaw State University

Melanie Middlemist
Colorado State University

Debby Bloom
Boston University

James Hansen
North Dakota State University

Steve Campbell
University of Idaho

Pamela Stuerke
Case Western Reserve

Tom English
Boise State University

Johanna Lyle
Kansas State University

Dianna Schallenburger
Central Methodist University

Linda Johnson
Georgia State University

A special thanks goes out to:

Kris J. Clark
Georgia State University

Kim Charland
Kansas State University

Ronald Peterson
University of Wyoming

Rodney Vogt
Kansas State University

About the Authors

Penne Ainsworth

University of Wyoming

Penne Ainsworth, Ph.D., CPA, CMA, and CIA. Penne received her Ph.D. from the University of Nebraska and is the Chairperson and professor in the Department of Accounting and Associate Dean for the College of Business at the University of Wyoming. She received the *Senior Teaching Award* in the College of Business in 1998, 2000, and 2003 and the *John P. Ellbogen Meritorious Classroom Teaching Award* for the University of Wyoming in 2001. She also received the *Kansas State Bank Outstanding Teacher Award* in 1993. Penne coauthored the original application for the grant Kansas State University received from the Accounting Education Change Commission (AECC) and authored three additional grants for accounting education and assessment. Her research focuses on managerial accounting, accounting education, and assessment. Penne's work has been published in *Issues in Accounting Education* and other journals. She is a member of the AAA, the IMA, and the Wyoming Society of CPAs.

Dan Deines

Kansas State University

Dan Deines received his undergraduate degree in history from Fort Hays State University, a masters in business from Emporia State University, and his Ph.D. in accounting from the University of Nebraska. He has been at Kansas State University since 1982 and currently is the Ralph Crouch, KPMG Professor of Accounting. Dan received the College of Business's *Outstanding Educator Award* in 1987 and in 1994 received the College of Business's *Outstanding Advising Award.* He was the co-coordinator for Kansas State University's accounting curriculum revision sponsored by the American Education Change Commission. Dan was president of the Kansas Society of CPAs for 2003–2004; he was designated an academic pathfinder by the AICPA and in May 2007 received the AICPA's *Distinguished Achievement in Accounting Education Award.* He is a member of the AAA and a cofounder of the Banner Road Hunt Club of Collyer, Kansas.

Brief Contents

Contents

Prologue

Throughout this textbook we use Apple Computer, Inc., to illustrate the concepts we examine and the issues we address. Apple's financial statements and accompanying notes, including its required officer certifications, which were part of its 2008 SEC Form 10-K, are included in the Appendix to this textbook. We refer to these financial statements and accompanying notes and discuss specific aspects of them throughout the text. For now, you might want to glance through them to get a feel for what is included.

WHO IS APPLE?

Apple Computer, Inc. (referred to simply as Apple) is an international computer and portable digital media player designer, developer, and manufacturer. Its hardware brands include Mac Pro and Mac mini (desktop computers), MacBook and MacBook Pro (portable computers), and iMac (all-in-one desktop computers). Its media products include the iPod shuffle (portable digital music player), the iPod classic and iPod nano (portable digital music and video players), and the iPod touch (portable media player with built-in Web browser), as well as Apple TV (digital media receiver), the iTunes Music Store (an online music download store), and its very successful iPhone. Apple also designs and manufactures certain peripheral products to support its Apple-branded computers.

Apple ignited the personal computer revolution in the 1970s with the Apple II and reinvented the personal computer in the 1980s with the Macintosh. Today, Apple continues to lead the industry in innovation with its award-winning computers, OS X operating system and iLife and professional applications. Apple is also spearheading the digital media revolution with its iPod portable music and video players and iTunes online store, and entered the mobile phone market in 2007 with its revolutionary iPhone.

Environmental protection is a top priority for Apple. According to Apple:

> *Apple is constantly working to minimize its impact on the environment. We've learned that the best way to do this is by making our products more energy efficient and environmentally friendly overall.*
>
> *In October 2008, Apple began providing customers with an estimate of the greenhouse gas emissions generated by every new product we sell. For example, manufacturing and using a MacBook—our most popular notebook—results in 460kg of CO_2 emissions over four years of use. According to the EPA, that's about the same amount the average car emits in a month.*
>
> *Apple's Environment team arrived at this estimate using a sophisticated life cycle analysis of carbon emissions at each phase of production, starting with the mining of raw materials. We account for the manufacturing of the product as well as its packaging. Then we add up the emissions related to transporting it to market, the power consumption during the product's use, and the energy required for eventual recycling. Apple also factors in the environmental impact of our offices and other business operations, which account for about 5 percent of total emissions.*

Apple is also very concerned with ethical business practices. Apple's mission statement and Supplier Code of Conduct reflect that attitude. According to Apple:

> *Apple ignited the personal computer revolution in the 1970s with the Apple II and reinvented the personal computer in the 1980s with the Macintosh. Today, Apple continues to lead the industry in innovation with its award-winning computers, OS X operating system and iLife and professional applications. Apple is also spearheading the digital media revolution with its iPod portable music and video players and iTunes online store, and has entered the mobile phone market with its revolutionary iPhone*
>
> *Apple requires our suppliers to adhere to our Supplier Code of Conduct. We insist they provide safe working conditions, treat employees fairly, and use environmentally responsible*

manufacturing processes. We drive compliance to the Code through an aggressive monitoring program that includes factory audits, corrective action plans, and verification measures.

In addition to audit procedures, Apple communicates the importance of social responsibility through regular business reviews. During this process, Apple executives review items such as audit results, audit cooperation, progress on corrective action plans, key performance indicators, and overall compliance status.

We recognize that many Apple employees—such as quality engineers and purchasing managers—are on site at supplier factories and can serve as ad hoc monitors of social responsibility. We are expanding our education program for Apple staff, training them to identify potential Code violations. We've also developed an online ticket system, making it easy for our employees to report any concerns or issues they observe.

Many workers in supplier factories have aspirations to continue their education and grow their careers. To support these aspirations, Apple launched a pilot initiative called the Supplier Employee Education and Development (SEED) program. Working with one of our final assembly suppliers in China, we have made available a flexible, computer-based learning curriculum, set in a classroom environment on a manufacturing campus.

Apple's common stock is traded on the NASDAQ Global Select Market under the symbol AAPL and on the Frankfurt Stock Exchange under the symbol APCD. Apple currently (2008) does not pay dividends.

BRIEF HISTORY OF APPLE

Steven Wozniak, who had worked for Hewlett-Packard, and his friend Steven Jobs, who had worked for Atari, designed and built Apple I in Steven Jobs's garage in 1976. On April 1 (yes, April Fools Day), Apple Computer was born. The friends did over $100,000 of "garage business" that first year and sought out venture capital. On January 3, 1977, Apple Computer was incorporated in California. Six months later, Apple II emerged. It sold for just under $1,000 and included color graphics (the first computer to do so). Three out of four early Apple buyers had never used a computer before and bought it for its "user-friendliness."

WHY WE CHOSE APPLE

Apple isn't the largest computer manufacturer; in fact, it's not even in the top three. But Apple is leading the way when it comes to digital music, video technology, and personal communications. In Chapter 20, we will compare Apple to its leading competitors. Be sure to visit Apple's Web site: **www.apple.com.**

PART ONE

I

Introduction: Business Operating Activities

CHAPTER ONE

1 Accounting and Business

Learning Objectives

LO 1 Describe the development of business and accounting.

LO 2 Explain the elements of accounting (assets, liabilities, owners' equity, revenue, expense, and net income).

LO 3 Identify the differences among the basic types of businesses and business organization structures.

LO 4 Identify the purpose and relationship among the four financial statements and the report of the independent accountant.

Accounting: Who Needs It?

Who needs accounting? Everyone. People use accounting information every day. When you write a check, use a credit card, or pay for merchandise with cash, you utilize an accounting information system. When you pay your income taxes, invest in the stock market, or take out a loan to buy a new car, you utilize accounting information. When you estimate your take-home pay, plan for your retirement, or save for next year's vacation, you utilize accounting information. As we saw in the financial meltdown in 2008, an understanding of accounting is crucial to survival in today's global economy. As you will see, accounting has evolved in response to users' needs for information. To explore the role of accounting, you must understand what a business is and what functions exist within a business.

Business is the exchange of goods or services on an arm's-length basis (that is, fair trade between unrelated parties) resulting in mutual benefit for both parties involved. People who engage in business believe that the rewards (possible future benefits) are greater than the risks (possible future sacrifices). To be successful, a business must have capable employees empowered to do their jobs. Employees perform five basic functions for a business: marketing, human resources, production and operations, finance, and accounting and information systems. All these functions require accounting information to some extent.

The **marketing function** determines the wants and needs of consumers and devises a system for distributing goods and services to meet customer demand. Marketing is customer focused and governed by the four Ps: product, price, promotion, and physical distribution. That is, marketing concentrates on the quality and functionality of the product, its selling price, how it is promoted, and how it is distributed. It is concerned with issues such as the nature of local, national, and global markets and customer satisfaction. Marketing uses accounting information to help determine selling prices, to evaluate alternative distribution channels, and to evaluate marketing success, among other things.

The **human resources function** is responsible for ensuring that capable employees are given opportunities to succeed in a safe work environment. Human resources management is concerned with issues such as continuing education for employees, health and safety of the workforce, and diversity in the workforce. Human resources managers use accounting information to determine employees' monthly, retirement, and vacation earnings. In addition, human resources personnel rely on accounting information to show compliance with health and safety regulations.

The **production and operations function** is responsible for planning, organizing, directing, and controlling the day-to-day activities of the business. For example, a firm's production and operations function may make a variety of different brands for regional and nationwide distribution. Production and operations management is concerned with issues such as efficiency and timeliness. It uses accounting information to determine the goals of operating activities and to evaluate the success or failure of those activities.

The **finance function** is responsible for managing the financial resources of the business. It is concerned with issues such as when and how to raise capital as well as where to invest that capital. Finance uses accounting information to evaluate investment proposals, to determine the cost of alternative financing strategies, and to manage the amount and timing of cash flows.

Finally, the **accounting and information systems function** is responsible for providing useful information to the other functional areas and external parties. It must ensure that users receive the information they need, when they need it, and in a form that is appropriate to their needs. Accounting and information systems are the backbone of the business—the infrastructure. We discuss this need for information and the role of accounting in providing it throughout the text. (See Of Interest: Specialties in Accounting.)

In this information age, more and more of today's businesses use cross-functional teams to replace the four functional areas just discussed. For example, if a company wanted to introduce a new line of computers, it might use a team of members from each of the functional areas to coordinate these functions. Marketing personnel would determine the extent of customer demand and a proposed selling price. Production would identify the resources needed to make the new computers and coordinate activities with suppliers. Human resources would provide

OF INTEREST Specialties in Accounting

Accounting is hot! It is one of the fastest growing career fields and it is projected to continue to grow in the next several years. Bright, articulate people are needed to major in accounting; yet, research indicates that many young people make up their minds about accounting based on incorrect stereotypes long before they get to college. Accounting is not about number crunching and desk work. Accountants have financial knowledge and analytical skills needed by every company. This "Of Interest" discusses a few things that you can do in accounting. A great interactive Web site you might be interested in is **www.startheregoplaces.com**.

FINANCIAL ACCOUNTING

Financial accounting reports the results of a company's operating activities to the investing public and other external users. Financial accountants must ensure that the company follows GAAP (generally accepted accounting principles). When a new issue arises, the financial accountant must determine the best manner to report it. Financial accountants are invaluable to business. They're responsible for ensuring the proper recording and reporting of all the business's transactions.

TAX ACCOUNTING AND TAX PLANNING

The Sixteenth Amendment to the U.S. Constitution established a system of federal income taxation that requires the periodic determination of income by individuals and businesses. It has had a profound effect on the accounting profession because it requires records to support the determination of taxable income. Today, all businesses must compute and report taxable income; however, only corporations actually pay tax on that income. Sole proprietorship and partnership income is taxed at the individual level. Generally, businesses and individuals do not want to pay more taxes than they are required to pay. Therefore, tax planning is essential to legally minimize the impact of taxes.

REGULATORY ACCOUNTING

Companies are required to comply with various laws at the federal, state, and local level. Because there are a large number of these laws, an accounting specialty has developed to ensure compliance with these regulations. Regulatory accounting provides the required information to regulatory agencies such as the Securities and Exchange Commission and others. For example, a regulatory accountant might prepare reports for the Occupational Safety and Health Administration to show compliance with its rules. Or reports might be filed with the Environmental Protection Agency to indicate compliance with pollution standards.

MANAGEMENT ACCOUNTING

Management accountants provide useful information for internal decision makers. They must understand the particular needs of their users and design appropriate reports for them. Often management accountants serve as a part of the management team and, therefore, are often fairly high on the corporate ladder. Many management accountants possess a Certified Management Accountant (CMA) certificate. For more information about the CMA, see **www.imanet.org**.

INFORMATION SYSTEMS

Accountants also help companies purchase, design, and control information technology. Because much of the information used by companies is financial, it is natural that accountants are involved in decisions concerning information technology. Information

input on the new product line's impact on the current workforce, and finance would assess the amount of capital needed to support research and development as well as production operations. Accounting and information systems would be responsible for providing financial and other data in a timely manner to promote the collaboration necessary to enable project success. By using the cross-functional approach the efforts of each functional area are focused on achieving the company's goals. Thus when we discuss a functional area of business, we refer to the *decisions made,* not necessarily a specific department making the decisions.

Business Today

Now that you understand the functions within a business, we look at how businesses operate today. You must understand how businesses operate currently and how they have changed recently so that you can adapt to changes in the future. In addition, you must understand how business operates to appreciate the role of accounting in business. The most recent dramatic changes in business are, in part, driven by technology. Technology allows businesses to more readily ascertain customers' needs, gain access to global markets, improve products quicker and easier, and operate more efficiently. We group the changes into four areas: (1) customer-focused operations, (2) global markets, (3) manufacturing and communication advances, and (4) e-business.

systems specialists help their businesses analyze accounting information systems to determine if systems should be modified or replaced. They help design new systems or modifications to existing systems.

AUDITING

Auditing is the practice of determining whether the information presented in accounting reports fairly represents the financial condition of the company. In addition, auditors provide many other useful services to their clients. Auditors can be internal or external to the company.

Internal Auditing

An internal auditor works for the particular company and is responsible for ensuring the integrity of the accounting system. In addition, internal auditors often engage in performance and financial audits where they monitor a process and try to suggest improvements. Internal auditors often work closely with external auditors to ensure a timely, cost-effective audit. Many internal auditors are Certified Internal Auditors. For more information about the CIA, see **www.theiia.org.**

External Auditing

An external auditor works for a public accounting firm and attests to the fairness of its clients' externally released financial statements. The CPA issues an audit report indicating whether a company's financial statements are prepared in accordance with GAAP. Companies whose financial statements are found in accordance with GAAP are presumed to be fair. An annual audit by an external, licensed auditor is required for all companies registered with the Securities and Exchange Commission (SEC). An external auditor must be a Certified Public Accountant (CPA). For more information about the CPA, see **www.aicpa.org.** Audits must be conducted in accordance with the standards issued by the Public Company Accounting Oversight Board, which resulted from the passage of the Sarbanes-Oxley Act. These standards require that audits be conducted to obtain reasonable assurance about whether financial statements are free from material misstatement.

GOVERNMENTAL AND NOT-FOR-PROFIT ACCOUNTING

The rules governing the preparation of external reports for not-for-profit and governmental entities are different than those for profit-seeking entities. A governmental or not-for-profit accountant must understand these rules and be able to assist the entities in achieving their objectives. These accountants follow procedures outlined by the Governmental Accounting Standards Board (GASB).

FORENSIC ACCOUNTING/FRAUD AUDITING

Forensic accounting and fraud auditing are specializations within accounting concerned with the detection, investigation, and prevention of fraud. A forensic accountant/fraud auditor often prepares documents and other visual aids that can be used in trial to show a paper trail. Thus, a forensic accountant must not only understand accounting but also know methods of evidence gathering and criminal investigation. Forensic accountants are hired by the FBI, the CIA, the DEA, and the ATF as well as by private companies. For instance, forensic accountants are investigating the financial networks of terrorist organizations throughout the world. Many forensic accountants and fraud auditors possess CFE (Certified Fraud Examiner) certificates. For more information about the CFE see **www.cfenet.com.**

Customer-Focused Operations

Although businesses have always been interested in their customers, the business climate has changed. Today, businesses are customer-focused. This means that the whole operation of the business is based on knowing who the company's customers are and providing them what they want, when they want it.

For example, back when Intel Corporation introduced the 386SX, it did not sell well. Intel's customers, computer manufacturers such as Dell, Inc., were not interested in the new technology because the old technology worked fine in their products. But Intel knew that if it did not upgrade from the 286 to the 386SX, clones would soon control the market. Thus, Intel did something considered radical at the time. Instead of trying to convince computer manufacturers that the 386SX was better, Intel redefined its customers and aimed its marketing campaign at computer users. When convinced that the new technology was better, computer users began to demand it in their computers. This demand convinced companies such as Dell to include the new technology in their computers.[1]

This attitude of knowing your customers and giving them what they want also has resulted in the just-in-time philosophy. **Just-in-time (JIT)** stipulates that products (inventory) should be received by customers just as they are needed and in the quantities needed. When

[1] Sally Helgesen, *The Web of Inclusion* (New York: Doubleday, 1995).

FAST FACT

Did you know that Apple's ad campaign comparing PCs to Macs was one of the most successful in its history? It was designed to impress upon computer users that Macs are "ready to go" and easy to use without requiring expensive add-ons for things that computer users want to do, like videoconferencing.

products are received as needed, customers do not have to carry as much inventory. As we discuss later, this saves money. Therefore, JIT is a customer-focused philosophy: Get the customers what they want, when they want it, at a price they are willing to pay for it. For example, Apple Computer Inc., determined that a partnership with AT&T would enable it to market its iPhone by enabling customers to buy the phone through Apple or through AT&T, thus increasing visibility. A company like Apple must understand its customers and their buying habits so that it can develop products they desire.

Products must be user friendly so that they not only meet the needs of customers but also are easy to use and reliable. Businesses seek to achieve excellence in products and processes because just selling a reliable product is no longer sufficient. Today's businesses must also provide customer support before and after the sale. Businesses can win or lose customers due to their customer support (or the lack of it). Many companies advertise their customer support as much, if not more, than they advertise their products. For instance, Apple advertises its AppleCare Service and Support for iPods/iTunes, Macs, and iPhones.

For manufacturing companies, customer focus means that products must be manufactured with zero defects. A zero defect policy is accomplished by building quality into the product rather than inspecting it in. Companies believe that it is less expensive to build a quality product at the outset than to rework or fix an inferior product. By designing products with fewer parts, companies have lessened the opportunity for mistakes to occur. Vendors that supply parts to manufacturers are also becoming involved in the production process. Because they can see how their supplied parts fit into the final product, vendors help manufacturers design products that can be made more easily and more cost effectively. At the same time, vendors can ensure that quality raw materials are coming into the production process; thus, defects due to poor materials are reduced or eliminated. Finally, many companies have adopted quality circles or other employee-empowerment ideas that reward employees for finding and correcting defects before the products leave the manufacturing facilities.

Global Markets

In terms of time, the world seems to be getting smaller. We can now travel from country to country in less time than it once took to get from one state to another. Transportation and communication also are getting cheaper. In 1776 it took Thomas Jefferson days to travel from Virginia to Philadelphia. Today, he could fax or e-mail his copy of the Declaration of Independence in a matter of seconds and save the trip.

Countries have formed free-trade blocs that eliminate tariffs and permit goods to be traded between these countries without restrictions. For example, the United States, Canada, and Mexico entered into the North American Free Trade Agreement (NAFTA), which allows free trade among them while trade with nonmembers is still restricted. Restrictions allow member countries to protect industries within the trading bloc by implementing tariffs for outside purchases, thus effectively raising the price of goods from nonmember nations. Some economists foresee a time when free trade will be the rule rather than the exception.

Manufacturers must consider global markets when they design and market their products. The Internet provides a means of reaching consumers in every country in the world. Therefore, they must understand the economic environment and the culture of countries with which they do business. For example, Chevrolet launched an unsuccessful marketing campaign for its Nova in Spanish-speaking countries because *nova* in Spanish means "do not go." The global market also affects the labor supply. International companies such as Apple's may operate in many countries—sometimes to find cheaper labor but more often to develop markets for products.

Manufacturing and Communication Advances

Technology has dramatically affected manufacturing and communication processes. Companies can now phone, fax, and e-mail to almost anywhere in the world. Bar coding allows companies to monitor inventory levels on a real-time basis. For example, when a clerk scans an item purchased by a customer at Wal-Mart, the scan does three things: First, it determines the selling price for the customer as indicated by the checkout register. Second, it signals the removal of that item from Wal-Mart's inventory. And third, it electronically forwards an order to suppliers so that Procter & Gamble, for example, can fill the order and ship the products, and Wal-Mart can replace the goods on its shelves. Manufacturers also use bar coding to signal when raw materials are placed in production. In this way, orders for additional raw materials can be placed to ensure the uninterrupted flow of goods through the factory.

Additional changes in manufacturing include the following:

1. Computer-assisted design (CAD) that tests products before they are produced.
2. Computer-assisted manufacturing (CAM) that improves the speed and precision of production processes.
3. Computer-integrated manufacturing (CIM) that uses computers and robotics to control production from the ordering of raw materials through processing and shipment of goods to customers.

All these changes in technology require significant investments in equipment. Therefore, it is increasingly important for companies to gather information concerning customer preferences. Determining customers' wants and needs helps ensure that the expensive, specialized equipment is used effectively.

Customer and vendor input is crucial in an environment of shortened product life cycles. **Product life cycle** is the time span from the conception of the product until consumers no longer demand it. For some products this time period is very short—a few months perhaps; for others, it is much longer. For example, in computer manufacturing, a new operating system, such as the OSX, progresses through four phases during its life cycle. First, in the design phase, an idea is formulated, product specifications are determined, and a prototype is built. Second, the operating system is developed. In the development phase, the product is manufactured, and the design is modified to ensure defect-free, efficient processing. At this point, marketing typically begins. Third, during the production phase, the product is produced and sold to customers. Fourth, the product is phased out. During the phaseout period, production ceases, and the remaining products are sold, perhaps during a close-out sale. Then the cycle starts all over again, with a new and improved model.

E-Business

E-business is the use of information technology and electronic communication networks to exchange business information and conduct transactions in an electronic, paperless form. Advances in manufacturing and communication led to business conducted electronically. Today most companies are either conducting business electronically or considering adoption of electronic communication networks. Retail electronic sales are growing rapidly. For example, in 2006 alone, 70.8 percent of music and videos were sold online. In addition, 69 percent of electronics and appliances and 61.9 percent of office equipment and supplies were purchased through e-commerce networks.[2] The rapid growth of e-business indicates that its benefits outweigh its risks. Some of the benefits of e-business are (1) increased sales opportunities, (2) improved communication, and (3) lower costs.

[2] 2006 Annual Retail Trade Survey, U.S. Census Bureau.

Increased sales opportunities are created through Internet sales in addition to, or instead of, brick-and-mortar sales. Apple is an excellent example. Apple computers are sold on the Internet, over the phone, and in traditional stores. Many people enjoy the flexibility of shopping over the Internet, as companies such as Apple are open 24 hours a day, 7 days a week. Providing product information and customer support for B2C (business-to-consumer) transactions over the Internet also increases sales opportunities for many companies.

E-business is less expensive than paper transactions. For example in 2005, a teller-based bank transaction cost approximately $1.07; an ATM transaction cost $0.39; while an online transaction cost only $0.01.[3] Recruiting and hiring costs are also reduced through e-business. Many companies now offer an online application process allowing potential employees to submit resumes and engage in a prescreening process. Finally costs can be reduced through smaller inventories. Companies that engage in B2B often reduce inventory levels by significant amounts.

E-business is not without risks however. Whenever outsiders are allowed inside a company's information infrastructure, risk increases. Denial-of-service attacks are intentional attacks by outsiders to slow down or halt a company's communication system. E-business has also created an environment that has spawned the growth of identity theft. This impacts not only the consumer but also the companies that mistakenly provide goods or funds to the identity thief. It has become such a threat that on May 10, 2006, President Bush signed an executive order creating an identify theft task force to address this growing problem. The task force was co-chaired by the attorney general and the chairman of the Federal Trade Commission.

Warehousing and distribution is a major issue for e-business companies. For example, a few years ago a mail-order would take seven or more days to arrive. Now Amazon.com and Eddie Bauer can ship products within 24 hours. Failure to meet customers' expectations regarding delivery can be fatal, however. For example, many e-business companies actually went out of business during the late 1990s due to their inability to ship products in a timely manner during the holiday season.

Business and Accounting: Together Forever

For as long as people have engaged in business, there has been some form of accounting. Accounting is the means of keeping track of the results of business transactions. Accounting is called the language of business because it enables interested parties to obtain useful information about businesses. A more formal definition of accounting follows:

> ***Accounting*** is the information infrastructure of the firm/economy that permits it to achieve its objectives.[4]

What are the objectives of business? A for-profit business enterprise such as Apple is designed to provide needed goods or services at a price that customers are willing to pay and to provide a return to its owners. That is, Apple must sell its products and services at a price that is greater than the cost of the goods or services. This excess is used to pay its creditors (people and entities that loan it money) and provide a return (a profit or gain on an investment) to its shareholders (people and entities that own Apple's stock). A not-for-profit business enterprise such as the United Way provides needed goods and services at a price that customers can pay without exceeding the amount of resources entrusted to it by donors. Accounting provides a business with information required to achieve its goals. An accountant enables an entity to achieve its objectives through the strategic use of information and information systems.

[3] S. M. Glover, S. W. Liddle, and D. F. Prawitt, *E-Business: Principles and Strategies for Accountants,* 2nd ed. (Upper Saddle River, NJ: Prentice Hall, 2002), p. 8.
[4] Bob Elliot, "Assurance Service Opportunities: Implications for Academia," AICPA Special Committee on Assurance Services, American Accounting Association National Meeting, August 1997.

Changes in the way business is conducted dramatically impact the accounting profession. No longer do accountants sit behind desks recording data—the computers can do that. Today's accountant is an information intermediary as the accountant's role has evolved to keep pace with the evolution of business. To understand this evolution we must take a trip back in time. During the first leg of our journey, we stop in Babylonia, around 2000 B.C. to examine accounting in an illiterate society.

Ancient Babylonia

The first stop on our journey takes us to the first dynasty of Babylonia (2286–2242 B.C.), a rich farming area located between the Tigris and Euphrates rivers in what is now Iraq. Babylonia's law is based on the Code of Hammurabi, which requires merchants trading goods to give buyers a sealed memorandum quoting prices, or the trade is not legally enforceable. Thus the Code of Hammurabi reduces a source of conflict between parties to business transactions that in turn facilitates commerce and benefits Babylonian society. For example, the law protects buyers from unscrupulous sellers who might quote one price but demand a higher price when the goods are delivered. However, there is one problem—most of the citizens of Babylonia are illiterate.

Assume you are a merchant in Babylonia. How do you conduct business? You are operating as a **sole proprietorship**—that is, a business owned by one person whose personal wealth is at risk if the business fails. You are also operating as a **merchandising company**—that is, a business that obtains and distributes goods to customers. To conduct business, you must find a customer or customers who possess the goods you want and who want the goods you have to trade. But how do you record your business transactions when you are illiterate?

First, you must find a scribe, who is probably sitting outside the city gates. Second, you explain to him your agreed-upon transaction and he records it in a small mound of clay. Then, since neither you nor your trading partner can read or write, you each affix your "signatures" to the agreement by impressing your signature amulet on the clay document.[5] The clay tablet is allowed to dry in the sun, or, if the transaction is very important, the record can be kiln-dried. The clay tablet serves as a record of the transaction and provides control to protect each party. Obviously, the integrity of the scribe is crucial. The scribe is the predecessor to the modern accountant. The next leg of our historical journey takes us to northern Italy. We make two stops here. The first stop is during the 12th century where we find partnerships forming. Our second stop is during the 15th century where we discover a man who becomes known as the "Father of Accounting."

Commerce in Old Italy

The first stop on this leg of our journey lands us in the trading centers of northern Italy that developed as a result of the Crusades from the 11th to the 13th centuries. Literacy is more widespread, Arabic numerals are used as a result of trade with the Near East allowing columns of numbers to be added and subtracted, an international banking system functions, and the use of credit is prevalent. A bank is a **service firm**—a business that exists to provide services to customers (clients). In this case, the services are loaning money, finding investors, and other services for which the bank receives fees.

As business grows, it is commonplace for two or more people to pool their resources and form a partnership for a single venture. A **partnership** is a business owned by two or more individuals whose personal wealth is at risk if the business fails. How do you conduct business in this environment? First, you must find a partner, or partners. So a partnership, like a sole proprietorship, is easy to form; you just do it. Second, each of you contributes assets to the partnership. **Assets** are rights to use resources that have expected future economic

Assets
Rights to use resources that have expected future economic benefits.

[5] Every male citizen was required to have a signature amulet to conduct business (women were not allowed to conduct business). The amulet was worn around the man's neck and buried with him when he died.

FAST FACT

Did you know that Al Capone, the infamous Chicago mobster, was actually brought to justice not for murder, but rather for tax evasion? Elmer Irey, a forensic accountant for the IRS, put together enough evidence from Capone's bank statements and other financial records to indict him on income tax evasion for which he was subsequently sentenced to prison.

Liabilities
Obligations to transfer economic resources to suppliers of money, goods, and services at some point in the future.

Owners' equity
Claims on the business to transfer the residual interest (net assets) to the owners.

benefits. That is, the business has the right to use something of value. Perhaps your partner contributes the boat for shipping goods to other lands, while you contribute the goods to be traded. Once contributed, the boat and the goods are assets of the business. Then, since more capital is needed, your partnership obtains a loan from the bank. This loan is a **liability**—the obligation to transfer economic resources to suppliers of money, goods, and services at some point in the future. That is, the partnership must repay the bank for the money borrowed (plus interest) at some predetermined date in the future. Note, however, that both you and your partner are liable for this loan should the partnership fail. This is known as mutual agency and unlimited liability. **Mutual agency** means that each partner has the power to act for, and legally obligate, all other partners. **Unlimited liability** means that once the business's assets are exhausted, the personal assets of the owners can be used to satisfy liabilities of the business.

Next, you hire an agent to trade the goods with others in foreign lands. When the ship returns, the partnership must sell the goods traded for, repay the loan (plus interest) to the bank, pay the agent, and allocate the remaining assets of the partnership to the partners. These remaining assets are **net assets** (assets minus liabilities) and represent the owners' equity of the business. **Owners' equity** represents the claims on the business to transfer the residual interest (net assets of the business) to the owners. That is, after all the business's liabilities (obligations) are met, any remaining assets (net assets) belong to the owners.

How can you tell if your partnership venture is successful? How can you tell how much to return to each partner? Your accounting system provides the information to help you determine the success of the business. Let's see what we know. You and your partner invested an amount of assets in the business venture and borrowed an additional amount from the bank. When the venture was completed, the obligations of the business were met—that is, the bank loan (plus interest) and the agent were paid. The remaining assets were then divided among the partners and the partnership ceased. To determine how to divide the remaining assets, you refer to your **partnership agreement,** which outlines the rights and obligations of each partner. If your wealth increased, that is, if you received more assets (in terms of value, not quantity) than originally invested, the business venture was successful.

Gradually, such one-venture partnerships give way to businesses organized with the idea of continuing for more than one venture, as people do not liquidate the assets but instead keep them invested in the business. In addition, businesses grow in size and become more geographically dispersed as the population becomes more mobile. Now accounting systems are needed to determine each partner's share of an ongoing business and to control business associates located in remote locations.

At this point, we see the development of two very important accounting concepts: the business entity concept and the going concern concept. The **business entity concept** requires that an accounting system reflect only information about economic events that pertain to a particular entity. That is, the business records should be separate and distinct from the personal records of the business owners. This concept is particularly important so that the success or failure of the business can be determined. The **going concern concept** assumes that, absent any information to the contrary, the business entity will continue into the foreseeable future. That is, the business is not expected to terminate after each venture. This concept is particularly crucial because it allows business records to continue from one venture and time period to another.

Now assume you continue doing business with your partner. Since you want the partnership to continue beyond the current venture, you must find a way to measure the partnership's success or failure while it is still operating. Again, your accounting system provides this information. When you want to know how the partnership is doing, you determine the value of all the partnership's assets and subtract the liabilities of the partnership. This amount represents the net assets (equity) of the partnership. Therefore, during this time period, the success (failure) of the business is determined by the increase (decrease) in the net assets of the business. Also during this period, we notice that each business transaction is recorded twice—once to represent what was received and once to represent what was given. For example, if your partnership buys a new boat with a loan from the bank, your accounting system reflects both the boat received and the liability incurred. This duality of recording developed into what we now call double-entry accounting.

Pacioli and the Method of Venice

Our second stop is in 15th century Venice, Italy, where business is commonly conducted using currency rather than barter. The Arabic number system is widely used, enabling addition and subtraction to be done easily, and literacy is widespread. The double-entry accounting system—in which for every *debet dare* (should give) there exists a *debet habere* (should have or should receive)—has evolved to the point where it is similar in form to its 21st century counterpart. The double-entry concept leads to the following fundamental **accounting equation:**

$$\text{Assets} = \text{Liabilities} + \text{Owners' equity}$$

That is, the rights of the business are equal to the obligations of the business plus the owners' equity in the business. The business is simply a conduit to transfer goods and services from one or more parties to others. If we rearrange the equation as follows, we observe that owners' equity is the residual interest (what's left for the owners) in the company:

$$\text{Assets} - \text{Liabilities} = \text{Owners' equity}$$

In 15th century Venice, you meet Luca Pacioli, a Franciscan monk. He has just completed his fifth book, entitled *Summa de Arithmetica, Geometria, Proportioni et Proportionalita (Everything about Arithmetic, Geometry, and Proportion)*. In his book are 36 short chapters on bookkeeping. Pacioli does not claim to have invented this method of bookkeeping, known as the Method of Venice; rather, he describes procedures generally in use at the time.

In the *Summa,* Luca states that to be successful every merchant needs three things: sufficient cash or credit, good bookkeepers, and an accounting system to view the business affairs at a glance.[6] He discusses three books in the *Summa:* the memorandum, the journal, and the ledger. The memorandum is the book where all transactions are recorded, in the currency in which they are conducted, at the time they are conducted. The memorandum, prepared in chronological order, is a narrative description of the business's economic events. The memorandum is necessary because there are no documents (invoices, bank statements, and so on of the modern world) to support transactions. The second book, the journal, is the merchant's private book. The entries made here are in one currency, in chronological order, and in narrative form.[7]

The last book, known as the ledger, is an alphabetic listing of all the business's accounts along with a running balance of each particular account. What is interesting is that Pacioli never discusses **financial statements,** that is, statements prepared to communicate the results of business activities to interested users. Financial statements are unnecessary because businesses are still closely controlled by owners who can examine the business's records. However, Pacioli does advocate an annual balancing to determine the success or failure of the business and to find errors.

During Pacioli's time two other important accounting concepts emerge: the monetary unit concept and the periodicity concept. The **monetary unit concept** asserts that money is the common measurement unit of economic activity. This concept is crucial because it allows things to

[6] A. C. Littleton, "Evolution of the Ledger Account," *The Accounting Review,* December 1926.

[7] Michael Chatfield, *A History of Accounting Thought,* Robert E. Krieger Publishing Company, Huntington, New York, 1977.

be measured in a common denominator. For example, rather than recording the number of cows or sheep available for trade, the accounting system reflects the monetary value of the livestock. Thus the merchant can total his assets rather than merely list them. Since these businesses were going concerns but needed to monitor their success (or failure), the periodicity concept developed. The **periodicity concept** requires that the success or failure of the business be determined at regular intervals. This means the business does not have to cease before the profits of the business can be determined. This concept enables businesses to grow because admission and departure of partners can be accomplished without interrupting the business operations.

At this point in history, income is the measurement of the success or failure of the business. Income in the 15th century is the difference between the cash received from customers and the cash paid to employees and other suppliers of goods and services. (In the 21st century, we call this **cash basis accounting.**)

So what have we learned during this leg of our journey? Accounting is changing as business needs change. The success or failure of the business, once measured by the changes in the net assets, is now measured by the income of the business. Four basic concepts underlie accounting: business entity, going concern, monetary unit, and periodicity. Pacioli, who did not invent accounting, helped people understand its underlying logic. Again, people are engaging in business because the perceived rewards (increase in income) are greater than the perceived risks (potential loss).

The final leg of our journey begins during the 18th century when important economic and institutional changes take place. The Industrial Revolution that started in England has been responsible for technological developments that eventually led to changes in the systems of production, marketing, and financing. After describing the environment, we make our final stop—the 1929 stock market crash—before returning to the present.

Advent of the Corporation

During the Industrial Revolution, we see that **manufacturing firms** organized to convert raw materials into finished goods are commonplace. Specialization is more common and distribution systems are increasingly sophisticated. The development and use of steam-powered machinery allow for mass production of inexpensive goods. Revolutions in transportation, led by the railroad industry, create access to new markets for goods. These changes precipitate the need for additional sources of capital, and financial institutions grow correspondingly to meet this need. More elaborate accounting systems evolve to respond to the requirements of management and owners as well as those of creditors.

Enhance Your Understanding

Is Apple a service, merchandising, and/or manufacturing company?

Answer: Apple is primarily a manufacturing company. It makes computers and related products that it sells to other businesses. However, because it provides services it is also a service company, and it has retail and online stores, so it is also a merchandising firm.

As business increases, it is possible for individuals to accumulate wealth and have funds available for investment purposes. Corporations emerge to provide opportunities for investing in business without the obligation of overseeing day-to-day business operations. A **corporation** is a business entity that is legally separate and distinct from its owners. Thus forming a corporation is a legal process. Corporations are attractive business ventures because they provide investors with **limited liability**—that is, the assets invested in the corporation are at risk but investors' personal possessions are not at risk if the business fails. The most the investor can lose is the amount of his or her investment. Professional managers often run these corporations, which leads to the separation of owners and managers.

The evolution of the corporation firmly entrenched the four basic accounting concepts of business entity, going concern, monetary unit, and periodicity. The corporation is legally separate from its owners and, therefore, has a life that extends beyond its owners. In addition, because the owners are not involved in the day-to-day operations, the corporation places additional burdens on the accounting system to provide these owners with information concerning the ongoing activities of the business on a periodic basis. The **accrual basis of accounting** is widely adopted. In the accrual basis of accounting, income is the difference between the sales (revenues) *earned* and the expenses *incurred* during the period, regardless of when cash is paid or received. A sale is earned when the seller has transferred resources or services to the buyer. An expense is incurred when the buyer has used resources or services. Thus we can define a **revenue** as the amount earned from providing services or transferring resources to customers. An **expense** is the amount incurred from using resources or services in the effort to generate revenue. **Net income,** then, is the company's total revenues less its total expenses for a period of time. For example, if the business provides services to clients who will pay for these services in a later period, the business has earned revenue at the time the service is rendered even though it has not yet received the cash. Likewise, if the business uses services but has not yet paid for them, the business has incurred an expense, even though it has not yet paid cash. At the end of a designated time period the net income is the difference between the total revenues and total expenses for the period.

Revenue
The amount earned from providing services or transferring resources to customers.

Expense
The amount incurred from using resources or services in the effort to generate revenue.

Net income
Total revenue less total expenses for a period of time.

To illustrate the accrual concept, assume a company provided $60,000 of services to its customers but received only $50,000 in cash from them. Is its accrual basis revenue $60,000 or $50,000? The answer is $60,000 because the company provided services of $60,000. Now assume the same company used $45,000 of services from its vendors but paid only $40,000 for them in this time period. Is its accrual basis expense $45,000 or $40,000? The answer is $45,000 because this is the amount of services used. Now, given these answers, what is the company's accrual basis income for the period? It is $15,000 ($60,000 revenue earned − $45,000 expense incurred). What is the cash basis income? It is $10,000 ($50,000 cash received − $40,000 cash paid).

The Stock Market Crash of 1929

We now cross the Atlantic Ocean to reach America, where the Industrial Revolution has had a profound effect. In the 1920s after World War I, the public is investing in the stock market (an organized exchange for buying and selling stocks). Production and employment are high, American capitalism is lively, and many people are investing in rapidly growing business enterprises. Commonly stocks are sold on a margin of 10 percent allowing investors to buy stocks with a 10 percent down payment and a promise to pay the remainder at a later date. Because the market prices of stocks are increasing rapidly, everyone assumes they will be able to sell their stocks for more than they still owe and make a huge profit. But this bubble is about to burst.

On Sunday, October 20, 1929, a depression may be looming. *The New York Times* headline reads "Stocks Driven Down as Wave of Selling Engulfs the Market." Monday is worse. The volume of stock sold is 6,091,870 shares—the third largest in history—and prices are falling. By Wednesday, the stock market is nervous. While the New York Stock Exchange opens quietly enough, 2.6 million shares are sold during the final trading hour at falling prices. Thursday, October 24, marks the beginning of the panic as 12.9 million shares of stock change hands! Outside the Exchange, crowds begin to gather. At one point, a workman appears on an outside ledge and the crowd assumes he is going to jump. Later in the day, the stock market rebounds, but because there are no computers in the 1920s, not everyone realizes this fact. The effects of "Black Thursday" are not fully known until after midnight. Conditions do not improve on Friday or Saturday. On Monday, October 28, the nightmare continues. Trading volume is large—over 9 million shares sold—and losses are larger. On Tuesday, October 29, selling begins as soon as the market opens. By the time the market closes, 16.4 million trades have been recorded, and market watchers believe that many more go unrecorded! The *Times* Industrial Average (a measure of stock market value) is down 43 points, erasing in one day all the gains of the previous boom year![8] As Exhibit 1.1 illustrates, the Dow Jones Industrial Average reached its peak at 381 in September. On October 29, it closed at 230. By November, the Dow was below 50.

[8] John Kenneth Galbraith, *The Great Crash 1929* (Boston: Houghton Mifflin, 1988).

EXHIBIT 1.1
1929 Stock Market Crash

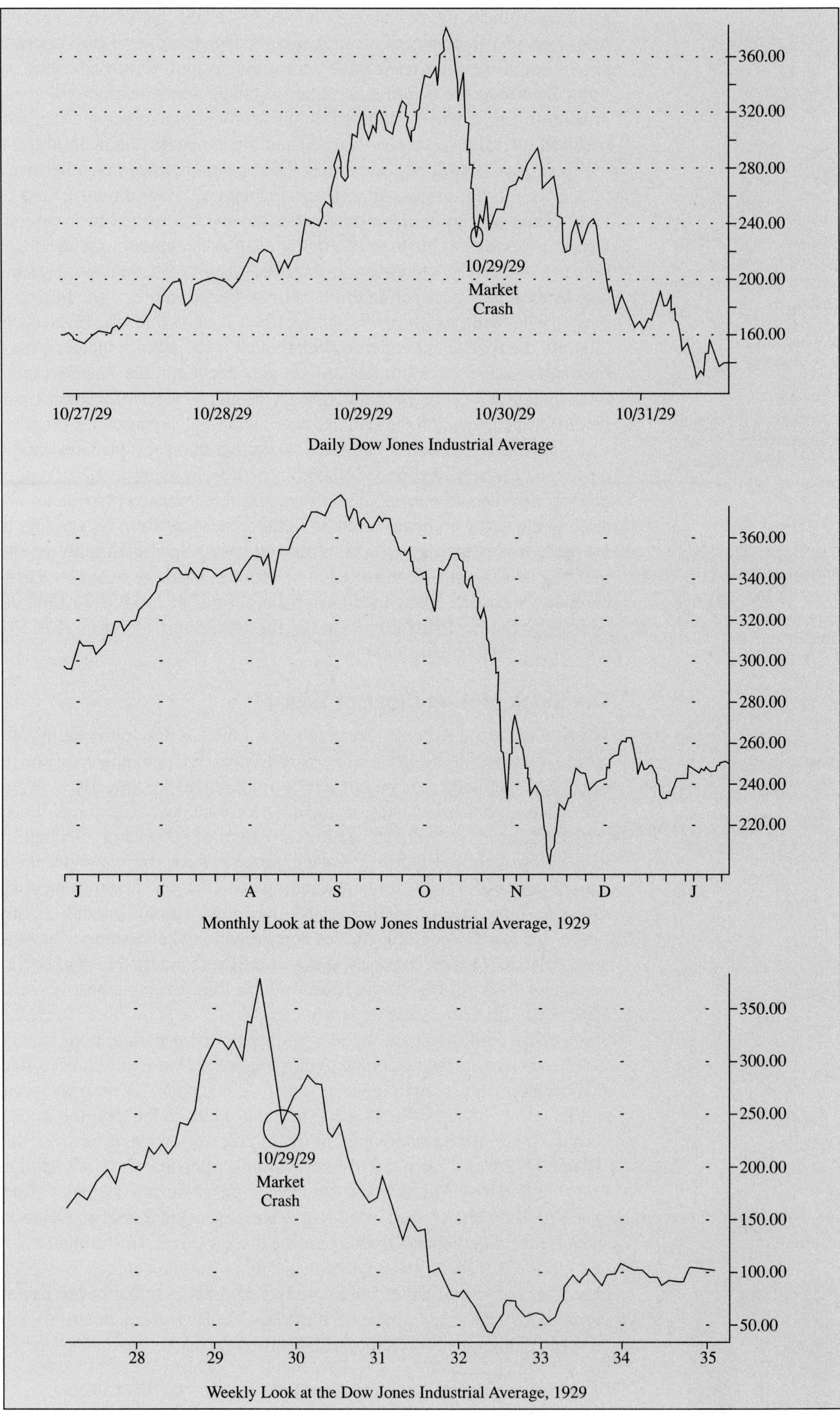

Many historians believe that the stock market crash was caused, in part, by the lack of quality information about businesses. Although accounting reports were available at this time, accounting methods were determined by the reporting company, leading to a lack of consistency in the application of accounting methods from reporting period to reporting period and reducing the comparability between companies.

The stock market crash of 1929, followed by the Great Depression in the 1930s, led to federal regulation of the securities market. The Securities Act of 1933 required that all companies issuing stock to the public register with the Federal Trade Commission (FTC). In addition, each company must file and disclose to the public certain financial information. The Securities Exchange Act of 1934 required submission of audited, annual financial information for all publicly owned companies and established the Securities and Exchange Commission (SEC). The SEC limited the reporting options available to companies and required full disclosure of financial results so investors could compare companies. In addition, although the SEC has the legal power to set accounting principles, it formally recognized the accounting profession—and not the federal government—as the authoritative body to determine accounting rules for the preparation of financial statements.

What have we learned during this leg of our journey? Accounting has changed again to meet the needs of its users. Corporations emerged and put additional pressures on accounting. Internally, accounting was used to monitor the cost of production and the efficiency of operations. Externally, the accrual concept of accounting was adopted. The stock market crash of 1929 led to the regulation of corporations and accounting in the United States to provide investors with reliable information. Accounting regulation also led to the formalization of generally accepted accounting principles (discussed in the next major section).

Return to the Present

What does the business environment look like today? According to the Internal Revenue Service, there were 2,763,625 partnership tax returns, 5,671,257 corporation tax returns, and 21,467,566 nonfarm sole proprietorship tax returns, for a total of 29,902,448 business returns, filed in 2005.[9] Why are so few businesses operated as partnerships? One reason may be that partnerships are much like marriages. Each partner must compromise regarding the other's strengths and weaknesses. Recall that in a partnership, mutual agency gives each partner the power to act for all other partners, making partnerships very risky. A partnership agreement that outlines each partner's duties and responsibilities as well as the division of partnership profits is essential. If the partners do not prepare an agreement, the affairs of the partnership are addressed in the Uniform Partnership Act, which governs the rights and obligations of partners.

Corporations are popular because they have a better ability to raise capital due to owners' limited liability. On the other hand, corporations are subject to **double taxation** in which the profits earned by the corporation are taxed twice—once at the business level and again at the owner level if the profits are distributed as dividends. Exhibit 1.2 summarizes the characteristics of sole proprietorships, partnerships, and corporations.

In recent years, a number of other business forms that combine various characteristics of sole proprietorships, partnerships, and corporations have emerged. For example, a **limited**

EXHIBIT 1.2
Characteristics of Business Ownership Structures

Characteristic	Sole Proprietorship	Partnership	Corporation
Business entity	Yes	Yes	Yes
Double taxation	No	No	Yes
Ease of formation	Easy	Easy	Legal process
Legal entity	No	No	Yes
Limited liability for owners	No	No	Yes
Maximum number of owners	1	Unlimited	Unlimited
Minimum number of owners	1	2	1
Mutual agency	No	Yes	No
Unlimited liability	Yes	Yes	No

[9] www.irs.gov.

partnership is a partnership composed of one or more general partners and one or more limited partners. The general partners are personally liable for the business, while the limited partners' personal risk is limited to the amount of their investments. An **S corporation** is a small business corporation owned by no more than 100 individuals. In an S corporation, the profits earned by the business are not taxed at the corporate level; instead, the profits flow through to the owners and are taxed on the owners' personal tax returns regardless of whether the profits have been distributed. This eliminates double taxation. A **limited liability partnership (LLP)** is a partnership in which the individual partners are liable only for their own actions and the actions of those individuals under their control. Therefore, one partner in an LLP cannot be held responsible for the negligence of another partner. This reduces the impact of mutual agency. Another form of business—the **limited liability company (LLC)**—eliminates the impact of unlimited liability for all the owners, does not limit the number of owners as required by the S corporation, and does not limit participation in the management of the firm as limited partnerships do. Like the limited partnerships, S corporations, and LLPs, the profits pass through to the owners before they are taxed. Not all states recognize these hybrid organizational structures, so it is important to check all state and local regulations.

A significant issue facing businesses is how to fairly report the financial condition of the company to its owners and other interested third parties such as bankers and potential investors. As we have seen, this issue came to a peak in the United States during the Great Depression. Today the fairness of external financial reports is determined by whether a company is in compliance with *generally accepted accounting principles.* Generally accepted accounting principles are necessary so that all publicly held companies use the same set of rules when preparing their external financial statements. Without generally accepted accounting principles, companies would be free to present whatever information they desired in whatever form they desired and, therefore, comparing one company to another would be virtually impossible.

Generally Accepted Accounting Principles

Generally accepted accounting principles (GAAP) are the set of reporting standards applicable to all companies that issue financial reports for external users. Currently, the group responsible for determining GAAP in the United States is the **Financial Accounting Standards Board (FASB).** The FASB is a nongovernmental organization consisting of seven, full-time, paid professionals and a support staff. After obtaining input from businesspersons and other accounting professionals, the board determines the manner in which particular accounting events are disclosed to external users of accounting information. The SEC requires that all publicly traded companies that file their financial reports with them must be in compliance with GAAP as defined by the FASB. The FASB is funded by fees collected by the SEC from publicly traded companies.

The pronouncements of the FASB are called Statements of Financial Accounting Standards (SFAS). However, GAAP includes statements and accounting principles developed by its predecessors, the Committee on Accounting Procedures (1938–1959) and the Accounting Principles Board (1959–1973). GAAP assures financial statement users that the same rules are followed by all externally reporting companies.

Statements of Financial Accounting Concepts

The Statements of Financial Accounting Concepts (SFAC) provide a broad overview of accounting and serve as a foundation for future accounting standards. The seven statements are as follows:

No. 1 Objectives of Financial Reporting by Business Enterprises

No. 2 Qualitative Characteristics of Accounting Information

No. 3 Superceded by No. 6

No. 4 Objectives of Financial Reporting by Nonbusiness Organizations

No. 5 Recognition and Measurement in Financial Statements of Business Enterprises

No. 6 Elements of Financial Statements

No. 7 Using Cash Flow Information and Present Value in Accounting Measurements

Concepts Statement No. 1

According to Concepts Statement No. 1, financial reporting should provide information that is useful for making investment, credit, and similar decisions; that helps assess the amounts, timing, and uncertainty of cash flows; and that indicates the company's economic resources and claims to those resources. These objectives are accomplished by providing external users with a set of financial information known collectively as the financial statements.

Concepts Statement No. 2

Concepts Statement No. 2 discusses the characteristics that accounting information should possess. As shown in Exhibit 1.3, the FASB has prioritized these characteristics. Accordingly, the benefits received from accounting information must exceed the cost of providing the information. Accounting information must be understandable and useful for decision making. The information should be relevant—that is, it must make a difference in decision making—and it must be reliable—that is, decision makers can depend on the information.

Concepts Statement No. 4

Concepts Statement No. 4 discusses the objectives of reporting by nonbusiness organizations. The United Way, religious organizations, and other not-for-profit organizations fall in this category. While the content of this statement falls outside the realm of this text, note that the objectives of nonbusiness organizations are similar to those of business enterprises—to provide useful information to external decision makers.

Concepts Statement No. 5

Concepts Statement No. 5 addresses what information should be presented in financial statements and when that information should be presented. (We discuss financial statements in the next section.)

Concepts Statement No. 6

Concepts Statement No. 6 discusses the elements of financial statements. It defines 10 interrelated elements that measure the performance and financial position of a company. These elements are assets, liabilities, equity or net assets, investments, distributions, comprehensive income, revenues, expenses, gains, and losses. These basic elements are the foundation on which accounting and business are based.

Concepts Statement No. 7

Concepts Statement No. 7 is the most recent. It indicates how to measure the value of estimated future cash flows. Concepts Statement No. 7 provides the general principles that govern the use of present value computations that we discuss in Chapter 11.

International Accounting Standards

The International Accounting Standards Board assumed the responsibility for setting international accounting standards in 2001. **International Financial Reporting Standards (IFRS)** is a set of global accounting standards for the preparation and reporting of public company financial statements. As of 2008, 113 countries required or permitted IFRS for domestic companies filing on their respective stock exchanges. In 2008, the SEC announced that it was leaning toward mandating IFRS adoption by all companies publicly traded in the United States.

The SEC's move to switch to IFRS is driven by the growth in the global economy and capital market. Accounting systems that produce financial reports based on common reporting requirements will help the United States compete in the world economy two ways. First

EXHIBIT 1.3

A Hierarchy of Accounting Qualities

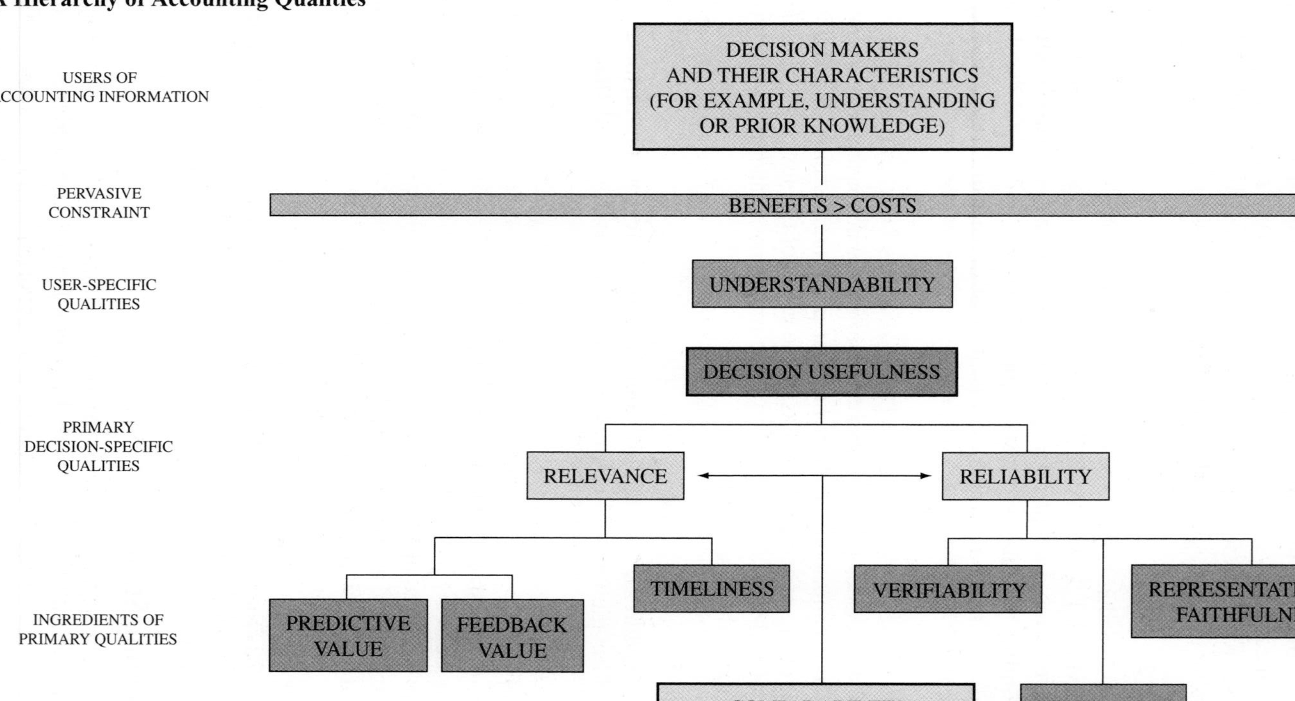

Source: Financial Accounting Standards Board, *Statements of Financial Accounting Concepts* (Stamford, CT: FASB, 1986), p. 44.

it will increase cross-border commerce, and it will help U.S. companies to raise capital abroad in addition to within the United States.

The Commission has laid out a road map for adopting IFRS and by 2011 will determine whether to proceed with rules requiring adoption of IFRS. If it does so, U.S. public companies would be required to file under IFRS beginning in fiscal 2014 by presenting three years of financial statements (discussed below); thus, the effective date of implementation for public companies would be 2012.[10] Some multinational companies like United Technologies, the aerospace manufacturer in Hartford, Connecticut, already use IFRS. Companies can volunteer to start submitting IFRS-based financial reports to the SEC by 2011, and many companies are expected to become early adopters.

The biggest difference between IFRS and U.S. GAAP is that IFRS is more principles-based and, thus, provides significantly fewer detailed rules than does GAAP. For example, IFRS currently has about 2,500 pages and fits into one, two-inch-thick book while U.S. GAAP is many volumes measuring over nine inches and consisting of about 25,000 pages.[11] In cases where specific guidance is not available under IFRS, disclosure is encouraged in footnotes and management discussion and analysis. The FASB and the IASB have made great strides to minimize the differences between U.S. GAAP and IFRS, but significant differences, most of which are beyond the scope of this text, do still exist. For example, IFRS does not allow Last-in, First-out for inventory costing which we will study in Chapter 10. For the latest information on the progress on IFRS, students are encouraged to go to **www.ifrs.com** and **www.sec.gov.**

Financial Statements

Today's publicly held companies prepare four basic financial statements, the (1) income statement, (2) statement of cash flows, (3) balance sheet or statement of financial position, and (4) statement of owners' (shareholders') equity and the accompanying notes. These financial statements are one of the company's primary means of communicating with its stakeholders. **Stakeholders** are those people and entities (both internal and external to the company) that have a stake, or interest, in the outcomes of the company. We briefly discuss the purpose and content of each of these statements next. Throughout this text, you will learn more about each of these statements; the last four chapters examine financial statements and financial statement analysis, in detail. The notes that accompany financial statements are crucial to understanding the content of the statements because they provide details not disclosed on the statements themselves. In addition, the report of the auditors (discussed below) should be reviewed. We use financial statements of Apple to illustrate these four financial statements. Please note that these statements are referred to as consolidated statements (for example, consolidated statement of cash flows). Apple is a corporation that owns or controls other corporations that are also separate legal entities but the financial reports of all these legal entities are consolidated and reported as one economic entity. GAAP requires consolidated financial statements to capture the economic substance of the parent or controlling corporation. Also note the date on the financial statements. This date reflects the end of the company's fiscal year (business year). (Apple's 2008 financial statements and accompanying notes from its SEC Form 10-K are located in the Appendix to the text.)

Income Statement

The **income statement** is designed to show the net income (total revenues less total expenses) of the company for a period of time (typically one year). In addition, it contains information concerning the types and sources of revenues and expenses. For example, the Appendix illustrates the income statement of Apple for the fiscal year ended September 27, 2008. Note that the statement is titled Consolidated Statement of Operations. This reflects the idea that operations generate profits. Companies also commonly refer to the income statement as the profit and loss statement or simply the P & L.

[10] www.sec.gov.

[11] www.ifrs.com.

Notice that the income statement (see Appendix p. 55 of the 10-K) begins with "*Net Sales*" (the amounts earned from providing products/services) and deducts expenses (the amounts incurred in an effort to generate revenues). Expenses include:

- *Cost of sales*—this is the cost of producing the products sold by Apple during the period.
- *Operating expenses*—this is the cost of selling products/services and other general expenses.
- *Provision for income tax*—this represents the cost of generating profits. Recall that a corporation is a legal entity. Thus corporations pay income taxes just as individuals do.

The net income of Apple for 2008 is $4,834 million (note that all of the statements are presented in millions). Apple provides information for the current period (left column) as well as the previous two periods. This allows users to compare current period results to those of prior periods without the need to obtain earlier financial statements. Apple increased its sales by $13,164 million from 2006 to 2008 ($32,479 − $19,315) while its net income increased $2,845 million in this same time period ($4,834 − $1,989). These data are important to financial statement users who compare current results to prior results and look for meaningful relationships in the financial statement numbers.

Statement of Owners' (Shareholders') Equity

The **statement of owners' equity** shows the changes that occurred in owners' equity during the period of time covered by the income statement. This statement is somewhat complicated so we defer a discussion of it until the second half of the text. Apple's statement, entitled Consolidated Statement of Changes in Shareholders' Equity, is shown in the Appendix (p. 56 of the 10-K.) Notice, for now, that this statement has a column entitled retained earnings. As we mentioned, retained earnings are earnings reinvested by Apple; thus, retained earnings represent all past net income not distributed to shareholders as dividends. Notice that at the end of 2008 Apple had a retained earnings balance of $13,845 million. This means that Apple's past net incomes have exceeded its past net losses and dividends by $13,845 million.

Statement of Cash Flows

The **statement of cash flows** (see Appendix p. 57 of the 10-K) shows the cash inflows and outflows of the company for the same period of time as the income statement. By classifying cash flows as operating, investing, or financing, companies show interested parties the types of activities that provided or used cash. Let's look at the statement of cash flows of Apple in the Appendix to the text. Notice that this statement has three main parts—cash flows from operating activities, cash flows from investing activities, and cash flows from financing activities. We discuss operating, investing, and financing activities in detail in Chapter 2. Remember the statement of cash flows shows cash paid and received; therefore, items such as *Purchases of short-term investments* and *Payments for acquisition of property, plant and equipment* denote cash paid. Likewise items such as *Proceeds from sales of investments* and *Proceeds from maturities of short-term investments* denote cash received during the period. In addition, companies are required to disclose the amount of cash paid for interest and income taxes. Apple discloses this amount, $1,267 million of cash paid for income taxes, at the bottom of the cash flow statement (note that no cash was paid for interest in 2008). Finally, note that net cash flows from operating activities is $9,596 million. This is not the same as "net income," $4,834 million. Why? Because revenues are recognized when earned, regardless of when they are received and expenses are recognized when incurred, regardless of when they are paid. *Thus net income is not the same as cash!*

Balance Sheet (Statement of Financial Position)

The **balance sheet** is designed to show the amounts of the company's assets, liabilities, and owners' equity at the end of the fiscal year. Recall that total assets must equal total liabilities plus total owners' equity; therefore, the balance sheet must balance (hence, the name). We examine Apple's consolidated balance sheet next (see Appendix p. 54 of the 10-K).

Assets

Notice that assets are divided into **current assets** (those likely to be used or consumed within one year) and **nonconcurrent (long-term) assets** (those assets that are likely to provide economic benefits for more than one year). The latter category includes *property, plant and equipment* (physical assets used in the business) as well as *goodwill and acquired intangible assets* (assets without physical substance that provide legal and other future economic benefits). Some items to note in the asset section:

- *Cash and cash equivalents*—this is the right to use money in the future. In note 1 (see Appendix p. 58 of the 10-K), Apple indicates that cash equivalents are highly liquid investments with maturities of three months or less.
- *Accounts receivable*—this represents the right to receive money from customers in the future. This right arises because Apple sells its products/services on account; that is, customers of Apple can receive products in one period and pay for them in a subsequent period. Note that accounts receivable, $2,422 million, is not the same as sales, $32,479 million, because sales represent all amounts earned during the period; that is, amounts received by and amounts still owed to Apple. Accounts receivable, on the other hand, represents the amounts still owed to Apple by customers at the end of the period.
- *Inventories*—this represents the right to use inventories (raw materials and finished goods) in the future.
- *Property, plant and equipment (net)*—this represents the long-term assets used by Apple. *Net* means that accumulated depreciation has been subtracted from the cost of the assets. (*Depreciation* is that portion of the cost of long-term assets that has been used to this point in time in an effort to generate revenue.)

Liabilities

Likewise liabilities are divided into **current liabilities** (those likely to be paid or otherwise discharged within one year) and **noncurrent (long-term) liabilities** (those obligations that extend beyond one year). Long-term liabilities include long-term borrowings from creditors. Some items to note in the liabilities section:

- *Accounts payable*—this represents the amounts owed to suppliers of goods/services. The accounts payable obligation arises because suppliers allow Apple to buy products/services on account. That is, Apple can receive products/services in one period and pay for them in a subsequent period. Note that accounts payable ($5,520 million) does not equal cost of sales ($21,334 million). Cost of sales represents the cost of the products/services that Apple provided to customers regardless of when these costs have been paid. Accounts payable represents the amounts still owed by Apple for goods/services received from suppliers.
- *Accrued expenses*—this represents amounts owed by Apple that are due within one year.

Owners' Equity

The shareholders' equity (owners' equity) section of the balance sheet indicates the contributions made to Apple by owners (shareholders) and earnings reinvested by Apple (retained earnings). Recall that when individuals (and other entities) purchase corporation stock, they become owners of the corporation. From the corporation's point of view, the owners have contributed capital for the company to use. Thus common stock represents initial contributions from owners. Of course, owners are free to sell their stock on organized exchanges such as the New York Stock Exchange. These subsequent sales by owners do not affect the balance sheet of the company. We discuss stock in more detail in the second part of the text.

Recall that corporations are legal entities. Their income belongs to the owners; however, corporations rarely return each year's income to the owners in the form of dividends. Usually the corporations retain a portion of the annual earnings for growth. The amount shown on the balance sheet as retained earnings represents the earnings reinvested to this point for growth.

Enhance Your Understanding

If, on September 27, 2008, Apple had sold all its assets and then paid all its obligations, would the shareholders have received the amount shown on the balance sheet as "total shareholders' equity"?

Answer: It is doubtful that Apple could have sold its assets for the exact amounts represented on the balance sheet. The balance sheet, in general, represents the amounts incurred to receive the asset, not the asset's current worth. Therefore shareholders could receive more or less than the amount shown as shareholders' equity on the balance sheet.

Report of the Independent Accountant (Auditor)

All publicly held companies must issue audited financial statements. The audit determines whether the company followed GAAP when preparing the financial statements and whether the assertions made by management are reliable.

In the wake of the Enron and WorldCom failures, the Sarbanes-Oxley Act of 2002 created the Public Company Accounting Oversight Board (PCAOB) and authorized it to establish auditing and attestation standards, to establish standards for quality and ethics, and to establish standards for independence for public accounting firms. Any accounting firm auditing publicly held companies is regulated by the PCAOB and must abide by its standards.

The audit of such companies is a complex process that includes an analysis of whether the company followed GAAP when preparing its financial statements. In addition, the auditing firm expresses an opinion on management's assessment of the effectiveness of internal controls (discussed in Chapter 2).

The Appendix (p. 88 of the 10-K) shows Apple's report of independent accountants. Let's examine this report. First, note the title. The responsible auditor must be independent from the company being audited. That is, the auditor cannot have any relationship with the client that might impair the auditor's impartiality. Second, the report states an opinion on whether the financial statements reflect the financial position of the company in accordance with GAAP.

> In our opinion, the consolidated financial statements . . . present fairly, in all material respects, the financial position of Apple, Inc. . . . in conformity with U.S. generally accepted accounting principles.

Third, the report outlines the responsibilities of management and the auditor. Management is responsible for the content of the financial statements, while the auditor is responsible for conducting an audit in conformance with generally accepted auditing standards (rules for conducting audits) and expressing an opinion on the financial statements.

> These consolidated financial statements are the responsibility of the Company's management. Our responsibility is to express an opinion on these consolidated financial statements based on our audits.

Finally, note, the last paragraph:

> We have also audited, in accordance with the standards of the Public Company Accounting Oversight Board (United States), Apple, Inc.'s internal control over financial reporting . . . .

Relationship of the Financial Statements

The financial statements, together, are designed to provide a picture of the performance of the company. These statements are related and interconnected as we discuss in future chapters. For example, on the income statement, net income is $4,834 million. This same amount is shown on the statement of changes in shareholders' equity as increase in retained earnings. The amount shown as the ending balance of retained earnings, $13,845 million,

EXHIBIT 1.4
Primary Components of Financial Statements

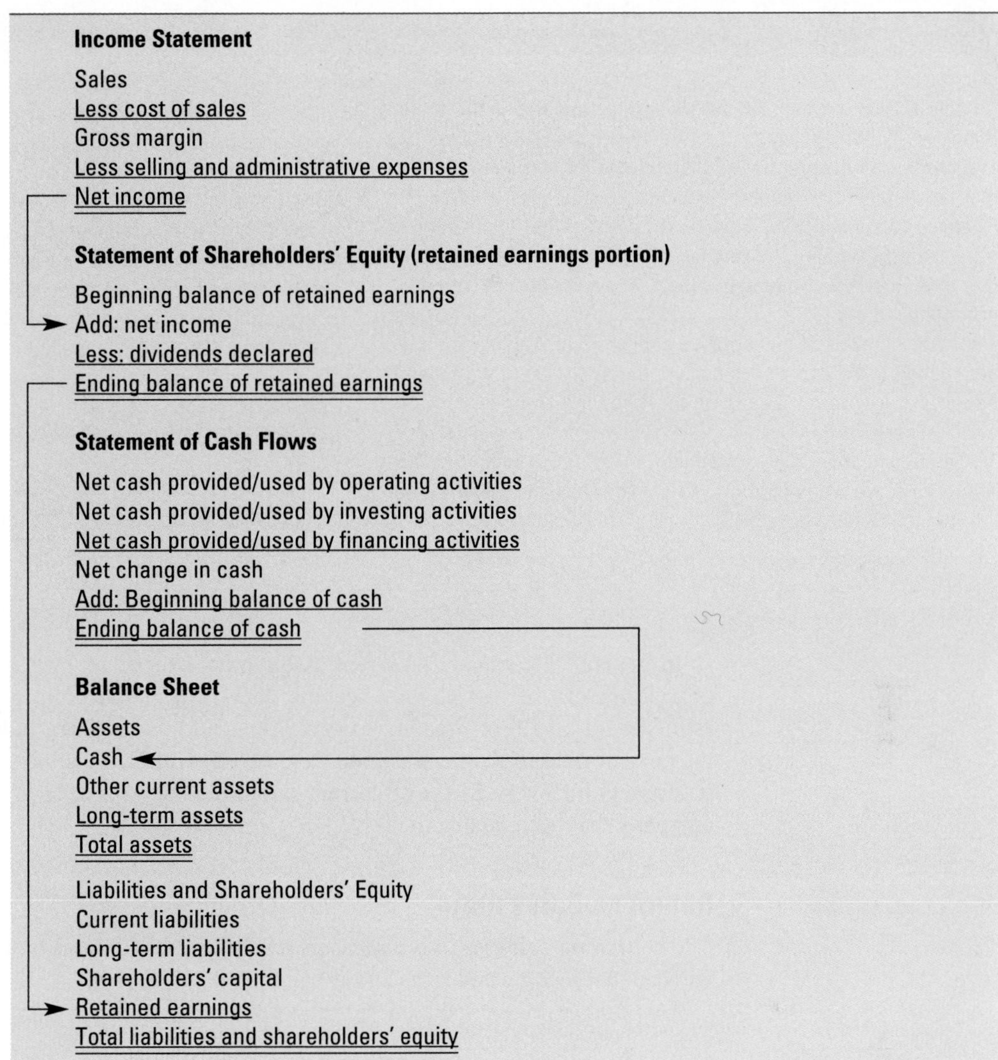

on the statement of changes in shareholders' equity is also shown on the balance sheet in the owners' equity section. Finally, the amount shown as the ending balance of cash, \$11,875 million, on the statement of cash flows is also shown on the balance sheet in the asset section. The basic components of financial statements and their interrelationships are illustrated in Exhibit 1.4. Note how amounts from one statement are tied to another.

As we learned, the financial statements are related. So, too, are items within and between statements. Financial statement users such as stockholders and creditors often calculate ratios to measure relationships between financial statement items. Next we look at three such ratios that examine company liquidity, profitability, and solvency. Throughout this text we look at additional ratios. When evaluating a company using ratios, always compare the company to others in the same industry during the same time period. In addition, compare the current period ratios to the company's ratios in the past.

Income Statement
Sales
Less cost of sales
Gross margin
Less selling and administrative expenses
Net income
Statement of Shareholders' Equity (retained earnings portion)
Beginning balance of retained earnings
Add: net income
Less: dividends declared
Ending balance of retained earnings
Statement of Cash Flows
Net cash provided/used by operating activities
Net cash provided/used by investing activities
Net cash provided/used by financing activities
Net change in cash
Add: Beginning balance of cash
Ending balance of cash
Balance Sheet
Assets
Cash
Other current assets
Long-term assets
Total assets
Liabilities and Shareholders' Equity
Current liabilities
Long-term liabilities
Shareholders' capital
Retained earnings
Total liabilities and shareholders' equity

Current Ratio

The **current ratio** is a measure of company liquidity. It indicates the relationship between current assets and current liabilities and is calculated as:

$$\frac{\text{Current assets}}{\text{Current liabilities}}$$

OF INTEREST Codification

On July 1, 2009, accounting and reporting standards in the United States were dramatically restructured when the FASB Accounting Standards Codification became the single official source of authoritative generally accepted accounting principles (GAAP). The Financial Accounting Standard Board created the Codification to organize and simplify the tangled web of accounting standards that existed before. No longer is there a laundry list of accounting pronouncements (APB Opinions, EITFs, ARBs, FASs and SOPs) with varying levels of authoritative support. The Codification does not change GAAP but makes it much easier for users to research specific accounting issues online knowing their finding are authoritative GAAP.

The Codification is organized into about 90 accounting topics. The topics are organized into four broad areas: Presentation (guide on financial statement presentation) Financial Statement Accounts, Broad Transactions, and Industries (guidance for specific industries). In turn each topic is divided into subtopics, sections, subsections, paragraphs, and subparagraphs. Also included in the Codification is relevant SEC guidance that follows the same topical structure. The new system reduces the time and effort to research and resolve an accounting issue and also reduces the risk of a company using an accounting treatment that is not in compliance with GAAP. In addition, the Codification is a real-time system so the most recent guidance will be incorporated quickly into the database. The Codification will also facilitate the convergence of U.S. GAAP and international accounting standards.

In general, a company's current assets must exceed its current liabilities so that current obligations can be met as they become due. Thus a good rule of thumb is that the current ratio should be 1.0 or greater; however, this rule varies from industry to industry. In 2008 the current ratio of Apple was 2.46 ($34,690/$14,092). This means Apple had $2.46 of current assets for every $1.00 of current liabilities and was able to pay the obligations of the company that became due in 2009.

Return on Sales Ratio

The **return on sales ratio** is a measure of company profitability. It indicates the relationship between net income and sales and is calculated as:

$$\frac{\text{Net income}}{\text{Sales}}$$

Return on sales indicates whether the company is generating profits from its sales activity. A low return on sales could indicate poor selling price decisions or relatively high expenses. Apple's return on sales ratio is 14.88 percent ($4,834/$32,479 × 100) in 2008. This means that Apple generated a 14.88 percent return (profit) per dollar of sales ($0.15 of every dollar of sales is profit).

Debt-to-Equity Ratio

The **debt-to-equity ratio** is a measure of the company's solvency and its ability to meet its short- and long-term obligations. This ratio measures the relative proportions of financing from debt (borrowing) and financing from shareholders (owners). In general, the more debt a company has, the more profits it must generate to pay the interest; thus, the greater the risk for shareholders. The debt-to-equity ratio is calculated as:

$$\frac{\text{Total debt}}{\text{Total shareholders' equity}}$$

Debt-to-equity ratios vary dramatically across industries, so you must be careful when evaluating a company's debt-to-equity position. A debt-to-equity ratio of 1 to 1 means that half of the company's assets are financed with debt and half with shareholders' equity. Apple's debt-to-equity ratio for 2008 was 0.88 to 1 ($18,542/$21,030). This means that Apple had $0.88 of (current and long-term) debt for every $1.00 of shareholders' equity.

XBRL Filing

In 2008, the SEC unanimously voted to propose public companies to begin filing financial statements using eXtensible Business Reporting Language (XBRL). **XBRL** is an interactive data format that uses computer "tags" to identify individual items in a company's financial statements so that those items may be easily searched on the Internet and downloaded into spreadsheets and databases for intercompany comparisons by investors, analysts, and others. According to the consortium's Web site, the idea behind XBRL is simple, "instead of treating financial information as a block of text—as in a standard Internet page or a printed document—it provides an identifying tag for each individual item of data. This is computer readable. For example, company net profit has its own unique tag."[12] When adopted, the first interactive data under mandatory reporting (a voluntary program has been in place since 2005) would be available in 2009 for the largest public companies reporting under U.S. GAAP. The remaining public companies using U.S. GAAP would provide XBRL disclosures within the next two years and those U.S. companies using IFRS would provide XBRL disclosures for fiscal periods ending later 2010.[13]

Summary

Business has evolved as technology has changed and as the population has become more mobile. Accounting likewise has developed over time as the needs of its users, both internal and external to the organization, have changed. The basic concepts of accounting have evolved over time as businesses, investors, and managers have become more sophisticated. Business today is characterized as global in nature with rapidly changing technology. Accounting today, as in earlier times, is an integral part of business, providing the information infrastructure that permits business to achieve its objectives.

- The five basic functions within business are marketing, human resources, production and operations, finance, and accounting and information systems.
- The four concepts crucial to accounting are the business entity, going concern, periodicity, and monetary unit concepts.
- The three business organizational structures are sole proprietorships, partnerships, and corporations.
- The three types of businesses are service, merchandising, and manufacturing firms.
- Business and accounting are regulated. The Financial Accounting Standards Board has been given the authority by the Securities and Exchange Commission to develop accounting standards.
- The basic financial statements are (1) the income statement, (2) the statement of cash flows, (3) the balance sheet, and (4) the statement of owners' equity.

Key Terms

Accounting The information infrastructure of the firm/economy that permits it to achieve its objectives, *8*
Accounting and information systems function The function that is responsible for providing useful information to the other functional areas and external parties, *3*
Accounting equation Assets equal liabilities plus owners' equity, *11*
Accrual basis of accounting A system in which income is measured as the difference between the sales (revenues) earned and the expenses incurred during the period, regardless of when cash is paid or received, *13*

[12] www.xbrl.org.
[13] www.sec.gov.

Assets The rights to use resources that have expected future economic benefits, *9*
Balance sheet The financial statement designed to show the ending amounts of the company's assets, liabilities, and owners' equity, *20*
Business The exchange of goods or services on an arm's-length basis that results in mutual benefit for both parties involved, *3*
Business entity concept The concept that requires an accounting system to reflect only information about economic events that pertain to a particular entity, *10*
Cash basis accounting A system in which income is measured as the difference between the cash received from customers and the cash paid to employees and other suppliers of goods and services, *12*
Corporation A business entity that is legally separate and distinct from its owners, *12*
Current asset An asset likely to be used or consumed within one year, *21*
Current liability A liability likely to be paid or otherwise discharged within one year, *21*
Current ratio A measure of company liquidity; the relationship between current assets and current liabilities, *23*
Debt-to-equity ratio A measure of company solvency and its ability to meet its long-term obligations, *24*
Double taxation A situation in which the profits earned by the corporation are taxed twice—once at the business level and again at the owner level if the profits are distributed as dividends, *15*
Expense An amount incurred from using resources or services in the effort to generate revenue, *13*
Finance function The function that is responsible for managing the financial resources of the business, *3*
Financial Accounting Standards Board (FASB) The group the SEC holds responsible for determining accounting standards in the United States, *16*
Financial statements Statements prepared to communicate the results of business activities to interested users, *11*
Generally accepted accounting principles (GAAP) The set of reporting standards applicable to all U.S. companies that issue financial reports for external users, *16*
Going concern concept The concept that assumes that, absent any information to the contrary, the business entity will continue into the foreseeable future, *10*
Human resources function The function that is responsible for ensuring that capable employees are given opportunities to succeed in a safe work environment, *3*
Income statement The financial statement designed to show the net income of the company for a period of time, *19*
International Financial Reporting Standards (IFRS) The set of global reporting standards for the preparation of public financial statements, *17*
Just-in-time (JIT) A philosophy that stipulates products should be received by customers just as they are needed and in the quantities needed, *5*
Liability The obligation to transfer economic resources to suppliers of goods and services at some point in the future, *10*
Limited liability A situation in which the money invested in a corporation is at risk but investors' personal possessions are not at risk if the business fails, *12*
Limited liability company (LLC) Eliminates the impact of unlimited liability for all the owners, does not limit the number of owners as required by the S corporation, and does not limit participation in the management of the firm like limited partnerships, *16*
Limited liability partnership (LLP) A partnership in which the individual partners are liable only for their own actions and the actions of those individuals under their control, *16*
Limited partnership A partnership composed of one or more general partners and one or more limited partners; only the general partners' personal possessions are at risk if the business should fail, *16*
Long-term asset See noncurrent asset, *21*
Long-term liability See noncurrent liability, *21*
Manufacturing firm A business organized to convert raw materials into finished goods, *12*

Marketing function The function of business that determines the wants and needs of consumers and devises a system for distributing the goods and services customers demand, *3*
Merchandising company A business that obtains and distributes goods to customers, *9*
Monetary unit concept The concept that asserts money is the common measurement unit of economic activity, *11*
Mutual agency A situation whereby each partner has the power to act for all, and legally obligate, other partners, *10*
Net assets Assets minus liabilities, *10*
Net income A company's total revenues less its total expenses for a period of time, *13*
Noncurrent asset An asset that is likely to provide economic benefits for more than one year, *21*
Noncurrent liability An obligation that extends beyond one year, *21*
Owners' equity Represents the claims on the business to transfer the residual interest (net assets of the business) to the owners, *10*
Partnership A business owned by two or more individuals whose personal possessions are at risk if the business fails, *9*
Partnership agreement An agreement that outlines the rights and obligations of each partner, *10*
Periodicity concept The concept that requires that the success or failure of the business be determined at regular intervals, *12*
Product life cycle The time span from the conception of the product until it is no longer demanded by consumers, *7*
Production and operations function The function that is responsible for planning, organizing, directing, and controlling the operations of the business, *3*
Return on sales ratio A measure of company profitability; the relationship between net income and sales, *24*
Revenue An amount earned from rendering services or transferring resources to customers, *13*
S corporation A small business corporation owned by no more than 75 individuals; its profits are taxed at the individual level rather than the corporate level, *16*
Service firm A business that exists to provide services such as loaning money, finding investors, and other services for which it charges fees, *9*
Sole proprietorship A business owned by one person whose personal possessions are at risk if the business fails, *9*
Stakeholders Those people and entities (both internal and external to the company) that have a stake, or interest, in the outcomes of the company, *19*
Statement of cash flows The financial statement designed to show the cash inflows and cash outflows for the period of time covered by the income statement, *20*
Statement of owners' equity The financial statement designed to show the changes that occurred in owners' equity during the period of time covered by the income statement, *20*
Unlimited liability A situation where once the assets of a business are exhausted, the personal assets of the owners can be used to satisfy liabilities of the business, *10*
XBRL (eXtensible Business Reporting Language) An interactive data format that uses computer tags to identify financial statement items, *25*

Questions

1. What is a business and why does it exist?
2. What is accounting and why does it exist?
3. Explain the different functions within business.
4. What is JIT?
5. Explain the differences among sole proprietorships, partnerships, and corporations.
6. Explain the differences among service, merchandising, and manufacturing firms.
7. Explain the role of accounting in ancient times.
8. Explain the role of accounting in the 11th through 15th centuries in Italy.
9. What is an asset? Give an example.

10. What is a liability? Give an example.
11. What are net assets?
12. What is owners' equity?
13. Why is a partnership agreement important?
14. Explain the business entity concept and how it affects accounting.
15. Explain the going concern concept and how it affects accounting.
16. What is the fundamental accounting equation?
17. Who was Pacioli and why is he important?
18. What is the purpose of financial statements?
19. Explain the monetary unit concept.
20. Explain the periodicity concept.
21. How is income measured using the cash basis of accounting?
22. What is limited liability? Is it desirable? Why or why not?
23. How is income measured using the accrual basis of accounting?
24. How did the 1929 stock market crash affect accounting and business?
25. What are generally accepted accounting principles? Who is responsible for them?
26. Explain the purpose of the FASB concepts statements.
27. What are International Financial Reporting Standards?
28. Explain the product life cycle and give an example.
29. Why did limited partnerships, S corporations, limited liability companies, and limited liability partnerships arise?
30. What are the four basic financial statements and what is the purpose of each?
31. What is the purpose of the PCAOB?
32. Explain the purpose of the current ratio, the return on sales ratio, and the debt-to-equity ratio.

Exercises

E1.1 LO 3 Classify each of the following businesses by type (service, merchandising, and/or manufacturing):

A. MasterCard
B. KPMG, LLP (accounting firm)
C. Frontier Airlines
D. International Business Machines Corp. (IBM)
E. Accenture (consulting firm)
F. Microsoft Corp.
G. Sears, Inc.
H. Target Stores

LO 3 **E1.2** Classify each of the following businesses by type (service, merchandising, and/or manufacturing):

A. H&R Block, Inc.
B. Walt Disney Company
C. Ford Motor Co.
D. eBay
E. PepsiCo, Inc.
F. Dell, Inc.
G. Wal-Mart Stores, Inc.
H. Amazon.com

LO 3 **E1.3** Describe companies from your hometown that have the following ownership structures: (1) sole proprietorship, (2) partnership, and (3) corporation.

LO 3 **E1.4** List four well-known companies that have the following ownership structures: (1) partnership and (2) corporation.

LO 2 **E1.5** Aullman Company has $3 million in assets and $1.2 million in liabilities. What is its owners' equity?

LO 2 **E1.6** Swaby Company has $800,000 in liabilities and $100,000 of owners' equity. What are its total assets?

LO 4 **E1.7** Refer to E1.6. What is the debt-to-equity ratio for Swaby Company?

LO 2 **E1.8** Hoppal Company has $5 million in assets and $3.2 million in liabilities. What are its net assets?

LO 4 **E1.9** Refer to E1.8. What is the debt-to-equity ratio of Hoppal Company?

LO 1 **E1.10** Noe Company has hundreds of owners located throughout the country. Once a month, Noe sends financial statements to its owners. These statements report the results of operations as measured in dollars. What basic accounting concepts does this practice illustrate?

LO 1 **E1.11** Misty Briggs, owner of Briggs Machine Shop, maintains two checking accounts—one for personal affairs and one for the business. What basic accounting concept does this arrangement illustrate?

LO 2 **E1.12** Henman Company made sales of $350,000 to customers, of which it received $200,000 in cash from customers. Henman incurred $210,000 in operating expenses, of which it paid $160,000 in cash. What was Henman's accrual basis income?

LO 2 **E1.13** Collins Company made sales totaling $500,000 but received only $350,000 in cash from sales to customers. It paid $400,000 in cash for operating expenses but incurred only $200,000 of expenses this period. What was Collins Company's cash basis income (loss)?

LO 2 **E1.14** Classify each of the following as assets or liabilities for Shenefield Company:

A. Shenefield Company owes its suppliers $50,000.
B. Shenefield Company's customers owe it $40,000.
C. Shenefield Company has $100,000 in its checking account.
D. Shenefield Company owes the bank $20,000 on a five-year loan.
E. Shenefield Company owns a building costing $500,000.
F. Shenefield Company's employees have worked all week but have not been paid the $5,000 owed to them.
G. Shenefield Company has developed a new process that is protected by a patent costing $16,000.

LO 4 **E1.15** Refer to E1.14. What is the current ratio of Shenefield Company?

LO 2 **E1.16** Classify each of the following as assets, liabilities, or owners' equity for Kiren Company:

A. Kiren Company's owners have contributed $100,000 to the company.
B. Kiren Company owes $10,000 to the bank on a three-year note payable.
C. Kiren Company bought and has not yet sold $50,000 of inventory.
D. Kiren Company owns a piece of land costing $175,000 for a future building site.
E. Kiren Company owes the Internal Revenue Service $2,000 for taxes.
F. Kiren Company has office and other supplies costing $1,500.
G. Kiren Company owes the utility company $1,250 for services received last month.

LO 4 **E1.17** Refer to E1.16. What is the current ratio of Kiren Company?

LO 2 **E1.18** Classify the following as revenues or expenses assuming Bowen Company uses the accrual basis of accounting:

A. Bowen Company provides $4,500 in services to a client and sends the client a bill.
B. Bowen Company provides $1,500 in services to a client who pays in cash.
C. Bowen Company receives a bill for $200 for utilities from the power company.
D. Bowen Company pays $250 in cash for this week's advertising.

E. Bowen Company's employees work all week earning $4,000. Bowen pays its employees monthly.
F. Bowen Company provides $8,000 in services to a client. The client has no money so he gives Bowen some computer equipment instead.

LO 4 **E1.19** Refer to E1.18 and calculate the return on sales ratio for Bowen Company.

LO 1 **E1.20** Interview a marketing, management, or finance instructor at your school to determine the accounting information used by individuals with these particular backgrounds. Describe what you discover.

LO 2 **E1.21** Prepare a list of your personal assets and liabilities. What is your net asset position?

LO 3 **E1.22** Assume you and your friends are going to start a business. Should you organize as a sole proprietorship, partnership, or corporation? Why?

Problems

P1.1 LO 2 Classify each of the following items as affecting assets or liabilities and revenues or expenses for Madsen Company. Each item affects both an asset or liability and a revenue or an expense. Assume Madsen uses the accrual basis of determining income.

A. Madsen Company's employees have worked 500 hours, earning $7,500, and have not been paid.
B. Madsen Company provided $20,000 of service to customers who promised to pay for the services next month.
C. Madsen Company used $1,000 of office supplies.

LO 2 **P1.2** Refer to P1.1. If these were the only items affecting the company during the period, what would Madsen's net income be?

LO 2 **P1.3** Classify each of the following events as affecting assets, liabilities, or owners' equity (contribution by owners or distributions to owners) for Buckingham Company. Note that these events impact more than one element. Assume Buckingham uses the accrual basis of income determination.

A. Buckingham Company borrows $200,000 from the bank.
B. Buckingham Company buys a building for $125,000 in cash.
C. One of the owners of Buckingham Company contributes $15,000 in computer equipment to the company.
D. Buckingham Company distributes a $5,000 cash dividend to the owners.

LO 2 **P1.4** Refer to P1.3. If these were the only items affecting the company during the period, what would its assets be?

LO 2 **P1.5** Merritt, Inc., has revealed the following items:

Amounts owed by Merritt, Inc., to employees, $3,000
Amounts owed by Merritt, Inc., to suppliers, $50,000
Amounts owed to Merritt, Inc., by customers, $75,000
Building owned by Merritt, Inc., $500,000
Cash in the bank, $40,000
Raw materials owned by Merritt, Inc., $10,000

Required:
A. What are Merritt's total assets?
B. What are Merritt's total liabilities?
C. What is Merritt, Inc.'s, owners' equity amount?

LO 4 **P1.6** For each of the following items **(A–L)**, indicate on which financial statement you would expect to find it and briefly explain why. For one item, two answers will be needed.

1. Income statement
2. Statement of cash flows
3. Balance sheet

_______ A. Service fees earned
_______ B. Accumulated depreciation on equipment
_______ C. Cost of sales
_______ D. Cash balance at the end of the period
_______ E. Accounts receivable
_______ F. Accounts payable
_______ G. Inventory
_______ H. Cash received from customers
_______ I. Depreciation expense
_______ J. Equipment
_______ K. Cash paid for equipment
_______ L. Retained earnings

LO 4 **P1.7** Refer to P1.6. For any item on the balance sheet determine whether it is a current asset, a long-term (noncurrent asset), a current liability, a long-term (noncurrent) liability, or an owners' equity item.

LO 4 **P1.8** For each of the following items **(A–L),** indicate on which financial statement you would expect to find it and briefly explain why.

1. Income statement
2. Statement of cash flows
3. Balance sheet

_______ A. Cash paid to suppliers
_______ B. Provision for income taxes (income tax expense)
_______ C. Sales, both cash and on account
_______ D. Dividends paid during the period
_______ E. Buildings
_______ F. Net income
_______ G. Cash received from sale of building
_______ H. Common stock
_______ I. Operating expenses
_______ J. Note payable, due in 5 years
_______ K. Patents
_______ L. Retained earnings

LO 4 **P1.9** Refer to P1.8. For any item on the balance sheet determine whether it is a current asset, a long-term (noncurrent) asset, a current liability, a long-term (noncurrent) liability, or an owners' equity item.

LO 2 **P1.10** Farwell Company has the following information available from its most recent fiscal year. Use the relevant information to determine the net income (loss) for the period.

A. Cash sales, $40,000
B. Employee salary expense, $30,000
C. Common stock issued for cash, $100,000
D. Sales on account, $58,000
E. Utility expense, $1,500
F. Long-term loan received, $50,000
G. Interest earned on investments, $100
H. Property tax expense, $10,000
I. Inventory purchased for resale, $120,000
J. Cost of inventory sold, $102,000
K. Insurance purchased for the next year, $4,800
L. Rent expense, $12,000

LO 1 **P1.11** Determine which of the basic accounting concepts apply to each of these situations.

1. Business entity
2. Going concern

3. Monetary unit
4. Periodicity

A. A company trades a delivery truck for computer equipment. The truck is valued at $5,000.
B. A company has 10,000 shareholders. Subsequently 2,000 shareholders sell their shares to others. The company's financial statements are not affected.
C. A company continues in business even though its founder died.
D. A company prepares annual financial statements.
E. A major supplier for the company declares bankruptcy. The company's financial statements are not affected.

Cases

C1.1 LO 2 LO 3 LO 4 Select a company you are interested in and obtain a copy of its most recent annual report. Keep this report for use throughout this book. Based on the information in this report, answer the following questions:

A. What type of business is this company (service, merchandising, or manufacturing)?
B. Does the company conduct business internationally?
C. What are the company's primary products and/or services?
D. Who is the chief executive officer of the company?
E. Who is the auditor for the company?
F. Did the company have positive or negative income during the period?
G. What are the total assets at the end of the most recent period?
H. What are the total liabilities at the end of the most recent period?
I. What are the cash flows from operating activities for the most recent period?
J. What are the current, return on sales, and debt-to-equity ratios for the most recent period?

LO 3 **C1.2** Consider the businesses in the town where your college is located. Select one that interests you and prepare written responses to the following questions:

A. What type of business is this company (service, merchandising, or manufacturing)?
B. Does the company conduct business internationally?
C. What are the company's primary products and/or services?
D. What is the organizational structure of this company (sole proprietorship, partnership, or corporation)?
E. Is the company independently owned or is it part of a larger company?

Critical Thinking

CT1.1 LO 3 Critically evaluate these statements: "The business of business is to do business. Businesses should not be involved in social issues. It is the role of government to control pollution and unemployment. It is the role of business to make money for its owners."

LO 1 **CT1.2** The JIT philosophy stipulates that products (inventory) should arrive just as needed. Discuss the risks for a business that adopts this philosophy.

LO 2 **CT1.3** Although employees are usually considered to be, and are often referred to as, a company's most valued asset, they do not appear as assets on the balance sheet. Prepare an argument supporting or refuting this practice.

LO 1 **CT1.4** Compare and contrast the stock market crash of 1929 to the market crash of 2008.

Ethical Challenges

EC1.1 LO 1 In 2008 Congress voted to bail out many financial institutions that faced bankruptcy due to bad loans. During the same year, it refused to bail out the "Big 3" automakers which also faced bankruptcy citing "bad management" as the cause for the automakers' troubles. Discuss this issue from the point of view of the businesses requesting the federal loans.

LO 1 **EC1.2** A student was interviewing for a full-time position with a firm. The on-campus interview went very well and the student was invited to visit the offices which were located some distance away. The firm bought the student's airline ticket, made and paid for the hotel reservations, and planned the office visit for the following month. Two days before the office visit the student called and told the firm that s/he could not come to the office visit because s/he had accepted a job with another firm. Discuss this issue from the point of view of the student and the firm.

Computer Applications

CA1.1 (LO 3, LO 4) Search the Internet for information about Intel. Find its company history and a description of its products. Download Intel's most recent financial statements. Write a brief report on your findings.

CA1.2 (LO 3, LO 4) Search the Internet for information about IBM. Find its company history and a description of its products. Download IBM's most recent financial statements. Write a brief report on your findings.

CA1.3 (LO 1) Search the Internet for information about careers in accounting. Try the Web sites for the AICPA (American Institute of Certified Public Accountants), the IMA (Institute of Management Accountants), and the IIA (Institute of Internal Auditors) to begin. Write a brief report on your findings.

CA1.4 (LO 1) Search the Internet for information about the WorldCom bankruptcy in 2002. Write a brief report on your findings.

Visit the text Online Learning Center at **www.mhhe.com/ainsworth6e** for additional problem material that accompanies this chapter.

CHAPTER TWO

2 Business Processes and Accounting Information

Learning Objectives

LO 1 Explain the management cycle and the four basic business processes.

LO 2 Describe the balanced scorecard approach and its four perspectives.

LO 3 Discuss what internal controls are and why they are important.

LO 4 Perform a two-column bank reconciliation.

In Chapter 1 we discovered how businesses are organized and how they report their activities on four basic financial statements. In this chapter we describe the management cycle and the four primary business processes and the activities undertaken in these processes. Then we look at the internal controls necessary to safeguard assets and ensure the accuracy of the information provided by the company's accounting system. In Chapter 3 we consider the analysis and control of operating activities.

Management Cycle

Businesses make and implement decisions in the three phases depicted in Exhibit 2.1. In the planning phase, management determines its objectives and the means of achieving those objectives. The performing phase occurs when management implements the plans by actually doing the planned activities. Finally, in the evaluating phase, management compares the results of performing activities with the plan to determine whether it achieved the company's objectives. Regardless of their ownership structure or the economic market in which they operate, businesses have overlapping management cycles that follow this sequence of planning, performing, and evaluating decisions.

Planning Phase

Planning is an essential part of a successful business. Without plans, a business might not be able to produce goods or customers might not receive the goods or services they want.

EXHIBIT 2.1
The Management Cycle

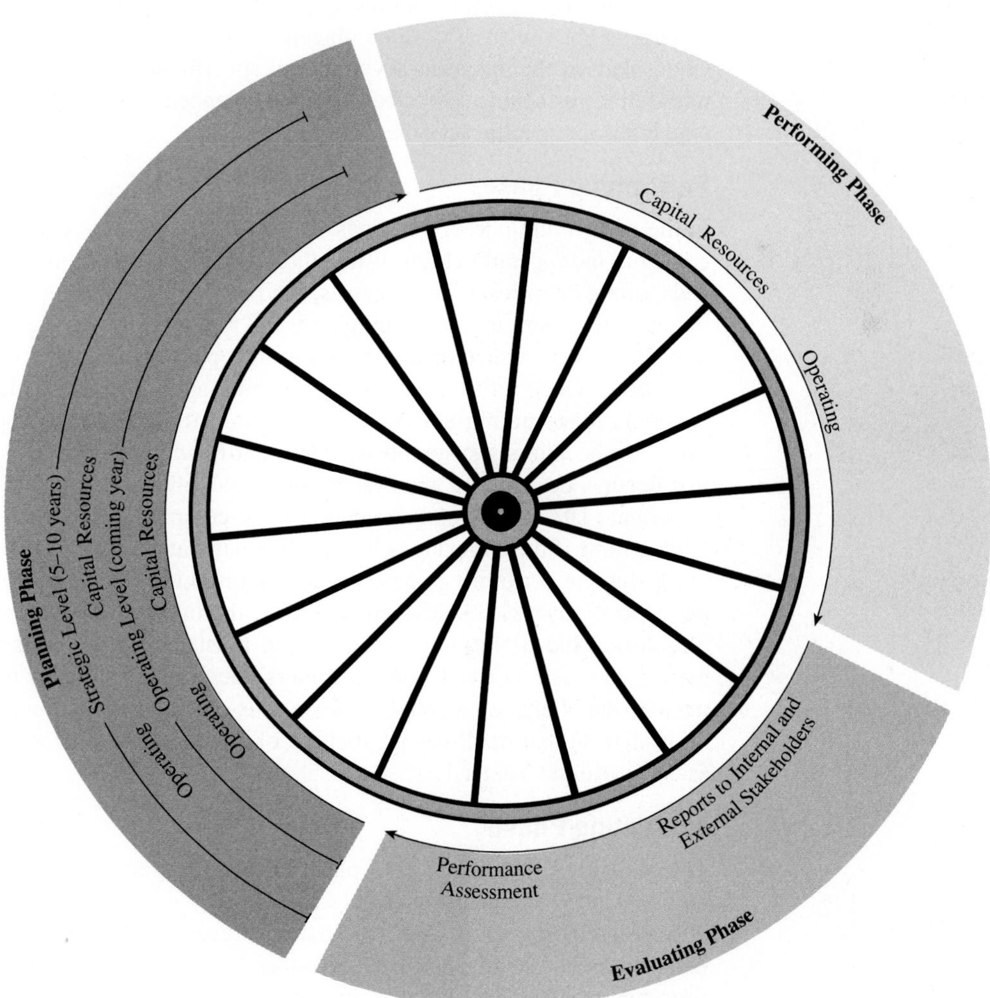

Within the planning phase there are two levels of planning: strategic and operating. Strategic plans set the broad course for the business based on its goals—for example, what products to sell or services to offer, whether to build facilities and make what they sell, or to buy products for resale from someone else, and whether to use debt or equity financing. Strategic plans cover a relatively long period of 5 to 10 years, while operating-level plans used to accomplish the strategic objectives usually apply to only a year at a time.

Successful management of a business requires both strategic and operating planning for the overall strategy of the business and for the shorter time periods, including day-to-day functioning of the business. Strategic plans become a framework within which management formulates its operating plans to guide shorter-term decisions. Strategic plans identify the sales level the firm expects in the future (operating processes) and the plant capacity needed to meet consumers' needs (capital resources process).

At the operating level, plans must be compatible with the strategic plans of the firm. For example, projected sales for the coming period cannot exceed the actual productive capacity of the firm plus the inventory the business has on hand. Productive capacity is determined during strategic planning when management chooses the size of the production plant. However, if the strategic plan calls for building a new plant during the year to meet increased demand for the product, the firm also plans for these investing activities at the operating level. At the operating level, the business plans the construction activities and when its increased capacity will be available. Similarly, at the strategic level the firm may plan to finance the new plant with debt, but at the operating level the firm must anticipate possible sources of debt financing (where it can borrow from) as well as the terms of the debt agreement.

To make planning manageable, businesses should begin by setting objectives that are measurable and specific. Setting objectives that are too vague, such as to make a lot of money, is not very useful. Such objectives do not serve as guides for what actions to take. Good plans at the operating level lay out specific actions that must be taken in the near future. Later this chapter describes how the balanced scorecard approach provides measurable objectives for specific actions.

Performing Phase

In the performing phase, a business actually completes its planned business processes (discussed in more detail below). While the planning phase begins with operating processes and ends with capital resource processes, the performance phase reverses the sequence. Financing activities, both debt and equity, are the first as the company raises the necessary capital to operate. Next, the company invests in the operating infrastructure necessary for the firm's operations. Once a firm has sufficient capital and its operating infrastructure is in place, it conducts its operating activities. Throughout the performance phase of the management cycle, the accounting system is used to identify and collect data and to analyze the processes that occur. For example, the system monitors collections from customers to see if any customers are late in making payments. Or the company might monitor its financing activities to determine if the company is finding financing at acceptable interest rates.

During the performing phase the accounting information system plays a key role in internal control (discussed below) by recording the impact of events on the company. For example, during the performing phase, Apple must record the dollar amount of sales revenue earned, the cash received from customers, the purchases of raw materials, and the payments made to suppliers, to name a few items. It is crucial that accounting records are accurate and up-to-date so that the financial position of the company is properly reported to stakeholders as discussed in Chapter 1.

Evaluating Phase

The evaluating phase is the final phase of the management cycle and provides information to internal and external users about the company's performance. Evaluating operations involves comparing actual operating activity results with planned results and with other standards to assess performance. Differences between planned and actual activities can stem from two sources: the plan was good but the activities were not performed well, or the plan

FAST FACT Dow Jones Industrial Average

What is the Dow Jones Industrial Average (DJIA)? The DJIA is the most commonly quoted market indicator, yet many people have no idea what it is or how it is calculated. The DJIA, commonly referred to simply as the Dow, is the oldest measure of whether the stock market is generally moving up or down. Originally it was a simple arithmetic average of 12 stocks: add up the prices and divide by 12. Today the DJIA is a weighted average of 30 stocks, often referred to as blue chips. These 30 stocks and their respective weights in the DJIA are shown below:

Company	Weight
IBM	7.70
ExxonMobil	7.20
Chevron	6.75
McDonald's	5.62
Procter & Gamble	5.54
Johnson & Johnson	5.35
3M	5.22
Wal-Mart	5.04
United Technologies	4.84
Caterpillar	4.14
Coca-Cola	4.05
Boeing	3.99
Hewlett-Packard	3.25
Verizon Communications	3.05
JPMorgan Chase	2.76
Merck	2.73
AT&T	2.59
Kraft Foods	2.41
DuPont	2.31
Home Depot	2.13
Disney	2.11
Microsoft	1.79
American Express	1.70
Pfizer	1.61
General Electric	1.50
Intel	1.34
Bank of America	1.26
Alcoa	1.07
Citigroup	0.63
General Motors	0.32

was not very good and the activities were done well. These two sources have different implications for planning future activities. If the plan was bad, there is a need to examine the assumptions and bases for the plan in order to improve them and thus provide for better predictions. On the other hand, if the plan was good, then management and employees need to identify any performance problems they observed or experienced to make the necessary changes for improvement.

Although operating activities are constantly monitored during the performing phase, events are not formally summarized and communicated until the evaluating phase. The nature of the communicated information varies depending on the level of detail a person needs at his or her level within the organization.

The information provided by the accounting system is used in the evaluating phase for two important business functions: to evaluate the company's processes and to plan for the next iteration of the management cycle. During the evaluating phase the company assesses its performance against the plan and provides a basis for planning the next year's activities. It is necessary to examine activities that did not turn out as planned to determine why they did not work. In addition, those activities that worked better than planned are examined to see why they worked so well. Next we examine the four basic business processes.

Business Processes

A **business process** is a collection of activities that takes one or more kinds of input and creates an output that is of value to the customer.[1] Because business processes involve more than one functional area within the business, many companies utilize cross-functional teams

[1] M. Hammer and J. Champy, *Reengineering the Corporation: A Manifesto for Business Revolution* (New York: HarperBusiness, 1993).

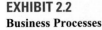

EXHIBIT 2.2
Business Processes

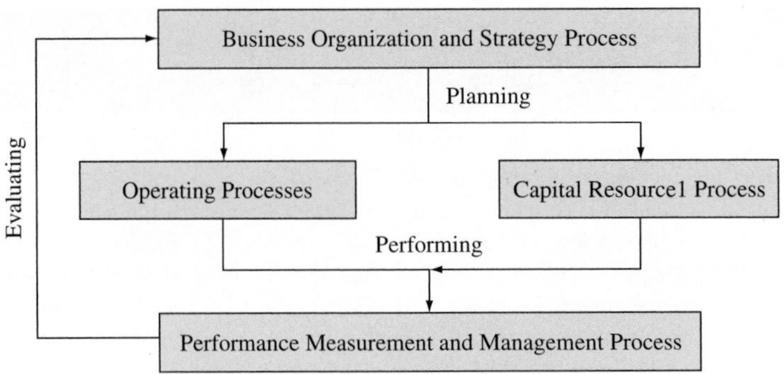

to solve business problems. Businesses define their processes differently, but four processes are common. These processes are (1) business organization and strategy, (2) operating, (3) capital resources, and (4) performance measurement and management.

The business organization and strategy process concerns the fit between a company's internal and external environment. The operating process is divided into two or three subprocesses depending on whether the company is engaged in manufacturing activities. The three subprocesses are (1) marketing/sales/collection/customer service, (2) purchasing/human resources/payment, and (3) conversion. The marketing/sales/collection/customer service subprocess relates to the revenue-generating activities of the business. The purchasing/human resources/payment subprocess involves acquiring and paying for goods and services, including employees, to generate revenue. The conversion subprocess concerns the manufacturing process that converts inputs to finished products. The capital resources process relates to raising and investing capital to create long-term value. Finally, the performance measurement and management process is concerned with measuring and analyzing the results of the other processes to ensure that the company's strategy is achieved.

This chapter focuses on the last process—performance measurement—to set the stage for the planning and performing chapters to come. We also revisit the performance measurement process at the end of the text as an evaluating process. We look at the details of the operating processes in Chapter 3 and the remainder of the first half of this text. The business organization and strategy process is examined in both halves of the text while the capital resources process is examined in more detail in the latter half as it primarily concerns long-term financing and investing activities.

Exhibit 2.2 indicates the relationship among these four basic business processes. Notice that the organization and strategy process determines the firm's plans of action. The operating and capital resources processes indicate how these plans are carried out. Finally, the performance measurement and management process provides information for management to determine how well the plans were met. Thus the business processes mirror the management cycle—planning, performing, and evaluating.

Business Organization and Strategy Process

The organization and strategy process determines the plans of action for the company. **Organizational strategy** is a company's long-term plan for using its resources—physical and human. An organization's strategy as well as its organizational structure must fit its external environment. The external environment can be considered a continuum with certainty at one end and uncertainty at the other end. A certain environment is characterized as one where the products and customers are established, the competition is known, and cost control is a primary concern. Companies operating in a certain environment tend to focus inward. That is, they tend to treat the external environment as given and concentrate on ways to improve operating efficiency. These companies typically have a **mechanistic organizational structure** in which activities and employees are arranged by functions (marketing, human resources, production/operations, finance, and accounting). Control is maintained at the top of the hierarchy and decision making is centralized. Companies in this environment tend to adopt an **efficiency strategy** focusing primarily on the reduction or containment of costs, improvements in productivity, and penetration of their products and services in the market due to their low cost. For example, a manufacturer of nuts and bolts for electrical applications, follows an efficiency strategy because it is in a relatively certain external environment.

On the other hand, an uncertain environment is characterized as one having rapidly changing products and/or customers, with incoming and outgoing competitors making creativity a primary concern. Companies operating in this environment tend to focus outward. That is, they concentrate on customer satisfaction and new product development. These companies typically have an **organic organizational structure** in which activities and people are arranged in cross-functional teams—that is, a team consists of employees from marketing, human resources, production/operations, finance, and accounting. Decision making is typically decentralized throughout the organization. Companies in this environment tend to adopt a **flexibility strategy** that adapts to changing market conditions by developing new products/services, markets, and technologies. Electronics companies tend to follow flexibility strategies in part due to the environment. They strive to provide the latest in computer and digital products to customers and focus heavily on customer satisfaction.

Operating processes/ activities
The profit-making activities of the company.

Operating Processes

Operating processes/activities are the profit-making activities of the business. These activities are planned as part of the business organization and strategy process and controlled as part of the performance measurement and management process. Recall from Chapter 1 that a business's net income (profit) results when revenues earned exceed expenses incurred for a given period. Operating processes include those processes that generate revenues—the marketing/sales/collection/customer service process as well as those processes that result in expenses—the purchasing/human resources/payment process. Finally, for manufacturing companies, activities of the conversion process are also operating because they result in products available for the company to sell in the marketing/sales/collection/customer service process by using resources from the purchasing/human resources/payment process. Exhibit 2.3 shows the interrelationship of these three operating subprocesses. Notice that the resources provided by the purchasing/human resources/payment process are inputs to the conversion process. The outputs of the conversion process are products that are sold as part of the marketing/sales/collection/customer service process. Also notice that these processes are circular. The marketing/sales/collection/customer service process provides resources for the purchasing/human resources/payment process and the whole cycle starts again. We examine these processes in detail in Chapter 3.

Investing processes/ activities
The activities involving purchasing and selling of long-term assets.

Capital Resources Process

The capital resources process involves the investing and financing activities of the business. **Investing processes/activities** involve the purchase and sale of long-term assets and other major

EXHIBIT 2.3
Operating Processes

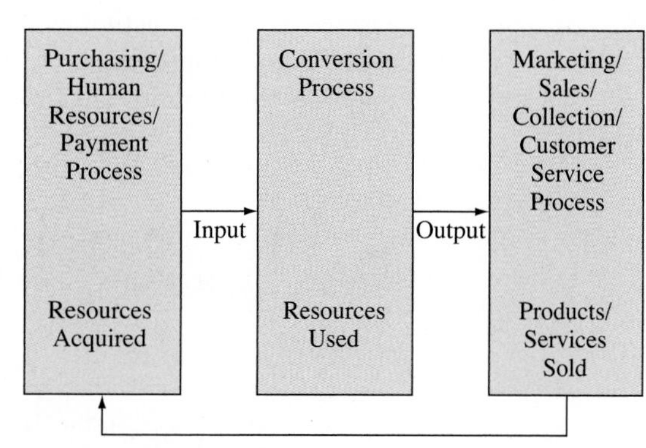

items used to achieve the business's strategy. For example, purchasing equipment and buildings that a company expects to use over a period of years is an investing process. However, actually using the buildings and equipment to provide a product or service to customers is an operating process. **Financing processes/activities** involve obtaining the cash or other resources to pay for investments in long-term assets, to repay monies borrowed from creditors, and to provide a return to owners (shareholders). Financing decisions determine the means of paying for the business's strategic plans. We examine investing and financing activities, in detail, in the latter half of this text.

Financing processes/activities
The activities involving obtaining and repaying cash and other capital resources.

Performance Measurement and Management Process

A company's performance measurement and management process must also match its strategy. Since the mid-1990s many companies have adopted a performance measurement and management process known as the balanced scorecard approach. The **balanced scorecard approach** translates a company's strategy (from the business organization and strategy process) into measurable objectives (for the operating and capital resources processes). This approach has four perspectives: (1) financial, (2) internal, (3) customer, and (4) learning and growth. The balanced scorecard is a holistic approach to planning and evaluating business success. That is, the balanced scorecard approach plans and evaluates business success using financial *and other measures* of success. The balanced scorecard approach provides various measures of success that, in turn, are used to evaluate performance and plan for the future. This is important because as we will see these other measures impact the financial performance of the company in future periods. Thus the balanced scorecard approach is a forward-looking planning and evaluating tool.

Balanced Scorecard Approach

Exhibit 2.4 illustrates the balanced scorecard approach. Notice that the four perspectives are interrelated. For example, as part of the customer perspective Apple might monitor customer satisfaction with the quality of its iPhones. While customer satisfaction in this period may not have a direct impact on profit, in the long run if customers are not happy with Apple's products and services, its sales and profits will decrease. As part of the internal process perspective Apple might monitor employee satisfaction. Again, employee satisfaction in the current period may not have a direct impact on profit. But in the long run, if employees are not happy it may impact productivity, which, in turn, impacts profits. Next we examine financial and nonfinancial measures for each of the four perspectives of the balanced scorecard.

Financial perspective
The part of the balanced scorecard concerned with the financial health of the company.

Financial Perspective

Financial measures of performance are critical to the survival of the company. A company must create profits to remain attractive to investors and creditors, so companies use a variety of financial measures to control activities and measure results of the operating and capital resources processes. For example, the ratios discussed in Chapter 1 (current ratio, return on sales ratio, and debt-to-equity ratio) are financial measures companies can use for planning

EXHIBIT 2.4
Balanced Scorecard

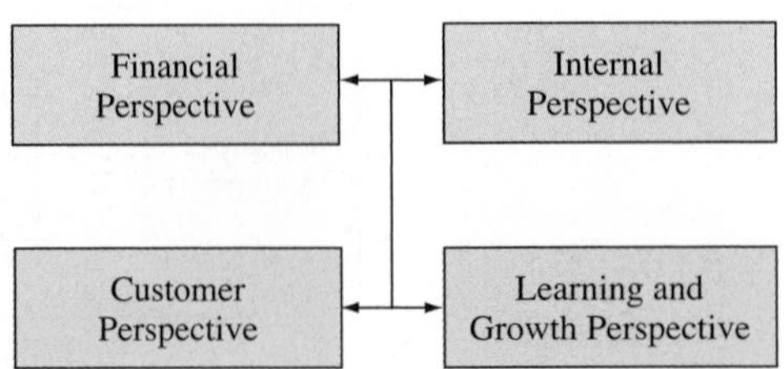

and control. In addition, companies assess the growth in stock prices as an indication of financial performance. Internally, a widely used financial measurement is return on investment. The **return on investment ratio** is the return generated per dollar of total investment. Often it is calculated by dividing the profit of a project, a division, or the whole company by the average amount of assets devoted to that project, division, or company.[2] Therefore the return on investment ratio for a company is

$$\frac{\text{Net income}}{\text{Average total assets}}$$

For example, by using Apple's financial statements in the Appendix to the text we can calculate the return on investment for this firm in 2008. (See the Consolidated Statement of Operations and the Consolidated Balance Sheet.) First, find the net income (on the Statement of Operations). It is $4,834 million. Next, find the ending balance of total assets for 2008 and 2007 (on the Consolidated Balance Sheet). The total assets are $39,572 million and $25,347 million, respectively. The return on investment ratio, in millions, is

$$\$4{,}834/[(\$39{,}572 + \$25{,}347)/2] = \$4{,}834/\$32{,}459.5 = .1489 \text{ or } 14.89\%$$

This means that Apple generated an asset return of 14.89 percent after taxes. Or put another way, Apple earned $14.89 for every $100 investment in assets. Is that good? We don't really know. Remember, when evaluating results using ratios we should always compare our company to others in the industry and to the past. In addition to the ratios introduced in Chapter 1 and the return on investment ratio, companies often calculate the quick ratio, the return on owners' equity ratio, and the gross margin ratio as measures of financial performance.

The **quick ratio,** like the current ratio, is a measure of a company's ability to meet its current obligations as they become due. The quick ratio is a more reliable measurement of liquidity because it considers only cash and assets that are quickly converted to cash as "quick" assets. Inventory and other current assets, such as prepaid insurance, may not be liquid enough to meet short-term obligations. The quick ratio is:

$$\frac{\text{Cash + Short-term investments + Receivables}}{\text{Current liabilities}}$$

The quick ratio of Apple for 2008 (using the Consolidated Balance Sheet) in millions is

$$(\$11{,}875 + \$12{,}615 + \$2{,}422)/\$14{,}092 = \$26{,}912/\$14{,}092 = 1.91$$

This means Apple has $1.91 of liquid assets for every $1.00 of current liabilities. Or put another way, Apple's quick assets are 191 percent of its current liabilities. Is this good? Again, we don't really know. We should compare this ratio to the quick ratio of others in the industry as well as to Apple in the past. We discuss this process in detail in Chapter 20.

The **return on owners' equity ratio** measures the return generated per dollar of owners' equity. This ratio is often used to assess whether the company is generating a sufficient return for its owners (shareholders). The return on owners' equity ratio is

$$\frac{\text{Net income}}{\text{Average owners' equity}}$$

The firm's return on owners' equity ratio for 2008 (see the Consolidated Statement of Operations and the Consolidated Balance Sheet) in millions is

$$\$4{,}834/[(\$21{,}030 + \$14{,}532)/2] = \$4{,}834/\$17{,}781 = .2719 \text{ or } 27.19\%$$

This means Apple has generated a return of 27.19 percent of every dollar of owners' equity. Or Apple earned $27.19 for every $100 invested by owners (shareholders). Whether this is sufficient depends on the needs of shareholders, other comparable companies, and the past.

[2] Later chapters discuss other ways of calculating return on investment.

The **gross margin ratio** measures the gross profit of the company's products. It is a very important ratio because it examines the relationship between sales and cost of goods sold. The gross margin is calculated as sales less cost of goods sold and represents the dollar amount that is available to cover the rest of the company's operating expenses. The gross margin ratio is

$$\frac{\text{Gross margin}}{\text{Sales}}$$

Apple's gross margin for 2008 (see the Consolidated Statement of Operations in the Appendix to this text) in millions is $11,145. Therefore the gross margin ratio for 2008 is

$$\$11{,}145/\$32{,}479 = .3431 \text{ or } 34.31\%$$

This means that for every dollar of sales, Apple's gross margin is $0.34. Or, put another way, for every dollar of sales, $0.66 is the cost of the product sold and $0.34 is available to cover the other expenses and generate net income. Remember, you must compare this ratio to past gross margin ratios for Apple and to gross margin ratios for the firm's competitors before making any conclusions.

Companies use these ratios to plan activities as well as to evaluate the results of these activities. For example, Apple could plan to increase its gross margin to 40 percent in 2009. Or it could decide that a return on owners' equity of 30 percent would be desirable in 2009. In addition to ratios, other measurements of the financial perspective include net income (income statement); cash flows from operating, financing, and investing activities (statement of cash flows); and financial position (balance sheet).

Internal perspective
The part of the balanced scorecard concerned with the internal operations of the company.

Internal Perspective

The internal perspective looks at the internal operations of the company and, therefore, is used primarily to plan and control operating processes. It seeks to find measures of improvement in both the way work is done and the manner in which people are utilized. Two areas for analysis in the internal perspective are time and quality.

Time Measurements

Companies often monitor time and classify it as value-added or nonvalue-added. **Value-added time** is time spent on activities that add value to the company's products/services or processes. For example, the time spent producing iPhones is value-added time. **Nonvalue-added time** is time spent on activities that do not add value to the company's products/services or processes. For example, the time spent moving raw materials such as circuits from the storeroom to the factory is nonvalue-added time. The process would be more efficient if circuits did not require storage and, subsequently, have to be moved. Thus time spent storing and moving finished products is nonvalue-added time. Likewise any time products spend waiting for available equipment or people (queue time) is nonvalue-added. Apple continually seeks to reduce its nonvalue-added activities because it realizes that these activities add cost but do not add value.

Customer response time is the amount of time that elapses between a customer placing and receiving an order. Typically a customer order proceeds through a number of steps. As we will see, customer response time often includes nonvalue-added time. For a simple example, consider Apple's competitor, Dell Computer, that manufactures products only after they have been ordered by customers. First, the customer places the order. Second, the order is assigned to production. Third, the order is produced and stored until it is shipped. Dell customer response time then is the total of the following:

- *Order response time*—the time that elapses between when the customer places an order and the order is assigned to production.
- *Processing time*—the time it takes to actually manufacture the order.
- *Queue time*—any time during the process when the order is waiting for processing.

- *Storing time*—the time that elapses between when the order is finished processing and when it is shipped.
- *Shipping time*—the time it takes to deliver the order to the customer.

Think about these times from the customer's viewpoint. *The only time that adds value to the product is processing time.* All the other time is nonvalue-added. Thus companies must monitor customer response time to ensure that resources are not wasted on nonvalue-added activities.

In addition to monitoring customer response time, companies calculate activity ratios to plan and monitor the time required for important internal operations. The three most common activity ratios are the accounts receivable turnover (and days in the collection cycle), the inventory turnover (and days in the selling cycle), and the accounts payable turnover (and days in the payment cycle). We discuss each of these, in turn, below.

The **accounts receivable turnover** and resulting measure of days in the collection cycle measures the speed at which the company is receiving cash from its customers. It is very important because while the company wants to grant credit to worthy customers, it does expect to receive cash from these customers in a timely fashion. We discuss this in more detail in Chapter 3. The accounts receivable turnover and days in the collection cycle are:

$$\frac{\text{Sales}}{\text{Average accounts receivable}} = \text{Turnover} \qquad \frac{365}{\text{Turnover}} = \text{Days}$$

For 2008, Apple's accounts receivable turnover and days in the collection cycle are determined as:

$$\frac{\$32{,}479}{(\$2{,}422 + \$1{,}637)/2} = 16.00 \qquad \frac{365}{16.00} = 22.81 \text{ days}$$

This means that it takes, on average, 23 days for Apple to collect its accounts receivables from customers. Apple would compare this ratio to the credit terms it sets for customers. For example, if it expects customers to pay in 30 days, then this ratio is quicker than expectation. In addition, Apple should compare this result to the past, to the internal perspective goals, and to ratios of the competition before determining whether the result is good or bad.

The **inventory turnover** and resulting days in the selling cycle measures the speed at which the company sells its inventory. These measures are important because the company must ensure that inventory does not sit idle—it must be delivered to customers in a timely manner so that cash can be received by the company. We discuss the selling cycle in more detail in Chapter 3. The inventory turnover and days in the selling cycle are:

$$\frac{\text{Cost of sales}}{\text{Average inventory}} = \text{Turnover} \qquad \frac{365}{\text{Turnover}} = \text{Days}$$

Apple's 2008 inventory turnover and days in the selling cycle are determined as follows:

$$\frac{\$21{,}334}{(\$509 + \$346)/2} = 49.90 \qquad \frac{365}{49.90} = 7.31$$

This means that it takes Apple, on average, seven days to sell its inventory! Inventory turnover ratios should be analyzed with regard to the type of inventory held and whether the company is practicing JIT. For example, a grocer should have a higher inventory turnover than an appliance retailer. An inventory turnover of seven days would indicate that Apple is practicing JIT. Again, Apple should compare this ratio to its internal perspective goals and objectives, its past performance, and its competitors before deciding whether seven days is adequate.

The **accounts payable turnover** and days in the payment period measure the speed at which the company pays its obligations to suppliers. These measures are important because the company must maintain good relationships with suppliers and paying obligations when they are due is crucial to building supplier relationships. We will discuss the payment process in more detail in Chapter 3. The accounts payable turnover and days in the payment period are calculated as:

$$\frac{\text{Cost of sales}}{\text{Average accounts payable}} = \text{Turnover} \qquad \frac{365}{\text{Turnover}} = \text{Days}$$

We use "cost of sales," also known as "cost of goods sold," as a surrogate for "purchases." If the company, internally, has purchase records, it would use "purchases" in the numerator rather than "cost of sales," since it is the amount of the purchases that create obligations to suppliers. For 2008, Apple's accounts payable turnover and days in the payment period are 4.07 and 90, respectively, as shown below:

$$\frac{\$21{,}334}{(\$5{,}520 + \$4{,}970)/2} = 4.07 \qquad \frac{365}{4.07} = 89.74$$

This means that it takes Apple, on average, 90 days to pay its suppliers. The accounts payable turnover should be analyzed by looking at the credit terms granted by suppliers. If suppliers expect payment in 30 days, then Apple is a little slow in meeting its supplier obligations. On the other hand, if payment is expected in 90 days, Apple is paying its bills, on average, when they are due. And, of course, Apple must compare these results to the balanced scorecard goals, the past, and the competition.

Quality Measurements

Another important internal perspective concerns quality and the costs incurred to have quality in processes and products. Typically companies monitor four types of quality costs: (1) prevention, (2) appraisal, (3) internal failure, and (4) external failure. Companies voluntarily incur prevention and appraisal costs while internal and external failure costs are incurred involuntarily.

- **Prevention cost**—the cost incurred to prevent mistakes from occurring, such as the cost incurred to engineer products for easy assembly or the cost incurred to train customer-support personnel so that customers are given correct information.
- **Appraisal cost**—the cost incurred to detect mistakes as early in the process as possible, such as the cost incurred to monitor customer phone calls to ensure that employees are pleasant and informative, or the cost incurred to inspect incoming materials to ensure quality before the materials are used in production.
- **Internal failure cost**—the cost incurred to fix mistakes before the mistakes become known to the customer, such as the cost incurred to rework defective products.
- **External failure cost**—the cost incurred to fix mistakes after the mistakes become known to the customer, such as the cost incurred to settle product liability lawsuits, warranty costs, and the costs associated with customer ill will.

Note that customer ill will includes the cost of losing the customer, the potential to lose future customers, and the damage to the company's reputation. For example, recall the pet food crisis of 2007. Wal-Mart, Iams, and many other companies sold pet food containing contaminated wheat gluten from China that resulted in kidney failure and death for a number of pets. Because these external failure costs are potentially devastating to companies, they strive to increase prevention and appraisal costs in an effort to reduce those costs. Companies often monitor quality costs by determining the cost as a percentage of sales. For example, rather than stating that prevention quality cost is $500,000, a company might say prevention quality costs are 10 percent of sales. By stating quality as a percentage of sales the company is implying that quality costs should be evaluated in relationship to the level of sales. That is, knowing the absolute dollars spent on quality may not be meaningful if one does not know the amount of sales generated.

Note that quality refers to both products and processes. As we have seen, in today's market quality products are a necessary but not the only condition for success. Today's companies must also provide excellent customer support.

The final dimension of the internal perspective concerns employees. Companies realize that without qualified, motivated employees, success is fleeting. Thus companies often monitor employee satisfaction, employee retention, and employee productivity. Some common measurement tools include employee satisfaction surveys (anonymous), exit interviews, absenteeism and tardiness counts, and revenue generated per employee.

Customer perspective
The part of the balanced scorecard concerned with the customer base of the company.

Customer Perspective

The customer perspective relates to monitoring the company's largest unrecorded asset—its customer base. Companies develop strategies and measurable objectives that increase the value of their customer base by increasing market share (the percentage of total sales in a market that a particular company generates), acquiring more or larger customers, and increasing customer satisfaction and loyalty. To increase market share, the company must add value by providing products/services that customers demand at prices they are willing to pay. To increase customer satisfaction, the company must add value by providing quality in a timely manner. Thus the relationship between the internal and customer perspectives is clear.

Companies monitor the customer perspective by tracking the number of new customers acquired, the amount of profit generated by new customers, and the growth in market share. Customer satisfaction is measured through customer surveys and firms monitor the number of customer complaints, as well as the time and effort required to resolve them. In addition, companies often monitor phone calls between customer-service representatives and customers to ensure prompt, courteous service. Finally since it is usually less expensive to keep a current customer than it is to obtain a new customer, companies measure customer retention. Common measurements include the number of customers lost, customer loyalty (determined through surveys), customer growth (increase in revenue generated by a particular customer), and changes in customer buying habits.

Amazon.com is an excellent example of a company that monitors customers closely. It establishes customer profiles based on buying habits. For example, if you buy a book from Amazon.com by John Grisham, you might receive an e-mail message when Grisham's latest novel is available. Or you might receive an e-mail suggesting that customers who have purchased Grisham novels in the past have also purchased novels by Sue Grafton. This way Amazon.com is hoping to generate additional sales and maintain contact with you, the customer.

Learning and growth perspective
The part of the balanced scorecard concerned with the company's ability to ensure its future.

Learning and Growth Perspective

The final perspective of the balanced scorecard is the learning and growth perspective. The learning and growth perspective concerns the company's ability to take actions now to ensure its future. The company's future, in part, depends on its current expenditures for research and development, employee growth, and information systems.

To monitor research and development, companies look at the amount of research and development dollars spent, the number of new products introduced, and the time it takes to get new products to the market. Recall that product life cycles are shorter now so getting products to the market sooner is important for long-term survival. To monitor employee growth companies look at the dollars spent on employee education and training, the number of employees receiving training/education, and the number of employees promoted or recognized for achievement.

Finally companies must consider their information systems. As mentioned in Chapter 1, e-business has dramatically changed the way companies interact with their customers and their suppliers. A company must constantly monitor its information systems to ensure compatibility with suppliers and customers and to keep up with changes in technology.

Now that you understand the four basic business processes, we examine the issue of internal control. Internal control is crucial to ensure that the company's strategies are properly carried out and that information is generated to evaluate and manage performance.

Internal Control

As part of effectively running a business, management should ensure that the business has a good system of internal controls. An **internal control system** is the set of policies and procedures designed to meet three objectives: (1) promote operational efficiency, (2) ensure the accuracy of accounting information, and (3) encourage management and employee compliance with applicable laws and regulations.

While having a system of internal controls is a good business practice, it is also a legal requirement. The Foreign Corrupt Practices Act requires that all publicly owned companies maintain accurate and detailed accounting records and a documented system of internal controls. In addition, as mentioned previously, the Sarbanes-Oxley Act requires publicly held companies to have their internal control systems audited by CPAs. In a simplified sense, the procedures employed in internal control systems include (1) requiring proper authorization for transactions, (2) separating incompatible duties, (3) maintaining adequate documents and records, (4) physically controlling assets and information, and (5) providing independent checks on performance.

Requiring Proper Authorization

Every business has objectives that serve as a framework for its daily activities—for example, the level of profit it wants to attain or the level of quality in its products. The means of achieving these objectives are part of the company's policies and are determined during the business organization and strategy process.

One way to be sure that employees follow company policies is to ensure that the persons responsible for certain activities have the authority to enforce the policies associated with those activities. By giving an employee the authority to carry out a particular policy, the company can hold that person accountable for its implementation. In this way the company can pinpoint the person responsible when a problem occurs. For example, Apple might assign the authority for determining which customers can pay on account to one person in the credit function. Then, if a problem arises, Apple knows exactly who is responsible for that policy function.

For major transactions involving capital resource processes, the authority to approve transactions often rests at the highest level of the organization. In a corporation, the authority to engage in major transactions, such as issuing stock, rests with the board of directors. While owners and boards of directors remain ultimately responsible for all business policies and related actions, they often delegate responsibility and authority for many day-to-day transactions to lower management and operating personnel.

Separation of Duties

When one employee performs certain combinations of jobs, it sometimes is too easy and inviting to violate company policies. For example, assume that an employee is responsible for not only recording the cash received in the accounting records, but also depositing cash in the bank account. This combination of duties makes it very easy for the employee to record less cash than was received in the accounting records, to deposit the recorded lower amount, and to keep the difference. Dividing duties that have the potential for one person to violate company policies among two or more employees is called separation (or segregation) of incompatible duties.

To determine which employee duties are incompatible, divide any business transaction into four phases: (1) approval, (2) execution, (3) custody, and (4) recording. In the approval phase, an employee with authority agrees to allow another employee to initiate a transaction. The execution phase involves a person who has approval to legally commit the business to a transaction, such as when the individual makes an agreement to purchase goods or services with an outside party. Custody includes actually possessing the asset, such as cash or inventory items. The recording phase requires entering transactions into the accounting system.

A good system of internal controls prevents employees from performing more than one phase of any business transaction. Note that in small companies there usually are not enough employees to segregate all the incompatible duties. In such cases, other control procedures can ensure that the effect of segregation occurs, such as forcing employees to take mandatory vacations, which allows an opportunity for checks on the vacationing employee's work. Another effective control in small businesses is the usual presence of the owners at the workplace, which makes it easier to detect employee wrongdoing.

Maintaining Adequate Documentation

Recording transactions is an important control procedure because employees know that the actions they take on behalf of the company are recorded in the company's records. In addition, properly recording transactions allows managers to trace responsibility for transactions so that they can maintain employee accountability. Therefore, a good internal control system includes documents that capture all the necessary information about a transaction in the most efficient and effective way possible. At a minimum, necessary information for a purchase, for example, includes a description of the product as well as the price, date, parties involved, and terms of the transaction.

Whether the documents are paper and manually completed or images of documents on a computer screen, they should make it easy for employees to provide the required information and ensure that everything necessary is included. One important control procedure is prenumbering paper documents so that all numbers in a sequence must be accounted for. Therefore, an employee could not use a prenumbered document without potentially being held accountable for it. Prenumbering documents and limiting access to authorized employees helps ensure that documents are not misused as part of unauthorized transactions.

Physically Controlling Assets and Information

Part of the role of an internal control system is to safeguard both human and physical resources. For human resources, safeguarding means enforcing policies and regulations regarding workplace safety. Companies protect physical assets and accounting records by limiting access to them by unauthorized personnel. Limiting physical access includes, for example, using cash registers that produce a written receipt and record of transactions, locking storerooms, and using fireproof safes. Even fences around company buildings and storage lots for company equipment are examples of physical safeguards of assets. Passwords and firewalls are protections for electronic data. In addition, companies must safeguard company data and information systems against viruses and denial-of-service attacks as discussed in Chapter 1.

Providing Independent Checks on Performance

Companies strengthen their internal control systems by providing independent checks on the performance of employees; this includes having another employee who was not involved in the original activity check the work. For example, when an independent person compares the amount recorded as cash receipts in the accounting records with the records of the bank, the comparison helps to ensure that all the cash the company received was deposited in the bank. Independent checks not only guard against intentional theft and fraud but also reveal cases where employees perform certain procedures incorrectly. The independence of the person providing the check is critical because people checking their own work have no reason to report any problems or wrongdoing.

For publicly held companies an annual audit is required as an independent check on performance. As you know, the audit is conducted by a licensed certified public accounting firm and is designed to determine whether the company followed generally accepted accounting principles (GAAP) when preparing its financial statements. As part of the audit, the CPA also analyzes the company's internal control system.

Enhance Your Understanding

An employee takes a prenumbered document and uses it to make a personal purchase. Will prenumbering documents prevent this misappropriation? Why? What type of internal control might prevent this from happening?

Answer: No, prenumbering will not stop the theft of the document. Prenumbering may deter the theft if employees know that prenumbering will allow the company to detect that the document is missing. Physically securing the documents to limit access is the best protection against document theft.

Applying Internal Control to Protect Cash

Security over cash is critical because possession implies ownership. It is impossible to determine who owns cash by simply looking, and there is no realistic way of tracking ownership of cash outside the banking system. Thus controls over cash receipts and disbursements are an important part of a company's internal control system.

Cash Receipts

Activities in the operating process are the principal source of cash receipts. The procedures to protect cash receipts include physically safeguarding the cash, separating the duties of those with custody of cash from those who keep the accounting records, assigning duties so that cash is deposited and recorded as soon as possible after receipt, and having independent checks on cash balances and cash handling procedures.

Many of the sales transactions at stores like Wal-Mart are cash sales. The cash register used to hold cash and checks is an example of physically protecting assets. For each sales transaction, one copy of a sales slip is given to the customer. Sales slips (or sales receipts) provide two control procedures: adequate documentation of the transaction and an opportunity for an independent check by the customer.

You have probably seen stores with this sign at the cash register: "If you are not offered a receipt, your purchase is free." This is done because only rarely are clerks adequately supervised to ensure that all the cash they receive is placed in the register. Such a policy allows owners and managers who cannot observe whether the money is put in the cash register to safeguard the cash received. To give the customer a receipt, the clerk must record the transaction in the register. Someone independent from such transactions can compare the amount of money in the register at the end of a shift with the recorded sales. This serves as a check to ensure that receipts (cash, checks, and charge slips) equal the amount of sales. Another good control is to deposit the receipts from the register into the bank each day. Securing the cash in this way results in keeping only a minimum amount of cash at risk in the register.

Cash (checks) received from credit sales or in advance of sales requires different controls.[3] These cash receipts arrive in the company's mailroom, along with part of the customer invoice known as a remittance advice, which indicates the amount paid, or remitted, by the customer. The mail clerk should separate the checks from the remittance advice and make a list of both the checks received and who sent them. A person who does not have access to the accounting system should deposit the cash into the bank as soon as possible. Someone without access to the cash itself should record the cash receipts. This segregation of duties is a control that makes it unlikely that one person acting alone can divert the company's cash without being detected because it prevents access to both the cash itself and the accounting records related to the cash received.

One means of both protecting cash receipts and speeding the availability of cash receipts is by using a *lockbox collection system.* Large businesses with geographically dispersed customers, such as major oil companies and retailers whose customers make credit purchases with the business's credit card, use lockbox systems to collect cash receipts from customers.

In a **lockbox system,** the business establishes bank accounts at various locations around the area where its customers live. Then the customers mail their payments to the post office (locked box) of the business's bank nearest to them. Each day the bank collects the cash receipts, deposits the cash into the business's account, and sends the business a listing of the customer receipts. This provides good cash control because it segregates the duties of cash handling and depositing from the business personnel's other duties. And it makes the cash available to the business quicker than if customers mailed payments to the company itself.

[3] Cash should never be sent through the mail; however, some companies continue to receive cash in the mail from customers.

Cash Disbursements

The operating process also includes making cash disbursements. As a business receives goods and services, it usually either pays in cash or promises to pay later by purchasing on credit. The main concern with cash disbursements is that all expenditures should be made only for items the business has approved. Control procedures over cash disbursements include separating the responsibilities of check writing, check signing, check mailing, keeping the accounting records, and ensuring that payments are properly authorized.

The segregation of the various duties in paying obligations serves the same role that it does elsewhere in the control system—that is, it makes it difficult for one person to divert company assets. The strongest control over cash disbursements is to have a company policy requiring proper authorization for payments. Often different purchase amounts require different levels of authorization. Small purchase decisions are often decentralized and, thus, are authorized by various persons throughout an organization, while purchases of major investments require recommendation of the CEO and approval by the company's board of directors.

Controls over cash are essential, and the segregation of incompatible duties is a very effective control for both receipts and disbursements. Physical protection is particularly necessary for cash receipts, while for cash disbursements it is important that proper authorization is secured. Now we'll describe how to determine whether the company's records reflect the correct amount of the company's cash.

Bank Reconciliation

Most businesses depend on their system of internal controls to ensure that cash transactions are properly recorded in their accounting records. However, it is good to periodically compare any company's records against the records of outside parties as an independent check on accuracy, especially regarding the important area of cash.

Several procedures in accounting systems can do this. For example, monthly statements of accounts sent to customers who can independently verify balances are a good check on the accuracy of the recorded balances at a certain point in time. To verify the amount recorded as cash, a business periodically compares the amount that it has recorded in its records with the balance recorded by the bank responsible for handling the checking accounts. The **bank reconciliation** is a control procedure performed periodically by a company to adjust the recorded cash amount and to reflect any differences between its cash balance and the cash balance according to the bank.

Bank Statement

Bank statements are reports sent by banks to the businesses and individuals who have accounts showing all the transactions in each account for the period (typically a month). These include (1) the beginning and ending balance of the account according to the bank's books; (2) the total amount deposited in the account during the period, together with a detailed listing of the individual deposits; (3) the total amount withdrawn from the account during the period, along with the amounts of individual checks and other withdrawals; and (4) any additional charges against or additions to the account according to the bank, such as service charges or interest earned.

Exhibit 2.5 shows a bank statement sent by Coastal National Bank to one of its customers, Eagle Electronics Company. Let's take a moment to look at this statement. Notice that it records all the deposits made and checks written on Eagle's account. It shows the checks processed by number and by day so that Eagle can determine if all the checks it has written have been processed by the bank.

The bank statement that Eagle received also shows some of the common adjustments made by banks to their customers' accounts. The bank's **service charge** (fee charged by the bank for services to customers) of $25.50, shown on the bank statement, has been deducted

EXHIBIT 2.5
Bank Statement

Coastal National Bank
Tampa, Florida 34092

Statement Period	**Account Number**	**Account Description**
1/14/2009 thru 2/14/2009	9212321-9	Checking

Eagle Electronics Company
7293 West 10th Avenue
Tampa, FL 24998

Summary
26,882.66 beginning balance
95,294.77 additions
112,657.03 subtractions
9,520.40 ending balance

Date	**Amount**	**Description**
1/15	15,306.20	deposit
1/17	20,941.88	deposit
1/21	22,119.13	deposit
1/23	17,876.62	deposit
1/28	19,010.09	deposit
2/4	500.00	NSF check
2/4	15.00	NSF fee
2/12	90.85	interest
2/14	25.50	service chg.

CK.	**Amount**	**Day**	**CK.**	**Amount**	**Day**	**CK.**	**Amount**	**Day**
9852	20,983.00	13	9853	18,350.32	18	9854	2,851.19	20
9855	28,132.27	22	9856	3,311.91	27	9859	3,008.20	31
9860	988.43	03	9861	16,707.76	05	9863	17,783.45	09

from Eagle's bank balance. The amount shown on the bank statement as interest earned has been added by the bank to Eagle's bank balance. (Not all accounts earn interest, particularly those with small average balances.) If any **nonsufficient funds (NSF) checks** were deposited by the company, they are returned for lack of funds. When NSF checks reach the bank shortly before the bank statements are mailed to the business customers, the bank includes them when it mails the statement. In this case, both the NSF check for $500.00 and the $15.00 NSF fee are deducted from Eagle's cash balance.

Bank Reconciliation Process

The bank reconciliation process ensures that all checks and deposits are recorded properly in the business records. Reconciling the business's cash balance with the balance recorded by the bank highlights any differences due to the timing of withdrawals, deposits, and other account increases and decreases. Any unrecorded items not reflected in the records of the business and the bank are caught and other errors are corrected. A bank reconciliation is an important internal control procedure because it allows for the detection of errors, either in the business's books or its account at the bank.

There are a variety of approaches to preparing a bank reconciliation. We show the two-column approach where both the cash balance according to the bank and the cash balance according to the books are reconciled to an adjusted correct balance. If the reconciliation is done correctly, and if there are no undetected errors in either the business's or the bank's books, the adjusted bank and the adjusted book balances are equal after reconciliation. Keep in mind that one of the main purposes of a bank reconciliation is to discover the undetected errors and to correct them.

Exhibit 2.6 shows the detailed cash records kept by Eagle Electronics that include the dates and amounts of deposits and checks written by Eagle. To perform a bank reconciliation we compare each check written by Eagle with the checks processed by the bank. Then we verify each deposit recorded by Eagle against each deposit processed by the bank.

EXHIBIT 2.6
Eagle Electronics Cash Records

Date	Transaction Description	Increase	Decrease	Balance
1/6	Check #9852—Minute Electrical Supply		$20,983.00	$5,899.66
1/11	Check #9853—H&H Wire and Supply		18,359.32	(12,459.66)
1/12	Deposit	$15,306.20	2,846.54	
1/12	Check #9854—Accurate Meters, Inc.		2,851.19	(4.65)
1/17	Deposit	20,941.88	20,937.23	
1/20	Check #9855—H&H Wire and Supply		28,132.27	(7,195.04)
1/21	Deposit	22,119.13	14,924.09	
1/21	Check #9856—Elegant Fixtures		3,311.91	11,612.18
1/23	Deposit	17,876.62	29,488.80	
1/28	Check #9857—City of Tampa		209.74	29,279.06
1/28	Deposit	19,010.09	48,289.15	
1/29	Check #9858—Accurate Meters		695.01	47,594.14
1/29	Check #9859—Wier Electrical Wholesale		3,008.20	44,585.94
1/31	Check #9860—Bell Atlantic		988.43	43,597.51
2/1	Check #9861—Chuck's Used Cars		16,707.76	26,889.75
2/7	Check #9862—Diamond Electric		2,415.76	24,473.99
2/7	Check #9863—Elegant Fixtures		17,783.45	6,690.54
2/14	Deposit	389.74		7,080.28

By comparing the list of individual deposits and checks recorded in Eagle's account by the bank with the company's cash records, we note the following things:

- Three checks totaling $3,320.51 (check numbers 9857, 9858, and 9862) have not cleared the bank and, thus, are not deducted from the balance according to the bank's records. These **outstanding checks** are written and mailed by the business and deducted from the business's cash records, but the bank has not processed them yet. Therefore, the amount of outstanding checks must be *deducted from the bank balance* to reconcile.

- The bank has not recorded a deposit of $389.74 made by Eagle. **Deposits in transit** are bank deposits that the business has recorded in its cash records and sent to the bank or put in the night depository. However, the bank has not received and recorded the amounts of these deposits in transit before it sent the bank statement to the business. Therefore the amount of the deposit must be *added to the bank balance* to reconcile.

- The service charge and NSF check shown on the bank statement (Exhibit 2.5) must be *subtracted from the company's balance* and the interest earned must be *added to the company's balance* to reconcile.

- The cash balance according to the bank is $9,520.40. The bank made a $50 error when adding up the additions to the account. (Add the deposits plus the interest earned on the account and the amount is $95,344.77; however the bank added only $95,294.77 to Eagle's account.) This error must be *added to the bank balance* to reconcile.

- The cash balance according to the company is $7,080.28. However an investigation reveals that check number 9853 recorded in Eagle's records as $18,359.32 was actually written by Eagle and processed by the bank for $18,350.32. This error must be *added to the company's balance* to reconcile.

Exhibit 2.7 shows the reconciliation for Eagle Electronics. After adjusting for the outstanding checks, the deposit in transit, and the error, the balance per the bank reconciles to $6,639.63. After adjusting for the service charge, the NSF check and fee, the interest earned, and the error, the balance per books reconciles to $6,639.63. Notice, however, that the current balance recorded as cash in Eagle's records is $7,080.28. Therefore, Eagle will need to adjust its recorded cash balance to reflect the correct cash balance. Any item added to or deducted from the balance per the books in the reconciliation requires an adjustment to the recorded amount of cash. In this case, Eagle should do the following:

EXHIBIT 2.7
Bank Reconciliation

EAGLE ELECTRONICS COMPANY
Bank Reconciliation
February 14, 2009

Balance per bank		$9,520.40	Balance per books		$7,080.28
Add: Deposits in transit	$389.74		Add: Interest Earned	$ 90.85	
Error	50.00	439.74	Error—check #9853	9.00	99.85
Deduct: Outstanding checks		(3,320.51)	Deduct: Service charge	$ 25.50	
Adjusted balance per bank		$6,639.63	NSF check	500.00	
			NSF check fee	15.00	(540.50)
			Adjusted balance per books		$6,639.63

- Add the $90.85 in interest earned to its cash balance and deduct the $25.50 service charge.
- The NSF check for $500.00 must be deducted from Eagle's cash balance (as well as the NSF fee charged by the bank). The check was originally recorded as an increase in cash when it was received. Since the check is not good, the customer who wrote it still owes Eagle Electronics $500. In addition, Eagle will charge the customer for the NSF fee, so the customer now owes Eagle an additional $15, for a total of $515.
- Add $9.00 to correct the recording error. Eagle recorded the amount as $18,359.32 (i.e., this amount has been deducted from the cash account), which is $9.00 more than the actual amount.

Note that an error may be made by the bank, the company, or both. When the bank makes an error, the company should request an immediate correction from the bank. For example, when Eagle discovered the error, it would notify the bank and later verify that the error was corrected. As part of good control over cash, companies should have their bank reconciliation done on a regular basis by an employee who is not involved in the receipt or the deposit of cash, nor the approval or payment of cash payments for liabilities. This segregation of duties serves as an effective check on the persons writing the checks or making deposits at the bank because the person doing the bank reconciliation would detect any irregularities.

During the reconciliation process, the person performing the reconciliation would look for checks for unauthorized purposes. These include unauthorized checks to employees or checks to pay obligations that were not debts of the business. Reconciliations may reveal the amounts deposited differ from the amounts that should have been deposited. If the proper amount was not deposited, an independent person would report any differences found because this person would not have been involved in misappropriation.

Summary

In general, there are four basic business processes: (1) business organization and strategy, (2) operating, (3) capital resources, and (4) performance measurement and management. The performance measurement and management process ensures that the business organization and strategy process is achieved.

- The three subprocesses of the operating process are (1) marketing/sales/collection/customer service, (2) purchasing/human resources/payment, and (3) conversion.
- The balanced scorecard has four perspectives: (1) financial, (2) internal, (3) customer, and (4) learning and growth.
- The policies and procedures found in the internal control system are designed to (1) promote operational efficiency, (2) ensure the accuracy of accounting information, and (3) encourage compliance with applicable laws and regulations.
- Internal controls over cash are important because ownership of cash is almost impossible to prove.

Key Terms

Appraisal cost The cost incurred to detect mistakes as early in the process as possible, *44*

Accounts payable turnover A measure of the speed at which the company pays its obligations to suppliers, *43*

Accounts receivable turnover A measure of the speed at which the company receives cash from its customers, *43*

Balanced scorecard approach A process for translating a company's strategy into measurable objectives and plans organized into four perspectives, *40*

Bank reconciliation A control procedure performed periodically by a company to adjust the recorded cash amounts and to reflect any differences between its cash balance and the cash balance according to the bank, *49*

Bank statements Reports sent by banks to the businesses and individuals who have an account at the bank showing all transactions in each cash account for the period, *49*

Business process A collection of activities that takes one or more kinds of input and creates an output that is of value to the customer, *37*

Customer response time The amount of time that elapses from when a customer places an order until the customer receives that order, *42*

Deposits in transit Bank deposits that the business has recorded in its cash records and sent to the bank or put in the night depository, but that the bank has not received and recorded before it sent the bank statement to the business, *51*

Efficiency strategy A strategy that focuses primarily on the reduction or containment of costs, improvements in productivity, and penetration of products/services in the market by having the lowest cost, *39*

External failure cost A cost incurred to fix mistakes after the mistakes become known by the customer, *44*

Financing processes/activities Activities that involve obtaining the cash or other resources as means to pay for investments in long-term assets, to repay money borrowed from creditors, and to provide a return to owners (shareholders), *40*

Flexibility strategy A strategy in which a company strives to adapt to changing market conditions by developing new products/services, markets, and technologies, *39*

Gross margin ratio A ratio used to monitor the profitability of the company's products, *42*

Internal control system The set of policies and procedures designed to promote operational efficiency, ensure the accuracy of accounting information, and encourage management and employee compliance with applicable laws and regulations, *45*

Internal failure cost A cost incurred to fix mistakes before the mistakes become known to the customer, *44*

Inventory turnover A measure of the speed at which the company sells its inventory, *43*

Investing processes/activities Activities involving the purchase and sale of long-term assets and other major items to achieve the business's strategy, *39*

Lockbox system A control system where the business establishes bank accounts at various locations around the area where customers live, *48*

Mechanistic organizational structure A structure in which activities and people are arranged by functions, *38*

Nonsufficient funds (NSF) check A check received and deposited by the company that has been returned for lack of funds, *50*

Nonvalue-added time Time spent on activities that do not add value to the company's products/services or processes, *42*

Operating processes/activities The profit-making activities of a business enterprise, *39*

Organic organizational structure A structure in which activities and people are arranged in cross-functional teams, *39*

Organizational strategy A company's long-term plan for using its resources, both physical and human, *38*

Outstanding checks Checks written and mailed by the business and deducted from the business's cash records, but that the bank has not processed yet, *51*

Prevention cost A cost incurred to prevent mistakes from occurring, *44*

Quick ratio A measure of the company's ability to meet its current obligations as they become due, *41*

Return on investment ratio The return generated per dollar of total investment, *41*

Return on owners' equity ratio The return generated per dollar of owners' equity, *41*

Service charge A fee charged by the bank for services to customers, *49*

Value-added time Time spent on activities that add value to the company's products/services or processes, *42*

Questions

1. Describe the four basic business processes.
2. Discuss the business processes that are considered operating processes.
3. Describe the balanced scorecard approach.
4. What are the four perspectives of the balanced scorecard approach?
5. Describe some measurements used in the financial perspective.
6. Describe some measurements used in the internal perspective.
7. Describe some measurements used in the customer perspective.
8. Describe some measurements used in the learning and growth perspective.
9. Explain the three objectives of an internal control system.
10. Explain the five procedures employed in an internal control system.
11. Explain the importance of internal controls.
12. How is a company's organizational strategy related to its environment and structure?
13. What are the three phases of the management cycle and how are these phases related?
14. What is a lockbox system and why is it used?
15. Why is internal control over cash so important?
16. What is a bank reconciliation?
17. What is the purpose of a bank statement?
18. Explain the items that are used as adjustments to the balance per bank in a two-column bank reconciliation.
19. Explain the items that are used as adjustments to the balance per books in a two-column bank reconciliation.
20. What is the distinction between strategic and operating planning?

Exercises

E2.1 LO 1 Refer to PepsiCo, Inc. **(www.pepsico.com).** Based on your knowledge of this company, determine its environment, organizational structure, and strategy.

Environment	Certain versus uncertain
Structure	Mechanistic versus organic
Strategy	Efficiency versus flexibility

LO 1 **E2.2** Refer to Walt Disney Company **(www.disney.com).** Based on your knowledge of this company, determine its environment, organizational structure, and strategy.

Environment	Certain versus uncertain
Structure	Mechanistic versus organic
Strategy	Efficiency versus flexibility

LO 1 **E2.3** Refer to Dell Computer **(www.dell.com).** Based on your knowledge of this company, determine its environment, organizational structure, and strategy.

Environment	Certain versus uncertain
Structure	Mechanistic versus organic
Strategy	Efficiency versus flexibility

LO 1 **E2.4** For each of the following events, indicate whether the event would occur in the planning, performing, or evaluating phase.

A. Signed a five-year note payable with the bank.
B. Decided to finance 40 percent of the company with debt financing.
C. Decided to offer customers a lifetime warranty on products.
D. Made sales to customers.
E. Compared planned sales to actual sales.

LO 1 **E2.5** For each of the following events, indicate whether the event would occur in the planning, performing, or evaluating phase.

A. Determined the level of production for the coming year.
B. Prepared a report on sales for the period by geographic area.

C. Purchased a new factory that increased production to planned levels.
D. Prepared the income statement.
E. Decided to organize employees into cross-functional teams.

LO 3 **E2.6** Describe the internal control problem(s) in the following situation. The mail clerk opens the mail, records the receipts, and turns this record and the receipts over to the bookkeeper who deposits the receipts in the bank. The bookkeeper then records the receipts in the customer accounts.

LO 3 **E2.7** Describe the internal control problem(s) in the following situation. A company allows a cashier to make small payments for various miscellaneous items with cash from the cash register. The cashier is required to make a note of the amount and the reasons for the payments.

LO 3 **E2.8** Describe the internal control problem(s) in the following situation. All employees share a cash register and no passwords are required.

LO 3 **E2.9** Describe the internal control problem(s) in the following situation. An office manager, who is authorized to sign checks in the absence of the owner, has been stealing money from the company.

LO 4 **E2.10** Garn Industries's bank statement had a balance of $17,252 on April 30. Its cash records showed a balance of $16,243. What is the amount of its outstanding checks if the only other reconciling items are service charges of $12, an NSF check of $56, and deposits in transit of $562?

LO 4 **E2.11** At the end of September, Rose had a cash balance of $9,060. The bank statement on September 30 showed a balance of $8,610. What is the amount of deposits in transit, assuming the only other reconciling items consist of a service charge of $7 and outstanding checks of $825?

LO 4 **E2.12** Swope Company had the following information available on May 31. Prepare a two-column bank reconciliation.

A. Cash balance is $8,700
B. Ending balance on the bank statement is $8,939.
C. Deposit made after the close of banking hours on May 31, $856.
D. Checks issued by the company but not yet cleared through the bank, $1,110.
E. Charge on the bank statement for serving the account in May, $15.

LO 4 **E2.13** Wulf Company had the following information available on November 30. Prepare a two-column bank reconciliation.

A. Balance per books, $1,289
B. Balance per bank, $824
C. Deposits in transit, $900
D. Outstanding checks, $573.50
E. Service charge, $15
F. Interest earned, $40.50
G. NSF check returned, $124

LO 1 **E2.14** The following activities occurred at Berg Legal Services during the period. Determine whether each of the activities occurred in the operating or capital resources process. If the latter, also state whether the activity is investing or financing.

A. A stockholder contributes money to the company.
B. Interest is earned on the company's checking account.
C. Payments are received from clients.
D. Computer equipment is purchased for billing clients.

LO 1 **E2.15** The following activities occurred at All Day Women's Clothing store. Determine whether each of the activities occurred in the operating or capital resources process. If the latter, also state whether the activity is investing or financing.

A. Clothing is purchased for resale.
B. A bank loan is obtained to buy new shelving.
C. New shelving and display racks are purchased.
D. Clothing is sold to customers.

LO 1 **E2.16** The following activities occurred at Applegarth Manufacturing. Determine whether each of the activities occurred in the operating or capital resources process. If it is capital resources, determine whether the activity is financing or investing.

A. Materials are purchased to be used in manufacturing.
B. A new factory building is purchased.

C. Factory equipment is sold.
D. Products are manufactured.

LO 2 **E2.17** Wallace Company experienced the following operating times during the last month:

Order response time	0.8 day
Storing time	3.5 days
Shipping time	2.0 days
Processing time	6.8 days
Queue time	4.5 days

What is the customer response time for Wallace Company? What is the value-added time for Wallace Company?

LO 2 **E2.18** Pauley Enterprises requires 1.3 days to respond to a customer's order. Then it takes Pauley five days of processing time and three days of shipping time to produce and distribute the order to the customer. On average, one day of queue time and one-half day of storing time are also required. What is the customer response time for Pauley Enterprises? What action could Pauley take to reduce this time?

Problems

P2.1 Information related to the cash account of Stubbs Limited for July follows:

LO 4

A. The balance per books is $12,732.36.
B. The bank statement balance on July 31 is $11,920.91.
C. The following checks are outstanding on July 31: check number 758 for $316.34, 762 for $89.36, and 765 for $461.30.
D. A memo for $212.87 included in the bank statement is for an NSF check from Joan Everett.
E. Included among the checks paid by the bank is check number 735 for $153.60, which had been stolen. The check was paid by the bank after Stubbs had issued a stop payment order to the bank.
F. A deposit of $815.63 on July 23 was properly recorded by the bank, although it was erroneously recorded in the books as $851.63. These were collections on customer accounts.

Required: Prepare a bank reconciliation for July.

LO 4 **P2.2** The following information was obtained from the books of Burghduff Products for the month of March:

Cash Account Information:

Balance on February 28	$2,223.00
Receipts	1,715.00
Payments	2,015.00
Balance on March 31	$??

Cash Receipts

Date	Amount
Mar. 4	$ 282.00
Mar. 8	187.00
Mar. 14	329.00
Mar. 20	256.00
Mar. 25	342.00
Mar. 31	319.00

Cash Payments

Date	Check Number	Amount
Mar. 3	415	$ 357.00
Mar. 9	416	88.00
Mar. 13	417	106.00
Mar. 18	418	$335.00
Mar. 21	419	59.00
Mar. 28	420	450.00
Mar. 29	421	250.00
Mar. 31	422	370.00

Bank Account Information:

Sentinel National Bank
1443 Woodlawn Avenue

In account with: Burghduff Products
1804 Oak Street

Date	Deductions	Deposits	Balance
March 1	Balance forwarded		$2,316.00
March 1		$265.00	2,581.00
March 4	$358.00	282.00	2,505.00
March 8	357.00	187.00	2,335.00
March 14	88.00	329.00	2,576.00
March 14	106.00		2,470.00
March 19	335.00		2,135.00
March 20		256.00	2,391.00
March 25	59.00	342.00	2,674.00
March 29	NSF 150.00		2,524.00
March 31	450.00		2,074.00
March 31	SC 45.00		2,029.00

Additional Information:

A. The reconciliation on February 28 included the following two items:

Outstanding check number 412	$358
Deposit in transit	$265

B. The service charge includes a $15 fee for the nonsufficient funds check.

C. The nonsufficient funds check from Mark Edgerston was included in Burghduff Products's deposit on March 14.

Required: Prepare the bank reconciliation for March.

LO 4 **P2.3** Loveland Company had the following bank reconciliation at March 31, 2009.

Balance per bank	$46,500
Add: deposits in transit	10,300
Deduct: outstanding checks	12,600
Adjusted balance per bank	$44,200

Information found on the bank statement on April 30, 2009:

Deposits	$58,400
Disbursements	49,700

All reconciliation items at March 31, 2009, cleared through the bank in April. Outstanding checks at April 30, 2009, totaled $7,500. What is the amount of cash disbursements in Loveland Company's books in April 2009? *(CPA Adapted)*

LO 2 **P2.4** Refer to PepsiCo, Inc. **(www.pepsico.com).**

Required:

A. Based on your knowledge of this company, prepare a balanced scorecard.

B. Calculate the following ratios: (1) quick, (2) return on investment, (3) return on owners' equity, and (4) gross margin.

LO 2 **P2.5** Refer to Walt Disney Company **(www.disney.com).**

A. Based on your knowledge of this company, prepare a balanced scorecard.

B. Calculate the following ratios: (1) quick, (2) return on investment, (3) return on owners' equity, and (4) gross margin.

LO 2 **P2.6** Refer to Dell Computer **(www.dell.com).**

A. Based on your knowledge of this company, prepare a balanced scorecard.

B. Calculate the following ratios: (1) quick, (2) return on investment, (3) return on owners' equity, and (4) gross margin.

LO 2 **P2.7** The financial statements for Faulkender Company are as follows:

FAULKENDER COMPANY
Comparative Balance Sheets
December 31, 2009, and 2008

	2009	2008
Cash	$ 22,000	$ 20,000
Accounts receivable	41,500	39,000
Inventory	72,000	64,000
Plant and equipment	288,000	265,000
Accumulated depreciation	(80,000)	(72,000)
Total assets	$343,500	$316,000
Accounts payable	$ 24,000	$ 37,000
Wages payable	3,500	4,000
Taxes payable	6,750	8,500
Bonds payable	100,000	100,000
Common stock	80,000	80,000
Retained earnings	129,250	86,500
Total liabilities and shareholders' equity	$343,500	$316,000

FAULKENDER COMPANY
Income Statement
For the Year Ended December 31, 2009

Sales		$400,000
Cost of goods sold		248,000
Gross margin		$152,000
Operating expenses:		
Selling expense	$39,000	
Rent expense	45,000	
Depreciation expense	11,000	
Bad debt expense	1,715	
Interest expense	15,000	111,715
Income from operations		$ 40,285
Loss on sale of equipment		(1,000)
Income before taxes		$ 39,285
Income tax expense		11,785
Net income		$ 27,500

Required: Calculate the appropriate ratios for the financial and internal perspectives of the balanced scorecard. Be sure to include the ratios from Chapter 1.

P2.8 These are the condensed financial statements of Pedersen Company for 2009 and 2008. (Pedersen prepares an Income Statement that shows how cost of goods sold is calculated: Beginning inventory plus purchases made during the period minus ending inventory equals cost of goods sold for the period.)

PEDERSEN COMPANY
Income Statement
For the Years Ended December 31, 2009, and 2008

	2009	2008
Sales	$140,000	$130,000
Cost of goods sold:		
Inventory, January 1	$ 12,250	$ 10,250
Add: Purchases	83,000	76,500
Goods available for sale	$95,250	$86,750
Inventory, December 31	14,100	12,400
Cost of goods sold	$81,150	$74,350
Gross margin	$58,850	$55,650
Operating expenses	42,000	41,600
Net income before taxes	$ 16,850	$ 14,050
Income taxes	5,055	4,215
Net income	$ 11,795	$ 9,835

PEDERSEN COMPANY
Statement of Financial Position
December 31, 2009, and 2008

	2009	2008
Cash	$ 10,900	$ 10,400
Accounts receivable	19,600	18,800
Inventory	28,200	24,800
Property, plant and equipment, net	85,700	84,600
Total assets	$144,400	$138,600
Current liabilities	$ 25,000	$ 23,800
Long-term liabilities	22,000	22,000
Owners' equity	97,400	92,800
Total liabilities and owners' equity	$144,400	$138,600

Required: Calculate the appropriate ratios for the financial and internal perspectives of the balanced scorecard. Be sure to include the ratios from Chapter 1.

LO 2 **P2.9** Classify each of the following costs as appraisal **(A)**, prevention **(P)**, internal failure **(I)**, or external failure **(E)**. Give a justification for your answer.

________ A. Cost of field service
________ B. Customer ill will
________ C. Depreciation of test equipment
________ D. Depreciation on computerized manufacturing equipment
________ E. Disposal of defective products
________ F. Downtime
________ G. Employee quality circles
________ H. Final product testing
________ I. Increased labor due to rework
________ J. Liability claims
________ K. Maintenance of test equipment
________ L. Product design
________ M. Product recalls
________ N. Quality data gathering and analysis
________ O. Quality engineering
________ P. Retesting of reworked products
________ Q. Returns due to poor quality

________ R. Rework
________ S. Scrap
________ T. Setups for testing
________ U. Spoilage
________ V. Supplies used in testing
________ W. Systems development
________ X. Technical support provided to suppliers
________ Y. Testing of incoming materials
________ Z. Warranty repairs

Cases

C2.1 LO 1 Based on your knowledge of the company you chose in C1.1, summarize the company's business processes. What is that firm's strategy? What are its operating processes? What are its capital resources processes?

LO 4 **C2.2** You are currently the only bookkeeper at a small business. You are going on vacation, so the company will hire a temporary person to replace you while you are away. Unfortunately, you are leaving today and the new person cannot start work until tomorrow. Prepare an instruction sheet that explains how the temporary person should perform the monthly bank reconciliation.

Critical Thinking

CT2.1 LO 2

FLEISCHMAN COMPANY
Balance Sheet
December 31, 2009, 2008, and 2007

	2009	2008	2007
Current assets:			
Cash	$ 42,000	$ 41,000	$ 39,000
Temporary investments	14,000	10,000	9,000
Accounts receivable, net	192,000	178,000	152,000
Inventories	248,000	301,000	316,000
Total current assets	$ 496,000	$ 530,000	$516,000
Property, plant and equipment:			
Land	75,000	75,000	75,000
Buildings, net of depreciation	430,000	445,000	305,000
Equipment, net of depreciation	28,000	29,000	32,000
Total assets	$1,029,000	$1,079,000	$928,000
Accounts payable	$ 98,000	$ 106,000	$110,000
Notes payable, current	38,000	60,000	60,000
Other current liabilities	42,000	41,000	39,000
Total current liabilities	$ 178,000	$ 207,000	$209,000
Long-term liabilities	90,000	90,000	90,000
Owners' equity	761,000	782,000	629,000
Total liabilities and owners' equity	$1,029,000	$1,079,000	$928,000

FLEISCHMAN COMPANY
Income Statement
For the Years Ended December 31, 2009, 2008, and 2007

	2009	2008	2007
Sales	$2,085,000	$1,920,000	$1,880,000
Cost of goods sold	1,409,000	1,297,000	1,165,000
Gross margin	$ 676,000	$ 623,000	$ 715,000
Operating expenses	616,000	558,000	652,000
Net income	$ 60,000	$ 65,000	$ 63,000

Required:

A. Calculate the ratios for the financial and internal perspectives of the balanced scorecard for 2009 and 2008.
B. Comment on any trend you see from your ratio analysis.
C. Develop scorecard measurements for the customer, internal process, and learning and growth perspectives of the balanced scorecard.

LO 3 **CT2.2** Niyongere, Inc., uses a central collection system to process its cash receipts from customers. Currently it takes an average of five days for mailed checks to be received, one day for them to be processed, and two days for the checks to clear the bank. A lockbox system would cost $6,000 per month and would reduce the mail and processing time to three days. The average daily collections are $300,000 and the money market rate of interest is 5 percent. Should Niyongere adopt the lockbox system? Why?

Ethical Challenges

EC1.1 LO 2 Since many companies profess that "employees are our most valuable asset," some people feel that employees should be given information contained within the balanced scorecard so that the employees might make better decisions. Discuss this idea from the point of view of both the employees and the potential investors.

LO 2 **EC1.2** In light of XBRL, it would be easier than ever before for companies to disclose balanced scorecard information to shareholders by simply "tagging" the information so that it would be released in the XBRL format. Do you think this is a good idea? Discuss this from the point of view of both management and shareholders.

Computer Applications

CA2.1 LO 2

JACOBSEN COMPANY
Balance Sheet
December 31, 2009, 2008, and 2007

	2009	2008	2007
Current assets:			
Cash	$ 42,000	$ 41,000	$ 39,000
Temporary investments	14,000	10,000	9,000
Accounts receivable, net	192,000	178,000	152,000
Inventories	248,000	301,000	316,000
Total current assets	$ 496,000	$ 530,000	$516,000
Property, plant and equipment:			
Land	75,000	75,000	75,000
Buildings, net of depreciation	430,000	445,000	305,000
Equipment, net of depreciation	28,000	29,000	32,000
Total assets	$1,029,000	$1,079,000	$928,000
Accounts payable	$ 98,000	$ 106,000	$110,000
Notes payable, current	38,000	60,000	60,000
Other current liabilities	42,000	41,000	39,000
Total current liabilities	$ 178,000	$ 207,000	$209,000
Long-term liabilities	90,000	90,000	90,000
Owners' equity	761,000	782,000	629,000
Total liabilities and owners' equity	$1,029,000	$1,079,000	$928,000

JACOBSEN COMPANY
Income Statement
For the Year Ended December 31, 2009, 2008, and 2007

	2009	2008	2007
Sales	$2,085,000	$1,920,000	$1,880,000
Cost of goods sold	1,409,000	1,297,000	1,165,000
Gross margin	$ 676,000	$ 623,000	$ 715,000
Operating expenses	616,000	558,000	652,000
Net income	$ 60,000	$ 65,000	$ 63,000

Required: A. Develop a spreadsheet to calculate the ratios for the financial and internal perspectives of the balanced scorecard for 2009 and 2008.
B. Comment on any trend you see from your ratio analysis.

 **CA2.2** Search the Internet for articles concerning the balanced scorecard approach and write a two- to three-page essay describing what you discovered.

Visit the text Online Learning Center at **www.mhhe.com/ainsworth6e** for additional problem material that accompanies this chapter.

CHAPTER THREE

3 Operating Processes: Planning and Control

Learning Objectives

LO 1 Identify the activities in the three operating subprocesses.

LO 2 Describe fixed, variable, and mixed costs and revenues.

LO 3 Use the high/low method to determine fixed and variable costs and revenues.

LO 4 Apply linear regression analysis to determine fixed and variable costs and revenues.

In Chapter 2 we examined the four basic business processes: (1) business organization and strategy, (2) operating, (3) capital resources, and (4) performance measurement and management. We focused on the performance measurement and management process and learned that the balanced scorecard is used for planning and for evaluation. We also learned that the operating processes are the profit-making activities of the company and thus concern revenues and expenses (costs). We learned that the operating process consists of three subprocesses: (1) marketing/sales/collection/customer service, (2) purchasing/human resources/payment, and (3) conversion. In this chapter we examine the activities of these three subprocesses looking closely at the information needed for planning and control. For ease in communication (since some of these processes have long names) we refer to the marketing/sales/collection/customer service process as the *revenue process*. We refer to the purchasing/human resources/payment process as the *expenditure process*. Throughout this discussion we consider the internal control issues involved. Then we turn our attention to identifying and predicting costs and revenues.

Revenue Process

Revenue process
The activities in which the company interacts with its customers to generate revenue.

The **revenue process** consists of a series of interrelated activities designed to generate revenue. These activities involve an interaction between the company and its customers. The complexity of the revenue process depends on factors such as how the company obtains orders, the customer-credit policies established, and the customer support provided. The goals of the revenue process are to (1) provide customers with the product/service they want at a price they are willing to pay, (2) receive payment from customers in a timely fashion, and (3) provide customer support to ensure future sales. The primary activities in the revenue process are

- Determine marketing and distribution channels to generate sales.
- Receive and accept orders for goods and services.
- Deliver goods and/or services.
- Receive payment from customers.
- Provide customer support.

Generate Sales

Changes in business practices are revising the nature of generating customer orders, which is the beginning of the revenue process. Until the mid-1980s, companies made products first and then began the process of marketing them to potential customers. In today's business environment, marketing a product begins even before it is developed.

Companies often use two important sources of information to determine which products and services meet customers' needs: a marketing analysis of customer buying habits and surveys of customer preferences. Related customer-focused issues, such as quality of the products and services, are essential to successful marketing of products and, consequently, to the profitability of the business. Another important part of marketing is distribution. The company must determine whether to engage in Internet sales as Apple does, brick-and-mortar sales, and/or personal sales. In addition, the company determines how to deliver its goods to the customers.

Although sales transactions between the business and its customers occur in a variety of forms, the two basic forms are cash sales and credit sales. Customers often initiate cash sales when they go to the business, but cash sales also occur in other settings. For example, consider door-to-door book sales made by students, cosmetic sales made by cosmetic company representatives, or personal fitness trainers who visit clients' homes. Cash sales are the simplest sales transactions in that they require a direct exchange of cash for goods or services. In such cases, there is no need for shipping products and billing or for subsequent collections from customers.

FAST FACT

Speaking of sales, did you know that Apple has partnered with Nike to help you with your workout? A customer simply gets an iPod nano or iPod touch, a pair of Nike+ shoes, and the Nike + iPod Sport Kit or Sensor. The customer then connects the receiver to the iPod nano. (iPod touch includes built-in support for Nike+, so no receiver is necessary.) The sensor tracks the run and then sends the data to the iPod. This is another example of responding to customer needs.

Source: www.apple.com

Credit sales can result from personal contact, either with the customer in a retail store or with a sales representative who calls on the customer at his or her business. When making credit sales, an employee writes a sales order, which starts the process of filling the customer's request. Customers initiate credit sales by placing an order in person, by mail, or by telephone.

When the customer uses an outside credit card, such as Visa, MasterCard, or American Express, the business, such as Wal-Mart, treats the transaction as a cash sale. The amount of the sale minus a processing fee, typically 1½ to 5 percent, is deposited in the seller's bank account in two to three business days. When a customer uses the business's charge card, such as using a Sears card at Sears, the transaction is treated as a credit sale. The reason for the distinction between the outside credit card sale being treated as a cash sale and the company's credit card being treated as a credit sale is that the business is not subject to the risk of nonpayment with an outside card. When a customer uses an outside charge card, the credit card company pays the business in cash for the amount of the sale minus the card company's fee. Then the credit card company assumes the risk of collection. When a business issues its own credit cards, it bears the risk of nonpayment and all costs of collection, which can be significant.[1]

In some cases, customers invite bids and specify what they want to buy, which can range from major construction projects, such as ships or buildings, to large lots of supplies used in offices or in production. The advantage of the bidding process to the customer is that it explicitly encourages competition among suppliers who are vying to make the sale and, therefore, who are focused on the customer's specific needs. This approach to sales transactions is very common in service industries like architecture and engineering, or even for contracts involving services such as janitorial services.

When a personal sales call is made to generate orders, certain information is captured in the company's information system. This information should include the (1) date, time, location, and duration of the sales call; (2) products/services promoted; and (3) customer's characteristics such as business size or number of employees. In addition, many companies ask potential customers about which marketing efforts would attract them. Finally any expenditures made by the sales personnel must be recorded and linked to the sales call. Other internal controls include requiring proper authorization before certain sales calls and/or sales expenditures are made. For example, an Apple salesperson might need written authorization before making an overseas trip to obtain a customer.

Receive and Accept Orders

The next step in the revenue process is to receive and accept orders. When an order is received the company must do two things: (1) determine the credit and payment policies for the customer and (2) determine if the goods are available.

[1] Also recall that many businesses allow their customers to buy goods/services on account. In these cases the seller sends a bill to the buyer and no credit cards are used.

The best way to reduce the risk of nonpayment by a customer is to obtain credit approval. This usually involves a background check of how well the potential customer has paid debts in the past by reviewing the customer's credit history. Obtaining credit approval for customers usually is necessary only for the initial sale. After that, the customer is preapproved and can make purchases for amounts within approved limits without additional credit checks.

In addition to determining which customers are allowed to purchase goods and services on credit, the business must also determine its discount policies. When a company wants to induce its customers to pay their bills early, it offers a **sales discount.** That is, the company allows the customer to pay less than the full invoice amount if the customer remits (sends in) payment within a specified period of time. Recall that receiving cash from customers is an internal processes goal.

For example, assume Apple makes a $20,000 sale to a school with terms: 3/30, n/60. This means a 3 percent discount is available if payment is remitted within 30 days; otherwise the entire amount is due in 60 days. If the school pays within the discount period, it sends Apple a check for $19,400 ($20,000 × 0.97). Sales discounts are more common in B2B sales than in businesses that sell goods to nonbusiness consumers (B2C sales).

In addition to checking customer information to determine selling terms, the company must determine whether the goods are available (or services can be scheduled). If the company warehouses inventory before sale, the inventory manager must determine whether the product is currently in stock or must be ordered. If the company does not carry inventory, it must determine how quickly the product can be obtained. For example, Dell Computer does not carry an inventory of finished goods. So when an order is placed with Dell, it must determine how quickly the product can be produced and delivered to the customer. On the other hand, Amazon.com has large warehouses to increase the likelihood that its products will be in stock when needed.

When a company receives and accepts (or declines) an order, it must collect certain information for internal control. This customer information includes (1) name, address, and contact information; (2) credit information, including sales discounts offered, if applicable; and (3) distribution information, that is, how the goods will reach the customer (discussed next). The order information collected includes (1) inventory ordered, (2) prices quoted, and (3) delivery date. Additional internal controls include *physical control of inventory* and *separation of duties.* Physical control of inventory is necessary to prevent theft and to ensure that goods are available when needed. Finally the person taking the sales order should not be the person who approves the customer for credit and sales discounts.

Deliver Goods and/or Services

Many sales occur where the customer is not present, such as when the customer places a phone order. In these cases, employees remove the goods from storage and ship them to the customer. Shipping can be done on common carriers like freight companies or on the company's trucks. When using a common carrier, the business usually includes the freight charges as part of the sales agreement with the customer. Often whoever owns the goods during transit determines who incurs freight charges, and ownership in transit depends on the shipping terms.

The shipping agreement between the business and the common carrier is known as a **bill of lading.** It sets out the rates that the carrier will charge and the degree of responsibility that each party has for lost or damaged goods. This document can be used to trace lost shipments using the carrier's accounting system. The terms of the bill of lading may indicate that the goods were shipped **free on board (FOB) destination,** which means that the legal title to the goods does not pass until the customer receives the goods (see Exhibit 3.1). Therefore, FOB destination implies that the seller of the goods pays any related freight charges required to move the goods to the customer. On the other hand, goods shipped **free on board (FOB) shipping point** legally belong to the customer when they are picked up by the common carrier because that is the point at which legal title transfers (see Exhibit 3.1). In such cases, the customer is responsible for payment of freight charges, although shipping charges are often negotiated between buyers and sellers.

EXHIBIT 3.1 **Shipping Terms Determine When Title to the Goods Passes from the Seller to the Customer**

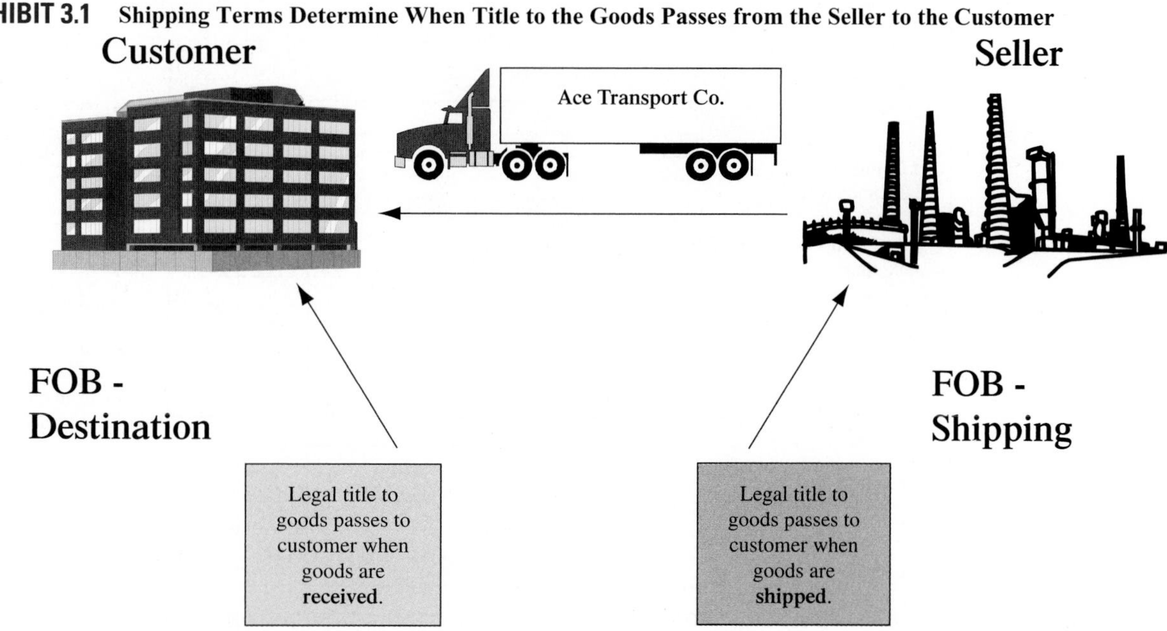

The terms of shipment—FOB destination or FOB shipping point—have two important implications. One implication involves measuring a period's income and ending inventories. If goods are sold FOB destination at the end of a fiscal year, then the sale is not included in determining the seller's current year's income because the transaction is not complete until the customer has title to the goods. In this case the inventory still belongs to the seller. If the same goods were sold FOB shipping point at the end of the accounting period, the seller would include the sale as part of the current year's income and would exclude the inventory from the balance sheet. As an example, suppose a company ships $200,000 of computers on December 30, 2009. If the merchandise is shipped FOB shipping point, the company has a $200,000 sale in fiscal year 2009. However, if the goods are shipped FOB destination, the company cannot recognize this sale until fiscal year 2010 when the goods are received by, and legal title passes to, the buyer.

Shipping terms have another implication for goods damaged or lost during shipping. If title does not pass until the customer receives the goods, then goods that are damaged or lost during shipping are the seller's responsibility. The seller must deal with the shipping company to find the lost items or file the required insurance claims with its insurance company. When title passes at the shipment point, the buyer is responsible for dealing with these problems.

Companies use *separation of duties* and *information records* to control delivery activities. For example, the person who removes the goods from the selling company's facilities should not be the same person who delivers the goods to the buyer. Furthermore the date, time, and person removing the goods for shipping should be recorded as well as the quantity of goods shipped. A unique tracking number should be assigned to the order and the bill of lading must be recorded. Often companies also send a shipping notice to the customer. For example, Apple and Amazon.com notify customers via e-mail when their products are shipped. This not only notifies the customer of an upcoming delivery but also aims to improve customer satisfaction.

Receive Payment from Customers

Billing is an essential step in the process of making credit sales. Exhibit 3.2 shows an example of the **sales invoice** that sellers send (via mail or electronically) to customers as bills. The seller includes on the invoice information about the quantity and type of goods the customer is expected to pay for and the price and terms of the sales agreement. The invoice

EXHIBIT 3.2
Sales Invoice

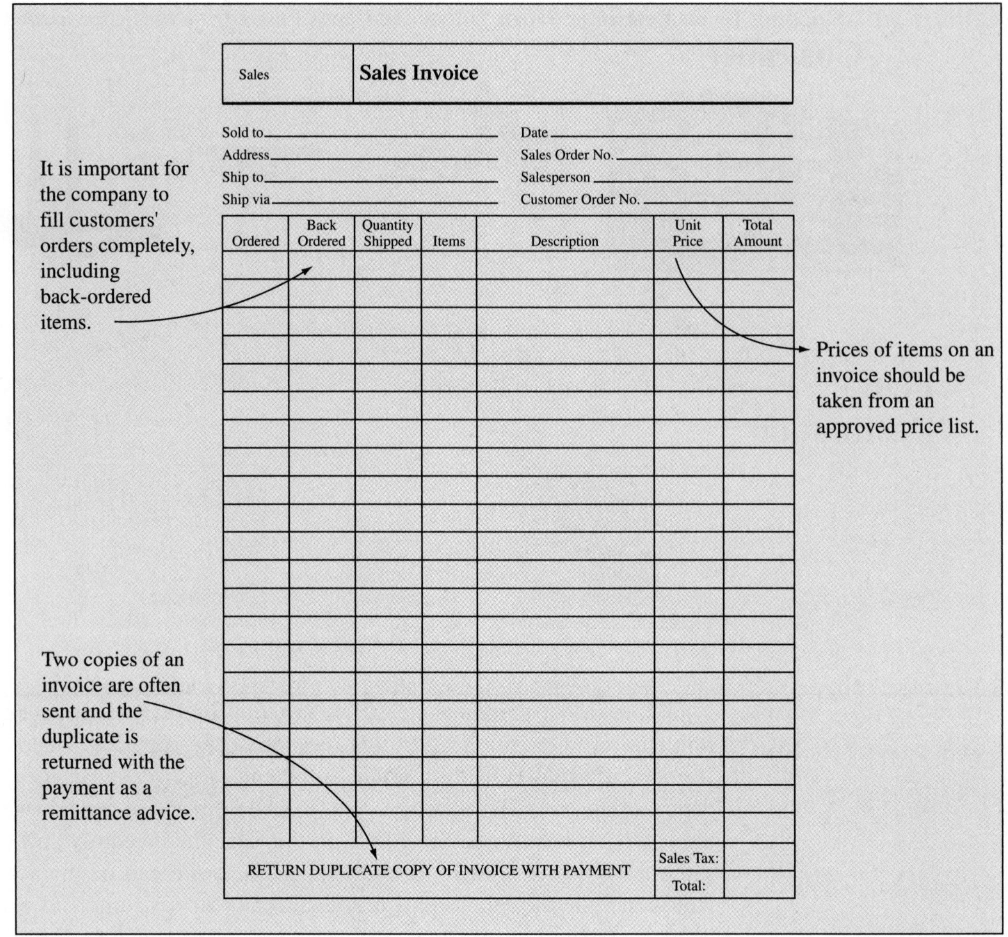

Sales | **Sales Invoice**

Sold to ____ Date ____
Address ____ Sales Order No. ____
Ship to ____ Salesperson ____
Ship via ____ Customer Order No. ____

Ordered	Back Ordered	Quantity Shipped	Items	Description	Unit Price	Total Amount

RETURN DUPLICATE COPY OF INVOICE WITH PAYMENT | Sales Tax: | Total:

It is important for the company to fill customers' orders completely, including back-ordered items.
Prices of items on an invoice should be taken from an approved price list.
Two copies of an invoice are often sent and the duplicate is returned with the payment as a remittance advice.

often includes the customer's purchase order number, which the customer can easily use to trace the order from its inception through the receipt of the goods and approval of the invoice for payment. (Recall that revenues are recognized when title passes, regardless of when the customer pays the bill.)

When the customer remits payment (by check or electronically) the company must record the receipt and credit the customer's account. It is important to both the customer and the business that the business records payments properly to give the customer credit for payments made. The customer does not want to be billed more than once for purchases that have been paid for. Double billing does not reflect well on the business and hurts customer relations. So the business wants an internal control system that avoids the expense of trying to straighten out problems such as potentially lost customers caused by double billing.

After winning a competitive bid to provide services under a long-term contract, a company engages in periodic billing and collection. Typically as part of the contract, the parties agree to progress billings. The firm providing the service, such as an architecture or accounting firm, periodically sends invoices during the term of the contract. These cover a portion of the total amount due and equal unbilled work performed to date. In addition, both firms agree on the measures to use regarding the service provided, like hours worked, because receipt of services is harder to measure than receipt of goods.

Unfortunately, despite careful credit checks, companies occasionally have customers who do not pay their bills. Typically in these situations the company turns the customer's account over to a collection agency (external or internal) or writes off the uncollected amount.

Separation of duties is critical here. The person who made the sale should never have authorization to write off a customer's account for nonpayment. For example, if an employee could make sales and write off accounts, he or she could make fictitious sales in order to earn bonuses and later write those amounts off as uncollectible.

Provide Customer Support

The final activity in the revenue process is providing service before and after the sale. Even though these services are free to the customer, the services provided and any costs incurred must be recorded. Customer support before the sale includes distribution of information regarding products and services. Often this information is provided on the company's Web site. Customer support after the sale includes customer 800-numbers, customer training, and, on occasion, repairs or returns from customers.

A good information system requires a record of **sales returns** by customers as well as any **sales allowances** given to unhappy customers. (Sometimes companies give customers an allowance, a reduction from the selling price, as compensation if the customer is upset with the product or service.) This allows management to track the costs as well as the revenue generated by that customer. Sometimes companies find that some customers are just too expensive to keep!

Relationship of the Revenue Process and the Information System

The information system plays a key role in making decisions in the revenue process. Exhibit 3.3 indicates the primary decisions made and the data collected or accessed during each activity in the revenue process. We discuss planning for the activities in the revenue process in Chapter 6. Recall that both planning and evaluating are part of the balanced scorecard approach.

EXHIBIT 3.3
Decisions Made and Data Collected or Accessed during the Revenue Process

Activity	Decisions Made Include	Information System Data Collected or Accessed
Determine marketing and distribution channels	How can we market and distribute our product? What sales calls were made, where, when, by whom?	Sales call data Sales expenditure data
Receive and accept orders	Should we grant this customer credit? What did the customer order at what price? Are the goods available?	Customer data Customer order data
Deliver goods/services	What goods were shipped? How were the goods shipped? Are the goods on back order?	Inventory data Shipping data Back order data
Receive payment from customers	How much sales revenue was generated? How much money was received? Is the account uncollectible?	Sales data Receipt data Sales discount data Uncollectible accounts data
Provide customer support	What was returned and why? Did we give a price discount and why? What additional services were required and at what cost?	Sales returns data Price allowances (discounts) data Other customer support Expenditures data

Expenditure Process

Expenditure process
The activities in which the company interacts with its suppliers of goods and services to enable it to generate revenues.

The **expenditure process** consists of a series of interrelated activities designed to enable the company to generate revenues. These activities involve an interaction between the company and its suppliers (including employees). The complexity of the expenditure process depends on factors such as the company's ordering policies, its payroll activities, and the support it receives from its suppliers. The goals of the expenditure process are to (1) receive the highest-quality goods/services at the lowest cost, (2) pay for goods/services in a timely manner, and (3) develop good relationships with suppliers of goods/services. The primary activities in the expenditure process are

- Determine the need for goods/services.
- Select suppliers and order goods/services.
- Receive goods/services.
- Pay suppliers for goods/services.

For purposes of discussion, we focus on the expenditure process related to goods. The process related to services, including employees, is similar.

Determine the Company's Need for Goods

Chaos would abound if all the employees in a business could order goods and services from suppliers. Orders might be duplicated or never placed. Small companies, usually those with fewer than 40 or 50 employees, can use less formal procedures for ordering goods or services than larger companies. In a small company, it may be sufficient to tell the person authorized to make the purchase to do so. However, as companies increase in size and become more geographically dispersed, their purchasing procedures need to become formalized.

Large companies, such as Apple, utilize people experienced in both the legal and logistical aspects of purchasing for large organizations. To make sure that proper ordering procedures are followed, the purchasing manager has authority to purchase for the other areas in the business. When various business functions need items, they use a **purchase requisition** to communicate their needs to the purchasing manager. The purchasing requisition (electronic or paper) includes the type and quantity of items needed. If the purchase requisition is authorized, a supplier is selected and goods are ordered. Notice how the internal control system handles this activity—*one person requests goods but a different person approves the request.*

Exhibit 3.4 presents a purchase requisition that includes information about the type and quantity of goods or services needed and the date they are required. Notice the control features incorporated in the purchase requisition: They are serially numbered so that the person responsible for them knows if documents are missing. Also, the authorized person must sign the request so that the purchasing department can verify the signature to avoid unauthorized requests. Purchase requisitions are commonly electronic documents today.

Select Suppliers and Order Goods

Upon receiving a purchase requisition from the requesting department, the purchasing manager selects the supplier of the needed goods or services. As a result of the recent emphasis on product quality, relationships between businesses and their suppliers have become even more important than in the past. Businesses want the goods they purchase to be exactly as specified and to be as free of defects as possible. Businesses also need to ensure that goods are available when needed and in the quantities needed. Thus the business supplier selection process assesses service and quality as well as price. In addition, many companies realize the benefits of maintaining a good working relationship with suppliers. As a result of these closer relationships, businesses and suppliers often work together in product design and production scheduling.

Obtaining the right quantity and quality of goods when needed may conflict with buying those goods at the lowest possible price. For example, suppliers usually offer lower prices per unit for larger quantities purchased (volume discounts). However, purchasing larger quantities may require the business to receive more goods than it actually needs. This could lead to lost,

EXHIBIT 3.4 Purchase Requisition

Once a vendor is selected, that information plus the purchase order number is added to the requisition.

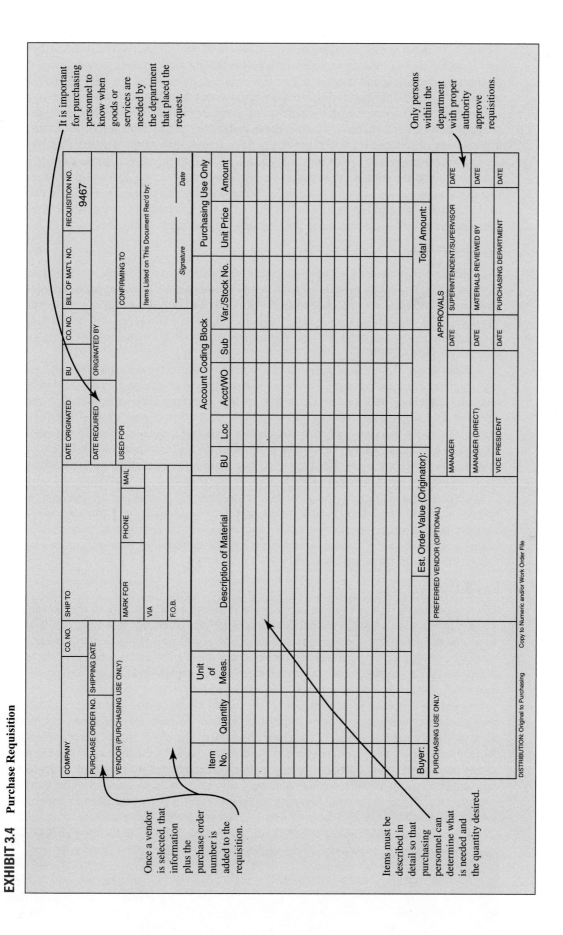

It is important for purchasing personnel to know when goods or services are needed by the department that placed the request.

COMPANY	CO. NO.	SHIP TO			DATE ORIGINATED	BU	CO. NO.	BILL OF MAT'L NO.	REQUISITION NO. 9467
PURCHASE ORDER NO.	SHIPPING DATE				DATE REQUIRED	ORIGINATED BY			
VENDOR (PURCHASING USE ONLY)		MARK FOR	PHONE	MAIL	USED FOR			CONFIRMING TO	
		VIA						Items Listed on This Document Rec'd by:	
		F.O.B.						Signature	Date

Item No.	Quantity	Unit of Meas.	Description of Material	Account Coding Block BU	Loc	Acct/WO	Sub	Var./Stock No.	Purchasing Use Only Unit Price	Amount
Buyer:			Est. Order Value (Originator):						Total Amount:	

PURCHASING USE ONLY	PREFERRED VENDOR (OPTIONAL)	APPROVALS			
		MANAGER	DATE	SUPERINTENDENT/SUPERVISOR	DATE
		MANAGER (DIRECT)	DATE	MATERIALS REVIEWED BY	DATE
		VICE PRESIDENT	DATE	PURCHASING DEPARTMENT	DATE

DISTRIBUTION: Original to Purchasing Copy to Numeric and/or Work Order File

Items must be described in detail so that purchasing personnel can determine what is needed and the quantity desired.

Only persons within the department with proper authority approve requisitions.

damaged, or stolen goods. In addition, large amounts of goods may require warehouse space for excess inventories. Managers responsible for purchasing must balance these conflicts when determining the timing and quantity of goods to purchase. We discuss this issue in more detail in Chapter 5. Recall that monitoring inventory turnover is part of the internal perspective.

Once the supplier is selected, the purchasing manager remits a purchase order to the supplier electronically or via mail. The **purchase order** stipulates the quantity and description of the goods or services requested as well as other terms, such as the delivery date. By accepting the purchase order, two important things occur: (1) the supplier enters into a legal contract binding the supplier to provide the goods or services, and (2) the purchaser agrees to pay the supplier the agreed-upon price. Thus the purchase order not only is a means of communicating but also has legal standing as a contract. Purchase orders can also communicate other terms of the agreement, such as the delivery date and credit terms.

Receive Goods

After the supplier delivers the requested goods, the business must inspect, store, and secure the assets. The inspection process ensures that the goods meet the agreed-upon terms of the transaction, including the type and quantity of items; and that the goods are in acceptable condition. The company's employees in the receiving function record this information on the receiving report and send it to the department responsible for making payments to the supplier (usually accounting).

Another result of the closer relationships between suppliers and businesses today is that now suppliers are working to provide goods that are free of defects and do not need to be inspected. Receiving goods for production that are free of defects means that manufacturers do not have production delays due to inferior goods. It also reduces the chance that the company's customers will receive goods that are not high quality. Goods that do not meet the company's specifications may need to be returned to the supplier **(purchase return).** Or the company may accept the goods but request a **purchase allowance** (this is simply a sales allowance from the buyer's point of view).

Once goods are inspected, strong internal controls require that they be *secured and stored* so that only authorized people have access to them. In addition, it is often necessary to consider storage under special physical conditions, such as appropriate temperature and humidity. For example, electronic components may be damaged by heat and dust, so manufacturers must store them in a cool, clean place prior to use.

Pay Suppliers

Paying suppliers for the goods and services received is the final activity in the expenditure process. The supplier's invoice is a bill that the supplier sends after shipping the goods. It shows the quantity of goods sent, the description of the goods, and the price billed to the customer. The person responsible for paying the invoice cross-checks the quantity and description of the goods or services on the purchase order, the completed receiving report, and the supplier's invoice to ensure that only goods ordered, received, and authorized for payment are paid for.

One critical aspect of paying invoices is the timing of the payment. Recall that suppliers offer discounts to encourage buyers to pay their bills in a timely fashion. From the buyer's point of view, these discounts are **purchase discounts.** The buyer should delay payment of the invoice until the latest possible time in the discount period, yet pay it early enough to be able to take the discount. Although paying early requires that the business give up the use of cash before it legally has to, there is a significant advantage to the business in taking purchase discounts. Recall that monitoring accounts payable turnover is part of the internal perspective.

Enhance Your Understanding

If a company purchased, on average, $50,000 every month and took a 2 percent discount on every purchase, how much would it save every year?

Answer: This company would save $12,000 over the course of a year ($50,0000 × 0.02 × 12). If the company invested the money, the company could earn even more.

EXHIBIT 3.5
Decisions Made and Data Collected or Accessed during the Expenditure Process

Activity	Decisions Made Include	Information System Data Collected or Accessed
Determine the need for goods/services	What goods are needed? When are the goods needed?	Purchase requisition data
Select suppliers and order goods/services	From whom should we order? What has been ordered, from whom, at what price?	Supplier data Purchase order data
Receive goods/services	What was received? Were the goods in acceptable condition?	Receiving data Purchase return data Purchase allowance data
Pay suppliers of goods/services	Are we paying only for goods ordered, received, and accepted?	Purchase invoice data Purchase discount data Payment data

Relationship of the Expenditure Process and the Information System

As we have discussed, the information system plays an important role for making decisions in the expenditure process. Exhibit 3.5 indicates the decisions made and the data collected or accessed during the expenditure process. We discuss planning for the expenditure process in Chapter 6.

Conversion Process

Conversion process
An internal process whereby a company converts raw materials into finished products to be sold to customers.

The conversion process is found only in manufacturing companies. It requires the use of machines and other equipment along with employee labor to convert raw materials into products to be sold. The raw materials are acquired through the expenditure process while the finished goods produced by the company are sold through the revenue process.

The **conversion process** consists of a series of interrelated activities designed to produce the goods the company sells. These activities, unlike those of the revenue and expenditure processes, are internal. The complexity of the conversion process is directly related to the complexity and flexibility of the production process. For example, computer manufacturers like Apple make their products in a matter of days while airplane manufacturers such as Boeing Company require a much longer conversion process. The goals of the conversion process are to (1) manufacture the highest-quality products and (2) utilize labor and other manufacturing resources in an efficient and effective manner. There are four primary activities in the conversion process:

- Schedule production.
- Obtain raw materials.
- Use labor and other manufacturing resources to make products.
- Store finished goods until sold.

Schedule Production

Manufacturers try to process raw materials in a systematic and controlled way that minimizes costs. Because various machines make a wide variety of products, scheduling the use of machines and the arrival of materials is an important part of controlling and reducing costs. Production managers who understand the details of the production process make these scheduling decisions using estimates of product demand from the sales and marketing departments. These important decisions have significant bearing on the manufacturer's profitability.

Scheduling production would not be a problem if a business made only one product, knew when customers wanted the product, and had only a few suppliers from whom to arrange delivery. Because most manufacturers have many products and suppliers and do not know exactly when a customer wants the product, scheduling production is not a simple problem. How well scheduling is done can greatly affect the cost of the product. For example, a company with 800 production workers, each paid $18 an hour, will lose $14,400 in labor costs alone for every hour that it has to stop production due to shortages of raw materials.

Many manufacturers use each of their machines to make a variety of different products. Using the same machine to make different products requires changing its setup. Machine setups are adjustments made to machines to get them ready to manufacture the next type of product; for example, changing parts like drill bits so that the machine meets the design requirements of the next product. When machines were manually operated, this process took hours, even days. Increasingly we find that because computers control machine setups, setup times are dropping. For example, many companies report that they have reduced setup time from hours to a matter of minutes.

In addition, manufacturers are organizing their production floors into cells so that machines related to the production of certain products or types of products are close to each other to reduce travel time between machines. For example, consider a pharmaceutical firm that makes antibiotics sold in capsules. The firm could organize its production into cells by locating the machines for mixing the compounds, putting the mixed product into the capsules, and packaging the capsules close together on the production floor. This would make the production process more efficient. Schedulers also use mathematical models to determine the optimal length of production runs (the number of a given product made at one time) based on factors like setup times and the organization of the production floor.

The overriding factor in scheduling production is the demand for the product. A manufacturer wants inventories of both raw materials and finished goods to be as small as possible. It wants to produce the amount of product required when the product is needed. Predictions of customer demand for the product based on sources such as surveys conducted in places that sell the product play a critical role in production scheduling. Customer demand for products can fluctuate with the season, or even daily, and the production process needs to adapt its output to the expected level of demand. JIT inventory management, discussed in Chapter 1, is an efficient approach to scheduling production. Companies that produce only when customers place orders use sales call data and customer order data to schedule production.

The complexity of the products and the production process itself, as well as the number of different products produced, can affect scheduling. Manufacturing products like cars and appliances is complicated because of the many different parts they require; therefore, a bill of materials that lists all the materials required for a particular product is crucial for control purposes. In manufacturing products such as these, getting the parts where they are needed when they are needed can be a difficult scheduling task. Products requiring a complicated sequence of processes also can make production scheduling difficult. For example, refining crude oil into gasoline involves a complicated series of chemical transformations and, consequently, sophisticated scheduling of production activities.

In addition to making a wide array of products, manufacturers sometimes must package a product, or products, in a variety of different forms. For example, McNeil Consumer Products, maker of Tylenol, packages a brand like Tylenol in a variety of different strengths and package sizes, all of which complicate scheduling the production process. Other factors affecting scheduling include the availability of raw materials, the length of production runs, the time and complexity of machine setups, and lead times for delivery, including packaging and shipping times. Actual production begins when the scheduler issues a production order (electronic or paper) to the production function.

Obtain Direct Materials

Direct materials and other supplies (inventories) used in the production process are acquired through the expenditure process and stored in a secure place until they are needed on the production floor. Direct materials, such as the steel used in making cars or the crude oil used in making gasoline, and supplies, such as the glue used in making furniture or the solder

FAST FACT

It pays to pay attention to quality in your manufacturing processes. In 1903, 21-year-old William S. Harley and 20-year-old Arthur Davidson produced the first Harley-Davidson motorcycle. Their factory was a 10 × 15 foot wooden shed with the words "Harley-Davidson Motor Company" written on the door. By 1920, Harley-Davidson (HD) was the largest motorcycle manufacturer in the world. In 1969, HD merged with American Machine & Foundry Company (AMF) and quality began to suffer. Throughout the 1970s, HD had the dubious reputation of poor quality resulting in motorcycles prone to breaking down on the highway. In 1981, 13 senior executives sought to buy back the company from AMF and return HD to its former glory. By 1986 the buy-back was complete and HD renewed its commitment to quality manufacturing. In 2001, *Forbes* magazine named Harley-Davidson its company of the year. In 2008, more than 250,000 people came to Milwaukee to celebrate the 105th anniversary of Harley, some riding more than 5,000 miles to be there.

Source: www.harleydavidson.com.

used in making electric appliances, are then requisitioned into the manufacturing process as they are needed.

When there is a need for direct materials in production, an authorized employee from the production department obtains the needed materials from storage. To maintain control over the materials, the employee getting the materials uses a *materials requisition form.* This document indicates what is needed in production and shows that the person requesting the goods has the authority to do so. Thus the accountability for these materials shifts from storage to production at the time of the materials requisition. Therefore, any damage or theft after the materials leave storage and before they are moved to finished goods is the responsibility of the production department.

Use Labor and Other Manufacturing Resources to Make Products

Manufacturing processes for making products are as varied as the products we see every day. Production orders provide information to the production workers about the required schedule and identify the products or batches of products as they go through the production process. In addition, many companies prepare an operations list that details the sequence of operations required. Being able to identify when and where defective products were produced allows quality control—that is, monitoring quality to ensure adherence to standards—to be included in the production process. In addition, knowing where specific items or batches are in the process improves prediction of the need for raw materials and machine time, as well as the completion time for the goods.

Companies hire individuals to supply the labor required to make products. These employees provide a variety of human resources for the production of goods. Employees provide labor for operating manufacturing machines or for transforming the raw materials into finished products manually. In addition, employees provide labor in the form of supervisory, janitorial, and other services used in the manufacturing process. Labor is tracked by using *time tickets* that indicate who worked on particular jobs. Exhibit 3.6 shows the combination of production inputs in the conversion process to manufacture finished products.

Manufacturing overhead is the cost of all manufacturing resources used to make products that are not directly associated with production. Manufacturing overhead includes items such as the rent on the manufacturing facilities; insurance on the direct materials inventory; and heat, light, and power used to manufacture products. A growing category of overhead costs includes the engineering costs of designing products and scheduling the production process. Associating engineering and other overhead costs with products helps make the operating and strategic decisions about those products more economically sound. As companies become more automated, the amount of manufacturing overhead relative to materials and labor increases. For many manufacturing companies, manufacturing overhead is 70 percent or more of the costs of total production. Therefore, accurate overhead allocation for product costing is crucial for making sound business decisions.

EXHIBIT 3.6
The Conversion Process

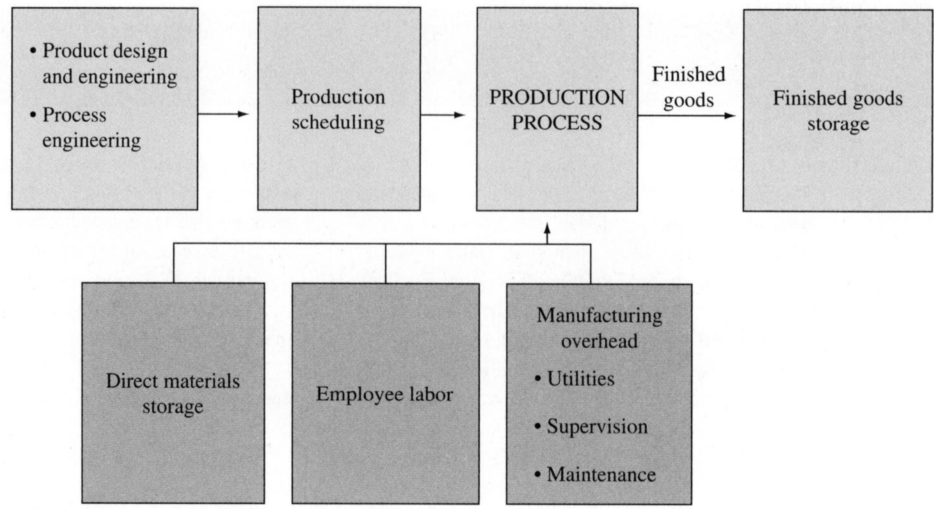

Store Finished Goods Until Sold

After the manufacturing process is complete, finished products move from the production floor to storage until a shipping order is received. An efficient business stores these products for as short a time as possible to minimize the storage costs and the investment in finished, unsold goods. A warehouse list is often maintained when different products require different types of storage. Selling finished goods involves activities previously described in the revenue cycle. Demand-pull production, based on the just-in-time (JIT) philosophy, requires companies to develop flexible manufacturing processes so that products are manufactured only as customers order them. Demand-pull production eliminates the need for a finished goods inventory, thereby dramatically reducing costs. Companies that adopt demand-pull production must maintain the highest standards of quality production. Imagine, for example, a company that manufactures products only as the customers demand them. This means that a product manufactured incorrectly cannot be shipped to the customer. Because the company does not have any finished goods inventory, the customer will not receive the order when desired. (We discuss this in greater detail in Chapter 5.)

Relationship between the Conversion Process and the Information System

As we discussed, the information system plays a key role for making decisions in the conversion process. Exhibit 3.7 indicates the primary decisions made and the data collected or accessed during each activity in the conversion process. We discuss planning for the activities in the conversion process in Chapter 6. Both planning and evaluating reflect the balanced scorecard approach.

We have described the activities in the revenue, expenditure, and conversion processes. Clearly, management must plan its activities, ensure that the results of those activities are properly recorded, and then compare the actual results to the plans to determine if changes are necessary. Activity analysis is the primary tool for planning and controlling operating activities. Simply put, activity analysis is the evaluation of the business operating activities to determine (1) cost and revenue behavior and (2) cost and revenue drivers.

Cost and Revenue Behavior

Cost behavior refers to how a cost reacts to changes in the level of operating activity, while **revenue behavior** refers to how a revenue reacts to changes in the level of operating activity. To predict and control costs and revenues in the future, we must understand how costs and

EXHIBIT 3.7
Decisions Made and Data Collected or Accessed during the Conversion Process

Activity	Decisions Made Include	Information System Data Collected or Accessed
Schedule production	What needs to be made? How will it be made? What is the demand for the product? What packaging is required?	Sales call data Marketing surveys Production order
Obtain raw materials	What materials are needed?	Bill of materials Materials requisition
Use labor and other manufacturing resources to make products	What labor is needed? What other resources are needed?	Operations list Time tickets
Store finished goods until sold	Where are goods stored? How are goods stored? How long are goods stored?	Warehouse list Shipping order

revenues change in response to changes in operating activity. Furthermore, understanding cost and revenue behavior is important to estimating profit at different levels of operating activity. For example, if Apple sells 20 percent more products next year than it did this year, will the profits increase by 20 percent? The answer is no, because some costs and revenues do not change proportionately with increases in the number of units sold.

"Well, shoot. I just can't figure it out. ... I'm movin' over 500 doughnuts a day, but I'm still just barely squeakin' by."

EXHIBIT 3.8
Linear Behavior

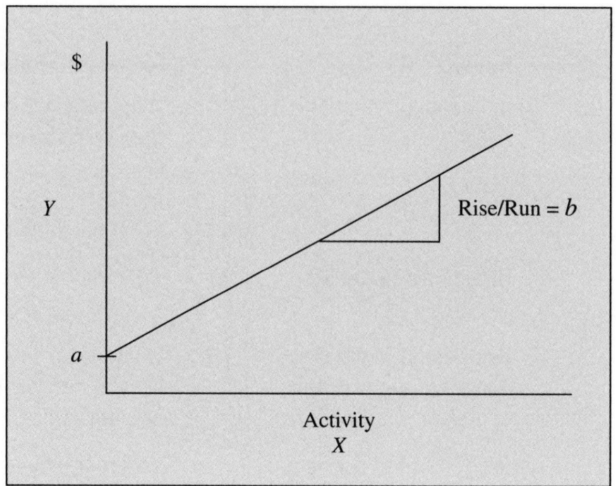

Behavior Patterns

Cost and revenue behavior patterns are reflected as linear relationships represented by the formula $Y = a + b \times X$ where Y represents dollars, a is the intercept, b is the slope, and X represents activity. Exhibit 3.8 illustrates this relationship graphically. Keep in mind, however, that many costs and revenues do not exhibit a linear relationship over a wide range of activity. For example, due to efficiencies in production, costs may decrease over time or level of activity or costs may increase due to required equipment or building purchases beyond a certain level of activity. For example, if a company can produce 50,000 units of a product per machine, it will have to purchase another machine to produce 50,001 units. Likewise revenues are not necessarily linear over time or level of activity. For example, sales prices may have to be lowered to increase the number of customers beyond a certain level of activity. Nevertheless, over a given range of activity, known as the *relevant range,* we can define costs and revenues linearly.

Relevant Range

When establishing cost and revenue behavior patterns, we limit the description to a specific range of activity called the relevant range. The **relevant range** is the span of operating activity that is considered normal for the company. Assume, for example, that a computer retailer normally sells between 200 and 500 computers per month. If we define operating activity as the number of computers sold, the relevant range is 200 to 500 computers—the normal activity range for the store. Since the store is not contemplating sales of 15,000 computers per month, analysis of costs and revenues at this level is inappropriate because cost and revenue behavior patterns are only valid for the range of activity analyzed. In other words, the relevant range of activity establishes the $Y = a + b \times X$ relationship between the activity and the dollar amount of costs and revenues. Exhibit 3.9 illustrates the concept of the relevant range.

Activity Measures

Recall that operating activities are the profit-making activities of the company. Understanding operating activities is crucial to profit planning and analysis because activities provide and consume resources. Different costs and revenues change in relation to different operating activities. For example, shipping costs may change with the number of orders shipped, while receiving costs may change with the number of orders received. In both cases the activity, orders shipped or orders received, consumes resources. On the other hand, revenues provide resources. Revenues may change with the number of units sold, the number of hours billed, or the number of customers.

We measure activity using different bases that reflect the consumption or provision of resources. These bases are called **activity drivers.** Because activities, as measured by activity

EXHIBIT 3.9
Relevant Range

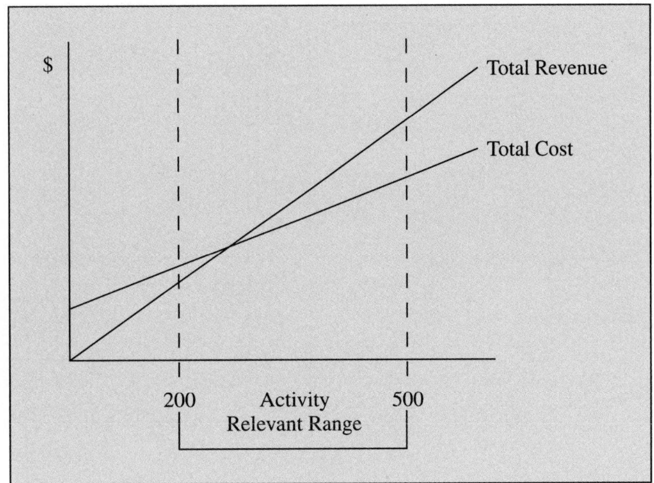

drivers, provide or consume resources, as measured by costs and/or revenues, changes in the amount of the activity driver ultimately cause, or drive, changes in costs and/or revenues. Exhibit 3.10 indicates some common activity and activity driver relationships. For example, if Apple wanted to measure the resources consumed by the activity *purchasing,* it might use an activity driver such as the *number of purchase orders processed.* If Apple wanted to measure the resources provided by the activity *promoting products,* it might use an activity driver such as the *amount of advertising.* Note that activity drivers are simply numerical measures of activities. *The key point is that changes in the activity driver are assumed to cause changes in the related cost or revenue.*

Now that we understand the relationship between activities and activity drivers, we focus our attention on defining cost and revenue behavior patterns. We discuss three identifiable linear behavior patterns: (1) fixed, (2) variable, and (3) mixed.

Fixed cost (fixed revenue) A cost (revenue) that remains constant throughout the relevant range.

Fixed Costs and Revenues

A **fixed cost** or **fixed revenue** does not change in total as the amount of the activity driver changes throughout the relevant range. For example, assume that Apple pays a Webmaster a salary to maintain its Web site. Further assume that we define activity as the number of

EXHIBIT 3.10
Activity and Activity Drivers

Cost Activities	Activity Drivers
Setting up machines	Number of production runs
Purchasing	Number of purchase orders processed
Opening a new store	Number of stores opened
Educating employees	Number of employees
Using warehouses	Number of warehouses
Assembling	Number of products produced
Marketing	Number of product lines
Inspecting	Number of batches
Developing new products	Hours of development time
Revenue Activities	**Activity Drivers**
Selling products	Number of units sold
Providing services	Number of customers
	Hours of service provided
Expanding markets	Number of territories
Promoting products	Amount of advertising

EXHIBIT 3.11
Fixed Cost or Fixed Revenue

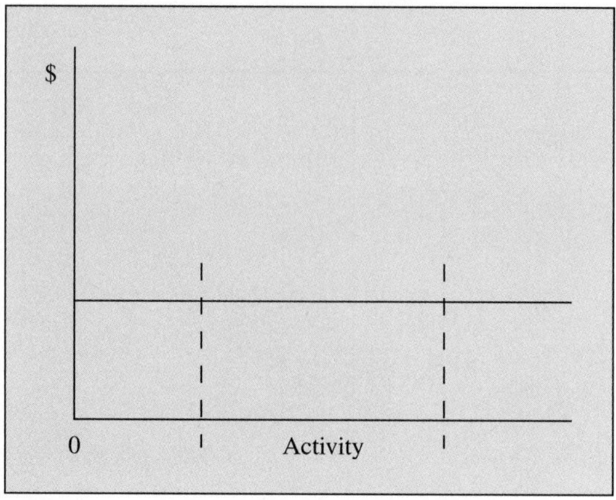

B2B sales orders generated online. The Webmaster's salary, then, is a fixed cost because it does not change based on the number of online sales. As another example, assume that Apple provides promotional support to customers for a set fee per month. Further assume that Apple defines activity as the number of hours of support provided to customers per month. This fee is a fixed revenue because it does not change based on the number of hours of support provided. Exhibit 3.11 shows how a fixed cost or revenue looks throughout the relevant range.

Although a fixed cost or revenue does not change in total as the activity driver changes, when measured on a per-activity basis, the amount of fixed cost or revenue does change. For example, assume a computer store pays its employees salaries totaling $10,000 per month and it defines activity as *sales in dollars* within the relevant range of $180,000 to $300,000 per month. (Note that activities are not always defined as physical actions; for instance, sales in dollars is an activity measure.) Exhibit 3.12 indicates that as sales increase, the salary cost as a *percentage of sales* decreases.

Variable cost (variable revenue)
A cost (revenue) that changes in direct proportion to changes in the activity driver throughout the relevant range.

Variable Costs and Revenues

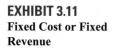

A **variable cost** or **variable revenue** changes in direct proportion to the change in the amount of activity driver throughout the relevant range. For example, assume that Apple pays its sales personnel a commission based on the dollar amount of sales made. Commissions, then, are a variable cost because the total amount varies proportionately with the dollar amount of sales. Similarly, assume that Apple sells an iPhone to customers for $300 each. This revenue is variable because it increases in total as the number of iPhone sold to customers increases. Exhibit 3.13 illustrates how a variable cost or revenue appears throughout the relevant range.

Although a variable cost or revenue changes in total throughout the relevant range, when measured on a per-activity basis, the amount of variable cost or revenue does not change. For example, assume the computer store offers training for $10 per hour. If we define activity as the *number of hours of training* provided, the revenue per hour remains constant while the total revenue increases as the number of hours increase as shown in Exhibit 3.14.

EXHIBIT 3.12
Fixed Costs per Activity

(1) Activity Level (Sales)	(2) Total Fixed Cost (Salaries)	(3) = (2)/(1) × 100 Fixed Cost per Activity
$180,000	$10,000	5.56%
240,000	10,000	4.17
280,000	10,000	3.57
300,000	10,000	3.33

EXHIBIT 3.13
Variable Cost or Variable Revenue

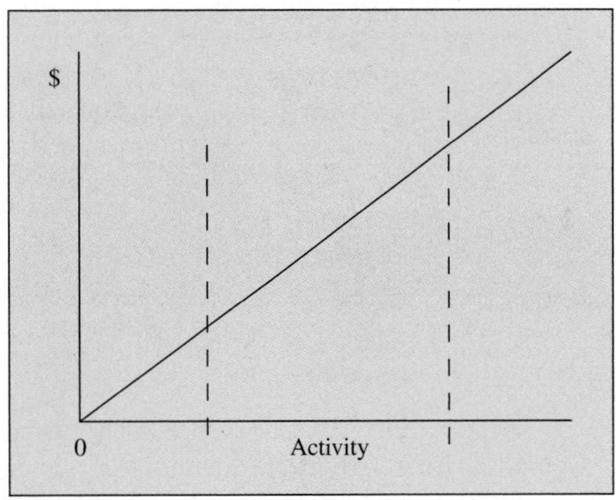

EXHIBIT 3.14
Variable Revenue per Activity

(1) Activity Level (Training Hours)	(2) Total Variable Revenue (Service Fees)	(3) = (2)/(1) Variable Revenue per Activity
100	$1,000	$10
200	2,000	10
300	3,000	10
400	4,000	10

Mixed cost (mixed revenue)
A cost (revenue) that has both a fixed and a variable component in the relevant range.

Mixed Costs and Revenues

A **mixed cost** or **mixed revenue** varies, but not proportionately, to a change in activity throughout the relevant range. For example, assume Apple pays its Webmaster a salary of $10,000 per month plus a commission based on the number of hits on the Web site. In this case, the total compensation is a mixed cost because the total amount depends partly on the number of hits per month. Likewise, if Apple sold computers to schools based on a flat amount plus an additional amount per hour of training provided, this revenue would be a mixed revenue. Exhibit 3.15 illustrates a mixed cost or revenue. Note that the mixed cost/revenue has a variable component, the slope, and a fixed component, the intercept.

EXHIBIT 3.15
Mixed Cost or Mixed Revenue

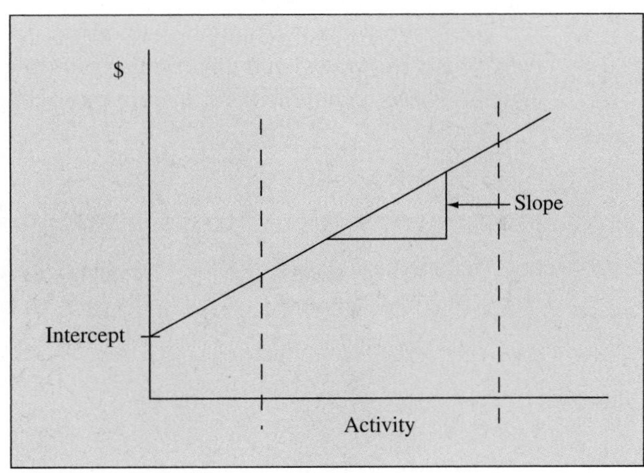

EXHIBIT 3.16
Mixed Cost per Activity

(1) Activity Level (Sales)	(2) Total Mixed Cost (Salaries and Commissions)	(3) = (2)/(1) × 100 Mixed Cost per Activity
$180,000	$15,400	8.56%
240,000	18,400	7.67
280,000	20,400	7.29
300,000	21,400	7.13

Since a mixed cost/revenue has both a fixed and a variable component, it changes in total and per activity throughout the relevant range. For example, assume a computer store pays its eight employees a salary of $800 and a commission of 5 percent of sales dollars each month. Thus total salary and commission cost = ($800 × 8) + 0.05 × sales in dollars. In this case, the total salary cost depends, in part, on the amount of sales per month. As Exhibit 3.16 indicates, the *salary cost as a percentage of sales (activity)* decreases throughout the relevant range.

So, when activity is $180,000 of sales, the salary plus commission cost is $15,400 [($180,000 × 0.05) + (8 × $800)] or 8.56 percent of sales ($15,400/$180,000 × 100). But when activity is $300,000, the salary plus commission cost is $21,400 [($300,000 × 0.05) + (8 × $800)] or 7.13 percent of sales ($21,400/$300,000 × 100).

A different pattern emerges for mixed revenues. Assume the computer store offers private training to school districts for $500 for the first 100 hours (per month) and $10 per hour for any additional hours. Thus total revenue = $500 + $10 × number of training hours (over 100). Service revenue, then, is a mixed revenue because it depends, in part, on the number of hours of training provided. As indicated in Exhibit 3.17, the *revenue per hour (activity)* increases throughout the relevant range.

Thus, when activity is 100 hours of training, the service fees earned are $500 [$500 + (100 − 100) × $10] and the mixed revenue per hour is $5 ($500/100). However, when the activity is 400 hours of training, the service fees earned are $3,500 [$500 + (400 − 100) × $10] and the mixed revenue per hour is $8.75 ($3,500/400).

As this discussion indicates, it is crucial that companies understand the relationships between costs, revenues, and activities. As we noted, some costs/revenues are fixed, some are variable, and some are mixed. When we think about a company as a whole, it probably incurs fixed, variable, and mixed costs and earns fixed, variable, and mixed revenues. Therefore we need a method to predict future costs/revenues that recognizes multiple cost/revenue behavior patterns. We turn to this topic next.

Cost/Revenue Estimation Methods

We use cost/revenue estimation methods to determine the relationship between total (company) costs (revenues) and a particular activity driver to estimate (predict) future costs (revenues). These techniques use information about past costs (revenues) and past levels of

EXHIBIT 3.17
Mixed Revenue per Activity

(1) Activity Level (Training Hours)	(2) Total Mixed Revenue (Service Fees)	(3) = (2)/(1) Mixed Revenue per Activity
100	$ 500	$5.00
200	1,500	7.50
300	2,500	8.33
400	3,500	8.75

activity *to estimate future costs (revenues)* given expected future activity levels. Remember, however, that cost (revenue) behavior patterns are valid only within the relevant range; thus, we cannot predict costs (revenues) *outside the relevant range.* We examine two cost (revenue) estimation methods next. Throughout this discussion we focus on costs, but these methods work equally well for revenue estimation.

High/Low Method

The high/low method of cost or revenue estimation uses only two data points to determine the total cost/revenue formula. It uses the highest and the lowest levels of activity driver to define the relevant range and determine the total cost or revenue line because these two data points give the widest relevant range. Since estimations are valid only for the relevant range, using the highest and lowest levels is crucial. In addition, since we are attempting to predict normal operating activity, no unusual events can have occurred in the time period used for data collection. For example, assume Apple attempts to predict costs using the number of B2B hits to its Web site each month for the past year as an activity driver. Further assume that during one month last year, Apple suffered a denial of service attack, rendering the Web site inoperable. Obviously the relationship between the number of hits and costs is not normal during this month. The number of hits would be well below normal while the costs would be well above normal as the Web site is repaired.

To use the high/low method we need to collect past data about costs (revenues) and the associated activity drivers. Assume a computer retailer wishes to predict total costs based on the number of computers sold. Exhibit 3.18 illustrates the data regarding monthly costs and the number of computers sold for the past year. We use these data to develop the linear relationship between costs and the number of computers that allows us to predict the future.

First, we must find the highest and lowest levels of activity. Looking down the column labeled "number of computers sold," we discover that June is the month with the lowest level of activity while December is the month with the highest level of activity. Second, we must determine the total costs of these two months. As seen in Exhibit 3.18, total costs in June were $210,500 while in December total costs were $487,900. *The key point is that the high and low points are based on activity since we assume that activity changes cause cost (or revenue) changes.*

Selecting High and Low
Choose the high and low points based on activity.

Third, we calculate the variable cost per computer sold using the change in cost (rise) divided by the change in activity (run) to find the slope:

$$\frac{\text{Rise}}{\text{Run}} = \frac{\text{Highest cost} - \text{Lowest cost}}{\text{Highest activity} - \text{Lowest activity}} = \text{Slope}$$

$$\frac{\$487{,}900 - \$210{,}500}{490 - 210} = \frac{\$277{,}400}{280} = \$990.7143$$

EXHIBIT 3.18
Total Cost and Number of Computers Sold

Month	Total Cost	Number of Computers Sold
January	$315,000	310
February	419,000	432
March	360,500	350
April	281,000	276
May	256,000	290
June	210,500	210
July	377,100	328
August	398,500	385
September	380,100	360
October	444,000	435
November	437,000	470
December	487,900	490

Now that we have the variable cost per computer sold, we can use that information to determine the fixed cost per month. We take the variable cost just determined and apply it to the cost formula represented by either the highest or the lowest level of activity. (Do not go back to the original data or use any other activity level.) Assuming we use the lowest activity level, our cost formula is

$$\text{Total cost} = \text{Fixed cost} + (\text{Variable cost} \times \text{Lowest activity level})$$

$$\$210{,}500 = \text{Fixed cost} + (\$990.7143 \times 210)$$

$$\$2{,}450.00 = \text{Fixed cost}$$

Enhance Your Understanding

What is the fixed cost if the highest level of activity is used?

Answer: The fixed cost is the same, \$2,450. It is calculated as \$487,900 = Fixed cost + (490 × \$990.7143); therefore, fixed cost is \$2,450.

Now that we know the variable cost and the fixed cost, we can write our total cost formula and use it to predict costs in the future. The total cost formula is

$$\text{Total cost} = \$2{,}450.00 + (\$990.71 \times \text{Number of computers sold})$$

If we believe that 220 computers will be sold next month, we predict total costs at:

$$\text{Total cost} = \$2{,}450.00 + (\$990.71 \times 220)$$

$$\text{Total cost} = \$220{,}406.20$$

If we believe that 462 computers will be sold next month, we predict total costs at:

$$\text{Total cost} = \$2{,}450.00 + (\$990.71 \times 462)$$

$$\text{Total cost} = \$460{,}158.02$$

Exhibit 3.19 illustrates these data and the resulting cost line using the high/low method. Notice that except for the highest and lowest, the data points do not fall on the cost formula line. The high/low method is very simple to use because it requires only two data points and very little math. This strength is also a weakness, because it ignores most of the data gathered; the results may not appropriately reflect the cost/activity relationship. For example, look at Exhibit 3.19. Since most of the data points are above the cost line, the cost line may not adequately reflect the relationship between number of computers sold and total cost. Given this problem you should use the high/low method with caution.

EXHIBIT 3.19
High/Low Method

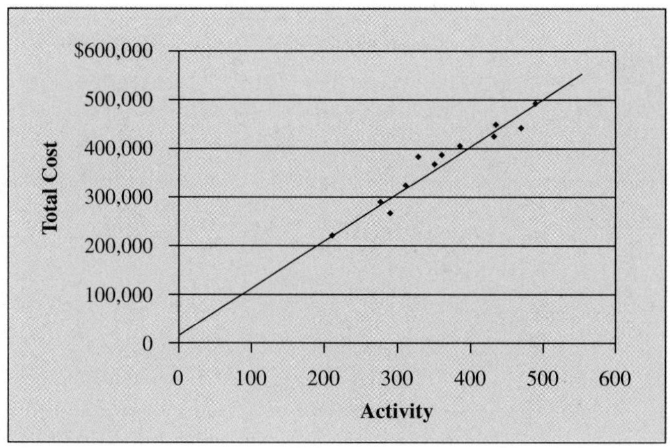

OF INTEREST Using Spreadsheets for Regression Analysis

If you understand some basic concepts, linear regression is fairly easy to perform on most any computer spreadsheet package. Typically, the independent variable is simply referred to as *X*, and the dependent variable is referred to as *Y*. Then it is simply a matter of indicating the location of *X* and *Y* and requesting the appropriate analysis.

Let's examine how to perform regression analysis using Excel and the following data:

Independent Variable Number of Orders Filled	Dependent Variable Cost of Packing Supplies
160	$18,000
250	26,000
170	20,000
240	28,000
210	24,000
180	22,000

First, enter all the observations of the independent variable, *X*, in column A, and the corresponding observations of the dependent variable, *Y*, in column B (omit the dollar sign). Next, locate the "Formulas" pull-down menu. Now you should see a "More Functions" option. From the "Function Category" menu, choose "Statistical." Then from the "Function Name" menu, choose "intercept" to calculate the fixed cost and click "OK." You must indicate the location of the known *Y* and *X* observations, cells B1.B6 and A1.A6, in this case. Then click "OK" and the value 3924.706 should be calculated as the intercept, or fixed cost. Then repeat the above procedure (Formulas/More Functions/Statistical), and choose "slope" from the "Function Name" menu. The calculated value of 94.58824 is returned as the slope, or variable cost. Finally, to determine the strength of this regression analysis, repeat the procedure and choose "RSQ" to determine R^2. The value of 0.905345 is returned. This indicates that the strength of the relationship between the independent and dependent variables is very strong. Therefore, we can be confident using the number of orders filled to predict the cost of packing supplies.

For more sophisticated analysis to determine T statistics and other measures, Excel offers a regression analysis package in its Data Analysis Add-ins.

Linear Regression Analysis

One of the most commonly used statistical techniques for estimating costs or revenues is called linear regression analysis or least squares regression. Linear regression analysis uses multiple data points and statistical analysis to determine the total cost or revenue formula. It is called least squares regression because it allows determination of the total cost (revenue) formula by minimizing the sum of the squared deviations of the data points around the line.

Companies benefit from using linear regression because it utilizes *all* the available data, thus overcoming the limitation of the high/low method. Another benefit of linear regression is that in addition to determining the cost or revenue formula, the linear regression software indicates measures of the strength of the cost (revenue) and activity relationship. The formula representing the cost (revenue) and activity relationship obtained using linear regression is the most accurate representation of the linear relationship between the activity driver and the cost (revenue). If you haven't had a statistics class yet, don't worry. All the computer is doing for us is using all the data we "feed" it to determine the formula for a straight line. We will go slowly through all the "jargon" associated with statistics and you will see that linear regression analysis is not that complicated.

Most spreadsheet programs and many handheld calculators perform linear regression. The Of Interest box in this chapter discusses how to perform linear regression using Excel. Our purpose here is to focus on the data needed to perform regression and how to interpret the output of the regression program.

As we did with the high/low method, we must begin by gathering data about the activity driver (number of computers sold, in this case) and the costs or revenues we wish to analyze (total costs, in this case). As with the high/low method we must ensure that the data used reflect normal operating activity. Recall that these data are shown in Exhibit 3.18. Next we need to enter these data into a spreadsheet in the same format as shown in Exhibit 3.18 except that the column containing months is not relevant and need not be entered.

The total cost data are called the **Y variable** or **dependent variable,** depending on the statistical package used. Recall that the Y variable refers to the Y-axis on a graph. The dependent variable means that the amount of this variable depends on some other variable. For our purposes, we believe that the total cost depends on the number of computers sold. The number of computers sold is called the **X variable** or **independent variable,** depending on the statistical package used. The X refers to the X-axis on a graph while the term *independent* means that the amount of this variable does not depend on any other variable.

Depending on the statistical program used, the output of a linear regression analysis includes information reflecting the formula representing the cost (revenue) and activity driver relationship and additional information to evaluate the dependability of the formula.

The output of Excel reveals the following:

	Coefficients	Standard Error	T Statistic
Intercept	20,542.3984		
X Variable	950.2055	82.8231	11.4727

Recall that the intercept represents the fixed cost and, therefore, the X variable represents the variable cost. The term *coefficient* simply means "amount." Thus, according to the linear regression output our total cost formula is

$$\text{Total cost} = \$20{,}542.40 + (\$950.21 \times \text{Number of computers sold})$$

Stat Talk = English
Dependent = Y = Cost/revenue
Independent = X = Activity
Coefficient = Amount
R square = Strength

The standard error is a measure of variability around the mean (statistical average of a variable). Thus the larger the standard error, the greater the variability and, therefore, the *less reliable the prediction of cost.* The T statistic is a statistical measure of the significance of the slope of the regression line. Think for a moment why this is important. If the slope is not significant, the relationship between the activity and the cost (or revenue) is primarily fixed and, therefore, we cannot use knowledge about the level of activity to predict costs (or revenues). Thus it is important that the T statistic indicates a significant slope. Since we typically deal with small sample sizes in accounting (less than 30 observations) a T statistic that is greater than 2 indicates significance.

If your statistical package does not provide a T statistic, one can easily be calculated. The T statistic measures the reliability of the X coefficient so it is equal to the X coefficient divided by the standard error of the X coefficient. For our results, the T statistic would be determined as $950.2055/82.8231 = 11.4727$. The difference is due to rounding, which the computer output shows but did not do internally.

Additional information provided by Excel indicates the following:

Multiple R	0.9640
R square	0.9294
Observations	12

First, observations tells us that 12 data points (the activity and the associated cost are one data point) were processed. You should always check this to make sure it agrees with the number of data points you believe you analyzed. Since we used one year of monthly data, the number of observations is appropriate. The Multiple R is a measure of correlation. A positive correlation means that as the amount of the X variable (number of computers sold) increases, the amount of the Y variable (total cost) also increases. A negative correlation means that as the amount of the X variable (number of computers sold) increases, the amount of the Y variable (total cost) decreases. You should always check to make sure this makes sense for your situation. In this case, it does: as the number of computers increases, the total cost increases. The R square is literally the Multiple R squared (multiplied by itself). It indicates the strength of the relationship between the independent (number of computers sold) and dependent (total cost) variables. R square ranges from 0 to 1 and the larger the number is, the stronger the relationship. Since we have an R square of 0.9294, the relationship between the number of computers sold and total cost is very strong. This is important because it indicates that if the past can be used to predict the future our predictions should be fairly accurate within the relevant range of activity.

EXHIBIT 3.20
Linear Regression Method

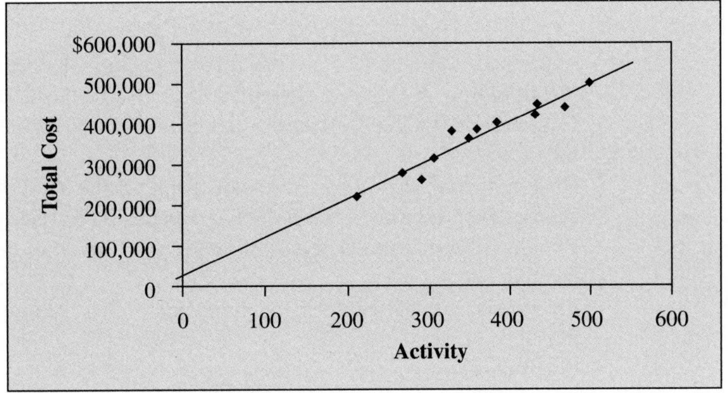

Now that we know the variable cost and the fixed cost, the significance of the slope, and the strength of the cost/activity driver relationship, we can predict costs in the future. Recall that the total cost formula is

$$\text{Total cost} = \$20{,}542.40 + (\$950.21 \times \text{Number of computers sold})$$

If we believe that 220 computers will be sold next month, we predict total costs at:

$$\text{Total cost} = \$20{,}542.40 + (\$950.21 \times 220)$$

$$\text{Total cost} = \$229{,}588.60$$

If we believe that 462 computers will be sold next month, we predict total costs at:

$$\text{Total cost} = \$20{,}542.40 + (\$950.21 \times 462)$$

$$\text{Total cost} = \$459{,}539.42$$

Exhibit 3.20 illustrates these data and the resulting cost line using the linear regression method. Notice that the data points fall very close to the line because all the data were considered when developing the total cost formula.

Summary

The marketing/sales/collection/customer support, purchasing/human resources/payment, and conversion process are all operating processes. The activities of these processes are undertaken to generate revenue. The marketing/sales/collection/customer support process is commonly called the revenue process while the purchasing/human resources/payment process is commonly referred to as the expenditure process. The activities of the revenue and expenditure processes involve the company interacting with others outside the company—customers and suppliers. The activities of the conversion process are internal to the company. Understanding the relationship between costs and activities as well as between revenues and activities is crucial to planning and controlling the operating process.

- There are five primary activities in the revenue process, four primary activities in the expenditure process, and four primary activities in the conversion process.
- Costs and revenues exhibit three types of behaviors—fixed, variable, and mixed.
- The high/low and linear regression methods are used to separate mixed costs (revenues) into their fixed and variable components.

Key Terms

Activity drivers Bases that reflect the consumption or provision of resources, *78*
Bill of lading A shipping agreement between the business and the common carrier, *66*
Conversion process A series of interrelated activities designed to produce the goods a company sells, *73*
Cost behavior How a cost reacts to change in the level of operating activity, *76*
Dependent variable A variable that depends on another variable, *85*
Expenditure process A series of interrelated activities designed to enable the company to generate revenue, *70*
Fixed cost A cost that does not change in total as the amount of the activity driver changes throughout the relevant range, *79*
Fixed revenue A revenue that does not change in total as the amount of the activity driver changes throughout the relevant range, *79*
Free on board (FOB) destination A situation where legal title to goods passes to the customer when the goods are received, *66*
Free on board (FOB) shipping point A situation where legal title to goods passes to the customer when the goods are picked up by the common carrier, *66*
Independent variable A variable that does not depend on another variable, *86*
Manufacturing overhead The cost of all manufacturing resources used to make products that are not directly associated with production, *75*
Mixed cost A cost that varies, but not proportionately, to a change in activity throughout the relevant range, *81*
Mixed revenue A revenue that varies, but not proportionately, to a change in activity throughout the relevant range, *81*
Purchase allowances Discounts given to unhappy customers (buyer's perspective), *72*
Purchase discounts Discounts offered to induce customers to pay their bills early (buyer's perspective), *72*
Purchase order A document sent from a buyer to a vendor to request items for purchase, *72*
Purchase requisition A document used by an internal party to communicate their needs to the purchasing manager, *70*
Purchase returns Goods returned to the seller by the buyer (buyer's perspective), *72*
Relevant range The span of operating activity that is considered normal for the company, *78*
Revenue behavior How a revenue reacts to change in the level of operating activity, *76*
Revenue process A series of interrelated activities designed to generate revenue, *64*
Sales allowances Discounts given to unhappy customers (seller's perspective), *69*
Sales discounts Discounts offered to induce customers to pay their bills early (seller's perspective), *66*
Sales invoice A document sent from a seller to a customer as a bill, *67*
Sales returns Goods returned to the seller by the buyer (seller's perspective), *69*
Variable cost A cost that changes in direct proportion to the change in the amount of activity driver throughout the relevant range, *80*
Variable revenue A revenue that changes in direct proportion to the change in the amount of activity driver throughout the relevant range, *80*
X variable See independent variable, *86*
Y variable See dependent variable, *85*

Questions

1. Describe the activities in the revenue process and the types of decisions that must be made.
2. Describe the activities in the expenditure process and the types of decisions that must be made.
3. Describe the activities in the conversion process and the types of decisions that must be made.
4. Contrast FOB destination and FOB shipping point. Why is this distinction important?
5. How does a company treat a sale when a customer uses a bankcard? How does a company treat a sale when a customer uses a company-issued card?
6. How has automation affected the conversion process?
7. What is the relationship between a sales return and a purchase return? What is the relationship between a sales discount and a purchase discount? What is the relationship between a sales allowance and a purchase allowance?
8. Why is activity analysis important?

9. Define and give an example of each of the following costs for a merchandising company: (*a*) fixed cost, (*b*) variable cost, and (*c*) mixed cost.
10. Define and give an example of each of the following revenues for a service company: (*a*) fixed revenue, (*b*) variable revenue, and (*c*) mixed revenue.
11. Define and give an example of each of the following costs for a manufacturing company: (*a*) fixed cost, (*b*) variable cost, and (*c*) mixed cost.
12. Give an example of a cost that might vary with each of the following cost drivers: (*a*) number of orders placed, (*b*) number of units produced, (*c*) number of tests performed, and (*d*) number of square feet.
13. Explain the importance of the relevant range concept.
14. What is an activity driver?
15. What does each element in the equation $Y = a + b\,(X)$ indicate in terms of costs?
16. What does each element in the equation $Y = a + b\,(X)$ indicate in terms of revenues?
17. Explain how to use the high/low method to estimate costs and/or revenues.
18. What are the advantages and disadvantages of the high/low method?
19. Define the following terms used in regression analysis: (*a*) independent variable, (*b*) dependent variable, (*c*) T statistic, and (*d*) R square.
20. Is an R square of 0.9 good? Why or why not?
21. Explain how to use the output of linear regression analysis to define the cost (or revenue) line.
22. What are the advantages and disadvantages of using linear regression analysis to define cost (or revenue) lines?

Exercises

E3.1 LO 1 On December 29, 2009, Wolfe Company ships $100,000 of merchandise by common carrier to the Audio Midwest Company. The terms of the sale are 2/15, n/30, FOB destination. It takes five days for the merchandise to arrive at Audio Midwest. Wolfe and Audio Midwest have December 31 year-ends. Which company should report the merchandise on their balance sheet? Why?

LO 1 **E3.2** Refer to E3.1. What is the available sales/purchase discount? When is it available?

LO 1 **E3.3** On December 30, 2009, Parker Company ships $250,000 of merchandise by common carrier to Jackson, Inc. The terms of the sale are 2/10, n/60, FOB shipping point. It takes four days for the merchandise to arrive at Jackson, Inc. Both Parker and Jackson have December 31 year-ends. Can Parker report a sale on its income statement for fiscal 2009? Why?

LO 1 **E3.4** Refer to E3.3. What is the available sales/purchase discount? When is it available?

LO 1 **E3.5** Eddie Bauer accepts Visa, MasterCard, Discover, and American Express as well as its own Eddie Bauer charge cards. Assume that Visa and MasterCard charge a 1.8 percent processing fee while Discover and American Express charge a 3.5 percent processing fee. During the period, the following charge card sales occurred at a particular Eddie Bauer store (no payments were made by customers):

Visa	$ 8,650
MasterCard	10,625
Discover	6,175
American Express	2,130
Eddie Bauer	25,843

What is the net amount of cash received from charge sales during the period?

LO 1 **E3.6** Shea, a regional jewelry store, issues its own charge cards to customers. It bills its customers on the first day of every month for purchases made during the previous month. In addition, Shea accepts Visa and MasterCard, both of which charge a 1.8 percent processing fee. The following sales were made during the period:

Visa	$ 5,490
MasterCard	3,401
Shea card	10,980
Cash sales	2,695
Sales paid by check	6,400

What is the net amount of cash received from the sales made during the period (assume 10% NSF checks)?

LO 2 **E3.7** Trollinger is an automotive parts retail store. It sells motor oil, oil filters, automotive batteries, and other automotive equipment. Assume that activity is defined as the *number of products sold.* Identify each of the following costs as variable, fixed, or mixed. Use **V** for variable, **F** for fixed, and **M** for mixed.

________ A. Cost of automotive batteries
________ B. Wages paid to employees who deliver parts to customers
________ C. Cost of shelving for the showroom
________ D. Utilities: water, electricity, and heat
________ E. Freight paid to receive parts from the warehouse
________ F. Insurance paid on shipments from the factory to Trollinger
________ G. Insurance paid on retail store
________ H. Computer costs for inventory maintenance
________ I. Wages paid to employees who wait on customers
________ J. Cost of oil

LO 2 **E3.8** Leasure Locks is a hair styling salon. The following is a list of costs connected with the salon. Identify each of the costs as variable, fixed, or mixed. Assume that activity is measured as the *number of customers.* Use **V** for variable, **F** for fixed, and **M** for mixed.

________ A. Hair products sold to customers
________ B. Computer costs for inventory maintenance
________ C. Stylists' wages and commissions
________ D. Hair dryers
________ E. Combs, brushes, and miscellaneous hair supplies
________ F. Perming solution
________ G. Laundry service for towels and gowns
________ H. Shampoo and rinse
________ I. Utilities: water, electricity, and heat
________ J. Rent on the facilities

LO 2 **E3.9** Woznick offers clients a variety of legal services. Some clients pay Woznick a monthly retainer, while others are billed as services are rendered. Identify each of the revenues below as variable, fixed, or mixed. Use **V** for variable, **F** for fixed, and **M** for mixed. Activity is measured as the number of *hours of legal service provided.*

________ A. Nicky hires Woznick to handle her divorce. She is billed for the hours worked.
________ B. Paul hires Woznick for estate planning. He is billed a research fee plus time worked.
________ C. Michelle hires Woznick to handle her real estate transactions. This is an ongoing situation for which Michelle pays a monthly fee.
________ D. David hires Woznick for legal advice as he incorporates his business. Woznick charges David a flat fee to prepare the documents plus a fee per hours worked.
________ E. Katie hires Woznick to write a partnership agreement. Woznick charges a flat fee for this service.
________ F. Jason hires Woznick to obtain local permits to operate his business. Woznick bills Jason for time worked.

LO 2 **E3.10** Duckworth is a manufacturing firm that makes ping-pong paddles. Each ping-pong paddle consists of a handle, a wooden paddle, and a rubber backing for the wooden paddle. As the paddles progress through the assembly process, workers attach the handles and glue on the rubber backing. Identify each of these costs as variable, fixed, or mixed. Use **V** for variable, **F** for fixed, and **M** for mixed. Activity is measured as the *number of ping-pong paddles produced.*

________ A. Cost of shipping crates
________ B. Cost of glue
________ C. Cost of wooden paddles
________ D. Production supervisor's salary
________ E. Cost of rubber backing for the ping-pong paddles
________ F. Utilities for the production facilities: water, electricity, and heat
________ G. Commission of sales personnel
________ H. Rent on production facilities
________ I. Wages of assembly workers
________ J. Cost of handles for the paddles

LO 3 E3.11 Mitchem Fleet, Inc., has incurred the following maintenance costs on its fleet of taxicabs during the past six months. Use the high/low cost estimation method to determine the expected cost if 12,000 miles are logged in one month.

Month	Total Miles Logged	Maintenance Cost
1	13,255	$26,000
2	8,650	17,000
3	12,250	21,400
4	18,200	31,600
5	9,120	19,400
6	12,750	24,000

LO 4 E3.12 Refer to E3.11. These data were entered into a regression program, resulting in the following output. Use this output to determine the expected cost if 12,000 miles are logged in one month. What is the T statistic and what does it indicate?

Intercept	5013.585
X coefficient	1.473
R square	0.952
Standard error	0.1658

LO 3 E3.13 The engineering costs and the number of machine setups for each month during the first half of the year at Decklever Company follow. Using the high/low cost estimation method, determine the cost equation.

Month	Engineering Cost	Number of Setups
1	$2,400	6
2	2,325	5
3	3,600	8
4	3,450	7
5	4,200	10
6	4,050	9

LO 4 E3.14 Refer to E3.13. These data were entered into a regression program, resulting in the following output. Determine the cost equation and evaluate its strength.

Intercept	235.7143
X coefficient	413.5714
Standard error	59.0356
R square	0.9246
T statistic	7.0055

LO 3 E3.15 Wagner Company incurred the following shipping costs during the past six months. Use the high/low method to determine the expected cost of shipping 1,000 items in one month.

Month	Total Items Shipped	Total Shipping Cost
1	850	$720
2	900	750
3	1,100	900
4	1,200	940
5	750	625
6	1,150	920

LO 4 E3.16 Refer to E3.15. These data were entered into a regression program, resulting in the following output. Use this output to determine the expected cost if 1,000 items are shipped in one month.

Intercept	113.5162
X coefficient	0.7015
Multiple R	0.9952
T statistic	20.2805

LO 3 E3.17 Howe provided the following revenue and client data for the past six months. Use the high/low method to predict revenues when Howe has 25 clients in a month.

Month	Number of Clients	Revenue Generated
1	28	$35,800
2	20	24,500
3	32	39,870
4	43	50,120
5	14	18,340
6	38	43,500

LO 4 E3.18 Refer to E3.17. These data were entered into a linear regression program, resulting in the following output. Use this output to predict revenues when Howe has 25 clients in a month.

Intercept	3570.8771
X coefficient	1089.7414
Standard error	59.0182
Observations	6
Multiple R	0.9942

LO 4 E3.19 Refer to E3.18. What are the R square and T statistic for this analysis? Evaluate the strength of the linear regression analysis.

LO 4 E3.20 Refer to E3.16. What are the R square and the standard error? Evaluate the strength of this linear regression relationship.

LO 3 E3.21 Batchelor, LLP, an accounting firm, has customers who pay flat monthly fees for services, others who pay by the hour, and still other customers who pay flat fees plus hourly fees. Batchelor wants to understand the relationship between hours worked and fees earned. He has gathered the following data for you. Use the high/low method to determine Batchelor's revenue formula.

Month	Revenues	Hours Worked
January	$53,350	470
February	34,500	325
March	23,450	250
April	37,840	365
May	43,250	435
June	48,975	460
July	54,500	490
August	55,000	525
September	66,000	600
October	54,600	630
November	52,600	560
December	35,800	510

LO 4 E3.22 Refer to E3.21. These data were entered into a regression program, resulting in the following output. What is Batchelor's revenue formula according to the regression analysis?

Intercept	4406.8576
X coefficient	90.2104
Multiple R	0.8499
R square	0.7224
Observations	12
Standard error	17.6834
T statistic	5.1014

LO 3 LO 4 E3.23 Refer to E3.21 and E3.22. If Batchelor anticipates working 500 hours, what is the predicted level of revenue using the high/low method? What is the predicted level of revenue using the linear regression method? Evaluate the strength of the linear regression analysis.

Problems

P3.1 LO 2 Examine these cost graphs. Identify the cost and revenue behavior pattern shown for each graph and provide at least one example of a cost and a revenue that fits the pattern.

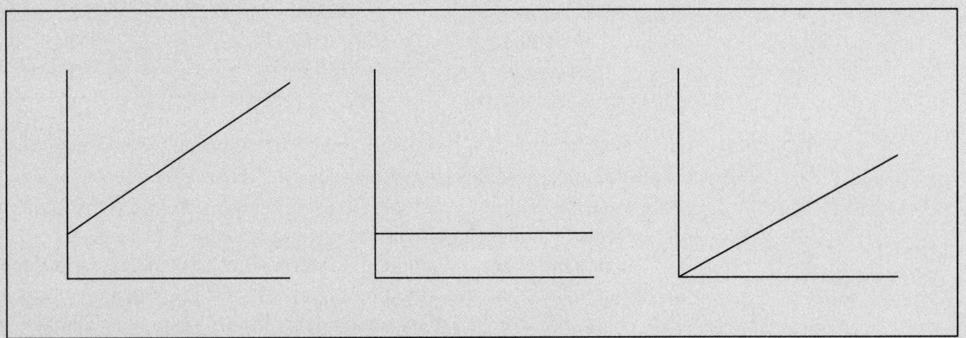

P3.2 LO 3 Forster is estimating costs for the last half of the year based on activity during the first half of the year. The results from January through June are as follows:

Month	Units	Production Costs
January	3,500	$ 56,700
February	6,200	81,800
March	4,600	69,800
April	12,500	128,900
May	8,100	95,800
June	9,800	122,100

Required:

A. Using the high/low cost estimation method, determine the total variable cost per unit made.
B. Using the high/low cost estimation method, determine the total fixed cost per month.
C. What is the cost estimation equation?
D. Estimate the total cost if 11,000 units are made during July using the equation developed in part **(C)**.
E. Why are the high and low points chosen based on units?

P3.3 LO 4 Refer to P3.2. The following is the output of a regression analysis applied to these data.

Regression Statistics	
Multiple R	0.9821
R square	0.9645

	Coefficients	Standard Error	*T* Stat
Intercept	30142.6956		
Units	8.3723	0.8035	10.4196

Required:

A. What is the dependent variable in the regression application?
B. What is the independent variable in the regression application?
C. Using the results, determine the cost equation.
D. Estimate the total cost if 11,000 units are made during July.
E. Is this regression analysis reliable? Why?

P3.4 LO 3 Wickstrom currently uses labor hours to predict overhead. However, the accountant at Wickstrom has suggested that machine hours would be a better predictor of overhead cost than labor hours. The following data have been provided to you from the past year:

Month	Overhead Cost	Labor Hours	Machine Hours
January	$54,500	1,600	2,100
February	53,400	1,900	1,950
March	63,800	1,850	3,100
April	70,000	2,000	4,000
May	62,700	2,100	3,200
June	68,900	1,950	3,600
July	80,100	2,500	4,850
August	82,200	2,400	5,100

Month	Overhead Cost	Labor Hours	Machine Hours
September	$69,900	1,800	3,950
October	59,600	1,700	2,600
November	71,500	2,300	4,100
December	77,400	2,450	4,700

Required:
A. Using the high/low estimation method, determine the cost equation when direct labor hours is used as the independent variable.
B. Using the high/low cost estimation method, determine the cost equation when machine hours is used as the independent variable.
C. What is the estimated amount of overhead if 2,200 direct labor hours are worked next month?
D. What is the estimated amount of overhead if 4,200 machine hours are worked?
E. Which of these variables, direct labor hours or machine hours, do you believe is more useful? Why?

LO 4 **P3.5** Refer to the information in P3.4. The following regression results were obtained using these data:

Direct Labor Hours

Regression Statistics	
Multiple R	0.835394694
R square	0.697884295

	Coefficients	Standard Error	*T* Stat
Intercept	14970.91994	11109.00128	1.347638691
Labor hours	25.83906154	5.376153673	4.806235667

Machine Hours

Regression Statistics	
Multiple R	0.994679721
R square	0.989387748

	Coefficients	Standard Error	*T* Stat
Intercept	35542.95886	1097.278139	32.39193201
Machine hours	8.959179043	0.293419334	30.53370388

Required:
A. What is the estimated amount of overhead if 2,200 direct labor hours are worked next month?
B. What is the estimated amount of overhead if 4,200 machine hours are worked next month?
C. Which of these variables, direct labor hours or machine hours, do you think is more useful? Why?

LO 1 **P3.6** Your company is experiencing a cash shortage this month and can only pay up to $150,000 of invoices. You received the following list of invoices currently due.

	Amount	Terms
1	$50,800	2/10, n/30
2	37,500	3/15, n/30
3	79,100	n/60
4	20,300	2/10, n/30
5	39,000	1/10, n/60
6	52,800	1/15, n/60

Required:
A. Determine the invoices to pay this month (i.e., in the next 30 days) and what the total cash disbursement is. (Assume no partial payments are allowed.)
B. Would your answer to part **A** change if any of these suppliers were to charge a 1 percent fee for overdue accounts?

LO 3 **P3.7** Scott, LLC, has gathered the following information regarding the number of tax schedules prepared and the revenue generated.

Period	Revenue Generated	Number of Tax Schedules Prepared
1	$38,400	6,550
2	36,750	5,400
3	35,885	3,700
4	36,780	4,300
5	39,000	5,450
6	39,875	6,575

Required:
A. Determine the revenue formula using the high/low method.
B. What is the estimated revenue if 5,600 tax schedules are prepared in one period?
C. What is the estimated revenue if 2,200 tax schedules are prepared in one period?
D. Does the relevant range concept impact your answer to part **(C)?**

LO 4 **P3.8** Refer to P3.7. The following linear regression results were obtained using these data:

Regression Statistics	
Multiple R	0.841205359
R square	0.707626455

	Coefficients	Standard Error	*T* Stat
Intercept	31837.18587	1948.130283	16.34243
Number of schedules	1.115461604	0.358502044	3.111451

Required:
A. Determine the revenue formula using the linear regression ouput.
B. What is the estimated revenue if 5,600 tax schedules are prepared in one period?
C. What is the estimated revenue if 2,200 tax schedules are prepared in one period?
D. Does the relevant range concept impact your answer to part **(C)?**
E. Evaluate the strength of the linear regression analysis.

LO 3 **P3.9** Dewine Medical wants to analyze its revenue per patient day. A patient day is one patient staying for one day. The following information has been provided to you:

Period	Revenue	Patient Days
1	$20,325	768
2	19,829	699
3	20,035	702
4	17,805	641
5	18,895	634
6	18,466	565

Required:
A. Determine the revenue formula using the high/low method.
B. What is the estimated revenue if 600 patient days are used?
C. What is the estimated revenue if 700 patient days are used?

LO 4 **P3.10** Refer to P3.9. The following linear regression results were obtained using these data:

Regression Statistics	
Multiple R	0.81513775
R square	0.66444956

	Coefficients	Standard Error	*T* Stat
Intercept	11515.4303	2752.206095	4.184073
Patient days	11.5396404	4.100248498	2.814376

Required:
A. Determine the revenue formula using the linear regression output.
B. What is the estimated revenue if 600 patient days are used?

C. What is the estimated revenue if 700 patient days are used?
D. Evaluate the strength of the linear regression analysis.

Cases

C3.1 LO 1 Refer to C1.1. Based on your knowledge of this company, describe its revenue, expenditure, and conversion (if applicable) processes.

LO 1 C3.2 Custom Cabinets manufactures custom kitchen cabinets. The company employs a general manager, two production designers, 45 cabinetmakers, a bookkeeper, and two office assistants. Customers place orders in consultation with one of the production designers. Each order is then assigned to one or more cabinetmakers depending on the size of the order. The selling price of the order is determined by totaling the costs of materials and labor and adding an amount to cover overhead and an amount for profit.

Required:
A. Describe the conversion process for this company.
B. Describe the information needs of this company.
C. Describe how the total cost of an order will be tracked.

Critical Thinking

CT3.1 LO 4 The shipping manager of Sullivan is concerned about the recent increase in shipping costs. He is finding it difficult to predict shipping costs from one warehouse to the next or from one month to the next. After investigation, you determine that shipping costs are driven by one of the following activities:

- The number of shipments received
- The weight of the shipments received
- The dollar value of the shipments received

Based on this investigation, data on each activity were gathered for regression analysis and the following results were obtained:

Regression 1:	Number of Shipments
Intercept	628,680
Slope	−1,127.8
R square	0.95

Regression 2:	Weight of Shipments
Intercept	271,610
Slope	150.8
R square	0.927

Regression 3:	Value of Shipments
Intercept	236,790
Slope	0.123
R square	0.912

Additional Information:
1. Management is expecting a 10 percent increase in product costs next year.
2. Only 80 percent of the warehouses have scales to weigh the shipments. Scales will have to be purchased for the other warehouses at a cost of $1,200 each.
3. The number of shipments varies widely between the warehouses, from a low of 17 shipments per month to a high of 102 shipments per month.

Required:
A. Explain the rationale behind each of the cost driver–cost relationships.
B. Analyze this information and explain which variable (number of shipments, weight of shipments, or value of shipments) should be used to predict shipping costs in the future.

LO 1 CT3.2 Watkins has a $15,800 invoice that is due in 60 days. If Watkins pays the invoice in 10 days, it can take advantage of a 2 percent cash discount offered by the supplier. Alternatively, Watkins can invest the money and earn a 6 percent annual return. Should Watkins pay the invoice in 10 days? Why?

Ethical Challenges

EC3.1 LO 3,4 In Chapter 1, we examined the FASB Concept Statement 2 that indicated that the benefits of accounting information should outweigh the costs of providing the information in order for information to be useful. Discuss the use of the high/low method versus the linear regression method to determine fixed and variable costs given that the benefits often accrue to management while the costs are incurred by accounting.

EC3.2 LO 1 Many companies have moved operations overseas in an attempt to reduce costs. For example, order fulfillment and customer service call centers are often located in nondomestic locations. Discuss this issue from three points of view—customers, employees, and shareholders.

Computer Applications

CA3.1 LO 4 Olana Company is estimating costs for the last half of the year based on activity during the first half of the year. The results from January through June are as follows:

Month	Units	Direct Materials	Direct Labor	Overhead
January	2,920	$11,680	$17,520	$27,550
February	5,000	20,000	30,000	31,810
March	3,625	14,500	21,750	33,640
April	8,720	34,880	52,320	41,760
May	5,986	23,944	35,916	36,000
June	7,986	31,944	47,916	42,840

Required:

A. Use linear regression analysis to determine the cost formula for Olana Company.
B. What is the estimated total cost if 6,000 units are produced?
C. What is the estimated total cost if 8,000 units are produced?

LO 4 **CA3.2** Labrie Hospital wants to analyze its revenue per patient day. A "patient day" is one patient staying for one day. The following information has been provided to you:

Period	Revenues	Patient Days
1	$20,325	768
2	20,580	703
3	19,829	699
4	19,917	790
5	20,035	702
6	16,705	558
7	17,805	641
8	21,358	802
9	18,895	634
10	18,466	565

Required:

A. Determine the revenue formula using the linear regression.
B. What is the estimated revenue if 600 patient days are used?
C. What is the estimated revenue if 700 patient days are used?

Visit the text Online Learning Center at **www.mhhe.com/ainsworth6e** for additional problem material that accompanies this chapter.

PART TWO

II

Planning: Operating Activities

CHAPTER FOUR

4

Short-Term Decision Making

Learning Objectives

LO 1 Describe the differences among product, nonproduct, unit-related, batch-related, product-sustaining, and facility-sustaining costs.

LO 2 Explain the purpose of, and perform, cost-volume-profit (CVP) analysis.

LO 3 Define and analyze a short-term special order decision.

LO 4 Explain and analyze a short-term outsourcing decision.

LO 5 Discuss and analyze a short-term product mix decision.

In Chapter 1 we learned that businesses use accounting information to make decisions regarding operating as well as capital resources. In Chapter 2 we examined the activities involved in the operating process and discovered that the operating process consists of three subprocesses: (1) revenue, (2) expenditure, and (3) conversion. In Chapter 3 we studied how costs and revenues vary with activities and how we can use models to predict cost and revenue behavior. Chapter 4 begins a sequence where we examine planning issues for the operating subprocesses. In this chapter we examine how cost/revenue behavior can be modeled to make short-term operating decisions. In subsequent chapters we examine how the revenue, expenditure, and conversion processes are planned and budgeted.

Short-Term Decisions

The extent to which an individual company faces short-term decisions varies dramatically. Some companies' operations are stable and these opportunities arise infrequently. For others, short-term decisions are recurring. For example, consider a grocery store chain. Its business is fairly stable and it does not experience a great deal of uncertainty in its purchasing and selling activities. But what would happen if the grocer had the opportunity to purchase a large quantity of some grocery item, perhaps soda, at a substantial discount? The grocer must decide whether there is sufficient storage space for the soda and whether the soda can be sold. This is a short-term operating decision because expanding the physical capacity of the grocery store is not possible in the time frame the decision must be made. Likewise, consider a restaurant that has the opportunity to host a large banquet for the management team of Apple Computer. In this case, the restaurant must determine whether the revenues generated by the banquet exceed the cost of hosting the banquet. In addition, the restaurant manager must evaluate the potential of losing revenues if regular clientele must be turned away while the banquet is being held. Again, this is a short-term operating decision because expanding the physical capacity of the restaurant is not possible in the time frame during which the decision must be made.

Short-term operating decisions are different from the types of decisions made by managers in the business organization and strategy process and the capital resource process in one crucial way: *Short-term operating decisions assume that capacity is fixed.* That is, in the short term, the company cannot increase its physical capacity to operate by building new facilities, putting on an additional shift of workers, or relocating to a new area. Therefore, during the time when the decision must be made, capacity cannot be increased or decreased. Recall that neither the grocer nor the restaurant manager could increase the physical capacity of their stores to take advantage of the opportunity. But managers must be aware that decisions made in the short term can impact the firm's future long-term decisions, a situation examined later in the chapter.

Short-term operating decisions also differ from other operating decisions in two other important ways. First, short-term operating decisions are ad hoc; that is, they cannot be planned during the company's normal planning process. These decisions arise due to changes in the business environment and must be addressed in a timely manner. The grocer did not know during the normal ordering process that soda might be available at a discounted price, and the restaurant manager did not know about the banquet until approached by the customer.

Second, short-term operating decisions are unique. Each decision must be analyzed as a distinct opportunity. That is, each decision has relevant variables that are particular to that decision. The grocer had to analyze revenues and costs that are different from those analyzed by the restaurant manager. Therefore, the key to making short-term operating decisions is to understand how to use decision-making models.

A **model** is a representation of reality. Models are useful for short-term operating decisions because they help decision makers organize and sort information and, therefore, provide a decision-making tool for analysis. In this chapter we consider two particular short-term operating models (analyses): cost-volume-profit analysis and relevant variable analysis, both of which make use of the ideas we learned in Chapter 3.

FAST FACT

When planning, it is critical to know who your competitors are. For Apple, competitors include computer manufacturers such as Hewlett-Packard, IBM, and Dell. But, other competitors would include companies that make electronic products and cell phones for consumers, such as Sony, Motorola, and LG. Since technology changes rapidly, it is crucial that Apple keep its eye on what consumers are demanding and what new start-up companies are emerging. After all, Apple started in a garage not that long ago.

Cost-Volume-Profit Analysis

Cost-volume-profit (CVP) analysis is the study of how costs, revenues, and profits change in response to changes in the volume of goods or services provided to customers. This is a valuable tool for planning because management must assess whether the company can sell a given product in sufficient volume to cover the costs of manufacturing, or purchasing, the product and distributing it. Cost-volume-profit analysis also can be helpful in determining selling prices if it is possible to estimate the quantity demanded. However, cost-volume-profit analysis is a model that simplifies reality in order to make predictions without considering every factor connected with the decision. Users must understand the assumptions under which CVP operates because the assumptions establish the limits of CVP applicability and its effectiveness in forecasting.

We already know from Chapter 3 that we can identify cost and revenue behavior patterns within a relevant range of activity. This same assumption applies to cost-volume-profit analysis, only *CVP assumes that the activity driver is the number of units produced and sold.* The assumptions of cost-volume-profit analysis are as follows:

- Selling price remains constant per unit regardless of the volume sold. The total revenue formula is represented by a straight line where *total revenue changes in direct proportion to changes in volume of units sold.* There are no volume discounts (a reduced price when large quantities are ordered), nor are prices changed at various volume levels.
- Variable cost remains constant per unit regardless of the volume produced and sold. The variable cost portion of the total cost function is represented by a straight line where *total variable costs (versus variable cost per unit) change in direct proportion to changes in the volume of units produced* (or purchased, for merchandising firms). There are no volume production efficiencies resulting in a lower cost per unit as more units are produced, nor are extremely high- or low-volume units more expensive to produce and sell.
- Fixed cost remains constant in total regardless of the volume produced and sold throughout the relevant range. *The fixed cost portion of the total cost function is represented by a straight line where total fixed cost does not increase or decrease with changes in volume of units produced and sold.* Additional capacity cannot be obtained, nor can facilities be abandoned in the short run.
- For manufacturing firms, the number of units produced equals the number of units sold during the period; for merchandising firms, the number of units purchased equals the number of units sold during the period. As a result of this assumption, there are no changes in the inventory levels from the beginning to the end of the period. Therefore, *the volume number used for cost determination is the same volume number used for revenue determination.*
- If more than one type of product is sold, the **sales mix** (the relative proportions of units sold) remains constant. At all levels of activity, the mix of product sales remains the same. For example, if 100 units of product A and 50 units of product B are sold at lower

EXHIBIT 4.1
CVP Graph

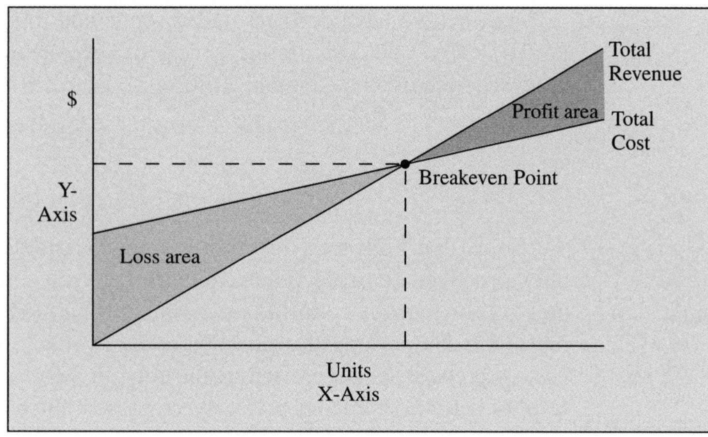

volume levels, then twice as much product A (200 units) as product B (100 units) is also sold at higher volume levels. (This situation is beyond the scope of this text.)

While these assumptions may seem limiting, they are sufficiently realistic within the relevant range to provide a useful first approximation of reality.

In CVP analysis, straight lines represent both total revenues and total costs; activity is measured as units produced (purchased) and sold. Exhibit 4.1 shows both the total revenue and total cost line on the same graph. Notice that the total revenue line begins at the origin because if no units are sold, no revenue is earned. On the other hand, the total cost line does not begin at the origin because fixed costs are incurred even if no units are produced and sold.

Breakeven point
The volume of sales where the company makes no profit nor incurs any loss; therefore, total revenues equal total costs.

The point where the total cost line intersects with the total revenue line is called the **breakeven point.** It can be measured in dollars on the Y-axis or in units on the X-axis. Because total revenues equal total costs at the breakeven point, it is the point where the company does not make a profit or incur a loss. Any volume changes from this point result in either a profit or a loss. Therefore, when the volume exceeds the breakeven point, the difference between the total revenue line and the total cost line is the profit for that particular volume. However, when the volume is below the breakeven point and the total cost line is above the total revenue line, the difference between the lines reflects the loss for that particular level of volume.

Graphs are useful for visualizing the CVP relationship because they allow us to see the breakeven point as well as the profit and loss areas. When managers use CVP as a planning tool, they use a mathematical model based on these linear relationships. The first step in CVP analysis is to define revenue as a linear relationship between the selling price and the quantity sold. That is:

$$\text{Total revenue} = \text{Selling price per unit} \times \text{Number of units sold}$$

Or,

$$TR = SP \times Q$$ [1]

Next we define total cost as a linear relationship based on the number of units purchased or produced. Analysts determine the total amount of fixed costs over the relevant range and the variable cost per unit produced or purchased by using a cost estimation technique such as the high/low method or linear regression analysis discussed in Chapter 3. This results in the following equation:

$$\text{Total cost} = (\text{Variable cost per unit} \times \text{Number of units produced}) + \text{Fixed costs}$$

Or,

$$TC = (VC \times Q) + FC$$

[1] We use Q to define units rather than X because X was previously used to define activity.

Now that we have defined total revenue and total cost, it is possible to determine profit. Profit, in CVP analysis, is the excess of revenues over costs. Because both revenues and costs are stated in a mathematical form, so is profit:

$$\text{Total revenue} - \text{Total cost} = \text{Profit}$$

Or,

$$(SP \times Q) - (VC \times Q) - FC = P$$

Contribution margin per unit
Selling price per unit less variable costs per unit; therefore, total contribution margin at a given volume level is total sales less total variable costs.

Notice that both total revenue and total variable cost are dependent on the number of units produced and sold. The difference between selling price per unit and variable cost per unit is known as the **contribution margin per unit** (SP – VC = CM). It is so named because it represents the portion of each sales dollar available to contribute to fixed costs. Once fixed costs are covered, the **contribution margin** (total sales less total variable costs at a given level of activity) becomes profit. We represent the CVP relationship as follows:

$$(SP \times Q) - (VC \times Q) - FC = P$$

$$(SP - VC) \times Q - FC = P$$

$$CM \times Q - FC = P$$

$$CM \times Q = FC + P$$

$$Q = (FC + P)/CM$$

Thus (FC + P)/CM = Q is a quicker way to calculate the number of units that must be produced and sold to cover the fixed costs and contribute to profit. It is known as the *contribution margin approach* to CVP analysis.

To illustrate CVP, we consider starting an outdoor restaurant operating in a kiosk to sell hamburgers at college sporting events:

- The material cost of $0.60 per hamburger consists of one hamburger patty, a hamburger bun, condiments (ketchup, mustard, pickle), wrapping, and a napkin.
- To encourage employees to work hard, the business will pay them $0.50 per hamburger sold rather than paying them by the hour.
- The university charges a concession fee of $600 per game.
- The grill rental fee is $100 per game.
- Miscellaneous supplies (salt, pepper, etc.) are estimated at $3 per game.
- The selling price for the hamburgers is $3.00 each.

Based on this information, the CVP elements are as follows:

- SP = $3.00
- VC = $1.10 ($0.60 materials + $0.50 labor)
- CM = $1.90 ($3.00 selling price per unit less $1.10 variable cost per unit)
- FC = $703 ($600 concession fee + $100 equipment rental + $3 miscellaneous supplies)

Determining the Breakeven Point

At the breakeven point, profit is zero. Breakeven, then, is represented as SP × Q − VC × Q − FC = 0 or (FC + 0)/CM = Q. Using the preceding data, the number of hamburgers that the business must sell to break even is

$$(\$3.00 \times Q) - (\$1.10 \times Q) - \$703 = \$0$$

$$(\$3.00 - \$1.10) \times Q - \$703 = \$0$$

$$\$1.90 \times Q - \$703 = \$0$$

$$\$1.90 \times Q = \$703$$

$$Q = 370$$

Or, using the contribution margin approach:

$$(\$703 + \$0)/\$1.90 = 370$$

Accordingly, if 370 hamburgers are sold, the profit will be zero. Therefore, if we do not believe we can sell at least 370 hamburgers per game, we should not operate. But, if we sell 371 hamburgers, we will make $1.90 of profit because the contribution margin on the first 370 hamburgers was used to cover the fixed costs so the $1.90 on the 371st hamburger contributes to profit.

We can also state the breakeven point in dollars rather than units to answer the question, "How many dollars of sales are required to break even?" We express breakeven in dollars of revenue using the contribution margin ratio approach. The **contribution margin ratio** is the contribution margin per unit divided by the selling price per unit. The contribution margin ratio is .6333 or 63.33 percent ($1.90/$3.00), so the breakeven point in sales dollars is

$$(\$703 + \$0)/0.6333 = \$1{,}110$$

This means that we must sell $1,110 worth of hamburgers to break even. That is, 370 hamburgers at $3.00 each (370 × $3.00 = $1,110).

Determining the Target Profit Level

A company cannot survive if it only breaks even because it needs profit to grow, to pay off debt, and to distribute dividends to owners. Therefore, for planning purposes, it is necessary to determine a certain targeted profit level. Using the hamburger business example, assume that we want to make a profit of $150 per game. How many hamburgers must we sell?

$$(\$3.00 \times Q) - (\$1.10 \times Q) - \$703 = \$150$$

$$\$1.90 \times Q - \$703 = \$150$$

$$\$1.90 \times Q = \$853$$

$$Q = 448.95$$

Using the contribution margin approach alternatively gives the following:

$$(\$703 + \$150)/\$1.90 = 448.95$$

Results indicate that we must sell 449 hamburgers each game to earn $150 per game. Again, we would use this information to decide whether to operate. If the goal is to have a profit of $150 to earn an adequate return, and we do not believe that we can sell 449 hamburgers per game, the business should not open.

Determining the Target Profit Level After Taxes

Corporations in the United States and many other countries must pay income taxes on profit. Fortunately, we can easily incorporate taxes into cost-volume-profit analysis. To have a particular amount of profit after taxes, a company must earn more profit before taxes. We calculate the level of before-tax profit, or the amount of profit a company earns prior to the deduction of taxes, as follows:

$$\text{After-tax profit} = \text{Before-tax profit} - (\text{Before-tax profit} \times \text{Tax rate})$$

$$\text{After-tax profit} = \text{Before-tax profit} \times (1 - \text{Tax rate})$$

Therefore,

$$\text{After-tax profit}/(1 - \text{Tax rate}) = \text{Before-tax profit}$$

Now, assuming we want to make a profit of $150 per game and that the business is subject to a 15 percent tax rate, how many hamburgers must we sell to earn $150 per game after taxes?

EXHIBIT 4.2
Profit Report When 463 Hamburgers Are Produced and Sold

Sales (463 × \$3.00)	\$1,389.00
Less: variable cost per hamburger (463 × \$1.10)	509.30
Contribution margin	\$ 879.70
Less fixed costs	703.00
Profit before taxes	\$ 176.70
Less taxes (15%)	26.51
Profit after taxes	\$ 150.19*

*Difference due to rounding.

$$(\$3.00 \times Q) - (\$1.10 \times Q) - \$703 = \$150/(1 - 0.15)$$
$$\$1.90 \times Q - \$703 = \$176.47$$
$$\$1.90 \times Q = \$879.47$$
$$Q = 462.88$$

Or, using the contribution margin approach:

$$\{\$703 + (\$150/[1 - 0.15])\}/\$1.90 = 462.88$$

According to these calculations, we must sell 463 hamburgers to make a profit of \$150 after taxes. Take a moment to examine the profit report in Exhibit 4.2 that confirms this result. It shows that when 463 hamburgers are sold, total sales are \$1,389 and total variable costs are \$509, resulting in a total contribution margin of \$880. After deducting fixed costs, the profit before taxes is \$177; subtracting taxes of 15 percent results in the desired after-tax profit of \$150.

Cost-volume-profit analysis is a useful tool for planning because decision makers can use it to determine the breakeven point, the target profit level, and the after-tax profit level. CVP analysis provides a useful explanation of some otherwise complex interrelationships, such as analyzing the sensitivity of profit to changes in (1) selling price, (2) variable cost per unit, (3) fixed cost, and (4) tax rate. It is also possible to use CVP analysis to analyze multiple-product CVP relationships.

Sensitivity Analysis

Sensitivity analysis is the process of changing the key variables (but not the assumptions) in CVP analysis to determine how sensitive the CVP relationships are to changes in these variables. Usually, the values of key variables are estimates; therefore, it is useful to know how sensitive the results are to changes in these variables. Thus analysts using sensitivity analysis increase or decrease the amount of key variables, such as selling price, variable cost per unit, fixed cost, or the tax rate, to determine the effects on profit. Generally, we change variables one at a time to isolate the sensitivity of the results to that particular variable. Be sure to review Exhibit 4.3, which shows how a change in a key variable affects breakeven, the contribution margin, and desired profit. Examples of sensitivity analysis follow.

Change in Selling Price

A change in the selling price causes a change in both the contribution margin and the breakeven point. An increase in the selling price causes an increase in the contribution margin and, therefore, a decrease in the breakeven point. On the other hand, a decrease in the selling price triggers a decrease in the contribution margin and a subsequent increase in the breakeven point.

Let's return to our example of selling hamburgers at college sporting events: Suppose that another vendor at college games is selling hot dogs for \$2.00 each, so we decide to lower our hamburger's selling price by \$0.50 to become more competitive. Then the new contribution margin is \$1.40 (\$2.50 − \$1.10), so it is now necessary to sell 503 (versus 370) hamburgers to break even:

$$(\$703 + \$0)/\$1.40 = 502.14$$

EXHIBIT 4.3
Sensitivity Analysis

Change in Variable	Contribution Margin Change	Breakeven Point Change	Units Needed for Desired Profit Change
Increase in selling price per unit	Increase	Decrease	Decrease
Decrease in selling price per unit	Decrease	Increase	Increase
Increase in variable cost per unit	Decrease	Increase	Increase
Decrease in variable cost per unit	Increase	Decrease	Decrease
Increase in fixed cost (total)	No change	Increase	Increase
Decrease in fixed cost (total)	No change	Decrease	Decrease
Increase in tax rate	No change	No change	Increase
Decrease in tax rate	No change	No change	Decrease

A decrease in selling price per unit also requires that more units be sold to obtain a particular desired profit after taxes. Assume that we want to maintain a profit of \$150 per game after taxes of 15 percent. Due to its reduced selling price, we must now sell 629 (versus 463) hamburgers:

$$\{\$703 + [\$150/(1 - 0.15)]\}/\$1.40 = 628.19$$

Change in Variable Cost

A change in the variable cost per unit also causes a change in both the contribution margin and the breakeven point. An increase in the variable cost per unit causes a decrease in the contribution margin and, therefore, an increase in the breakeven point. A decrease in the variable cost per unit triggers an increase in the contribution margin and a subsequent decrease in the breakeven point.

For example, suppose we are able to lower our variable cost per hamburger by \$0.05. Our new variable cost per hamburger is \$1.05; therefore, our new contribution margin per unit is \$1.95 (\$3.00 − \$1.05), resulting in a new breakeven point of 361 hamburgers:

$$\$703/\$1.95 = 360.51$$

A decrease in variable cost per unit also means that fewer units need to be sold to achieve a desired after-tax profit. Assuming that \$150 is the desired after-tax profit, the variable cost decrease of \$0.05 requires that 452 hamburgers be sold:

$$\{\$703 + [\$150/(1 - 0.15)]\}/\$1.95 = 451.01$$

Change in Fixed Cost

A change in fixed cost causes a change in the breakeven point but not in the contribution margin. If fixed costs increase, the breakeven point increases because it requires more unit sales to cover fixed costs. Conversely, if fixed costs decrease, the breakeven point decreases.

For example, suppose that the college increases the concession fee by \$50 per game. Now we must sell 397 (versus 370) hamburgers to break even:

$$\$753/\$1.90 = 396.32$$

An increase in fixed costs also increases the number of units that must be sold to obtain a desired profit after taxes. To obtain a profit of \$150 per game after taxes of 15 percent, we must now sell 490 hamburgers per game:

$$\{\$753 + [\$150/(1 - 0.15)]\}/\$1.90 = 489.2$$

Change in Tax Rate

A change in the tax rate affects only the number of units that must be sold to obtain a desired profit after taxes. It does not affect the breakeven point because the tax rate impacts only profits created after the breakeven point is reached. If the tax rate increases, it is necessary to

OF INTEREST Using Excel for Sensitivity Analysis

Using Excel (or another spreadsheet package) is a fast and easy way to perform sensitivity analyses. You simply set up cells for each variable in the cost-volume-profit formula and then write a formula to have Excel calculate the number of units. For example, the spreadsheet shown represents the CVP information in the chapter. In cell A6 we enter the following formula: ((E3/(1–D3))+C3)/(A3–B3) and the result is the number of units required to have a profit of $150 after taxes.

Now to perform sensitivity analysis, we copy this information to cells A8 through E13 and change a cell representing the variable of interest. For example, assume the selling price is reduced to $2.50, we simply change cell A10 to $2.50 and the results tell us that we must sell 629 units to have a profit of $150 after taxes with a selling price of $2.50 per unit.

	A	B	C	D	E
1	Selling	Variable	Fixed	Tax	Target
2	Price	Costs	Costs	Rate	Profit
3	3	1.1	703	0.15	150
4					
5	Cost-volume-profit analysis				
6	462.897				
7					
8	Selling	Variable	Fixed	Tax	Target
9	Price	Costs	Costs	Rate	Profit
10	2.5	1.1	703	0.15	150
11					
12	Cost-volume-profit analysis				
13	628.193				

sell more units to obtain the same desired after-tax profit. Conversely, if the tax rate decreases, fewer units must be sold to obtain the desired after-tax profit. For example, assume the tax rate is increased to 20 percent. How many units must be sold to obtain $150 after taxes?

$$\{\$703 + [\$150/(1 - 0.20)]\}/\$1.90 = 468.68$$

According to our calculations, if the tax rate increases by 5 percent, the number of hamburgers that must be sold to generate a profit of $150 after taxes increases to 469 (versus 463 before).

Sensitivity analysis is useful for assessing the effects of changes in the cost-volume-profit variables. Businesses often use computer spreadsheets for these analyses because they make it quick and easy to see the effects of changes in one, or several, variables.

Relevant Variable Analysis

Nonproduct costs
Those costs related to selling the product/services or running the company.

Product costs
Those costs related to obtaining or manufacturing the product.

Companies incur many different operating costs. Costs related to selling the product and services or administering the company are **nonproduct costs.** Costs related to obtaining or manufacturing the product are **product costs.**

Nonproduct costs are typically either selling (marketing) costs or administrative costs. Selling costs include the salaries and commissions paid to salespersons, the cost of maintaining delivery vehicles, and the cost of advertising. Administrative costs include the salaries paid to executives, rent on office space, and income taxes paid on profits. Notice that in all cases, nonproduct costs are related to activities involved in selling and administration.

For a merchandising firm, product costs are all the costs incurred to purchase and receive the product. For example, when a grocery store purchases soda, the product cost is the cost of the soda purchased plus any freight incurred to receive the items plus any insurance incurred while the items were in transit. Therefore, if the grocer purchased $1,000 of soda and paid $50 in freight, the total product cost is $1,050 for these items.

For a manufacturing firm such as Apple, product costs are those incurred to make the product. We typically discuss three types of manufacturing product costs:

- **Direct materials**—the cost of materials that are directly traceable to the product and that are costly enough to warrant tracing them; for example, sheet metal in a car, lumber in a table, or microprocessors in a computer. Conversely, **indirect materials** are production materials that either cannot be traced to the product or are not costly enough to warrant tracing; for example, grease in a car, glue in a table, or soldering in a computer.

Manufacturing product costs
Direct materials (cost of materials traceable to product); direct labor (cost of labor traceable to product); and manufacturing overhead (indirect/necessary manufacturing [product] cost).

- **Direct labor**—the cost of employees who manufacture the product; for example, assembly-line workers producing cars, woodcrafters making tables, or computer assemblers. Conversely, **indirect labor** is the cost of production employees who do not physically manufacture the product; for example, quality-control inspectors in a car manufacturing plant, supervisors in a furniture manufacturer, or sanitation engineers in a computer manufacturer.
- **Manufacturing overhead**—all costs incurred to manufacture products other than direct materials and direct labor. Therefore, manufacturing overhead includes indirect materials, indirect labor, and other costs necessary to manufacture products such as utilities for the factory and insurance paid on the factory building and equipment.

Notice that product costs are incurred in connection with the production of goods rather than the selling of those goods. For example, when a company uses long-term assets, it must spread the cost of those assets over the period the assets are used. The resulting cost for the time period is called **depreciation.** If a company uses a delivery vehicle to get its products to customers, depreciation on the delivery vehicle is a selling cost while depreciation on production machinery is a product cost (manufacturing overhead). Depreciation is not relevant in short-term decision making because it represents the recovery of the cost of the asset over the periods it is used.

As another example, consider Apple. The costs incurred to make iPhones are product costs. The costs incurred to sell the iPhones and administer the corporation are nonproduct costs. Let's examine the product costs closer.

The plastic case is a direct material in an iPhone, while glue is an indirect material. Although we could physically trace the amount of glue used in each iPhone, its cost is not sufficient to warrant such treatment. People assembling iPhones are considered direct labor while the janitorial staff, supervisors, and quality-control inspectors are indirect labor because their job descriptions do not include making iPhones. Finally, in addition to the indirect materials and indirect labor, supplies used in the factory, utilities, rent, insurance, property taxes, and other costs related to manufacturing iPhones are included in manufacturing overhead.

Enhance Your Understanding

If Apple rented a building and used the space for both offices and manufacturing, is the rent a product cost or a nonproduct cost?

Answer: The cost is both a product cost and a nonproduct cost. Apple would need to divide the rent cost between the two using some rational basis such as the number of square feet occupied.

Levels of cost behavior
Unit—vary with units produced or sold
Batch—vary with batches
Product-sustaining—vary with the number of product lines
Facility-sustaining—provide capacity

In addition to knowing whether a cost is a product cost or a nonproduct cost, you must understand its cost behavior to determine whether it is relevant in a given situation. Recall from Chapter 3 that costs vary with many different activities. We typically analyze four levels of cost behavior: unit-related, batch-related, product-sustaining, and facility-sustaining.

Costs that vary with the number of units, such as direct materials and shipping, are **unit-related costs.** Costs that vary with the number of batches regardless of how many units are in each batch, such as setup costs and ordering costs, are **batch-related costs.** Costs that vary with the number of product lines, such as advertising or research and development, are **product-sustaining costs.** Finally, costs incurred to maintain the company's capacity to operate, such as rent on buildings and insurance paid on office equipment, are **facility-sustaining costs.**

For example, at Apple the cost of plastic cases is a unit-related cost because it depends on the number of iPhones produced. The cost incurred to order plastic cases is a batch-related cost because it depends on the number of orders, not the size of the order. Advertising is a product-sustaining cost because it is incurred to promote a particular product line, regardless of how many units are sold. Finally, the heat and lighting cost for the factory is a facility-sustaining cost because it sustains Apple's ability to manufacture its products.

Enhance Your Understanding

Identify each of the following costs as unit-related, batch-related, product-sustaining, or facility-sustaining:

Freight paid per unit ordered

Freight paid per order

Costs incurred to service Product A

Costs incurred to hire a new CEO

Answer: Freight paid per unit order—unit-related

Freight paid per order—batch-related

Cost incurred to service Product A—product-sustaining

Costs incurred to hire a new CEO—facility-sustaining

Once costs are identified, the next step is to determine which costs (and revenues) are relevant to the operating decision.

A **relevant variable** is a cost or revenue that will occur in the future and that differs among the alternatives considered. For example, the grocer can accept or reject the opportunity to buy a large quantity of soda at a reduced price. The cost to purchase the large quantity of soda is relevant, but the cost to purchase soda last week is not. Likewise, the restaurant manager can accept or reject the banquet. The revenue generated by the banquet as well as the potential lost revenue from turning away other customers are relevant. Because each decision is unique, the relevant variables are also unique.

Sunk cost
Past cost; never relevant.

Sunk Costs Are Never Relevant

A **sunk cost** is a past cost and never relevant in a short-term operating decision. Sunk costs arise from past decisions and represent items that have already been purchased. Sunk costs are important because occasionally managers incorrectly include them in decision-making models. Perhaps you have heard the phrase "throwing good money after bad." This refers to a situation where an individual has made a bad decision and attempts to fix it by putting more money into the project. If this fix is due to the mistaken idea that the project cannot be abandoned because so much money has already been spent on it, the fix may not work. The money already spent on the project is sunk and must not be considered when deciding how, or if, to fix the project. The only costs that should be considered are those to be incurred in the future. For the grocer, the past cost of soda and the cost of shelves for storing and displaying the soda are sunk. For the restaurant manager, the cost to sponsor a banquet last month and the cost of tablecloths already purchased are sunk. Let's reconsider depreciation. As stated earlier, depreciation is the recovery of a prior cost. So, since the cost was incurred in the past, the depreciation for the period is essentially a sunk cost and irrelevant. So for the grocer, the depreciation on the shelves is irrelevant and for the restaurant manager the depreciation on the kitchen equipment is irrelevant.

Opportunity cost
Benefit forgone; always relevant.

Opportunity Costs Are Always Relevant

An **opportunity cost** is the benefit forgone when choosing one alternative over another. Since accepting one alternative means rejecting other alternatives, the opportunity cost is the benefit provided by the next best alternative. For example, if the grocer accepts the soda offer, the opportunity to use the shelf space for potato chips is forgone. Therefore, the profit that could be made from potato chip sales is the opportunity cost of accepting the soda offer. Likewise, for the restaurant manager, if the banquet is hosted, the restaurant may forgo the opportunity to serve other customers. The profit that could be made from the other customers is the opportunity cost of accepting the banquet offer.

Incremental Costs and Revenues May Be Relevant

The term *increment* means "additional." **Incremental revenue** is the additional revenue expected from an alternative. **Incremental cost** is the additional cost associated with an alternative. Therefore **incremental profit** is the difference between the incremental revenues and incremental costs of a particular alternative. Remember, however, that we look only at the revenues and costs that differ between alternatives. Therefore, if two alternatives have the same incremental revenues (costs), those revenues (costs) are irrelevant for the decision situation.

Consider the following decision situations: Assume the grocer stocks either Pepsi products or Coke products, but not both. Further assume that the products do not cost the same, but they are sold for the same price. If the grocer thinks that the same amount of each product will be sold, the incremental revenues from the sales of either soda are not relevant because they do not differ between the alternatives. However, the incremental costs are relevant. Now consider the restaurant manager. Assume the restaurant can host one of two possible banquets. One banquet party has requested chicken as the main entrée, while the other party has requested a vegetarian entrée. Both banquets will require a wait staff of 10. Although the labor cost associated with the banquets is an incremental cost, it is not relevant because it does not differ between the alternatives. However, other costs and the incremental revenues would be relevant in this situation.

There are three steps in a relevant variable analysis:

1. Identify the possible alternative actions.
2. Determine the relevant revenues, costs, and/or profits of each alternative.
3. Choose the best alternative.

Next we discuss each of these steps. Then we apply this analysis to three, specific short-term operating decision situations.

Identify the Alternative Actions

The first step in a decision situation is choosing between at least two alternatives. Whether there are only two alternatives or many, the goal is the same—choose the best alternative. For example, assume that a computer manufacturer wants to introduce a new personal digital assistant/phone to compete with the iPhone. The company has the resources available to produce only one type of phone so it must decide which is best. One possibility is to produce a super digital phone we'll call SDP. Another possibility is a regular digital phone, RDP. The final alternative is an economy digital phone, EDP. Are these the only alternatives available? No, the computer manufacturer can also choose not to make any of these products. Therefore, the four opportunities available are (1) make SDP, (2) make RDP, (3) make EDP, or (4) make none of these.

Determine the Relevant Revenues, Costs, and Profit

The second step in a relevant variable analysis is to determine the relevant revenues, costs, and profits of the alternatives. Exhibit 4.4 indicates the expected selling prices, variable costs, and quantities of the three players considered.

Assume further that the computer manufacturer must spend \$80,000, \$60,000, and \$50,000, respectively, for research and development on SDP, RDP, and EDP (product-sustaining cost). In addition, production of SDP requires the computer manufacturer to rent specialized equipment for \$20,000 per month (product-sustaining cost). Also assume that SDP can be manufactured using 15 production runs per month, RDP 12, and EDP 15. The computer company estimates its setup and other costs at \$10,000 per production run (batch-related cost). Finally, assume that insurance, rent, and other costs on the factory facilities will be \$500,000 per month (facility-sustaining cost).

EXHIBIT 4.4
Selling Prices, Unit-Variable Costs, and Quantities of Players

	SDP	RDP	EDP
Selling price per unit	$800	$600	$250
Unit-related cost	$300	$200	$100
Estimated unit sales	1,200	1,700	2,000

What Are the Relevant Costs and Revenues in This Situation?

Revenue is relevant because the selling prices and quantities demanded are different. Unit-related costs are relevant because the *unit costs* and the *quantities* are different. Batch-related costs are relevant because the *number of production runs* required is different. Product-sustaining costs are relevant because *research and development* is different among the alternatives and SDP requires specialized equipment. However, the rent, insurance, and other costs for the factory are not relevant. These facility-sustaining costs will be incurred regardless of the decision made and, therefore, are irrelevant to the decision. Exhibit 4.5 shows the relevant cost analysis for this decision.

Thus, according to our analysis, the relevant profits of SDP, RDP, and EDP are $350,000, $500,000, and $100,000, respectively. What is the relevant profit of the alternative of not producing any of these products? It is zero; if none of these products are produced, no incremental revenue is earned and no incremental costs are incurred.

Choose the Best Alternative

The third step is realizing that some decisions involve both relevant revenues and costs. Then, the best alternative is the one that has the highest relevant profit. Other decisions involve only relevant revenues, in which case the best alternative is the one that has the highest relevant revenue. Finally, some decisions involve only relevant costs, in which case the best alternative is the one that has the lowest relevant cost. Our example involves both relevant revenues and costs. Therefore, we should pick the alternative with the highest relevant profit—RDP in this case.

No decision should be made based on quantitative factors alone; qualitative factors are important, too. Managers must consider the effect of a decision on customers, employees, competitors, suppliers, shareholders, creditors, and existing product lines. As you can see, decision making is more complicated than it appears. We look at these qualitative factors in more detail as we apply a relevant variable analysis to two short-term operating decisions next.

To illustrate short-term operating decisions we again consider our hamburger kiosk. Assume now, however, that our business has been successful and that we have expanded our product line to include soft drinks, ice cream cones, and french fries.

- Employees work on a commission basis, earning 20 percent of sales.
- The college concession fee is $700 per game per kiosk.
- The rental fees for the soft drink machine, ice cream freezer, fryer, and grill are $60, $70, $85, and $85, respectively.

EXHIBIT 4.5
Relevant Variable Analysis

	SDP	RDP	EDP
Relevant revenue (selling price × units)	$960,000	$1,020,000	$500,000
Relevant unit-related costs (unit cost × units)	360,000	340,000	200,000
Relevant batch-related costs	150,000	120,000	150,000
Relevant product-sustaining costs	100,000	60,000	50,000
Relevant profit (revenues minus costs)	$350,000	$ 500,000	$100,000

EXHIBIT 4.6
Profit Report for Hamburger Kiosk

	Hamburger	French Fries	Ice Cream Cones	Soft Drinks	Kiosk Total
Selling price per item	$3.00	$1.00	$1.50	$1.00	
Unit-related cost (direct materials)	0.60	0.10	0.20	0.05	
Unit-related cost (direct labor)*	0.60	0.20	0.30	0.20	
Contribution margin per item	$1.80	$0.70	$1.00	$0.75	
Items sold	400	400	80	320	
Total contribution margin	$720.00	$280.00	$80.00	$240.00	$1,320
Product-sustaining cost	85.00	85.00	70.00	60.00	300
Total product line profit	$635.00	$195.00	$10.00	$180.00	$1,020
Facility-sustaining costs					820
Kiosk profit per game					$200

*Labor is paid a commission of 20 percent of sales made.

- The rent for a deep freezer is $100 per game.
- Other miscellaneous supplies are estimated at $20 per game.
- Estimated material costs:

Hamburgers	$0.60
French fries (per order)	0.10
Ice cream and cones	0.20
Soft drinks	0.05

- Our selling prices:

Hamburgers (each)	$3.00
French fries (per order)	1.00
Ice cream cone (each)	1.50
Soft drinks (per glass)	1.00

We show a current product line profit report in Exhibit 4.6. Examine this report carefully as we refer to it during the discussion that follows. Note that each product line incurred unit-related (direct materials and direct labor) and product-sustaining (equipment rental) costs. However, since facility-sustaining costs (concession fees, freezer rental, and miscellaneous supplies) are incurred to support the company, we deduct these from the kiosk column only.

Key Point: Internal decision making requires cost information divided into unit-related, batch-related, product-sustaining, and facility-sustaining costs. For external decision making, costs are typically divided into product and nonproduct. Therefore, if external information is provided, we must convert it into a form better suited for internal decision making. This is why you must understand both product and nonproduct costs and unit-related, batch-related, product-sustaining, and facility-sustaining costs.

Special Order (Accept-or-Reject) Decision

Typically, a customer initiates a special order situation. A customer may request a large quantity of product at a reduced price, or the customer may request a large quantity of product and ask that the supplier prepare a bid. If the customer is asking for a reduced price, the decision maker must decide whether to accept or reject the customer's offer. If the customer is asking for a bid, the company must determine an acceptable bid price. If the price is too high, the customer will reject the bid, but if the bid is too low, the company might lose

EXHIBIT 4.7
Relevant Variable Analysis—Special Order Decision

	Hamburgers	French Fries
Selling price offered	$1.50	$0.50
Unit-related cost (direct materials)	$0.60	$0.10
Unit-related cost (direct labor)*	$0.15	$0.05
Contribution margin	$0.75	$0.35
Items requested	500	500
Total contribution margin	$375.00	$175.00
Product-sustaining costs†	$170.00	$170.00
Profit on order	$205.00	$5.00

*Labor is paid a 10 percent commission on this order.
†Two additional grills and two additional fryers must be rented.

money. In both situations, a relevant cost analysis provides the quantitative answer to the question.

Assume the alumni association has contacted us regarding next week's game. They would like to purchase 500 hamburgers and 500 orders of fries. If we accept this order, we must rent two more grills ($85 each) and two additional fryers ($85 each). Because employees did not make this sale, the commission rate will be cut to 10 percent. The alumni association is willing to pay $1.50 per hamburger and $0.50 for each order of fries. Should we accept this order?

Exhibit 4.7 shows the relevant variable analysis of this situation. The selling price offered less the unit-related costs (direct materials and direct labor) results in a contribution margin of $0.70 for each hamburger and $0.35 for each order of fries. After subtracting the additional product-sustaining costs (grills and fryers), the resulting profit is $205 for hamburgers and $5 for fries. Since this is $210 in additional profit, we should accept the order.

Operating Decision Rule: Accept a special order if the relevant profit is positive and reject a special order if the relevant profit is negative.

What other factors should we consider before accepting the customer's offer? First, we must consider how this short-term decision impacts the long-term profitability of the company. For example, will the alumni association expect similar treatment for the next game? Also, we cannot sell our hamburgers and fries for this price in the long run because this price does not cover our total costs and provide the profit we want. Second, we must consider our other customers. Will other customers demand the same selling price? If we do not give other customers the same price, is this price discrimination?[2] These are just a sample of the additional considerations that must be addressed in a special order decision.

Outsourcing (Make-or-Buy) Decision

In an outsourcing decision, the company must determine whether it should do something internally or outsource the activity to another company. For example, a company might consider whether it should make a component of the main product itself or temporarily hire an outside manufacturer to make the component. A company might also consider whether it should do its own accounting or temporarily hire an outside accounting firm. In both cases, the company must determine which option is less expensive. Revenues are not relevant.

Assume that we are rethinking our ice cream sales because we are not making much profit. We have contacted an ice cream company and we could purchase ice cream bars for $0.10 each. If we outsource the ice cream we will not have to rent an ice cream freezer, but we will rent an additional smaller deep freezer for $50 per game. We would sell the ice cream bars for $1.50 each. Should we outsource ice cream or continue to make ice cream cones?

[2] Price discrimination results when different customers are charged different prices without economic justification.

EXHIBIT 4.8
Relevant Variable Analysis—Outsourcing Decision

	Make Ice Cream Cones	Buy Ice Cream Bars
Direct materials	$0.20	NA
Purchase price	NA	$0.10
Total unit cost	$0.20	$0.10
Units needed	80	80
Total unit cost	$16.00	$8.00
Ice cream freezer rental	70.00	NA
Deep freezer rental	NA	50.00
Total relevant cost	$86.00	$58.00

In Exhibit 4.8 you can see the relevant variable analysis of this situation. Notice that selling prices and direct labor costs are irrelevant because they do not differ between our alternatives. Therefore the relevant costs are direct materials, the purchase price of the ice cream bars, and the freezer rentals. According to our analysis, we should outsource ice cream because the relevant cost to make ice cream cones is greater than the relevant cost to buy ice cream bars.

Operating Decision Rule: Make a product internally if the relevant cost of making the item is less than the relevant cost of buying the item externally. Buy an item externally if the relevant cost of buying the item is less than the relevant cost of making the item.

What other factors should we consider? First, we should consider the quality of the supplier's product and processes. Will the ice cream bars be the same high quality as the ice cream cones we produce? Will the ice cream bars be available when needed? If the ice cream bars are defective (melted, for example) or not received in time, we could lose sales. Second, we must consider how this short-term decision might impact the long term. Do we want to develop a long-term relationship with this supplier rather than using it only temporarily? Will this supplier be around in the long term? These are a few of the qualitative factors that companies should consider in a make-or-buy decision situation.

Product Mix (Keep-or-Drop) Decision

In a product mix decision, the company must determine whether it should keep selling a product line or discontinue offering it in the short term. The product may be reintroduced later. For example, a company may have a product line that appears to be losing money or at least not making a large profit. The company may want to discontinue this product line. Before making the decision, managers must consider the revenues that would be lost if the product line is discontinued as well as the costs that would be saved.

Assume that we are again rethinking our ice cream sales. Rather than outsourcing ice cream we are considering dropping the product line altogether. See Exhibit 4.9 for the relevant variable analysis of this situation. Notice that if ice cream cones are discontinued we lose $120 in revenue. On the other hand we save our unit-related costs and our product-sustaining costs, for a total savings of $110. Notice that facility-sustaining costs are irrelevant as they continue regardless of whether or not we sell ice cream cones. Since we will lose more revenue than we will save in costs, we should not drop the ice cream line at this time.

EXHIBIT 4.9
Relevant Variable Analysis—Discontinue a Product Line

Relevant Variables	Revenues Lost	Costs Saved
Selling price × units sold	80 × $1.50 = $120	
Unit-related costs × units sold		80 × $0.50 = $40
Product-sustaining costs		$ 70
Total	$120	$110

FAST FACT

When considering whether to discontinue a product line, a company must evaluate the long-term impact of the decision. In the early 1990s, Ford Motor Company considered dropping the Ford Mustang. Sales were down and executives believed that the Mustang had lost its appeal. However, Ford decided to give the Mustang one more chance. In 1994, the Mustang was redesigned to appeal to sports car enthusiasts by retaining the styling of the earlier muscle cars of the 1960s. Ford included modifications to appeal to 1990s buyers such as dual airbags, antilock brakes, and an improved handling system. The new Mustang was not invented in a drawing room, however. Ford listened to its customers and improved its production process to make the "new" Mustang one of the hottest selling cars.

Operating Decision Rule: Keep a product line if the relevant revenues lost exceed the relevant costs saved from discontinuing the product line. Drop a product line if the relevant revenues lost are less than the relevant costs saved from discontinuing the product line.

What other factors should we consider? First, we must consider the impact that not serving ice cream would have on our other product sales. Will we lose hamburger sales because ice cream is not available? Second, we must consider how this short-term decision might impact the long term. Do we want to continue to grow our product lines or do we want to focus instead on a few, high-quality products? Finally we must consider our image. Do we want to be known as a full-service kiosk or one with limited offerings? These are just a few qualitative factors that must be addressed in addition to the quantitative analysis.

Another (More Difficult) Example

In this example we must convert externally focused data for internal decision making. Assume Example Company has the capacity to produce 300,000 pocket calculators in a period. A customer wants to place an order for 50,000 calculators. The customer wants to purchase these calculators for $8 each; however, our normal selling price is $12 per calculator ($3,000,000/250,000). If we accept this order it will require two additional production runs. This is the profit report for the production and sale of 250,000 calculators (normal activity level):

Sales	$3,000,000
Less cost of goods sold	1,750,000
Gross margin	$1,250,000
Less selling and administrative costs	750,000
Profit	$ 500,000

Notice that this profit report divides costs into product and nonproduct costs. But for internal decision making we need to consider which activities cause our costs to change. Assume that further investigation reveals the following:

- Cost of goods sold consists of unit-related, batch-related, and facility-sustaining costs while selling and administrative costs consist of unit-related, product-sustaining, and facility-sustaining costs.
- Facility-sustaining cost of goods sold is $500,000 and batch-related costs are $1,500 per batch with a batch size of 0 to 25,000 (maximum).
- Facility-sustaining selling and administrative costs are $250,000 and product-sustaining selling and administrative costs are $20,000.

In Exhibit 4.10 we illustrate the reclassification of external data (product/nonproduct) to internal data (unit-related, batch-related, product-sustaining, and facility-sustaining).

EXHIBIT 4.10
Conversions of Product/Nonproduct Data

		Cost of Goods Sold		Selling and Administrative
Total costs (given p. 116)		$1,750,000		$750,000
Less: facility-sustaining		$500,000		$250,000
Less: product-sustaining		$0		$20,000
Less: batch-related				
Number of batches*	10			
Cost per batch	$1,500			
Total batch-related cost†		$15,000		$0
Total unit-related cost‡		$1,235,000		$480,000
Number of units	250,000		250,000	
Cost per unit§	$4.94		$1.92	

*250,000 units total divided by 25,000 units per batch.
†10 batches multiplied by $1,500 per batch.
‡Total cost less facility-sustaining, product-sustaining, and batch-related costs.
§Total unit cost divided by 250,000 units. ($1,235,000/250,000 = $4.94; $480,000/250,000 = $1.92).

EXHIBIT 4.11
Relevant Variable Analysis: Special Order Decision

Selling price offered (given p.116)	$8
Unit-related cost ($4.94 + $1.92)	$6.86
Contribution margin per unit	$1.14
Items requested by customer	× 50,000
Total contribution margin	$57,000
Batch-related cost (2 batches × $1,500)	($3,000)
Profit on order	$54,000

Notice that we have reclassified cost of goods sold into facility-sustaining, batch-related, and unit-related costs and we reclassified selling and administrative into facility-sustaining, product-sustaining, and unit-related costs. Study this exhibit carefully.

Next we must determine which costs are relevant to this decision. First, we consider capacity—can we physically produce the number of calculators the customer wants? Yes, our capacity is 300,000 and we are currently producing 250,000 calculators. Second, we determine which costs are relevant to this decision. Are facility-sustaining costs relevant? No, they do not change whether we accept or reject this offer. Are product-sustaining costs relevant? No, the customer came to us—we did not have to advertise nor do research and development. Are batch-related costs relevant? Yes, producing the extra calculators will require two more production runs. Are unit-related costs relevant? Yes, we will be producing and selling 50,000 additional calculators.

In Exhibit 4.11 we show the relevant variable analysis of this problem. According to this analysis we should accept the customer's offer because the relevant profit is greater than zero.

Summary

Short-term decisions assume that capacity is fixed so the company must determine the best course of action given existing long-term resources. Short-term operating decisions are ad hoc and unique; thus, they cannot be planned in advance. Rather, the company must use a model to determine the proper course of action. Cost-volume-profit analysis and relevant variable analysis are two such models used for short-term decision making. Cost-volume-profit analysis assumes that costs vary only with units produced and sold. Relevant variable analysis examines all variables that will occur in the future and that are different between alternatives. It recognizes that both product and nonproduct costs can be unit-related, batch-related, product-sustaining, or facility-sustaining.

- There are five basic assumptions underlying the cost-volume-profit model.
- To be relevant, a variable must occur in the future and differ between alternatives.

- Special order, outsourcing, and product mix decisions are common short-term operating decisions.
- Decision makers must consider qualitative facts in addition to quantitative analyses when making short-term decisions.

Key Terms

Batch-related cost A cost that varies with the number of batches regardless of how many units are in each batch, *109*
Breakeven point The point where the total cost line intersects the total revenue line, *103*
Contribution margin Total sales less total variable costs at a given level of activity, *104*
Contribution margin per unit The selling price per unit less the variable cost per unit, *104*
Contribution margin ratio The contribution margin per unit divided by the selling price per unit, *105*
Cost-volume-profit (CVP) analysis The study of how costs and profits change in response to changes in the volume of goods and services provided to customers, *102*
Depreciation The cost of a long-term asset spread over the period the assets are used, *109*
Direct labor The cost of employees who manufacture the product, *109*
Direct material The cost of materials that are directly traceable to the product and that are costly enough to warrant tracing them, *108*
Facility-sustaining cost A cost incurred to maintain the company's capacity to operate, *109*
Incremental cost The additional cost associated with an alternative, *111*
Incremental profit The difference between the incremental revenues and incremental costs of a particular alternative, *111*
Incremental revenue The additional revenue associated with an alternative, *111*
Indirect labor The cost of production employees who do not physically manufacture the product, *109*
Indirect material The cost of production materials that either cannot be traced to the product or whose cost is not enough to warrant tracing, *108*
Manufacturing overhead All costs other than direct materials and direct labor that are incurred to manufacture products, *109*
Model A representation of reality, *101*
Nonproduct cost A cost that is related to selling the products and services or administering the company, *108*
Opportunity cost A benefit forgone when choosing one alternative over another, *110*
Product cost A cost that is incurred to obtain or manufacture a product, *108*
Product-sustaining cost A cost that varies with the number of product lines, *109*
Relevant variable A cost or revenue that will occur in the future and that differs among the alternatives considered, *110*
Sales mix The relative proportions of units of products sold in a multiple-product company, *102*
Sensitivity analysis The process of changing key variables in CVP analysis to determine how sensitive the CVP relationships are to changes, *106*
Sunk cost A past cost; therefore, never relevant in short-term operating decisions, *110*
Unit-related cost A cost that varies with the number of units, *109*

Questions

1. Explain how short-term operating decisions differ from other decisions made by managers.
2. How is activity defined in cost-volume-profit analysis?
3. Describe the five basic assumptions of cost-volume-profit analysis.
4. Explain the breakeven point in units. How is it related to the breakeven point in dollars?
5. Explain each of the following: contribution margin per unit and contribution margin ratio.
6. Explain how to calculate before-tax profit by using after-tax profit.
7. How can cost-volume-profit analysis determine the number of units that must be sold to achieve a certain profit after taxes?
8. Explain the difference between product and nonproduct costs.
9. Explain the three types of product costs and give an example of each.

10. Explain the difference among unit-related, batch-related, product-sustaining, and facility-sustaining costs and give an example of each.
11. What are the two attributes of a relevant variable?
12. Explain the concept of sunk cost. Are sunk costs ever relevant in short-term operating decisions? Why or why not?
13. Explain the concept of opportunity cost. Are opportunity costs ever relevant in short-term operating decisions? Why or why not?
14. Explain the term *incremental*. How are incremental revenues, costs, and profits used in short-term operating decisions?
15. What are the steps in a relevant variable analysis?
16. What is a special order decision? What variables are relevant in a special order decision?
17. What factors other than relevant costs and revenues must be considered when making a special order decision?
18. What is a make-or-buy decision? What are the relevant variables in a make-or-buy decision?
19. How are opportunity costs incorporated into make-or-buy decisions?
20. What factors other than costs must be considered before making a make-or-buy decision?
21. What is a keep-or-drop decision? What are the relevant variables in a keep-or-drop decision?
22. What factors other than costs and revenues must be considered when making a keep-or-drop decision?

Exercises

E4.1 **LO 2** Use the following information to determine the profit equation:

Selling price per unit	$ 65
Variable cost per unit	24
Fixed cost per year	260,000

LO 2 **E4.2** Examine the following graph. Identify each of the items listed.

Line *AB*	________
Line *CD*	________
Point *E*	________
Area *AEC*	________
Area *DEB*	________
Line segment *FG*	________

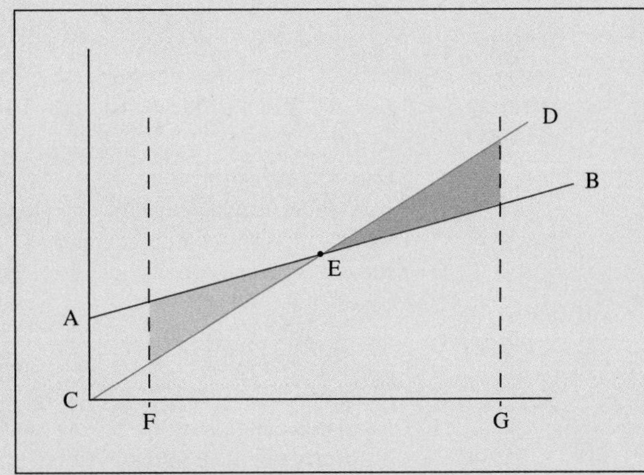

LO 2 **E4.3** Weber, Inc., sells its one product for $120 per unit. The variable cost per unit is $30. The fixed cost per year is $900,000.

A. What is the contribution margin per unit?
B. What is the breakeven point in units?

C. What is the contribution margin ratio?
D. What is the breakeven point in dollars?

LO 2 **E4.4** Meeker Company is developing a new product. The selling price has not yet been determined, nor are the variable costs per unit known. The fixed costs are $600,000. Management plans to set the selling price so that variable cost is 55 percent of the selling price.

A. What is the contribution margin ratio?
B. What is the breakeven point in dollars?
C. If management desires a profit of $50,000, what will total sales be?

LO 2 **E4.5** Crow, Inc., a not-for-profit company, has a product contribution margin of $40. The fixed costs are $800,000. Crow, Inc., has set a target profit of $35,000 per year.

A. What is the breakeven point in units?
B. How many units must be sold to achieve the target profit?
C. If fixed costs decrease 10 percent, how many units must be sold to achieve the target profit?

LO 2 **E4.6** Longpre Company distributes insect repellent. Each can of repellent sells for $4.00. The variable cost per can of repellent is $0.75. The fixed selling and distribution costs are $80,000. The after-tax target profit level is $15,000. Longpre Company is subject to an income tax rate of 20 percent.

A. What is the breakeven point in units?
B. What is the breakeven point in dollars?
C. To achieve the profit goal, what must the before-tax profit be?
D. How many units must be sold to achieve the profit goal after taxes?

LO 2 **E4.7** Gorman Company has the following cost-volume-profit relationships.

Breakeven point in units sold	1,000
Variable cost per unit	$2,000
Fixed cost per period	$750,000

A. What is the contribution margin per unit?
B. What is the selling price per unit?
C. What is the total profit if 1,001 units are sold?

LO 2 **E4.8** Ukaegbu, Inc., currently sells its product for $3.25 per unit. The variable cost per unit is $0.60 and fixed costs are $90,000. Purchasing a new machine will increase fixed costs by $6,000, but variable costs will be cut by 20 percent.

A. What is the breakeven point before the new machine is purchased?
B. What is the breakeven point after the new machine is purchased?
C. Should Ukaegbu, Inc., purchase the new machine? Why or why not?

LO 2 **E4.9** Refer to the basic assumptions of the CVP discussion in the chapter. Without using any numbers, prepare a graph that illustrates the first four assumptions.

LO 1 **E4.10** Roberts Shirts is a producer of men's, women's, and children's shirts. Roberts expects to incur the following production costs. Determine whether each of the costs is direct materials, direct labor, or manufacturing overhead. Use **DM** for direct materials, **DL** for direct labor, and **MOH** for manufacturing overhead.

________ A. Salary of the pattern cutter
________ B. Wages of the sewing machine operators
________ C. Cost of patterns used in production
________ D. Setup costs incurred to change production from one type of shirt to another
________ E. Cost of cloth
________ F. Costs incurred to develop patterns
________ G. Costs incurred to order and receive fabric
________ H. Cost of buttons
________ I. Cost of depreciation on the sewing machines
________ J. Cost of rent on the production facilities
________ K. Cost of thread used to sew shirts
________ L. Costs incurred to develop flame-retardant materials for children's clothing
________ M. Salary of quality control inspector
________ N. Salary of production supervisors—one supervisor for each clothing line
________ O. Salary of vice-president of manufacturing
________ P. Insurance on the factory facilities

LO 1 **E4.11** Refer to E4.10. Classify each of the costs as unit-related, batch-related, product-sustaining, or facility-sustaining. Use **U** for unit-related, **B** for batch-related, **P** for product-sustaining, and **F** for facility-sustaining.

LO 1 **E4.12** Murphy, a firm that produces ping-pong paddles, expects to incur the following costs in its manufacturing process. The ping-pong paddles it manufactures consist of a wooden paddle, a handle, and a rubber backing for the paddle. Determine whether each of the following costs is a product cost or a nonproduct cost. Use **P** for product cost and **NP** for nonproduct cost.

________ A. Cost of handles for the paddles
________ B. Wages of the assembly-line workers
________ C. Rent on the production facilities
________ D. Utilities for the production facilities
________ E. Wages of sales personnel
________ F. Cost of the wooden paddles
________ G. Cost of glue used to adhere the rubber backing
________ H. Cost of shipping crates
________ I. Cost of office supplies
________ J. Cost of rubber backing
________ K. Cost of supervisor in production facilities
________ L. Depreciation on the delivery trucks
________ M. Office workers' salaries
________ N. Cost of janitorial staff in production facilities
________ O. Cost of workers who cut the rubber backing

LO 3 **E4.13** Capellen Manufacturing Corporation produces and sells quality wooden wall clocks that are priced at $340 each. Capellen has just received a request for a special order for 1,500 clocks at a price of $215 each. The current unit cost to produce a clock is $210 (direct materials, $90; direct labor, $70; unit-related overhead, $50). Capellen has the capacity to produce the special order; however, four additional production runs will be required costing $1,500 each. Should the order be accepted? Why or why not?

LO 3 **E4.14** Gooch Catering Company has received an offer from a very important client to work a large party next month. The client has requested service for 1,000 people at $120 per person. Gooch normally charges $185 per person for catering services. Assuming that facility costs will not change if the order is taken and that unit-variable costs are $110 per person, should the offer be accepted? Why or why not?

LO 3 **E4.15** Gashler Company sells motor oil by the case to automobile repair shops and dealerships. Each case of oil costs Gashler $15. The facility costs are $150,000 per period. Each period, Gashler sells approximately 100,000 cases of motor oil at $25 per case. California Classic Cars is requesting an order of 30,000 cases of motor oil in the next period at a price of $20 per case. Since Gashler has no excess capacity, accepting this order means that only 70,000 cases of motor oil can be sold through normal channels. Should Gashler accept this offer? Why or why not? Would your answer change it Gashler had excess capacity of 20,000 cases? Why or why not?

LO 4 **E4.16** Terpening Enterprises manufactures 1,000 units of pottery annually. The production costs for 1,000 vases are as follows:

Direct materials	$ 20,000
Direct labor	55,000
Unit-related overhead	35,000
Batch-related overhead	5,000
Allocated facility-sustaining overhead	30,000
Total	$145,000

A supplier has offered to provide all 1,000 vases at a price of $175 per vase. If Terpening accepts the offer, it will rent the released space for an annual rental fee of $50,000. Should Terpening make or buy the vases? Why?

LO 4 **E4.17** Roccabruna Corporation currently produces 5,000 tablecloths per period. The production cost per tablecloth is:

Direct materials	$5
Direct labor	2
Unit-related overhead	1
Total	$8

Batch-related overhead is $1,000 per batch and 5 batches are normally used to produce 5,000 tablecloths. Facility-sustaining overhead is $300,000 per period, and 10 percent is allocated to the tablecloth product line. A private contractor has offered to supply all of the labor needed for production at a cost of $2.50 per tablecloth. If this offer is accepted, direct laborers will be laid off and unit-related overhead will decrease by 70 percent. Should Roccabruna accept the contractor's offer? Why or why not? What other factors should Roccabruna consider?

LO 4 **E4.18** Refer to E4.17. Assume the contractor has changed its offer. It now proposes to supply all the tablecloths needed at a price of $9.50 per tablecloth. If Roccabruna accepts this offer, it will use the released space to produce 1,500 more napkins. The contribution margin per napkin is $3. To produce 1,500 additional napkins, one more production run will be needed at a cost of $200. Should Roccabruna accept the contractor's latest offer? Why or why not? What additional factors should Roccabruna consider?

LO 5 **E4.19** Chanson Retail Sales Company sells products A, B, and C. After reading the following profit report, decide whether Chanson should drop Product C. Why? Show a quantitative analysis. What additional factors should Chanson consider?

	Product A	Product B	Product C
Sales	$10,000	$8,000	$12,000
Cost of products	6,000	5,000	10,000
Product margin	$ 4,000	$3,000	$ 2,000
Facility-sustaining costs	3,000	3,000	3,000
Profit	$ 1,000	—	$(1,000)

LO 5 **E4.20** Norvell Lawn Care offers three lawn care services to its clients. The revenues and costs associated with each service follow:

	Full Service	Complete Service	Minimum Service
Revenues	$60,000	$72,000	$48,000
Cost of sales	42,000	43,200	25,000
Product margin	$18,000	$28,800	$23,000
Facility-sustaining costs	20,000	20,000	20,000
Profit	$(2,000)	$ 8,800	$ 3,000

Norvell wants to discontinue Full Service. The facility-sustaining costs are related to depreciation on the equipment and insurance and are allocated equally across all product lines. Cost of sales includes wages, gasoline, and lawn chemicals consumed. Should Norvell drop Full Service? Why?

LO 5 **E4.21** Refer to E4.20. If Norvell can increase Complete Service revenues by 40 percent by discontinuing Full Service should it discontinue the Full Service line? Why?

Problems

P4.1 LO 3 Refer to the Example Company on page 116 and answer these questions.

Required:

A. What is the minimum price Example Company can accept for the special order and maintain the same profit as last year?
B. If the customer increases its order to 100,000 calculators and offers to pay $8 each, should the order be accepted? Why or why not?
C. Discuss three additional factors Example Company should consider before accepting or rejecting this offer.

LO 3 **P4.2** The Jacobs Corporation produced and sold 20,000 cowbells last year. Jacobs's profit report follows:

Sales	$50,000
Less:	
Direct materials	10,000
Direct labor	5,000
Unit-related overhead	6,000
Selling costs per unit	10,000
Contribution margin	$19,000
Less:	
Batch-related costs	4,000
Product-sustaining costs	1,000
Facility-sustaining costs	12,000
Profit	$ 2,000

This year Jacobs again expects to sell 20,000 cowbells through normal channels. It has also received an order for 5,000 cowbells at $1.75 each. The selling cost per unit will not be incurred on this order because no commission will be paid; however, an additional production run will be required at a cost of $1,000. Product-sustaining costs will not be incurred. The company has the capacity to produce the order.

Required:
A. What is the relevant cost of the special order?
B. Should Jacobs accept or reject the special order?
C. How could this decision be affected by Jacobs's other customers?
D. How could this decision be affected by legal factors?

LO 4 **P4.3** Hahn Enterprises, which produces and sells to wholesalers a very successful line of skiwear, has decided to diversify its product line. It is considering the production of sunscreen that will be sold in small plastic tubes. The sunscreen will be sold to wholesalers in boxes of 100 tubes for $10 per box. Due to available capacity, no additional facility-sustaining costs will be incurred to manufacture the sunscreen; however, $200,000 of facility-sustaining overhead will be allocated to the new product line. Hahn estimates that production and sales of sunscreen will be 200,000 boxes during the first year and that 1,000 production runs costing $100 each will be required. The estimated cost per box is as follows:

Direct labor	$2.00
Direct materials	3.50
Total overhead	2.25
Total unit cost	$7.75

As an alternative, Hahn is discussing the possibility of purchasing the plastic tubes for the sunscreen from an outside supplier. The purchase price of the empty tubes will be $1.60 per box of 100 tubes. If Hahn purchases the tubes, it is estimated that direct labor, direct materials, and unit-related overhead will decrease by 25, 60, and 20 percent, respectively. (*Hint:* Total overhead per unit is $2.25 if and only if 200,000 boxes are produced. Divide overhead into its facility-sustaining, batch-related, and unit-related components.)

Required:
A. What is the relevant cost of the make alternative?
B. What is the relevant cost of the buy alternative?
C. Should Hahn make or buy the tubes?
D. If the supplier raises the price of the tubes to $3.00 per box, should Hahn make or buy the tubes?
E. Refer to part **D.** If Hahn can rent the space needed for producing tubes to another company for $60,000, should it make or buy the tubes?
F. What factors other than cost should Hahn consider before making this decision?

LO 4 **P4.4** Burt Company makes a product that includes a component part, Item XJ7. Presently, the company purchases XJ7 from an outside supplier for $48 each. Burt Company is considering manufacturing XJ7 itself. Estimated total manufacturing costs for the yearly requirement of 1,000 units of XJ7 follow. Burt anticipates producing XJ7 in 5 batches.

Direct materials	$ 7,000
Direct labor	8,000
Unit-related overhead	5,000
Batch-related overhead	30,000
Facility-sustaining overhead*	36,000
Total	$86,000

*Facility-sustaining overhead is allocated to each product line throughout the company based on relative sales in dollars.

Required:
A. Should Burt Company make or buy component XJ7?
B. If the company could reduce the number of batches needed from 5 to 2, would your answer change? Why or why not?
C. Discuss the additional factors Burt should consider before making this decision.

LO 2 **P4.5** Dirt Devils is a partnership that specializes in office cleaning. The charge per office averages $175 per visit. The variable costs per visit are $65. The fixed operating costs are $90,000. The management of Dirt Devils wants to maintain a profit of 10 percent of total sales revenue. (*Hint:* Define the desired profit as a percentage of sales rather than a dollar amount.)

Required:
A. What is the profit equation?
B. How many offices must be cleaned to achieve the profit goal?

C. If the price charged for office cleaning is increased by 20 percent, how many offices must be cleaned to achieve the profit goal?
D. What are the problems that might be encountered by changing the price charged for office cleaning? Why?

LO 2 **P4.6** Aberra Corporation sells widgets for $15 each. For the month of June, Aberra sold 8,000 widgets and reported variable costs of $24,000 and fixed costs of $78,000. Assume that Aberra increased its selling price by 20 percent on July 1.

Required:
A. How many widgets have to be sold in July to break even?
B. How many widgets have to be sold to earn a before-tax profit of $44,000?
C. If Aberra is subject to an income tax rate of 30 percent, how many widgets have to be sold to earn an after-tax profit of $44,000?
D. How many widgets have to be sold to earn a before-tax profit of 20 percent of sales? (*Hint:* Define the desired profit as a percentage of sales rather than a dollar amount.)
E. How many widgets have to be sold to earn an after-tax profit of 20 percent of sales?

LO 2 **P4.7** Be Thin is a weight control center in Dallas. Clients are charged a fee of $800 for the weight control, counseling, and maintenance program. The average client spends 15 weeks in the program. In addition, each client must purchase a weekly food allowance at the center during the 15-week program. The average cost per client per week for food is $75. The variable costs per client per program average $80. This includes the cost of initial paperwork, insurance, and administrative costs. The variable costs per client per week average $20. This includes the cost of food, utilities, and counselors' salaries. The fixed costs of operations including rent, property insurance, and other fixed administrative costs amount to $9,000 per 15-week period.

Required: Assume independent situations.
A. How many clients must Be Thin have each 15-week period to break even?
B. If Be Thin desires a before-tax profit of $8,000 per 15-week period, how many clients are needed?
C. If Be Thin has 50 clients each 15-week period, what is the profit before taxes?
D. If the program fee per client is increased by 15 percent, how many clients are needed to break even each 15-week period?
E. If the program fee per client is increased by 15 percent and the number of clients per 15-week period falls to 40, what is the profit before taxes each 15-week period? Should the program fee be increased? Explain.
F. If the variable costs per client per week are decreased by $2, how many clients are needed each 15-week period to break even?
G. If the variable costs per client per week are decreased as in part **(F)** and Be Thin has 55 clients each 15-week period, what is the before-tax profit each 15-week period?

LO 2 **P4.8** Buchanan Enterprises has projected its income before taxes as follows:

Sales (800,000 units)	$16,000,000
Variable costs	2,000,000
Contribution margin	$14,000,000
Fixed costs	8,000,000
Income before taxes	$6,000,000

Required:
A. What is the selling price per unit?
B. What is the variable cost per unit?
C. What is the contribution margin per unit?
D. What is the contribution margin ratio?
E. What is the breakeven point in units?
F. What is the breakeven point in dollars?

LO 5 **P4.9** Quinton Corporation produces and sells two types of chili: 1-Alarm and 5-Alarm. Operating performance for the most recent quarter is:

	1-Alarm	5-Alarm
Units produced and sold	100,000	300,000
Sales	$229,000	$837,000
Cost of goods sold	191,000	631,000
Gross margin	38,000	206,000
Selling and administrative costs	31,000	225,000
Profit	$ 7,000	$ (19,000)

Management is puzzled by these results because they spent $120,000 on advertising 5-Alarm Chili last quarter (included in selling and administrative costs) and increased sales by 50,000 jars. The accountant investigated the cost structure and discovered the following about the 5-Alarm Chili.

- Cost of goods sold consists of unit-related, batch-related, product-sustaining, and allocated facility-sustaining costs. Unit-related costs are $0.75 per jar, batch-related costs are $800 per batch (batch size is 2,500 jars), and ongoing research and development costs are $10,000 per quarter. Facility-sustaining costs of $400,000 per quarter are allocated to the product lines based on the number of units produced.
- Selling and administrative costs consist of unit-related, product-sustaining, and facility-sustaining costs. Unit-related costs are $0.15 per jar. Advertising is the only product-sustaining cost and facility-sustaining costs of $80,000 per quarter are allocated to the product lines based on the number of units sold.

Required: A. Should the 5-Alarm Chili line be discontinued? Why?
B. What other factors should Quinton consider before making this decision?

LO 5 P4.10 Crawford sells three types of games to national toy companies. These games are known internally as Gamma, Omega, and Lambda. Recently the Gamma and Lambda lines have not shown acceptable profits. The most recent monthly results are:

	Gamma	Omega	Lambda
Unit sales	1,800	400	1,500
Sales	$900	$1,200	$1,500
Cost of goods sold	810	600	1,245
Gross margin	90	600	255
Selling and administrative cost	204	218	240
Profit	$(114)	$ 382	$ 15

Additional analysis reveals that $150 per month in facility-sustaining selling and administrative cost is charged to each product line. The remaining costs are assumed to vary directly with the number of units sold. Crawford is analyzing the following alternatives:

1. Discontinue the Gamma line and increase advertising at a cost of $10 per month for the Lambda line. This is expected to increase Lambda sales by 20 percent.
2. Discontinue the Gamma and Lambda lines and focus solely on the Omega line. This is expected to increase Omega sales by 40 percent.
3. Increase promotion of both the Gamma and Lambda lines. The promotion will increase selling costs by $25 per month for each line. Unit sales of Gamma are expected to increase by 15 percent while unit sales of Lambda are expected to increase by 10 percent.
4. Do nothing. Leave the Gamma, Lambda, and Omega lines as they are.

Required: A. Evaluate each alternative. Which alternative is best for Crawford Company?
B. What additional factors should Crawford consider before making this decision?

Cases

C4.1 **LO 1** Refer to the annual report of the company you chose in C1.1. Based on your knowledge of this company, which of the decisions discussed in this chapter might the company you chose face? Is there any specific information in the annual report about any such decisions? Using your knowledge of this company and what you have learned in this chapter, classify the expenses on the income statement as fixed, variable, or mixed costs. You may need to read some of the notes to gain a better understanding of the income statement items.

LO 3 C4.2 The Stiefvater Company manufactures a variety of industrial valves and pipe fittings that are sold to customers in the region. Currently the company is operating at about 70 percent of capacity and is earning a satisfactory profit.

Glascow Industries, Ltd., of Scotland has approached Stiefvater with an offer to buy 120,000 units of pressure valves. Glascow normally produces its own valves, but a fire in one of its plants has caused a temporary shortage. Glascow needs the 120,000 valves over the next four months to meet commitments to its regular customers. It is prepared to pay $19 for each valve.

Stiefvater's product cost for the pressure value is as follows:

Direct materials	$ 5.00
Direct labor	6.00
Unit-related overhead	6.00
Facility-sustaining overhead	7.00
Total cost	$24.00

Additional costs incurred in connection with sales of the pressure valve include sales commissions of 5 percent (excluded for this order) and freight expense of $1.00 per unit. Stiefvater normally sells the pressure valves at a markup on unit-related manufacturing cost of 75 percent. Production management believes that it can handle the Glascow order without disrupting its scheduled production. The order would, however, require additional batch-related overhead of $12,000 per month. If management accepts this order, 30,000 pressure valves will be manufactured and shipped to Glascow each month for the next four months. (*CMA Adapted*)

Required:
A. What are the relevant variables for this decision?
B. Should Stiefvater accept this order?
C. What factors other than those identified in part **(A)** should Stiefvater consider before making this decision?

Critical Thinking

CT4.1 LO 1

Wendy's was founded on the concept of old-fashioned hamburgers. Each hamburger is a square patty, which is served directly from the grill when a customer places an order. During peak periods, cooks must estimate demand and have a sufficient supply of hamburgers cooking when customers arrive. Hamburgers that become too well done cannot be served because they don't meet Wendy's specifications for "hot and juicy." Thus Wendy's invented Wendy's chili made with overdone hamburgers.

Wendy's chili is made daily by the assistant manager or an experienced crew member. It takes four to six hours to cook the chili and, during this time, it must be stirred once each hour to prevent burning. It takes 10 to 20 minutes to prepare a batch of chili using the following ingredients:

48 hamburger patties (equals 12 pounds of meat)	$1.25/pound
1 can crushed tomatoes	1.70/can
5 cans tomato sauce	0.51/can
2 cans red beans	1.32/can
1 Wendy's seasoning packet	0.45/each

This recipe yields 57 bowls of chili. Ten percent of the time it is necessary to cook hamburgers specifically for the chili. The remainder of the time, overdone hamburgers, which have been refrigerated until needed, are used. It takes 10 minutes to cook 48 hamburger patties. Then the patties must be chopped into smaller pieces, which takes about five minutes. Mixing the ingredients takes approximately five minutes.

Other chili costs include the following:

Serving bowls	$0.035 each
Lids for carry out	0.025 each
Spoons	0.010 each

Labor costs are:

Assistant manager	$4.08 per hour
Management trainee	3.98 per hour
Crew member	2.90 per hour

Required: Determine the cost of a bowl of chili.

LO 2 **CT4.2** Millett, Inc., compiled the following information for this year:

Sales (10,000 units)	$5,000,000
Variable costs	1,000,000
Contribution margin	$4,000,000
Fixed costs	1,500,000
Before-tax profit	$2,500,000
Tax (40%)	1,000,000
After-tax profit	$1,500,000

Required:

A. What is the breakeven point in units? What is the breakeven point in dollars?
B. How many units must Millett, Inc., sell to earn a profit after taxes of $2,000,000?
C. Millett has learned that its total fixed costs will increase by $750,000 next year. If Millett increases its selling price per unit by 20 percent next year, how many units must it sell to earn the same before-tax profit as this year?
D. What factors should Millett, Inc.'s, management consider prior to increasing its selling price by 20 percent?
E. If Millett, Inc., can reduce its variable cost by 20 percent rather than increasing its selling price to offset the increase in fixed costs of $750,000, what is the new breakeven point?
F. If Millett, Inc., can reduce its variable cost by 20 percent to offset the increase in fixed costs of $750,000, should it also decrease its selling price? Why?

Ethical Challenges

EC4.1 LO 1

Mr. Ed, the manager of Stick Horses Manufacturing, wants to treat all depreciation as a product cost arguing that without the buildings (administrative as well as manufacturing), the company could not produce the product; therefore, depreciation on administrative facilities should be treated as a product cost and allocated to the production process and thereby cost of goods sold. He further argues that it makes no difference in the long run, a cost is a cost and all costs end up on the income statement. Do you agree with his argument? Why or why not?

EC4.2

In the 1980s, Ford Motor Company was taken to court to defend its safety practices concerning the Pinto in the 1970s. Apparently, the Pinto could burst into flames in crashes at 30 miles per hour if hit just right. According to the court records, Ford was aware of the problem and conducted a cost/benefit analysis of fixing the Pintos. Without getting into all the numbers, the benefits Ford considered were savings from the accidents that would not occur and any resulting deaths, burns to people, and burns to vehicles. Ford used governmental numbers for the cost of a person and for a burn injury, and their own estimate of the cost to fix the burned vehicles. The estimates were 180 deaths, 180 burns to people, and 2,100 burned vehicles. The costs considered were the unit costs to fix 11 million cars and 1.5 million light trucks. Needless to say, Ford determined that the costs outweighed the benefits and did not fix the problem. Subsequently, people died and Ford was sued. Discuss Ford's decision-making processes. What items did it forget to include in the analysis?

Computer Applications

CA4.1 LO 2

MyWare is a computer software retailer located in Portland. Its product is a state-of-the-art software package, with a $300 selling price. The fixed operating costs are $40,000 per period. The variable cost per software package is $100. Use a computer spreadsheet. Assume independent situations.

Required:

A. How many software packages must be sold to break even?
B. How many software packages must be sold to earn $3,000 per period before taxes?
C. How many software packages must be sold to earn $3,000 per period after taxes of 40 percent?
D. If fixed costs increase by 10 percent, how many software packages must be sold to break even?
E. If variable costs increase by 15 percent, how many software packages must be sold to break even?
F. If the selling price decreases by 5 percent, how many software packages must be sold to break even?

CA4.2

Homewatch Company is a security firm that offers house-sitting services during owners' vacations and other absences. The daily fees are $20 and variable costs are $7. The fixed operating costs are $1,850 per period. Use a computer spreadsheet.

Required:

A. What is the breakeven point in customer days (one customer for one day)?
B. If Homewatch desires a before-tax profit of $600 per period, how many customer days are needed?
C. If Homewatch desires a profit of $600 per period after taxes of 30 percent, how many customer days are needed?
D. If the selling price is increased by 10 percent, what is the breakeven point?
E. If the fixed costs are decreased by $850, what is the breakeven point?

Visit the text Online Learning Center at **www.mhhe.com/ainsworth6e** for additional problem material that accompanies this chapter.

CHAPTER FIVE

5

Strategic Planning Regarding Operating Processes

Learning Objectives

LO 1 Describe the process of determining selling prices and demonstrate how various strategies are used to determine selling price.

LO 2 Explain the process of determining the inventory model and demonstrate how the EOQ and JIT models are used.

LO 3 Discuss the process of determining the compensation package offered to employees and calculate wages and bonuses paid to employees.

In Chapters 1 through 3, we examined business, business processes, and operating processes. In Chapter 2 we described how the business organization and strategy process are concerned with the company's long-term plan for using its resources. Thus strategic decisions must be made regarding operating processes before we plan and budget the activities in these processes. We examine three such strategic decisions in this chapter. We also explained in Chapter 2 that the balanced scorecard is a holistic approach to planning and evaluating a company's business processes. The balanced scorecard consists of four perspectives: (1) customer, (2) internal processes, (3) learning and growth, and (4) financial. As shown below these perspectives are not independent; rather they are linked and each affects the others. Therefore when we plan operating processes we must consider measurements in each perspective and how these perspectives are linked to the financial success of the company.

Customer ⟶ Internal Processes ⟶ Learning and Growth ⟶ Financial

In Chapter 4 we learned how managers use models to make short-term, ad hoc decisions concerning the operating processes. For example: Using CVP analysis we learned to answer the question: Will this product break even at this selling price and this variable cost? Using relevant variable analysis we learned to answer questions such as: Can we accept this special order from a customer? Should we make or buy this item? In this chapter we examine three strategic decisions regarding operating activities: (1) determining the selling price, (2) determining the inventory model, and (3) determining the employee compensation package. In Chapter 6 we study how managers plan and budget using the balanced scorecard perspectives for ongoing revenue, conversion, and expenditure process activities.

DILBERT®/ by Scott Adams

Revenue Process: Determining the Selling Price

Recall that the activities in the revenue process (marketing/sales/collection/customer service process) are (1) determine marketing and distribution channels to generate orders, (2) receive and accept orders, (3) deliver goods and services, (4) receive payment from customers, and (5) provide customer support.

A significant part of marketing is setting the selling prices for products/services offered to customers. Setting the selling price is an operating decision that has long-term consequences. The selling price may affect and be affected by the quantity demanded by customers; the quantity supplied by competitors; legal, social, and political factors; and the company's costs in the long run. For example, if Apple Computer, Inc., sets its prices too high, customers may not buy its computers and other products offered; instead, they may purchase these items from competitors such as Dell. On the other hand, if Apple has prices that are too low, profits may not be sufficient to cover operating costs or to provide sufficient returns to investors. When setting selling prices, a company must consider its customers (customer perspective), its competitors (learning and growth perspective), legal and social issues (learning and growth perspective), and cost (internal perspective) as well as profitability (financial perspective).

Customers: Customer Perspective

A customer's willingness to purchase goods and services depends, in part, on the selling prices the company charges for them. In simple terms, if the selling price of the product increases, the quantity of the product demanded decreases. If the selling price of the product decreases, the quantity of the product demanded increases.

These rules do not apply equally to all products, however. A company may be able to increase the selling price of a product if customers are *loyal* and unwilling to substitute other products. If the price of coffee, for example, increases substantially due to a crop failure, the quantity of coffee demanded may not fall even when the selling price increases if people are unwilling to substitute another product, such as tea, for coffee. Consider also the case of a product that is considered to be a staple (necessity) versus one that is considered to be a luxury. A staple's selling price does not affect the quantity demanded as much as the price of a luxury item does. Consider a staple grocery product, such as hamburger meat, versus a luxury item such as filet mignon (steak). The quantity of hamburger demanded does not decrease dramatically in response to increases in selling price. However, the quantity of filet mignon demanded is more sensitive to price increases because people are willing to forgo purchasing such a luxury food item and may purchase a substitute product when the price of the luxury item increases dramatically.

Finally, the quantity demanded is influenced heavily by product quality and *service*. Products with perceived high quality and service are in greater demand than products with lower quality and service that sell at the same, or perhaps even slightly lower, prices. In the 1980s Japanese automobiles, such as Toyota and Honda, sold at much higher prices than comparably equipped American automobiles due to the perceived high quality of Japanese cars. Most companies try to differentiate their products in terms of quality and service. Apple Computer, for example, markets its AppleCare services because Apple believes that this differentiates it from competitors such as Dell and Gateway.

Competitors: Learning and Growth Perspective

The selling price charged by a particular company is also influenced by the quantity of the product supplied by competitors and/or the selling prices charged by those competitors. Thus it is important to *monitor and learn from the competition*. Some companies operate in an environment where there is an abundance of suppliers whose products are almost identical. Companies in this situation are price takers—that is, the company "takes" the selling price from the market based on total supply and demand. In these markets, an individual company has little or no influence on the selling price. In the agricultural industry, for example, wheat produced by individual farming operations is almost identical. Therefore, wheat sellers are price takers who receive the price for wheat that the market determines. This type of environment, where a large number of sellers produce and distribute virtually identical products and services, is **pure competition.**

Other companies operate in an environment where many companies produce similar, but not identical, products. In this environment, called **monopolistic competition,** the market has a large impact on, but no control over, prices. Individual companies operating within this type of market can influence selling prices by advertising quality and service as well as price. For example, the selling prices of Apple computers and Dell computers may differ, not so much because the computers differ, but because Apple and Dell try to differentiate their products through advertising.

In a monopolistic competition environment, a firm must constantly monitor its competitors to note changes in their operating strategies that might affect the firm's sales. The market analyst must be aware of actions taken by the company's competitors that may affect the company. Airlines often engage in price wars whereby one company lowers its price and the other company is forced to do the same or risk losing customers. This behavior is common in a monopolistic competition environment.

Legal and Social Forces: Learning and Growth Perspective

Legal and social forces also impact selling prices, usually by constraining the price that can be charged for products and, thus, the company must *monitor and learn* from these external forces. These forces affect all companies, but there is a greater impact on large companies that have the ability to restrain trade and on companies in certain industries.

The government imposes legal constraints on companies that have exclusive control over a product, service, or geographic market. A company in this market is called a **monopoly.** In certain circumstances, monopolies are allowed to operate because competition is not in the best interests of consumers. Consider utility companies that often are given monopoly rights because the cost of starting and operating a utility is so high that few companies are willing to undertake such a venture. The danger posed by monopolies is that the company can set any selling price it chooses since it is the sole provider of that particular product or service. Therefore, the government has stepped in to regulate monopolies in an attempt to ensure that they do not overcharge customers or discriminate in their products, service, or distribution.

Legal constraints also are imposed on companies that operate in an **oligopoly.** This business environment exists when a few firms control the types of products and services and their distribution. The government monitors companies in an oligopolistic market to ensure that they do not form a cartel, which is a monopolistic combination of businesses, and practice price fixing. **Price fixing** occurs when a group of companies agree to limit supply and charge identical (usually high) prices for their goods and services. For example, in the early 1970s, an oil embargo by OPEC (Oil Producing and Exporting Countries) caused the price of gasoline to skyrocket when the OPEC cartel limited supply and raised crude oil prices. (Note that while cartels are illegal in the United States, they are legal in other countries.)

Finally, social constraints may be placed on businesses due to the products they sell or the market in which they sell their products. For example, following the 9/11 attack on America in 2001, some service stations in the Midwest raised their prices for gasoline dramatically. Once this practice was discovered, the public outcry was so great that the stations were forced to lower their prices. In addition, the attorneys general of the states charged the companies with price gouging. **Price gouging** is the practice of setting an excessively high price with the intent of reaping short-term excessive profits. But what is excessive? Ultimately the public and possibly the courts decide this issue and the company must learn from these actions.

Cost: Internal Process Perspective

The cost to produce and distribute a product also has an impact on selling price. Cost is determined, in part, by a company's internal processes, that is, *how it produces and markets its products.* Ultimately, a company must set a high enough selling price for its products to cover all its costs and provide a profit to owners. By all costs, we mean the costs to buy or produce and distribute the product as well as the costs incurred to operate the company, such as building and equipment costs, wages and salaries, and interest on debt. To ensure that they earn a profit, companies add a **markup,** or an additional amount, to the cost of their products and services. Obviously, a company must understand its cost behavior (Chapter 3) when setting selling prices based on cost. When a company sets its selling price based on cost, it is using a cost-based pricing policy where

$$\text{Selling price} = \text{Cost} + (\text{Cost} \times \text{Markup percentage})$$

The size of the markup percentage varies among industries. For example, jewelry is typically marked up more than 200 percent, while some grocery items may be marked up as little as 10 percent due to the nature of their costs. Suppose Apple determines that it must mark up iPhones 50 percent. Therefore, if the cost of an iPhone were \$200, the selling price would be as follows:

$$\text{Selling price} = \$200 + (\$200 \times 0.5) = \$300$$

At this selling price, the **selling margin** (selling price less cost) is \$100. The selling margin percentage for the iPhone is 33 percent:

$$\text{Selling margin/Selling price} = \$100/\$300 = 0.33 \text{ or } 33\%$$

The selling margin allows the company to cover other costs such as advertising, salaries, interest on debt, investment in assets, and research and development. If, due to supply and demand or legal, political, and social forces, the company cannot sell its product at a price that yields a sufficient selling margin, it may choose not to offer the product.

Pricing Strategies

In most industries, selling prices are heavily influenced by both external or market factors, such as customers and competitors, legal/social factors, and internal factors, such as costs. In most cases, companies determine prices based on one of two strategies:

- They set prices based on the market, subject to the constraint that it is necessary to cover the long-run costs of the company.
- They set prices based on costs, subject to the constraints of customers, competitors, and legal/social factors.

Within these two strategies are a variety of pricing schemes that companies use to compete in the marketplace. These schemes involve a combination of the balanced scorecard perspectives. We look at four of these schemes next.

Penetration Pricing

Penetration pricing Setting an initial selling price low in an attempt to gain a market share.

Early in the product's life cycle (recall our discussion in Chapter 1), the company may set its selling price low in an attempt to gain a share of the total market for its goods and services. Such a pricing strategy is known as **penetration pricing** because the company tries to penetrate the market to gain a share of the market from its competitors. Later in the product's life cycle, after establishing the market for the product, the company intends to increase its selling price. This type of pricing is common in the household products and food industries. For example, if Burger King introduced a new burger variety, it might set the initial selling price low to entice individuals to try the product and gain a share of the market. Penetration pricing is legal because it aims to gain market share by introducing the product at a low price. However, when using penetration pricing, a company must not practice predatory pricing, which is illegal in many states. **Predatory pricing** is the practice of selling products below cost in an attempt to drive out the competition, control the market, and then raise the price. Each state that has specific laws against predatory pricing defines it differently; however, the one common element is intent. If the courts determine that the intent of low pricing is to harm and drive out the competition, the company is guilty of predatory pricing. In the international market predatory pricing is called dumping. **Dumping** occurs when a company sells its products below cost in foreign countries. Companies found guilty of dumping in the United States are subject to tariffs and trade restrictions.

Skimming Pricing

Skimming pricing Setting an initial selling price high in an attempt to make early profits.

Penetration pricing is the opposite of **skimming pricing,** a pricing strategy in which the company initially sets a high price for its product. The idea behind skimming pricing is to appeal to those individuals who want to be the first to own a product and who are willing to pay more for it, thus generating more profit for the company. Later, when the novelty of the product wears off, the company lowers the selling price. This type of pricing is common in industries such as electronics and fashion in which products change frequently and customers value products for status as well as functionality.

For example, when laptop computers were first introduced, the selling price was high, but many people bought laptops to be one of the first to own such a computer. Likewise, consider the Beta Max (the forerunner to the VCR). When Sony first introduced the Beta Max it sold for more than $2,000 because there was nothing else like it on the market. It gave people the ability to watch one television program while recording another, which, at the time, was a novel idea! Companies practicing skimming pricing must be careful to avoid the appearance of price gouging discussed previously.

Life-cycle pricing
A pricing strategy based on the estimated total cost of the product over its life.

Life-Cycle Pricing

With the pricing strategy known as **life-cycle pricing**, a company attempts to establish a selling price based on costs that will earn it a return over the life of the product. Therefore, the company's initial selling prices may be below its initial costs based on the idea that costs will decrease over the product's life cycle. Because a product normally becomes less expensive to produce and sell in the later stages of its life due to operating efficiencies, the selling margin in a life-cycle pricing system increases as the product's cost declines. This pricing strategy is different from penetration pricing because the company does not intend to raise its prices once there is an established market for its products or services. A company using life-cycle pricing must understand and estimate all the costs over the product life cycle, from research and development through customer service. Thus, this pricing strategy focuses on the internal processes and learning and growth perspectives of the balanced scorecard. Typically the company must estimate the following costs:

- Research and development—the costs incurred to develop the idea for the product.
- Design—the costs incurred to design the product for manufacturing.
- Supply—the costs incurred to supply the raw materials for the product.
- Production—the costs of the raw materials, labor, and overhead required to manufacture the product.
- Marketing—the costs incurred to sell the product.
- Distribution—the costs incurred to get the product to the customer.
- Customer service—the costs incurred to support the customer.

After the company estimates these costs they are summed to calculate the total product life-cycle costs. Then the company must estimate the number of units it expects to sell over the product's life cycle. Next the company divides the estimated product life-cycle cost by the estimated units to determine the cost per unit. Finally the markup is determined and the selling price is set. Life-cycle pricing begins with an analysis of cost to set the selling price and, therefore, understanding cost behavior and the internal perspective of the balanced scorecard is crucial, but the customer perspective cannot be ignored.

For example, assume that a computer manufacturer has developed the following cost estimates to design, produce, and service 1,000,000 new lightweight laptop computers it plans to sell over the new computer's two-year life:

Research and development	$300,000,000
Design	205,000,000
Supply	20,000,000
Production	60,000,000
Marketing	80,000,000
Distribution	40,000,000
Customer service	90,000,000
Total	$795,000,000

The estimated cost per unit is

$$\frac{\$795{,}000{,}000}{1{,}000{,}000} = \$795 \text{ per unit}$$

Then the computer maker must determine a selling price based on this cost that provides an adequate return over the life of the product.

Target pricing
A pricing strategy where the company first estimates the selling price and then subtracts the required markup to determine the target cost.

Target Pricing

Target pricing is also a long-term pricing strategy that considers the product's life cycle. However, target pricing is market based (customer perspective). Companies often use target pricing to determine whether to introduce a product or service. With **target pricing** the company first determines the selling price of the product based on market surveys (customer perspective). Second, it determines the markup needed to provide a sufficient return to shareholders (learning and growth perspective). Third, it takes the selling price less the required markup to determine the target cost (internal processes perspective). The target cost, then, is the maximum that the product can cost to generate a sufficient return to owners. Now the company must determine how to manufacture the product so that costs do not exceed the target cost. The idea behind target pricing is to produce products in a cost-effective manner to achieve an adequate return for the owners.

For example, suppose that an electronics company is planning to introduce a new portable DVD recorder. Market research determines that it is possible to sell such a recorder for \$800. Further assume that the company desires a 70 percent selling margin percentage to return profit to the owners. The target selling price is \$800. The required markup is 70 percent or \$560 (\$800 × 0.7). Therefore the target cost is found as follows:

Target selling price	\$800
Less required markup	(560)
Target cost	\$ 240

Then the company must find a means of producing the recorder for \$240 (internal processes perspective), or it should not produce the recorder at all. Since target costing considers the market first, its use can save the company from making a potentially disastrous decision. For example, research suggests that up to 80 percent of a product's total cost is committed before the first unit comes off the production line. With target costing a company only commits to products that can be sold at a price that provides an adequate return, thus monies can be saved by knowing when not to produce. Obviously understanding revenue behavior and the customer perspective of the balanced scorecard is essential to target costing. In addition, understanding the internal and learning and growth perspectives is also crucial so that products with potential are pursued while products with little future are abandoned before excessive resources are committed.

Enhance Your Understanding

What pricing strategy do you believe Apple uses?

Answer: While it is difficult to know for sure, it is likely that Apple uses some form of target pricing because the computer manufacturing industry is so competitive.

Conversion Process: Determining the Inventory Model

As you know, the conversion process consists of four primary activities: (1) scheduling production, (2) obtaining raw materials, (3) using labor and other resources, and (4) storing finished goods. Thus the activities of the conversion process reflect primarily the internal process perspective of the balanced scorecard. One of the concerns in conversion process planning is determining the amount and timing of finished goods, work-in-process, and raw materials inventories. Maintaining adequate supplies of inventory to meet the quantity demanded is necessary; however, holding inventory usually generates significant costs.

Reasons to Maintain Inventory

Generally companies maintain inventories for four primary reasons: (1) to meet customer demand, (2) to smooth production scheduling, (3) to take advantage of quantity discounts, and (4) to hedge against price increases. Let's take a look at each of these reasons.

For companies that produce and sell standardized products and for most retail companies, inventory must be available to meet customer demand. Customers rarely order out-of-stock items; rather they are more likely to go to the competition to get the items they want. Thus anticipating customer demand is crucial for these companies.

Some manufacturing companies maintain a certain level of raw materials so that production can be scheduled without fear of inventory shortages that shut down production. In addition, having inventory on hand protects the company in case a portion of the raw materials inventory is defective and, therefore, cannot be used in production. For these companies scheduling production is crucial so that excessive inventories are avoided.

Some companies buy inventory in volume because suppliers offer substantial quantity discounts. A **quantity discount** is a reduced purchase price due to volume. Thus the buyer is actually paying less per unit purchased. For some companies these discounts outweigh the additional costs incurred to store the inventory (discussed shortly). For these companies expenditure planning is crucial.

Occasionally companies will buy extra inventory because a price increase is anticipated in the future. In this case the company attempts to save money in the future by buying more inventory than is needed currently. For these companies, weighing the costs of storing the inventory against the anticipated cost savings is vital.

Reasons to Not Maintain Inventory

Proponents of just-in-time or JIT (introduced in Chapter 1 and expanded on below) believe that companies shouldn't hold inventory due to the costs incurred to maintain inventory and because inventory hides problems.

Companies incur many costs associated with holding inventory. For example, if large amounts of inventory are maintained a separate warehouse may be needed. Companies may need to insure inventories against theft or acts of nature such as fires or floods. In addition, in some states, inventories are subject to property tax. Some companies find that the costs to hold inventory are so great that they maintain only minimal inventories.

Proponents of minimal inventories argue that the most significant reason not to hold inventory is that it hides problems. That is, companies that maintain inventories of finished goods don't need to worry about quality as much as companies that do not maintain finished goods inventories. Why is that? Imagine a company that has a weekly demand of 10,000 units of its product and, therefore, produces 10,000 units every week. Now assume that in Week 4, 3,000 of these units are defective and cannot be shipped. If the company doesn't have any finished goods inventory, it cannot meet this Week 4 demand. So is the company's problem that it did not have inventory and, therefore, could not meet demand? No, its real problem is quality control because it should not have produced 3,000 defective units! If the company has an inventory of finished goods, it covers up the real problem by shipping replacement products from inventory.

Balancing Ordering and Carrying Costs

In large organizations, inventory planning is the responsibility of the purchasing and production functions and is a process of balancing the costs of ordering inventory against the costs of carrying inventory.

Ordering Costs

In the short run, inventory ordering costs are the costs incurred to place one additional order for inventory—that is, the costs that vary with the number of orders placed and received.

Ordering costs include shipping costs per order, the costs incurred to fax or otherwise place an order, and insurance costs per order. Thus in the short run, ordering costs are considered a *batch-related cost*. In the long run, ordering costs also include the product-sustaining and facility-sustaining costs associated with ordering, such as the cost of company vehicles used to transport inventory from the warehouse to the production facilities as well as the costs involved to maintain supplier relationships. For example, if a supplier demands at least 50 percent of all the company purchases, this demand has long-run consequences because it limits the company's ability to choose its suppliers, but it does not vary with the number of orders placed.

Carrying Costs

In the short run, inventory carrying costs are the costs incurred to carry one additional unit in inventory for the period—that is, *the costs that vary with the number of units carried in inventory*. Carrying costs include insurance costs based on the number of units held in storage during the period; the estimated costs of spoilage or obsolescence during the period; and the unit-related costs of storing a unit, such as inspection costs. In the long run, inventory carrying costs also include the batch-related, product-sustaining, and facility-sustaining costs associated with carrying inventory, such as the cost of the warehouse used for storing inventory as well as the cost of the security guard for the warehouse. For example, the cost to a company of renting a warehouse to maintain a certain inventory level is considered a long-run carrying cost, but the amount of the cost does not vary with the number of units held. Both in the short and long run, carrying costs also include stockout costs. **Stockout costs** include the cost of production slowdowns or stoppages and lost sales as well as customer ill will that may result in lost sales in the future.

Inventory Models

A variety of inventory models have been developed to deal with the trade-off between ordering and carrying costs of inventory. We examine two such models next.

Economic Order Quantity (EOQ) Model

The economic order quantity (EOQ) model is a mathematical model that minimizes the total of short-term ordering costs plus short-term carrying costs for the period. It indicates the size of order to place every time inventory is ordered. Because EOQ is a model, it is based on certain assumptions:

- Demand is uniform throughout the year; that is, there is no seasonal fluctuation in demand.
- Lead time (discussed below) is constant throughout the year, regardless of the supplier.
- The entire order is received at the same time; partial orders are not possible.
- No quantity discounts are available. EOQ assumes that inventory costs are the same regardless of the size of the order.
- Inventory size is not limited; orders of any size are possible.
- Batch-related, product-sustaining, and facility-sustaining storage costs are irrelevant. EOQ is a short-term model, so it assumes that these costs (storage) do not change with the number of units stored.

For some companies, the assumptions of EOQ are impractical. For example, EOQ does not work well for automobile manufacturers because, among other things, nonunit storage costs are not irrelevant. Apple Computer would not use the EOQ model either because it often produces computers to order; thus, demand is not uniform throughout the year. However, for companies with low nonunit storage costs and for which the other assumptions are not limiting, the EOQ model works very well. The EOQ model assumes that inventory ordering and inventory usage occur in uniform cycles throughout the period. Exhibit 5.1 illustrates two inventory cycles. Notice the cycle begins with an order of size Q. This inventory

EXHIBIT 5.1
Inventory Usage Cycles

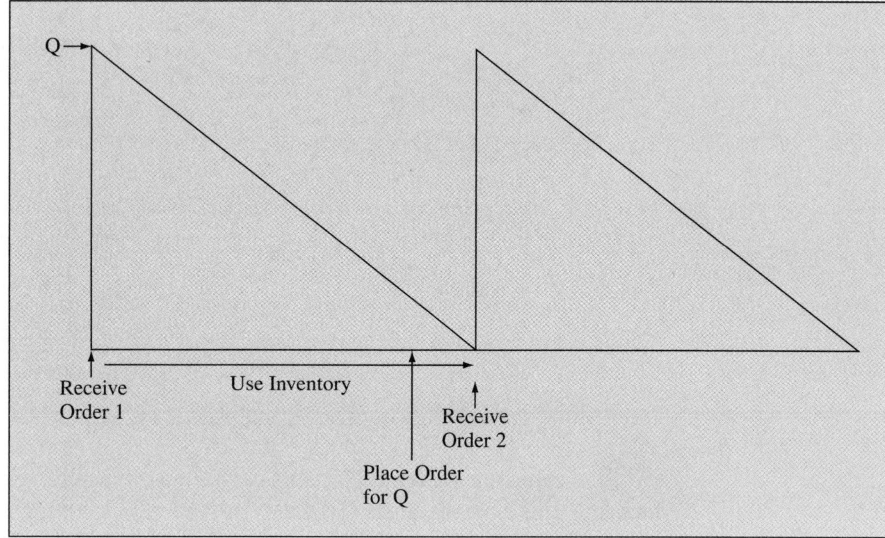

is consumed at the daily usage rate. When the inventory level falls to a certain point, another order is placed for size Q. When this second order is received no inventory from the first order remains in stock.

The formula for the EOQ model is as follows:

$$Q = \sqrt{\frac{2DO}{C}}$$

where:

D = Annual demand for inventory in units

O = Cost to place one additional order (batch-related cost)

C = Cost to carry one additional unit in inventory (unit-related cost)

We illustrate the economic order quantity model graphically in Exhibit 5.2. Notice the economic order quantity occurs at the intersection of the total carrying cost and total ordering cost lines. At this point, the total cost is minimized.

To illustrate the EOQ model, assume that a company's annual demand for its product is 400,000 units, the ordering cost is \$52 per order, and the carrying cost is \$4 per unit in inventory per year. The economic order quantity is determined as follows:

$$Q = \sqrt{\frac{2 \times 400{,}000 \times \$52}{4}} = 3{,}224.9031$$

This implies that the company should order 3,225 units each time it places an order. Total ordering costs for the period would be determined as follows:

$$\text{Annual demand} \,/\, Q = \text{Number of orders to place}$$

$$\text{Number of orders to place} \times O = \text{Total ordering cost}$$

$$400{,}000 \,/\, 3{,}225 = 124.031 \times \$52 = \$6{,}450$$

Total carrying costs would be:

$$(Q + 0) \,/\, 2 = \text{Average inventory on hand}$$

$$\text{Average inventory on hand} \times C = \text{Total carrying cost}$$

$$3{,}225 \,/\, 2 = 1{,}612.5 \times \$4 = \$6{,}450$$

EXHIBIT 5.2
EOQ Model

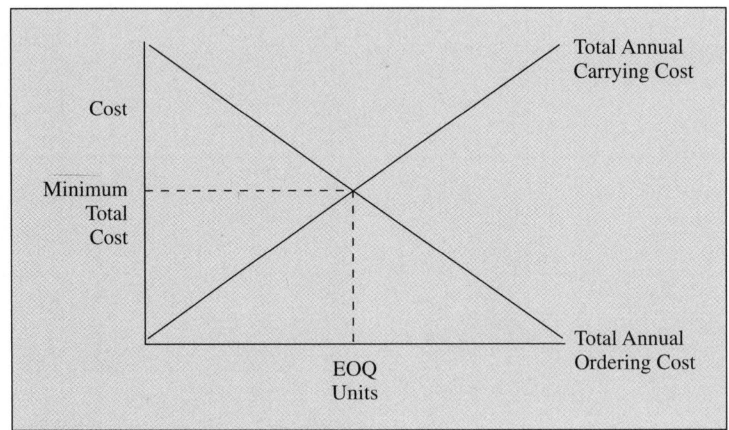

If the company orders 3,225 units each time it places an order, it minimizes the total of its ordering plus carrying costs ($6,450 + $6,450 = $12,900). Note: It is not an accident that the total ordering cost equals the total carrying cost at EOQ. The proof of the EOQ result is shown in Exhibit 5.3. If the order size decreases to 3,000 units, the carrying cost decreases ($6,000 versus $6,450) because fewer units are carried in inventory, but the ordering cost increases ($6,933 versus $6,450) because more orders must be placed. The increase in the ordering cost is greater than the decrease in the carrying cost, so the total cost increases to $12,933. Conversely, if the order size increases to 4,000 units in this example, the carrying cost increases ($8,000 versus $6,450) because more units are carried in inventory, but the ordering cost decreases ($5,200 versus $6,450) because fewer orders must be placed. The increase in the carrying cost is greater than the decrease in the ordering cost, so the total cost increases to $13,200.

Once the size of the order is determined, the next issue is to determine the **reorder point**—that is, the inventory level that, when reached, indicates the need to place an order for additional inventory. To address this issue, it is necessary to determine requirements for daily demand and lead time. **Daily demand** is the amount of inventory needed each business day and is calculated as annual demand (*D*) divided by the number of business days in the year. To determine the reorder point, it is necessary to multiply the daily demand by the **lead time,** or the number of days elapsing from the time an order is placed until the order is received.

Enhance Your Understanding

What is the relationship between lead time and customer response time discussed in Chapter 2?

Answer: Customer response time and lead time are the same concepts from different viewpoints. Both measure the time that elapses from when the buyer places an order until that order is received.

For example, assume that the company estimates that lead time is two days. If the company operates 320 days per year, its reorder point would be calculated as follows:

$$400{,}000/320 = 1{,}250 = \text{Daily demand}$$

$$1{,}250 \times 2 = 2{,}500 = \text{Reorder point}$$

EXHIBIT 5.3
Proof of the Economic Order Quantity Model

Quantity	Ordering Cost D / Q × O	Carrying Cost Q / 2 × C	Total Ordering Cost + Carrying Cost
3,225	400,000 / 3,225 × $52 = $6,450	3,225 / 2 × $4 = $6,450	$6,450 + $6,450 = $12,900
3,000	400,000 / 3,000 × $52 = $6,933	3,000 / 2 × $4 = 6,000	$6,933 + $6,000 = $12,933
4,000	400,000 / 4,000 × $52 = $5,200	4,000 / 2 × $4 = $8,000	$5,200 + $8,000 = $13,200

The reorder point indicates that the company should place an order for 3,225 units when the quantity of inventory on hand falls to 2,500 units. By the time the order arrives there would be no units left in inventory.

Earlier we discussed the issue of stockout cost, or the cost of running out of inventory. To guard against stockout costs, many companies maintain a **safety stock,** or a small amount of inventory kept on hand to avoid stockouts. The level of safety stock does not affect the EOQ calculation, but it does impact the reorder point. To calculate the reorder point when a company maintains a safety stock, we use the following formula:

$$(\text{Daily demand} \times \text{Lead time}) + \text{Safety stock} = \text{Reorder point}$$

To illustrate, assume that the company wants to maintain a safety stock of 30 units. The reorder point in this case would be ([1,250 × 2] + 30) = 2,530. This means that when the new order of inventory arrives there will be 30 units left. If the order is delayed, these units may prevent stockout.

Just-in-Time Model (JIT)

The just-in-time (JIT) inventory model is a long-run model based on the principle that inventory should arrive just as needed for production in the quantities needed. It operates on the assumption that carrying costs should include the nonunit costs of storage such as rent and insurance on warehouse facilities because, in the long run, these costs are relevant. For many companies, the long-run costs of carrying inventory outweigh the long-run costs of ordering inventory, so, according to the JIT model, the best decision is to maintain zero or minimal inventories. This implies that products should be produced when needed, in the quantities needed by customers, so there is little need for work-in-process or finished goods inventories. In addition, raw materials should arrive when needed, in the quantities needed, for production. JIT is a pull system; that is, production is determined by (pulled by) customer demand, and the need for raw materials is determined by (pulled by) production. Exhibit 5.4 illustrates this concept. Accordingly, storing inventory is a nonvalue-added activity that a company should try to reduce or eliminate.

EXHIBIT 5.4
Push and Pull Systems

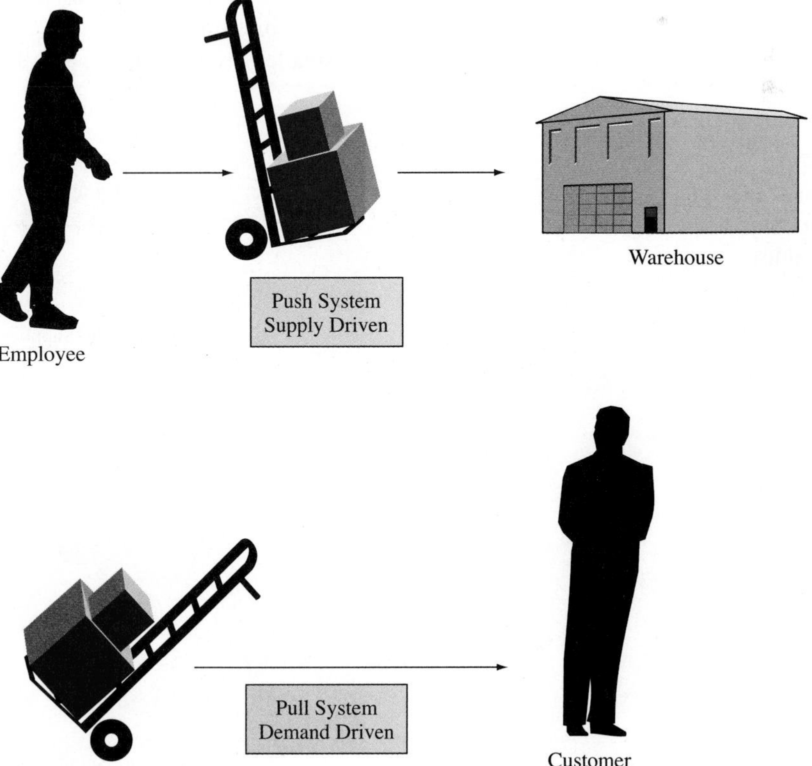

Adopting a JIT inventory model has significant implications for a company. First, because little or no inventory is maintained, the sales estimates must be accurate so the production can be completed when customers demand the products. Along these same lines, production must be completed with zero, or very few, defects. Because the company carries very little inventory in a JIT system, if defects occur in the production process, customer orders may be delayed as defective products are reworked. In other words, a company using a JIT system cannot use inventory to cover up problems and, therefore, must eliminate defects in products and processes.

JIT requires a company to have a strong relationship with its suppliers. Because orders are placed frequently, sometimes more than once a day, the company using JIT must choose suppliers that can meet the frequent delivery schedules on time, every time, with high-quality raw materials. The company must also have faith in the freight carriers used because a strike or accident that shuts down transportation lines also halts production. In a traditional purchasing system, the company places orders with many different suppliers. In a JIT system, the company has one or two primary suppliers that, in turn, have a few secondary suppliers. Exhibit 5.5 illustrates the difference between a traditional and a JIT company/supplier relationship. There are also risks associated with having only a few suppliers. For example, what would happen if one of the suppliers declared bankruptcy? Careful selection of suppliers and cultivation of supplier relationships are crucial for JIT implementation.

A company that adopts JIT must have a good relationship with its employees. A JIT company often relies more heavily on its employees to detect and correct defects as soon as possible, rather than hiring a quality control inspector whose job is to inspect the final product. It is easier, and typically cheaper, to correct defects early in the production process. In addition, a strike or work slowdown by employees can be devastating to a JIT company. For example, when a subassembly plant at General Motors went on strike, causing the final assembly plant to shut down within the same week, it ran out of electronic components for its automobiles. Companies adopting JIT typically cross-train employees to ensure smooth and flexible production flows. This cross-training must be planned as part of the learning and growth perspective. There are risks here, too. Employees who are well trained are more mobile and may leave the company. Therefore careful selection of employees and careful monitoring of employee relationships are crucial for JIT companies.

Recall that JIT companies often arrange employees and equipment into cells to ensure smooth production with smaller production runs. A JIT system is often a kanban system.

EXHIBIT 5.5
Traditional and JIT Company/Supplier Relationships

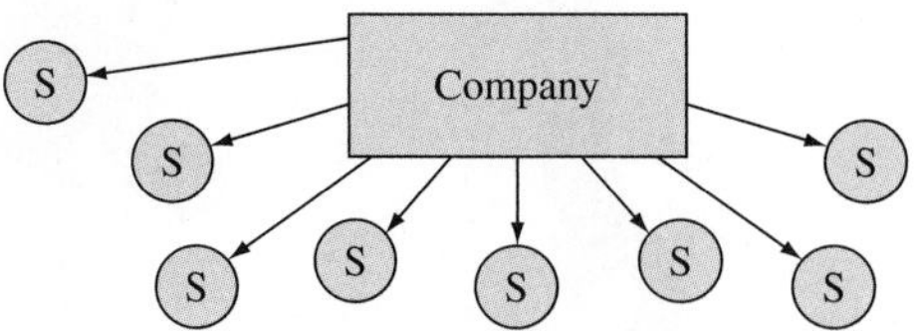

Traditional Company/Supplier Relationship

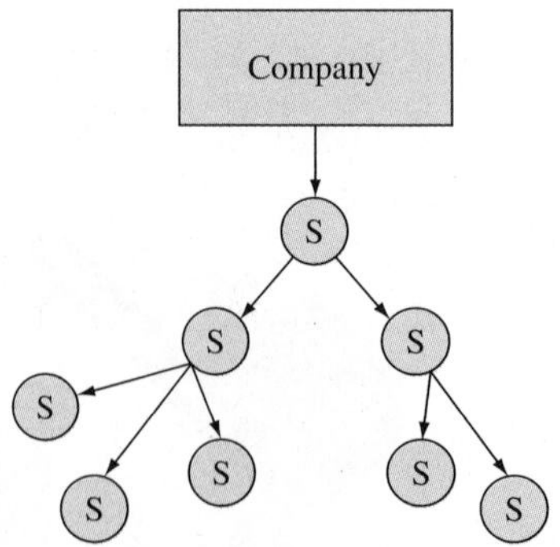

JIT Company/Supplier Relationship

Kanban is a Japanese word meaning visual or signal. Thus a **kanban system** is a pull system that uses cards to visually signal the need for inventory. For example, raw materials are kept in bins and within each bin are containers holding a specified number of parts. When a manufacturing cell needs materials, a designated employee goes to the bin to retrieve the materials and withdraws a container holding the specified number of parts. The employee then removes the kanban card attached to the container and posts it in a designated area where it is clearly visible. The stock employee in charge of the materials sees the kanban card and understands that the raw materials bin should be replenished with another container holding the specified number of parts. Thus demand for parts triggers replenishment.

Finally, to implement a just-in-time inventory system, a manufacturing company must have a good relationship with and understand its customers. Because finished goods are produced only as needed by customers, and because raw material is received only as it is needed by production, customers who change their orders at the last minute cause production slowdowns for a just-in-time company. For example, a customer who at the last minute increases the size of an order may cause other customers' orders to be delayed as resources are redeployed to meet the additional quantity demanded. Thus the company must understand its customers and provide incentives for customers not to change orders at the last minute.

Companies that have successfully implemented just-in-time systems find that costs decrease because large quantities of raw materials and finished goods are not necessary. Therefore, they can eliminate many nonunit storage costs. In addition, many companies have found that customer satisfaction is enhanced once a JIT system with few or no defects is implemented because customers get a defect-free product on time, every time. As you can see, JIT is more than an inventory management system. JIT is a philosophy—a way of doing business that relies on zero defects, quality suppliers, and well-trained employees. The goals of JIT are to achieve smooth, rapid production by:

- Eliminating disruptions in production.
- Reducing or eliminating nonvalue-added activities.
- Minimizing inventory.

Disruptions in production are caused by a variety of factors such as equipment breakdowns, defective products, and/or late deliveries of raw materials. As you know, nonvalue-added activities should be reduced or eliminated because the customer is unwilling to pay for it. Finally, JIT systems seek to minimize inventory to reduce storage costs and to reduce defects.

Although adopting JIT usually results in cost savings, JIT is not desirable for every company. Typically, companies in established markets where demand can be predicted fairly accurately are good candidates for JIT. For example, automobile manufacturers such as Ford and Toyota have successfully adopted JIT. Those companies whose demand fluctuates greatly, whose suppliers are unreliable, or whose customers frequently change orders are not good candidates for JIT adoption. Merchandising companies such as JC Penney or Eddie Bauer are not good candidates for JIT because if the clothing is not on the racks, the sale is lost. In addition, the selling period for a particular style of clothing is typically very short, which may make JIT adoption less desirable.

Enhance Your Understanding

Based on your knowledge of Apple Computer, do you believe it uses an EOQ or JIT system? Why?

Answer: In Chapter 2 we discovered that Apple's selling period is only seven days; thus, its inventory levels are very low, indicating JIT.

Comparison of Inventory Models

As we have indicated, some companies prefer the EOQ model and others like the JIT model. Exhibit 5.6 shows a comparison of these models. EOQ considers only short-term carrying and ordering costs. JIT, on the other hand, is a long-term model. EOQ is a mathematical

EXHIBIT 5.6
Comparison of Inventory Models

	Economic Order Quantity	Just in Time
Planning horizon	Short term	Long term
Type of model	Mathematical	Visual
Reorder trigger	Predetermined reorder point	Kanban card
Relevant costs analyzed	Batch-related ordering and unit-related carrying	All levels

model that determines the optimal order size. JIT is a visual or electronic model that uses a kanban system to trigger the need for inventory. The EOQ system considers batch-related ordering costs and unit-related carrying costs. JIT considers all levels of cost and focuses on reducing or eliminating nonvalue-added costs.

Expenditure Process: Determining the Employee Compensation Package

As you know from Chapter 3, the expenditure process consists of four activities: (1) determining the need for goods/services, (2) selecting suppliers and ordering goods/services, (3) receiving goods/services, and (4) paying suppliers of goods/services. Thus in the expenditure process we must consider both goods and services used as well as the employees we need. Expenditure process planning reflects the internal, learning and growth, and financial perspectives of the balanced scorecard. One of the crucial areas of expenditure process planning is determining the employee compensation package.

In addition to the regular wages and salaries paid to employees, many companies also provide other benefits such as health and life insurance, paid leave, and bonuses for employees. Whether employees are accountants, production workers, or upper-level managers, the wages and other benefits paid them are part of the cost of obtaining and maintaining the company's human capital. Therefore, employee benefits must be carefully planned as part of the overall investment in human resources. We first look at compensation plans that define how a company pays its current employees. Second, we examine other benefits for current employees such as insurance, paid leave, and cash bonuses based on performance.

Paid Compensation

Companies pay their employees using a variety of plans. Some companies pay employees **piece-rate pay.** That is, the employee receives compensation based on the number of items completed. For example, in the clothing manufacturing industry, it is common for employees to be paid based on the number of articles of clothing manufactured. A variation of piece-rate pay is **commission pay.** A commission, typically used for sales personnel, is a percentage of revenue generated. Commissions are usually based on net sales or contribution margin. Companies use piece-rate pay to encourage productivity; therefore, the company expects compensation costs to increase as productivity increases. The most common form of compensation is **hourly pay.** The employee is paid a certain amount per hour with, perhaps, more per hour for overtime. In this situation, the amount of pay is not based on the amount of work completed. Finally, some employees receive **salary pay,** compensation based on a fixed amount per period, typically one month. In this situation, the amount of pay is independent of the number of hours worked or the amount of work done.

An individual company may use any one or a combination of these compensation plans. For example, sales personnel are often paid a fixed salary plus a commission to encourage productivity. Companies often use hourly pay and salaries to encourage time-on-task. Therefore, the company expects compensation costs of hourly employees to increase only if more time is required to accomplish the objectives of the company.

The full amount the employee earns is known as **gross pay.** But from this amount the employer is required to withhold federal income taxes mandated by the Internal Revenue Code, and social security taxes dictated by the Federal Insurance Contributions Act (FICA). In addition, in some locations, the employer is also responsible for withholding state and local income taxes. Other deductions are for voluntary withholdings, pensions, charitable contributions, medical and life insurance, and union dues. That is, the employee agrees to have the company withhold these amounts from gross pay and to remit them to the proper organizations at a later date. Thus the employee's take-home pay, known as **net pay,** is less than gross pay.

For example, let's assume that Apple's gross payroll for January was $500,000 and that the FICA rate is 7.65 percent, the federal income tax rate (average) for Apple's employees is 20 percent, and the state income tax rate is 10 percent. What would the net pay due to employees be?

Gross pay	$ 500,000
Less: withholdings	
FICA taxes (0.765 × $500,000)	(38,250)
Federal income taxes (0.2 × $500,000)	(100,000)
State income taxes (0.1 × $500,000)	(50,000)
Net pay	$ 311,750

The employer also has costs connected with payroll. In addition to paying the employees their net pay and remitting their voluntary and involuntary withholdings to the proper organizations, the employer incurs payroll taxes. The Federal Income Contributions Act requires that employers pay social security taxes equal to the amount withheld from the employees. The Federal Unemployment Tax Act (FUTA) requires employers to pay payroll-related taxes to support the federal government's administration of unemployment benefits. The State Unemployment Tax Act (SUTA) requires employers to pay payroll-related taxes to the state to fund unemployment benefits.

Continuing with the example above, let's determine Apple's taxes for a gross payroll of $500,000. Assume that the FUTA rate is 0.8 percent and the SUTA rate is 5.4 percent.

FICA taxes (0.765 × $500,000)	$38,250
FUTA taxes (0.008 × $500,000)	4,000
SUTA taxes (0.054 × $500,000)	27,000
Total employer taxes	$69,250

Health and Life Insurance

In general, when a business buys an insurance policy, it is buying protection for its assets. For example, a flood insurance policy protects the company from substantial loss of property due to floods because the company receives insurance proceeds to replace the assets lost. A fire insurance policy protects the company from substantial loss of property due to fire because the company receives insurance proceeds in the event of loss. A life insurance policy on a key executive protects the company from substantial loss in the event of the executive's untimely death because the company receives insurance proceeds for such a loss. However, in most cases when a company provides health and life insurance for its employees, it is not the beneficiary of the policy.

Why do companies pay for health and life insurance for their employees and subsidize insurance payments for the employees' families? The best answer is that by offering these forms of compensation in addition to wages and salaries, companies can recruit and retain better employees at a lower overall cost to the company. If a company offered its employees a wage rate high enough to allow them to buy their own insurance, it would cost more than

OF INTEREST Does One Person Really Make a Difference?

If your name is Steve Jobs, it would appear that the answer is "yes." As you know, Steve Jobs was one of the founders of Apple Computers after starting the business in his garage. But in 1996, he was dismissed from the company and Apple struggled. Jobs however, went on to start another computer company called Next. He then proceeded to take over an animation company known as Pixar. Subsequently, Apple took over Pixar and Steve Jobs came back to the helm of Apple. In 2001, Apple launched a new operating system for its computers, the OS X, which was described as a cross between a Porsche and an Abrams tank. Then Apple really began to introduce new, innovative products—the iPod, the iPhone, and iTunes. But in January 2009, Steve Jobs announced that he was taking a medical leave of absence from Apple until June (he had previously suffered from pancreatic cancer). Apple stock dropped 7 percent upon the news and trading was suspended for a time. The next day, the stock opened $5 lower than the previous day's close. Yes, one person can make a difference!

offering lower wages to employees and buying health and life insurance policies directly. It is less expensive for companies to buy health and life insurance because they purchase at group insurance rates that are lower than individual rates. Therefore, the cost of paying lower wages plus insurance is lower than the cost of paying higher wages. In addition, employees may be reluctant to leave positions where health and life insurance benefits are provided; a company thereby saves recruitment, selection, and training costs. Based on these facts, it seems that companies do, in fact, receive benefits from insuring employees and their families.

Paid Leave

Most businesses pay employees during certain times when they are not working. For example, companies pay sick leave, family leave, and vacation leave. Sick leave and vacations are typically paid leave. That is, employees receive wages and salaries as if they had been working. Family leave—that is, leave for family reasons such as the birth or adoption of a child, the care of elderly parents, or the illness of a spouse—may be paid or unpaid. Some companies pay employees for a certain amount of family leave; others simply ensure employees their jobs until the family leave expires. In both cases, however, there is a cost to the company. When employees are on leave, others must complete their work. These persons may be employees of the company, or, as is increasingly common, temporary workers may be hired. As with insurance benefits, companies offer paid or unpaid leave based on the belief that these benefits help attract and retain better employees.

Contingent Compensation: Bonuses

A **bonus** is a fringe benefit, or a part of the company's compensation plan, that is contingent on the occurrence of some future event. For example, sales employees may be given bonuses if their individual or group sales exceed some targeted amount. Production employees receive bonuses if production quotas are met. In these cases, the individual or group performance is fairly easy to measure (the dollar amount of sales or the number of units produced), so the link between performance and reward is clear. However, the link between effort and performance of upper-level managers is more difficult to measure. An upper-level manager spends time supervising, making decisions, thinking, networking, and planning. The output of these activities is typically not "directly" measurable in quantitative terms. Thus upper-level managers' bonuses often are based on broader organizational measures such as net income. In this way, the manager is encouraged to increase the profitability of the company. When the company's profits increase, the bonus payment increases. From the company's perspective, there is an additional consideration, however. The bonus payment is an expense to the company. Thus the bonus, itself, affects net income and, therefore, income taxes, as shown in the following condensed income statement:

Sales
Less: cost of goods sold
Gross margin
Less: operating expenses other than bonuses
Income before bonus and income taxes
Less: bonus
Income before income taxes
Less: income taxes
Net income

Companies must consider the effect of the bonus on net income and cash flows when they set the bonus rate and bonus base. The **bonus rate** is the percentage the bonus will pay; for example, 5 percent or 10 percent. The **bonus base** is the form of income the bonus rate is applied to; for example, income before bonus and income taxes, income before income taxes, or net income.

The following sections use this information to illustrate the impact three bonus bases have on the company's net income and cash outflows. For this illustration, we assume that all bonuses and income taxes are paid in cash in the period incurred.

- Income before bonus or income taxes $1,000,000
- Income tax rate 30%
- Bonus rate 10%

Bonus Based on Income before Bonus or Income Taxes

If the bonus is based on income before the bonus or income taxes, the bonus base is $1 million. The resulting bonus is $100,000 ($1,000,000 × 10%). The company's net income and cash outflows associated with the bonus and income taxes are

Income before bonus and income taxes	$1,000,000
Less bonus (0.10 × $1,000,000)	100,000
Income before income taxes	$ 900,000
Less income taxes (0.30 × $900,000)	270,000
Net income	$ 630,000
Cash paid for bonuses	$ 100,000
Cash paid for income taxes	270,000
Total cash outflows	$ 370,000

This situation is fairly straightforward and the calculations are not difficult. But when the bonus is based on income after the bonus, the computations are more complex.

Bonus Based on Income before Income Taxes

Let's return to the original information. If the bonus is 10 percent of income before income taxes (but after the bonus), the bonus formula is

$$\text{Bonus} = (\text{Income before bonus} - \text{Bonus}) \times \text{Bonus rate}$$

Therefore, the bonus amount is $90,909, as follows:

$$\text{Bonus} = (\$1{,}000{,}000 - \text{Bonus}) \times 0.10$$

$$\text{Bonus} = \$100{,}000 - 0.10 \times \text{Bonus}$$

$$1.1 \times \text{Bonus} = \$100{,}000$$

$$\text{Bonus} = \$90{,}909$$

The resulting net income and cash outflows associated with the bonus and income taxes are calculated as follows (all amounts are rounded to the nearest dollar):

Income before bonus and income taxes	$1,000,000
Less bonus	90,909
Income before income taxes	$ 909,091
Less income taxes (0.30 × $909,091)	272,727
Net income	$ 636,364
Cash paid for bonuses	$ 90,909
Cash paid for income taxes	272,727
Total cash outflows	$ 363,636

Notice that by basing the bonus on income after the bonus, the company is able to increase its net income and decrease its total cash outflows when compared to the first bonus alternative.

Bonus Based on Net Income

What happens if the bonus is based on net income (i.e., after bonus and after taxes)? We have two formulas to work with: one to calculate the bonus and another to calculate the income taxes:

[1] Bonus = (Income before bonus and income taxes − Bonus − Income taxes) × Bonus rate

[2] Income taxes = (Income before bonus and income taxes – Bonus) × Tax rate

Using this information, we know the following:

[1] Bonus = ($1,000,000 − Bonus − Income taxes) × 0.10

[2] Income taxes = ($1,000,000 − Bonus) × 0.30

Now we simplify the income tax equation [2] and insert it into the bonus equation [1] for the income taxes variable as follows:

[2] Income taxes = ($1,000,000 − Bonus) × 0.30

Income taxes = $300,000 − 0.30 × Bonus

[1] Bonus = ($1,000,000 − Bonus − [$300,000 − 0.30 × Bonus]) × 0.10

Bonus = ($1,000,000 − Bonus − $300,000 + 0.30 × Bonus) × 0.10

Bonus = $100,000 − 0.10 × Bonus − $30,000 + 0.03 × Bonus

Bonus = $70,000 − 0.07 × Bonus

1.07 × Bonus = $70,000

Bonus = $65,421

The resulting net income and cash outflows associated with the bonus and income taxes are calculated as follows:

Income before bonus and income taxes	$1,000,000
Less bonus	65,421
Income before income taxes	$ 934,579
Less income taxes (0.30 × $934,579)	280,374
Net income	$ 654,205
Cash paid for bonuses	$ 65,421
Cash paid for income taxes	280,374
Total cash outflows	$ 345,795

Note that with this bonus plan, the company's net income is larger and its cash outflows are smaller than with the previous two plans.

Comparison of Bonus Plans

The table below shows a comparison of the resulting net income and cash outflows of the three options calculated previously.

	Income before Bonus and Taxes	Income before Taxes (after Bonus)	Net Income (after Bonus and Taxes)
Net income	$630,000	$636,364	$654,205
Cash paid to employees (bonus)	$100,000	$ 90,909	$ 65,421
Cash paid to government (taxes)	$270,000	$272,727	$280,374
Total cash outflow	$370,000	$363,636	$345,795

From the company's perspective the bonus based on net income (after bonus and after taxes) is best because the *total* cash outflows decreased and the net income was larger than with the other two options. However, from the perspective of those receiving the bonus, this would be the least favored option because the bonus amount was the smallest under this option ($65,421 compared to 90,909 and $100,000).

Summary

To plan operating processes a company must consider its customers, its employees, and its internal processes as well as its financial goals. Therefore the balanced scorecard approach is an excellent tool for planning operating activities. Before planning and budgeting operating activities, a company must make some strategic decisions that concern its long-term plans for using its resources. Three crucial decisions that managers must plan are (1) determining the selling price, (2) determining the inventory model, and (3) determining the employee compensation package.

- There are four primary influences on selling price: (1) customers, (2) competitors, (3) legal and social factors, and (4) cost.
- Two common inventory management models are EOQ and JIT. EOQ is a short-term model while JIT is a long-term model.
- In addition to paying employees, companies often provide health and life insurance and paid leave. Upper-level managers are often given bonuses based on net income.

Key Terms

Bonus A fringe benefit contingent on the occurrence of some future event, *144*
Bonus base The form of income on which the bonus is based, *145*
Bonus rate The percentage the bonus will pay, *145*
Commission pay Payment for services rendered based on a percentage of revenue generated, *142*
Daily demand The amount of inventory needed each business day, *138*
Dumping Selling products below cost in a foreign market, *132*
Gross pay The full amount an employee earns, *143*
Hourly pay Payment for services rendered based on the number of hours worked, *142*
Kanban system A pull system that uses cards to visually signal the need for inventory, *141*
Lead time The number of days elapsing from the time an order is placed until the order is received, *138*
Life-cycle pricing A pricing strategy where the company attempts to set a selling price for the life of the product based on its total life-cycle costs, *133*
Markup An additional amount over cost that is added to determine selling price, *131*
Monopolistic competition An environment in which there are many companies whose products/services are similar but not identical, *130*
Monopoly A company that has exclusive control over a product, service, or geographic market, *131*

Net pay The employee's take-home pay, *143*
Oligopoly An environment where a few firms control the types of products and services and their distribution, *131*
Penetration pricing A pricing strategy where a company sets its initial selling price low in an attempt to gain a share of the market from its competitors, *132*
Piece-rate pay Payment for services rendered based on the number of items completed, *142*
Predatory pricing The practice of selling products below cost in an attempt to drive out competition, control the market, and then raise prices, *132*
Price fixing When a group of companies agree to limit supply and charge identical prices, *131*
Price gouging The practice of setting excessively high prices, *131*
Pure competition An environment where a large number of sellers produce and distribute virtually identical products and services, *130*
Quantity discount A reduced purchase price due to the amount purchased, *135*
Reorder point The inventory level that, when reached, indicates the need to place an order for additional inventory, *138*
Safety stock A small amount of inventory kept on hand to avoid stockouts, *139*
Salary pay Payment for services rendered based on a fixed amount per period, *142*
Selling margin Selling price less cost, *132*
Skimming pricing A pricing strategy in which the company sets its initial selling price high in an attempt to appeal to those individuals who want to be the first to have the product and who are not concerned about price, *132*
Stockout cost The opportunity cost of not having inventory on hand when needed, *136*
Target pricing A pricing strategy where the company first determines the selling price of the product and then decides whether to enter the market, *134*

Questions

1. Describe the four influences on selling price and how each is related to the balanced scorecard.
2. Describe the four economic environments and how each impacts the setting of selling prices.
3. What is price fixing?
4. What is price gouging?
5. Describe how markup pricing is done.
6. Compare and contrast penetration pricing and predatory pricing.
7. Compare and contrast skimming pricing and price gouging.
8. Compare and contrast life-cycle pricing and target pricing.
9. What is dumping?
10. Discuss reasons to hold inventory.
11. Discuss reasons to not hold inventory.
12. What is the difference between a quantity discount and a purchase discount (Chapter 3)?
13. What is a stockout cost and why is it important?
14. What is the difference between short-run and long-run ordering costs?
15. What is the difference between short-run and long-run carrying costs?
16. What type of company would use an EOQ system?
17. What type of company would use a JIT system?
18. When the EOQ formula is solved, what does the result indicate?
19. How do you determine the reorder point in an EOQ system?
20. What are the goals of a JIT system?
21. How does the adoption of a JIT system impact the company/supplier relationship?
22. How does the adoption of a JIT system impact the company/employee relationship?
23. How does the adoption of a JIT system impact the company/customer relationship?
24. How does a kanban system work?
25. Explain the differences among piece-rate, commission, hourly, and salary pay.
26. What is the difference between gross pay and net pay?
27. What is the difference between voluntary and involuntary withholdings?

28. Why do companies provide health and life insurance for employees?
29. Define the following terms: (*a*) bonus, (*b*) bonus rate, and (*c*) bonus base.

Exercises

E5.1 **LO 2** Use the following information to determine the economic order quantity for Albert Company.

Units required during the year	20,000
Cost to place an order	$60
Cost of carrying a unit in inventory	$12

LO 2 **E5.2** Clark has determined its economic order quantity to be 1,500 units. Demand for the year is 54,000. Five days elapse between the time an order is placed until it is received. Clark conducts business 360 days per year. What is the reorder point?

LO 2 **E5.3** Kallsen has calculated its economic order quantity at 200 units. The ordering cost is $40 and the carrying cost is $6. What is the expected demand for the year?

LO 2 **E5.4** Peek, Inc., has calculated its economic order quantity at 500 units when its annual demand is 3,125 units. The cost to place an order is $10 and the cost to carry one unit in inventory is $0.25. What is the total ordering plus carrying cost for the year?

LO 2 **E5.5** Vigil Company uses 32,000 units each year during the 240 days the company operates. The cost to hold one unit in inventory is $0.50 and the ordering cost is $20. What is the economic order quantity?

LO 2 **E5.6** Ward, Inc., needs 180,000 units each year to meet its production requirements. The costs incurred to place an order are $10 and the cost of carrying a unit in inventory is $2. What is the economic order quantity?

LO 2 **E5.7** Refer to E5.6. If Ward, Inc., operates 300 days per year and its lead time is 2 days, what is the reorder point?

LO 2 **E5.8** Nelson operates 300 days per year. In the past, demand for its product has been fairly steady at 50 units per day. Recently however, customer orders have been inconsistent, ranging from 25 to 150 units per day. It costs Nelson $0.50 per day to store one unit in inventory while its facility-sustaining warehousing costs are $50,000 per year. Should Nelson adopt a just-in-time inventory system? Why?

LO 2 **E5.9** Fortura Company is considering adopting a JIT system. Fortura estimates that facility-sustaining and product-sustaining inventory costs will decrease by $300,000 if JIT is adopted. However, Fortura anticipates a $240,000 increase in prevention and appraisal quality costs to reduce external failure costs by $50,000. Finally, Fortura estimates that a one-time cost of $100,000 will be required to install a kanban system. Should Fortura adopt JIT? Why?

LO 2 **E5.10** Describe the anticipated cost increases when adopting JIT. Describe the anticipated cost decreases when adopting JIT. How should a company determine whether to adopt JIT?

LO 3 **E5.11** Weede Company's expected gross payroll for the period is $250,000. Assuming that its FICA rate is 7.65 percent, its FUTA rate is 0.8 percent, and its SUTA rate is 5.4 percent, what is the expected payroll tax for the period?

LO 3 **E5.12** Leithead, Inc., expects its gross payroll for the period to be $60,000. It expects to withhold 7.65 percent of gross payroll for FICA taxes, 15 percent for federal income taxes, and 5 percent for state income taxes. What is the expected net pay for the period?

LO 3 **E5.13** Refer to E5.12. Assuming Leithead remits the taxes to the proper authorities during the same period as the employees are paid, what is the expected cash outflow for Leithead (ignore employer taxes)?

LO 3 **E5.14** McQuary Enterprises plans to pay its managers a bonus to encourage performance. The bonus rate is 12 percent and the bonus base is net income before bonus or taxes. McQuary's expected income before bonus or taxes is $400,000. Its tax rate is 30 percent. Determine the amount of the expected bonus.

LO 3 **E5.15** Refer to E5.14. Determine the amount of the expected cash outflow assuming that taxes and bonus are paid in the budgeting period. Determine the net income expected.

LO 3 **E5.16** Ebzery Company plans to pay its managers a bonus to encourage performance. The bonus rate is 15 percent and the bonus base is net income after bonus but before taxes. Ebzery's expected income before bonus or taxes is $400,000. Its tax rate is 30 percent. Determine the amount of the expected bonus.

LO 3 **E5.17** Refer to E5.16. What is the expected cash outflow for bonus and taxes if the bonus and the taxes are paid in the budgeting period? What is the expected net income?

LO 3 **E5.18** Downs, Inc., plans to pay its managers a bonus to encourage performance. The bonus rate is 10 percent and the bonus base is net income after bonus and after taxes (net income). Downs's expected income before bonus or taxes is $300,000. Its tax rate is 30 percent. Determine the amount of the expected bonus.

LO 3 **E5.19** Refer to E5.18. What is the expected cash outflow for bonus and taxes if the bonus and the taxes are paid in the budgeting period? What is the expected net income?

LO 1 **E5.20** Cavanagh Company estimates its cost per unit at $375. Its markup is 80 percent. What is the selling price? What is the selling margin? What is the selling margin percentage?

LO 1 **E5.21** Murphy Enterprises has set its selling price at $400. At this price, its selling margin is $300. What is Murphy's cost per unit? What is its selling margin percentage?

LO 1 **E5.22** Roester, Inc., set its selling price at $120. Its markup percentage is 60 percent. What is Roester's cost per unit? What is its selling margin? What is its selling margin percentage?

Problems

P5.1 LO 1 LO 2 LO 3 Refer to Walt Disney Company **(www.disney.com).** Based on your knowledge of this company, answer the following questions:

A. Describe its customers, competitors, and legal/social environment.
B. Do you believe this company sets its selling prices based primarily on market factors or primarily on cost? Why?
C. Describe Disney's short-term and long-term carrying costs and ordering costs.
D. Describe its suppliers.
E. What inventory method do you believe Disney uses? Why?
F. What type of compensation package do you think it provides for its employees? Why?
G. What does the annual report tell you about executive compensation?

LO 1 LO 2 LO 3 **P5.2** Refer to PepsiCo **(www.pepsico.com).** Based on your knowledge of this company, answer the following questions:

A. Describe its customers, competitors, and legal/social environment.
B. Do you believe Pepsi sets its selling prices based primarily on market factors or primarily on cost? Why?
C. Describe its short-term and long-term carrying costs and ordering costs.
D. Describe its suppliers.
E. What inventory method do you believe it uses? Why?
F. What type of compensation package do you think Pepsi provides for its employees? Why?
G. What does the annual report tell you about executive compensation?

LO 1 LO 2 LO 3 **P5.3** Refer to Dell Computer **(www.dell.com).** Based on your knowledge of this company, answer the following questions:

A. Describe its customers, competitors, and legal/social environment.
B. Do you believe Dell sets its selling prices based primarily on market factors or primarily on cost? Why?
C. Describe Dell's short-term and long-term carrying costs and ordering costs.
D. Describe its suppliers.
E. What inventory method do you believe it uses? Why?
F. What type of compensation package do you think Dell provides for its employees? Why?
G. What does the annual report tell you about executive compensation?

LO 2 **P5.4** Bunkowske Company plans to introduce a new product next year. This product has a two-year life and an estimated demand of 20,000 units annually. The product will be produced 50 weeks each year. Bunkowske estimates the following costs:

- Direct materials will be $16 per unit.
- Setup costs will be $200 per week. Ten setups will be required per week.
- Design costs will be $40,000 in total.
- Specialized equipment must be rented for $15,000 per week.
- Research and development costs are estimated at $500,000.
- Labor will be paid $20 per hour. Five employees will be assigned to this product and each employee will work 35 hours on the product.

Bunkowske Company uses cost-plus pricing whereby the selling price of each of its products are 150 percent of the life-cycle costs. Determine the selling price of this product.

LO 3 **P5.5** Rossetter, Inc., has 10 employees. Jan and Fred are each paid a salary of $4,000 per month. Joe, Betty, Frankie, and Donita are paid $10 per hour. Abby, Norman, Bill, and Erika are paid on a commission basis at a rate of 2 percent of their individual sales. During January, the following occurred:

	Hours Worked		Sales Made
Joe	160	Abby	$150,000
Betty	180	Norman	$170,000
Frankie	145	Bill	$180,000
Donita	150	Erika	$185,000

Determine the gross payroll for Rossetter, Inc., for January.

LO 3 **P5.6** Refer to P5.5. Determine the net pay due to employees (in total) assuming a 7.65 FICA rate and a 15 percent federal income tax rate.

LO 3 **P5.7** Grauberger Company has provided the following budgeting information for you to determine its expected bonus payments and cash outflows. Grauberger's bonus rate is 15 percent and its tax rate is 30 percent.

Sales	$6,000,000
Less cost of goods sold	3,500,000
Gross margin	$2,500,000
Less operating costs	1,000,000
Expected income before bonus or taxes	$1,500,000

Required:
A. If Grauberger's bonus base is income before bonus or taxes, what is the expected bonus amount?
B. If Grauberger's bonus base is income before taxes (after bonus), what is the expected bonus amount?
C. If Grauberger's bonus base is net income (after taxes, after bonus), what is the expected bonus amount?
D. What are the expected cash outflows for bonus and taxes for each of the above alternatives?
E. What is the expected net income for each alternative?

LO 3 **P5.8** Refer to P5.7. Assume Grauberger changes the bonus rate to 10 percent.

Required:
A. If Grauberger's bonus base is income before bonus or taxes, what is the expected bonus amount?
B. If Grauberger's bonus base is income before taxes (after bonus), what is the expected bonus amount?
C. If Grauberger's bonus base is net income (after taxes, after bonus), what is the expected bonus amount?
D. What are the expected cash outflows for bonus and taxes for each of the above alternatives?
E. What is the expected net income for each alternative?

LO 1 **P5.9** Praeuner Company has surveyed the market and set a target selling price of $2,000 per unit for its product. Praeuner believes it can sell 100,000 units of this product over its two-year life. Praeuner requires a 20 percent return on selling price. Therefore its target cost per unit is $1,600. Praeuner has gathered the following budgeted cost data:

Unit cost	$ 1,200
Batch cost (batch size = 1,000)	15,000
Product-sustaining cost (annual)	480,000
Facility-sustaining cost (annual)	900,000

In addition to the previous costs, Praeuner will incur $5,000,000 in research and development costs before the product is manufactured.

Required:
A. What is the total target cost for this product's life?
B. What is the total budgeted cost for this product over its two-year life?
C. Should Praeuner develop this product? Why?

LO 2 **P5.10** Engelhaupt Company is considering a switch to JIT. It has gathered the following data:

Increase in prevention quality costs	$140,000
Increase in appraisal quality costs	234,000
Increase in employee training costs	125,600
Increase in ordering costs	95,740
Decrease in carrying costs	480,000
Decrease in internal failure costs	110,800

In addition, Engelhaupt estimates that its relationship with its customers will improve by 10 percent. Because it will use fewer suppliers, however, there is a greater risk associated with purchasing.

Required:
A. What is the total cost savings associated with switching to JIT?
B. How should you determine the costs or cost savings associated with increased customer satisfaction and purchasing risk?
C. Should Engelhaupt make the switch to JIT? Why?

Cases

C5.1 LO 1 LO 2 LO 3 Refer to the company you selected in C1.1. Based on your knowledge of this company, answer the following questions.

A. Describe its customers, competitors, and legal/social environment.
B. Do you believe the company sets its selling prices based primarily on market factors or primarily on cost? Why?
C. Describe its short-term and long-term carrying costs and ordering costs.
D. Describe its suppliers.
E. What inventory method do you believe it uses? Why?
F. What type of compensation package do you think it provides for its employees? Why?
G. What does the annual report tell you about executive compensation?

C5.2 LO 1 LO 2 LO 3 In Chapter 2 we learned that the business organization and strategy process concerned the company's long-term plan for using its resources. In this chapter we looked at three strategic decisions that must be made before the company can plan its operating processes activities. What other strategic decisions regarding operations must be made prior to planning operating activities? Be sure to consider strategic decisions related to the revenue process, the conversion process, and the expenditure process.

Critical Thinking

CT5.1 LO 2 Write a paper comparing and contrasting the EOQ and JIT inventory methods. Make sure you compare *and* contrast.

CT5.2 LO 2 Grainer, a wholesale distributor of candy, leases space in a warehouse and is charged according to the average number of cases stored. Management is concerned about the high ordering costs incurred last year. The company employs temporary personnel to process purchase orders and invoices upon receipt of the candy. Managers, supervisors, and shipping clerks are full-time employees.

The company placed 200 orders last year. Data for the high-activity month (30 orders) and the low-activity month (10 orders) for the purchasing and warehouse operations are

	High-Activity Month (30)	Low-Activity Month (10)
Purchasing Department		
Manager	$1,600	$1,600
Clerks	300	100
Supplies	60	20
Warehousing Department		
Supervisor	1,550	1,550
Receiving clerks	360	120
Shipping clerks	2,800	2,800
Total	$6,670	$6,190

The company purchased 160,000 cases of candy last year. Information on the high-storage month (4,000 cases) and the low-storage month (2,500 cases) follows:

	High-Inventory Month (4,000)	Low-Inventory Month (2,500)
Warehouse charges:		
Rent	$ 6,000	$3,750
Property taxes	2,000	1,250
Insurance	4,000	2,500
Total	$12,000	$7,500

Last year it took three days to receive candy from suppliers after the order was placed. The company does business 320 days per year. It wants to maintain a safety stock of 1,000 cases of candy.

Required:

A. Determine the economic order quantity.
B. Determine the reorder point.
C. Explain why ordering costs were too high last year.
D. Show proof that the economic order quantity results in the lowest possible carrying plus ordering costs. (Ignore safety stock in your calculations.)

LO 2 **CT5.3** JIT has gained in popularity throughout the business world. Yet we also see companies such as Amazon.com building huge warehouses. Conduct Internet research on the topic of JIT and write a four-to-five-page paper arguing for or against adopting JIT for a company such as Barnes & Noble.

Ethical Challenges

EC5.1 LO 3 During the financial crisis of 2008, Congress was particularly upset by the high salaries paid to CEOs of financial institutions that were losing money. Members of Congress argued that CEO compensation should be tied to profits such that in good times the CEO makes money, but in bad times s/he does not. Companies argue that such a practice would not only be impractical because no CEO would work under such conditions, but, furthermore, it is unethical because the CEO cannot control market conditions. Discuss the ethics of this situation.

LO 1 **EC5.2** Large companies such as Wal-Mart have been accused in the past of predatory pricing. The accusers argue that a company such as Wal-Mart comes into a smaller community and because of its buying power can set its prices much lower. Accusers go on to state that Wal-Mart will deliberately undersell small companies within the community until these companies are forced to close, at which time Wal-Mart will raise its prices. Wal-Mart, on the other hand, argues that its pricing practices are not predatory, rather it prices products in accordance with its ability to buy and distribute its products nationally, thus keeping prices low. Discuss the ethics of this situation.

LO 2 **EC5.3** If a company wishes to use JIT successfully, it must make a lot of demands on its suppliers for more frequent deliveries of smaller batches. This, in turn, increases distribution costs for the supplier. Is this ethical? How would you negotiate such a change in inventory management?

Computer Applications

CA5.1 LO 2 The following information has been gathered by Miller Company to determine its economic order quantity.

Annual demand	2,000,000
Cost to place an order	$9.50
Cost to carry a unit in inventory	2.75

Required: Use a computer spreadsheet to answer the following questions. Treat each situation independently. Do not round your answers to the nearest whole unit.

A. What is the economic order quantity?
B. If demand increases by 25 percent, what is the economic order quantity?
C. If the cost to place an order increases by $2.00, what is the economic order quantity?
D. If the cost to carry a unit in inventory increases by $0.50, what is the economic order quantity?
E. If Miller decides to maintain a safety stock of 200 units, what is the economic order quantity?

LO 2 **CA5.2** Refer to CA5.1. Prepare a spreadsheet that proves using the economic order quantity minimizes total inventory ordering costs plus inventory carrying costs. Use Exhibit 5.3 as a guide. Do not round your answers to the nearest whole unit.

Visit the text Online Learning Center at **www.mhhe.com/ainsworth6e** for additional problem material that accompanies this chapter.

CHAPTER SIX

6

Planning, the Balanced Scorecard, and Budgeting

Learning Objectives

LO 1 Describe the purposes, strategies, and approaches to budgeting.

LO 2 Explain the process of revenue process planning and prepare the resulting budgets and schedules.

LO 3 Discuss the process of conversion process planning and prepare the resulting budget.

LO 4 Explain the process of expenditure process planning and prepare the resulting budgets and schedules.

As we have learned, planning is crucial for any business. Without planning, a business has no direction or objectives to accomplish. Companies plan to coordinate their activities; without planning, managers and employees would not know what they are supposed to accomplish in the coming period. For example, assume that Apple did not plan its activities. How would they know what customers want? How would they know how many plastic cases to purchase? How would the marketing manager know which computers were most profitable? How would the human resources manager determine how many employees to hire? Planning is necessary to answer all of these questions. In Chapter 5 we examined three strategic decisions that must be made before operating processes can be planned and budgeted. In this chapter we examine the planning and budgeting process.

Budgeting and Goal Setting

Budgeting
The process of expressing the company's goals in quantitative terms.

A **budget** is a plan for the future expressed in quantitative terms. **Budgeting** is the process of expressing a company's goals and objectives from its balanced scorecard perspectives in quantitative terms and, therefore, is a crucial part of the planning process. Businesses, not-for-profit organizations, and individuals need budgets to plan for future activities. For example, a business plans for the future to satisfy the needs of its customers, employees, suppliers, and owners. Not-for-profit organizations plan for the future to meet their goals in an effective and efficient manner. Individuals plan for meeting day-to-day obligations as well as for making other major but infrequent expenditures, such as buying a house or car and saving for retirement. All of these groups benefit from the financial planning provided by the budgeting process. An organization budgets as long as the benefits derived from budgeting exceed the costs incurred. We discuss these issues next.

Planning

The primary purpose of a budget is to present and describe the financial ramifications of plans for the future. The budgeting process requires individuals to consider possible future courses of action and the resources needed to accomplish the various activities. For example, key planners at Apple would consider the types of products and product features they want to sell in the future. They must determine the number of customers they expect in the future and the financial and physical resources needed to provide service to those customers. Failure to do so may impact the profitability of the company. That is, if Apple does not consider its customers (customer perspective) in the planning process, it may lose those customers.

Communication and Coordination

The budgeting process promotes communication and coordination among divisions or functions within a company. To function effectively, the firm's managers and other employees must understand the interaction among the departments and how the actions of one department affect another. Then managers must communicate their plans to each other to coordinate the activities of the organization as a whole. This coordination is part of the budgeting process. Again, communication and coordination affect profitability. Functions and divisions must work together for the company to operate effectively and efficiently (internal perspective).

For example, before Apple's production function determines which types of iPhones to manufacture, it must consult the marketing function to determine the types of iPhones that customers want. Also, when Apple plans to introduce a new type of product, the marketing function must plan how to promote sales of this product. Finally, if iPhone production is expected to increase dramatically, the human resources function might plan for the hiring of additional temporary workers. Budgetary communication and coordination help ensure that all functions or cross-functional teams are working toward common strategic and operating goals of the company.

Resource Allocation

Businesses operate with limited resources that require some type of allocation. Budgeting aids resource allocation by ensuring that information is available to help managers determine which activities should receive the limited resources of the company. In addition, through the budgeting process, companies can analyze activities to determine if they add value to the company as discussed in Chapter 2. Since resources are limited, some activities cannot be undertaken, others may need reduction, and yet other activities may need increased financial support. Understanding value-added versus nonvalue-added activities is important so that scarce resources are allocated to those activities that add value to the company. Nonvalue-added activities should be reduced if not eliminated, thereby releasing scarce resources for use in value-added activities (learning and growth perspective).

Evaluation and Control

Finally, a budget serves as a useful benchmark against which to evaluate and control actual performance. The evaluation process consists of comparing actual performance results to the budget to determine what areas deviated from planned activities and whether to take corrective actions. When actual and budgeted results do not match, the financial and operating activities of the firm may need to be adjusted, the budget may need to be revised, or both. Thus the evaluation process serves to control operations by determining when and where a company did not achieve planned balanced scorecard results. Then management uses this information to determine the causes for budget variations. Companies must learn from both their mistakes and their successes. A company that has a learning and growth perspective is more likely to increase its profits in the future.

The budgeting process requires time and other resources, such as people. The results of the process impact the activities of departments and individuals. Thus we discuss the costs of budgeting in terms of three important aspects: (1) time and resource requirements, (2) adaptability of departments and segments of the business, and (3) motivation and behavior of individuals.

Time and Resource Requirements

Budgeting is time-consuming. A typical yearly budgeting sequence may take as long as three or four months. During this time, management must coordinate its activities with others in the organization. A large organization typically appoints a budget director, often the controller, who determines how to collect the data and prepare the budget. The budget director works closely with various department managers who provide the information necessary to complete the budgets. The budget director typically reports to a budget committee, a group of key executives responsible for overseeing the budget process. Because many people are involved in the budgeting process, in terms of human capital the cost is large (financial perspective).

Adaptability of Departments and Segments

Another cost associated with budgeting occurs when the budget is so rigidly adhered to that it inhibits a function or business segment from responding to the changes in the environment. For example, if a business segment is only allocated a specific amount of resources, it may be forced to forgo profitable opportunities due to lack of available resources (internal perspective).

To illustrate, suppose that after the budgeting process is complete, the marketing function at Apple wants to accept an order from a customer for an additional 5,000 computers during the coming period. The production function may be reluctant to accept this order that will cause its costs to exceed the budgeted amount for production. In this case, production may refuse the order, not because it is unprofitable but, rather, because the budget might not be met if the company accepts the order. This type of rigid adherence to a budget limits the ability of functions or segments to take advantage of profitable opportunities, such as those discussed in Chapter 4, as they arise.

The opposite problem may exist if a company continues to allocate resources to product lines that are unprofitable. For example, a product line may be continued despite declining sales if the company does not consider changes in the environment during the period covered by the budget. If, instead, the company continues to follow the budgetary plans, profits may be adversely affected.

Motivation and Behavior of Individuals

The budget also has an effect on the motivation and behavior of individuals, both during the budgeting process and after the budget has been formalized. During the budgeting process, individuals who develop budgets (employees, lower-level managers, and/or upper-level managers) are affected by it. If communication between functions is inadequate, the budgeting process can result in inaccurate functional budgets. For example, if the marketing and the production functions at Apple do not communicate effectively, either, or both, of their functional budgets may not reflect the expected activities of the coming period.

In addition, the budgeting process may lead to dysfunctional behavior on the part of those individuals involved in determining the budget numbers. When meeting or beating the budget is used as a measurement of performance, managers and other employees may be motivated to report budget numbers that they know are not accurate representations of future expectations. We call this **budgetary slack,** which is the difference between what a person with input into the budgeting process chooses as an estimate of revenues or expenses and what is actually a realistic estimate. In other words, budgetary slack is deliberately introduced bias by those who fear the consequences of not meeting the budget.

For example, a marketing manager at Apple who is fairly sure that 250,000 units of a certain computer can be sold during the coming period might report an estimated sales number of only 200,000 units to ensure that sales are not overestimated. The difference between what the manager actually expects (250,000) and what the manager reports (200,000) is budgetary slack. Budgetary slack is potentially dangerous to companies. Consider what might happen to Apple in this scenario. If the marketing manager reports a sales estimate of 200,000 units, the human resources manager may hire only enough workers to produce 200,000 units. Therefore, Apple might lose sales because the computers could not be produced when the customers wanted them.

Another form of introducing bias into budgets occurs when budgetees overestimate the time or cost to complete an activity to protect themselves from unanticipated cost increases. For example, a purchasing manager at Apple who anticipates that plastic cases will cost $4 each might report a cost of $4.50 each, just to be safe. That is, the manager makes sure that the costs do not exceed the department budget. Or a production manager at Apple who is fairly sure that it will take six hours of labor time to produce a computer workstation might report that it will take eight hours to allow for unanticipated delays. The additional two hours per batch is budgetary slack. Again, this situation may be serious. If Apple allocates to production scarce employee resources that, in reality, are not needed, these resources are not available for other uses. Thus profits could be affected because resources are misallocated and wasted.

People engage in the types of budget manipulation just mentioned for many reasons. For example, top management might place emphasis on "meeting or beating" the budget to obtain bonuses or other rewards. In such a case, the person preparing the budget estimates might have an incentive to overestimate expenses or underestimate revenues to ensure meeting the budgetary goals. People also might be motivated to engage in budget manipulation because they anticipate budget number adjustments by upper-level management. That is, they might expect estimated expenses to be decreased and estimated revenues to be increased as part of upper management's budgetary input. Thus employees might overestimate expenses or underestimate revenues to counteract management's reaction to their estimates. Since people take these actions in order to avoid negative repercussions, management must create an environment that minimizes fear and encourages understanding that making the company better creates financial and psychic rewards for everyone in the business.

After the budget is formalized, individuals are also affected by budgetary requirements. The budget places certain requirements on functional and individual work performance to meet budgetary goals. Individuals may resist the budget requirements for several reasons. For example, they might believe that the goals are unrealistic and, therefore, that any attempt to reach the budgetary goals is futile. Or they might resist the budgetary requirements if they think that upper management has not considered their input. This is one reason the balanced scorecard approach is successful—by having many different measures of success, the desire and ability to manipulate budget numbers are reduced.

As you can see, every budgeting process has benefits and costs. A successful budgeting process occurs when the benefits gained from budgeting exceed the costs incurred. Businesses adopt a variety of different budgeting strategies in an attempt to ensure a successful budgeting process. A budgetary strategy is the manner in which a company approaches the budgeting process. The strategy adopted by the company impacts who is involved in the budgeting process and how the budget numbers are derived. Each of the various budgeting strategies is an attempt to minimize the motivational and behavioral costs associated with budgeting. We discuss several of these strategies next.

Mandated versus Participatory Budgeting

Mandated and participatory budgeting are diametric approaches used to determine who is involved in the budgeting process. They can be considered as the two extreme points on the budgeting process continuum. At the one extreme, only upper-level managers are involved in budgeting; this is known as mandated budgeting. At the other extreme, all employees are involved in budgeting; this is known as participatory budgeting. In the business world, most companies use a combination of mandated and participatory budgeting.

Mandated budgeting Top-down budgeting; the budget is prepared by upper management based on predetermined standards.

Mandated Budgeting

Mandated budgeting relies on predetermined standards set by upper-level managers for its budget levels. It is also known as top-down budgeting because top management develops the budgets and passes them down the organizational hierarchy to various divisions and/or departments without input from lower levels of management and employees.

The purpose of mandated budgeting is to set operating budgets that are in line with the goals and objectives of upper-level management. The predetermined standards on which such budgets are based are estimates of the quantity and cost of operating inputs and can be either ideal or normal. An **ideal standard** can be achieved if operating conditions are almost perfect; it does not allow for any operating inefficiencies. A **normal standard** can be achieved under practical operating conditions and allows for some normal operating inefficiencies.

For example, suppose the upper-level management at Apple determines that a certain computer workstation can be manufactured using six hours of machine time if the production line runs continuously. On the other hand, if normal work stoppages and estimated breakdowns are considered, it should take eight hours to complete this computer workstation. In this case, six hours is considered an ideal standard, while eight hours is a normal standard.

A company uses mandated budgeting because it believes that the advantages of this approach exceed the disadvantages. The advantages are twofold: First, mandated budgeting eliminates the potential problems associated with budgetary slack. Second, upper-level managers often have a better vision of where the company needs to go and what activities it must accomplish to achieve its goals. On the other hand, employees subject to mandated budgets may resist them and, therefore, the company's goals may not be achieved.

Participatory budgeting Bottom-up budgeting; the budget is coordinated by upper management based on input from lower-level employees.

Participatory Budgeting

Participatory budgeting allows individuals affected by the budget to have input into the budgeting process. It is also known as bottom-up budgeting because the budgeting process begins at lower levels of the organizational hierarchy and continues up through the organization to top management. Upper-level management and the budget director are responsible for coordinating the information received from the employees and for developing a comprehensive budget plan.

For example, suppose that rather than having upper management determine the standard time allowed to produce a computer workstation, the production managers at Apple asked production employees for their input. Because the employees affected by the budget are given input into the process, this is a participatory budget process.

A company that uses participatory budgeting does so because it believes that the advantages outweigh the disadvantages. Perhaps the most significant advantage of participatory budgeting is the wealth of information that is gathered from employees. However, if this information is biased, the problems associated with budgetary slack may exist. In addition, employee motivation normally increases in a participatory environment because employees believe that their ideas are valued by upper-level management.

Incremental Budgeting versus Zero-Based Budgeting

The second aspect of budgeting strategy concerns how to determine the budget numbers. Some companies begin a period's budgeting process by referring to the current period's budget, while others begin each budgeting period anew.

Incremental Budgeting

Incremental budgeting is a strategy whereby the company uses the prior period's budget as a starting point in preparing this period's budget. The resource requirements of the prior period are increased or decreased based on the changes expected during this period. The advantage of this strategy is that it is less time-consuming and may involve fewer individuals within the organization. Because much budgeting activity is the same from period to period, this strategy saves time and money because managers are not required to create each budget from scratch. This is particularly important because one of the significant costs of budgeting is the time and resources required. The disadvantage of incremental budgeting is that an increase in resource requirements is often proposed without considering whether the increase is really necessary. Thus some companies find themselves engaged in an activity commonly known as "use it or lose it." That is, the division or department thinks that if it does not spend all of its budgeted resources in one period, its budget allocation for the subsequent period will be cut. This attitude often leads departments into buying items that are not currently needed; thus resources are wasted, and profitability is affected.

Zero-Based Budgeting

In contrast, a **zero-based budgeting** strategy, in which the company begins each budget period with a zero budget, requires consideration of every activity undertaken by the department or segment. Rather than beginning with the current period's budget, the manager must determine if the activity is necessary (value-added versus nonvalue-added), the alternative ways of conducting the activity, and the amount of resources needed to conduct the activity.

The advantage of zero-based budgeting is that it requires managers to carefully consider the activities undertaken by their respective functions and to determine if activities add value. The disadvantage of zero-based budgeting is that it is very time-consuming and, therefore, requires more resources than incremental budgeting. Another potential disadvantage of zero-based budgeting is that it may cause managers to vie against one another in an attempt to protect their turf. For example, since each manager must justify all requests for resources, they may have an incentive to withhold information and, therefore, communication between functions is hampered. If this results in a misallocation of resources, future profitability is impacted.

Enhance Your Understanding

If you were a manager of Apple, what budget approach and budget strategy would you adopt? Why?

Answer: A manager at Apple might adopt a participatory budgeting strategy to obtain input and ideas from employees and use zero-based budgeting in a three-to-five year cycle with incremental budgeting in between.

Master Budget

Master budget
The compilation of all the operating budgets and schedules culminating in the budgeted financial statements.

The **master budget** is the compilation of all the budgets and schedules prepared in planning for the revenue, conversion, and expenditure processes. Such planning culminates with the budgeted financial statements as shown in Exhibit 6.1. As you can see, planning for the revenue process results in four budgets/schedules: (1) sales budget, (2) cash receipts schedule, (3) accounts receivable schedule, and (4) marketing and distribution budget. This planning provides input to conversion process planning. Conversion process planning results in one budget, the production budget. Conversion process planning leads to expenditure process planning. Expenditure process planning results in five budgets/schedules: (1) direct materials purchases budget, (2) direct labor/overhead budget, (3) administrative budget, (4) cash disbursements schedule, and (5) accounts payable schedule. Finally note that all planning processes are linked to the budgeted (a.k.a. pro forma) financial statements. Before these financial statements are prepared, companies often prepare a budgeted schedule of cost of goods sold and finished goods. Thus the goals and objectives of the customer, internal processes, and learning and growth perspectives reflected in the budgets and schedules are ultimately linked to the financial perspective of the balanced scorecard. In this chapter we examine the budgets and schedules of the operating processes. Budgeted financial statements and the related schedules are beyond the scope of this text.

To illustrate the planning process throughout this chapter, we open a computer manufacturing company called PCs to Go. To begin, we adopt a penetration pricing strategy and sell only tablet PCs. We will sell our PCs to regional electronics stores. Once we have established ourselves in the market we intend to expand by offering additional electronic devices. At this time we will also raise our prices. We will organize our company as a corporation

EXHIBIT 6.1
Planning Process and Budgeted Statements

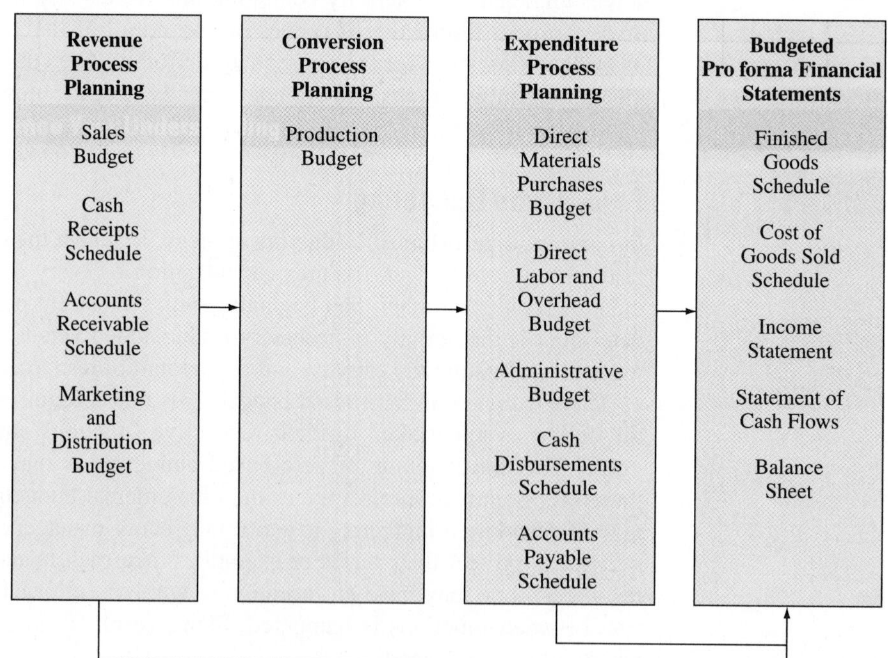

EXHIBIT 6.2
Planning Information for PCs to Go

Expected selling price per unit	$1,500
Anticipated sales per month:	
Month one	300
Month two	350
Month three	400
Month four	450
Month five	500
Month six	500
Expected cash collection schedule:	
30 percent cash sales	
40 percent paid within the discount period (terms 2/10, n/30)*	
25 percent paid in the month of billing but after the discount period	
5 percent paid in the month after billing	
Direct materials per PC:**	
1 processor	$200
2 component parts (1 keyboard and 1 screen)	$25/each
Marketing and distribution costs:	
Salaries and commissions	10 percent of sales
Advertising and promotion	3 percent of sales
Equipment rental	$12,000 per month
Manufacturing costs:	
Direct labor	$2 per unit (15 minutes per unit @ $8 per hour)
Indirect materials	$160 per unit
Unit-related overhead	$1 per unit
Batch overhead	$1,600 per month
Product-sustaining overhead	$3,500 per month
Facility overhead per month:	
Rent on facilities	$2,000 per month
Depreciation on equipment	$1,500 per month ($180,000/120 = $1,500)
Indirect labor	$2,148 per month
Other administrative costs:	
Interest on loan	$500 per month ($100,000 × 0.06 × 1/12 = $500)
Miscellaneous	$300 per month
Salaries	$2,000 per month

*PCs to Go sends invoices on the first of each month for charge sales made in the previous month.
**For simplicity we assume only two direct materials.

and finance it by issuing stock for $200,000 and borrowing $100,000 at 6 percent simple interest from the bank. We must purchase equipment at a cost of $180,000 with an expected useful life of 10 years.

Exhibit 6.2 indicates the expected selling prices, sales volume, and operating costs of PCs to Go necessary to budget for the first quarter. We refer to this exhibit throughout the discussion that follows in this chapter, so you may want to bookmark this page.

Revenue Process Planning

The first step in revenue process planning is to estimate the volume of sales of goods or services given the expected selling price (see Chapter 5). For example, a service organization must estimate how many clients it will serve in the coming period. Both merchandising and manufacturing firms must estimate how many units of product will be sold during the coming period. This planning reflects the customer perspective of the balanced scorecard. In addition, it is necessary to estimate cash receipts from customers and the resulting accounts receivable as part of revenue cycle planning. Finally, the marketing and distribution activities of the company must be planned and budgeted. For some companies, the planning of marketing activities precedes the planning of sales because the number of units sold and the selling prices result from marketing efforts. For purposes of discussion, however, we consider the marketing and distribution budget last in the revenue process. These latter processes reflect the internal perspective of the balanced scorecard.

Balanced Scorecard Goals

Companies monitor the customer perspective along two dimensions: customer satisfaction and customer loyalty. To measure customer satisfaction, companies can develop specific, measurable goals for (1) increasing the number of customers, (2) increasing market share—the number of customers relative to the competition, and (3) enhancing company image. Enhancing company image might be measured by monitoring the number of customer complaints or through customer surveys. To measure customer loyalty, companies can develop specific measurable goals for (1) increasing customer retention and (2) increasing revenue per customer. For example, Apple might set a goal of reducing the number of customers lost by 3 percent. Or it might want to increase the revenue generated per customer by 15 percent.

Understanding customers' wants and needs is crucial so customer surveys are frequently used to develop customer-perspective goals. For example, assume Apple conducts a customer survey that reveals a need for portable video players. Apple could plan research and development (learning and growth) activities to meet this demand. This, in turn, could impact the internal processes of Apple in the future. As you can see from this example, developing goals in one perspective impacts other perspectives.

Sales Budget

After considering all of these issues, the revenue planning team develops the sales budget. The **sales budget** shows the expected sales for the period in both physical (quantity) and financial (dollar) amounts for a particular product line, geographic area, or sales manager. Therefore, the number of sales budgets depends on the number of product lines, geographic areas, or sales managers the company has. The company must develop its budgets in light of the balanced scorecard measures it wants to use. For example, Apple might develop sales budgets for every product line because it is interested in increasing market share for all its products. As you will discover, the accuracy of the sales budget is important because it drives all the other operating plans.

Using the information concerning sales volume and selling prices, our sales budget is shown in Exhibit 6.3. Notice that the budget indicates sales in both units and dollars. Since we intend to sell only one product in one region at this time, we have only one sales budget. In addition, the budget shows that we intend to maintain the same selling price per unit during the first quarter.

Cash Receipts Schedule

Once the sales budget is determined, the next step in revenue cycle planning is to estimate cash receipts. When companies sell their products on account, cash receipts may be different from their sales. Therefore, part of revenue process planning includes planning the billing to and collecting from customers who purchased items using credit. To determine the expected cash receipts, the company must address two important issues: what amount will be collected from customers and when it will be collected. Therefore, as part of cash planning, the company must consider whether to offer cash discounts and whether to expect uncollectible credit sales. This analysis is part of internal process planning because it reflects the company's credit policies as well as its willingness to offer sales discounts to customers.

A **cash receipts schedule** shows the anticipated cash collections from customers for the period. According to Exhibit 6.2, we anticipate collecting 30 percent of sales at the time the sale is made. We believe that the remaining sales will be on account and that 40 percent of total sales will be collected in the discount period. Another 25 percent of the total sales will be collected at the end of the billing month and 5 percent will be collected in the month after billing. Based on this information, the cash receipts schedule for PCs to Go is shown in Exhibit 6.4.

OF INTEREST Using Spreadsheets for Budgeting

Preparing budgets can sometimes be a time-consuming process. However, spreadsheets make the task much easier. By using copy commands, you can dramatically reduce the time it takes to prepare a budget. And as long as your beginning formula is correct, you need not worry about mathematical errors in your budgets. A simple example will illustrate this point. Let's assume that you are preparing a cash receipts schedule based on the following assumptions:

Month	1	2	3	4	5	6
Sales in dollars	$10,000	$11,000	$12,000	$13,000	$14,000	$15,000

Expected collection pattern:

20% in the month of sale

50% in the month following the sale less a 2% discount

28% in the second month following the sale

First, you must design your spreadsheet. You want the columns to represent months and the rows to represent the cash collections. Column A will describe the cells and you will need a heading for your schedule. Using Excel you can enter the following data in Column A, rows 1–2: (1) Example Company and (2) Cash Receipts Schedule. You can then center this over Columns A–G (Merge and Center). Next, enter your descriptions in Column A, rows 3–7: (3) Total sales, (4) Collections in the month of sale, (5) Collections in the month following sale, (6) Collections in the second month following sale, and (7) Total collections from customers. You may also want to bold these headings as well as your schedule headings.

Now you are ready to enter data. Enter the sales data given into cells B3–G3. Do not worry about formatting; you'll do that later. Next, enter the following formulas into these cells:

B4: =b3*.2
C5: =b3*.5*.98
D6: =b3*.28

You will save yourself much time by using the copy command. Copy cell B4 and paste into cells C4–G4. Copy cell C5 and paste into cells D5–G5. Finally, copy cell D6 and paste into cells E6–G6. The last item to be calculated is the total. To complete your data entry, enter zeros into cells B5, B6, and C6. Next, use the Sum function to determine the total of rows 4, 5, and 6 of Column B, then copy cell B7 and paste into C7–G7. Finally, format your spreadsheet in dollars with zero decimal places. Your finished product should look like the example below.

For a more sophisticated spreadsheet, you can use an input page that contains all the information such as percentage of sales collected in a given time period. Then each of the budget formulas references a cell or group of cells on the input page. This way, you can simply change the information on the input page and the budgets change automatically.

Example Company

Cash Receipts Schedule

Total sales	**$10,000**	**$11,000**	**$12,000**	**$13,000**	**$14,000**	**$15,000**
Collections in the month of sale	$2,000	$2,200	$ 2,400	$ 2,600	$ 2,800	$ 3,000
Collections in the month following sale	$ 0	$4,900	$ 5,390	$ 5,880	$ 6,370	$ 6,860
Collections in the second month following sale	$ 0	$ 0	$ 2,800	$ 3,080	$ 3,360	$ 3,640
Total collections from customers	$2,000	$7,100	$10,590	$11,560	$12,530	$13,500

EXHIBIT 6.3
PCs to Go Sales Budget

	Month One	Month Two	Month Three
Sales in units	300	350	400
Selling price per unit	$ 1,500	$ 1,500	$ 1,500
Sales in dollars	$450,000	$525,000	$600,000

EXHIBIT 6.4
PCs to Go Cash Receipts Schedule

	Month One	Month Two	Month Three
Cash sales (30% × current month)	$135,000	$ 157,500	$ 180,000
Charge sales paid in discount period (40% × prior month)	0	176,400	205,800
Charge sales paid in billing month (25% × prior month)	0	112,500	131,250
Charge sales paid in month after billing (5% × 2 months prior)		0	22,500
Total estimated cash receipts	$ 135,000	$ 446,400	$ 539,550
Cash discounts given	$ 0	$ 3,600	$ 4,200

Let's see how some of the amounts in Exhibit 6.4 were determined. In Month Three, we anticipate collecting the following:

30 percent cash sales ($600,000 × 0.3)	$180,000
40 percent sales on account from Month Two	
less 2 percent discount ($525,000 × 0.4 × 0.98)	205,800
25 percent sales on account from Month Two ($525,000 × 0.25)	131,250
5 percent sales on account from Month One ($450,000 × 0.05)	22,500
Total estimated cash receipts	$539,550

We should also calculate the estimated cash discounts expected each month as shown in Exhibit 6.4. For Month Three, this amount is determined as $525,000 × 0.4 × 0.02 = $4,200. Since we do not anticipate any uncollectible credit sales, we do not need to make this particular calculation. At some point in our company's future, unfortunately, this may be necessary.

Enhance Your Understanding

How were the amounts in Exhibit 6.4 for Month Two calculated?

Answer: Month Two is calculated as:

Cash sales ($525,000 × 0.30)	$157,500
On account sales from Month One less 2 percent discount ($450,000 × 0.40 × 0.98)	176,400
On account sales from Month One ($450,000 × 0.25)	112,500
Total	$446,400

Accounts Receivable Schedule

Since we allow customers to buy computers in one period and pay for them in another, we must also consider the status of our accounts receivable. Recall that accounts receivable is an asset representing the amounts owed by customers. It is important to plan accounts receivable because it has a dramatic impact on certain ratios (current ratio, quick ratio and accounts receivable turnover) that we use to measure performance. An **accounts receivable schedule** indicates the changes expected in the balance of accounts receivable during the budget period. Planning and controlling accounts receivable is an important aspect of the internal perspective. We calculate the estimated ending balance of accounts receivable as:

  Beginning balance of accounts receivable (amounts owed from previous months)
+ Credit sales during the month
= Total amount due from customers
− Cash received from credit customers during the month
− Cash (sales) discounts taken by customers during the month
− Estimated uncollectible credit sales for the month
= Ending balance of accounts receivable

Exhibit 6.5 shows the accounts receivable schedule for PCs to Go. Take a moment to study this schedule. In Month Two, the beginning balance of accounts receivable represents what we expect customers to owe us. Notice that this is the same amount as the ending balance of Month One. The beginning balance is increased by credit sales for the month to determine the total amount due from customers. Then this amount is reduced by payments from credit

EXHIBIT 6.5
PCs to Go Accounts Receivable Schedule

	Month One	Month Two	Month Three
Beginning balance	0	$315,000	$390,000
Add: charge sales (Exhibit 6.3 × 0.7)	$315,000	$367,500	$420,000
Total amount due from customers	$315,000	$682,500	$810,000
Less charge sales paid in discount period (Exhibit 6.4)	0	176,400	205,800
Less charge sales paid in billing month (Exhibit 6.4)	0	112,500	131,250
Less charge sales paid in month after billing (Exhibit 6.4)	0	0	22,500
Less cash discounts given (Exhibit 6.4)	0	3,600	4,200
Ending balance	$315,000	$390,000	$446,250

EXHIBIT 6.6
PCs to Go Marketing and Distribution Costs Budget

	Month One	Month Two	Month Three
Salaries and commissions (10% of sales)	$45,000	$52,500	$60,000
Advertising and promotional materials (3% of sales)	13,500	15,750	18,000
Equipment rental	12,000	12,000	12,000
Total estimated marketing and distribution costs	$70,500	$80,250	$90,000

customers and discounts given to customers. (Recall, we don't anticipate any uncollectible credit sales.)

Therefore, for Month Two, the ending balance is determined as follows:

Beginning balance (ending balance from Month One)	$315,000
Add: credit sales from Month Two (Sales from Month Two × 0.70)	367,500
Less: cash receipts from credit customers Month Two (Exhibit 6.4)	288,900
Less: cash discounts from Month Two (Exhibit 6.4)	3,600
Ending balance	$390,000

Marketing and Distribution Budget

Finally, a company must plan its marketing and distribution activities (internal processes perspective). Management must plan how to market, advertise, and sell its products/services. In addition, distribution and customer service activities must be determined. For example, do we plan Internet sales? Will we promote service after the sale? The **marketing and distribution budget** indicates the planned expenditures for these marketing and distribution activities.

We plan personal contact sales; therefore, we will pay our sales force a commission to encourage personal contacts. As shown in Exhibit 6.2, we plan to pay our sales force a 10 percent commission based on sales. We believe that advertising and promotion costs will vary with sales at the rate of 3 percent. Also, we were able to rent office equipment for $12,000 per month. Exhibit 6.6 is the marketing and distribution costs budget that reflects these plans. Note that the commission and the advertising and promotion costs vary with the expected level of sales (unit-related cost). On the other hand, the equipment rental is fixed over our range of activity (facility-sustaining cost).

Conversion Process Planning

After determining the inventory model (Chapter 5) that establishes the relationship between production and raw materials, the next step in conversion process planning is to develop goals with regard to efficiency and quality (internal process perspective).

EXHIBIT 6.7
PCs to Go Production Budget

	Month One	Month Two	Month Three	Month Four
Sales in units	300	350	400	450
Add: desired ending inventory				
(2% of next month)	7	8	9	10
Total units needed	307	358	409	460
Less: beginning inventory	0	7	8	9
Tablet PCs to produce	307	351	401	451

Balanced Scorecard Goals

Efficiency can be measured by determining and monitoring customer response time (see Chapter 2) and quality can be controlled by planning the relative expenditures for prevention and appraisal quality costs versus internal and external failure quality costs (see Chapter 2). For example, a company might set a goal of increasing production efficiency by 8 percent during the current period. Or the company might plan to increase spending for prevention and appraisal quality costs by 20 percent with the goal of reducing internal failure costs by 30 percent. A company might also set goals related to its turnover ratios. For example, if it wants to increase cash inflows it would set a goal to increase the accounts receivable turnover. If it wanted to decrease its inventory levels, it might set a goal to increase its inventory turnover ratio. The goals set for efficiency (time) and quality are, in turn, reflected in the production budget (that follows) and the expenditure budgets.

To plan production levels the company must determine the quantity of finished goods to produce and when to produce them. Because production is planned to meet demand, the sales quantity information in the sales budget is a key input to the production planning process. The anticipated demand plus the desired level of finished goods make up the production budget, which shows the expected level of production for the period. After the production budget is completed, the company can prepare its cost of goods sold and finished goods schedules.

Production Budget

The **production budget** uses information from the sales budget plus the company's desired ending inventory level to determine the quantity of finished goods to produce each period. Now we must determine our desired ending inventory level. Since we want to minimize inventory levels, we will maintain a minimal inventory of 2 percent of next month's anticipated sales. That is, if we believe that we will sell 100 units next month, we desire an ending inventory of 2 units (100 × 0.02) this month. Recall that our anticipated sales are Month One, 300 units; Month Two, 350 units; Month Three, 400 units; and Month Four, 450 units.

Based on this information, our production budget is illustrated in Exhibit 6.7. Note several items on the production budget: First, the production budget is prepared entirely in units; no monetary amounts are shown. Second, the desired ending inventory is stated as a percentage of next month's anticipated sales. Third, the beginning inventory in a given month is the previous month's ending inventory. That is, the ending inventory in Month One is the beginning inventory in Month Two, and so on. Let's look closer at Month Three. In Month Three we need to produce enough units to meet Month Three's anticipated sales (400 tablet PCs). We want an ending inventory equal to 2 percent of Month Four's anticipated sales; therefore, we need an ending inventory of 9 computers (450 × 0.02). However, we anticipate beginning Month Three with 8 computers (Month Two ending inventory). Thus, we need to produce 401 tablet PCs in Month Three (400 + 9 − 8 = 401). Also note that the production budget extends to Month Four for reasons that will become clear later.

Expenditure Process Planning

After determining the compensation package offered to employees (Chapter 5), expenditure process planning considers the use and payment for services and goods. Therefore the company must develop internal process and learning and growth goals.

Balanced Scorecard Goals

For example, Apple might plan to reduce labor time by 10 percent. Or it may set a goal to increase the amount of continuing education for employees by 25 percent. The company might also have goals regarding cash payments. Perhaps it wants to increase the efficiency of the payment process by ensuring that all purchase discounts are taken. Or perhaps the company determines that it is actually paying its bills too quickly. In this case, it might develop a goal to pay all bills when due, but never early. With regard to purchasing, various goals may be established. For example, the company might want to develop supplier relationships. Or it might want to increase the quality of raw materials received. Once these goals are established, the company must budget for the cost of implementing the plans. Thus we must plan and budget for human resources, manufacturing overhead, and administrative costs that arise from internal process and learning and growth goals.

Budgeting for Human Resources

Human resources costs are reflected in a number of budgets. For employees who are part of the selling function, their expected salaries (per month, per hour, or commission) and other benefits for the coming period are reflected in the marketing and distribution budget. Recall this budget in Exhibit 6.6. For employees who are part of the administrative function, their expected salaries (per month or per hour) and other benefits are reflected in the administrative budget. For employees who are part of the conversion function, their salaries (piece-rate, per hour, or per month) and other benefits are reflected in the direct labor and manufacturing overhead budget. In addition, amounts incurred for payroll taxes (FICA, FUTA, and SUTA) are included in these budgets. We consider these latter two budgets next.

Administrative Budget

The **administrative budget** reflects the expected administrative costs, including administrative labor. Thus the administrative budget should reflect the costs of activities not considered in the revenue or conversion processes. As you can see in Exhibit 6.8, other administrative costs consist of interest on the loan, miscellaneous costs, and salaries (and payroll costs). Recall that we plan to borrow $100,000 at 6 percent simple interest. Our monthly interest cost, therefore, will be $\$100{,}000 \times 0.06 \times 1/12 = \$500$. We assume that this interest, but no principal, is paid each month. Notice that the total budget remains the same each month and, therefore, these costs can be considered facility-sustaining costs.

Direct Labor and Manufacturing Overhead Budget

The **direct labor and manufacturing overhead budget** reflects the expected costs of the conversion process. Since these costs are paid in the expenditure process, we have deferred discussion until now. Because there is a need for both labor and manufacturing overhead resources to convert direct materials into finished products, the information in the production budget (in Exhibit 6.7) is input into the direct labor and manufacturing overhead planning process. As shown in Exhibit 6.2 direct labor (and payroll cost) is $2 per computer. Exhibit 6.2 also indicates that manufacturing costs consist of indirect materials of $160 per computer, unit-related overhead of $1 per computer, batch-related overhead of $1,600 per month,

EXHIBIT 6.8
PCs to Go
Administrative Budget

	Month One	Month Two	Month Three
Interest on loan	$ 500	$ 500	$ 500
Miscellaneous costs	300	300	300
Salaries	2,000	2,000	2,000
Total administrative costs	$2,800	$2,800	$2,800

EXHIBIT 6.9
PCs to Go Direct Labor and Manufacturing Overhead Budget

	Month One	Month Two	Month Three
Direct labor ($2 per unit produced)	$ 614	$ 702	$ 802
Indirect materials ($160 per unit produced)	49,120	56,160	64,160
Unit-related overhead ($1 per unit produced)	307	351	401
Batch-related overhead	1,600	1,600	1,600
Product-sustaining overhead	3,500	3,500	3,500
Rent on facilities	2,000	2,000	2,000
Indirect labor	2,148	2,148	2,148
Total cash manufacturing costs	$59,289	$66,461	$74,611
Depreciation on equipment	1,500	1,500	1,500
Total manufacturing cost	$60,789	$67,961	$76,111

product-sustaining overhead of $3,500 per month, and facility-sustaining overhead of $5,648 per month. Exhibit 6.9 illustrates the direct labor and manufacturing overhead budget for the first quarter. Notice that direct labor, indirect materials, and unit-related overhead vary with the number of units produced, while batch-related overhead varies with the number of batches planned. Also note that depreciation (a noncash cost) is listed separately.

Therefore, for Month Two, the direct labor and manufacturing overhead amounts are:

Direct labor (351 × $2)	$ 702
Indirect materials (351 × $160)	56,160
Unit-related overhead (351 × $1)	351
Batch-related overhead	1,600
Product-sustaining overhead	3,500
Rent	2,000
Indirect labor	2,148
Depreciation	1,500
Total direct labor and manufacturing overhead	$67,961

Direct Materials Purchases Budget

The **direct materials purchases budget** reflects the expected cost of direct material purchases during the period. It depends on the inventory model (Chapter 5) adopted by the company as well as its plans for efficiency improvements during the period (internal processes perspective). Since materials are purchased for use in production, the information from the production budget is a key input to the materials planning process. In addition, the desired ending inventory of materials must be planned. Therefore, the direct materials purchases budget, which shows the expected quantity and cost of direct materials purchases for the period, looks very similar to the production budget except the final amount is stated in dollars because direct materials are purchased, not made.

For simplicity, we assume only two direct materials—processors and component parts.[1] Let's assume that our processor supplier will offer us credit terms of 2/10, EOM. This means we can take a 2 percent discount if we pay for all the processors purchased by the end of the month in which we purchase them. Further assume that we have determined that a 10 percent ending inventory of processors is desirable. This means that we want to have on hand at the end of Month One 10 percent of what we need to meet production in Month Two, and so on. Our parts supplier does not offer credit terms. However, the component parts supplier does not require payment until the month after the purchase is made. Therefore, component parts purchases made in Month One will be paid in Month Two, and so on. We have determined that a 20 percent ending inventory of component parts is appropriate.

Exhibit 6.10 shows the direct materials purchases budget for the processors. Notice that the budget indicates the number of processors needed for production (1 processor per unit), then adds to this the desired ending inventory (10 percent multiplied by the next month's production needs). Therefore, the desired ending inventory for Month One is 351 units × 0.10 = 35.

[1]Component parts consist of the keyboard and the screen.

EXHIBIT 6.10
PCs to Go Direct Materials Purchases Budget: Processors

	Month One	Month Two	Month Three
Number of processors needed for production	307	351	401
Add: desired ending inventory (10% of next month)	35	40	45
Total processors needed	342	391	446
Less: beginning inventory	0	35	40
Number of processors to purchase	342	356	406
Processor purchases in dollars	$68,400	$71,200	$81,200

EXHIBIT 6.11
PCs to Go Direct Materials Purchases Budget: Component Parts

	Month One	Month Two	Month Three
Number of component parts needed for production	614	702	802
Add: desired ending inventory (20% of next month)	140	160	180
Total component parts needed	754	862	982
Less: beginning inventory	0	140	160
Number of component parts to purchase	754	722	822
Component parts purchases in dollars	$18,850	$18,050	$20,550

From this amount we subtract the beginning inventory (zero for Month One) to calculate the number of processors to purchase. Finally, this amount is multiplied by the purchase price ($200) to determine the processor purchases in dollars.

Enhance Your Understanding

How is the amount of processor purchases for Month Three calculated?
Answer: 401 + (451 × 0.1) − 40 = 406 × $200 = $81,200

Exhibit 6.11 shows the direct materials purchases budget for the component parts. Notice that the budget indicates the number of component parts needed for production (2 component parts [1 keyboard and 1 screen] per unit), then adds to this amount the desired ending inventory (20 percent multiplied by the next month's production needs). From this amount, the beginning inventory is subtracted to determine the number of component parts to buy. When this result is multiplied by the purchase price ($25), we know the estimated component parts purchases in dollars. Footnote 2 describes the purchases budget for a merchandising company.[2]

Cash Disbursements Schedule

Recall that the expenditure process concludes with the payment for goods and services. Therefore, the last step in expenditure process planning is to determine when and how much to pay

[2] Merchandising Company's Purchases Budget: A merchandising company plans purchases to meet budgeted sales rather than budgeted production. Like a manufacturing company, a merchandising company must also determine the desired ending inventory level. A merchandising purchases budget then begins with sales in dollars. These amounts are converted to cost of goods sold numbers (recall the company's cost of the products it sells is called cost of goods sold). Then the desired ending inventory is added and the beginning inventory is subtracted and the purchases required are determined. For example, assume a convenience store intends to stock candy bars. It believes it can sell $1,500 of candy bars in Month Two and $2,250 of candy bars in Month Three. The store's cost of goods sold is two-thirds of the selling price; therefore, the budgeted cost of goods sold for Month Two is $1,000 and the budgeted cost of goods sold for Month Three is $1,500. If the store desires an ending inventory of 10 percent of next month's expected cost of goods sold, the desired ending inventory in Month Two would be $150 ($1,500 × 0.10). Putting this information together (assuming no beginning inventory) would result in a purchases budget for Month Two as follows:

Sales	$1,500
Cost of goods sold (⅔ of sales)	$1,000
Add: desired ending inventory	150
Less: beginning inventory	–0–
Purchases required	$1,150

EXHIBIT 6.12
Cash Disbursements Schedule

	Month One	Month Two	Month Three
Marketing and distribution costs (Exhibit 6.6)	$ 70,500	$ 80,250	$ 90,000
Administrative costs (Exhibit 6.8)	2,800	2,800	2,800
Direct labor and manufacturing overhead costs (Exhibit 6.9)	59,289	66,461	74,611
Direct material purchases: processors (98% of Exhibit 6.10)	67,032	69,776	79,576
Direct material purchases: component parts (Exhibit 6.11)	0	18,850	18,050
Total cash disbursements	$199,621	$238,137	$265,037
Cash discounts taken (2% of Exhibit 6.10)	$ 1,368	$ 1,424	$ 1,624

for goods and services used. This is an internal perspective because it reflects the company's goals regarding the payments to suppliers of goods and services. We determine the amount of payments by using information from the other budgets. The direct materials purchases, direct labor and manufacturing overhead, administrative, and the marketing and distribution budgets all contain information regarding the planned operating expenditures during the period.

Examine each of these budgets, in turn. Take a moment to think about all the goods and services we plan to use during the coming period. Are there any items listed in these budgets that do not require cash payments? The direct labor and manufacturing overhead budget contains depreciation. Because depreciation is the allocation of the cost of an asset to the time periods in which the asset is used, it does not require a cash payment. All other items shown on the budgets do require cash payments; therefore, it is necessary to determine a cash payment schedule for them.

Recall from Chapter 3 that the best policy is to take advantage of purchase discounts whenever possible and to delay paying bills until the last possible date within the discount period. Typically labor and overhead items must be paid as incurred but materials (and sometimes supplies) can be purchased on account. In these cases, we must determine the terms of sale. For example, our processor supplier will allow us a 2 percent discount.

Once we determine how much money is owed and when it is due, we can prepare our **cash disbursements schedule** that shows the expected cash outflows during the period. Exhibit 6.12 shows the cash disbursements budget for PCs to Go for the first quarter. Take a moment to make sure you can trace these amounts back to the appropriate budgets. Note that the payments for processors are 98 percent of the total processor purchases and that component parts are paid for in the month after purchase. All other payments are made in the month incurred. Therefore our Month Two cash disbursements are

Marketing and distribution costs (Exhibit 6.6 Month Two)	$ 80,250
Administrative costs (Exhibit 6.8 Month Two)	2,800
Direct labor and manufacturing overhead (Exhibit 6.9 Month Two)	66,461
Processors (Exhibit 6.10 Month Two × 0.98)	69,776
Component parts (Exhibit 6.11 Month One)	18,850
Total cash disbursements	$238,137

Accounts Payable Schedule

Because companies are able to purchase items in one period and pay for them in a different period, they must also consider their liabilities and their goals for increasing, decreasing, or maintaining their accounts payable turnover ratio.[3] As you know, accounts payable is a

[3] Recall from Chapter 1 that companies also monitor the amount of liabilities relative to the amount of shareholders' equity (debt-to-equity ratio).

EXHIBIT 6.13
Accounts Payable Schedule

	Month One	Month Two	Month Three
Beginning balance	0	$ 18,850	$ 18,050
Add: direct material purchases (Exhibits 6.10 and 6.11)	$87,250	$ 89,250	$101,750
Total amount owed to suppliers	$87,250	$108,100	$119,800
Less: cash paid for processors (Exhibit 6.12)	67,032	69,776	79,576
Less: cash paid for component parts (Exhibit 6.12)	0	18,850	18,050
Less: cash discounts taken (Exhibit 6.12)	1,368	1,424	1,624
Ending balance	$18,850	$ 18,050	$ 20,550

liability reflecting the amounts owed to suppliers of goods and services. The estimated ending balance in accounts payable is determined as follows:

Beginning balance of accounts payable
\+ Purchases on account during the month
= Total amount owed to suppliers
– Cash paid to suppliers on account during the month
– Cash (purchase) discounts for the month
= Ending balance of accounts payable

An **accounts payable schedule** indicates the expected changes in the balance of accounts payable during the period. Exhibit 6.13 shows our schedule of accounts payable for each month. In Month Two, our accounts payable schedule reflects the beginning balance of accounts payable (Month One purchases of component parts = $18,850) plus the purchases of processors and component parts in Month Two ($89,250). This sum is then reduced by payments made in Month Two ($69,776 + $18,850) and the cash discount taken ($1,424) to determine the ending balance of accounts payable ($18,050).

Enhance Your Understanding: Budgets Needed by Merchandising Firms

Merchandising firms prepare the same budgets as manufacturing firms in the revenue process planning phase. However, they do not have a conversion process, and in the expenditure process a merchandising firm would prepare an inventory purchases budget (or budgets) based on its sales budget. A merchandising firm would also prepare a labor and operating expenses budget as part of the expenditure process planning before preparing its cash disbursements and accounts payable schedules. Therefore, the most noticeable difference is that a merchandising firm does not prepare a production budget or a direct labor and manufacturing overhead budget and its material purchases budget (inventory purchases) is linked to its sales budget rather than to a production budget.

Summary

To plan and budget operating processes, a company must consider its customers, its employees, and its internal processes as well as its financial goals. In addition, the strategic decisions made regarding operating processes must be reflected in the plans and budgets of the current period. The master budget is the compilation of the budgets and schedules prepared as part of the revenue, conversion, and expenditure processes planning.

- Revenue process planning results in the sales budget, cash receipts schedule, accounts receivable schedule, and marketing and distribution budget.
- Conversion process planning results in the production budget.
- Expenditure process planning results in the direct materials purchases budget, direct labor/overhead budget, administrative budget, cash disbursements schedule, and accounts payable schedule.

Key Terms

Accounts payable schedule A schedule that indicates the expected changes in the balance of accounts payable during the period, *171*

Accounts receivable schedule A schedule that indicates the changes expected in the balance of accounts receivable during the budget period, *164*

Administrative budget A budget that reflects the expected administrative costs, including administrative labor, *167*

Budget A plan for the future expressed in quantitative terms, *155*

Budgetary slack A difference between reported budget numbers and realistic budget numbers, *157*

Budgeting The process of expressing the company's goals and objectives in quantitative terms, *155*

Cash disbursements schedule A schedule that shows the expected cash outflows during the period, *170*

Cash receipts schedule A schedule that shows the anticipated cash collections from customers for the period, *162*

Direct labor and manufacturing overhead budget A budget that reflects the expected costs of the conversion process, *167*

Direct materials purchases budget A budget that reflects the expected cost of direct material purchases during the period, *168*

Ideal standard A standard that can be achieved only if operating conditions are almost perfect, *158*

Incremental budgeting A budgeting strategy whereby the company uses the prior period's budget as a starting point in preparing this period's budget, *159*

Mandated budgeting A budgeting approach that relies on predetermined standards set by upper-level management; top-down budgeting, *158*

Marketing and distribution budget A budget that indicates the planning expenditures for the marketing and distribution activities, *165*

Master budget The compilation of all the budgets/schedules prepared in planning for the revenue, conversion, and expenditure processes, *160*

Normal standard A standard that can be achieved under practical operating conditions, *158*

Participatory budgeting A budgeting approach that allows individuals who are affected by the budget to have input into the budgeting process; bottom-up budgeting, *158*

Production budget A budget that uses information from the sales budget plus the company's desired ending inventory level to determine the quantity of finished goods to produce each period, *166*

Sales budget A budget that shows the expected sales for the period in both physical and financial amounts, *162*

Zero-based budgeting A budgeting strategy in which the company begins each budget period with a zero budget and considers every activity undertaken by the department or segment, *159*

Questions

1. What is the purpose of budgeting?
2. Describe the benefits of budgeting.
3. Describe the costs of budgeting.
4. Describe budgetary slack.
5. Compare and contrast mandated and participatory budgeting.
6. What is the difference between an ideal and a normal standard?
7. Compare and contrast incremental and zero-based budgeting.
8. What are the budgets/schedules that result from revenue process planning?
9. What is the relationship between the sales budget and the cash receipts schedule?
10. What is the relationship between the cash receipts schedule and the accounts receivable schedule?
11. What is the relationship between the accounts receivable schedule and the sales budget?
12. What is the relationship between the marketing and distribution budget and the sales budget?
13. How can balanced scorecard measures be used for revenue process planning?
14. Develop a set of nonfinancial balanced scorecard measures for the revenue process.
15. How is the production budget related to the sales budget?
16. How can balanced scorecard measures be used for conversion process planning?
17. Develop a set of nonfinancial balanced scorecard measures for the conversion process.

18. What is the purpose of the administrative budget?
19. What is the purpose of the direct labor and manufacturing overhead budget?
20. What is the purpose of the direct materials budget?
21. How does a purchases budget for a manufacturing company differ from a purchases budget for a merchandising company?
22. What information is needed to prepare a cash disbursements schedule and where is this information found?
23. How is the accounts payable schedule related to the cash disbursements schedule?
24. How can balanced scorecard measures be used for expenditure process planning?
25. Develop a set of nonfinancial balanced scorecard measures for the expenditure process.

Exercises

E6.1 LO 2 Gerstenberger, Inc., operates a children's day care center in a major metropolitan area. It offers three child care services: full-day, half-day, and after-school care. Gerstenberger charges $200 per week for full-day care, $100 per week for half-day care, and $75 per week for after-school care per child. Projected enrollments for the next six weeks follow. Use this information to estimate the revenue per week for Gerstenberger.

Week	Full-Day Care	Half-Day Care	After-School Care
1	30	25	20
2	30	30	25
3	30	26	31
4	30	30	30
5	35	25	27
6	35	27	28

LO 2 **E6.2** O'Connell sells two products: Dynamo and Craylon. It estimates that two Craylons are sold each period for every Dynamo sold. A Dynamo sells for $7.50 and a Craylon sells for $5. O'Connell estimates that sales of Dynamo per quarter for the year will be 30,000; 45,000; 35,000; and 48,000, respectively. What is the estimated sales revenue per quarter for O'Connell for the year?

LO 2 **E6.3** Zaragoza Enterprises produces and sells a ceiling fan to retail outlets. Each fan costs Zaragoza $40 to produce and $5 to sell. Zaragoza charges its customers $90 per fan. Estimated sales for the first quarter are 50,000 fans and sales are expected to increase by 10 percent per quarter for the first two years. What is the expected sales revenue per quarter for Zaragoza for the first two years?

LO 2 **E6.4** To aid in preparing its budget for March 2008, Gotfredson Company has provided the following information:

Amount owed by customers, March 1, 2008	$ 400,000
Estimated sales for March 2008	1,400,000
Estimated amount owed by customers, March 31, 2008	525,000

What are the estimated cash receipts for March 2008?

LO 2 **E6.5** Niedringhaus Corporation's sales revenue follows:

	November (Actual Sales)	December (Projected Sales)	January (Projected Sales)
Cash sales	$ 80,000	$100,000	$ 60,000
Credit sales	340,000	460,000	380,000

Niedringhaus's management estimates that 65 percent of credit sales will be collected in the month of sale with a 2% discount taken, and that 34 percent will be collected in the month following sale. What are the expected cash collections for December and January?

LO 2 **E6.6** Soderlund Company has a balance in its accounts receivable of $35,000 at the beginning of the year. Credit sales for the year are expected to be $675,000. It is estimated that Soderlund will collect the entire beginning balance of accounts receivable plus 70 percent of the credit sales. What are the expected cash receipts from sales on account?

LO 2 **E6.7** Refer to E6.6. What is the expected ending balance of accounts receivable?

LO 2 **E6.8** Amadio, Inc., has a beginning accounts receivable balance of $20,000. It expects the following sales for the first quarter:

January	$140,000
February	150,000
March	160,000

Based on past experience, Amadio believes that 60 percent of sales will be collected in the month of sale receiving a 2 percent discount. The remaining sales will be collected in the month after that sale. What are the estimated cash receipts for January through March?

LO 2 **E6.9** Refer to E6.8. Prepare an accounts receivable schedule for January through March.

LO 2 **E6.10** McKown plans to sell 5,000 units of Herbal Wash in the first month, 4,500 units in the second month, and 5,500 units in the third month, at $2 each. Commissions are 2 percent of sales and other unit-related marketing costs are 7 percent of sales. Depreciation of delivery equipment and warehouse rent is $15,000 per quarter. Prepare a sales budget by month for the quarter for McKown.

LO 2 **E6.11** Refer to E6.10. Prepare a marketing and distribution budget by month for the quarter for McKown.

LO 2 **E6.12** Barcenilla has a beginning accounts receivable balance of $140,000. Barcenilla expects sales to be $460,000; $500,000; and $520,000, respectively, for each month in the next quarter. Based on past experience, Barcenilla estimates that 65 percent of sales will be collected in the month of sale with the remaining amount collected in the month following the sale. Barcenilla estimates that marketing costs will average 8 percent of sales while distribution costs will be 2 percent of sales plus $8,000 per month. What are Barcenilla's estimated cash receipts by month for the next quarter?

LO 2 **E6.13** Refer to E6.12. What is Barcenilla's anticipated accounts receivable balance at the end of each month for next quarter?

LO 2 **E6.14** Refer to E6.12. Prepare a marketing and distribution budget, by month, for next quarter.

LO 2 **E6.15** Refer to E6.12. Assume Barcenilla sells its product for $100 each. Prepare a sales budget, by month, for next quarter.

LO 2 **E6.16** Hoch Company, a flower nursery, has estimated these sales:

April	$678,000
May	945,000
June	840,000

Based on past experience, Hoch estimates the following marketing and distribution costs:

Advertising	1 percent of sales
Delivery	3 percent of sales
Customer support	$2,000 per month
Customer analysis	$1,200 per month
Packaging	½ percent of sales

What are the estimated marketing and distribution costs for Hoch by month?

LO 2 **E6.17** Kallsen Enterprises, in its first year of operations, has provided the following estimated sales information:

Month One	$150,000
Month Two	160,000
Month Three	170,000

Based on past experience with similar companies, the manager believes that 55 percent of sales will be collected in the month of sale while the remaining 45 percent will be collected in the month following the sale. What is the expected accounts receivable balance each month?

LO 2 **E6.18** Refer to E6.17. If Kallsen gives customers who pay within the month of sale a 2 percent discount, does this change your answer? Why?

LO 2 **E6.19** Refer to E6.17. Assume that Kallsen pays its sales personnel a commission of 4 percent of sales and that other marketing costs are estimated at $20,000 per month. What is the expected marketing cost each month?

LO 3 E6.20 Otto Enterprises produces ceiling fans for industrial use. Otto estimates quarterly sales of 50,000; 45,000; 60,000; 55,000; and 65,000 for the next five quarters. Otto desires an ending finished goods inventory equal to 10 percent of the expected sales in the next quarter. Otto Enterprises currently has an inventory of 10,000 ceiling fans. How many ceiling fans should Otto produce each quarter next year?

LO 3 E6.21 Barrows Company estimates sales of 40,000 next month and expects a 5 percent increase in sales each month for next year. Barrows Company's beginning finished goods inventory is 2,000 and it desires an ending inventory of 10 percent of the expected sales in the next month. Prepare the production budget, by month, for the first quarter.

LO 3 E6.22 He, Inc., estimates sales of 20,000; 22,000; 24,000; and 26,000 units, respectively, for the next four months. He currently has 3,000 units in ending inventory but would like to reduce this amount to 10 percent of the expected sales in the next month. How many units should be produced in each of the next three months?

LO 4 E6.23 Mathison Enterprises has a balance in accounts payable of $34,500 at the beginning of the budgeting period. Mathison expects to purchase $890,000 of direct materials during the period and intends to pay its suppliers for amounts owed from last period plus 90 percent of material purchases during the budgeted period. What is the expected cash disbursement?

LO 4 E6.24 Refer to E6.23. What is the expected ending balance of accounts payable?

LO 4 E6.25 Codner, Inc., plans to purchase $800,000 and $850,000 of direct materials in Months One and Two, respectively. The accounts payable balance at the beginning of Month One is $50,000. Codner pays for 75 percent of its purchases in the month of purchase because a 2 percent discount is available. The remaining purchases are paid in the month following purchase. What is the expected ending balance of accounts payable?

LO 4 E6.26 Schuh, Inc., plans to produce 6,000 units in Month One and 7,000 units in Month Two. Each unit requires 3 pounds of direct materials that can be purchased for $2 per pound. At the beginning of Month One there are 2,000 pounds of direct materials on hand. Schuh desires an ending inventory of direct materials equal to 10 percent of the next month's direct materials needs. What is the expected cost of direct materials purchases for Month One?

LO 4 E6.27 Murphy Company plans to produce 50,000 units in Quarter One and 60,000 units in Quarter Two. Each unit requires 6 pounds of direct materials that can be purchased for $4 per pound. At the beginning of Quarter One there are 70,000 pounds of direct materials on hand. Murphy desires an ending inventory of direct materials equal to 20 percent of the next quarter's direct materials needs. What is the expected cost of direct materials purchases for Quarter One?

Problems

P6.1 LO 2 Sun Company has studied the collection pattern of sales for the past year and management has developed the following collection schedule:

55 percent in the month of sale with a 1 percent discount
30 percent in the month following the sale
15 percent in the second month following the sale

Actual sales for the past six months are:

January	$200,100
February	220,450
March	300,700
April	251,200
May	275,890
June	180,460

Expected sales for the next six months are:

July	$175,800
August	194,500
September	186,300
October	210,750
November	349,000
December	375,900

Required: A. Determine the expected cash receipts by month for July through September.
B. Determine the expected cash discounts by month for July through September.
C. Determine the expected ending balance of accounts receivable by month for July through September.

LO 2 **P6.2** Gatcheva, Inc., shows a cash balance of $24,000 on January 1, 2008. The expected sales (in units) of its product by month for the first quarter are

January	600,000
February	400,000
March	500,000

Sales are collected 75 percent in the month of sale and 25 percent in the month following the sale. Actual sales (in units) by month for the previous quarter follow:

October	550,000
November	700,000
December	800,000

Gatcheva sells its product for $2 each.

Required: A. Determine the expected unit and dollar sales by month for the first quarter.
B. Determine the expected cash receipts by month for the first quarter.
C. Determine the anticipated accounts receivable balance by month for the first quarter.

LO 2 **P6.3** Green Thumb Lawn Care Service provides lawn care service to clients located throughout the region. It offers two levels of service—full service (watering, mowing, fertilizing, trimming, and edging) and budget service (fertilizing and mowing only). Green Thumb charges $1,500 per quarter for full service and $800 per quarter for budget service. Clients are asked to pay for services in advance. Green Thumb estimates that marketing costs average 1 percent of sales. In addition, Green Thumb estimates product-sustaining costs of $100 per full-service client per quarter and $50 per budget client per quarter. Green Thumb has developed the following estimates of clients per quarter for next year:

	Quarter 1	Quarter 2	Quarter 3	Quarter 4
Full-service clients	$100	$300	$300	$150
Budget clients	500	650	700	400

Required: A. Prepare a sales budget by quarter for each Green Thumb level of service.
B. Prepare a marketing and distribution budget by quarter for Green Thumb.

LO 3 LO 5 **P6.4** Craven Company plans to sell 20,000; 22,000; 30,000; and 34,000 units per month for the next four months. The desired ending finished goods inventory is 5 percent of the expected sales in the next month. Beginning inventory is 2,000 units.

Required: Prepare the production budget, by month, for the first three months.

LO 4 **P6.5** Frausto, Inc., plans to produce 22,000; 24,000; 26,000; 28,000; 30,000; and 32,000 units for the first six months, respectively, of the coming year. Each unit requires 2 liters of direct materials that cost $3 per liter. Frausto indicates that the beginning inventory of direct materials is 5,000 liters, but Frausto wants to reduce inventory to 5 percent of what is needed for the next month's production. Frausto pays for 70 percent of its purchases in the month of purchase, taking a 3 percent discount. The remaining purchases are paid in the month following purchase. Frausto indicates that the beginning accounts payable balance is $24,000.

Required: A. Prepare Frausto's direct materials purchases budget by month for the first quarter.
B. Prepare Frausto's cash disbursements schedule by month for the first quarter.
C. Prepare Frausto's accounts payable schedule by month for the first quarter.

LO 4 **P6.6** Refer to P6.5. Each unit requires one-half hour of direct labor time at $20 per hour. Unit-related overhead is $5 per machine hour and each unit requires 3 machine hours. Batch-related overhead is $1,600 per batch with a batch-size of 500 units. Facility overhead, including depreciation of $7,000, is $35,000 per month.

Required: Prepare Frausto's direct labor and manufacturing overhead budget by month for the first quarter.

LO 3 LO 5 **P6.7** McGary, Inc., expects the following sales, by month, for the next six months:

January	$600,000
February	400,000
March	500,000
April	550,000
May	700,000
June	800,000

McGary currently has 100,000 units in ending inventory and it wants to decrease its ending inventory by 10 percent each month until it reaches a desired ending inventory level of 50,000. Each unit produced by McGary uses 2 liters of direct materials, 3 hours of direct labor, and one-half hour of machine time. McGary expects to pay $4 per liter for materials and $12 per hour for labor. Its estimated unit-related overhead is $10 per machine hour. Other overhead (batch-related and facility-sustaining) has been calculated at $20 per unit.

Required:
A. Prepare the production budget, by month, for the first three months.
B. Prepare the direct labor and manufacturing overhead budget for the first three months.

LO 4 **P6.8** Shumway Enterprises has the following production planned for the first six months of next year:

January	50,000
February	45,000
March	55,000
April	60,000
May	65,000
June	70,000

Each unit produced requires 5 pounds of direct materials at $6 per pound. Shumway wants to maintain an inventory balance equal to 10 percent of what is needed to meet next month's production. Shumway pays for 90 percent of its purchases in the month of purchase to receive a 2 percent cash discount. The remaining purchases are paid in the month following purchase. Shumway indicates the following beginning balances:

Accounts payable	$600,000
Direct materials	$300,000 (50,000 pounds)

Required:
A. Prepare Shumway's direct materials purchases budget by month for the first quarter.
B. Prepare Shumway's cash disbursements schedule by month for the first quarter.
C. Prepare Shumway's accounts payable schedule by month for the first quarter.

LO 4 **P6.9** Refer to P6.8. Each unit requires 3 hours of direct labor time at $12 per hour. Unit-related overhead is $10 per machine hour and each unit requires one-half machine hour. Batch-related overhead is $3,000 per batch with a batch-size of 1,000 units. Facility overhead, including depreciation of $17,000, is $59,000 per month.

Required: Prepare Shumway's direct labor and manufacturing overhead budget by month for the first quarter.

LO 1 LO 2 LO 3 LO 4 **P6.10** Refer to PepsiCo, Inc. **(www.pepsico.com).** Based on your knowledge of this company, answer the following.

A. What budgeting strategy do you think it uses?
B. What budgeting approach do you think it uses?
C. How do you think its sales budget is organized (i.e., by product, by region)?
D. What do you think is the composition of its marketing and distribution costs?
E. How do you think its production budget (if applicable) is organized (i.e., by product, by facility)?
F. How do you think its purchases budgets are organized (i.e., by product, by supplier)?
G. Do you believe this company would prepare a direct labor and manufacturing overhead budget? Why?
H. What other balanced scorecard measures do you think this company uses?

LO 1 LO 2 LO 3 LO 4 **P6.11** Refer to Walt Disney Company **(www.disney.com).** Based on your knowledge of this company, answer the following:

A. What budgeting strategy do you think it uses?
B. What budgeting approach do you think it uses?

C. How do you think its sales budget is organized (i.e., by product, by region)?
D. What do you think is the composition of its marketing and distribution costs?
E. How do you think its production budget (if applicable) is organized (i.e., by product, by facility)?
F. How do you think its purchases budget(s) is organized (i.e., by product, by supplier)?
G. Do you believe this company would prepare a direct labor and manufacturing overhead budget? Why?
H. What other balanced scorecard measures do you think this company uses?

LO 1 LO 2 LO 3 LO 4 **P6.12** Refer to Dell Computer **(www.dell.com).** Based on your knowledge of this company, answer the following:

A. What budgeting strategy do you think it uses?
B. What budgeting approach do you think it uses?
C. How do you think its sales budget is organized (i.e., by product, by region)?
D. What do you think is the composition of its marketing and distribution costs?
E. How do you think its production budget (if applicable) is organized (i.e., by product, by facility)?
F. How do you think its purchases budget(s) is organized (i.e., by product, by supplier)?
G. Do you believe this company would prepare a direct labor and manufacturing overhead budget? Why?
H. What other balanced scorecard measures do you think this company uses?

Cases

C6.1 LO 1 LO 2 LO 3 LO 4 Refer to the company you selected in C1.1. Based on your knowledge of this company, answer the following:

A. What budgeting strategy do you think it uses?
B. What budgeting approach do you think it uses?
C. How do you think its sales budget is organized (i.e., by product, by region)?
D. What do you think is the composition of its marketing and distribution costs?
E. How do you think its production budget (if applicable) is organized (i.e., by product, by facility)?
F. How do you think its purchases budgets are organized (i.e., by product, by supplier)?
G. Do you believe this company would prepare a direct labor and manufacturing overhead budget? Why?
H. What other balanced scorecard measures do you think this company uses?

LO 3 **C6.2** Li and Rory, two Introduction to Accounting students, have decided to give a midsemester party. They will serve hamburgers, hot dogs, chips, dip, and sodas. Since their refrigerator space is limited, they do not want a lot of leftover food after the party. Li and Rory have decided to invite 75 guests; each guest is permitted to bring a significant other to the party. Li and Rory estimate that 80 percent of the guests will be accompanied by someone else. Li estimates that they will need one bag of chips for every two people and one container of dip for every two bags of chips. Rory believes that, on average, each guest will eat one quarter-pound hamburger and one hot dog. They think that six sodas per guest is adequate. After looking in their refrigerator and cupboards, they discover two pounds of hamburger patties, 20 sodas, and one package of hot dog buns (8 per package).

Required: Determine the food and drink that need to be purchased for the party. Assume that hot dogs come in packages of 10 while hot dog and hamburger buns come in packages of 8. Soda will be purchased in 12-packs.

Critical Thinking

CT6.1 LO 4 Clark, Inc., a merchandising company, has hired you to help it determine the amount and timing of purchases of office products for resale next year. The marketing function has forecasted sales of office products by quarter of $65,000; $75,000; $59,000; and $90,000 for next year. After examining last year's accounting records, you determine that the cost of goods sold is 40 percent of sales. In the past, Clark has always maintained an ending inventory of 50 percent of next quarter's expected cost of goods sold. However, due to increasing storage costs, the company has decided to decrease ending inventories to 25 percent of the next quarter's cost of goods sold, beginning with the first quarter of the planning period. Clark would like an ending inventory for the year of $9,000. After examining last year's purchase invoices, you discovered that suppliers require payment within 30 days (i.e., within the quarter of purchase) but offer a cash discount of 3 percent for payments made within 10 days of purchase.

Required: A. Prepare a purchases budget for each quarter of next year.
B. Prepare a cash disbursements schedule for each quarter of next year.

LO 4 **CT6.2** Bateman Company is an electronic parts distributor with the following expected sales:

January	$5,400,000
February	7,000,000
March	6,400,000
April	6,600,000
May	7,000,000
June	7,500,000
July	6,900,000
August	7,300,000

Bateman's cost of goods sold averages 65 percent of sales. Seventy percent of parts are received by Bateman one month prior to sale while the remaining 30 percent are received in the month of sale. Historically, Bateman has paid 80 percent of its accounts payable one month after receipt of the purchased parts and the remaining 20 percent two months after receipt of the purchased part.

Required: A. Prepare a purchases budget, by month, for the second quarter.
B. Prepare a cash disbursements schedule, by month, for the second quarter.

Ethical Challenges

EC6.1 LO 1 LO 2 You have recently been hired by a large firm and after a major promotion have just completed your first sales budget by yourself. You and your best friend set a date to go out and celebrate on Friday. The following conversation takes place:

Friend: "You look a little down. I thought this was supposed to be a celebration."

You: "I think I made a mistake with the budget. I checked the numbers again and I think I doubled the expected sales from our overseas branch, resulting in a 50 percent increase in overall budgeted sales."

Friend: "Are you sure? Maybe you miscalculated something else."

You: "I'm sure. I checked and rechecked the numbers. I just messed it up completely."

Friend: "Well maybe demand will pick up overseas and your budget will be met naturally. I wouldn't panic about something like this; after all, it's just a budget. It's not like you were preparing the actual financial statements. Why raise an issue now when everything might just work itself out? I would just sit tight and let things play out."

What are you going to do on Monday?

LO 1 **EC6.2** Many of the issues involved in budgetary slack, etc., are caused because performance is measured against the budget. Given what you have learned about the balanced scorecard, discuss the appropriateness and suggest other means of measuring performance of middle and upper managers.

Computer Applications

CA6.1 LO 2 Skordas Company has studied the collection pattern of sales for the past year and management has developed the following collection schedule:

40 percent in the month of sale with a 1 percent discount
30 percent in the month following the sale
15 percent in the second month following the sale
8 percent in the third month following the sale
5 percent in the fourth month following the sale

Actual sales for the past six months are:

January	$200,100	April	$251,200
February	220,450	May	275,890
March	300,700	June	180,460

Expected sales for the next six months are:

July	$175,800	October	$210,750
August	194,500	November	349,000
September	186,300	December	375,900

Required: Use a spreadsheet package.

A. Determine the expected cash receipts for July through September.
B. Determine the expected cash discounts for July through September.
C. Determine the expected uncollectible sales for July through December. Assume uncollectible sales are budgeted in the month of sale.
D. Determine the expected ending balance of accounts receivable for July through September. The beginning balance on July 1 is $229,607.

LO 2 CA6.2 Ochittree, Inc., shows a cash balance of $24,000 on January 1, 2007. Expected sales of model dune buggies by month for the first six months are:

January	$600,000	April	$450,000
February	400,000	May	750,000
March	500,000	June	825,000

Sales are collected 75 percent in the month of sale and 25 percent in the month following the sale. Actual sales by month for the last quarter are:

October	$550,000
November	700,000
December	800,000

Ochittree sells dune buggies for $30 each.

Required: Use a spreadsheet package.

A. Determine the expected sales by month for the first three months of the year.
B. Determine the expected cash receipts by month for the first three months of the year.
C. Determine the anticipated accounts receivable balance by month for the first three months of the year.

Visit the text Online Learning Center at **www.mhhe.com/ainsworth6e** for additional problem material that accompanies this chapter.

PART THREE

III

Recording and Evaluating: Operating Activities

CHAPTER SEVEN

7

Accounting Information Systems

Learning Objectives

LO 1 Explain the impact of accounting events on the accounting equation and demonstrate how to make and post journal entries.

LO 2 Describe the impact of adjusting events on the accounting equation and demonstrate how to make and post adjusting journal entries.

LO 3 Discuss the impact of closing events on the accounting equation and demonstrate how to make and post closing journal entries.

LO 4 Explain and show how accounting events are reported on the financial statements.

LO 5 Compare and contrast manual accounting systems to computer-based transaction systems and database systems.

In Chapters 1 through 3 we learned about business, business processes, and operating activities. In Chapters 4 through 6, we explored how operating activities are planned. Chapters 7 through 10 examine how companies record and control operating activities.

As you know from Chapter 1, financial statements for external users are prepared in accordance with generally accepted accounting principles (GAAP). GAAP is a set of rules concerning how a company *reports* its economic activity to shareholders and other interested parties. GAAP, however, does not control how companies *record* economic activity. Companies can record information in any manner deemed appropriate as long as an adequate system of internal controls (see Chapter 2) is in place. When deciding on an accounting system, a company must consider its processes (Chapters 1 through 3) and the activities it has planned (Chapters 4 through 6) and then design a system appropriate for recording those activities. In general terms, companies use three types of accounting information systems to record the results of economic transactions: (1) manual systems, (2) computer-based transactional systems, and (3) database systems. We briefly examine the basics of these latter two systems after learning the manual system that is the foundation of computerized and database accounting systems.

Manual Accounting Systems

As you know from Chapter 1, Luca Pacioli is often referred to as the "Father of Double-Entry Accounting." Double-entry accounting is the foundation of a manual accounting system and is based on the accounting equation: *Assets = Liabilities + Owners' equity.* In a double-entry system, each accounting event is recorded twice and, therefore, the accounting equation remains in balance. Let's explore how this system works.

Accounting Events

First, an accounting event must have three characteristics related to the four accounting concepts introduced in Chapter 1. First, an accounting event must be *specific to the entity for which the accounting records are kept.* This characteristic arises from the business entity concept. Second, an accounting event must be *measurable in monetary terms.* This characteristic, obviously, arises from the monetary unit concept. Finally, an accounting event must *impact the entity's assets, liabilities, and/or owners' equity.* This final characteristic is related to the business entity, going concern, and periodicity concepts. That is, the event must impact the company's assets, liabilities, and/or owners' equity (business entity). Because the company is assumed to continue into the future, assets, liabilities, and owners' equity represent rights and obligations extending into the future. Finally, because we need to determine income periodically, revenues and expenses are recognized as part of owners' equity. Because the accounting equation (A = L + OE) must remain in balance, the following nine basic combinations of accounting events are possible:

	Assets	=	Liabilities	+	Owners' Equity
Assets increase; Assets decrease	+/−				
Assets increase; Liabilities increase	+		+		
Assets increase; Owners' equity increases	+				+
Assets decrease; Liabilities decrease	−		−		
Assets decrease; Owners' equity decreases	−				−
Liabilities increase; Liabilities decrease			+/−		
Liabilities increase; Owners' equity decreases			+		−
Liabilities decrease; Owners' equity increases			−		+
Owners' equity increases; Owners' equity decreases					+/−

Other, more complex combinations are also possible. Let's look at an example of each of these accounting events. Note that as one element of the equation changes, a second change is required to balance the equation; hence, the term *double-entry system.*

Event	Example	Analysis
Asset increase; Asset decrease	Cash is used to purchase inventory	Cash is the decreasing asset (−) and inventory is the increasing asset (+).
Asset increase; Liability increase	Inventory is purchased on account	Inventory is the increasing asset (+) and "on account" represents an increase in a liability to a supplier (+)—an obligation to pay the supplier in the future.
Asset increase; Owners' equity increase	Services are provided to a client on account	"On account" represents an increase in an asset (+)—the right to receive the customer's money in the future; since services are provided, revenue has been earned, therefore owners' equity increased (+).*
Asset decrease; Liability decrease	An obligation to the bank is paid	Cash is the asset decreased (−) and the obligation to the bank is the liability decreased (−).
Asset decrease; Owners' equity decrease	A bill for utilities is received and immediately paid	Since the bill is paid, cash (an asset) decreases (−). The bill was received because services have been used and an expense was incurred, which means owners' equity decreased (−).*
Liability increase; Liability decrease	A note payable is given to a supplier to pay off an account payable	Since the account payable is paid off, liabilities (accounts payable) decrease (−). Since a note payable is given to the supplier, liabilities (notes payable) increase (+).
Liability increase; Owners' equity decrease	A bill is received but not paid	Since the bill is not paid, a liability is created increasing total liabilities (+). The bill was received because services have been used and, therefore, an expense was incurred, which means owners' equity decreased (−).*
Liability decrease; Owners' equity increase	An obligation to a customer is fulfilled	Since the obligation has been fulfilled, the liability is decreased (−). Since the company has performed for the customer, revenue has been created, which means owners' equity is increased (+).*
Owners' equity increase; Owners' equity decrease	Common stock is issued in exchange for preferred stock	One type of capital stock is issued, which increases owners' equity (+), in exchange for a different type of capital stock, which decreases owners' equity (−).†

*We discuss these events in more detail later in this chapter.
†We discuss these types of events in the second half of this text.

Chart of Accounts

Because double-entry accounting was developed before people had calculators, accountants needed a system to separate events affecting specific items and to separate increases from decreases. Therefore each specific item in the accounting equation was given an **account**—a place where the results of events affecting that item could be recorded. For example, we

FAST FACT

A chart of accounts is as individualized as the business itself. However, certain accounts are common to all businesses: cash, accounts receivable, and accounts payable. There are also certain accounts that are common to specific industries. When setting up a chart of accounts it is often helpful to consult trade magazines in your industry for ideas about developing your company's chart of accounts.

have a Cash account, an Accounts Receivable account, an Accounts Payable account, and a Capital Stock account. These accounts are organized into a **chart of accounts** that is used like an index to help people find the account by classifying each account as an asset, liability, or owners' equity. Assets are listed first in the chart of accounts followed by liabilities and owners' equity. Revenue and expense accounts are listed after owners' equity because they measure net income and net income is considered part of owners' equity because it belongs to the owners.

Next increases were separated from decreases in each account. Each item in the accounting equation has a left and a right side, as follows:

Assets		=	Liabilities		+	Owners' Equity	
Left	Right		Left	Right		Left	Right

Then beginning on the left side of the accounting equation, we apply the following rule, *increases to assets are recorded on the left because they are on the left side of the equation.* Therefore, decreases to assets would be recorded on the right. Now think what happens when we go to the other side of the equal sign; recall that pluses and minuses switch. Therefore, *increases to liabilities and owners' equity are recorded on the right because they are on the right side of the equation* while decreases would be recorded on the left. This left and right system is based on *subtraction by opposition* rather than subtracting directly from an amount as we do today. Subtraction by opposition means that items on the right side of an asset account are subtracted from the amounts on the left side of the asset balance to determine the final balance. Likewise, amounts on the left of liabilities and owners' equity accounts are subtracted from amounts on the right side of the liability or owners' equity to arrive at the final balance of the account.

Assets		=	Liabilities		+	Owners' Equity	
Left	Right		Left	Right		Left	Right
+	–		–	+		–	+

Debits and credits
Increase an asset with a debit (left).
Increase a liability or owners' equity with a credit (right).

Early accountants did not refer to positions as left and right. Rather, they called the left side of an account a *debet habere* (should have) and the right side of an account a *debet dare* (should give). Today we know these terms as **debit** and **credit,** abbreviated as DR and CR, respectively. Thus accountants today do not typically speak of lefts and rights, but rather of debits and credits. But remember, *debit simply means left and credit simply means right.*

The accounting equation must remain in balance after each accounting event; therefore, for each transaction recorded, the debits must equal the credits if the left side of the equation is to equal the right side of the equation. Let's look at the nine basic accounting events in this debit/credit way:

	Assets		= Liabilities		+ Owners' Equity	
	DR	**CR**	**DR**	**CR**	**DR**	**CR**
Assets increase; Assets decrease	+	−				
Assets increase; Liabilities increase	+			+		
Assets increase; Owners' equity increases	+					+
Assets decrease; Liabilities decrease		−	−			
Assets decrease; Owners' equity decreases		−			−	
Liabilities increase; Liabilities decrease			−	+		
Liabilities increase; Owners' equity decreases				+	−	
Liabilities decrease; Owners' equity increases			−			+
Owners' equity increases; Owners' equity decreases					−	+

Notice that after each type of accounting event, the accounting equation would balance. For example, if we increase an asset and decrease another asset, total assets remain the same, and the equation remains in balance. If we increase an asset and increase a liability, both sides of the accounting equation increase by the same amount, and the equation remains in balance. If we increase a liability and decrease an owners' equity, the right side of the equation would increase and decrease by the same amount, and the equation remains in balance.

Now let's expand the accounting equation by creating a separate account for cash (since we have a separate statement for it—the statement of cash flows) and separating owners' equity into a Contributed Capital account and a Retained Earnings account (again reflecting a separate statement—the statement of owners' equity):

Cash		+ Other Assets		= Liabilities		+ Contributed Capital		+ Retained Earnings	
Left	Right	Left	Right	Left	Right	Left	Right	Left	Right
+	−	+	−	−	+	−	+	−	+
DR	CR	DR	CR	DR	CR	DR	CR	DR	CR

Now recall that retained earnings represents the accumulated net incomes of the company not distributed as dividends. Therefore, revenues earned and expenses incurred are part of retained earnings (and are reflected in a separate statement—the income statement). Let's expand the accounting equation one more time by adding a revenue account and an expense account:

Cash		+ Other Assets		= Liabilities		+ Contributed Capital		+ Retained Earnings	
Left	Right	Left	Right	Left	Right	Left	Right	Left	Right
+	−	+	−	−	+	−	+	−	+
DR	CR	DR	CR	DR	CR	DR	CR	DR	CR

Revenue		Expense	
Left	Right	Left	Right
−	+	+	−
DR	CR	DR	CR

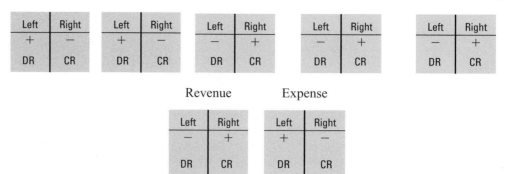

Now let's consider revenues and expenses. Revenues increase net income; net income belongs to the owners; therefore, revenues increase on the right side—the credit side. On the other hand, expenses decrease net income; net income belongs to the owners; therefore, expenses increase on the left side—the debit side. Now let's revisit the transaction examples (excluding the last) using debits and credits. Note that each transaction changes the amounts in the accounts affected (either adding or subtracting depending on the left or right side balance in the account) while keeping the accounting equation in balance.

Event	Example	Debit and Credits
Asset increase; Asset decrease	Cash is used to purchase inventory	Debit inventory Credit cash
Asset increase; Liability increase	Inventory is purchased on account	Debit inventory Credit accounts payable
Asset increase; Owners' equity increase	Services are provided to a client on account	Debit accounts receivable Credit revenue (or fees earned)
Asset decrease; Liability decrease	An obligation to the bank is paid	Debit notes payable Credit cash
Asset decrease; Owners' equity decrease	A bill for utilities is received and immediately paid	Debit utilities expense Credit cash
Liability increase; Liability decrease	A note payable is given to a supplier to pay off an account payable	Debit accounts payable Credit note payable
Liability increase; Owners' equity decrease	A bill is received but not paid	Debit expense Credit accounts payable
Liability decrease; Owners' equity increase	An obligation to a customer is fulfilled	Debit unearned revenue Credit revenue (or fees earned)

Journalizing

So how does a manual accounting system work? To begin, events involving external parties typically have source documents such as those we discussed in Chapter 3: sales invoices, purchase invoices, payroll checks, and so on. Accountants use source documents to validate the existence of the event and to determine the effects of specific transactions on the accounting equation. Then this effect is recorded in a journal in chronological order. This process is called **journalizing** (step one in the accounting cycle, discussed later) and the outcome is called a **journal entry.**

Manual accounting systems typically have a general journal and one or more special journals. In the **general journal** we record both the accounts to be debited and the accounts to be credited. Let's suppose our company purchases $5,000 of supplies on account from an office supply warehouse on March 31, 2010. Supplies are assets (we have the right to use the supplies for any legal purpose) and we are increasing assets by making a purchase. Since we did not pay for the purchase, we owe the supplier, thus, a liability—accounts payable—is increased. This event is recorded in the general journal as follows:

General Journal

Date	Description	DR	CR
3-31-10	Supplies	5,000.00	
	Accounts Payable		5,000.00

Notice that position is used to signify debit/credit in two ways. In the description column, the account being debited is listed first and recorded beginning on the left margin. The account being credited is listed last and indented to signify "right." The amounts are denoted in left and right columns denoted DR (debit) and CR (credit).

Let's try another event. Assume that on April 5, 2010, we purchase land costing $120,000 and a building for $80,000 by making a down payment of $50,000 cash and signing a note payable for the balance. We are obtaining two assets (land and building) by giving up another asset (cash) and incurring a liability (notes payable). This event is recorded in the general journal as follows:

General Journal

Date	Description	DR	CR
4-5-10	Building	80,000.00	
	Land	120,000.00	
	Cash		50,000.00
	Note Payable		150,000.00

What have we learned from this latter journal entry? When we say that debits must equal credits, we mean that the dollar amount of the debits listed must equal the dollar amount of the credits listed in the journal entry and, therefore, the accounting equation remains balanced. In this case the two debits total $200,000, the dollar amount of the two credits.

Posting

After the accounting event is journalized, the effect of the event must be posted to the appropriate accounts in the general ledger. A **general ledger** is simply a collection of specific asset, liability, and owners' equity accounts from the chart of accounts. **Posting** (step two in the accounting cycle, discussed later) is the process of recording the appropriate part of a journal entry to the affected account. Thus, each ledger account keeps track of the changes in that account over time and gives the balance at any point in time. Let's post our previous two examples—buying supplies and buying a building and land. The first event must be posted to two accounts—supplies (an asset) and accounts payable (a liability).

Supplies Account

Date	Description	DR	CR	Balance
	Beginning balance			00.00
3-31-10		5,000.00		5,000.00

Accounts Payable Account

Date	Description	DR	CR	Balance
	Beginning balance			00.00
3-31-10			5,000.00	5,000.00

The second event must be posted to four accounts—building (an asset), land (an asset), cash (an asset), and notes payable (a liability).

Cash Account

Date	Description	DR	CR	Balance
	Beginning balance (assumed)			180,000.00
4-5-10			50,000.00	130,000.00

Building Account

Date	Description	DR	CR	Balance
	Beginning balance			00.00
4-5-10		80,000.00		80,000.00

Land Account

Date	Description	DR	CR	Balance
	Beginning balance			00.00
4-5-10		120,000.00		120,000.00

Notes Payable Account

Date	Description	DR	CR	Balance
	Beginning balance			00.00
4-5-10			150,000.00	150,000.00

Normal balance
The normal balance of an account is always the side (debit or credit) on which it increases.

Notice that the balance column does not indicate whether the balance is a debit or a credit. That is why you must understand the accounting equation and the rule: assets increase with a debit. The **normal balance** of an account is the increase side of the account or the side of the accounting equation the account is on. *Thus an asset account has a normal debit balance because it increases with a debit and is on the left side of the accounting equation while a liability account and an owners' equity account have normal credit balances because they increase with credits and are on the right side of the accounting equation.* Recall however, that expenses decrease owners' equity; therefore, expenses have normal debit balances. Revenues, on the other hand, increase owners' equity and have a normal credit balance.

Enhance Your Understanding

If cash has a credit balance, what does this imply?

Answer: If cash has a credit balance, it indicates that the company is overdrawn.

Why do we record accounting events in two places—once in the general journal and once in the general ledger? Internal control. In the journal we record the entire event at the time the event occurred. In the ledger we record the effect of the event on the specific item. Typically posting is not done immediately following journalizing. The general journal is kept up-to-date and posting is done periodically as time allows. However, all posting must be finished before the financial statements are prepared.

*A note on general ledger account representation: Often accountants use a T-account to represent a general ledger account. A **T-account** is simply an informal representation of a general ledger account. For example, the following cash T-account reflects the events posted above.*

Cash		
	DR	CR
Beginning	180,000	50,000
Ending	130,000	

Enhance Your Understanding

When the bank records a deposit to a customer's checking account, it typically credits the account and customers use debit cards to withdraw money from their accounts. Does this use of debit and credit make sense in light of what we have just discussed?

Answer: Remember a bank is an entity and, therefore, maintains records for its accounting events. When you deposit a check, the bank receives cash, but the cash belongs to you—thus, the bank has a liability to you, hence, the credit to your account. Likewise when you use your debit card to withdraw money, it decreases the bank's liability to you, hence the debit.

Adjusting Entries

Journalizing and posting
Journalizing (recording events in the general journal) and posting (recording the appropriate part of the journal entry to the affected account) are continuous processes throughout the accounting cycle. These are the first two steps in the accounting cycle.

Let's review what we have learned so far in this chapter. The accountant, in a manual system, uses source documents to determine the effect of accounting events. The event is then recorded in the *general journal* in chronological order. As time allows, the accountant posts the effect of these events in the appropriate *general ledger* accounts. This process continues throughout the **accounting cycle** (the time period between financial statements). At the end of the accounting cycle the accountant prepares financial statements.

We already know that all journal entries must be posted prior to preparing financial statements, but is there anything else that must be done? Yes, because not all accounting events are supported by source documents. Therefore, before preparing financial statements, the accountant must record these other events. Before preparing these entries, the accountant typically prepares a **trial balance.** A trial balance is simply a listing of all the general ledger account balances to ensure that debits equal credits.

Why aren't source documents available for some accounting events? Because some events are internal to the company, and thus, outside verification in the form of source documents is not available. For example, assume that on January 2, 2010, we pay our rent for the entire year in the amount of $24,000. On January 2, 2010, we record the following in the general journal:

General Journal

Date	Description	DR	CR
1-2-10	Prepaid Rent	24,000.00	
	Cash		24,000.00

Notice that this event is recorded as an increase to an asset called prepaid rent and a decrease to another asset, cash. Why is prepaid rent an asset? Because the company has the right to occupy the rental space for one year—this right is an asset. Subsequently we post this event to the appropriate accounts in the general ledger as follows:

Cash Account

Date	Description	DR	CR	Balance
	Beginning Balance (assumed)			180,000.00
1-2-10			24,000.00	156,000.00

Prepaid Rent Account

Date	Description	DR	CR	Balance
	Beginning Balance			00.00
1-2-10		24,000.00		24,000.00

Now assume that the end of the accounting period is January 31, 2010. On January 31, 2010, does the company still have an asset representing the right to rental space for one year? No. Since one month has passed and a portion of the asset has been used, the asset must be reduced so that it represents only 11 months of prepaid rent. Therefore, prepaid rent must be decreased or credited. What should we debit? Since we used the rental space in an attempt to generate revenue, the cost of one month's rent is an expense—rent expense. (Remember expenses increase with debits.) We would journalize and post this internal event as:

General Journal: Adjusting Entry

Date	Description	DR	CR
1-31-10	Rent Expense	2,000.00	
	Prepaid Rent		2,000.00

Prepaid Rent Account

Date	Description	DR	CR	Balance
	Beginning Balance			00.00
1-2-10		24,000.00		24,000.00
1-31-10			2,000.00	22,000.00

Rent Expense Account

Date	Description	DR	CR	Balance
	Beginning Balance			00.00
1-31-10		2,000.00		2,000.00

This latter type of entry, an internal entry, is known as an **adjusting entry** because it is required to adjust the accounts for internal events prior to preparing financial statements. Notice that after posting this journal entry, the asset account balance is stated properly and the expense has been recognized in the period incurred.

The four types of adjusting entries are shown in the following table:

Type of Entry	Impact of Entry
Revenue accrual	Increase assets; increase revenue (increase owners' equity)
Revenue deferral	Decrease liabilities; increase revenue (increase owners' equity)
Expense accrual	Increase liabilities; increase expense (decrease owners' equity)
Expense deferral	Decrease assets; increase expense (decrease owners' equity)

Let's examine each of these entry types. A **revenue accrual** is recorded when revenues are earned in one accounting period and payment is received in a later period. For example, assume a company has a note receivable from a customer. This note earns interest each day, but the company only needs to record the interest prior to financial statement preparation. Let's assume that the company loaned a supplier \$10,000 cash for 90 days at 6 percent interest on November 1, 2010. The entry to record the note receivable is:

General Journal

Date	Description	DR	CR
11-1-10	Note Receivable	10,000.00	
	Cash		10,000.00

Because the accounting period ends on December 31 (before the note is due) an adjusting entry is necessary to recognize the interest earned since November 1. Interest = Principal $\times$ Rate $\times$ Time, in this case \$10,000 $\times$ 0.06 $\times$ 60/365 = \$98.63. The earned interest increases the assets and revenues as the entry below illustrates.

General Journal: Adjusting Entry

Date	Description	DR	CR
12-31-10	Interest Receivable	98.63	
	Interest Earned		98.63

A **revenue deferral** occurs when a company has been paid in advance by a client for services to be performed in the future, that is, revenue recognition has been deferred. For example, assume a company is paid \$9,000 on December 1 for services to be performed during December and January. On December 1, the company makes the following entry:

General Journal

Date	Description	DR	CR
12-1-10	Cash	9,000.00	
	Unearned Revenue		9,000.00

The account, Unearned Revenue, is a liability account. That is, the company owes services to the client or the company must give the money received back. Now assume that on December 31 (fiscal year-end) the company estimates it has completed two-thirds of the work for the client. Thus, on December 31, the company has earned two-thirds of the revenue. This adjusting entry records the revenue earned and reduces the company's obligation to the client:

General Journal: Adjusting Entry

Date	Description	DR	CR
12-31-10	Unearned Revenues	6,000.00	
	Service Fees Earned		6,000.00

An **expense accrual** is recorded when expenses are incurred in one accounting period and payment is made in a later period. For example, assume that the company borrows \$12,000 cash on November 10, 2010, and signs a 7 percent, 150-day note. The entry to record this event is:

General Journal

Date	Description	DR	CR
11-10-10	Cash	12,000.00	
	Note Payable		12,000.00

Adjusting process
Steps four and five in the accounting cycle—adjust the accounting records by making and posting appropriate journal entries; then take a trial balance to ensure that debits equal credits.

Further assume that the end of the accounting period (December 31) occurs 50 days after the note is signed. Since the company has incurred the interest expense ($\$12{,}000 \times 0.07 \times 50/365 = \$115.07$) but has not paid it, the following journal entry is needed:

General Journal: Adjusting Entry

Date	Description	DR	CR
12-31-10	Interest Expense	115.07	
	Interest Payable		115.07

Finally an **expense deferral** occurs when a company uses previously purchased assets in an attempt to generate revenue in future periods, that is, expense recognition has been deferred. For example, assume a company purchased a delivery truck with a five-year life and no salvage value on January 2, 2010. The company paid $35,000 for the truck. This entry records the purchase of the truck in 2010:

General Journal

Date	Description	DR	CR
1-2-10	Truck	35,000.00	
	Cash		35,000.00

Recall that depreciation is the allocation of the cost of the long-term asset over its useful life and is calculated as cost divided by useful life. Therefore the annual depreciation is $35,000 / 5 = $7,000 and the required adjusting entry follows. Accumulated depreciation is the account used to accumulate the depreciation expense taken over the life of the asset. This account is called a **contra account** because its balance is opposite (contra to) the normal balance of its associated account, truck, in this case.

General Journal: Adjusting Entry

Date	Description	DR	CR
12-31-10	Depreciation Expense	7,000.00	
	Accumulated Depreciation		7,000.00

Enhance Your Understanding

Refer to the adjusting entry example for prepaid rent on page 190. What type of adjusting entry is it? How does it impact the accounting equation?

Answer: Since prepaid rent is consumed in an effort to generate revenue, the adjusting entry recognizes an expense that was deferred.

Closing Entries

Exhibit 7.1 illustrates the accounting cycle in a manual system. Let's review what we have learned thus far. Source documents provide information that accountants use to prepare journal entries in the general (or special) journal. The effects of journal entries are subsequently posted to the appropriate general ledger (and subsidiary ledger, if appropriate) accounts. We discuss special journals and subsidiary ledgers in the next three chapters. Periodically the accounts must be adjusted prior to preparing financial statements. Prior to preparing closing entries, accountants typically prepare an adjusted trial balance. An **adjusted trial balance** is simply a trial balance done after the adjusting entries have been made and posted to the appropriate accounts. This takes us through step five of the accounting cycle. Then since we need to keep the results

EXHIBIT 7.1 **The Eight Steps in the Accounting Cycle**

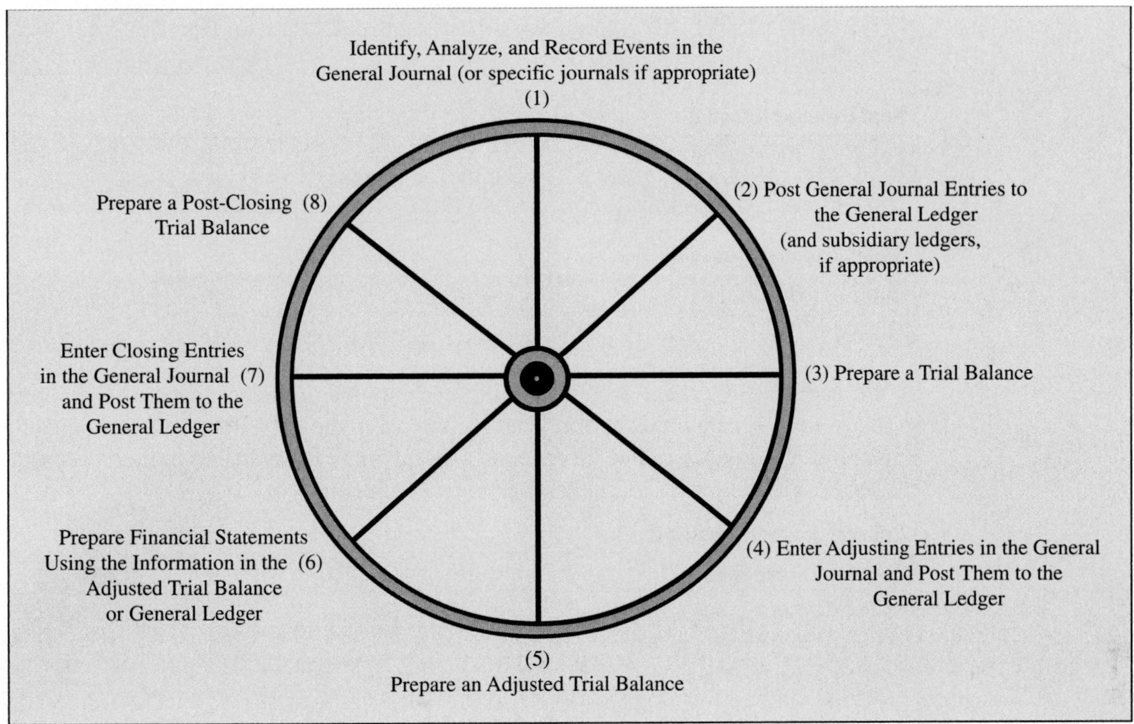

Closing process
Preparing and posting closing entries to zero-out income statement accounts and transfer the balances to owners' equity.

of one accounting period separate from those of another period (recall the periodicity concept) we must prepare financial statements and closing entries. A **closing entry** is prepared to close (zero-out) income statement accounts (this is step seven in the accounting cycle). Recall that net income belongs to the owners; therefore, a closing entry transfers the balance in an income statement account to an account classified as owners' equity. Remember that in a corporation, this account is called Retained Earnings because it represents earnings (revenues minus expenses) that have not been distributed to owners (shareholders) as dividends. In a sole proprietorship or partnership, account balances are transferred to the owners' capital accounts because the income flows through to the owners and, therefore, need not be separated in the accounting records.

Let's think about revenue and expenses. Revenues increase with a credit and represent an increase in owners' equity, which is on the right side of the accounting equation. Therefore, revenues have credit balances. Expenses increase with a debit and represent a decrease in owners' equity. Therefore, expenses have debit balances. So at the end of the accounting period, we have many revenue accounts with credit balances and expense accounts with debit balances. We need to zero-out these accounts and transfer their balances to retained earnings. How can we do this?—how can we zero-out an account with a credit balance? How can we zero-out an account with a debit balance? To close a revenue account with its credit balance (using subtraction by opposition) we would debit the account with the amount of the credit balance. To close an expense account with a debit balance we would credit the account with the amount of the debit balance. When a revenue account is debited, an offsetting credit to Retained Earnings transfers the revenue to Retained Earnings. When the expense account is credited a corresponding debit is made to Retained Earnings to reduce the owners' equity account. The difference between the increase in Retained Earnings due to closing the revenue account and the decrease in Retained Earnings due to closing the expense accounts is the net income that belongs to the owners. Let's look at an example. Assume that on December 31, 2010, our income statement accounts appeared as follows:

Fee Revenue Account

Date	Description	DR	CR	Balance
12-31-10				50,000.00

Depreciation Expense Account

Date	Description	DR	CR	Balance
12-31-10				30,000.00

Rent Expense Account

Date	Description	DR	CR	Balance
12-31-10				2,000.00

Salary Expense Account

Date	Description	DR	CR	Balance
12-31-10				8,000.00

We need to close these accounts so that we can determine net income for the period and so that we can separate this period's net income from the net incomes of subsequent periods. Remember the balance in Fee Revenue is a credit while the balances in the expense accounts are debits. The following journal entries must be prepared:

General Journal: Closing Entries

Date	Description	DR	CR
12-31-10	Fee Revenue	50,000.00	
	Retained Earnings		50,000.00
12-31-10	Retained Earnings	40,000.00	
	Depreciation Expense		30,000.00
	Rent Expense		2,000.00
	Salary Expense		8,000.00

Notice that Fee Revenue is debited and Retained Earnings is credited to transfer the balance of the Fee Revenue account to the Retained Earnings account. The Retained Earnings account is debited and the specific expenses are credited to transfer their balances to Retained Earnings. Let's consider the impact of these transactions. Retained Earnings increased by the amount of revenue and decreased by the amount of expenses. Thus this $10,000 change in Retained Earnings represents the net income for the period. Some companies close their revenue and expense accounts to another account, called Income Summary. Income Summary, in turn, is closed to Retained Earnings (or owners' capital). Although this process requires extra work, many companies prefer it because the balance in the Income Summary account prior to closing it to Retained Earnings is the net income (loss) for the period (hence, the name, Income Summary). The closing entries are then posted as follows:

Retained Earnings Account

Date	Description	DR	CR	Balance
1-1-10				00.00
12-31-10			50,000.00	50,000.00
12-31-10		40,000.00		10,000.00

Fee Revenue Account

Date	Description	DR	CR	Balance
				50,000.00
12-31-10		50,000.00		00.00

Depreciation Expense Account

Date	Description	DR	CR	Balance
				30,000.00
12-31-10			30,000.00	00.00

Rent Expense Account

Date	Description	DR	CR	Balance
				2,000.00
12-31-10			2,000.00	00.00

Salary Expense Account

Date	Description	DR	CR	Balance
				8,000.00
12-31-10			8,000.00	00.00

After all the closing entries have been posted to the appropriate accounts, a **post-closing trial balance** is prepared to ensure that debits equal credits to begin the new accounting period (step eight in the accounting cycle). Additionally the financial statements are prepared. (Note that many companies prepare financial statements prior to preparing closing entries.) Remember we have four financial statements: (1) income statement, (2) statement of owners' equity [we are considering only the retained earnings portion for now], (3) statement of cash flows, and (4) balance sheet. We examine these statements in the comprehensive example that follows.

Comprehensive Example

Assume a merchandising company experienced the following events during its first month of operations:

01-1 Issued $500,000 of capital stock to owners.

01-2 Obtained a loan for $200,000 from the bank.

01-3 Equipment was purchased for $400,000 cash.

01-4 Merchandise inventory was purchased for $250,000 on account.

01-15 Employees who earned $5,000 this period were paid.

01-16 A utility bill for $1,500 was received, but not paid.

01-17 Merchandise inventory costing $100,000 was sold to customers for $175,000 on account.

01-26 Customers paid $80,000 on their accounts.

01-29 Dividends of $5,000 were paid.

And it used the following adjusting information:

01-31 Depreciation on the equipment is estimated at $4,000.

01-31 Accrued interest on the loan is $1,875.

Step One: Let's analyze these events (through the 29th) before we journalize them.

01-1 Cash (asset) increases and capital stock (owners' equity) increases.

01-2 Cash (asset) increases and bank loan payable (liability) increases.

01-3 Equipment (asset) increases and cash (asset) decreases.

01-4 Inventory (asset) increases and accounts payable (liability) increases.

01-15 Salary expense increases (owners' equity—decreases) and cash (asset) decreases.

01-16 Utility expense increases (owners' equity—decreases) and utilities payable (liability) increases.

01-17 Accounts receivable (asset) increases and sales (owners' equity) increases by $175,000. Cost of goods sold increases (owners' equity—decreases) and inventory (asset) decreases by $100,000.

EXHIBIT 7.2
Journal Entries—General Journal

Date	Description	DR	CR
01-1	Cash	500,000	
	Capital Stock		500,000
01-2	Cash	200,000	
	Bank Loan Payable		200,000
01-3	Equipment	400,000	
	Cash		400,000
01-4	Inventory	250,000	
	Accounts Payable		250,000
01-15	Salary Expense	5,000	
	Cash		5,000
01-16	Utility Expense	1,500	
	Utilities Payable		1,500
01-17	Accounts Receivable	175,000	
	Sales		175,000
	Cost of Goods Sold	100,000	
	Inventory		100,000
01-26	Cash	80,000	
	Accounts Receivable		80,000
01-29	Retained Earnings	5,000	
	Cash		5,000

01-26 Cash (asset) increases and accounts receivable (asset) decreases.

01-29 Retained earnings (owners' equity) decreases and cash (asset) decreases.

Try Journalizing these events yourself before looking at Exhibit 7.2, which shows the entries for these events. Make sure you study these events carefully.

Exhibit 7.3 illustrates the general ledger accounts after posting the journal entries from Exhibit 7.2 (step two). Take a few moments to examine the general ledger carefully. Notice that the balance of retained earnings is bracketed, signifying that the balance is not a normal balance. Why does retained earnings have an abnormal balance? Because revenues and expenses haven't been closed to retained earnings yet. Let's prepare a trial balance before preparing the adjusting entries. Exhibit 7.4 (see page 198) shows the trial balance after the journal entries (step one) were prepared and posted (step two). Now we are ready to prepare the adjusting entries. Let's analyze the adjusting information given on page 195. Step Three:

01-31 Depreciation expense increases (owners' equity decreases) and accumulated depreciation increases (asset decreases).

01-31 Interest expense increases (owners' equity decreases) and interest payable (liability) increases.

On page 198, Exhibit 7.5 shows the adjusting journal entries and Exhibit 7.6 shows those general ledger accounts after posting. Carefully study these exhibits. This completes

EXHIBIT 7.3
General Ledger after Posting

Cash Account

Date	Description	DR	CR	Balance
01-1		500,000		500,000
01-2		200,000		700,000
01-3			400,000	300,000
01-15			5,000	295,000
01-26		80,000		375,000
01-31			5,000	370,000

Accounts Receivable Account

Date	Description	DR	CR	Balance
01-17		175,000		175,000
01-26			80,000	95,000

Inventory Account

Date	Description	DR	CR	Balance
01-4		250,000		250,000
01-17			100,000	150,000

Equipment Account

Date	Description	DR	CR	Balance
01-3		400,000		400,000

Accounts Payable Account

Date	Description	DR	CR	Balance
01-4			250,000	250,000

Utilities Payable Account

Date	Description	DR	CR	Balance
01-16			1,500	1,500

Bank Loan Payable Account

Date	Description	DR	CR	Balance
01-2			200,000	200,000

Capital Stock Account

Date	Description	DR	CR	Balance
01-1			500,000	500,000

Retained Earnings Account

Date	Description	DR	CR	Balance
01-31		5,000		(5,000)

Sales Account

Date	Description	DR	CR	Balance
01-17			175,000	175,000

Cost of Goods Sold Account

Date	Description	DR	CR	Balance
01-17		100,000		100,000

Salary Expense Account

Date	Description	DR	CR	Balance
01-15		5,000		5,000

Utilities Expense Account

Date	Description	DR	CR	Balance
01-16		1,500		1,500

step four in the accounting cycle. Now we prepare an adjusted trial balance; this is shown in Exhibit 7.7 on page 199. Notice that the only difference between this trial balance and the one illustrated in Exhibit 7.4 is the addition of the adjusting information.

All that's left is to prepare the financial statements from information in the general ledger accounts (step six). Recall that the income statement represents the revenues earned and expenses incurred during the period. Thus sales, cost of goods sold, salary expense, utilities expense, depreciation expense, and interest expense are used to determine net income for the period. The increases and decreases in the cash account must be explained on the statement of

EXHIBIT 7.4
Trial Balance after Posting Journal Entries

Trial Balance
January 31

	DR	CR
Cash	$ 370,000	
Accounts receivable	95,000	
Inventory	150,000	
Equipment	400,000	
Accounts payable		$ 250,000
Utilities payable		1,500
Bank loan payable		200,000
Capital stock		500,000
Retained earnings	5,000	
Sales		175,000
Cost of goods sold	100,000	
Salary expense	5,000	
Utility expense	1,500	
Total	$1,126,500	$1,126,500

EXHIBIT 7.5
Adjusting Journal Entries

Date	Description	DR	CR
01-31	Depreciation expense	4,000	
	Accumulated depreciation		4,000
01-31	Interest expense	1,875	
	Interest payable		1,875

EXHIBIT 7.6
General Ledger Accounts after Posting

Accumulated Depreciation Account

Date	Description	DR	CR	Balance
01-31			4,000	4,000

Interest Payable Account

Date	Description	DR	CR	Balance
01-31			1,875	1,875

Depreciation Expense Account

Date	Description	DR	CR	Balance
01-31		4,000		4,000

Interest Expense Account

Date	Description	DR	CR	Balance
01-31		1,875		1,875

cash flows. The changes in the retained earnings account must be explained on the statement of retained earnings (part of the statement of owners' equity). Finally, recall that the balance sheet indicates the ending balance in each permanent general ledger account. A **permanent account** is an asset, liability, or owners' equity account whose balance is carried over from year to year. All of these statements are prepared by using information taken from the ledger. Then we can prepare the closing entries and post them (step seven) and prepare a post-closing trial balance (step eight).

Exhibit 7.8 (page 200) illustrates the income statement, statement of retained earnings, statement of cash flows, and balance sheet. Carefully examine each of these statements. Notice that the income ($62,625) on the income statement is also included on the statement of retained earnings. Notice that the ending balance of retained earnings ($57,625) from the

EXHIBIT 7.7
Adjusted Trial Balance

Adjusted Trial Balance
January 31

	DR	CR
Cash	$ 370,000	
Accounts receivable	95,000	
Inventory	150,000	
Equipment	400,000	
Accumulated depreciation		$ 4,000
Accounts payable		250,000
Utilities payable		1,500
Interest payable		1,875
Bank loan payable		200,000
Capital stock		500,000
Retained earnings	5,000	
Sales		175,000
Cost of goods sold	100,000	
Salary expense	5,000	
Utility expense	1,500	
Depreciation expense	4,000	
Interest expense	1,875	
Total	$1,132,375	$1,132,375

statement of retained earnings is also included on the balance sheet. Finally, look at the statement of cash flows. Notice that cash flows are classified as operating, investing, or financing. Recall our previous discussion in Chapter 2 regarding this issue. Also note that the ending balance of cash on this statement is also reflected on the balance sheet.

Exhibit 7.9 shows the closing entries. Note that the revenue account (sales) is debited to close it to retained earnings while the expense accounts (cost of goods sold, salary expense, etc.) are credited to close them to retained earnings. The increase to the retained earnings account, $62,625 ($175,000 – $112,375) is the net income for the period. Confirm that this amount is the same as that shown on the income statement in Exhibit 7.8. Exhibit 7.10 illustrates the accounts after the closing entries are posted. Notice that all the temporary accounts now have zero balances—which is exactly the outcome we desired. Finally, Exhibit 7.11 illustrates the post-closing trial balance that shows the equality of debits and credits after the closing process.

Computer-Based Transaction Systems

Because manual systems rely on human processing, they are labor intensive and may be inefficient in today's complex business environment.[1] In addition, because manual systems rely on human processing, they are error prone. For example, an entry made in the journal could be posted to the wrong account. Debits would still equal credits, but the accounting records would be incorrect. Or an entry for $10,000 could be posted for $1,000. Again, debits would equal credits, but the accounting records would be incorrect.

To overcome these deficiencies, many companies have computerized their accounting processes. A computer-based transaction system maintains accounting data stored separately from other operating data. That is, the accounting records are kept separately from the records required for the expenditure processes (supplier information, inventory reorder points, etc.), revenue processes (customer information, credit terms, etc.), and conversion processes (bill of materials, master production schedule, etc.). Thus a computer-based

[1] For some small businesses, manual accounting systems still work very well. Software such as Quick Books Pro is available for small businesses to computerize their accounting functions.

EXHIBIT 7.8
Financial Statements

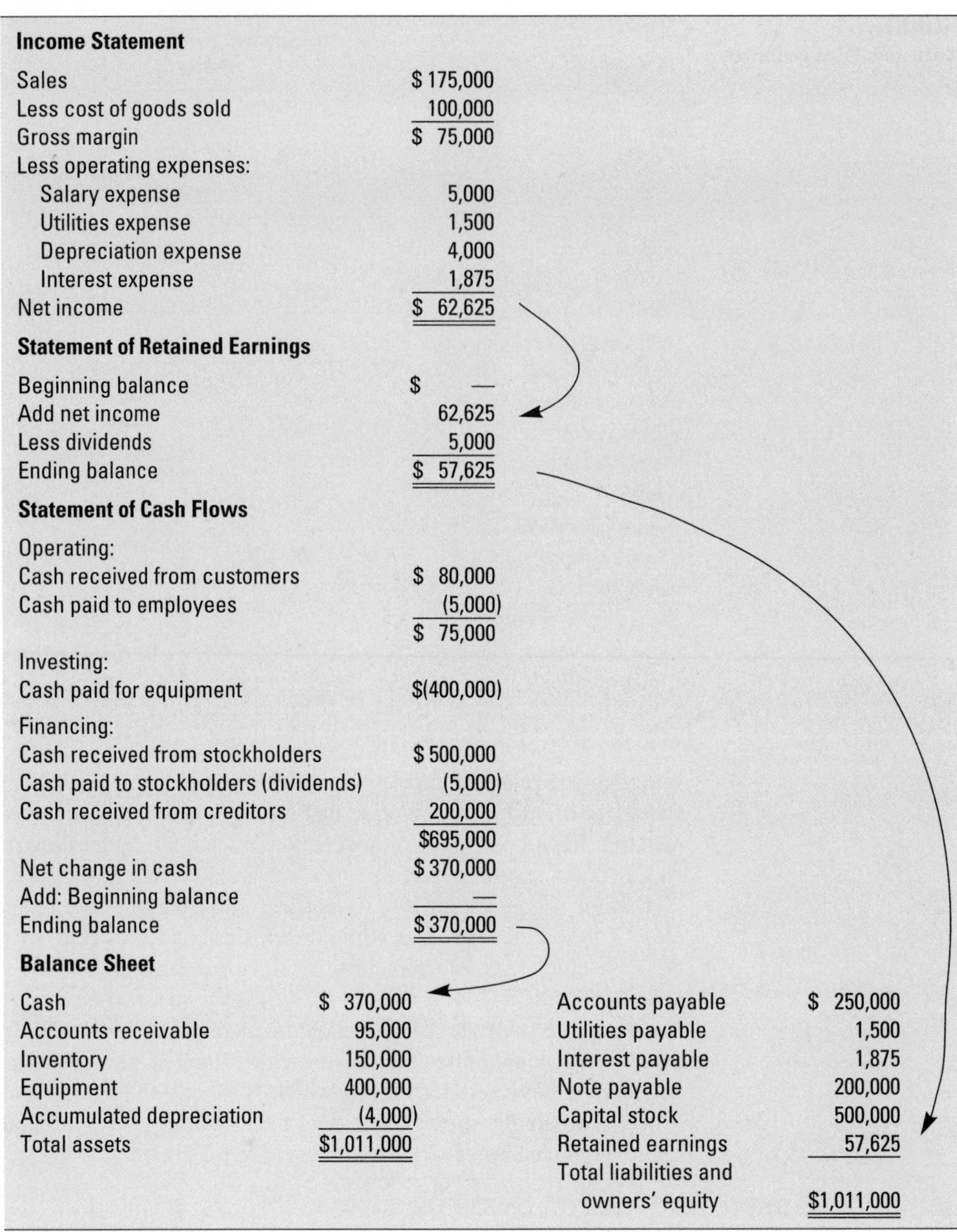

Income Statement

Sales	$ 175,000
Less cost of goods sold	100,000
Gross margin	$ 75,000
Less operating expenses:	
Salary expense	5,000
Utilities expense	1,500
Depreciation expense	4,000
Interest expense	1,875
Net income	$ 62,625

Statement of Retained Earnings

Beginning balance	$ —
Add net income	62,625
Less dividends	5,000
Ending balance	$ 57,625

Statement of Cash Flows

Operating:	
Cash received from customers	$ 80,000
Cash paid to employees	(5,000)
	$ 75,000
Investing:	
Cash paid for equipment	$(400,000)
Financing:	
Cash received from stockholders	$ 500,000
Cash paid to stockholders (dividends)	(5,000)
Cash received from creditors	200,000
	$695,000
Net change in cash	$ 370,000
Add: Beginning balance	—
Ending balance	$ 370,000

Balance Sheet

Cash	$ 370,000	Accounts payable	$ 250,000
Accounts receivable	95,000	Utilities payable	1,500
Inventory	150,000	Interest payable	1,875
Equipment	400,000	Note payable	200,000
Accumulated depreciation	(4,000)	Capital stock	500,000
Total assets	$1,011,000	Retained earnings	57,625
		Total liabilities and owners' equity	$1,011,000

transaction system treats information in the same manner as a manual system—only the transaction data are entered into the computerized set of accounting records.

Maintaining accounting records on a computerized transaction-based system is very similar to a manual system, but there are some terminology differences. First, computerized systems utilize special journals (which we discuss in subsequent chapters) so typically a

EXHIBIT 7.9
Closing Entries

Date	Description	DR	CR
01-31	Sales	175,000	
	Retained Earnings		175,000
01-31	Retained Earnings	112,375	
	Cost of Goods Sold		100,000
	Salary Expense		5,000
	Utilities Expense		1,500
	Depreciation Expense		4,000
	Interest Expense		1,875

EXHIBIT 7.10
Closing Entries Posted

Retained Earnings Account

Date	Description	DR	CR	Balance
01-31		5,000		(5,000)
01-31			175,000	170,000
01-31		112,375		57,625

Sales Account

Date	Description	DR	CR	Balance
01-17			175,000	175,000
01-31		175,000		00

Cost of Goods Sold Account

Date	Description	DR	CR	Balance
01-17		100,000		100,000
01-31			100,000	00

Salary Expense Account

Date	Description	DR	CR	Balance
01-15		5,000		5,000
01-31			5,000	00

Utilities Expense Account

Date	Description	DR	CR	Balance
01-16		1,500		1,500
01-31			1,500	00

Depreciation Expense Account

Date	Description	DR	CR	Balance
01-31		4,000		4,000
01-31			4,000	00

Interest Expense Account

Date	Description	DR	CR	Balance
01-31		1,875		1,875
01-31			1,875	00

computerized system has five or more journals referred to as **transaction files.** Second, computerized systems access data from general and subsidiary ledgers (discussed in subsequent chapters) typically referred to as **master files.** What is different is that the transaction listing (journal) is *an output not an input* to the process.

EXHIBIT 7.11
Post-Closing Trial Balance

Post-Closing Trial Balance
January 31

	DR	CR
Cash	$ 370,000	
Accounts receivable	95,000	
Inventory	150,000	
Equipment	400,000	
Accumulated depreciation		$ 4,000
Accounts payable		250,000
Utilities payable		1,500
Interest payable		1,875
Bank loan payable		200,000
Capital stock		500,000
Retained earnings		57,625
Total	$1,015,000	$1,015,000

OF INTEREST Let's Review the Accounting Cycle

The process of recording accounting events in the journals and ledgers is not intuitive for everyone. If you are one of those people for whom this process seems a bit nebulous, this review is FOR YOU! Let's think of the accounting cycle as three major processes: (1) the recording process—steps one through three—journalizing, posting, and preparing a trial balance; (2) the adjusting process—steps four and five—entering and posting adjusting entries and preparing an adjusting trial balance; and (3) the closing process—steps six through eight—preparing financial statements, entering and posting closing entries, and preparing a post-closing trial balance.

Before we review the basics of each process, notice what each has in common—each ends with a trial balance to ensure that debits equal credits. This equality is an important internal control device in a manual accounting system; while it doesn't ensure that the entries have been prepared correctly (you could debit the wrong account, for example), it does ensure that an account wasn't debited twice for the same event. So let's review each process, starting at the beginning.

THE RECORDING PROCESS

The recording process is a continuous process of taking source documents, analyzing the information, and recording it in the accounting records. Remember, we record information twice—once in the journal as the event occurs (a chronological record) and again in the ledger to show the impact of the event on the specific account. At the end of the period, we prepare a trial balance to ensure that debits equal credits before preparing adjusting entries.

THE ADJUSTING PROCESS

The adjusting process is typically done only once during an accounting cycle, just prior to preparing financial statements. The purpose is to bring the accounting records up-to-date so that the financial statements will reflect all the events of the period (even if those events didn't result in source documents). Once adjusting events are analyzed, we make the appropriate entry in the general journal and post the entries to the appropriate accounts in the general ledger. When we are finished we prepare an adjusted trial balance to ensure that debits equal credits before proceeding to prepare financial statements.

THE CLOSING PROCESS

The closing process is done at the end of the accounting cycle and consists of two basic activities—preparing financial statements and preparing the accounting records for the next accounting cycle. The information in the adjusted trial balance (plus additional information about cash activities—we will discuss this more in later chapters) is used to prepare the financial statements. Once the financial statements are prepared, we must get ready for a new accounting cycle, so we close the temporary accounts—the income statement accounts—and transfer the balances to retained earnings (if the company is a corporation). Then we prepare a post-closing trial balance to again ensure that debits equal credits (we don't want to start the new accounting cycle with records that don't balance!).

Database Systems

Relational database systems such as enterprise resource planning (ERP) depart from the assets = liabilities + owners' equity method of organizing data. These systems capture data about an entity's activities and store that information in a data warehouse. In ERP systems both financial and nonfinancial information are captured and stored so that various users can access the data they need for particular decisions. These event-driven systems change the scope of accounting because the company, not the accounting equation, is used to determine which events to record. As you know, an accounting event must impact the company's assets, liabilities, and/or owners' equity. A **business event,** on the other hand, is one that management wants to plan and evaluate. Thus making a sales call is a business event, but it is not an accounting event because the company's assets, liabilities, and/or owners' equity do not change. Similarly, recording the number of defects found in a process is a business event, but not an accounting event.

While an in-depth description of relational database systems is beyond the scope of this text, it is important that you understand the logic behind these systems. As you know from our discussion in Chapter 3, the three primary operating processes are the (1) marketing/sales/collection/customer service process, (2) conversion process, and (3) purchasing/receipt/payment process. In Chapters 4 through 6 we planned for activities in these processes. *All of these activities are business events and, therefore, would be recorded in an ERP system.* We address this in Chapters 8 through 10.

Database systems eliminate redundancies in the company's information system. Since accounting event and business event data are maintained in the same data warehouse, redundant data are eliminated. For example, in many companies, customer information is maintained in several places—marketing needs data to make sales calls, production needs information regarding special requests, and accounting needs information about customer account balances. Think how many times the customer's name is recorded if these information systems are maintained separately. As another example, human resources maintains employee data, but payroll maintains data on employee salaries, withholdings, and so forth. Production maintains data regarding what jobs employees are working on and how many hours were worked. Again, when these systems are not linked, a lot of redundancies occur.

Summary

Accounting information systems are designed to capture information regarding accounting events to prepare financial statements. Manual systems utilize paper-based journals (general and special) and ledgers (general and subsidiary). Computer-based transaction systems replace paper records with computer records. Database systems embed accounting data within the business event data on which they are based. In all cases, the system must meet the company's need to plan and control activities.

- An accounting event must (1) be specific to the entity, (2) be measurable, and (3) impact the entity's assets, liabilities, and/or owners' equity.
- Journalizing is the process of recording events, in chronological order, in the journal while posting is the process of recording event data in the account impacted by the event.

Key Terms

Account A place where the results of events affecting that item are recorded, *184*
Accounting cycle The time period between financial statements, *189*
Adjusted trial balance A trial balance done after adjusting entries have been made and posted, *192*
Adjusting entry An internal entry made to adjust the accounts for internal events prior to preparing financial statements, *190*
Business event An event that management wants to plan and evaluate, *202*
Chart of accounts An organizational scheme used to classify accounts as assets, liabilities, or owners' equity, *185*
Closing entry An entry made to close out a temporary account, transfer the balance to retained earnings, and determine net income, *193*
Contra account An account with an opposite balance to the normal balance of its associated account, *192*
Credit The right side of an account, *185*
Debit The left side of an account, *185*
Expense accrual An adjusting entry that occurs when expenses are incurred in one accounting period and payment is made in a later period, *191*
Expense deferral An adjusting entry that occurs when a company uses previously purchased assets in an attempt to generate revenue in future periods, *192*
General journal The journal used to record both the account(s) to be debited and the account(s) to be credited, *187*
General ledger A collection of specific asset, liability, and owners' equity accounts, *188*
Journal entry The recorded effect of an accounting event, *187*
Journalizing The process of recording a journal entry, *187*
Master file A ledger in a computer-based transaction system, *201*
Normal balance The normal balance of an account is always the side (debit or credit) on which it increases, *189*
Permanent account An asset, liability, or owners' equity account whose balance is carried over from year to year, *198*
Post-closing trial balance A trial balance prepared after the closing entries have been posted, *195*
Posting The process of recording the appropriate part of a journal entry to the affected account, *188*
Revenue accrual An adjusting entry that occurs when revenues are earned in one accounting period and payment is received in a later period, *191*
Revenue deferral An adjusting entry that occurs when a company has been paid in advance for services to be performed in a future period, *191*
T-account An informal representation of a general ledger account, *189*
Transaction files A journal in a computer-based transaction system, *201*
Trial balance A listing of all general ledger accounts and their respective balances to ensure that debits equal credits, *189*

Questions

1. What is GAAP?
2. What is the accounting equation and why is it important?
3. What are the three characteristics required for an accounting event?
4. What does debit mean?
5. What does credit mean?
6. What is meant by subtraction by opposition?
7. To decrease an asset account, is a debit or credit required?
8. To decrease a liability account, is a debit or credit required?
9. What is an account and where is it located in a manual accounting system?
10. What is the difference between a general journal and the ledger and why is each needed in the accounting system?
11. What is the difference between journalizing and posting? Which occurs first?
12. What is the accounting cycle?
13. What is the purpose of adjusting entries?
14. What is the difference between an expense and a revenue accrual?
15. What is the difference between a revenue and an expense deferral?
16. What is a contra account? If an account is a contra liability, what is its normal balance?
17. What is the difference among a trial balance, an adjusted trial balance, and a post-closing trial balance?
18. What is the purpose of closing entries?

Exercises

E7.1 LO 1

The following list of events occurred in the first month of business at a local auto parts supplier. Indicate which of the events are accounting events and provide a short justification for your answer.

A. The owner purchases supplies (paper, pens, etc.) on an open account.
B. The manager hires a receptionist and several salespeople. The receptionist will be paid on an hourly basis. Each salesperson will receive a commission and salary.
C. A customer pays for a part that she just received.
D. The customer orders a part that was not in stock.
E. The owner contacts a supplier to be the exclusive provider of auto parts for the store.
F. All employees have worked for two weeks. Employees are paid on a monthly basis.
G. The owner finds out that a competitor across the street is offering 20 percent off on all parts for the following week.

LO 1 **E7.2**

Specify in the space provided the effect of each of the following accounting events on assets, liabilities, and owners' equity. Use **I** for Increase, **D** for Decrease, and **NA** for Not Applicable.

Assets	Liabilities	Owners' Equity	
________	________	________	A. Borrowed cash from the bank by signing a note payable.
________	________	________	B. Paid a dividend to the owners of the business.
________	________	________	C. Employees earned, but were not paid, one week's salary.
________	________	________	D. Paid an obligation to the IRS for taxes.
________	________	________	E. Supplies were used in the business.
________	________	________	F. Purchased land and a building for cash.

LO 1 **E7.3**

Specify in the space provided the effect of each of the following accounting events on assets, liabilities, and owners' equity. Use **I** for Increase, **D** for Decrease, and **NA** for Not Applicable.

Assets	Liabilities	Owners' Equity	
________	________	________	A. Issued capital stock for cash.
________	________	________	B. Purchased supplies on open account.
________	________	________	C. Purchased office equipment for cash.
________	________	________	D. Returned some of the supplies purchased on open account to the seller because the wrong items were received.
________	________	________	E. Obtained a bank loan.
________	________	________	F. Purchased additional office equipment by making a cash down payment with the balance owed on open account.

LO 1 **E7.4** For each of the accounting events that follow (**A–F**), indicate in the space provided the appropriate number designating the effect of that event. If none of the options applies, use **NA** for not applicable.

1. Increases assets, increases owners' equity.
2. Increases assets, increases liabilities.
3. Increases assets, decreases assets.
4. Decreases assets, decreases liabilities.
5. Decreases assets, decreases owners' equity.

_________ A. Paid an obligation of $1,300.
_________ B. Paid rent of $4,200 in advance for the year.
_________ C. Purchased office supplies costing $1,500 on account.
_________ D. Obtained a loan of $5,000 from First Bank.
_________ E. Provided services to a customer on account.
_________ F. Collected $500 cash from a customer who had previously been billed.

LO 4 **E7.5** For each of the accounting elements that follow (**A–F**), indicate in the space provided the appropriate number designating the financial statements where the element would appear. Some elements may appear on more than one statement.

1. Income statement
2. Statement of owners' equity
3. Balance sheet
4. Statement of cash flows

_________ A. Accounts receivable
_________ B. Cash sales
_________ C. Utilities payable
_________ D. Note payable, due in five years
_________ E. Sales on account
_________ F. Utilities expense

LO 5 **E7.6** For each of the accounting elements that follow (**A–F**), indicate in the space provided the appropriate number of the financial statement(s) where the element would appear.

1. Income statement
2. Statement of owners' equity
3. Balance sheet
4. Statement of cash flows

_________ A. Services provided on account
_________ B. Inventory purchased on account
_________ C. Accounts payable
_________ D. Cost of good sold
_________ E. Equipment purchased with cash
_________ F. Depreciation expense

LO 1 **E7.7** Various accounts are affected differently by debits and credits. For each of these accounts, state whether it is increased or decreased by a debit or credit. The first account is an example.

Accounts	Increased by	Decreased by	Normal Balance
A. Cash	Debit	Credit	Debit
B. Salaries Payable			
C. Buildings			
D. Accounts Receivable			
E. Sales			
F. Capital Stock			
G. Prepaid Insurance			
H. Acounts Payable			
I. Utilities Expense			
J. Retained Earnings			

LO 1 **E7.8** For each of the following entries, describe the event that gave rise to the entry:

A. Accounts Payable	1,300	
Cash		1,300
B. Prepaid Rent	4,200	
Cash		4,200
C. Office Supplies	1,500	
Accounts Payable		1,500

D. Cash	5,000	
Unearned Revenue		5,000
E. Accounts Receivable	500	
Fee Revenue		500
F. Telephone Expense	200	
Cash		200

LO 2 **E7.9** For each of the following situations, prepare the adjusting entry for the month ended October 31 and indicate the effect each adjustment would have on net income:

A. Wingenbach Plumbing had a $35,000 contract with a construction company to perform plumbing services for a home under construction. Payment was to be received at the end of the job. As of October 31, $8,000 worth of services had been performed.
B. Hutchison State Bank made a $10,000 loan to a customer on October 1. The terms called for principal and interest of 8 percent to be paid at the end of one year. Hutchison State Bank prepares monthly financial statements.
C. Davis, Inc., a real estate company, rents office space to a lawyer for $1,200 per month. The invoice for October had not been sent as of October 31.

LO 2 **E7.10** For each of the following situations, prepare the adjusting entry for the month ended February 28 and indicate the effect each adjustment would have on net income:

A. On February 1, Doan Company received a $6,000 retainer from a client. By the end of February, Doan had earned $4,500 of the retainer.
B. During January, $24,000 in magazine subscriptions was received by MG Corp. The subscriptions were for 12 monthly issues of *Summer Sport,* beginning with the month of February. MG Corp. prepares monthly financial statements.
C. Weisz Insurance Company sells policies that run on a calendar-year basis. It sold $60,000 of insurance policies and collected the cash in early January. Weisz prepares monthly financial statements.

LO 2 **E7.11** For each of the following situations, prepare the adjusting entry for the month ended May 31 and indicate the effect each adjustment would have on net income:

A. The May telephone bill for Scheele Company arrived in the accounting department on June 8. The invoice totaled $210.
B. Bailey, Inc., had an arrangement with a local newspaper to run a full-page advertisement every Sunday. The cost of each ad was $350. The newspaper sends Bailey a bill on the 15th of the next month. There were four Sundays in the month of May.
C. Santoni borrowed $50,000 on October 1. The terms of the note called for repayment of principal and interest of 7 percent one year from the date of the note. Santoni prepares monthly financial statements.

LO 2 **E7.12** For each of the following situations, prepare the adjusting entry for the month ended July 31 and indicate the effect each adjustment would have on net income:

A. Delgado, Inc., purchased a three-year insurance policy on January 2 for $6,000. Delgado prepares quarterly financial statements.
B. On July 1, Rottman Company had a $390 balance in its supplies account. During July, $1,450 of additional supplies were purchased. An inventory at July 31 showed $275 of supplies still on the shelves.
C. Last year, Apple Enterprises purchased some equipment at a total cost of $75,000. The estimated useful life of the equipment is five years. Apple prepares semiannual financial statements.

LO 2 **E7.13** Prepare the adjusting entry for each of the following situations:

A. On May 1, Unicover Services, Inc., had a $7,820 debit balance in its supplies account. During May, $4,250 of additional supplies were purchased. At the end of the month, a count of supplies revealed $2,430 left on hand.
B. Best Sports Enterprises, which produces a monthly magazine, received $9,600 in payments from its customers for two-year subscriptions. The subscriptions start with the June issue this year. The company prepares financial statements annually on December 31.

LO 2 **E7.14** Each of the following combinations of effects results from making adjusting entries:

1. Increases assets, increases revenues, and increases owners' equity.
2. Decreases assets, increases expenses, and decreases owners' equity.
3. Increases liabilities, increases expenses, and decreases owners' equity.
4. Decreases liabilities, increases revenues, and increases owners' equity.

Select one of the preceding items **(1–4)** to match the effect achieved by each of the following adjusting entries:

A. Salaries earned by employees but unpaid amount to $7,850.
B. Depreciation expense on equipment is $3,250.
C. Prepaid insurance expired during the period totals $1,300.
D. Interest earned, but not yet received, amounts to $800.
E. Of the revenue received and previously recorded as unearned, $13,675 has been earned this period.
F. Property taxes accrued, but not yet paid, amount to $6,700.
G. Supplies used during the period total $2,100.
H. Interest owed on long-term debt totals $1,500.

LO 4 E7.15 Given this adjusted trial balance for Wagner Services, Inc., prepare the income statement and statement of retained earnings for the month ended August 31, 2010. Dividends of $2,500 were paid during the month and there were no additional capital stock transactions during the month.

WAGNER SERVICES, INC.
Adjusted Trial Balance
August 31, 2010

	Debits	Credits
Cash	$ 4,600	
Supplies	400	
Prepaid rent	650	
Equipment	5,600	
Accumulated depreciation—equipment		$ 1,200
Furniture	2,700	
Accumulated depreciation—furniture		900
Accounts payable		800
Note payable		3,000
Interest payable		150
Capital stock		6,000
Retained earnings		(2,500)
Service fee revenue		5,800
Supplies expense	150	
Rent expense	650	
Interest expense	25	
Depreciation expense	300	
Postage expense	125	
Telephone expense	50	
Utilities expense	100	
Total	$15,350	$15,350

LO 4 E7.16 Refer to E7.15. Prepare the balance sheet for Wagner Services, Inc., as of August 31, 2010.

LO 3 E7.17 Refer to E7.15. Prepare the closing entries for Wagner Services, Inc., on August 31, 2010.

LO 3 E7.18 The adjusted trial balance of Murphy's Taxi Service, Inc., follows. Determine the net income or loss for the month of May and the balance in the Retained Earnings account that would appear on the balance sheet.

MURPHY'S TAXI SERVICE, INC.
Adjusted Trial Balance
May 31, 2010

	Debits	Credits
Cash	$ 1,920	
Prepaid insurance	690	
Automobiles	29,500	
Accumulated depreciation—automobiles		$12,800

MURPHY'S TAXI SERVICE, INC. (continued)
Adjusted Trial Balance
May 31, 2010

Capital stock		15,000
Retained earnings		3,720
Passenger fee revenue		4,250
Salary expense	2,400	
Fuel expense	485	
Depreciation expense	615	
Repairs and maintenance expense	160	
Total	$35,770	$35,770

E7.19 Your company has decided to switch from a manual accounting system to a computerized transaction-based system with a March 31 fiscal year-end. The system your company is adopting utilizes increases and decreases rather than debits and credits. Your boss has asked you to analyze each of the following events by determining which master files would be affected and whether they would be increased or decreased by the event and the year-end adjusting/closing process.

A. On January 1 your company paid its insurance premiums for the next two years, $2,400.
B. On February 1 your company accepted an advance payment from a customer for services to be provided uniformly over the next nine months, $7,200.
C. On March 1 your company borrowed $100,000 on a simple interest loan with an 8 percent annual rate. The loan and the interest will be repaid on March 1 of next year.
D. On January 1 your company loaned $50,000 to a shareholder on a simple interest loan with a 10 percent annual rate. The loan and the interest will be repaid by the shareholder on January 1 of next year.
E. On January 1 your company bought equipment costing $80,000 with an eight-year useful life. The equipment will be expensed uniformly over its life.

E7.20 Your company has decided to switch from its computerized transaction-based accounting system to an ERP system. Your boss understands that this system is capable of tracking accounting and other business event information. Describe the other business event information that could be tracked (recorded) in each of the following processes:

A. Revenue process
B. Conversion process
C. Expenditure process

Problems

P7.1

Biando Corporation began operations on May 1, 2010, and completed the following transactions during its first month of operations.

A. Sold capital stock for $30,000.
B. Purchased land and a building valued at $35,000 and $165,000, respectively, by paying $10,000 cash and signing a 20-year mortgage for the balance.
C. Purchased office equipment on account, $7,500.
D. Billed a customer for services performed, $5,000.
E. Received an $800 deposit from a customer for services to be performed next month.
F. Made a partial payment on account for the office equipment purchased in transaction (**C**), $1,500.
G. Performed a service and immediately collected $2,000.
H. Received and immediately paid the telephone bill for the month, $380.
I. Paid a dividend to owners, $3,000.
J. Received, but did not pay, the monthly utility bill, $450.

Required:

1. Determine the effect of each of the preceding events on the accounting equation.
2. Prepare the general journal entries to record each of these events. Note: You may want to set up T-accounts to keep track of some accounts. Do not prepare adjusting entries.
3. Prepare the income statement for the period.
4. Prepare the statement of retained earnings for the period.
5. Prepare the statement of cash flows for the period.

6. Prepare the balance sheet at the end of the period.
7. Prepare the closing entries.

LO 1 LO 2 LO 3 LO 4 **P7.2** The following accounting events (**A–I**) affected the assets, liabilities, and owners' equity of Buckingham Company during the fiscal year ended December 31, 2010.

A. Purchased $26,000 in merchandise inventory on open account.
B. Sold $60,000 in merchandise inventory on open account to a customer for $89,400.
C. Purchased $36,000 in merchandise inventory for cash.
D. Sold $63,600 in merchandise inventory for $85,040 cash.
E. Received and immediately paid the monthly utility bill, $2,150.
F. Paid employees $8,200 for wages earned.
G. Received a partial payment from a customer on account, $58,000.
H. Paid rent for the current month, $12,000.
I. Recorded depreciation on store equipment, $6,000.

Required:

1. Determine the effect of each of the preceding events on the accounting equation.
2. Prepare the general journal entries to record each of these events. Note: You may want to set up T-accounts (see page 189) to keep track of some accounts.
3. Prepare the income statement for the period.
4. Prepare the statement of cash flows for the period (ignore beginning balance).

LO 1 LO 4 **P7.3** The following accounting events (**A–I**) affected the assets, liabilities, and owners' equity of Pauley Enterprises during the year ended September 30, 2010.

A. Capital stock sold for $25,000 cash.
B. Raw materials are purchased on account for $50,000.
C. Raw materials of $42,000 are issued into production.
D. Assembly workers' wages of $11,500 are paid in cash.
E. Manufacturing overhead of $17,700 is incurred, but not paid.
F. Products costing $47,500 are finished.
G. Products costing $36,250 are sold for $50,750 in cash.
H. Selling expenses of $7,500 are paid in cash.
I. A dividend of $2,500 is paid to the owners.

Required:

1. Determine the effect of each of the preceding events on the accounting equation.
2. Prepare the general journal entries to record each of these events. Note: You may want to set up T-accounts (see page 189) to keep track of some accounts.
3. Prepare the income statement for the period.
4. Prepare the statement of cash flows for the period (ignore beginning balance).

LO 1 LO 2 **P7.4** Analyze the following events and complete the requirements.

A. Yarber Industries purchased buildings costing $240,000 and land costing $190,000 by paying $43,000 in cash and signing a note payable for the balance.
B. Cui Manufacturing has an obligation on its books for $15,000 owed to a supplier. Cui purchased an additional $8,000 in equipment from this supplier making an immediate cash payment of $23,000 to pay for both the current and previous purchases.
C. GPS Systems has a right to receive $3,000 from a customer for purchases previously made on open account. GPS Systems sells $8,000 in materials to this customer and receives a check for $11,000 at that time to pay for both the current and previous purchases. The materials had cost GPS Systems $2,000.
D. Kelsey Company purchased merchandise on open account at a cost of $19,500. Kelsey then sold the merchandise to a customer for $34,125 cash.

Required:

1. Determine the effect of each of the preceding events on the accounting equation.
2. Prepare the general journal entries to record each of these events.

LO 4 **P7.5** Monger Company has the following information available from fiscal 2010. Use the relevant information to prepare the income statement and statement of cash flows (ignore beginning balance) for the year ended July 31, 2010, for Monger Company.

A. Cash received from clients for services rendered in June, $65,000.
B. Incurred employee wages expense, $43,000.
C. Capital stock issued for cash, $80,000.
D. Depreciation expense incurred, $5,300.

E. Services performed on credit, $85,000.
F. Received cash by signing a long-term note payable, $40,000.
G. Interest earned on short-term investments, $200.
H. Purchased supplies for cash, $12,000.
I. Insurance purchased for the following year, $4,800.
J. Rent expense, $24,000.

LO 4 **P7.6** For each of the following items (**A–L**), indicate on which financial statement you would expect to find it and briefly explain why you chose that particular statement. Some items may appear on more than one statement.

1. Income statement
2. Statement of retained earnings
3. Balance sheet
4. Statement of cash flows

_________ A. Accumulated depreciation on equipment
_________ B. Cash received from capital stock issued during the period
_________ C. Cash paid for buildings during the period
_________ D. Cost of merchandise sold during the period
_________ E. Depreciation expense
_________ F. Ending cash balance
_________ G. Ending retained earnings
_________ H. Interest payable, due in 30 days
_________ I. Interest receivable
_________ J. Interest revenue
_________ K. Note payable, due in 10 years
_________ L. Note receivable, due in 60 days

LO 4 **P7.7** For each of the following items (**A–L**), indicate on which financial statement you would expect to find it and briefly explain why you chose that particular statement. Some items may appear on more than one statement.

1. Income statement
2. Statement of retained earnings
3. Balance sheet
4. Statement of cash flows

_________ A. Accounts payable
_________ B. Accounts receivable
_________ C. Beginning retained earnings
_________ D. Cash paid to employees
_________ E. Cash received from customers
_________ F. Dividends paid during the year
_________ G. Equipment
_________ H. Inventory
_________ I. Land
_________ J. Net loss
_________ K. Revenue from services
_________ L. Selling expenses

LO 1 **P7.8** Painter Supplies buys paint and supplies wholesale as needed for contracting jobs, but it also maintains a stock of paint and miscellaneous supplies. The accountant for Painter Supplies provided the following journal entries for events that occurred during July. The president cannot understand these entries and would like you to describe the events for her.

	Debit	Credit
A. Cash	$920	
Accounts Receivable		$920
B. Supplies	75	
Cash		75
C. Cash	380	
Revenue		380

D. Inventory	425	
Accounts Payable		425
E. Accounts Payable	875	
Cash		875
F. Accounts Receivable	765	
Revenue		765
G. Expense	300	
Cash		300
H. Note Payable	425	
Cash		425
I. Expense	425	
Inventory		425
Accounts Receivable	600	
Revenue		600

P7.9 Adjustment data and the unadjusted trial balance have been gathered by Farlow Corporation.

Adjustment data:

LO 2 LO 3 LO 4

A. Unused supplies on hand, $230.
B. Unexpired rent, $1,000.
C. Depreciation on buildings, $1,500.
D. Depreciation on equipment, $800.
E. Unearned fees still unearned, $740.
F. Salaries earned but not yet paid, $740.
G. Accrued interest on the note, $240.
H. Fees earned but not recorded and not received, $570.

FARLOW CORPORATION
Unadjusted Trial Balance
March 31, 2010

	Debits	Credits
Cash	$ 7,280	
Accounts receivable	1,700	
Supplies	940	
Prepaid rent	2,400	
Land	52,000	
Buildings	94,000	
Accumulated depreciation—buildings		$ 16,600
Equipment	41,500	
Accumulated depreciation—equipment		13,500
Accounts payable		3,480
Unearned fees		2,970
Note payable		60,000
Capital stock		45,000
Retained earnings		39,150
Fee revenue		29,300
Salary expense	9,320	
Telephone expense	260	
Utilities expense	410	
Miscellaneous expense	190	
Total	$210,000	$210,000

Required:

1. Prepare the adjusting entries. In some instances, it will be necessary to establish new accounts.
2. Prepare an adjusted trial balance.
3. Prepare the closing entries.
4. Determine the net income or loss for the period.
5. Prepare a post-closing trial balance.

LO 2 LO 3 LO 4 **P7.10** This unadjusted trial balance of Wesaw Delivery Service, Inc., is followed by information for adjustments.

WESAW DELIVERY SERVICE, INC.
Unadjusted Trial Balance
June 30, 2010

	DR	CR
Cash	$ 6,340	
Accounts receivable	1,410	
Supplies	890	
Prepaid insurance	1,900	
Land	48,000	
Buildings	82,000	
Accumulated depreciation—buildings		$ 18,960
Equipment	53,000	
Accumulated depreciation—equipment		16,800
Accounts payable		2,550
Unearned delivery fees		2,100
Mortgage payable		58,000
Capital stock		50,000
Retained earnings		21,630
Fee revenue		33,460
Salary expense	9,060	
Telephone expense	120	
Utilities expense	350	
Repairs expense	430	
Total	$203,500	$203,500

Adjustment data:

A. Supplies used, $560.
B. Expired insurance, $250.
C. Depreciation on buildings, $750.
D. Depreciation on equipment, $350.
E. Unearned delivery fees earned this month, $900.
F. Salaries earned but not yet paid, $280.
G. Interest on the mortgage, $500.
H. Delivery fees earned but not recorded and not received, $560.

Required:

1. Prepare the adjusting entries. In some instances, it will be necessary to establish new accounts for items not shown on the unadjusted trial balance.
2. Prepare an adjusted trial balance.
3. Prepare the closing entries.
4. Determine the net income or loss for the period.
5. Prepare a post-closing trial balance.

Cases

C7.1 LO 4 Refer to the company you chose in C1.1. Examine this company's financial statements and answer the following questions:

Required:

1. Examine the balance sheet of this company. Which accounts have debit balances and which accounts have credit balances?
2. Trace the net income from the income statement to the statement of owners' equity.
3. Trace the ending balance of retained earnings from the statement of owners' equity to the balance sheet.
4. Trace the ending balance of cash from the statement of cash flows to the balance sheet.
5. What is the date for the end of the accounting cycle?

LO 1 LO 2 LO 3 LO 4 **C7.2** Hillary Curran set up her psychology practice on March 1. The following transactions occurred during March:

1	Deposited $25,000 in an account in the name of the business.
2	Paid $5,400 for three months' rent of an office.
5	Purchased office supplies for cash, $900.
8	Purchased $4,800 of office furniture on account.
10	Paid $250 for advertising in the local newspaper.
12	Completed counseling with a client and sent a bill for $850 for services rendered.
15	Performed counseling services for a local DJ and immediately collected $350.
18	Paid the March insurance premium of $300.
20	Received a $5,000 deposit for counseling services to be performed for the employees of Reny Company beginning next week.
21	Received a partial payment of $200 from the client billed on March 12.
25	Paid $1,000 of the amount owed from the purchase of office furniture on March 8.
27	Withdrew $2,000 for personal living expenses.
31	Paid the receptionist's salary of $1,200.

Required:

1. Prepare journal entries for each of the previous transactions.
2. Post the entries to the general ledger. Use T-accounts (see page 189) to represent general ledger accounts and determine the ending balance of each account.
3. Using this information, prepare the necessary adjusting entries and post them to the T-accounts:
   A. One month's rent has expired.
   B. An inventory of supplies showed $250 still on hand.
   C. The office furniture is estimated to have a 10-year useful life.
   D. Of the Unearned Revenue, $400 had been earned by March 31.
   E. The telephone bill for March, for $130, was received on April 3.
   F. A client counseled on March 31 was sent an invoice for $350 on April 2.
4. Prepare an income statement, statement of owners' equity, balance sheet, and statement of cash flows.
5. Prepare the closing entries and post them to the T-accounts.

Critical Thinking

CT7.1 LO 5 In Chapter 6 we planned the operating activities of our start-up company, PCs to Go. Review the budgets developed for this company and prepare a chart of accounts for PCs to Go.

CT7.2 LO 4 Your best friend, who knows little about accounting, recently started a landscaping business. During one of your conversations he made the following statements:

I don't need financial statements prepared by an accountant. All I really need to know is how much money is in my business's bank account so I can pay the bills when they come in. If I need a loan, the bank will demand appraisals of all my property. Why would I need financial statements that list what I paid for the property instead of what it's worth today?

Respond to your friend's statements. Be prepared to present your opinions to the class.

Ethical Challenges

EC7.1 LO 4 During the banking "crisis" in 2008, many financial institutions blamed their problems on an accounting rule called mark-to-market which essentially requires companies to report certain assets at their market (current) value rather than historical cost (what was paid for the item). Thus, the argument went, since the financial institutions were holding many mortgages that were worthless (the so-called sub-prime mortgages) and were required to write these assets down (thus reducing both the assets of the financial institutions as well as owners' equity), it was the accounting rule that caused the financial institutions' balance sheets to look bad. Discuss whether you believe that following an accounting process can cause a company to experience economic problems.

LO 4 **EC7.2** A bookkeeping client of yours made the following journal entry to record the purchase of a piece of equipment to be used in the sales office. The useful life of the equipment is estimated at five years.

Supplies	8,000	
Accounts payable		8,000

You have told the client that the journal entry is incorrect, but the client does not want to fix it, arguing that "an asset is an asset." You have learned that the client is seeking a bank loan. Discuss what you should do in this situation.

Computer Applications

CA7.1 LO 2 LO 5

Companies often make use of computerized spreadsheets to help determine the impact of various adjusting entries before they are formally recorded. By using a spreadsheet, managers can perform calculations to quickly determine the effect of various adjusting entries on account balances.

Unadjusted Trial Balance

	Debits	Credits
Cash	$1,600	
Accounts receivable	1,100	
Supplies	300	
Equipment	3,000	
Accumulated depreciation—equipment		$ 900
Accounts payable		600
Unearned revenue		700
Capital stock		1,500
Retained earnings		800
Service fee revenue		3,300
Salary expense	1,500	
Utilities expense	100	
Insurance expense	200	
Total	$7,800	$7,800

Required: Use a spreadsheet package.

A. Set up a spreadsheet with debit and credit columns and enter the debit and credit data. Then set up debit and credit columns for the adjustments and the adjusted trial balance. Your spreadsheet should now have seven columns.

B. In the adjustments columns, make the following adjustments and then write a formula in the adjusted trial balance columns so that the correct after-adjustment amount is determined.

1. Supplies used during the period were $150.
2. Depreciation on the equipment was $250.
3. Unearned revenue earned during the period was $300.
4. Revenue earned but not recorded for the period was $400.

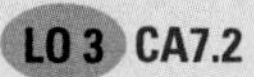

CA7.2 Refer to CA7.1. Set up a spreadsheet with debit and credit columns and enter the adjusted trial balance. Then set up debit and credit columns for closing and the post-closing trial balance.

Required:

A. Enter the closing information.

B. Write a formula to determine the correct post-closing amounts.

Visit the text Online Learning Center at **www.mhhe.com/ainsworth6e** for additional problem material that accompanies this chapter.

CHAPTER EIGHT

8

Purchasing/Human Resources/Payment Process: Recording and Evaluating Expenditure Process Activities

Learning Objectives

LO 1 Describe the difference between the periodic and perpetual inventory systems and record inventory activities using each system.

LO 2 Discuss the difference between the net price and gross price methods for recording inventory and record inventory activities using each method.

LO 3 Explain the payroll reporting process and record payroll and payroll taxes.

LO 4 Explain how to analyze other expenditure process activities and record these activities in the accounting system.

LO 5 Describe how expenditure process activities are reported on the financial statements.

In Chapter 2 we found out that the management cycle consists of planning, performing, and evaluating phases. In addition we learned about the four basic business processes and how they are interrelated. In Chapter 3, we discovered that the expenditure process provides the inputs to the conversion process. The conversion process, in turn, provides the products that are sold in the revenue process. We examined the activities in these processes in detail and learned about the decisions made and the information needed to make these decisions. In Chapter 4 we learned how companies use models to make decisions in these operating processes. In Chapters 5 and 6 we discovered how companies plan, and then budget, for their operating activities. In Chapters 8 through 10 we explore the performing and evaluating phase of the management cycle. We examine how the accounting system captures and reports information gathered during the performance of each operating process for evaluation and control purposes. We begin with the expenditure process since it provides the input to the conversion process. In Chapter 9 we explore the conversion process, and in Chapter 10 we examine the revenue process.

Expenditure Process

As you know the expenditure process consists of the following activities:

- Determine the need for goods/services.
- Select suppliers and order goods/services.
- Receive goods/services.
- Pay suppliers of goods/services.

All of these activities are business events, but only the last two are accounting events. That is, determining the need for goods/services and selecting suppliers do not change the company's assets, liabilities, and/or owners' equity and, therefore, are not accounting events.

A company must have an information system that captures data needed to report the effects of accounting events and to provide information to management to plan and control the activities of the business. Data for *all* the activities just listed are captured regardless of whether the company uses a transaction-based system or a database system. In a database system, this information is maintained with the information concerning accounting events. In a manual or computer-based transactional system, information concerning the first two activities is typically maintained outside the formal accounting information system.

Exhibit 8.1 illustrates the documents and records maintained for inventory purchase activities in a transaction-based accounting system. The system illustrated is a manual system, but a computer-based system is similar in utilizing transaction and master files. Let's examine this exhibit. Note that six functions are represented in this diagram—inventory control, purchasing, receiving, accounts payable, general ledger, and cashier/control. Recall that these functions are not necessarily housed in six separate departments within the company. Note all the activity records (purchase requisition, purchase order, receiving report, vendor's invoice, and check) that are maintained outside the formal accounting system. A document is represented by the symbol:

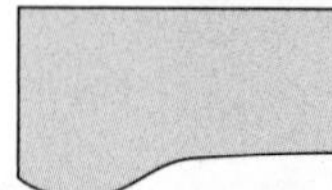

Note the use of special journals (purchases journal, cash disbursements journal) and subsidiary ledgers (inventory, accounts payable). We discuss special journals and subsidiary ledgers in the next section. These journals and ledgers are represented by the symbol:

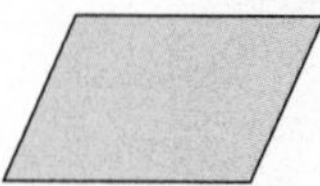

EXHIBIT 8.1 Traditional Inventory Purchase Flowchart

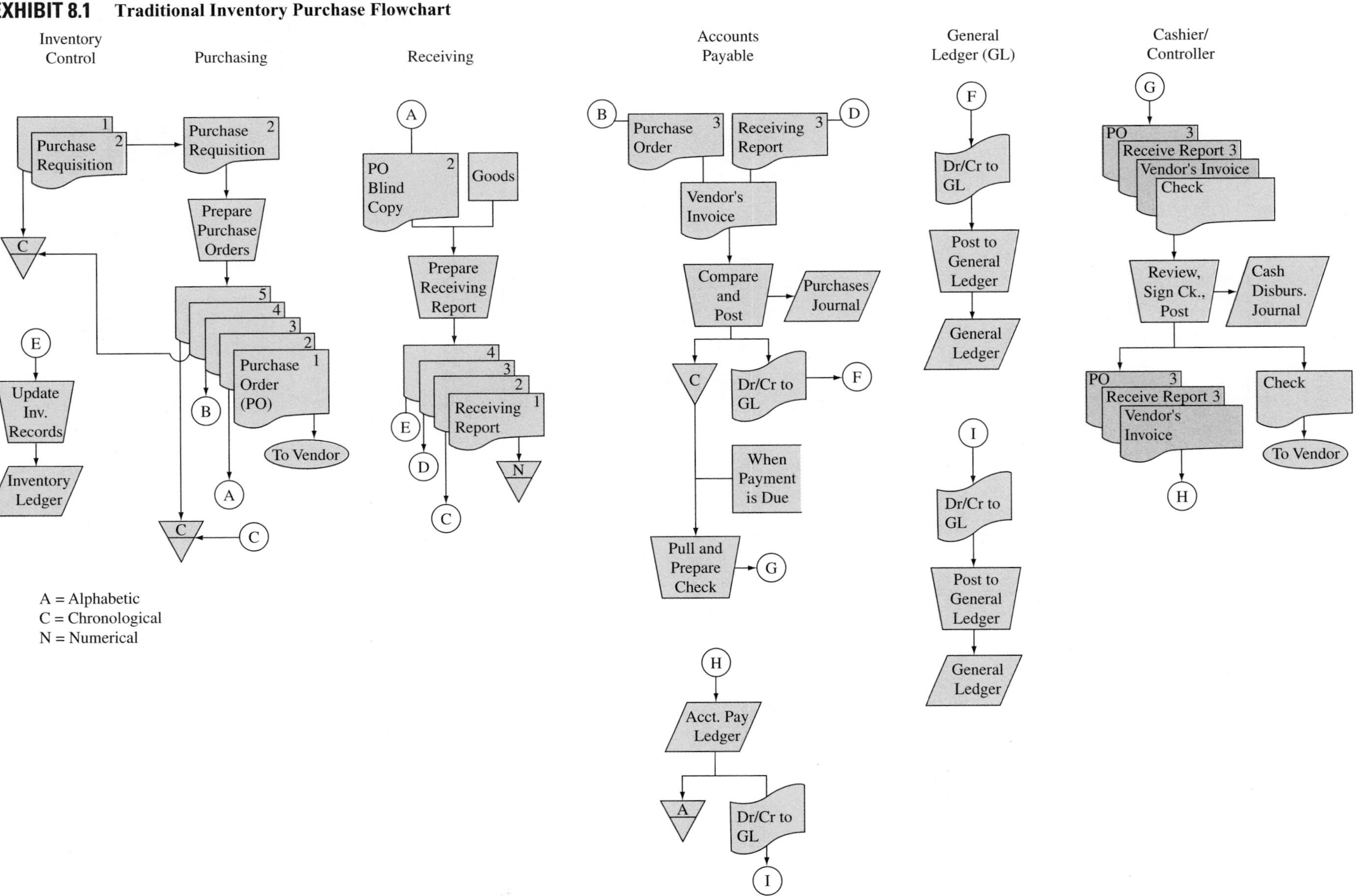

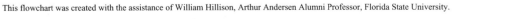

This flowchart was created with the assistance of William Hillison, Arthur Andersen Alumni Professor, Florida State University.

Source: A. S. Hollander, E. L. Denna, and J. O. Cherrington, *Accounting Information, Technology, and Business Solutions,* 2nd ed. (New York: McGraw-Hill, 2000), p. 302.

Finally, actions are represented by the symbol:

Next, we focus on two activities that concern the inventory (purchases), accounts payable, and cash records of the company as illustrated in Exhibit 8.1. After a brief discussion of special journals and subsidiary ledgers, we consider purchases of inventory; then, we examine human resources and other expenditures.

Special Journals and Subsidiary Ledgers

In Chapter 7, we learned how companies use the general journal to record accounting events. The accounting events are subsequently posted to the appropriate general ledger accounts. Some companies also maintain special journals and subsidiary ledgers in addition to the general ledger and general journal.

Special Journals

Accountants use a **special journal** for transactions that occur frequently and in the same manner. For example, if a company always purchases its inventory on account, it would make many entries throughout the period increasing (debiting) inventory and increasing (crediting) accounts payable. Or consider a company that always provides services to clients on account. It would make many entries throughout the period increasing (debiting) accounts receivable and increasing (crediting) revenue. Since these types of entries occur again and again throughout the period, many companies find it convenient to develop special journals to record these frequently recurring transactions and continue to use the general journal for less repetitious events. Typically companies develop the following special journals:

Type of Journal	Purpose
Cash disbursements	Record payments of cash
Cash receipts	Record receipts of cash
Purchases	Record purchases of inventory on account
Sales	Record sales to customers on account

For example, an inventory purchases journal might look like the following:

Inventory Purchases Journal

Date	Description	Amount
1-7-10		10,000.00
1-14-10		15,000.00
1-21-10		13,000.00
1-28-10		12,000.00
1-31-10	Total	50,000.00

Note that this journal has only one column for the amount. Since the journal is used only to record purchases on account, at the end of a predetermined time period (one month for this example) the total amount will be posted twice—once to inventory (debit) and once to accounts payable (credit). However, the individual transaction amounts are posted to the accounts payable subsidiary ledger, discussed next, every time a purchase is made on account. As you can see the two primary advantages of using special journals are, first, repetitious entries are recorded in one place so it is easy to track these events and, second, time is saved in making entries and in posting.

Note that an entry in a special journal replaces one in the general journal. Thus if a company used all the special journals listed earlier, the general journal would be used only for entries that did not belong in one of the special journals.

OF INTEREST Reading the Inventory Purchase Flowchart

Flowcharts can be a bit intimidating at first, but with a little patience and practice, you can learn to read one. And the results are well worth the effort because there is a wealth of information on a flowchart concerning the flow of documents and the internal controls throughout a process. Let's look closer at the flowchart in Exhibit 8.1. Starting in the left column we see that the Inventory Control function must determine a need for inventory and then complete a document called a *purchase requisition*. This purchase requisition is sent to the Purchasing function, which prepares a *purchase order* (multiple copies). One copy of the *purchase order* is sent to the vendor (supplier), one copy goes back to the Inventory Control function so that they know the inventory has been ordered, one copy goes to the Receiving function so that they know inventory will be arriving, another copy goes to the Accounts Payable function so that they know a bill will be arriving, and the final copy is filed in chronological order (notice the little C in the triangle denoting a file). Moving now to the Receiving function we notice that when the goods are received, they prepare a *receiving report* (again, multiple copies). One copy of the *receiving report* is filed in the Receiving function (numerically) and another copy is sent back to the Purchasing function where it is attached to the related *purchase order* and filed. The third copy of the receiving report is sent to the Accounts Payable function and the last copy is sent to the Inventory Control function so that they can update the inventory subsidiary records to reflect the receipt of the inventory. Did you notice the separation of duties, appropriate authorization, and the maintenance of records through here? This is internal control!

Now let's move to the Accounts Payable function. Remember accounts payable is what the company owes its suppliers of goods and services, so this function is responsible for ensuring that bills are paid in time to take advantage of discounts when offered or by the due date when no discounts are available. The Accounts Payable function compares the *purchase order* received from the Purchasing function to the *receiving report* from the Receiving function to the *vendor's invoice* from the vendor. What are they looking for? They need to be sure that only the goods ordered and received are billed by the vendor. If everything checks out a *journal entry is made to record the purchase and the resulting liability*. Isn't it amazing that all this activity has taken place and all these documents have been completed, and this is the first accounting event that has occurred! According to this flowchart, the journal entry is made in a special journal—the purchases journal. At some later point, the event (as part of the total purchasing activity of the period) is posted to the general ledger. The purchase order, receiving report, and vendor's invoice are filed in chronological order and pulled when needed to prepare the check to be sent to the vendor. At that time they are sent to the Cashier/Controller function. The check is written to the vendor and approved and another accounting event is recorded. The *journal entry is made to record the payment and subsequent decrease in the liability, accounts payable*. Again, this flowchart reflects a special journal—the cash disbursements journal. The check is sent to the vendor, the purchase order, receiving report, and vendor invoice combo is filed, and the event is posted to the general ledger. Again, notice the internal controls at work—separation of duties, appropriate authorization, and maintenance of records.

Subsidiary Ledgers

In addition to special journals, companies often utilize **subsidiary ledgers** to record details for specific general ledger accounts. For example, assume a company purchases supplies from many different vendors. For purposes of preparing the financial statements, the company needs only to know the total amount owed to vendors. But for purposes of paying bills, the company needs to know exactly how much is owed to each vendor. Or consider a company that provides services on account to many different customers. For financial statement purposes, it needs to know the total accounts receivable balance, but for internal control purposes, it needs information to determine how much each individual customer owes. Common subsidiary ledgers are:

General Ledger Account	Purpose of Subsidiary Ledger
Accounts Payable	Charges and payments made to specific suppliers
Accounts Receivable	Charges and payments made by specific customers
Inventory	Increases and decreases to specific inventory items

For example, an accounts payable subsidiary ledger might look like the following:

Plastics, Inc., Accounts Payable Subsidiary

Date	Description	DR	CR	Balance
1-7-10			10,000.00	10,000.00
1-21-10			13,000.00	23,000.00

Therefore, this subsidiary ledger shows how much is owed to Plastics, Inc., at a particular date and how much the company has purchased from and paid to this supplier of goods and services.

Note that a subsidiary ledger provides details for, but does not replace, the general ledger. The total of all subsidiary ledger accounts for a particular general ledger account must balance to (equal) the general ledger total. Determining whether the subsidiary ledger total agrees with the general ledger total is part of the internal control system.

Also note that the use of special journals and subsidiary ledgers does not change the basic accounting process. Events are first recorded in a journal (general or special) and then posted to the ledger (general and, if appropriate, subsidiary).

Inventory

To capture data concerning purchases and payments of inventory the company has to make a couple of decisions. First, the company must decide whether it should maintain an up-to-date inventory record or update inventory records periodically (recall our discussion in Chapter 5). Second, the company must decide whether to record inventory at the net-of-discount amount or the gross amount.

Perpetual versus Periodic Inventory Systems

Perpetual inventory system
All inventory events are reflected in the Inventory account so a running balance of cost of goods available is maintained.

Periodic inventory system
All inventory events are reflected in temporary accounts, which are closed at the end of the accounting cycle.

Two types of inventory systems account for the purchase and sale (Chapter 10) of inventory: the perpetual system and the periodic system. The **perpetual inventory system** is used by companies that want to keep a running balance of the cost of inventory available for sale and the cost of goods sold during the period. The **periodic inventory system** is used by companies that need to determine the balance in inventory and the cost of goods sold only at specific points in time (the end of the accounting cycle).

In a perpetual inventory system, any accounting event that affects the balance of inventory is recorded in the inventory account. Thus all purchases of inventory are recorded as increases to the inventory account and all sales of, returns of, discounts on, and allowances for inventory are recorded as decreases to the inventory account.

In the periodic system, purchases of inventory are recorded in a temporary account, called **Purchases.** Purchase returns and allowances are recorded in another temporary account called **Purchase Returns and Allowances.** Purchase discounts (using the gross price method discussed later) are recorded in another temporary account, **Purchase Discounts.** The cost of the inventory sold is not recorded in the accounting records until the end of the period when a physical count of inventory is done.[1]

Let's compare the planning and control aspects of these two systems. The perpetual system maintains a running balance of inventory. Thus at the end of the period, a physical count of inventory can be compared to the accounting records for control purposes. The periodic system records purchases, purchase returns and allowances, and purchase discounts (gross price method) in separate accounts. With this system it is easy to determine exactly how much inventory was returned, how many discounts were taken, and how much inventory was purchased during the period. Thus both systems have benefits, so how does a company decide which system to use? Typically a company maintains a perpetual inventory for more expensive inventory items and a periodic inventory system for less expensive items. However, because technology has made maintaining perpetual systems easier and cheaper, they are becoming more prevalent.

Purchases of Inventory

Let's look at the perpetual and periodic systems. Assume that Apple maintains its direct materials inventories (for plastic cases) using a perpetual system, but its supplies inventory (for glue) is maintained using a periodic system. Since direct materials are used to make iPhones, we use an inventory account called **Direct Materials Inventory** to record

[1] If the company pays freight and/or insurance on purchases it may have one or more additional temporary accounts. For example, Freight-in is a common temporary account for recording the cost of freight on purchases.

direct material inventory events. (A merchandising company uses an inventory account called **Merchandise Inventory** or simply **Inventory** but the purchasing process illustrated next is the same.)

Assume Apple purchases $21,500 of plastic cases. (Since this is Chapter 8, Example 1, we will use 8–1 for the date.) Because Apple has the right to use the inventory for any legal purpose, its assets increase. Since Apple is not paying for the inventory at this time, its liabilities also increase. Thus,

$$\text{Assets} = \text{Liabilities} + \text{Owners' equity}$$
$$+21{,}500 \quad +21{,}500$$

In the general journal Apple would record the following:

General Journal

Date	Description	DR	CR
8–1	Direct Materials Inventory	21,500	
	Accounts Payable		21,500

Now assume that Apple purchases $500 of glue on account. Again, because Apple has the right to use the glue for any legal purpose, its assets increase. But we will use a temporary account, Purchases, to record this asset.

General Journal

Date	Description	DR	CR
8–2	Purchases	500	
	Accounts Payable		500

Notice the difference between these two inventory systems. When the perpetual system is used, the inventory account is increased (directly) for the purchase. When the periodic system is used, the purchase is recorded in a special temporary account, Purchases.

Purchase Returns and Allowances

Let's expand this example. Assume that the direct material supplier inadvertently sent Apple $2,000 of the wrong color of plastic cases. Apple must return the plastic cases and request that the supplier fix the mistake. Further assume that the type of glue Apple requested wasn't in stock so the glue vendor will give Apple a 20 percent allowance on its $500 purchase. Because Apple is not sending the glue back, the supplier will reduce Apple's bill by $100 ($500 × 0.2). What is the effect of these events? First, since Apple is sending back $2,000 of plastic cases, it needs to reduce its inventory and liabilities (you don't want to pay for something sent back).

$$\text{Assets} = \text{Liabilities} + \text{Owners' equity}$$
$$(2{,}000) \quad (2{,}000)$$

In the general journal Apple records:

General Journal

Date	Description	DR	CR
8–3	Accounts Payable	2,000	
	Direct Materials Inventory		2,000

Second, Apple needs to record the 20 percent price allowance on the $500 purchase granted by the glue vendor. This allowance also decreases liabilities. In the general journal Apple records the following:

General Journal

Date	Description	DR	CR
8–4	Accounts Payable ($500 × 0.2)	100	
	Purchase Returns and Allowances		100

Again, notice the difference between these two systems. When the perpetual system is used, the inventory account is reduced (directly) when the inventory is returned to the supplier. When the periodic system is used, the allowance (a return would work the same way) is recorded in a special temporary account, Purchase Returns and Allowances.

What have we learned about the perpetual and periodic inventory systems? With a perpetual system *all* events that affect inventory are recorded as increases or decreases to the inventory account. With a periodic system all events that affect inventory are recorded in separate temporary accounts. Therefore, with the periodic inventory system we must make an adjusting entry at the end of the period to update the inventory records. We discuss this entry later in this chapter.

Gross versus Net Price Methods

The second inventory system decision a company must make concerns what price to record for inventory. The total cost of inventory purchases is the purchase price of the inventory plus any freight paid to receive the inventory (recall the discussion of FOB shipping point versus FOB destination) plus any insurance paid on the inventory while it is in transit. So if a company purchased $10,000 of inventory, paid $300 in freight costs, and paid $200 to insure the inventory while in transit, the total cost of the inventory is $10,500. Also recall that suppliers often offer cash discounts to encourage customers to pay their bills promptly. Thus a company must decide whether to record the full cost (total cost) or the discounted cost (total cost less discount available) of the inventory. Companies use the **gross price method** to record the purchase of inventory at its full or gross price. With this method the assumption is that discounts, when received, are reductions in the purchase price of the inventory. Therefore, a purchase discount is recorded if, and only if, it is taken.

Gross price method
Inventory is recorded at its full (gross) price and discounts are recorded when taken.

Net price method
Inventory is recorded at its discounted (net) price and discounts lost are recorded if discount periods are missed.

Companies use the **net price method** to record the purchase of inventory at its discounted, or net, price. With this method the assumption is that all discounts should be taken; therefore, the cost of the inventory is the minimum amount due to the supplier. If the company fails to take the discount, the additional amount paid is, essentially, a financing charge.

Let's compare the planning and control aspects of these two methods. The gross price method records purchase *discounts when taken.* At the end of the period it is easy to determine the total *discounts taken* during the period. The net price method records *discounts lost.* Therefore at the end of the period it is easy to determine the total amount of *discounts not taken* during the period. The system chosen by the company depends on its goals and objectives. If the company assumes that all discounts should be taken and, therefore, it wants a record of any *discounts lost,* it should use the net price method. If the company assumes that discounts are a price reduction, it wants a record of all *discounts taken;* therefore, it should use the gross price method.

Purchasing Inventory

Let's examine the recording process using these two pricing methods. The journal entries in examples 8–1 to 8–4 use the gross price method, that is, the Direct Materials Inventory account or the Purchases account and the associated Accounts Payable account were recorded at the full (undiscounted) amount of the purchase.

Now let's compare the net price method to the gross price method. Let's assume that Apple decides to maintain its inventories using the net price method and that its suppliers allow a 2 percent discount. The journal entries in examples 8–5 and 8–6 reflect the purchase and return of direct materials using the net price method versus the gross price method (examples 8–7 and 8–8). Notice that the only difference is the dollar amount recorded.

Net price method, Perpetual system: Purchase and return of inventory

Date	Description	DR	CR
8–5	Direct Materials Inventory ($21,500 × 0.98)	21,070	
	Accounts Payable		21,070
8–6	Accounts Payable ($2,000 × 0.98)	1,960	
	Direct Materials Inventory		1,960

Gross price method, Perpetual system: Purchase and return of inventory (previously entries 8–1 and 8–3)

Date	Description	DR	CR
8–7	Direct Materials Inventory	21,500	
	Accounts Payable		21,500
8–8	Accounts Payable	2,000	
	Direct Materials Inventory		2,000

What if Apple had used the net price method periodic system to record glue purchases? The following entries would result:

Net price method, Periodic system: Purchase and return of inventory

Date	Description	DR	CR
8–9	Purchases	490	
	Accounts Payable		490
8–10	Accounts Payable	98	
	Purchase Returns and Allowances		98

Gross price method, Periodic system: Purchase and return of inventory (previously entries 8–2 and 8–4)

Date	Description	DR	CR
8–11	Purchases	500	
	Accounts Payable		500
8–12	Accounts Payable	2,100	
	Purchase Returns and Allowances		2,100

Paying for Inventory

Now let's see what happens when Apple pays the bill. Let's assume it pays for the direct materials within the discount period as planned. Is it entitled to take the cash discount? Yes. Has the discount been recorded? If Apple uses the net price method, the answer is yes. We recorded the inventory at the discounted amount so we need only record the payment now. If Apple uses the gross price method, the answer is no. Thus we must record the *discount taken* when we make the payment. Let's look at the resulting journal entries in each case.

Net price method: Payment within the discount period (see entries 8–5 and 8–6)

Date	Description	DR	CR
8–13	Accounts Payable ($21,070 – $1,960)	19,110	
	Cash		19,110

Gross price method: Payment within the discount period (see entries 8–7 and 8–8)

Date	Description	DR	CR
8–14	Accounts Payable ($21,500 – $2,000)	19,500	
	Cash ($19,500 × 0.98)		19,110
	Direct Materials Inventory ($19,500 × 0.02)		390

Note that in both cases, the Cash account was reduced by the amount owed—$19,110. The Accounts Payable account was reduced by the amount previously recorded as the obligation ($19,110 if the net price method is used or $19,500 if the gross price method is used). The purchase *discount taken* ($390) was recognized under the gross price method. Finally the Direct Materials Inventory is recorded at its discounted amount under both methods ($19,500 − $390 gross price method).

Now let's assume that something happened and Apple did not pay its glue supplier within the discount period. Is it entitled to the discount? No. Has the discount been recorded? If we use the net price method, the answer is yes, so we must now recognize the *discount lost.* If we use the gross price method, the answer is no, so we simply record the payment. Let's look at the resulting journal entries with each method.

Net price method: Payment after the discount period has expired (see entries 8–9 and 8–10)

Date	Description	DR	CR
8–15	Accounts Payable	392	
	Discounts Lost	8	
	Cash		400

Gross price method: Payment after the discount period has expired (see entries 8–11 and 8–12)

Date	Description	DR	CR
8–16	Accounts Payable	400	
	Cash		400

Note that in both cases, the Cash account was reduced by the amount owed—$400. The Accounts Payable account was reduced by the amount previously recorded as the obligation ($392 if the net price method is used or $400 if the gross price method is used). The **Discount Lost** ($8) was recognized under the net price method.

Let's think about recording inventory using the net price versus gross price methods (regardless of whether we use a perpetual or a periodic inventory system). In the above examples, under the net price method the plastic cases were recorded at $19,110 (see entries 8–5 and 8–6) and the glue inventory was recorded at $392 (see entries 8–9 and 8–10). On the other hand, under the gross price method, the plastic cases were recorded at $19,500 (see entries 8–7 and 8–8) while the glue inventory was recorded at $400 (see entries 8–11 and 8–12). These events are reflected in the table below:

Event	Perpetual		Periodic	
Goods	Net	Gross	Net	Gross
Purchase	21,070	21,500	490	500
Return	1,960	2,000	98	100
Balance	19,110	19,500	392	400

So does this imply that inventory is more "valuable" when we use the gross price method? Absolutely not! The same event took place under both scenarios. If the inventory is paid for during the discount period, the cost of the inventory will be further reduced by the *Discount Taken* (notice entry 8–14). But under the net price method, the inventory cost is not increased by *Discounts Lost;* rather this amount is treated as a financing cost.

Enhance Your Understanding

Where does the Discount Lost appear on the financial statements?

Answer: For internal reporting purposes, it would be a line-item on the income statement. For external reporting, it would become part of selling and administrative expenses.

Reporting Inventory Purchase and Payment Events

Inventory purchases are not reported directly on any of the financial statements; rather the balance sheet indicates the inventory on hand at the end of the accounting period. (Recall our discussion in Chapter 3 regarding shipping terms and when title passes.) Regardless of whether the perpetual or periodic inventory system is used, a physical count of inventory should be done at the end of the period and this amount should be reported on the balance sheet.

Perpetual System

If the company uses the perpetual inventory system, and the ending balance of the Inventory account does not agree with the physical count, an adjusting entry must be made. For example, assume a merchandising company's physical count of inventory reveals $50,000 of inventory on hand while the perpetual inventory system shows a $52,000 balance in the Inventory account. Clearly we must reduce the asset by $2,000 but what else happened? Since the inventory is not available to generate revenue, we must also recognize a reduction in Owners' Equity:

Assets	=	Liabilities	+	Owners' equity
(2,000)				(2,000)

The journal entry to record this loss of inventory is:

General Journal

Date	Description	DR	CR
8–17	Loss on Inventory	2,000.00	
	Merchandise Inventory		2,000.00

A loss, like an expense, reduces owners' equity because it decreases profits. Therefore, **Loss on Inventory** is a temporary account that is reported on the income statement. The difference between a loss and an expense is that a loss was not incurred in an attempt to generate revenue. Note that this is another advantage of the perpetual inventory system—losses on inventory are more easily determined because the accounting records are reconciled with the physical count of inventory.

Periodic System

If the company uses the periodic inventory system, the amount determined through physical count must be recorded as the ending balance in the Merchandise Inventory account and all the temporary accounts must be closed. For example, assume a merchandising company using the gross price method has the following account balances at the end of the year:

Merchandise inventory (beginning balance)	$ 35,000
Purchases	650,000
Purchase returns and allowances	10,000
Purchase discounts (for discounts taken)	8,000

Further assume that a physical count of merchandise inventory reveals $30,000 of inventory on hand at the end of the period. So at this point, the ledger accounts reveal the following information:

Merchandise inventory, beginning inventory	$ 35,000
Add: Purchases less returns and allowances and discounts	632,000
Cost of goods available for sale	$667,000

Now we need the accounting system to capture two things. The first is the amount of ending inventory that needs to appear on the balance sheet, and the second is the amount of cost of goods sold that needs to appear on the income statement. Since the periodic system does not capture the cost of goods sold at the time the sale is made, we must count the ending inventory ($30,000) and then determine the cost of goods sold by subtracting ending inventory from cost of goods available for sale as shown below.

Merchandise inventory, beginning inventory	$ 35,000
Add: Purchases less returns and allowances and discounts	632,000
Cost of goods available for sale	$667,000
Less: Ending inventory	30,000
Cost of goods sold	$637,000

Now we need to make a journal entry to reflect the cost of goods sold we have determined and to record the ending inventory. This journal entry will also close the temporary accounts used in the periodic system—purchases, purchase returns and allowances, and purchase discounts—so that they are ready for use in the coming period. That is, these accounts need to have a zero balance at the start of the next period. Since Purchases currently has a debit balance, we must credit the account for its balance to close it. Since Purchase Returns and Allowances and Purchase Discounts have credit balances, we will debit these accounts in the amount of their respective balances to close them. Then we will credit the Merchandise Inventory for the amount of the beginning balance to remove that balance and debit Merchandise Inventory for the amount of the ending balance to record that balance. (Note we could just adjust the account for the change, but removing the beginning balance and establishing the ending balance is a better way of indicating the purpose of the entry.)

The following entry accomplishes our objectives:

Periodic System (Closing Entry)

Date	Description	DR	CR
8–18	Merchandise Inventory (ending balance)	30,000.00	
	Purchase Returns and Allowances	10,000.00	
	Purchase Discounts	8,000.00	
	Cost of Goods Sold	637,000.00	
	Purchases		650,000.00
	Merchandise Inventory (beginning balance)		35,000.00

Note that when the periodic inventory system is used, the company can still determine if there is a loss of inventory. However the process is more complicated as it requires a comparison of purchasing records in the accounting system with sales records maintained outside the accounting system. This is one reason that companies typically maintain periodic inventory systems only for less expensive inventories.

Other Reporting Issues

If a company uses the net price method, the Discounts Lost amount is reported on the income statement. Regardless of the inventory system or costing method used, the cash paid for inventory is reported on the statement of cash flows.

A note on financial statements: Items such as Loss on Inventory and Discounts Lost are not typically reported separately on external financial statements. Rather these items are combined with other miscellaneous items and reported as a lump-sum amount. However, internally, it is important that these items are reported separately for planning and control purposes.

Enhance Your Understanding

Why would a company be reluctant to report Loss on Inventory and Discounts Lost on its external income statement?

Answer: Recall that external financial statements are publicly available. That means the company's customers and competitors have access to these statements. The company might not want its customers or competitors to know about these losses. Furthermore, for most companies these amounts are relatively small and, therefore, do not warrant a separate disclosure.

Human Resources

In Chapters 5 and 6 we discussed the planning issues concerning human resources and we learned that employees have amounts voluntarily and involuntarily withheld from their paychecks and that employers must remit these amounts to the proper authorities. In addition, employers are required to remit payroll taxes. Exhibit 8.2 illustrates the documents and records maintained for payroll activities in a transaction-based accounting system. The system illustrated is a manual system, but a computer-based system similarly utilizes transaction files and master files. Let's examine this exhibit. First note that many functions are represented in this diagram—personnel, timekeeping, payroll, and accounts payable to name a few. Next, note all the activity records (employee records, supervisor reviews, time cards, etc.) that are maintained outside the formal accounting system. Note the use of a register (a detailed listing)—the payroll register, rather than a special journal. Finally note how complicated this process is. This is one reason that payroll is typically the first computerized function in a company.

EXHIBIT 8.2 **Traditional Manual Payroll Process Flowchart**

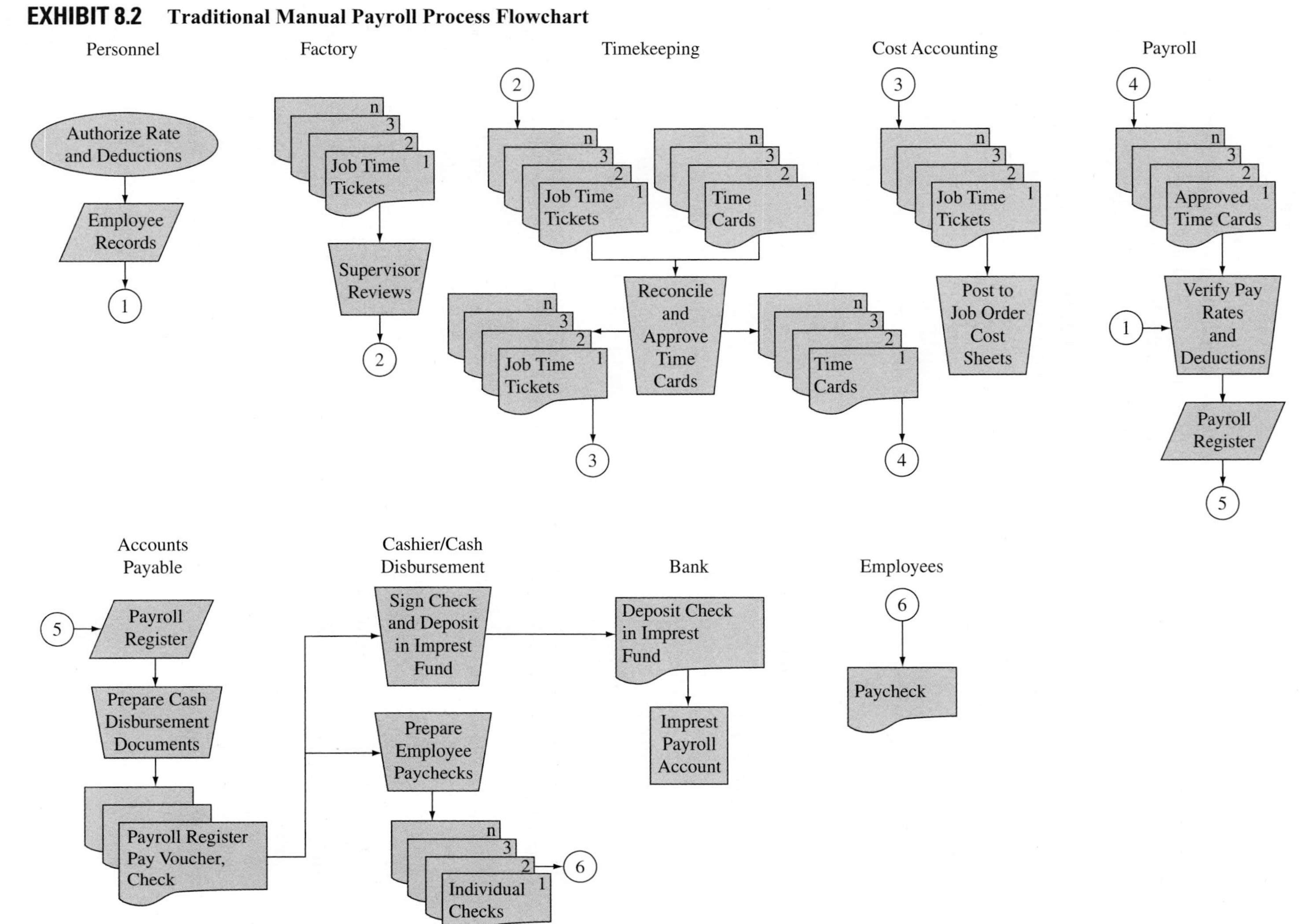

Source: A. S. Hollander, E. L. Denna, and J. O. Cherrington, *Accounting Information, Technology, and Business Solutions,* 2nd ed. (New York: McGraw-Hill, 2000), p. 342.

Withholdings from Employees

The Federal Insurance Contributions Act (FICA) requires most companies to withhold portions of employees' earnings to contribute to social security and Medicare. The 2009 withholding rates were 6.2 percent on the first $102,000 for social security and 1.45 percent for Medicare. Companies remit FICA withholding quarterly to the proper governmental agency.

Federal law and many state and local laws require employers to withhold amounts from employees for the payment of the employees' income taxes. The amount withheld depends on the amount that each individual employee earns, the length of the pay period, and the number of exemptions claimed by the employee on Form W-4. Each exemption represents a specific dollar amount by which a taxpayer can reduce the income subject to tax on the tax return. It is also used to determine the amount withheld from an employee's pay for income tax. The greater the number of exemptions claimed by the employee, the less the amount withheld from the employee's gross pay. Note that the Internal Revenue Service assesses a penalty for underwithholding, so it is important to claim your exemptions carefully. At the end of the calendar year, the employer prepares Form W-2 for each employee. It indicates the gross pay the employee earned and the amounts withheld for social security, Medicare, and income taxes during the year. This is an important internal control function because it holds the company accountable for remitting the withheld amounts to the government agencies. Income tax withholding is remitted quarterly to the proper governmental agency.

An employee may request that other amounts be withheld from gross pay for charitable contributions, retirement savings, union dues, and so forth. Again, the employer is responsible for remitting such amounts withheld to the proper authorities and reporting to the employee the amounts withheld for the year.

Employer Taxes

In addition to FICA taxes that the employer must match, employers also pay unemployment taxes. The Federal Unemployment Tax Act (FUTA) and the State Unemployment Tax Act (SUTA) require that employers pay taxes to fund and support the administration of unemployment benefits. The SUTA rate varies from state to state. It is currently approximately 5.4 percent (0.054) of each employee's first $8,000 of gross pay. SUTA credits may be granted depending on the type of industry and the company's employment history. That is, a company that has a history of infrequent layoffs will pay lower unemployment taxes. The state uses this incentive to encourage companies to minimize employee layoffs. If a company is granted the maximum SUTA tax, then the FUTA rate is 0.8 percent (0.008) of each employee's first $7,000 of gross pay. FUTA and SUTA taxes are also remitted quarterly.

There are many different laws and regulations surrounding payroll that require the use of different tax rates, schedules, and tables. This is another reason why payroll is typically one of the first activities computerized within a company.

Accounting Events in the Payroll Process

Let's assume that administrative and marketing employees at Apple earned $50,000 during the period. Further assume that the appropriate federal income tax withholding rate is 15 percent, the state rate is 5 percent, and FICA is withheld at 7.65 percent. What is the employees' net pay? Recall that net pay is gross pay less withholding as shown below:

Gross pay		$50,000
Less:	Federal income taxes	7,500 ($50,000 × 0.15)
	State income taxes	2,500 ($50,000 × 0.05)
	FICA taxes	3,825 ($50,000 × 0.0765)
Net pay		$36,175

What is the salary and wage expense for Apple—the gross pay or the net pay? It is the gross pay. The company cannot keep the amounts withheld from the employee; therefore, the entire amount earned by the employee is the expense for the company. The amounts withheld represent liabilities—the employer must remit them to the proper authorities on behalf of the employees. Thus, the company's assets are reduced by $36,175 (the amount of

FAST FACT

It pays to remember what a liability is. In 2002 a woman in Massachusetts was sentenced to six months of imprisonment for failure to submit tax withholdings to the Internal Revenue Service (IRS). According to the court, she was a proprietor of a business with 10 to 15 employees. She correctly withheld taxes from the employees' checks but then failed to submit the withholdings to the IRS. To make matters worse, she filed quarterly payroll reporting forms with the IRS indicating that she had made the payments. The investigation that led to these charges was conducted by special agents of the IRS.

Source: PR Newswire Association, April 22, 2002.

the checks written to the employees), the liabilities are increased by $13,825 (the amounts withheld from the employees), and the owners' equity is decreased by $50,000 (the amount earned by the employees—the company's salary and wage expense). Therefore,

Assets	=	Liabilities	+	Owners' equity
(36,175)		+13,825		(50,000)

The following journal entry is needed:

General Journal

Date	Description	DR	CR
8–19	Salary and Wage Expense	50,000	
	Federal Income Tax Withheld ($50,000 × 0.15)		7,500
	State Income Tax Withheld ($50,000 × 0.05)		2,500
	FICA Taxes Withheld ($50,000 × 0.0765)		3,825
	Cash		36,175

Further assume that Apple is subject to a FUTA rate of 0.8 percent and a SUTA rate of 5.4 percent. Remember it must also match the FICA withholding. So Apple owes a total of $6,925 in payroll taxes as shown here:

FUTA taxes	$ 400 ($50,000 × 0.008)
SUTA taxes	2,700 ($50,000 × 0.054)
FICA taxes	3,825 ($50,000 × 0.0765)
Total	$6,925

But unless today is the end of a quarter, Apple will not remit these amounts today, so it must record the appropriate liabilities and recognize the expense. (Companies use employees in an effort to generate revenues; therefore, payroll taxes are an expense to the company.) Thus,

Assets	=	Liabilities	+	Owners' equity
		+6,925		(6,925)

The following is the appropriate journal entry:

General Journal

Date	Description	DR	CR
8–20	Payroll Tax Expense	6,925	
	FUTA Taxes Payable ($50,000 × 0.008)		400
	SUTA Taxes Payable ($50,000 × 0.054)		2,700
	FICA Taxes Payable ($50,000 × 0.0765)		3,825

Later, when the liabilities created by this process are paid, the balances in the FICA, SUTA, FUTA, and the federal and state withholding accounts are reduced by debiting the respective accounts and crediting cash.

Reporting Human Resource Events

The amounts paid to employees are reported on the statement of cash flows as cash outflows from operations. The salary and wage expense for nonmanufacturing employees and the payroll tax expense would be reported on the income statement. (We discuss manufacturing employees in Chapter 9.) Finally any payroll-related liabilities that remain at the end of the period are reported on the balance sheet as current liabilities.

Other Expenditure Process Activities

Companies have a multitude of other expenditure process activities. For example, the company must either own or rent a place to operate from. The company uses advertising, supplies, and utilities in an effort to generate revenue. For all these items the expenditure process is, essentially, the same: (1) determine the need, (2) select a supplier and order, (3) receive the good/service, and (4) pay the supplier. As you know, sometimes the cash payment precedes the expense, sometimes the cash payment occurs after the expense, and sometimes the cash payment and the expense occur at the same time.

Cash Outflow before Expense (Assets Created)

A company that acquires a good or service but does not use it immediately has the right to use it in the future (asset). Once the company uses the good/service in an effort to generate revenue, the asset must be reduced and the expense recognized. Let's assume Apple pays its rent ($3,000 each month) for one year in advance. Has the company used this rent in an effort to generate revenue? No. Does it have the right to use this rental space for any legal purpose? Yes. Therefore,

Assets	= Liabilities	+ Owners' equity
+36,000		
(36,000)		

And,

General Journal

Date	Description	DR	CR
8-21	Prepaid Rent	36,000.00	
	Cash		36,000.00

As time passes this Prepaid Rent asset is used in an effort to generate revenue. Thus prior to preparing financial statements Apple must adjust the balance of the asset and recognize the expense as discussed in Chapter 7. Let's assume the fiscal year ends three months after the rent is paid. Therefore, the deferral adjusting entry is:

Assets	= Liabilities	+ Owners' equity
(9,000)		(9,000)

And,

General Journal

Date	Description	DR	CR
8-22	Rent Expense	9,000.00	
	Prepaid Rent		9,000.00

Let's look at another example. Assume that Apple had a zero balance in its Promotional Supplies account and it purchases $20,000 of promotional supplies on account at the beginning of the period. It pays for these promotional supplies 30 days later. At the end of the period a count of promotional supplies reveals $4,000 on hand. What happened to the other $16,000 of promotional supplies? They were used in an effort to generate revenue and, thus, at the end of the period, an expense must be recognized (as discussed in Chapter 7). Let's examine these events. First, promotional supplies (an asset) were purchased on account (a liability), therefore,

Assets	= Liabilities	+ Owners' equity
+20,000	+20,000	

And,

General Journal

Date	Description	DR	CR
8–23	Promotional Supplies	20,000.00	
	Accounts Payable		20,000.00

Then the obligation (a liability) was paid using cash (an asset); hence,

Assets	= Liabilities	+ Owners' equity
(20,000)	(20,000)	

And,

General Journal

Date	Description	DR	CR
8–24	Accounts Payable	20,000.00	
	Cash		20,000.00

Finally a count at year-end reveals $4,000 of promotional supplies on hand and, therefore, $16,000 of promotional supplies have been used. Thus, the deferral adjusting entry is:

Assets	= Liabilities	+ Owners' equity
(16,000)		(16,000)

General Journal

Date	Description	DR	CR
8–25	Promotional Supplies Expense	16,000.00	
	Promotional Supplies		16,000.00

As a final example, assume Apple purchases office equipment for $48,000. This equipment has a useful life of six years, after which Apple plans to donate it to charity. Since the equipment is used to generate revenue, we must recognize a portion of the cost of the equipment each period as an expense. Let's assume the equipment was purchased at the beginning of the accounting period for cash. Therefore,

Assets	= Liabilities	+ Owners' equity
+48,000		
(48,000)		

And,

General Journal

Date	Description	DR	CR
8–26	Office Equipment	48,000.00	
	Cash		48,000.00

At the end of the period, we must recognize depreciation expense and indirectly reduce the asset by using a contra asset account, Accumulated Depreciation, to reflect its use. Annual depreciation expense is $48,000/6 = $8,000. Thus, another deferral adjusting entry is:

Assets = Liabilities + Owners' equity

(8,000) (8,000)

And,

General Journal

Date	Description	DR	CR
8–27	Depreciation Expense	8,000.00	
	Accumulated Depreciation		8,000.00

Expense before Cash Outflow (Liabilities Incurred)

If a company uses a good or service but does not pay for it at the time, a liability must be recognized. Assume that Apple receives, but does not pay, a utility bill for the month of $1,500. Has the company incurred an expense? Yes. Apple used the services of the utility company in an effort to generate revenue. Have the services been paid? No. Therefore, Apple must record its obligation to pay this bill in the future. Therefore,

Assets = Liabilities + Owners' equity

+1,500 (1,500)

And,

General Journal

Date	Description	DR	CR
8–28	Utility Expense	1,500.00	
	Utilities Payable		1,500.00

Later when the bill is paid,

Assets = Liabilities + Owners' equity

(1,500) (1,500)

And,

General Journal

Date	Description	DR	CR
8–29	Utilities Payable	1,500.00	
	Cash		1,500.00

Let's try another event. Assume Apple uses a local accountant to provide bookkeeping services. The accountant bills the company each month for services provided and allows Apple to pay the bill in the following month. Assume that the services provided in Month One were $3,000; then,

Assets = Liabilities + Owners' equity

+3,000 (3,000)

Why? Because Apple used the services in an effort to generate revenue, an expense has been incurred. Because the company has not paid for the services provided, a liability is recognized.

Later when the accountant's bill is paid:

Assets = Liabilities + Owners' equity

(3,000) (3,000)

Enhance Your Understanding

Make sure you can make the journal entries to reflect the bookkeeping expense Apple incurred.

Answer:

Bookkeeping Expense	3,000	
Accounts Payable		3,000
Accounts Payable	3,000	
Cash		3,000

Expense Concurrent with Payment

Often companies use a good or service and immediately pay for the good or service. For example, assume that Apple pays $600 for advertising this month. Since the right will be used up in the current month, the company should recognize an expense and a cash payment. Therefore,

Assets	=	Liabilities	+	Owners' equity
(600)				(600)

And,

General Journal

Date	Description	DR	CR
8–30	Advertising Expense	600.00	
	Cash		600.00

Reporting Other Expenditure Process Activities

As with inventory purchases and human resources, the ending balance of any related asset or liability is reported on the balance sheet. The associated expenses are reported on the income statement and the cash paid is reported on the statement of cash flows as an outflow in the operating section. Exhibit 8.3 summarizes expenditure process reporting.

A note on account titles: As you have probably noticed we have expanded the types of accounts used to reflect accounting events. Each company develops its own chart of accounts to reflect the type of activities conducted. In general, account titles reveal whether the account is an asset, a liability, or an owners' equity account and give a one-word descriptor of the account. For Utility Expense, expense tells us that the account is an owners' equity account and utility tells us why the expense was incurred. The account title, FICA Taxes Payable, tells us that it is a liability (payable) for FICA taxes. As you become more familiar with accounting you will be better able to develop descriptive account titles.

EXHIBIT 8.3
Reporting Expenditure Process Events

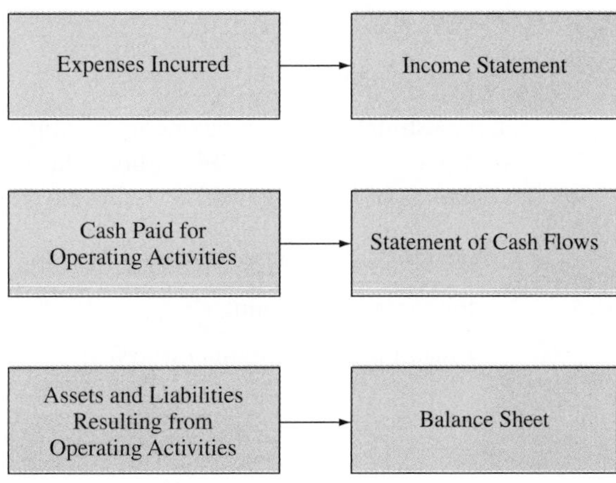

FAST FACT

To generate revenues you need a good image. Some companies spend billions of dollars to create a new image. For example, IBM in the mid-1990s changed its image from computer maker to business consultant. But not all such image changes work. In the mid-1980s, Coca-Cola tried to reinvent itself with the introduction of New Coke. But New Coke wasn't a big hit with consumers and the new image failed. Some companies build image through joint ventures, for example, Apple's joint venture with Nike (see Chapter 3).

Financial Statements and the Expenditure Process

Take a few minutes to examine Apple's financial statements (see Appendix). The income statement indicates selling, general and administrative expense of $3,761 million for fiscal 2008. The balance sheet reports in the current asset section ending inventories of $509 million and an ending balance in other current assets of $5,822 million. In the current liabilities section, Apple reports accounts payable of $5,520 million and accrued expenses of $8,572 million.

Notice that the statement of cash flows does not indicate the amount of cash paid for inventory during the period. But we can make a *very* rough estimate of this amount by examining the changes in the inventory and accounts payable accounts.

Estimating Cash Paid for Inventory

Recall that the inventory account represents:

Beginning balance
\+ Net purchases on account
= Inventory available for sale or use
− Cost of goods sold
= Ending inventory

The accounts payable account represents:

Beginning balance
\+ Net purchases on account
= Maximum amount owed to suppliers
− Cash paid to suppliers
= Ending balance

Let's estimate the cash payments of Apple to suppliers. On the income statement we find cost of goods sold is $21,334 million. On the balance sheet we find the beginning and ending balances of inventory and accounts payable. Then,

Inventory, beginning balance	$ 346
+ Purchases on account	?
= Cost of goods available for sale	$?
− Cost of goods sold (cost of sales)	21,334
= Inventory, ending balance	$ 509

With a little bit of algebra we find that purchases on account are $21,497 million ($509 + $21,334 = $21,843; $21,843 − $346 = $21,497). Now let's look at the accounts payable account.

Accounts payable, beginning balance	$ 4,970
+ Purchases on account (determined above)	21,497
= Maximum amount owed to suppliers	$26,467
− Cash paid to suppliers	?
= Accounts payable, ending balance	$ 5,520

Thus we estimate that Apple paid $20,947 ($26,467 − $5,520 = $20,947) million to suppliers for inventory during the period.

Estimating Cash Paid for Operating Expenses

We can also estimate the amount of cash paid for other operating expenses. Let's assume that XYZ Company has the following information available on its financial statements:

	Ending Balance	Beginning Balance
Prepaid insurance	$ 331,000	$ 607,000
Salaries payable	1,708,000	3,081,000
Interest payable	601,000	750,000
Insurance expense	712,000	
Salary expense	2,433,000	
Interest expense	829,000	

Let's analyze the relationship between these balance sheet and income statement accounts to estimate the cash paid to suppliers of goods and services. We will begin with Prepaid Insurance. This account represents the cash paid in advance for insurance resources to be used in the future. Therefore, the account increases when cash is paid and decreases as the resources are used (time passes) as shown below.

Prepaid insurance, beginning balance	$607,000
+ Cash paid for insurance	?
= Maximum insurance available for use	$
− Insurance expense	712,000
= Prepaid insurance, ending balance	$331,000

Using algebra, we find the amount of cash paid for insurance to be $436,000 ($331,000 +$712,000 − $607,000).

Now Let's Analyze Salaries Payable This account represents the amounts owed to employees for services provided by them for which they have not yet been paid. Therefore, the account increases when salary expense is incurred by the company and decreases when cash is paid out to the employees as shown below:

Salaries payable, beginning balance	$3,081,000
+ Salary expense	2,433,000
= Maximum amount owed to employees	$5,514,000
− Cash paid to employees	?
= Salaries payable, ending balance	$1,708,000

Thus, cash paid to employees is $3,806,000 ($5,514,000 − $1,708,000).

Finally, Consider Interest Payable This account represents the amount of interest owed to those creditors who have loaned XYZ Company money but have not yet been paid the interest due to them. Thus, the account increases when interest expense is incurred (time passes) and decreases when cash is paid to creditors for interest.

Interest payable, beginning balance	$ 750,000
+ Interest expense	829,000
= Maximum amount of interest owed	$1,579,000
− Cash paid for interest	?
= Interest payable, ending balance	$ 601,000

And, we discover that cash paid for interest is $978,000 ($1,579,000 − $601,000).

Internal Evaluation of Expenditure Process Events

In Chapters 5 and 6 we explored expenditure process planning and discovered among other things that companies develop measurable balanced scorecard goals. At the end of the accounting period (or other appropriate times) the company must compare its results against these goals. Thus, for example, the company would compare its efficiency against its goals for efficiency. It might determine the number of employees trained during the period and compare that against its plans for employee training. To measure the financial perspective the company would compare its budgeted financial results to its actual financial results. These types of comparisons help companies plan for the future by learning from successes as well as failures. We examine a tool to analyze purchases in Chapter 9.

Other items that should be evaluated include the number and amount of discounts lost (if the net price method is used) or the number and amount of discounts taken (if the gross price method is used). This evaluation is used to monitor the internal processes perspective.

Summary

In the expenditure process companies must record the results of the following accounting events: (1) receive [use] goods/services and (2) pay suppliers of goods/services. Companies must determine the type of inventory system and the pricing method to use to record inventory events. Companies must also record human resource events and other operating activities in the accounting system.

- The perpetual inventory system is used to keep a running balance of inventory while the periodic system relies on temporary accounts to track inventory.
- The gross price method is used to record inventory at its full, undiscounted cost while the net price method is used to record inventory at its discounted amount.
- The gross pay earned by employees and the payroll taxes associated with having employees are expenses to the employer.

Key Terms

Direct Materials Inventory An inventory account used in a manufacturing company to record the direct materials on hand, *220*
Discount Lost An account used under the net price method to record discounts lost, *224*
Gross price method A method used to record inventory purchases at the full price, *222*
Inventory See Merchandise Inventory, *221*
Loss on Inventory A temporary account used to report losses of inventory, *225*
Merchandise Inventory An inventory account used by a merchandising company, *221*
Net price method A method used to record inventory purchases at the discounted price, *222*

Periodic inventory system A system used by companies that need to determine the balance in inventory and the cost of goods sold only at specific points in time, *220*
Perpetual inventory system A system used by companies that want to keep a running balance of the cost of inventory available for sale and the cost of goods sold during the period, *220*
Purchase Discounts A temporary account used to record purchase discounts taken, *220*
Purchase Returns and Allowances A temporary account used to record purchase returns and purchase allowances, *220*
Purchases A temporary account used to record purchases of inventory, *220*
Special journal A journal used for transactions that occur frequently and in the same manner, *218*
Subsidiary ledger A ledger used to record details for specific general ledger accounts, *219*

Questions

1. What is the purpose of a special journal? Does it replace the general journal?
2. What is the purpose of a subsidiary ledger? Does it replace the general ledger?
3. What is the difference between a perpetual and a periodic inventory system?
4. Explain the purpose of each of the following accounts: (*a*) Purchases, (*b*) Purchase Discounts, and (*c*) Purchase Returns and Allowances.
5. What is the difference between Direct Materials Inventory and Merchandise Inventory?
6. What is the difference between the gross price method and the net price method of recording inventory purchases?
7. What is the difference between a discount taken and a discount lost?
8. What is the difference between a loss and an expense?
9. Does a company's Salary and Wage Expense reflect employees' gross pay or net pay? Why?
10. Who pays FICA taxes, the employee or the employer? Why?
11. What is the difference between prepaid rent and rent expense?
12. What is the difference between supplies and supplies expense?
13. What is the purpose of the account Accumulated Depreciation?
14. What is the difference between utilities expense and utilities payable?
15. Assume a company began the period with $5,000 of prepaid insurance. During the period, the company paid an additional $8,000 for insurance. At the end of the period, the company determined that insurance expense for the period was $12,000. On which financial statement would each of these numbers be reported?
16. A company's Inventory account increased during the period. Is cost of goods sold greater than or less than the amount of net purchases during the period? Why?
17. A company's Accounts Payable—Merchandise Inventory account decreased during the period. Were the net purchases on account greater than or less than the cash paid for purchases? Why?
18. How does a company decide whether to use a perpetual or a periodic inventory system?
19. How does a company decide whether to use the gross or net price method to record inventory?
20. Why would a company compare its actual financial results to its budgeted financial results?

Exercises

E8.1 LO 4

On January 1, 2010, the start of its fiscal year, the Stamper Company had these account balances.

	Debit	Credit
Office Supplies	$2,780	
Prepaid Insurance	2,000	
Utilities Payable		$2,200

During the year, the company was involved in the following operating events:

Jan. 14 Paid the $2,200 due on the utilities.

Mar. 15 Purchased $5,000 of office supplies on account.

Apr. 1 Paid the amount due on the office supplies.

July 1 Renewed the insurance policy by making a $6,400 cash payment for one year's premium.

Dec. 31 Received December's utility bill for $3,600, which is due January 15, 2011. A count of the office supplies indicates that $2,500 of office supplies are on hand.

Make the entries for operating events listed above and make the appropriate adjusting entries on December 31, 2010.

LO 3 **E8.2** An abbreviated payroll register for the Achermann Corporation for the week ending August 18, 2010, follows:

Employee	Gross Earnings	Federal Income Tax	FICA	Retirement Contribution
Dean	$740.00	$148.00	$56.61	$74.00
Schmidt	705.00	141.00	53.93	70.00
Lacey	580.00	104.00	44.37	50.00

Prepare the journal entry to record the following:

1. Payment of the weekly payroll.
2. The payroll taxes for this time period (SUTA is 5.4 percent and FUTA is 0.8 percent of gross earnings).

LO 3 **E8.3** At the end of the fiscal year on June 30, 2010, Weisz Industries had unpaid accrued wages of $260,000. Assuming a FICA tax rate of 7.65 percent, a FUTA tax rate of 0.8 percent, and a SUTA tax rate of 5.4 percent, prepare the adjusting entry to record Weisz's payroll tax expense.

LO 1 **E8.4** Provide the missing data for each of these three cases:

	Case 1	Case 2	Case 3
Beginning inventory	$54,000	$ 37,000	$?
Goods purchased	72,000	?	67,000
Cost of goods available for sale	$?	$?	$?
Ending inventory	41,000	13,000	26,000
Cost of goods sold	$?	$172,000	$88,000

LO 1 **E8.5** Determine the amounts in question in the following schedule:

	Company A	Company B	Company C
Beginning inventory	$ 667,800	$ 388,200	$?
Merchandise purchased	4,776,200	?	647,600
Merchandise available for sale	$?	$2,940,700	$?
Ending inventory	819,900	?	163,900
Cost of goods sold	$?	$1,457,900	$534,800

LO 1 LO 2 **E8.6** Using perpetual inventory procedures, journalize the following transactions on the books of Murray Company for August. Assume Murray Company uses the net price method of recording direct material purchases.

8 Murray Company purchased $26,800 in direct materials from Bartunek Company; terms 2/10, n/30.

12 One group of items in the August 8 purchase was not up to the purchase specifications. Murray Company requested and was granted an $1,600 allowance on the gross price of those items.

16 Murray Company paid Bartunek Company for the purchase and took advantage of the cash discount.

LO 1 LO 2 **E8.7** Refer to E8.6. Make the journal entries assuming Murray uses the gross price method.

LO 1 LO 2 **E8.8** Refer to E8.6. Make the journal entries assuming Murray uses a periodic inventory system and the net price method.

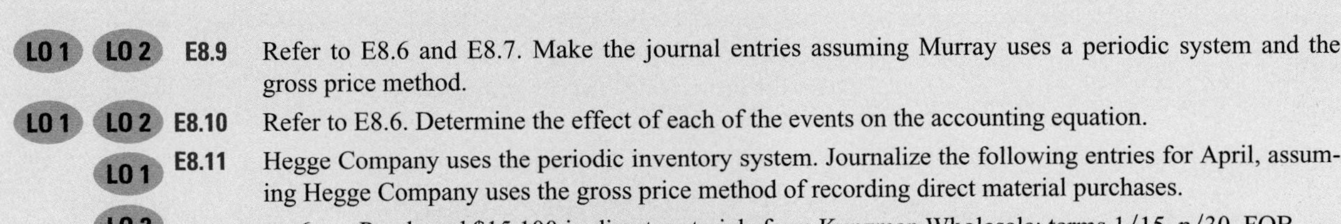

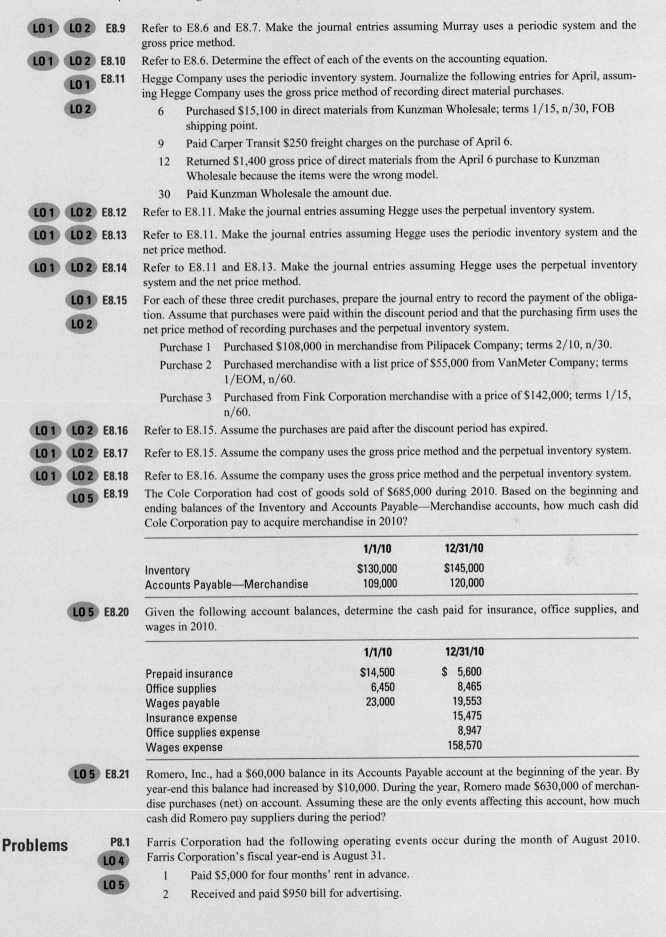

LO 1 LO 2 **E8.9** Refer to E8.6 and E8.7. Make the journal entries assuming Murray uses a periodic system and the gross price method.

LO 1 LO 2 **E8.10** Refer to E8.6. Determine the effect of each of the events on the accounting equation.

LO 1 LO 2 **E8.11** Hegge Company uses the periodic inventory system. Journalize the following entries for April, assuming Hegge Company uses the gross price method of recording direct material purchases.

6 Purchased $15,100 in direct materials from Kunzman Wholesale; terms 1/15, n/30, FOB shipping point.

9 Paid Carper Transit $250 freight charges on the purchase of April 6.

12 Returned $1,400 gross price of direct materials from the April 6 purchase to Kunzman Wholesale because the items were the wrong model.

30 Paid Kunzman Wholesale the amount due.

LO 1 LO 2 **E8.12** Refer to E8.11. Make the journal entries assuming Hegge uses the perpetual inventory system.

LO 1 LO 2 **E8.13** Refer to E8.11. Make the journal entries assuming Hegge uses the periodic inventory system and the net price method.

LO 1 LO 2 **E8.14** Refer to E8.11 and E8.13. Make the journal entries assuming Hegge uses the perpetual inventory system and the net price method.

LO 1 LO 2 **E8.15** For each of these three credit purchases, prepare the journal entry to record the payment of the obligation. Assume that purchases were paid within the discount period and that the purchasing firm uses the net price method of recording purchases and the perpetual inventory system.

Purchase 1 Purchased $108,000 in merchandise from Pilipacek Company; terms 2/10, n/30.

Purchase 2 Purchased merchandise with a list price of $55,000 from VanMeter Company; terms 1/EOM, n/60.

Purchase 3 Purchased from Fink Corporation merchandise with a price of $142,000; terms 1/15, n/60.

LO 1 LO 2 **E8.16** Refer to E8.15. Assume the purchases are paid after the discount period has expired.

LO 1 LO 2 **E8.17** Refer to E8.15. Assume the company uses the gross price method and the perpetual inventory system.

LO 1 LO 2 **E8.18** Refer to E8.16. Assume the company uses the gross price method and the perpetual inventory system.

LO 5 **E8.19** The Cole Corporation had cost of goods sold of $685,000 during 2010. Based on the beginning and ending balances of the Inventory and Accounts Payable—Merchandise accounts, how much cash did Cole Corporation pay to acquire merchandise in 2010?

	1/1/10	12/31/10
Inventory	$130,000	$145,000
Accounts Payable—Merchandise	109,000	120,000

LO 5 **E8.20** Given the following account balances, determine the cash paid for insurance, office supplies, and wages in 2010.

	1/1/10	12/31/10
Prepaid insurance	$14,500	$ 5,600
Office supplies	6,450	8,465
Wages payable	23,000	19,553
Insurance expense		15,475
Office supplies expense		8,947
Wages expense		158,570

LO 5 **E8.21** Romero, Inc., had a $60,000 balance in its Accounts Payable account at the beginning of the year. By year-end this balance had increased by $10,000. During the year, Romero made $630,000 of merchandise purchases (net) on account. Assuming these are the only events affecting this account, how much cash did Romero pay suppliers during the period?

Problems

LO 4 LO 5 **P8.1** Farris Corporation had the following operating events occur during the month of August 2010. Farris Corporation's fiscal year-end is August 31.

1 Paid $5,000 for four months' rent in advance.

2 Received and paid $950 bill for advertising.

5 Purchased $300 of office supplies on account.

15 Paid $700 for life insurance on the company president. This is a semiannual premium and the first time the company has insured the president.

21 Received phone bill for $240 to be paid on August 30.

26 Paid $365 postage to mail advertising brochures to customers.

30 Paid phone bill.

Additional Information: Account balances August 1:

Office supplies	$3,100
Information for adjusting entries:	
Office supplies on hand, August 31, 2010	1,250

Required:
A. Make the appropriate entries for the events in August.
B. Show how the results of these events are presented on Farris Corporation's financial statements.

LO 3 **P8.2** Gross pay for the employees of Adams Supply Company for September 2010 is as follows:

Office salaries	$ 56,000
Sales salaries	128,000
Warehouse salaries	112,000
Total salaries	$296,000

Information on withholding and taxes:

1. Federal income tax withheld, $62,000.
2. FICA taxes withheld on employees, $22,644.
3. State income tax withheld, $6,820.
4. Health insurance premiums withheld, $5,100.
5. Pension contributions withheld, $13,200.
6. SUTA taxes are $15,984 and FUTA taxes are $2,368.

Required:
A. Make the journal entry to record the September payroll.
B. Record the journal entry for the employer's payroll taxes.

P8.3 Dixon Company experienced the following transactions during the month of November 2010:

3 Purchased $90,200 in merchandise from Maris Manufacturing Company; terms 2/10, n/30, FOB shipping point.

11 Paid $350 freight charges to Intercontinental Transit for merchandise purchased from Maris Manufacturing Company on November 3.

15 Bought inventory items totaling $65,400 from Massoth, Inc.; terms 2/10, n/30, FOB destination.

20 Returned $8,000 (gross price) of merchandise to Massoth, Inc.

25 Sent amount due to Massoth, Inc.

28 Paid Maris Manufacturing Company amount due for inventory items purchased on November 3.

Required:
A. Make the journal entries to record the events assuming Dixon Company uses the perpetual inventory system and the net price method for recording inventory.
B. Make the journal entries to record the events assuming Dixon Company uses the perpetual inventory system and the gross price method for recording inventory.
C. Make the journal entries to record the events assuming Dixon Company uses the periodic inventory system and the net price method for recording inventory.
D. Make the journal entries to record the events assuming Dixon Company uses the periodic inventory system and the gross price method for recording inventory.

P8.4 Piesik Company had the following transactions during May 2010:

LO 2

3 Purchased direct materials from Holtman Company, $8,600; terms 1/10, n/30, FOB destination.

10 Purchased direct materials from Lambson Company with a price of $7,200; terms n/30, FOB shipping point.

12 Paid Holtman Company for the purchase of May 3.

13 Paid $150 freight and $60 for insurance on shipment from Lambson Company.

15 Returned $1,000 list price of direct materials purchased from Lambson Company because the items were damaged.

16 Purchased direct materials from Allan Company for $8,300; terms 2/10, n/60, FOB destination.

28 Paid Allan Company the amount due on the purchase of May 16.

Required:

A. Make the journal entries to record these events assuming Piesik uses the perpetual inventory system and the gross price method to record purchases.
B. Make the journal entries to record these events assuming Piesik uses the perpetual inventory system and the net price method to record purchases.
C. Make the journal entries to record these events assuming Piesik uses the periodic inventory system and the gross price method to record purchases.
D. Make the journal entries to record these events assuming Piesik uses the periodic inventory system and the net price method to record purchases.

LO 5

P8.5 The following partial income statement and partial balance sheet are for Baker Company. From this information, calculate the cash paid for inventory and for each of the operating expenses.

BAKER COMPANY
Partial Income Statement
For the Period Ending December 31, 2010

Sales		$956,000
Cost of goods sold		537,000
Gross margin		$419,000
Operating expenses:		
Wages expense	$195,000	
Advertising expense	29,000	
Rent expense	21,000	
Insurance expense	4,000	
Office supplies expense	7,000	
Payroll tax expense	21,000	
Depreciation expense	60,000	337,000
Operating income before income taxes		$ 82,000
Tax expense (30% tax rate)		24,600
Net income		$ 57,400

BAKER COMPANY
Partial Comparative Balance Sheets
At December 31, 2010, and 2009

	12/31/10	12/31/09
Current assets:		
Inventory	$85,000	$95,000
Prepaid rent	12,000	13,000
Prepaid insurance	1,700	1,200
Office supplies	800	500
Current liabilities:		
Accounts payable—merchandise	47,000	41,000
Wages payable	13,000	16,000
Income taxes payable	20,100	18,000
Employee income tax payable	5,500	4,000
FICA taxes payable	2,000	1,200
FUTA taxes payable	800	900
SUTA taxes payable	1,400	1,300

LO 3 LO 5 **P8.6** Sondeno Company has gathered the following payroll data for the month of July 2010.

Administrative salaries	$ 50,000
Sales commissions earned	60,000
Executive salaries	280,000

Assume the following rates: FICA, 7.65 percent (no employees have reached the maximum withholding for social security); federal income taxes for administrative and sales 15%, executives 25%; state income taxes, 10 percent of the federal income tax withholding; FUTA taxes, 0.8 percent; and SUTA, 5.4 percent. Assume that employees are paid at the end of each month.

Required:
A. What is the net pay for Sondeno's employees?
B. What is the total payroll-related liability for Sondeno?
C. What is the payroll-related expense for Sondeno?
D. What are the amounts to be shown on the income statement, statement of cash flows, and balance sheet?

LO 4 LO 5 **P8.7** Storey Enterprises has provided you the following information:

	Beginning Balance	Ending Balance
Prepaid rent	$ 5,000	$ 6,000
Prepaid insurance	4,000	1,500
Utilities payable	2,400	3,000
Accrued liabilities	6,800	4,300

An analysis of Storey's records reveals the following payments:

Rent paid in advance	$ 48,000
Insurance paid in advance	36,000
Payments for utilities	50,000
Payments for miscellaneous expenses	620,000

Required: Determine the expenses during the period.

LO 4 **P8.8** Refer to P8.7. Make the journal entries for the cash payments and expenses during the period.

LO 1 LO 2 **P8.9** Duthie Company had the following transactions during May 2010:

3 Purchased direct materials from Holt Company, $19,600; terms 1/10, n/30, FOB destination.

10 Purchased direct materials from Lamb Company with a price of $18,200; terms n/30, FOB shipping point.

12 Paid Holt Company for the purchase of May 3.

15 Returned $1,000 list price of direct materials purchased from Lamb Company because the items were damaged.

16 Purchased direct materials from Ellen Company for $18,800; terms 2/10, n/60, FOB destination.

31 Paid Ellen Company the amount due on the purchase of May 16.

Required:
A. Prepare the journal entry for each of the preceding events assuming Duthie uses the perpetual inventory system and the gross price method to record purchases.
B. Prepare the journal entry for each of these events assuming Duthie uses the perpetual inventory system and the net price method to record purchases.

LO 4 LO 5 **P8.10** Following are a partial income statement and a partial balance sheet for Marcy Corporation. From this information, calculate the cash paid for inventory and for each of the operating expenses.

MARCY CORPORATION
Partial Income Statement
For the Period Ending December 31, 2010

Sales	$478,000
Cost of goods sold	268,500
Gross margin	$209,500

MARCY CORPORATION (continued)
Partial Income Statement
For the Period Ending December 31, 2010

Operating expenses:		
Wages expense	$97,500	
Advertising expense	14,500	
Rent expense	10,500	
Insurance expense	2,000	
Office supplies expense	3,500	
Payroll tax expense	10,500	
Depreciation expense	30,000	168,500
Operating income before income taxes		$ 41,000
Tax expense (30% tax rate)		12,300
Net income		$ 28,700

MARCY CORPORATION
Partial Comparative Balance Sheets
At December 31, 2010, and 2009

	12/31/10	12/31/09
Current assets:		
Inventory	$95,000	$85,000
Prepaid rent	13,000	12,000
Prepaid insurance	1,200	1,700
Office supplies	500	800
Current liabilities:		
Accounts payable—merchandise	41,000	47,000
Wages payable	16,000	13,000
Income taxes payable	18,100	20,000
Employee income tax payable	4,500	5,000
FICA taxes payable	1,000	2,200
FUTA taxes payable	900	800
SUTA taxes payable	1,300	1,400

Cases

C8.1 LO 5 Refer to the company you chose in C1.1. Based on your knowledge of this company, answer the following.

A. Estimate the cash paid for inventory.
B. Estimate the cash paid for operating expenses.
C. What additional information is disclosed in the notes concerning inventories, human resources, and operating expenses?

LO 4 LO 5 **C8.2** Refer to the income statement and balance sheet of Gateway in Exhibits 8.4 and 8.5 on the next page.

Required:

A. Using the Accounts Payable account, estimate the cash paid for inventory in 2000.
B. Using the Accrued Liabilities and Other (current assets) accounts, estimate the cash paid for operating expenses in 2000.

Critical Thinking

CT8.1 LO 1 LO 5 The Jenkins Corporation, a merchandising company, wants to include the cost of operating its warehouse in the cost of inventory. The company's controller argues that the cost of the warehouse is a reasonable and necessary cost of getting the inventory ready for sale and, therefore, should be included in the cost of the inventory. What impact will this decision have on the firm's income statement and balance sheet? Do you think the controller is justified in his actions? Why?

LO 3 **CT8.2** Design a payroll register.

Ethical Challenges

EC8.1 LO 2 Mr. X, the owner of XYZ Company is having some cash flow problems. He is unable to take discounts on inventory and, in fact, is having trouble paying his inventory invoices as they become due. The XYZ Company maintains its inventory using the perpetual inventory system and the net price method.

EXHIBIT 8.4
Gateway's Consolidated Income Statements

	2000	1999	1998
Net sales	$9,600,600	$8,964,900	$7,703,279
Cost of goods sold	7,541,606	7,127,678	6,290,227
Gross profit	2,058,994	1,837,222	1,413,052
Selling, general and administrative expenses	1,547,701	1,241,552	918,825
Operating income	511,293	595,670	494,227
Other income (loss), net	(102,693)	67,809	47,021
Income before income taxes	408,600	663,479	541,248
Provision for income taxes	155,266	235,535	194,849
Net income before cumulative effect of change in accounting principle	253,334	427,944	346,399
Cumulative effect of change in accounting principle, net of tax	(11,851)	—	—
Net income	$ 241,483	$ 427,944	$ 346,399
Net income per share before cumulative effect of change in accounting principle:			
Basic	$ 0.79	$ 1.36	$ 1.11
Diluted	$ 0.76	$ 1.32	$ 1.09
Net income per share after cumulative effect of change in accounting principle:			
Basic	$ 0.75	$ 1.36	$ 1.11
Diluted	$ 0.73	$ 1.32	$ 1.09
Weighted average shares outstanding:			
Basic	321,742	313,974	311,084
Diluted	331,320	324,421	317,857

For the years ended December 31, 2000, 1999, and 1998 (in thousands, except per share amounts).

EXHIBIT 8.5
Gateway's Consolidated Balance Sheets

	2000	1999
Assets		
Current assets:		
Cash and cash equivalents	$ 483,997	$1,127,654
Marketable securities	130,073	208,717
Accounts receivable, net	544,755	646,399
Inventory	315,069	191,870
Other	793,166	522,225
Total current assets	2,267,060	2,696,805
Property, plant and equipment, net	897,414	745,660
Intangibles, net	165,914	52,302
Other assets	822,156	459,921
	$4,152,544	$3,954,688
Liabilities and Shareholders' Equity		
Current liabilities:		
Accounts payable	$ 785,345	$ 898,436
Accrued liabilities	556,323	609,132
Accrued royalities	138,446	153,840
Other current liabilities	150,920	148,302
Total current liabilities	1,631,034	1,809,710
Other long-term liabilities	141,171	127,860
Total liabilities	1,772,205	1,937,570
Commitments and contingencies		
Shareholders' equity:		
Preferred stock, $.01 par value, 5,000 shares authorized; none issued and outstanding	—	—
Class A common stock, nonvoting, $.01 par value, 1,000 shares authorized; none issued and outstanding	—	—
Common stock, $.01 par value, 1,000,000 shares authorized; 323,955 shares and 320,016 shares issued in 2000 and 1999, respectively	3,239	3,200
Additional paid-in capital	741,646	656,870
Common stock in treasury, at cost, 552 shares and 730 shares in 2000 and 1999, respectively	(21,948	(51,796)
Retained earnings	1,650,335	1,408,852
Accumulated other comprehensive income (loss)	7,067	(8)
Total shareholders' equity	2,380,339	2,017,118
	$4,152,544	$3,954,688

December 31, 2000, and 1999 (in thousands, except per share amounts).

Mr. X wants to switch to the periodic inventory systems and the gross price method because he believes that doing so will make his balance sheet look better. Is it ethical and/or logical for XYZ Company to make this switch? Why or why not?

LO 3 EC8.2 When a company computes an employee's withholdings for income taxes, they use the information provided by the employee on the employee's W4, which indicates the employee's filing status (married, single, etc.) and the number of dependents. An employee is not allowed to determine a flat amount to be deducted each payroll period. Assume that you are working in the payroll department of a large corporation and you notice that a new employee has filled out a W4 claiming 10 dependents. You went to high school with this particular person and happen to know that s/he is single and has no children. What should you do?

Computer Applications

CA8.1 LO 3 Jordan Enterprises is preparing its biweekly payroll. The company has 10 employees. Each employee earns $10 per hour but Jordan pays an overtime premium of 50 percent of the hourly wage for any hours exceeding 80 in a pay period. The company would like you to set up a spreadsheet that it can use to prepare payroll in the future. The following rates apply:

Federal income tax	15%
State income tax	10% of the federal withholding
Social security	6.2%
Medicare	1.45%
Federal unemployment tax	0.8%
State unemployment tax	5.4%

Hours worked:

Scott	85
David	90
Stan	80
Sandy	70
Janice	100
Suzanne	83
Ryan	84
Laverne	89.5
Laura	75.5
Ema	80

LO 5 CA8.2 Set up a spreadsheet that can be used to estimate cash paid for inventory. Then determine the cash paid for inventory with the following parameters:

A.	Inventory, beginning	$ 10,000
	Inventory, ending	20,000
	Accounts Payable, beginning	8,000
	Accounts Payable, ending	12,000
	Cost of Goods Sold	450,000
B.	Inventory, beginning	$ 20,000
	Inventory, ending	30,000
	Accounts Payable, beginning	16,000
	Accounts Payable, ending	24,000
	Cost of Goods Sold	900,000
C.	Inventory, beginning	$ 20,000
	Inventory, ending	10,000
	Accounts Payable, beginning	12,000
	Accounts Payable, ending	8,000
	Cost of Goods Sold	450,000
D.	Inventory, beginning	$ 70,000
	Inventory, ending	80,000
	Accounts Payable, beginning	38,000
	Accounts Payable, ending	50,000
	Cost of Goods Sold	875,000

LO 3 CA8.3 Go to the IRS Web site (**www.irs.gov**) and determine what an EIN is and why it is important.

Visit the text Online Learning Center at **www.mhhe.com/ainsworth6e** for additional problem material that accompanies this chapter.

CHAPTER NINE

Recording and Evaluating Conversion Process Activities

Learning Objectives

LO 1 Explain the different types of manufacturing costs and how manufacturing costs are different than nonmanufacturing costs.

LO 2 Describe manufacturing cost flows for direct materials and direct labor and record these activities.

LO 3 Explain the process of applying manufacturing overhead and record these activities.

LO 4 Discuss the purpose of and prepare a cost of goods manufactured report.

LO 5 Conduct a variance analysis for direct materials and direct labor.

In Chapter 8 we examined the recording process in the expenditure process. In this chapter we continue our discussion of the recording process by examining the conversion process. As you know, the conversion process consists of the following activities:

- Schedule production.
- Obtain direct materials (internal transfer).
- Use labor and other manufacturing resources to convert direct materials into finished goods.
- Store finished goods until sold.

As we learned in Chapter 7, all of these activities are business events, but the first one is not an accounting event because it doesn't have an impact on the company's assets, liabilities, and/or owners' equity. The latter three events impact the company's assets, liabilities, and owners' equity as the company adds value by converting direct materials first into work-in-process and then into finished goods. As we discussed in Chapter 7 information regarding all business events is maintained by the company. In a database (ERP) system this information is integrated. In a transaction-based system (manual or computerized) information concerning accounting events is maintained in the accounting system while other information is maintained outside the formal accounting system.

Exhibit 9.1 illustrates the conversion process in a manual accounting system. Note the activity records (materials requisition, production order, job ticket) maintained outside the accounting system. Also note the basic flow of information. Production is scheduled (production control) and materials are requisitioned (requested) from inventory. In cost accounting departments costs are recorded, while in the factory goods are manufactured. Because the activities of the conversion process are internal to the company and do not have outside verification, internal controls are extremely important. Let's examine some of these internal control documents.

- Production order—issued by the production function, prenumbered; production cannot begin without a production order.
- Materials requisition—issued by the production function, verified by the inventory control function; materials are released only when the requisition is received.
- Job cost record—maintained by the cost accounting function, updated daily, verified with the general ledger records discussed below and the production function.

Manufacturing Inventories

A manufacturing firm typically maintains three types of inventory accounts in the general ledger, each of which reflects a different aspect of the manufacturing process:

- **Direct Materials Inventory**—the costs incurred to purchase and receive direct materials (introduced in Chapter 8).
- **Work-in-Process Inventory**—the costs of products started but not yet completed.
- **Finished Goods Inventory**—the costs of products completed but not yet sold.

These three accounts, called *control accounts,* actually reflect a summary of individual costs for many items maintained in separate subsidiary ledgers. For example, the Direct Materials Inventory account of Apple represents the costs of all direct materials stored for use in production, such as plastic cases, components, and processors. The Work-in-Process Inventory account represents the costs of all products, such as computers and iPhones, which are still in the production process. The Finished Goods Inventory account represents the cost of these same products that are finished but not sold.

Exhibit 9.2 illustrates the cost flows through the various manufacturing inventories during the conversion process and the related product flows from suppliers to customers. Notice that the cost flows mirror the physical product flows. As direct materials are physically

EXHIBIT 9.1 **Conversion Process**

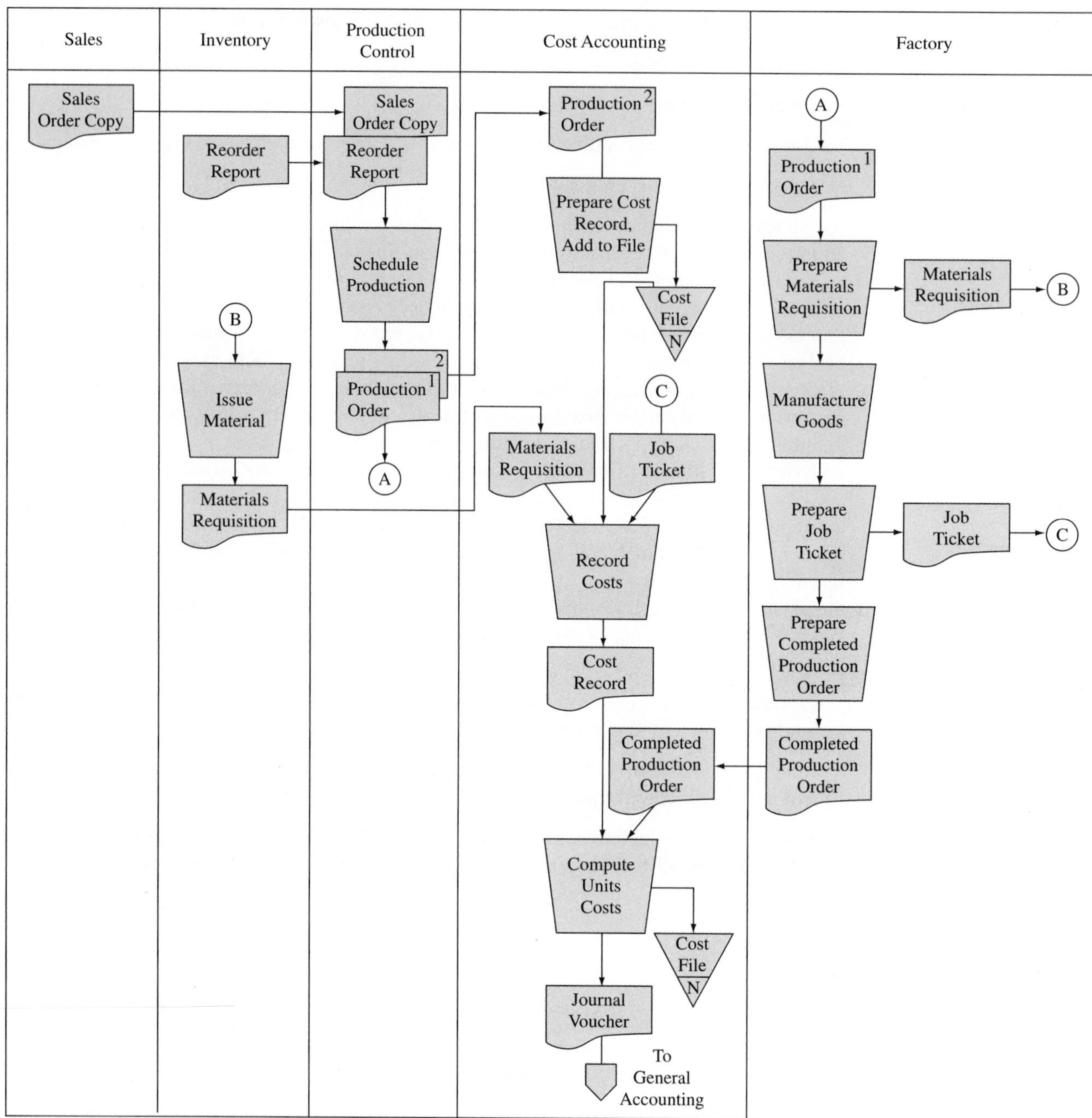

Source: J. L. Boockholdt, *Accounting Information Systems,* 5th ed. (New York: McGraw-Hill, 1999), p. 666.

moved from the storeroom to the factory where they are issued into production, their cost is transferred from Direct Materials Inventory to Work-in-Process Inventory. As products are finished and physically transferred from the factory to the finished goods warehouse, their cost is transferred from Work-in-Process Inventory to Finished Goods Inventory. Note also that product costs become expenses (cost of goods sold) when the products are sold.

To keep track of the items making up the control accounts, companies like Apple maintain subsidiary ledgers, which we introduced in Chapter 8. For example, as Exhibit 9.3 illustrates, Apple might maintain one subsidiary ledger for plastic cases, another for components,

EXHIBIT 9.2
Cost Flows and Product Flows in the Conversion Cycle

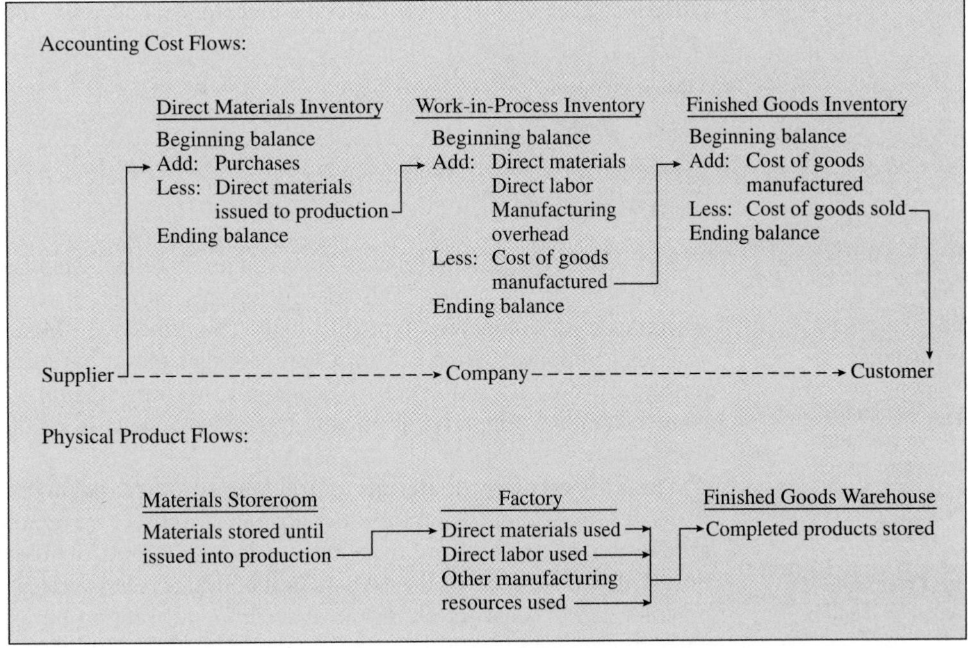

EXHIBIT 9.3
Work-in-Process Control and Subsidiary Ledgers

Control Account

Direct Materials Inventory

Beginning balance	8,000		
Purchases	100,000	80,000	Issued into production
Ending balance	28,000		

Subsidiary Ledgers (see Note below)

	Plastic Cases		**Components**		**Processors**	
Beginning balances	5,000	50,000	2,500	25,000	500	5,000
Purchases	60,000		30,000		10,000	
Ending balances	15,000		7,500		5,500	

Note: The total of ending balances in the subsidiary ledgers for plastic cases, components, and processors ($15,000 + $7,500 + $5,500) equals the ending balance in the Direct Materials Inventory control account ($28,000).

and a third for processors. The total of all the ending balances in the individual direct materials subsidiary ledgers equals the total of the Direct Materials Inventory control account. The same is true for each of the other inventory control accounts, which we discuss below as we analyze conversion process events.

Now that you understand the cost and product flow of conversion activities in manufacturing firms, we will examine the analysis and recording of the conversion process events in a company's accounting system. We look first at the analysis and recording of materials and labor costs; then we turn our attention to analyzing and recording manufacturing overhead.

Recording Raw Material Activities

As indicated in Chapter 8, when companies purchase materials, the costs of acquiring them along with any related freight or insurance charges are recorded as inventory (perpetual system)—in this case as Direct Materials Inventory. To review let's assume that Apple purchases $102,500 of direct materials inventory on account; the following journal entry is needed:

General Journal

Date	Description	DR	CR
9–1	Direct Materials Inventory	102,500	
	Accounts Payable		102,500

Direct materials
Materials that are physically traceable and expensive enough to warrant tracing.

Indirect materials
Recorded as supplies.

The direct materials purchases costs remain in Direct Materials Inventory until the production department requisitions these materials into production. When indirect materials are purchased, companies typically debit "Supplies" or "Manufacturing Overhead." We will use "Supplies." Recall from Chapter 4 that **direct materials** are physically traceable to the final product and expensive enough to warrant tracing. On the other hand, **indirect materials** either cannot be physically traced or the cost is small enough that tracing is not warranted.

The cost of direct materials is transferred to Work-in-Process Inventory when the items are requisitioned into production. Since indirect materials are not traced directly to production, their costs are assigned to manufacturing overhead when they are requisitioned. The allocation of these costs to the product is discussed later. If Apple treats components and processors as direct materials and treats glue as an indirect material, the entry to transfer $150,000 of components, $25,000 of processors, and $5,000 of glue into production is:[1]

General Journal

Date	Description	DR	CR
9–2	Work-in-Process Inventory ($150,000 + $25,000)	175,000	
	Manufacturing Overhead	5,000	
	Direct Materials Inventory		175,000
	Manufacturing Supplies		5,000

Once materials are issued into production, the company uses labor and manufacturing overhead to convert these materials into finished goods. We look at the labor component of the conversion process next.

Recording Labor Activities

Direct labor
The cost of employees who actually work on the product.

Indirect labor
The cost of employees who support manufacturing operations.

As you know, the cost of labor is the sum of the employees' gross wages. In addition, other employee-related costs, such as employer taxes and the costs of on-the-job training provided to employees, and the fringe benefits they receive are labor costs.

Like materials, labor must be classified as direct or indirect. Recall that **direct labor** refers to those employees who actually manufacture the product. **Indirect labor,** on the other hand, refers to those employees whose services support manufacturing, such as janitorial services in the factory. As labor is used in the production process, the total labor cost is recorded in the Work-in-Process Inventory account for direct labor and in the Manufacturing Overhead account for indirect labor.

Recall that in Chapter 8 we recorded the wages employees earn in an account called Salary and Wage Expense. Manufacturing wages are different, however, because we assume that this cost adds value to the product, and thus, it must be recorded as an asset until the product is sold.

For example, assume that on Friday, January 25, manufacturing employees of Apple submit their timecards for the hours worked that week. Further assume that there are two

[1] Another company might treat glue as a direct material. A company must determine whether a given material is direct or indirect based on its ability and willingness to trace the cost of the material.

groups providing labor. One group, direct labor, worked 6,000 hours at $12 per hour, for a total of $72,000 direct labor cost. The other group, indirect labor, earned a salary of $3,000 for the week. We show the related journal entry to record the payment of the manufacturing payroll, ignoring withholdings that we examined in Chapter 8. As is the case for indirect materials, indirect labor is not traced to specific products; therefore, its cost is assigned to manufacturing overhead.

General Journal

Date	Description	DR	CR
9–3	Work-in-Process Inventory	72,000	
	Manufacturing Overhead	3,000	
	Wages Payable		75,000

Enhance Your Understanding

What is the impact if direct labor wages are incorrectly recorded as salary and wage expense?

Answer: Work-in-Process Inventory (and Finished Goods Inventory discussed later) and Cost of Goods Sold would be understated and Operating Expenses would be overstated. In addition, if the company sets its selling prices based on the cost of its products (Chapter 5) it might set its selling prices too low.

Recording Manufacturing Overhead Events

Manufacturing overhead is a temporary account used to reflect the indirect manufacturing costs of the period. Recall that indirect manufacturing costs are all product costs other than direct material and direct labor. In addition to indirect materials and indirect labor, the category includes many other costs incurred in the manufacturing process that are not directly traceable to specific products. These costs include items such as supplies used to maintain the production equipment, utilities used in the manufacturing process, and property taxes paid on the production facilities. To keep track of these various costs, companies maintain one or more temporary accounts known collectively as manufacturing overhead. Next we look at how companies use these accounts during the conversion cycle.

Actual Manufacturing Overhead

Actual manufacturing overhead
The amount of overhead incurred during the accounting cycle.

As companies incur manufacturing overhead costs (rent, supplies, depreciation, etc.) during the period, the manufacturing overhead accounts are increased (debited) and the related cash, payable, or other relevant accounts are credited for the actual cost incurred. **Actual manufacturing overhead,** then, is the amount of overhead incurred during the period, recorded as debits to Manufacturing Overhead when the cost is incurred.

For example, assume that Apple incurs the following manufacturing overhead costs, in addition to indirect materials and indirect labor, during the month:

Production utilities paid	$ 5,600
Rent paid on production facilities	12,000
Depreciation on production equipment	20,000
Insurance used for production facilities	3,000
Total manufacturing overhead	$40,600

Apple would make the following journal entry in its accounting records to reflect these costs, assuming that the insurance was prepaid and that the utilities and rent are paid in cash:

General Journal

Date	Description	DR	CR
9–4	Manufacturing Overhead	40,600	
	Cash ($5,600 + $12,000)		17,600
	Accumulated Depreciation—Equipment		20,000
	Prepaid Insurance		3,000

Notice that the manufacturing overhead costs incurred are recorded in the Manufacturing Overhead account rather than in the Work-in-Process Inventory account because they are indirect costs. The debit side of the Manufacturing Overhead account reflects the actual costs incurred for overhead items. It is then necessary to somehow assign overhead costs to the products themselves. The process of assigning manufacturing overhead to work-in-process inventory is called *applying manufacturing overhead,* which we discuss next.

Again, recall the events in Chapter 8. When we used rent and depreciation, they were recorded as expenses. However when these costs are incurred in connection with production of a product, it is assumed that the cost adds value to the product and, therefore, the cost is recorded as an asset until the product is sold.

Applied Manufacturing Overhead

The difficulty dealing with actual overhead is that it occurs sporadically during the accounting period, whereas production is more continuous throughout the period. We need a system, then, that will match the overhead costs with the production activities. The process of applying overhead to production serves to smooth the overhead costs throughout the conversion process and match the costs with the activities that cause them. Therefore, the amount applied during the production process is an estimate of the actual cost that will be incurred during the production period.

Applied manufacturing overhead
The amount of overhead allocated to the work-in-process during the accounting cycle.

Applied manufacturing overhead is the amount of manufacturing overhead applied to work-in-process during the period, recorded as credits to Manufacturing Overhead. The following entry applies $56,700 of manufacturing overhead to the Work-in-Process Inventory account. Because this entry applies estimated overhead to production, it is not dependent on the actual incurrence of an overhead cost and can be done throughout the accounting period whenever it is convenient and necessary. Note that the Manufacturing Overhead account was debited for the actual overhead while the account is credited for the applied overhead.

General Journal

Date	Description	DR	CR
9–5	Work-in-Process Inventory	56,700	
	Manufacturing Overhead		56,700

The application of overhead is the responsibility of the accounting function, which relies heavily on the purchasing, production, and human resources functions for information about cost drivers and estimated overhead costs. We now discuss this application process.

Overhead Application Process Using ABC

Recall from Chapter 3 that different costs vary with different activities and that activities are measured using cost drivers. **Activity-based costing (ABC)** is a system for assigning costs (overhead, in this case) to cost objects (Work-in-Process inventory, in this case) based on the consumption of cost drivers. Thus an activity-based costing system uses more than one predetermined overhead rate to assign overhead costs to production. This ensures that the amount of overhead assigned is representative of the resources consumed.

ABC Application Process Steps

We illustrate the ABC manufacturing overhead application process next. The process of applying manufacturing overhead to production in an ABC system has six steps. The first five steps occur prior to the start of the period, while the last step occurs throughout the period.

Step 1: Identify and Classify Production Activities by Level When companies use an activity-based costing system, they first assign estimated manufacturing overhead costs to cost pools. A **cost pool** is a group of costs that change in response to the same cost driver. For example, all the costs associated with producing computers could be grouped into one cost pool while the costs associated with research and development of iPhones would be grouped into a different cost pool. The company also must choose an appropriate cost driver; that is, the cost driver that best measures the activity in the conversion process that causes conversion process costs to change. Also recall that costs and their cost drivers are typically identified at four different levels: facility-sustaining, product-sustaining, batch-related, and unit-related. Exhibit 9.4 identifies various activities, types of costs, and cost drivers that pertain to manufacturing operations.

Step 2: Determine the Appropriate Cost Driver for Each Activity Because cost drivers are measures used for the activities being performed, they must relate as closely as possible to the activities examined. For example, designing products is a product-sustaining activity that develops products for consumers. Therefore, an appropriate cost driver to use for this activity might be the number of design hours required to develop a product. In another case, owning buildings is a facility-sustaining activity because it maintains the company's ability to produce products. Therefore, the number of square feet used is an appropriate cost driver because it measures the size of the facilities. Finally, cutting or drilling products is a unit-related activity because it must be done on each individual unit produced. The number of machine hours is an appropriate cost driver if the cutting or drilling is done by machines.

Step 3: Estimate the Amount of Overhead Related to Each Cost Driver After the company identifies the costs and cost drivers, it must estimate how much of each will be incurred during the coming period. Based on this estimate, the overhead application rates are calculated.

EXHIBIT 9.4 **Activity-Based Costs and Cost Drivers**

Activity Level	Type of Activity	Type of Cost	Type of Cost Driver
Facility-sustaining	Owning buildings	Depreciation	Number of square feet
	Occupying buildings	Property taxes	Number of square feet
	Using buildings	Utilities	BTUs of heat required
	Maintaining buildings	Insurance	Number of square feet
Product-sustaining	Testing products	Equipment costs	Number of tests required
	Designing products	Engineering salaries	Number of hours of design time
	Maintaining parts inventory	Carrying costs	Number of distinct parts required
	Using specialized machinery	Depreciation	Number of specialized processes required
Batch-related	Ordering parts	Ordering costs	Number of orders placed
	Setting up machines	Setup costs	Number of production runs
	Handling materials	Moving costs	Number of moves required
	Requisitioning parts	Requisition costs	Number of requisitions made
Unit-related	Cutting/drilling units	Power costs	Machine time used
	Assembling units	Indirect labor	Complexity of process
	Painting units	Indirect materials	Painting time required
	Inspecting units	Rework costs	Number of units reworked

Step 4: Estimate the Amount of Each Cost Driver to Be Used Estimating the quantities of cost drivers to use requires input from those in charge of the related activities. Normally this occurs as part of the planning and budgeting process.

Step 5: Determine the Predetermined Overhead Rate for Each Cost Driver Calculating the **predetermined overhead rate** (overhead application rate) for each cost driver involves dividing the estimated total manufacturing overhead amount for the cost pool by the estimated amount of the appropriate cost driver. The predetermined overhead rate is used throughout the period as the estimate of manufacturing overhead per unit of cost driver. The number of predetermined overhead rates, then, depends on the number of cost pools used. When determining how many cost pools to use and, therefore, how many overhead rates to calculate, the accountant must weigh the benefits of more accurate costing against the costs incurred to provide additional information.

Step 6: Apply Manufacturing Overhead to Work-in-Process Inventory Using the Predetermined Overhead Rate Finally, during the conversion process, the accounting department applies manufacturing overhead to the Work-in-Process Inventory account as the cost driver is used, not as the overhead is incurred. We apply overhead by multiplying the predetermined overhead rate by the actual amount of the cost driver used and then adding this amount to the Work-in-Process Inventory account.

ABC Illustration

We use the following simplified example to illustrate the application of manufacturing overhead to production using activity-based costing. Exhibit 9.5 shows the activities, the estimated costs, and the appropriate cost drivers for the coming period in connection with the production of iPhones.

Step 1: Identify Levels and Activities For simplicity we assume one facility-sustaining activity, one product-sustaining activity, one batch-related activity, and one unit-related activity for this example.

Step 2: Choose Cost Drivers Take a minute to analyze why each cost driver shown in Exhibit 9.5 is appropriate. For example, the number of production runs is an appropriate cost driver for setting up and inspecting production because each production run must be analyzed to ensure that it meets quality standards.

Step 3: Estimate Costs The activities identified in Step 1 result in four cost pools, with four respective cost drivers.

Step 4: Estimate Cost Driver Usage Assume that a budgeting analysis of iPhones and the other Apple products reveals the following:

- Total production facilities (for iPhones and other products) occupy 200,000 square feet.
- The product development department estimates using 1,000 tests (total for all product lines).

EXHIBIT 9.5
Activity-Based Costing for iPhones

Activity Level	Type of Activity	Estimated Cost	Appropriate Cost Driver
Facility-sustaining	Using building	$500,000	Number of square feet
Product sustaining	Developing products	200,000	Number of tests required
Batch-related	Setting up and inspecting production	240,000	Number of production runs
Unit-related	Using machines	80,000	Number of machine hours required

- 160 production runs are planned, in total, for all products.
- Machinery is expected to operate 5,000 hours, in total, during the coming period.

Step 5: Calculate Predetermined Overhead Rate To calculate the predetermined overhead rates, divide the amount of each estimated cost pool by its estimated cost driver. Using the numbers presented in steps 3 and 4, we calculate the predetermined overhead rates for each cost driver as follows:

Building costs:	\$500,000/200,000 square feet = \$2.50 per square foot occupied
Product development costs:	\$200,000/1,000 tests = \$200 per test
Setup and inspection costs:	\$240,000/160 production runs = \$1,500 per production run
Machine costs:	\$80,000/5,000 machine hours = \$16 per machine hour

Step 6: Apply Overhead Assume that during the period, the production of iPhones actually required the following resources:

- 20,000 square feet of building space
- 180 tests
- 12 production runs
- 400 machine hours

Using the predetermined overhead rates calculated in step 5, manufacturing overhead is applied to the production of iPhones as follows:

Building costs:	20,000 square feet × \$2.50 = \$50,000
Product development costs:	180 tests × \$200 = \$36,000
Setup and inspection costs:	12 production runs × \$1,500 = \$18,000
Machine usage costs:	400 machine hours × \$16 = \$6,400

The accounting department would reflect the application of these costs to the Work-in-Process Inventory account by making the following summary entry:

General Journal

Date	Description	DR	CR
9–6	Work-in-Process Inventory—iPhones	110,400	
	Manufacturing Overhead—Building		50,000
	Manufacturing Overhead—Product Development		36,000
	Manufacturing Overhead—Setup and Inspection		18,000
	Manufacturing Overhead—Machine Usage		6,400

This summary entry reflects all the entries made during the year. The actual number of entries made depends on the accounting system and when the necessary information becomes available. For example, machining overhead would be applied whenever the production function reports the number of machine hours used, perhaps daily. Product development overhead would be applied whenever the product development function reports the number of tests performed, probably weekly. Building overhead might be applied monthly because it is convenient and efficient for the accounting department to do this as part of the monthly reporting process.

Over- and Underapplied Manufacturing Overhead

As you have seen, a company records both actual and applied overhead in the same manufacturing overhead account for each individual cost pool. Let's review:

- *Actual overhead* (debit to Manufacturing Overhead) is the actual amount of overhead incurred for the various overhead items consumed during the entire production process.
- *Applied overhead* (credit to Manufacturing Overhead) is the estimated consumption of overhead resources based on the actual usage of the various cost drivers.

Rarely does the amount of actual overhead equal the amount of applied overhead, so the individual manufacturing overhead accounts show balances at the end of the accounting period. If there is a debit balance in the account, the actual manufacturing overhead for the period is greater than the applied manufacturing overhead. In this case, overhead is *underapplied* for that overhead cost pool. **Underapplied overhead** implies that the amount of overhead applied to Work-in-Process Inventory throughout the period was not as much as the actual amount of manufacturing overhead cost incurred to produce the products. Therefore, the cost of the products manufactured during the period is *understated.*

Conversely, a credit balance in the manufacturing overhead account would indicate that the amount of applied overhead was greater than the actual overhead, and, therefore, that overhead is *overapplied* for that cost pool. With **overapplied overhead,** the amount of overhead applied to Work-in-Process Inventory is greater than the actual amount of overhead for that cost pool. Thus the cost of the products manufactured during the period is *overstated.*

In either case, the balance in the manufacturing overhead account must be closed because it is a temporary account. If the balance is small, it is closed to Cost of Goods Sold because the amount of over- or understating is not large enough to warrant tracing it to partially completed products (Work-in-Process Inventory), completed products (Finished Goods Inventory), and products sold (Cost of Goods Sold).[2]

Now that you understand how to analyze and record direct materials, direct labor, and manufacturing overhead, we examine how to analyze and record the cost of finished products.

Recording Finished Goods

As the production process is completed, it is necessary to transfer the cost of manufacturing the products, called **cost of goods manufactured,** from Work-in-Process Inventory to Finished Goods Inventory. Cost of goods manufactured includes costs of direct materials, direct labor, and applied manufacturing overhead. Assume that, during the period, Apple completed the production of 6,000 iPhones at a cost of $842,000. The following summary entry reflects the transfer of costs from Work-in-Process Inventory to Finished Goods Inventory when the product is completed:

General Journal

Date	Description	DR	CR
9–8	Finished Goods Inventory	842,000	
	Work-in-Process Inventory		842,000

Enhance Your Understanding

What is the cost of goods manufactured per iPhone in the example?

Answer: $140.33 ($842,000/6,000)

In Chapter 10 we examine the final operating process—selling the finished goods to customers. External reporting of inventory requires **full-absorption costing,** a costing system in which

[2] If the balance is large, it is closed to Cost of Goods Sold, Work-in-Process Inventory, and Finished Goods Inventory based on the balances in these accounts because the over- or understating of the cost of products represented by these three accounts is considered significant.

OF INTEREST Backflush Costing Systems

Many manufacturing companies that adopt the just-in-time philosophy use a product costing system known as *backflush costing.* This system reflects the assumption that the amount of direct materials purchased, direct labor used, and manufacturing overhead applied in the period will be expensed during the period. If, at the end of the period, any inventory remains on hand, it is necessary to make an entry to adjust the Cost of Goods Sold account to reflect the cost of the remaining inventory. The cost of these small ending inventories, whether direct materials, work-in-process, or finished goods, are combined in one current asset account called *Direct and In-Process Inventory.* This eliminates the need for separate Direct Materials, Work-in-Process, and Finished Goods Inventory accounts, so it saves recordkeeping time and cost.

For example, assume that Apple adopts a backflush costing system and during the period incurs the following costs in connection with the production of iPhones:

Direct materials purchased	$240,000
Direct labor used	345,000
Manufacturing overhead applied	860,000

During the period, the following summary journal entries are made in connection with these costs. Notice that all costs are recorded as Cost of Goods Sold on the assumption that they will be transferred to the income statement during the period:

Cost of Goods Sold	240,000	
Accounts Payable		240,000
To record the purchase of direct materials.		
Cost of Goods Sold	345,000	
Wages Payable		345,000
To record the labor used in production.		
Cost of Goods Sold	860,000	
Manufacturing Overhead		860,000
To record the overhead applied to production.		

Assume that at the end of the period, the cost of iPhones still in process is $25,000 and there are $2,000 of direct materials stored. This means that $27,000 of costs assigned to Cost of Goods Sold for the period must be "backflushed" into inventory. This requires the following entry:

Direct and In-Process Inventory	27,000	
Cost of Goods Sold		27,000

In the next period, the amount backflushed into Direct and In-Process Inventory is expensed to Cost of Goods Sold. Then direct materials purchases, direct labor cost, and manufacturing overhead are expensed as incurred. At the end of the period, the costs of remaining inventories are again backflushed.

all production costs are applied to the products manufactured during the period. The reason that full-absorption costing is required for external reporting is the belief that production costs (direct labor and manufacturing overhead) add value to direct materials and, therefore, should be added to the cost of the product. If these products are still in process or finished but waiting to be sold, they are assets to the producing company. Thus, product costs as we have seen are added to the inventory accounts because they add "value," the future economic benefit to the inventory that the company holds. However, for internal reporting purposes, the company must determine which costs are assigned to inventory and which costs are expensed during the period.

Reporting Conversion Process Events

Since conversion process events are internal, they are not generally reported on the company's external financial statements. However, internally many companies prepare a **cost of goods manufactured report** to show the changes that occurred in the Direct Materials Inventory and Work-in-Process Inventory accounts during the period.

The cost of goods manufactured report shows the total direct materials, direct labor, and manufacturing overhead consumed in the production process during the period. It allows comparison of the cost of manufacturing products during the period with the budgeted production costs as part of the evaluation process. The cost of goods manufactured report shows the summary of the events during the period that affected the Direct Materials Inventory and Work-in-Process Inventory accounts.

Exhibit 9.6 shows an assumed cost of goods manufactured report for iPhones based on the following information:

EXHIBIT 9.6
Cost of Goods Manufactured Report

iPhones **Cost of Goods Manufactured**	
Beginning balance of direct materials	$ 148,650
Add: direct materials purchased during period	662,600
Direct materials available for use	$ 811,250
Less ending balance of direct materials	144,580
Direct materials issued into production	$ 666,670
Beginning balance of work-in-process	$ 106,440
Add: Direct materials issued into production	666,670
Direct labor used in production	102,350
Manufacturing overhead applied to production	800,410
Total work-in-process	$1,675,870
Less ending balance of work-in-process	50,820
Cost of goods manufactured	$1,625,050

Purchases of direct materials	$662,600
Direct labor used	102,350
Manufacturing overhead applied	800,410

Further assume that Apple had the following balances in the inventory records related to iPhones:

Direct materials inventory, beginning	$148,650
Direct materials inventory, ending	144,580
Work-in-process inventory, beginning	106,440
Work-in-process inventory, ending	50,820

Notice that the report illustrates the cost flows for the period through the Direct Materials Inventory and Work-in-Process Inventory accounts. Direct Materials Inventory increases by the amount of purchases of materials ($662,600) to determine the amount of direct materials available for use. This amount then decreases by the amount of materials on hand at the end of the period (ending balance of $144,580) to show the amount of direct materials issued into production ($666,670). Also note that the beginning Work-in-Process Inventory ($106,440) increases by the costs added to production for direct materials, direct labor, and applied manufacturing overhead ($666,670, $102,350, and $800,410, respectively) and decreases by the ending balance of Work-in-Process Inventory ($50,820) to derive the cost of goods manufactured ($1,625,050).

Internal Evaluation of Conversion Process Events

As we discussed in Chapter 8, companies gather information to evaluate each of their balanced scorecard goals. In the conversion process we are very concerned with efficiency and quality. Quality might be monitored by calculating quality costs (Chapter 2), determining the number of defects in the period, and monitoring the number of returns from customers. One way to evaluate the efficiency of the conversion (and expenditure) process is to calculate variances. A **variance** is the difference between the standard and actual amounts of inputs. Recall that a standard is the amount required to make a unit or the budgeted cost per item purchased. For example, if a unit requires three pounds of materials that should cost $5.00 per pound, three pounds is the standard amount and $5.00 is the standard price.

To evaluate the conversion (and expenditure) process we must determine variances for production inputs. These variances are used to hold people accountable for efficiency and cost control. However, as we will see in the discussion that follows, we must be careful about assigning responsibility until the underlying cause of the variance is known. The following variances are typically analyzed:

- Price and usage variances for labor.
- Price, usage, and inventory variances for materials.
- Cost pool and cost driver variances for overhead (beyond the scope of this text).

To illustrate the process of calculating and analyzing variances, we will return to the company we started in Chapter 6. Recall that PCs to Go makes tablet PCs. The standards call for the following:

- Direct materials
  1 processor at $200 each
  2 components at $25 each
- Direct labor 15 minutes (¼ hour) at $8.00 per hour

Now assume that during the month we produced 3,000 tablet PCs and used the following production inputs:

- Direct materials
  3,500 processors purchased at a total cost of $735,000 (3,050 used)
  8,000 components purchased at a total cost of $192,000 (6,000 used)
- Direct labor 800 hours worked at $7.50 per hour

Exhibit 9.7 illustrates a comparison between the actual results and the budgeted results for the 3,000 PCs produced. Let's analyze each of the inputs to see if we can pinpoint the source of this difference. We begin with direct labor.

Direct Labor Variance Analysis

When the actual amount of direct labor is different than the budgeted amount of direct labor there are three possible explanations. First, the wage rate per hour was different than the standard. Second, the number of hours used was different than the standard allowed for the actual level of production. Or, third, both the wage rate and the number of hours allowed were different than the standard. To analyze these explanations we calculate a direct labor price variance and a direct labor usage variance.

Direct Labor Price Variance

The **direct labor price variance** indicates the difference in labor cost due to a change in the average wage rate paid to direct labor. It is the difference between the actual and standard rates multiplied by the actual number of hours worked:

Direct labor price variance = (Actual price per hour − Standard price per hour) × Actual number of hours worked

If the actual price is greater than the standard price per hour, the direct labor price variance is a positive number, indicating an unfavorable (U) variance. If the actual price is less than the standard price per hour, the direct labor price variance is a negative number, indicating a

EXHIBIT 9.7
Comparison of Budgeted and Actual Results

Actual		Budgeted	
Processors (3,500 purchased × $210)	$735,000*	3,000 × 1 × $200 =	$600,000
Components (8,000 purchased × $24)	192,000**	3,000 × 2 × $25 =	150,000
Direct labor (800 hours × $7.50)	6,000	3,000 × 15/60 × $8 =	6,000
Total	$933,000		$756,000

*$735,000/3,500 = $210 per processor.
**$192,000/8,000 = $24 per component.

favorable (F) variance.[3] The terms *favorable* and *unfavorable* should not be construed to mean good and bad. Until the cause of a variance is determined we cannot know if it is good or bad.

Let's calculate the direct labor price variance (DLPV) for PCs to Go.

$$\text{DLPV} = (\$7.50 - \$8.00) \times 800 \text{ hours} = \$400 \text{ F}$$

This variance is favorable because PCs to Go paid $0.50 per hour less than the standard. Remember this is not necessarily good. Perhaps the workers will become unmotivated because their wages are not what they expected. Or perhaps they will leave if other companies in the area pay more than $7.50 per hour.

DLPV = (AR−SR) × AH
DLUV = (AH−SHa) × SR
Where:
AR = actual rate per hour
SR = standard rate per hour
AH = actual hours worked
SHa = standard hours allowed for the actual number of units produced

Direct Labor Usage Variance

The **direct labor usage variance** indicates the difference in labor cost due to a change in the number of hours worked per unit produced. It is the difference between the actual and the standard hours allowed for the number of units produced multiplied by the budgeted wage rate as shown here:

$$\text{Direct labor usage variance} = (\text{Actual hours worked} - \text{Standard hours allowed for the actual number of units produced}) \times \text{Standard price}$$

If the actual hours worked are greater than the standard hours allowed, the direct labor usage variance is a positive number, indicating an unfavorable (U) variance. If the actual hours worked are less than the standard hours allowed, the direct labor usage variance is a negative number, indicating a favorable (F) variance. Again, the terms *favorable* and *unfavorable* should not be construed to mean good or bad. Until the cause of a variance is determined we cannot know if it is good or bad.

Let's calculate the direct labor usage variance (DLUV) for PCs to Go (see Exhibit 9.7).

$$\text{DLUV} = (800 \text{ hours} - 750 \text{ hours}^4) \times \$8.00 = \$400 \text{ U}$$

This variance is unfavorable because PCs to Go used 50 more hours than allowed to make 3,000 tablet PCs.

Direct Materials Variances

When the actual amount of direct materials is different than the budgeted amount of direct materials there are four possible explanations. First, the amount paid to purchase materials was different than the standard price. Second, the amount of materials used was different than the standard amount allowed for the actual number of units produced. Third, the amount of materials purchased was different than the amount used. Or, fourth, some combination of the above. To analyze these explanations we calculate a direct materials price variance, a direct materials usage variance, and a direct materials inventory variance.

Direct Materials Price Variance

The **direct materials price variance** indicates the difference in material cost due to a change in the amount paid to purchase materials. It is the difference between the actual and standard purchase price multiplied by the actual amount of material purchased:

$$\text{Direct materials price variance} = (\text{Actual price per item purchased} - \text{Standard price per item purchased}) \times \text{Actual amount of material purchased}$$

If the actual price is greater than the standard price, the direct materials price variance is a positive number, indicating an unfavorable (U) variance. If the actual price is less than the

[3] We will not show negative numbers in variances, just F, denoting favorable.
[4] 3,000 units × 15 minutes (1/4 hour) per unit = 750 hours

standard price, the direct materials price variance is a negative number, indicating a favorable (F) variance. Again, the terms *favorable* and *unfavorable* should not be construed to mean good or bad. Let's calculate the direct materials price variances (DMPV) for PCs to Go (see Exhibit 9.7).

$$\text{DMPV (processors)} = (\$210 - \$200) \times 3{,}500 = \$35{,}000\text{ U}$$

$$\text{DMPV (components)} = (\$24 - \$25) \times 8{,}000 = 8{,}000\text{ F}$$

These variances indicate that PCs to Go paid more for processors than planned but less for components than planned. Remember this is not necessarily good or bad. Perhaps the materials obtained were of higher or lower quality than planned.

Direct Materials Usage Variance

The **direct materials usage variance** indicates the difference in material cost due to a change in the amount of materials used per unit produced. It is the difference between the actual and standard amount of materials allowed for the actual number of units produced multiplied by the budgeted purchase price:

Direct materials usage variance = (Actual amount of materials used – Standard amount of materials allowed for the actual number of units produced) × Standard purchase price

$\text{DMPV} = (\text{AP}-\text{SP}) \times \text{AQp}$
$\text{DMUV} = (\text{AQu}-\text{SQa}) \times \text{SP}$
$\text{DMIV} = (\text{AQp}-\text{AQu}) \times \text{SP}$
Where:
AP = actual price
SP = standard price
AQp = actual quantity purchased
AQu = actual quantity used
SQa = standard quantity allowed for the actual number of units produced

If the actual amount of materials used is greater than the standard amount of materials allowed, the direct materials usage variance is a positive number, indicating an unfavorable (U) variance. If the actual amount used is less than the standard amount allowed, the direct materials usage variance is a negative number, indicating a favorable (F) variance.

Let's calculate the direct materials usage variances (DMUV)[5] for PCs to Go (see Exhibit 9.7).

$$\text{DMUV (processors)} = (3{,}050 - 3{,}000) \times \$200 = \$10{,}000\text{ U}$$

$$\text{DMUV (components)} = (6{,}000 - 6{,}000) \times \$25 = \$0$$

These variances indicate that PCs to Go used more processors than planned but it used the appropriate number of components.

Direct Materials Inventory Variance

The **direct materials inventory variance** indicates the change in direct materials cost due to purchasing a different quantity of materials than what was used. Recall that one of the goals of JIT is to receive materials just when needed and, therefore, reduce the amount of direct material inventory. Thus, calculating a direct materials inventory variance is an important evaluation technique. The direct materials inventory variance is the difference between the amount of materials purchased and the amount of materials used in production multiplied by the standard purchase price:

Direct materials inventory variance = (Actual amount of materials purchased – Actual amount of materials used in production) × Standard purchase price

Let's calculate the direct materials inventory variance for PCs to Go. The direct materials inventory variance (DMIV) is:

$$\text{DMIV (processors)} = (3{,}500 - 3{,}050) \times \$200 = \$90{,}000\text{ U}$$

$$\text{DMIV (components)} = (8{,}000 - 6{,}000) \times \$25 = \$50{,}000\text{ U}$$

This implies that the cost of direct materials during the period was $140,000 higher because some materials were purchased and not used.

Now we can show why the budgeted costs and the actual costs are different this period. Exhibit 9.8 illustrates this comparison. To read Exhibit 9.8 start with the actual column

[5] The standard amounts of materials allowed are determined as follows:
Processors = 3,000 PCs × 1 processor per PC = 3,000 processors
Components = 3,000 PCs × 2 components per PC = 6,000 components

OF INTEREST A Visual Approach to Calculating Variances

Many students find that the equation approach to variance analysis is not very comfortable. If you are one of those students, then this Of Interest is for YOU! Another way to calculate variances is to use a variance diagram, which will be illustrated below. The items to remember about the diagram are (1) the amount of the variance is the total difference between the two columns, (2) the U or F is determined by looking at what changes between the two columns, and (3) keep items in alphabetical order as you work your way from left to right. Let's start with direct labor:

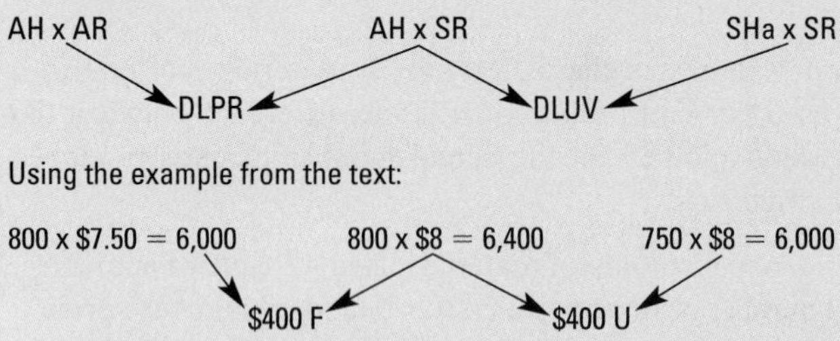

The $400 DLPR is the difference between column one and column two. It is favorable because the actual rate is less than the standard rate. Apply that same analysis to columns two and three to determine the amount of direction of the variance. Now let's try direct materials.

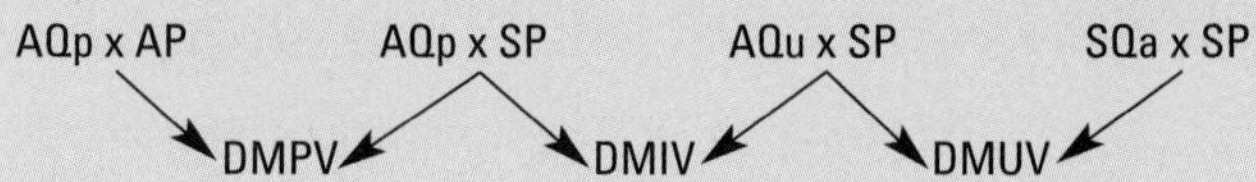

Again, notice that the items within the columns are alphabetical as we go from left to right. Now let's do the calculations using the information from the text example for processors:

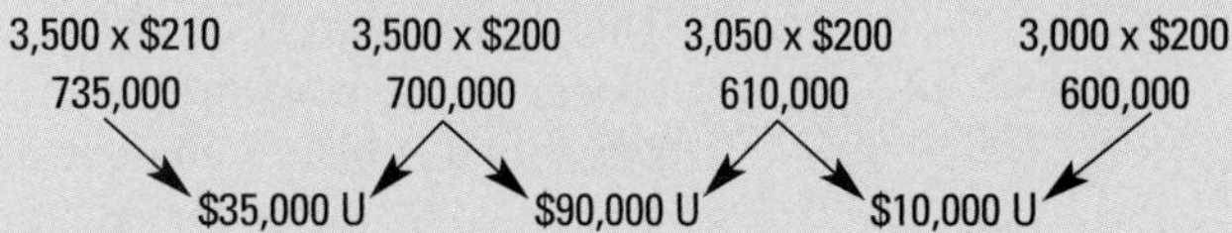

The $90,000 DMIV is the difference between column two and column three. It is unfavorable because the amount of inventory purchased is greater than the amount of inventory used. Apply this same analysis to columns one versus two and columns three versus four to determine the DMPV and DMUV.

EXHIBIT 9.8
Using Variances to Explain the Difference between Budgeted and Actual Results

	Actual Results	Price Variance	Inventory Variance	Usage Variance	Budgeted Results
Processors	$735,000	$35,000 U	$90,000 U	$10,000 U	$600,000
Components	192,000	8,000 F	50,000 U	0	150,000
Direct labor	6,000	400 F		400 U	6,000
Total	$933,000	$26,600 U	$140,000 U	$10,400 U	$756,000

and subtract unfavorable variances and add favorable variances to arrive at the budgeted results.

Notice that the variances explain the difference between the actual amounts incurred for the inputs and the budgeted amounts. This analysis is important so that management can plan for the future.

Summary

A manufacturing company maintains three inventory accounts (Direct Materials, Work-in-Process, and Finished Goods) to reflect events occurring during the conversion process. The Direct Materials account is decreased when direct materials are requisitioned into production. The Work-in-Process account is increased by the amount of direct materials, direct labor, and applied overhead used in production during the period. The Work-in-Process account is decreased by the cost of goods manufactured during the period. The Finished Goods account is increased by cost of goods manufactured and decreased by cost of goods sold.

Manufacturing overhead consists of all indirect product costs. Actual manufacturing overhead is recorded in a temporary account called Manufacturing Overhead. Applied manufacturing overhead is allocated to production through the Work-in-Process account. At the end of the period, cost of goods sold is adjusted for the difference between actual and applied manufacturing overhead.

A cost of goods manufactured report is used internally to monitor conversion process costs. Variance analysis is used to monitor the efficiency of the conversion process.

Key Terms

Activity-based costing (ABC) A system for assigning costs to cost objects, *252*
Actual manufacturing overhead The amount of overhead incurred during the period, *251*
Applied manufacturing overhead The amount of overhead applied to work-in-process during the period, *252*
Cost of goods manufactured The total cost of products manufactured during the period, *256*
Cost of goods manufactured report A report showing changes that occurred in the Raw Materials Inventory and Work-in-Process Inventory accounts, *257*
Cost pool A group of costs that change in response to the same cost driver, *253*
Direct labor price variance A variance that indicates the difference in labor cost due to a change in the average wage rate paid to direct labor, *259*
Direct labor usage variance A variance that indicates the difference in labor cost due to a change in the number of hours worked per unit produced, *260*
Direct Materials Inventory An account that represents the costs incurred to purchase and receive direct materials, *247*
Direct materials inventory variance A variance that indicates the change in direct material cost due to purchasing a different quantity of materials than what was used, *261*
Direct materials price variance A variance that indicates the difference in material cost due to a change in the amount paid to purchase materials, *260*
Direct materials usage variance A variance that indicates the difference in material cost due to a change in the amount of materials used per unit produced, *261*
Finished Goods Inventory An account that represents the costs of products completed but not yet sold, *247*
Full-absorption costing A costing system in which all production costs are applied to the products manufactured during the period, *256*
Manufacturing overhead A temporary account used to reflect the indirect manufacturing costs of the period, *251*
Overapplied overhead The amount of overhead applied to production is greater than the actual amount of overhead incurred, *256*
Predetermined overhead rate The estimated amount of overhead divided by the estimated amount of cost driver; used to apply overhead to work-in-process, *254*
Underapplied overhead The amount of overhead applied to production is less than the actual amount of overhead incurred, *256*
Variance The difference between the standard and actual amounts of inputs, *258*
Work-in-Process Inventory An account that represents the costs of products started but not completed, *247*

Questions

1. Explain the purpose of each of the three inventory accounts used in a manufacturing company such as Ford Motor Company.
2. If the Direct Materials Inventory account decreased during the period, were purchases greater than or less than the amount of materials issued into production? Why?
3. If Work-in-Process Inventory increased during the period, was cost of goods manufactured greater than or less than the total product costs transferred into Work-in-Process during the period? Why?
4. If the Finished Goods account decreases during the period, is cost of goods manufactured greater than or less than cost of goods sold? Why?
5. Explain the difference between direct and indirect materials and give examples of each for a manufacturing company such as Levi Strauss.
6. Explain the difference between direct and indirect labor and give examples of each for a manufacturer such as Boeing Company.
7. What is the difference between actual and applied manufacturing overhead? When are they recorded?
8. There are four levels of production activities. What are they and why are they important?
9. Explain the concept of a cost driver and how to determine an appropriate cost driver for a given activity.
10. Explain the concept of cost pool and how to determine cost pools.
11. How do companies use the predetermined overhead rate to assign overhead to work-in-process?
12. Explain the process of applying manufacturing overhead to Work-in-Process Inventory.

13. Explain the difference between over- and underapplied manufacturing overhead. Assuming the amount is small, what is the implication of each type of manufacturing overhead on (*a*) product costs and (*b*) net income for the period?
14. What is the difference between a favorable and an unfavorable variance? Are favorable variances good and unfavorable variances bad?
15. What do the direct labor price and direct labor usage variance indicate?
16. If the actual wage rate is greater than the standard wage rate, is the direct labor price variance favorable or unfavorable? Why?
17. What do the direct materials price, direct materials usage, and direct materials inventory variances indicate?
18. If the actual price paid for direct materials is less than the standard price, is the direct materials price variance favorable or unfavorable? Why?

Exercises

E9.1 LO 1

Winters, Inc., is a manufacturing firm that makes table tennis paddles. Each paddle consists of a handle, a wooden paddle, and a rubber backing for each side of the wooden paddle. As the paddles progress through the assembly process, workers attach the handles and glue the rubber backing into place. Classify the following costs as one of the following four options by placing the number of the correct answer in the space provided.

1. Direct materials cost
2. Direct labor cost
3. Manufacturing overhead cost
4. Selling and administrative cost

________ A. Cost of glue
________ B. Cost of handles
________ C. Cost of rubber packing for the handles
________ D. Cost of shipping crates
________ E. Cost of wooden paddles
________ F. Depreciation on the delivery trucks
________ G. Depreciation on the factory equipment
________ H. Office workers' salaries
________ I. Production supervisors' salaries
________ J. Rent on finished goods warehouse
________ K. Rent on production facilities
________ L. Rent on direct materials materials warehouse
________ M. Utilities for the production facilities
________ N. Wages of assembly workers
________ O. Wages of sales personnel

LO 1 **E9.2**

The following costs are for Booth, Inc., a manufacturer of labels used in the packaging of a variety of products. Classify the costs as one of the following four options by placing the number of the correct answer in the space provided.

1. Direct materials cost
2. Direct labor cost
3. Manufacturing overhead cost
4. Selling and administrative cost

________ A. Salary of production foreman
________ B. Property taxes on corporate office building
________ C. Vacation pay for factory employees
________ D. Salespersons' commissions
________ E. Advertising expense
________ F. Boxes used to ship finished labels
________ G. Cost of electricity to operate factory machinery
________ H. Income tax expense
________ I. Insurance on manufacturing facilities
________ J. Wages paid to machine operator
________ K. Paper for labels

_________ L. Rent on finished goods warehouse
_________ M. Depreciation on the factory building
_________ N. Salary of the corporate controller
_________ O. Ink used in printing labels

LO 2 **E9.3** Tyrell Company had inventories at the beginning and end of June 2010 as follows:

	June 1, 2010	June 30, 2010
Direct materials inventory	$15,000	$ 8,000
Work-in-process inventory	46,000	26,000
Finished goods inventory	30,000	19,000

During June, Tyrell purchased direct materials of $400,000, incurred direct labor costs of $150,000, and applied manufacturing overhead of $250,000 to production. Show the flow of costs through the company's inventory accounts during June 2010.

LO 2 **E9.4** Hamilton, Inc., incurred the following costs during fiscal 2010:

Direct materials	$330,000
Direct labor	160,000
Manufacturing overhead applied	440,000

During 2010, cost of goods manufactured totaled $920,000 while cost of goods sold was $930,000. Inventory balances at January 1, 2010, were as follows:

Work-in-process	$16,000
Finished goods	30,000

Show the flow of costs through the company's inventory accounts during 2010.

LO 2 **E9.5** Prepare journal entries for these transactions of Brayton Company using the gross price method and the perpetual inventory system.

Apr. 8 Purchased $15,800 in direct materials; terms 1/10, n/30, FOB shipping point.
11 $3,080 direct materials were requisitioned from the direct materials warehouse.
15 Filled indirect materials requisition, $800. These materials are recorded as supplies.
17 $380 in direct materials requisitioned on April 11 were not used in production and were returned to the warehouse.
17 Paid for direct materials purchased April 8.

LO 2 **E9.6** Given the following information, prepare journal entries for Spainhower Manufacturing to record the monthly payroll at March 31, 2010 (ignore payroll withholding).

President	$30,000
Factory supervisor	6,000
Machinist	4,000

LO 2 **E9.7** Carlson Company incurred the following manufacturing overhead costs during the month of June 2010. Prepare the journal entry to record the costs.

Depreciation, building	$7,000
Wages earned but not yet paid, janitor	600
Electricity used and paid, factory	350
Rent on equipment previously paid	900

LO 3 **E9.8** Erickson Company applies unit-related manufacturing overhead on the basis of machine hours. The following unit-related overhead data were accumulated by the accounting department:

	Estimated	Actual
Machine hours	450,000	500,000
Overhead costs	$900,000	$950,000

What is the amount of over- or underapplied overhead?

LO 3 **E9.9** Chamberlain Manufacturing produces three models of water softeners: the standard model, the super model, and the deluxe model. The models differ in the features offered and the warranties given to customers. The deluxe model has the most features and the best warranty. Chamberlain applies product-sustaining overhead to each product based on the number of hours of engineering time. It estimates that a total of 7,500 engineering hours will be required in the coming period and that product-sustaining overhead costs will be $225,000.

At the end of the period, it was discovered that the standard model required 1,200 engineering hours, the super model used 2,000 engineering hours, and the deluxe model required 5,800 engineering hours. The actual product-sustaining overhead for the period was $250,000. Determine the amount of overhead applied to each product line during the year. Determine the amount of over- or underapplied overhead.

LO 3 **E9.10** Lexie, a clothing manufacturer, incurs the following types of costs. Classify the costs **(A–G)** as one of the following four options **(1–4)** by placing the number of the correct answer in the space provided.

1. Facility-sustaining
2. Product-sustaining
3. Batch-related
4. Unit-related

________ A. Occupying the factory
________ B. Designing clothing
________ C. Inspecting production
________ D. Using specialized cutting equipment
________ E. Maintaining materials inventory
________ F. Setting up sewing machines
________ G. Using sewing machines

LO 3 **E9.11** Anderson has identified the following operating activities for its company, the estimated overhead costs associated with each activity, an appropriate cost driver for each activity, and the estimated usage of the cost driver for the coming period. Using this information, determine the appropriate overhead rates.

Activity	Cost	Cost Driver	Estimated Usage
Occupying facilities	$800,000	Square feet	100,000
Testing quality	50,000	Production runs	100
Carrying inventory	125,000	Pounds of material	1,500
Setting up machines	60,000	Production runs	100
Packing containers	400,000	Units made	200,000
Using machines	200,000	Machine hours	100,000

LO 4 **E9.12** Using the following information, determine the cost of goods manufactured and the ending direct materials inventory balance for Steele Company during August 2010. Assume that over- or underapplied manufacturing overhead is closed to Cost of Goods Sold at the end of the period.

Direct materials inventory, Aug. 1, 2010	$21,000
Direct materials inventory, Aug. 31, 2010	?
Work-in-process inventory, Aug. 1, 2010	4,000
Work-in-process inventory, Aug. 31, 2010	16,000
Finished goods inventory, Aug. 1, 2010	8,000
Finished goods inventory, Aug. 31, 2010	10,000
Direct materials used	30,000
Direct labor used	20,000
Direct materials purchased	35,000
Indirect materials used (supplies)	6,000
Indirect labor used	25,000
Manufacturing overhead, other	29,000
Administrative salaries	15,000
Sales salaries and commissions	10,000
Depreciation on sales and office equipment	14,000
Manufacturing overhead, applied	65,000

LO 3 LO 2 **E9.13** Refer to E9.12. Determine the cost of goods sold for the period.

LO 5 **E9.14** Based on the standard set by Tish Company, 5,500 direct labor hours should have been used in production this period at a cost of $20 per hour. The actual results indicate that 5,400 hours were used at a total cost of $113,400. What are the direct labor price and direct labor usage variances?

LO 5 **E9.15** Swanson Company has set the following standards for direct labor:

Assembly line workers	30 minutes per unit at $10 per hour

During the period, assembly line workers worked 8,100 hours and earned $74,925 in total. Swanson Company produced 18,000 units during the period. What are the direct labor price and direct labor usage variances?

LO 5 **E9.16** Henry Enterprises reports the following direct labor information for the month of December when production was 18,000 units. What is the standard price for direct labor per hour?

Actual direct labor hours used	40,000
Actual direct labor rate per hour	$16.25
Direct labor price variance	$10,000 F
Direct labor usage variance	$64,000 U

LO 5 **E9.17** Jorrey Company manufactures bookcases. Direct materials standards are 20 board feet of lumber per bookcase at a cost of $2.50 per board foot. During the month of July, Jorrey purchased 25,000 board feet of lumber at a total cost of $60,000. Production during July used 21,000 board feet of lumber to manufacture 1,000 bookcases. What are the direct materials price, usage, and inventory variances?

LO 5 **E9.18** Madsen Enterprises's direct materials costs for March follow. What are the direct materials price, usage, and inventory variances?

Actual quantity purchased	5,000 pounds
Actual quantity used in production	4,900 pounds
Quantity allowed for production	4,800 pounds
Actual price per pound	$13
Standard price per pound	$12

LO 5 **E9.19** Patton, Inc., has the following information available concerning direct materials:

Direct materials price variance	$17,500 F
Direct materials inventory variance	$18,000 U
Direct materials usage variance	$12,000 U

Patton standards allow for 6 liters of direct materials for each unit produced. During the period, Patton produced 25,000 units and used 160,000 liters of direct materials. Patton purchased 175,000 liters of direct materials. What was the standard purchase price per liter for direct materials?

Problems

P9.1 LO 5 Edwards Company manufactures a product with the following standard materials costs:

Material A	30 pounds at $2.50 per pound
Material B	40 pounds at $2.90 per pound

During the month of May, 18,000 pounds of material A were purchased at a cost of $2.76 per pound, of which 10,000 pounds were used in production. During the period, 20,000 pounds of material B were purchased at a cost of $2.98 per pound; 27,000 pounds were used in production. The actual production for the month of May was 500 units.

Required:

A. Compute the direct materials price variance for each material.
B. Compute the direct materials usage variance for each material.
C. Compute the direct materials inventory variance for each material.
D. Interpret each of these variances and determine who is responsible for them.

LO 5 **P9.2** Hayley produces a product that requires two types of labor: assembly and finishing. The standard and actual cost data for the month of October are as follows:

	Standard Cost per Unit	Actual Hours	Actual Cost
Assembly	25 hours at $7 per hour	5,100	$38,250
Finishing	17 hours at $11 per hour	3,450	33,810

A total of 200 units of finished product were produced during October.

Required:
A. Compute the direct labor price variance for each type of labor.
B. Compute the direct labor usage variance for each type of labor.
C. Interpret each variance and determine who is responsible for them.

LO 5 **P9.3** Rompola Corporation manufactures futons with the following standard costs per unit:

Direct materials	80 yards at $2.00 per yard
Direct labor	20 hours at $20 per hour

The actual results for the year were as follows:

Direct materials	120,000 yards purchased at a total cost of $264,000; 118,000 yards used
Direct labor	32,000 hours worked at a total cost of $604,800
Production	1,500 units

Required:
A. Compute the following variances:
1. Direct materials price variance
2. Direct materials usage variance
3. Direct materials inventory variance
4. Direct labor price variance
5. Direct labor usage variance

B. Interpret each of the variances calculated.

LO 5 **P9.4** Martin Manufacturing manufactures ready-mix cement with the following standard costs:

Direct materials	2.5 pounds at $2.40 per pound
Direct labor	1.5 hours at $18.00 per hour

Actual results for the month of September were as follows:

Units produced	6,500
Materials purchased (18,000 pounds)	$36,000
Materials used	17,500 pounds
Labor used (9,500 hours)	$180,500

Required:
A. Calculate the following variances for the month of September:
1. Direct materials price variance
2. Direct materials usage variance
3. Direct materials inventory variance
4. Direct labor price variance
5. Direct labor usage variance

B. Interpret each of the variances calculated.

LO 5 **P9.5** The following information is available for Lowham Company:

Direct materials price variance	$9,000 U
Direct materials usage variance	6,000 U
Direct labor price variance	1,300 U
Direct labor usage variance	3,000 U

During the period, 4,500 pounds of direct materials costing $99,000 were purchased and used, 3,250 direct labor hours were worked at a total cost of $40,300, and 2,000 finished units were produced.

Required:
A. Compute the actual cost per pound of materials purchased and used.
B. Compute the actual cost per direct labor hour.
C. Compute the standard cost per pound of materials used.
D. Compute the standard cost per direct labor hour.
E. Compute the standard number of pounds of materials per unit of finished product.
F. Compute the standard number of direct labor hours per unit of finished product.

LO 2 **LO 3** **P9.6** The following events occurred during the month of June at the Phipps Company, manufacturers of golf clubs. Prepare the appropriate journal entries. Phipps uses the gross price method and the perpetual inventory system.

1. Purchased $55,000 of direct materials and $45,000 of indirect materials (supplies), both on account.
2. Sold 10,000 shares of capital stock for $50,000.
3. Direct materials of $60,000 were issued into production.
4. Indirect materials of $45,000 were issued into production.
5. Collected $12,000 on accounts receivable.
6. Paid $31,000 in wages to employees: $17,000 was direct labor and $14,000 was indirect labor. (Ignore payroll taxes.)
7. Paid the electricity bill for the factory when received, $3,000.
8. Manufacturing overhead of $54,000 was applied to production.
9. Paid selling and administrative expenses of $17,000.
10. Paid $32,000 in wages to employees: $18,000 was direct labor and $14,000 was indirect labor. (Ignore payroll taxes.)
11. Manufacturing overhead of $63,000 was applied to production.
12. Completed jobs costing $175,000.

LO 2 LO 3 LO 4 **P9.7** Refer to the transactions in P9.6.

Additional information:

1. Depreciation expense for the month was $15,000 on the factory building and $5,000 on the manufacturing equipment.
2. Depreciation expense for the month was $3,000 on selling and administrative equipment.
3. Overhead is closed to cost of goods sold after the adjusting entries are made.
4. The account balances before the P9.6 entries were made are presented in the following trial balance:

Trial Balance

	Debits	Credits
Cash	$ 82,300	
Accounts receivable	20,000	
Direct materials inventory	21,000	
Work-in-process inventory	100,000	
Finished goods inventory	165,000	
Manufacturing equipment	300,000	
Accumulated depreciation—manufacturing equipment		$ 188,000
Factory building	1,100,000	
Accumulated depreciation—factory building		612,000
Selling and administrative equipment	20,000	
Accumulated depreciation—selling and administrative equipment		5,000
Accounts payable		34,000
Taxes payable		22,000
Long-term notes payable		500,000
Capital stock		250,000
Retained earnings		197,300
	$1,808,300	$1,808,300

Required:

A. Use the trial balance and open the appropriate T-accounts.
B. Post the journal entries prepared in P9.6 to the accounts. (Additional accounts will be required.)
C. Prepare a preliminary trial balance.
D. Prepare the adjusting entries as needed and post to the appropriate accounts.
E. Prepare a schedule of cost of goods manufactured for the month.

LO 2 **P9.8** The following information was obtained from the accounting records of Feddersen Company:

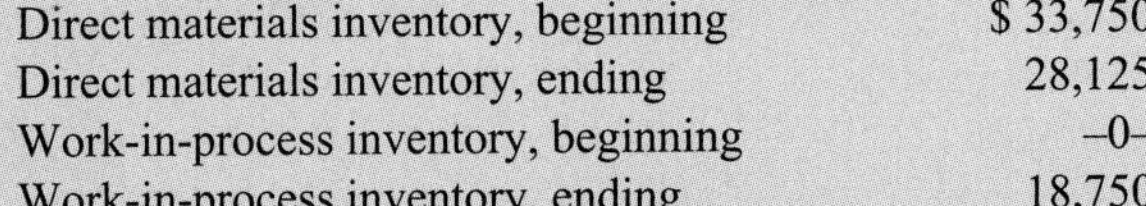

Direct materials inventory, beginning	$ 33,750
Direct materials inventory, ending	28,125
Work-in-process inventory, beginning	–0–
Work-in-process inventory, ending	18,750

Finished goods inventory, beginning	16,875
Finished goods inventory, ending	18,750
Direct materials purchased	187,500
Direct labor	122,500
Indirect labor	40,000
Depreciation, factory	33,750
Depreciation, factory machinery	17,500
Utilities, factory and machinery	20,000
Insurance, factory and machinery	12,500
Selling and administrative expenses	70,000
Property taxes, factory	25,000
Manufacturing overhead, applied	147,000

Required:
A. Determine the over- or underapplied overhead for the period.
B. Prepare a cost of goods manufactured report.

LO 2 LO 3 LO 4 **P9.9** Reemts Company manufactures bookcases. Unit-related manufacturing overhead is applied based on the number of direct labor hours worked. Estimated unit-related manufacturing overhead for the year is $320,000. Employees are expected to work 40,000 direct labor hours during the year. Batch-related overhead is applied on the basis of the number of production runs. Estimated batch-related manufacturing overhead for the coming year is $400,000. There are 1,000 production runs planned for the year. Reemts uses a perpetual inventory system. The following events occurred during the month of April:

1. Purchased 70,000 board feet of lumber at $0.30 per board foot.
2. Requisitioned 50,000 board feet of lumber into production (cost $0.25 per board foot).
3. Indirect materials (held as supplies) in the amount of $4,500 were placed into production.
4. Twelve production runs producing 1,200 bookcases and requiring a total of 6,100 hours of direct labor at $6.00 per direct labor hour were completed during the month. Overhead is applied to production at this time.
5. Indirect labor costs incurred totaled $30,000.
6. Utility bill for the factory received and paid, $600.
7. Depreciation on the factory for April, $6,000.
8. A bill for advertising was received, but not paid, in the amount of $120.
9. Other manufacturing overhead totaling $21,500 was incurred.
10. Bookcases with a cost of $75,000 were completed during the month and transferred to the finished goods warehouse.

Additional information:

Balance at April 1:

Direct materials inventory	$10,000
Work-in-process inventory	40,000
Finished goods inventory	30,000

Required:
A. Calculate the predetermined overhead rates.
B. Prepare the journal entries to record the information given.
C. Determine the over- or underapplied overhead, in total, for the period.
D. Prepare a cost of goods manufactured schedule.

LO 2 LO 3 LO 4 **P9.10** The following information was provided by Alley Manufacturing for the month of August 2010:

	Beginning Balance	Ending Balance
Direct materials inventory	$ 60,000	$ 80,000
Work-in-process inventory	100,000	110,000
Finished goods inventory	110,000	140,000

Additional information:

Direct materials purchased	$450,000
Direct labor costs incurred	$150,000
Machine hours worked	33,000
Actual unit-related manufacturing overhead	$370,000
Applied unit-related manufacturing overhead	$11 per machine hour

Required: Calculate the following amounts:

A. Direct materials used in production.
B. Applied manufacturing overhead.
C. Cost of goods manufactured.
D. Over- or underapplied manufacturing overhead.

Cases

C9.1 LO 3 The following annual budgeted information is available for Speckner Company, which manufactures folding tables, chairs, and footstools:

Activity	Estimated Cost	Cost Driver	Usage
Setting up machines	$ 90,000	Number of production runs	150
Processing orders	150,000	Number of orders	300
Handling materials	60,000	Pounds of materials	12,000
Using machines	180,000	Number of machine hours	20,000
Managing quality	150,000	Number of inspections	60
Packing and shipping	120,000	Number of units shipped	30,000
Using building	600,000	Square feet occupied	300,000
Total cost	$1,350,000		

During the current month, the following cost drivers were used:

	Tables	Chairs	Footstools
Number of production runs	2	4	8
Number of orders	8	8	4
Pounds of materials	400	200	200
Number of machine hours	500	300	300
Number of inspections	2	2	4
Number of units shipped	1,000	500	300
Square feet occupied	60,000	40,000	100,000

Required: A. Classify each of the activities as facility-sustaining, product-sustaining, batch-related, or unit-related.
B. Determine the types of costs included in each activity.
C. Calculate the overhead rate for each cost driver.

LO 3 **C9.2** Refer to C9.1 and complete the following.

A. Determine the overhead applied to each product line.
B. Determine the overhead cost per unit assuming the number of units produced equaled the number of units shipped.

Critical Thinking

CT9.1 LO 3 Refer to C9.1 and C9.2. The manager of Speckner Company likes the old way of allocating overhead based on the number of direct labor hours used. Additional information is available:

Direct labor hours expected during the year	4,000
Direct labor hours used during the month:	
For table production	200
For chair production	100
For footstool production	60

Required: A. Determine the manufacturing overhead rate based on direct labor hours.
B. Determine the applied overhead cost for each product.
C. Explain why direct labor hours are, or are not, an inappropriate overhead allocation basis for this company.

LO 3 **CT9.2** Dawson Company manufactures three types of computer games: Skyhawk, Seahawk, and Sharks. It allocates overhead to the games based on the number of direct labor hours worked on each product. The results of the most recent period follow:

	Skyhawk	Seahawk	Sharks
Units produced and sold	9,000	8,000	7,000
Selling price	$45.00	$30.00	$25.00
Less:			
Direct materials per unit	5.50	4.25	3.00
Direct labor cost per unit	9.00	2.00	3.00
Manufacturing overhead per unit	27.00	6.00	9.00
Gross margin	$ 3.50	$17.75	$10.00
Less:			
Selling cost per unit	2.25	1.50	1.25
Administrative cost per unit	3.75	3.00	2.75
Net income (loss) per unit	$ (2.50)	$13.25	$ 6.00

The manager of Dawson Company is concerned that the Skyhawk game seems to be a net loser and he is considering whether to discontinue it. He has asked you to analyze the situation and make a recommendation. Your analysis reveals that Dawson Company has three levels of overhead—facility-sustaining, batch-related, and unit-related—and that the appropriate overhead rates are $6.00 per square foot, $1,000 per production run, and $4 per unit, respectively. Resource usage during the past period follows. In addition, you discover that administrative costs are fixed while selling costs are variable per unit.

	Skyhawk	Seahawk	Sharks
Square feet occupied	10,000	12,500	15,000
Production runs	9	12	12

Required: Requires prior study of Chapter 4.

A. Determine whether Dawson Company should drop any game.

B. Write a memo to the manager with your recommendation.

Ethical Challenges

EC9.1 LO 3 Under a traditional manufacturing overhead allocation system, a company simply estimates total manufacturing overhead for the company and selects a cost driver, typically direct labor hours or machine hours. The predetermined overhead rate is the total estimated overhead divided by the total estimated direct labor hours (machine hours). This system is obviously much easier because only one manufacturing overhead allocation must be done rather than the various allocations we made using ABC. Discuss the ethical implications to the traditional allocation system if the company has different managers in charge of different, widely diverse product lines.

LO 5 EC9.2 Mark-Wright, Inc. (MWI), is a specialty frozen food processor located in the Midwest. Since its founding in 1982, MWI has enjoyed a loyal clientele that is willing to pay premium prices for the high-quality frozen foods it prepares from specialized recipes. In the past two years, the company has experienced rapid sales growth in its operating region and has had many inquiries about supplying its products on a national basis. To meet this growth, MWI expanded its processing capabilities, which resulted in increased production and distribution costs. Furthermore, MWI has been encountering pricing pressure from competitors outside its normal marketing region.

As MWI desires to continue its expansion, Jim Condon, CEO, has engaged a consulting firm to assist MWI in determining its best course of action. The consulting firm concluded that, while premium pricing is sustainable in some areas, if sales growth is to be achieved, MWI must make some price concessions. Also, in order to maintain profit margins, costs must be reduced and controlled. The consulting firm recommended the institution of a standard costing system that would facilitate a flexible budgeting system to better accommodate the changes in demand that can be expected when serving an expanding market area.

Condon met with his management team and explained the recommendations of the consulting firm. Condon then assigned the task of establishing standard costs to his management team. After discussing the situation with their respective staffs, the management team met to review the matter.

Jane Morgan, purchasing manager, advised that meeting expanded production would necessitate obtaining basic food supplies from other than traditional MWI sources. This would entail increased raw materials and shipping costs and could result in lower-quality supplies. Consequently, the increased costs would need to be made up by the processing department if current cost levels were to be maintained or reduced.

Stan Walters, processing manager, countered that the need to accelerate processing cycles to increase production, coupled with the possibility of receiving lower-grade supplies, can be expected to result in a slip in quality and a greater product rejection rate. Under these circumstances, per unit labor utilization might not be maintained or might be reduced, and forecasting future unit labor content would become very difficult.

Tom Lopez, production engineer, advised that if the equipment is not properly maintained and thoroughly cleaned at prescribed intervals, it can be anticipated that the quality and unique taste of the frozen food products would be affected.

Jack Reid, vice president of sales, states that if quality cannot be maintained, MWI cannot expect to increase sales to the levels projected.

When Condon was apprised of the problems encountered by his management team, he advised them that if agreement could not be reached on appropriate standards, he would arrange to have them set by the consulting firm and everyone would have to live with the results.

Required:

A. Discuss the major advantages of using standards to control behavior.
B. Identify those who should participate in setting the standards and describe the benefits of their participation in the standard-setting process.
C. What could be the consequences if Jim Condon has the standards set by the outside consulting firm?

(CMA Adapted)

Computer Applications

CA9.1 

The following annual budgeted information is available for Beavis Company, which manufactures picnic tables, lawn chairs, and table umbrellas:

Activity	Estimated Cost	Cost Driver	Usage
Setting up machines	$ 180,000	Number of production runs	225
Processing orders	300,000	Number of orders	450
Handling materials	120,000	Pounds of materials	18,000
Using machines	360,000	Number of machine hours	30,000
Managing quality	300,000	Number of inspections	90
Packing and shipping	240,000	Number of units shipped	45,000
Using building	1,200,000	Square feet occupied	450,000
Total cost	$2,700,000		

During the current month, the following cost drivers were used:

	Tables	Chairs	Umbrellas
Number of production runs	4	8	16
Number of orders	16	16	8
Pounds of materials	800	400	400
Number of machine hours	1,000	600	600
Number of inspections	4	4	8
Number of units shipped	1,000	600	600
Square feet occupied	120,000	80,000	250,000

Required: Use a computer spreadsheet.

A. Calculate the overhead rate for each cost driver.
B. Determine the overhead applied to each product line.

LO 5 **CA9.2** Tykes Bykes has the following standard costs for its direct materials and direct labor in the production of tricycles:

Direct materials	3 wheels at $0.50 each
	1 metal frame at $2.50 each
	1 handlebar set at $1.00 per set
Direct labor	3/4 of an hour at $8.00 per hour

Actual results for each month of the first quarter are as follows:

	January	February	March
Tricycles produced	10,600	11,100	10,800
Wheels purchased	35,000	35,000	35,000
Wheel cost	$21,000	$21,000	$22,750
Wheels used	31,950	33,300	32,500
Frames purchased	12,000	11,000	11,500
Frame cost	$33,000	$29,400	$26,250
Frames used	10,600	11,500	10,800
Handlebars purchased	10,000	12,500	13,500
Handlebar cost	$11,000	$12,500	$14,850
Handlebars used	11,000	11,900	13,500
Direct labor hours used	8,500	8,300	8,000
Direct labor cost	$65,000	$70,550	$68,850

Required: Use a spreadsheet package.

A. Determine the direct materials price variance for each month for each material.
B. Determine the direct materials usage variance for each month for each material.
C. Determine the direct labor price variance for each month.

Visit the text Online Learning Center at **www.mhhe.com/ainsworth6e** for additional problem material that accompanies this chapter.

CHAPTER TEN

10

Marketing/Sales/Collection/Customer Support Process: Recording and Evaluating Revenue Process Activities

Learning Objectives

LO 1 Describe how revenue activities are analyzed and recorded in the accounting system.

LO 2 Explain how cost of goods sold activities are analyzed and recorded in the accounting system using FIFO and/or LIFO costing.

LO 3 Discuss how uncollectible accounts are recorded.

LO 4 Explain how revenue process activities are reported on the financial statements.

LO 5 Discuss how revenue process activities are evaluated internally.

In Chapter 9 we studied the conversion process. In this chapter we examine the revenue process; this completes our discussion of the operating processes. As you know, the revenue process consists of the following actions:

- Determine marketing and distribution channels.
- Receive and accept orders.
- Deliver goods and services.
- Receive payment from customers.
- Provide customer support.

As we learned in Chapter 7, all of these activities are business events, but the first two are not accounting events because they do not have an impact on the company's assets, liabilities, and/or owners' equity. (The second event—receive and accept orders—may have an expenditure process event if expenses are incurred in the process.) The last three events are accounting events because the company's assets, liabilities, and/or owners' equity will be affected. As we learn in this chapter, the fourth event (receive payment) sometimes precedes the third event (deliver goods/services). Finally, note that the last event (provide support) may have an expenditure process impact as well. As we discussed in Chapter 7, businesses maintain information regarding all business events. In a database (ERP) system this information is integrated. In a transaction-based system, information concerning accounting events is maintained in the accounting system and supporting documents capture information regarding other, nonaccounting events.

Exhibit 10.1 illustrates the sales/collection part of the revenue process in a manual accounting system. Let's examine this exhibit to better understand the records involved in the revenue process. First, notice that the exhibit is divided into two separate processes: sales (Exhibit 10.1A) and collections (Exhibit 10.1B). Second, notice that the activity records are maintained outside the formal accounting system (customer order, sales order, shipping notice, packing slip, bill of lading, remittance advice, and deposit slip). Third, notice the use of special journals (sales journal, cash receipts journal) and subsidiary ledgers (accounts receivable, inventory).

We have four primary issues to address in the revenue process. First, when is revenue recognized? Second, what cost is assigned to cost of goods sold? Third, how do we record uncollectible credit sales? Fourth, how do we evaluate revenue process activities? We examine each of these issues next.

Revenue Recognition

According to the FASB, revenues are recognized when they have been *earned* and *realized.* But what do each of these components mean? *SFAC No. 5* declares that revenues are earned when an "entity has substantially accomplished what it must do to be entitled to the benefits represented by the revenues."[1] This generally means that revenues are earned when a company has done everything it has promised to do for the customer, that is, delivered products or rendered services to a customer. Revenues are realized when an exchange has taken place and the company receives cash, a claim to cash, or some other increase in net assets. Recall that net assets are total assets less total liabilities. Thus, revenues are also realized when a company receives some other noncash asset or has its liabilities reduced. Companies base the amount of revenue recognized on the dollar amount of cash received or the cash equivalent value of the increase in net assets resulting from the transaction. *Cash equivalent value* refers to the cash price for which a noncash asset could be sold. For example, if a company accepts a piece of equipment valued at $15,000 in exchange for services rendered, it will record revenue of $15,000 because it has performed all services necessary to earn the revenue and it has received a noncash asset with a cash equivalent value of $15,000.

[1] Financial Accounting Standards Board, *Concepts Statement #5* (New York: McGraw-Hill, 1998), p. 181.

EXHIBIT 10.1A

Traditional Manual Sales/Collection Process Flowchart—Part I

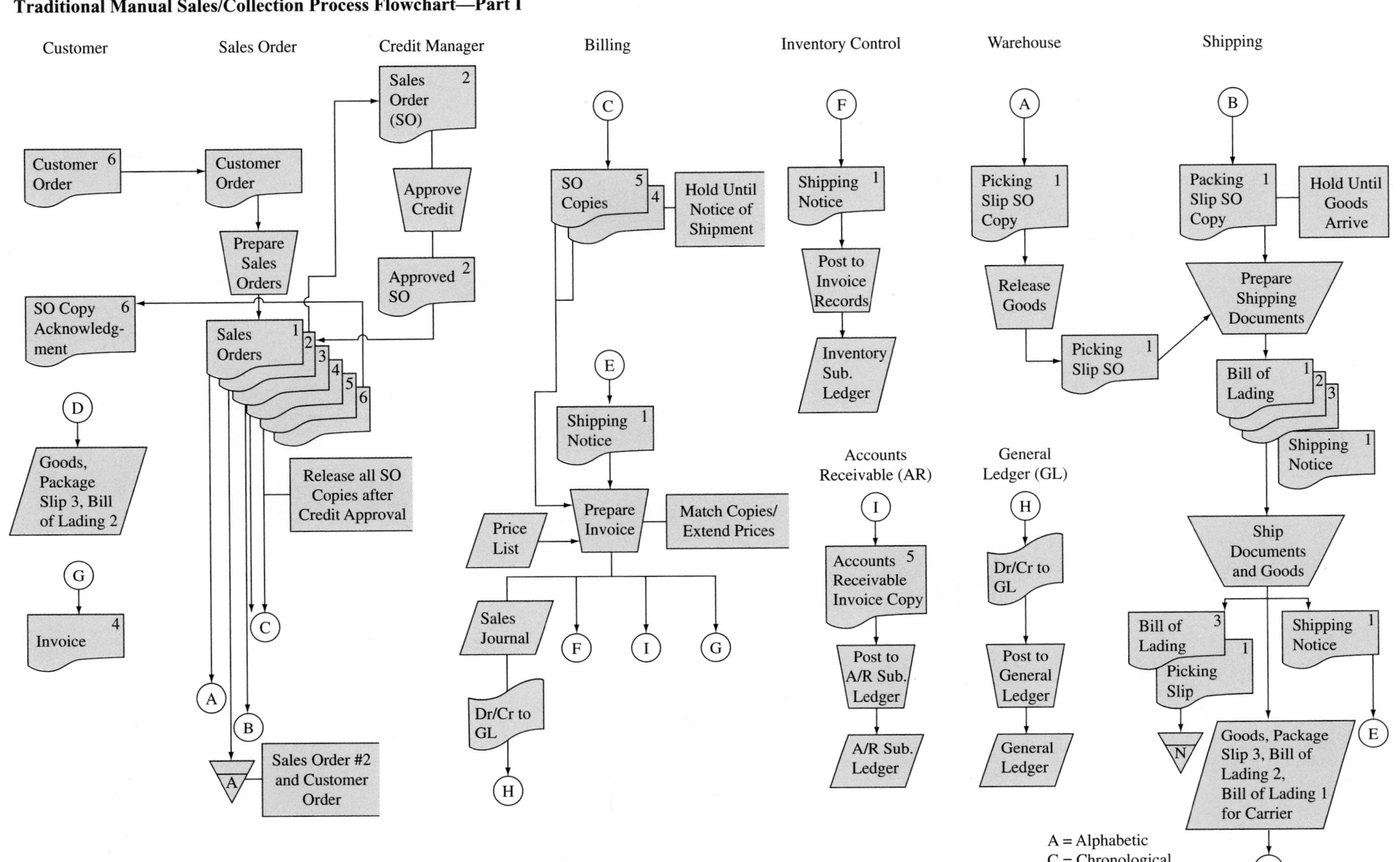

Source: A. S. Hollander, E. L. Denna, and J. O. Cherrington, *Accounting Information, Technology, and Business Solutions,* 2nd ed. (New York: McGraw-Hill, 2000), p. 234.

EXHIBIT 10.1B
Traditional Manual Sales/Collection Process Flowchart—Part II

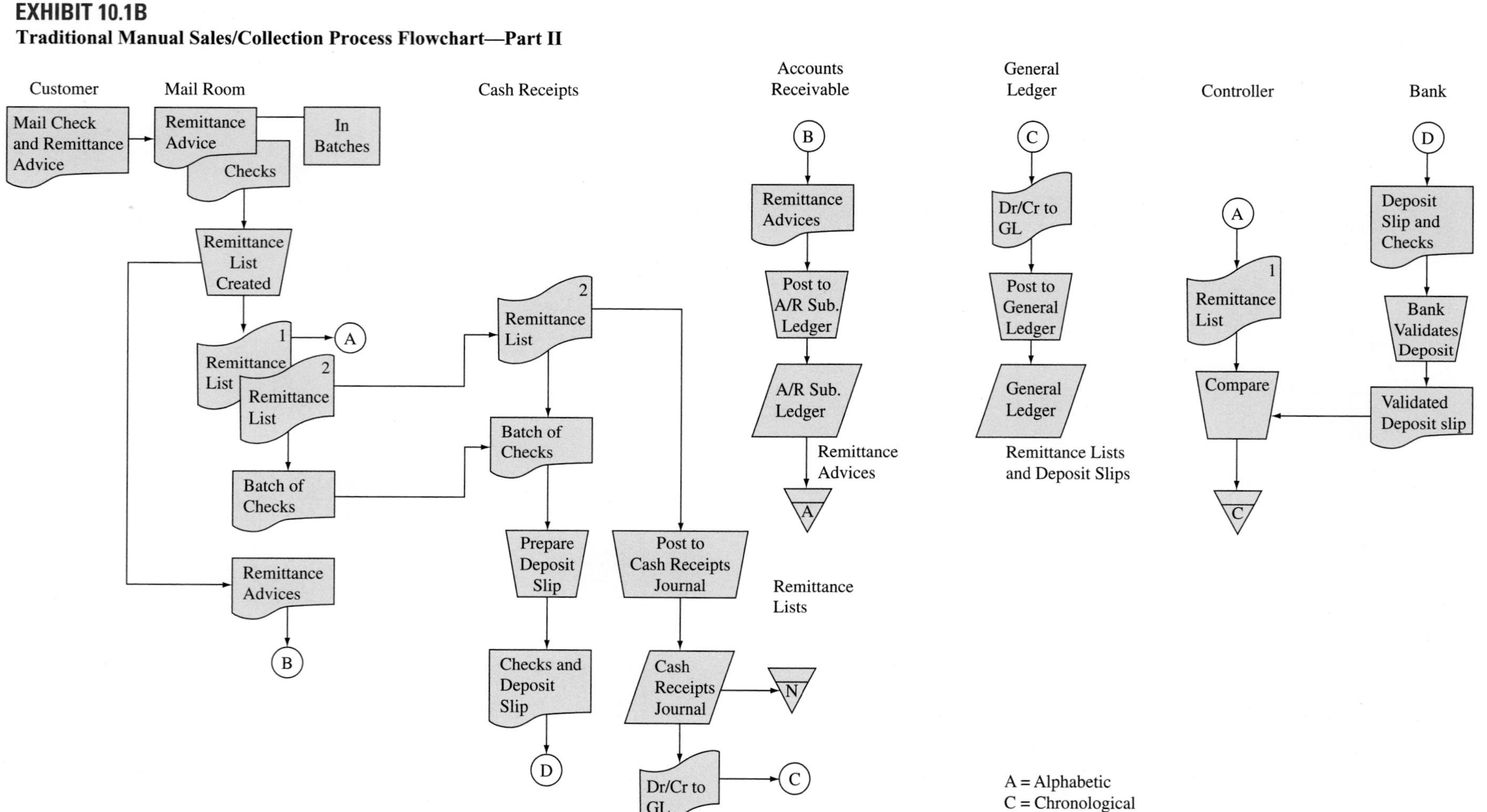

Source: A. S. Hollander, E. L. Denna, and J. O. Cherrington, *Accounting Information, Technology, and Business Solutions,* 2nd ed. (New York: McGraw-Hill, 2000), p. 235.

We know that revenue can be recognized (1) at the time cash is collected, (2) before cash is collected, or (3) after cash is collected. We discuss and illustrate each of these possibilities next.

Revenue Recognized When Cash Collected

When a company performs a service or sells a product and immediately collects cash in return, revenue is recorded at the same time cash is collected, because the revenue is both earned and realized. For example, assume that Apple sells a $2,000 computer to a customer and immediately collects a cash payment of $2,000. The revenue recognition and collection of cash are concurrent, the transaction is complete, and the accounting records reflect that fact. Thus,

Assets	=	Liabilities	+	Owners' equity
+2,000				+2,000

General Journal

Date	Description	DR	CR
10-1	Cash	2,000	
	Sales		2,000

Revenue Recognized before Cash Collected (Asset Created)

Companies frequently perform a service or sell a product and send the customer a bill that must be paid within some specified time period. For example, assume Apple sells $20,000 of computers to a school and agrees to send a bill for the computers at the end of the month. Since Apple has delivered the product and received an asset (a legitimate promise to pay from the school), the revenue is recognized because it has been earned and realized. Thus,

Assets	=	Liabilities	+	Owners' equity
+20,000				+20,000

General Journal

Date	Description	DR	CR
10-2	Accounts Receivable	20,000	
	Sales		20,000

Later, when the school pays Apple,

Assets	=	Liabilities	+	Owners' equity
+20,000				
(20,000)				

General Journal

Date	Description	DR	CR
10-3	Cash	20,000	
	Accounts Receivable		20,000

Revenue Recognized after Cash Received (Liability Incurred)

Companies often collect cash before revenue is earned. For example, customers usually pay for magazine subscriptions at the beginning of the subscription period; insured parties frequently pay for insurance premiums before the start of the policy period; and, in some situations, lawyers, accountants, and doctors collect money from clients before performing services.

In these situations the receipt of cash from the customer precedes the earning process so revenue recognition must wait. Instead, the customer payment creates an obligation (a liability) for the business to perform a service, deliver a product, or return the cash to the customer in the future.

Assume that Apple collects a $2,400 deposit from a customer on March 1, 2010, for a computer to be delivered in April. This deposit represents unearned revenue (a liability), thus:

$$\text{Assets} = \text{Liabilities} + \text{Owners' equity}$$
$$+2{,}400 \qquad +2{,}400$$

General Journal

Date	Description	DR	CR
10-4	Cash	2,400	
	Unearned Revenue		2,400

Later, when Apple delivers the computer, the earnings process is complete and the revenue is recognized because net assets are increased as the liability is decreased,

$$\text{Assets} = \text{Liabilities} + \text{Owners' equity}$$
$$(2{,}400) \qquad +2{,}400$$

General Journal

Date	Description	DR	CR
10-5	Unearned Revenue	2,400	
	Sales		2,400

Note concerning external financial statements: The liability created by the collection of advance payments from customers may appear in a company's balance sheet under other various titles. Some common examples are Advances from Customers, Revenue Received in Advance, or Deferred Revenue. Often the details are reported only in the notes that accompany the financial statements.

Sales Returns and Allowances

The revenue process does not necessarily end once companies recognize and record revenue. For example, if sales are made on account, the company must collect the cash owed by customers. Problems of customer dissatisfaction and support also may require attention. These three important events related to revenue recognition affect the amount of revenue reported for a given time period: sales returns, sales allowances, and sales discounts.

When a product is sold, there is a chance the customer will not be satisfied because, for example, the merchandise may be damaged or a clothing item purchased may be the wrong size. When this occurs, most vendors either allow the customer to return the merchandise (a sales return) or negotiate with the customer to keep the merchandise and pay a reduced price (a sales allowance). (We described these transactions from the purchasing company's viewpoint as purchase returns and allowances in Chapter 8.)

To run a company effectively, managers need to know the portion of merchandise sales that is returned or defective. Changes in this ratio from one year to the next may indicate positive or negative developments that require attention. Also, the cost involved in handling returned merchandise must be factored into the prices charged for all merchandise sold. Therefore, the company reflects these events in its records by debiting a temporary account related to sales, titled **Sales Returns and Allowances.** This contra revenue account represents returns by customers and price allowances granted to customers.

For instance, assume that Apple sells a $3,000 computer system on account to a customer. Subsequently, because the customer complains about the functionality of the system received, Apple agrees to a price allowance (reduction in the amount due) of 10 percent. Apple would make the following entry in the general journal to record the sales allowance:

General Journal

Date	Description	DR	CR
10-6	Sales Returns and Allowances	300	
	Accounts Receivable		300

If the customer had returned the computer, Apple would also debit Sales Returns and Allowances (for $3,000 however) and credit Accounts Receivable for $3,000. In addition, Apple would record the return of the inventory (debit Inventory) and it would credit Cost of Goods Sold for the cost of the inventory returned (assuming a perpetual inventory system). We discuss inventory cost below.

Sales Discounts

Recall that companies often offer customers a cash discount in return for prompt payment of account balances. This discount, which is stated as a percentage of the gross sales amount, is available to a customer only when payment is made within a specified discount period. The invoice sent to the customer specifies the discount terms, which might appear as 2/10, n/30. Whereas buyers refer to these discounts as *purchase discounts* (see Chapter 8), from the seller's perspective they are sales discounts.

To illustrate the accounting for sales discounts, assume that Apple makes a credit sale of $30,000 to a customer. Terms of sale are 3/15, n/45. Thus,

Assets	=	Liabilities	+	Owners' equity
+30,000				+30,000

And,

General Journal

Date	Description	DR	CR
10-7	Accounts Receivable	30,000	
	Sales		30,000

Let's assume the customer pays for the merchandise within the discount period. How much does the customer owe Apple? Since the customer is entitled to a 3 percent discount, it owes Apple 97 percent of the gross selling price. Thus, the customer will pay Apple $29,100 ($30,000 × 0.97).

Assets	=	Liabilities	+	Owners' equity
+29,100				
(30,000)				(900)

Apple would record the sales discount taken by the customer in a temporary account, **Sales Discount.** And Apple would make the following entry in the general journal to record the cash received from the customer.

Cash Received within the Discount Period

Date	Description	DR	CR
10-8	Sales Discounts	900	
	Cash	29,100	
	Accounts Receivable		30,000

In examining this entry, note that we recorded the cash received, $29,100, as well as the sales discount taken by the customer. Finally we credited the customer's account for the full amount owed since she did not owe Apple any additional amounts from this sale.

Now let's explore the process when the customer pays the bill after the discount expires. In this case the customer must pay the entire bill, thus:

Assets	=	Liabilities	+	Owners' equity
+30,000				
(30,000)				

And,

Cash Received after the Discount Period Has Expired

Date	Description	DR	CR
10-9	Cash	30,000	
	Accounts Receivable		30,000

Enhance Your Understanding

In Chapter 8 we learned that some companies use the net price method to record purchases. Why don't we use a net price method to record sales?

Answer: Some people would reply that at the end of the period, a company needs to evaluate its credit policies and, therefore, it needs to know the *sales discounts taken* during the period. A better answer is that recording sales at the gross price and discounts when taken results in better information for management. Although the company can control whether purchase discounts are taken, it cannot control whether sales discounts are taken. Therefore recording sales at the net amount is not appropriate.

The temporary accounts—Sales Returns and Allowances and Sales Discounts—are *contra revenue* accounts because they are subtracted from gross sales revenue to obtain net sales revenue for presentation on the income statement. By using separate Sales Returns and Allowances and Sales Discounts accounts, managers can keep track of the cost to the company of returns and allowances and of receiving prompt payments. This helps management monitor quality (internal perspective) and it helps determine whether the benefits of offering cash discounts outweigh the costs (internal perspective).

Enhance Your Understanding

Many companies simply report net sales on their external financial statements. Why do you think companies would be reluctant to report sales returns and allowances and sales discounts externally?

Answer: Because external financial statements are publicly available, customers and competitors can receive this information. The company might not want its customers and/or competitors to know the extent of its sales returns and allowances or sales discounts.

As we discussed in Chapters 8 and 9, companies often use special journals and subsidiary ledgers to enhance their accounting systems. A sales journal might look like the following:

Sales Journal

Date	Description	Amount

Like the purchases journal illustrated in Chapter 8, this journal has only one amount column. Thus this total amount is posted twice to the general ledger at the end of a specified time period—once to Accounts Receivable and once to Sales (it is posted individually to the Accounts Receivable subsidiary ledger every time a credit sale is made).

An accounts receivable subsidiary ledger provides details concerning the accounts receivable general ledger account. An accounts receivable subsidiary ledger might look like the following:

Joe Customer Accounts Receivable Subsidiary Account

Date	Description	DR	CR	Balance

FAST FACT

Accounting systems have become very sophisticated. Some restaurants can tell you revenues and cost of goods sold by table, by hour, or by wait-staff. This allows the restaurant to determine if specific items sell better at specific times of day, if certain areas within the restaurant are more desirable, and yes, if certain employees generate higher sales. Talk about specific identification!

Like the accounts payable subsidiary ledger introduced in Chapter 8, an accounts receivable subsidiary ledger is used to record sales to, payments received by, and write-offs (discussed later) of specific customers' accounts.

Cost of Goods Sold

In Chapter 8 we discussed the process of purchasing inventory. In Chapter 9 we examined the process of producing inventory. Now it is time to consider the sale of inventory. We use the perpetual inventory system throughout the discussion that follows.

Specific Identification Method

When a business has a heterogeneous inventory and identifies each inventory item with the date of its purchase (or production) and the price paid to purchase or make the item, the price of that item is transferred from the Inventory account to the Cost of Goods Sold account when the company sells the individual item. This costing system is known as the **specific identification method.** For example, in a car dealership, each item of inventory (car, truck, or van) has an identification code that enables management to monitor the status of each vehicle. The identification code indicates to management the amount the dealership paid for the vehicle and any additional costs incurred to prepare the vehicle for sale. The dealership expenses the costs identified by the identification code for a specific vehicle, to cost of goods sold, when the vehicle is sold.

In most businesses, specific identification is difficult because, once an item is purchased or made and stored as inventory, it loses its physical identification. For example, assume that a company buys and sells one type of shirt. Further assume that it purchased shirts on January 15, February 7, and March 1. On March 7, a customer purchases a shirt. Did this customer purchase a shirt from the group bought on January 15, February 7, or March 1? It is hard to tell because the shirt has lost its identification with a particular purchase date and its specific purchase price because it looks like the other shirts. If the prices paid for the shirts were the same, determining which group was sold first, second, or third would not be an issue. However, when the price paid for each group of shirts differs, determining the cost of the shirts sold becomes an issue because we can't determine what group it came from. Because these shirts represent a homogeneous inventory that has different costs, management must adopt a cost flow assumption—that is, a rational and systematic allocation of inventory cost between the Cost of Goods Sold and Inventory accounts based on presumptions made about the order in which the company expenses its inventory cost.

One alternative is to average the cost of inventory purchased (or made). However, this method requires more bookkeeping because the cost per unit changes with every purchase made (or product produced) at a different price. Most companies use the first-in, first-out (FIFO) or last-in, first-out (LIFO) costing methods that assume an order in which inventory items are sold rather than recalculating inventory cost.[2] To illustrate FIFO and LIFO cost flow assumptions, we use the data presented in Exhibit 10.2.

First-In, First-Out (FIFO) Method

The **first-in, first-out (FIFO)** cost flow assumption means that costs are charged to cost of goods sold in chronological order. The first inventory costs recorded are the first costs

[2] LIFO costing is not allowed under IFRS.

EXHIBIT 10.2
Inventory Events

Date	Event	Inventory			
		Number of Units		Unit Price	Total Cost
		Transferred In	Sold		
Oct. 1	Beginning inventory	1,200		$5.00	$ 6,000
Oct. 5	Sale*		800		
Oct. 6	Transfer	600		5.10	3,060
Oct. 9	Transfer	500		5.25	2,625
Oct. 15	Sale*		800		
Oct. 21	Sale*		600		
Oct. 24	Transfer	600		5.30	3,180
Oct. 26	Transfer	200		5.40	1,080
Oct. 28	Sale*		300		
Total		3,100	2,500		$15,945

*All units sell for $8.00 each.

FIFO
A cost flow assumption whereby costs are allocated to cost of goods sold in chronological order.

expensed to Cost of Goods Sold and, therefore, the remaining inventory balance consists of the most recent costs. FIFO approximates the physical flow of the inventory because, generally, companies sell the oldest items first, leaving the most recent purchases in inventory. In periods of rising prices, use of the FIFO cost flow assumption results in the older, lower prices appearing on the income statement as Cost of Goods Sold and the newer, higher prices appearing on the balance sheet as Inventory. We discuss the implications of this cost flow assumption for the users of financial statements later in the chapter.

In a perpetual inventory system, the cost of goods sold is calculated and recorded at the time a sale is made. Using the information presented in Exhibit 10.2, we analyze the entries and record the transfer of cost from Work-in-Process Inventory to Finished Goods Inventory (Chapter 9) and the cost of goods sold for the month of October below. We label FIFO entries (A) throughout this discussion and we use (B) when we switch to LIFO. When using a perpetual inventory system, the company might prepare an inventory register for each inventory item (see Exhibit 10.3), which is a supplemental, internal record designed to keep track of the units sold and the inventory on hand for a particular item on a continual basis. Thus, at any point in time, the inventory balance will reflect all purchases and sales made to date. To illustrate these events we use the Acme Company which produces and sells iPhone accessories.

EXHIBIT 10.3
FIFO Perpetual Inventory Register for Finished Goods (A Entries)

Date	Inventory Transferred In	Inventory Sold	Finished Goods
10/1	Beginning bal.		1,200 × $5.00
10/5		800 × $5.00 = $4,000	400 × $5.00
10/6	600 × $5.10 = $3,060		400 × $5.00 600 × $5.10
10/9	500 × $5.25 = $2,625		400 × $5.00 600 × $5.10 500 × $5.25
10/15		400 × $5.00 400 × $5.10 } = $4,040	200 × $5.10 500 × $5.25
10/21		200 × $5.10 400 × $5.25 } = $3,120	100 × $5.25
10/24	600 × $5.30 = $3,180		100 × $5.25 600 × $5.30
10/26	200 × $5.40 = $1,080		100 × $5.25 600 × $5.30 200 × $5.40
10/28		100 × $5.25 200 × $5.30 } = $1,585	400 × $5.30 200 × $5.40
Total or Ending Balance	$9,945	$12,745	$3,200

October 5 Sold 800 units on account for $8.00 each. Because the only units available on October 5 come from the beginning inventory of 1,200 units, cost of goods sold is $4,000 (800 units at $5.00 each). The journal entries on October 5 are:

General Journal

Date	Description	DR	CR
10-5 A	Accounts Receivable	6,400	
	Sales		6,400
	Cost of Goods Sold	4,000	
	Finished Goods Inventory		4,000

October 6 Transferred 600 units costing $5.10 each from Work-in-Process Inventory to Finished Goods Inventory.

General Journal

Date	Description	DR	CR
10-6 A	Finished Goods Inventory	3,060	
	Work-in-Process Inventory		3,060

October 9 Transferred 500 units costing $5.25 each from Work-in-Process Inventory to Finished Goods Inventory.

General Journal

Date	Description	DR	CR
10-9 A	Finished Goods Inventory	2,625	
	Work-in-Process Inventory		2,625

October 15 Sold 800 units on account for $8.00 each. Because the first costs recorded are the first costs expensed (FIFO assumption), the remaining beginning inventory costs (400 at $5.00) are expensed first, followed by the costs recorded on October 6, of which 400 units are expensed. Thus, Cost of Goods Sold is $4,040 [(400 × $5.00) + (400 × $5.10)]. The journal entries on October 15 are:

General Journal

Date	Description	DR	CR
10-15 A	Accounts Receivable	6,400	
	Sales		6,400
	Cost of Goods Sold	4,040	
	Finished Goods Inventory		4,040

October 21 Sold 600 units on account for $8.00 each. The oldest costs remaining on October 21 were recorded on October 6 (200 units at $5.10) and the next oldest were recorded on October 9, of which 400 units at $5.25 will be expensed. Cost of Goods Sold is $3,120 [(200 × $5.10) + (400 × $5.25)]. The journal entries on October 21 are

General Journal

Date	Description	DR	CR
10-21 A	Accounts Receivable	4,800	
	Sales		4,800
	Cost of Goods Sold	3,120	
	Finished Goods Inventory		3,120

October 24 Transferred 600 units costing $5.30 each from Work-in-Process Inventory to Finished Goods Inventory. The journal entry is:

General Journal

Date	Description	DR	CR
10-24 A	Finished Goods Inventory	3,180	
	Work-in-Process Inventory		3,180

October 26 Transferred 200 units costing $5.40 each from Work-in-Process Inventory to Finished Goods Inventory. The journal entry is:

General Journal

Date	Description	DR	CR
10-26 A	Finished Goods Inventory	1,080	
	Work-in-Process Inventory		1,080

October 28 Sold 300 units on account for $8.00 each. The oldest costs remaining on October 28 include 100 units from October 9 and 600 units from October 24. Because 300 units are sold on October 28, Cost of Goods Sold is $1,585 [(100 × $5.25) + (200 × $5.30)]. The journal entries on October 28 are:

General Journal

Date	Description	DR	CR
10-28 A	Accounts Receivable	2,400	
	Sales		2,400
	Cost of Goods Sold	1,585	
	Finished Goods Inventory		1,585

For the month of October, using the FIFO cost flow assumption for inventory, the total cost of goods sold is $12,745 ($4,000 + $4,040 + $3,120 + $1,585), and the ending balance of the Finished Goods Inventory account in the general ledger is $3,200. The inventory register reflects the dollar amounts to record in Cost of Goods Sold because it keeps a running balance of inventory on hand. The accounts for Inventory and Cost of Goods Sold summarize the flow of costs from the inventory accounts to cost of goods sold.

Work-in-Process Inventory Account

Date	Description	DR	CR	Balance
10-1A	Beginning Balance (assumed)	14,345		
10-6A			3,060	11,285
10-9A			2,625	8,660
10-24A			3,180	5,480
10-26A			1,080	4,400

Finished Goods Inventory Account

Date	Description	DR	CR	Balance
10-1A	Beginning balance			6,000
10-5A			4,000	2,000
10-6A		3,060		5,060
10-9A		2,625		7,685
10-15A			4,040	3,645
10-21A			3,120	525
10-24A		3,180		3,705
10-26A		1,080		4,785
10-28A			1,585	3,200

Cost of Goods Sold Account

Date	Description	DR	CR	Balance
10-5A		4,000		4,000
10-15A		4,040		8,040
10-21A		3,120		11,160
10-28A		1,585		12,745

LIFO
A cost flow assumption whereby costs are allocated to cost of goods sold in reverse chronological order.

Last-In, First-Out (LIFO) Method

In contrast to the FIFO cost flow assumption method of accounting for inventory, the **last-in, first-out (LIFO)** cost flow assumption assumes that costs are charged to cost of goods sold in reverse chronological order. The last inventory costs recorded are the first costs expensed to Cost of Goods Sold, and the inventory balance consists of the oldest inventory costs. While LIFO does not correspond to the physical flow of the goods, it does provide benefits that we discuss later.

Using the information presented in Exhibit 10.2 and the LIFO inventory register shown in Exhibit 10.4, the entries to record transfers and sales of inventory for the month of October 2008 are analyzed as follows.

October 5 Sold 800 units on account for $8.00 each. Because the only units available on October 5 come from the beginning inventory of 1,200 units, cost of goods sold is $400 (800 units at $5.00 each). The journal entries on October 5 are:

General Journal

Date	Description	DR	CR
10-5 B	Accounts Receivable	6,400	
	Sales		6,400
	Cost of Goods Sold	4,000	
	Finished Goods Inventory		4,000

EXHIBIT 10.4
LIFO Perpetual Inventory Register for Finished Goods (B Entries)

Date	Inventory Transferred In	Inventory Sold	Finished Goods
10/1	Beginning balance		12 × $5.00
10/5		800 × $5.00 = $4,000	400 × $5.00
10/6	600 × $5.10 = $3,060		400 × $5.00 600 × $5.10
10/9	500 × $5.25 = $2,625		400 × $5.00 600 × $5.10 500 × $5.25
10/15		500 × $5.25 300 × $5.10 } = $4,155	400 × $5.00 300 × $5.10
10/21		300 × $5.10 300 × $5.00 } = $3,030	100 × $5.00
10/24	600 × $5.30 = $3,180		100 × $5.00 600 × $5.30
10/26	200 × $5.40 = $1,080		100 × $5.00 600 × $5.30 200 × $5.40
10/28		200 × $5.40 100 × $5.30 } = $1,610	100 × $5.00 500 × $5.30
Total or Ending Balance	$9,945	$12,795	$3,150

October 6 Transferred 600 units costing $5.10 each from Work-in-Process Inventory to Finished Goods Inventory.

General Journal

Date	Description	DR	CR
10-6 B	Finished Goods Inventory	3,060	
	Work-in-Process Inventory		3,060

October 9 Transferred 500 units costing $5.25 each from Work-in-Process Inventory to Finished Goods Inventory.

General Journal

Date	Description	DR	CR
10-9 B	Finished Goods Inventory	2,625	
	Work-in-Process Inventory		2,625

October 15 Sold 800 units on account for $8.00 each. Because the last costs recorded are the first costs expensed (LIFO assumption), the inventory transferred on October 9 is expensed first, followed by the costs recorded on October 6. Thus, cost of goods sold is $4,155 [(500 × $5.25) + (300 × $5.10)]. The journal entries on October 15 are:

General Journal

Date	Description	DR	CR
10-15 B	Accounts Receivable	6,400	
	Sales		6,400
	Cost of Goods Sold	4,155	
	Finished Goods Inventory		4,155

October 21 Sold 600 units on account for $8.00 each. The newest costs on October 21 were recorded on October 6 (300 units at $5.10) and the next newest are part of beginning inventory of which 300 units at $5.00 will be expensed. Cost of goods sold is $3,030 [(300 × $5.10) + (300 × $5.00)]. The journal entries on October 21 are:

General Journal

Date	Description	DR	CR
10-21 B	Accounts Receivable	4,800	
	Sales		4,800
	Cost of Goods Sold	3,030	
	Finished Goods Inventory		3,030

October 24 Transferred 600 units costing $5.30 each from Work-in-Process Inventory to Finished Goods Inventory. The journal entry is:

General Journal

Date	Description	DR	CR
10-24 B	Finished Goods Inventory	3,180	
	Work-in-Process Inventory		3,180

October 26 Transferred 200 units costing $5.40 each from Work-in-Process Inventory to Finished Goods Inventory. The journal entry is:

General Journal

Date	Description	DR	CR
10-26 B	Finished Goods Inventory	1,080	
	Work-in-Process Inventory		1,080

October 28 Sold 300 units on account for $8.00 each. The newest costs on October 28 resulted from transfers made October 26 and 24. Because 300 units are sold on October 28, cost of goods sold is $1,610 [(200 × $5.40) + (100 × $5.30)]. The journal entries on October 28 are:

General Journal

Date	Description	DR	CR
10-28 B	Accounts Receivable	2,400	
	Sales		2,400
	Cost of Goods Sold	1,610	
	Finished Goods Inventory		1,610

For the month of October, total cost of goods sold using the LIFO cost flow assumption is $12,795 ($4,000 + $4,155 + $3,030 + $1,610), and the cost of ending inventory is $3,150. The information on the inventory register reflects the amount to record in the Cost of Goods Sold account for each sale by keeping a running balance of the number and cost of goods available for sale at any time. These transactions are summarized as follows:

Work-in-Process Inventory Account

Date	Description	DR	CR	Balance
10-1B	Beginning balance (assumed)			14,345
10-6B			3,060	11,285
10-9B			2,625	8,660
10-24B			3,180	5,480
10-26B			1,080	4,400

Finished Goods Inventory Account

Date	Description	DR	CR	Balance
10-1B	Beginning balance			6,000
10-5B			4,000	2,000
10-6B		3,060		5,060
10-9B		2,625		7,685
10-15B			4,155	3,530
10-21B			3,030	500
10-24B		3,180		3,680
10-26B		1,080		4,760
10-28B			1,610	3,150

Cost of Goods Sold Account

Date	Description	DR	CR	Balance
10-5B		4,000		4,000
10-15B		4,155		8,155
10-21B		3,030		11,185
10-28B		1,610		12,795

Exhibit 10.5 compares gross margins and ending inventories using both the FIFO and LIFO methods. Notice that because the transfer costs of inventory were increasing in this example, the FIFO cost flow assumption results in the lower cost of goods sold amount, the higher gross margin, and the higher ending inventory. If the price of producing the inventory had decreased during the period, the opposite effects would occur.

EXHIBIT 10.5
Comparison of FIFO and LIFO

	FIFO	LIFO
Sales	$20,000	$20,000
Less cost of goods sold:		
Feb. 5	4,000	4,000
Feb. 15	4,040	4,155
Feb. 21	3,120	3,030
Feb. 28	1,585	1,610
Total cost of goods sold	$12,745	$12,795
Gross margin	$ 7,255	$ 7,205
Ending inventory	$ 3,200	$ 3,150

While LIFO reflects less income during a period of rising prices, a company may want to adopt a LIFO cost flow assumption because it generates a higher cost of goods sold and, therefore, a lower net income. This results in a smaller income tax expense. To illustrate, use the information in Exhibit 10.5 and assume that operating expenses were $2,000 and that the company is subject to a 40 percent average tax rate. The resulting net incomes under FIFO and LIFO are $3,153 and $3,123, respectively, as shown in Exhibit 10.6.

Recall that companies also must be concerned with cash flows. Assume that the cash for all sales is collected and all production costs and operating expenses are paid in cash during the period. As shown in Exhibit 10.6, the resulting cash flows under FIFO and LIFO before taxes are the same ($20,000); however, after taxes cash flows are $5,953 and $5,973, respectively. This illustrates why a company may adopt LIFO in a period of rising prices. While the net income under LIFO is smaller, the cash flows are larger because LIFO saves the company money on income taxes.

Periodic Inventory System and Cost Flow Assumptions

Recall from Chapter 8 that companies using the periodic inventory system determine the balance of inventory and cost of goods sold only at the end of the period. After physically counting the inventory, the FIFO or LIFO cost flow assumption is applied to determine the ending inventory balance. Once ending inventory is known, cost of goods sold can be determined as we did in Chapter 8.

To illustrate this process, refer to the previous example and Exhibit 10.2. Note the following: beginning inventory is $6,000, transfers into finished goods during the period were $9,945, and there are 600 units in ending inventory. Using FIFO, the cost of ending inventory would be the newest costs (the oldest costs have been expensed) at the end of the period. Thus the ending inventory would be $3,200 (200 units at $5.40 and 400 units at $5.30). Therefore, Cost of Goods Sold is $12,745 ($6,000 + $9,945 − $3,200).

EXHIBIT 10.6
Comparison of Cash Flows Using FIFO and LIFO

	FIFO	LIFO
Gross margin (Exhibit 10.5)	$ 7,255	$ 7,205
Less operating expenses	2,000	2,000
Net income before tax	$ 5,255	$ 5,205
Less income taxes (40%)	2,102	2,082
Net income	$ 3,153	$ 3,123
Cash receipts from sales	$20,000	$20,000
Less cash payments:		
Production costs	(9,945)	(9,945)
Operating expenses	(2,000)	(2,000)
Income taxes	(2,102)	(2,082)
Net cash flows	$ 5,953	$ 5,973

Using LIFO, the cost of ending inventory would be the oldest costs (the newest costs have been expensed) at the end of the period. Thus the ending inventory would be $3,000 (600 units at $5.00). Cost of Goods Sold using LIFO is $12,945 ($6,000 + $9,945 − $3,000).

FIFO, LIFO, and GAAP External Reporting

Companies could conceivably switch back and forth between FIFO and LIFO to take advantage of changing prices. However, changing inventory methods eliminates the consistency of the financial statements from year to year. As a result, generally accepted accounting principles require the consistent application of cost flow assumptions. A publicly held company that switches cost flow methods must disclose the impact of the change in its financial reports to the public. This disclosure must include a justification for the change. In addition, the Internal Revenue Service (IRS) requires that any company using LIFO for tax purposes also use LIFO for financial statement reporting purposes. In other words, a company cannot use different inventory costing methods to report a higher net income to its stockholders and a lower net income to the IRS. Again, recall that LIFO is not allowable under International Financial Reporting Standards.

The IRS allows the use of FIFO for tax purposes and LIFO for reporting on financial statements. However, it is very unlikely that a firm's management would select this option in periods of inflation, because a company would report more taxable income and pay more taxes to the IRS but report less income to its shareholders.

Estimating Uncollectible Credit Sales

As we saw in Chapter 6, when a company makes credit sales, it is an unfortunate fact that some accounts will prove to be uncollectible. Managers must allow for this in their budgets. They also need an accounting system that provides detailed and relevant information regarding the benefits of granting credit (increased sales) versus the cost of granting credit (the amount of losses from uncollectible accounts). An overly restrictive credit policy might result in too many lost sales, while overly generous policies might result in a large proportion of sales that will never be collected.

Enhance Your Understanding

Are there situations in which 100 percent collections from customers might not be considered a good result?

Answer: Yes, 100 percent collections could imply that the company's credit policies are too restrictive and, therefore, it may be missing potential sales. Thus the company must always weigh the cost of possible uncollectible accounts against the benefit of increased sales.

When preparing financial statements for external stakeholders, companies should consider two primary objectives: proper income measurement and proper asset valuation.

Proper Income Measurement

It is important to match the revenues recognized during a given period with all related expenses incurred to earn those revenues. Therefore, it would be inappropriate to record revenue from credit sales in one year and the expense resulting from related uncollectible accounts in the next. This matching requirement creates a problem because some year-end accounts receivable balances resulting from current year sales are not specifically identified as uncollectible until the following year.

To solve this problem, at each year-end companies must estimate the portion of the current year's credit sales they anticipate will eventually prove uncollectible and deduct this estimated expense on the current year's income statement.

Proper Asset Valuation

The estimated uncollectible accounts expense deducted on the income statement has a corresponding impact on the balance sheet. Like any expense, it reduces owners' equity, which, in turn, means that some asset account must decrease or liability account must increase to maintain the equation Assets = Liabilities + Owners' equity. Because uncollectible accounts are related to accounts receivable, the other balance sheet item affected is Accounts Receivable. We must reduce Accounts Receivable to its **net realizable value,** the net dollar amount the company expects to eventually collect after making allowances for estimated uncollectible accounts.

Recording Estimated Uncollectible Accounts

Assume that at September 27, 2010, the end of its fiscal year, Apple has a $300,000 balance in its Accounts Receivable account but estimates that $15,000 will prove uncollectible. Since that $15,000 is not collectible, the assets are overstated and must be reduced. In addition we must recognize an expense related to noncollection. Thus,

Assets	=	Liabilities	+	Owners' equity
(15,000)				(15,000)

And,

General Journal

Date	Description	DR	CR
09-27-10	Uncollectible Accounts Expense	15,000	
	Allowance for Uncollectible Accounts		15,000

The debit to Uncollectible Accounts Expense reduces net income by $15,000. Allowance for Uncollectible Accounts is a *contra asset* that, when subtracted from the year-end Accounts Receivable balance of $300,000, yields the $285,000 estimated net realizable value of accounts receivable to be reported on the balance sheet. This might be shown in the current asset section of the balance sheet as follows:

Accounts receivable	$300,000
Less allowance for uncollectible accounts	15,000
Net accounts receivable	$285,000

Or, more frequently, the balance sheet simply presents the $285,000, identifying it as the net accounts receivable.

Recording Actual Uncollectible Accounts

In subsequent accounting periods, the company monitors customer subsidiary ledger accounts to identify specific balances that are not going to be paid. For instance, a customer's account balance may be designated as uncollectible if the customer declares bankruptcy or if that particular customer's account remains unpaid after repeated attempts at collection. A company must make appropriate entries (known as a write-off) to remove these uncollectible balances from the company's accounting records.

Assume that on January 31, 2011 (the next accounting year), Apple determines that one of its customers is unable to pay its $5,000 accounts receivable balance. So, we must decrease Accounts Receivable by $5,000 because we assume this amount will never be collected. But what is the other effect? Recall that the Allowance for Uncollectible Accounts is a contra asset representing the estimated uncollectible accounts. Since we now know that a specific account is uncollectible, the amount is no longer an estimate; therefore, the allowance account should be reduced:

General Journal

Date	Description	DR	CR
01-31-11	Allowance for Uncollectible Accounts	5,000	
	Accounts Receivable		5,000

Let's examine the impact of this entry on the net Accounts Receivable balance:

	Before Write-Off	After Write-Off
Total accounts receivable	$300,000	$295,000
Less allowance for uncollectible accounts	15,000	10,000
Net accounts receivable	$285,000	$285,000

Appropriately, the net Accounts Receivable balance has not changed. Remember that Apple already reduced the net realizable value of Accounts Receivable at the end of fiscal 2010 when the company recorded its uncollectible accounts expense for the year. To reduce the amount of accounts receivable a second time would record the effect of the same expense twice, and in two different periods. Instead, when Apple identifies a specific account as uncollectible, it removes that account receivable balance from its records and reduces the Allowance for Uncollectible Accounts by the same amount, yielding no change in net Accounts Receivable. The company also reduces (credits) the customer's accounts receivable account in the subsidiary ledger and denotes it as a write-off rather than a payment.

Enhance Your Understanding

Why might a company be reluctant to report its Allowance for Uncollectible Accounts or write-offs of customer accounts on the balance sheet?

Answer: Remember an external financial statement is available to the public. Thus the company's customers and competitors as well as its shareholders have access to these statements. The company might not want its customers and competitors to know the proportion of Accounts Receivable deemed uncollectible.

On rare occasions, companies eventually collect amounts due previously on accounts that have been written off. When this occurs, the company reverses the entry originally made to record the write-off of the account. Then the company records the collection of the account in the same manner as the collection of any Accounts Receivable balance due.

Reporting Revenue Process Events

Let's recap what we have learned about the revenue process in this chapter. We know that revenues are recognized when earned and realized. And we know that the revenues for the period are reported on the income statement. We learned that cost of goods sold is determined by applying a cost flow assumption (FIFO or LIFO) and that the cost of goods sold for the period is also reported on the income statement. Finally we learned that companies estimate the amount of uncollectible credit sales and recognize the expense on the income statement and the resulting net realizable value of accounts receivable on the balance sheet. Cash received from customers during the period is reported on the statement of cash flows. Exhibit 10.7 summarizes revenue process reporting.

Let's examine Apple's financial statements in the Appendix. On the income statement Apple reports net sales of $32,479 million and cost of sales (cost of goods sold) of $21,334 million. (Note 1 in Apple's Annual Report reveals that this firm uses the FIFO cost flow assumption, p. 59) On the balance sheet we note that Accounts Receivable, net of Allowance for Uncollectible Accounts, is $2,422 million. Note, however, that the statement of cash flows does not reveal the amount of cash received from customers during the period.

Estimating Cash Receipts from Customers

We can estimate this amount based on our knowledge of the Accounts Receivable account. We know that:

EXHIBIT 10.7
Reporting Revenue Process Events

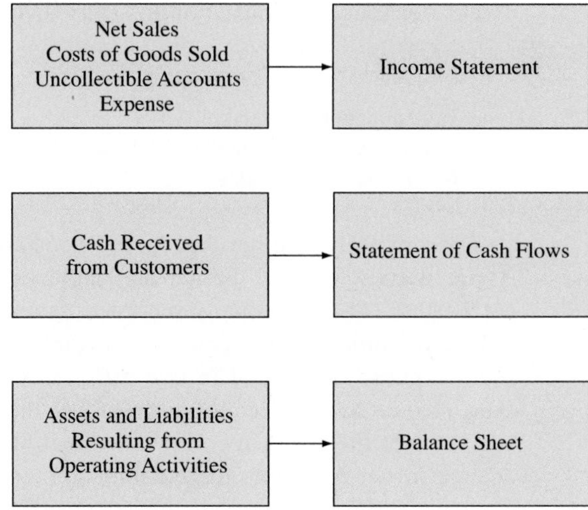

Beginning accounts receivable, net
+ Net sales (sales less sales returns and allowances and less sales discounts)
= Maximum amount owed to the company by customers
− Cash received from customers
= Ending accounts receivable, net

Let's estimate Apple's cash receipts from customers. On the income statement we find net sales of $32,479 million. On the balance sheet we find the beginning and ending balances of accounts receivable of $1,637 and $2,422 million, respectively. So,

Accounts receivable, beginning balance	$ 1,637
+ Net sales	32,479
= Maximum amount owed by customers	$34,116
− Cash received from customers	?
= Accounts receivable, ending balance	$ 2,422

Thus we estimate that Apple received $31,694 million ($34,116 − $2,422) from customers during fiscal 2008.

Internal Evaluation of Revenue Process Events

Earlier we explored revenue process planning and discovered that companies develop balanced scorecard measures to monitor the revenue process. At the end of the accounting period (or at other appropriate times) the company must compare its actual results against these goals. Thus if the company had a goal to increase the number of customers by 10 percent, it would need to determine, at the end of the period, the number of customers and compare this amount to the number of customers at the beginning of the period. Or, if the company planned to increase customer satisfaction during the period, it would need to determine whether this goal had been reached at year-end. In addition, it should compare its budgeted revenues to its actual revenues for the period, which we discuss next. Companies also monitor sales discounts taken by customers to evaluate their internal credit policies. Sales returns and allowances are monitored to evaluate quality (internal perspective).

Another evaluation companies often undertake to analyze both their expenditure process and their revenue process is to compare their planned activity ratios against their activity ratios. Recall from Chapter 2 that companies typically calculate an accounts receivable turnover (and days in the collection period) to plan and monitor the speed at which they collect accounts receivable from customers. An inventory turnover (and days in the selling period) is commonly calculated to plan and monitor the speed at which inventory is sold. Finally, an accounts payable turnover (and days in the payment period) indicates the speed at which the company pays its suppliers. Planning and then evaluating all these ratios is a crucial part of monitoring the internal process perspective in addition to the revenue variances discussed below.

Revenue Variances

In Chapter 9 we learned how managers use production variances to evaluate the conversion (and expenditure) process. Similarly revenue variances are useful to evaluate the revenue process. When the actual amount of revenues earned is different than the planned amount of revenues there are three explanations. First, the selling price was different than budgeted. Second, the number of units sold was different than planned. Third, both the selling price and the number of units sold were different than planned. The **sales price variance** indicates the difference in revenue due to a change in selling price. The **sales quantity variance** indicates the difference in revenue due to a change in sales volume. The sales price variance is determined as follows:

SPV = (ASP − BSP) × AS
SQV = (AS − BS) × BSP
where:
ASP = actual selling price
BSP = budgeted selling price
AS = actual units sold
BS = budgeted sales (units)

Sales price variance = (Actual selling price per unit − Budgeted selling price per unit) × Actual number of units sold

If the actual selling price is greater than the budgeted selling price, the result is a positive number indicating a "favorable" variance. If the actual selling price is less than the budgeted selling price, the result is a negative number indicating an "unfavorable" variance.[3] Recall, however, that the terms *favorable* and *unfavorable* do not necessarily mean good or bad. Until we understand the cause of the variance, we cannot determine whether it is good or bad.

The sales quantity variance is determined as follows:

Sales quantity variance = (Actual number of units sold − Budgeted number of units to sell) × Budgeted selling price

If the actual number of units sold is greater than the budgeted number of units, the result is a positive number indicating a favorable variance. If the actual number of units sold is less than the budgeted number of units, the result is a negative number indicating an unfavorable variance. Again, the terms *favorable* and *unfavorable* do not necessarily mean good or bad.

Enhance Your Understanding

In Chapter 9 when the actual amount was greater than the budgeted amount, the variance was unfavorable. Why is a revenue variance favorable when the actual amount is greater than the budgeted amount?

Answer: Production variances concern inputs; therefore, when the actual amount of input consumed is greater than that budgeted, the variance is unfavorable. Revenue variances concern outputs; therefore, when the actual output is greater than budgeted, the variance is favorable.

Let's return to our company, PCs to Go, to illustrate these variances. In Chapter 6 we budgeted sales for the quarter at $1,500 per tablet PC as follows:

	PC	Revenue
Month One	300	$ 450,000
Month Two	350	525,000
Month Three	400	600,000
	1,050	$1,575,000

Now assume that actual sales for the quarter were 1,100 tablet PCs at an average selling price of $1,550 (total revenue = $1,705,000 [1,100 × $1,550]). Our sales price and sales quantity variances are:

Sales price variance = ($1,550 – $1,500) × 1,100 = $55,000 F
Sales quantity variance = (1,100 – 1,050) × $1,500 = $75,000 F

[3] As we did in Chapter 9, we will not show negative numbers in variances. Rather, we denote them with a U for unfavorable and an F for favorable.

This means that our actual revenue was $55,000 more than budgeted due to the increased selling price and $75,000 more than budgeted due to the increased number of PCs sold. We can reconcile actual revenue to budgeted revenue as shown here:

Actual revenue	$1,705,000
Less favorable sales price variance	(55,000)
Less favorable sales quantity variance	(75,000)
Budgeted revenue	$1,575,000

Again, an analysis such as this is important so that management can plan for the future.

Summary

In this chapter we examined the final operating process—the revenue process. Revenues are recognized when earned and realized. This may be when cash is received, before cash is received, or after cash is received. Sales returns and allowances and sales discounts are called contra revenues because they reduce the gross revenue reported on the income statement. When a company sells homogeneous products it must adopt a cost flow assumption to determine which costs to expense (cost of goods sold) during the period. Finally companies must estimate the amount of uncollectible accounts for the period to match the expense (uncollectible accounts expense) to the revenue (sales) in the same period.

- FIFO cost flow assumes that the oldest costs are expensed first. On the other hand, LIFO assumes that the newest costs are expensed first.
- The sales price and sales quantity variances help explain the difference between actual and budgeted revenues.

Key Terms

First-in, first-out (FIFO) A cost flow assumption where costs are charged to Cost of Goods Sold in chronological order, *283*
Last-in, first-out (LIFO) A cost flow assumption where costs are charged to Cost of Goods Sold in reverse chronological order, *287*
Net realizable value The net dollar amount of receivables the company expects to eventually collect after making allowances for estimated uncollectible accounts, *292*
Sales Discount A temporary account used to record cash discounts taken by customers, *281*
Sales price variance A variance that indicates the difference in revenue due to a change in selling price, *295*
Sales quantity variance A variance that indicates the difference in revenue due to a change in sales volume, *295*
Sales Returns and Allowances A temporary account that represents the returns by customers and price allowances granted to customers, *280*
Specific identification method A costing system where the price paid for an item is specifically identified with the item and expensed when the item is sold, *283*

Questions

1. What two conditions must be met for a company to recognize revenue?
2. Define a cash equivalent value.
3. What two contra accounts are related to sales and what is the purpose of each?
4. What is the difference between a sales return and a sales allowance?
5. What is meant by the phrase "cost flow assumption" as it relates to inventories?
6. Assume a company has two items for sale. Item 1 was produced on January 15 at a cost of $50,000 and Item 2 was produced on January 31 at a cost of $60,000. If the company sells Item 2 on February 5 and uses the specific identification method, what is the amount of cost of goods sold?
7. What does the term *first-in, first-out* mean? What is the impact of this cost flow assumption on the income statement and balance sheet?
8. What does the term *last-in, first-out* mean? What is the impact of this cost flow assumption on the income statement and balance sheet?

9. Assume a company has two items for sale. Item 1 was produced on January 15 at a cost of $50,000 and Item 2 was produced on January 31 at a cost of $60,000. If the company sells Item 2 on February 5 and uses the FIFO method, what is the amount of cost of goods sold?
10. If a company uses the periodic inventory system, it determines the FIFO or LIFO cost of ending inventory rather than the cost of goods sold. Why?
11. In a period of rising prices would a company prefer FIFO or LIFO costing? Why?
12. Can a company use LIFO for tax reporting and FIFO for external reporting? Why?
13. What are the external reporting objectives in accounting for uncollectible accounts?
14. What is meant by the term *net realizable value* as it pertains to accounts receivable?
15. What is the impact on the financial statements of writing off a specific customer's account receivable?
16. If a company's Accounts Receivable account increases during the period, were cash collections from customers greater than or less than net sales?
17. What does the sales price variance indicate?
18. What does the sales quantity variance indicate?
19. If the actual quantity sold is less than the budgeted sales quantity, is the sales quantity variance favorable or unfavorable?
20. If the actual selling price is greater than the planned selling price, is the sales price variance favorable or unfavorable?

Exercises

E10.1 **LO 1** In each of the following situations, determine the month in which the business should recognize the revenue:

A. On June 5, Jacquie Monahan, an editor, received an advance from a publisher. She performed the work during the period July 8 through July 22. On August 9, Jacquie sent the publisher an accounting of her hours.
B. On February 27, Paul's Plumbing placed an advertisement with the *Kansas City Tribune.* The full-page ad ran during the week of March 15–22. The *Tribune* billed Paul's Plumbing for the ad on March 7, with payment terms of n/30. Payment was received by the *Tribune* on April 4.
C. On November 25, Bookworm, Inc., sold an encyclopedia to Children's Learning Center on account. Payment was due on December 25 but was not received until January 15.

LO 1 **E10.2** In each of the following situations, determine the dollar amount of the revenue to be recognized:

A. Metric Corporation received $10,000 from a customer as a deposit on a special order.
B. Pearldine, Inc., shipped a machine to a customer and billed the customer for the remaining amount owed, $30,000. The customer had made a deposit of $8,000 two weeks prior to the shipment date.
C. Catherine Dole, a doctor, received $200 in copayments from various patients during the month. She also billed several insurance companies $3,500 for services rendered to these patients. The insurance companies usually pay within 60 days of receipt of the bills.

LO 1 **E10.3** Given the following events, prepare the necessary journal entries for Morrison:

A. Kathleen Morrison, a CPA, received $3,000 from a client for services to be performed next month.
B. Kathleen performed the services for the client.
C. An accounting of the work performed was sent to the client.

LO 1 **E10.4** Given the following events, prepare the necessary journal entries on behalf of ABC Company:

A. Jeff Gray placed an order for merchandise and made a $2,000 deposit.
B. ABC Company notified Jeff that his order was ready for pickup.
C. Jeff picked up his order and paid the balance due, $5,000.

LO 1 **E10.5** Journalize the following transactions for the Prado Company:

Oct. 8 Sold $9,200 of merchandise to Zen, Inc., on account, terms 2/10, n/60. The merchandise had a cost of $6,000.

Oct. 10 Zen, Inc., returned some of the merchandise, receiving an $800 credit from Prado Company. The merchandise, which originally cost Prado $500, was put back into inventory.

Oct. 23 Received payment from Zen, Inc., for the merchandise purchased on October 8, less the return and any appropriate discount.

LO 1 **E10.6** Journalize the following transactions using the perpetual inventory system on the books of Drietz Company:

A. June 5, sold $10,200 of merchandise to Bailey Company on account, terms 2/10, n/30. The merchandise had a cost of $8,000.

B. June 8, Bailey requested a reduction in the selling price of the merchandise because of some slight imperfections. Drietz granted a $600 allowance.

C. June 14, received payment from Bailey for the merchandise purchased on June 5, less the allowance and the discount.

LO 3 E10.7 Carpenter Company estimated uncollectible accounts expense for the year ended June 30, 2010, at $4,500. During July 2010, Carpenter identified the Wong account as uncollectible and wrote off the balance of $375. Give the journal entries to record these events. What is the effect of each entry on net accounts receivable?

LO 3 E10.8 Technics Corporation wrote off $28,700 of accounts receivable during the year ended November 30, 2010. The balance of Allowance for Uncollectible Accounts at December 1, 2009, was $34,200, and at November 30, 2010, it was $29,500. Determine the amount of uncollectible accounts expense for the year ended November 30, 2010.

LO 3 E10.9 A review of the financial statements of Micromania, Inc., revealed a beginning and ending Allowance for Uncollectible Accounts balance of $32,500 and $28,600, respectively. If the uncollectible accounts expense for the period was $15,530, what was the total dollar amount of accounts written off during the period?

LO 2 E10.10 Matthews, Inc., is in its first year of operating as a wholesale company. During the accounting period just completed, it experienced consistently rising prices on the products it buys and sells. The following partial income statement information was developed by its chief accountant using two different cost flow assumptions, FIFO and LIFO.

	Case 1	Case 2
Sales	$1,500,000	$1,500,000
Cost of goods sold	975,000	996,000
Gross margin	$ 525,000	$ 504,000

Determine which case is FIFO and which is LIFO. State which case would result in the higher inventory value on the balance sheet and indicate why.

LO 2 E10.11 Johnston Industries uses the perpetual inventory system for some of its products. From the following information, prepare the journal entries to record the cost of goods sold under FIFO and LIFO. What is the ending inventory under each cost flow assumption?

Date	Transaction	Quantity	Unit Cost
Jan. 1	Beginning inventory	40	$50
Jan. 8	Purchase	90	$75
Jan. 12	Sale	105	—

LO 2 E10.12 The following information is taken from the records of the Perry Company. Perry uses a perpetual inventory system.

Date	Transaction	Number of Units	Unit Cost
May 1	Beginning inventory	28	$5.00
4	Sale	10	
12	Purchase	16	$4.00
16	Sale	6	
21	Sale	14	
25	Purchase	8	$3.00
31	Sale	17	

Determine the cost of goods sold for the month using FIFO and LIFO cost flow assumptions. How many units are in ending inventory and what is the cost of ending inventory under each assumption?

LO 2 E10.13 The following information is taken from the records of the Strauch Company. Strauch uses a perpetual inventory system.

Date	Transaction	Quantity	Unit Cost
May 1	Beginning inventory	28	$5
4	Sale	10	
12	Purchase	12	$6
16	Sale	8	
21	Sale	13	
25	Purchase	8	$7
31	Sale	12	

Determine the cost of goods sold for the month using FIFO and LIFO cost flow assumptions. How many units are in ending inventory and what is the cost of ending inventory under each assumption? (The perpetual inventory registers in Exhibit 10.3 and Exhibit 10.4 may be helpful in solving this exercise.)

LO 4 **E10.14** The statement of cash flows for Steinhoff Corporation for the year ended June 30, 2010, reported cash received from customers of $5,680,000. Steinhoff's comparative balance sheets for June 30, 2009, and 2010, reported net accounts receivable balances of $690,000 and $765,000, respectively. Determine the net sales reported by Steinhoff for the year ended June 30, 2010.

LO 4 **E10.15** The accountant at Zetec, Inc., gathered the following information:

	12/31/09	12/31/10
Accounts receivable, net	$9,600	$17,200

If net sales for the year ended December 31, 2010, were $783,200, determine the amount of cash received from customers during the year.

LO 4 **E10.16** The Rodgers Company reported $284,700 of cash received from customers on its statement of cash flows for the year ended September 30, 2010. However, the income statement for the same time period reported net sales totaling $231,400. Explain why these two numbers are not equal.

LO 5 **E10.17** Manley Company planned to sell 140,000 units this year at $6.00 per unit. Actual results indicate that 142,000 units were sold at $6.25 per unit. What are the sales price and sales quantity variances?

LO 5 **E10.18** Peterson, Inc., sold 260,000 units last year, which was 20 percent less than expected. Its average selling price was $6 per unit, which was 20 percent higher than planned. What are the sales price and sales quantity variances?

LO 5 **E10.19** Rasmussen, CPAs, completed 1,800 tax returns for clients during 2008. The average price paid per return was $165. The firm's master budget indicated expected tax return revenues of $308,000 based on 2,000 expected returns. What are the sales price and sales quantity variances?

LO 5 **E10.20** Hills Dog Food generated revenues of $5,000,000 during 2010 by selling 1,000,000 bags of dog food. The master budget of Hills shows expected sales of 1,200,000 bags of dog food generating $5,760,000 in revenue. What are the sales price and sales quantity variances?

Problems

P10.1 LO 4 For each of these three cases, determine the missing amounts indicated by question marks.

	Case 1	Case 2	Case 3
Sales	$?	$95,000	$?
Finished goods inventory, beginning	19,480	9,000	34,000
Work-in-process inventory, beginning	?	8,000	18,000
Direct materials	134,650	19,000	86,000
Direct labor	76,420	30,000	38,000
Manufacturing overhead applied	157,830	26,000	?
Work-in-process inventory, ending	28,845	?	34,000
Cost of goods manufactured	350,175	66,000	146,000
Finished goods inventory, ending	?	32,000	?
Cost of goods sold	352,095	?	132,000
Gross margin	177,715	?	36,000
Operating expenses	?	19,000	28,000
Net income (loss)	(39,707)	33,000	?

LO 2 **P10.2** Data from Trail Bikes, Inc.'s perpetual inventory records for a tire it produces and sells follow:

	Number of Units	Cost per Unit
Beginning inventory	6,000	$12.25
Transfers to Finished Goods:		
Mar. 3	12,000	12.20
June 28	15,000	12.10
Sept. 12	11,000	12.05
Nov. 30	17,000	11.95
Sales:		
Mar. 7	11,000	
July 8	18,000	
Oct. 12	8,000	
Dec. 7	16,000	

The company sold 53,000 tires during the year at $20 each.

Required:
A. Compute the cost of the ending inventory and the cost of goods sold using both FIFO and LIFO.
B. In your opinion, which of the two methods is a better representation of the balance sheet value for the inventory? Why?
C. What is the gross margin using each method?
D. Which method do you think is more representative of the firm's income? Why?

LO 2 **P10.3** Refer to P10.2. Assume the company uses a periodic inventory system.

LO 1 LO 2 **P10.4** Franzen Company uses a perpetual inventory system. During the month of February of the current year, the company experienced the following transfers and sales on one item in the stock of goods. The sale price of the product is $6. Assume that all sales are for cash.

Date	Transaction	Number of Units	Unit Cost
Feb. 1	Beginning inventory	300	$4.00
3	Sale	200	
9	Transfer to Finished Goods	600	$4.10
15	Sale	500	
24	Transfer to Finished Goods	400	$4.20
28	Sale	300	

Required:
A. Make the entries for these transactions using FIFO.
B. Make the entries for these transactions using LIFO.
C. What are the cost of goods sold and the cost of ending inventory under each of these assumptions? Explain why the two methods generate different amounts.

LO 2 **P10.5** Refer to P10.4. Assume the company uses a periodic inventory system.

LO 1 LO 2 **P10.6** The Patterson Company sells two products, Tog and Uni. Tog sells for $850 per unit, and Uni has a price of $1,300. Patterson uses the perpetual inventory system and uses the net price method of accounting for purchase discounts. On December 1, 2010, Patterson had 70 units of Tog at a cost of $400 each and 20 units of Uni at a cost of $740 each. During the month of December 2010, Patterson had the following transactions:

Dec. 1 Purchased 20 units of Tog from Quirin Corporation on account for $410 each; terms 2/10, n/30, FOB destination.
3 Sold six units of Uni to Mahoney Corporation on account; terms n/EOM (end-of-month) and FOB destination.
4 Paid $88 freight on the shipment to Mahoney.
5 Purchased 25 units of Uni from Deitz Co. on account for $760 each; terms 1/15, n/30, FOB destination.
15 Sold 30 units of Tog to the Utica Corporation on account; terms n/30, FOB shipping point.
16 Returned five units of Uni that were defective to Deitz Co.
20 Paid the amount due to Deitz Co.

22 Sold 25 units of Uni to Tasco Corp. for cash.
30 Collected amount due from Mahoney Corporation from December 3 sale.
31 Paid amount due to Quirin Corporation.

Required:
A. Make the entries for these transactions using the FIFO cost flow assumption.
B. Make the entries for these transactions using the LIFO cost flow assumption.
C. What is the amount of gross margin and ending inventory under FIFO?
D. What is the amount of gross margin and ending inventory under LIFO?
E. What is the difference in the gross margin, ending inventory, and cash flows between these two methods?

LO 4 **P10.7** The Rust Corporation has gathered the following information for activities during 2010:

Credit sales	$3,500,000
Cash sales	1,100,000
Sales discounts	35,000
Sales returns and allowances	150,000
Uncollectible account written off	5,000
Beginning accounts receivable balance	70,000
Ending accounts receivable balance	50,000

Required:
A. Calculate net sales during 2010.
B. Calculate estimated cash receipts from customers during 2010.

LO 5 **P10.8** Mulcahy Enterprises produces and sells three models of video disc players. Budgeted and actual information follow.

Model Type	Budgeted Units	Budgeted Sales	Actual Units	Actual Sales
Model A 2356	4,000	$ 800,000	4,100	$ 902,000
Model B 2875	5,000	925,000	4,850	911,800
Model C 2742	2,000	660,000	2,400	780,000
Total		$2,385,000		$2,593,800

Required:
A. Compute the sales price variances for each video disc model.
B. Compute the sales quantity variances for each video disc model.
C. Prove that the total of the variances explains the difference between actual and budgeted sales for the period.

LO 1 LO 4 **P10.9** Heath Enterprises operates a chain of retail stores in California specializing in paintings by local artists. Heath uses a perpetual inventory system and the specific identification method to determine cost of goods sold. During the month of July, the following transactions occurred:

July 3 Sold a $1,500 painting to Dawn Associates on account, terms 2/10, n/30. The painting had a cost of $800.
6 Received a $1,000 deposit from D&W Industries for a painting that was to be reframed. The balance of $500 will be collected at the time of pickup.
10 Sold a painting for $950 cash. The painting had a cost of $320.
12 Received payment from Dawn Associates for the painting purchased on July 3, less the applicable discount.
15 D&W picked up the reframed painting and paid the balance due.
17 Sold a $3,200 painting to Universal Corporation on account, terms 1/10, n/60. The painting had a cost of $1,100.
20 Universal requested a reduction in the price of the painting because of a defect in the frame. Heath granted a $200 allowance to Universal.
27 Received payment from Universal for the July 17 sale, less the allowance and the discount.

Required:
A. Prepare journal entries to record these transactions.
B. Determine the total amount of net revenue reported by Heath for the month of July. What is the gross margin for July?

LO 1 LO 4 **P10.10** McGinty Consulting & Placement provides personnel services to clients in the Boston area. During the month of November, McGinty engaged in the following transactions:

Nov. 4	Received a $6,000 retainer from Morac & Associates for services to be rendered in January.
8	Sent JM Corporation a bill for $3,400 for services rendered during the week ended November 7, terms 2/10, n/30.
13	Provided services to Dillard Company and mailed an invoice for $1,900, terms 1/15, n/60.
17	Received a check from JM Corporation for services billed on November 8, less the applicable discount.
20	Received $5,700 from Natick Industries in full settlement of its account, after the discount period had elapsed.
28	Payment was received from Dillard Company for the invoice dated November 13, less the applicable discount.

Required:
A. Prepare journal entries to record these transactions.
B. Determine the amount of net revenue reported by McGinty for the month of November.
C. Determine the cash received from customers during the month of November. Would you expect it to be the same as net revenue? Why?

Cases

C10.1 LO 4 

Refer to the company you chose in C1.1. Based on your knowledge of this company, answer the following:

A. Estimate the cash received from customers.
B. Calculate the inventory turnover.
C. Calculate the accounts receivable turnover.
D. Calculate the accounts payable turnover.
E. What additional information is provided in the notes concerning revenue recognition, uncollectible accounts, and the company's inventory costing method?

LO 4 **C10.2**

Lockhart Enterprises recently completed its first fiscal year and developed the following income statement. M. J., the manager, cannot understand why it is showing a net loss when the number of units sold exceeded expectations. Analyze the following income statement and other information given and write a memo to M. J. explaining your findings.

LOCKHART ENTERPRISES
Income Statement
For the Year Ended September 30, 2010

Sales (120,000 units)		$1,800,000
Less operating expenses:		
Administrative salaries	$110,000	
Advertising expense	54,000	
Batch-related overhead applied	185,500	
Depreciation on office equipment	34,500	
Depreciation on factory	108,000	
Direct labor salaries	200,000	
Heat, light, and power for offices	20,000	
Heat, light, and power for factory	48,000	
Insurance expense for offices	18,000	
Insurance expense for factory	36,000	
Purchases of direct materials	800,000	
Product-sustaining overhead applied	250,000	
Sales salaries	180,000	
Selling expenses	12,000	
Transportation out expense	30,000	
Unit-related overhead applied	100,000	
Total expenses		2,186,000
Net loss		$ (386,000)

Additional information:

1. The ending balances of Direct Materials Inventory, Work-in-Process Inventory, and Finished Goods Inventory were $200,000, $381,750, and $76,350, respectively.
2. There were no indirect materials used in production.

3. Facility-sustaining overhead consists of depreciation on factory; heat, light, and power for factory; and insurance for factory.
4. There was no over- or underapplied overhead at any level.

Critical Thinking

CT10.1 LO 1

Hightech Company offers its customers credit terms of 2/10, n/30. Most customers take advantage of the cash discount, mailing their payments to arrive on the 10th day following the date of the invoice. However, Lowmart Company, Hightech's largest customer, has recently begun sending payments to arrive on the 30th day after invoice, while still taking the 2 percent discount. Hightech's collection department has been in touch with Lowmart regarding the taking of the discount outside the discount period, and Lowmart's response is that it deserves to take the discount whenever payment is made. After all, it is Hightech's biggest customer.

Required: Identify Hightech's possible courses of action as well as the consequences of these actions.

LO 1 **CT10.2**

Xanetics, Inc., recently received a $150,000 special order from Lartech, Inc., for some customized equipment. A 50 percent deposit accompanied the order, with the remaining $75,000 payment to be made at delivery. Xanetics manufactured the equipment and was ready to ship it to Lartech when it was notified that Lartech had declared bankruptcy.

Required: Identify the accounting issues related to the above scenario. Has Xanetics earned a revenue? Has it been realized? Should the company recognize any revenue?

Ethical Challenges

EC10.1 LO 1

Your company has just signed several long-term contracts for several million dollars. Since the contracts are legally binding, your boss wants you to record these contacts as a debit to accounts receivable and a credit to contract revenue earned. Discuss the ethical implications of your boss's request.

LO 5 **EC10.2**

Managing a company's product mix is crucial to the long-term strategy of the company. For retail companies like grocery stores, "loss leaders" are often advertised to entice customers into the store in hopes that, while there, the customer will buy more than just what was advertised. Discuss the ethical implications of this type of advertising from the point of view of the store and the customer.

Computer Applications

CA10.1 LO 5

Ex

Yummi Company makes five types of cookies. The budgeted and actual sales and selling prices follow.

Budgeted revenues:	
Chocolate chip (45,000 boxes at $7.40 per box)	$333,000
Oatmeal raisin (25,000 boxes at $6.20 per box)	155,000
Coconut (10,000 boxes at $6.60 per box)	66,000
White chocolate (15,000 boxes at $7.60 per box)	114,000
Macadamia nut (5,000 boxes at $12.00 per box)	60,000
Total budgeted revenues	$728,000

Actual revenues:	
Chocolate chip (57,600 boxes at $7.50 per box)	$432,000
Oatmeal raisin (28,000 boxes at $6.00 per box)	168,000
Coconut (9,600 boxes at $6.20 per box)	59,520
White chocolate (13,200 boxes at $7.50 per box)	99,000
Macadamia nut (11,600 boxes at $11.00 per box)	127,600
Total actual revenues	$886,120

Required: Prepare a spreadsheet that explains, using variances, the difference between budgeted and sales revenues.

LO 4 **CA10.2**

Set up a spreadsheet that can be used to estimate cash received from customers. Then determine the cash received from customers with the following parameters:

A. Accounts receivable, beginning	$ 8,000
Accounts receivable, ending	12,000
Sales	450,000

B.	Accounts receivable, beginning	$ 20,000
	Accounts receivable, ending	30,000
	Sales	900,000
C.	Accounts receivable, beginning	$ 12,000
	Accounts receivable, ending	8,000
	Sales	450,000
D.	Accounts receivable, beginning	$ 38,000
	Accounts receivable, ending	50,000
	Sales	875,000

Visit the text Online Learning Center at **www.mhhe.com/ainsworth6e** for additional problem material that accompanies this chapter.

PART FOUR

IV

Introduction: Capital Resource Process Activities

CHAPTER ELEVEN

11

Time Value of Money

Learning Objectives

LO1 Explain the risk/return relationship.

LO2 Use the time value of money concepts to solve present and future value problems.

Chapters 1 through 3 described the four basic business processes: (1) business organization and strategy, (2) operating, (3) capital resources, and (4) performance evaluation and control. And we examined the subprocesses (revenue, conversion, and expenditure) within the operating process. The first half of the text focuses on how accounting information is used to plan (Chapters 4 through 6) and then record the results of and evaluate operating processes (Chapters 7 through 10).

In Chapters 11 through 16 we discuss the capital resources processes and how they relate to the business organization and strategy process. Recall that the capital resources process involves the investing and financing activities of the company. Investing activities concern the *purchase, use, and sale of long-term assets* while financing activities involve *raising cash by borrowing and by issuing an ownership interest in the business and paying cash to repay monies borrowed from creditors and to provide a return to owners.* In addition, cash generated from operating activities is also used to acquire assets, repay creditors, and provide a return to owners. In Chapters 17 through 20 we bring everything together by explaining the performance evaluation and control of all business processes.

In Chapter 2 we described the management cycle of planning, performing, and evaluating. This cycle is illustrated again in Exhibit 11.1. At the strategic level, companies conduct long-term planning for operating and capital resources processes, which in turn impacts the short-term planning at the operating level. At the operating level, the company first plans the firm's operating processes based on expected customer demand for the company's goods and services. These planning activities were discussed in Chapters 4 through 6. In the second step, decision makers ascertain the investments in long-term assets necessary to support

EXHIBIT 11.1
The Management Cycle

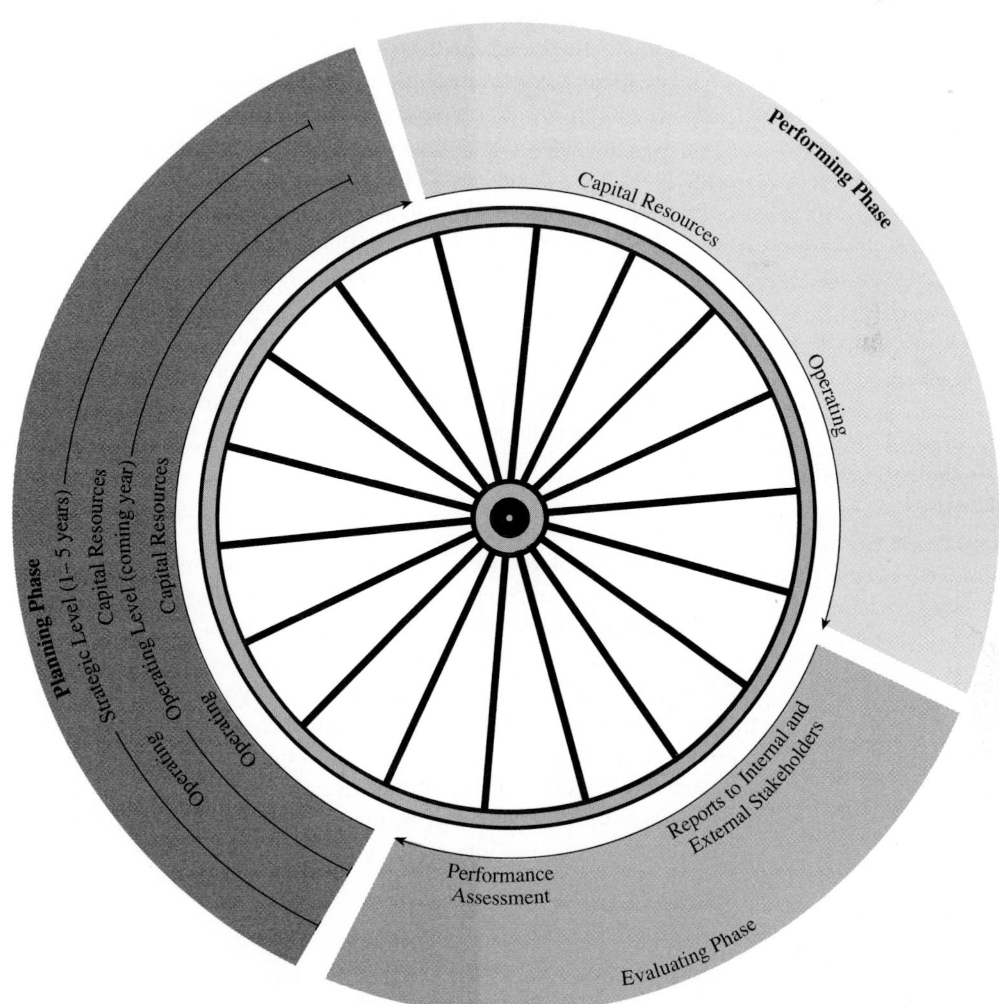

the operating processes planned for the firm. We discuss this process in Chapter 12. The third step involves determining how to finance these investments. After determining the amount of funds needed to acquire the assets, planners must decide on the source of the financing—debt financing (creditors) or equity financing (owners' contributions). We discuss these issues in Chapters 13 and 14. While the planning phase starts with operating processes and ends with capital resources processes, the performance phase reverses the sequence.

In a start-up company, financing activities are the first captured by the accounting system as the company raises the necessary capital. The accounting system is used to record these events and makes a distinction between debt and equity financing. Next companies invest in the operating infrastructure necessary for the firm's operations. The accounting system is used to record these events and notes the difference in the type of assets acquired. Finally, the firm begins operating and the accounting system captures the operating activities as described in Chapters 8 through 10.

Management's goal is to utilize the company's resources effectively and efficiently so the operating activities generate an operating profit. Companies use operating profits in three ways: (1) to pay the interest on borrowed funds and repay the borrowed funds when they come due, (2) to reward the owners with dividends (or in the form of withdrawals in proprietorships and partnerships), and (3) to reinvest funds in the firm to maintain the existing operational capacity and to finance additional long-term investments in the firm.

The evaluating phase provides information about a firm's performance to internal and external stakeholders. In the first half of the text we saw how the balanced scorecard can be used internally to provide measurable goals against which performance can be measured. In addition, we also examined how operating process results are communicated to external users in the annual report. In Chapters 17 through 20 we examine the reporting and evaluating process in greater detail.

The planning, performing, evaluating cycle starts again when the management team begins planning for the operating and capital resources processes of the next time period. The amount and sources of funds needed for new investments depend on management's operating plans and the long-term assets needed to successfully implement the plans. If additional investments are needed to support planned operating activity, managers must decide whether to borrow from creditors, solicit contributions from new or existing owners, or use the funds generated by last year's operations.

Before going any further, however, it is imperative that you understand the fundamental concepts underlying capital resource decisions. In this chapter we introduce the concept of the time value of money, an essential tool for making capital resources (financing and investing) decisions. With this tool, you can make informed financing and investing decisions for a business enterprise or for yourself.

Return

The concept of return is associated with investing decisions involving the acquisition of assets, such as certificates of deposit, government bonds, and new equipment. The two types of return are return *of* investment and return *on* investment. When assessing investment alternatives, investors expect to receive a **return of investment**—that is, the return of the amount initially invested. For example, if you invest $1,000 in a savings account for one year, you expect, at a minimum, to receive $1,000 at the end of the year. The $1,000 you receive at the end of the year is your return *of* investment. **Return on investment** is money received in excess of the initial investment. If the $1,000 in the savings account generates $1,050 at the end of one year, there is a return of the initial $1,000 investment and a return *on* the investment of interest of $50.

Time Considerations

Return on investment is not adequate to differentiate among investments because it does not consider the length of time that investments are held or the amount of the initial investment. For example, investments X and Y, shown in Exhibit 11.2, generate a return on investment

EXHIBIT 11.2
Return on Investment

Investment X		**Investment Y**	
January 1, 2010, Invest	$(1,000)	January 1, 2010, Invest	$(1,000)
January 1, 2011, Receive	1,300	July 1, 2011, Receive	1,400
Return on investment on January 1, 2011	$ 300	Return on investment on July 1, 2011	$ 400

of $300 and $400, respectively. How would you choose between the two investments based on the dollar amount of the return? You might select investment Y because its return is $100 greater than investment X. However, this does not consider the length of time investments X and Y were held. If the $1,300 accumulated by investment X on January 1, 2011, is reinvested and held as long as investment Y (until July 1, 2011), it could generate an additional return that equals or exceeds the $100 difference between the two investments.

Initial Investment Considerations

Even when investments are held for the same period of time, the amounts of the initial investment can distort comparisons. Consider investments X, Y, and Z in Exhibit 11.3. One might choose to make investment Z because it has the largest dollar amount of return on investment of the three investments. However, this choice does not take into account the differences in the size of the initial investments—$1,000, $2,000, and $3,000, respectively.

What we need to analyze the investments realistically is a common-size measure of performance; that is, a measure that allows us to compare and rank the performance of investments regardless of the size of the initial investment.

Rate of Return

The **rate of return** (a percentage) measures the performance of investments on a common-size basis and eliminates any distortion caused by the size of the initial investment. Exhibit 11.3 uses the following rate of return formula to determine the rate of return for investments X, Y, and Z. We calculate rate of return as follows:

$$\frac{\text{Dollar amount of return on investment}}{\text{Dollar amount of initial investment}} = \text{Rate of return}$$

In these cases, the 10 percent rate of return on investment X is greater than those on investments Y (8 percent) and Z (6 percent). The rate of return on investments is usually expressed as an annual (one-year) rate even if the life of the investment is greater or less than one year. The return percentage in Exhibit 11.3 is based on a one-year time period and is called the **annual rate of return.**

Investments have a negative rate of return when they do not recover the initial investment; that is, when the investor fails to get a return of investment. For example, if an investment returns only $800 of the $1,000 initially invested, the $200 difference is described as a 20 percent negative rate of return [($800 − $1,000)/$1,000].

EXHIBIT 11.3
Rate of Return

	Investments		
	X	**Y**	**Z**
January 1, 2010, Invest	$(1,000)	$(2,000)	$(3,000)
January 1, 2011, Receive	1,100	2,160	3,180
Return on investment	$ 100	$ 160	$ 180
Rate of return calculation	$ 100 / $ 1,000	$ 160 / $ 2,000	$ 180 / $ 3,000
Annual rate of return	10%	8%	6%

EXHIBIT 11.4
Expected Outcomes and Probabilities

Possible Outcomes	Possible Returns	Rate of Return If Event Occurs	Probability of Outcome
Best	$1,000,000	1,000%	0.01
Better	150,000	150	0.20
Good	50,000	50	0.40
Worst	(100,000)	(100)	0.39

Expected rate of return (ERR) = (0.01 × 1,000%) + (0.2 × 150%) + (0.4 × 50%) + (0.39 × −100%) = 21%

In Exhibit 11.3, we measured the performance of the investments by calculating the rates of return on investment after the returns were generated by the investments. However, most investments are made before investors know what their actual rates of return will be. How can potential investors measure the performance of investments before knowing the actual rate of return the investments will generate?

Expected Rate of Return

Expected rate of return
The estimated/predicted rate of return before making the investment.

Unfortunately, individuals make investment decisions without the benefit of clairvoyance and, as a result, they must predict rates of return on investments they are considering. The predicted return rate is known as the **expected rate of return,** a summary measure of an investment's performance, stated as a percentage, based on the possible rates of return and the likelihood of those rates of return occurring. The expected rate of return is a useful measure for choosing among investment alternatives.

To ascertain an investment's expected rate of return, it is necessary to (1) forecast the investment's possible rates of return, (2) establish a probability that each forecasted rate of return will occur, and (3) multiply each forecasted return by its respective probability and sum the resulting products.

To illustrate, assume that an investor has the opportunity to buy an investment for $100,000. Exhibit 11.4 lists the four possible outcomes to expect in terms of dollars and rates of return on the investment. The exhibit also shows the probability of the four outcomes occurring. The investor believes that there is 1 chance in 100, or a 1 percent chance, of getting a 1,000 percent rate of return ($1,000,000/$100,000). At the other extreme, there are 39 chances in 100, or a 39 percent chance, of a negative 100 percent rate of return (−$100,000/$100,000). The expected rate of return for this investment is 21 percent, as calculated in Exhibit 11.4.

The investment's 21 percent expected rate of return does not mean that the investment will earn a 21 percent rate of return. Instead, it summarizes the possible rates of return. Do not confuse the expected rate of return with the actual rate of return on an investment. *An investor estimates the expected rate of return before making the investment, while the actual rate of return on an investment is calculated at some future date after the outcome of the investment is revealed.*

The concepts of return of investment, return on investment, rate of return, and expected rate of return are fundamental when making any investment decision. However, investors do not automatically select the investment alternative that generates the highest expected rate of return. Before selecting an investment, it is necessary to appraise not only the expected return but also the risk of the investments under consideration.

Risk

Risk
One's exposure to possible unfavorable outcomes.

Risk is exposure to the chance that an unfavorable outcome will occur at some future point in time. Typically, people take risks because some monetary or psychic reward is possible. For example, people go to Las Vegas and gamble even though they know that casinos are profitable because most people lose money. However, many people are willing to put their money at risk in the hope of beating the odds and winning. The likelihood of losing money is offset by the belief that it is possible to beat the odds and by the enjoyment of actually taking the risk itself.

Attitudes toward Risk

The amount of risk people are willing to assume depends on their attitudes toward risk and the decision under consideration. People who enjoy risky situations are called risk seekers, whereas those who avoid risk are called risk avoiders. However, the decision under consideration may change the decision maker's normal attitude toward risk. For example, in terms of taking physical risks, rock climbers are risk seekers; however, the climbers might be risk avoiders when making investment decisions affecting their ability to finance the next climbing expedition.

Risk is associated with the uncertainty of an unfavorable outcome actually occurring. To illustrate, assume that an alternative to the previous investment is buying a $100,000 one-year U.S. government security that yields a 5 percent rate of return. Because the U.S. government has never defaulted on its debt, there is little doubt that the government will return the initial investment of $100,000 and pay an actual return on investment of $5,000 ($100,000 × 0.05). This investment, therefore, has very little risk because there is very little chance of an unfavorable outcome occurring. In contrast, investing in a gold mine could generate a chance for a significantly higher rate of return than 5 percent but there is also a much higher chance of losing some of your initial investment. Which investment is better depends on the investor's willingness to accept the risk.

Types of Risk

When making investment decisions three primary sources of risk must be considered. We discuss inflation risk, business risk, and liquidity risk next.

Inflation Risk

Inflation causes the purchasing power of the monetary unit to decline. For example, suppose $3.00 buys a loaf of bread on January 1, 2009, but at the end of the year the same loaf of bread costs $3.15. The purchasing power of the dollar declined by 5 percent ($0.15/$3.00 = 0.05, or 5%) during 2009 because it now takes $3.15 instead of $3.00 to buy the same loaf of bread at the end of the period. **Inflation risk,** then, is the chance of a decline in the purchasing power of the monetary unit during the time money is invested. It is factored into every investment decision to allow for the chance of inflation during the investment period.

Business Risk

Business risk is the risk associated with the ability of a particular company to continue in business. A business fails when its revenues do not cover its operating expenses or when cash flows are insufficient to pay the interest or principal on the business's debt. The business risk factor reflects the likelihood of a company ceasing normal operations. For example, a company in financial difficulty has to pay a higher rate of interest on its debt than a financially sound company because its financial difficulty increases the chance that the business may not be able to continue its operations. A bank's prime interest rate is the interest rate charged to the bank's most financially sound customers. The rate of interest on borrowed funds increases as the chance of business failure increases. For example, an airline company such as American, which filed for bankruptcy protection in 2002, has a higher business risk than Southwest Airlines, which has never faced similar financial difficulties.

Liquidity Risk

Investments that are quickly converted into cash are considered to be liquid. **Liquidity risk** is the chance that an investment cannot be readily converted into cash. For example, a holder of 100 shares of McDonald's stock could quickly sell the shares on the New York Stock Exchange; therefore, such an investment is considered to be liquid. On the other hand, if an

FAST FACT

In early May 2005 both General Motors Corporation's and Ford Motors Corporation's credit ratings were downgraded by Standard & Poor's to junk bond status. Analysts indicated that slumping SUV sales and increasing healthcare costs made the downgrade necessary. The drop to junk bond status made the cost of borrowing for both companies much more costly. In 2008, these same companies appealed to Congress for bailout monies.

investor purchased 100 shares of Utica State Bank stock that is not traded on any organized stock exchange, a quick conversion of the stock to cash would be difficult. If the investor needs cash immediately, she might have to reduce the price of the stock substantially to attract a buyer. On the other hand, she could borrow money until she finds a buyer willing to pay the higher price. Then the investor would repay the principal and interest on the loan from the proceeds of the sale of the stock.

Risk/Return Relationship

Risk and return are directly related; that is, the greater the risk, the greater the return the investor expects. When choosing among investment alternatives, investors want the investment with the highest return, but they must also consider the risk of the investment. Typically, investors select investments with the highest expected return for a given level of risk. Thus the expected rate of return includes **risk premiums** to compensate for the inflation, business, and liquidity risks and is called the **risk-adjusted expected rate of return.**

Investors who are risk avoiders and assume greater risk want a greater expected rate of return on their investments. Keep in mind that the notions of risk and return are based on investors' beliefs about the likelihood of future events. Therefore, the assessment of risk and return and the resulting valuation of investments are the result of subjective assessments and the ability of the buyer and seller of the investment to agree on a price.

Risk Premiums

All investors expect some return on their investment, even if an investment has no risk. The determination of the expected return on any investment begins with an assumption called the **risk-free rate of return,** or the rate of return that a virtually risk-free investment produces. Risk premiums for risk factors associated with particular investments are added to the risk-free rate to determine the risk-adjusted expected rate of return of an investment.

To illustrate how risk factors work, assume that an investor is considering the purchase of Utica State Bank stock. Assume that the investor expects a 4 percent inflation rate and that estimates for the business risk and liquidity risk premiums for Utica State's stock are 3 percent and 1 percent, respectively. If the risk-free rate of return is 3 percent, the risk-adjusted expected rate of return for Utica State's stock is 11 percent, as shown here:

Risk-free rate of return	3%
Inflation risk premium	4
Business risk premium	3
Liquidity risk premium	1
Risk-adjusted expected rate of return	11%

Thus, to compensate for the respective risks anticipated, the investor needs an 11 percent risk-adjusted expected rate of return to make the Utica State Bank investment worthwhile.

Key point: To earn a higher rate of return, investors must assume more risk. All investors want to obtain the greatest return possible on their invested funds but must temper their investment decision by the amount of risk they are willing to assume.

Risk/Return and Investors' Money

A company's management team makes similar return-risk assessments as it invests the resources of the firm. However, its investment decisions cannot be based exclusively on the team members' personal attitudes toward risk. The risk that management assumes must be consistent with the risk preferences of the firm's owners because managers act on the owners' behalf.

Businesses use borrowed funds in the expectation of earning a greater return on the funds they invest than the cost of borrowing the funds (interest). Therefore, businesses want to minimize the interest on the borrowed funds. To do so, these businesses must convince their creditors (lenders) that the investments made with the borrowed funds will generate a return sufficient to pay the interest and principal on the loan. The lower the probability that a firm will default on the payment of interest or principal on a loan, the lower the rate of interest creditors will charge for borrowed funds. A lower interest rate improves the chance of increasing the rate of return on the business owners' investment. The business, in such situations, would net more on its borrowed funds, with the excess return going to the owners.

Borrowing money, soliciting contributions from owners, and investing these funds all involve evaluating dollar amounts at different points in time. Understanding the relationship of money and time is critical to all investing and financing decisions.

Time Value of Money

The expectation that investments generate returns over time implies that a dollar today, given that it can generate a return on investment over time, is worth more than a dollar one year from today. This concept is known as the *time value of money.*

The **time value of money** is the tool used to solve problems involving the comparison of cash flows that occur at different points in time. The time value of money allows individuals and businesses to determine the cash equivalent today of cash flows that will occur at some point in time in the future. The interest rates assumed determine the size of the cash equivalent values given a particular period of time.

For example, if an investor could receive 10 percent interest on his investments, \$100 on January 1, 2010, is the cash equivalent of \$110 on January 1, 2011. Thus any amount less than \$110 on January 1, 2011, is not as valuable as \$100 on January 1, 2010. It follows that any amount greater than \$110 on January 1, 2011, is more valuable than the \$100 on January 1, 2010, because the most the \$100, 10 percent investment could generate on January 1, 2011, is \$110. Our illustration describes the concept of cash equivalent values and the role that interest rates play in determining cash equivalent values. However, before going any further, it is necessary to understand the two alternative methods for calculating interest on an investment.

Simple and Compound Interest

As you know, interest is the cost of borrowing money and can be calculated on either a simple or compound basis. **Simple interest** is interest calculated only on the amount borrowed. The amount of interest depends on the amount loaned or borrowed (principal), the annual interest rate, and the amount of time the principal is used. Recall that the formula for calculating interest is:

$$\text{Principal} \times \text{Rate} \times \text{Time} = \text{Interest}$$

For example, assume that you borrow \$1,000 for two years at 10 percent simple interest. The amount of each year's interest is computed using the original \$1,000. The calculation of simple interest for the two-year period is:

Year 1 $1,000 × 0.10 × 1 =	$ 100
Year 2 $1,000 × 0.10 × 1 =	100
Total simple interest	$ 200
Add: Principal	1,000
Total amount due on note	$1,200

The total amount you owe on the note on its maturity date is $1,200, or $1,000 of principal plus $200 of interest.

Compound interest is interest based on a principal amount that includes interest from previous time periods. Like simple interest, compound interest is interest calculated on the principal in the first interest period. However, at the start of the second interest period, the interest from the first period is added to the principal and becomes part of the principal on which interest is calculated for the second period. The process of adding interest to the principal is called **compounding** and is repeated at the start of each subsequent interest period. In other words, compound interest includes interest paid on interest.

To illustrate, assume that you borrow $1,000 for two years at a 10 percent interest rate that is compounded annually. The total amount of interest due at the end of two years is $210 and the total amount due is $1,210.

Year 1 $1,000 × 0.10 × 1 =	$ 100
Year 2 $1,100 × 0.10 × 1 =	110
Total compound interest	$ 210
Add: Principal	1,000
Total amount due on note	$1,210

The difference between the amount of compound and simple interest is the $10 interest charged on Year 1's interest of $100. Note that the first year's interest of $100 becomes part of the principal on which the second year's interest of $110 is calculated [($1,000 + $100 interest) × 0.10 × 1 = $110].

This illustration shows how to compound interest annually; however, it is possible to compound interest more frequently. By increasing the frequency of the compounding, more interest accumulates on the note. To illustrate, suppose the 10 percent interest on the $1,000 note is compounded semiannually. Thus the interest on the note is added to the principal every six months. Consequently, the total amount of interest on the note for two years is $215.51, as follows:

Year 1:		
First six months	$1,000 × 0.10 × ½ =	$ 50.00
Second six months	$1,050 × 0.10 × ½ =	52.50
Year 2:		
Third six months	$1,102.50 × 0.10 × ½ =	55.13
Fourth six months	$1,157.63 × 0.10 × ½ =	57.88
Total compound interest		$ 215.51
Add: Principal		1,000.00
Total amount due on note		$1,215.51

The $215.51 of interest for two years is $5.51 more than the interest incurred when the interest was compounded annually. After six months, $50 of interest is added to principal and, as a result, interest for the first year is $2.50 higher than the $100 interest incurred when compounding the 10 percent rate annually. *Therefore, as the frequency of compounding increases, the total amount of interest increases.* Interest can be compounded quarterly, monthly, daily, hourly, or even continuously.

Based on the concept of compounding, you can use four basic tools to determine cash equivalent values of cash flows that occur at different points in time. These four tools are (1) the future value of the amount of $1, (2) the present value of the amount of $1, (3) the future value of an annuity, and (4) the present value of an annuity. Throughout the discussion that follows we use the following notation:

OF INTEREST Using Financial Calculators

Of the variety of financial calculators on the market today, one of the most popular and affordable is the Hewlett-Packard 10B II. Recall that time value of money problems have six elements that we can relate to this calculator:

Element	HP Keys
PV = present value	PV
FV = future value	FV
ANN = annuity	PMT
r = annual interest rate	I/YR
n = total number of payments/compoundings	N
c = compoundings/payments per year	P/YR

Enter the interest rate as a whole number. Enter the number first and then press the function key. Enter the present value and annuities as negative numbers signifying cash outflows. Notice the +/− key to convert positive numbers to negative numbers or negative numbers to positive numbers.

Let's try a couple of examples. Assume you invest $100 every month starting one month from today for 10 years and earn 12 percent. How much money will you have at the end of 10 years? What do we know?

$ANN = 100$; $c = 12$; $n = 120$; $r = 12$; $PV = 0$; $FV = ?$

HP Keys

(100)	PMT
12	P/YR
10* 12	N
12	I/YR
0	PV
	FV

Answer: 23,003.869

Let's try another one. Assume you want to buy a car for $25,000. The dealer will give you financing at 10 percent for five years. What is your monthly payment? What do we know?

$PV = 25{,}000$; $c = 12$; $y = 5$; $n = 60$; $r = 10$; $FV = 0$; $ANN = ?$

HP Keys

(25000)	PV
12	P/YR
5* 12	N
10	I/YR
0	FV
	PMT

Answer: 531.176

FV = lump-sum amount at some point in the future

PV = lump-sum amount currently

ANN = an annuity (an equal payment over equal intervals)

r = annual rate of return

c = number of compoundings/payments per year

n = total number of payments/compoundings over the entire time period

Throughout this chapter and the chapters to follow we assume the use of a financial calculator. If a financial calculator is not available, you can use published tables to perform time value of money calculations. However, the calculations that can be performed are limited by the data in the tables; therefore, we suggest that you invest in a financial calculator. The appendix to this chapter contains time value of money tables. The Of Interest feature for this chapter discusses one of the most popular financial calculators. Note that when using a financial calculator you should enter a zero for any component that is not used in a given situation. We will follow this convention throughout the discussion that follows.

Future Value of the Amount of $1

We have shown how to calculate the total amount due on a note at some point in the future. The combination of principal and interest on the principal at some specified date in the future (due date) is the note's future value. By using the following formula for the future value of the amount of $1 it is possible to quickly calculate future values.

The future value of the amount of $1 is

$$FV = PV \times (\$1 + r/c)^n$$

The **future value of the amount of $1** is the amount that $1 becomes at a future date, if invested at a specified annual interest rate (r) and compounded a certain number of times per year (c) over the investment period (n). The future value of the amount of $1 is a means of determining the amount of money in the future that is equivalent to an amount today.

Let's try an example. If we invest $1,000 today, at 10 percent annual interest compounded semiannually, what is it worth in two years? What do we know?

$$PV = \$1{,}000;\ r = 10;\ c = 2;\ n = 4;\ ANN = 0;\ FV = ?$$

Using the formula we find:

$$FV = \$1{,}000 \times (\$1 + 0.10/2)^4$$

$$FV = \$1{,}215.51$$

For example, suppose an employee of Apple wants to invest $5,000 in a retirement plan for her daughter on the child's fifth birthday. The investor wants to know how much her daughter will have in her retirement account on her 55th birthday. If we assume an 8 percent rate of return, compounded quarterly for 50 years, the daughter's account will have a balance of $262,424.49 upon her 55th birthday, as follows:

$$PV = \$5{,}000;\ r = 8;\ c = 4;\ n = 200;\ ANN = 0;\ FV = ?$$

$$FV = \$5{,}000 \times (\$1 + 0.08/4)^{200}$$

$$FV = \$262{,}424.49$$

Let's try another example. Assume you have $1,000 to invest today. If you earn 15 percent annually in the stock market (don't you wish?), what will your investment be worth when you graduate in three years? What do we know?

$$PV = 1{,}000;\ ANN = 0;\ r = 15;\ c = 1;\ n = 3;\ FV = ?$$

Therefore, we solve for the future value and find that you will have $1,520.88 if the above assumptions prove to be true.

Present Value of the Amount of $1

The cash equivalent today of some specified amount of cash at a specified date in the future is called the present value of that future amount. It is equivalent to the future amount less the interest that has accumulated over the intervening time period. For example, the present value of $110 one year from today is $100 if the interest rate is 10 percent compounded annually [$110 – ($100 × 0.10 × 1)].

The **present value of the amount of $1** represents the amount of money that, if invested today at some compounded interest rate for a specified time period, will equal $1 at the end of that time period. The present value of the amount of $1 is

$$PV = FV \times 1 / (\$1 + r/c)^n$$

The present value of the amount of $1 is the reciprocal of the future value of the amount of $1. The present value of $1 two years from today is $0.8227. That is, $0.8227 invested today at 10 percent interest compounded semiannually will become $1 in two years.

Likewise, by using the formula for the present value of the amount of $1, we can determine that the present value of $10,000 at 10 percent interest compounded semiannually for two years is $8,227.02.

$$FV = \$10{,}000;\ r = 10;\ c = 2;\ n = 4;\ ANN = 0;\ PV = ?$$

$$PV = \$10{,}000 \times 1 / (\$1 + 0.10/2)^4$$

$$PV = \$8{,}227.02$$

Like future values, the number of compoundings affects the size of the present value. However, present values decrease as the number of compoundings increases. For example, what is the present value of $10,000 at 10 percent for two years compounded quarterly?

$$FV = \$10{,}000;\ r = 10;\ c = 4;\ n = 8;\ ANN = 0;\ PV = ?$$

$$PV = \$10{,}000 \times 1 \,/\, (\$1 + 0.10/4)^8$$

$$PV = \$8{,}207.47$$

Note that increasing the number of compoundings each year decreases the dollars needed today to achieve the same future value. Let's look at another example. Assume that the same Apple employee wants to know how much she has to invest on her daughter's fifth birthday so that her daughter will have $50,000 for college on her 18th birthday. If we assume that the investment will earn 8 percent compounded quarterly for 13 years, the employee must invest $17,855.05 as shown here:

$$FV = \$50{,}000;\ r = 8;\ c = 4;\ n = 52;\ ANN = 0;\ PV = ?$$

$$PV = \$50{,}000 \times 1 \,/\, (\$1 + 0.08/4)^{52}$$

$$PV = \$17{,}855.05$$

Let's try another situation. Assume you want to buy a car when you graduate with your Ph.D. How much money should you invest today to have $30,000 in 10 years if you can earn 8 percent annually? Again, let's organize what we know.

$$FV = 30{,}000;\ ANN = 0;\ r = 8;\ c = 1;\ n = 10;\ PV = ?$$

Solving for present value reveals that you need to invest $13,895.80 to have $30,000 in 10 years if the assumptions above hold true.

Annuities

As you probably noticed in the preceeding examples, *ANN* was always = 0. That is because those examples involved lump sums only, not periodic payments. An **annuity** is a series of equal cash payments made at equal intervals. Car or house payments are examples of annuities. Understanding the future or present value of annuities is essential in making financing and investment decisions. For example, suppose a consultant completed a project for a client and sent a bill for $15,000. The client offers to pay the bill by making payments of $5,000 a year for the next three years. Because the consultant understands the time value of money, she rejects this offer. However, if she extends this client credit, how does the consultant determine the amount of the yearly payments that would be the equivalent of $15,000 cash today? We will examine the future and present values of annuities to answer this type of question.

Future Value of an Annuity

The **future value of an annuity** is the amount of money that accumulates at some future date as a result of making equal payments over equal intervals of time and earning a specified interest rate over that time period. The amount of money that accumulates is a function of (1) the size of the payments, (2) the frequency of the payments, and (3) the interest rate used over the life of the annuity. Businesses and individuals use the future value of annuities to determine the amount to save on a regular basis to buy new assets or retire debt at some future date.

Exhibit 11.5 illustrates the future value of an annuity. Notice that the three $1,000 payments plus the compound interest accumulate to a future value of $3,310. An annuity assumes that the final payment is made on the future value date; consequently, there is one less interest period than the number of payments. *As a result of this relationship, the number of payments over the life of the annuity (3) and not the number of years (2) is used as a basis for determining the future value of the annuity.*

The formula for the future value of an annuity is:

$$FV = ANN \times \frac{[(\$1 + r/c)^n - \$1]}{r/c}$$

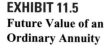

EXHIBIT 11.5
Future Value of an Ordinary Annuity

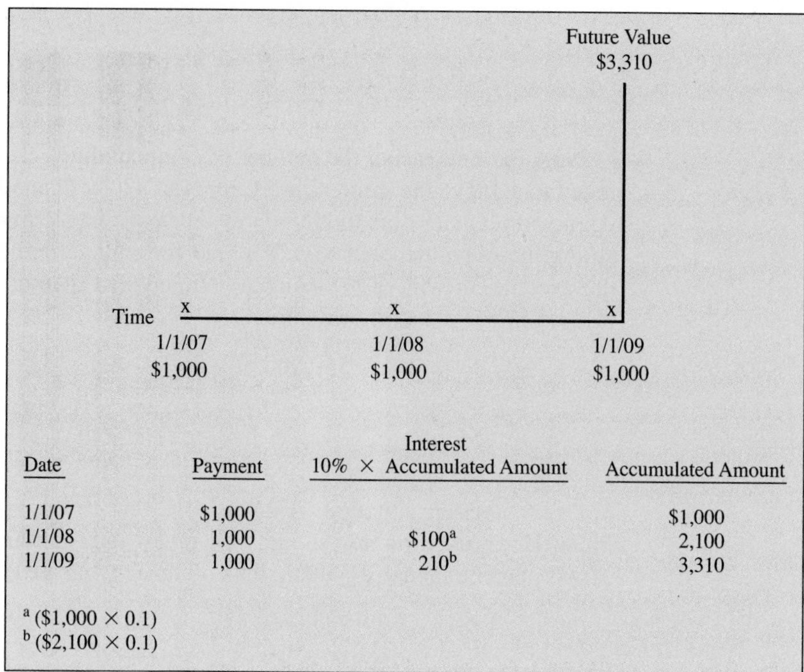

Date	Payment	Interest 10% × Accumulated Amount	Accumulated Amount
1/1/07	$1,000		$1,000
1/1/08	1,000	$100[a]	2,100
1/1/09	1,000	210[b]	3,310

[a] ($1,000 × 0.1)
[b] ($2,100 × 0.1)

As you can see, the formula has gotten rather complicated. This is why time value of money problems are typically solved using financial calculators or time value of money tables. It is important to note that the formula assumes that the number of compoundings in a year is the same as the number of payments during a year (monthly payments assume 12 compoundings) and that n is the number of payments over the time period in question. To illustrate, let's find the future value of a six-payment, $1,000, semiannual annuity that earns 10 percent interest. We know

$$ANN = \$1{,}000;\ r = 10;\ c = 2;\ n = 6;\ PV = 0;\ FV = ?$$

$$FV = \$1{,}000 \times \frac{[(\$1 + 0.10/2)^6 - \$1]}{0.10/2}$$

$$FV = \$6{,}801.91$$

Let's try another example. If we invest $1,000 each quarter and earn 12 percent, how much money will we have after 100 payments?

$$ANN = \$1{,}000;\ r = 12;\ c = 4;\ n = 100;\ PV = 0;\ FV = ?$$

$$FV = \$1{,}000 \times \frac{[(\$1 + 0.12/4)^{100} - \$1]}{0.12/4}$$

$$FV = \$607{,}287.73$$

One more try. Assume you want to buy a stereo system for your car. Unfortunately you have no money today and do not want to borrow. How much money must you save every month starting one month from today, assuming you can earn 12 percent, to have $3,000 in two years? First, organize what you know. Then, solve for the unknown.

$$PV = 0;\ FV = 3{,}000;\ c = 12;\ r = 12;\ n = 24;\ ANN = ?$$

Therefore, you must save $111.22 each month. What would happen if you began saving today, rather than waiting one month?

$$PV = 0;\ FV = 3{,}000;\ c = 12;\ r = 12;\ n = 25;\ ANN = ?$$

Since you can save for one extra month, your monthly savings requirement drops to $106.22.

Present Value of an Annuity

The **present value of an annuity** is the amount of money that, if invested at some interest rate today, will generate a set number of equal periodic payments that are made over equal time intervals. Exhibit 11.6 shows the cash flows and interest of the present value of an annuity.

Note that the first $1,000 payment occurs one period after the present value date and that the number of payments (three) equals the number of interest periods (three). If the present value of $2,486.85 earns 10 percent interest compounded annually, then the present value amount can generate three $1,000 payments. Each $1,000 payment consists of (1) 10 percent interest earned on the present value amount at the beginning of the period and (2) the return of a portion of the present value (principal). Every payment reduces the present value amount until the last payment brings the present value balance to zero.

The formula for the present value of an annuity is:

$$PV = ANN \times \frac{[\$1 - \$1/(\$1 + r/c)^n]}{r/c}$$

Let's try an example. Suppose that after graduating you want to borrow some money to furnish your new apartment. After setting up a budget, you conclude that you can afford annual payments of $1,000 for the next three years. If the interest rate available for the loan is 10 percent, what is the maximum amount you can borrow?

$$ANN = \$1{,}000;\ r = 10;\ c = 1;\ n = 3;\ FV = 0;\ PV = ?$$

$$PV = \$1{,}000 \times \frac{[\$1 - \$1/(\$1 + 0.10/1)^3]}{0.10/1}$$

$$PV = \$2{,}486.85$$

Let's explore how this loan would work (refer to Exhibit 11.6a and b). Pay close attention to this as you will use it again in Chapter 14. You will borrow $2,486.85. One year from now you will make a payment of $1,000. Part of this payment is for interest and part of it

EXHIBIT 11.6
Present Value of an Ordinary Annuity

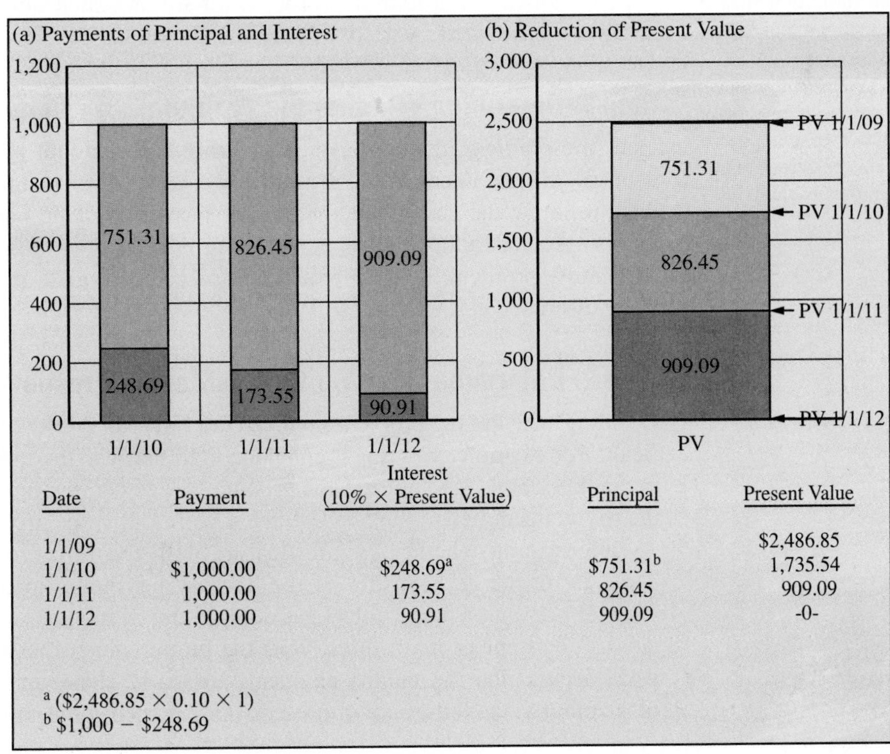

Date	Payment	Interest (10% × Present Value)	Principal	Present Value
1/1/09				$2,486.85
1/1/10	$1,000.00	$248.69[a]	$751.31[b]	1,735.54
1/1/11	1,000.00	173.55	826.45	909.09
1/1/12	1,000.00	90.91	909.09	-0-

[a] ($2,486.85 × 0.10 × 1)
[b] $1,000 − $248.69

repays the principal. Interest is the principal of the loan multiplied by the annual interest rate. So the interest on your first payment is (see column 1, Exhibit 11.6a):

$$\text{Interest (year 1)} = \$2{,}486.85 \times 0.1 = \$248.69$$

Therefore, the amount of principal repayment is $751.31 ($1,000 − $248.69).

How does the second payment work? Interest is calculated on the remaining principal (PV) ($2,486.85 − $751.31) so (see Exhibit 11.6b),

$$\text{Interest (year 2)} = \$1{,}735.54 \times 0.10 = \$173.55$$

And the amount of the principal repayment in the second year of the loan is $826.45 ($1,000 − $173.55) (see Exhibit 11.6a).

Finally, in the third year you will make your final payment of $1,000. This payment covers the interest for the third year ($909.09 × 0.10 = $90.91) plus the remaining principal ($1735.54 − $826.45 = $909.09).

Let's try one more example. Assume you want to buy a car today that costs $15,000. You can obtain financing at 10 percent for five years beginning one month from today. How much is your monthly payment going to be? Again, organize what you know and solve for the unknown value.

$$PV = 15{,}000;\ FV = 0;\ r = 10;\ c = 12;\ n = 60;\ ANN = ?$$

Your monthly payment would be $318.71.

More Practice with Time Value of Money Problems

Annuity problems may seem rather straightforward at this point, but they can become confusing rather quickly. Take, for instance, the problem presented at the start of the annuity section about payment of $15,000 of consulting fees over three years. Clearly the consultant should reject the first offer of three annual payments of $5,000 in lieu of the $15,000 fee. However, how can she determine the amount of three future payments that would be acceptable in lieu of $15,000 today?

After looking at a four-step process for solving such time value of money problems, we apply this process to a variety of business situations.

All time value of money problems have six elements
PV, FV, ANN, r, n, c; one of which will be an unknown. Note, however, that one might also be zero if not a factor in the problem.

Step 1. Determine Whether the Problem Is an Annuity

Does the problem involve payments of the same amount made over equal periods of time using a constant interest rate? If the answer is yes, it is an annuity problem. In this case, you want to know the size of the three equal payments made one year apart. Also, one interest rate is assumed, although it is not stated at this point, so it is an annuity problem. If it is not an annuity problem, it is either a future or present value of the amount of $1 problem like those discussed earlier.

Step 2. Determine Whether the Problem Is Present or Future Value

Deciding whether the problem involves the future or present value is essential, but often difficult. For example, you might conclude that, because the unknown annuity payments occur in the future, this is a future value problem. However, the problem of determining the size of the payments in lieu of the $15,000 fee is a present value problem.

Determining whether we are dealing with the future or present value of an annuity depends on the relationship of the annuity payments to the lump sum. Every annuity, whether present or future value, has a large sum of money or an asset with a specified monetary value as one of its features. With the future value of an annuity, the lump sum or future value occurs after the annuity payments are made. However, in the case of the present value of an annuity, the lump sum or present value precedes the annuity payments.

Key point: With annuities, if the lump sum occurs after the periodic payments, it is a future value problem. If the lump sum occurs before the periodic payments, it is a present value problem.

Exhibit 11.7 illustrates the relationship between the timing of the annuity payments and the lump sums for both future and present value problems. By identifying the relationship of the timing of the annuity payments to the annuity's lump sum, we can determine the type of annuity. The $15,000 consulting fee charged is the lump sum, and the payments come after the lump sum; therefore, this is a present value of an annuity problem.

Step 3. Identify the Missing Element

As you know, all time value of money problems involve six fundamental elements:

$PV =$ lump-sum payment currently (present value)

$FV =$ lump-sum payment in the future (future value)

$ANN =$ equal payments over equal intervals

$r =$ annual interest rate

$c =$ number of compoundings/payments per year

$n =$ total number of payments/compoundings over the entire time period

Your job is to determine which item is unknown. In the case of the $15,000 fee, only four of the six elements are known:

$PV = \$15{,}000$

$FV = 0$ (there is no lump sum at the end of the period)

$c = 1$

$n = 3$

The consultant must determine an interest rate to calculate the annual payments. Let's assume the consultant wants a 9 percent return on her money; then $r = 9$.

Step 4. Solve for the Missing Element

We know the following:

$$PV = \$15{,}000;\ FV = 0;\ c = 1;\ n = 3;\ r = 9;\ ANN = ?$$

Thus,

$$ANN = \$5{,}925.82$$

EXHIBIT 11.7
Lump Sums and Payment Periods

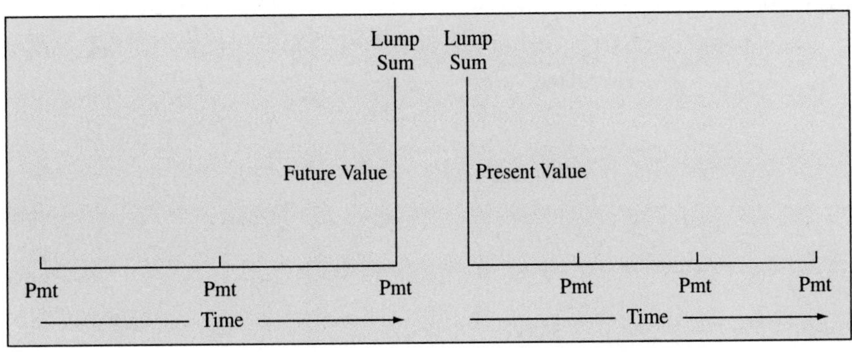

FAST FACT

If you invest only $1,000 today and earn 8 percent annually, you will have $46,901.61 in 50 years.

This analysis indicates that the consultant would accept three $5,925.82 annual payments because they are the equivalent of $15,000 today, assuming a 9 percent interest rate. Another way to think of this is that the consultant is lending her client the value of her services for three years. If the client makes three $5,925.82 payments, this will ensure the recovery of the $15,000 fee and also generate a 9 percent rate of return on the loan.

More Time Value of Money Problems

1. You want to buy a used car. You can afford payments of no more than $400 per month for two years. If you can obtain financing at 12 percent, what is the maximum car you can afford? This is an annuity problem because you are making monthly payments. This is a present value problem because you want to obtain the car (lump sum) today and the payments are after the lump sum (*PV*) amount. We know:

$$ANN = 400;\ FV = 0;\ r = 12;\ c = 12;\ n = 24;\ PV = ?$$

Therefore,

$$PV = \$8{,}497.35$$

2. You just won the lottery. They will give you annual payments of $5,000,000 for the next 20 years. Assuming you can invest at 15 percent compounded annually, what are your winnings worth today? This is an annuity problem because you will receive annual payments. This is a present value problem because the lump sum is before the annual payments (*ANN*). We know:

$$ANN = 5{,}000{,}000;\ c = 1;\ n = 20;\ r = 15;\ FV = 0;\ PV = ?$$

Therefore,

$$PV = \$31{,}296{,}657.37$$

3. You want to retire in 40 years with $5 million. If you can invest at 11 percent, how much money do you need to put aside each month starting one month from today? This is an annuity problem because you will put aside money every month. This is a future value problem because the monthly payments (*ANN*) are before the lump sum ($5,000,000), which occurs in the future (40 years from now). We know:

$$FV = 5{,}000{,}000;\ c = 12;\ n = 480;\ r = 11;\ PV = 0;\ ANN = ?$$

Therefore,

$$ANN = \$581.39$$

Summary

The management cycle reflects the interrelationship of a firm's planning, performing, and evaluating activities. Planning the firm's operating and capital resources processes and then executing these plans are based on the belief that the firm will generate a return *of* and a satisfactory return *on* the investments made by the creditors and owners of the firm. Risk is considered in the expected return of an investment. Investments are exposed to three types of risk: inflation risk, business risk, and liquidity risk. Each type of risk is factored into the risk assessment of any investment. Management must consider the relationship of both return and risk when trying to invest funds at its disposal and when trying to acquire funds from owners and creditors.

Considering the time value of money is essential before making long-term investing and financing decisions. The future value of a dollar is the amount that a dollar will become if invested today for a specific period of time at a specific rate of interest. The present value of a dollar is the amount today that is equivalent to a dollar at some specified future time when invested at a specified rate of interest. Present and future values also can be calculated for annuities.

- The rate of return is a common-size measure of the return on an investment and presumes the return of and a return on the investment. The expected rate of return of an investment is a summary measure of possible rates of return the investment might generate that investors use to evaluate alternative investments.
- A person's willingness to make risky investments depends on whether he or she is a risk seeker or a risk avoider. Risk avoiders want an additional return called a risk premium for accepting any additional risk.
- A firm's management invests the firm's resources in an attempt to maximize the return of the firm at a level of risk that is acceptable to the firm's owners. However, when borrowing funds, management tries to minimize the risk of the firm to lower the cost of using borrowed funds.
- The time value of money is a tool that uses compound interest to determine the cash equivalent values for single or multiple cash flows that occur at different points in time.

Key Terms

Annual rate of return Rate of return based on a one-year time period, *309*

Annuity A series of equal cash payments made at equal intervals, *317*

Business risk The risk associated with the ability of a particular company to continue in business, *311*

Compound interest Interest that is based on a principal amount that includes interest from previous time periods, *314*

Compounding The process of adding interest to principal for purposes of interest calculation, *314*

Expected rate of return A summary measure of an investment's performance, stated as a percentage, based on the possible rates of return and on the likelihood of those rates of return occurring, *310*

Future value of an annuity The amount of money that accumulates at some future date as a result of making equal payments over equal intervals of time and earning a specified rate of interest over that time period, *317*

Future value of the amount of $1 The amount that $1 becomes at a future date, if invested at a specified annual interest rate and compounded a certain number of times per year over the investment period, *316*

Inflation risk The chance of a decline in the purchasing power of the monetary units during the time money is invested, *311*

Liquidity risk The chance that an investment cannot be readily converted to cash, *311*

Present value of an annuity The amount of money that, if invested at some rate of interest today, will generate a set number of equal periodic payments that are made over equal time intervals, *319*

Present value of the amount of $1 The amount that, if invested today at some compound interest rate for a specified period of time, will equal $1 at the end of that time period, *316*

Rate of return A percentage measurement of the performance of investments on a common-size basis, *309*

Return of investment The return of the amount initially invested, *308*

Return on investment The money received in excess of the initial investment, *308*

Risk Exposure to the chance that an unfavorable outcome will occur at some future point in time, *310*

Risk-adjusted expected rate of return An expected rate of return including the risk premium, *312*

Risk-free rate of return The rate of return that a virtually riskless investment produces, *312*

Risk premium An increase in the rate of return expected by an investor for assuming greater investment risk, *312*

Simple interest Interest calculated only on the amount borrowed, *313*

Time value of money A tool used to solve problems involving the comparison of cash flows that occur at different points in time, *313*

Appendix

Time Value of Money Tables

Time value of money tables can be used to solve many time value of money calculations. There are four common time value of money tables: (1) future value of \$1, (2) present value of \$1, (3) future value of an annuity, and (4) present value of an annuity. In each case the amounts shown in the table represent a combination of n as the rows and i (r/c) as the columns to determine the factor that represents the mathematical formula in the time value of money equation. Let's examine these tables.

Table 1 Is the Future Value of \$1 Let's use it to solve the following problem. Assume you will invest \$1,000 for 2 years at 10 percent compounded quarterly. What do we know? $PV = 1{,}000$; $c = 4$; $n = 8$; $r = 10$; $i = 2.5$. Therefore, we go down the 2.5 percent column to the periods = 8 row and we find the number 1.2184. This number represents the $(\$1 + r/c)^n$ in the FV formula:

$$FV = PV \times (\$1 + r/c)^n$$

Therefore,

$$FV = 1{,}000 \times 1.2184; FV = \$1{,}218.40$$

Table 2 Is the Present Value of \$1 Let's use this table to solve the following problem: Assume you will receive \$10,000 in five years. If you can invest at 8 percent compounded semiannually, what is the \$10,000 worth today? We know: $FV = 10{,}000$; $c = 2$; $n = 10$; $r = 8$; $i = 4$. Go down the 4% column to the periods = 10 row. The present value factor is 0.6756. This number represents the $1/(\$1 + r/c)^n$ in the present value formula. Therefore, $10{,}000 \times 0.6756 = \$6{,}756 = PV$.

Table 3 Is the Future Value of an Annuity Again the table values replace the compounding part of the future value of an annuity formula. Let's try the following example. You will invest \$1,000 every quarter beginning one quarter from today for 10 years. If you earn 12 percent on your investment, how much money will you have at the end of 10 years? We know: $ANN = 1{,}000$; $c = 4$; $n = 40$; $r = 12$; $i = 3$. What column and row should we use? We will use the 3% interest column and the periods = 40 row. The future value of an annuity factor is 75.4013. Therefore,

$$FV = 1{,}000 \times 75.4013 = \$75{,}401.30$$

Table 4 Is the Present Value of an Annuity As you know, the table values replace the compounding part of the present value of an annuity formula. Assume that you want to borrow \$8,000 for 4 years at 12 percent interest. You will make monthly payments to repay the principal and interest. What do we know? $PV = 8{,}000$; $c = 12$; $n = 48$; $r = 12$; $i = 1$. The present value of an annuity factor found at the intersection of $i = 1$ and $n = 48$ is 37.9740. Therefore, since we are looking for the *ANN*, not the *PV*, our calculation is

$$8{,}000 = ANN \times 37.974$$

$$ANN = \$210.67$$

TABLE 1 Future Value of the Amount of $1

Periods	1.0%	1.5%	2.0%	2.5%	3.0%	4.0%	5.0%	6.0%	7.0%	8.0%	9.0%
1	1.0100	1.0150	1.0200	1.0250	1.0300	1.0400	1.0500	1.0600	1.0700	1.0800	1.0900
2	1.0201	1.0302	1.0404	1.0506	1.0609	1.0816	1.1025	1.1236	1.1449	1.1664	1.1881
3	1.0303	1.0457	1.0612	1.0769	1.0927	1.1249	1.1576	1.1910	1.2250	1.2597	1.2950
4	1.0406	1.0614	1.0824	1.1038	1.1255	1.1699	1.2155	1.2625	1.3108	1.3605	1.4116
5	1.0510	1.0073	1.1041	1.1314	1.1593	1.2167	1.2763	1.3382	1.4026	1.4693	1.5386
6	1.0615	1.0934	1.1262	1.1597	1.1941	1.2653	1.3401	1.4185	1.5007	1.5869	1.6771
7	1.0721	1.1098	1.1487	1.1887	1.2299	1.3159	1.4071	1.5036	1.6058	1.7138	1.8280
8	1.0829	1.1265	1.1717	1.2184	1.2668	1.3686	1.4775	1.5938	1.7182	1.8509	1.9926
9	1.0937	1.1434	1.1951	1.2489	1.3048	1.4233	1.5513	1.6895	1.8385	1.9990	2.1719
10	1.1046	1.1605	1.2190	1.2801	1.3439	1.4802	1.6289	1.7908	1.9672	2.1589	2.3674
11	1.1157	1.1779	1.2434	1.3121	1.3842	1.5395	1.7103	1.8983	2.1049	2.3316	2.5804
12	1.1268	1.1956	1.2682	1.3449	1.4258	1.6010	1.7959	2.0122	2.2522	2.5182	2.8127
13	1.1381	1.2136	1.2936	1.3785	1.4685	1.6651	1.8856	2.1329	2.4098	2.7196	3.0658
14	1.1495	1.2318	1.3195	1.4130	1.5126	1.7317	1.9799	2.2609	2.5785	2.9372	3.3417
15	1.1610	1.2502	1.3459	1.4483	1.5580	1.8009	2.0789	2.3966	2.7590	3.1722	3.6425
16	1.1726	1.2690	1.3728	1.4845	1.6047	1.8730	2.1829	2.5404	2.9522	3.4259	3.9703
17	1.1843	1.2880	1.4002	1.5216	1.6528	1.9479	2.2920	2.6928	3.1588	3.7000	4.3276
18	1.1961	1.3073	1.4282	1.5597	1.7024	2.0258	2.4066	2.8543	3.3799	3.9960	4.7171
19	1.2081	1.3270	1.4568	1.5987	1.7535	2.1068	2.5270	3.0256	3.6165	4.3157	5.1417
20	1.2202	1.3469	1.4859	1.6386	1.8061	2.1911	2.6533	3.2071	3.8697	4.6610	5.6044
21	1.2324	1.3671	1.5157	1.6796	1.8603	2.2788	2.7860	3.3996	4.1406	5.0338	6.1088
22	1.2447	1.3876	1.5460	1.7216	1.9161	2.3699	2.9253	3.6035	4.4304	5.4365	6.6586
23	1.2572	1.4084	1.5769	1.7646	1.9736	2.4647	3.0715	3.8197	4.7405	5.8715	7.2579
24	1.2697	1.4295	1.6084	1.8087	2.0328	2.5633	3.2251	4.0489	5.0724	6.3412	7.9111
25	1.2824	1.4509	1.6406	1.8539	2.0938	2.6658	3.3864	4.2919	5.4274	6.8485	8.6231
26	1.2953	1.4727	1.6734	1.9003	2.1566	2.7725	3.5557	4.5494	5.8074	7.3964	9.3992
27	1.3082	1.4948	1.7069	1.9478	2.2213	2.8834	3.7335	4.8223	6.2139	7.9881	10.2451
28	1.3213	1.5172	1.7410	1.9965	2.2879	2.9987	3.9201	5.1117	6.6488	8.6271	11.1671
29	1.3345	1.5400	1.7758	2.0464	2.3566	3.1187	4.1161	5.4184	7.1143	9.3173	12.1722
30	1.3478	1.5631	1.8114	2.0976	2.4273	3.2434	4.3219	5.7435	7.6123	10.0627	13.2677
31	1.3613	1.5865	1.8476	2.1500	2.5001	3.3731	4.5380	6.0881	8.1451	10.8677	14.4618
32	1.3749	1.6103	1.8845	2.2038	2.5751	3.5081	4.7649	6.4534	8.7153	11.7371	15.7633
33	1.3887	1.6345	1.9222	2.2589	2.6523	3.6484	5.0032	6.8406	9.3253	12.6760	17.1820
34	1.4026	1.6590	1.9607	2.3153	2.7319	3.7943	5.2533	7.2510	9.9781	13.6901	18.7284
35	1.4166	1.6839	1.9999	2.3732	2.8139	3.9461	5.5160	7.6861	10.6766	14.7853	20.4140
36	1.4308	1.7091	2.0399	2.4325	2.8983	4.1039	5.7918	8.1473	11.4239	15.9682	22.2512
37	1.4451	1.7348	2.0807	2.4933	2.9852	4.2681	6.0814	8.6361	12.2236	17.2456	24.2538
38	1.4595	1.7608	2.1223	2.5557	3.0748	4.4388	6.3855	9.1543	13.0793	18.6253	26.4367
39	1.4741	1.7872	2.1647	2.6196	3.1670	4.6164	6.7048	9.7035	13.9948	20.1153	28.8160
40	1.4889	1.8140	2.2080	2.6851	3.2620	4.8010	7.0400	10.2857	14.9745	21.7245	31.4094
41	1.5038	1.8412	2.2522	2.7522	3.3599	4.9931	7.3920	10.9029	16.0227	23.4625	34.2363
42	1.5188	1.8688	2.2972	2.8210	3.4607	5.1928	7.7616	11.5570	17.1443	25.3395	37.3175
43	1.5340	1.8969	2.3432	2.8915	3.5645	5.4005	8.1497	12.2505	18.3444	27.3666	40.6761
44	1.5493	1.9253	2.3901	2.9638	3.6715	5.6165	8.5572	12.9855	19.6285	29.5560	44.3370
45	1.5648	1.9542	2.4379	3.0379	3.7816	5.8412	8.9850	13.7646	21.0025	31.9204	48.3273
46	1.5805	1.9835	2.4866	3.1139	3.8950	6.0748	9.4343	14.5905	22.4726	34.4741	52.6767
47	1.5963	2.0133	2.5363	3.1917	4.0119	6.3178	9.9060	15.4659	24.0457	37.2320	57.4176
48	1.6122	2.0435	2.5871	3.2715	4.1323	6.5705	10.4013	16.3939	25.7289	40.2106	62.5852
49	1.6283	2.0741	2.6388	3.3533	4.2562	6.8333	10.9213	17.3775	27.5299	43.4274	68.2179
50	1.6446	2.1052	2.6916	3.4371	4.3839	7.1067	11.4674	18.4202	29.4570	46.9016	74.3575

10.0%	11.0%	12.0%	13.0%	14.0%	15.0%	16.0%	17.0%	18.0%	19.0%	20.0%	Periods
1.1000	1.1100	1.1200	1.1300	1.1400	1.1500	1.1600	1.1700	1.1800	1.1900	1.2000	1
1.2100	1.2321	1.2544	1.2769	1.2996	1.3225	1.3456	1.3689	1.3924	1.4161	1.4400	2
1.3310	1.3676	1.4049	1.4429	1.4815	1.5209	1.5609	1.6016	1.6430	1.6852	1.7280	3
1.4641	1.5181	1.5735	1.6305	1.6890	1.7490	1.8106	1.8739	1.9388	2.0053	2.0736	4
1.6105	1.6851	1.7623	1.8424	1.9254	2.0114	2.1003	2.1924	2.2878	2.3864	2.4883	5
1.7716	1.8704	1.9738	2.0820	2.1950	2.3131	2.4364	2.5652	2.6996	2.8398	2.9860	6
1.9487	2.0762	2.2107	2.3526	2.5023	2.6600	2.8262	3.0012	3.1855	3.3793	3.5832	7
2.1436	2.3045	2.4760	2.6584	2.8526	3.0590	3.2784	3.5115	3.7589	4.0214	4.2998	8
2.3579	2.5580	2.7731	3.0040	3.2519	3.5179	3.8030	4.1084	4.4355	4.7854	5.1598	9
2.5937	2.8394	3.1058	3.3946	3.7072	4.0456	4.4114	4.8068	5.2338	5.6947	6.1917	10
2.8531	3.1518	3.4785	3.8359	4.2262	4.6524	5.1173	5.6240	6.1759	6.7767	7.4301	11
3.1384	3.4985	3.8960	4.3345	4.8179	5.3503	5.9360	6.5801	7.2876	8.0642	8.9161	12
3.4523	3.8833	4.3635	4.8980	5.4924	6.1528	6.8858	7.6987	8.5994	9.5964	10.6993	13
3.7975	4.3104	4.8871	5.5348	6.2613	7.0757	7.9875	9.0075	10.1472	11.4198	12.8392	14
4.1772	4.7846	5.4736	6.2543	7.1379	8.1371	9.2655	10.5387	11.9737	13.5895	15.4070	15
4.5950	5.3109	6.1304	7.0673	8.1372	9.3576	10.7480	12.3303	14.1290	16.1715	18.4884	16
5.0545	5.8951	6.8660	7.9861	9.2765	10.7613	12.4677	14.4265	16.6722	19.2441	22.1861	17
5.5599	6.5436	7.6900	9.0243	10.5752	12.3755	14.4625	16.8790	19.6733	22.9005	26.6233	18
6.1159	7.2633	8.6128	10.1974	12.0557	14.2318	16.7765	19.7484	23.2144	27.2516	31.9480	19
6.7275	8.0623	9.6463	11.5231	13.7435	16.3665	19.4608	23.1056	27.3930	32.4294	38.3376	20
7.4002	8.9492	10.8038	13.0211	15.6676	18.8215	22.5745	27.0336	32.3238	38.5910	46.0051	21
8.1403	9.9336	12.1003	14.7138	17.8610	21.6447	26.1864	31.6293	38.1421	45.9233	55.2061	22
8.9543	11.0263	13.5523	16.6266	20.3616	24.8915	30.3762	37.0062	45.0076	54.6487	66.2474	23
9.8497	12.2392	15.1786	18.7881	23.2122	28.6252	35.2364	43.2973	53.1090	65.0320	79.4968	24
0.8347	13.5855	17.0001	21.2305	26.4619	32.9190	40.8742	50.6578	62.6686	77.3881	95.3962	25
1.9182	15.0799	19.0401	23.9905	30.1666	37.8568	47.4141	59.2697	73.9490	92.0918	114.4755	26
13.1100	16.7386	21.3249	27.1093	34.3899	43.5353	55.0004	69.3455	87.2598	109.5893	137.3706	27
14.4210	18.5799	23.8839	30.6335	39.2045	50.0656	63.8004	81.1342	102.9666	130.4112	164.8447	28
15.8631	20.6237	26.7499	34.6158	44.6931	57.5755	74.0085	94.9271	121.5005	155.1893	197.8136	29
17.4494	22.8923	29.9599	39.1159	50.9502	66.2118	85.8499	111.0647	143.3706	184.6753	237.3763	30
19.1943	25.4104	33.5551	44.2010	58.0832	76.1435	99.5859	129.9456	169.1774	219.7636	284.8516	31
21.1138	28.2056	37.5817	49.9471	66.2148	87.5651	115.5196	152.0364	199.6293	261.5187	341.8219	32
23.2252	31.3082	42.0915	56.4402	75.4849	100.6998	134.0027	177.8826	235.5625	311.2073	410.1863	33
25.5477	34.7521	47.1425	63.7774	86.0528	115.8048	155.4432	208.1226	277.9638	370.3366	492.2235	34
28.1024	38.5749	52.7996	72.0685	98.1002	133.1755	180.3141	243.5035	327.9973	440.7006	590.6682	35
30.9127	42.8181	59.1356	81.4374	111.8342	153.1519	209.1643	284.8991	387.0368	524.4337	708.8019	36
34.0039	47.5281	66.2318	92.0243	127.4910	176.1246	242.6306	333.3319	456.7034	624.0761	850.5622	37
37.4043	52.7562	74.1797	103.9874	145.3397	202.5433	281.4515	389.9983	538.9100	742.6506	1020.6747	38
41.1448	58.5593	83.0812	117.5058	165.6873	232.9248	326.4838	456.2980	635.9139	883.7542	1224.8096	39
45.2593	65.0009	93.0510	132.7816	188.8835	267.8635	378.7212	533.8687	750.3783	1051.6675	1469.7716	40
49.7852	72.1510	104.2171	150.0432	215.3272	308.0431	439.3165	624.6264	885.4464	1251.4843	1763.7259	41
54.7637	80.0876	116.7231	169.5488	245.4730	354.2495	509.6072	730.8129	1044.8268	1489.2664	2116.4711	42
60.2401	88.8972	130.7299	191.5901	279.8392	407.3870	591.1443	855.0511	1232.8956	1772.2270	2539.7653	43
66.2641	98.6759	146.4175	216.4968	319.0167	468.4950	685.7274	1000.4098	1454.8168	2108.9501	3047.7183	44
72.8905	109.5302	163.9876	244.6414	363.6791	538.7693	795.4438	1170.4794	1716.6839	2509.6506	3657.2620	45
80.1795	121.5786	183.6661	276.4448	414.5941	619.5847	922.7148	1369.4609	2025.6870	2986.4842	4388.7144	46
88.1975	134.9522	205.7061	312.3826	472.6373	712.5224	1070.3492	1602.2693	2390.3106	3553.9162	5266.4573	47
97.0172	149.7970	230.3908	352.9923	538.8065	819.4007	1241.6051	1874.6550	2820.5665	4229.1603	6319.7487	48
106.7190	166.2746	258.0377	398.8813	614.2395	942.3108	1440.2619	2193.3464	3328.2685	5032.7008	7583.6985	49
117.3909	184.5648	289.0022	450.7359	700.2330	1083.6574	1670.7038	2566.2153	3927.3569	5988.9139	9100.4382	50

TABLE 2 Present Value of the Amount of $1

Periods	1.0%	1.5%	2.0%	2.5%	3.0%	4.0%	5.0%	6.0%	7.0%	8.0%	9.0%
1	0.9901	0.9852	0.9804	0.9756	0.9709	0.9615	0.9524	0.9434	0.9346	0.9259	0.9174
2	0.9803	0.9707	0.9612	0.9518	0.9426	0.9246	0.9070	0.8900	0.8734	0.8573	0.8417
3	0.9706	0.9563	0.9423	0.9286	0.9151	0.8890	0.8638	0.8396	0.8163	0.7938	0.7722
4	0.9610	0.9422	0.9238	0.9060	0.8885	0.8548	0.8227	0.7921	0.7629	0.7350	0.7084
5	0.9515	0.9283	0.9057	0.8839	0.8626	0.8219	0.7835	0.7473	0.7130	0.6806	0.6499
6	0.9420	0.9145	0.8880	0.8623	0.8375	0.7903	0.7462	0.7050	0.6663	0.6302	0.5963
7	0.9327	0.9010	0.8706	0.8413	0.8131	0.7599	0.7107	0.6651	0.6227	0.5835	0.5470
8	0.9235	0.8877	0.8535	0.8207	0.7894	0.7307	0.6768	0.6274	0.5820	0.5403	0.5019
9	0.9143	0.8746	0.8368	0.8007	0.7664	0.7026	0.6446	0.5919	0.5439	0.5002	0.4604
10	0.9053	0.8617	0.8203	0.7812	0.7441	0.6756	0.6139	0.5584	0.5083	0.4632	0.4224
11	0.8963	0.8489	0.8043	0.7621	0.7224	0.6496	0.5847	0.5268	0.4751	0.4289	0.3875
12	0.8874	0.8364	0.7885	0.7436	0.7014	0.6246	0.5568	0.4970	0.4440	0.3971	0.3555
13	0.8787	0.8240	0.7730	0.7254	0.6810	0.6006	0.5303	0.4688	0.4150	0.3677	0.3262
14	0.8700	0.8118	0.7579	0.7077	0.6611	0.5775	0.5051	0.4423	0.3878	0.3405	0.2992
15	0.8613	0.7999	0.7430	0.6905	0.6419	0.5553	0.4810	0.4173	0.3624	0.3152	0.2745
16	0.8528	0.7880	0.7284	0.6736	0.6232	0.5339	0.4581	0.3936	0.3387	0.2919	0.2519
17	0.8444	0.7764	0.7142	0.6572	0.6050	0.5134	0.4363	0.3714	0.3166	0.2703	0.2311
18	0.8360	0.7649	0.7002	0.6412	0.5874	0.4936	0.4155	0.3503	0.2959	0.2502	0.2120
19	0.8277	0.7536	0.6864	0.6255	0.5703	0.4746	0.3957	0.3305	0.2765	0.2317	0.1945
20	0.8195	0.7425	0.6730	0.6103	0.5537	0.4564	0.3769	0.3118	0.2584	0.2145	0.1784
21	0.8114	0.7315	0.6598	0.5954	0.5375	0.4388	0.3589	0.2942	0.2415	0.1987	0.1637
22	0.8034	0.7207	0.6468	0.5809	0.5219	0.4220	0.3418	0.2775	0.2257	0.1839	0.1502
23	0.7954	0.7100	0.6342	0.5667	0.5067	0.4057	0.3256	0.2618	0.2109	0.1703	0.1378
24	0.7876	0.6995	0.6217	0.5529	0.4919	0.3901	0.3101	0.2470	0.1971	0.1577	0.1264
25	0.7798	0.6892	0.6095	0.5394	0.4776	0.3751	0.2953	0.2330	0.1842	0.1460	0.1160
26	0.7720	0.6790	0.5976	0.5262	0.4637	0.3607	0.2812	0.2198	0.1722	0.1352	0.1064
27	0.7644	0.6690	0.5859	0.5134	0.4502	0.3468	0.2678	0.2074	0.1609	0.1252	0.0976
28	0.7568	0.6591	0.5744	0.5009	0.4371	0.3335	0.2551	0.1956	0.1504	0.1159	0.0895
29	0.7493	0.6494	0.5631	0.4887	0.4243	0.3207	0.2429	0.1846	0.1406	0.1073	0.0822
30	0.7419	0.6398	0.5521	0.4767	0.4120	0.3083	0.2314	0.1741	0.1314	0.0994	0.0754
31	0.7346	0.6303	0.5412	0.4651	0.4000	0.2965	0.2204	0.1643	0.1228	0.0920	0.0691
32	0.7273	0.6210	0.5306	0.4538	0.3883	0.2851	0.2099	0.1550	0.1147	0.0852	0.0634
33	0.7201	0.6118	0.5202	0.4427	0.3770	0.2741	0.1999	0.1462	0.1072	0.0789	0.0582
34	0.7130	0.6028	0.5100	0.4319	0.3660	0.2636	0.1904	0.1379	0.1002	0.0730	0.0534
35	0.7059	0.5939	0.5000	0.4214	0.3554	0.2534	0.1813	0.1301	0.0937	0.0676	0.0490
36	0.6989	0.5851	0.4902	0.4111	0.3450	0.2437	0.1727	0.1227	0.0875	0.0626	0.0449
37	0.6920	0.5764	0.4806	0.4011	0.3350	0.2343	0.1644	0.1158	0.0818	0.0580	0.0412
38	0.6852	0.5679	0.4712	0.3913	0.3252	0.2253	0.1566	0.1092	0.0765	0.0537	0.0378
39	0.6784	0.5595	0.4619	0.3817	0.3158	0.2166	0.1491	0.1031	0.0715	0.0497	0.0347
40	0.6717	0.5513	0.4529	0.3724	0.3066	0.2083	0.1420	0.0972	0.0668	0.0460	0.0318
41	0.6650	0.5431	0.4440	0.3633	0.2976	0.2003	0.1353	0.0917	0.0624	0.0426	0.0292
42	0.6584	0.5351	0.4353	0.3545	0.2890	0.1926	0.1288	0.0865	0.0583	0.0395	0.0268
43	0.6519	0.5272	0.4268	0.3458	0.2805	0.1852	0.1227	0.0816	0.0545	0.0365	0.0246
44	0.6454	0.5194	0.4184	0.3374	0.2724	0.1780	0.1169	0.0770	0.0509	0.0338	0.0226
45	0.6391	0.5117	0.4102	0.3292	0.2644	0.1712	0.1113	0.0727	0.0476	0.0313	0.0207
46	0.6327	0.5042	0.4022	0.3211	0.2567	0.1646	0.1060	0.0685	0.0445	0.0290	0.0190
47	0.6265	0.4967	0.3943	0.3133	0.2493	0.1583	0.1009	0.0647	0.0416	0.0269	0.0174
48	0.6203	0.4894	0.3865	0.3057	0.2420	0.1522	0.0961	0.0610	0.0389	0.0249	0.0160
49	0.6141	0.4821	0.3790	0.2982	0.2350	0.1463	0.0916	0.0575	0.0363	0.0230	0.0147
50	0.6080	0.4750	0.3715	0.2909	0.2281	0.1407	0.0872	0.0543	0.0339	0.0213	0.0134

10.0%	11.0%	12.0%	13.0%	14.0%	15.0%	16.0%	17.0%	18.0%	19.0%	20.0%	Periods
0.9091	0.9009	0.8929	0.8850	0.8772	0.8696	0.8621	0.8547	0.8475	0.8403	0.8333	1
0.8264	0.8116	0.7972	0.7831	0.7695	0.7561	0.7432	0.7305	0.7182	0.7062	0.6944	2
0.7513	0.7312	0.7118	0.6931	0.6750	0.6575	0.6407	0.6244	0.6086	0.5934	0.5787	3
0.6830	0.6587	0.6355	0.6133	0.5921	0.5718	0.5523	0.5337	0.5158	0.4987	0.4823	4
0.6209	0.5935	0.5674	0.5428	0.5194	0.4972	0.4761	0.4561	0.4371	0.4190	0.4019	5
0.5645	0.5346	0.5066	0.4803	0.4556	0.4323	0.4104	0.3898	0.3704	0.3521	0.3349	6
0.5132	0.4817	0.4523	0.4251	0.3996	0.3759	0.3538	0.3332	0.3139	0.2959	0.2791	7
0.4665	0.4339	0.4039	0.3762	0.3506	0.3269	0.3050	0.2848	0.2660	0.2487	0.2326	8
0.4241	0.3909	0.3606	0.3329	0.3075	0.2843	0.2630	0.2434	0.2255	0.2090	0.1938	9
0.3855	0.3522	0.3220	0.2946	0.2697	0.2472	0.2267	0.2080	0.1911	0.1756	0.1615	10
0.3505	0.3173	0.2875	0.2607	0.2366	0.2149	0.1954	0.1778	0.1619	0.1476	0.1346	11
0.3186	0.2858	0.2567	0.2307	0.2076	0.1869	0.1685	0.1520	0.1372	0.1240	0.1122	12
0.2897	0.2575	0.2292	0.2042	0.1821	0.1625	0.1452	0.1299	0.1163	0.1042	0.0935	13
0.2633	0.2320	0.2046	0.1807	0.1597	0.1413	0.1252	0.1110	0.0985	0.0876	0.0779	14
0.2394	0.2090	0.1827	0.1599	0.1401	0.1229	0.1079	0.0949	0.0835	0.0736	0.0649	15
0.2176	0.1883	0.1631	0.1415	0.1229	0.1069	0.0930	0.0811	0.0708	0.0618	0.0541	16
0.1978	0.1696	0.1456	0.1252	0.1078	0.0929	0.0802	0.0693	0.0600	0.0520	0.0451	17
0.1799	0.1528	0.1300	0.1108	0.0946	0.0808	0.0691	0.0592	0.0508	0.0437	0.0376	18
0.1635	0.1377	0.1161	0.0981	0.0829	0.0703	0.0596	0.0506	0.0431	0.0367	0.0313	19
0.1486	0.1240	0.1037	0.0868	0.0728	0.0611	0.0514	0.0433	0.0365	0.0308	0.0261	20
0.1351	0.1117	0.0926	0.0768	0.0638	0.0531	0.0443	0.0370	0.0309	0.0259	0.0217	21
0.1228	0.1007	0.0826	0.0680	0.0560	0.0462	0.0382	0.0316	0.0262	0.0218	0.0181	22
0.1117	0.0907	0.0738	0.0601	0.0491	0.0402	0.0329	0.0270	0.0222	0.0183	0.0151	23
0.1015	0.0817	0.0659	0.0532	0.0431	0.0349	0.0284	0.0231	0.0188	0.0154	0.0126	24
0.0923	0.0736	0.0588	0.0471	0.0378	0.0304	0.0245	0.0197	0.0160	0.0129	0.0105	25
0.0839	0.0663	0.0525	0.0417	0.0331	0.0264	0.0211	0.0169	0.0135	0.0109	0.0087	26
0.0763	0.0597	0.0469	0.0369	0.0291	0.0230	0.0182	0.0144	0.0115	0.0091	0.0073	27
0.0693	0.0538	0.0419	0.0326	0.0255	0.0200	0.0157	0.0123	0.0097	0.0077	0.0061	28
0.0630	0.0485	0.0374	0.0289	0.0224	0.0174	0.0135	0.0105	0.0082	0.0064	0.0051	29
0.0573	0.0437	0.0334	0.0256	0.0196	0.0151	0.0116	0.0090	0.0070	0.0054	0.0042	30
0.0521	0.0394	0.0298	0.0226	0.0172	0.0131	0.0100	0.0077	0.0059	0.0046	0.0035	31
0.0474	0.0355	0.0266	0.0200	0.0151	0.0114	0.0087	0.0066	0.0050	0.0038	0.0029	32
0.0431	0.0319	0.0238	0.0177	0.0132	0.0099	0.0075	0.0056	0.0042	0.0032	0.0024	33
0.0391	0.0288	0.0212	0.0157	0.0116	0.0086	0.0064	0.0048	0.0036	0.0027	0.0020	34
0.0356	0.0259	0.0189	0.0139	0.0102	0.0075	0.0055	0.0041	0.0030	0.0023	0.0017	35
0.0323	0.0234	0.0169	0.0123	0.0089	0.0065	0.0048	0.0035	0.0026	0.0019	0.0014	36
0.0294	0.0210	0.0151	0.0109	0.0078	0.0057	0.0041	0.0030	0.0022	0.0016	0.0012	37
0.0267	0.0190	0.0135	0.0096	0.0069	0.0049	0.0036	0.0026	0.0019	0.0013	0.0010	38
0.0243	0.0171	0.0120	0.0085	0.0060	0.0043	0.0031	0.0022	0.0016	0.0011	0.0008	39
0.0221	0.0154	0.0107	0.0075	0.0053	0.0037	0.0026	0.0019	0.0013	0.0010	0.0007	40
0.0201	0.0139	0.0096	0.0067	0.0046	0.0032	0.0023	0.0016	0.0011	0.0008	0.0006	41
0.0183	0.0125	0.0086	0.0059	0.0041	0.0028	0.0020	0.0014	0.0010	0.0007	0.0005	42
0.0166	0.0112	0.0076	0.0052	0.0036	0.0025	0.0017	0.0012	0.0008	0.0006	0.0004	43
0.0151	0.0101	0.0068	0.0046	0.0031	0.0021	0.0015	0.0010	0.0007	0.0005	0.0003	44
0.0137	0.0091	0.0061	0.0041	0.0027	0.0019	0.0013	0.0009	0.0006	0.0004	0.0003	45
0.0125	0.0082	0.0054	0.0036	0.0024	0.0016	0.0011	0.0007	0.0005	0.0003	0.0002	46
0.0113	0.0074	0.0049	0.0032	0.0021	0.0014	0.0009	0.0006	0.0004	0.0003	0.0002	47
0.0103	0.0067	0.0043	0.0028	0.0019	0.0012	0.0008	0.0005	0.0004	0.0002	0.0002	48
0.0094	0.0060	0.0039	0.0025	0.0016	0.0011	0.0007	0.0005	0.0003	0.0002	0.0001	49
0.0085	0.0054	0.0035	0.0022	0.0014	0.0009	0.0006	0.0004	0.0003	0.0002	0.0001	50

TABLE 3 Future Amount of an Annuity of $1

Payments	1.0%	1.5%	2.0%	2.5%	3.0%	4.0%	5.0%	6.0%	7.0%	8.0%	9.0%
1	1.0000	1.0000	1.0000	1.0000	1.0000	1.0000	1.0000	1.0000	1.0000	1.0000	1.0000
2	2.0100	2.0150	2.0200	2.0250	2.0300	2.0400	2.0500	2.0600	2.0700	2.0800	2.0900
3	3.0301	3.0452	3.0604	3.0756	3.0909	3.1216	3.1525	3.1836	3.2149	3.2464	3.2781
4	4.0604	4.0909	4.1216	4.1525	4.1836	4.2465	4.3101	4.3746	4.4399	4.5061	4.5731
5	5.1010	5.1523	5.2040	5.2563	5.3091	5.4163	5.5256	5.6371	5.7507	5.8666	5.9847
6	6.1520	6.2296	6.3081	6.3877	6.4684	6.6330	6.8019	6.9753	7.1533	7.3359	7.5233
7	7.2135	7.3230	7.4343	7.5474	7.6625	7.8983	8.1420	8.3938	8.6540	8.9228	9.2004
8	8.2857	8.4328	8.5830	8.7361	8.8923	9.2142	9.5491	9.8975	10.2598	10.6366	11.0285
9	9.3685	9.5593	9.7546	9.9545	10.1591	10.5828	11.0266	11.4913	11.9780	12.4876	13.0210
10	10.4622	10.7027	10.9497	11.2034	11.4639	12.0061	12.5779	13.1808	13.8164	14.4866	15.1929
11	11.5668	11.8633	12.1687	12.4835	12.8078	13.4864	14.2068	14.9716	15.7836	16.6455	17.5603
12	12.6825	13.0412	13.4121	13.7956	14.1920	15.0258	15.9171	16.8699	17.8885	18.9771	20.1407
13	13.8093	14.2368	14.6803	15.1404	15.6178	16.6268	17.7130	18.8821	20.1406	21.4953	22.9534
14	14.9474	15.4504	15.9739	16.5190	17.0863	18.2919	19.5986	21.0151	22.5505	24.2149	26.0192
15	16.0969	16.6821	17.2934	17.9319	18.5989	20.0236	21.5786	23.2760	25.1290	27.1521	29.3609
16	17.2579	17.9324	18.6393	19.3802	20.1569	21.8245	23.6575	25.6725	27.8881	30.3243	33.0034
17	18.4304	19.2014	20.0121	20.8647	21.7616	23.6975	25.8404	28.2129	30.8402	33.7502	36.9737
18	19.6147	20.4894	21.4123	22.3863	23.4144	25.6454	28.1324	30.9057	33.9990	37.4502	41.3013
19	20.8109	21.7967	22.8406	23.9460	25.1169	27.6712	30.5390	33.7600	37.3790	41.4463	46.0185
20	22.0190	23.1237	24.2974	25.5447	26.8704	29.7781	33.0660	36.7856	40.9955	45.7620	51.1601
21	23.2392	24.4705	25.7833	27.1833	28.6765	31.9692	35.7193	39.9927	44.8652	50.4229	56.7645
22	24.4716	25.8376	27.2990	28.8629	30.5368	34.2480	38.5052	43.3923	49.0057	55.4568	62.8733
23	25.7163	27.2251	28.8450	30.5844	32.4529	36.6179	41.4305	46.9958	53.4361	60.8933	69.5319
24	26.9735	28.6335	30.4219	32.3490	34.4265	39.0826	44.5020	50.8156	58.1767	66.7648	76.7898
25	28.2432	30.0630	32.0303	34.1578	36.4593	41.6459	47.7271	54.8645	63.2490	73.1059	84.7009
26	29.5256	31.5140	33.6709	36.0117	38.5530	44.3117	51.1135	59.1564	68.6765	79.9544	93.3240
27	30.8209	32.9867	35.3443	37.9120	40.7096	47.0842	54.6691	63.7058	74.4838	87.3508	102.7231
28	32.1291	34.4815	37.0512	39.8598	42.9309	49.9676	58.4026	68.5281	80.6977	95.3388	112.9682
29	33.4504	35.9987	38.7922	41.8563	45.2189	52.9663	62.3227	73.6398	87.3465	103.9659	124.1354
30	34.7849	37.5387	40.5681	43.9027	47.5754	56.0849	66.4388	79.0582	94.4608	113.2832	136.3075
31	36.1327	39.1018	42.3794	46.0003	50.0027	59.3283	70.7608	84.8017	102.0730	123.3459	149.5752
32	37.4941	40.6883	44.2270	48.1503	52.5028	62.7015	75.2988	90.8898	110.2182	134.2135	164.0370
33	38.8690	42.2986	46.1116	50.3540	55.0778	66.2095	80.0638	97.3432	118.9334	145.9506	179.8003
34	40.2577	43.9331	48.0338	52.6129	57.7302	69.8579	85.0670	104.1838	128.2588	158.6267	196.9823
35	41.6603	45.5921	49.9945	54.9282	60.4621	73.6522	90.3203	111.4348	138.2369	172.3168	215.7108
36	43.0769	47.2760	51.9944	57.3014	63.2759	77.5983	95.8363	119.1209	148.9135	187.1021	236.1247
37	44.5076	48.9851	54.0343	59.7339	66.1742	81.7022	101.6281	127.2681	160.3374	203.0703	258.3759
38	45.9527	50.7199	56.1149	62.2273	69.1594	85.9703	107.7095	135.9042	172.5610	220.3159	282.6298
39	47.4123	52.4807	58.2372	64.7830	72.2342	90.4091	114.0950	145.0585	185.6403	238.9412	309.0665
40	48.8864	54.2679	60.4020	67.4026	75.4013	95.0255	120.7998	154.7620	199.6351	259.0565	337.8824
41	50.3752	56.0819	62.6100	70.0876	78.6633	99.8265	127.8398	165.0477	214.6096	280.7810	369.2919
42	51.8790	57.9231	64.8622	72.8398	82.0232	104.8196	135.2318	175.9505	230.6322	304.2435	403.5281
43	53.3978	59.7920	67.1595	75.6608	85.4839	110.0124	142.9933	187.5076	247.7765	329.5830	440.8457
44	54.9318	61.6889	69.5027	78.5523	89.0484	115.4129	151.1430	199.7580	266.1209	356.9496	481.5218
45	56.4811	63.6142	71.8927	81.5161	92.7199	121.0294	159.7002	212.7435	285.7493	386.5056	525.8587
46	58.0459	65.5684	74.3306	84.5540	96.5015	126.8706	168.6852	226.5081	306.7518	418.4261	574.1860
47	59.6263	67.5519	76.8172	87.6679	100.3965	132.9454	178.1194	241.0986	329.2244	452.9002	626.8628
48	61.2226	69.5652	79.3535	90.8596	104.4084	139.2632	188.0254	256.5645	353.2701	490.1322	684.2804
49	62.8348	71.6087	81.9406	94.1311	108.5406	145.8337	198.4267	272.9584	378.9990	530.3427	746.8656
50	64.4632	73.6828	84.5794	97.4843	112.7969	152.6671	209.3480	290.3359	406.5289	573.7702	815.0836

10.0%	11.0%	12.0%	13.0%	14.0%	15.0%	16.0%	17.0%	18.0%	19.0%	20.0%	Payments
1.0000	1.0000	1.0000	1.0000	1.0000	1.0000	1.0000	1.0000	1.0000	1.0000	1.0000	1
2.1000	2.1100	2.1200	2.1300	2.1400	2.1500	2.1600	2.1700	2.1800	2.1900	2.2000	2
3.3100	3.3421	3.3744	3.4069	3.4396	3.4725	3.5056	3.5389	3.5724	3.6061	3.6400	3
4.6410	4.7097	4.7793	4.8498	4.9211	4.9934	5.0665	5.1405	5.2154	5.2913	5.3680	4
6.1051	6.2278	6.3528	6.4803	6.6101	6.7424	6.8771	7.0144	7.1542	7.2966	7.4416	5
7.7156	7.9129	8.1152	8.3227	8.5355	8.7537	8.9775	9.2068	9.4420	9.6830	9.9299	6
9.4872	9.7833	10.0890	10.4047	10.7305	11.0668	11.4139	11.7720	12.1415	12.5227	12.9159	7
11.4359	11.8594	12.2997	12.7573	13.2328	13.7268	14.2401	14.7733	15.3270	15.9020	16.4991	8
13.5795	14.1640	14.7757	15.4157	16.0853	16.7858	17.5185	18.2847	19.0859	19.9234	20.7989	9
15.9374	16.7220	17.5487	18.4197	19.3373	20.3037	21.3215	22.3931	23.5213	24.7089	25.9587	10
18.5312	19.5614	20.6546	21.8143	23.0445	24.3493	25.7329	27.1999	28.7551	30.4035	32.1504	11
21.3843	22.7132	24.1331	25.6502	27.2707	29.0017	30.8502	32.8239	34.9311	37.1802	39.5805	12
24.5227	26.2116	28.0291	29.9847	32.0887	34.3519	36.7862	39.4040	42.2187	45.2445	48.4966	13
27.9750	30.0949	32.3926	34.8827	37.5811	40.5047	43.6720	47.1027	50.8180	54.8409	59.1959	14
31.7725	34.4054	37.2797	40.4175	43.8424	47.5804	51.6595	56.1101	60.9653	66.2607	72.0351	15
35.9497	39.1899	42.7533	46.6717	50.9804	55.7175	60.9250	66.6488	72.9390	79.8502	87.4421	16
40.5447	44.5008	48.8837	53.7391	59.1176	65.0751	71.6730	78.9792	87.0680	96.0218	105.9306	17
45.5992	50.3959	55.7497	61.7251	68.3941	75.8364	84.1407	93.4056	103.7403	115.2659	128.1167	18
51.1591	56.9395	63.4397	70.7494	78.9692	88.2118	98.6032	110.2846	123.4135	138.1664	154.7400	19
57.2750	64.2028	72.0524	80.9468	91.0249	102.4436	115.3797	130.0329	146.6280	165.4180	186.6880	20
64.0025	72.2651	81.6987	92.4699	104.7684	118.8101	134.8405	153.1385	174.0210	197.8474	225.0256	21
71.4027	81.2143	92.5026	105.4910	120.4360	137.6316	157.4150	180.1721	206.3448	236.4385	271.0307	22
79.5430	91.1479	104.6029	120.2048	138.2970	159.2764	183.6014	211.8013	244.4868	282.3618	326.2369	23
88.4973	102.1742	118.1552	136.8315	158.6586	184.1678	213.9776	248.8076	289.4945	337.0105	392.4842	24
98.3471	114.4133	133.3339	155.6196	181.8708	212.7930	249.2140	292.1049	342.6035	402.0425	471.9811	25
109.1818	127.9988	150.3339	176.8501	208.3327	245.7120	290.0883	342.7627	405.2721	479.4306	567.3773	26
121.0999	143.0786	169.3740	200.8406	238.4993	283.5688	337.5024	402.0323	479.2211	571.5224	681.8528	27
134.2099	159.8173	190.6989	227.9499	272.8892	327.1041	392.5028	471.3778	566.4809	681.1116	819.2233	28
148.6309	178.3972	214.5828	258.5834	312.0937	377.1697	456.3032	552.5121	669.4475	811.5228	984.0680	29
164.4940	199.0209	241.3327	293.1992	356.7868	434.7451	530.3117	647.4391	790.9480	966.7122	1181.8816	30
181.9434	221.9132	271.2926	332.3151	407.7370	500.9569	616.1616	758.5038	934.3186	1151.3875	1419.2579	31
201.1378	247.3236	304.8477	376.5161	465.8202	577.1005	715.7475	888.4494	1103.4960	1371.1511	1704.1095	32
222.2515	275.5292	342.4294	426.4632	532.0350	664.6655	831.2671	1040.4858	1303.1253	1632.6698	2045.9314	33
245.4767	306.8374	384.5210	482.9034	607.5199	765.3654	965.2698	1218.3684	1538.6878	1943.8771	2456.1176	34
271.0244	341.5896	431.6635	546.6808	693.5727	881.1702	1120.7130	1426.4910	1816.6516	2314.2137	2948.3411	35
299.1268	380.1644	484.4631	618.7493	791.6729	1014.3457	1301.0270	1669.9945	2144.6489	2754.9143	3539.0094	36
330.0395	422.9825	543.5987	700.1867	903.5071	1167.4975	1510.1914	1954.8936	2531.6857	3279.3481	4247.8112	37
364.0434	470.5106	609.8305	792.2110	1030.9981	1343.6222	1752.8220	2288.2255	2988.3891	3903.4242	5098.3735	38
401.4478	523.2667	684.0102	896.1984	1176.3378	1546.1655	2034.2735	2678.2238	3527.2992	4646.0748	6119.0482	39
442.5926	581.8261	767.0914	1013.7042	1342.0251	1779.0903	2360.7572	3134.5218	4163.2130	5529.8290	7343.8578	40
487.8518	646.8269	860.1424	1146.4858	1530.9086	2046.9539	2739.4784	3668.3906	4913.5914	6581.4965	8813.6294	41
537.6370	718.9779	964.3595	1296.5289	1746.2358	2354.9969	3178.7949	4293.0169	5799.0378	7832.9808	10577.3553	42
592.4007	799.0655	1081.0826	1466.0777	1991.7088	2709.2465	3688.4021	5023.8298	6843.8646	9322.2472	12693.8263	43
652.6408	887.9627	1211.8125	1657.6678	2271.5481	3116.6334	4279.5465	5878.8809	8076.7603	11094.4741	15233.5916	44
718.9048	986.6386	1358.2300	1874.1646	2590.5648	3585.1285	4965.2739	6879.2907	9531.5771	13203.4242	18281.3099	45
791.7953	1096.1688	1522.2176	2118.8060	2954.2439	4123.8977	5760.7177	8049.7701	11248.2610	15713.0748	21938.5719	46
871.9749	1217.7474	1705.8838	2395.2508	3368.8380	4743.4824	6683.4326	9419.2310	13273.9480	18699.5590	26327.2863	47
960.1723	1352.6996	1911.5898	2707.6334	3841.4753	5456.0047	7753.7818	11021.5002	15664.2586	22253.4753	31593.7436	48
1057.1896	1502.4965	2141.9806	3060.6258	4380.2819	6275.4055	8995.3869	12896.1553	18484.8251	26482.6356	37913.4923	49
1163.9085	1668.7712	2400.0182	3459.5071	4994.5213	7217.7163	10435.6488	15089.5017	21813.0937	31515.3363	45497.1908	50

TABLE 4 Present Value of an Annuity of $1

Payments	1.0%	1.5%	2.0%	2.5%	3.0%	4.0%	5.0%	6.0%	7.0%	8.0%	9.0%
1	0.9901	0.9852	0.9804	0.9756	0.9709	0.9615	0.9524	0.9434	0.9346	0.9259	0.9174
2	1.9704	1.9559	1.9416	1.9274	1.9135	1.8861	1.8594	1.8334	1.8080	1.7833	1.7591
3	2.9410	2.9122	2.8839	2.8560	2.8586	2.7751	2.7232	2.6730	2.6243	2.5771	2.5313
4	3.9020	3.8544	3.8077	3.7620	3.7171	3.6299	3.5460	3.4651	3.3872	3.3121	3.2397
5	4.8534	4.7826	4.7135	4.6458	4.5797	4.4518	4.3295	4.2124	4.1002	3.9927	3.8897
6	5.7955	5.6972	5.6014	5.5081	5.4172	5.2421	5.0757	4.9173	4.7665	4.6229	4.4859
7	6.7282	6.5982	6.4720	6.3494	6.2303	6.0021	5.7864	5.5824	5.3893	5.2064	5.0330
8	7.6517	7.4859	7.3255	7.1701	7.0197	6.7327	6.4632	6.2098	5.9713	5.7466	5.5348
9	8.5660	8.3605	8.1622	7.9709	7.7861	7.4353	7.1078	6.8017	6.5152	6.2469	5.9952
10	9.4713	9.2222	8.9826	8.7521	8.5302	8.1109	7.7217	7.3601	7.0236	6.7101	6.4177
11	10.3676	10.0711	9.7868	9.5142	9.2526	8.7605	8.3064	7.8869	7.4987	7.1390	6.8052
12	11.2551	10.9075	10.5753	10.2578	9.9540	9.3851	8.8633	8.3838	7.9427	7.5361	7.1607
13	12.1337	11.7315	11.3484	10.9832	10.6350	9.9856	9.3936	8.8527	8.3577	7.9038	7.4869
14	13.0037	12.5434	12.1062	11.6909	11.2961	10.5631	9.8986	9.2950	8.7455	8.2442	7.7862
15	13.8651	13.3432	12.8493	12.3814	11.9379	11.1184	10.3797	9.7122	9.1079	8.5595	8.0607
16	14.7179	14.1313	13.5777	13.0550	12.5611	11.6523	10.8378	10.1059	9.4466	8.8514	8.3126
17	15.5623	14.9076	14.2919	13.7122	13.1661	12.1657	11.2741	10.4773	9.7632	9.1216	8.5436
18	16.3983	15.6726	14.9920	14.3534	13.7535	12.6593	11.6896	10.8276	10.0591	9.3719	8.7556
19	17.2260	16.4262	15.6785	14.9789	14.3238	13.1339	12.0853	11.1581	10.3356	9.6036	8.9501
20	18.0456	17.1686	16.3514	15.5892	14.8775	13.5903	12.4622	11.4699	10.5940	9.8181	9.1285
21	18.8570	17.9001	17.0112	16.1845	15.4150	14.0292	12.8212	11.7641	10.8355	10.0168	9.2922
22	19.6604	18.6208	17.6580	16.7654	15.9369	14.4511	13.1630	12.0416	11.0612	10.2007	9.4424
23	20.4558	19.3309	18.2922	17.3321	16.4436	14.8568	13.4886	12.3034	11.2722	10.3711	9.5802
24	21.2434	20.0304	18.9139	17.8850	16.9355	15.2470	13.7986	12.5504	11.4693	10.5288	9.7066
25	22.0232	20.7196	19.5235	18.4244	17.4131	15.6221	14.0939	12.7834	11.6536	10.6748	9.8226
26	22.7952	21.3986	20.1210	18.9506	17.8768	15.9828	14.3752	13.0032	11.8258	10.8100	9.9290
27	23.5596	22.0676	20.7069	19.4640	18.3270	16.3296	14.6430	13.2105	11.9867	10.9352	10.0266
28	24.3164	22.7267	21.2813	19.9649	18.7641	16.6631	14.8981	13.4062	12.1371	11.0511	10.1161
29	25.0658	23.3761	21.8444	20.4535	19.1885	16.9837	15.1411	13.5907	12.2777	11.1584	10.1983
30	25.8077	24.0158	22.3965	20.9303	19.6004	17.2920	15.3725	13.7648	12.4090	11.2578	10.2737
31	26.5423	24.6461	22.9377	21.3954	20.0004	17.5885	15.5928	13.9291	12.5318	11.3498	10.3428
32	27.2696	25.2671	23.4683	21.8492	20.3888	17.8736	15.8027	14.0840	12.6466	11.4350	10.4062
33	27.9897	25.8790	23.9886	22.2919	20.7658	18.1476	16.0025	14.2302	12.7538	11.5139	10.4644
34	28.7027	26.4817	24.4986	22.7238	21.1318	18.4112	16.1929	14.3681	12.8540	11.5869	10.5178
35	29.4086	27.0756	24.9986	23.1452	21.4872	18.6646	16.3742	14.4982	12.9477	11.6546	10.5668
36	30.1075	27.6607	25.4888	23.5563	21.8323	18.9083	16.5469	14.6210	13.0352	11.7172	10.6118
37	30.7995	28.2371	25.9695	23.9573	22.1672	19.1426	16.7113	14.7368	13.1170	11.7752	10.6530
38	31.4847	28.8051	26.4406	24.3486	22.4925	19.3679	16.8679	14.8460	13.1935	11.8289	10.6908
39	32.1630	29.3646	26.9026	24.7303	22.8082	19.5845	17.0170	14.9491	13.2649	11.8786	10.7255
40	32.8347	29.9158	27.3555	25.1028	23.1148	19.7928	17.1591	15.0463	13.3317	11.9246	10.7574
41	33.4997	30.4590	27.7995	25.4661	23.4124	19.9931	17.2994	15.1380	13.3941	11.9672	10.7866
42	34.1581	30.9941	28.2348	25.8206	23.7014	20.1856	17.4232	15.2245	13.4524	12.0067	10.8134
43	34.8100	31.5212	28.6616	26.1664	23.9819	20.3708	17.5459	15.3062	13.5070	12.0432	10.8380
44	35.4555	32.0406	29.0800	26.5038	24.2543	20.5488	17.6628	15.3832	13.5579	12.0771	10.8605
45	36.0945	32.5523	29.4902	26.8330	24.5187	20.7200	17.7741	15.4558	13.6055	12.1084	10.8812
46	36.7272	33.0565	29.8923	27.1542	24.7754	20.8847	17.8801	15.5244	13.6500	12.1374	10.9002
47	37.3537	33.5532	30.2866	27.4675	25.0247	21.0429	17.9810	15.5890	13.6916	12.1643	10.9176
48	37.9740	34.0426	30.6731	27.7732	25.2667	21.1951	18.0772	15.6500	13.7305	12.1891	10.9336
49	38.5881	34.5247	31.0521	28.0714	25.5017	21.3415	18.1687	15.7076	13.7668	12.2122	10.9482
50	39.1961	34.9997	31.4236	28.3623	25.7298	21.4822	18.2559	15.7619	13.8007	12.2335	10.9617

10.0%	11.0%	12.0%	13.0%	14.0%	15.0%	16.0%	17.0%	18.0%	19.0%	20.0%	Payments
0.9091	0.9009	0.8929	0.8850	0.8772	0.8696	0.8621	0.8547	0.8475	0.8403	0.8333	1
1.7355	1.7125	1.6901	1.6681	1.6467	1.6257	1.6052	1.5852	1.5656	1.5465	1.5278	2
2.4869	2.4437	2.4018	2.3612	2.3216	2.2832	2.2459	2.2096	2.1743	2.1399	2.1065	3
3.1699	3.1024	3.0373	2.9745	2.9137	2.8550	2.7982	2.7432	2.6901	2.6386	2.5887	4
3.7908	3.6959	3.6048	3.5172	3.4331	3.3522	3.2743	3.1993	3.1272	3.0576	2.9906	5
4.3553	4.2305	4.1114	3.9975	3.8887	3.7845	3.6847	3.5892	3.4976	3.4098	3.3255	6
4.8684	4.7122	4.5638	4.4226	4.2883	4.1604	4.0386	3.9224	3.8115	3.7057	3.6046	7
5.3349	5.1461	4.9676	4.7988	4.6389	4.4873	4.3436	4.2072	4.0776	3.9544	3.8372	8
5.7590	5.5370	5.3282	5.1317	4.9464	4.7716	4.6065	4.4506	4.3030	4.1633	4.0310	9
6.1446	5.8892	5.6502	5.4262	5.2161	5.0188	4.8332	4.6586	4.4941	4.3389	4.1925	10
6.4951	6.2065	5.9377	5.6869	5.4527	5.2337	5.0286	4.8364	4.6560	4.4865	4.3271	11
6.8137	6.4924	6.1944	5.9176	5.6603	5.4206	5.1971	4.9884	4.7932	4.6105	4.4392	12
7.1034	6.7499	6.4235	6.1218	5.8424	5.5831	5.3423	5.1183	4.9095	4.7147	4.5327	13
7.3667	6.9819	6.6282	6.3025	6.0021	5.7245	5.4675	5.2293	5.0081	4.8023	4.6106	14
7.6061	7.1909	6.8109	6.4624	6.1422	5.8474	5.5755	5.3242	5.0916	4.8759	4.6755	15
7.8237	7.3792	6.9740	6.6039	6.2651	5.9542	5.6685	5.4053	5.1624	4.9377	4.7296	16
8.0216	7.5488	7.1196	6.7291	6.3729	6.0472	5.7487	5.4746	5.2223	4.9897	4.7746	17
8.2014	7.7016	7.2497	6.8399	6.4674	6.1280	5.8178	5.5339	5.2732	5.0333	4.8122	18
8.3649	7.8393	7.3658	6.9380	6.5504	6.1982	5.8775	5.5845	5.3162	5.0700	4.8435	19
8.5136	7.9633	7.4694	7.0248	6.6231	6.2593	5.9288	5.6278	5.3527	5.1009	4.8696	20
8.6487	8.0751	7.5620	7.1016	6.6870	6.3125	5.9731	5.6648	5.3837	5.1268	4.8913	21
8.7715	8.1757	7.6446	7.1695	6.7429	6.3587	6.0113	5.6964	5.4099	5.1486	4.9094	22
8.8832	8.2664	7.7184	7.2297	6.7921	6.3988	6.0442	5.7234	5.4321	5.1668	4.9245	23
8.9847	8.3481	7.7843	7.2829	6.8351	6.4338	6.0726	5.7465	5.4509	5.1822	4.9371	24
9.0770	8.4217	7.8431	7.3300	6.8729	6.4641	6.0971	5.7662	5.4669	5.1951	4.9476	25
9.1609	8.4881	7.8957	7.3717	6.9061	6.4906	6.1182	5.7831	5.4804	5.2060	4.9563	26
9.2372	8.5478	7.9426	7.4086	6.9352	6.5135	6.1364	5.7975	5.4919	5.2151	4.9636	27
9.3066	8.6016	7.9844	7.4412	6.9607	6.5335	6.1520	5.8099	5.5016	5.2228	4.9697	28
9.3696	8.6501	8.0218	7.4701	6.9830	6.5509	6.1656	5.8204	5.5098	5.2292	4.9747	29
9.4269	8.6938	8.0552	7.4957	7.0027	6.5660	6.1772	5.8294	5.5168	5.2347	4.9789	30
9.4790	8.7331	8.0850	7.5183	7.0199	6.5791	6.1872	5.8371	5.5227	5.2392	4.9824	31
9.5264	8.7686	8.1116	7.5383	7.0350	6.5905	6.1959	5.8437	5.5277	5.2430	4.9854	32
9.5694	8.8005	8.1354	7.5560	7.0482	6.6005	6.2034	5.8493	5.5320	5.2462	4.9878	33
9.6086	8.8293	8.1566	7.5717	7.0599	6.6091	6.2098	5.8541	5.5356	5.2489	4.9898	34
9.6442	8.8552	8.1755	7.5856	7.0700	6.6166	6.2153	5.8582	5.5386	5.2512	4.9915	35
9.6765	8.8786	8.1924	7.5979	7.0790	6.6231	6.2201	5.8617	5.5412	5.2531	4.9929	36
9.7059	8.8996	8.2075	7.6087	7.0868	6.6288	6.2242	5.8647	5.5434	5.2547	4.9941	37
9.7327	8.9186	8.2210	7.6183	7.0937	6.6338	6.2278	5.8673	5.5452	5.2561	4.9951	38
9.7570	8.9357	8.2330	7.6268	7.0997	6.6380	6.2309	5.8695	5.5468	5.2572	4.9959	39
9.7791	8.9511	8.2438	7.6344	7.1050	6.6418	6.2335	5.8713	5.5482	5.2582	4.9966	40
9.7991	8.9649	8.2534	7.6410	7.1097	6.6450	6.2358	5.8729	5.5493	5.2590	4.9972	41
9.8174	8.9774	8.2619	7.6469	7.1138	6.6478	6.2377	5.8743	5.5502	5.2596	4.9976	42
9.8340	8.9886	8.2696	7.6522	7.1173	6.6503	6.2394	5.8755	5.5510	5.2602	4.9980	43
9.8491	8.9988	8.2764	7.6568	7.1205	6.6524	6.2409	5.8765	5.5517	5.2607	4.9984	44
9.8628	9.0079	8.2825	7.6609	7.1232	6.6543	6.2421	5.8773	5.5523	5.2611	4.9986	45
9.8753	9.0161	8.2880	7.6645	7.1256	6.6559	6.2432	5.8781	5.5528	5.2614	4.9989	46
9.8866	9.0235	8.2928	7.6677	7.1277	6.6573	6.2442	5.8787	5.5532	5.2617	4.9991	47
9.8969	9.0302	8.2972	7.6705	7.1296	6.6585	6.2450	5.8792	5.5536	5.2619	4.9992	48
9.9063	9.0362	8.3010	7.6730	7.1312	6.6596	6.2457	5.8797	5.5539	5.2621	4.9993	49
9.9148	9.0417	8.3045	7.6752	7.1327	6.6605	6.2463	5.8801	5.5541	5.2623	4.9995	50

Questions

1. What is the management cycle and how does it relate to strategic and short-term planning?
2. What is the sequence in the planning phase of the management cycle and how does it differ from the sequence in the performing phase?
3. What are a business's operating profits generated for?
4. What is the distinction between return of investment and return on investment?
5. How does time impact investment decisions?
6. How does the size of the investment impact investment decisions?
7. How does rate of return on an investment differ from return on investment? What are the advantages of using a rate of return on investment when choosing among alternative investments?
8. Under what conditions does a negative rate of return occur?
9. What is risk?
10. How does a person's attitude toward risk affect his or her decision-making process?
11. Contrast expected rate of return on an investment with the actual rate of return on an investment.
12. What is the relationship between risk and return?
13. What is a risk premium? Describe the three factors that generate risk premiums and give an example of each.
14. Explain what is meant by the time value of money.
15. How does simple interest differ from compound interest?
16. Describe the six time value of money elements.
17. What is the future value of an amount of $1 and when is this concept used?
18. What is the present value of an amount of $1 and when is this concept used?
19. How are the future value of an amount of $1 and the present value of an amount of $1 similar?
20. What are the characteristics of an annuity?
21. What is the difference between the future value and present value of an annuity?
22. Describe the four-step process for solving time value of money problems.

End-of-chapter time value of money exercises and problems that can be completed using the tables in the chapter appendix are indicated by **.

Exercises

E11.1 **LO 1** Each of the following three investments costs $400,000. Calculate the expected rates of return on these investments. Each possible outcome will occur at the end of one year.

	Possible Outcome	Probability
Investment A	$40,000	0.3
	50,000	0.4
	60,000	0.3
Investment B	$50,000	0.1
	55,000	0.4
	60,000	0.3
	65,000	0.2
Investment C	$60,000	0.4
	70,000	0.3
	80,000	0.3

LO 1 **E11.2** Refer to E11.1. How, if at all, does your answer change if the investments cost $500,000? Why?

LO 2 **E11.3** **How much will an investment of $10,000 be worth at the end of five years if it earns:

A. 10 percent interest compounded annually?
B. 10 percent interest compounded semiannually?
C. 10 percent interest compounded quarterly?
D. Why do the answers above change?

LO 2 **E11.4** **What is the present value of $10,000 five years from today if interest is:

A. 10 percent compounded annually?
B. 10 percent compounded semiannually?
C. 10 percent compounded quarterly?
D. Why do the answers above change?

LO 2 **E11.5** **What will be the maturity value of $30,000 deposited in a three-year certificate of deposit that earns 8 percent interest compounded semiannually?

LO 2 **E11.6** **Determine the future value of the following annuities; assume each annuity can earn 10 percent interest.

A. Six annual payments of $15,000 beginning one year from today.
B. 12 semiannual payments of $7,500 beginning six months from today.
C. 24 quarterly payments of $3,750 beginning three months from today.
D. Explain why the results differ.

LO 2 **E11.7** **Determine the present value of the following annuities if the annuity earns 8 percent.

A. Five annual payments of $10,000 beginning one year from today.
B. 20 quarterly payments of $2,500 beginning three months from today.
C. 10 semiannual payments of $5,000 beginning six months from today.
D. Explain why the results differ.

LO 2 **E11.8** **If $7,500 was invested five years ago and has accumulated to $11,019.75, what rate of interest was earned if the interest was compounded annually?

LO 2 **E11.9** **If $60,000 was invested at 8 percent and has grown to $85,692, how many years has the money been invested if interest was compounded quarterly?

LO 2 **E11.10** **If $30,000 is invested today at 6 percent compounded quarterly, how long will it take to accumulate $40,407?

LO 2 **E11.11** **If $8,000 is invested today and will accumulate to $30,957.60 in 10 years, what annual interest rate compounded semiannually will generate this amount?

LO 2 **E11.12** **How long will it take to double an investment of $4,300 if the investment can generate an 8 percent return that is compounded semiannually?

LO 2 **E11.13** How much will an investment of $8,000 be worth at the end of five years if it earns:

A. 3 percent interest compounded monthly?
B. 4 percent interest compounded monthly?
C. 3 percent interest compounded semimonthly?
D. 4 percent interest compounded semimonthly?
E. Explain the difference between part **A** and part **C.**

LO 2 **E11.14** What is the present value of $8,000 five years from today if interest is:

A. 3 percent compounded monthly?
B. 4 percent compounded monthly?
C. 3 percent compounded semimonthly?
D. 4 percent compounded semimonthly?
E. Explain the difference between part **A** and part **C.**

LO 2 **E11.15** Ashley just borrowed $15,000. Her monthly payment for five years will be $293.49. What interest rate is Ashley paying?

LO 2 **E11.16** David just borrowed $50,000 at 8 percent. If he makes monthly payments of $650.94, how long will it take him to pay off this loan?

LO 2 **E11.17** Matthew wants to buy a new touring bus for $250,000. His bank is willing to loan him the money for 12 years at 7 percent. What is his monthly payment?

LO 2 **E11.18** **Katie needs to borrow $50,000, but she cannot make periodic payments. Instead she would like to make a lump-sum payment in 10 years. Assuming that Katie and the bank agree on 8 percent interest compounded quarterly, how much money will Katie owe in 10 years?

LO 2 **E11.19** Joshua needs to borrow some money. The bank agrees to let him make quarterly payments of $2,500 and a final payment of $200,000 in 10 years. If the bank and Joshua agree on a 6 percent rate of interest, compounded quarterly, how much money will Joshua receive?

Problems

P11.1 LO 2 **Levi McArthur graduated with a masters of accountancy degree and has accepted a staff accounting position with a firm; he will receive a salary of $50,000. The firm guarantees that Levi will receive a 5 to 9 percent raise each year for the next five years depending on his performance. What will

Levi's salary be in five years if he gets a 5 percent raise each year? What would his salary be in five years if the annual raise is 9 percent?

LO 2 P11.2 The Grooms Diner has just purchased a counter and stools for $45,000. Nick paid $5,000 down and is going to borrow the remaining $40,000. The Manhattan National Bank will loan him the money for four years if he agrees to make monthly payments.

A. What are the monthly payments if the bank charges 5 percent interest?
B. What are the monthly payments if the bank charges 7 percent interest?
C. What are the monthly payments if the bank charges 9 percent interest?

LO 2 P11.3 **Michael Paul wants to start his own business when he graduates from college in three years and he needs $600,000 to do so. How much money must he put aside today under the following conditions?

A. He can earn 8 percent compounded semiannually.
B. He can earn 8 percent compounded annually.
C. He can earn 8 percent compounded quarterly.

LO 2 P11.4 **Albany County wants to raise $4,000,000 to finance the construction of a new high school. The school board wants to make quarterly payments to repay the loan over the next 10 years. What will be the amount of the payments assuming these interest rates?

A. 10 percent
B. 8 percent
C. 6 percent

LO 2 P11.5 **Davidsmeier Corporation just sold inventory with a cost of $150,000. In exchange for the inventory, Davidsmeier received $40,000 cash and a note promising to pay $250,000 in five years (there is no interest rate specified on the note).

A. How much profit did Davidsmeier make on this sale if it usually loans money at 10 percent interest compounded annually?
B. How much profit did Davidsmeier make on this sale if it usually loans money at 12 percent interest compounded annually?
C. How much profit did Davidsmeier make on this sale if it usually loans money at 8 percent interest compounded annually?
D. Explain how the interest rate assumed on a note like this affects the income of the company.

LO 2 P11.6 Josh Jacobsen just received $1,000,000 from winning the lottery. He has decided to spend $200,000 immediately and to invest the remaining $800,000 for 10 years.

A. If he can get an 5 percent rate of return that is compounded quarterly, how much will he have at the end of 10 years?
B. If he can get a 7 percent rate of return that is compounded quarterly, how much will he have at the end of 10 years?
C. If he can get an 9 percent rate of return that is compounded quarterly, how much will he have at the end of 10 years?

LO 2 P11.7 Tara Storey can afford car payments of $400 per month for five years. The interest rate on car loans is 6 percent.

A. How much can she spend for a car?
B. How much can she spend for a car if she could get an interest rate of 4 percent?
C. How would your answer to part **A** change if she could make a $2,000 down payment?
D. How would your answer to part **B** change if she could make a $2,000 down payment?

LO 2 P11.8 **Freyensee just acquired office furniture that had a list price of $400,000. The furniture store said that it would finance the entire price at 0 percent interest by letting the company make eight quarterly payments of $50,000 starting three months from the date of purchase.

A. If Freyensee Company can borrow money at 8 percent, what is the cost of the office furniture?
B. What is the cost of the office furniture if Freyensee Company usually borrows money at 6 percent?
C. What is the cost of the office furniture if Freyensee Company agrees to make four semiannual payments of $100,000 each if it usually borrows money at 8 percent?

LO 2 P11.9 James Marcy just signed a contract to purchase some land in the Laramie Valley. The contract requires James to make monthly payments of $19,001.37 for 10 years at 9 percent interest.

A. What price did James pay for the land?
B. What would the monthly payments be if the interest rate were dropped to 8 percent?
C. What would the monthly payments be if James extended the loan to 15 years at 8 percent?

LO 2 P11.10 Michelle Paul has acquired a new computer system at a price of $240,000 and is considering two financing alternatives. If National Bank makes the loan, Michelle will make monthly payments of $2,545.57 for 10 years to repay the debt. If First State Bank makes the loan, the monthly payments will be $2,925.43 for eight years.

A. What is the interest rate charged by National Bank?
B. What is the interest rate charged by First State Bank?
C. What other factors should Michelle take into consideration when deciding which bank to use?

LO 2 P11.11 **George Mackay has identified two buildings that are suitable for his new office. For building A, George will have to pay $245,000 a year for 10 years, while building B will cost $175,000 a year for 15 years. The interest rate on both loans is 9 percent.

A. Which building is less expensive?
B. Which building is less expensive if building A has payments of $150,000 for 20 years and the interest rate is 9 percent?

LO 2 P11.12 Kevin Finnegan, CPA, has just billed a customer $35,000 for services rendered. The customer wants to pay for this bill by making monthly payments over the next three years.

A. Determine the amount of the customer's monthly payments if Kevin wants an 6 percent annual return on the loan.
B. Determine the amount of the customer's monthly payments if Kevin wants a 7 percent annual return on the loan.
C. Assume Kevin wants an 6 percent return, but the customer wants to make quarterly payments over the next three years. Determine the amount of the payment that Kevin would find acceptable in this situation.

LO 2 P11.13 Jeff Johnson wants to have $2,000,000 in his retirement account when he retires on his 65th birthday. He is 24 today and will make annual payments once he starts paying into the retirement fund. How much will Jeff have to pay monthly to achieve his goal if he can get an 8 percent annual rate of interest and he starts payments at:

A. Age 25?
B. Age 35?
C. Age 45?
D. What is the moral of this story?

LO 2 P11.14 Refer to P11.13. Jeff is confident he can achieve his goal of accumulating $2,000,000 by his 65th birthday. Now he wants to know how much he can withdraw from his investment account each month after he retires.

A. How much cash will Jeff receive if he can earn 10 percent interest and if he withdraws the cash over five years?
B. How much cash will Jeff receive if he can earn 10 percent interest and if he withdraws the cash over 10 years?
C. How much cash will Jeff receive if he can earn 10 percent interest and if he withdraws the cash over 15 years?

LO 2 P11.15 **Jamie Sorensen was given the assignment of finding suitable office space for her company. She found a great office in an upscale office park that requires a three-year lease. There are two options to pay for this lease. The first is to pay $160,000 on the first day of the lease, and the second is to make quarterly payments of $15,800 for three years starting three months from today. She must decide which of the two payment methods is the most economical for her company. Jamie knows the firm usually borrows money at 12 percent interest. Which payment plan should Jamie select? Why?

Cases

C11.1 LO 2 Ray Corporation, a small manufacturing firm, wants to establish a pension fund for its 10 employees who range from 28 to 51 years of age. Ray wants each employee who retires from the firm at age 65 to receive an annual pension on the retirement date that is 70 percent of the employee's annual wage at retirement. What factors must Ray Corporation take into consideration to determine how much the firm must contribute to the pension fund each year to meet the terms of its retirement plan?

LO 2 C11.2 John Dean is trying to buy a new Ford pickup and has been negotiating with two dealerships on identical trucks with sticker prices of $42,200. The first dealer is offering to finance the truck at 0 percent interest for the next 36 months. The second dealer has offered to sell John the truck for $36,000 and will finance the price with a bank loan over the next 36 months at a 12 percent annual rate of interest. Which of the two deals is better for John if 12 percent is the going truck loan interest rate? Why would the first dealer be willing to loan money at 0 percent interest?

Critical Thinking

CT11.1 LO 2 **Jill Walters, your boss at Walters's Waterbeds & Futons, has seen the zero percent interest advertising of other furniture stores and wants to use this promotion to attract new customers. Currently, her cost to buy a futon is $200 and she is selling them for $550. She is also charging 18 percent interest for customers who buy on credit. Jill wants to offer 24 months' interest-free financing. What price must she charge if she wants to maintain her current profit margin and still make 18 percent interest?

LO 2 **CT11.2** **On September 1, 2009, the Little Broadway Players signed a note to raise cash to buy a theater. The terms of the note call for seven annual payments of $5,000 and an interest rate of 9 percent. However, because the Players are just starting this enterprise, the bank has agreed to defer the first of the seven payments until September 1, 2012. How much cash will the bank loan the Little Broadway Players given the terms of this note?

Ethical Challenges

EC11.1 LO 2 In December 2008, Bernie Madoff was arrested and charged with one count of securities fraud for allegedly stealing up to $50 billion from investors. He was convicted and sentenced to 150 years in prison for his Ponzi scheme that defrauded investors including Steven Spielberg and Kevin Bacon. What is a Ponzi scheme? How does it work?

EC11.2 LO 2 Many home furnishing retailers advertise that they will finance your purchases for a certain period of time at zero percent interest. Given what you have just learned about the time value of money, do you believe that this is a "genuine" offer? Suppose the offer was zero percent interest or a $500 rebate. Under these circumstances are you really paying zero percent if you forego the rebate? Explain. Are these types of advertisements ethical? Explain.

Excel and other spreadsheet packages can be used to solve time value of money problems. Use Excel (or another spreadsheet package) to answer each of the following.

Computer Applications

CA11.1 LO 2 Meghan Bonner wants to save $100 each month starting one month from today for the next 20 years. What will her investment be worth if she earns

A. 6 percent?
B. 8 percent?
C. 10 percent?

LO 2 **CA11.2** Ryan Fornstrom wants to buy a house costing $150,000. He can make monthly payments for the next 20 years. What will his monthly payment be if the bank charges

A. 4 percent?
B. 6 percent?
C. 8 percent?

Visit the text Online Learning Center at **www.mhhe.com/ainsworth6e** for additional problem material that accompanies this chapter.

PART FIVE

V

Planning: Capital Resource Process Activities

CHAPTER TWELVE

12 Planning Investments: Capital Budgeting

Learning Objectives

- **LO1** Explain the concept of and calculate a company cost of capital.
- **LO2** Use NPV analysis to make investment decisions for a not-for-profit entity.
- **LO3** Use NPV analysis to make investment decisions assuming uniform depreciation.
- **LO4** Use NPV analysis to make investment decisions assuming tax depreciation.

In Chapter 11 we learned a valuable tool for making investing and financing decisions. In this chapter we apply that tool for capital budgeting analysis. **Capital budgeting** is a process used for analysis and selection of the long-term investments of a business. Because the amounts spent on long-term investments—such as buildings, equipment, and even other businesses—are usually quite large, they affect the long-term profitability of the company. Therefore, they require systematic and careful consideration.

The Capital Budgeting Process

The capital budgeting process requires cooperative input from functions throughout the organization. For example, without the marketing function's forecast of demand for the company's services or products in the operating stage of the planning phase, it would be difficult for a company to assess its potential need for plant expansion. Without the production function's recommendations for the timely acquisition of machines to cut costs and improve product quality, it might be difficult to maintain efficiency. The finance function fulfills an important capital budgeting function by monitoring the cost and sources of funds needed to pay for selected projects. Finally, the accounting/information systems function collects, organizes, analyzes, and distributes the information necessary to facilitate capital budgeting decisions. In addition, it is very important that capital budgeting decisions are tied to the company's business organization and strategy process.

While the capital budgeting process itself is unique to each company or enterprise, its four basic processes apply in all situations. Notice that the capital budgeting process is involved in the planning, performing, and evaluating phases of the management cycle:

1. Identifying long-term investment opportunities.
2. Selecting appropriate investments.
3. Financing the selected investments (Chapters 13 and 14).
4. Recording the purchase and use of the investments (Chapter 16).
5. Evaluating the investments (Chapter 16).

The capital budgeting process usually involves the acquisition of operational investments. These assets provide the infrastructure of the business enterprise—that is, the facilities, equipment, software, and information systems necessary for a company to conduct its basic business activities. For example, an electronics merchant needs a store and a parking lot in order to sell electronics. Apple needs equipment to produce its computers and patents to protect the company from duplication of its products by other companies. Physicians need offices and medical equipment to provide quality healthcare services to their patients.

The cost of an investment is the purchase price plus one-time costs necessary and reasonable to get it ready for its intended use.

Identifying Long-Term Investment Opportunities

To identify investment opportunities, managers must recognize what is included in the cost of the company's long-term investments. In addition, they must understand both their motives for making these investments and the organizational and other mechanisms that identify the need for operational investments.

Expenditures that you might not normally think of as being part of an investment are included in its cost. In addition to the purchase price of an asset, the related sales tax, freight charges, brokerage fees, and installation costs all become part of an investment's (asset's) cost when they are reasonable and necessary to get the asset ready for its intended use. For example, if Apple pays $200,000 for new equipment, $500 for freight charges, and $10,000 for installation, the cost of the equipment would be $210,500 because all of these expenditures are reasonable and necessary to get the equipment ready for its intended use. (Recall we used a similar definition of cost in Chapter 8 regarding inventory.) Identifying this cost establishes the basis for determining whether future cash flows are generating both a return *of* and a return *on* investment.

Companies make capital investments for four significant reasons: The first is the need to replace worn-out or unproductive operating assets, such as buildings, machinery, and equipment.

The critical factor in deciding to replace assets is knowing what constitutes a worn-out or unproductive asset. This decision must come from operating personnel who are familiar with the capabilities of the old assets and their proposed replacements. As part of the internal perspective, improving operating efficiency may be a planned goal for the period.

The second reason to make a capital expenditure is to expand the business's operating capacity based on long-term strategic decisions made by the company. This decision is stimulated by increased demand for existing products and services or the demand for new products or services. Usually, the marketing function identifies these opportunities in the planning phase of the management cycle. Once the marketing function quantifies the production necessary to meet the increased demand, it informs the company's production managers. The production managers use the marketing function's projections to determine the specifications of the asset(s) that can meet the increased demand. This would be considered part of the learning and growth goals of the company.

The third reason to make a capital expenditure is to keep up with changing technology. Since technology is changing so rapidly, it is important that companies keep up-to-date. Skipping a generation of computer technology is not generally recommended. It is easier, and ultimately less expensive, to keep up with technology. For example, imagine a company switching from a manual accounting system to an ERP system. The differences are so great that implementation and employee-training costs skyrocket. Therefore continual updates and changes are generally recommended. This, however, is not universally true. Some companies have found that a complete overhaul of their systems is preferable to constant updating. Regardless of the process adopted—gradual change or overhaul—significant investments must be made in technology and technology-related training. Again, this is a learning and growth perspective issue that requires careful consideration and planning.

Finally, the fourth reason is that capital expenditures are often made to comply with mandates of the government. To comply with environmental or safety regulations, companies are often required to make capital expenditures that alter their normal operating activities. For example, power companies that use coal-fired generating plants are required to install costly scrubbers to reduce the pollutants emitted from their power plants that cause acid rain, smog, and other environmental hazards. This could be considered an internal perspective since compliance may alter normal operating processes. On the other hand as part of a company's learning and growth goals, a company may desire ISO 9000 or ISO 14000 certification. ISO (International Organization for Standardization) awards certifications in quality assurance processes and environmental assurance. ISO 9000 is a series of quality guidelines to ensure quality at every step of the production process. ISO 14000 is a series of standards for managing environmental impacts of products and processes. Obtaining ISO certification is not only prestigious; it is also necessary to conduct business with many other companies.

Tie to Business Organization and Strategy Process

An organization's strategic planning document, which covers a 5-to 10-year time period, is one means of identifying long-term investment opportunities. Such documents reflect top management's vision of how the organization will grow and change during the period of the plan. Long-term plans identify and include the required capital expenditures associated with changes anticipated by management—for example, replacement of existing equipment or plant expansions.

Suppose Apple created a five-year plan in 2010 that called for the construction of a new manufacturing plant in 2015. The plan would outline management's assumptions about both the demand for computers and other products and the profitability of the company for the specified period. While the goals in the five-year plan are subject to change as each year passes, the document helps management focus its efforts on the basic company goals. The planning document is rolled forward each year when management reassesses its long-term commitments in relation to the company's yearly performance.

Because businesses exist in a dynamic environment, management must be able to identify and evaluate business opportunities whenever they occur, even if they are unexpected. For example, suppose Apple becomes aware of a new processing technique that can reduce processing time while maintaining quality. Apple would begin the capital budgeting process to determine if it should replace its existing processing techniques, even though normal equipment replacement might not have been planned until some time in the future.

Selecting Appropriate Investments

Once management identifies a potential capital expenditure, it evaluates the investment to assess whether it is capable of generating a satisfactory rate of return for the company. Any return that is greater than or equal to the company's cost of capital is considered a satisfactory return.

A company's **cost of capital** is often calculated as the weighted average cost of its debt and equity financing. It represents the amount of return that the assets of the company must generate to satisfy both creditors and owners. The cost of debt financing is the rate of interest the creditors receive for the use of their money, and the cost of equity financing is the rate of return the owners receive for the use of their money. Owners expect the company to provide a return on their investment, and, if they are not satisfied, they can dispose of their holdings in the company or vote to replace the management of the company.

Calculating the amount of return that owners expect is unique to each company. Calculating a company's cost of capital is complicated, and the following example simplifies the process to illustrate the concept. Assume that Benchmark Corporation is financed with $1,000,000 of debt and $3,000,000 of shareholders' equity. If the debt has an interest rate of 12 percent, and the shareholders demand a 16 percent rate of return, what is the cost of capital? Exhibit 12.1 shows that Benchmark's cost of capital is 15 percent. This amount is the weighted average of the returns demanded by the creditors and owners and represents the minimum rate of return that the company's assets must generate to keep both creditors and shareholders satisfied. Thus any investments made by the company must generate a return that meets or exceeds the company's weighted average cost of capital.

When making capital budgeting decisions, the company must compare its weighted average cost of capital to the expected return on investment. **Return on investment** is calculated as:[1]

$$\frac{\text{Profit before interest and taxes}}{\text{Asset investment}}$$

EXHIBIT 12.1
Benchmark Corporation's Cost of Capital

Capital Structure:

Assets	=	Liabilities	+	Owners' Equity
$4,000,000		$1,000,000		$3,000,000

Required Returns:

Liabilities	12%
Owners' equity	16%

Financing Proportions:

Liabilities	$1,000,000	1/4
Owners' equity	3,000,000	3/4
Total	$4,000,000	

Cost of capital = Weighted average cost of financing
Cost of capital = Liability proportion × Liability required return + Owners' equity proportion × Owners' equity required return

Cost of Capital = (1/4 × 12%) + (3/4 × 16%) = 15%

[1] Recall that we calculated a simplified return on investment ratio in Chapter 2. Return on investment is often calculated using profit before interest and taxes to examine the return generated by the assets regardless of how the assets are financed.

That is, for planning purposes we want to estimate the return generated by the company's assets regardless of how those assets are financed. Then we compare this return to the weighted average cost of capital. To illustrate assume that Benchmark plans to invest $700,000 in assets for one year and that these assets are expected to generate a profit of $98,000 before interest or taxes. Thus this investment has an expected return of 14 percent:

$$\$98{,}000/\$700{,}000 = 14\%$$

This return is not sufficient to satisfy both the creditors and the stockholders, as demonstrated in Exhibit 12.2. As Exhibit 12.2 shows, prior to this investment, Benchmark's expected profit before interest and taxes was $600,000. This generates the required 12 percent return for the creditors ($1,000,000 [Exhibit 12.1] × 0.12 = $120,000) and the required 16 percent return for the stockholders ($3,000,000 [Exhibit 12.1] × 0.16 = $480,000). Now look what happens if this investment is undertaken. The profit of the company is expected to be $698,000 ($600,000 + $98,000) and the assets would be increased to $4,700,000 ($4,000,000 + $700,000). Assuming that the capital structure of the company remains one-quarter debt and three-quarters equity, the new liabilities and owners' equity of the company would be:

Assets	=	Liabilities	+	Owners' equity
$4,700,000		$1,175,000		$3,525,000

Therefore the required return of the creditors is $1,175,000 × 0.12 = $141,000. Leaving $557,000 ($698,000 − $141,000) for the shareholders. Thus the return for the shareholders is 15.8 percent ($557,000/$3,525,000), not the required 16 percent return.

This illustrates the importance of a company's cost of capital in management's decisions regarding acceptable investments in the capital budgeting process. The cost of capital is also commonly called a **hurdle rate.** Unless management's analysis indicates that the expected rate of return on a long-term asset investment meets or exceeds the hurdle rate, the investment in the asset would not be able to satisfy both the creditors' and owners' desire for a satisfactory return.

As you know, capital budgeting decisions usually involve long-term projects; thus, the illustration that assumed a one-year time period is not realistic. To estimate the rate of return of a potential investment, decision makers must be able to estimate the future cash inflows and outflows attributable to the investment if it is acquired. These cash flows represent the future costs and benefits of acquiring the asset. Management must estimate cash flows with as much care and precision as possible because the accuracy of the estimates directly affects the quality of the investment decision. Once the future cash flows are estimated, we apply the time value of money concepts learned in Chapter 11 to make our investment decision. There are several methods used to aid capital budgeting decisions—we

EXHIBIT 12.2
Benchmark's Return on Investment

Return on Investment Before:

Income before interest and taxes	$600,000
Less: Interest ($1,000,000 × 0.12)	120,000
Income before taxes	$480,000

Return on liabilities	$120,000/$1,000,000 = 12%
Return on owners' equity	$480,000/$3,000,000 = 16%

Return on Investment After:

Income before interest and taxes	$698,000
Less: Interest ($1,175,000 × 0.12)	141,000
Income before taxes	$557,000

Return on liabilities	$141,000/$1,175,000 = 12%
Return on owners' equity	$557,000/$3,525,000 = 15.8%

consider the net present value method. Throughout this discussion we use the same notation as in Chapter 11:

PV = present value

FV = future value

c = number of compoundings/payments per year

n = total number of payments/compoundings in the time period

r = annual interest rate (hurdle rate, cost of capital)

ANN = annuity

We will make a few simplifying assumptions as we learn this new decision-making technique. First, we will assume that all cash flows will occur at the end of the period. Second, we assume that compounding will occur annually. Finally, we assume that all items are taxed at the same rate. That is, gains and losses are not taxed differently than revenues and expenses. As you take more business courses you may find that one or more of these assumptions are relaxed in future capital budgeting analyses that you undertake.

Net Present Value Analysis

Net present value analysis is a method of evaluating investments that uses the time value of money to assess whether the investment's expected rate of return is greater than the company's cost of capital. If the expected rate of return is greater than the company's cost of capital, the company should acquire the asset. Since we must make the decision to invest in the present, we must find the present value of all expected future cash flows.

The net present value method requires that decision makers find the present value of an investment's estimated future cash flows by using the company's cost of capital as the interest rate. If the cost of the investment is less than the present value of the estimated future cash flows, the investment's return, assuming that the future cash flows occur as projected, is greater than the company's cost of capital, making it a favorable investment.

The net present value (NPV) method includes the following four steps:

1. Identify (estimate) the timing and amount of all cash inflows and outflows associated with the potential investment over its anticipated life.
2. Calculate the present value of the expected future cash flows using the company's cost of capital as the discount rate.
3. Compute the net present value by subtracting the initial cash outflows necessary to acquire the asset from the present value of the future cash flows.
4. Decide to accept or reject the investment in the capital asset. If the net present value is zero or positive, the proposed investment is acceptable. If the NPV is negative, the company should reject the project.

The following simplified example illustrates the net present value method. Assume that Apple is considering the acquisition of new equipment that costs $750,000 and has a useful life of four years. Management estimates that the equipment will save Apple $250,000 per year over its life. If Apple's cost of capital is 10 percent, should it acquire the equipment?

Exhibit 12.3 illustrates the four steps in the NPV method of analysis used to resolve this capital budgeting decision. Step 1 identifies the initial cash outflow of $750,000 necessary to acquire the equipment and the $250,000 estimated cash inflows Apple expects in each of the next four years. Step 2 calculates the present value of the expected future cash flows using the 10 percent cost of capital, $792,466. Step 3 calculates the net present value by

EXHIBIT 12.3
Net Present Value Analysis Steps

Step One: Identify the cash flows

	N = 0	N = 1	N = 2	N = 3	N = 4
Cash to acquire	(750,000)				
Cash inflows		250,000	250,000	250,000	250,000

Step Two: Find the present value of the future cash flows

$ANN = 250{,}000$; $c = 1$; $n = 4$; $FV = 0$; $r = 10$; $PV = 792{,}466.36$

Step Three: Compute the net present value

Present value of future cash flows	$792,466
Less: initial investment	750,000
Net present value	$ 42,466

Step Four: Accept or reject the proposal

Accept because the NPV is positive.

subtracting the initial cash outflow from the present value of the future cash flows, $42,466. In Step 4 Apple will decide to make the investment if it expects the investment to generate a return greater than the cost of capital. In this case the NPV is positive, which means that if the cash inflows occur as expected, the equipment will generate a return greater than the cost of capital and Apple should acquire the machine. The decision, in this case, is to acquire the equipment because its NPV is positive, $42,466 (Step 3). If the cash flows occur as projected, the new equipment will have a greater return than the 10 percent cost of capital (hurdle rate) of Apple.

Why does a positive NPV indicate that the rate of return is greater than the cost of capital? The answer lies in understanding Step 2 of the analysis illustrated in Exhibit 12.3. The present value of the future cash flows represents the maximum price that Apple would pay for the equipment because it is based on the minimum rate of return, 10 percent, that Apple would accept. Stated another way, if Apple invested $792,466 in an asset and received $250,000 each year for four years, it would recover its original investment and receive a 10 percent return on its investment.

Looking at Exhibit 12.4, the cash flows expected (column 2) would provide both a 10 percent return on a $792,466 investment (column 3) and the return of the $792,466 initial investment (column 4). The maximum price that Apple would pay for the equipment is $792,466 given the projected cash flows and Apple's desired minimum rate of return of 10 percent (hurdle rate). If Apple pays an amount greater than $792,466, and the $250,000 cash flows occur as projected, the investment in the new equipment will yield a rate of return that is less than the required 10 percent. If Apple pays any amount less than $792,466, and the $250,000 cash flows occur as expected, the new equipment will yield a rate of return greater than 10 percent. The positive NPV of $42,466 means that Apple is paying less than the amount required to generate a 10 percent return and, therefore, will receive a rate of return higher than 10 percent. Thus, if an investment of $792,466 that produces $250,000 cash

EXHIBIT 12.4
Proof of NPV

Years	Expected Cash Inflow	10 Percent Return on Investment	Return of Investment	Investment
0				$792,466.36
1	$250,000.00	$79,246.64	$170,753.36	621,713.00
2	250,000.00	62,171.30	187,828.70	433,884.30
3	250,000.00	43,388.43	206,611.57	227,272.73
4	250,000.00	22,727.27	227,272.73	0.00

at the end of each year for the next four years yields a 10 percent return, then Apple's investment of $750,000 that generates the same cash flows must earn more than a 10 percent return on the investment.

Key point: The net present value technique does not indicate the expected return of the investment or the amount of its profitability, only that the expected return is greater (positive NPV) or less (negative NPV) than the cost of capital or hurdle rate.

Assumptions of NPV

Exhibit 12.4 presents a simplified illustration of the NPV method. Before we consider more realistic applications, it is important to understand the assumptions underlying the NPV method. Remember NPV is a model, and like CVP, EOQ, or any other model, it has certain assumptions that may limit its usefulness. Three common assumptions underlie NPV analysis:

1. All cash flows are known with certainty. Although cash flow projections are really estimates and, therefore, are subject to uncertainty, we are willing to accept this assumption. The net present value method can adjust for the risk of uncertainty without increasing the complexity of the model.

2. Cash flows are assumed to occur at the end of the time period. Although cash flows occur throughout the year, any distortion caused by this assumption is not sufficient to significantly affect the decision.

3. Cash inflows are immediately reinvested in another project that earns a return for the company. This assumption does not take into consideration the fact that cash flows might be distributed to shareholders or creditors. The NPV method assumes that the cash flows are reinvested at a rate equal to the hurdle rate (cost of capital).

These assumptions, while not always realistic, provide the structure that makes net present value an effective capital budgeting tool, if the decision maker considers these limitations. Now that we have examined the assumptions underlying the NPV model, we look at the details of the NPV method.

Source of Cash Flows

The NPV method incorporates cash flows into the model because the acquisition and operation of capital assets produce cash flows. What is not always obvious about this process is the source of these cash flows. The following description reviews the typical cash inflows and outflows used in capital budgeting projects.

The initial cash outflows are the expenditures made to acquire the asset in addition to other acquisition costs such as freight charges, sales tax, and installation costs. Another possible related cash outflow that could occur is an increase in working capital. *Working capital, or the excess of current assets over current liabilities,* increases when a project requires more cash on hand, supplies, and inventories. When acquiring a new manufacturing facility, for example, a company might need additional cash and inventory to operate the facility on a day-to-day basis.

Cash inflows occur during the investment's life because the investment generates revenues, decreases operating expenses, or both. For capital budgeting purposes, a decrease in operating expenses is considered to be a cash inflow because it increases the cash flows of the company. At the end of the investment's life, cash inflows occur when the amount of working capital necessary to operate the facility is reduced and the investment is sold for salvage.

Key point: Savings = Cash inflows

In NPV analysis, the cash flows can be either certain and precise or quite uncertain and imprecise. For example, there is little uncertainty about the amount of cash outflows necessary to acquire the asset. However, the amount of cash inflows from the sale of the asset at the end of its useful life is much more uncertain. Managers should make their cash flow projections with the best information possible, including information obtained from prior experience, to help evaluate cash flow projections and improve the process of projecting cash flows.

Uneven Cash Flows

The preceding NPV illustration used equal cash flows each period. In reality, cash flows generated by operating assets are seldom constant over time. In these cases, each future cash flow is a future value that must be discounted at the cost of capital (hurdle rate) to determine the present value. We now illustrate how to use the net present value method when estimated cash flows are uneven.

Assume that the $750,000 equipment proposal Apple is considering is expected to generate the following cash flows:

Year 1	$300,000
Year 2	260,000
Year 3	240,000
Year 4	200,000

Exhibit 12.5 shows the present value of all the future cash flows and represents the maximum price Apple should pay for the equipment given the cash flows expected. The remaining steps of the net present value method show that the net present value of $54,522 is positive and that the initial cost of the asset is less than the maximum price of $804,522 Apple should pay. Therefore, Apple should buy the equipment.

Income Taxes

Income taxes can significantly affect capital budgeting decisions because they change the amount of both cash inflows and cash outflows used in the capital budgeting process. Understanding how income taxes affect net present value analysis is essential to the proper use of this method. Because income taxes are paid based on the amount of income a business generates, they typically represent cash outflows. Proposed capital expenditures will affect the company's income and, therefore, the tax liability of the company.

EXHIBIT 12.5
Net Present Value with Uneven Cash Flows

Step Two: Find the present value of future cash flows

c	*n*	*r*	*ANN*	*FV*	*PV*
1	1	10	0	300,000	272,727
1	2	10	0	260,000	214,876
1	3	10	0	240,000	180,316
1	4	10	0	200,000	136,603
Total					804,522

Step Three: Compute the NPV

Present value of cash flows	$804,522
Less: Initial investment	750,000
NPV	$ 54,522

Step Four: Accept or reject

Accept because the NPV is positive.

After-tax cash flows are the estimated cash flows associated with a potential investment after considering the impact of income taxes. Determining the after-tax cash flows is the first step in NPV analysis in for-profit businesses. Since the profits of the company are taxable, operating cash inflows are taxable and operating cash outflows reduce the company's tax liability.

Since cash inflows are taxed, the company receives only 1 minus the tax rate; therefore, cash inflows must be multiplied by (1 − Tax rate) before determining the present value.

After-Tax Cash Inflows

An after-tax cash inflow is the difference between the taxable cash inflow and the amount of tax paid on it. An after-tax cash inflow can be calculated using one of the following two methods:

Cash inflow	Cash inflow
× Tax rate	− Tax paid on cash inflow
= Tax paid on cash inflow	= *After-tax cash inflow*

Or,

Cash inflow
× (1 − Tax rate)
= *After-tax cash inflow*

The (1 − Tax rate) portion of the latter formula represents the portion of $1 of pretax cash inflows that would remain after paying the tax due on $1. Recall that we made a similar calculation in Chapter 4 when we determined target profit before taxes in CVP analysis. For example, assume Apple estimates a $250,000 cash inflow each year for four years. Further assume that Apple is subject to a 20 percent average income tax rate. Thus the tax liability associated with this $250,000 cash inflow is $250,000 × 0.2 = $50,000. We can find the present value of this cash inflow two ways:

1. Cash inflow $250,000
   Tax paid on cash inflow 50,000
   After-tax cash inflow $200,000; thus,
   $ANN = 200{,}000;\ c = 1;\ n = 4;\ r = 10;\ FV = 0;$ $PV = 633{,}973$

Or,

2. Net cash inflow: 250,000 × 0.8 = 200,000; thus,
   $ANN = 200{,}000;\ c = 1;\ n = 4;\ r = 10;\ FV = 0;$ $PV = 633{,}973$

Since cash outflows save taxes (that is, the tax bill would have been higher without the outflow), we must multiply the outflow by (1 − Tax rate) to find the after-tax outflow before determining the present value.

After-Tax Cash Outflows

Cash outflows associated with capital expenditures after acquisition normally include cash expenditures made to operate or maintain the asset. After-tax cash payments are smaller than pretax cash payments because pretax cash payments reduce the income subject to tax and, therefore, the company's tax liability.

An after-tax cash operating outflow is the difference between the taxable deductible cash outflow and the amount of tax savings because of it. An after-tax cash outflow can be calculated using one of the following two methods:

Cash outflow	Cash outflow
× Tax rate	− Tax saved
= Tax saved	= *After-tax cash outflow*

Or,

Cash outflow
× (1 − Tax rate)
= *After-tax cash outflow*

Here the (1 − Tax rate) represents the after-tax cost of spending $1. When multiplied by the deductible cash outflows, it yields the after-tax cash outflows. For example, assume that Apple expects cash operating outflows of $60,000 each year for four years. Again, assume a 20 percent tax rate. Because this cash outflow is tax deductible, the tax savings associated with the outflow is $60,000 × 0.2 = $12,000. We can determine the net cash operating outflow one of two ways:

1. Cash outflow: $60,000
   Tax saved on cash outflow 12,000
   After-tax cash outflow $48,000; thus,
   $ANN = 48{,}000; c = 1; n = 4; r = 10; FV = 0;$ $PV = 152{,}154$

Or,

2. Net cash outflow: 60,000 × 0.8 = 48,000; thus,
   $ANN = 48{,}000; c = 1; n = 4; r = 10; FV = 0;$ $PV = 152{,}154$

Tax Shield

Think of a "shield" as something that provides protection; in this case, it provides "protection" from taxes. That is, the shield saves taxes; therefore, we must multiply the shield (the amount of annual depreciation) by the tax rate to determine the tax savings.
Savings = Inflow
Then, determine the present value of the savings.

Depreciation, and other noncash expenses, does not directly decrease cash, but it reduces income subject to tax and the related amount of income taxes due on income. Therefore, depreciation provides a **tax shield** because it reduces the potential amount of a company's tax liability by reducing its taxable income without affecting its pretax cash flows. Tax shields keep companies from being taxed on the recovery of the cost of their investments.

For example, assume Apple's potential investment will be depreciated uniformly over its life. Therefore, annual depreciation will be $750,000/4 = $187,500. Each year's depreciation reduces taxable income because it represents the portion of the income that is a return of the initial investment and only a return on investment is subject to income tax. Because depreciation is tax deductible, this $187,500 expense will reduce Apple's taxes each year. The tax shield of $187,500 creates a tax savings of $187,500 × 0.2 = $37,500 and the present value of the tax savings (inflow) is:

$$ANN = 37{,}500; c = 1; n = 4; r = 10; FV = 0; \text{ therefore: } PV = 118{,}870$$

When projecting the amount of cash flows for a project, the tax savings generated by the tax shield created by depreciation are a critical part of the process. The only uncertainty involved in projecting these cash savings is whether the tax rates will remain the same over the life of the asset.

MACRS Depreciation

When determining taxable income, companies can use accelerated depreciation methods approved by the Internal Revenue Service. These tax depreciation methods allow more (accelerated) depreciation in the first years of an asset's life and, therefore, create larger tax shields earlier in the asset's life and smaller tax shields later in the asset's life. Our current tax depreciation system is referred to as the **modified accelerated cost recovery system (MACRS).** The MACRS classifies assets according to the period of time over which the Internal Revenue Code requires those assets to be depreciated. For example, three-year property includes race horses that are more than two years old when placed in service. (Yes, even horses are sometimes treated as depreciable assets!) The IRS considers automobiles, trucks, computers, and typewriters to be five-year property. The normal depreciation period allowed for office desks and files is seven years, and for residential buildings the period is 27.5 years. Note that the actual useful life of an asset will probably be different (typically longer) from what the tax depreciation schedules allow. Assume that Apple's potential investment is considered to be three-year property by the IRS.[2] Then the following depreciation schedule would be used:

[2] Note that IRS depreciation is one year longer than the property class of the asset being depreciated. Therefore, 3-year property is depreciated over 4 years; 5-year property is depreciated over 6 years; and 7-year property is depreciated over 8 years.

Year 1	33.33%
Year 2	44.45
Year 3	14.81
Year 4	7.41

This means that Apple can deduct depreciation expense of 33.33 percent of the cost of the investment in the first year; 44.45 percent of the cost in the second year, and so on. Since the amount of depreciation changes each year, the associated tax savings also change each year. Let's assume a 20 percent tax rate and calculate the tax savings associated with the IRS depreciation on this proposed $750,000 investment.

Year	Depreciation Rate	Depreciation Amount	Tax Rate	Tax Savings
1	33.33%	$249,975	20%	$49,995
2	44.45	333,375	20	66,675
3	14.81	111,075	20	22,215
4	7.41	55,575	20	11,115

Because the tax savings created by depreciation's tax shield are different amounts occurring at different points in the future, we must determine the present values as follows:

Year 1: $FV = 49{,}995$; $c = 1$; $n = 1$; $r = 10$; $ANN = 0$; $PV = \$\ 45{,}450$

Year 2: $FV = 66{,}675$; $c = 1$; $n = 2$; $r = 10$; $ANN = 0$; $PV = 55{,}103$

Year 3: $FV = 22{,}215$; $c = 1$; $n = 3$; $r = 10$; $ANN = 0$; $PV = 16{,}690$

Year 4: $FV = 11{,}115$; $c = 1$; $n = 4$; $r = 10$; $ANN = 0$; $PV = 7{,}592$

$124,835

Although using IRS depreciation schedules is more accurate, many companies calculate uniform depreciation over the life of the project because it is less complex. In addition, if a project generates a positive net present value using uniform depreciation, it will usually generate an even larger net present value using MACRS depreciation (see Enhance Your Understanding).

Enhance Your Understanding

Why is the present value of the IRS tax shield more than the present value of the tax savings created by uniform depreciation even though the total depreciation expense in both cases is $750,000?

Answer: Recall that the further away cash flows are, the lower the present value. Since the IRS depreciation allows greater depreciation early in the asset's life, the present value of the cash flows is greater.

Gains and Losses on Disposal of Assets

In capital budgeting decisions, the disposal of assets occurs when organizations either replace old assets or sell the proposed assets at the end of their useful lives. When a company disposes of such assets, there are usually two sources of cash flows: (1) the proceeds of the sale and (2) the change in the amount of taxes due when the asset is sold for a gain or a loss.

To determine whether an asset is sold at a gain or a loss we must compare the proceeds from the sale to the book value (not the original cost) of the asset. The book value of an asset represents the undepreciated portion of the asset's original cost rather than the market value of the asset, or the amount for which the company could sell the asset on the market. A **gain on disposal** occurs if the proceeds from the sale of an asset exceed its book value at the date of disposal. A **loss on disposal** occurs if the proceeds from the sale of an asset are less than its book value at the date of the sale.

Enhance Your Understanding

Why are these proposed increases and decreases in the company's net assets called gains and losses rather than revenues and expenses?

Answer: Recall that revenues are earned in the normal course of operations and expenses are incurred in an effort to generate revenues. Because these disposals involve the long-term assets of the company (as opposed to inventory), they are not part of operations and are not revenues/expenses.

When an asset is sold at a gain or loss there are two cash flows: (1) The *proceeds* from the sale and (2) the tax *paid* if gain resulted or the tax *saved* if a loss resulted. Net these two cash flows and then determine the PV.

To illustrate the cash flows surrounding the disposal of an asset, we describe both a gain and a loss on disposal. Assume that Apple has a piece of equipment that originally cost $10,000 and that at the point of sale the equipment has accumulated depreciation of $8,000, giving it a book value of $2,000. Assume that Apple will dispose of this asset immediately if the potential investment is undertaken. Recall that Apple's assumed tax rate is 20 percent.

Gain on Disposal

If the equipment is sold for $3,000 cash, there would be a gain on disposal of $1,000:

Cash proceeds from the sale	$3,000
Less: book value of equipment	2,000
Gain on disposal	$1,000

Since a gain is a taxable event, we must determine the taxes owed:

Gain on disposal	$1,000
× Tax rate	0.2
Taxes paid on disposal	$ 200

Thus the net cash inflow from this event is $2,800: the $3,000 cash proceeds less the $200 tax paid on the disposal.

Cash proceeds from the sale	$3,000
Less: tax paid on disposal	200
Net cash inflows	$2,800

Since this disposal will take place immediately, the $2,800 is the present value. However, if this sale were expected at some point in the future, we would determine the present value.

Loss on Disposal

Now assume that the equipment is sold for $1,500 cash; then there would be a loss on disposal of $500:

Cash proceeds from the sale	$1,500
Less: book value of equipment	2,000
Loss on disposal	$ (500)

The loss saves the company taxes, so we must determine the tax savings from this event:

Loss on disposal	$500
× Tax rate	0.2
Taxes saved on disposal	$100

Thus the net cash inflow from this event is $1,600: the $1,500 cash proceeds plus the $100 tax savings on disposal.

Cash proceeds from the sale	$1,500
Add: tax savings on disposal	100
Net cash inflows	$1,600

Again, the $1,600 is the present value because the disposal takes place immediately.

Comprehensive Example

This comprehensive illustration reviews most of the capital budgeting topics covered to this point. In the example assume that PCs to Go (our company from Chapter 6) is considering the acquisition of $900,000 in new processing equipment on January 1, 2011, and will use the net present value method to assess the potential investment. PCs to Go anticipates a tax increase so we will use a 30 percent tax rate. The following facts are related to this capital budgeting proposal:

- The processing equipment will increase the speed and accuracy of PCs to Go production processes and will benefit PCs to Go for *seven* years.
- The greater efficiency of the equipment will increase revenues by $180,000 each year of its life, but it requires a one-time $100,000 increase in the amount of direct material inventory to avoid running out of stock. This working capital increase will be released at the end of the project.
- The equipment will reduce labor costs by $35,000 each year but cause utility costs to increase $20,000 each year (Net change = $15,000).
- The equipment is depreciated uniformly over six years. (The IRS considers it five-year property.)
- The book value of the old equipment that will be replaced if the new equipment is purchased is $120,000; its market value is $80,000.
- The new equipment can be sold at the end of Year 7 (1/1/2018) for $160,000.
- PCs to Go has a 12 percent cost of capital (hurdle rate).

Let's calculate the net present value of this proposal. Cash outflows are denoted with parentheses.

Events anticipated at the beginning of the proposal:

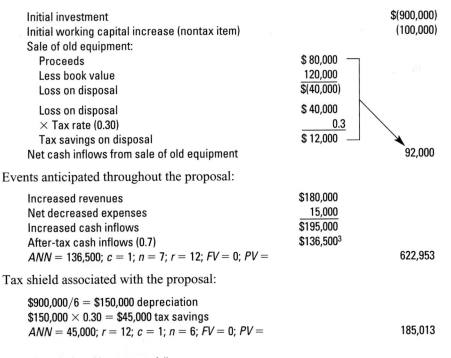

Initial investment		$(900,000)
Initial working capital increase (nontax item)		(100,000)
Sale of old equipment:		
Proceeds	$ 80,000	
Less book value	120,000	
Loss on disposal	$(40,000)	
Loss on disposal	$ 40,000	
× Tax rate (0.30)	0.3	
Tax savings on disposal	$ 12,000	
Net cash inflows from sale of old equipment		92,000

Events anticipated throughout the proposal:

Increased revenues	$180,000	
Net decreased expenses	15,000	
Increased cash inflows	$195,000	
After-tax cash inflows (0.7)	$136,500[3]	
ANN = 136,500; *c* = 1; *n* = 7; *r* = 12; *FV* = 0; *PV* =		622,953

Tax shield associated with the proposal:

$900,000/6 = $150,000 depreciation	
$150,000 × 0.30 = $45,000 tax savings	
ANN = 45,000; *r* = 12; *c* = 1; *n* = 6; *FV* = 0; *PV* =	185,013

[3] You can also calculate this amount as follows:

Cash inflows	$195,000
Less tax paid (0.3)	58,500
After-tax cash inflows	$136,500

OF INTEREST Using Excel for NPV Analysis

To calculate NPV using Excel we set up a time line to analyze our cash flows. Then we put this information into an Excel spreadsheet and use the function =NPV(rate, value 1, value 2, . . .). Let's use the comprehensive example in the chapter to set up our time line. Recall that our initial investment is $900,000 and that we need an increase in working capital of $100,000 but will sell the old equipment at the beginning of the project for a net cash inflow of $92,000. Throughout the life of the project we anticipate net cash inflows of $136,500. For Years 1 through 6 we anticipate a tax shield of $45,000. Finally at the end of the project we anticipate a release of $100,000 of working capital and we will sell the investment for a net cash inflow of $112,000. These facts are reflected on this time line:

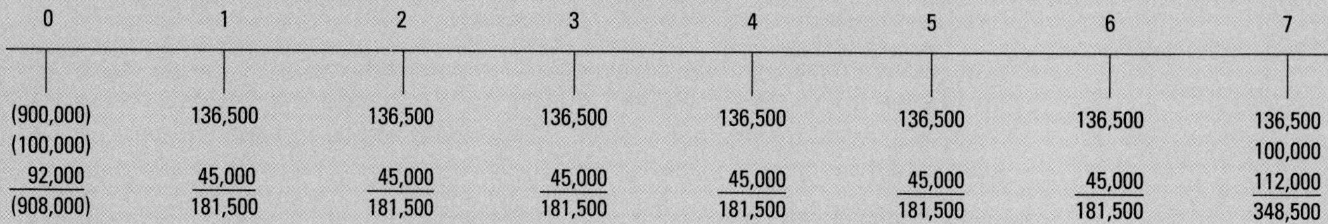

0 1 2 3 4 5 6 7
(900,000) 136,500 136,500 136,500 136,500 136,500 136,500 136,500
(100,000) 100,000
92,000 45,000 45,000 45,000 45,000 45,000 45,000 112,000
(908,000) 181,500 181,500 181,500 181,500 181,500 181,500 348,500

Next, we put this information along with our cost of capital (hurdle rate) into an Excel spreadsheet as shown here.

	A	B
1	Year 0	–908,000
2	Year 1	181500
3	Year 2	181500
4	Year 3	181500
5	Year 4	181500
6	Year 5	181500
7	Year 6	181500
8	Year 7	348500
9	Interest rate	12%
10		
11	($4,135.87)	

Then, in cell A11, enter the following: =NPV(B9,B2:B8)+B1.

This tells Excel that the appropriate interest rate is in cell B9, the cash flows for Years 1 through 7 are in cells B2 through B8, and the initial cash outflow is in cell B1. The result of this calculation is shown in cell A11: ($4,135.87).

Sensitivity analysis can be performed by changing the cash flows, the interest rate, or both.

Events anticipated at the end of the proposal:

Working capital decrease $FV = 100{,}000$; $n = 7$; $ANN = 0$; $r = 12$; $PV =$		45,235
Disposal of proposal equipment:		
Proceeds	$160,000	
Less book value	-0-	
Gain on disposal	$160,000	
Gain on disposal	$160,000	
× Tax rate (0.30)	0.3	
Tax paid on disposal	$ 48,000	
Net cash inflows $FV = \$112{,}000$; $n = 7$; $ANN = 0$; $r = 12$; $PV =$		50,663
Net present value		$ (4,136)

The proposal shows a negative net present value of $4,136. If PCs to Go acquires the equipment and the cash flows remain as projected, the rate of return on the equipment will be less than PCs to Go's cost of capital (hurdle rate) or minimum acceptable rate of return. Therefore, PCs to Go should not consider purchasing the equipment.

Now PCs to Go has a dilemma. It used uniform depreciation, which is known to be less accurate, and came to a negative NPV. At this point, it should probably redo the analysis to see if the more accurate depreciation would change the decision. Recall that the IRS considers this equipment to be five-year property, so the following depreciation schedule is appropriate:

Year 1	20.00%	Year 2	32.00%	Year 3	19.20%
Year 4	11.52%	Year 5	11.52%	Year 6	5.76%

The only difference is the tax shield associated with the proposal. We will replace the $185,013 tax shield calculated with the following:[4]

Year 1: $180,000 × 0.3 = $54,000 = *FV*; *n* = 1; *ANN* = 0; *r* = 12; *PV* =	$ 48,214
Year 2: $288,000 × 0.3 = $86,400 = *FV*; *n* = 2; *ANN* = 0; *r* = 12; *PV* =	68,878
Year 3: $172,800 × 0.3 = $51,840 = *FV*; *n* = 3; *ANN* = 0; *r* = 12; *PV* =	36,899
Year 4: $103,680 × 0.3 = $31,104 = *FV*; *n* = 4; *ANN* = 0; *r* = 12; *PV* =	19,767
Year 5: $103,680 × 0.3 = $31,104 = *FV*; *n* = 5; *ANN* = 0; *r* = 12; *PV* =	17,649
Year 6: $ 51,840 × 0.3 = $15,552 = *FV*; *n* = 6; *ANN* = 0; *r* = 12; *PV* =	7,879
Total	$199,286

The tax shield difference is $14,273 ($199,286 − $185,013); therefore, the new, more accurate NPV is $10,137 and PCs to Go should consider purchasing the equipment. Thus, using the easier uniform depreciation method is not always desirable.

Other Issues

Calculating the net present value of the equipment yielded a measure that helps management decide whether to acquire this capital asset. However, the apparent mathematical precision of this process should not obscure the fact that it is based on human judgment and uncertainty and that we must consider the impact of qualitative factors. These issues are the focus of the rest of this chapter.

Human Judgment

NPV analysis and accrual accounting are based on different assumptions. NPV analysis considers only the amount and timing of cash flows, whereas accrual accounting measures the results of accounting events, whether or not cash was a part of the transaction. When bonuses (see Chapter 5) or other rewards are based on accounting income while capital budgeting decisions are based on net present value, the potential for goal incongruence exists. **Goal incongruence** arises because an employee acts in his or her own best interests even if that action is not in the company's best interest; thus, the goals of the employee and the company are not congruent.

For example, assume a division manager of Apple is opposed to the acquisition of a new plant for which the manager will be responsible, even though it has a positive net present value. The manager, we call him Bob, bases his opposition on the fact that the projected accounting income of the plant during its four-year life shows that the plant would have a net loss or zero income in the first two years. The negative or zero income in these first two years will have a significant impact on the division's income, and Bob's performance is evaluated based on the division's accounting earnings. His yearly bonus is 5 percent of the division's income before bonus and taxes.

Exhibit 12.6 depicts the effects of the apparent conflict between NPV and accrual basis accounting income. Assume that the cost of capital (hurdle rate) for Apple is 10 percent and the

[4] Depreciation is determined as $900,000 × 0.20 = $180,000; $900,000 × 0.32 = $288,000; $900,000 × 0.192 = $172,800, etc.

EXHIBIT 12.6
Net Present Value Bonus Conflict

Net Present Value Analysis

Step One: Identify the cash flows

	0	1	2	3	4
Initial investment	(200,000)				
Pretax cash inflows		12,500	50,000	175,000	187,500
Tax paid on inflows		(2,500)	(10,000)	(35,000)	(37,500)
Tax savings on tax shield*		10,000	10,000	10,000	10,000

Step Two: Find the present value of future cash flows

After-tax cash flows:

$c = 1; r = 10; ANN = 0; n = 1; FV = 10{,}000;\ PV =$	9,091
$c = 1; r = 10; ANN = 0; n = 2; FV = 40{,}000;\ PV =$	33,058
$c = 1; r = 10; ANN = 0; n = 3; FV = 140{,}000; PV =$	105,184
$c = 1; r = 10; ANN = 0; n = 4; FV = 150{,}000; PV =$	102,452

Tax savings on tax shield:

$c = 1; r = 10; ANN = 10{,}000; n = 4; FV = 0; PV =$	31,699
Total present value of future cash flows	$281,484

Step Three: Compute the NPV

Present value of cash flows (above)	$281,484
Less: initial investment	200,000
NPV	$ 81,484

Step Four: Accept or reject

Accept because the NPV is positive.

Accounting Income and Bonus

	0	1	2	3	4
Revenues		12,500	50,000	175,000	187,500
Depreciation		50,000	50,000	50,000	50,000
Income before bonus and tax		(37,500)	-0-	125,000	137,500
Bonus (5%)		-0-	-0-	6,250	6,875

*Tax savings from tax shield = $200,000/4 = $50,000 × 0.2 = $10,000.

tax rate is 20 percent. You can see that the NPV of the new plant is a positive $81,484, which indicates that the plant would be a favorable investment for Apple. However, the accounting income generated in the first year is a loss of $37,500 and the accounting income in the second year is zero. Therefore Bob will not receive a bonus in either year. Although Bob will receive bonuses in years 3 and 4, he may not be willing to wait; thus he will reject this proposal.

The evaluation system encourages the division manager to oppose the acquisition of this plant, despite the fact it is a good decision for the company. If Apple acquires the plant Bob is penalized by losing a potential bonus in Years 1 and 2. This illustrates another reason that bonuses should be tied to balanced scorecard goals and not merely accounting income.

Uncertainty

Capital budgeting relies upon the use of many technical tools to facilitate the decision-making process. What is often lost in the process of applying these tools is the realization that informed speculation is a necessary component of the capital budgeting process. What do we mean by informed speculation? Because making capital budgeting decisions requires the personal judgment of decision makers, forecasting can be affected by personal perceptions of the decision maker. Sensitivity analysis is one way to deal with the uncertainty inherent in the capital budgeting process.

Sensitivity analysis, which we described in Chapter 4, reflects the results of changing a key element in a decision model. Capital budgeting uses sensitivity analysis to evaluate how a change in estimated cash flows or discount rates might affect the capital budgeting decision.

To illustrate, assume that Apple has a 10 percent cost of capital and is considering two $100,000 investments, A and B, shown in Exhibit 12.7. Apple's accountants have suggested that the cash flow estimates may vary downward by as much as 10 percent. Exhibit 12.7 illustrates how a 10 percent fluctuation might affect the investment decision.

For investment A, the possible fluctuation in cash flows from $32,000 per year (line 2) to $28,800 (line 3) would not affect the decision to acquire the investment because both possible cash flows have positive net present values of $21,305 and $9,175, respectively. Investment B, on the other hand, has a small NPV, $2,351, and a 10 percent drop in the projected cash flows from $27,000 to $24,300 would result in a negative NPV of ($7,884), leading to the suggestion that Apple should reject the investment. The closer the NPV is to zero and the greater the uncertainty about the cash flows, the greater the chance of making an incorrect investment decision. Sensitivity analysis helps clarify this type of risk.

Another form of risk that should be considered in capital budgeting decisions is operating leverage. **Operating leverage** is the proportion of fixed costs associated with a project. Recall that fixed costs do not vary with activity; therefore, the higher the proportion of fixed costs, the higher the risk if sales are less than expected. If a company believes its operating leverage is high, it might want to use a higher hurdle rate to compensate for the increased risk.

EXHIBIT 12.7
Sensitivity Analysis

Investment A

Price	$100,000
Estimated annual cash inflows	32,000
Estimated cash flows reduced 10 percent	28,800

Present value of annual cash flows:

$c = 1$; $n = 5$; $r = 10$; $FV = 0$; $ANN = 32{,}000$; $PV = 121{,}305$

Present value of decreased cash flows:

$c = 1$; $n = 5$; $r = 10$; $FV = 0$; $ANN = 28{,}800$; $PV = 109{,}175$

Net Present Values:

	Estimated Cash Flows	Reduced Cash Flows
Present value	$121,305	$109,175
Initial investment	(100,000)	(100,000)
NPV	$ 21,305	$ 9,175

Investment B

Price	$100,000
Estimated annual cash inflows	27,000
Estimated cash flows reduced 10 percent	24,300

Present value of annual cash flows:

$c = 1$; $n = 5$; $r = 10$; $FV = 0$; $ANN = 27{,}000$; $PV = 102{,}351$

Present value of decreased cash flows:

$c = 1$; $n = 5$; $r = 10$; $FV = 0$; $ANN = 24{,}300$; $PV = 92{,}116$

Net Present Values:

	Estimated Cash Flows	Reduced Cash Flows
Present value	$102,351	$ 92,116
Initial investment	(100,000)	(100,000)
NPV	$ 2,351	$ (7,884)

FAST FACT

You can also perform NPV analysis using your Hewlett-Packard financial calculator. We must know the cost of capital (hurdle rate) (I/YR) and the cash flows each year (CFj). Using the comprehensive example in the chapter and featured in the Of Interest, do the following:

12	I/YR	(cost of capital)
1	P/YR	(payments per year)
−908000	CFj	(cash flow 1—time zero)
181500	CFj	(cash flow 2—time one)
181500	CFj	(cash flow 3—time two)
181500	CFj	(cash flow 4—time three)
181500	CFj	(cash flow 5—time four)
181500	CFj	(cash flow 6—time five)
181500	CFj	(cash flow 7—time six)
348500	CFj	(cash flow 8—time seven)

NPV −4,135.87

Alternatively, since the $181,500 cash flow occurs repeatedly, we can do the following (be sure to clear your calculator):

12	I/YR	(cost of capital)
1	P/YR	(payments per year)
−908000	CFj	(cash flow 1—time zero)
181500	CFj	(cash flow 2—time one through six)
6	Nj	(number of periods for cash flow 2)
348500	CFj	(cash flow 3—time seven)

NPV −4,135.87

Qualitative/Ethical Factors

In addition to the uncertainty about future cash flows, managers must also consider qualitative factors that affect capital expenditure decisions. For example, suppose a company is considering the construction of a new parking garage, and NPV analysis indicates that the parking garage will yield a return well above the company's cost of capital (hurdle rate). However, the construction of the parking garage would require the destruction of an important historic landmark. The decision to build the garage must take into consideration this qualitative factor as well as the financial considerations.

In some cases, the nature of the investment may deter its acquisition despite a positive net present value. For example, a chemical company might reject the acquisition of a commercial fishing operation even though the computations of net present value indicate that it would exceed the company's cost of capital (hurdle rate). Management might reject this investment opportunity because it has no expertise in the fishing business.

The company must also consider its other balanced scorecard goals when making capital budgeting decisions. For example, refer to PCs to Go's equipment proposal. The net present value of this proposal was positive so we chose to accept it. But what if this equipment would cause PCs to Go to layoff one-half of the workers in the long run? How do we put a dollar value on employee morale/satisfaction? We can estimate the costs associated with laying off workers, but estimating the "hidden" costs due to the loss of employee loyalty is much more difficult. Another way to analyze this issue is to ask ourselves: Do we believe that the decrease in employee satisfaction outweighs the decision to accept this proposal? If the answer is yes, the proposal might be rejected despite its positive net present value.

Capital Expenditures and Budgeting

The capital investment decision impacts the budgeted financial statements of the company as shown in Exhibit 12.8. The anticipated cash outflows would be shown on the statement of cash flows as an investing activity and the anticipated cash inflows this period would be shown as an operating activity. The investment also impacts the budgeted balance sheet—book value of the asset (cost less depreciation). The depreciation each year impacts the

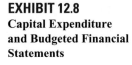

EXHIBIT 12.8
Capital Expenditure and Budgeted Financial Statements

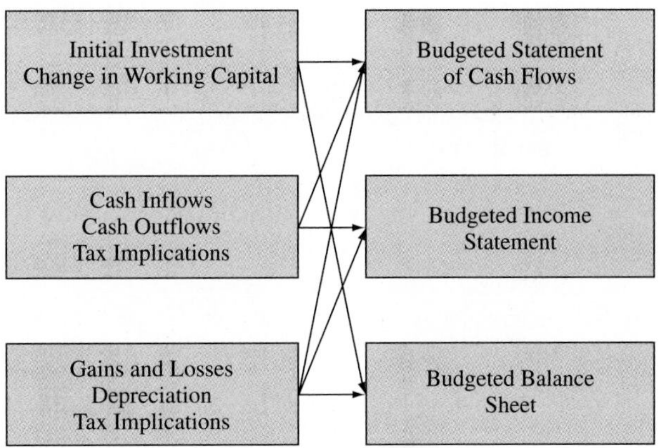

budgeted income statement. When companies have many capital investments planned for a given period, they often prepare a separate capital expenditures budget that indicates the expenditures planned and the timing of these expenditures. This latter budget is used to help management plan the financing of these investments—the topic we examine in Chapters 13 and 14.

Summary

Capital budgeting is an important process used for analysis and selection of a company's long-term investments. To be effective, it requires input from many functional areas in the company. Capital budgeting is the process used to select the long-term investments of a business and involves identifying the company's long-term investment needs, determining the investment alternatives that can satisfy its needs, deciding which investments to acquire, and evaluating the performance of the investments after acquisition.

- The cost of capital is the minimum acceptable return for a company's assets and serves as a hurdle rate for screening potential investments.
- NPV uses the cost of capital or hurdle rate to find the present value of the projected cash flows of an investment and to determine the maximum price a company should pay for an asset and still generate a satisfactory return. If the cost of the investment exceeds this price, the investment should be rejected.
- NPV analysis is based on assumptions that (1) all cash flows are known with certainty, (2) cash flows occur at the end of the time period, and (3) cash inflows are immediately reinvested in another project that earns a return at the same rate for the company.
- Income taxes reduce cash revenues and expenses, and depreciation provides tax shields from taxes. The tax effect of gains and losses reduces and increases, respectively, the proceeds from the disposal of assets.

Key Terms

Capital budgeting A process used for analysis and selection of long-term investments, *341*
Cost of capital Often the weighted average cost of debt and equity financing, *343*
Gain on disposal When the proceeds from the sale exceed the book value of the asset disposed of, *351*
Goal incongruence A condition whereby an employee acts in his or her own best interests even if the action is not in the company's best interest, *355*
Hurdle rate Cost of capital, *344*
Loss on disposal When the proceeds from the sale are less than the book value of the asset disposed of, *351*

Modified accelerated cost recovery system (MACRS) The laws that currently govern the calculation of depreciation for federal tax purposes, *350*
Net present value analysis A method of evaluating investments that uses the time value of money to assess whether the investment's expected rate of return is greater than the company's cost of capital, *345*
Operating leverage The proportion of fixed costs associated with a project, *357*
Return on investment The profit before interest and taxes divided by the asset investment, *343*
Tax shield A reduction in tax liability by reducing taxable income without affecting pretax cash flows, *350*

Questions

1. What is the purpose of capital budgeting and why is it important?
2. How is capital budgeting related to the business organization and strategy perspective of the balanced scorecard?
3. List and briefly explain the first two steps of the capital budgeting process.
4. What is a company's cost of capital and what role does it play in the capital budgeting process?
5. What is the return on investment and how is it related to the cost of capital?
6. What does a positive net present value tell the person making a capital budgeting decision?
7. Describe the four steps used in the net present value method.
8. What is the decision rule used to accept or reject a potential investment when using the net present value method? Why does it work?
9. Identify and explain the three key assumptions underlying net present value analysis.
10. How are uneven cash flows treated in net present value analysis?
11. How do income taxes impact the cash flows of capital budgeting decisions?
12. How does a noncash expense create a tax shield?
13. What is the benefit of IRS depreciation over uniform depreciation?
14. What causes gains and losses from the disposal of assets?
15. Describe how taxes impact the cash flows generated by the disposal of assets.
16. Why must human judgment be considered in capital budgeting analyses?
17. Why is sensitivity analysis useful in capital budgeting?
18. What constitutes a qualitative factor in a capital budgeting problem?
19. How do balanced scorecard goals impact the capital budgeting decision?
20. If a company projected a negative net present value would it always reject the proposal? Why?

Exercises

E12.1 LO 1 Russell Corporation's capital structure consists of $5,000,000 of assets and $2,000,000 of liabilities. Joe Russell, the corporation's CEO and largest shareholder, says that the debt has an average interest rate of 9 percent and that shareholders want a 16 percent return. What is Russell Corporation's cost of capital?

LO 1 **E12.2** Refer to E12.1. If the average interest rate on debt is 11 percent, what is the cost of capital?

LO 2 **E12.3** Gerard, a not-for-profit entity, is considering the acquisition of a baseball winder that costs $56,200. The baseball winder has an expected life of 10 years and is expected to reduce production costs by $9,000 a year. Gerard's hurdle rate is 12 percent. What is the net present value of this project? Should Gerard undertake this investment? Why?

LO 2 **E12.4** The United Way is considering purchasing a new machine with a cost of $9,000, no salvage value, and a useful life of five years. The machine is expected to generate $2,850 in cash inflows during each year of the machine's five-year life. Assuming the United Way's hurdle rate is 14 percent, what is the maximum price the United Way should pay for this machine? Why? Compute the net present value of the machine. Should the United Way acquire the machine? Why?

LO 2 **E12.5** Liz Perry is the chief financial officer of the Pasta House, a not-for-profit entity that provides hot meals to the homeless. She is considering the acquisition of a pasta processor with a cost of $936,000 and an installation cost of $22,000. Her analysis suggests that the pasta processor will save the Pasta

House $192,850 a year for the next eight years. What is the net present value of this investment using a 12 percent hurdle rate? Should Liz buy the pasta processor?

LO 2 **E12.6** Murdock Company, a not-for-profit enterprise, is contemplating the acquisition of a new copier on December 30, 2009. The copier costs $42,600, has an estimated life of six years, and is expected to save paper and time, as well as reduce repair cost. The cash Murdock expects to save as a result of buying the copier over the next six years is as follows:

2010	$14,000	2013	$8,000
2011	12,000	2014	6,000
2012	10,000	2015	4,000

What is the maximum price Murdock should pay for the copier if its hurdle rate is 15 percent? Calculate the net present value of the new copier using a 12 percent hurdle rate. Should Murdock Company buy the copier? Why?

LO 2 **E12.7** Clerihew Kennels, a no-kill, not-for-profit, animal shelter, is considering replacing its manual accounting system with a computerized accounting system. As of January 1, 2011, the software package and related equipment will cost the company $300,000 and are expected to have a useful life of five years. Clerihew's analyst has forecast that efficiencies created by the new system will reduce the cost of operating the accounting system by the following amounts:

2011	$ 60,000
2012	90,000
2013	150,000
2014	75,000
2015	75,000

Assuming that Clerihew uses a 13 percent hurdle rate, what is the net present value of the software package and related equipment? Should Clerihew purchase the accounting system? Why?

LO 3 **E12.8** Calculate the annual tax shield for a seven-year investment of $840,000 assuming uniform depreciation and a 25 percent tax rate.

LO 4 **E12.9** Calculate the annual tax shield on a $900,000 investment assuming a 25 percent tax rate and the following IRS depreciation schedule:

Year 1	14.29%	Year 5	8.93%
Year 2	24.49	Year 6	8.92
Year 3	17.49	Year 7	8.93
Year 4	12.49	Year 8	4.46

LO 3 **E12.10** Howard Corporation's sales for the year are expected to be $1,500,000 and operating expenses were $600,000. Included in the operating expenses is $100,000 of depreciation expense. If Howard's tax rate is 30 percent, what are its projected after-tax cash flows?

LO 4 **E12.11** Johnson Company is considering the purchase of a new delivery van for $28,000 that it expects to use for four years. The new van will increase delivery revenue each year by $10,700. The projected gas and repair expense and accelerated depreciation expense for each of the next four years are as follows:

	Gas and Repair Expense	Accelerated Tax Depreciation
Year 1	$2,700	$ 9,332
Year 2	3,250	12,446
Year 3	4,000	4,147
Year 4	4,500	2,075

If Johnson's tax rate is 30 percent, what is the tax shield created by the depreciation for each year? What are the after-tax cash flows for each year?

LO 3 **E12.12** If Scott Construction Company purchases a new steamroller, it will sell its old steamroller. The cost of the old steamroller is $215,000 and the accumulated depreciation on the old steamroller is $150,700. Scott's tax rate is 30 percent. What is the book value of the steamroller? If the steamroller sold for $84,000 cash, what is the after-tax cash inflow from the sale of the steamroller? If the steamroller sold for $54,000 cash, what is the after-tax cash inflow from the sale of the steamroller?

LO 3 E12.13 As of January 1, 2011, Alvarado Company wants to acquire a new machine costing $196,000. The machine has an estimated useful life of seven years and no salvage value. Alvarado's tax rate is 30 percent and the depreciation is calculated uniformly. The expected pretax cash flows are as follows:

	Pretax Cash Revenues	Pretax Cash Expenses
2011	$64,000	$22,000
2012	72,000	24,000
2013	80,000	30,000
2014	66,000	20,000
2015	60,000	28,000
2016	69,000	18,000
2017	50,000	16,000

If Alvarado Company has an 11 percent cost of capital, what is the maximum price Alvarado should pay for the machine? Why? Calculate the net present value of this project. Should Alvarado buy the machine? Why? Hint: Net the cash revenues with the cash expenses.

LO 3 E12.14 In 2011, Hoffman Corporation is considering investing in a new five-year project that will require an initial cash outlay of $650,000. When the project is undertaken, Hoffman will sell old equipment with an initial cost of $400,000 and accumulated depreciation of $275,000 for $50,000 cash. Hoffman management anticipates that the new project will generate $280,000 of cash revenue and require $88,000 of cash expenses in each of the five years. Depreciation associated with the project is calculated uniformly. Hoffman has an 11 percent cost of capital and a 30 percent tax rate. Calculate the project's net present value. Should Hoffman undertake the project? Why?

LO 4 E12.15 Refer to E12.14. Determine the net present value if depreciation is calculated according to the following IRS schedule. Should Hoffman undertake the project? Why?

Year 1	20.00%	Year 4	11.52%
Year 2	32.00	Year 5	11.52
Year 3	19.20	Year 6	5.76

LO 3 E12.16 Northrop Corporation is trying to decide whether to make the following two investments: The first is a piece of equipment that costs $40,000 but will save the company $9,000 after taxes (including the tax shield) in each year of its 10-year life. The second is a patent that costs $60,000 but will generate $9,400 in after-tax cash flows (including the tax shield) over its 17-year life. Northrop's cost of capital is 15 percent. Calculate the net present value of each investment. Should the company acquire one, both, or neither investment?

LO 3 E12.17 In January 2010 Chin Imports generated the following data about investments A and B, which the company is considering. Chin's cost of capital is 12 percent, and its tax rate is 20 percent.

	Investment A	Investment B
Initial cost	$104,000	$300,000
Annual depreciation	26,000	50,000
Net pretax cash inflows:		
2010	38,000	48,000
2011	42,000	46,000
2012	34,000	60,000
2013	36,000	51,000
2014		53,000
2015		52,000

What is the net present value of each investment? Would you recommend that Chin purchase one, both, or neither investment? Why?

LO 3 E12.18 In 2011 Sprague Corporation is considering the acquisition of a new $1,040,000 diagnostic machine and has projected the after-tax cash flows related to the machine. Sprague's manager has decided to use multiple cost of capital figures to calculate the net present value of this potential investment. The cash flows and cost of capital figures follow. Calculate the net present value of the investment. Should Sprague buy the diagnostic machine? Why?

Cost of Capital	Years	After-Tax Cash Flows
12%	2011	$240,000
12	2012	260,000
12	2013	253,000
14	2014	290,000
14	2015	310,000
14	2016	222,000
15	2017	240,000
15	2018	220,000

LO 3 **E12.19** Lonny Radford, a manager for the Albany Company, has projected these after-tax cash flows for a $131,000 machine he wants to buy in December 2010. The cash flows represent a worst-case scenario for the machine.

	After-Tax Cash Flows
2011	$31,650
2012	34,050
2013	34,500
2014	33,750
2015	34,500
2016	34,600

Another Albany Company manager feels that the projected cash flows are much too conservative and that they should be higher by as much as 5 percent each year. Albany's cost of capital is 12 percent. Calculate the net present value of the machine based on the given projections. Should Albany Company buy the machine?

LO 3 **E12.20** In 2011 the Tricola Company is considering whether to replace its old de-icer with a more efficient de-icer that costs $100,000. The old de-icer has a book value of $16,000 and can be sold for $20,000. The new de-icer will save $28,000 of operating cash flows before taxes in each of the next five years. Tricola will take $20,000 of depreciation in each of the next five years. It has a 30 percent tax rate and a 14 percent cost of capital. Calculate the NPV of this potential investment. Should Tricola buy the new de-icer?

Problems

P12.1  LO 2 The following cash savings are expected to occur if the city of Manhattan, Kansas, buys new trash trucks that cost $190,000 at the start of 2011. The city of Manhattan pays no taxes and uses a hurdle rate of 8 percent to evaluate investments.

2011	$56,000	2014	$58,000
2012	52,000	2015	55,000
2013	54,000	2016	52,000

Required:

A. What is the maximum price the city should pay for the trash trucks?
B. Calculate the net present value of the trash trucks.
C. Should the city of Manhattan acquire the trash trucks? Explain your answer.

LO 4 **P12.2** Ray, Inc., is considering replacing an existing machine with a new machine. The existing machine originally cost $45,000 and has a book value of $22,000 today. The old machine costs $37,000 per year to operate and can be sold today for $20,000. The purchase price of the new machine is $40,000 and will be depreciated at the following IRS rates for three-year equipment. The new machine is expected to cost $26,000 per year to operate. Ray's cost of capital is 15 percent and its tax rate is 30 percent.

Year 1	33.33%
Year 2	44.45
Year 3	14.81
Year 4	7.41

Required:

A. Calculate the net present value of the new machine.
B. Should Ray replace its machine? Explain your answer.

LO 3 P12.3 O'Dell Enterprises manufactures lenses for telescopes. O'Dell is considering replacing a machine that grinds lenses and has received a proposal from a vendor for the new lens grinder. O'Dell has a 12 percent cost of capital and a 30 percent tax rate. The vendor will sell the company a new machine for $310,000 and buy the old machine, which has a $20,000 book value, for $30,000. The new machine is expected to generate $80,000 of pretax cash inflows, and the company calculates depreciation expense uniformly over its five-year life.

Required:
A. Calculate the net present value of the new machine.
B. Should O'Dell buy the new machine? Explain your answer.

LO 4 P12.4 At the end of 2010, Williams Corporation is planning to buy a new machine for $80,000. The pretax cash flows and the tax purposes depreciation rates follow. Williams's tax rate is 30 percent and its cost of capital is 14 percent.

	Pretax Cash Flows	Tax Depreciation Rates
2011	$21,500	14.29%
2012	25,000	24.49
2013	22,000	17.49
2014	20,000	12.49
2015	19,000	8.93
2016	17,500	8.92
2017	16,000	8.93
2018	14,000	4.46

Required:
A. Calculate the net present value for the new machine.
B. Should Williams buy the new machine? Why?

LO 4 P12.5 As of January 2012, McRae Boat Cruises is considering the acquisition of a new skiing boat that costs $100,000. If the new boat is purchased, an old boat with a book value of $28,000 will be sold for $32,000. The pretax cash flows and depreciation rates follow. At the end of the boat's useful life McRae estimates the new boat can be sold for $20,000. McRae Boat Cruises has a cost of capital of 15 percent and a tax rate of 30 percent.

	Pretax Cash Inflows	Pretax Cash Outflows	Depreciation Rates
2012	$67,500	$30,000	20.00%
2013	84,000	45,000	32.00
2014	73,500	37,500	19.20
2015	67,500	34,500	11.52
2016	62,000	30,000	11.52
2017	59,000	32,000	5.76

Required:
A. Calculate the net present value for the new boat. (Net the inflows and the outflows).
B. Should McRae Boat Cruises buy the new boat? Explain your answer.

LO 3 P12.6 Luft Products is considering a proposal to open another operation in Sheridan, Wyoming. The following information has been compiled for you.

1. The initial investment is $400,000 to equip the facility.
2. The facility will be operated for eight years and depreciated uniformly over its life.
3. At the end of the eight-year period, Luft will spend $40,000 to clean up the facility and return it to the city. (This is a tax-deductible expense.)
4. The pretax net cash flows are expected to be $75,000 annually.
5. To operate the new facility, Luft will require an additional inflow of working capital in the amount of $60,000. This working capital will be released at the end of the eight-year period.
6. The equipment will be sold at the end of the period for an estimated $20,000.
7. Luft's tax rate is 30 percent and its cost of capital is 10 percent.

Required:
A. Calculate the net present value of the new facility.
B. Should Luft invest in the new facility? Why?

LO 3 P12.7 Barton Company wants to replace a machine that has a zero book value and a market value of $12,800 in January 2011. The new machine Barton is considering has a cost of $50,000 and an estimated useful life of five years. The new machine will create cost savings of $14,500 per year. The machine will require an additional investment in working capital of $4,000, which would be recovered at the end of the machine's life. The new machine would be depreciated uniformly over its useful life. Barton has a 25 percent tax rate and a 14 percent cost of capital.

Required: A. Calculate the net present value of the new machine.
B. Should Barton Company buy the machine? Explain your answer.

LO 4 **P12.8** In January 2011, the Jamal Corporation has projected these pretax cash flows for an investment that will cost $450,000. For tax purposes, this investment is considered three-year property and, therefore, is depreciated over four years according to the following schedule. If Jamal's tax rate is 40 percent and its cost of capital is 14 percent, calculate the net present value for this investment. Should Jamal undertake this investment? Why?

	Pretax Cash Inflows	Pretax Cash Outflows	Tax Depreciation Schedule
2011	$220,000	$350,000	33.33%
2012	400,000	320,000	44.45
2013	600,000	280,000	14.81
2014	620,000	240,000	7.41
2015	520,000	230,000	

LO 4 **P12.9** Refer to P12.8. Would your answer be the same if this investment was considered five-year property by the IRS and depreciated according to the following schedule? Why?

Year 1	20.00%	Year 4	11.52
Year 2	32.00	Year 5	11.52
Year 3	19.20	Year 6	5.76

LO 3 **P12.10** In January 2012, Herdt Company is trying to decide whether to buy one, both, or neither of the following investments. Herdt Company's cost of capital is 16 percent and its tax rate is 30 percent. Neither investment has a salvage value.

	Investment A	Investment B
Price	$860,000	$860,000
Annual depreciation	172,000	172,000
Projected pretax cash flows:		
2012	296,200	254,000
2013	326,200	283,400
2014	383,400	312,000
2015	440,800	340,400
2016	496,000	368,600

Required: A. Compute the net present value for both investments.
B. Assume that the cash flows could vary up and down by as much as 10 percent. Given the potential fluctuations, which investment would you consider acceptable? Explain your decision.

Cases

LO 3 LO 4 **C12.1** Refer to the company you chose in C1.1. Examine this company's statement of cash flows. Did the company undertake any long-term investments during the period? If so, what additional information can you find in the notes regarding these acquisitions?

LO 4 **C12.2** Adams Products, Inc., manufactures a product it sells for $25. Adams sells all of the 24,000 units per year it is capable of producing at the current time, and a marketing study indicates that it could sell 14,000 more units per year. To increase its capacity, Adams must buy a machine that has the capacity to produce 50,000 units of its product annually. The existing equipment can produce the product at a unit cost of $16. Today it has a book value of $80,000 and a market value of $60,000. The new equipment could produce 50,000 units at a unit cost of $12. The new equipment would cost $500,000 and would be depreciated uniformly over its five-year life. If the new machine is purchased, fixed operating costs will decrease by $20,000 per year. If Adams's cost of capital is 18 percent and its tax rate is 30 percent, should Adams buy the new machine? Why?

Critical Thinking

CT12.1 LO 3 As of January 2, 2012, you have just completed a discounted cash flow analysis on a $250,000 investment. You calculated after-tax cash flows (including the following tax shield). You then determined that the project has a positive net present value using the company's cost of capital of 15 percent. You reported your findings to your supervisor and recommended that the company make the investment. To your surprise, the supervisor rejected the acquisition. He said that company policy was to not invest in any project in which the cash flows do not recover the initial investment in three years. He points out that of the $250,000 expended, only $190,000 would be recovered in three years.

	After-Tax Cash Flows
2012	$ 20,000
2013	50,000
2014	120,000
2015	100,000
2016	100,000
2017	90,000
2018	80,000

Required:
A. Complete the net present value analysis showing that the investment should be undertaken.
B. Write a memo explaining why the company should make this investment and why the company should scrap its three-year payback rule.

LO 3 **CT12.2** Mercil Corporation is going to buy one of the following two machines. Each machine meets the specifications for a particular task in the company. Mercil's tax rate is 30 percent and its cost of capital is 15 percent. Which machine should Mercil buy and why?

Machine A: Costs $90,000 to acquire and $12,000 cash a year to operate in each year of its 10-year life. Annual depreciation is $9,000, and the machine has no salvage value.

Machine B: Costs $50,000 to acquire and $24,600 a year to operate in each year of its 10-year life. Annual depreciation is $5,000, and the machine has no salvage value.

LO 3 LO 4 **CT12.3** Your supervisor has just completed a discounted cash flow analysis on a 15-year, $3,000,000 project. She is upset that the net present value was negative and is getting ready to report her findings to senior management and recommend that the company abandon the project. Upon reviewing the computations, you discover that the net present value on this $3,000,000 project was a negative $3,510. What additional factors would you suggest that your supervisor consider before she makes her report recommending the abandonment of this project?

Ethical Challenges

EC12.1 LO 3 LO 4 Wal-Mart Stores has run into opposition when it has tried to open stores in certain New England and Pennsylvania towns. Wal-Mart's capital budgeting process has determined that these locations would be profitable for the corporation. However, these communities have successfully fought to keep Wal-Mart from opening stores. The communities argue that a Wal-Mart store will destroy the downtown businesses of the community and hurt the town's quality of life. Despite being rebuffed by the citizens of these towns, Wal-Mart has continued its efforts to locate stores in these communities. Should Wal-Mart continue or stop its efforts to open stores in these communities? Why?

LO 3 LO 4 **EC12.2** Oaks Company is a small company that employs 15 people in a town with a population of about 9,000. Oaks's plant manager is considering the acquisition of a new machine that will cost $474,500. The machine will replace five long-time employees and is expected to generate savings of $105,600 in after-tax cash flows for the next 10 years. Oaks's cost of capital is 18 percent. Based on the net present value of the machine, should Oaks buy the machine? Are there qualitative factors that he should consider in his decision? Why?

LO 3 LO 4 **EC12.3** The Snethen Corporation has the opportunity to manufacture a new chemical but will have to buy a new machine that costs $350,000 to produce the chemical. The net present value of the new machine is $2,500. However, you have learned that in calculating the net present value, the cost of disposing of a waste product that the EPA has labeled mildly hazardous was excluded. Snethen disputes the EPA's claim that the waste product is toxic. Therefore, Snethen management decided it could avoid the disposal cost by dumping the waste with other trash. Should Snethen buy the new machine? Why?

Computer Applications

CA12.1 LO 4

Achord Company wants to determine whether it should invest in a piece of equipment that costs $1.5 million and is expected to last 10 years. At the end of the 10-year period, the equipment will be scrapped and have no salvage value. Achord has a 12 percent cost of capital. These are the expected after-tax net cash flows of the equipment (excluding the tax shield) and the applicable tax depreciation rates:

Year	After-Tax Cash Flows	Tax Depreciation Rates
1	$ 225,000	14.29
2	200,000	24.49
3	250,000	17.49
4	250,000	12.49
5	(300,000)	8.93
6	250,000	8.92
7	250,000	8.93
8	225,000	4.46
9	125,000	
10	50,000	

Required:

A. Set up a spreadsheet to calculate the present value of the future cash flows assuming a 20 percent tax rate.
B. What is the net present value of this equipment?
C. Should Achord invest in the equipment? Why?

LO 3 **CA12.2**

Terry, Inc., wants to buy a new printing press. The cost of the press is $300,000, it is expected to last for 10 years after which it will be scrapped with no salvage value, and it will be depreciated uniformly over its life. Terry has an 8 percent cost of capital. Terry, Inc., is subject to a 40 percent tax rate. The pretax net cash inflows are:

Year	Pretax Cash Flow	Year	Pretax Cash Flow
1	$ 80,000	6	$90,000
2	90,000	7	75,000
3	100,000	9	60,000
4	110,000	8	50,000
5	100,000	10	25,000

Required:

A. Set up a spreadsheet to calculate the present value of the future cash flows.
B. What is the net present value of this equipment?
C. Should Terry invest in the equipment? Why?

Visit the text Online Learning Center at **www.mhhe.com/ainsworth6e** for additional problem material that accompanies this chapter.

CHAPTER THIRTEEN

13 Planning Equity Financing

Learning Objectives

- **LO 1** Explain how companies plan for debt versus equity financing.
- **LO 2** Describe how partnership profits and losses are allocated.
- **LO 3** Discuss the process of raising capital through equity financing in a corporation.
- **LO 4** Explain the process of giving shareholders a return on investment.
- **LO 5** Compare and contrast stock dividends and stock splits.

Chapter 12 described how capital budgeting helps plan for the acquisition of the long-term investments that will profitably support the company's operations. In the next two chapters we consider the planning required to finance these investments. In addition we examine how the capital resources process (investing and financing) is tied to the business organization and strategy process.

Tie to Business Organization and Strategy Process

Recall that a business is organized to achieve certain objectives—to provide goods and services that customers want and to provide a return to the owners. As we have learned, a business's strategy is its long-term plan for using its resources (physical and human) to achieve its objectives. Thus the long-term assets a business chooses to invest in (Chapter 12) as well as the type of financing a business chooses to use (Chapters 13 and 14) are tied to its strategy. We have also seen that organizational structure is tied to strategy. Thus when we consider the sources of capital available to a business we must also consider how those capital sources fit with the business's organization and strategy for achieving its objectives. Finally we must consider how financing decisions impact our budgeted financial statements.

Companies acquire funds from three sources: (1) owners' contributions, (2) earnings generated by the company's operating activities, and (3) debt. We classify the three sources of funds into two financing categories: equity and debt. **Equity financing** is a means for companies to obtain funds in exchange for an ownership interest in the company. Companies raise equity funds when owners acquire a financial interest in the company and when management elects to reinvest the company's earnings that would otherwise be distributed to the owners in the company. **Debt financing** arises when a company obtains funds (cash) in exchange for a liability to repay the borrowed funds. Exhibit 13.1 illustrates how the various sources of capital are provided by and used in the company.

Debt versus Equity Financing

When deciding whether to raise capital using equity financing or debt financing, the company must consider the risks and rewards of debt versus equity financing. We examine these issues next.

Risk of Debt Financing

The risk of debt financing, called **financial risk,** is the chance that a company will fail because it defaults on its debt. A company defaults if it is unable to meet (make) either the interest or principal payments that come due on the debt. When this occurs, the lender has the legal right to require the debtor to pay the principal and the interest due immediately.

EXHIBIT 13.1
Sources and Uses of Funds

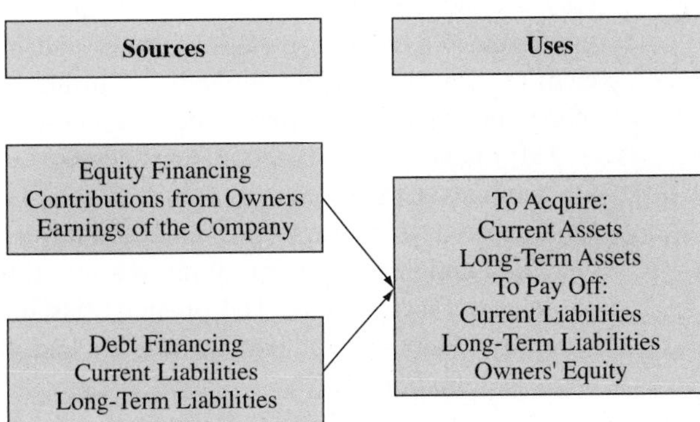

In some situations the debtor may have to liquidate (sell) its assets to raise the cash necessary to pay the debt. Liquidating the company's assets may drive the enterprise out of business.

Debt-to-Equity Ratio

Debt financing increases the exposure of shareholders to the risks of default just described. As you know from Chapter 1, the debt-to-equity ratio measures the relationship between the amount of debt and the amount of owners' equity used to finance the company. Recall the debt-to-equity ratio is calculated as total liabilities divided by total owners' equity. A debt-to-equity ratio of 1 means that equal amounts of debt and owners' equity finance the company. The larger the debt-to-equity ratio, the greater the amount of debt used to finance the company and, therefore, the greater the financial risk. As a company's debt increases, it needs more earnings to cover the interest incurred on its debt and, as a result, the financial risk of the company increases.

When companies plan to use debt financing, the debt-to-equity ratio is an excellent tool to assess the impact of the new debt on the company's risk. In general, a ratio of 1 or less is considered a safe level of financial risk. However, a company can get a better assessment of its current and potential financial risk in two ways. The first is to compare the size of its planned debt-to-equity ratio with the amount and trend of ratios in prior years and the debt-to-equity ratios of peer companies. The second is to assess the company's ability to meet its interest obligations.

Times Interest Earned Ratio

One of the concerns a company has when considering debt financing is whether the company can meet its interest obligations. The **times interest earned ratio** measures a company's ability to service its debt by comparing earnings before deducting interest and taxes to the amount of interest expense for the period. Planners use the times interest earned ratio to determine whether the interest on new debt will put the company at risk of not meeting its interest obligations. The formula for the times interest earned ratio is

$$\frac{\text{(Earnings before interest and taxes)}}{\text{Interest expense}}$$

So if a company has a times interest earned ratio of 1 (very unlikely) it means that its income before interest and taxes is exactly equal to its interest expense and would therefore have no income. With a times interest earned ratio of 1, any anticipated decrease in net income would indicate that the company's income would be insufficient to meet its interest obligations. Therefore companies strive to have times interest earned ratios that are well above 1.

Therefore, a company with a high debt-to-equity ratio and a low times interest earned ratio has increased risk because the amount of debt relative to owners' equity is high and, thus, the owners are at risk of the company not meeting its debt obligations. Furthermore, a low times interest earned ratio indicates that the earnings of the company may not be sufficient to meet the interest obligations, further supporting the idea that the owners are at risk of the company not meeting its debt obligations.

The financial risk of a company depends not only on the size of its debt-to-equity and times interest earned ratios but also the volatility of its sales, that is, the tendency of its sales to increase or decrease dramatically from one period to the next. In general, when a company has a high debt-to-equity ratio, a low times interest earned ratio, and volatile sales, it has greater financial risk. The financial risk increases because a decline in sales would substantially reduce the company's earnings and, therefore, might cause the company to default on its debt obligations.

Reward of Debt Financing

Consider, however, the reward for using debt financing. When companies generate a return on their borrowed funds that is greater than the cost to them of using the borrowed funds, the owners of the companies benefit. Any excess return on the borrowed funds belongs to the owners and, therefore, increases their return on investment. When this occurs, we say that the owners used financial leverage to increase the rate of return on their investment.

Financial leverage is a financing strategy designed to increase the rate of return on owners' investment by generating a greater return on borrowed funds than the cost of using the funds. To illustrate the concept, suppose that two companies, Benchmark Corporation and Comparison Company, each have $1,000,000 in assets and receive a 20 percent return on these assets before deducting interest and taxes. The only difference between these companies is how the assets of Benchmark Corporation and Comparison Company are financed. Benchmark Corporation finances 100 percent of its $1,000,000 in assets by using only its owners' money. Comparison Company, on the other hand, borrows $700,000 at 8 percent annual interest, creating a $700,000 liability, and uses $300,000 of its owners' money.

	Assets	= Liabilities + Owners' equity
Benchmark Corporation	$1,000,000	= $ –0– + $1,000,000
Comparison Company	1,000,000	= 700,000 + 300,000

We show the effects of the different financing arrangements in Exhibit 13.2. Note that both companies generate $200,000 earnings before interest and taxes as a result of the 20 percent return on the $1,000,000 of assets (Rate of return on assets = Income before interest and taxes/Total assets). Comparison Company's net income, however, is further reduced by the $56,000 of interest expense ($700,000 × 0.08) charged for the use of the borrowed funds. Both companies are subject to a tax rate of 40 percent, but Comparison Company will pay $22,400 less in taxes than Benchmark Corporation because the $56,000 of interest expense is tax deductible. This means that the after-tax cost to Comparison Company of borrowing the funds is $33,600 ($56,000 − $22,400), or 4.8 percent [($56,000 − $22,400)/$700,000]. While Benchmark Corporation's net income, $120,000, is greater than Comparison Company's net income of $86,400, Comparison Company's owners have less money invested in the company than Benchmark Corporation's owners. To see how financial leverage works we calculate a return on owners' equity ratio.

EXHIBIT 13.2
Financial Leverage

	Benchmark Corporation	Comparison Company
Income before interest and taxes ($1,000,000 × 20%)	$ 200,000	$200,000
Interest expense	–0–	56,000
Income before taxes	$ 200,000	$144,000
Tax expense (40%)	80,000	57,600
Net income	$ 120,000	$ 86,400
Rate of return on owners' equity	$ 120,000 / $1,000,000 = 12%	$ 86,400 / $300,000 = 28.8%

After-Tax Cost of Debt:

Interest on $700,000 debt at 8%		$ 56,000
Tax without interest	$80,000	
Tax with interest	57,600	
Tax saving from interest		$ 22,400
After-tax cost of debt		$ 33,600
After-tax rate of interest		$ 33,600 / $700,000 = 4.8%

Return on Owners' Equity Ratio

The **return on owners' equity ratio (ROE)** measures the performance of the company in terms of the owners' investment. The return on owners' equity is

$$\frac{\text{Net income}}{\text{Owners' equity}}$$

This ratio measures the return per dollar of owners' equity of the company. The higher the return, the more the owners are earning, and thus, the better their investment. We return to the example of Benchmark Corporation and Comparison Company to see how leverage affects a company's return on owners' equity. It might appear that because Benchmark Corporation's net income is higher ($120,000) than Comparison Company's ($86,400), Benchmark Corporation has the more desirable financing structure. However, common-size measures, such as the return on owners' equity ratio, are the preferred way to compare performance. Look again at Exhibit 13.2; Comparison Company's return on owners' equity is 28.8 percent ($86,400/$300,000). This is greater than Benchmark Corporation's return on owners' equity of 12 percent ($120,000/$1,000,000). Now examine Exhibit 13.3; Comparison Company's return on assets, $200,000 ($1,000,000 × 0.20), is the same dollar amount as Benchmark Corporation's return. However, by financing $700,000 of the assets with borrowed funds, Comparison Company has leveraged its return on owners' equity from 12 percent to 28.8 percent as shown in Exhibit 13.3.

Enhance Your Understanding

Since a company can use financial leverage to increase its return, why don't companies simply finance with 100 percent debt?

Answer: Each company must have owners or it doesn't exist; thus, 100 percent debt financing is not possible. (While a corporation could not exist without contributing shareholders, a partnership or sole proprietorship could exist with no equity if it could convince someone or some institution to loan them the money. After a business begins operations it is possible for equity to become zero or a deficit, in which case the creditors are financing 100 percent of the company, and with a deficit there is more debt than assets in the firm.) Furthermore, as the company increases the amount of debt relative to equity, the company's risk increases and, therefore, the debt and equity holders will want a higher rate of return. Higher interest rates and rates of return for owners in turn raise a company's cost of capital and, therefore, impact its investment decisions.

Reward of Equity Financing

Before a business can begin, the owners of the company commit their resources to the enterprise in the expectation that the business will produce a satisfactory return on their initial investment. Ownership is attractive because the return the business generates on owners' investment is limited only by the performance of the company. In addition to realizing financial rewards, many owners enjoy the psychological reward of knowing they own a business enterprise.

EXHIBIT 13.3
Comparison Company's Return

	Owners' Funds	Borrowed Funds	Total
Assets	$300,000	$700,000	$1,000,000
Rate of return (20%)	0.20	0.20	0.20
Return on assets	$ 60,000	$140,000	$ 200,000
Interest on debt	-0-	56,000	56,000
Income before taxes	$ 60,000	$ 84,000	$ 144,000
Taxes (40% of income)	24,000	33,600	57,600
Income after taxes	$ 36,000	$ 50,400	$ 86,400

$$\text{Rate of return on owners' equity} = \frac{\$36,000 + \$50,400}{\$300,000} = 28.8\%$$

Risk of Equity Financing

Owners of a business entity face the risk of not receiving a satisfactory return on their invested funds or of losing some or all of their investment if the business fails. The owners' risk is directly related to the company's ability to sell goods and services, cover operating expenses, and generate sufficient net income to provide a satisfactory return on their investment. Obviously, companies that consistently provide a satisfactory return on the owners' investment have less risk than those whose earnings and returns are more erratic.

Now that we have looked at the risks and rewards of debt versus equity financing we examine the types of equity financing and consider the risks and rewards of different ownership structures. In Chapter 14 we examine the types of debt financing available.

Equity Financing

Regardless of the legal form of business entity, owner financing comes from people or other entities acquiring an ownership interest in the company or the company reinvesting the company's earnings. The first source includes the investors' contribution of assets to the company in exchange for an ownership interest in the business entity. Initial contributions provide the funds necessary to begin the company's operations, while subsequent contributions are used for expansion. The second source of owner financing is reinvested earnings. The net income of a company represents the increase in the net assets of the company as a result of its operations. The net income, or earnings, belongs to the owners and is either distributed to them or reinvested in the company. When the earnings are reinvested in the business entity, the owners are keeping the funds in the entity and, thereby, increasing their interest in the company.

THE FAR SIDE® By GARY LARSON

Early business failures

Contributions by owners are often used to acquire long-term assets such as buildings, equipment, land, patents, and franchises that provide the infrastructure for the company's operations. Owner contributions also are used to retire long-term debt and, therefore, reduce the company's risk of defaulting on its long-term debt. The earnings reinvested in the company are used to support the daily operations, acquire long-term assets, or retire long-term debt, based on recommendations by management.

Sole Proprietorships and Partnerships

Selecting a business ownership structure is one of the first and most important planning activities. As you know, the three basic forms of business entities are the sole proprietorship, partnership, and corporation; each has its advantages and disadvantages. Sole proprietorships and partnerships have three important advantages. The first is their ease of formation. Because they are not separate legal entities, they do not have the costly and time-consuming registration requirements of corporations. The second advantage is that the income generated by sole proprietorships and partnerships is taxed only once. That is, the income generated by a sole proprietorship or partnership is reported as taxable income on each owner's Form 1040. (Partnerships must complete an informational partnership return, but their income is reported as taxable income on each partner's Form 1040.) In contrast, income generated by a corporation, as we discuss shortly, is taxed twice. Finally, sole proprietors and partners are more likely to manage the business and be involved in its operations; they choose these forms of organization because they enjoy the psychological and financial rewards they offer.

Sole proprietorships and partnerships share two disadvantages. The first is the risk associated with unlimited liability; that is, owners can lose not only what they have invested in the company but also their personal assets when the assets of the company do not satisfy the creditors' claims. The second disadvantage is the inability to raise large amounts of equity capital. The equity capital raised by sole proprietorships and partnerships is limited to the personal resources of the owners. While partnerships can generate more capital by increasing the number of partners, the risk posed by mutual agency (see Chapter 1) probably limits the amount of capital the company can raise from its owners' contributions. For example, when one partner signs a contract and the deal goes bad, the loss puts the assets of the business and the personal assets of all partners at risk. Mutual agency also applies to the performance of each partner. For example, a partner in a manufacturing company who signs a large contract with a very unreliable supplier without the consent of his fellow partners binds all the partners of the company. If the supplier fails to deliver, the losses could put the personal assets of the other partners at risk if the company's assets are not sufficient to cover the loss.

Corporations

Corporations have three major advantages that are all tied to the fact that a corporation is a separate legal entity. The first advantage is limited liability, which means that owners of a corporation can lose only the amounts they invested in the company. The second advantage is the corporation's ability to raise large amounts of capital by selling its stock (one unit of ownership). Unlike partnerships, individual shareholders cannot bind the corporation because the corporation is a separate legal entity; only those authorized by the corporation can bind the corporation to a contract. The third advantage is unlimited life. Unlike sole proprietorships and partnerships, which are limited to the life of the owner(s), a corporation's life is limited only by its ability to remain a going business concern.

Corporations have two disadvantages. The first is the time and money it takes to become incorporated and then satisfy the regulatory requirements necessary to maintain the corporate status. For example, Apple must file reports with California's secretary of state, get and maintain permission to operate in other states, and, because its stock is publicly traded,

OF INTEREST Other Ownership Structures

Four alternative ownership structures are used to resolve the taxation and liability problems of traditional partnership and corporate structures: the limited partnership, the limited liability partnership (LLP), the Subchapter S corporation (S corporation), and the limited liability company (LLC).

LIMITED PARTNERSHIP

A limited partnership has one or more general partners and one or more limited partners. While the general partners are personally responsible for the debts of the firm (unlimited liability), the limited partners are liable only for their investment in the partnership. However, limited partners do not have the same rights as a general partner; that is, the limited partner cannot manage the firm or enter into contracts on behalf of the firm. Limited partners who take such action lose their limited liability status. Like any partnership, the income of the partnership is taxed only once. In most states, the limited partnership must be registered with the secretary of state in accordance with the Revised Uniform Limited Partnership Act.

LIMITED LIABILITY PARTNERSHIP (LLP)

In states that recognize LLPs, a limited liability partnership follows the same basic structure as a general partnership but allows partners to benefit from partial limited liability. Partners in an LLP are personally liable for their own wrongful acts and the acts of those they directly supervise, but they are not personally responsible for the wrongful acts of another partner. Creditors and others with claims against the partnership still have recourse against the partnership assets and the individual partner's personal assets. As in the case of the limited partnership, the income of the firm is taxed only once. If an existing general partnership decides to become an LLP, it should be aware that some states will not release the partnership from obligations that existed under the general partnership.

SUBCHAPTER S CORPORATION (S CORPORATION)

Subchapter S of the Internal Revenue Code allows corporations that meet certain criteria to pass their earnings through to shareholders and, therefore, have the earnings of the enterprise taxed only once at the federal level. S corporation shareholders, like other corporations, have limited liability and, therefore, have only their investment in the corporation at risk. To obtain S corporation status, the corporation must meet several criteria that may offset the tax advantages. For example, S corporations are limited to no more than 100 shareholders, none of the shareholders can be a nonresident alien, and they can issue only one class of stock. These restrictions may limit the firm's ability to raise equity capital. A disadvantage of the S corporation occurs when it generates earnings but does not pay dividends. The earnings are passed through to the shareholders who must pay the tax on their share of the earnings out of their personal assets.

LIMITED LIABILITY COMPANY (LLC)

In states that recognize LLCs, limited liability companies have several advantages. The first advantage is that, unlike limited partnerships that require at least one general partner, all of an LLC's owners have limited liability and, therefore, their personal assets are not at risk. The second advantage is that the LLC's earnings are taxed only once. That is, like partnerships, the LLC's net income passes through to the owners before it is subject to tax. An advantage of the LLC over the S corporation is that the number of owners in an LLC is not limited to 100. Finally, all owners of an LLC are free to participate in the operation of the firm. Recall that in a limited partnership, limited partners can lose their limited liability status if their actions regarding the operation of the firm are construed to be those of a general partner.

An LLC has two disadvantages. The first is that it does not have continuity of life. The second is that LLC owners, unlike corporate shareholders, cannot easily transfer their ownership interest to another person or entity. However, for members of CPA firms, law firms, or any group of professionals, the ability to obtain limited liability without increasing the tax burden on the firm's earnings through double taxation far outweighs these disadvantages.

report annually (Form 10-K) and quarterly (Form 10-Q) to the Securities and Exchange Commission. The second disadvantage of incorporating is double taxation. Due to its status as a legal entity, the corporation's profits are taxed first at the corporate level and then again when they are distributed to the owners in the form of dividends.

Planning for Partnership Equity

Due to the limited number of owners, sole proprietorships and partnerships measure the dollar amount of each individual owner's interest in the company. The value of each owner's interest consists of the owner's contribution and his or her share of the company's undistributed earnings; however, only the total of the two is disclosed on the pro forma balance sheet.

Thus it is important for a partnership (and some sole proprietorships) to prepare a **budgeted (pro forma) statement of owners' (partners') equity.** This budgeted statement reflects the following relationships:

Beginning capital
\+ Anticipated contributions by the partner
− Anticipated withdrawals by the partner
+/− Estimated income allocation to the partner
= Ending capital

In the following section, we discuss how a partner's capital can change. Tracking the changes in each partner's capital is important because it ultimately is the basis for distributing the company's assets. For example, when a partner leaves the company, the amount of cash or other assets the partner receives is based on the amount of equity the partner has accumulated to the date of withdrawal.

Partnership Income Allocations

Because determining the equity of each partner is critical, planning for the allocation of the company's income is most important. In the absence of an agreement to the contrary, the Uniform Partnership Act provides that partners share profits and losses equally. However, partners typically do not do this because each partner's involvement in the company varies. For example, a partner who contributes $10,000 to a company and is not involved with its operations would not receive the same allocation of the profits as a person who contributes $50,000 and manages the company's activities on a daily basis. Therefore, the allocation of the partnership's earnings and losses usually reflects the nature of each partner's involvement.

A company's partnership agreement should describe in detail how the partners agree to allocate the profits and losses of the company. Whenever the partners deem it appropriate, they can change their agreement. The following are commonly used methods for the allocation of earnings:

- Fixed ratio.
- Ratio of capital account balances.
- Salary allowances and some determination of allocation of any remainder.
- Interest allowance on capital balances and some determination of allocation of any remainder.
- Combination of salary and interest allowance and some determination of allocation of any remainder.

Note that unless otherwise specified, partnership losses are allocated using the same method by which profits are allocated. When using the salary allowance, interest allowance, or combination method to allocate a partnership's net loss, it is possible for some partners' capital accounts to increase. We illustrate this paradox later.

To describe the possible ways to allocate income, we use a partnership called AD Company that offers accounting services. The partners are Stuart, Finley, Janice, and Jo. In planning for the allocation of partnership income, they want to examine each of the methods just described.

Fixed Ratio

The partners (Stuart, Finley, Janice, and Jo) agree to allocate income or loss in a fixed ratio of 4:2:1:1. Since 4 + 2 + 1 + 1 = 8, Stuart will get 4/8, or 1/2, of the total; Finley 2/8, or 1/4; and Janice and Jo 1/8 each. If AD is expected to generate $48,000 of net income, using the fixed ratio method of allocating profits would increase Stuart's capital account by $24,000, Finley's capital account by $12,000, and Janice's and Jo's capital accounts by $6,000 each:

Stuart	(1/2 × $48,000)	$24,000
Finley	(1/4 × $48,000)	12,000
Janice	(1/8 × $48,000)	6,000
Jo	(1/8 × $48,000)	6,000
Total income allocation		$48,000

Note that this allocation does not imply that Stuart received $24,000 in cash from the partnership, or that Finley received $12,000, or that Janice received $6,000, or that Jo received $6,000. An income allocation is merely a means of allocating the profits (the increase in the owners' equity created by operating activities that increase the assets of the company) among the partners (to determine who must report what on their individual Form 1040); it does not reflect any distributions of assets that may or may not have taken place during the year.

Ratio of Capital Account Balances

Sometimes the amount of net income is closely related to the amount invested by the individual partners in the partnership entity. Consequently, a method of allocating earnings based on the relationship of the amounts of the partners' investments offers a fair approach to allocate the company's income. However, because of withdrawals and additional investments made during the accounting period, the capital balances may change. In such circumstances, partners must agree on which capital balances to use as a basis for earnings allocation—beginning, ending, or some average for the period.

Assume that the partners agree to allocate income based on the beginning capital balances. Further assume that their beginning capital balances were: Stuart, $15,000; Finley, $10,000; Janice, $45,000; and Jo, $30,000. The allocation is computed using the ratio of each individual's capital balance to the total of the capital balances and then multiplying the amount of the profits by that ratio.

For example, the ratio of Stuart's capital to total capital is 15 percent ($15,000/$100,000) and, therefore, Stuart is allocated $7,200 ($48,000 × 0.15). The income allocation using the ratio of capital balances follows.

A	B	C	D	E
Partner	**Capital Balance**	**Percentage (B/$100,000)**	**Income**	**Allocation (C × D)**
Stuart	$ 15,000	15%	$48,000	$ 7,200
Finley	10,000	10	48,000	4,800
Janice	45,000	45	48,000	21,600
Jo	30,000	30	48,000	14,400
Total	$100,000	100%	$48,000	$48,000

Salary Allowances

If a partner spends all or part of his or her time on partnership business while others are not as involved in operations, the partners may agree to recognize the value of these services. A salary allowance is a method of allocating partnership earnings based on the amount of time respective partners spend operating the business enterprise.

Key point: The salary allowance is a means of allocating income. It is not an expense of the business, it is not shown as an expense on the income statement, and it is not tax deductible.

Suppose Stuart and Finley run the accounting service on a full-time basis, while Janice and Jo provide tax expertise only for selected clients. In these circumstances, they agree

EXHIBIT 13.4
Allocation of Net Income with Salary Allowances

Item	Stuart	Finley	Janice	Jo	Amount Allocated	Amount Remaining
Estimated net income						$48,000
Salary allowance	$15,000	$10,000	$ -0-	$ -0-	$25,000	23,000
Remainder	5,750	5,750	5,750	5,750	23,000	-0-
Total allocation	$20,750	$15,750	$5,750	$5,750	$48,000	$ -0-

that Stuart and Finley are to receive salary allowances, with any additional amounts of profit or loss allocated equally. For example, assume that Stuart gets a salary allowance of $15,000 and Finley receives one of $10,000, with any remainder allocated equally among the four partners. Assume again that AD Company expected to generate net income of $48,000. After allocating the salary allowances of $25,000, the $23,000 remainder is divided by four and allocated to each partner. After both the salary and the remainder are allocated, Stuart's capital would increase by $20,750, Finley's capital would increase by $15,750, and Janice's and Jo's capital accounts would increase by $5,750 each. Exhibit 13.4 presents the computations showing the allocation of net income with these salary allowances.

When Stuart's salary allowance is $15,000 and Finley's is $10,000, any amount of net income less than $25,000 will result in a negative remainder. The amount of the remainder, whether positive or negative, is always allocated according to the terms of the partnership agreement. For example, if the expected net income is only $21,000, the negative remainder of $4,000 would be allocated among all four partners. As Exhibit 13.5 shows, after the $25,000 salary allowance is awarded, each partner's allocation is reduced by $1,000, or their equal shares of the negative residual. Notice that the $14,000 increase in Stuart's capital is the result of a $15,000 salary allowance minus his $1,000 share of the negative remainder. Finley's capital increased $9,000 because he was allocated $10,000 for the salary allowance minus his $1,000 share of the negative remainder. Since neither Janice nor Jo has a salary allowance, they would be allocated only their share of the negative remainder and, therefore, their capital is reduced by $1,000 each. It may seem unusual to decrease a partner's capital when the company made a profit, but the practice follows the terms of the partnership agreement. (The partnership agreement must be written specifically to avoid this paradox.)

Interest Allowance on Capital Balances

The interest allowance method uses an interest rate multiplied by each partner's capital balance to allocate partnership earnings. This method of allocating income is an incentive designed to reward partners who invest and maintain capital in the business. Just as in the case of the salary allowance, the interest on capital balances is merely one step in the method of computing the allocation of earnings; it is not an expense of the company and it is not tax deductible.

The partnership agreement must specify the interest rate, the capital balance (beginning, ending, or average) that the rate applied to, and the basis for allocating any residual income

EXHIBIT 13.5
Allocation of Net Income with a Negative Remainder

Item	Stuart	Finley	Janice	Jo	Amount Allocated	Amount Remaining
Estimated net income						$21,000
Salary allowance	$15,000	$10,000	$ -0-	$ -0-	$25,000	(4,000)
Remainder	(1,000)	(1,000)	(1,000)	(1,000)	(4,000)	-0-
Total allocation	$14,000	$ 9,000	$(1,000)	$(1,000)	$21,000	$ -0-

or losses. Assume that the partners have agreed to apply a 10 percent rate to the average capital balances for the period. Their average capital balances are shown in column B of the following table. The interest allowance is, therefore, $9,000 ($90,000 total average capital × 0.10) and the income allocation would be:

A	B	C	D
Partner	**Average Capital Balance**	**Percentage**	**Interest Allocation (B × C)**
Stuart	$13,000	10%	$1,300
Finley	9,000	10	900
Janice	40,000	10	4,000
Jo	28,000	10	2,800
Total	$90,000		$9,000

Further assume that the partners agree to allocate any remainder after interest allowances in a ratio of 4:2:1:1. Exhibit 13.6 shows the allocation among the partners, again assuming an expected net income of $48,000.

Once the initial $9,000 allowance for interest is allocated, Stuart would be allocated an additional $19,500 (4/8 of $39,000), Finley would be allocated $9,750 (2/8 of $39,000), while Janice and Jo each would be allocated $4,875 (1/8 of $39,000). Each partner's capital would increase by the amounts shown in the total line in Exhibit 13.6. Given the capital balances and the 10 percent rate in this example, any loss or an income figure less than the $9,000 amount of interest allowance would result in a negative remainder that must be allocated among the partners.

Let's walk through Exhibit 13.7. First, allocate the salary allowances ($15,000); next allocate the interest allowances ($9,000); and then subtract these two amounts from the net income of the partnership. The result, whether positive or negative ($24,000 in this case), is then allocated equally to the partners.

Combination of Salary and Interest Allowance

Some partnership agreements provide both salary and interest allowances as well as an agreement for allocating the remainder. For example, assume that Stuart receives a salary allowance of $10,000, Finley receives a salary allowance of $5,000, and all the partners are allowed a 10 percent interest allowance on their average capital balances. Exhibit 13.7 shows the resulting allocation if expected profits are $48,000 and any remainder after salary and interest allowance is to be allocated equally. Stuart's, Finley's, Janice's, and Jo's capital accounts will increase by $17,300, $11,900, $10,000, and $8,800, respectively, as a result of

EXHIBIT 13.6
Allocation of Net Income with Interest Allowances

Item	Stuart	Finley	Janice	Jo	Amount Allocated	Amount Remaining
Estimated net income						$48,000
Interest allowance	$ 1,300	$ 900	$4,000	$2,800	$ 9,000	39,000
Remainder	19,500	9,750	4,875	4,875	39,000	-0-
Total allocation	$20,800	$10,650	$8,875	$7,675	$48,000	$ -0-

EXHIBIT 13.7
Allocation of Net Income with Salary and Interest Allowances

Item	Stuart	Finley	Janice	Jo	Amount Allocated	Amount Remaining
Estimated net income						$48,000
Salary allowance	$10,000	$ 5,000			$15,000	33,000
Interest allowance	1,300	900	$ 4,000	$2,800	9,000	24,000
Remainder	6,000	6,000	6,000	6,000	24,000	-0-
Total allocation	$17,300	$11,900	$10,000	$8,800	$48,000	$ -0-

EXHIBIT 13.8
Budgeted Statement of Owners' Equity

	Stuart	Finley	Janice	Jo	Total
Beginning capital balance	$15,000	$10,000	$45,000	$30,000	$100,000
Add: planned contributions from partner	2,000	0	0	3,000	5,000
Less: planned withdrawals by partners	(10,000)	(3,000)	(1,000)	0	(14,000)
Add: estimated income allocation (Exhibit 13.7)	17,300	11,900	10,000	8,800	48,000
Budgeted ending capital balance	$24,300	$18,900	$54,000	$41,800	$139,000

this partnership agreement. Again, notice that the income allocation does not indicate the cash that the partner did or did not withdraw from the partnership. We discuss anticipated partner withdrawals and contributions next.

Other Changes in Capital

The previous discussion focused on partnership income allocations, but income allocations are not the only reason a partner's capital changes. Throughout the period the partner may make additional contributions to the partnership and/or make withdrawals of cash and other assets from the partnership. For planning purposes it is important that the partnership consider these withdrawals and contributions so that the business knows how much owner capital should be available to invest in assets, pay debts, and so forth. To illustrate, we return to the AD Company. Assume that the partners agree to allocate profits as illustrated in Exhibit 13.7. Further assume that Stuart plans to contribute $2,000 to the partnership in March but anticipates withdrawing cash each month for living expenses. He plans to withdraw a total of $10,000 over the period. Finley does not plan to contribute any additional funds to the partnership this year, but he does plan to withdraw $3,000 in September to pay his son's tuition. Janice plans to withdraw $1,000 during the summer for her vacation and does not plan to contribute any additional funds this year. Jo plans to contribute an additional $3,000 in April and does not plan to withdraw any monies during the year. Based on these facts, the budgeted (pro forma) statement of owners' (partners') equity that indicates the anticipated changes in each partner's capital is illustrated in Exhibit 13.8.

As Exhibit 13.8 indicates, the partnership can expect total partner capital at the end of the year of $139,000. Stuart has an anticipated capital balance of $24,300 while Jo has a planned ending capital balance of $41,800. In addition, the amounts shown as contributions to and withdrawals from the partnership would be reflected in the financing section of the budgeted statement of cash flows for the partnership.

Planning Corporate Equity

Corporations that have a large number of owners must issue shares of capital stock to indicate an owner's interest in the corporation and to allow the owners to increase or decrease their interest in the organization without the consent of the other owners. This section discusses the characteristics of the financial instruments used by corporations for equity financing. Understanding the characteristics of the financial instruments is essential when planning to use the corporate structure for financing a business. In general, a corporation issues two classes of stock—common and preferred—although it may have different types of each.

Common Stock

If a corporation has only one class of stock, it is called common stock. **Common stock** represents the basic ownership unit of the corporation, and, unless specifically noted in the corporation's charter and bylaws, it confers all the rights of ownership. Common stock represents the residual ownership interest in the corporation because the common shareholders, upon liquidation of the corporation, receive benefits only after the corporation satisfies all creditors' and other owners' claims. Thus the common shareholders receive the remainder, or residual, interest in the corporation.

Common shareholders have the right to vote on significant events that affect the corporation and they elect members of the board of directors who, in turn, hire the corporation's professional managers. Common shareholders normally have other rights that include the right to declared dividends, the right to the residual assets upon liquidation of the corporation, the right to dispose of the shares by sale or gift, and the preemptive right.

The **preemptive right** gives common shareholders the right to maintain their percentage interest in the corporation when it issues new shares of common stock. For example, suppose that a common shareholder owns 10 percent of the shares of Apple and that Apple is going to issue 200,000 new shares of common stock. The preemptive right requires that the corporation offer this shareholder the right to buy 20,000 (200,000 × 0.10) shares of the new issue to maintain the shareholder's 10 percent interest in the company. The trend today is for most large corporations to eliminate the preemptive right, but it is common in smaller corporations.

Some corporations have more than one class of common stock (Class A common stock and Class B common stock). The difference between the classes of stock usually involves the voting rights associated with each class of stock and is described in the corporation's charter and bylaws.

Preferred Stock

Preferred stock represents an ownership interest in a corporation with special privileges or preferences as to liquidation and dividends. Upon liquidation of the corporation, the preferred shareholders are paid before the common shareholders. In addition, preferred shareholders are entitled to receive dividends before common shareholders receive dividends. Thus the preference conferred on preferred shareholders is in reference to common shareholders, not creditors.

In exchange for these preferences, preferred shareholders usually give up the right to vote, and the dividends they receive are usually limited to a set amount per share of stock. Preferred stock dividends are stated in either *predetermined dollar amounts* or as a *percentage of par value* (defined and discussed later in the chapter). For example, stock that is termed $5.50 preferred would receive a dividend of $5.50 per share before common shareholders would receive any dividends. If a preferred stock has a $100 par value and a 10 percent dividend rate, each preferred shareholder would receive a $10 dividend ($100 par × 0.10) for every share held before common shareholders could receive dividends.

Companies often issue preferred stock with one or more of the following five features: (1) cumulative, (2) participating, (3) callable, (4) redeemable, and (5) convertible. Each feature is designed to make the preferred stock more attractive to investors and can be used individually or in combination.

Cumulative preferred stock accumulates unpaid dividends over time. When cumulative preferred stock dividends are not paid when stipulated they are called **dividends in arrears.** If a corporation does not pay dividends in a given year, the next time dividends are paid, all the preferred dividends skipped in prior years plus the preferred dividend due for the current year must be paid before the common shareholders can receive any dividends. Note that dividends in arrears are not a liability unless and until dividends are declared by the board of directors. This provides preferred shareholders some assurance that preferred dividends, if missed in one year, will be paid in a subsequent year. To illustrate, assume that Example Corporation has preferred stock but does not pay its normal stated amount of preferred stock dividend of $100,000 in 2009. In 2010, if the Example Corporation pays dividends of $250,000, the preferred shareholders will receive $200,000 ($100,000 for 2009 and $100,000 for 2010), and the common shareholders will receive the residual $50,000.

Enhance Your Understanding

When preferred stock is guaranteed a certain percentage dividend and this stock is cumulative, does the preferred stock begin to take on the characteristics of debt financing?

Answer: Many people think so. Since the amount of the dividend is known and, if dividends are paid, the amount of the dividend is guaranteed, it begins to look like an interest payment. However, there are two significant differences—dividends do not have to be paid, but interest does, and interest is tax deductible for the corporation, while dividends are not.

Participating preferred stock allows preferred shareholders the right to receive an amount in excess of the stated dividend rate or amount. After common shareholders have received a dividend, any dividend remaining is shared between preferred and common shareholders. The amount of the residual dividends that each class of shareholders receives depends on the terms of the participation outlined in the corporation's charter. For example, assume the Example Corporation has participating preferred stock and declares a $500,000 dividend. If the normal preferred stock dividend is $100,000, and the common shareholders' equivalent share of the dividends is $200,000, then the residual dividend of $200,000 [$500,000 − ($100,000 + $200,000)] is divided between the preferred and common shareholders. The amount of the residual that each class of shareholder receives depends on the terms of participation outlined in the corporate charter. In many cases the division is based on the ratio of the preferred to common stock par values (par values are discussed later in the chapter).

Callable preferred stock gives the corporation the right to repurchase its preferred stock at a stipulated price. If the corporation decides it wants to reduce the number of shares of preferred stock or eliminate all preferred shareholders, it can *call* or buy back some or all of the preferred stock. When the corporation *calls* the preferred stock, the preferred shareholders must relinquish their shares. The corporation must compensate the preferred shareholders for the shares relinquished. Normally, call prices are listed on the preferred stock at a certain dollar amount. Corporations call their preferred stock and liquidate the preferred shareholders' interest in the corporation when this action will benefit the common shareholders of the corporation. By eliminating preferred shareholders, the common shareholders will receive the dividends normally given to preferred shareholders. In some cases, the preferred stock is called in order to use another less expensive source of financing. For example, if a company had issued preferred stock with a 10 percent dividend and can now issue long-term debt at 7 percent, it might be to its advantage to call the preferred stock and replace the equity financing with cheaper debt financing.

Redeemable preferred stock is similar to callable preferred stock except it gives the shareholder the option to turn in (redeem) the stock for cash at the shareholder's option. If the shareholder no longer wishes to hold preferred stock, he or she can redeem or sell the stock to the corporation for a predetermined price per share. Of course, preferred shareholders also could sell the stock in the secondary market at any time. The redemption price assures the preferred shareholder of a guaranteed minimum price for the stock. For example, suppose Example Corporation issues 5,000 shares of redeemable preferred stock with a redemption price of $50. If shareholders present 1,000 of the shares for redemption, Example Corporation must give each shareholder $50 per share or a total of $50,000.

Convertible preferred stock gives shareholders the right to convert (exchange) preferred shares for other forms of capital, as stated in the corporate charter, at the option of the preferred shareholder. Preferred stock is normally convertible into common stock, although occasionally it is convertible into debt instruments. When preferred stock is convertible into common stock, the conversion is normally stated as a number of shares, such as "convertible into four shares of common stock." This feature is attractive to both the prospective investor and the company. The prospective investor sees the option as a way to increase the return on his or her investment and is willing to pay a higher price for the security. Companies find convertible preferred stock attractive because it sells at a higher price and is more marketable. To illustrate, assume Example Corporation issues 5,000 shares of $20 par, 5 percent convertible preferred stock that is convertible into two shares of common stock. If later the preferred stock has a market price of $30 per share and common stock is selling for $20 per share, many preferred shareholders will convert their preferred stock for two shares of common stock worth $40. When the preferred stock is converted, it is retired (discussed later) and the common stock issued.

Return on Common Equity

When planning whether to issue preferred stock or common stock, the return on common equity ratio is often used. The **return on common equity ratio** represents the portion of income available to provide a return for common shareholders. The return on common equity ratio is similar to the return on owners' equity ratio except the numerator is reduced by the guaranteed preferred stock dividends (cumulative preferred stock) and the denominator represents only the common equity of the corporation. The common equity of the corporation is the total shareholders' equity less the liquidating value (stated on the stock certificate) of the preferred stock. The return on common equity ratio is

$$\frac{\text{Net income} - \text{Preferred stock dividends}}{\text{Shareholders' equity} - \text{Liquidating value of preferred stock}}$$

So when a company issues additional shares of preferred stock, the return on common equity is reduced. Since common shareholders are the residual owners of the corporation, maintaining a "reasonable" return on common equity is desirable. Recall however that we must compare a planned ratio to those in the past and to our competitors before we can determine what is reasonable.

Stock Shares

When referring to the number of shares of stock associated with a corporation, we refer to the number of shares the corporation has authorized, issued, and outstanding. These three terms give financial planners and external investors some idea about the equity financing potential of the corporation. The terms also help describe the current status of equity financing.

When a company files its articles of incorporation with the secretary of state of the incorporating state, it specifies the number of shares it wants to be able to sell. The number of **authorized shares** is the total number of shares the state has approved for a corporation to sell. The corporation can issue more than the number of authorized shares only by obtaining permission from the incorporating state. The number of shares authorized is usually set high enough so additional authorization from the state is unnecessary. Apple, for example, had 1.8 billion shares of common stock authorized as of fiscal 2008.

A corporation raises money to fund its investments by selling its stock to individuals, groups, or businesses that want to have an ownership interest in the corporation. When the corporation sells its stock initially, it has issued its shares. The number of **issued shares** refers to the number of authorized shares a corporation has sold to shareholders. After the corporation issues stock, shareholders are free to buy and sell the issued shares. Secondary markets such as the New York Stock Exchange and NASDAQ exist to facilitate the shareholders' desire to trade these securities. The number of shares issued is unaffected when the corporation's stock is traded in secondary markets because investors are merely trading existing shares of stock. The number of shares issued changes when the corporation sells more of its authorized shares or buys back *and retires* some of its issued shares.

Treasury stock is NOT an asset because the company cannot own itself (remember, treasury stock is the company's stock that it purchased in the secondary market).

The number of outstanding shares is the number of shares issued and currently held outside the corporation. Because a corporation is a legal entity, it can buy its own stock in the secondary market. Typically, a corporation buys its own shares in anticipation of reissuing the stock at a higher price at a later date and, therefore, raising additional capital. In addition, corporations purchase their stock to give to their executives as compensation and to protect against hostile takeovers. **Treasury stock** are the shares of a corporation's issued stock that the corporation has repurchased and intends to reissue at a later date. When a corporation buys treasury stock, it is liquidating an existing shareholders' interest in the corporation by giving them the corporation's cash in exchange for their ownership interest. Thus, the corporation is not buying an asset; rather, it is reducing its shareholders' equity by reducing the number of shares outstanding (discussed next).

The number of **outstanding shares** is the number of shares issued less the number of shares of treasury stock held by the corporation. In other words, it is the number of issued shares held outside the corporation. If the corporation has no treasury shares, the number of shares outstanding and the number issued are the same. On September 27, 2008, Apple had 888,325,973 shares issued and outstanding (see the Consolidated Balance Sheet in the Appendix to the text). Since the number of shares issued is the same as the number of shares outstanding, we know that Apple did not have any treasury stock on September 27, 2008.

The corporation can sell its treasury stock in the market at any time. When treasury stock is sold (reissued) the corporation receives cash or other assets and the number of shares outstanding increases, but the number of shares issued remains the same because selling treasury stock is not a new issue of stock.

A corporation can buy its issued shares and then retire the shares. **Retired shares** are repurchased (or converted) issued shares that the corporation will never reissue. When shares are retired, both the number of shares issued and outstanding are decreased. In most states, the number of shares a company is allowed to repurchase is limited to 20 percent of the number of shares issued to protect corporate creditors. Because corporations have limited liability, creditors of a corporation have claim only to the assets of the corporation. If the corporation could buy all of its stock back, the shareholders would receive their interest in the corporation (cash payment for the repurchased stock) before the creditors, and the assets remaining might not be sufficient to satisfy the claims of the creditors upon liquidation.

Stock Values

While the number of shares authorized, issued, and outstanding provides some insight into the capital structure of the company, monetary values must be attached to these shares to gain a complete picture of a corporation's ownership structure. Capital stock has two important values depending on the context in which it appears. The first is par value, which is established to comply with the legal requirements of issuing stock. The second is a stock's market value, which represents the economic value of capital stock.

Par value is an arbitrary value assigned to shares of capital stock; this value is approved by the state in which the business is incorporated. The par value is specified in the corporation's charter and is printed on the stock certificates. In most states, the par value is the minimum price the stock can sell for when it is initially issued by the corporation. Because the par value of common stock is a purely arbitrary amount, and because a high par value might impair the company's ability to sell its shares, most par values of common stock are quite low.

The **legal capital** of the corporation is the portion of shareholders' equity required by state law to be retained for the protection of the corporation's creditors. In many states it is calculated by multiplying the par value times the number of shares of stock issued. The corporation cannot pay dividends that cause its total assets to drop below the sum of its legal capital and the total liabilities of the corporation, thus providing some protection for the creditors of the corporation. For instance, suppose Example Corporation has total assets of $1,200,000, total liabilities of $800,000, legal capital of $100,000, and retained earnings of $300,000. Example Corporation can pay dividends of only $300,000 because any dividends in excess of $300,000 would mean the corporation is providing a return *of* the shareholders' equity ahead of the creditors' claim on the assets. Because corporate creditors can be paid only from the corporation's assets, paying dividends that reduce Example Corporation's legal capital may impair the creditors' ability to recover their investment.

The amount of proceeds received from stock issuance in excess of the par value of the stock is called paid-in capital in excess of par or contributed capital in excess of par. This classification makes the distinction between monies received that satisfy legal capital requirements (par values) and the amounts that are in excess of the legal minimum.

No-par stock does not have a minimum price assigned to each share of stock. Its initial purpose was to overcome two problems associated with par value shares: the possible need to issue stock below par value, and the confusion that existed about par values and any relationship they might have to the market values of the stocks. The legal capital of corporations that issue no-par stock is often specified by the state. Apple's common stock is no-par. **No-par, stated value stock** is stock that has a minimum price or stated value established by the corporation's board of directors but no par value specified in the charter. In effect, a stated value stock makes a no-par stock function the same way as par value stock. This type of stock allows creditors to have the assurance that a minimum amount of capital is available in the corporation to protect their interest. The advantage of stated value stock is that the board of directors decides whether to establish a stated value on the no-par stock. This creates more flexibility for the corporation than when a stock has its par value established in its articles of incorporation.

The **market value** of a share of stock is the price agreed to by an unrelated willing buyer and seller. For stocks traded in organized secondary markets, the market values of stock are readily available from listings in financial news sources such as *The Wall Street Journal* and *Barron's*. For stocks that are not traded on organized exchanges, individuals who are making trades determine market values. Unlike par values, which are determined prior to the issuance of the stock and cannot be changed without approval of the incorporating state, the market value of stock is constantly changing based on willing buyers' and sellers' estimates of the value of the corporation.

The market price a corporation receives in the initial issue market determines the amount of cash the corporation receives from investors to finance its operations. Corporations continue to monitor the market value of their stock in the secondary market after the initial sale of the stock. Increasing or decreasing market values reflect the investors' perceptions of the corporation's financial condition and future profit potential. Rising stock prices reflect increasing investor confidence in future profitability, while declining prices indicate erosion of their confidence in the company's future profitability. The market price of stock in the secondary market gives the corporation's management an idea of the amount of cash it could raise if additional stock issues are planned. One item that has a significant impact on investors' perception of future profitability is the amount and timing of the company's dividends.

Dividends

As you know, dividends are a distribution of the assets of the corporation to the owners of the corporation. Typically, these distributions are made from the earnings of the company, providing shareholders with a return *on* their investment. However, if the dividends exceed the accumulated earnings of the company, they are called *liquidating dividends* because they are a return *of* the shareholders' investments.

Cash Dividends

Dividends usually are distributed in the form of cash; however, corporations routinely issue stock dividends, and they can issue property dividends. A **cash dividend** is a cash distribution paid by sending checks to shareholders as of a certain date. The advantage of cash dividends is that most investors prefer this type of distribution. The disadvantage of cash dividends is that they reduce a source of equity financing. Many corporations offer what are referred to as DRIP accounts to encourage the reinvestment of the company's dividends. A **dividend reinvestment program (DRIP)** is a program that allows current shareholders to use their cash dividends to buy more shares of the company's stock. Shareholders like the program because they can acquire more shares of stock without paying brokerage fees. Companies like the program because it keeps their shareholders happy while reinvesting the cash that would otherwise be paid out as dividends.

Remember when determining dividends that preferred shareholders receive their dividend distribution before common shareholders. For example, let's assume that Example Corporation has 10,000 shares of $100 par preferred stock with a 6 percent dividend rate and 100,000 shares of $1 par common stock. Example Corporation plans a $90,000 dividend. How would the dividend be divided between preferred and common shareholders? First, we determine the preferred shareholders' dividend. The remainder goes to common:

Preferred: 10,000 shares × \$100 par × 0.06 dividend rate = \$60,000 dividend

Common: \$90,000 total dividend − \$60,000 preferred dividend = \$30,000 dividend

Stock Dividends

When a corporation issues a **stock dividend,** it distributes additional shares of the corporation's stock to existing shareholders. Stock dividends have no effect on the assets of the company because each shareholder receives more shares of stock rather than corporate assets. Although each investor has more shares as a result of a stock dividend, his or her percentage interest in the corporation does not change. When planning a stock dividend, management must be aware that as the size of the stock dividend increases, the market price of the outstanding shares will decrease.

For instance, if Example Corporation issues a 10 percent stock dividend on the number of shares issued, a shareholder who owns 100 shares of stock will receive 10 new shares (100 shares × 0.10). However, because the number of shares that every Example Corporation shareholder owns will increase by 10 percent, no single shareholder will have a greater interest in the company than he or she did before the stock dividend. However, the number of shares issued and outstanding will increase by 10 percent. As a result, the price of the stock should decrease about 10 percent to reflect the increase in the number of shares. The advantage of a stock dividend is that in many cases the stock price drops less than the dividend percentage and, therefore, increases the shareholders' wealth. This keeps the shareholders satisfied without having to distribute the assets of the company.

Property Dividends

A **property dividend** typically involves the distribution of specific noncash assets, such as inventory or investments in other corporations' securities, to shareholders. Property dividends usually are given in corporations with just a few shareholders. They are not as popular with shareholders as cash dividends due to the difficulty of receiving and disposing of the corporation's property. In the 1950s, tobacco companies would send packs of cigarettes to their shareholders!

Dividend Dates

Three dates related to dividends are important to remember: the (1) date of declaration, (2) date of record, and (3) date of payment. Exhibit 13.9 shows the sequence with assumed dates, which we describe next in detail.

The **date of declaration** is the date on which the board of directors announces its decision to pay a dividend. The board of directors usually declares dividends after the company has generated sufficient earnings and has cash on hand to provide shareholders with a return on their investment. On the date of declaration, the board of directors sets the amount of the

EXHIBIT 13.9
Dividend Dates

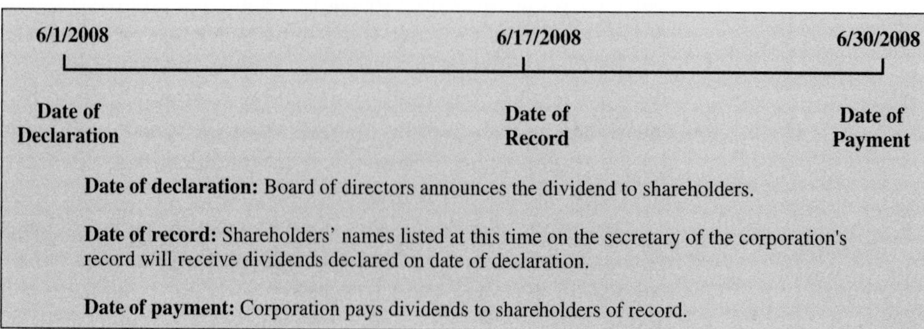
6/1/2008
6/17/2008
6/30/2008
Date of Declaration
Date of Record
Date of Payment
Date of declaration: Board of directors announces the dividend to shareholders.
Date of record: Shareholders' names listed at this time on the secretary of the corporation's record will receive dividends declared on date of declaration.
Date of payment: Corporation pays dividends to shareholders of record.

dividend and the date to distribute it. For cash and property dividends, once the board declares the dividend, the corporation incurs the obligation to pay the dividend on the date of payment, which gives rise to a related liability. However, because stock dividends involve the distribution of shares of stock rather than the company's assets, no liability is incurred on the date of declaration for stock dividends.

The **date of record** is the date on which the secretary of the corporation examines the stock ownership transfer book to determine who is officially registered as a shareholder of the corporation and, therefore, eligible to receive the corporation's dividends. Those persons listed in the ownership book on this date will receive the dividends. Shareholders can sell their stock after this date but before the date of payment and still receive the declared dividend. The date of record is announced at the time the board of directors declares the dividend.

The **date of payment** is the date that the company pays the dividends to shareholders of record. Normally, no more than 90 days elapse from the date of declaration until the date of payment. Once the corporation has distributed the dividend, it has met its dividend obligation created on the date of declaration.

Stock Splits

A **stock split** occurs when a corporation calls in its old shares of stock and issues a larger number of new shares of stock in their place.[1] However, each shareholder retains the same percentage interest in the company after the stock split because the par or stated value of the stock also changes to reflect the number of new shares on the market. Assume that Example Corporation has 400,000 shares of common stock issued and outstanding with a par value of $3 per share. With its total par value at $1,200,000 (400,000 issued shares × $3 par value), the board of directors approves a three-for-one stock split. To implement the split, the company will call in all the old $3 par value common stock and replace it with 1,200,000 (400,000 × 3) shares of $1 ($3/3) par value common stock. Notice that the stock split increases (triples) the number of shares issued and decreases the par value to one-third of its original amount.[2] However, the legal capital remains the same, $1,200,000 (1,200,000 issued shares × $1 par value).

Companies enter into stock splits for a variety of reasons. The most common reason is to lower the market price of the company's stock to make the price more affordable to a wider group of potential investors. When a stock splits, the market price of the stock is reduced to reflect the size of the split. For instance, if Example Corporation's stock were selling for $60 per share before the split, its price after the split would be around $20 per share. This occurs because while each shareholder owns a greater number of shares, each shareholder's proportional ownership of the company remains unchanged.

A **reverse stock split** occurs when a corporation calls in its old shares and replaces them with a reduced number of shares with a higher par value. Assume Example Corporation has 400,000 shares of common stock issued and outstanding ($3 par value) when it declares a one-for-four reverse stock split. To implement the split, the company will call in all the old $3 par value common stock and replace it with 100,000 (400,000/4) shares of $12 ($3 × 4) par value common stock. Notice that the reverse stock split decreases the number of shares issued (by one-fourth) and increases the par value to four times its original amount. However, the legal capital issued remains the same, $1,200,000 (100,000 issued shares × $12 par value). Why would a company do such a thing? The most common reason is to increase the selling price of the stock. Many stock exchanges require that the stock sell for a certain minimum amount or the stock will be delisted. Delisting means that the stock cannot be sold on that exchange. Obviously this is something corporations seek to avoid.

[1] A corporation typically does not physically call in its old shares because in today's electronic market stock certificates are rarely distributed to shareholders.

[2] This also requires filing with the secretary of the incorporating state because of the change in par value.

EXHIBIT 13.10
Equity Activities and the Budgeted Financial Statements

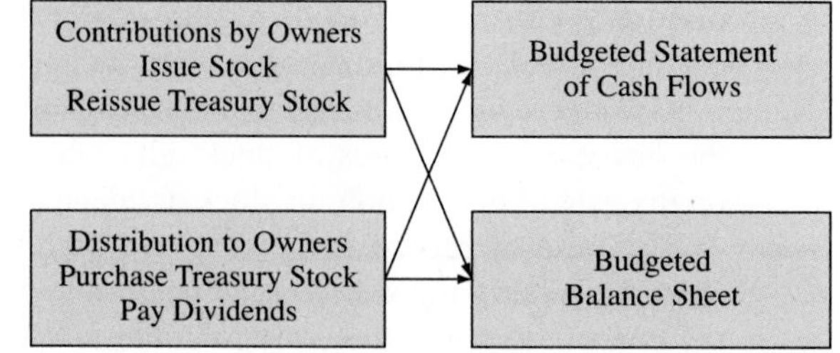

FAST FACT

Sirius (XM) satellite-radio company, early in 2009, sought to head off a delisting by NASDAQ by approving a plan to issue 3.5 billion new shares and then do a reverse stock split of up to 50-to-1 in an attempt to boost the share price. It was hoped that this reverse split could head off the delisting as Sirius's stock price had been below $1 for three months.

Source: www.usatoday.com, January 28, 2009.

Corporate Equity Planning and Budgeting

Once the corporation has planned all its equity financing activities for the period, it needs to reflect the anticipated results of these activities on its budgeted financial statements. In addition, if a lot of activity is planned, the company might prepare a separate financing budget (we discuss this in Chapter 14). Exhibit 13.10 illustrates the relationship between equity events and the budgeted financial statements. As you can see, equity activities impact the statement of cash flows if contributions (stock issues) from or distributions (dividends and treasury stock purchases) to owners are planned. In addition, the expected ending balances of the owners' equity items (common stock, preferred stock, treasury stock, etc.) should be shown on the budgeted balance sheet.

Summary

Companies must consider the risks and rewards of debt versus equity financing when planning financial structure. Equity financing is provided by owners who accept the risks in exchange for financial and psychological rewards. There are two sources of equity financing. The first source consists of the contributions owners make in exchange for an ownership interest. The second is the cash generated by the company's operations that is reinvested in the company. Sole proprietorships and partnerships are easily formed but have unlimited liability. While partnerships can generate more capital, mutual agency and unlimited liability create additional risks for the members of the partnership.

- The amount of a partner's capital depends on the interest granted to him or her when he or she is admitted to the partnership and how the partnership divides its income.
- Common stock represents the residual ownership in the corporation, while preferred stock represents an ownership interest with special privileges as to dividends and liquidation.
- Treasury stock is the corporation's stock that the corporation repurchases for the purpose of either reissuing it to key employees as compensation or selling it at a higher price in the market at a later date.
- The market price of stock is the price investors are willing to pay for an ownership interest in a corporation.

- Corporations reward their shareholders by distributing to them cash, property, and stock dividends. The board of directors declares dividends on the date of declaration; dividends are distributed on the date of payment to the shareholders who are registered owners on the date of record.
- A stock split occurs when a corporation calls in all its old shares of stock and issues a larger number of new shares. A reverse stock split occurs when a corporation calls in its old shares of stock and issues a smaller number of new shares.
- The impact of planned equity activities should be reflected in the budgeted financial statements. For partnerships, a budgeted statement of owners' equity is often prepared in addition to the budgeted statement of cash flows and balance sheet to reflect equity activity.

Key Terms

Authorized shares The total number of shares the state has approved for a corporation to sell, *383*

Budgeted (pro forma) statement of owners' (partners') equity A statement that indicates the anticipated changes in each partner's capital, *376*

Callable preferred stock Preferred stock that gives the issuing corporation the right to repurchase the preferred stock at a stipulated price, *382*

Cash dividend A cash distribution in the form of a check drawn on the corporation's bank account that is sent to each shareholder as of a certain date, *385*

Common stock The basic ownership unit of a corporation, *380*

Convertible preferred stock Preferred stock that gives the shareholder the right to convert (exchange) the preferred shares for other forms of capital, as stated in the corporate charter, at the option of the preferred shareholder, *382*

Cumulative preferred stock Preferred stock that accumulates unpaid dividends over time, *381*

Date of declaration The date on which the board of directors announces its decision to pay a dividend, *386*

Date of payment The date on which the corporation formally pays dividends to shareholders of record, *387*

Date of record The date on which the secretary of the corporation examines the stock ownership transfer book to determine who is officially registered as a shareholder of the corporation and, therefore, eligible to receive the corporation's dividends, *387*

Debt financing When a company obtains funds (cash) in exchange for a liability to repay the borrowed funds, *369*

Dividend reinvestment program (DRIP) A program that allows current shareholders to use their cash dividends to buy more shares of the company's stock, *385*

Dividends in arrears The amount of cumulative preferred stock dividends not paid in full when stipulated, *381*

Equity financing A means for a company to obtain funds in exchange for an ownership interest in the company, *369*

Financial leverage A financing strategy designed to increase the rate of return on the owners' investment, *371*

Financial risk The chance that a company will fail because it defaults on its debt, *369*

Issued shares The number of authorized shares a corporation has sold to shareholders, *383*

Legal capital The portion of shareholders' equity required by state law to be retained for the protection of the corporation's creditors, *384*

Market value Price agreed to by a willing unrelated buyer and seller, *385*

No-par, stated value stock Stock with a minimum issue price or stated value established by the corporation's board of directors but no par value specified in the charter, *385*

No-par stock Stock that does not have a minimum price assigned to each share of stock, *385*

Outstanding shares The number of shares issued and held outside the corporation, *384*

Par value An arbitrary value assigned to shares of capital stock that is approved by the state in which the business is incorporated, *384*

Participating preferred stock Preferred stock that allows preferred shareholders the right to receive an amount in excess of the stated dividend rate or amount, *382*
Preemptive right A right of common shareholders that allows them to maintain their percentage interest in the corporation when it issues new shares of common stock, *381*
Preferred stock An ownership interest in a corporation with special privileges or preferences as to liquidation and dividends, *381*
Property dividend The distribution of specific noncash assets to the shareholders of a corporation, *386*
Redeemable preferred stock Preferred stock that allows a shareholder to turn in (redeem) the preferred stock for cash at the shareholder's option, *382*
Retired shares Repurchased issued shares that the corporation will never reissue, *384*
Return on common equity ratio A ratio that measures the proportion of income available to provide a return for common shareholders, *383*
Return on owners' equity (ROE) ratio A ratio that measures the performance of the company in terms of the owners' investment, *372*
Reverse stock split The corporation's recall of its old shares of stock and issuance of a smaller number of new shares in their place, *387*
Stock dividend The distribution of additional shares of the corporation's stock to existing shareholders, *386*
Stock split The corporation's recall of its old shares of stock and issuance of a larger number of new shares in their place, *387*
Times interest earned ratio A measure of the company's ability to service its debt, *370*
Treasury stock The shares of a corporation's issued stock that the corporation has repurchased and intends to reissue at a later date, *383*

Questions

1. Describe the three sources of funds and how they are used in a business.
2. Describe the two sources of financing available to a company.
3. What are the risks and rewards of debt financing?
4. How are ratios used to assess the risk and reward of debt financing?
5. What are the rewards and risks of equity financing?
6. How is equity financing used?
7. What are the advantages of a sole proprietorship and a partnership?
8. What is mutual agency and why is it risky?
9. What is unlimited liability and why is it considered a disadvantage for a partnership?
10. What are the advantages and disadvantages of a corporate ownership structure?
11. Why is a salary allowance used in the allocation of income in a partnership?
12. Why is an interest allowance used in the allocation of income in a partnership?
13. Are salary and interest allowances considered partnership expenses? Why?
14. Why is it possible for a partner's equity to increase when the partnership generates a loss?
15. Compare and contrast common stock versus preferred stock.
16. Compare and contrast cumulative versus participating preferred stock.
17. Compare and contrast callable versus redeemable preferred stock.
18. What is treasury stock and why is it acquired?
19. Distinguish among authorized shares, issued shares, and outstanding shares of stock.
20. What is the distinction between the par value and market value of a stock?
21. What are the four key dividend dates? Why is each important?
22. How does a cash dividend differ from a stock dividend or a property dividend?
23. What is the distinction between stock splits and stock dividends?

Exercises

E13.1 LO 1 Bergman Corporation has planned to have $4,000,000 in assets and $1,000,000 in liabilities at the end of the year. What is its planned debt-to-equity ratio?

E13.2 LO 1 Lindberg Company expects to earn income before interest and taxes of $600,000 during 2011. Its estimated interest expense is $40,000 and its estimated tax expense is $92,000. What is its planned times interest earned ratio? Is it satisfactory?

LO 2 E13.3 Einstein Company currently has $800,000 owners' equity and no long-term debt. Its expected income for 2011 is $120,000 and it is subject to a 20 percent tax rate. What is Einstein's planned return on equity?

LO 1 E13.4 Refer to E13.3. If Einstein issues $200,000 in debt it anticipates that the interest expense will be $14,000. However it expects to use this money and increase sales such that the income before interest and taxes will be $180,000. If Einstein issues the debt what is its planned return on equity?

LO 2 E13.5 Richard and Liz are in a partnership and have agreed to share profits and losses in a ratio of 4:6, respectively. Determine how much their capital will increase or decrease if the partnership has (*a*) net income of $65,000 and (*b*) a net loss of $62,000.

LO 2 E13.6 In their partnership agreement, Bogie and McCall agreed that Bogie should receive a salary allowance of $40,000 per year and that McCall should receive a salary allowance of $60,000. Any remainder is allocated equally between the partners. How much should each partner's capital change if the partnership generates (*a*) net income of $102,000, (*b*) net income of $28,000, and (*c*) a net loss of $48,000?

LO 2 E13.7 Larry, Mo, and Curly have agreed to allocate profits and losses as follows: 10 percent interest on beginning capital and the remainder allocated equally. The beginning capital amounts are Larry, $120,000; Mo, $60,000; and Curly, $80,000. Determine the projected ending balance in each partner's capital account if the partnership generated (*a*) net income of $71,000, (*b*) net income of $11,000, and (*c*) a net loss of $34,000.

LO 3 E13.8 Longfellow is authorized to issue 1,500,000 shares of its $1 par value common stock and 400,000 shares of $50 par value preferred stock. Longfellow plans to sell 20,000 shares of common stock at $35 and 1,000 shares of its preferred stock at $55 per share. How much capital will Longfellow generate by this sale? What would be Longfellow's legal capital?

LO 3 E13.9 Dante Corporation plans to issue 7,500 shares of its $1 par value common stock for $52 per share and 800 shares of its $30 par value preferred stock for $63 per share. What would Dante's legal capital be? What would be the amount of capital received in excess of the par value of common and preferred stock? Why is a distinction made between legal capital and total capital?

LO 3 E13.10 Monet, Inc., is authorized to issue 1,500,000 shares of no-par common stock and 800,000 shares of $40 par value 6 percent preferred stock. During its first year of operation, the company plans to issue 800,000 shares of common stock for $6,400,000 and 20,000 shares of its preferred stock for $1,100,000. The company anticipates net income of $550,000 for the year and plans to pay dividends of $150,000 during the year. What would be the total amount of the company's shareholders' equity at the end of the year? How much of the company would be financed by contributions by its owners and how much by its operations?

LO 3 E13.11 Rembrandt Corporation has 5,000 shares of $100 par value 8 percent cumulative preferred stock included in its total owners' equity of $1,800,000. Its budgeted income for the period is $300,000. If the preferred stock has a liquidating value of $400,000, what is the expected return on common equity?

LO 3 E13.12 Refer to E13.11. How would your answer change if the preferred stock were not cumulative? Why?

LO 4 E13.13 The board of directors of Rose Company is going to pay a dividend of $56,000 to its common shareholders. Describe what will happen on each of the dates below in relation to this $56,000 dividend.

A. Date of declaration
B. Date of record
C. Date of payment

LO 4 E13.14 The board of directors of Newton Industries is contemplating a dividend of $500,000. The corporation had 60,000 shares of 10 percent, $40 par value cumulative preferred stock outstanding. There were 400,000 shares of $1 par value common stock outstanding at the time Newton declared dividends. Determine the dividends the preferred and common shareholders will receive if the preferred stock is one year in arrears.

LO 4 E13.15 The board of directors of Picasso Manufacturing, Inc., may declare a dividend this year but has not declared a dividend for the past two years. The corporation has 800,000 shares of $1 par value common stock authorized and 200,000 shares issued and outstanding. It also has 40,000 shares of 5 percent, $10 par value cumulative preferred stock authorized, of which 40,000 shares are issued and outstanding. Compute the amount of dividends available for common and preferred shareholders if the dividend declaration is $80,000.

LO 4 E13.16 Calculate the proposed distribution of dividends in E13.15 assuming that the preferred stock is noncumulative.

LO 5 E13.17 Zulu Corporation has 5,000,000 shares of $0.03 par value common stock authorized, of which 750,000 shares were issued for $3,550,000 and are currently selling for $90 in the stock market. Zulu

Corporation is considering a three-for-one stock split. What will be the impact of the stock split on Zulu Corporation?

LO 5 **E13.18** Alpha, Inc., has 250,000 shares of $1 stated value common stock issued and outstanding. The stock has a market value of $32 per share on October 14 when the board of directors is considering a 10 percent stock dividend to holders of record on October 20. If the board declares the dividend, the new shares will be issued on November 1. Explain the impact of the proposed stock dividend on Alpha issued and outstanding stock.

LO 5 **E13.19** Washington Corporation has 1,000,000 shares of common stock issued and outstanding with a $1 par value. If Washington declares a one-for-four reverse stock split, how many shares will be issued and outstanding and what will the par value be after the split?

LO 5 **E13.20** Refer to E13.19. If Washington declares a four-for-one stock split, how many new shares will be issued, what will the par value be, and what will the legal capital of the corporation be?

Problems

P13.1  LO 2 Letterman, Leno, and Carson all are partners in the WB Company and have the following amounts of capital: Letterman, $120,000; Leno; $80,000; and Carson, $100,000. The partners currently share all profits and losses equally but are considering allocating profits and losses in a ratio of beginning capital balances.

Required: Show how income of $100,000 and a loss of $30,000 would be allocated under the current plan and the proposed plan. Determine the projected ending capital balances.

LO 2 **P13.2** Assume the partners in P13.1 want to consider the following methods of allocating WB Company's profits and losses:

1. Salary allowances of $20,000 to Letterman and $40,000 to Leno, with any residual allocated equally.
2. Interest of 10 percent on beginning capital balances, with any residual allocated equally.
3. Interest of 10 percent on beginning capital balances; salary allowances of $20,000 to Letterman, $40,000 to Leno, with any residual allocated equally.

Required: For each of the three alternatives just described, show how the following amounts would be allocated to the partners and determine the projected ending capital balances.

A. Net income of $100,000.
B. Net loss of $30,000.

LO 2 **P13.3** Huey, Louie, and Dewey are forming a dental partnership and are concerned about how to allocate the partnership's income. Once the partnership is formed, Huey will have $200,000 of capital, while Louie and Dewey will have capital of $100,000 and $50,000, respectively. The partnership is considering the following two methods of allocating the company's income:

Method 1 Salaries: Huey, $30,000; Louie, $15,000; and Dewey, $10,000
Interest of 10 percent on beginning capital balances of all partners
Residual allocated on a 3:2:1 basis

Method 2 Salaries: Huey, $15,000; and Louie, $10,000
Interest on beginning capital balances: Huey, 20 percent; Louie, 10 percent; and Dewey, 5 percent
Residual allocated equally

Required:

1. Show how the following income and loss amounts would be allocated under each of the two methods.
2. Determine the projected ending capital balances that would result after the allocations from part (1) above.
3. Discuss some reasons the partners might have used to justify each of these income allocation methods.

A. Net income of $150,000.
B. Net income of $50,000.
C. Net loss of $30,000.

LO 3 LO 4 LO 5 **P13.4** Match the following terms with the appropriate description.

A. Authorized shares	E. Stock split	I. Treasury stock
B. Common stock	F. Stock dividend	J. Par value
C. Preemptive right	G. Dividends in arrears	K. Reverse stock split
D. Preferred stock	H. Outstanding shares	L. Date of record

________ 1. When a corporation buys its own shares in the secondary market.
________ 2. Minimum price a share of stock can be sold for in the initial issue market.
________ 3. Basic unit of ownership in a corporation.
________ 4. Stock that gets paid dividends first but typically does not have the right to vote.
________ 5. Last chance to buy stock and still get the dividend.
________ 6. Maximum number of shares a corporation can sell.
________ 7. Number of shares issued that are not held by the corporation.
________ 8. When a corporation fails to pay cumulative preferred dividends.
________ 9. Changes the par value of the stock to a higher value.
________ 10. Assures common shareholders they can maintain their percentage of ownership when new shares are issued.

LO 4 LO 5 **P13.5** Lauer Company has 700,000 shares of $1 par value common stock outstanding and 12,000 shares of $100 par value preferred stock outstanding. Earlier in the year, Lauer's common stock had been selling around $8 per share, but for the past two months, the share price has dropped to $1.25 per share (on average). Lauer is contemplating a one-for-four reverse stock split on its common stock.

Required:

A. What is the legal capital of Lauer Company currently?
B. If Lauer undertakes the reverse stock split, what will the legal capital of the company be following the split?
C. How many common shares will be outstanding and what will the par value be after the split?
D. If Lauer's strategy is successful, what should happen to the selling price of its common stock following the split?

LO 4 **P13.6** Harry Potter Corporation had the following stocks issued and outstanding when the board of directors proposed a $150,000 dividend:

Preferred stock: 45,000 shares issued and 40,000 shares outstanding, 8 percent, $10 par value
Common stock: 60,000 shares issued and 50,000 outstanding, $1 par value

Required:

A. Determine the amount of dividends each class of stock would receive given the following assumptions:
   1. Preferred stock is noncumulative.
   2. Preferred stock is cumulative (one year in arrears).
   3. Preferred stock is cumulative (two years in arrears).
B. What is the dividend per share for preferred and common stock in each of the scenarios described in part **A**?

LO 3 LO 4 LO 5 **P13.7** The following information is about Jennings Corporation's shareholders' equity. For each of the following proposed events, determine the impact on each of the items described and keep a running balance of the changes.

Event	Par Value Per Share	Authorized Shares	Issued Shares	Outstanding Shares	Total Par Value
	$1	2,000,000	600,000	600,000	$600,000
1. Issue 10,000 shares of common stock					
2. Purchase 5,000 shares of Jennings common stock					
3. Sell 1,000 shares of treasury stock					
4. Declare and distribute a 2-for-1 stock split					

LO 2 **P13.8** Bert and Ernie formed a partnership in 2003 to produce and sell puppets. At the time the partnership was formed, it was agreed that Bert would oversee the day-to-day operations for which he would receive a salary allowance of $30,000. Ernie, on the other hand, provided most of the capital to start the business, so he will receive an interest allowance of 9 percent of his beginning capital balance. Finally, the partners agreed that the remainder would be allocated in the proportion of the ending capital

balances before allocation. The beginning capital balances and expected ending capital balances of the partners before income allocation are

	Bert	Ernie
Beginning capital	$100,000	$420,000
Add: expected contributions	–0–	–0–
Less: expected withdrawals	40,000	–0–
Expected ending capital	$ 60,000	$420,000

Required:

A. Determine expected ending capital balances if the partners predict a business income of $150,000 for the period.
B. Determine expected ending capital balances if the partners predict a business income of $50,000 for the period.
C. Determine expected ending capital balances if the partners predict a business loss of $40,000 for the period.

LO 1 **P13.9** Lisa Meuli is a sole proprietor offering cooking classes for clients throughout the region. She is considering starting a syndicated television cooking show for one year. She estimates that she will need $500,000 to start this venture. She believes the television show will earn her $50,000 this year. Lisa can borrow money at 8 percent annual interest. If the venture is successful Lisa will expand her television show to a national audience. Should she use debt or equity financing for this one-year venture? Why?

LO 2 **P13.10** Tom Thumb, a sole proprietor, is budgeting for the coming year. He will start the year with a $50,000 balance in his capital account. During the year Tom anticipates that he will withdraw $30,000 from the business for living expenses. However he anticipates a tax refund in May so he will contribute $20,000 to the business at that time. Tom predicts that the business income for the year will be $120,000. What is the estimated balance in Tom's capital account at the end of the year? How much will Tom report on his Form 1040 for tax purposes?

Cases

C13.1 LO 3 LO 4 Suzie Lee, your long-time friend, owns 1,000 shares of $1 par value common stock in Electronics, Inc. There are 1,000,000 shares of common stock authorized, and 100,000 shares are issued and outstanding. Recently, the company was authorized to issue 20,000 shares of $50 par value preferred stock. These shares have a dividend rate of 6 percent based on par, and they are cumulative. The company expects to sell 5,000 shares of the preferred stock in the near future to finance the acquisition of more production facilities. Suzie has studied the company's annual reports in an effort to determine the effects the new stock issue will have on her dividends. She is confused because her $1 par value common stock has a market value of $32 per share. She has received a $4 dividend per share in recent years. The company has consistently maintained a policy of paying out 60 percent of its after-tax net income as dividends, a policy management expects to continue into the foreseeable future. Aside from being confused about the difference between par value and market value, Suzie is concerned that the company will not make enough net income to maintain her $4 per share dividend.

Required:

A. Explain to Suzie in memo form the difference between par value and market value.
B. Show Suzie how to compute the minimum amount of after-tax net income the company must earn in order for her to receive a $4 per share dividend if the 5,000 shares of preferred stock are sold.
C. Would you recommend that Suzie keep the stock?

LO 3 LO 4 **C13.2** Rickhaus Company is authorized to issue 10 million shares of $1 par value common stock and 800,000 shares of $10 par value 7 percent cumulative, convertible, preferred stock. For simplicity assume these are the only relevant events that occurred during the years noted.

1. If Rickhaus issues 1,000,000 shares of common stock for $15 per share and 200,000 shares of preferred stock for $30 per share on January 1, 2006, what would be the amount of legal capital shown on the pro forma balance sheet?
2. If on December 15, 2006, the board of directors declares a cash dividend of $500,000 to shareholders of record on December 23, payable on December 31, what is the amount of the dividend that would be received per share for common shareholders?
3. Assume that Rickhaus distributes a 10 percent common stock dividend on September 1, 2007. How many shares of common stock would be authorized, issued, and outstanding after the dividend?
4. Assume that Rickhaus buys back 50,000 shares of common stock for $50 per share on October 1, 2008. How many shares of common stock would be authorized, issued, and outstanding after the treasury stock is purchased?
5. Assume that all the preferred stock is converted at the rate of 1 to 20 for common stock on March 1, 2009. How many shares of common stock are authorized, issued, and outstanding after the conversion?

Critical Thinking

CT13.1 LO 2 Mitch Holtus and Stan Weber are partners in a company called Sports Voice. Greg Sharp has approached the partners about joining the company, and he wants to buy a 20 percent interest in the company. Sports Voice has $80,000 in liabilities. Holtus has a capital balance of $108,000; Weber's capital balance is $92,000. They share profits and losses equally. How much money will Sharp have to contribute to the company to obtain a 20 percent interest?

CT13.2 The Melano Corporation was authorized to issue 1,000,000 shares of $1 par common stock and 100,000 shares of $100 par, 10 percent cumulative preferred stock. To date, Melano has issued 300,000 shares of common stock and no preferred stock. Melano is contemplating the acquisition of a new plant and wants to issue stock to raise the $1,000,000 cash to finance its acquisition. The company is trying to decide whether to issue 25,000 shares of common stock or 10,000 shares of preferred stock. Describe the advantages and disadvantages of issuing each type of stock.

Ethical Challenges

EC13.1 LO 4 Property dividends, although rare, are occasionally distributed by corporations. As you know from the chapter, a property dividend is a distribution of the corporation's assets other than cash. Given that dividends are taxable to shareholders, would you rather receive a cash dividend or a property dividend? What are the ethical implications of a corporation issuing property dividends?

EC13.2 The Of Interest box in this chapter discussed several "hybrid" types of business organizational forms. Assume that you have started a business but are now looking for additional sources of financing. What are the advantages and disadvantages of each of these hybrid forms of organization? Do you see any ethical issues involved with attracting investors with any of these organizational forms?

Computer Applications

CA13.1 LO 2 L&E Consulting has four partners: Jodi, Rachel, Tyler, and Chad. Its budgeted net income for this period is $90,000. The partners are currently debating how the company's net income should be divided among themselves. The partners are considering the following four alternatives:

1. Divide net income in the ratios of the partners' average capital balances during the year.
2. Give a $10,000 salary allowance to Jodi and a $5,000 salary allowance to Rachel and divide the remainder in the ratios of their average capital balances.
3. Give each partner an interest allowance equal to 10 percent of his or her average capital balance during the year and divide the remainder equally among the partners.
4. Divide the net income among Jodi, Rachel, Tyler, and Chad—25 percent, 10 percent, 35 percent, and 30 percent, respectively.

The average capital balances for Jodi, Rachel, Tyler, and Chad during the past year were $20,000, $10,000, $30,000, and $40,000, respectively.

Required: Use a computer spreadsheet package.

A. Determine each partner's share of net income using alternative 1.
B. Determine each partner's share of net income using alternative 2.
C. Determine each partner's share of net income using alternative 3.
D. Determine each partner's share of net income using alternative 4.

CA13.2 LO 3 LO 4 Using the SEC's EDGAR database (**www.sec.gov/edgar**) find the following for five corporations:

A. Common and preferred stock the corporation is authorized to issue.
B. The par value of each class of stock.
C. The number of shares authorized, issued, and outstanding of each class of stock.
D. The amount of contributed capital.
E. The amount of reinvested earnings.
F. The number and dollar value of treasury shares held by the corporation.

Visit the text Online Learning Center at **www.mhhe.com/ainsworth6e** for additional problem material that accompanies this chapter.

CHAPTER FOURTEEN

14 Planning Debt Financing

Learning Objectives

LO 1 Describe and calculate the impact of a periodic payment note payable on the company's budgeted financial statements.

LO 2 Discuss and calculate the impact of a lump-sum payment note payable on the company's budgeted financial statements.

LO 3 Explain and calculate the impact of a periodic and lump-sum payment note payable on the company's budgeted financial statements.

In Chapter 13 we learned about the risks and rewards of equity versus debt financing and how the ownership structures of sole proprietorships, partnerships, and corporations impact a company's ability to raise money for the business entity. This chapter examines long-term debt financing and how companies plan for the impact of these long-term financing decisions. To begin, we examine the characteristics of financial instruments used to borrow funds, how market interest rates affect the cash inflows generated by these notes, and the sources of debt financing. Then we examine how debt and equity financing impact a company's plans to finance its long-term investments.

Debt finances a company's day-to-day operations and is often used to acquire the assets that provide the infrastructure that supports operations. In general, short-term, or current, liabilities, such as accounts payable, salaries payable, and trade notes payable, finance the daily operations of the company. Companies use long-term liabilities to finance the acquisition of long-term assets such as buildings, equipment, land, and patents that support their operations. The cash flows these assets generate over their useful lives make it possible to meet the obligations of the long-term debt used to finance their acquisition. Recall that a company must consider its business organization and strategy process when it makes debt financing decisions.

Debt Financing

Debt financing is a means for a company to obtain funds (cash), goods, and/or services in exchange for a liability to repay the borrowed funds. Typically, liabilities require the repayment of an amount of cash that is greater than the amount of the original obligation. From the borrower's point of view, this excess amount is interest expense and represents the cost of using borrowed funds. From the lender's point of view, this additional amount is interest revenue and is the return on the investment necessary to justify lending money to the company.

When long-term debt is issued, both the borrower and lender must be careful to formalize the terms of the debt. In corporations, the board of directors must approve the issuance of long-term debt. Lenders may place certain restrictions on the borrowing company called **covenants,** which they document in the debt agreement to protect the lenders' interest. For example, a lender may limit the amount of additional long-term debt the company can issue to provide the lender some assurance that the company's debt will not become too large and impair the company's ability to service its present debt commitments. In addition a lender may require that the borrower maintain certain ratios such as those discussed in Chapters 1, 2, and 13.

Understanding the cash flow obligations of debt instruments allows planners to match the debt instrument with the cash flows expected from the assets being acquired (see Chapter 12). As you know, notes are written promises of companies that borrow funds. Each note describes the cash flows the borrower, or **maker of the note,** is willing to pay in return for the use of the lender's, or **holder of the note's,** funds. The **face value of the note** indicates the amount that the note's maker will ultimately pay the note's holder. The **face rate on the note** determines the amount of cash interest the maker will periodically pay the holder of the note. The amount of cash raised from the issuance of the debt is called the **proceeds of the note.** The *actual* interest rate charged for the use of the proceeds of the note is called the **market, or effective, interest rate.**

Key point: The market (effective) rate may or may not be the face rate of interest printed on the note.

The market (effective) interest rate is negotiated between the borrower and the lender. The borrower wants the use of the funds at the lowest possible cost, while the lender wants the highest possible return for the risk assumed. For example, suppose our PC company, PCs to Go, needs to borrow $500,000 for a long-term project and is willing to pay 7 percent interest. Citibank is interested in making the loan but wants an 8 percent rate on the loan. If Citibank agrees to our terms, the market rate of interest would be 7 percent, but if we agree to Citibank's terms, the market rate of interest would be 8 percent. If both parties compromise and agree to 7.5 percent, then 7.5 percent would be the market rate of interest.

When choosing between available debt instruments, managers consider how the debt impacts the budgeted income statement (interest expense), statement of cash flows (initial receipt of cash and repayment of debt), and the remaining liability on the balance sheet **(carrying value of debt).** The impact on the financial statements may affect bonuses, tax liabilities, financial ratios, and other balanced scorecard goals and/or debt covenants so it is important to carefully plan both the amount and type of debt financing.

Long-Term Debt Instruments

When companies plan to use long-term debt financing, they typically select one of three basic types of notes. These notes are classified based on their promised cash flows and are described next. As we examine each of these notes we consider the impact of the note on the budgeted (pro forma) statement of cash flows, income statement, and balance sheet.

Periodic Payment (Installment) Note

A **periodic payment note** is a debt instrument that contains a promise to make a series of equal payments consisting of *both interest and principal* at equal time intervals over a specified time period. Typically these are called *installment notes.* Since we are paying both interest and principal after receiving the use of funds, this is a present value of an annuity problem. For example, assume our PC company, PCs to Go, plans to borrow $500,000 on January 1, 2011, by signing a note with a $500,000 face value and agreeing to repay the money semiannually over the next four years at an annual face rate of 7 percent. Note that with an installment note the face rate and the market rate of interest are the same. Since we need the money today, $500,000 (the face value) is the present value. The amount of the semiannual payments, $72,738.32, is determined as:

$$PV = 500{,}000;\ FV = 0;\ c = 2;\ n = 8;\ r = 7;\ \text{therefore: } ANN = 72{,}738.32$$

This means that PCs to Go would make eight payments of $72,738.32 each for a total of $581,906.56 over the life of the note. The difference between the total amount repaid ($581,906.56) and the face amount of the note ($500,000) is the *interest expense for the entire four-year period.* Because each payment that is made includes the interest for the last installment period, the remainder is repayment of the principal. (A monthly car payment is an example of an installment note.)

Let's see how this loan works. We know that PCs to Go will receive the present value of the note ($500,000) and the first cash payment of $72,738.32 will be due on June 30, 2011. Of the first payment, $17,500 will be for interest ($500,000 × 0.07 × 1/2) and the remainder ($55,238.32 = $72,738.32 − $17,500) will reduce the principal or carrying value of the note. Therefore, at the end of the first payment period, the new carrying value will be $444,761.68 ($500,000 − $55,238.32).

Exhibit 14.1 illustrates this note. Notice that the carrying value of the note decreases over time, the payment is the same over time, and the interest portion of the payment decreases while the principal portion of the note increases over time.

So, what happens in the second semiannual period? Our cash payment is the same, $72,738.32. But the interest is based on the new carrying value; therefore, our interest for the second semiannual period is $444,761.68 × 0.07 × 1/2 = $15,566.66. So our principal payment is $72,738.32 − $15,566.66 = $57,171.66. At the end of the second semiannual period, December 31, 2011, the carrying value would be $444,761.68 − $57,171.66 = $387,590.02.

How is this information reflected on the budgeted financial statements of PCs to Go? Assuming that PCs to Go prepares annual budgeted financial statements, the interest expense for the year (two semiannual periods) would be $33,066.66 ($17,500 + $15,566.66). On the annual budgeted statement of cash flows, PCs to Go would report a financing inflow of $500,000 and

EXHIBIT 14.1
Periodic Payment (Installment) Note Payable

Period	Payment	Interest	Principal	Carrying Value
1/1/11				$500,000.00
6/30/11	$72,738.32	$17,500.00	$55,238.32	$444,761.68
12/31/11	72,738.32	15,566.66	57,171.66	387,590.02
6/30/12	72,738.32	13,565.65	59,172.67	328,417.35
12/31/12	72,738.32	11,494.61	61,243.71	267,173.64
6/30/13	72,738.32	9,351.08	63,387.24	203,786.40
12/31/13	72,738.32	7,132.52	65,605.80	138,180.60
6/30/14	72,738.32	4,836.32	67,902.00	70,278.60
12/31/14	72,738.32	2,459.75	70,278.57	0.03*

*rounding

Using the same notation learned in Chapter 11 and applying it to the periodic payment note:

PV = proceeds
FV = 0
ANN = payment
r = market rate of interest
c = number of payments per year
n = total number of payments

two semiannual payments totaling $145,476.64.[1] Finally, the budgeted balance sheet would show the carrying value of the note at the end of the budgeting period, $387,590.02. The part of this carrying value that will be paid in 2012 will be shown as a current liability, while the remainder will be shown as a long-term liability. This distinction is important because it impacts ratios such as the current and quick ratios that are often used in debt covenants. The portion of the note that would be shown as a current liability on the budgeted balance sheet is $120,416.38 (principal payments for June 30 and December 31, 2012). Thus the long-term liability for this note would be $267,173.64 ($387,590.02 − $120,416.38).

Key Points for Periodic Payment (Installment) Notes:

1. *The initial carrying value of the note = proceeds = present value = face value.*
2. *The face rate of interest = market rate of interest.*
3. *The future value of the note is zero because we are paying back the face value of the note over its life.*
4. *Interest expense for a period is: carrying value × market rate × 1/c.*
5. *Payments are for interest and principal (face value) each period.*
6. *The carrying value of the note decreases over time as the principal (face value) is paid off.*

Lump-Sum Payment (Noninterest-Bearing) Note

A **lump-sum payment note** is a debt instrument that contains a promise to pay a specific amount of money at the end of a specific period of time. Lump-sum payment notes are often called *noninterest-bearing notes* because the note specifies only a face value and a due date. Thus the note does not have a face interest rate; it specifies only the amount the borrower *promises to pay back at a future date.* The face value of a noninterest-bearing note depends on the amount of money the borrower wants to use and the market interest rate the borrower and lender agree upon. With this type of note, the face value is the future value (amount owed at the end of the loan period).

Assume PCs to Go wants to borrow $500,000 on January 1, 2011, for four years from the Bank of America by issuing a noninterest-bearing note. To determine the face value of the note, assume that the bank and PCs to Go agree to a 7 percent market rate that is compounded semiannually. Since we need the money today, the $500,000 is the present value of the note. The face value of the note is calculated as follows:

$$PV = 500{,}000;\ c = 2;\ n = 8;\ r = 7;\ ANN = 0;\ \text{therefore: } FV = 658{,}404.52$$

This means that the Bank of America will loan us $500,000 if we promise to pay it $658,404.52 in four years. If we comply with the terms of the note, Bank of America will earn a 7 percent return, while we will incur 7 percent interest expense.

[1] Technically we should divide the cash flows into operating (interest) and financing (principal) but for planning purposes this distinction is not important so we defer this discussion to Chapter 15.

Let's see how this note works. On January 1, 2011, we receive the initial cash inflow from the proceeds of the note. Unlike the installment note, the cash we receive is not the same as the note's face value. The face value represents the only other cash flow associated with the note that occurs when we repay the bank on December 31, 2014. The difference between the two cash flows (the present value and the future value, or $658,404.52 − $500,000) is the interest incurred by PCs to Go over the four-year life of the note.

Exhibit 14.2 illustrates this note. Because interest is compounded semiannually, the first interest calculation on June 30, 2011, is $500,000 × 0.07 × 1/2 = $17,500. Since we make no periodic payments on this type of note, the interest is added to the carrying value of the note, so that the new carrying value on June 30, 2011, would be $517,500 ($500,000 + $17,500). Thus the interest for the second compounding period ending December 31, 2011, would be $517,500 × 0.07 × 1/2 = $18,112.50 and the resulting carrying value would be $535,612.50 ($517,500 + $18,112.50).

How is this information reported on the annual budgeted financial statements for PCs to Go? The interest expense for the year, $35,612.50 ($17,500 + $18,112.50), is disclosed on the budgeted income statement. On the budgeted statement of cash flows, we would show only a financing inflow of cash of $500,000 because we will not make any periodic payments with this type of note. The budgeted balance sheet on December 31, 2011, would report the note as a long-term liability of $535,612.50. In contrast to the installment note, no portion of the noninterest-bearing note is reported as a current liability because PCs to Go would not be required to pay any portion of the note's carrying value in the next fiscal year, 2012.

Let's examine the second year of the note's life. Interest on the note for the period ending June 30, 2012, would be $18,746.44 ($535,612.50 × 0.07 × 1/2), which would increase the carrying value of the note to $554,358.94 ($535,612.50 + $18,746.44). The June 30, 2012, carrying value, in turn, serves as the basis for determining the interest that would be incurred for the period ending December 31, 2012, $19,402.56 ($554,358.94 × 0.07 × 1/2). So total interest expense expected in 2012 would be $38,149 ($18,746.44 + $19,402.56) and the carrying value of the note at the end of 2012 is expected to be $573,761.50 ($554,358.94 + $19,402.56).

Using the same notation learned in Chapter 11 and applying it to the lump-sum payment note:

PV = proceeds
FV = face value repaid
ANN = 0
r = market rate of interest
c = number of interest periods per year
n = total number of interest periods

Again, the budgeted income statement would indicate the interest expense expected for 2012, $38,149, and the budgeted balance sheet would show the carrying value of the note expected at the end of 2012, $573,761.50. Nothing regarding this note would be reported on the budgeted statement of cash flows for 2012.

This type of note can be confusing because the borrower does not receive the $658,404.52 face value when the note is issued. *Care must be taken not to confuse the face value with the proceeds of the note.* Remember, the note merely specifies the cash flows promised by the note's maker. The cash proceeds of the note depend on the market rate of interest used to find the present value of the promised cash flows. In this case, the $500,000 of proceeds are the present value of the $658,404.52 promised in four years by the maker of the note assuming a 7 percent annual market rate that is compounded semiannually.

EXHIBIT 14.2
Lump-Sum Payment (Noninterest-Bearing) Note Payable

Period	Payment	Interest	CV Adjustment	Carrying Value
1/1/11				$500,000.00
6/30/11	$0.00	$17,500.00	$17,500.00	517,500.00
12/31/11	0.00	18,112.50	18,112.50	535,612.50
6/30/12	0.00	18,746.44	18,746.44	554,358.94
12/31/12	0.00	19,402.56	19,402.56	573,761.50
6/30/13	0.00	20,081.65	20,081.65	593,843.15
12/31/13	0.00	20,784.51	20,784.51	614,627.66
6/30/14	0.00	21,511.97	21,511.97	636,139.63
12/31/14	0.00	22,264.89	22,264.89	658,404.52

Key Points for Lump-Sum (Noninterest-Bearing) Notes:

1. *Initial carrying value of the note = proceeds = present value.*
2. *There is NO face rate of interest, only a market rate.*
3. *There are NO periodic payments.*
4. *The future value = face value of the note.*
5. *Interest expense for a period is: carrying value × market rate × 1/c.*
6. *The carrying value of the note increases over time as interest expense (not paid) is added to the carrying value.*

Periodic Payment and Lump-Sum Note

A **periodic payment and lump-sum note** is a debt instrument that combines periodic cash payments and a final lump-sum cash payment. It has a face rate of interest and a face value that indicates that the maker promises to make periodic cash interest payments *and* a lump-sum payment on the date the note matures. Because an interest rate (face rate) is printed on the note, this type of note is often referred to as an *interest-bearing note.* To determine the periodic cash payments, multiply *the face rate of interest by the face value of the note.* For example, suppose that on January 1, 2011, PCs to Go issues a $500,000, four-year note that has a face interest rate of 8 percent that is paid semiannually. The note is the maker's (PCs to Go) written promise to pay $20,000 ($500,000 × 0.08 × 1/2) every six months for four years, in addition to $500,000 at the end of the four years. Therefore, the maker of this note makes *two promises*—a promise to repay the face value ($500,000) of the note at the end of four years and a promise to pay interest ($20,000) every six months.

The face rate and face values are used to determine the cash flows promised by PCs to Go. But the amount of proceeds that PCs to Go receives for the note depends on the *market rate of interest at the time the note is issued.* The market rate of interest depends, in part, on the perceived riskiness of the borrower. When notes are prepared, the market rate and the face rate may be the same; but before the note is issued to the lender, the market rate may change. If the market rate increases, the lender would want the higher market rate; if the market rate decreases, the borrower would want the lower market rate. We will examine how the proceeds of a note are affected when (1) the market rate is greater than the face rate, (2) the market rate is less than the face rate, and (3) the market rate is equal to the face rate.

Market Rate Greater Than Face Rate

When the market rate of interest is *greater* than the face rate of interest, the proceeds of the note will be *less* than the face value of the note. Under these circumstances, the note will be issued at a **discount;** that is, the present value (cash proceeds) will be less than the face value, to make the note yield the market interest rate. To illustrate, assume that PCs to Go takes the $500,000 note described above to Citicorp. The banker thinks that, due to PCs to Go's level of risk, it needs a 9 percent interest rate before it can lend money. Remember, the note is already printed signifying an 8 percent face rate of interest. To make the 8 percent face rate note yield the desired 9 percent market rate, the bank determines the proceeds of the note by finding the present value of the two cash flows specified on the note using the 9 percent market rate. Remember, PCs to Go is making *two* promises:

$$FV = 500{,}000;\ ANN = 20{,}000;\ c = 2;\ n = 8;\ r = 9;\ \text{therefore: } PV = 483{,}510.28$$

This means that Citicorp will loan PCs to Go $483,510.28 and PCs to Go, in turn, will pay Citicorp $20,000 every six months *plus* $500,000 at the end of four years. The $16,489.72 discount ($500,000 − $483,510.28) represents the additional interest expense that PCs to Go will incur over the life of the note because the market rate of interest, 9 percent, is greater than the face rate of interest, 8 percent.

EXHIBIT 14.3
Periodic and Lump-Sum Payment Note Payable

Period	Payment	Interest	CV Adjustment	Carrying Value
1/1/11				$483,510.28
6/30/11	$20,000.00	$21,757.96	$1,757.96	485,268.24
12/31/11	20,000.00	21,837.07	1,837.07	487,105.31
6/30/12	20,000.00	21,919.74	1,919.74	489,025.05
12/31/12	20,000.00	22,006.13	2,006.13	491,031.18
6/30/13	20,000.00	22,096.40	2,096.40	493,127.58
12/31/13	20,000.00	22,190.74	2,190.74	495,318.32
6/30/14	20,000.00	22,289.32	2,289.32	497,607.64
12/31/14	20,000.00	22,392.34	2,392.34	499,999.98*

*rounding

Let's see how this note works by referring to Exhibit 14.3. On January 1, 2011, PCs to Go will receive the proceeds of the note, $483,510.28, which is the present value of the two cash flows promised by PCs to Go at the market rate of 9 percent. In exchange for this loan, PCs to Go has promised to make eight semiannual payments of $20,000 starting June 30, 2011, and a lump-sum payment of $500,000 on December 31, 2014. The interest incurred over the life of the note is $176,480.72, which is the difference between the proceeds of the note and the total amount repaid on the loan ($500,000 + [8 × $20,000] = $660,000). As you can see in Exhibit 14.3, this interest is allocated over the life of the note as we discuss below.

On June 30, 2011, the first payment will be made for $20,000. However, the interest incurred for this period is $21,757.96 ($483,510.28 × 0.09 × 1/2). The difference between the two, $1,757.96, increases the carrying value of the note to $485,268.24. Why? Because the cash payment is less than the interest incurred during this time period, the additional interest is added to the carrying value and, thus, in effect, paid at the end of the note's life. (Recall we are paying back more than we initially received.) On December 31, 2011, this process will be repeated. The cash payment will remain at $20,000. The interest incurred for the period will be determined as carrying value × market rate × $1/c$ (as always) so the interest is $21,837.07 ($485,268.24 × 0.09 × 1/2). The difference between the payment and the interest, $1,837.07, will increase the carrying value of the note to $487,105.31 ($485,268.24 + $1,837.07).

On the budgeted income statement for the fiscal 2011 period, PCs to Go would report interest expense of $43,595.03 ($21,757.96 + $21,837.07). The budgeted statement of cash flows would show a financing inflow of $483,510.28 and an operating cash outflow of $40,000. This outflow is operating because the cash is paid for interest only. The budgeted balance sheet at the end of the fiscal 2011 period would show the carrying value of the note, $487,105.31, as a long-term liability.

Let's look at 2012. Interest for the six months ending June 30, 2012, would be:

$$\$487{,}105.31 \times 0.09 \times 1/2 = \$21{,}919.74$$

The cash payment is still $20,000. So the carrying value adjustment is $1,919.74 ($21,919.74 − $20,000). The new carrying value on June 30, 2012, would be $489,025.05. So, the interest for the six months ending December 31, 2012, would be:

$$\$489{,}025.05 \times 0.09 \times 1/2 = \$22{,}006.13$$

The cash payment is $20,000. The carrying value adjustment is $2,006.13, and the December 31, 2012, carrying value would be $491,031.18 ($489,025.05 + $2,006.13), reported as a long-term liability.

Key Points for Periodic and Lump-Sum Payment (Bonds) Notes When Market Rate > Face Rate:

1. *Initial carrying value of the note = proceeds = present value.*
2. *The payment (ANN) = face value × face rate ×* $1/c$.

3. *Face value of the note = future value.*
4. *Interest expense for a period is: carrying value × market rate × 1/c.*
5. *The difference between the interest expense on the income statement and the interest payment on the statement of cash flows is the adjustment to the carrying value of the note on the balance sheet.*
6. *The carrying value of the note* increases *over time as the adjustment (see #5) is added to the carrying value.*

Market Rate Less Than Face Rate

Discounts and premiums
Think of discounts as being "less than" as in the "proceeds are less than the face value of the note." Likewise, think of premiums as being "more than" as in the "proceeds are more than the face value of the note."

When the market rate of interest is *less* than the face rate of interest on the note, the proceeds of the note will be *greater* than the face value of the note. This means that the note is issued at a *premium* to make the note yield the market rate of interest, which is less than the face rate of interest. A **premium,** then, is the amount that the present value (cash proceeds) of a note exceeds its face value because the market rate of interest is less than the face rate of interest.

To illustrate, assume that PCs to Go takes the same $500,000 note to Citicorp when the market rate of interest is 7 percent. In this case, PCs to Go will not incur 8 percent because the market rate of interest is 7 percent. To determine the proceeds of this note, the lender finds the present value of the two promised cash flows using the 7 percent market rate; that is, the promise to pay $20,000 every six months and the promise to pay $500,000 in four years. We know:

$$FV = \$500{,}000;\ ANN = 20{,}000;\ c = 2;\ n = 8;\ r = 7;\ \text{therefore: } PV = 517{,}184.89$$

This means that Citicorp will loan PCs to Go $517,184.89 and PCs to Go, in turn, will pay Citicorp $20,000 every six months plus $500,000 at the end of four years. But why would Citicorp be willing to give PCs to Go more than the face value of the note? The answer lies in the difference between the market rate of interest and the face rate of interest. The $17,184.89 ($517,184.89 − $500,000) represents the amount PCs to Go's interest will be reduced over the life of the note because the market rate of interest, 7 percent, is less than the face rate of interest, 8 percent. In other words, PCs to Go will get to use $517,184.89 and repay only $500,000 at the maturity date as a way to get the 8 percent face rate to yield the 7 percent market rate that both Citicorp and PCs to Go agree is appropriate.

Exhibit 14.4 shows how this note works. On January 1, 2011, PCs to Go would receive the proceeds of the note, $517,184.89, which is the present value of the two cash flows promised by PCs to Go at the agreed upon market value of 7 percent. Recall that these two cash flows are the eight semiannual payments of $20,000 plus the lump-sum payment of $500,000 promised on December 31, 2014. The interest incurred over the life of the note is $142,815.11, which is the difference between the proceeds of the note, $517,184.89, and

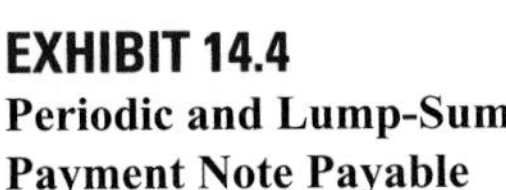

EXHIBIT 14.4
Periodic and Lump-Sum Payment Note Payable

Period	Payment	Interest	CV Adjustment	Carrying Value
1/1/11				$517,184.89
6/30/11	$20,000.00	$18,101.47	$1,898.53	515,286.36
12/31/11	20,000.00	18,035.02	1,964.98	513,321.38
6/30/12	20,000.00	17,966.25	2,033.75	511,287.63
12/31/12	20,000.00	17,895.07	2,104.93	509,182.70
6/30/13	20,000.00	17,821.39	2,178.61	507,004.09
12/31/13	20,000.00	17,745.14	2,254.86	504,749.23
6/30/14	20,000.00	17,666.22	2,333.78	502,415.45
12/31/14	20,000.00	17,584.54	2,415.46	499,999.99*

*rounding

the total amount PCs to Go will repay Citicorp, \$660,000 (\$500,000 + [8 × \$20,000]). As Exhibit 14.4 indicates, the total interest is allocated over the life of the note as we discuss below.

On June 30, 2011, the first payment of \$20,000 will be made. However, interest incurred for this six-month period is only \$18,101.47 (\$517,184.89 × 0.07 × 1/2). The difference between the cash payment and the interest incurred, \$1,898.53, is the adjustment to the carrying value (a decrease this time) necessary because the market rate of interest and the face rate of interest are different. On June 30, 2011, the new carrying value would be \$515,286.36 (\$517,184.89 − \$1,898.53). On December 31, this process would be repeated. The cash payment would be \$20,000. But the interest incurred would be determined as the new carrying value × market rate × $1/c$, or \$515,286.36 × 0.07 × 1/2 = \$18,035.02. Again, the difference, in this time period \$1,964.98, will decrease the carrying value to \$513,321.38 at December 31, 2011.

How will the impact of this note be reported on the budgeted financial statements for the year 2011? The interest expense shown on the budgeted income statement would be \$36,136.49 (\$18,101.47 + \$18,035.02). On the statement of cash flows, PCs to Go would report estimated cash inflows from financing activities of \$517,184.89 and estimated cash outflows from operating activities of \$40,000. Lastly, on the budgeted balance sheet, we would report the carrying value on December 31, 2011, of \$513,321.38 as a long-term liability.

Now that we have completed these calculations a few times, let's step back and examine this process a bit further. How does this compare to the previous situation when the market rate was greater than the face rate? In that circumstance, we incurred interest expense that was greater than the amount of cash paid, so we added the difference between the interest expense incurred and the cash paid to the carrying value of the debt. In this case, the amount of interest incurred is less than the amount of cash paid, so we deduct the difference between the cash paid and the interest incurred from the carrying value of the debt. Another way to look at this is to remember that we received the present value but we will repay the future value at the end of the note's life. If the present value (initial carrying value) is less than the future value, it must increase over the life of the note as in the previous example. If the present value (initial carrying value) is greater than the future value, it must decrease over the life of the note as in this example.

Using the same notation learned in Chapter 11 and applying it to the periodic and lump-sum payment note:

PV = proceeds
FV = face value repaid
ANN = payment
r = market rate of interest
c = number of payments per year
n = total number of payments

Key Points for Periodic and Lump-Sum Payment (Bonds) Notes When Market Rate < Face Rate:

1. *Initial carrying value of the note = proceeds = present value.*
2. *The payment* (ANN) = *face value × face rate × 1/*c.
3. *Face value of the note = future value.*
4. *Interest expense for a period is: carrying value × market rate × 1/*c.
5. *The difference between the interest expense on the income statement and the interest payment on the statement of cash flows is the adjustment to the carrying value of the note on the balance sheet.*
6. *The carrying value of the note* decreases *over time as the adjustment (see #5) is deducted from the carrying value.*

Market Rate Equal to Face Rate

When the market rate of interest is the same as the face rate, the proceeds of the note will be the same as the face value of the note. To illustrate, assume that PCs to Go took the same \$500,000 note to Citicorp when the market rate is 8 percent. We know:

$$FV = 500{,}000;\ ANN = 20{,}000;\ c = 2;\ n = 8;\ r = 8;\ \text{therefore: } PV = 500{,}000$$

EXHIBIT 14.5
Periodic and Lump-Sum Payment Note Payable

Period	Payment	Interest	CV Adjustment	Carrying Value
1/1/11				$500,000.00
6/30/11	$20,000.00	$20,000.00	$0.00	500,000.00
12/31/11	20,000.00	20,000.00	0.00	500,000.00
6/30/12	20,000.00	20,000.00	0.00	500,000.00
12/31/12	20,000.00	20,000.00	0.00	500,000.00
6/30/13	20,000.00	20,000.00	0.00	500,000.00
12/31/13	20,000.00	20,000.00	0.00	500,000.00
6/30/14	20,000.00	20,000.00	0.00	500,000.00
12/31/14	20,000.00	20,000.00	0.00	500,000.00

No premium or discount exists because the face rate and the market rate of interest are the same and, therefore, the *present value of the note's promised cash flows is equal to the note's face value.* On the budgeted statement of cash flows we would show a cash payment of $20,000. (An initial cash inflow of $500,000 is shown on the first period's budgeted statement of cash flows.) On the budgeted income statement we would show interest expense of $20,000 ($500,000 carrying value × 0.08 market rate × 1/2) every period. Since the cash paid for interest is the same as the interest expense, the carrying value shown on the budgeted balance sheet will not change. Exhibit 14.5 shows this note.

Enhance Your Understanding

On the budgeted statement of cash flows, are the cash flows associated with the notes classified as operating, financing, or investing cash flows?

Answer: The initial inflow of cash is financing. Interest payments are operating and principal payments are financing.

Comparison of the Three Types of Notes

When selecting a debt instrument to finance a project, the financial planner should consider the impact on the company's budgeted financial statements and try to match the cash outflows of the debt instrument to the cash inflows expected from the project being financed (Chapter 12). For example, if the capital budgeting analysis indicates that the project will not yield any cash inflows for the first five years, the company might consider a noninterest-bearing note since it does not require any periodic payments. On the other hand, if the capital budgeting analysis indicates small cash inflows throughout the project and a large cash inflow at the end of the project, the company might consider a periodic and lump-sum payment note.

In addition, financial planners should consider the impact of the proposed debt financing on the income statement since that impacts the amount of taxes paid and the amount of bonuses based on income. In addition, the company may need to maintain certain ratios such as return on equity that are impacted by the interest expense. Finally the impact on the balance sheet (carrying value) must be considered if, for example, covenants require a certain debt-to-equity ratio. Exhibit 14.6 summarizes the impact of the three types of notes on the budgeted financial statements.

If the company expects to have a lot of financing activity during the period, it might prepare a separate financing budget that would show the sources and amounts of financing expected during the period. Another option is to prepare a capital resources budget that would

EXHIBIT 14.6
Budgeted Financial Statements and Notes Payable

	Income Statement Interest Expense	Statement of Cash Flows, Inflows, and Outflows	Balance Sheet Carrying Value
Installment Note (Periodic Payment Note)	$CV \times FR \times$ Time Decreases over life of note	Inflow = *PV* Outflow: Constant payment over life; No lump-sum payment	Decreases over life of note by amount of principal payment
Noninterest-Bearing Note (Lump-Sum Payment Note)	$CV \times MR \times$ Time Increases over life of note	Inflow = *PV* Outflow = *FV* No periodic payment	Increases over life of note by the amount of interest expense
Periodic and Lump-Sum Payment Note at Discount	$CV \times MR \times$ Time Increases over life of note	Inflow = *PV* Outflow: Constant payment over life; *FV* at end	Increases over life of note by the difference between interest expense and cash payment
Periodic and Lump-Sum Payment Note at Premium	$CV \times MR \times$ Time Decreases over life of note	Inflow = *PV* Outflow: Constant payment over life; *FV* at end	Decreases over life of note by the difference between cash payment and interest expense

Legend:
PV = present value
FV = future value
FR = face rate
MR = market rate

show both the investments expected (Chapter 12) and the financing for those investments (Chapters 13 and 14).

Sources of Debt Financing

To this point we have discussed the characteristics of debt financing. Now we will examine the sources of debt financing available to companies. Long-term debt financing is available from a variety of sources that are classified as nonpublic and public. The nonpublic sources include individuals and institutions, such as banks and other financial institutions, other companies, and insurance companies. The public source of debt financing is the bond market.

Nonpublic Funding

Nonpublic debt financing occurs when a company enters into an agreement with a person or institution to borrow funds. For most businesses, nonpublic debt financing is the most common source of long-term debt. While companies sometimes approach individuals to borrow funds, banks and other financial institutions are the most common nonpublic sources of debt financing because they are in business specifically to lend money and want to make loans to qualified companies and individuals. Insurance companies are also a source of long-term debt financing because they need to generate a return on the premiums they receive from their policyholders.

Companies may use any of the three types of notes described earlier—periodic payment notes, lump-sum payment notes, and periodic payment and lump-sum notes—to acquire financing. The form of the note the company plans to use depends on the cash inflows generated after the borrowed funds are invested and the impact of the note on the budgeted financial statements. In addition to describing the face value of the note, the face rate of interest, if any, and its repayment period, the note may include covenants that protect the claims of the holder of the note.

FAST FACT

Commercial paper is a type of debt instrument issued by large, creditworthy companies. Commercial paper is typically issued in denominations of $100,000 and is typically sold to other businesses, insurance companies, pension plans, and mutual funds. Commercial paper is short-term debt with maturities less than 270 days (five months is the average).

Collateral

A typical means of protecting creditors' claims is to require the borrower to use some assets as collateral for the note. **Collateral** is an asset or group of assets specifically named in a debt agreement to which the creditor has claim if the borrower fails to comply with the terms of the note. For example, for most car loans, the car that is acquired is collateral for the note. If the car buyer fails to make the installment payments, the lending institution can repossess the car and sell it to satisfy the debt. In most cases, the company borrowing the money cannot dispose of the collateral unless it reaches an agreement with the lending institution about paying off the loan or providing another asset as collateral. A **mortgage** is a long-term note that is secured with real estate, such as land or buildings, as collateral.

Leases

In recent years, extensive use has been made of leasing as another way for a company to secure the use of an asset. A **lease** is an agreement to convey the use of a tangible asset from one party to another in return for rental payments. The agreement usually covers a specified period of time. It is, in effect, a contract whereby the owner (the lessor) agrees to rent an asset to another party (the lessee) in return for rental payments. There are a wide variety of lease agreements but, in general, they fall into two classifications: operating leases and capital leases.

Typically, an **operating lease** is a rental agreement for a period of time that is substantially shorter than the economic life of the leased asset. When a lessee (user) company acquires such a substantial interest in the leased property that the lessee company, for all practical purposes, owns the asset, there is recognition of the acquisition of an asset and a related liability by the lessee. This type of lease is called a **capital lease.** A lease classified as a capital lease recognizes the substance of the economic event over the legal form of the transaction. The economic substance of the lease transaction, the lessee's control of the asset for its useful life, takes precedence over legal requirements (the formal transfer of the title from the seller to the buyer) used to determine when the transfer of ownership occurs. When a company enters into a capital lease, it recognizes the leased property as an asset and reflects the related liability incurred. The value of the asset is the present value of the lease payments, using the company's market rate of interest.

To illustrate a capital lease, let's assume that PCs to Go signs a five-year lease on equipment that has an estimated useful life of five years. PCs to Go agrees to pay $50,000 today and $55,481.95 per year, for five years, starting one year from today. PCs to Go has entered into a capital lease because in economic substance it has purchased the equipment, since the lease term is the same as the life of the equipment. On the date it signs the lease, PCs to Go will have a long-term liability of $200,000, which is the present value of the $55,481.95, five-payment annuity at PCs to Go's market rate of interest, 12 percent. PCs to Go also would recognize a leased asset in the amount of $250,000, which is the present value of the lease payments, $200,000, plus the initial $50,000 payment. This liability is a periodic payment note, described earlier in the chapter.

OF INTEREST Derivatives

Derivatives are financial products whose value is based on an asset. Derivatives are a means for a risk-adverse investor to move risk (and the expected rewards) to a risk-seeking investor. Although derivatives are complicated, the following "Hen House" story illustrates three common types of derivatives.

1. Futures Contracts

Gail, the owner of Healthy Hen Farms (HEN), is worried about the volatility of the chicken market with all the sporadic reports of bird flu coming out of the east. Gail wants a way to protect her business against another spell of bad news. Gail meets with an investor who enters into a *futures contract* with her. The investor agrees to pay $30 per bird when the birds are ready for slaughter, say, in six months time, regardless of the market price. If, at that time, the price is above $30, the investor will get the benefit as he or she will be able to buy the birds for less than market cost and sell them onto the market at a higher price for a gain.

If the price goes below $30, then Gail will be receiving the benefit because she will be able to sell her birds for more than the current market price, or what she would have gotten for the birds in the open market. By entering into a *futures contract,* Gail is protected from price changes in the market, as she has locked in a price of $30 per bird. She may lose out if the price flies up to $50 per bird on a mad cow scare, but she will be protected if the price falls to $10 on news of a bird flu outbreak.

2. Swapping

Gail has decided that it's time to take Healthy Hen Farms to the next level. She has already acquired all the smaller farms near her and is looking at opening her own processing plant. She tries to get more financing, but the lender, Lenny, rejects her. The reason is that Gail financed her takeovers of the other farms through a massive variable-rate loan and the lender is worried that, if interest rates rise, Gail won't be able to pay her debts. He tells Gail that he will only lend to her if she can convert the loan to a fixed rate. Unfortunately, her other lenders refuse to change her current loan terms because they are hoping interest rates will increase too.

Gail gets a lucky break when she meets Sam, the owner of a chain of restaurants. Sam has a fixed-rate loan about the same size as Gail's and he wants to convert it to a variable-rate loan because he hopes interest rates will decline in the future. For similar reasons, Sam's lenders won't change the terms of the loan. Gail and Sam decide to *swap loans.* They work out a deal by which Gail's payments go toward Sam's loan and his go toward Gail's loan. Although the names on the loans haven't changed, *their contract allows them both to get the type of loan they want.* This is a bit risky for both of them because if one of them defaults or goes bankrupt, the other will be snapped back into his or her old loan, which may require a payment for which neither Gail of Sam may be prepared.

3. Options

Years later, Gail and Sam are both looking forward to retirement. Over the years, Sam bought quite a few shares of Gail's company, HEN. In fact, he has more than $100,000 invested in the company. Sam is getting nervous because he is worried that some shock, another case of bird flu for example, might wipe out a huge chunk of his retirement money. Sam starts looking for someone to take the risk off his shoulders. Lenny, financier extraordinaire and an active *writer of options,* agrees to give him a hand.

Lenny outlines a deal in which Sam pays Lenny a *fee to for the right (but not the obligation) to sell* Lenny the HEN shares in a year's time at their current price of $25 per share. If the share prices plummet, Lenny protects Sam from the loss of his retirement savings. Lenny is OK because he has been collecting the fees and can handle the risk. This is called a *put option,* but it can be done in reverse by someone agreeing to buy a stock in the future at a fixed price (called a *call option*).

Source: www.investorpedia.com. Author: Andrew Beattie

Public Funding: Bonds

Bonds are long-term debt instruments issued by corporations to raise money from the public. Bonds usually take the form of periodic payment and lump-sum notes. However, rather than being in the form of one note, a **bond issue** typically consists of a group of $1,000 face value notes (bonds) with a specified face interest rate, often paid semiannually, that mature in 10 or more years. For example, a $5,000,000, 10-year bond issue with a 10 percent face interest rate that is paid semiannually consists of 5,000 bonds, each with a $1,000 face value. Each $1,000 bond has a 10-year life and a 10 percent face interest rate paid semiannually. These terms would be printed on a note called a **bond certificate.**

As with any note, the 5,000 bond certificates are the corporation's promise to pay the bondholders the cash flows indicated on the bond certificate. In this example, a person holding one bond would receive $50 ($1,000 × 0.1 × 1/2) every six months for 10 years and $1,000 at the end of 10 years. In total, the corporation promises to pay $250,000 ($5,000,000 × 0.1 × 1/2) cash interest every six months and $5,000,000 at the end of 10 years. The amount of cash the corporation can borrow by issuing bonds, like any other note payable, is based on the present value of the promised cash flows using the market interest rate at the time of issuance.

Corporations issue bonds because individual financial institutions are unwilling or unable to accept the risk of making very large long-term loans to one corporation. However, because individual bonds are relatively small investing units, many investors can lend funds to the corporation. This enhances the company's ability to borrow large amounts of funds. Individual investors, banks, insurance companies, and other corporations can lend the corporation money by acquiring as many bonds as they deem prudent. The bond contract is called a **bond indenture.** This contract specifies the amount of the bond issue, the life of the bond, the face value of each bond, and the face interest rate of the bond issue. The bond indenture also may have covenants that place restrictions on the issuing corporation. Many covenants limit the amount of long-term debt a corporation can have.

Normally, the corporation's board of directors must give formal approval before the company can issue bonds. In cases where the bonds are publicly traded on organized bond exchanges, the Securities and Exchange Commission also must approve the bond issue. Once the corporation obtains all of the necessary approvals, it can offer the bonds to the public. An underwriter at an investment banking company typically handles the initial bond issuance. The investment banking company can buy the entire bond issue from the corporation and then resell the bonds to the public. However, if the investment banking company does not want to underwrite (buy) the entire bond issue, it can sell the bonds and take a percentage of the proceeds of the bond issue as a commission before remitting the cash to the corporation. In some cases, the company issuing bonds sells them directly to specific financial institutions or individuals without using an underwriter. This is called a *private (direct) placement of a bond issue.*

Regardless of whether a bond issue is underwritten, sold on a commission basis, or privately placed, the corporation obtains the use of money from a bond sale just as if it borrowed money from a bank in a traditional lending process. However, because the lender is the public, and because investment bankers must convince a variety of potential lenders to loan the corporation money, the process of borrowing the money by issuing bonds takes on the form of a sale. The buyers are acquiring, and the corporation is selling, the right to a set of future cash flows promised in each bond.

Selling the bond issue and transferring the proceeds of the sale to the corporation take place in an initial issue market. After the bonds are sold in the initial issue market, they are bought either from another individual, through bond brokers, or in a bond market like the New York Bond Exchange, called the *secondary bond market.* This secondary market allows bondholders to sell their bonds and receive cash from their investment without waiting for the bonds to mature.

Bond prices in the secondary market are quoted as a percentage of the face value of the bond. For example, a $1,000 bond with a price of 98 1/2 is selling for 98.5 percent of its $1,000 face value, or $985. A bond quoted at a price of 101 3/4 is selling for $1,017.50, or 101.75 percent of its $1,000 face value.

Bond Provisions

Although the contractual arrangements of bonds vary greatly, we describe bond issues in terms of how their provisions relate to ownership, repayment, and security. Each bond may have several of the following provisions. These provisions are important when planning to issue bonds because the provisions of the bond impact investors' assessment of the risk of the bond issue, which in turn impacts the market interest rate of the bond issue.

Ownership Provisions

Registered bonds are numbered and made payable in the name of the bondholder. The issuing company or its appointed agent maintains a list, called the bond register, of the individuals or institutions that own the bonds. If a bond changes ownership, it is endorsed on the back and sent to the registrar for recording and reissue, and the issuing company is notified of that change. Interest on these bonds is generally paid by a check made payable to the registered owner on the interest date.

Bearer bonds are made payable to the bearer or person who has physical possession of the bond. Interest is paid by means of coupons attached to the bond. Each coupon is dated and has a dollar value shown on it. The number of coupons and the amount on each coupon depend on the face rate of interest on the bond and the frequency of interest payments during the year. For example, a 10-year, $1,000 bearer bond with a 10 percent face rate that is paid semiannually has 20 $50 coupons attached to it ($1,000 × 0.1 × 1/2). On the date printed on the coupon, the coupon is detached from the bond and deposited in a bank in the same way a check is deposited. Bearer bonds are sometimes referred to as *coupon bonds* due to their interest payment procedures. While bearer bonds still exist in the secondary market, the 1984 Tax Reform Act prohibited any further issuance of bearer bonds due to the difficulty the IRS had in identifying the interest income received by the bearers. These bonds were also susceptible to theft because possession is proof of ownership.

Repayment Provisions

Callable bonds give the company issuing the bonds the right to buy them back before the maturity date at a specified price. Corporations use the call feature when they want to ensure the retirement of all or part of their bond issue. The call feature specifies the dates on which the debtor company may call, or buy back, a bond. If a bond has a call feature, the bond indenture must also state the price (usually expressed as a percentage of the face value) that the company will pay for the bonds on those dates. For example, if a $1,000 bond has a call price of 105, the issuing company can buy the bond back at $1,050, or 105 percent of the bond's face value ($1,000 × 1.05). Calling the bonds in for redemption is at the option of the debtor company, and the bond owner must surrender the securities for the call price; therefore, the call price is always greater than the face value of the bond. When planning for the repayment of the bond issue, the call price gives the issuing company more flexibility by creating another option to retire the bond issue.

Convertible bonds allow bondholders to exchange their bonds for common or preferred stock. The bond indenture describes both the time at which the conversion may take place and the number of shares of stock that the bondholder can obtain. The privilege of converting the bonds into other specific securities rests with the bondholder. Once the bonds are converted to common or preferred stock, the bonds no longer exist, and the company is no longer responsible for the cash flows promised by the bond. Convertible bonds generally have lower market interest rates because conversion gives the investors a second option that could generate higher cash flows than those promised by the bond. However, when planning to use the conversion feature, the issuing company must consider whether the additional shares issued upon conversion will dilute the existing shareholders' interest in the company.

Bondholders only convert bonds into common stock if the stock has the potential of generating a greater return than the bond. For example, suppose a $1,000, 12 percent bond has a 50-to-1 conversion ratio; that is, when the bond is converted, the bondholder will receive 50 shares of common stock for each bond converted. If the price of the common stock is $10, the bondholder is unlikely to convert the bond, because the value of the stock received upon conversion will be only $500 ($10 × 50). However, if the common stock price rises to $40 per share, the bondholder probably would convert the bond because the value of the converted stock ($2,000) is greater than the value of the bond.

A **serial bond** is a bond issue that has specified portions of the bond issue coming due periodically over the life of the bond issue. For example, a $20 million, 20-year bond that has $5 million of its face value maturing every 5 years over its 20-year life is a serial bond. This type of bond is useful when planned cash flows from the bond-financed project are sufficient to repay the principal earlier in the life of the bond issue.

Security Provisions

Secured bonds have some part of the issuing corporation's assets serving as security for the loan. Quite often these bonds are secured by a mortgage on the corporation's real estate (buildings or land), in which case they may properly be called **mortgage bonds.** The object of the security feature is to assure bondholders that there are specific assets to which they have first claim in the event that the bond indenture is violated.

Unsecured bonds do not have any specific assets pledged as security against their repayment. Rather, their security rests on the general creditworthiness of the issuing company. Bondholders of unsecured bonds are general creditors of the company just like the accounts payable creditors. Unsecured bonds are usually called **debenture bonds.** Most bond issues are of this type.

Subordinated bonds are unsecured bonds whose rights to repayment are ranked after, or subordinated to, some other person or group of creditors. Subordinated bonds are unsecured debts that are usually the last obligation the company pays in the event the company is liquidated. Their claims do, however, continue to rank ahead of the owners' claims.

Now that we have examined the planning process for investing and financing decisions, we put these activities together in a comprehensive example so that we can examine how investing decisions impact financing decisions. In addition, the business organization and strategy process impacts this capital resource process.

Comprehensive Example: Chapters 12 through 14

PCs to Go has the opportunity to invest in equipment that will allow it to expand its product line. PCs to Go estimates that the initial cost to purchase and install the equipment will be $100,000. It further estimates that the net cash inflows after taxes would be $26,000 each year. The equipment is expected to last five years, at which time it will be discarded at an after-tax cost of $5,000. PCs to Go will depreciate the equipment uniformly over its useful life. Assume that PCs to Go uses a 15 percent hurdle rate and is subject to a 30 percent tax rate. The first question is whether PCs to Go should invest in the new equipment. Let's complete a capital budgeting analysis. We know that $c = 1$, $n = 5$, and $r = 15$.

Initial investment	$(100,000)
Cash inflows (after tax):	
26,000 = *ANN; FV* = 0; *PV* =	87,156
Tax shield:	
100,000/5 = 20,000 (depreciation)	
20,000 × 0.3 = 6,000 = *ANN; FV* = 0; *PV* =	20,113
Disposal cost:	
FV = 5,000; *ANN* = 0; *PV* =	(2,486)
NPV	$ 4,783

Based on our capital budgeting decision it appears that this is an acceptable project because the NPV indicates that the expected return given the projected cash flows will be greater than the cost of capital or hurdle rate. Therefore, PCs to Go needs to raise $100,000 today.

The second question is how should PCs to Go finance this project? Assume that PCs to Go estimates that the market interest rate is 8 percent, so it opts to borrow money because the net present value is positive using a 15 percent hurdle rate. Thus, if the project works out as planned, the project will earn more than 15 percent. Since the company estimates it can borrow at 8 percent, the additional return will increase the company's return on owners' equity. In addition, since PCs to Go is a relatively new company (recall we created it in Chapter 6) management does not believe that issuing additional shares of common stock is possible at this time. Thus PCs to Go decides to borrow rather than issue additional shares of stock. Assume that PCs to Go decides to borrow $100,000 that it can repay over five years. The bank, after evaluating PCs to Go's risk, determines a market rate of interest of 7 percent.

The final question is which type of note should PCs to Go use to finance this project. For each option, we examine the budgeted financial statements over the life of the project.

Option 1 Obtain a five-year annual-payment installment note from the bank. With this type of note, the present value is the face value. The periodic payments made throughout the life of the note pay the interest plus the principal; thus, at the end of the life of the note, the future value is zero. Therefore,

$$PV = 100{,}000;\ c = 1;\ n = 5;\ FV = 0;\ r = 7;\ \text{therefore: } ANN = \$24{,}389.07$$

With this option PCs to Go receives $100,000 today and pays $24,389.07 annually for five years. Exhibit 14.7 illustrates this note. Based on this information we know our annual cash outflows will be $24,389.07. Our annual interest expense will decrease over the life of the loan and our liability will decrease over the life of the loan.

Option 2 Obtain a noninterest-bearing note with annual compounding. With this option, PCs to Go will not make any payments during the five-year period but will pay the face value of the note at the end of five years. Since PCs to Go needs $100,000 today, we know the present value and we need to determine the future value of this note (recall this is also the face value).

$$PV = 100{,}000;\ c = 1;\ n = 5;\ ANN = 0;\ r = 7;\ \text{therefore: } FV = 140{,}255.17$$

With this option PCs to Go receives $100,000 today and pays $140,255.17 in five years. Exhibit 14.8 illustrates this note. Based on this information we know there will not be any annual cash outflow, but we will make a final payment of $140,255.17 at the end of five years. Our interest expense and our liability will both increase over the life of the loan.

Option 3 Issue bonds with a face rate of 8 percent (recall this is the rate that PCs to Go estimated). Therefore, it prepares its promissory papers using a face rate of 8 percent paid annually. As it turns out when PCs to Go goes to the bank, it obtains a market rate of interest of 7 percent. So PCs to Go will receive more than the face value because the face rate of interest is more than the market rate of interest. PCs to Go will make interest payments of $8,000 ($100,000 × 0.08 × 1) annually and pay $100,000 at the end of five years. The amount received is:

$$FV = 100{,}000;\ ANN = 8{,}000;\ c = 1;\ n = 5;\ r = 7;\ \text{therefore: } PV = 104{,}100.20$$

With this option PCs to Go will receive $104,100.20 today and make annual payments of $8,000, with a final payment of $100,000 in five years. Exhibit 14.9 illustrates this note. Based on this information we know that our annual payment will be $8,000 and we must make a final payment of $100,000 at the end of five years. Our interest expense and our liability will decrease over the life of this loan.

EXHIBIT 14.7
Installment Note Payable

Period	Payment	Interest	CV Adjustment	Carrying Value
				$100,000.00
1	$24,389.07	$7,000.00	$17,389.07	$82,610.93
2	24,389.07	5,782.77	18,606.30	64,004.63
3	24,389.07	4,480.32	19,908.75	44,095.88
4	24,389.07	3,086.71	21,302.36	22,793.52
5	24,389.07	1,595.55	22,793.52	0.00

EXHIBIT 14.8
Noninterest-Bearing Note Payable

Period	Payment	Interest	CV Adjustment	Carrying Value
				$100,000.00
1	$0.00	$7,000.00	$7,000.00	107.000.00
2	0.00	7,490.00	7,490.00	114,490.00
3	0.00	8,014.30	8,014.30	122,504.30
4	0.00	8,575.30	8,575.30	131,079.60
5	0.00	9,175.57	9,175.57	140,255.17

EXHIBIT 14.9
Bonds Payable

Period	Payment	Interest	CV Adjustment	Carrying Value
				$104,100.20
1	$8,000.00	$7,287.01	$712.99	103,387.21
2	8,000.00	7,237.10	762.90	102,624.32
3	8,000.00	7,183.70	816.30	101,808.02
4	8,000.00	7,126.56	873.44	100,934.58
5	8,000.00	7,065.42	934.58	100,000.00

So which option should PCs to Go choose? Exhibit 14.10 compares these three notes. The installment note requires the largest annual payment of the three notes. The noninterest-bearing note shows the greatest interest expense of the three notes. The bonds indicate the most constant liability of the three notes. Unlike the other two, the installment note will impact current and quick ratios during years one, two, and three.

Since we have no information regarding covenants or other restrictions, we should make our decision by matching the cash inflows from the investing to the cash outflows of the financing. Recall that the capital budgeting analysis indicated a steady stream of cash inflows for the five-year period. Thus either the installment note or the bond payable would match the cash outflows with the cash inflows. However, the lump-sum payment at the end of the bond might be a problem. In addition, since the company's anticipated cash inflows ($26,000 per year) will cover both a principal and interest payment ($24,389.07), it seems that the installment note would be best.

EXHIBIT 14.10
Comparison of Notes for Comprehensive Example

	Installment Note	Noninterest-Bearing Note	Bonds
Cash Outflows			
Year 1	$24,389.07	$0.00	$8,000.00
Year 2	24,389.07	0.00	8,000.00
Year 3	24,389.07	0.00	8,000.00
Year 4	24,389.07	0.00	8,000.00
Year 5	24,389.07	0.00	8,000.00
Year 5		$140,255.17	$100,000.00
Interest Expense			
Year 1	$ 7,000.00	$ 7,000.00	$ 7,287.01
Year 2	5,782.77	7,490.00	7,237.10
Year 3	4,480.32	8,014.30	7,183.70
Year 4	3,086.71	8,575.30	7,126.56
Year 5	1,595.55	9,175.57	7,065.42
Liability at Year-End			
Year 1			
Current	$18,606.30	$ 0.00	$ 0.00
Long-term	64,004.63	107,000.00	103,387.21
Year 2			
Current	19,908.75	0.00	0.00
Long-term	44,095.88	114,490.00	102,624.32
Year 3			
Current	21,302.36	0.00	0.00
Long-term	22,793.52	112,504.30	101,808.02
Year 4			
Current	22,793.52	131,079.60	100,934.58
Long-term	0.00	0.00	0.00
Year 5			
Current	0.00	0.00	0.00
Long-term	0.00	0.00	0.00

Summary

Debt financing is provided by creditors and creates the risk that the company's inability to meet interest and principal obligations will result in foreclosure on the company's assets. Financial leverage associated with debt financing creates the potential for boosting the owners' return on investment. Accounting provides vital information to internal and external decision makers about prior financing decisions and the financing alternatives available to the company in the future.

- The three basic notes used as debt instruments are the periodic payment note, the lump-sum note, and the periodic payment and lump-sum note. Each of these notes is the creditor's promise to make a particular set of payments. The present value of the cash flows using the market rate of interest determines the cash proceeds or cash equivalent of these notes.
- Debt financing is acquired from nonpublic and public sources. Nonpublic sources are banks, insurance companies, leasing companies, and individuals. Bonds are the debt instruments used to acquire debt financing from the public.
- The planning process involves examining the impact of the proposed financing alternatives on the company's cash flows, income, and its budgeted balance sheet.

Key Terms

Bearer bond A bond that is payable to the bearer or person who has physical possession of the bond, *410*

Bond A long-term debt instrument issued by corporations to raise money from the public, *408*

Bond certificate The note given to bondholders, *408*

Bond indenture The bond contract, *409*

Bond issue A group of bonds, *408*

Callable bond A bond that gives the company issuing the bond the right to buy it back before the maturity date at a specified price, *410*

Capital lease A lease in which a company acquires such a substantial interest in the leased property that, for all practical purposes, the lessee company owns the asset, *407*

Carrying value of debt Remaining liability on the pro forma balance sheet, *398*

Collateral An asset or group of assets specifically named in a debt agreement to which the creditor has claim if the borrower fails to comply with the terms of the note, *407*

Convertible bond A bond feature that allows bondholders to exchange the bonds for common or preferred stock, *410*

Covenants Restrictions that lenders place on the borrowing company to protect the lender's interest, *397*

Debenture bonds Unsecured bonds; bonds with no specific assets pledged as collateral, *411*

Discount on a note The excess of the face value of a note over its present value (cash proceeds), *401*

Face rate on the note Used to determine the cash interest the borrower pays, *397*

Face value of the note The amount the borrower will repay the lender for principal, *397*

Holder of the note The lender, *397*

Lease An agreement to convey the use of a tangible asset from one party to another in return for rental payments, *407*

Lump-sum payment note A debt instrument that contains a promise to pay a specific amount of money at the end of a specified period of time, *399*

Maker of the note The borrower, *397*

Market, or effective, interest rate The actual interest rate charged on a note's proceeds, *397*

Mortgage A long-term note secured with real estate, such as land or buildings, as collateral, *407*

Mortgage bond A bond that is secured with real estate, *411*

Operating lease A rental agreement for a period of time substantially shorter than the economic life of the leased asset, *407*

Periodic payment and lump-sum note A debt instrument that combines periodic payments and a final lump-sum payment, *401*

Periodic payment note A debt instrument that contains a promise to make a series of equal payments consisting of both interest and principal at equal time intervals over a specified time period, *398*

Premium on a note The amount that the present value (cash proceeds) of a note exceeds its face value, *403*

Proceeds of the note The amount of cash raised from issuance of a note, *397*

Registered bonds Bonds that are numbered and made payable in the name of the bondholder, *409*

Secured bond A bond that has some part of the issuing corporation's assets serving as security for the loan, *410*

Serial bond A bond issue that has specified portions of the bond issue coming due periodically over the life of the bond issue, *410*

Subordinated bonds Unsecured bonds whose rights to repayment are ranked after, or subordinated to, some other person or group of creditors, *411*

Unsecured bond A bond that does not have any specific assets pledged as security against its repayment, *411*

Questions

1. Distinguish between the market rate of interest and the face rate of interest on a note.
2. Describe the cash inflows and outflows of a periodic payment (installment) note shown on the budgeted statement of cash flows.
3. Describe the cash inflows and outflows of a lump-sum payment (noninterest-bearing) note shown on the budgeted statement of cash flows.
4. Describe the cash inflows and outflows of a periodic and lump-sum payment note shown on the budgeted statement of cash flows.
5. Describe the interest expense reflected on the budgeted income statement over the life of a periodic payment (installment) note.
6. Describe the interest expense reflected on the budgeted income statement over the life of a lump-sum payment (noninterest-bearing) note.
7. Describe the interest expense reflected on the budgeted income statement over the life of a periodic and lump-sum payment note.
8. Describe the carrying value shown on the budgeted balance sheet over the life of a periodic payment (installment) note.
9. Describe the carrying value shown on the budgeted balance sheet over the life of a lump-sum payment (noninterest-bearing) note.
10. Describe the carrying value shown on the budgeted balance sheet over the life of a periodic and lump-sum payment note.
11. Why does a discount on a note arise?
12. Why does a premium on a note arise?
13. What is the difference between an operating and a capital lease?
14. What distinguishes a bond from other types of debt instruments?
15. Describe how a corporation raises money by issuing bonds.
16. Describe the difference between a debenture and a mortgage bond.
17. When planning to issue a bond, why would a company use a call feature?
18. When planning to issue a bond, why would a company use a conversion feature?
19. What is the distinction between a bearer bond and a registered bond?
20. What factors should be considered when choosing a debt instrument?

End-of-chapter exercises and problems that can be completed using the time value of money tables in the appendix to Chapter 11 are indicated by**.

Exercises

E14.1 LO 1 On April 1, Bailey Products borrowed $150,000 at 7 percent on a five-year installment loan. Annual payments are $36,583.60. How much of the first payment is principal and how much is interest? How much of the second payment is principal and how much is interest? Describe the cash inflows and outflows associated with the note.

E14.2 **On November 1, Turner Company borrowed $30,000. Turner signed a three-year installment note that calls for 12 quarterly payments and a 8 percent interest rate. How much cash will Turner pay each quarter? How much of the first payment will be interest expense and how much will be principal?

LO 2 E14.3 **On January 1, Harrison Enterprises borrowed $40,000 for three years. Harrison signed a noninterest-bearing note. Assuming that the market rate of interest is 9 percent on the date the note is made and that interest is compounded annually, what is the face value of the note? What is the amount of interest expense shown on the budgeted income statement for the first two years? Describe the cash inflows and outflows Harrison must plan for with this note.

LO 2 E14.4 **Fouch Corporation wants to borrow $80,000 and use a noninterest-bearing note with a five-year life. If the market interest rate is 8 percent and the interest is compounded semiannually, what is the face value of the note? How much interest expense will Fouch Corporation show on its budgeted income statement for the first year of the note's life? Describe the cash inflows and outflows Fouch must plan for with this note.

LO 3 E14.5 **Fleak Corporation borrows money by issuing a three-year periodic and lump-sum payment note payable with a face value of $300,000 and a face rate of 7 percent that is paid annually. The market rate of interest is 6 percent when Fleak takes this note to the bank. What will be the cash inflows shown on the budgeted statement of cash flows? What will be the cash outflows shown on the budgeted statement of cash flows for the first year? What is the amount of interest expense shown on the budgeted income statement for the first year? Why is this latter amount different than the cash outflows for the first year?

LO 3 E14.6 **Kerby Company will issue a $400,000, five-year, 7 percent periodic and lump-sum payment note when the market interest rate is 8 percent. The face rate of interest is paid semiannually. Determine the amount of cash the company will receive from the note. Describe the cash outflows Kerby will pay on the note over its life. What is the interest expense shown on the budgeted income statement for the first year?

LO 3 E14.7 **Romine Delivery Corporation is planning to issue $10,000,000 in 10-year, 10 percent bonds. The bonds are dated May 1, 2011, and interest is payable annually on May 1. If the bonds are sold on May 1, 2011, to yield the 8 percent market rate of interest, how much cash will Romine Delivery raise by issuing the bonds? How much interest expense will Romine Delivery incur during the first year of the bonds' life? How much cash will the corporation pay out during the first year of the bonds' life? Describe the cash outflows of the bonds for the life of the bond issue.

LO 3 E14.8 **Using the information in E14.7, how much cash will Romine Delivery Corporation receive if the bonds are issued to yield a 12 percent market rate of interest? How much interest expense will Romine Delivery incur during the first year of the bonds' life? How much cash will the corporation pay out during the first year of the bonds' life? Describe the bonds' cash outflows for the life of the bond issue.

LO 3 E14.9 Determine the cash received from a $1,000,000 bond issue if the bonds were issued at each of the following prices:

A. 93 7/8
B. 97 3/4
C. 102 3/8
D. 105 1/4

LO 3 E14.10 **On December 1, the Weber Corporation plans to issue bonds with a face value of $8,000,000. The bonds mature in 10 years and have a face rate of 10 percent interest that is paid semiannually. If the market rate of interest when the bonds are issued is 8 percent, how much cash will Weber receive? What will be the interest expense shown on the budgeted income statement for the first year of the bonds' life? How much cash is paid out in the first year of the bonds' life?

LO 3 E14.11 The Harter Corporation has issued bonds with a face value of $4,000,000 that are convertible on a 50:1 basis (50 shares of common stock for one bond) and have a call price of 104. Describe the cash flows if the bonds are called when their carrying (book) value is $3,900,000. Describe the cash flows if the bonds are instead converted to common stock.

LO 3 E14.12 Knoepfle Corporation's bonds have a face value of $11,000,000 and a call price of 103. On February 1, 2012, the bonds have a carrying value of $11,200,000 on Knoepfle's books and a market price of 98 3/4 in the secondary market. If Knoepfle wants to retire the entire bond issue, how much will it have to pay if it calls the bonds? How much will it pay if it buys the bonds in the secondary bond market?

LO 1 E14.13 **On October 1, Snyder Technologies plans to sign a capital lease for machinery with a fair market value of $152,865 for a six-year period. The company will make the first of seven $27,865 annual payments when it signs the lease. The interest rate is 9 percent. What is the amount of the liability generated by this capital lease? How much interest expense will Snyder incur in the first year of the lease?

LO 1 LO 2 LO 3 E14.14 **Dietz Company's capital expenditure budget calls for a $1,500,000 addition to an existing plant. The company plans to issue a three-year note and is debating whether to use a three-payment, 8 percent annual installment note; a three-year, 8 percent, $1,500,000 interest-bearing note (interest paid annually); or a three-year noninterest-bearing note (interest compounded annually). If the market interest rate is 8 percent, describe the cash inflows and outflows for each year of each note's life.

LO 1 E14.15 Klamm Company needs to borrow $100,000. It plans to sign an installment note with a 6 percent interest rate and make monthly payments for the next eight years. How much is the monthly payment required? How much of the first month's payment is interest? What is the carrying value of the note at the end of the first month?

LO 2 E14.16 Glatt Enterprises needs to borrow $100,000. It plans to sign a noninterest-bearing note payable for eight years when the market rate of interest is 6 percent compounded quarterly. How much money will Glatt receive when it signs the note? How much money will Glatt pay the lender? What is the required quarterly payment? What is the interest expense for the first quarter?

LO 3 E14.17 Clifton, Inc., needs to borrow some money. It prepares a eight-year periodic and lump-sum payment note with a face value of $100,000 and a face rate of interest of 7 percent paid semiannually. If the market rate of interest is 6 percent, how much money will Clifton receive? How much is the periodic payment? What is the interest expense for the first period? What is the carrying value of the note at the end of the first period?

LO 3 E14.18 Refer to E14.17. Assume the market rate of interest is 8 percent.

LO 1 E14.19 For an installment note: (*a*) Describe the cash outflows shown on the budgeted cash flow statement over the life of the note. (*b*) Describe the change in the interest expense shown on the budgeted income statement over the life of the note. (*c*) Describe the change in the carrying value of the note on the budgeted balance sheet over the life of the note.

LO 2 E14.20 For a lump-sum payment note: (*a*) Describe the cash outflows shown on the budgeted cash flow statement over the life of the note. (*b*) Describe the change in the interest expense shown on the budgeted income statement over the life of the note. (*c*) Describe the change in the carrying value of the note on the budgeted balance sheet over the life of the note.

LO 3 E14.21 For a bond when the market rate of interest is greater than the face rate of interest: (*a*) Describe the cash outflows shown on the budgeted cash flow statement over the life of the note. (*b*) Describe the change in the interest expense shown on the budgeted income statement over the life of the note. (*c*) Describe the change in the carrying value of the note on the budgeted balance sheet over the life of the note.

LO 3 E14.22 For a bond when the market rate of interest is less than the face rate of interest: (*a*) Describe the cash outflows shown on the budgeted cash flow statement over the life of the note. (*b*) Describe the interest expense shown on the budgeted income statement over the life of the note. (*c*) Describe the carrying value of the note on the budgeted balance sheet over the life of the note.

Problems

P14.1 LO 1 On November 30, 2011, Harris Company arranged to purchase a $250,000 piece of equipment by making a 20 percent down payment and signing a 15-year installment loan contract with interest at 7 percent per year for the balance. The loan is to be repaid in monthly installments starting on December 31, 2011. Harris prepares its budgeted financial statements on a calendar-year basis.

Required:

A. What are the cash flows related to the loan shown on the budgeted statement of cash flows for 2011?
B. How much cash will the company pay over the life of the note?
C. How much interest expense will be shown on the budgeted income statement for 2011?
D. What is the carrying value of the note shown on the budgeted balance sheet for 2011?

LO 2 P14.2 Springer, Inc., plans to acquire a trenching machine on June 1, 2011, with a list price of $52,000, by paying $12,000 down and signing a four-year, $40,000 noninterest-bearing note. The market rate of interest is 9 percent, compounded annually. Springer prepares its budgeted financial statements on a calendar-year basis.

A. What price did Springer pay for the machine?
B. How much interest will Springer pay over the life of the note?
C. What are the cash flows related to the loan shown on the 2011 budgeted statement of cash flows?
D. What is the interest expense shown on the 2011 budgeted income statement?
E. What is the carrying value of the note shown on the budgeted balance sheet for 2011?

LO 3 P14.3 Messier Company is planning to finance several projects and wants you to determine the cash inflows and outflows of the following bonds. The market interest rate for Messier Company is 8 percent.

1. $100,000, 8 percent note, interest payable quarterly, due in eight years.
2. $500,000, 6 percent note, interest payable semiannually, due in 10 years.
3. $250,000, 10 percent note, interest payable semiannually, due in six years.

Required:

A. What is the cash Messier will receive from each note?
B. What are the annual cash outflows for each note?
C. What are the total cash outflows for each note?

LO 3 P14.4 Borthick Basketball Company is going to expand its manufacturing operations and plans to borrow some of the funds necessary for the expansion. Borthick wants to issue a 10-year, 9 percent, $600,000 note that pays interest semiannually but is concerned about the impact of the note. Assume the market interest rate is 8 percent.

Required:

A. What are the cash inflows from the note?
B. What are the cash outflows associated with the note each year?
C. What is the interest expense for the first year of the note?
D. How does the carrying value of the note change over the life of the note?

LO 1 P14.5 Giovinazzo Construction Company plans to buy a new dump truck that has a sticker price of $68,800. The dealer has offered to finance the truck on an installment note at 5 percent interest for 48 months.

Required:

A. What cost will be assigned to the truck and the note?
B. What is the monthly payment?
C. If Giovinazzo buys the truck on October 31, 2011, what is the interest expense shown on the budgeted income statement for calendar year 2011?
D. If Giovinazzo buys the truck on October 31, 2011, what is the carrying value of the note shown on the budgeted balance sheet for 2011?

LO 1 P14.6 Brown Leasing Service recently purchased drilling equipment for $218,705 and wants to lease it to Huss Excavation Company. If Huss accepts, it will sign the lease agreement on May 1, 2011. The equipment has an estimated useful life of five years, and the lease term is for five years. During the period of the lease, Huss will be responsible for all repairs and maintenance of the leased property. The lease agreement calls for Huss to make five annual lease payments of $56,227.41 starting May 1, 2012. The interest rate is 9 percent. Huss has asked you to help it plan for the impact of this lease.

Required:

A. What makes this lease qualify as a capital lease?
B. What is the value of the equipment and the amount of the liability generated by this transaction?
C. What are the cash flows associated with the first two years of the lease?
D. What is the interest cost incurred in each of the first two years of the lease?
E. How does the lease liability change over the first two years of the lease?

LO 3 P14.7 Larkins is planning to issue debentures with a face value of $2,000,000 on September 1, 2011. The debentures mature in 10 years and have a face interest rate of 8 percent that is paid semiannually on March 1 and September 1 of each year. Larkins is uncertain about what the market interest rate will be on those dates and has projected the following possibilities:

Situation 1: The market rate of interest is 9 percent.
Situation 2: The market rate of interest is 7 percent.
Situation 3: The market rate of interest is 8 percent.

Required:

A. How much cash will Larkins receive from the debentures for each interest rate?
B. What is the interest expense for the first year for each of the market interest rates?
C. What annual cash outflows will occur for each of the market interest rates?
D. How did the carrying value change each year under each scenario?

LO 3 P14.8 Mutchler Corporation plans a $12,000,000 bond issue that has a carrying value of $11,232,125 as of September 1, 2011. For each of the following assumptions, describe cash flows that occur and the impact each scenario would have on Mutchler's budgeted balance sheet. Consider each scenario an independent event.

Required:

A. Mutchler Corporation's bonds have a call price of 102 and on September 1, 2011, the corporation plans to exercise the call feature on the entire bond issue.
B. Mutchler Corporation's bonds have a 50-to-1 common stock conversion feature; that is, one bond is convertible into 50 shares of Mutchler Corporation's common stock. On September 1, 2011, Mutchler predicts that the bondholders will convert 25 percent of the bonds into common stock.

LO 1 LO 2 LO 3 P14.9 Sriram Corporation's capital expenditure budget calls for the construction of a new addition to the plant and the corporation's controller plans to borrow $8,000,000 to finance a portion of the construction. While the controller has decided to issue a three-year note, she is undecided on which debt instrument to use. She wants you to show the impact of the following alternatives on the company's budgeted statement of cash flows, income statement, and balance sheet over the life of the note: (*a*) a noninterest-bearing note (interest compounded annually), (*b*) a 9 percent installment note with annual payments, and (*c*) a 7 percent bond with annual payments. The market rate of interest is 9 percent.

LO 1 P14.10 Barden Company needs to borrow $400,000. It agrees to make monthly payments of principal and interest over the next 12 years. The bank agrees to loan Barden the money at 6 percent interest.

Required:

A. How much money will Barden receive from this loan?
B. How much is the monthly payment?
C. What amounts would be shown on the budgeted income statement for the first two months?
D. What amounts would be shown on the budgeted statement of cash flows for the first two months and how would it be classified?
E. What amounts would be shown on the budgeted balance sheet for the first two months?

LO 2 P14.11 Bullen needs to borrow $500,000. He agrees to sign a 15-year, noninterest-bearing note. The bank needs to earn 8 percent compounded quarterly. Bullen prepares its budgeted financial statements on a quarterly basis.

Required:

A. How much money will Bullen receive from this loan?
B. How much is the quarterly payment?
C. What amounts would be shown on the budgeted income statement for the first two quarters?
D. What amounts would be shown on the budgeted statement of cash flows for the first two quarters and how would it be classified?
E. What amounts would be shown on the budgeted balance sheet for the first two quarters?

Cases

C14.1 Sevcik Resort needs to acquire a new tour boat that costs $80,000 and is expected to be useful for approximately five years. There are three alternatives for financing the acquisition of the boat:

- Alternative 1: Lease the boat for five years as a capital lease. There would be five lease payments of $20,128 each, the first of which would be paid on the date the boat was acquired.
- Alternative 2: Purchase the boat outright for $80,000 from the proceeds of a $80,000, five-year, 8 percent note payable. The loan would require annual interest payments of $6,400 and repayment of the principal at the end of five years.
- Alternative 3: Sign a one-year lease for $20,128 with the option to renew the lease each year for the next five years. While the lease may be renewed, the amount of the lease may increase or decrease up to 10 percent.

Required: What are the advantages and disadvantages of each of these financing alternatives?

C14.2 LO 2 LO 3 Nathan Company has completed its capital budgeting analysis that indicated a positive net present value. Accordingly it has decided to purchase new equipment with a list price of $800,000 and a setup cost of $50,000. Now the question is how to finance the purchase. Nathan believes it can issue 10,000 shares of common stock for $30 per share but the rest of the money must be borrowed. The market rate of interest is predicted to be 5 percent when this deal is completed.

Required:

A. If Nathan finances this purchase with a 10-year quarterly installment note, how will the company's budgeted income statement, statement of cash flows, and balance sheet be impacted?
B. If Nathan finances this purchase with a 10-year noninterest-bearing note of $550,000, how will the company's budgeted income statement, statement of cash flows, and balance sheet be impacted?
C. If Nathan finances this purchase with a 10-year bond issue of $550,000 paying 6 percent semi-annually, how will the company's budgeted income statement, statement of cash flows, and balance sheet be impacted?

Critical Thinking

CT14.1 LO 1 LO 2 LO 3 Each of the following $5,000,000 debt instruments is subject to a 10 percent market rate of interest. When measured on a common-size basis, which of the following is the most expensive debt to use?

A. $5,000,000 noninterest-bearing, 10-year note (annual compounding).
B. $5,000,000 bond with an 8 percent face rate that is paid annually; the bond is due in 10 years.
C. $5,000,000 note payable, with a 10-year life and a 12 percent face rate of interest that is paid annually.

LO 1 CT14.2 LO 2 Gramling Inc. is considering an investment in new operating equipment with a 15-year life. The new equipment will cost $300,000 and a one-time cost of $15,000 will be incurred to remove the old equipment and install the new equipment. The old equipment that will be replaced originally cost $200,000 and has a current book value of $25,000. This old equipment will be sold for $8,000. The new equipment will be depreciated uniformly over its useful life. At the end of 15 years, this equipment will be removed and given to the local recycling center. The new equipment is expected to generate cash profits of $83,000 per year. Gramling uses an 11 percent hurdle rate (its market rate of interest) to evaluate long-term projects and is subject to a 30 percent tax rate.

Required:

A. Should Gramling invest in this equipment?

B. Assuming that Gramling does invest in the equipment, which of the following financing options would be best, a 10-year noninterest-bearing note (annual compounding) or a 10-year monthly installment note?

Ethical Challenges

EC14.1 

Refer to the Of Interest box in this chapter. Discuss the ethical implications of using derivatives to shift risk from one entity to another.

 **EC14.2**

XYZ Corporation plans to acquire a building (with a useful life of 10 years) by issuing a $5,000,000, 10-year, 3 percent note to the former owner of the building. XYZ will value the building and the note using the market interest rate of 10 percent. What impact will this decision have on XYZ's budgeted income in the first year of the note? If XYZ bases its upper-managers' bonuses on income, what is the impact of this action? Is this practice unethical? Be sure to consider all the stakeholders.

Computer Applications

CA14.1 

Hannan Company needs to borrow $15,000,000 to finance an addition to its manufacturing facilities. It has obtained an installment note at 8 percent interest for 15 years. Payments will be made monthly beginning one month from today.

Required:

A. What is the amount of each monthly payment?

B. Prepare a spreadsheet that indicates the amount of each payment, how much of each payment is interest, how much of each payment is principal, and the remaining balance on the loan for the first two years.

 **CA14.2**

Ransopher Corporation needs to buy a new computer system. Dwell Computers has agreed to sell Ransopher a computer system and accept a 10-year, noninterest-bearing note payable. The market rate of interest is currently 7 percent compounded annually and the value of the computer system is $53,000.

Required:

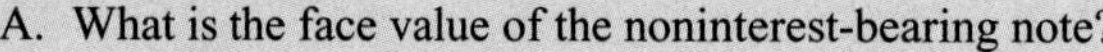

A. What is the face value of the noninterest-bearing note?

B. Prepare a spreadsheet that indicates the interest cost associated with the loan each year and the carrying value of the loan at the end of each year.

Visit the text Online Learning Center at **www.mhhe.com/ainsworth6e** for additional problem material that accompanies this chapter.

PART SIX

VI

Recording and Evaluating Capital Resource Processes

CHAPTER FIFTEEN

15

Recording and Evaluating Capital Resource Process Activities: Financing

Learning Objectives

LO 1 Explain, record, and report equity financing activities for a corporation.

LO 2 Describe, record, and report debt financing activities for a corporation.

In Chapters 13 and 14 we learned how companies plan their financing activities. We examined the relationship between debt and equity financing and how companies choose the type of debt and equity financing that is appropriate for them. In this chapter we examine how corporations record and evaluate these financing activities.

Review of Transaction-Based Accounting Systems

As we learned in Chapter 7, a manual accounting system and many computerized accounting systems are based on a system of debits and credits. A debit signifies the left-hand side of an account while a credit signifies the right-hand side of an account. We also know that because assets are on the left side of the accounting equation that they normally have debit balances and to increase an asset we must debit the account. We know:

Cash + Other assets = Liabilities + Contributed capital + Retained earnings

Cash		Other assets		Liabilities		Contributed capital		Retained earnings	
Left	Right	Left	Right	Left	Right	Left	Right	Left	Right
+	−	+	−	−	+	−	+	−	+
DR	CR	DR	CR	DR	CR	DR	CR	DR	CR

Revenue		Expense	
Left	Right	Left	Right
−	+	+	−
DR	CR	DR	CR

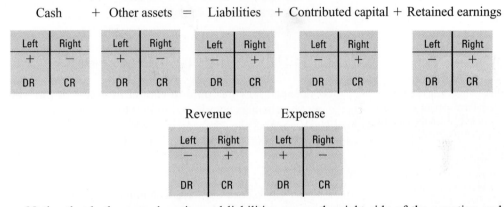

Notice that both owners' equity and liabilities are on the right side of the equation and normally have credit balances and are increased with credits and decreased with debits. In a corporation, the accounting system makes a distinction between the two principal sources of ownership funds: the contributions made by the shareholders in exchange for an ownership interest and the reinvested earnings of the firm. In addition the accounting system makes a distinction between the amounts owed to creditors for interest and the amounts owed on the principal of the debt. We will examine equity financing first, then we turn our attention to debt financing.

Equity Financing Activities

In this section we examine equity financing in a corporation. Accounting for sole proprietorship and partnership equity is similar because no distinction is made between the amounts contributed by owners and the amounts earned by the business. This is because the profits of the company are allocated to the owners who pay taxes on them (recall our discussion in Chapter 13). In a corporation we must separate owner contributions from the retained earnings of the company. The distinction between contributions and reinvested earnings allows creditors to determine if distributions to the shareholders are made from the corporation's earnings (a return on investment) or whether they are a return of the shareholders' investment.

Contributions by Owners (Shareholders)

For purposes of illustration let's assume that PCs to Go plans to expand and has received authorization to issue 1,000,000 shares of $1 par value common stock and 300,000 shares of $100 par value, 8 percent cumulative preferred stock.

Par Value Stock

When accounting for par value stock, the amount of the par value is credited to the capital stock account regardless of the amount paid for the shares. The total par value of the stock issued provides financial statement users with information about the amount of the corporation's *legal capital*.

If PCs to Go issues 250,000 shares of common stock for $14 per share and 12,000 shares of preferred stock for $125 per share, the total assets and total owners' equity of the company increase by $5,000,000 (250,000 × $14 + 12,000 × $125) as indicated here:

Assets = Liabilities + Owners' equity

+5,000,000 +5,000,000

But we must separate the legal capital from the capital contributed in excess of par value. Therefore the general journal entry is:

General Journal

Date	Description	DR	CR
15–1	Cash	5,000,000	
	Common Stock (250,000 × $1)		250,000
	Paid-in-Capital in Excess of Par Value—Common		3,250,000
	Preferred Stock (12,000 × $100)		1,200,000
	Paid-in-Capital in Excess of Par Value—Preferred		300,000

In a corporation, we must keep legal capital separate from excess capital and we must keep contributed capital separate from earned capital. Therefore, a corporation has separate accounts for common stock (preferred stock), paid-in capital, and retained earnings.

The amounts shown as **paid-in-capital in excess of par value** represent the additional net assets shareholders contributed to PCs to Go above the par value of the stock. Thus, the total legal capital of the company is $1,450,000 ($250,000 + $1,200,000) and the additional capital is $3,550,000 ($3,250,000 + $300,000).

No-Par Stock

Since no-par stock does not have a minimum legal issue price for each share, the amount credited to the capital stock account is the amount received for the shares. To illustrate the difference in accounting for no-par-value stock and par value stock, assume that PCs to Go's common stock is no-par. The following entry reflects the issuance of the common and preferred stock with this assumption.

General Journal

Date	Description	DR	CR
15–2	Cash	5,000,000	
	Common Stock (250,000 × $14)		3,500,000
	Preferred Stock (12,000 × $100)		1,200,000
	Paid-in-Capital in Excess of Par Value—Preferred		300,000

Notice that in both the par value and no-par cases, the $5,000,000 received by the corporation is credited to capital stock accounts. In the case of no-par stock, however, there is no Paid-in Capital in Excess of Par Value account associated with the common stock because the shares do not have par values.[1]

Noncash Stock Issue

Often corporations issue shares of stock, either in exchange for assets other than cash or in payment for services rendered. This raises the question of how to determine the dollar value of such a transaction. When the transaction does not involve cash, the fair market value of the stock issued or of the goods or services received, whichever is more readily determinable, provides the cash equivalent amount. To illustrate, suppose that PCs to Go issued

[1] When a corporation is authorized to issue no-par stated value stock, the amount credited to the Capital Stock account is the amount of the stated value, regardless of the amount of money received at the time of the sale of stock. Entries for the issuance of no-par stated value stock are the same as par value stock, except that the Paid-in Capital in Excess of Stated Value account is used instead of the Paid-in Capital in Excess of Par account.

20,000 shares of its $1 par value common stock in exchange for equipment having a fair market value of $240,000. Thus,

Assets	=	Liabilities	+	Owners' equity
+240,000				+240,000

The entry to reflect this event that separates legal capital from additional paid-in capital is

General Journal

Date	Description	DR	CR
15–3	Equipment	240,000	
	Common Stock (20,000 × $1)		20,000
	Paid-in-Capital in Excess of Par Value—Common		220,000

If PCs to Go could not determine the fair market value of the equipment, it would record the transaction using the fair market value of the shares of stock issued. Occasionally, the fair market value of the asset or stock is not determinable. When this occurs, the corporation records the transaction using either an appraised value of the asset or an amount set by the board of directors.

Corporate Earnings

Retained Earnings, or the amount of a corporation's earnings since its inception less all dividends distributed, appears on the balance sheet as part of the corporation's shareholders' equity. The account normally has a credit balance because the amount of net income usually exceeds the combined amount of net losses and dividends that would reduce the balance in the account. A credit balance in the Retained Earnings account represents the amount of earnings reinvested in the corporation rather than distributed to the shareholders as dividends. When the cumulative total of net losses plus dividends declared exceeds the cumulative total of net income, the Retained Earnings account will have a debit balance, which is referred to as a *deficit in retained earnings.* A deficit balance indicates that some portion of the shareholders' contributed capital was lost in the firm's attempt to generate income.

When a company generates net income, the firm has increased its net assets and the shareholders' interest in the firm as a result of its ongoing operations. As you know the revenue and expense accounts of the company are temporary accounts and their balances must be transferred to Retained Earnings at the end of each accounting period. Thus if the company generates net income, the total of the revenue and gain accounts (credit balances) exceeds the total amount of the expense and loss accounts (debit balances), and the normal credit balance of Retained Earnings increases. If the company generates net loss, the total of the expense and loss accounts (debit balances) exceeds the total amount of the revenue and gain accounts (credit balances), and the normal credit balance of Retained Earnings decreases. Thus if PCs to Go had revenues totaling $750,000, gains of $50,000, expenses of $420,000, and a loss of $80,000, its net income would be $300,000. Recall that the $300,000 represents the increase in the net assets of the firm during the year that belongs to the shareholders. The net income increases the balance in Retained Earnings $300,000 through the closing process as shown here.

General Journal

Date	Description	DR	CR
15–4	Revenue Accounts	750,000	
	Gain Accounts	50,000	
	Retained Earnings		800,000
	Retained Earnings	500,000	
	Expense Accounts		420,000
	Loss Accounts		80,000

Corporate Distributions

Chapter 13 described the three important dates associated with the payment of corporate dividends: (1) date of declaration, (2) date of record, and (3) date of payment. Accounting entries are made only on the date of declaration and the date of payment. Recall that on the date of declaration, the board of directors announces (1) the amount of the dividend, (2) the date on which investors must officially own the stock [the date of record] to receive the declared dividend, and (3) the date when the dividend will be paid [the date of payment].

Cash Dividends

Assume that PCs to Go declares a dividend of $180,000 on June 1 to shareholders of record on June 15, payable on June 25. PCs to Go preferred stock has an 8 percent dividend rate; thus, the dividend payable to preferred shareholders is $96,000 = 12,000 shares × $100 par value × 8 percent dividend rate. Then the dividend available for common shareholders is $84,000 ($180,000 − $96,000). On June 1, PCs to Go incurs a liability, thus:

Assets	=	Liabilities	+	Owners' equity
		+180,000		(180,000)

PCs to Go would record the following entry for the declaration of this dividend.

General Journal

Date	Description	DR	CR
15–5	Retained Earnings	180,000	
	Dividends Payable—Preferred Stock (12,000 × $100 × 0.08)		96,000
	Dividends Payable—Common Stock ($180,000 − $96,000)		84,000

On June 25 when the liability is paid,

Assets	=	Liabilities	+	Owners' equity
(180,000)		(180,000)		

And,

General Journal

Date	Description	DR	CR
15–6	Dividends Payable—Preferred Stock	96,000	
	Dividends Payable—Common Stock	84,000	
	Cash		180,000

Stock Dividends

Recall from Chapter 13 that stock dividends are issued to satisfy shareholders without distributing cash or other assets that may be needed in the business.

Small Stock Dividends If the additional number of shares to be issued in settlement of the stock dividend is small, usually 20 to 25 percent or less of the shares issued, the amount debited to Retained Earnings as a dividend is the *fair market value of the stock multiplied by the number of new shares issued.* The fair market value is used because it approximates the value of the transaction to the shareholders.

For example, if PCs to Go declared a 10 percent stock dividend, it would issue an additional 25,000 shares of stock (250,000 shares issued × 0.10). The amount of the debit to Retained Earnings would depend on the fair market value of the stock on the date of declaration. The amount credited to the **Stock Dividends Distributable** account on the date of declaration is the par value of the shares the corporation will issue on the date of payment. Any excess of the market price over par value is credited to Paid-in Capital in Excess of

Par—Common. If the fair market value of the stock on the date of declaration is $32 per share, the company would make the following entry:

General Journal: Date of Declaration

Date	Description	DR	CR
15–7	Retained Earnings (25,000 × $32)	800,000	
	Stock Dividends Distributable (25,000 × $1)		25,000
	Paid-in-Capital in Excess of Par Value—Common (25,000 × $31)		775,000

Stock Dividends Distributable is not a liability account because a stock dividend does not involve the distribution of the firm's assets. Rather, it is a *contributed capital account* because the company will issue the new shares of common stock on the date of payment. The next entry shows how to record the distribution of the additional shares:

General Journal: Date of Distribution

Date	Description	DR	CR
15–8	Stock Dividends Distributable	25,000	
	Common Stock		25,000

Large Stock Dividends A large stock dividend, one that is greater than 25 percent of the number of shares issued, requires the use of the *par value rather than the market value* of the stock to value the transaction. Using par value as opposed to market value is done because the issuance of such a large number of additional shares usually reduces the market value of the stock and makes it difficult to determine the appropriate market price.

To illustrate, assume that PCs to Go declared a 75 percent stock dividend; that is, it will issue 187,500 additional shares of common stock (250,000 × 0.75). Therefore, PCs to Go will transfer $187,500 of Retained Earnings to Common Stock. The company will record the same sequence of entries it used for the small stock dividends excluding the Paid-in Capital in Excess of Par account as follows:

General Journal: Date of Declaration

Date	Description	DR	CR
15–9	Retained Earnings (187,500 × $1)	187,500	
	Stock Dividends Distributable		187,500

General Journal: Date of Distribution

Date	Description	DR	CR
15–10	Stock Dividends Distributable	187,500	
	Common Stock		187,500

Another reason par values rather than market values are used to value large stock dividends is to prevent the impairment of retained earnings and the payment of cash dividends in the future. To illustrate, assume that PCs to Go had a $3,000,000 balance in Retained Earnings when the large stock dividend was declared. What impact would the stock dividend have on Retained Earnings if the market price instead of the par value had been used to record the transaction? Let's assume that the market price of the stock dropped from $32 to $18.75 as a result of the stock dividend and that we used $18.75 to value the transaction. Retained Earnings would be debited for $3,421,875 (187,500 new shares × $18.75) for the transaction and after posting would have a debit balance of $421,875 ($3,000,000 − $3,421,875). The deficit balance created by the stock dividend would preclude the company from declaring cash dividends until the deficit was removed with future earnings.

Treasury Stock

Recall from Chapter 13 that treasury stock is a company's own stock reacquired with the intent of issuing it again at a later date. Regardless of the reason a corporation buys its own stock, treasury stock is *not an asset* to the corporation. Rather, treasury stock represents the amount paid to liquidate one or more shareholders' interest in the corporation. The debit balance of the Treasury Stock account is reported as a contra equity account that reduces total shareholders' equity on a company's balance sheet.

Purchase of Treasury Stock When a firm purchases its own shares in the open market, the company debits the Treasury Stock (a contra owners' equity) account for the cost of those shares. For example, assume that PCs to Go purchased 1,000 shares of its own $1 par common stock for cash at $35 per share. Then,

Assets	=	Liabilities	+	Owners' equity
(35,000)				(35,000)

And the entry is

General Journal

Date	Description	DR	CR
15–11	Treasury Stock	35,000	
	Cash		35,000

Reissue of Treasury Stock Assume that some time after the purchase of those 1,000 shares of treasury stock, PCs to Go sells 350 shares at $38 per share. Because Treasury Stock is a shareholders' equity account and is not an asset, the difference between the sales price ($38) and the purchase price ($35) is recorded in a contributed capital account rather than being recognized as a gain. **Paid-in Capital from Treasury Stock** is the account that shows the additional capital generated from the reissue of treasury stock. Thus when PCs to Go reissues the treasury stock, its assets and owners' equity increase:

Assets	=	Liabilities	+	Owners' equity
+13,300				+13,300

The next entry illustrates the reissue of 350 shares of treasury stock by PCs to Go.

General Journal

Date	Description	DR	CR
15–12	Cash (350 × $38)	13,300	
	Treasury Stock (350 × $35)		12,250
	Paid-in-Capital from Treasury Stock (350 × $3)		1,050

When treasury stock is reissued at a price below its initial cost, the difference between the market price and the initial cost is debited to the Paid-in Capital from Treasury Stock. If the Paid-in Capital from Treasury Stock account has no balance, or if the balance is insufficient to offset the entire amount of the difference between the cost and the smaller reissue price, then it is necessary to subtract the remainder of the difference from Retained Earnings.

For example, if the remaining 650 shares of PCs to Go's treasury stock were sold for $27 per share, the Treasury Stock account ($22,750 = $35,000 − $12,250) would be reduced to zero, the Paid-in-Capital from Treasury Stock account ($1,050) would be reduced to zero,

OF INTEREST Partnership Accounting

Accounting for partnership and sole proprietorship equity events is very similar to the accounting for equity events in a corporation. There is one basic difference: Owners' contributions are not maintained separately from earnings retained by the company. So when a sole proprietor or a partner provides cash to the business, the company's assets are increased and the company's owners' equity (owner, capital) also increases. The reverse occurs when assets of the company are distributed to owners. In a partnership, the closing process is slightly different due to the income allocation process we discussed in Chapter 13. A partnership would close its revenue and expense accounts to an account called Income Summary. The balance in this account then would be allocated among the partners according to the partnership agreement. Refer back to Exhibit 13.7. If this net income ($48,000) resulted, the following general journal entry would be made:

Date	Description	DR	CR
01–1	Income summary	48,000	
	Stuart, capital		17,300
	Finley, capital		11,900
	Janice, capital		10,000
	Jo, capital		8,800

Partnership accounting becomes a bit more complicated when a new partner enters or an existing partner leaves the partnership and the *partnership's assets* are affected, that is, when the incoming or exiting partner is not buying an exiting interest in the partnership.

For example, let's assume that the AD partnership we studied in Chapter 13 has the following capital balances: Stuart, $24,300; Finley, $18,900; Janice, $54,000; and Jo, $41,800 (total $139,000) when they decide to admit Ron for a 1/5 interest with an investment of $34,750 ($139,000 = 4/5 interest; therefore, 1/5 interest = $34,750). The following general journal entry would be made:

Date	Description	DR	CR
01–2	Cash	34,750	
	Ron, capital		34,750

But what would happen if the partners really wanted Ron, so they offered him a 1/5 interest for an investment of only $25,000? The total capital after Ron's investment will be $164,000. Ron's capital account will be 1/5 of that amount, or $32,800, and the difference between his contribution ($25,000) and his interest ($32,800) is a reduction in the existing partners' capital accounts according to the partnership agreement (equally, in this case). The following general journal entry would be made:

Date	Description	DR	CR
01–3	Cash	25,000	
	Stuart, capital	1,950	
	Finley, capital	1,950	
	Janice, capital	1,950	
	Jo, capital	1,950	
	Ron, capital		32,800

If Ron's contribution had been greater than his interest, the existing partners' capital account balances would have increased by their share of the difference between the contribution and the interest given the income partner.

Now let's consider what happens when an existing partner leaves the partnership. Going back to the original partnership, let's assume that Stuart decides to leave the partnership and the partnership agrees to give him $15,200 for his partnership interest. The difference between the assets leaving the partnership ($15,200) and the decrease in partnership capital ($17,300) will be split among the remaining partners according to the partnership agreement (equally, in this case) and the following general journal entry would result:

Date	Description	DR	CR
01–4	Stuart, capital	17,300	
	Finley, capital		700
	Janice, capital		700
	Jo, capital		700
	Cash		15,200

If the partnership had agreed to give Stuart more assets than the balance in his partner capital account, the remaining partners' capital accounts would have been reduced.

It is not unusual for a partnership to revalue its assets before admitting a new partner or before an existing partner exits the partnership. This way any appreciation (or decline) in the value of the partnership may be recognized before the partnership is changed.

and the difference between cash received ($17,550) and the total of the stock accounts ($21,700 = $22,750 − $1,050) would be transferred from Retained Earnings. This entry reflects these facts:

General Journal: Reissue of Treasury Stock below Cost

Date	Description	DR	CR
15–13	Cash (650 × $27)	17,550	
	Paid-in-Capital from Treasury Stock (balance)	1,050	
	Retained Earnings	4,150	
	Treasury Stock (650 × $35)		22,750

By reducing Retained Earnings rather than a contributed capital account, the corporation reduces its dividend-paying ability rather than the initial contributions of the owners. By maintaining the corporation's initial contributed capital and, instead, reducing the amount of shareholders' equity available for distribution as dividends, creditors' interest in the firm is protected.

Financial Statements and Owners' Equity Activities

Owner financing activities are shown primarily on the statement of owners' equity and the balance sheet. Recall that one portion of the statement of owners' equity reports the changes in the Retained Earnings account. Any cash flows resulting from owners' equity activities are reported on the statement of cash flows as financing cash flows. At the end of this chapter, we examine this issue further when we look at Apple's financial statements.

Debt Financing Activities

Now that we have examined the process of recording equity financing activities, we turn our attention to debt financing. We examine each of the notes described and planned for in Chapter 14 separately. In each case we refer to an amortization table that indicates the payment, the interest expense, and the carrying value of the note. The second Of Interest feature for this chapter discusses the preparation of such tables.

Key point: Regardless of the type of debt instrument, debt is initially recorded at its face value.

Installment Notes Payable

Accounting for installment notes requires timely recognition of the interest expense on the notes and proper classification of the note itself as either a long-term or current liability. The following example illustrates how to account for an installment note.

Assume that on February 28, 2010, PCs to Go arranges to purchase a $100,000 piece of equipment by making a 10 percent down payment ($10,000) and signing a three-year installment note with an 8 percent annual interest rate and monthly payments. We know that: $PV =$ 90,000; $r = 8$; $c = 12$; $n = 36$; $FV = 0$; therefore, $ANN = 2{,}820.27$. Exhibit 15.1 illustrates the amortization table associated with this loan. Notice that each payment is the same (column B), but that the interest expense (column C) decreases and the principal payment (column D) increases over the life of the loan because the carrying value (column E) decreases over the life of the loan.

Let's examine the journal entries associated with this note. First, we must record the purchase of the equipment.

Assets	=	Liabilities	+	Owners' equity
+100,000		+90,000		
(10,000)				

General Journal

Date	Description	DR	CR
2-28-10	Equipment	100,000	
	Note Payable		90,000
	Cash		10,000

We know that when we make a payment on an installment note we pay interest and principal; thus when we make the first payment of $2,820.27 we pay interest expense of $600 ($90,000 × 0.08 × 1/12) and principal of $2,220.27 ($2,820.27 − $600.00). (Take a moment to locate these amounts on the amortization table.) Therefore,

Assets	=	Liabilities	+	Owners' equity
(2,820.27)		(2,220.27)		(600.00)

EXHIBIT 15.1
Installment Note Payable

	A	B	C	D	E
1	**Installment Note Payable**				
2	**Month**	**Payment**	**Interest**	**Principal**	**Carrying Value**
3					$90,000.00
4	March	$2,820.27	$600.00	$2,220.27	$87,779.73
5	April	$2,820.27	$585.20	$2,235.07	$85,544.66
6	May	$2,820.27	$570.30	$2,249.97	$83,294.69
7	June	$2,820.27	$555.30	$2,264.97	$81,029.71
8	July	$2,820.27	$540.20	$2,280.07	$78,749.64
9	August	$2,820.27	$525.00	$2,295.27	$76,454.37
10	September	$2,820.27	$509.70	$2,310.57	$74,143.80
11	October	$2,820.27	$494.29	$2,325.98	$71,817.82
12	November	$2,820.27	$478.79	$2,341.48	$69,476.33
13	December	$2,820.27	$463.18	$2,357.09	$67,119.24
14	January	$2,820.27	$447.46	$2,372.81	$64,746.43
15	February	$2,820.27	$431.64	$2,388.63	$62,357.80
16	March	$2,820.27	$415.72	$2,404.55	$59,953.25
17	April	$2,820.27	$399.69	$2,420.58	$57,532.67
18	May	$2,820.27	$383.55	$2,436.72	$55,095.95
19	June	$2,820.27	$367.31	$2,452.96	$52,642.99
20	July	$2,820.27	$350.95	$2,469.32	$50,173.67
21	August	$2,820.27	$334.49	$2,485.78	$47,687.89
22	September	$2,820.27	$317.92	$2,502.35	$45,185.54
23	October	$2,820.27	$301.24	$2,519.03	$42,666.51
24	November	$2,820.27	$284.44	$2,535.83	$40,130.68
25	December	$2,820.27	$267.54	$2,552.73	$37,577.95
26	January	$2,820.27	$250.52	$2,569.75	$35,008.20
27	February	$2,820.27	$233.39	$2,586.88	$32,421.32
28	March	$2,820.27	$216.14	$2,604.13	$29,817.19
29	April	$2,820.27	$198.78	$2,621.49	$27,195.70
30	May	$2,820.27	$181.30	$2,638.97	$24,556.73
31	June	$2,820.27	$163.71	$2,656.56	$21,900.18
32	July	$2,820.27	$146.00	$2,674.27	$19,225.91
33	August	$2,820.27	$128.17	$2,692.10	$16,533.81
34	September	$2,820.27	$110.23	$2,710.04	$13,823.77
35	October	$2,820.27	$92.16	$2,728.11	$11,095.65
36	November	$2,820.27	$73.97	$2,746.30	$ 8,349.36
37	December	$2,820.27	$55.66	$2,764.61	$ 5,584.75
38	January	$2,820.27	$37.23	$2,783.04	$ 2,801.71
39	February	$2,820.27	$18.68	$2,801.59	$0.12

And,

General Journal

Date	Description	DR	CR
3-31-10	Note Payable	2,220.27	
	Interest Expense	600.00	
	Cash		2,820.27

Notice that the credit to Cash is the same every month but the Interest Expense and the decrease to Note Payable for the principal payment change each month. This process will continue for another 35 months until the last payment is made. Note that the amortization table shows a balance of $0.12; therefore, the last payment on this installment note will be $2,820.39 ($2,820.27 + $0.12).

Assuming that PCs to Go has a December 31 year-end, the interest expense shown on the 2010 income statement would be $5,321.96 (total the interest expense column [C] through December [row 13]). The carrying value of this note shown on the 2010 balance sheet would be $67,119.24 (row 13, column E) but the portion due within one year $29,541.29 (total column D rows 14–25) would be shown in the current liabilities section and the remainder $37,577.95 (row 13, column E minus $29,541.29) would be shown as long-term debt. On the 2010 statement of cash flows we must separate the operating cash (interest) flows from the financing cash (principal) flows. Thus we would show:

Operating cash outflows	$5,321.96
Financing cash inflows	$90,000.00
Financing cash outflows	$22,880.74 (total column D through row 13)

Noninterest-Bearing Notes Payable

As we discussed in Chapter 14, the face value of a lump-sum payment note depends on the market rate of interest of the firm at the time the note is issued and the value of the asset acquired.

To illustrate, assume that on April 1, 2010, when the market interest rate was 8 percent PCs to Go issued a five-year noninterest-bearing note to acquire a parcel of land with a market value of $500,000. We know that $PV = 500{,}000$; $r = 8$; $n = 5$; $c = 1$; $ANN = 0$; therefore, $FV = 734{,}664.04$. Exhibit 15.2 illustrates the amortization table associated with this loan. Notice that there are no payments, but that the interest expense (column C) increases and the discount on notes payable (column D) decreases over the life of the loan because the carrying value (column E) increases over the life of the loan. **Discount on Notes Payable** is a *contra liability account* that represents the difference between the carrying value and the face value of the note due to the difference between the face rate of interest (0) and the market rate of interest (8 percent).

Because PCs to Go was able to exchange the note for the land, the assumption here is that the value of the property is the same as the present value of the note. In other words, PCs to Go could have gone to a bank with this $734,664.04 noninterest-bearing note and borrowed $500,000 in cash and then purchased the land. Therefore,

Assets	=	Liabilities	+	Owners' equity
+500,000		+500,000		

Let's make the entry to record the purchase of the land:

General Journal

Date	Description	DR	CR
4-1-10	Land	500,000.00	
	Discount on Notes Payable	234,664.04	
	Notes Payable		734,664.04

EXHIBIT 15.2
Noninterest-Bearing Note Payable

	A	B	C	D	E
1	**Noninterest-Bearing Note Payable**				
2			**Interest**	**Discount on**	
3	**Period**	**Payment**	**Expense**	**Notes Payable**	**Carrying Value**
4	April 2010			$234,664.04	$500,000.00
5	April 2011	$0.00	$40,000.00	$194,664.04	$540,000.00
6	April 2012	$0.00	$43,200.00	$151,464.04	$583,200.00
7	April 2013	$0.00	$46,656.00	$104,808.04	$629,856.00
8	April 2014	$0.00	$50,388.48	$54,419.56	$680,244.48
9	April 2015	$0.00	$54,419.56	$0.00	$734,664.04

Notice that the Discount on Notes Payable account has a $234,664.04 debit balance; thus, when put together with the Notes Payable account with a credit balance of $734,664.04, we have the carrying value of the note, $500,000.

Since this note requires no payments, we do not have to make any other journal entries until the end of the year. Recall that before preparing financial statements we must make adjusting entries to recognize revenues and expenses that have not yet been recorded. Let's think about PCs to Go's circumstances at year-end. We took out a loan on April 1 so we have been in debt for nine months. But we have not recognized any interest expense because we have not made any payments. Therefore we must determine the amount of, and make an entry for, the interest expense for 2010. Look at the amortization table in Exhibit 15.2. It shows that the interest expense for the 12-month period from April 2010 to April 2011 is $40,000 (row 5). We must recognize 9/12 of this interest as an expense in 2010 ($40,000 × 9/12 = $30,000). But are we going to pay this interest? The answer is no. At the end of the fifth year (April 2015), we will pay the carrying value (face value) of the note. Therefore, we do not want to recognize any interest payable; instead we reduce the Discount on Notes Payable account to increase the carrying value of the note. Thus,

Assets =	Liabilities +	Owners' equity
	+30,000	(30,000)

The entry is

General Journal

Date	Description	DR	CR
12-31-10	Interest Expense ($40,000 × 9/12)	30,000.00	
	Discount on Notes Payable		30,000.00

After this entry is posted the Discount on Notes Payable account will show a $204,664.04 ($234,664.04 – $30,000) balance but the Notes Payable account still has a balance of $734,664.04 as shown next. The resulting liability of $530,000 on December 31, 2010, represents the obligation to repay the $500,000 borrowed on April 1, 2010, and the $30,000 of interest incurred to date.

Discount on Notes Payable

Date	Description	DR	CR	Balance
4-1-10		234,664.04		234,664.04
12-31-10			30,000.00	204,664.04

Notes Payable

Date	Description	DR	CR	Balance
4-1-10			734,664.04	734,664.04

The balance sheet will indicate a carrying value on this note of $530,000 ($734,664.04 – $204,664.04). On the income statement for 2010, we will show interest expense of $30,000. And, finally, the statement of cash flows will show a cash inflow from financing activities of $500,000. We will not have to make another entry on this note until December 31, 2011. At that time we must recognize the remaining 3/12 of $40,000 interest (row 5) plus 9/12 of $43,200 interest (row 6) and reduce the Discount on Notes Payable account accordingly.

Long-term debt is recorded at its *face value* but reported on the balance sheet each fiscal period at its *carrying value*. With a lump-sum payment note carrying value represents two accounts:
Notes payable
Less: Discount on Notes Payable

The resulting entry for 2011 would be:

General Journal

Date	Description	DR	CR
12-31-11	Interest expense	42,400	
	Discount on Notes Payable		42,400

And, the resulting impact on the 2011 financial statements would be:

Income statement:	Interest expense	$ 42,400.00
Statement of cash flows:	Nothing	
Balance sheet:	Note payable	$734,664.04
	Less: Discount N/P	162,264.04
	Carrying value	$572,400.00

Bonds Payable: Market Rate Greater Than the Face Rate

When the market rate of interest is greater than the face rate of interest, the proceeds from the bond issue are smaller than the face value of the bond issue. That is, the bonds are issued at a discount. Let's assume that PCs to Go issues 2,000, 10-year bonds each with a face value of $1,000 and a face rate of interest of 10 percent paid semiannually. We issue the bonds on June 30, 2010, when the market rate of interest is 12 percent. We know that $FV = 2{,}000{,}000$; $c = 2$; $n = 20$; $ANN = 100{,}000$; $r = 12$; therefore, $PV = 1{,}770{,}601.58$. Exhibit 15.3 shows the amortization table for this note. Notice that the cash payment is the face value multiplied by the face rate of interest for one-half year while the interest expense is the carrying value multiplied by the market rate of interest for one-half year.

When PCs to Go issues the bonds:

Assets	=	Liabilities	+	Owners' equity
+1,770,601.58		+1,770,601.58		

EXHIBIT 15.3
Bonds Issued at a Discount

	A	B	C	D	E	F
1			Bonds Issued at a Discount			
2		Cash	Interest	Discount	Discount	Carrying
3	Period	Payment	Expense	Reduction	Remaining	Value
4					$229,398.42	$1,770,601.58
5	December 31	$100,000.00	$106,236.09	$6,236.09	$223,162.33	$1,776,837.67
6	June 30	$100,000.00	$106,610.26	$6,610.26	$216,552.06	$1,783,447.94
7	December 31	$100,000.00	$107,006.88	$7,006.88	$209,545.19	$1,790,454.81
8	June 30	$100,000.00	$107,427.29	$7,427.29	$202,117.90	$1,797,882.10
9	December 31	$100,000.00	$107,872.93	$7,872.93	$194,244.97	$1,805,755.03
10	June 30	$100,000.00	$108,345.30	$8,345.30	$185,899.67	$1,814,100.33
11	December 31	$100,000.00	$108,846.02	$8,846.02	$177,053.65	$1,822,946.35
12	June 30	$100,000.00	$109,376.78	$9,376.78	$167,676.87	$1,832,323.13
13	December 31	$100,000.00	$109,939.39	$9,939.39	$157,737.48	$1,842,262.52
14	June 30	$100,000.00	$110,535.75	$10,535.75	$147,201.73	$1,852,798.27
15	December 31	$100,000.00	$111,167.90	$11,167.90	$136,033.84	$1,863,966.16
16	June 30	$100,000.00	$111,837.97	$11,837.97	$124,195.87	$1,875,804.13
17	December 31	$100,000.00	$112,548.25	$12,548.25	$111,647.62	$1,888,352.38
18	June 30	$100,000.00	$113,301.14	$13,301.14	$98,346.48	$1,901,653.52
19	December 31	$100,000.00	$114,099.21	$14,099.21	$84,247.27	$1,915,752.73
20	June 30	$100,000.00	$114,945.16	$14,945.16	$69,302.10	$1,930,697.90
21	December 31	$100,000.00	$115,841.87	$15,841.87	$53,460.23	$1,946,539.77
22	June 30	$100,000.00	$116,792.39	$16,792.39	$36,667.84	$1,963,332.16
23	December 31	$100,000.00	$117,799.93	$17,799.93	$18,867.91	$1,981,132.09
24	June 30	$100,000.00	$118,867.93	$18,867.93	-$0.01	$2,000,000.01

Let's make the entry to record the issuance of the bonds:

General Journal

Date	Description	DR	CR
6-30-10	Cash	1,770,601.58	
	Discount on Bonds Payable	229,398.42	
	Bonds Payable		2,000,000.00

Notice that the Cash is the amount received (the present value of the bonds) and the bonds are recorded at their face (future) value. The **Discount on Bonds Payable** account represents the difference between the face value and the carrying value of the bonds. Like the Discount on Notes Payable account, it is a contra liability that when put together with the Bonds Payable account indicates the carrying value of the debt.

When is the next entry needed? The first periodic payment on these bonds is due December 31, 2010. The entry must recognize the interest expense, the cash payment, and the decrease in the discount necessary to increase the carrying value of the bonds. Let's look at Exhibit 15.3. Reading across row 5 gives us all the information we need to make this entry. The following entry indicates the cash paid, the interest expense incurred for the six-month period from June 30 through December 31, and the reduction in the discount due to the interest expense being larger than the cash payment (i.e., the carrying value of the debt increases).

General Journal

Date	Description	DR	CR
12-31-10	Interest Expense (column C)	106,236.09	
	Discount on Bonds Payable (column D)		6,236.09
	Cash (column B)		100,000.00

Because this entry is made on December 31 (PCs to Go's year-end) we don't need to make any adjusting entries to recognize interest expense associated with these bonds. The Discount on Bonds Payable and Bonds Payable accounts after these events are posted appear as:

Discount on Bonds Payable

Date	Description	DR	CR	Balance
6-30-10		229,398.42		229,398.42
12-31-10			6,236.09	223,162.33

Bonds Payable

Date	Description	DR	CR	Balance
6-30-10			2,000,000	2,000,000

Thus, the impact on the financial statements would be:

Income statement:	Interest expense	$ 106,236.09
Statement of cash flows:	Inflow (financing)	$1,770,601.58
	Outflow (operating)	$100,000.00
Balance sheet:		
Long-term liability	Bond payable	$2,000,000.00
	Less: Discount B/P	223,162.33
	Carrying value	$1,776,837.67

Since the cash payment is for interest only (no principal) the cash outflow is an operating cash flow. The carrying value of the bonds on the balance sheet reflects the balance in the previous two accounts. That is, the carrying value of the debt is $2,000,000.00 – $223,162.33 = $1,776,837.67.

Bonds Payable: Market Rate Less Than the Face Rate

When the market rate of interest is less than the face rate of interest, the proceeds from the bond are greater than the face value of the bond. That is, the bonds are issued at a premium. Let's assume that PCs to Go issues 2,000 10-year bonds each with a face value of $1,000 and a face rate of interest of 10 percent paid semiannually. We issue the bonds on May 31, 2010, when the market rate of interest is 8 percent. We know that $FV = 2{,}000{,}000$; $c = 2$; $n = 20$; $ANN = 100{,}000$; $r = 8$; therefore, $PV = 2{,}271{,}806.53$. Exhibit 15.4 shows the amortization table for this note.

When PCs to Go issues the bonds:

Assets	=	Liabilities	+	Owners' equity
+2,271,806.53		+2,271,806.53		

Let's make the entry to record the issuance of the bonds:

General Journal

Date	Description	DR	CR
5-31-10	Cash	2,271,806.53	
	Premium on Bonds Payable		271,806.53
	Bonds Payable		2,000,000.00

Notice that the cash is the amount received (the present value of the bonds) and the bonds are recorded at their face (future) value. The **Premium on Bonds Payable** account represents the difference between the face value and the carrying value of the bonds. The Premium on Bonds Payable is an *adjunct account,* which means it is *added* to the balance in the Bonds Payable account to indicate the carrying value of the debt.

EXHIBIT 15.4
Bonds Issued at a Premium

	A	B	C	D	E	F
1	Bonds Issued at a Premium					
2		Cash	Interest	Premium	Premium	Carrying
3	Period	Payment	Expense	Reduction	Remaining	Value
4					$271,806.53	$2,271,806.53
5	November	$100,000.00	$90,872.26	$9,127.74	$262,678.79	$2,262,678.79
6	May	$100,000.00	$90,507.15	$9,492.85	$253,185.94	$2,253,185.94
7	November	$100,000.00	$90,127.44	$9,872.56	$243,313.38	$2,243,313.38
8	May	$100,000.00	$89,732.54	$10,267.46	$233,045.92	$2,233,045.92
9	November	$100,000.00	$89,321.84	$10,678.16	$222,367.75	$2,222,367.75
10	May	$100,000.00	$88,894.71	$11,105.29	$211,262.46	$2,211,262.46
11	November	$100,000.00	$88,450.50	$11,549.50	$199,712.96	$2,199,712.96
12	May	$100,000.00	$87,988.52	$12,011.48	$187,701.48	$2,187,701.48
13	November	$100,000.00	$87,508.06	$12,491.94	$175,209.54	$2,175,209.54
14	May	$100,000.00	$87,008.38	$12,991.62	$162,217.92	$2,162,217.92
15	November	$100,000.00	$86,488.72	$13,511.28	$148,706.64	$2,148,706.64
16	May	$100,000.00	$85,948.27	$14,051.73	$134,654.90	$2,134,654.90
17	November	$100,000.00	$85,386.20	$14,613.80	$120,041.10	$2,120,041.10
18	May	$100,000.00	$84,801.64	$15,198.36	$104,842.74	$2,104,842.74
19	November	$100,000.00	$84,193.71	$15,806.29	$89,036.45	$2,089,036.45
20	May	$100,000.00	$83,561.46	$16,438.54	$72,597.91	$2,072,597.91
21	November	$100,000.00	$82,903.92	$17,096.08	$55,501.83	$2,055,501.83
22	May	$100,000.00	$82,220.07	$17,779.93	$37,721.90	$2,037,721.90
23	November	$100,000.00	$81,508.88	$18,491.12	$19,230.78	$2,019,230.78
24	May	$100,000.00	$80,769.23	$19,230.77	$0.01	$2,000,000.01

When is the next entry needed? The first periodic payment on these bonds is due November 30, 2010. The entry must recognize the interest expense, the cash payment, and the decrease in the premium necessary to decrease the carrying value of the bonds. Let's look at Exhibit 15.4. Reading across row 5 gives us all the information we need to make this entry. The next entry made on November 30, 2010, indicates the cash paid, the interest expense incurred for the six-month period from May 31 through November 30, and the reduction in the premium due to the interest expense being smaller than the cash payment (i.e., the carrying value of the debt decreases).

General Journal

Date	Description	DR	CR
11-30-10	Interest Expense	90,872.26	
	Premium on Bonds Payable	9,127.74	
	Cash		100,000.00

Do we need to make any other entries associated with these bonds in 2010? Yes, since the above entry was made on November 30 we need to recognize the interest expense associated with this debt for December. Let's examine the amortization table in Exhibit 15.4 again. It shows that the interest expense for the next payment period (six months) is $90,507.15 (row 6). Since we want the interest for only one out of six months, we must multiply this amount by one-sixth to determine the interest expense for December. Likewise, the cash payment shown in Exhibit 15.4 (row 6) is for the next six months. Since only one month is payable on December 31, we must recognize one-sixth of this amount as interest payable. Finally, the amortization schedule indicates that the premium will be reduced by $9,492.85 on the next payment, therefore, we recognize one-sixth of this amount during 2010 to properly report the carrying value of the bonds on the balance sheet. The following entry is needed on December 31, 2010:

General Journal

Date	Description	DR	CR
12-31-10	Interest Expense (90,507.15 × 1/6)	15,084.53	
	Premium on Bonds Payable (9,492.85 × 1/6)	1,582.14	
	Interest Payable (100,000 × 1/6)		16,666.67

After the previous entries are posted, the Premium on Bonds Payable, Bonds Payable, and Interest Expense accounts would appear as:

Premium on Bonds Payable

Date	Description	DR	CR	Balance
5-31-10			271,806.53	271,806.53
11-30-10		9,127.74		262,678.79
12-31-10		1,582.14		261,096.65

Bonds Payable

Date	Description	DR	CR	Balance
5-31-10			2,000,000	2,000,000

Interest Expense

Date	Description	DR	CR	Balance
11-30-10		90,872.26		90,872.26
12-31-10		15,084.53		105,956.79

Therefore for 2010 we would show the following information on the financial statements:

Income statement:	Interest expense	$ 105,956.79
Balance sheet:		
Current liability	Interest payable	$ 16,666.67
Long-term liability	Bond payable	$2,000,000.00
	Add: Premium on B/P	261,096.65
	Carrying value of debt	$2,261,096.65
Statement of cash flows:	Inflow (financing)	$2,271,806.53
	Outflow (operating)	$ 100,000.00

Now let's examine the entry that is required on May 31, 2011. According to the amortization table in Exhibit 15.4, the interest expense is $90,507.15; but we have already recognized one-sixth of this amount in 2010. Therefore, we must recognize the remaining five-sixths in 2011. Likewise, in 2010 we reduced the premium by one-sixth of $9,492.85 so we need to further reduce the premium by five-sixths of $9,492.85 in 2011. Finally, we must make a cash payment of $100,000 and remove the interest payable liability we recorded in 2010. The following entry is needed. Examine this entry very carefully.

General Journal

Date	Description	DR	CR
5-31-11	Interest Expense (90,507.15 × 5/6)	75,422.62	
	Interest Payable (100,000 × 1/6, see entry 12-31-10)	16,666.67	
	Premium on Bonds Payable (9,492.85 × 5/6)	7,910.71	
	Cash		100,000.00

Let's go ahead and finish the entries for 2011. On November 30, we need to recognize a six-month interest payment. Reading across row 7 on the amortization table:

General Journal

Date	Description	DR	CR
11-30-11	Interest Expense	90,127.44	
	Premium on Bonds Payable	9,872.56	
	Cash		100,000.00

On December 31, we need to make an adjusting entry for one month. Reading across row 8 and taking one-sixth of the amounts, we make the following entry:

General Journal

Date	Description	DR	CR
12-31-11	Interest Expense (89,732.54 × 1/6)	14,955.42	
	Premium on Bonds Payable (10,267.46 × 1/6)	1,711.24	
	Interest Payable (100,000.00 × 1/6)		16,666.66

Bonds are recorded at *face value* but reported on the balance sheet each fiscal period at the *carrying value*. If the bond was issued at a discount:
Bonds Payable
Less: Discount on Bonds Payable
If the bond was issued at a premium:
Bonds Payable
Add: Premium on Bonds Payable

So what amounts would appear on the 2011 financial statements? On the income statement, we would show interest expense from the May, November, and December entries ($75,422.62 + $90,127.44 + $14,955.42). On the statement of cash flows, we would show cash payments from the May and November entries ($100,000 + $100,000). Finally, on the balance sheet, we would show the interest payable from the December entry and the carrying value of the bonds at the end of 2011. The remaining premium is $241,602.14 ($261,096.65 − $7,910.71 − $9,872.56 − $1,711.24) as shown on the next page.

OF INTEREST Setting Up Amortization Schedules in Excel

Excel and other spreadsheet packages are very useful for setting up amortization tables for notes payable. All it takes is a little advance planning and the use of the "Copy" command and Excel does all the tedious work.

Let's set up the installment note discussed in the chapter and illustrated in Exhibit 15.1. We need the following columns: months, payment, interest, principal, and carrying value as shown in Exhibit 15.1. Then enter the initial carrying value in cell E3, the monthly payment amount in cell B4, and the names of the months or simply the numbers from 1 to 36 in column A cells 4 through 39. In cell C4 we need to write a formula to calculate monthly interest. We know that interest = CV * rate * 1/12 so we enter the following formula: = E3 * 0.08 * 1/12. In cell D4 we need to write a formula to calculate the portion of each payment that is principal so we enter the following: = B4 – C4. Finally, in cell E4 we must write a formula to determine the new carrying value, so we enter: = E3 – D4. Now simply copy B4: E4 and paste to B5: E39.

Let's set up the noninterest-bearing note discussed in the chapter and illustrated in Exhibit 15.2. We need the following columns: period, payment, interest, discount, carrying value. Enter the periods in column A. Then enter the initial discount on notes payable and carrying value in the appropriate columns (cells D4 and E4). We know there is no payment on this type of note so cell B5 is zero. Then we need to write a formula in cell C5 to calculate the annual interest expense. Remember interest expense = CV * rate * time, so we enter: = E4 * 0.08. Then in cell D5 we need a formula to calculate the remaining discount on notes payable so we enter = D4 – C5. Finally in cell E5 we write a formula to calculate the new carrying value, as: = E4 + C5. Now simply copy B5: E5 and paste to B6: E9.

Now let's set up the bonds issued at a premium discussed in the chapter and illustrated in Exhibit 15.4. Enter the periods in column A. In cells E4 and F4 enter the initial premium and carrying value of the bonds. In cell B5 enter the amount of the periodic payment. In cell C5 enter the formula to calculate the periodic interest expense: = F4 * 0.08 * 1/2. In cell D5 enter the formula to calculate the premium reduction. Remember the premium is reduced by the difference between the cash payment and the interest expense, so the formula is = B5 – C5. In cell E5 enter the formula to determine the remaining premium: = E4 – D5. And in cell F5 enter the formula to determine the new carrying value: = F4 – D5. Then copy cells B5: F5 and paste to B6: F24.

That's all there is to it! Enjoy!

Income statement:	Interest expense	$ 180,505.48
Statement of cash flows:	Operating outflow	200,000.00
Balance sheet:	Interest payable	16,666.66
	Bonds payable	2,000,000.00
	Add: Premium B/P	241,602.14
	Carrying value	$2,241,602.14

Bonds Payable: Market Rate Equal to the Face Rate

When the market rate of interest is equal to the face rate of interest, the proceeds from the bond are equal to the face value of the bond. Let's assume that PCs to Go issues 2,000 10-year bonds each with a face value of $1,000 and a face rate of interest of 10 percent paid semiannually on May 31 and November 30. We will issue the bonds on May 31, 2010, when the market rate of interest is 10 percent. We know that $FV = 2{,}000{,}000$; $c = 2$; $n = 20$; $ANN = 100{,}000$; $r = 10$; therefore, $PV = 2{,}000{,}000$. When PCs to Go issues the bonds:

Assets	=	Liabilities	+	Owners' equity
+2,000,000		+2,000,000		

Let's make the entry to record the issuance of the bonds:

General Journal

Date	Description	DR	CR
5-31-10	Cash	2,000,000.00	
	Bonds Payable		2,000,000.00

Notice that the Cash is the amount received (the present value of the bonds) and the bonds are recorded at their face (future) value. When is the next entry needed? The first periodic payment on these bonds is due November 30, 2010. The entry must recognize the interest expense and the cash payment but there will not be any change in the carrying value of the bonds. The following entry made on November 30 indicates the cash payment and the interest expense for the first six months.

General Journal

Date	Description	DR	CR
11-30-10	Interest Expense	100,000.00	
	Cash		100,000.00

Finally, this entry would be made to adjust the accounting records for the interest incurred but not paid during December.

General Journal

Date	Description	DR	CR
12-31-10	Interest Expense	16,666.67	
	Interest Payable		16,666.67

Therefore for 2010 we would show the following information on the financial statements:

Income statement:	Interest expense	$ 116,666.67
Balance sheet:		
Current liability	Interest payable	$ 16,666.67
Long-term liability	Bonds payable	$2,000,000.00
Statement of cash flows:	Inflow (financing)	$2,000,000.00
	Outflow (operating)	$ 100,000.00

Financial Statements and Financing Activities

As you know from our earlier discussion, financing activities impact the income statement (interest expense), the balance sheet (carrying value of debt and balances of owners' equity), the statement of cash flows (inflows and outflows), and the statement of owners' equity. Let's examine the financial statements of Apple for financing activities (see the Appendix).

Apple's income statement does not indicate the amount of interest expense incurred during fiscal 2008, but the statement of cash flows shows no cash paid for interest in 2008 (see Supplemental disclosures). On the balance sheet, Apple shows noncurrent liabilities of $4,450 million. Note 4 (page 70 of the 2008 annual report) indicates that most of this amount is deferred revenue.

In the shareholders' equity section, we notice that Apple has no par value common stock. It has 1.8 billion shares authorized and 888,325,973 issued and outstanding as of September 27, 2008. Therefore, Apple had no treasury stock at the end of fiscal 2008. Note 6 (page 74 of the annual report) also indicates that Apple has 5 million shares of preferred stock authorized, but not issued.

Note: In the shareholders' equity section, it is common for companies to combine their Paid-in Capital in Excess of Par Value accounts into one amount for reporting on the balance sheet. Thus a company might show Preferred Stock, then Common Stock, and then Paid-in Capital in Excess of Par Value. Also, note that if a company has treasury stock, it is typically shown last as a reduction of the shareholders' equity.

Internal Evaluation of Financing Activities

In addition to the information contained in the financial statements, management must also evaluate the results of financing activities against the balanced scorecard goals set for these activities. As part of this evaluation, management might calculate the debt-to-equity, times interest earned, return on equity, and return on common equity ratios and compare them against the planned ratios (Chapters 13 and 14). This evaluation is also necessary to ensure that debt covenants based on ratios are not violated and that operating activities are generating sufficient income to meet interest obligations and provide an adequate return to owners.

Summary

This chapter discusses how the accounting system captures and reports the financing activities of the business. The accounting treatment of a corporation's owners' equity reflects that it is a separate legal entity and that its owners have limited liability. The accounting treatment of long-term debt reflects the differing attributes of the three types of notes. In all cases the debt is initially recorded at its face value and reduced only as principal payments are made.

- Stock that is issued for noncash assets is valued at the fair market value of the asset or the stock, whichever is more reasonably determinable.
- Retained earnings typically represent the amount of earnings reinvested in the corporation. When the Retained Earnings account has a debit balance, it is referred to as a deficit in retained earnings.
- The Treasury Stock account is considered a contra equity account and is reported as a reduction of total shareholders' equity. When a company reissues treasury stock, the difference between the initial cost paid to acquire the stock and the reissue price will either increase or decrease shareholders' equity.
- The Discount on Notes (or Bonds) Payable account is a contra liability subtracted from the Notes (or Bonds) account to report the carrying value of the debt on the balance sheet. The Premium on Bonds Payable account is an adjunct account that is added to the Bonds Payable account to report the carrying value of the debt on the balance sheet.

Key Terms

Discount on Bonds Payable A contra liability account that represents the difference between the face value and the carrying value of the bonds, *435*

Discount on Notes Payable A contra liability account that represents the difference between the carrying value and the face value of the note; exists when the face value is greater than the carrying value, *432*

Paid-in Capital from Treasury Stock An account used to show the amount of additional capital generated from the reissue of treasury stock, *428*

Paid-in-Capital in Excess of Par Value An account used to reflect the difference between the net assets received and the par value of the stock issued, *424*

Premium on Bond Payable An account that represents the difference between the face value and the carrying value of the bonds; exists when the face value is less than the carrying value, *436*

Stock Dividends Distributable An account credited on the date of declaration of a stock dividend to show the par value of the shares the corporation will issue on the date of distribution, *426*

Questions

1. Why is the par value rather than the market value recorded in a stock account?
2. How do journal entries reflect the market value of par value stock when the stock is first issued?
3. What distinguishes par value from no-par stock in the shareholders' equity section of the balance sheet?

4. Explain the basis for determining the issue price of shares of stock when the stock is exchanged for a noncash asset.
5. What is the purpose of the Retained Earnings account, and what business events cause it to change during the year?
6. What does a deficit balance in Retained Earnings indicate?
7. Why would a company buy treasury stock? How is it reported on a firm's financial statements?
8. What does the Paid-in Capital from Treasury Stock account represent? How is it reported on a firm's financial statements?
9. What two accounts are debited when a company makes a payment on an installment loan?
10. When is an installment note classified as both a current liability and a long-term liability?
11. Describe what the Discount on Notes Payable represents.
12. Describe why and how the Discount on Notes Payable is reported on the balance sheet.
13. How does the entry to record the issuance of a bond at a premium differ from a bond issued at a discount?
14. How should a company report a premium on bonds payable on its balance sheet?
15. What constitutes the carrying value of a noninterest-bearing note?
16. What constitutes the carrying value of a bond?
17. Explain why and how the Premium and Discount on Bonds Payable affect interest expense.
18. Describe the difference in cash flows between two identical bonds when one is issued at a discount and the other is issued at a premium.

Exercises

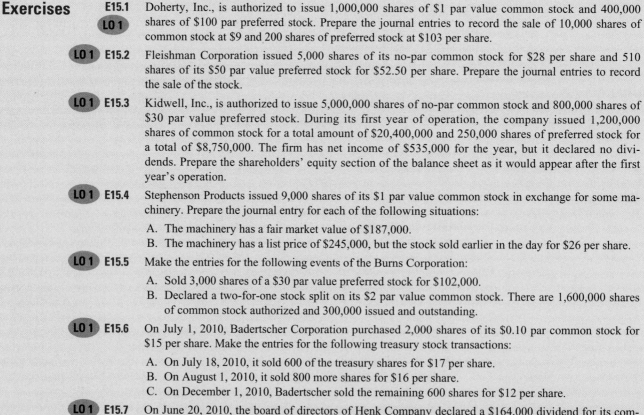

E15.1 LO 1 Doherty, Inc., is authorized to issue 1,000,000 shares of $1 par value common stock and 400,000 shares of $100 par preferred stock. Prepare the journal entries to record the sale of 10,000 shares of common stock at $9 and 200 shares of preferred stock at $103 per share.

LO 1 **E15.2** Fleishman Corporation issued 5,000 shares of its no-par common stock for $28 per share and 510 shares of its $50 par value preferred stock for $52.50 per share. Prepare the journal entries to record the sale of the stock.

LO 1 **E15.3** Kidwell, Inc., is authorized to issue 5,000,000 shares of no-par common stock and 800,000 shares of $30 par value preferred stock. During its first year of operation, the company issued 1,200,000 shares of common stock for a total amount of $20,400,000 and 250,000 shares of preferred stock for a total of $8,750,000. The firm has net income of $535,000 for the year, but it declared no dividends. Prepare the shareholders' equity section of the balance sheet as it would appear after the first year's operation.

LO 1 **E15.4** Stephenson Products issued 9,000 shares of its $1 par value common stock in exchange for some machinery. Prepare the journal entry for each of the following situations:

A. The machinery has a fair market value of $187,000.
B. The machinery has a list price of $245,000, but the stock sold earlier in the day for $26 per share.

LO 1 **E15.5** Make the entries for the following events of the Burns Corporation:

A. Sold 3,000 shares of a $30 par value preferred stock for $102,000.
B. Declared a two-for-one stock split on its $2 par value common stock. There are 1,600,000 shares of common stock authorized and 300,000 issued and outstanding.

LO 1 **E15.6** On July 1, 2010, Badertscher Corporation purchased 2,000 shares of its $0.10 par common stock for $15 per share. Make the entries for the following treasury stock transactions:

A. On July 18, 2010, it sold 600 of the treasury shares for $17 per share.
B. On August 1, 2010, it sold 800 more shares for $16 per share.
C. On December 1, 2010, Badertscher sold the remaining 600 shares for $12 per share.

LO 1 **E15.7** On June 20, 2010, the board of directors of Henk Company declared a $164,000 dividend for its common shareholders. The date of payment for the dividend is July 15, 2010, to shareholders of record on June 30, 2010. Record all the appropriate journal entries.

LO 1 **E15.8** Johnson Corporation decided to pay a dividend of $2.00 per share. The corporation has 2,500,000 shares authorized, 800,000 shares issued, and 750,000 shares outstanding on the date of declaration. Make the entries necessary for the dividend on the following dates:

- June 15, 2010 Date of declaration
- July 15, 2010 Date of record
- August 1, 2010 Date of payment

LO 1 **E15.9** Sprague, Inc., has 10,000,000 shares of $2 par value common stock authorized and 1,500,000 shares issued and outstanding. The stock had a fair market value of $20 per share on November 15, 2010, when the board of directors declared a 5 percent stock dividend to holders of record on November 27, 2010. The new shares were distributed on December 10, 2010. Make the journal entries to record the declaration and distribution of the stock dividend. How are the par value per share, retained earnings, total shareholders' equity, and number of shares authorized, issued, and outstanding affected by the stock dividend?

LO 1 **E15.10** Using the information in E15.9, how would your answer differ if Sprague, Inc., had declared a 50 percent stock dividend?

LO 2 **E15.11** The following schedules describe three notes:

Schedule 1

Date	Cash Payment	Interest Expense	Principal	Loan Balance
2/1/10				$40,000
8/1/10	$8,135	$2,400	$ 5,735	34,265
2/1/11	8,135	2,056	6,079	28,186
8/1/11	8,135	1,691	6,444	21,742
2/1/12	8,135	1,305	6,830	14,912
8/1/12	8,135	895	7,240	7,672
2/1/13	8,135	463	7,672	–0–

Schedule 2

Date	Cash Payment	Interest Expense	Discount	Carrying Value
4/1/10			$364,500.00	$ 635,500.00
4/1/11		$ 76,260.00	288,240.00	711,760.00
4/1/12		85,411.20	202,828.80	797,171.20
4/1/13		95,660.54	107,168.26	892,831.74
4/1/14		107,168.26	–0–	1,000,000.00
4/1/15	$1,000,000			–0–

Schedule 3

Date	Cash Interest	Interest Expense	No Discount or Premium	Carrying Value
3/1/10				$10,000,000
9/1/10	$500,000	$500,000		10,000,000
3/1/11	500,000	500,000		10,000,000
9/1/11	500,000	500,000		10,000,000
3/1/12	500,000	500,000		10,000,000

Required:

A. Which schedule describes a periodic payment and lump-sum note?
B. Which schedule describes a lump-sum payment note?
C. Which schedule describes a periodic payment note?
D. What are the annual interest rates on each of the notes?
E. Assuming each note was issued for cash, show the entry to record the issuance of each of the notes.

LO 2 E15.12 On September 1, 2010, Puriton Telescopes borrowed $100,000 cash at 6 percent on an eight-year installment note. Monthly payments start on October 1, 2010. Prepare an installment loan repayment schedule for the first three months of the note and make the entries for the three months.

LO 2 E15.13 The following partial payment schedule is for a $75,000 note the Steiner Corporation issued for cash on October 31, 2010. If Steiner has a December 31 fiscal year-end, make the entries for the issuance of the note and through December 31, 2010.

Period	Payment	Interest	Principal	Carrying Value
10/31/2010				$75,000.00
11/30/2010	$1,415.34	$312.50	$1,102.84	73,897.16
12/31/2010	1,415.34	307.90	1,107.44	72,789.72
1/31/2011	1,415.34	303.29	1,112.05	71,677.68
2/28/2011	1,415.34	298.66	1,116.68	70,560.99

LO 2 E15.14 Using the information in E15.13, show how the installment note is reported on Steiner Corporation's income statement, balance sheet, and statement of cash flows for the year ended December 31, 2010 (don't worry about current versus long-term debt).

LO 2 E15.15 On November 1, 2010, Phillips Corporation raised $2,382,041.19 by issuing a five-year, $3,500,000 noninterest-bearing note. The amortization table for the note follows. Make the entries for the note from November l, 2010, to December 31, 2011.

Period	Payment	Interest	Discount Left	Carrying Value
11/1/10			$1,117,958.81	$2,382,041.19
11/1/11	$0.00	$190,563.30	927,395.51	2,572,604.49
11/1/12	0.00	205,808.36	721,587.15	2,778,412.85
11/1/13	0.00	222,273.03	499,314.12	3,000,685.88
11/1/14	0.00	240,054.87	259,259.25	3,240,740.75
11/1/15	0.00	259,259.25	0.00	3,500,000.00

LO 2 E15.16 Using the information in E15.15, show how Phillips Corporation's income statement and balance sheet report the impact of this note for the years ended December 31, 2010, and December 31, 2011.

LO 2 E15.17 On June 1, 2010, Jorgensen Corporation purchased a piece of equipment with a list price of $200,000 and signed a five-year noninterest-bearing note. The market rate at the time the note was signed was 8 percent. Given the following amortization schedule for the note and the fact that Jorgensen has a December 31 fiscal year-end, make the entries necessary for 2010, 2011, and 2012.

Period	Payment	Interest	Discount Left	Carrying Value
6/1/10			$93,865.62	$200,000.00
6/1/11	$0.00	$16,000.00	77,865.62	216,000.00
6/1/12	0.00	17,280.00	60,585.62	233,280.00
6/1/13	0.00	18,662.40	41,923.22	251,942.40
6/1/14	0.00	20,155.39	21,767.83	272,097.79
6/1/15	0.00	21,767.83	0.00	293,865.62

LO 2 E15.18 The Brinkerhoff Company signed a $400,000, 6 percent, four-year bond dated May 1, 2011, when the market rate of interest was 6 percent. Interest on the bond is payable semiannually on November 1 and May 1 each year. The company closes its books annually on December 31. Prepare the entries for the issuance of the bond and for events related to the bond during the first year of the bond's life. How is the bond reported on Brinkerhoff's balance sheet, income statement, and cash flow statement for the year ended December 31, 2011?

LO 2 E15.19 Gland Corporation issued for cash a $400,000, 7 percent, three-year bond on September 1, 2010, that pays interest annually. Gland Corporation has a December 31 fiscal year-end. Make the entries for the first year of the note's life if the market rate of interest is 6.5 percent.

LO 2 E15.20 Using the information from E15.19 and assuming the market rate of interest was 7.5 percent, make the entries for the first year of the note's life.

LO 2 **E15.21** Scott Corporation issued a $100,000, eight-year, 7 percent note for cash on June 1, 2011. The note pays interest semiannually and the market rate of interest was 6 percent when the note was issued. Given this information, make the entries for the first year of the note's life if Scott Corporation has a December 31 fiscal year-end. Show how Scott reports the note on its income statement, balance sheet, and cash flow statement for the year ended December 31, 2011.

LO 2 **E15.22** Using the information from E15.21 and assuming the market rate of interest was 8 percent, make the entries for the first year of the bond's life and show how Scott would report its bond activities on its 2011 financial statements.

Problems

P15.1 LO 1 The charter of the Sanders Corporation authorizes the issuance of 1,500,000 shares of no-par common stock and 500,000 shares of 8 percent, $50 par value, cumulative preferred stock. These events affected shareholders' equity during the first year of operation:

1. 200,000 shares of common stock were sold for $15 per share.
2. 40,000 shares of preferred stock were sold at $52 per share.
3. A building with a fair market value of $560,000 was acquired for a cash payment of $150,000 and 17,000 shares of common stock.
4. 30,000 shares of common stock were issued for $690,000 cash.
5. A dividend of $1 per share for common and $4 per share for preferred stock was declared.

Required:
A. Record the transactions just described.
B. Prepare the shareholders' equity section of the balance sheet for December 31 assuming that Sanders generated $945,000 of income.

LO 1 **P15.2** McDougall Corporation is authorized to issue 500,000 shares of $40 par value, 10 percent cumulative preferred stock and 2,000,000 shares of $0.01 par value common stock. The following transactions summarize the events affecting its capital stock accounts during its first year of operations:

1. The company issued 800,000 shares of common stock for cash of $20 per share.
2. 100,000 shares of preferred stock were sold for cash of $44 per share.
3. McDougall repurchased and held as treasury stock 10,000 shares of its own common stock at $19 per share.
4. 2,000 shares of the treasury stock were reissued at $23 per share.

Required:
A. Make the entries to record these events.
B. Prepare the shareholders' equity section of McDougall's balance sheet assuming Retained Earnings has a credit balance of $276,000.

LO 1 **P15.3** The shareholders' equity section of Gilman Company's balance sheet appeared as follows on August 15, 2010:

Common stock—$1 par value, 1,000,000 shares authorized, 400,000 shares issued and outstanding	$ 400,000
Paid-in capital in excess of par	500,000
Total contributed capital	$ 900,000
Retained earnings	606,000
Total shareholders' equity	$1,506,000

1. On August 15, 2010, the board of directors declared a 5 percent stock dividend. The date of distribution was September 25, 2010, to the shareholders of record on September 1, 2010. The stock was selling for $10 per share on the date of declaration.
2. On November 30, 2010, Gilman Company repurchased and held as treasury stock 1,000 shares of its common stock at $11 per share.
3. Gilman generated $100,000 of net income in 2010.

Required:
A. Make the entries to record these equity events.
B. Prepare the shareholders' equity section of the balance sheet at December 31, 2010.

LO 2 **P15.4** The Glassburn Corporation made the following transactions in 2011 when its market rate of interest was 6 percent. Glassburn has a December 31 fiscal year-end.

Sep. 30 Purchased $42,000 of office equipment from Office World by paying $5,000 down and signing a two-year monthly installment note with a face interest rate of 6 percent.

Oct. 31 Purchased a piece of equipment for $62,000 and signed a two-year noninterest-bearing note (annual compounding).

Required: A. Make the amortization schedules for these notes.
B. Make the entries to record the preceding transactions for 2011.
C. Make the appropriate adjusting entries for the notes.
D. Show how the notes are reported on the December 31, 2011, balance sheet.
E. How much interest was reported on the 2011 income statement?
F. Is the cash paid for interest different than the amount reported on the income statement? Explain.
G. How much cash was paid to reduce the principal of the notes?

LO 2 **P15.5** Noble Corporation has a 7 percent market interest rate and a December 31 fiscal year-end. During 2010 the following notes were issued to acquire equipment:

June 1 Issued a $140,000, two-year, 6 percent note for a fabrication machine. The face interest is paid semiannually on December 1 and June 1.

Nov. 1 Issued a $140,000, two-year, 7 percent installment note for two trucks. The payments are due monthly beginning November 30.

Required: A. Make the amortization schedules for these notes.
B. Make the entries for the issuance of each of these notes.
C. Make the entries for the notes through December 31, 2010.

LO 2 **P15.6** Burrell Industries's board of directors authorized the issuance of $60,000,000 in 10-year, 9 percent bonds. The bonds are dated November 1, 2011, and interest is paid semiannually on May 1 and November 1. Burrell closes its books on June 30 each year. The bonds were issued on November 1, 2011, when the market rate of interest was 8 percent.

Required: A. Make the amortization schedule for this bond issue.
B. Prepare the journal entries for the issuance of the bonds and the first year of the bond's life.
C. Describe how the bonds are reported on Burrell's income statement, balance sheet, and statement of cash flows for the year ended June 30, 2012.

LO 2 **P15.7** On April 1, 2011, Arnwine Supply issued $50,000,000 in 15-year, 10 percent bonds that pay interest annually on April 1. The bonds were issued on April 1, 2009, when the market interest rate was 11 percent. Arnwine Supply's fiscal year ends December 31.

Required: A. Make the amortization schedule for this bond issue.
B. Prepare the journal entries for the first two years of the bond issue's life.
C. Show how Arnwine Supply reports the events involving the bond issue on its income statement, balance sheet, and statement of cash flows for the years ended December 31, 2011, and December 31, 2012.

LO 1 **P15.8** For each of the following, identify the impact of the proposed event on the assets, liabilities, and shareholders' equity by using + for increases, − for decreases, and 0 for no effect.

Event	Assets	Liabilities	Shareholders' Equity
1. Purchase of treasury stock			
2. Declare cash dividend			
3. Stock split distributed			
4. Issue common stock			
5. Issue a stock dividend			
6. Fail to pay cumulative preferred stock dividend			
7. Pay cash dividend previously declared			
8. Issue preferred stock			
9. Sell treasury stock previously purchased			
10. Board of directors determines par value			

LO 1 LO 2 **P15.9** Refer to PepsiCo, Inc. **(www.pepsico.com)**, and answer the following questions:

A. Does it have preferred stock? If so, how many shares are authorized, issued, and outstanding, and what is the par value?
B. Does it have common stock? If so, how many shares are authorized, issued, and outstanding, and what is the par (stated) value?
C. Does it have treasury stock? If so, how many shares and what is the total cost?
D. What is the balance in retained earnings?
E. Did it declare any dividends? If so, were they cash or stock dividends?
F. What is the composition of its long-term debt?

G. How much cash was received from financing activities during the most recent period?
H. How much cash was used for financing activities during the most recent period?

LO 1 LO 2 **P15.10** Refer to Dell Computer **(www.dell.com)** and answer the following questions:

A. Does it have preferred stock? If so, how many shares are authorized, issued, and outstanding, and what is the par value?
B. Does it have common stock? If so, how many shares are authorized, issued, and outstanding, and what is the par (stated) value?
C. Does it have treasury stock? If so, how many shares and what is the total cost?
D. What is the balance in retained earnings?
E. Did it declare any dividends? If so, were they cash or stock dividends?
F. What is the composition of its long-term debt?
G. How much cash was received from financing activities during the most recent period?
H. How much cash was used for financing activities during the most recent period?

LO 1 LO 2 **P15.11** Refer to Walt Disney Company **(www.disney.com)** and answer the following questions:

A. Does it have preferred stock? If so, how many shares are authorized, issued, and outstanding, and what is the par value?
B. Does it have common stock? If so, how many shares are authorized, issued, and outstanding, and what is the par (stated) value?
C. Does it have treasury stock? If so, how many shares, and what is the total cost?
D. What is the balance in retained earnings?
E. Did it declare any dividends? If so, were they cash or stock dividends?
F. What is the composition of its long-term debt?
G. How much cash was received from financing activities during the most recent period?
H. How much cash was used for financing activities during the most recent period?

Cases

C15.1 LO 1 LO 2 Refer to the company you selected in C1.1. Examine its financial statements and answer the following questions:

A. Does it have preferred stock? If so, how many shares are authorized, issued, and outstanding, and what is the par value?
B. Does it have common stock? If so, how many shares are authorized, issued, and outstanding, and what is the par (stated) value?
C. Does it have treasury stock? If so, how many shares, and what is the total cost?
D. What is the balance in retained earnings?
E. Did it declare any dividends? If so, were they cash or stock dividends?
F. What is the composition of its long-term debt?
G. How much cash was received from financing activities during the most recent period?
H. How much cash was used for financing activities during the most recent period?

LO 1 **C15.2** John Pepmeier, your longtime friend, owns 2,000 shares of $1 par value common stock in Sports Stuff Inc. There are 1,000,000 shares of common stock authorized, and 800,000 shares are issued and outstanding. Recently, the company was authorized to issue 200,000 shares of $50 par value preferred stock. These shares have a dividend rate of 8 percent based on par value, and they are cumulative. The company expects to sell 10,000 shares of the preferred stock in the near future to finance the acquisition of more production facilities. John has studied the firm's annual reports in an effort to determine the impact the new stock issue will have on his dividends. He is confused because his $1 par value common stock has a market value of $50 per share. He has received a $5 dividend per share in recent years. The company has consistently maintained a policy of paying out 70 percent of its after-tax net income as dividends, a policy management expects to continue into the foreseeable future. Aside from being confused about the difference between par value and market value, John is concerned that the company will not make enough net income to maintain his $5 per share dividend.

Required:

A. Explain to John in memo form the difference between par value and market value.
B. Show John how to compute the minimum amount of after-tax net income the company must earn for him to receive a $5 per share dividend if the 10,000 shares of preferred stock are sold.

Critical Thinking

CT15.1 LO 1 The Shepersky Corporation was authorized to issue 2,000,000 shares of $0.01 par value common stock and 200,000 shares of $50 par value, 10 percent preferred stock. To date, Shepersky has issued 600,000 shares of common stock and no preferred stock. Shepersky is contemplating the acquisition of a new piece of equipment and wants to issue stock to raise the $200,000 cash to finance its acquisition. The company is trying to decide whether to issue 10,000 shares of common stock or 4,000 shares of preferred stock.

Required:

A. Describe how the issue of each type of stock would affect the stockholders' equity of Shepersky Corporation.

B. If Shepersky generates about $3,600,000 of net income each year and the new machine can generate an additional $40,000 of after-tax income, how will the earnings of the common shareholders be affected if:

1. Preferred stock is issued?
2. Common stock is issued?

LO 2 CT15.2 The promotions manager of Waterbed World is interested in running a "36 months, no interest sale." He wants to offer customers the opportunity to buy waterbeds and to finance the purchase by merely dividing the price of the waterbed by 36 to determine the customer's monthly payment. However, he realizes that the sale price must somehow include the 12 percent interest usually charged to finance credit purchases. He has asked you to show him how to determine the sale price of a waterbed that normally sells for $1,000.

Ethical Challenges

EC15.1 LO 1 In 2002, Cynthia Cooper, Sherron Watkins, and Coleen Rowley were named *Time* Magazines Persons of the Year 2002. Each of these women faced personal risks to reveal the wrongdoings at WorldCom, Enron, and the FBI, respectively. Cynthia Cooper was the head of the internal audit department at WorldCom. She discovered the accounting irregularities at WorldCom that ultimately resulted in the largest bankruptcy in American history. According to the article written about Cynthia Cooper, "Shareholders have lost some $3 billion since the news broke, and soon at least 17,000 WorldCom employees will have lost their jobs." But Cynthia saw some good come from the downfall of WorldCom. She stated, "Internal audit departments are going to be taken more seriously." *(Note that Sarbanes-Oxley now requires public companies to maintain internal audit departments.)* Also according to the article, "She has received [as of 2002] more than 100 letters and e-mails from strangers who want to thank and encourage her. But she has not been personally thanked by a single senior executive at WorldCom . . . and there is grumbling that some employees think that WorldCom could have borrowed its way out of its problems and avoided bankruptcy if she had stayed quiet."

Required: Discuss the ethical situation faced by whistleblowers.

LO 1 EC15.2 In 2002, Cynthia Cooper, Sherron Watkins, and Coleen Rowley were named *Time* Magazines Persons of the Year 2002. Each of these women faced personal risks to reveal the wrongdoings at WorldCom, Enron, and the FBI, respectively. Although Sherron Watkins never really "blew" the whistle, she did write a letter to Ken Lay (then the CEO of Enron) that ultimately put into motion a series of events that led to the downfall of Enron. According to *Time,* "After nearly a decade at Enron she was high up enough, or grumpy enough, to send the boss a pull-no-punches, put-it-on-record letter telling him—for a very detailed seven pages—that his company was more or less a Ponzi scheme, and it sounds like she knew she wasn't telling him anything he didn't already know." Yet, Sherron did not leave Enron.

Required: Discuss the ethical situation faced by whistleblowers.

Computer Applications

CA15.1 LO 2 Tuell plans to issue $2 million of 10 percent, 20-year bonds. The market rate of interest at the time of issue is 9 percent. The bonds are issued on June 30, 2010, and pay interest semiannually on June 30 and December 31. Tuell has a December 31 year-end.

Required: Use a computer spreadsheet.

A. Determine the amount of cash Tuell will receive when the company issues the bonds.

B. Prepare a bond amortization schedule that indicates the amounts of cash, interest expense, amortization, and bond carrying value on each interest payment date.

LO 2 CA15.2 Refer to CA15.1. Assume that the market rate of interest at the time of issue is 12 percent.

Required: Use a computer spreadsheet.

A. Determine the amount of cash Tuell will receive when the bonds are issued.

B. Prepare a bond amortization schedule that indicates the amounts of cash, interest expense, amortization, and bond carrying value on each interest payment date.

Visit the text Online Learning Center at **www.mhhe.com/ainsworth6e** for additional problem material that accompanies this chapter.

CHAPTER SIXTEEN

16

Recording and Evaluating Capital Resource Process Activities: Investing

Learning Objectives

LO 1 Explain, record, and report long-term asset purchases.

LO 2 Describe, record, and report depreciation, depletion, and amortization of long-term assets.

LO 3 Discuss, record, and report long-term asset sales, disposals, and trade-ins.

In this chapter we discuss operational investments, which are long-term investments made to acquire the facilities necessary to conduct basic business activities. Operational investments fall into three major categories, which we discuss in turn: (1) plant assets, (2) natural resources, and (3) intangible assets. The benefits derived from investments in plant assets, natural resources, and intangible assets represent an important factor in the successful operation of most companies. Because of the importance of operational investments, it is vital that we understand not only what these assets represent but also how companies record and report their acquisition, use, and disposal.

Plant Assets

Plant assets, often referred to as property, plant, and equipment (PPE), are tangible assets acquired by a company primarily for use in the business over a time span covering more than one accounting period. This category includes land, buildings, and equipment employed to help create and deliver goods and services to customers. It represents the basic infrastructure of the business, without which successful business operations would be impossible.

Determining whether to categorize any tangible, long-term asset as PPE depends on its intended use. For example, if Apple acquires a parcel of land as the site for a new manufacturing facility, the land is a plant asset because of its intended use as a place to carry on the company's business. However, if the company acquires the same piece of land because it plans to hold the land vacant for several years and then sell it at a profit, it is not a plant asset because the company will not use the land to create any of the goods or services it provides. In this second case, the company would report the land as a long-term investment. The three stages to consider when describing the accounting process for PPE are: (1) acquisition, (2) use, and (3) disposal; we examine each stage next.

Acquisition of PPE

To understand why certain expenditures are added to or excluded from the acquisition cost of PPE, we must understand the difference between capital and revenue expenditures. A **capital expenditure** creates the expectation of future benefits that apply beyond the current accounting period. Because companies use PPE for more than one accounting period, expenditures to acquire plant assets are capital expenditures, which companies **capitalize,** or add to the cost of the plant asset rather than expensing it immediately. On the other hand, **revenue expenditures** (expenses) provide benefits exclusively during the current accounting period. Revenue expenditures include the costs of annual repairs and maintenance, as well as real estate taxes, utility bills, and most other day-to-day operating costs. Because revenue expenditures provide current benefits, companies generally expense them when incurred. Recall that we made these distinctions in Chapter 12 when we planned investment activities.

The accounting for construction costs helps illustrate the difference between capital and revenue expenditures. Remember that assets represent economic resources with expected future benefits and that assets become expenses as they are used up to generate current benefits. During construction of a building, all normal, necessary costs incurred provide future benefits and, therefore, are capital expenditures added to the cost of the building. These costs include labor and materials directly associated with construction, permits, architect's fees, and taxes paid. They also include indirect costs, such as wages paid to security personnel, insurance payments, and interest costs on money borrowed during construction. However, once a company begins to use the completed building, it derives current benefits from the asset's use; therefore, expenditures for normal repairs and maintenance to maintain these current benefits are revenue expenditures, which the company reflects as expenses as they are incurred.

Enhance Your Understanding

Why might a company have an incentive to call an expenditure a capital expenditure rather than a revenue expenditure?

Answer: Because a capital expenditure becomes part of the asset cost, it is expensed over time as the asset is used. A revenue expenditure, on the other hand, is expensed immediately, thereby reducing net income and possibly bonuses or other rewards associated with net income. Worldcom increased its net income by billions by capitalizing expenditures that should have been expensed.

Often a buyer pays one price to purchase land and a building together. When this occurs, the buyer must allocate the total purchase price between the two, because buildings and equipment are depreciable assets, *whereas land is not*. Allocation frequently occurs based on the relative dollar amount of separate appraisals completed for each asset. Or, to save money, small businesses may use real estate tax bills showing values assigned to the land and building by local tax assessors.

To demonstrate how this allocation works, assume that Apple paid $380,000 for a building sitting on one acre of land. An appraisal paid for by the company immediately prior to the transaction indicated that the land and building were worth $100,000 and $300,000, respectively. Apple might allocate the total purchase price based on the following calculation:

Asset	Appraised Value	Percentage of Appraised Value	Total Purchase Price	Allocated Purchase Price
Land	$100,000	100,000/400,000 = 25%	$380,000	$ 95,000
Building	$300,000	300,000/400,000 = 75%	$380,000	$285,000
Total	$400,000			$380,000

As a result of the allocation, the recorded cost of the land is $95,000, and the cost of the building is $285,000. These two amounts sum to the total purchase price of $380,000.

Recall that the cost of equipment normally includes the purchase price, freight charges, sales taxes paid, and installation costs. Any other normal, necessary costs, such as assembly and testing before use, are added to the cost of the equipment, and any discounts allowed, such as those for prompt payment, are deducted from the cost.

Many companies choose not to capitalize certain capital expenditures on the grounds that the dollar amount involved is insignificant. For example, if a company purchases a screwdriver for $5, even though the screwdriver may last for many years and is, therefore, theoretically a plant asset, the company will probably charge the $5 to an expense account. This is an application of the accounting concept of **materiality,** which relates to whether an item's dollar amount or its inherent nature is significant enough to influence a financial statement user. Now that we understand the factors affecting their recorded acquisition cost, let's examine how to account for the use of plant assets.

Use of PPE

After placing PPE in service, a company begins to receive benefits from its use, revenues, and/or reduced operating expenses; therefore, the firm must recognize the recovery of the cost of these benefits as an expense over the useful life of the asset. We also know from our previous discussions that the expense associated with using PPE is called depreciation and that it reduces the company's assets and owners' equity since the assets are used in an effort to generate revenue. Thus, for example, suppose PCs to Go purchased a piece of equipment for $1,000,000 with a five-year life. This would mean that the company expects to generate

OF INTEREST Nonoperational Investments

Companies often invest in debt and equity securities of other companies in order to earn a return on investment or to obtain an operating relationship with another company. These investments are called nonoperational investments and must be classified and accounted for based on the type of security (debt or equity) and management's intent regarding the security.

Debt securities: When a company invests in debt securities of another company, it has a creditor relationship with the other company. It classifies the securities based on management's intent as (1) trading securities, (2) available-for-sale securities, or (3) held-to-maturity securities. *Trading securities* are those that management plans to keep for only a very short time period. *Available-for-sale securities* are those that management plans to keep for a longer period of time, but not for the life of the security. *Held-to-maturity securities* consist of only debt securities that management plans to keep until the due date of the security (maturity date). On the balance sheet, trading and available-for-sale securities are shown at the market value. Because the market value may be greater than or less than the cost of the securities, an *unrealized holding gain or loss* may result. The gain or loss is unrealized because the investments have not been sold. We will discuss this more in Chapter 18. Held-to-maturity securities are shown at carrying value (cost less remaining discount or plus remaining premium, much like we did in Chapter 15 for long-term liabilities).

Equity securities: When a company invests in equity securities of another company, it has an investor relationship with the other company. It classifies the securities based on the percentage of the outstanding stock it holds as well as management's intent with regard to the securities. For example, when a company owns less than 20 percent of the outstanding stock of another company, it classifies it based on management's intent as (1) *trading securities* or (2) *available-for-sale securities* (the definitions are the same as for debt securities). Note that held-to-maturity is not a classification because stocks do not have due dates. When a company owns 20 to 50 percent of the outstanding stock of another company, it is assumed to have a significant economic influence on the investee company. Therefore, the investment is accounted for using the *equity method,* whereby the investor company recognizes proportionate changes in the value of the investee company's stockholders' equity. The details of this method are beyond the scope of this text. When a company owns more than 50 percent of the outstanding stock of another company, it controls the investee, and *consolidated financial statements* must be prepared.

The table below summarizes the accounting treatment for debt and equity investments of less than 20 percent of the outstanding stock.

Type of Security	Balance Sheet Classification	Balance Sheet Measurement
Trading securities—debt and equity	Current assets	Market value
Available-for-sale securities—debt and equity	Investments: a long-term asset classification	Market value
Held-to-maturity securities—debt only	Investments: a long-term asset (until due date is within one year)	Carrying value

benefits that will recover the cost of the investment over the next five years. This would result in $200,000 of depreciation expense recognized in each of the next five years.[1]

Assets	=	Liabilities	+	Owners' equity
(200,000)				(200,000)

And PCs to Go would record depreciation expense as follows:

General Journal

Date	Description	DR	CR
16–1	Depreciation Expense	200,000	
	Accumulated Depreciation		200,000

There is a separate accumulated depreciation account maintained for each asset or group of assets. Each separate accumulated depreciation account serves as a contra asset account and appears on the balance sheet as a deduction from the asset (or a group of assets) to which it relates. Whereas the depreciation expense account is closed out to retained earnings at the end of each period, accumulated depreciation is a permanent account, just like its related asset account. Its balance carries over and accumulates from one year to the next. Therefore, after three years of depreciating $200,000 per year the $1,000,000 piece of equipment PCs to Go purchased would appear on the balance sheet as follows:

Equipment (at cost)	$1,000,000
Less accumulated depreciation	(600,000)
Equipment, net	$ 400,000

[1] Recall that if the equipment is used to manufacture products, the expense is included in manufacturing overhead and, therefore, is expensed when the products are sold.

The $400,000 figure is variously referred to as the *carrying value, book value, or remaining undepreciated cost* of the equipment. Note that carrying value is not the same as market value because depreciation does not measure decline in value. Rather depreciation is the allocation of the cost of the asset to the time periods that the asset is used.

Depreciation

Before calculating depreciation for any given plant asset, it is necessary to know the following:

- Cost of the asset.
- Estimated useful life of the asset.
- Estimated salvage value of the asset.
- Method of depreciation.

We have already discussed those expenditures included in the cost of plant assets, so now we examine how the useful life, salvage value, and methods of depreciation impact the allocation of the cost of the assets.

As you know, useful life is the period of time over which a business expects to obtain economic benefits from the use of a plant asset or any other operational investment. Of necessity, it is an estimate based on information available to management at the date the company places an asset in service.

With the exception of land, the useful life of operational investments is limited due to two factors: (1) physical wear and tear resulting from use of the asset or the passage of time and (2) obsolescence. Obsolescence results from changing technology, tastes, and/or preferences. For example, businesses generally replace computers because improved hardware is available, not because the computers no longer function for their originally intended purpose. Or, even though an automobile could be used for 7 to 10 years, a company may have a policy of buying a new automobile every three years simply because of a preference for newer automobiles. Useful life can be expressed as a period of time or defined as the total number of units of output expected over the useful life of the asset, such as the estimated total miles an automobile will be driven.

The expected fair market value of a plant asset at the end of its useful life is referred to as the **salvage value,** or **residual value,** of the asset. Because the salvage value will be recovered at the end of the useful life of the asset, the portion of a plant asset's total cost that needs to be recovered and will be depreciated over the useful life is called its **depreciable cost.** It is calculated as follows:

$$\text{Cost} - \text{Salvage value} = \text{Depreciable cost}$$

Similar to useful life, the salvage value is based on an estimate made at the time an asset is placed in service. (Remember in Chapter 12 when we planned investment activities, we ignored salvage value because we focused on tax depreciation and the resulting cash inflows.)

Three common methods for calculating the amount of depreciation reported in financial statements are: (1) the straight-line method; (2) the units-of-production method; and (3) accelerated methods. We discuss each method in turn.

Straight-Line Depreciation Method

The **straight-line depreciation** method reflects the calculation of annual depreciation by allocating the depreciable cost of the asset to depreciation expense uniformly over its useful life based on the assumption that benefits are received uniformly. We calculate straight-line depreciation as follows:

$$\frac{\text{Cost} - \text{Salvage value}}{\text{Useful life (time)}} = \text{Depreciation expense per period}$$

For example, assume a delivery truck purchased by PCs to Go for a total cost of $22,000 has an anticipated useful life of five years and a salvage value estimated at $2,000. The company would calculate annual straight-line depreciation expense for the truck as follows:

$$\frac{(\$22{,}000 - \$2{,}000)}{5} = \$4{,}000$$

EXHIBIT 16.1
Comparison of Various Depreciation Methods

Assumptions

Asset description	Delivery truck
Cost of asset	$22,000
Useful life	5 years
Salvage value	$2,000

Panel A. Straight-Line Depreciation

Year	(1) Annual Depreciation Expense[a]	(2) Accumulated Depreciation as of Year-End	(3) Carrying Value as of Year-End
1	$4,000	$ 4,000	$18,000
2	4,000	8,000	14,000
3	4,000	12,000	10,000
4	4,000	16,000	6,000
5	4,000	20,000	2,000

Panel B. Units-of-Production Depreciation

Year	(1) Annual Depreciation Expense[b]	(2) Accumulated Depreciation as of Year-End	(3) Carrying Value as of Year-End
1	$0.20 × 14,000[c] = $2,800	$ 2,800	$19,200
2	0.20 × 23,000 = 4,600	7,400	14,600
3	0.20 × 18,700 = 3,740	11,140	10,860
4	0.20 × 21,300 = 4,260	15,400	6,600
5	0.20 × 23,000 = 4,600	20,000	2,000
	100,000 miles		

Panel C. Double-Declining-Balance (DDB) Depreciation (rounded to nearest whole dollar)

Year	(1) Annual Depreciation Expense[d]	(2) Accumulated Depreciation as of Year-End	(3) Carrying Value as of Year-End
1	$22,000 × 0.40 = $8,800	$ 8,800	$13,200
2	13,200 × 0.40 = 5,280	14,080	7,920
3	7,920 × 0.40 = 3,168	17,248	4,752
4	4,752 × 0.40 = 1,901	19,149	2,851
5	851[e]	20,000	2,000

[a]Annual depreciation expense = ($22,000 – $2,000)/5 years.
[b]Annual depreciation calculated in two steps:
1. ($22,000 – $2,000)/100,000 miles = $0.20/mile
2. $0.20/mile × Actual miles driven each year

[c]The mileage figures shown for each year are assumed.
[d]Annual depreciation expense calculated as follows:
1. Straight-line rate = 20%
Double-declining-balance rate = 2 × 20% = 40%
2. Depreciation for each year is equal to:
Carrying value at beginning of year × 0.40

[e]In year 5, the depreciation calculation yields the following: $2,851 × 0.40 = $1,140. However, if this amount is used, total depreciation taken over the useful life of the asset will exceed the $20,000 of total depreciation allowed. This is a common problem of DDB depreciation. When this happens, companies simply record the final year's depreciation as the amount that will bring total accumulated depreciation to the amount desired ($20,000, in this case).

Exhibit 16.1, panel A, shows annual straight-line depreciation expense (column 1), as well as the resulting accumulated depreciation (column 2) and asset carrying value (column 3) at the end of each year of the truck's useful life. Notice that the annual depreciation expense shown in column 1, which is deducted in calculating income each year, is a constant figure, while the amount of accumulated depreciation shown in column 2 increases by the amount of depreciation expense taken each year. The balance of accumulated depreciation at the end of each year is subtracted from the asset's cost to obtain the year-end carrying value shown in column 3 to be reported in the plant asset section of the company's balance sheet.

Units-of-Production Depreciation Method

Units-of-production depreciation is a way of calculating annual depreciation expense based on actual usage rather than the passage of time, which assumes that the benefit from the asset is tied to its use. Instead of defining the useful life of an asset in years, this depreciation method expresses an asset's useful life in total expected units of output. For example, a company might expect a piece of manufacturing equipment to last for a total of 20,000 hours of operating use. Or the company may assign an automobile a useful life of 100,000 miles. Thus we determine the depreciation rate per unit of output by dividing the depreciable cost of the asset by the expected total units of output. This rate is used to calculate annual depreciation based on the actual output for the period. Units-of-production depreciation involves calculating depreciation expense in two steps:

First, determine the depreciation rate per unit of output:

$$\frac{\text{Cost} - \text{Salvage value}}{\text{Useful life (units)}} = \text{Depreciation rate per unit}$$

Second, determine the depreciation for the period:

$$\text{Depreciation rate per unit} \times \text{Actual units of output} = \text{Depreciation expense per period}$$

If PCs to Go from the prior example expects its delivery truck to have a useful life of 100,000 miles, and it was actually driven 14,000 miles in its first year of use, depreciation expense for year 1, calculated using the units-of-production method, is

$$\frac{\$22{,}000 - \$2{,}000}{100{,}000 \text{ miles}} = \$0.20 \text{ depreciation rate per mile of use}$$

$$\$0.20/\text{mile} \times 14{,}000 \text{ miles} = \$2{,}800 \text{ depreciation for Year 1}$$

Exhibit 16.1, panel B, shows the calculation of depreciation expense for each year of the truck's use, based on the following assumptions:

Year	Actual Miles Driven
1	14,000
2	23,000
3	18,700
4	21,300
5	23,000

The advantage of the units-of-production method of depreciation is that it is a more accurate way to match the amount of expense recognized with actual rates of usage as illustrated in Exhibit 16.1, panel B. In our example, the rate of asset use and the corresponding benefit derived from that use are measured in terms of miles driven each year. Note that depreciation ceases when the asset's cost less accumulated depreciation equals salvage value even if the asset is still used.

Accelerated Depreciation Method

Most of the benefits of many assets are generated early in their lives and decline over the remainder of their lives. For example, a new computer functions at state-of-the-art efficiency, but after just a few years, the computer may no longer provide the same relative degree of benefit to the company. When benefits derived from the use of an asset tend to decline over time, companies use one of various **accelerated depreciation** methods designed to recognize relatively greater expense in early years of asset use and progressively less expense as time passes.

Declining-balance depreciation is a type of accelerated depreciation that reflects depreciation expense for each year based on a constant percentage of a declining balance. The declining balance amount is the remaining undepreciated cost of the asset at the start of each year. The asset's *undepreciated cost is its original cost less the total of any depreciation taken in prior years*. The multiplication of a constant rate by this declining balance yields the greatest amount of depreciation in the asset's first year of use and a declining amount in each subsequent year; thus the depreciation expense recorded each year declines along with the declining benefits of asset use.

Double-declining-balance (DDB) depreciation is a specific type of declining-balance depreciation that reflects annual depreciation expense using a constant percentage equal to twice the straight-line rate (1/useful life in years) of depreciation. For example, the double-declining-balance method would use a depreciation rate of 40 percent per year ($2 \times 1/5$ in this case).[2] The complete set of steps to calculate double-declining-balance depreciation follows:

1. Determine the straight-line rate of depreciation for the asset and double it.
2. Calculate depreciation for the first year by multiplying the rate determined in step 1 by the *original cost* of the asset. (Note: Do not reduce the cost by the salvage value of the asset.)
3. Determine depreciation for the second and all subsequent years by multiplying the rate from step 1 by the carrying value of the asset as of the beginning of the year, continuing until the asset's carrying value equals its salvage value.

Exhibit 16.1, panel C, illustrates this calculation for each year of the useful life of PCs to Go's delivery truck.

Although the depreciation expense in the early years of an asset's life is greater, accelerated depreciation does not increase the total amount of depreciation taken over the life of the asset, which is always limited to depreciable cost (Cost – Salvage value) of the asset. Notice in Exhibit 16.1 that total depreciation recorded under each of the three methods equals \$20,000 (\$22,000 original cost – \$2,000 salvage value). Because of this requirement, it is generally necessary to modify DDB depreciation taken during the last portion of an asset's useful life. In Exhibit 16.1, panel C, depreciation calculated for Year 5 under the DDB formula requires us to multiply \$2,851 (the carrying value of the truck at the beginning of the year) by 40 percent, which would result in Year 5 depreciation equal to \$1,140. However, this amount would cause total accumulated depreciation to exceed \$20,000 (and the carrying value would be less than the \$2,000 salvage value), so we must limit the amount of depreciation expense in Year 5 to \$851, the amount that will bring total accumulated depreciation to \$20,000. It is usually necessary to adjust the amount of double-declining-balance depreciation expense taken in the final portion of an asset's life so that total accumulated depreciation taken over the life of the asset equals the estimated net depreciable cost of the asset.[3]

Enhance Your Understanding

Does management have any incentives to choose one depreciation method over another?

Answer: Perhaps. Management can impact the net income by the type of depreciation method chosen. When rewards are tied to net income, management may have an incentive to increase or decrease income in a given period. Some research suggests that management tries to smooth earnings from period to period.

Other PPE Usage Issues

Midyear Convention

What if a company with a December 31 year-end purchases or disposes of a plant asset on April 5, 2010? If it uses the units-of-production depreciation method, the timing of the disposal is not an issue, because depreciation for any period is based on actual output or use for that period. But if the company uses either straight-line or accelerated depreciation, both of which define useful life in years, the fact that the asset was not used for a full 12-month period in 2008 will normally require a modification in the amount of depreciation expense recorded for that year.

[2] In addition to 200 percent declining-balance depreciation, 150 percent declining-balance depreciation is also common. Various other percentages are also used ranging up to 200 percent.

[3] Recall that we used MACRS depreciation in Chapter 12 to make capital budgeting decisions. However, MACRS is not allowed for financial accounting purposes.

There are several ways to deal with this issue. Companies making numerous plant asset purchases and disposals spread out evenly during the course of the fiscal year frequently use the **midyear convention,** which reflects depreciation expense for each asset as if it were purchased or disposed of exactly halfway through the company's fiscal year. (In fact, the IRS MACRS tables are based on the midyear convention. This is why three-year property is depreciated over four years and five-year property over six years.) This avoids the expense of tracking the exact date that the business places each asset in service, and so long as acquisitions and disposals of assets occur uniformly, it yields an annual depreciation expense that is not significantly different from the result that would have been obtained by tracking each asset individually.

Other companies record depreciation based on the actual number of months an asset was in service during the year. When following this approach, businesses that acquire assets on or before the 15th of each month record depreciation expense for these assets as if they were in service for the entire month. They treat assets acquired after the 15th of any month as being placed in service at the start of the next month. Similarly, assets disposed of after the 15th of any month get a full month's depreciation, while those disposed of on or before the 15th receive no depreciation for the month.

To illustrate, PCs to Go, with a December 31 year-end, purchases its delivery truck in April 2010 and expects to dispose of it five years later in April 2015. Straight-line depreciation for each fiscal year of use would be as follows:

(A) Year Ended	(B) Months Used	(C) Percentage of Year Used	(D) Annual Depreciation	(E) Depreciation Expense (C × D)
12-31-2010	9	9/12	$4,000	$ 3,000
12-31-2011	12	12/12	$4,000	$ 4,000
12-31-2012	12	12/12	$4,000	$ 4,000
12-31-2013	12	12/12	$4,000	$ 4,000
12-31-2014	12	12/12	$4,000	$ 4,000
12-31-2015	3	3/12	$4,000	$ 1,000
Total				$20,000

Revision of Estimates

The original useful life and salvage value assigned to any plant asset for financial reporting purposes are estimates. Due to the principle of materiality, companies do not worry if these projections are marginally inaccurate, as is normally the case. But what happens if a company originally assigns a useful life of seven years to a computer and, one year after the date of purchase, realizes that it will have to replace the computer after a total of three years? When it becomes clear that there were significant mistakes of judgment in estimating the useful life and/or salvage value of any asset, companies usually do the following: Depreciate the remaining carrying value of the asset over the asset's revised remaining useful life using the appropriate depreciation method and, when deemed necessary, a revised salvage value.

To illustrate, assume that on January 1, 2010, a company purchases and begins to use office equipment costing $12,000, with an expected useful life of 10 years and a salvage value of $2,000. Assuming the business uses the straight-line method of depreciation for the asset, accumulated depreciation at December 31, 2012, would be $3,000 [($12,000 − $2,000)/10 × 3 years]. The carrying value of the asset at that time would be $9,000 ($12,000 − $3,000). If, during the following year, the company realizes that the equipment will last only four more years, after which its estimated salvage value will be $3,000, then depreciation expense for each of the remaining four years of the asset's useful life would be calculated as follows:

$$\frac{\text{Carrying value} - \text{Revised salvage value}}{\text{Remaining useful life}} = \text{Depreciation expense}$$

$$\frac{\$9{,}000 - \$3{,}000}{4 \text{ years}} = \$1{,}500 \text{ Depreciation expense per year}$$

This change in depreciation is prospective—that is, it will affect only the current and future year financial statements.

Fully Depreciated PPE

The fact that an asset is fully depreciated does not mean that a company must stop using it. However, because total depreciation associated with the use of any asset cannot exceed the total cost of the asset (reduced by its salvage value), the company must stop recording annual depreciation expense.

Extraordinary Repairs and Betterments

After placing PPE in service, businesses record expenditures to maintain the asset in normal operating condition as expenses in the period incurred. However, some expenditures relating to the continued use of the asset may be capital in nature. These are classified as either extraordinary repairs or betterments. **Extraordinary repairs and betterments** are capital expenditures that extend the remaining useful life of an operational asset and/or improve its operating performance. When making such capital expenditures for a plant asset already in use, the company would add the amount of the expenditure to the depreciable cost of the asset (by debiting the asset or accumulated depreciation) and then depreciate it over the asset's remaining useful life. For example, $30,000 spent to add a new room onto an existing building with a remaining useful life of 15 years will increase straight-line depreciation expense by $2,000 ($30,000/15 years) per year for each of the last 15 years of the building's life, assuming the improvement does not change the building's expected salvage value.

Disposal of PPE

Eventually, it is necessary to dispose of depreciable assets, either because they have worn out or because management has determined that disposal is an economically desirable course of action. The asset may be discarded, sold, or exchanged for other assets. Whatever the method, the entries made to record disposals must generally accomplish the following:

- Record depreciation expense up to the date of disposal.
- Remove both the cost of the asset and its related accumulated depreciation from the accounting records.
- Record the fair market value of the asset(s) received, if any.
- Record any gain or loss, calculated as the difference between the carrying value of the disposed asset and the fair market value of any assets received in return. Gains increase owners' equity and, therefore, are recorded as credit entries. Losses reduce owners' equity and, therefore, are recorded as debits.

Discard PPE

Sometimes an asset with little or no value will be disposed of, with nothing at all received in return. When this happens, it is necessary to record a loss at the date of disposal. For example, let's assume that PCs to Go discards equipment that cost $50,000, with $40,000 of accumulated depreciation at the date of the last balance sheet. Depreciation expense for the current period up to the date of disposal is $2,000 and PCs to Go must pay $1,000 to have the equipment removed. First we must recognize the depreciation up to the disposal date:

Assets	=	Liabilities	+	Owners' equity
(2,000)				(2,000)

And,

General Journal

Date	Description	DR	CR
16–2	Depreciation Expense	2,000	
	Accumulated Depreciation		2,000

After this entry is posted, the Accumulated Depreciation account will have a $42,000 credit balance (previous balance of $40,000 plus $2,000 from the 16–2 entry). Second, we must recognize the removal of the equipment (book value = $8,000) and cash:

Assets	=	Liabilities	+	Owners' equity
(8,000)				(9,000)
(1,000)				

The next entry reflects this event as follows:

General Journal

Date	Description	DR	CR
16–3	Accumulated Depreciation	42,000	
	Loss on Disposal	9,000	
	Equipment		50,000
	Cash		1,000

Sell PPE

Plant assets may be sold for an amount equal to, less than, or greater than their carrying value. Terms of sale might require a cash payment of the selling price or an agreement in the form of a promissory note obligating the purchaser to make specified future cash payments or assets may be sold to satisfy obligations of the selling company. In any event, to determine the gain or loss on sale, simply compare the net assets received to the carrying value of the asset given up. Recall that when more net assets are received than are given up, a gain results. A loss results when fewer net assets are received than are given up. To illustrate the accounting for the various possibilities, assume that PCs to Go sells the following piece of equipment:

Cost of asset	$80,000
Accumulated depreciation through date of sale	(60,000)
Carrying value at date of sale	$20,000

Illustration 1: Sales Price $20,000

Since PCs to Go is receiving the same amount of net assets as it is giving up:

Assets	=	Liabilities	+	Owners' equity
+20,000				
(20,000)				

And,

General Journal

Date	Description	DR	CR
16–4	Cash	20,000	
	Accumulated Depreciation	60,000	
	Equipment		80,000

Illustration 2: Sales Price $27,000

Since PCs to Go is receiving more net assets than it is giving up:

Assets	=	Liabilities	+	Owners' equity
+27,000				+7,000
(20,000)				

And,

General Journal

Date	Description	DR	CR
16–5	Cash	27,000	
	Accumulated Depreciation	60,000	
	Equipment		80,000
	Gain on Sale of Equipment		7,000

Illustration 3: Sales Price $16,000

Since PCs to Go is receiving fewer net assets than it is giving up:

Assets	=	Liabilities	+	Owners' equity
+16,000				(4,000)
(20,000)				

And,

General Journal

Date	Description	DR	CR
16–6	Cash	16,000	
	Accumulated Depreciation	60,000	
	Loss on Sale of Equipment	4,000	
	Equipment		80,000

Exchange PPE

Companies occasionally exchange plant assets for other operational assets. In most cases these exchanges involve the payment or receipt of cash in addition to the exchanged assets. Cash is either *given or received* to make up the difference between the fair market values of the two noncash assets. For example, a business might trade an old automobile and cash for a new automobile. In this case, the cash given makes up the difference between the value of the old automobile and the new automobile. However, in some cases no cash is involved in the exchange. For example, a company might give a parcel of land in exchange for three pieces of equipment.

When noncash exchanges occur, the asset received is recorded at its fair value. There are two ways to determine this fair value. Either we can use the fair market value of the asset received or the fair market value of the asset given up plus (minus) any cash given (received). We choose the option that has the most readily determinable fair market value. The gain or loss on the exchange is always the difference between the fair market value and carrying (book) value of the asset given up.

Exchange with No Cash

Let's look at how asset exchanges work. For example, assume that Apple exchanges a building for land held by another company. The following is obtained regarding the building held by Apple:

Cost of building	$100,000
Less: Accumulated depreciation at the exchange date	35,000
Carrying value at date of exchange	$ 65,000

Assume further that the fair market value of the building on the date of exchange is difficult to determine, but that the land owned by the other company was recently appraised at $90,000. Thus the more readily determinable fair market value is that of the land. Therefore, Apple is receiving land valued at $90,000 and giving up a building with a carrying value of $65,000, resulting in a gain of $25,000 ($90,000 – $65,000). Thus,

Assets	=	Liabilities	+	Owners' equity
+$90,000				+$25,000
($65,000)				

And,

General Journal

Date	Description	DR	CR
16–7	Land	90,000	
	Accumulated Depreciation	35,000	
	Building		65,000
	Gain on Exchange		25,000

Note that the entry for the exchange records the land at its $90,000 fair market value. The carrying value of the building (cost and accumulated depreciation) is removed from the accounting records and the $25,000 gain is recognized.

Exchange with Cash Payment

Assume PCs to Go approaches an office equipment dealer offering to trade in an old copier for a new copier. The original cost of the old copier was $25,000 and the accumulated depreciation at the trade-in date is $15,000, yielding a carrying (book) value of $10,000. PCs to Go and the office equipment dealer agree to a price of $28,000 for the new copier and the dealer agrees to give PCs to Go an $8,000 trade-in allowance for the old copier. Therefore, PCs to Go must pay $20,000 in cash to make up the difference ($28,000 – $8,000) in order to buy the new copier. Because the $8,000 fair market value of the old copier is less than its $10,000 carrying value, PCs to Go has incurred a $2,000 loss on the exchange. In other words, it has given up more assets than it received [$28,000 – ($20,000 + $10,000)] which is the difference between the book value and fair value of the old asset. Thus,

Assets	=	Liabilities	+	Owners' equity
+$28,000				($2,000)
($20,000)				
($10,000)				

And,

General Journal

Date	Description	DR	CR
16–8	Copier (New)	28,000	
	Accumulated Depreciation	15,000	
	Loss on Exchange	2,000	
	Copier (Old)		25,000
	Cash		20,000

Now let's assume that instead of a trade-in allowance of $8,000, PCs to Go negotiated a trade-in allowance of $15,000. Now PCs to Go will pay only $13,000 in cash ($28,000 – $15,000) and will record a gain of $5,000. Why? Because the fair market value of the old copier is now assumed to be $15,000; which is $5,000 greater than its carrying value ($10,000). In other words, PCs to Go has given up less assets than it received [$28,000 – ($13,000 + $15,000)]. Thus,

Assets	=	Liabilities	+	Owners' equity
+$28,000				+$5,000
($13,000)				
($10,000)				

And,

General Journal

Date	Description	DR	CR
16–9	Copier (New)	28,000	
	Accumulated Depreciation	15,000	
	Gain on Exchange		5,000
	Copier (Old)		25,000
	Cash		13,000

Exchange with Cash Received

In many cases a company receives cash on an exchange. This means that the fair market value of the asset given is greater than the value of the asset received. As in all exchanges the new asset is recorded at its fair value and gains and losses are determined by comparing the carrying value of the asset given to its fair market value.

To illustrate, assume Electro Manufacturing has agreed to give one of its winch trucks and $10,000 cash in exchange for one of PCs to Go's forklifts. The forklift has a fair value of $30,000, originally cost $40,000, and has accumulated depreciation on the exchange date of $15,000. Electro Manufacturing is uncertain about the fair value of the winch truck so PCs to Go determines its fair value based on the fair market value of the forklift. In this case PCs to Go takes the $30,000 fair market value of the forklift and subtracts the $10,000 cash received from Electro Manufacturing to arrive at the winch truck's $20,000 fair market value. In other words, if PCs to Go's forklift is worth $30,000, then Electro Manufacturing must give PCs to Go assets worth $30,000; which in this case is cash plus its winch truck worth $20,000. This exchange creates a $5,000 gain because the $30,000 fair market value of the forklift is greater than the $25,000 carrying value of the forklift ($30,000 − $25,000 = $5,000 gain). Thus,

Assets	= Liabilities +	Owners' equity
+$20,000		+$5,000
+$10,000		
($25,000)		

And,

General Journal

Date	Description	DR	CR
16–10	Winch Truck	20,000	
	Accumulated Depreciation	15,000	
	Cash	10,000	
	Forklift		40,000
	Gain on Exchange		5,000

Let's change the scenario. Now assume that the forklift has a fair market value of $22,000 and Electro gives PCs to Go the winch truck and $5,000. The $17,000 fair market value of the winch truck is calculated by subtracting the $5,000 cash received from the $22,000 fair market value of the forklift ($22,000 − $5,000). In other words, if the forklift is worth $22,000, then Electro must give $22,000 of value ($5,000 of cash and a winch truck worth $17,000) to acquire it. This exchange creates a loss for PCs to Go of $3,000 because the fair market value of the forklift, $22,000, is less than its carrying value, $25,000 ($22,000 − $25,000 = $3,000 loss). Thus,

Assets	= Liabilities +	Owners' equity
+$17,000		($3,000)
+$5,000		
($25,000)		

OF INTEREST Impairments

When the fair value of an asset declines below its carrying value and management determines this is a permanent decline, the asset is said to be impaired and a loss is recorded. For example, assume a company purchased land in 2000 for $300,000 and today its fair value has declined to $50,000 due to geological conditions that limit its usefulness to the company. A loss of $250,000 is recorded ($50,000 fair market value − $300,000 carrying value) even though the company still owns the land, that is, even though no exchange has taken place.

And,

General Journal

Date	Description	DR	CR
16–11	Winch Truck	17,000	
	Accumulated Depreciation	15,000	
	Cash	5,000	
	Loss on Exchange	3,000	
	Forklift		40,000

Exchanges When No Gains and Losses Are Recorded

There are two circumstances where gains and losses are not recorded on exchanges. The first is in the unusual circumstance when neither the fair value of the noncash asset given nor the fair value of the asset received can be reasonably determined. When this occurs the new asset is recorded at the carrying value of the assets given plus (minus) cash paid (received). To illustrate, let us use the example above between PCs to Go and Electro Manufacturing (winch truck for a forklift) and assume that the fair value of neither the forklift nor the winch truck can be reasonably determined. In this case the winch truck would be recorded at $20,000, which is the carrying value of the forklift, $25,000 less the $5,000 cash received. Thus,

Assets	= Liabilities + Owners' equity
+$20,000	
+$5,000	
($25,000)	

And,

General Journal

Date	Description	DR	CR
16–12	Winch Truck	20,000	
	Accumulated Depreciation	15,000	
	Cash	5,000	
	Forklift		40,000

The second circumstance where gains and losses are not recorded is when the exchange lacks economic substance. This type of exchange receives the same treatment as exchanges with no determinable fair market values. That is, the acquired asset is recorded at the carrying value of the assets given plus (minus) cash paid (received). To illustrate, assume PCs to Go's forklift has a market value of $30,000. Assume that PCs to Go's management knows that Electro Manufacturing has the exact same forklift and contacts Electro's management and proposes a direct exchange. This exchange would yield a $5,000 gain for PCs to Go ($30,000 market value of the forklift − $25,000 carrying value = $5,000 gain). This exchange lacks economic substance because both companies are in the same position they were before the exchange and the exchange was done only to create the $5,000 gain. The accountant will not allow the gain to be recognized, thus,

The gain or loss on an exchange of assets is the difference between the fair market value and the carrying value (book value) of the assets given up.

Assets = Liabilities + Owners' equity

+$25,000
($25,000)

And,

General Journal

Date	Description	DR	CR
16–13	Forklift (New)	25,000	
	Accumulated Depreciation	15,000	
	Forklift (Old)		40,000

Natural Resources

Natural resources are nonrenewable assets such as coal mines and oil rights. A company's investment in natural resources is determined according to the same general rules established for assigning costs to plant assets; typically, the cost includes the purchase price of the asset and related legal fees, as well as items such as surveying and various development costs. As with PPE, the benefits associated with natural resources dissipate with use. Once coal or oil reserves are exhausted, they cannot be renewed. Therefore, the cost of these assets also must be allocated as an expense over the periods they benefit. This process is called **depletion.** Because benefits from natural resources usually correlate with usage rather than the passage of time, depletion is generally calculated using the *units-of-production method.* A contra asset account called Accumulated Depletion represents the amount of depletion accumulated over time.[4]

Intangible Assets

Intangible assets, unlike plant assets and natural resources, have no tangible or visible physical presence. However, they convey to their owner a legal right or benefit that is often vital to successful operations. Therefore, intangible assets usually represent some of the most important and valuable assets owned by a company. Let's look at some examples.

A **patent** is an intangible asset giving its owner the exclusive legal right to the commercial benefits of a specified product or process. In the United States, the U.S. Patent Office issues patents that last for a period of 20 years. However, even though they exist for 20 years, the economically useful life of patents may be much shorter if technological developments render the patented product or process obsolete. The cost of a patent includes the normal and necessary expenditures made to buy an existing patent from another entity, as well as legal costs directly incurred to obtain a patent. However, research and development costs incurred in an effort to obtain a patent are expensed during the period incurred since it was not known at the time whether these expenditures would result in an asset.

A **copyright** is an intangible asset that gives its owner an exclusive legal right to the reproduction and sale of a literary or artistic work. Copyrights last for the life of the creator plus 70 years. However, their economically useful life is almost always substantially less. Because the fee to initially establish a copyright is minimal, businesses usually write this cost off as an expense. However, when a company purchases a copyright from the original

[4] The amount of depletion each period is added to the cost of inventory because depletion is a product cost (see Chapter 4).

owner, the expenditure is often substantial; therefore, the company must capitalize the cost as an intangible asset.

A **trademark** is an intangible asset that identifies a particular company or product. The right to use a trademark remains with the originator for as long as it continues to be used. Trademarks are registered with the U.S. Patent and Trademark Office with indefinite renewals for intervals of 20 years. For example, McDonald's has a trademark for the Big Mac, McNuggets, and other products. The cost of a trademark includes the legal costs as well as other development costs. When a trademark is purchased, the capitalized cost is the amount paid. Although a company can renew a trademark indefinitely, trademarks are expensed over a period of no more than 40 years.

A **franchise** is an intangible asset representing the exclusive right to operate or sell a brand name product in a specified territory. A franchise is granted by one entity, called the franchisor, to another party, called the franchisee. Burger King and McDonald's are examples. If the franchisee pays an up-front fee for this right, it has an intangible asset to report on the balance sheet.

A **leasehold** is an intangible asset conveyed by a lease to use equipment, land, and/or buildings for a specified period of time. Periodic payments made on operating leases are generally expensed when paid but some leases require a down payment at the inception of the lease. If the amount of the down payment is material, companies will capitalize it by debiting an intangible asset account called Leasehold. This asset has a useful life equal to the term of the lease. Any amounts paid by a lessee to make physical improvements constituting an integral part of leased property are recorded as an intangible asset referred to as a **leasehold improvement.** Although the improvement represents tangible property, accountants consider this asset to be intangible because the lessee possesses only the *legal right* to use the improvement during the remaining life of the lease.

Goodwill is an intangible asset representing the value assigned to a company's ability to generate an above-average return on invested capital. This may result from a combination of many factors, including efficient management, good labor relations, superior product quality, and brand name recognition. Businesses record goodwill when they pay for it as part of the purchase price to acquire another company. Goodwill is the excess of the total price paid to purchase the company over the fair value of the purchased company's underlying net assets (all identifiable assets minus liabilities).

Key point: Internally generated goodwill is not an accounting asset reported on the balance sheet.

As they do for plant assets and natural resources, companies must expense the cost of intangible assets over the periods they benefit. This process, called **amortization,** is usually done using the *straight-line method.* However, goodwill is not amortized and instead must be revalued every accounting period and, if the value of goodwill has decreased, the reduction must be recognized in the current period.[5]

Reporting Investment Activities

Operational investment activities result in assets, expenses, and cash flows. These activities are communicated to both internal and external stakeholders. Cash paid or received from the sale of PPE and other long-term assets is reported on the statement of cash flows as "cash flows from investing activities." Gains and losses as well as depreciation and amortization expense are shown on the income statement. Finally the carrying value of the company's PPE, natural resources, and intangible assets is shown on the balance sheet. Exhibit 16.2 is a simple illustration of how the assets discussed in this chapter are reported on a balance sheet. You should also examine the notes accompanying the financial statements to determine the depreciation/ amortization method and the composition of the company's PPE.

Note that Trading Securities are reported at their market value as current assets right below cash because they are expected to be sold in the very near future. Both Available-for-Sale Securities and Held-to-Maturity Securities are reported as nonoperational investments.

[5] Unlike depreciation and depletion, there is no accumulated amortization account. Rather, companies reduce the asset directly to recognize the amortization expense for the period.

EXHIBIT 16.2
Partial Balance Sheet For the Year Ended 12/31/10

Current Asset:		
Cash		$ 50,000
Trading Securities—at market value		75,000
Investments:		
Available-for-Sale Securities—at market value		$125,000
Held-to-Maturity—at cost		200,000
Property Plant and Equipment:		
Land		$200,000
Building	$450,000	
Less: Accumulated Depreciation	125,000	325,000
Equipment	$150,000	
Less: Accumulated Depreciation	52,000	98,000
Oil Reserves	$600,000	
Less: Accumulated Depletion	250,000	350,000
Intangible Assets:		
Patent		$450,000
Trademark		210,000
Copyright		190,000
Goodwill		165,000

However, while Available-for-Sale Securities are reported at their market value because they are expected to be sold, the Held-to-Maturity Securities are debt securities and are reported at their cost because the company does not expect to sell these securities but instead hold on to them until they come due. The PPE classification shows the long-term operational assets at their cost. Land is reported at its undepreciated original cost. The building and equipment accounts are shown at their original cost less the accumulated depreciation (the total amount of depreciation taken on the assets to the balance sheet date). Oil Reserves is reported at its cost less the depletion taken on this natural resource to date. The net amount of each PPE account is referred to as the book value of these assets. The intangible assets classification reports four assets. The patent, trademark, and copyright accounts represent amortized book values of specific legal rights purchased by the company. While these assets have been amortized over their useful lives, there is no accumulated amortization account to report the amortization taken to date. Goodwill is the lone intangible asset that is not amortized but instead its original cost is reduced when its original value declines. As a result, the book value of goodwill reported on the balance sheet is either its original cost or the reduced value of the goodwill.

Now let's look at Apple's financial statements in the Appendix to see how a large corporation reports these types of assets on its financial statements.

Notice that depreciation/amortization expense is not listed separately on the income statement; however, the amount is listed on the statement of cash flows (for reasons we discuss below) as $473 million. Note 1 indicates that Apple uses the straight-line depreciation method and estimates the useful life of its buildings at 30 years, equipment up to 5 years, and leasehold improvements at the lease term or 10 years (page 59 of the annual report).

On the balance sheet, Apple shows property, plant, and equipment (net) of $2,455 million, goodwill of $207 million, and acquired intangible assets of $285 million. Note 3 (page 69 of the annual report) discloses the details of property, plant, and equipment (in millions). Note 4 (page 70 of the annual report) discusses the goodwill and acquired intangible assets.

The statement of cash flows indicates that Apple spent $1,091 million for purchases of property, plant, and equipment during fiscal 2008. Now let's consider the issue of depreciation on the statement of cash flows. We know from this chapter and Chapter 12 that when a company records depreciation it is not a cash expense. Why, then, does it appear on the statement of cash flows? This particular statement of cash flows is prepared using the indirect method (we will discuss this in more detail in Chapter 19). For now, you should know that under this method a company reconciles its net income to its cash flows from operations through a series of adjustments. One of these adjustments is for noncash expenses—that is, those expenses that while decreasing net income do not decrease cash flows from operating activities. Since the effect of the expense was to reduce net income, we add back the amount to reconcile to cash flows from operations. Thus, depreciation expense was added to net income on the statement of cash flows as an adjustment to determine cash flows from operating activities.

While we are examining the statement of cash flows, go down four lines and you will see a line item entitled, "Loss on disposition of property, plant, and equipment." Notice that the amount, $22 million, is added to net income to determine cash flows from operating activities. Why is it added? Because the loss reduced net income but did not reduce operating cash flows because a loss is an investing activity and the resulting cash flow is reported in the investing section of the statement of cash flows. A gain, therefore, would be subtracted from net income to determine cash flows from operations because a gain increases net income without any increase to operating cash flows.

Internal Evaluation of Investing Activities

In addition to evaluating the financial statement results, internal stakeholders must evaluate investing activities against the balanced scorecard goals. Managers must control both the acquisition and operating costs of the long-term assets purchased and ensure that assets are generating an adequate return for the owners. One common measure used to evaluate investing activities is the **return on assets ratio** (also known as the return on investment ratio as discussed in Chapter 12). Management would compare this ratio to the balanced scorecard goals to determine if changes are needed. In addition, companies typically conduct a post-audit of capital budgeting projects. A **post-audit** involves comparing the actual cash inflows and outflows of the project to the predicted cash inflows and outflows analyzed during the capital budgeting process. This provides management with valuable information not only regarding the project itself but also the capital budgeting process.

Summary

Operational investments represent some of the most significant long-term uses of a company's capital. This chapter presented information about plant assets, natural resources, and intangible assets and introduced some of the fundamental principles that determine how accountants record the acquisition, use, and disposal of these assets. Finally, we discussed and illustrated the manner in which companies report and evaluate information regarding operational investments to stakeholders.

- Operational investments are capital expenditures made to acquire the facilities necessary to conduct basic business activities. They include investments in plant assets, natural resources, and intangible assets.

- Depreciation is the process of systematically allocating the net cost of a plant asset to the various periods benefiting from the use of that asset. For financial statement reporting, depreciation can be calculated using the (1) straight-line method, (2) units-of-production method, or (3) accelerated methods.

- The gain or loss on the disposal of plant assets is the difference between the carrying value of the asset (Cost – Accumulated depreciation) and the fair market value of any net assets received in return. When a business sells assets for cash or exchanges dissimilar noncash assets, it records and reports all resulting gains and losses. For financial reporting purposes, when there is an exchange of similar assets, companies record losses but not gains.

- Natural resources are a company's investment in nonrenewable assets such as coal mines and oil rights. The expense resulting from the cost of these assets is called depletion and is usually calculated using the units-of-production method.

- Intangible assets have no physical presence that can be seen or touched. They convey a legal right or benefit to their owner. Intangible assets are amortized, generally by the straight-line method, over the expected useful life of the assets or their legal lives, whichever is shorter. Goodwill, however, is not amortized and is only reduced when evidence indicates its value has been impaired.

Key Terms

Accelerated depreciation A method of depreciation that recognizes relatively greater expense in early years of asset use and progressively less expense as time passes, *455*
Amortization The process of allocating the cost of intangible assets to an expense over the periods they benefit, *465*
Capital expenditure An expenditure that creates the expectation of future benefits that apply beyond the current accounting period, *450*
Capitalize To add an expenditure to the cost of an asset, rather than expensing it immediately, *450*
Copyright An intangible asset that gives its owner the exclusive legal right to the reproduction and sale of a literary or artistic work, *464*
Declining-balance depreciation A type of accelerated depreciation that reflects depreciation expense for each year based on a constant percentage of a declining balance equal to the remaining undepreciated cost of the asset at the start of each year, *455*
Depletion The process of allocating the cost of natural resources to an expense over the periods they benefit, *464*
Depreciable cost The portion of a plant asset's total cost that will be depreciated over its useful life, *453*
Double-declining-balance (DDB) depreciation A specific type of declining-balance depreciation that reflects annual depreciation expense using a constant percentage equal to twice the straight-line rate of depreciation, *456*
Extraordinary repairs and betterments Expenditures that extend the remaining useful life of an operational investment and/or improve performance capabilities, *458*
Franchise An intangible asset representing the exclusive right to operate or sell a brand name product in a specified territory, *465*
Goodwill An intangible asset representing the value assigned to a purchased company's ability to generate an above-average return on invested capital, *465*
Leasehold An intangible asset conveyed by a lease to use equipment, land, and/or buildings for a specified period of time, *465*
Leasehold improvement An intangible asset representing the amounts paid by a lessee to make physical improvements that are an integral part of leased property, *465*
Materiality An accounting concept that relates to whether an item's dollar amount or its inherent nature is significant enough to influence a financial statement user, *451*
Midyear convention The convention that reflects depreciation expense for each asset as if it were purchased or disposed of exactly halfway through the company's fiscal year, *457*
Natural resources Nonrenewable assets such as coal mines and oil rights, *464*
Patent An intangible asset giving its owner the exclusive legal right to the commercial benefits of a specified product or process, *464*
Plant assets Tangible assets acquired primarily for use in a business over a time span covering more than one accounting period, *450*
Post-audit A comparison of the actual cash inflows and outflows of the project to the predicted cash inflows and outflows analyzed during the capital budgeting process, *467*
Residual value See salvage value, *453*
Return on assets ratio A measurement of the relationship of earnings before interest and taxes to the average amount of asset investment, *467*
Revenue expenditure An expenditure that provides benefits exclusively during the current accounting period, *450*
Salvage value The expected fair market value of a plant asset at the end of its useful life; also referred to as residual value, *453*
Straight-line depreciation A method of calculating annual depreciation by allocating the depreciable cost of the asset evenly to depreciation expense over its useful life, *453*
Trademark An intangible asset that identifies a particular company or product, *465*
Units-of-production depreciation A method of calculating annual depreciation based on actual usage rather than the passage of time, *455*

Questions

1. What factors do companies consider in determining the cost of plant assets?
2. Distinguish between capital and revenue expenditures.
3. Should the cost of paving a parking lot be treated as a capital or revenue expenditure? Why?
4. If a company purchases 5,000 No. 2 lead pencils for $800 and plans to use the pencils for five years, are the pencils a plant asset? Why?
5. Describe how the cost of a multiple asset purchase is allocated to the individual assets in the purchase.
6. What is depreciation?
7. What is the carrying value of an asset?
8. Explain the difference between straight-line and units-of-production depreciation.
9. Explain how to calculate the rate used in double-declining-balance depreciation.
10. What is the midyear convention and why do companies use it?
11. When assets are exchanged, how do you determine the gain or loss?
12. How is the value of an asset received in an exchange determined?
13. Under what circumstances are gains and losses not recognized in a noncash exchange?
14. When gains and losses are not recognized in a noncash exchange, how is the cost of the new asset determined?
15. When is a loss on impairment recognized? (see, Of Interest)
16. What is a natural resource? What is depletion?
17. What is an intangible asset? What is amortization?
18. How are investing activities reported on the income statement?
19. How are investing activities reported on the statement of cash flows?
20. How are the results of investing activities reported on the balance sheet?

Exercises

E16.1 LO 1 For each of these situations, what account would be debited to record the expenditure?

A. Constructed a warehouse for storing merchandise.
B. Purchased 300 reams of 8 $\frac{1}{2}$-by-11-inch paper for the fax machine.
C. Purchased a parcel of land in a nearby town because of rumors that a new mall would be built on adjoining land. Management expects to sell the land in three years at a substantial profit.
D. Bought 20 used desks and 30 used chairs to be utilized at corporate headquarters in the accounting office.
E. Paid for a new battery installed in the delivery truck.

LO 1 **E16.2** For each of the following situations, indicate whether it is a capital **(C)** or revenue **(R)** expenditure.

________ A. Purchased land and a building at a cost of $750,000 by paying $200,000 down and signing a two-year note payable for the remainder.
________ B. Spent $325 on a tune-up for a truck used in making deliveries.
________ C. The owner of a restaurant paid a plumber $400 to install a new dishwasher in the kitchen.
________ D. Paid $1,300 in sales tax on a new delivery van when registering the van at the Registry of Motor Vehicles.
________ E. A new machine was accidently damaged during installation. The uninsured cost to repair the machine was $1,250.

LO 1 **E16.3** Baker Communications purchased land, a building, and several pieces of equipment for $5,400,000. An appraisal of the purchased items estimated the value of the land at $3,100,000, the building at $1,850,000, and the equipment at $650,500. Determine the portion of the total purchase price applicable to each asset.

LO 1 **E16.4** Winters Company purchased a new van to expand its business. The invoice price of the van was $35,400, with additional costs of $950 for dealer prep and $675 in destination charges. Winters also had the dealer install special roof racks at a cost of $1,450 and paid $2,255 in sales tax, $175 in annual registration fees, and $60 for the title. The annual insurance bill totaled $1,960, and Winters opted for an extended warranty package costing $935. Within one month's time, Winters spent $330 for gasoline. Determine the dollar amount that Winters should debit the Vehicles account.

LO 2 **E16.5** Dray Enterprises recently acquired a new machine at a cost of $59,000. The machine has an estimated useful life of six years or 45,000 production hours, and salvage value is estimated at $5,000. During the first two years of the asset's life, 8,000 and 7,500 production hours, respectively, were logged by the machine. Calculate the depreciation charge for the first two years of the asset's life using the (*a*) straight-line method, (*b*) units-of-production method, and (*c*) double-declining-balance method.

LO 2 **E16.6** Pexly Industries purchased a copier system with a cost of $62,000 and a salvage value estimated at $2,000. It was expected that the copier would last four years, over which time it would produce 6,000,000 copies. The copier actually produced 1,500,000 copies in Year 1, 1,900,000 copies in Year 2, 1,800,000 copies in Year 3, and 1,400,000 copies in Year 4. Calculate the depreciation expense and carrying value of the asset at year-end for each of the four years using the following methods: (*a*) straight-line method, (*b*) units-of-production method, and (*c*) double-declining-balance method.

LO 2 **E16.7** Bundy Company purchased several computerized cash registers on April 2, 2010, at a total cost of $36,600. Estimated useful life of the registers is four years, and their total expected salvage value is $1,600. Bundy uses the straight-line method of depreciation and has a December 31 year-end. Determine the amount of depreciation expense in 2008 assuming, alternatively, that (*a*) depreciation is calculated to the nearest month and (*b*) Bundy uses the midyear convention.

LO 2 **E16.8** Gandiaga owns a truck that it purchased two years ago at a total cost of $29,250. At that time it was estimated that the company would use the truck for six years and then sell it for $1,850. Recently, Gandiaga modified the truck at a cost of $4,500. This modification did not extend the life of the truck, nor did it change the estimated salvage value. Prepare journal entries to record the cost of the upgrade and the depreciation expense for the third year assuming that Gandiaga uses straight-line depreciation.

LO 2 **E16.9** Hutt Company purchased a building 12 years ago at a price of $850,000. At that time, useful life was estimated at 25 years with a $175,000 salvage value, and straight-line depreciation was used. After recording depreciation for the 12th year, Hutt decided that for future years it would revise its original estimate of the building's useful life from 25 to 39 years and salvage value from $175,000 to $150,000. Calculate the depreciation expense that Hutt should record for each of the remaining years of the building's life.

LO 3 **E16.10** Leavy Corporation owns a delivery van with an original cost of $36,500 and accumulated depreciation of $28,000. Determine the amount of gain or loss on the sale of the van under each of the following situations:

A. The van is sold for $10,000 cash.
B. The van is sold for $8,000 cash.
C. The van is sold for $2,000 cash plus a six-month $7,000 note receivable with a stated 8 percent interest rate.

LO 2 **E16.11** **LO 3** McKain, Inc., closes its books on October 31 and prepares depreciation adjustments annually. On July 27, 2010, McKain sold some equipment with an original cost of $36,250 for $18,500. The equipment was purchased on November 4, 2005, and was depreciated using the straight-line method and had an estimated useful life of eight years and a salvage value of $1,650. Prepare the entries to update the depreciation and record the sale of the equipment.

LO 3 **E16.12** Nelson Enterprises exchanged a building it owned in Grand Junction for a building in Canon City owned by Lamb Corporation. The buildings were both valued at $575,000, so there was no cash transferred between the companies. Just prior to the exchange, Nelson's accounts showed the cost of the original building as $425,000, with accumulated depreciation of $260,000. Lamb's Canon City building was on its books with a cost of $750,000 and accumulated depreciation of $160,000. Determine the gain or loss that each company should recognize. What dollar amount should each company assign to the building it acquired? If the exchange lacked economic substance, how would it be recorded?

LO 3 **E16.13** On July 1, Nutt Company exchanged a warehouse and some land for 50,000 shares of Zesco Corporation stock. The stock was selling for $12 per share, and a recent appraisal of the land and warehouse set their total value at $650,000. The warehouse and land originally cost $450,000 and $225,000, respectively. Accumulated depreciation on the warehouse was $320,000. Prepare the entry to record the exchange. What value did you assign to the stock acquired in the transaction? Why?

LO 3 **E16.14** Obssuth Company is trading in its old computer system for an ERP system. The old system is on the books at a cost of $1,270,000 with accumulated depreciation of $885,000. The ERP has a price of $4,500,000 installed and debugged, but the manufacturer has agreed to reduce this amount by $250,000 in return for Obssuth's old system. Prepare the journal entry to record the acquisition of the new ERP system.

LO 2 **E16.15** Kaltenheuser Corporation owns a patent with a 17-year legal life and a eight-year useful life. The patent cost $40,000. What is the amortization expense each year if Kaltenheuser uses the straight-line method?

LO 2 **E16.16** Refer to E16.15. How would the patent appear on Kaltenheuser's balance sheet after the third year?

LO 2 **E16.17** Refer to E16.15. If Kaltenheuser determined in year 2 that the patent's useful life was only five years, what would be the amortization expense for years 2 through 5?

LO 2 E16.18 Refer to E16.15. Assume Kaltenheuser spent $100,000 developing the process that led to the patent. What is the amortization expense each year? Why?

LO 2 E16.19 Worth Company recently purchased an oil well for $3.5 million. This well is expected to produce 700,000 barrels of oil over its life. What is the depletion rate if Worth uses the units-of-production method?

LO 2 E16.20 Refer to E16.19. If Worth Company produced 100,000 barrels of oil in its first year, what would be the accumulated depletion balance?

Problems

P16.1 LO 1 Downham Industries recently completed several transactions relating to plant assets. For each transaction described, determine the dollar amount to be capitalized as well as the account title to be used.

A. Downham purchased a parcel of land on which it will construct a manufacturing facility. The purchase price of $155,000 included survey fees of $2,700, a title document costing $800, and brokers' fees of $7,500. Downham also incurred $10,500 in blasting costs to prepare the land for construction of the building.
B. Downham constructed the manufacturing facility referred to in part **(A).** Materials and labor costs amounted to $278,000, the architect's fee was $18,500, and the necessary permits totaled $3,600. Insurance carried during the construction was $2,300, and interest on the construction loan amounted to $14,200.
C. Downham paid the following bills relating to the use of its plant assets: (1) annual real estate taxes, $14,250; (2) annual insurance premiums, $8,380; (3) annual mortgage payments, $124,800, of which $61,700 was interest; and (4) painting of the outside of the buildings, $7,200.

LO 2 P16.2 Baugh Travel, whose year-end is December 31, purchased $55,500 worth of office furniture on January 7, 2010. The company uses straight-line depreciation for financial statement purposes based on an estimated useful life of five years and a salvage value of $500. Baugh's tax return preparer follows the MACRS rules for income tax purposes.

A. Calculate depreciation expense for financial statement purposes for each year of the asset's life.
B. Why is it appropriate to use two different methods of depreciation for the same asset?

LO 2 P16.3 Gaub Corporation purchased a machine at a total cost of $400,000. As the accountant for the company, you estimated a useful life of seven years or 25,000 hours of operation, with a salvage value of $50,000. The president of the company wants to know what impact this capital expenditure will have on income over the next seven years. (Assume the computer is used 4,000 hours the first year and that its usage increases 10 percent in each succeeding year.)

Required:

A. Prepare a schedule showing the depreciation expense and year-end carrying value of the asset for each of the next four years under each of the following methods of depreciation:
   1. Straight-line method
   2. Units-of-production method
   3. Double-declining-balance method
B. Why would management select one method over another?

LO 1 LO 2 P16.4 Alexander, Inc., whose year-end is December 31, purchased a delivery truck on May 2, 2010. The invoice price was $63,500 and included dealer prep and destination charges of $4,850. Alexander also paid sales tax of $4,785, registration fees of $395, and a $100 fee to obtain a title. On May 5, 2010, the company installed air conditioning in the truck at a cost of $2,850. On January 10, 2013, the company installed a new transmission in the truck at a cost of $5,000 and paid $375 for a tune-up of the engine. Alexander uses straight-line depreciation and the midyear convention. The estimated useful life of the truck is eight years with a $6,000 salvage value.

Required:

A. Determine the dollar amount that should be capitalized to the Truck account in May 2010.
B. Calculate the depreciation expense to be recorded for 2010.
C. Should Alexander account for the expenditures made in January 2013 as capital or revenue expenditures?
D. If the useful life of the truck was extended two years by the installation of the new transmission, calculate the depreciation expense for 2013, assuming that the salvage value did not change.

LO 2 P16.5 Prager, Inc., acquired a mine for $870,000 at the beginning of the year. Of the total purchase price, $100,000 was allocated to the land while the remainder was allocated to the minerals in the mine itself. Prager estimates that 15,400,000 tons of ore are in the mine. During the year, Prager mined 2,500,000 tons of ore and sold 2,000,000 tons. During the year, Prager spent $240,000 developing a new process that resulted in a patent. On July 1, Prager obtained the patent, which has a useful life of eight years. The legal and filing fees associated with the patent totaled $32,000.

A. Determine the amortization rate per year and depletion rate per ton.
B. What is the amortization expense for the year?
C. What is total depletion for the year?
D. What is the total depletion charged to cost of goods sold for the year? *Hint:* See footnote 4.

LO 3 **P16.6** Cuomo Touring Company owns a luxury motorcoach it uses in long-distance tours. The motorcoach originally cost the company $685,000, and depreciation taken to date amounts to $274,000. Cuomo is considering several alternative methods of disposing of the motorcoach and is concerned about the financial statement impact. The alternative methods of disposal available are as follows. (Treat each alternative independently.)

1. The motorcoach will be sold for $365,000 cash.
2. The motorcoach will be exchanged for a stock investment in Recreation, Ltd. The value of the stock is estimated at $425,000.
3. The motorcoach will be traded in on a new model valued at $925,000. A trade-in allowance of $400,000 will be granted by the manufacturer with the balance paid in cash.
4. The motorcoach will be traded for a limousine owned by Barton Transportation Company. In exchange for the motorcoach, Barton will give Cuomo Touring $60,000 cash, a three-year $340,000 note with a face rate of 8 percent, and the limousine. The motorcoach has an appraised value of $450,000 but fair market value of the limousine is not clear.

Required: A. Determine the amount of gain or loss to be recognized in each of the alternatives.
B. Make the journal entries to record the events above.

LO 3 **P16.7** Shenefelt Medical Center wants to dispose of its CAT scan machine. The original cost of the machine was $445,000, and depreciation of $374,000 has been recorded to date. The purchasing manager is contemplating the following alternatives to dispose of the machine. (Treat each alternative independently.)

1. Mainland Medical Supply is willing to take the old machine and give Shenefelt a $85,000 trade-in allowance toward the purchase of a new CAT scan machine with a list price of $310,000. The balance of the price must be paid in cash.
2. Cornell Medical Supply is willing to give Shenefelt a $65,000 trade-in allowance on a new CAT scan machine with a list price of $325,000, the balance to be paid in cash.
3. Century Medical Center is willing to make an even exchange. Century will exchange its CAT scan machine for Shenefelt's CAT scan. Shenefelt's CAT scan has a fair market value of $80,000. The CPA for Shenefelt says this exchange has no commercial substance.
4. Saxony Medical Center is willing to give Shenefelt an ambulance with a fair market value of $65,000 and $20,000 cash for Shenefelt's CAT scan.

Required: A. Prepare Shenefelt's journal entry to record each of these alternatives for financial statement purposes.
B. Was the gain/loss recognized for each of the alternatives? If not, why not?

LO 1 LO 2 LO 3 **P16.8** Refer to Pepsico, Inc. (**www.pepsico.com**), and answer the following questions:

A. Which depreciation method is used?
B. Does the company have intangible assets? If so, how are they amortized?
C. What is the carrying value of its property, plant, and equipment? What is the balance of accumulated depreciation for property, plant, and equipment?
D. Did the company have any cash inflows from investing activities? If so, what was the dollar amount?
E. Did the company have any cash outflows from investing activities? If so, what was the dollar amount?

LO 1 LO 2 LO 3 **P16.9** Refer to Walt Disney Company (**www.disney.com**) and answer the following questions:

A. Which depreciation method is used?
B. Does the company have intangible assets? If so, how are they amortized?
C. What is the carrying value of its property, plant, and equipment? What is the balance of accumulated depreciation for property, plant, and equipment?
D. Did the company have any cash inflows from investing activities? If so, what was the dollar amount?
E. Did the company have any cash outflows from investing activities? If so, what was the dollar amount?

LO 1 LO 2 LO 3 **P16.10** Refer to Dell Computers (**www.dell.com**) and answer the following questions:

A. Which depreciation method is used?
B. Does the company have intangible assets? If so, how are they amortized?
C. What is the carrying value of its property, plant, and equipment? What is the balance of accumulated depreciation for property, plant, and equipment?
D. Did the company have any cash inflows from investing activities? If so, what was the dollar amount?
E. Did the company have any cash outflows from investing activities? If so, what was the dollar amount?

Cases

C16.1 LO 1 LO 2 LO 3 Refer to the financial statement of the company you selected in C1.1 and answer the following questions:

A. Which depreciation method is used?
B. Does the company have intangible assets? If so, how are they amortized?
C. What is the carrying value of its property, plant, and equipment? What is the balance of accumulated depreciation for property, plant, and equipment?
D. Did the company have any cash inflows from investing activities? If so, what was the dollar amount?
E. Did the company have any cash outflows from investing activities? If so, what was the dollar amount?

LO 2 **C16.2** Leziy Corporation owns a coal mine, an oil field, and a tract of timberland. Information regarding these assets follows:

1. The coal mine was purchased several years ago at a total cost of $865,000. The mine was estimated to contain 200,000 tons of ore and to have a $35,000 salvage value. During the current year, 53,000 tons of ore were mined.
2. The oil field was acquired in exchange for stock and was initially valued at $12,600,000. It was estimated to contain 500,000 barrels of oil and to have a salvage value of $100,000. During the current year, 127,000 barrels of oil were extracted.
3. The timberland was obtained through a land swap and was initially recorded at $1,350,000. The number of board feet of timber estimated to be available amounted to 120,000, and the salvage value of the land was estimated at $150,000. During the current year, 21,000 board feet of timber were cut.

Required:

A. Assuming Leziy uses the units-of-production method of depletion, determine the depletion rate per ton, barrel, and board foot.
B. Compute the amount of depletion for each of the assets for the current year.
C. Will the depletion charge appear on the financial statements as depletion expense? If not, where will it most likely appear?

LO 2 **C16.3** Whispering Recording Company (WRC) acquired the following assets at the beginning of 2006:

1. The patent to manufacture a revolutionary compact disc. The purchase price was $2,300,000, and there are 16 years remaining in the legal life of the patent.
2. The copyright to an album by the newest country western group, Best of the West. The total amount spent to obtain the copyright was $480,000. The album is expected to be produced for three years, but royalties from the album are expected to continue for 10 years.
3. The copyright to a music video by the hottest new female vocalist, Flamingo, was purchased by WRC for $1,000,000. The video is expected to be produced for two years. However, royalties from the video are expected to continue for six years.

Required:

A. Assuming WRC uses the straight-line method of amortization, determine the amortization expense for 2006 for each of these assets.
B. Give the journal entry to record the 2006 amortization expense for the patent.

Critical Thinking

CT16.1 LO 1  In each of the following situations, determine the age of each asset in either years or units, whichever is appropriate.

A. Equipment appears on the balance sheet at a cost of $28,500 with accumulated depreciation of $14,100. The salvage value was estimated at $5,000, the useful life was estimated at five years, and the straight-line method of depreciation is used.

B. The cost of the truck is $21,800 with $17,100 of accumulated depreciation. Salvage value was estimated at $2,800, and the truck would most likely be driven for 100,000 miles. The company uses the units-of-production method of depreciation.

C. Machinery was purchased for $64,500 and, at present, has accumulated depreciation of $23,220. The useful life was estimated at 10 years, with a salvage value of $9,500. The double-declining-balance method of depreciation is used.

LO 1 LO 2 **CT16.2** In each of the following situations, determine if the appropriate action was taken. If not, describe the financial statement impact of the error.

A. Recorded the $50,000 purchase of land acquired for investment purposes as a debit to the Land account.

B. A $450 tune-up to the delivery truck was capitalized to the Truck account.

C. Land to be used as the site for a new warehouse was purchased for $250,000 plus a broker's commission of $12,500. The Land account was debited for $250,000, and the $12,500 broker's commission was recorded as commission expense.

D. The $650 cost to install a new water heater was charged to plumbing repairs expense.

E. A patent was purchased for $475,000 and recorded in the Equipment account.

F. Depletion relating to the extraction of 200,000 barrels of oil was not recorded because the oil is still sitting in inventory and has not been sold.

Ethical Challenges

EC16.1 LO 1 Refer to the Of Interest: Nonoperational Investments. What incentives might management have to classify investments as trading securities versus available-for-sale securities? What are the ethical implications of classifying securities according to "management's intent"?

LO 2 **EC16.2** As you know, extraordinary repairs and betterments are recorded as capital expenditures while maintenance and normal repairs are recorded as expenses in the period incurred. What incentives might management have to classify expenditures as "extraordinary" or "ordinary"? What are the ethical implications of such practices?

Computer Applications

CA16.1 LO 2 Calande Corporation purchased five new assets at the beginning of its accounting period. The cost, salvage value, and estimated useful lives of these assets are

Asset	Cost	Salvage Value	Useful Life
1	$65,000	$3,500	7 years
2	34,400	0	3
3	45,200	1,200	6
4	58,900	1,900	6
5	88,200	2,500	5

Required: Use a computer spreadsheet package.

A. Set up a spreadsheet to calculate the straight-line depreciation on each asset for the first year.

B. Repeat part **(A)** using the double-declining-balance method.

LO 2 **CA16.2** Lambert Company purchased an asset for $525,000. It has an expected useful life of 10 years and no salvage value. Lambert uses the double-declining-balance depreciation method.

Required: Use a computer spreadsheet package.

A. Prepare a schedule that indicates the depreciation expense, ending balance of accumulated depreciation, and ending book value of each year of the asset's life. (Do not be alarmed if you still have a book value at the end of 10 years.)

B. Because double-declining-balance does not balance to zero, particularly when the cost of the asset is high and the salvage value is low, companies often switch to straight-line depreciation sometime during the life of the asset. Determine when Lambert should switch to the straight-line method and prepare a schedule as indicated in part **(A)**.

Visit the text Online Learning Center at **www.mhhe.com/ainsworth6e** for additional problem material that accompanies this chapter.

PART SEVEN

VII

Evaluating: Operating and Capital Resource Processes

CHAPTER SEVENTEEN

17 Company Performance: Profitability

Learning Objectives

LO 1 Discuss the importance of income from continuing operations and net income.

LO 2 Describe the purpose of, and calculate, earnings per share and diluted earnings per share.

LO 3 Explain the purpose of, and calculate, income using variable, absorption, and throughput costing for internal reporting purposes.

LO 4 Define the purpose of, and calculate, product-line (divisional) income and return on investment.

Throughout this text we have talked about business events that affect a company's profitability and that are reported on the income statement. In this chapter, we look at the income statement in its entirety, exploring issues such as what information the income statement and its related notes provide to users and some reporting issues income statement users should consider. We also introduce other ways of reporting profitability for internal users. To illustrate all the components of income we examine PCs to Go many years after formation. Then we relate these ideas to the financial statements and related notes of Apple.

Purpose of the Income Statement

The purpose of the income statement is to reflect the earnings (income) generated by the company during the accounting period. It is vital for both internal and external users to comprehend the components of reported earnings. Recall from Chapter 1 that the FASB's conceptual framework states that the three objectives of financial reporting are to provide information that is (1) useful for making investment and credit decisions; (2) useful for assessing cash flow prospects; and (3) relevant to evaluating enterprise resources, claims to those resources, and changes in the resources.

The income statement helps fulfill these three objectives by disclosing information about the earnings of the company during the current fiscal year. Investors and creditors use current earnings information to assess the future earnings potential of the firm. Such assessment of earnings also provides information that allows external users to evaluate the amounts, timing, and uncertainty of future cash flows from dividends or interest. The income statement also provides important information about changes in the company's resources and claims to those resources due to the operating activities of the company. Investors and creditors use this type of past operating performance information to predict the future performance of the company.

GAAP and Comprehensive Income

Generally accepted accounting principles (GAAP) require that external financial statements comply with the comprehensive concept of income. The elements of comprehensive income are

+	Revenues
−	Expenses
+	Gains
−	Losses
=	*Earnings (income from continuing operations)*
+/−	Discontinued operations (net-of-tax)
+/−	Extraordinary items (net-of-tax)
=	*Net income*
+/−	Other comprehensive income items (net-of-tax)
=	*Comprehensive income*

Comprehensive income often is not the same as earnings or net income. **Earnings** represent income from continuing operations and consist of revenues minus expenses and gains minus losses. Earnings are recurring, whereas the events included in net income are not necessarily recurring. **Net income** includes both the operating and other activities (excluding

OF INTEREST What Is GAAP?

As you know, GAAP stands for generally accepted accounting principles. GAAP consists of the pronouncements of the Financial Accounting Standards Board (FASB). These include Statements of Financial Accounting Standards (SFAS) and the bulletins, opinions, and principles issued by the Committee on Accounting Procedure (CAP) and the Accounting Principles Board (APB), the predecessors of the FASB. Standardization of the accounting profession began in 1913 with the passage of the 16th Amendment to the U.S. Constitution that allowed taxation of income. Following the passage of the Securities and Exchange Acts in 1933 and 1934, the first official accounting rule-making body (Committee on Accounting Procedure) was formed. CAP consisted of part-time members and it issued 51 bulletins during its tenure. In 1959 the APB replaced CAP. The APB also consisted of part-time members and it issued 31 opinions and 4 statements. The APB was unique in that it sponsored research studies to formulate postulates of accounting. In 1973 the FASB replaced the APB. The FASB consists of full-time, paid professionals who are responsible for developing accounting standards. What makes the FASB unique is that it actively seeks input from businesspersons outside the accounting profession as well as practicing accountants before it issues SFAS. To date the FASB has issued more than 150 Statements of Financial Accounting Standards and 7 Statements of Financial Accounting Concepts. As noted in Chapter 1, GAAP is now codified into one cohesive database.

dividends) that caused changes in retained earnings during the period. **Comprehensive income** reported externally should reflect *all* changes in owners' equity during the period except those resulting from investments by, or distributions to, owners and those resulting from the correction of errors made in previous periods. Comprehensive income is important because it reflects the recurring and nonrecurring accounting transactions during a time period and also nontransaction events such as changes in the fair value of securities investments that, when recognized, change the owners' equity of the firm. This gives financial statement users a better idea of how to predict future earnings and cash flows as well as how to evaluate management's actions for the current period. Companies can report their comprehensive income for the period on either the income statement, as a separate statement, or as part of the statement of owners' equity. Most companies choose to disclose comprehensive income on the statement of owners' equity, which is why we defer discussion of the details of comprehensive income until Chapter 18. In this chapter, we discuss those items that result in the calculation of net income as shown on the income statement.

Exhibit 17.1 shows the income statement for PCs to Go that we use as our road map for this chapter. We discuss the net income shown on the income statement in two sections: (1) earnings and (2) discontinued operations and extraordinary items. Following this discussion we look at the reporting of earnings per share.

What Are Earnings?

The earnings of the firm include its revenues minus expenses plus gains and minus losses. The business activities that result in income from continuing operations are assumed to be recurring. Revenue and expense events clearly are recurring events because they take place daily. Likewise, many gains and losses such as those from selling property, plant, and equipment occur often enough to be considered recurring events. Other gains and losses, such as those regarding discontinued operations, are not recurring events and are reported as other changes in equity. The recurring events are important to statement users because they can be used to predict future earnings of the company.

Exhibit 17.1 is an example of a multistep income statement that shows subdivided earnings (income) based on the types of company activities reported. In a multistep income statement, cost of goods sold ($2,629,226) is subtracted from sales ($3,687,240), which results in gross margin ($1,058,014). Gross margin, then, is the overall profitability of the company's products. Selling and administrative expenses ($636,204) are subtracted from gross margin to derive income from operations ($421,810). Income from operations reflects the overall profitability of the company's operating activities.

OF INTEREST Unrealized Holding Gains and Losses

In the Of Interest: Nonoperational Investments in Chapter 16 we discussed trading and available-for-sale securities (as well as held-to-maturity securities). Both of these securities are shown on the balance sheet at the market value at the end of the period. Typically a company compares the cost versus the market value of groups of like assets, for example, debt securities classified as trading securities. This process is often referred to as *mark-to-market* accounting because the value of the securities as shown on the balance sheet is adjusted (marked) to the market value. However, because these securities are still owned by the company, the resulting gain (market value greater than cost) or loss (market value less than cost) is *unrealized.*

When a company has an unrealized gain or loss on trading securities, it is reported as part of net income on the income statement (typically as part of "other income"). When a company has an unrealized gain or loss on available-for-sale securities, it is reported on the statement of owners' equity in comprehensive income and a running balance is maintained on the balance sheet in the stockholders' equity section under the title, "Accumulated other comprehensive income (loss)." We will discuss unrealized gains (losses) on available-for-sale securities in greater detail in the next chapter. The table below summarizes the accounting treatment of unrealized gains (losses).

Type of Security	Unrealized Holding Gains and Losses
Trading securities	Recognized in net income; shown on income statement
Available-for-sale securities	Recognized in comprehensive income; shown on the balance sheet and the statement of owners' equity

EXHIBIT 17.1
PCs to Go Income Statement

PCs to Go
Income Statement
For the Year Ended December 31, 2010

Sales	$3,687,240
Less cost of goods sold	(2,629,226)
Gross margin	$1,058,014
Less selling and administrative expenses	(636,204)
Income from operations	$ 421,810
Other revenues and gains:	
Interest income	920
Dividend income	302
Other expenses and losses:	
Interest expense	(675)
Loss on sale of equipment	(150)
Income from continuing operations before income taxes	$ 422,207
Income tax expense	(189,993)
Income from continuing operations	$ 232,214
Discontinued operations:	
Income from operations of division, net of applicable taxes	15,000
Loss on disposal of division, net of applicable taxes	(29,000)
Income before extraordinary items	$ 218,214
Extraordinary loss from flood, net of applicable taxes	(148,500)
Net income	$ 69,714
Earnings per share:	
Income from continuing operations	$7.44
Discontinued operations	–0.47
Income before extraordinary items	6.97
Extraordinary loss	–4.97
Net income	$2.00
Diluted earnings per share:	
Income from continuing operations	$6.35
Discontinued operations	–0.4
Income before extraordinary items	5.95
Extraordinary loss	–4.24
Net income	$1.71

Other revenues and gains ($920 and $302) are added and other expenses and losses ($675 and $150) are subtracted to calculate income from continuing operations before income taxes ($422,207). After taxes ($189,993) are subtracted, the resulting amount is called income from continuing operations ($232,214). Income from continuing operations represents the profitability of the company's ongoing activities.

Apple (see Appendix) shows 2008 net sales of $32,479 million, a gross margin of $11,145 million, an operating income of $6,275 million, and net income of $4,834 million. Apple does not report comprehensive income on the income statement. Notice that although some of the headings used are not exactly the same as PCs to Go (or are not given), you can determine their meaning once you understand the format of the income statement.

As you know, the notes to the financial statements are required because they provide valuable additional information for financial statement users. For example, by looking at the income statement, we see cost of sales of $21,334 million for Apple, but we cannot tell which cost flow assumption Apple used to determine cost of sales. Note 1 (page 59 of the annual report) reveals that Apple uses first-in, first-out (FIFO) to value its inventories. Furthermore, depreciation expense is calculated using straight-line (Note 1, page 59).

What Are Other Changes in Equity?

Other changes in equity resulting from discontinued operations and extraordinary items appear net of taxes after income from continuing operations, which is the basis for a company's income tax calculation. See Exhibit 17.1, which illustrates income from continuing operations before these items on the income statement. We discuss discontinued operations and extraordinary items in turn.

Discontinued operations result from a strategic decision to sell or dispose of a component of the operating entity.

Discontinued Operations

Discontinued operations are the result of a company selling or disposing of a *component of an entity*. A component of an entity consists of operations and cash flows that management has clearly distinguished, operationally and for financial reporting purposes, from the rest of the entity. Typically, these components are segments of the business that represent a line of the business's products. The results of discontinued operations are presented separately on the income statement because they are unique and infrequent and, thus, not a regular part of ongoing operations. However, discontinued operations do have ramifications on the future earnings potential and cash flows of the company and, therefore, provide useful information to income statement users.

When a segment of a business is discontinued, two items are reported, either on the income statement itself or in the notes to the financial statements. The first is the income or loss generated based on the operations of the segment from the beginning of the accounting period through the disposal date. The second item reported is the gain or loss resulting from the disposal of the segment's net assets. Separating these items allows income statement readers to assess management's actions concerning the current and future aspects of disposing of the segment.

To illustrate how discontinued operations appear on the income statement, assume that during 2010 PCs to Go disposed of the Video Tablet division of its operations that had income of $27,273 before taxes. Assuming a 45 percent tax rate, the income from operations, net of tax, reported on the income statement, is $15,000, as shown here:

Income from operations of division	$27,273
Less applicable taxes (45%)	12,273
Income from operations of division, net of applicable taxes	$15,000

The loss incurred by PCs to Go to dispose of the segment was $52,727 before taxes. The amount of the loss from disposing of the segment, net of tax, reported on the income statement is $29,000:

Loss from disposal	$52,727
Less tax savings (45%)	23,727
Loss from disposal of division, net of applicable tax	$29,000

Take a moment to locate these items in Exhibit 17.1. They are added and subtracted, respectively, from "income from continuing operations" to determine "income before extraordinary items." Typically, companies report a single line item, called discontinued operations, on the face of the income statement and provide additional information concerning the disposal in the notes, as mentioned earlier. An examination of the income statement of Apple reveals no discontinued operations from 2006 through 2008.

Extraordinary items result from unusual and infrequent, uncontrollable events affecting the operating entity.

Extraordinary Items

Extraordinary items are events that occurred during the accounting period that are both unusual and infrequent. Extraordinary events are often the result of a major casualty, such as assets that are expropriated by a foreign government or losses sustained from a disaster. Extraordinary items are important because they may have current and/or future cash flow implications. In addition, a financial statement user should evaluate the effect of an extraordinary item when predicting future earnings.

It is not always easy to determine if a particular event is an extraordinary item. For example, a California company's loss due to an earthquake is not an extraordinary item because earthquakes in that region are not unusual. On the other hand, a Tennessee company's loss due to an earthquake would probably be an extraordinary item because earthquakes are rare in that region of the United States.

Extraordinary items appear net of taxes, the details of which are often found in the notes. To illustrate extraordinary items, assume that PCs to Go suffered an uninsured loss from a flood during 2010. The total loss was $270,000; however, the amount shown on the income statement (see Exhibit 17.1) is only $148,500 due to the tax savings resulting from the loss, calculated as:

Loss due to flood	$270,000
Less tax savings (45%)	121,500
Extraordinary loss, net of applicable taxes	$148,500

An examination of its income statement reveals that Apple had no extraordinary events from fiscal 2006 through 2008.[1]

Net Income

Net income is the final item on the income statement and represents the net change in shareholders' equity due to the operating and nonoperating activities that occurred during the fiscal year. You may hear people refer to net income as the firm's bottom line; however, you should not dwell on just one number. An informed financial statement user knows that examining the components of net income is essential for anyone who wants to understand a firm's performance. For PCs to Go its bottom line or net income for 2010 was $69,714.

Earnings per Share

Fundamentally, **earnings per share** is a common-size measure of a company's earnings performance that allows financial statement users to compare the operating performance of large and small corporations on a per share basis. Earnings per share is the most frequently

[1] It is interesting to note that the losses sustained by the airlines as a result of September 11, 2001, were not considered extraordinary. The argument was that crashes are not unusual or infrequent events for airlines regardless of the cause.

quoted measure of firm performance in the financial press, and it is a required disclosure on the face of the income statement. It reflects the amount of the company's earnings belonging to each shareholder on a per share basis. Earnings per share is not the amount that each shareholder will receive as dividends because, as you know, companies typically do not pay out all their earnings in dividends.

Earnings per share are the earnings of the company available to common shareholders stated on a per share basis.

Calculating Earnings per Share

In its basic form, earnings per share is the current period's net income reported on a per share basis, or the net income of the current period available to common shareholders divided by the weighted average number of common shares outstanding. Earnings per share (EPS) is calculated as:

$$\frac{\text{Net income} - \text{Preferred stock dividends}}{\text{Weighted average number of common shares outstanding}}$$

Take a closer look at this formula. First, it is necessary to reduce net income by the amount of required preferred stock dividends because preferred shareholders have a prespecified first claim on the earnings of the firm if any of those earnings are paid out as dividends. The remaining amount is known as earnings available to common shareholders. Second, the company uses the weighted average number of common shares outstanding to measure the average number of shares held outside the company during the entire accounting period. It reflects an adjustment made for issuances and repurchases of shares during the period.

For example, suppose that on January 1, 2010, PCs to Go had 28,800 common shares outstanding. On June 1, 2010, it issued an additional 5,700 shares and on October 1, 2010, it repurchased 9,000 shares to hold as treasury stock through the end of the year. Using this information, we calculate the weighted average number of shares outstanding:

Time Period, 2010	Shares	Partial-Year Ratio	Weight
Jan. 1–May 31	28,800	5/12	12,000
June 1–Sept. 30	34,500	4/12	11,500
Oct. 1–Dec. 31	25,500	3/12	6,375
Weighted average number of shares outstanding			29,875

Assuming that net income is $69,714 (see Exhibit 17.1) and that preferred dividends are $10,000, the earnings per share is calculated as follows:

$$\frac{\$69{,}714 - \$10{,}000}{29{,}875} = \$2.00$$

This indicates to financial statement users that shareholders earned, on average, $2.00 per share held. Take a moment to examine Exhibit 17.1 and locate the earnings per share of $2.00.

Calculating Diluted Earnings per Share

How do securities that can be converted into common stock, such as convertible preferred stock and convertible bonds, affect earnings per share? What about stock options? A stock option is a type of compensation given to employees allowing them to buy the company's stock at a predetermined or exercise price within a given time period. The employees are compensated when the market price of the company's stock exceeds the exercise price, they exercise the option (buy the stock from the company at the exercise price), and then sell the stock at the market price. The amount of the compensation depends on whether the market price of the stock becomes larger than the option's exercise price and the market price of the stock when the employee exercises the option. Because earnings per share is often used as an indication of future earnings, it is necessary to show the maximum amount of dilution, or change, in earnings per share that would occur as a result of activities like conversions and the exercise of stock options. This figure is referred to as **diluted earnings per share.** Calculating diluted earning per share is complicated and beyond the scope of this text. For illustrative purposes, we look at a simple example of diluted earnings per share. Diluted earnings per share is important because it helps current and potential investors see the impact on their claims to the firm's earnings if new owners are created though the conversion process. A significant decline in earnings could drive the stock price down because there are more shares in the company and less earnings for each shareholder.

Assume that PCs to Go offers its employees stock options as additional compensation. Further suppose that if all these stock options were exercised, the weighted average number of shares outstanding would be 35,000 (versus the 29,875 calculated previously). Using this information, the diluted earnings per share would be:

$$\frac{\$69{,}714 - \$10{,}000}{35{,}000} = \$1.71$$

Take a moment to locate the amount of diluted earnings per share in Exhibit 17.1 and notice that it is lower than the amount of earnings per share because the existing shareholders' interests will be diluted if the options are exercised.[2] Diluted earnings per share also appear on the income statement with some details regarding the calculation disclosed in the notes to the financial statements.

Enhance Your Understanding

Could diluted earnings per share be antidilutive; that is, could diluted earnings per share be greater than earnings per share?

Answer: Actually this can happen. Consider a simple example: Assume that PCs to Go does not have stock options but that all of its preferred stock is convertible to common stock. Further assume that the effect of this conversion is that weighted average common shares outstanding would be 32,500. Then the diluted earnings per share would be:

$$\frac{\$69{,}714}{32{,}500} = \$2.15$$

Note that the preferred dividend is removed from the numerator, thereby increasing the numerator. Furthermore, the number of shares in the denominator is increased, but since the numerator increased proportionately more than the denominator, the diluted earnings per share are actually higher than the basic earnings per share. This phenomenon is relatively rare, but it does happen. GAAP does not allow antidilutive EPS to be reported.

Other Earnings per Share Disclosures

Companies must show the per share effects of extraordinary items and accounting changes so that users can assess, on a per share basis, the effects of these items on net income. For example, the income statement of PCs to Go (see Exhibit 17.1) indicates that earnings per share from continuing operations was $7.44 [($232,214 − $10,000)/29,875] and that the effect of the discontinued operations on a per share basis was ($0.47); thus, income before extraordinary items on a per share basis was $6.97 [($218,214 − $10,000)/29,875]. The per share effect of the extraordinary loss was ($4.97). This information is important because it allows shareholders and others to evaluate on a common-size basis the impact of specific items on earnings per share.

[2] If a company has dilutive, convertible securities, two adjustments are necessary. First, the weighted average number of common shares outstanding is adjusted. Second, the income available to common shareholders must be adjusted to reflect the fact that preferred dividends would not be required if preferred stock is converted into common stock. Or, in the case of convertible bonds, income must be adjusted by the amount of interest (net-of-tax) that would not be paid if the convertible bonds were converted into common stock.

Exhibit 17.1 indicates that diluted earnings per share from continuing operations was \$6.35 [(\$232,214 − \$10,000)/35,000] and that income before extraordinary items on a diluted per share basis was \$5.95 [(\$218,214 − \$10,000)/35,000].

Apple reports income per share (basic) of \$5.48 in 2008 and diluted income per share of \$5.36. Note 1 (pages 63 and 64 of the annual report) provides additional information concerning the calculation of earnings per share.

Other Required Income Statement Disclosures

Companies with multiple business segments usually report income on a combined basis; that is, the incomes of the various business units are combined and reported on one income statement. GAAP requires that such companies report segment information based on how management has organized the company. The company must report information about its products, geographic markets, and major customers. In addition, for any identifiable segment, the following items must be disclosed:

- Revenues from external customers.
- Revenues from internal customers (other segments of the same company).
- Interest revenue and/or expense.
- Depreciation, depletion, and amortization expense.
- Income tax expense.
- Segment profit or loss.
- Extraordinary items.
- Identifiable segment assets.
- Expenditures for segment assets.

Apple reports its segment information in Note 9 (pages 83–86 of the annual report). Apple manages its business primarily on a geographic basis and, therefore, its segments are the Americas, Europe, Japan, Retail, and Other. Page 84 of the annual report indicates the net sales, operating incomes, and assets of each segment, and on page 85 Apple reconciles segment operating income and assets to the consolidated financial statements. On page 86 of the annual report, Apple also shows net sales by product line. Note the phenomenal growth in iPhone sales!

Reporting Issues Concerning the Income Statement

No discussion of the income statement is complete without reference to its potential reporting issues. Because the income statement is based on historical costs and, for manufacturing firms, full-absorption costing, it is subject to certain assumptions that users must understand. We examine three reporting issues next: historical cost and conservatism, cost allocations, and full-absorption costing.

Historical Cost and Conservatism

We have discussed the concepts of return of and return on investment throughout the second part of this text. Investment pertains to the amount of capital invested in assets, and determining the return on investment depends on how capital is defined. When a company prepares its financial statements, it recognizes gains (profits) on inventory and property, plant, and equipment only when they are realized.

OF INTEREST How Are Changes in Accounting Principles Reported?

Consistency is one of the fundamental principles of accounting that says accounting reports are prepared using the same accounting treatments from one time period to the next. Consistency ensures that changes in the financial statements from one time period to the next represent changes in the actual operations and financial condition of the company and are not due to changes in accounting procedures. For example, suppose a company used the LIFO inventory method in 2008 and then switched to the FIFO inventory method in 2009. If this change were not disclosed, investors would be misled about the impact of the change on net income from 2008 to 2009 and also about the difference between the inventory amounts reported on the balance sheets in 2008 and 2009.

When a company's management changes its accounting principles, regardless of its motive, its company's financial statements are no longer consistent and, therefore, are not in compliance with GAAP. Companies legitimately make changes in their accounting principles when a new accounting treatment better reflects the financial condition of the company or in order to comply with new treatments mandated by the FASB. To keep investors from being misled, the FASB requires one of two treatments when accounting principles change. For most changes in accounting principles the FASB requires the retrospective approach. The *retrospective approach* requires that all financial statements presented on comparative financial statements be revised using the new accounting principle. Using the example above, assume the company that switched from LIFO to FIFO in 2009 prepares comparative financial statements. In 2009 the company would show the comparative financial statements for 2008 and 2009 based on the assumption that FIFO had been used for both years. In this way the financial statements are consistent from 2008 to 2009. The process to make this change and the accounting entries to support such change are beyond the scope of this text.

The second approach, called the prospective approach, is used when applying the retrospective approach is impractical. The *prospective approach* changes the current year's financial statements and those in the future to reflect the change in accounting principle. The prior year's financial statements are not revised. For example, assume a company switches from double-declining balance depreciation to straight-line depreciation in 2009. The new depreciation amount for 2009 is determined by using the carrying value of the assets based on the double-declining balance at the start of the year and then applying straight-line depreciation to that carrying value. This is the same procedure that was used in Chapter 16 when we accounted for a change in estimate.

Regardless of whether the retrospective or prospective approach is used, the company must disclose in the footnotes of the financial statements why the management of the company decided to make the change in accounting principle. Any additional information deemed necessary to explain the impact of the change on the financial statements is also disclosed in the footnotes.

Therefore, if a company has a building with a carrying value of $400,000 and a market value of $600,000, it will report the building on the balance sheet (next chapter) at $400,000 and will not report the unrealized gain of $200,000. Likewise, if the market value of the company's inventory is greater than its cost, it will report the inventory on the balance sheet at cost and will not report the unrealized gain. However, if the market value of the company's inventory is less than its cost, it will report the inventory on the balance sheet at its market value and will report the loss on the income statement. Recall that the Of Interest in Chapter 16 discussed the situation where losses are recognized on plant assets that are deemed "impaired" and are written down from their carrying value to the lower fair market value. This seeming inconsistency is due to the concept of conservatism that obligates companies to anticipate losses but not gains. However, exceptions do exist. Companies now report trading securities and available-for-sale securities at their fair market value. Recall the Of Interest in Chapter 16. Unrealized gains and losses created when trading securities are adjusted to their market value are reported on the income statement. Unrealized gains and losses created when available-for-sale securities are adjusted to market value are reported as part of other comprehensive income. (See Of Interest, p. 479.)

Cost Allocations

Another income statement issue that external users need to understand concerns cost allocations. As you know, depreciation (depletion and amortization) expense does not measure the economic deterioration of assets; it is merely the allocation of the cost of the asset over its expected useful life and reflects the return of the investment in a particular year. As you learned in Chapter 16, a variety of methods are available to allocate the cost of depreciable assets to the income statement. Therefore, readers of financial statements must look to the notes accompanying the financial statements to determine which depreciation method a company uses to compare companies.

Because companies use assets in different ways, alternatives are necessary to allow companies to describe and best reflect their operations. Therefore, knowing how management chooses to estimate its cost allocation is as important as knowing the actual amount of the estimate. Financial statement users must be aware that different companies use different allocation methods and should take this into account when reading financial statements and other information. Cost allocation information is normally disclosed only in the notes to the financial statements, so users should investigate note information when comparing companies. Likewise, users should determine the inventory costing method used by companies before comparing them.

Full-Absorption Costing

As discussed in Chapter 9, full-absorption costing, the required costing method for external reporting, assigns all production costs—such as direct materials, direct labor, and unit-related, batch-related, product-sustaining, and facility-sustaining manufacturing overhead—to the units produced during the period. The cost of goods sold, then, is the amount of beginning finished goods inventory plus the cost of goods manufactured minus the amount of ending finished goods inventory.

When a manufacturing company prepares an income statement for external users, it often calculates cost of goods manufactured and cost of goods sold by applying overhead to production based on the number of units produced. We know from earlier chapters, however, that many overhead cost items do not vary with the number of units produced. Therefore, distortions in income can result when overhead costs are treated as though they vary with the level of production.

To illustrate this issue, consider a very simple situation where two companies (Company A and Company B) in their first year of operations (2010) have only two types of overhead—unit-related and facility-sustaining. These companies are identical except that Company A produced 15,000 units and Company B produced 30,000 units during 2010. Relevant operating data for the two companies are shown in Exhibit 17.2.

Exhibit 17.3 shows the results of operations for Company A. Take a moment to study this exhibit. Using absorption costing, the cost of goods sold consists of all production costs on a per unit basis. Thus it includes an amount of facility-sustaining overhead per unit, $50 ($750,000 incurred/15,000 units produced) in this case.

Full-absorption costing implies that facility-sustaining overhead varies with the number of units produced rather than with a facility-related cost driver. What problems can result from this? Companies can increase income simply by increasing the number of units produced during the period, even if the number of units sold remains the same!

To illustrate, look at Exhibit 17.4, which shows the income statement for Company B. Notice that although the sales ($1,200,000), selling expenses ($24,000), and administrative expenses ($175,000) are the same as Company A's (compare Exhibit 17.3 to Exhibit 17.4), the gross margin and net income are each $300,000 greater due solely to an increase in production of 15,000 units! For Company B, cost of goods sold includes an amount of facility-sustaining overhead per unit of only $25 because more units were produced during the period ($750,000 incurred/30,000 units produced).

This $300,000 difference in income is due to the difference in the company's cost of ending inventory. Company A, which has only 3,000 units in ending inventory, shows a cost per unit of $62.50 ($4.25 direct materials + $1.75 direct labor + $6.50 unit-related overhead + $50.00 facility-sustaining overhead). Company B, however, which has 18,000 units in ending inventory, reports a cost per unit of $37.50 ($4.25 direct materials + $1.75 direct labor + $6.50 unit-related overhead + $25.00 facility-sustaining overhead). Therefore, Company A and Company B do not have a permanent difference in income; rather, the difference in this year's income is represented as an asset on the balance sheet. Does this imply that Company B's

EXHIBIT 17.2
Company A and Company B Data

	Company A	Company B
Units produced	15,000	30,000
Units sold	12,000	12,000
Selling price per unit	$ 100.00	$ 100.00
Direct materials cost per unit	4.25	4.25
Direct labor cost per unit	1.75	1.75
Unit-related overhead per unit	6.50	6.50
Variable selling cost per unit	2.00	2.00
Facility-sustaining overhead per year	750,000	750,000
Fixed administrative cost per year	175,000	175,000

EXHIBIT 17.3
Company A Income Statement

COMPANY A
Income Statement
For the Year Ended December 31, 2010

Sales (12,000 × $100)		$1,200,000
Less cost of goods sold:		
Direct materials (12,000 × $4.25)	$ 51,000	
Direct labor (12,000 × $1.75)	21,000	
Unit-related overhead (12,000 × $6.50)	78,000	
Facility-sustaining overhead* (12,000 × $50)	600,000	750,000
Gross margin		$ 450,000
Less other operating costs:		
Variable selling costs (12,000 × $2.00)	$ 24,000	
Fixed administrative costs	175,000	199,000
Net income		$ 251,000

*$750,000 overhead/15,000 units produced = $50.

EXHIBIT 17.4
Company B Income Statement

COMPANY B
Income Statement
For the Year Ended December 31, 2010

Sales (12,000 × $100)		$1,200,000
Less cost of goods sold:		
Direct materials (12,000 × $4.25)	$ 51,000	
Direct labor (12,000 × $1.75)	21,000	
Unit-related overhead (12,000 × $6.50)	78,000	
Facility-sustaining overhead* (12,000 × $25)	300,000	450,000
Gross margin		$ 750,000
Less other operating costs:		
Variable selling costs (12,000 × $2.00)	$ 24,000	
Fixed administrative costs	175,000	199,000
Net income		$ 551,000

*$750,000 overhead/30,000 units produced = $25.

inventory is worth more per unit than Company A's inventory? Absolutely not—the same costs were incurred by each company!

This simplified example illustrates that users must evaluate the change in cost of goods sold in relation to the change in inventory levels to judge whether the gross margin and ending inventory are larger than expected based on the past performance of the company. If the gross margin and ending inventory are larger than expected, this may indicate that the number of units produced far exceeded the number of units sold. Because inventories are costly to hold, a manager of a company that produces more than the amount sold may not be utilizing the company resources in an efficient and effective manner. This would be important for financial statement users to know because it has implications for the future earnings and cash flows of the company.

Now that we have looked at the reporting issues concerning the income statement, we turn to the topic of internal reporting of earnings.

Internal Profitability Reporting

As part of the balanced scorecard process, financial measurement is crucial. Financial measurement helps management determine whether the other balanced scorecard goals helped the company fulfill its responsibilities to shareholders. Internally, management needs to know not only the company's total income but also the revenues, costs, and profits of the company's various divisions, segments, and locations. These various portions of the total business are often evaluated as one of four types of responsibility centers:

- **Cost center**—responsible for controlling costs and providing a good or service in an efficient manner; example: manufacturing department.
- **Revenue center**—responsible for generating revenues and promoting the company's products and services effectively; example: marketing department.
- **Profit center**—responsible for making a profit; it must effectively generate revenues and efficiently control costs; example: major product line.
- **Investment center**—responsible for using assets in an effective and efficient manner to generate profits; example: overseas branch operation.

Notice that each of these centers is responsible for, and evaluated on, different items. Cost centers are evaluated on costs only and revenue centers are evaluated on revenues only. Thus, cost centers (depending on their function) are commonly evaluated based on variances such as those we calculated in Chapter 9: the direct material price, inventory, and usage variances and the direct labor price and usage variances. Revenue centers, on the other hand, are commonly evaluated based on variances such as those we calculated in Chapter 10: the sales price and quantity variances. But profit centers and investment centers are evaluated on profits. Therefore, two issues arise: how to measure profits internally and how to measure the profits of the division. We examine each of these issues next.

Variable and Throughput Costing Methods

Previously, we explored how a company can increase its reported income simply by producing more units. Why might management have an incentive to do such a thing? Recall from our previous discussions that management's bonuses are often based on net income. Thus managers might have an incentive to manage earnings to get or increase bonuses. One way to decrease this incentive is to report income internally (and compute bonuses) in a different manner.

One way of reporting income internally is known as the **variable costing method,** where only costs that vary with production are included in cost of goods sold. Using this method, facility-sustaining overhead costs are expensed, in total, in the period incurred. Another way of reporting income internally is with the **throughput costing method,** where only direct materials are included in cost of goods sold. All other production costs (labor and all types of overhead) are expensed, in total, in the period incurred.

To illustrate the differences among absorption, variable, and throughput accounting, we will again compare Company A and Company B introduced earlier. Relevant data are reproduced in Exhibit 17.5. Recall that using absorption costing, Company A and Company B reported the following (see Exhibits 17.3 and 17.4):

	Company A	Company B
Cost of goods sold	$750,000	$450,000
Net income	251,000	551,000
Ending inventory	187,500	675,000

Now let's see what happens if we use variable costing to determine profit. Under variable costing, cost of goods sold includes only costs that vary with production (direct materials, direct labor, and unit-related overhead). All other production costs (facility-sustaining overhead) are expensed in the year incurred. Therefore, a contribution margin format income report is frequently used.

Exhibit 17.6 shows the variable income reports of Company A and Company B. Notice that both Company A and Company B report the same contribution margin ($1,026,000) and the same profit ($101,000). Why does this occur? Because Company A and Company B have the same variable costs per unit and the same total facility-sustaining overhead, they will have the same contribution margin and profit. However, Company B shows a much larger ending inventory amount because it produced 30,000 units compared to the 15,000 units produced by Company A.

Also notice that the profit reported using variable costing is lower than that determined using absorption costing for both Company A ($101,000 versus $251,000) and Company B ($101,000 versus $551,000). This happens because the number of units produced was greater than the number of units sold. Because absorption costing calculates a higher unit cost, including facility-sustaining overhead in the cost figure, more costs are held in inventory. Managers whose bonuses are based on variable income will not be rewarded for overproducing inventory because facility-sustaining costs will be expensed regardless of how many units are produced.

If we use throughput accounting to determine profit, the results are even more dramatic. Exhibit 17.7 shows the throughput accounting income reports for Company A and Company B. Using throughput accounting, the costs of direct materials are subtracted from sales to determine the throughput margin. Then all other operating costs incurred during the period are subtracted to determine profit. Note that other operating costs are subtracted, in total, to determine profit. None of these costs are assigned to inventory.

Using throughput accounting, Company A and Company B report the same throughput margin ($1,149,000), but their profits are vastly different. Company A subtracts operating costs of $1,072,750 from its throughput margin, resulting in an operating profit of $76,250. On the other hand, Company B must subtract operating costs of $1,196,500 from its throughput margin, resulting in an operating loss of $47,500. Company B had higher operating costs because it produced more units and, using throughput accounting, these costs are not held in inventory.

Company B shows a larger ending inventory value than does Company A ($76,500 versus $12,750). Also notice that throughput costing results in the lowest reported profit, compared

EXHIBIT 17.5
Company A and Company B Data

	Company A	Company B
Units produced	15,000	30,000
Units sold	12,000	12,000
Selling price per unit	$ 100.00	$ 100.00
Direct materials cost per unit	4.25	4.25
Direct labor cost per unit	1.75	1.75
Unit-related overhead per unit	6.50	6.50
Variable selling cost per unit	2.00	2.00
Facility-sustaining overhead per year	750,000	750,000
Fixed administrative cost per year	175,000	175,000

EXHIBIT 17.6
Variable Income Reports

COMPANY A
Variable Income Report
For the Year Ended December 31, 2010

Sales (12,000 × $100)		$1,200,000
Less unit-variable costs:		
Direct materials (12,000 × $4.25)	$ 51,000	
Direct labor (12,000 × $1.75)	21,000	
Unit-related overhead (12,000 × $6.50)	78,000	
Variable selling costs (12,000 × $2.00)	24,000	174,000
Contribution margin		$1,026,000
Less other operating costs:		
Facility-sustaining overhead	$750,000	
Fixed administrative costs	175,000	925,000
Operating profit		$ 101,000
Ending inventory (3,000 × $12.50)		$ 37,500

COMPANY B
Variable Income Report
For the Year Ended December 31, 2010

Sales (12,000 × $100)		$1,200,000
Less unit-variable costs:		
Direct materials (12,000 × $4.25)	$ 51,000	
Direct labor (12,000 × $1.75)	21,000	
Unit-related overhead (12,000 × $6.50)	78,000	
Variable selling costs (12,000 × $2.00)	24,000	174,000
Contribution margin		$1,026,000
Less other operating costs:		
Facility-sustaining overhead	$750,000	
Fixed administrative costs	175,000	925,000
Operating profit		$ 101,000
Ending inventory (18,000 × $12.50)		$ 225,000

to absorption and variable costing. This is because throughput assigns the fewest costs to inventory and, therefore, expenses the greatest costs during the period. Throughput costing, even more than variable costing, discourages managers from overproducing inventory. Because the only costs held in inventory are direct materials, a manager who produces excess inventory will show more expenses on the income statement for labor and overhead during the current period. Clearly, there is no incentive for management to increase production if bonuses are based on throughput accounting.

Proponents of variable costing believe it is superior because it determines a contribution margin that can be used in cost-volume-profit analysis (see Chapter 4). Proponents of throughput costing believe it is superior because it determines cost of goods sold based only on direct materials, which according to many is the only truly variable cost. Which method a company uses internally reflects its philosophy concerning variable versus nonvariable costs.

Enhance Your Understanding

Why don't companies voluntarily report variable or throughput costing income to external users?

Answer: Recall that externally released information is available to the public, including the company's competitors. The company would not want its competitors to know its variable costs because this information could be used to gain an advantage in the market.

EXHIBIT 17.7
Throughput Income Reports

COMPANY A
Throughput Income Report
For the Year Ended December 31, 2010

Sales (12,000 × $100)		$1,200,000
Less direct materials (12,000 × $4.25)		51,000
Throughput margin		$1,149,000
Less other operating costs:		
Direct labor (15,000 × $1.75)	$ 26,250	
Unit-related overhead (15,000 × $6.50)	97,500	
Facility-sustaining overhead	750,000	
Variable selling costs (12,000 × $2.00)	24,000	
Fixed selling costs	175,000	1,072,750
Operating profit		$ 76,250
Ending inventory (3,000 × $4.25)		$ 12,750

COMPANY B
Throughput Income Report
For the Year Ended December 31, 2010

Sales (12,000 × $100)		$1,200,000
Less direct materials (12,000 × $4.25)		51,000
Throughput margin		$1,149,000
Less other operating costs:		
Direct labor (30,000 × $1.75)	$ 52,500	
Unit-related overhead (30,000 × $6.50)	195,000	
Facility-sustaining overhead	750,000	
Variable selling costs (12,000 × $2.00)	24,000	
Fixed selling costs	175,000	1,196,500
Operating loss		$ (47,500)
Ending inventory (18,000 × $4.25)		$ 76,500

Product Line (Divisional) Income Reports

Product line (divisional) income reports are specific-purpose reports designed to provide more detailed information than general-purpose segment disclosures of the results of operations for a product line or company division.

Internally, product line or divisional managers are often evaluated and rewarded as profit or investment centers. These product lines or divisions may not require external segment disclosure, but they may warrant internal disclosure. The goal of a good reward and control system is to assign responsibility for those items for which the manager has control. These income reports, then, are prepared to eliminate costs assigned to the product or division that the manager cannot control as well as to overcome the problems associated with full-absorption costing.

Exhibit 17.8 illustrates PCs to Go's income report on a divisional basis. Notice that there are many divisions of earnings, such as contribution margin (sales less variable costs), product margin (contribution margin less batch-related and product-sustaining overhead), and segment margin (product margin less other costs that are controllable by the manager).

As Exhibit 17.8 shows, the segment margins of the three divisions are $544,918, $487,481, and $306,961, respectively. Also notice that other fixed costs are deducted from the total margin of the company, not from the segment margins of the respective product lines or divisions. In this case, facility-sustaining overhead and other corporate expenses are not allocated to the divisions because their respective managers cannot control these costs. Therefore, the income from operations of the company is not the sum of the segment margins. Rather, it is the sum of the segment margins less the costs that were not assigned to the divisions.

EXHIBIT 17.8
Product Line Income Report

PCs to Go
Product Line Income Report
For the Year Ended December 31, 2010

	Segment 1	Segment 2	Segment 3	Company Total
Sales	$1,399,893	$1,234,394	$1,052,953	$3,687,240
Less unit costs:				
Direct materials	349,974	138,750	189,531	678,255
Direct labor	203,421	207,675	132,672	543,768
Unit-related overhead	5,898	270,571	39,801	316,270
Unit selling costs	87,493	61,470	59,178	208,141
Contribution margin	**$ 753,107**	**$ 555,928**	**$ 631,771**	**$1,940,806**
Less batch and product costs:				
Batch-related overhead	46,664	27,751	78,972	153,387
Product-sustaining overhead	146,937	27,796	236,913	411,646
Product margin	**$ 559,506**	**$ 500,381**	**$ 315,886**	**$1,375,773**
Less other controllable costs:				
Advertising	12,750	11,250	7,800	31,800
Market analysis	1,838	1,650	1,125	4,613
Segment margin	**$ 544,918**	**$ 487,481**	**$ 306,961**	**$1,339,360**
Less noncontrollable costs:				
Facility-sustaining costs				525,900
Other corporate overhead				391,650
Income from operations				**$ 421,810**

Finally, notice that these internal income reports do not use the net income concept used for external parties. That is, they do not reflect discontinued operations, extraordinary items, cumulative accounting adjustments, or other comprehensive income items that are assumed to be beyond the control of product line or divisional managers.

Return on Investment for the Division

If the division is evaluated as a profit center, the segment margins determined in the product-line income report are sufficient for evaluating segment success or failure. However, if the division is evaluated as an investment center, it is responsible for assets as well as profits. In these cases, it is necessary to determine the assets for which the divisional manager is responsible. Then we can calculate the return on investment for the division as shown here:

$$\frac{\text{Profit of the division}}{\text{Assets of the division}}$$

For example, assume that PCs to Go has determined that the manager of Segment 1 is responsible for $1,000,000 of assets, while the managers of Segments 2 and 3 are responsible for $800,000 and $500,000 of assets, respectively. The return on investment of each segment is determined as follows:

	Segment 1	Segment 2	Segment 3
Profit (segment margin)	$ 544,918	$487,481	$306,961
Assets	1,000,000	800,000	500,000
Return on investment	54.5%	60.9%	61.4%

Thus, although Segment 1 was the most profitable segment, Segment 3 generated the largest return on investment. Return on investment is a common measure of divisional performance because it reflects not only profits but also amounts that are invested in the division's operations.

Du Pont Method of Return on Investment

Another way of calculating return on investment for a division is the Du Pont method, named for the Du Pont Company. The Du Pont Company was one of the early examples of a very diversified company. It produced a number of different products requiring different raw materials and production processes. To assess the profitability of various production facilities, Du Pont developed the **Du Pont method of return on investment** that is a combination of return on sales ratio (a profitability measure) and asset turnover ratio (an activity measure). You learned the return on sales ratio in Chapter 1:

$$\frac{\text{Net income}}{\text{Net sales}}$$

The **asset turnover ratio** is an activity ratio that measures profitability because it relates a company's ability to generate sales to the amount of assets that the company uses. A high ratio indicates that management is utilizing assets well. The asset turnover ratio is calculated as:

$$\frac{\text{Net sales}}{\text{Average total assets}}$$

So, the Du Pont method of return on investment is calculated as:

$$\frac{\text{Net income}}{\text{Net sales}} \times \frac{\text{Net sales}}{\text{Average total assets}}$$

The advantage of the Du Pont method is that by breaking the return on investments into two components we can look at two potential causes for changes from period to period. Using the data from Exhibit 17.8 and the additional information concerning segment assets just described, we can calculate the Du Pont return on investment for each division:

	Segment 1	Segment 2	Segment 3
1. Net income (margin)	$544,918	$487,481	$306,961
2. Net sales	$1,399,893	$1,234,394	$1,052,953
3. Return on sales (#1/#2)	38.93%	39.49%	29.15%
4. Net sales	$1,399,893	$1,234,394	$1,052,953
5. Average total assets	$1,000,000	$800,000	$500,000
6. Asset turnover (#4/#5)	1.40	1.54	2.11
7. Return on investment (#3×#6)	54.5%	60.9%	61.4%

Notice that the return on investment is the same as we calculated earlier. However we have additional information from the Du Pont calculation. Notice that Segment 3 has the highest return on investment but the lowest return on sales. Therefore Segment 3 is profitable because it has a higher asset turnover. Its return on sales—in other words, its ability to generate profits from its products—is the lowest of the three divisions, which should be cause for concern for PCs to Go. Segments 1 and 2, on the other hand, are generating profits from sales of almost 40 percent, but their asset utilizations are very low (asset turnovers of 1.4 and 1.5, respectively). Management of PCs to Go may want to investigate the cause of this—perhaps some assets are not productive and should be sold.

Return on investment and the Du Pont method are useful for external financial statement users also. However, external financial statement users must be careful when comparing segments in this manner. Some segments require greater investments in assets and, therefore, may show a lower return on investment. Some segments may have older, more depreciated assets and, therefore, may show a higher return on investment. These are some of the issues involved when using return on investment as a measure of divisional performance. More advanced accounting and finance courses discuss additional issues involved in performance measurement.

Summary

The income statement is vitally important to both external and internal users in evaluating a company's operating activities. It is important for users to understand the actual components of income presented as well as the limitations of the income statement itself. Internally, these limitations are often corrected by preparing more detailed income reports.

- Comprehensive income is reported to external users to provide them with a complete picture of the recurring operating activities of the company during the period as well as other nonowner changes in equity that occurred during the period.
- Discontinued operations and extraordinary items are shown on the income statement after income from continuing operations. These items appear net of tax because income tax expense is based on income from continuing operations.
- Earnings per share is shown on the income statement as a common-size measure of company performance. Companies often report diluted earnings per share, which indicates the change in earnings per share if additional shares were outstanding.
- Companies are also required to disclose certain segment information in the notes to the financial statements.
- Internally, different profit-reporting formats and product line income reports are often used to provide additional information for decision making.

Key Terms

Asset turnover ratio An activity ratio that measures profitability because it relates a company's ability to generate sales to the amount of assets that the company uses, *493*

Comprehensive income Income that reflects all changes in owners' equity during the period except those resulting from investments by, or distributions to, owners and those resulting from errors made in previous periods, *478*

Cost center A center that is responsible for controlling costs and providing a good or service in an efficient manner, *488*

Diluted earnings per share Earnings per share that reflect the amount of change in earnings per share that would occur as a result of activities like conversions and the exercise of stock options, *483*

Discontinued operations The result of a company selling or disposing of a segment of its business, *480*

Du Pont method of return on investment A combination of return on sales ratio (a profitability measure) and asset turnover ratio (an activity measure), *493*

Earnings Income from continuing operations; consisting of revenues minus expenses and also gains minus losses, *477*

Earnings per share A common-size measure of a company's earnings performance; the reported net income of the company less preferred dividends for the period divided by the weighted-average number of common shares outstanding, *481*

Extraordinary items Events that occurred during the accounting period that are both unusual and infrequent, *481*

Investment center A center that is responsible for using assets in an effective and efficient manner to generate profits, *488*

Net income An income measure that includes both the operating and other nonowner activities that caused changes in retained earnings during the period, *477*

Product line (divisional) income reports Specific-purpose internal reports designed to provide more detailed information than general-purpose income statements regarding the results of operations for a product line or company division, *491*

Profit center A center that is responsible for making a profit; it must effectively generate revenues and efficiently control costs, *488*

Revenue center A center that is responsible for generating revenues and promoting the company's products and services effectively, *488*

Throughput costing method A method of determining profits in which only direct materials are included in cost of goods sold and all other production costs are expensed as incurred, *488*

Variable costing method A method of determining profits in which only costs that vary with production are included in cost of goods sold and facility-sustaining overhead costs are expensed as incurred, *488*

Questions

1. Explain the difference between earnings and comprehensive income. Why is this important?
2. What are the two types of other changes in equity? Why are they important?
3. Why are discontinued operations and extraordinary items shown net of tax on the income statement?
4. Why should the income (loss) from discontinued operations be disclosed separately from the gain (loss) on disposal of a segment? Where is this information usually found? Why?
5. Is a Georgia company's loss from a tornado an extraordinary item? Why?
6. When a company changes its method of accounting for depreciation, what must it do? Why?
7. What is earnings per share and how can it be diluted?
8. Explain why the historical cost and conservatism concepts are important to income statement users.
9. Why is cost allocation an issue for income statement users?
10. Explain how a company can increase net income by increasing production even though sales remain the same.
11. Explain how cost, revenue, profit, and investment centers, respectively, are evaluated.
12. Explain the advantages of a product line income report for internal users. Do you think this information would be useful for external users? Why?
13. Explain how production and nonproduction costs are treated using absorption costing.
14. Explain how variable and nonvariable costs are treated using the variable costing method.
15. Explain how direct materials and other operating costs are treated using the throughput costing method.
16. If a company produces more units than it sells in its first year of operations, which method (absorption, variable, or throughput) reports the highest profit? Why?
17. Why might a company report income differently for internal and external users? Is this ethical?
18. How is return on investment for a division determined? Why is this information important?
19. What is the Du Pont method for calculating return on investment? What is the advantage of this method?

Exercises

E17.1 LO 1

These accounts are from the Decker Company. Show how this information is presented on a multistep income statement.

Cost of goods sold	$110,000
Sales	305,000
Selling expenses	75,000
Administrative expenses	55,000
Depreciation expense	40,000
Loss on sale of equipment	18,000
Sales returns	10,000

LO 1 **E17.2**

The Riedl Corporation has the following information available on December 31, 2010. The tax rate is 30 percent. Show how this information is presented to external users in a multistep format.

Interest expense	$ 3,000
Sales salaries	120,000
Rental revenue	8,000
Accounts receivable	101,000
Administrative salaries	100,000
Sales	1,500,000
Depreciation (40% selling, 60% administrative)	30,000
Dividends paid	48,000
Cost of goods sold	850,000
Sales returns and allowances	15,000
Loss due to meteor damage	70,000
Loss on sale of equipment	79,000

LO 1 **E17.3** Hora Sporting Goods decided to sell its children's toy division during 2010. The following relevant information is available. Use this information to determine the income (loss) from operations of the division and the income (loss) upon disposal of the division.

Gain from operations of toy division	$800,000
Loss on disposal of toy division	500,000
Effective tax rate	30%

LO 1 **E17.4** Refer to E17.3. How does your answer change if the toy division showed a loss from operations of $800,000 and if Hora experiences a gain on disposal of the toy division of $500,000? Show your calculations.

LO 1 **E17.5** The Sakai Stores Corporation calculated its income before taxes and the extraordinary loss but wants you to advise it on how to present this information to external users. Determine the extraordinary loss, net of tax; calculate the net income for the year; and explain in a brief memo to the owners how to present this information on the income statement.

Earnings before income taxes and extraordinary items	$700,000
Tax rate	35%
Extraordinary loss due to an earthquake in Kansas	$250,000

LO 1 **E17.6** Leonard Corporation had assets of $1,000,000 expropriated in another country during 2010 with a resulting extraordinary loss on the expropriation of $600,000. Leonard's income tax rate is 40 percent. What is the extraordinary gain (loss) shown on the income statement for 2010? Show your calculations.

LO 2 **E17.7** Daniel Company has 500,000 shares of common stock issued and 300,000 shares of common stock outstanding. Determine the earnings per share for 2010 if its net income is $180,000.

LO 2 **E17.8** Pearson Corporation has 50,000 shares of common stock outstanding and 10,000 shares of $100 par value, 4 percent preferred stock outstanding. Determine the earnings per share for common stock for 2010 if net income is $350,000.

LO 2 **E17.9** Cox Enterprises had 200,000 shares of common stock outstanding on January 1, 2010, and issued an additional 50,000 shares on March 31, 2010. Determine the earnings per share for calendar 2010 if net income was $300,000.

LO 2 **E17.10** Guan Company had 200,000 shares of common stock outstanding on January 1, 2010, and repurchased 60,000 shares of common stock on March 31, 2010. Determine the earnings per share for calendar 2010 if net income was $400,000.

LO 4 **E17.11** Woollen, Inc., evaluates its divisions as investment centers. The sales, income, and assets of its three divisions follow. Calculate return on investment for each division. Which division is best?

	Division A	Division B	Division C
Sales	$800,000	$ 800,000	$ 800,000
Profit	80,000	160,000	320,000
Assets	600,000	7,900,000	4,000,000

LO 4 **E17.12** Refer to E17.11. Calculate the return on investment using the Du Pont method. What is revealed?

LO 4 **E17.13** Kaiama Clothing Store has three segments: Women's Wear, Men's Wear, and Children's Wear. Following are the sales, cost of goods sold, operating expenses, and identifiable assets of these segments. Determine the return on investment of each segment. Which segment is best?

	Women's	Men's	Children's
Sales	$3,000,000	$3,000,000	$5,000,000
Cost of goods sold	2,000,000	1,250,000	3,200,000
Operating expenses	200,000	200,000	200,000
Assets	1,600,000	1,500,000	1,900,000

LO 4 E17.14 Refer to E17.13. Assume the operating expenses are allocated from corporate headquarters and are not controllable by the segment managers. Determine the return on investment of each segment. Which segment is best?

LO 4 E17.15 Refer to E17.13. Calculate the return on investment using the Du Pont method. Which segment is best?

LO 3 E17.16 Gregson Enterprises, in its first year of operations, reported the following information:

Selling price per unit	$ 100
Direct materials per unit	5
Direct labor per unit	1
Unit-related overhead per unit	6
Selling cost per unit	2
Batch-related overhead for the year	500,000
Facility-sustaining overhead for the year	800,000
Fixed administrative cost for the year	650,000
Units produced	20,000
Units sold	15,000

What is Gregson's absorption costing gross margin and profit?

LO 3 E17.17 Refer to E17.16. What is Gregson's variable contribution margin and profit?

LO 3 E17.18 Refer to E17.16. What is Gregson's throughput margin and profit?

LO 3 E17.19 Refer to E17.16. What is Gregson's ending inventory using absorption costing?

LO 3 E17.20 Refer to E17.17. What is Gregson's ending inventory using variable costing?

LO 3 E17.21 Refer to E17.18. What is Gregson's ending inventory using throughput costing?

Problems

P17.1 **LO 1** **LO 2** Teruya Corporation provided the following relevant information for its fiscal year ending September 30, 2010:

Sales	$1,950,000
Cost of goods sold	1,231,600
Sales returns	41,000
Depreciation on sales equipment	6,500
Sales commissions	103,000
Sales salaries	62,300
Administrative salaries	98,200
Depreciation on office equipment	8,500
Bond interest expense	22,000
Selling expenses	168,900
Administrative expense	134,600
Loss on disposal of marine products division	80,000
Marine products division operating income	100,000
Dividend income	4,000
Entertainment expense	23,100
Dividends declared on preferred stock	10,000

On October 1, 2009, Teruya's retained earnings balance was $238,790. The tax rate for Teruya Corporation is 20 percent. There are 50,000 shares of common stock outstanding.

Required:

A. Prepare a multistep income statement for fiscal 2010.
B. Calculate the earnings per share for 2010.

LO 1 P17.2 This income statement was prepared by Bob's Bookkeeping Service for the Atlas Corporation:

ATLAS CORPORATION
Income Statement
At December 31, 2010

Sales	$1,200,000
Interest income	5,000
Less sales returns	9,000
Net sales	$1,196,000
Cost of goods sold	740,000
Gross margin	$ 456,000
Gain on sale of equipment	40,000
Total revenue inflows	$ 496,000
Administrative expenses	120,000
Selling expenses	45,000
Loss on sale of land	10,000
Operating income	$ 321,000
Interest expense	9,000
Extraordinary loss on building	20,000
Income from continuing operations	$ 292,000
Tax expense (30%)	$ 87,600
Net income	$ 204,400

Required: A. Make a list of all the errors found on this income statement and briefly describe what is wrong.
B. Prepare a correct multistep income statement for Atlas Corporation.

LO 1 LO 2 LO 4 **P17.3** Refer to the income statement of Pepsico, Inc. (**www.pepsico.com**), and answer the following questions:

A. What was the income from operations during the year?
B. What was the income from continuing operations during the year?
C. What was the net income?
D. Did the company discontinue any operations during the year? If so, what were they?
E. Did the company experience any extraordinary events during the year? If so, what were they?
F. What were the earnings per share for the year?
G. What were the diluted earnings per share for the year?
H. What is the overall return on investment using the Du Pont method?
I. Based on the income statement, would you advise someone to invest in this company? Why?

LO 1 LO 2 LO 4 **P17.4** Refer to the income statement of Walt Disney Company (**www.disney.com**) and answer the following questions:

A. What was the income from operations during the year?
B. What was the income from continuing operations during the year?
C. What was the net income?
D. Did the company discontinue any operations during the year? If so, what were they?
E. Did the company experience any extraordinary events during the year? If so, what were they?
F. What were the earnings per share for the year?
G. What were the diluted earnings per share for the year?
H. What is the overall return on investment using the Du Pont method?
I. Based on the income statement, would you advise someone to invest in this company? Why?

LO 1 LO 2 LO 4 **P17.5** Refer to the income statement of Dell Computer (**www.dell.com**) and answer the following questions:

A. What was the income from operations during the year?
B. What was the income from continuing operations during the year?
C. What was the net income?
D. Did the company discontinue any operations during the year? If so, what were they?
E. Did the company experience any extraordinary events during the year? If so, what were they?
F. What were the earnings per share for the year?
G. What were the diluted earnings per share for the year?
H. What is the overall return on investment using the Du Pont method?
I. Based on the income statement, would you advise someone to invest in this company? Why?

LO 1 **P17.6** The following alphabetical list of accounts was adopted from a recent PepsiCo annual report. Use these accounts to create Pepsi's income statement.

Amortization of intangible assets	147
Cost of sales	13,406
Discontinued operations, net of tax*	38
Interest expense	167
Interest income	74
Net revenue	29,261
Other income	380
Other operating expenses	150
Provision for income taxes	1,372
Selling, general, and administrative expenses	10,299

*This is a net gain item.

LO 1 **P17.7** Yang Company began operations in 2010. Its operating information follows:

LO 2

LO 4

Selling price per unit	$ 175	Units produced	50,000
Direct materials cost per unit	40	Units sold	30,000
Direct labor cost per unit	10		
Unit-related overhead per unit	15		
Unit selling cost	5		
Batch-related overhead per year	55,000		
Product-sustaining overhead per year	125,000		
Facility-sustaining overhead per year	750,000		
Fixed selling and administrative costs	400,000		

Required:

A. Using absorption costing, determine Yang's gross margin and profit for the year.
B. Using variable costing, determine Yang's contribution margin and profit for the year.
C. Using throughput costing, determine Yang's throughput margin and profit for the year.
D. Determine the differences in ending inventory using absorption, variable, and throughput costing.

LO 4 **P17.8** College Publishers produces three textbooks for various college campuses: *Introductory Marketing, Introductory Management,* and *Introductory Accounting.* Each book sells for $60. The manager of College Publishers is concerned that *Introductory Marketing* appears to be losing money. This is the most recent income report:

	Marketing	***Management***	***Accounting***	**Total**
Sales	$400,000	$500,000	$900,000	$1,800,000
Less expenses:				
Printing	160,000	200,000	360,000	720,000
Commissions	40,000	50,000	90,000	180,000
Warehousing	48,000	48,000	48,000	144,000
Salaries	34,000	34,000	34,000	102,000
Depreciation 1	36,000	36,000	36,000	108,000
Depreciation 2	24,000	24,000	24,000	72,000
Miscellaneous	34,000	34,000	34,000	102,000
Advertising	8,000	8,000	8,000	24,000
Shipping	48,000	60,000	108,000	216,000
Net income (loss)	$ (32,000)	$ 6,000	$158,000	$ 132,000

An analysis of the records reveals that printing, commissions, and shipping costs are traced directly to the product lines, while the remaining costs are allocated equally to the three product lines. Further analysis reveals the following:

1. The warehouse consists of 60,000 square feet of which 30,000 square feet are used for accounting books, 16,000 are used for management, and the remaining square feet are used to house marketing texts.

2. Depreciation 1 is depreciation on production equipment. During the past year, the production equipment operated a total of 2,500 hours, of which 1,250 hours were used to produce accounting texts, 750 hours were used for management texts, and 500 hours were used to produce marketing texts.
3. Depreciation 2, salaries, advertising, and miscellaneous costs, cannot be traced to any particular product line.

Required:
A. Prepare a product line income report.
B. Should College Publishers drop the marketing text? Why or why not?

LO 4 **P17.9** Refer to P17.8. Assume that management decides to drop the marketing text.

Required:
A. Determine the net income of the company.
B. Determine the product margins of the accounting and management texts.
C. Analyze your results.

LO 3 **P17.10** Wendell Products produces specialty alarm clocks that it sells to novelty stores throughout the mid-Atlantic. During the current period, the following results were obtained:

Sales		700,000 clocks at $40
Cost of goods manufactured		750,000 clocks at $28
Variable selling cost		700,000 clocks at $9
Fixed selling and administrative costs		$645,000
Cost of goods manufactured consists of:		
Direct materials	$ 5	
Direct labor	2	
Unit-related overhead	8	
Other nonvariable overhead	13	
	$28	

Other nonvariable overhead consists of depreciation on machinery and buildings, insurance, and other items that do not vary with the number of clocks produced during the period. The nonvariable overhead unit cost is calculated by dividing the total nonvariable overhead for the period by the number of clocks produced in the period as shown here:

$$\frac{\$9,750,000}{750,000} = \$13 \text{ per clock}$$

Required:
A. Determine the profit for the period using full-absorption costing.
B. Determine the profit for the period using variable costing.
C. Determine the profit for the period using throughput costing.
D. Determine the cost of ending inventory using each of the costing methods in parts **(A)** through **(C)**.

Cases

C17.1 Refer to the company you chose in C1.1 and answer the following questions:

LO 1 LO 2 LO 4

A. What was the income from operations during the year?
B. What was the income from continuing operations during the year?
C. What was the net income for the year?
D. Did the company discontinue any operations during the year? If so, what were they?
E. Did the company experience any extraordinary events during the year? If so, what were they?
F. What were the earnings per share for the year?
G. What were the diluted earnings per share for the year?
H. What is the overall return on investment using the Du Pont method?
I. Based on the income statement, would you advise someone to invest in this company? Why?

LO 1 LO 2 **C17.2** By consulting NEXIS, Disclosure, or a similar annual report database, determine the following:

A. How many companies reported discontinued operations during the period?
B. Of the companies that reported discontinued operations, did they report gains or losses?
C. How many companies reported extraordinary items during the period?
D. Of the companies that reported extraordinary items, did they report gains or losses?
E. How many companies reported a loss per share?

Critical Thinking

CT17.1 **LO 3** In the first year of operations, Naivete Company experienced a $500,000 net loss even though it sold 250,000 units. Management was very concerned about this outcome, so it hired an efficiency expert to turn the company's operations around. The efficiency expert guaranteed the company a profitable second year. The expert stressed, "I agree to work for you for one year at no salary. At the end of the year, if your net income is not at least $500,000, you pay me nothing. If your income is $500,000 or more, you pay me $500,000."

Naivete's income statement for the first year of operations is:

Sales (250,000 units at $16)		$4,000,000
Cost of goods sold:		
Beginning inventory	$ -0-	
Cost of goods manufactured	3,750,000	
Cost of goods available	$3,750,000	
Ending inventory	-0-	3,750,000
Gross margin		$ 250,000
Selling and administrative expenses		750,000
Net loss		$ (500,000)
Cost of goods manufactured is composed of the following:		
Direct materials		$ 750,000
Direct labor		500,000
Unit-related overhead		1,000,000
Other nonunit-related overhead		1,500,000
		$3,750,000

In the second year of operations, the same number of units were sold, but the company produced 750,000 units. The selling price and costs remained constant, which resulted in the following income statement:

Sales (250,000 units at $16)		$4,000,000
Cost of goods sold:		
Beginning inventory	$ -0-	
Cost of goods manufactured	8,250,000	
Cost of goods available	$8,250,000	
Ending inventory	5,500,000	2,750,000
Gross margin		$1,250,000
Selling and administrative expenses		750,000
Income before bonus		$ 500,000
Bonus		500,000
Net income		$ -0-

Required: Explain to the managers of Naivete Company, in detail, what happened to operations in the second year.

LO 3 **CT17.2** Hasselback, Inc., produced 175,000 units and prepared the following income report using absorption costing:

Sales (100,000 units)		$15,000,000
Less cost of goods sold:		
Direct materials	$1,200,000	
Direct labor	300,000	
Unit-related overhead	900,000	
Other overhead	4,000,000	6,400,000
Gross margin		$ 8,600,000
Less other operating costs:		
Variable selling and administrative costs		600,000
Fixed selling and administrative costs		2,000,000
Profit		$ 6,000,000

Required:

A. Determine Hasselback's profit using unit-variable costing.
B. Determine Hasselback's profit using throughput costing.
C. Which method do you think presents the most realistic picture of current earnings? Why?

Ethical Challenges

EC17.1 **LO 1** Refer to the Of Interest: Unrealized Holding Gains and Losses box (p. 479). Why might management have an incentive to classify securities as "trading" versus "available-for-sale"? What are the ethical implications of doing so?

LO 3 EC17.2 You have just been hired by a midsized manufacturing firm and part of your new job is to determine how income should be measured for internal reporting purposes. Discuss the benefits and drawbacks of absorption, throughput, and variable costing, being careful to consider the ethical implications of each.

Computer Applications

CA17.1 **LO 1** **LO 2** The following list of items (accounts) was obtained from an annual report of Braun's Fashions Corporation:

Depreciation and amortization	$ 2,052,707
Interest expense	210,678
Merchandise, buying, and occupancy expenses	56,406,679
Provision for income taxes	1,615,931
Selling, publicity, and administrative expenses	18,679,253
Net sales	81,301,766

The following additional information is available:

1. The beginning balance of Retained Earnings was a deficit of $(14,536,277).
2. Braun's has 3,664,625 common shares outstanding.
3. No dividends were declared during the period.

Required: Use a computer spreadsheet.

A. Determine net income.
B. Determine the earnings per share.
C. Assume that in the following year, net sales were 15 percent greater, merchandise and taxes remained at the same percentage rate, and all other expenses remained at the same dollar amount. What would be the amount of net income for this period?

LO 2 CA17.2 Use a computer spreadsheet program to determine earnings per share in each of the following independent situations. Assume a calendar year-end in each situation.

A. Net income is $500,000. There are 250,000 shares of common stock and 50,000 shares of $10 par, 8 percent preferred stock outstanding.
B. Net income is $600,000. There were 200,000 shares of common stock outstanding on January 1. On March 31, 100,000 additional shares were issued. On September 1, 50,000 additional shares were issued.
C. Net income is $250,000. There were 300,000 shares of common stock outstanding on January 1. On July 31, 50,000 shares of common stock were repurchased and held as treasury stock.
D. Net income is $425,000. There were 200,000 shares of common stock and 10,000 shares of $100 par, 6 percent preferred stock outstanding on January 1. On May 1, 60,000 shares of common stock were issued. On October 31, 10,000 shares of common stock were issued.

Visit the text Online Learning Center at **www.mhhe.com/ainsworth6e** for additional problem material that accompanies this chapter.

CHAPTER EIGHTEEN

18

Company Performance: Owners' Equity and Financial Position

Learning Objectives

LO 1 Discuss the importance of the statement of owners' equity.

LO 2 Describe the importance of balance sheet classifications.

LO 3 Explain why internal balance sheet information may be different from external balance sheet information.

In Chapter 17 we examined the income statement and how profits are reported to external and internal users. In this chapter we continue discussing how financial information is reported as we consider the statement of owners' equity (including comprehensive income) and the statement of financial position, more commonly known as the balance sheet. Again, throughout this chapter we illustrate the issues by examining PCs to Go many years after formation. Then we look at the financial statements of Apple.

Statement of Owners' Equity

The statement of owners' equity has three primary components—comprehensive income, if not included on the income statement, retained earnings, and other information regarding changes in owners' equity. This statement provides information concerning the changes in the owners' equity section of the balance sheet. Therefore, information concerning treasury stock transactions, common and preferred stock transactions, as well as comprehensive income and retained earnings are typically found on the statement. We examine comprehensive income and retained earnings first and then look briefly at the other disclosures. We use PCs to Go's statement of owners' equity shown in Exhibit 18.1 as our roadmap for this section.

Comprehensive Income

SFAS No. 130 requires that companies report comprehensive income in addition to net income. Items included in comprehensive income include: (1) foreign currency translation adjustments, (2) minimum pension liability adjustments, (3) derivative-related adjustments, and (4) unrealized gains and losses from certain debt and equity investment transactions.

Foreign currency translation adjustments may be required for companies operating in more than one country due to changes in currency exchange rates relative to the value of the U.S. dollar. Minimum pension liability adjustments may be required for companies that underfund their pension plan. These subjects and derivatives are beyond the scope of this text.

The final item of other comprehensive income is unrealized gains and losses from certain debt and equity transactions. As discussed in the Of Interest in Chapter 17, unrealized gains and losses from available-for-sale securities are reported in the current period as part of comprehensive, not net income. Recall from the Of Interest in Chapter 16 that available-for-sale securities are those that management does not intend to sell in the next year. Available-for-sale

EXHIBIT 18.1
PCs to Go Statement of Owners' Equity Information

PCs to Go
Statement of Owners' Equity
For the Year Ended December 31, 2010

	Preferred Stock Issued		Common Stock Issued			Treasury Stock			
	Shares	Amount	Shares	Amount	Additional Paid-in Capital	Shares	Amount	Compreh. Income	Retained Earnings
Balances, January 1, 2010	20,000	$200,000	28,800	$28,800	$1,416,988	0	$ 0	$ (0)	$250,000
Prior period adjustment									33,000
Adjusted balance									$283,000
Net income									69,714
Preferred stock dividends									(10,000)
Common stock dividends									(40,000)
Issuance of common stock			5,700	5,700	228,000				
Repurchase of common stock						9,000	288,000		
Unrealized gain on AFS								12,302	
Balances, December 31, 2010	20,000	$200,000	34,500	$34,500	$1,644,988	9,000	$288,000	$12,302	$302,714

securities are purchased by management as part of its long-term cash management strategy. Since the principal reason corporations hold these securities is not for short-term returns, fluctuations in their market value might distort current income. Therefore, by requiring that companies show these fluctuations as part of shareholders' equity, GAAP ensures that the corporation can show the market value of its investments without affecting the current period's reported income. Conversely, unrealized gains and losses on trading securities, those securities that management intends to sell within a very short period of time, are reported on the income statement as part of net income. Obviously, there is a potential for abuse here (a manager could claim an unrealized gain to increase net income), so auditors must carefully scrutinize all securities held by the company. For example, assume that PCs to Go had the following available-for-sale securities at the end of 2010:

	Cost	Market Value
Common stocks	$10,431	$33,982
Bonds	22,134	20,950
Total	$32,565	$54,932

Based on this information, PCs to Go has an unrealized gain (the market value exceeds the cost, but the assets have not been sold) before income taxes of $22,367 ($54,932 – $32,565). Assuming a 45 percent tax rate, the after-tax unrealized gain shown on the statement of owners' equity is determined as:

Unrealized gain before income taxes	$22,367
Less applicable taxes (45%)	10,065
Unrealized gain, net of applicable taxes	$12,302

This gain is the comprehensive income for the period. Notice this is revealed on the PCs to Go statement of owners' equity.

Retained Earnings

For corporations, the statement of retained earnings indicates the changes that occurred in the Retained Earnings account during the period. These changes arise from three sources: (1) net income or loss, (2) cash or stock dividends declared, and (3) prior period adjustments. Previously, we discussed how the balance of Retained Earnings increases or decreases during the closing process to reflect the net income or net loss of the period. In Chapter 15 we examined the effect of cash and stock dividends on retained earnings. Here we discuss prior period adjustments.

A **prior period adjustment** is a correction of a previously undetected material error that affected the net income or loss of a previous accounting period. The correction is made to beginning Retained Earnings because the net income or loss impacted by the error in a prior year was closed to Retained Earnings and, therefore, the beginning balance of Retained Earnings would be incorrect. When the error is discovered in the current year, companies report the impact of the error on Retained Earnings as an adjustment, net of tax.

For example, assume that PCs to Go discovered in April 2010 that land costing $60,000 was incorrectly recorded as depreciation expense rather than land in 2009. Thus PCs to Go's 2009 expenses were overstated and its income, total assets, and retained earnings were understated. If the entry had been made correctly, 2009 expenses would have been less, and assets would have been larger by $60,000 each, as shown here:

	Depreciation Expense	Land
Amounts actually recorded in error	$ 60,000	$ -0-
Amounts that should have been recorded	-0-	60,000
Correction needed	$(60,000)	$60,000

However, because depreciation expense was incorrectly recorded, the tax expense was smaller due to the smaller net income, so the 2009 tax expense (45 percent tax rate) and taxes payable were understated by $27,000 each ($60,000 × 0.45).

Because both the Depreciation Expense and Tax Expense accounts were closed into Retained Earnings at the end of 2009, the 2010 beginning balance of Retained Earnings must be increased by $33,000 ($60,000 − $27,000) as a result of this information:

Error	Correction to Retained Earnings
2009 depreciation expense overstated	Increase $60,000
2009 tax expense understated	Decrease 27,000
Net correction	Increase $33,000

The 2010 entry to record the correction of the error made in 2009 is

Date	Description	DR	CR
4-1-08	Land	60,000	
	Taxes payable		27,000
	Retained earnings		33,000

The following retained earnings disclosures are part of the statement of owners' equity in Exhibit 18.1. Notice that the beginning Retained Earnings balance is corrected for the $33,000 net error, which is a prior period adjustment. Then the balance is increased by the amount of net income generated during 2010 (Chapter 17) and decreased by the dividends declared in 2010 of $50,000. The dividends declared for each class of stock are determined as follows:

Total dividend declared	$50,000
Less preferred dividend (20,000 × $10 × 0.05)	10,000
Common stock dividends	$40,000

Other Disclosures

Other disclosures made on the statement of owners' equity typically concern stock—common stock, preferred stock, and treasury stock. The changes in the stock equity accounts in dollars, as well as the number of shares, are commonly shown. For example, in Chapter 17 we learned that PCs to Go issued additional shares of common stock on June 1 and purchased treasury stock on October 1. These events are disclosed on the statement of owners' equity along with retained earnings changes and changes in comprehensive income. Notice that the balances as of December 31, 2010, are reported on the balance sheet (discussed later in this chapter).

The Appendix shows the consolidated statement of changes in shareholders' equity of Apple for fiscal 2008 (page 56 of the annual report). Notice that the first two columns indicate changes in the Common Stock account in shares and in dollars. The next column shows information relative to deferred stock compensation. The next column shows the change in retained earnings. Notice that the amount of net income from the income statement, $4,834 million, is added to the beginning balance of retained earnings, $9,101 million, to determine the ending balance of retained earnings, $13,845 million (after subtracting the stock issue under stock plans). The next column indicates Apple's comprehensive income. For fiscal 2008, Apple had a loss in foreign currency translation of $11 million, an unrealized loss on available-for-sale securities of $63 million, and an unrealized gain on derivative investments of $19 million. Also note that all of these items are shown net of tax. Therefore, Apple's fiscal 2008 comprehensive income was ($55) million. Since comprehensive income hasn't been realized, it is carried on the balance sheet in the shareholders' equity section (as we will see next). The amount shown as the September 30, 2008, balance also appears on the balance sheet. In the next section, notice as we examine the balance sheet that all the ending balances shown on the statement of shareholders' equity are also shown on the balance sheet. Thus the purpose of this statement is to show the changes from one balance sheet date to the next.

Statement of Financial Position (Balance Sheet)

The balance sheet (the statement of financial position) along with its related disclosures reports the amount and type of assets the company controls and the claims the owners and creditors have on those assets on the last day of a reporting period. This financial statement is an important means of communication with parties inside and outside the business. The balance sheet describes for its readers three important characteristics of the company. The first is the portfolio of assets that the company has at its disposal to generate earnings. This helps readers assess the company's ability to generate profits in the future. Second, the balance sheet describes a company's solvency, that is, its ability to satisfy its obligations to its creditors. By examining the amount and type of a company's assets and the amount and timing (current versus long-term) of a company's obligations to creditors, readers can assess the firm's ability to satisfy its obligations. Finally, the balance sheet describes the financial flexibility of the company, that is, its ability to raise capital. In general, a company's financial flexibility decreases as the amount of its debt financing increases. For example, a company that finances 90 percent of its assets with debt and 10 percent with equity will have more difficulty raising capital than a company that finances 10 percent of its assets with debt financing.

In this chapter, the emphasis is on the external reporting rules embodied in GAAP. While we have described these rules throughout the book, here we provide a comprehensive overview of the balance sheet and expand upon previous discussions of the reporting rules for balance sheet items.

What Is Financial Position?

We know that a company's financial position is the summary of the relationship between its assets and the claims of its creditors, owners, and other suppliers of goods and services to those assets at a certain point in time. The concept of financial position conveys information about the nature of the company's resources and obligations, its ability to meet its obligations, and its prospects for future profitability. Measuring financial position differs from measuring profitability, as discussed in Chapter 17, because companies measure financial position at a *point in time,* while they measure profit (and cash flows) over a period of time.

Financial position, unlike earnings (net income) and cash flow, is measured at a point in time.

How does financial position reveal future profit potential? Assets reported as part of financial position are the economic resources that the company will have in the future to operate and generate future profits. Information about the quantities and types of assets a company has communicates the profit potential of the company. In addition, information about the claims on those assets by owners, creditors, and others reveals how the company might use its future profits. Possible uses could include providing a return to creditors in the form of interest, repaying amounts borrowed from creditors, or, for owners, either receiving a return in the form of dividends or reinvesting in additional assets.

Amounts appearing on a balance sheet are intended to provide statement users with enough information to make good assessments of the company's financial position without revealing more about the operations of the business than the company believes it should. One important assessment that external stakeholders make, particularly creditors, is the status of a company's short-term solvency. That is, how likely is the company to pay its obligations for the next year? Classifying assets and liabilities as current and noncurrent helps to answer that question.

Why Is the Distinction between Current and Noncurrent Items Important?

A company reflects its short-term liquidity and solvency on the balance sheet by the relationship of its current assets to its current liabilities. Liquidity refers to the time required for a company to convert its assets to cash, and solvency is simply the ability to meet obligations when they are due.

You already know that current assets include cash and other assets a company expects to convert into cash, sell, or use in one year or in the business's operating cycle, whichever is longer. Current liabilities are obligations that will become due in one year or within the operating cycle and will be paid with current assets or replaced with another current liability. Note that this definition includes not only the element of time but also the means by which the company will liquidate the debt. If a liability is due within one year and management intends to pay for it with noncurrent assets or refinance it with some form of long-term debt and can demonstrate the ability to refinance, the liability would be considered long term. Thus obligations due within one year may be classified as long term, depending on the means management intends to use to liquidate the debt.

The decision to classify a liability as either current or noncurrent also affects how investors and creditors perceive the solvency of the company. Classification of liabilities may seem straightforward, but managers must exercise care when doing this. For example, companies often sign one-year notes knowing that at the end of the year they will pay all of the accrued interest, but only part of the note's principal, and will then refinance the unpaid balance with another one-year note. Management's intention to repay the debt in more than one year using a series of one-year notes overrides the consideration of the form of the note and determines the substance of the transaction. Therefore the company should classify the note as long term.

Proper classification of current items also affects the assessment of short-term solvency ratios, such as the current and quick ratios. Keep in mind that a company's management realizes that reporting more assets as current and classifying liabilities as long term rather than short term enhances the appearance of the company's liquidity and solvency. Thus statement readers must consider the implications of such management decisions regarding the classification of current assets and liabilities as they study a company's balance sheet.

Balance Sheet Classifications

Those who use financial statements as their source of information about companies want to know more than the company's liquidity and short-term solvency. They also want to know useful information about the nature of the company's assets and its capital structure. One way accountants provide this information is by summarizing the accounts and recommending appropriate account classifications. The most commonly used classifications are

Assets	Liabilities	Owners' Equity
Current assets	Current	Contributed capital
Investments	Long-term debt	Retained earnings
Property, plant, and equipment	Other	Comprehensive income changes
Intangibles		Treasury stock
Other		

Companies are not required to use these specific classifications and may use alternatives to make the balance sheet more descriptive, as noted previously when discussing management's classification of assets and liabilities. Next we describe each of the major asset classifications and the related additional disclosures. As we discuss these items we examine the balance sheet of PCs to Go and relate it to the balance sheet and notes of Apple. Exhibit 18.2 shows the balance sheet of PCs to Go that we use as our roadmap throughout this discussion.

OF INTEREST Valuation on the Balance Sheet

In 1929 J. B. Canning discussed the processes of direct and indirect valuation of balance sheet items. His approach was based on the idea of discounting future cash flows to value assets and liabilities. From this approach, a framework for accounting valuation has been advocated to explain GAAP rules for valuation of monetary and nonmonetary items on the balance sheet.

As you can see in this framework, we begin by asking a simple question—can this item be reliably valued directly (present value of future cash flows)? If the answer to this question is yes, we use present value analysis to provide the balance sheet value. If the answer to this question is no, we must find another way to value the item and historical cost is our first choice. If historical cost is not acceptable, we have an exception or adaptation. For example, consider inventory. We cannot reliably value inventory using discounted cash flows because it is a nonmonetary item. Our next choice would be to value inventory using historical cost; however, since inventory is held for sale, not for use, we want to recognize when inventory has lost value. Therefore we value inventory at cost or market, whichever is lower.

Source: Frakes, Albert H., and Thomas R. Nunamaker, "A Fundamental Approach to Teaching Accounting Valuation," *Advances in Accounting Education* 5 (2003), pp. 43–54.

Complete Framework for Accounting Valuation

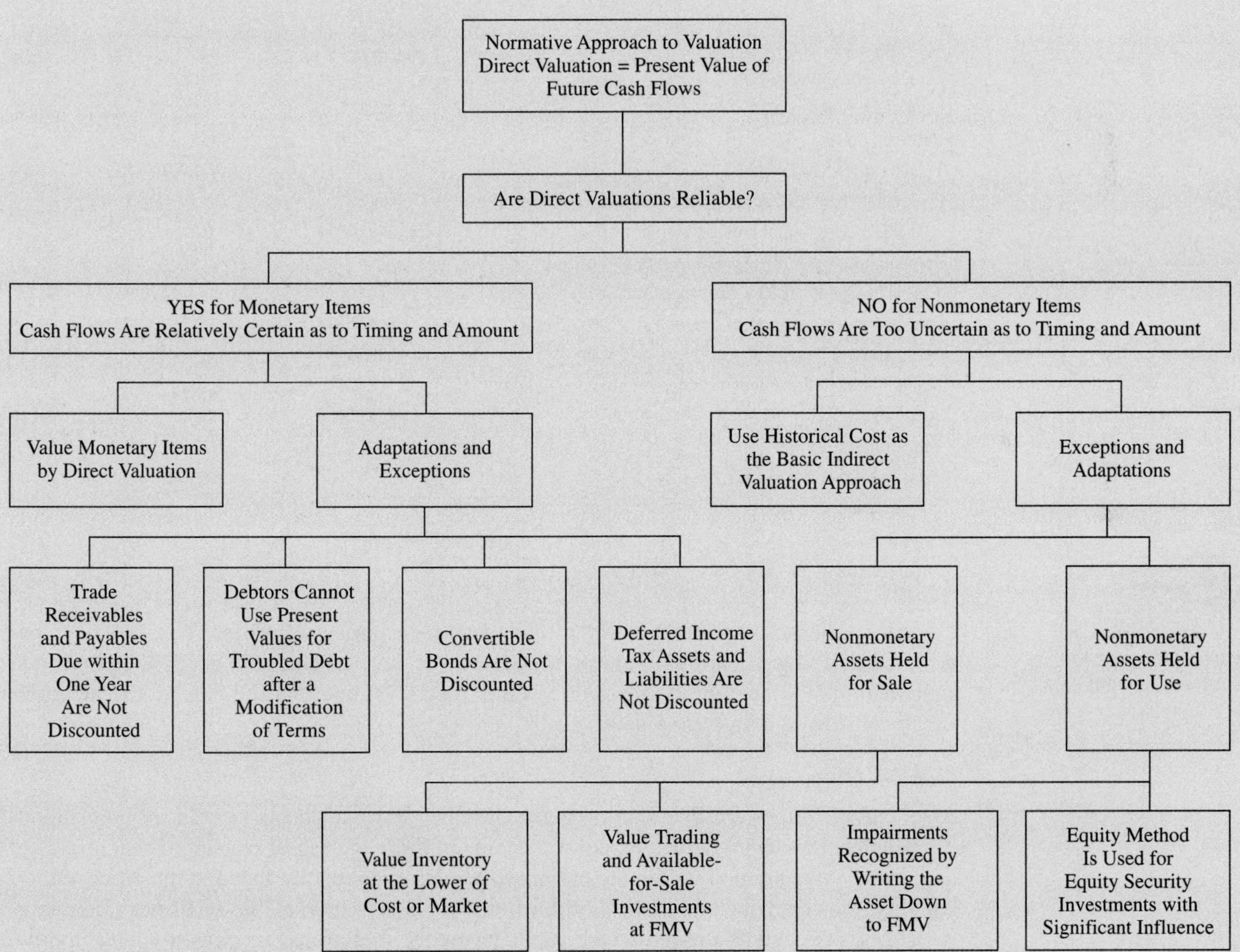

EXHIBIT 18.2
Balance Sheet

PCs to Go Balance Sheet As of December 31, 2010		
Assets		
Cash	$ 39,156	
Accounts receivable, net	263,189	
Inventories	438,575	
Prepaid expenses	43,597	
Total current assets		$ 784,517
Investments	$ 133,115	
Property, plant, and equipment, net	2,300,000	
Intangibles, net	$ 600,000	
Total long-term assets		3,033,115
Total Assets		**$3,817,632**
Liabilities and Owners' Equity		
Accounts payable	$ 241,125	
Accrued liabilities	120,003	
Current portion of long-term debt	$ 100,000	
Total current liabilities		$ 461,128
Long-term debt	$1,000,000	
Deferred taxes	450,000	
Total long-term liabilities		1,450,000
Preferred stock: $10 par, 5%; 500,000 shares authorized; 20,000 shares issued and outstanding	$ 200,000	
Common stock: $1 par; 500,000 shares authorized; 34,500 issued; 25,500 shares outstanding	34,500	
Paid-in capital in excess of par value	1,644,988	
Retained earnings	302,714	
Accumulated comprehensive income items	12,302	
Treasury stock	$ (288,000)	
Total owners' equity		1,906,504
Total liabilities and owners' equity		**$3,817,632**

Assets are listed on the balance sheet in order of liquidity.

Assets

Companies classify assets according to their purpose and/or useful life. Thus, most companies use five classifications: (1) current assets, (2) investments, (3) property, plant, and equipment, (4) intangible assets, and (5) other assets. Notice that the latter four categories are all considered long-term assets.

Current Assets

Asset classifications are listed on properly classified balance sheets in order of their liquidity, which is how quickly the company can convert them to cash or consume them as part of operations. Assets found within the current asset classification are listed in the order of their liquidity, too. They include cash, short-term investments in marketable securities (temporary investments), accounts and notes receivable, inventory, and prepaid expenses.

Cash Companies carry cash on the balance sheet at its stated value, assuming it is readily available to meet any current obligation. Companies should not classify as cash any deposits that are restricted for a particular use. Instead these amounts should be shown as other assets, which we discuss below. For example, some banks require that a company borrowing from the bank maintain a compensating balance in a checking account at the bank. A **compensating balance** is a minimum cash balance that the company (depositor) must maintain either to continue to earn interest on the amount deposited in the bank account or to avoid certain fees from the bank, such as service charges. Compensating balances may also be required by banks to maintain lines of credit or similar short-term lending arrangements. PCs to Go (see Exhibit 18.2) shows cash of $39,156 on hand.

Marketable Securities Short-term investments in marketable securities is the second item under the current assets classification. These securities are temporary investments that companies intend to convert to cash when needed, and they can be trading, available-for-sale, or held-to-maturity securities. Recall that the difference between trading securities and available-for-sale securities is determined by management's intent. Trading securities are those debt and equity securities that companies purchase with the intent of selling after a short period of time. Available-for-sale securities are those debt and equity securities that management intends to sell, as needed, to raise cash for particular projects. Held-to-maturity securities are debt securities that management intends to hold until maturity. However, when the maturity date is within the upcoming period, these securities are classified as current assets. Trading or available-for-sale securities appear on the balance sheet at their market value. This helps the reader understand the amount of cash that the company would realize if it sold the securities immediately.

Accounts and Notes Receivable Accounts and notes receivable appear after marketable securities on the balance sheet. As we explained in Chapter 10, companies show accounts receivable at their net realizable value, which represents the amount of accounts receivable currently due that the company estimates is collectible. When the company reports only the net accounts receivable on the balance sheet, it might disclose the amount of the allowance for uncollectible accounts in the notes to the financial statements. If accounts and notes receivable arise from persons who bought goods and services from the company, it often labels them as trade receivables. Companies must disclose the total amount of trade receivables as a separate item either on the balance sheet or in the notes. PCs to Go indicates that net accounts receivable are $263,189.

Inventory Inventory follows the receivables in the current asset section of the balance sheet. The balance sheet or related notes must disclose the inventory method used to determine the cost of the inventory (for example, FIFO or LIFO). If a company has an inventory of raw materials or work-in-process, it can show these amounts separately, although frequently the amounts are included with the inventory of merchandise available for sale. The details are then shown in the notes. Companies are required to show inventory on the balance sheet at the lower of cost or market, where market is the amount required to replace the old inventory. This rule is applied to individual inventory items, classes of items like computers or furniture, or the inventory as a whole. PCs to Go has inventories (raw materials and finished goods) of $438,575 on December 31, 2010.

Prepaid Expenses Prepaid expenses are classified as current assets because they support the operating activities of the company and are usually consumed during the operating cycle. They appear as current assets because they will be used up or consumed within the next year. Furthermore, prepayments made for items such as insurance and rent are considered current because, if the contract for either item is canceled, the company will receive a cash refund. If the prepaid item is not refunded when canceled, the portion that applies to periods of more than one year is considered long term and is reported as an other asset. PCs to Go indicates that its prepaid expenses are $43,597.

Take a moment to make sure you locate each of the current assets on the PCs to Go balance sheet in Exhibit 18.2. Now we look at the current assets and additional disclosures of Apple (see Appendix).

Apple shows cash and cash equivalents, short-term investments, accounts receivable (less allowance), inventories, deferred tax assets (discussed later), and other current assets in its current asset section. Note 1 (page 58 of the annual report) reveals that cash equivalents are "all highly liquid investments with maturities of three months or less at the date of purchase." Note 2 (page 65 of the annual report) shows the breakdown of these liquid investments and the composition of Apple's short-term investments. Note 2 (pages 66 and 67 of the annual report) also provides additional information concerning accounts receivable and the accompanying allowance for doubtful accounts (uncollectible accounts). Note 3 (page 69 of the annual report) provides additional information concerning Apple's other current assets.

Investments

Following the current assets section on the balance sheet is the investments section. The investment classification on the balance sheet describes the type and extent of the company's long-term, nonoperational investments. Acquiring long-term, nonoperational investments, such as stock or bonds of other companies, is an alternative to investing in operational assets such as production plants or equipment. Sometimes investing in nonoperating assets is a better management strategy because investing in operating assets might increase the company's productive capacity beyond the demand for the products and services the company provides. For financial statement users, a relatively detailed description of a company's long-term investments is often included in the notes to the financial statements. PCs to Go owns land that it is holding for speculation valued at $60,000 and available-for-sale securities reported at their market value of $73,115, for a total investment asset of $133,115 (Exhibit 18.2). This land is an investment because it is not being used for productive purposes. Apple reveals no investment assets.

Property, Plant, and Equipment (PPE)

Property, plant, and equipment follows the investments section and shows the tangible operational investments that support the operating infrastructure of the company. This balance sheet classification typically has the largest dollar amounts of any of the asset classifications and represents the largest and most diverse group of assets. The assets found most typically in property, plant, and equipment are land, buildings, and equipment.

Land in the property, plant, and equipment section represents the land acquired as a site for the company's operational activities. The building's classification summarizes the cost of the various structures used by the company to conduct its operations. Some companies subdivide this classification into more specific classifications such as manufacturing plants, office buildings, or retail outlets if such distinctions are deemed useful to the financial statement users. Buildings are depreciable assets and, therefore, companies show buildings at their book or carrying values—that is, net of their accumulated depreciation. This is accomplished either by showing the original cost of the buildings less the accumulated depreciation or by showing the net book value. Regardless of how net book (carrying) value is shown on the balance sheet, details such as major categories of property, plant, and equipment and the related amounts of accumulated depreciation are disclosed in the notes. PCs to Go shows property, plant, and equipment (net) of $2,300,000 as of December 31, 2010.

Leased Assets As discussed previously, leasing assets is an alternative to buying them. Assets leased under capital leases appear on the lessee's balance sheet as property, plant, and equipment. (Recall that operating leases are simply rental agreements whose asset and obligation are not recorded in a company's accounting records.) For capital leases, the economic substance of the lease agreement implies that the asset was purchased instead of leased, thus overriding the legal form of the lease itself.

Natural Resources Recall that natural resources are assets such as timber, oil fields, and diamond mines. As natural resources are consumed, the original cost of the asset is depleted. The original cost of the natural resource usually is maintained on the balance sheet, and the depletion taken to date is reported as a contra asset, accumulated depletion. A company can also show the net carrying value of the natural resource on the balance sheet and report accumulated depletion in the notes. Companies reveal the rate of depletion and how they determine its amount in the summary of significant accounting policies.

Let's examine the property, plant, and equipment disclosure of Apple. On the balance sheet, Apple shows a balance for property, plant, and equipment, net of $2,455 million. Note 3 (page 69 of the annual report) provides the following details (in millions):

Land and buildings	$ 810
Machinery, equipment, and internal-use software	1,491
Office furniture and equipment	122
Leasehold improvements	1,324
	$3,747
Accumulated depreciation and amortization	(1,292)
Net property, plant, and equipment	$2,455

Recall that Apple uses the straight-line depreciation method.

Intangible Assets

Intangible assets are operational investments that a company has acquired and that appear following property, plant, and equipment on a company's balance sheet. Intangibles have no physical substance but are expected to generate some economic benefit for the company in the future. Recall that intangibles include patents, copyrights, trademarks, and goodwill. Also recall that goodwill appears on the balance sheet only when one company purchases another company. Companies report intangible assets on the balance sheet at the original cost less the amortization taken on the assets up to that point in time. PCs to Go reports intangibles (net) of $600,000 (see Exhibit 18.2). Apple reports goodwill of $207 million and acquired intangible assets of $285 million on its fiscal 2008 balance sheet. Note 4 (page 70 of the annual report) describes its goodwill and intangible assets and its methods for amortizing the intangibles and adjusting the goodwill.

Other Assets

Companies use the last asset classification, other assets, for unusual items that do not fit in the previous asset classifications. The items in this classification vary in practice and include noncurrent receivables and special funds. Many accountants consider other assets to be too general a description and, therefore, recommend that items in this classification be placed in another, more specific asset classification. **Deferred charges** (deferrals) frequently are found in the other asset classification. Such charges are long-term prepayments that companies amortize over various lengths of time, depending on how long management believes the company will benefit from the expenditures. For example, the Capitalized Software and Development Cost is part of Apple's Other Assets and represents money spent for developing software for customers that includes licenses and attorneys' fees. This is an example of a deferred charge typically included in the "other assets" category. Apple reports total other assets of $1,935 million for 2008. Note 3 (page 69 of the annual report) discloses that these assets consist of:

Deferred costs under subscription accounting	$1,089
Long-term NAND flash memory prepayments	208
Deferred tax assets	138
Capitalized software development costs, net	67
Other assets	433
Total other assets	$1,935

Liabilities and Owners' (Shareholders') Equity

After describing the major classifications of assets, we look at the other side of the balance sheet that generally reflects the means a company has chosen to finance its assets. This portion of the balance sheet includes a company's obligations to creditors and other outside parties as well as its investments from owners. The three basic classifications of liabilities on the balance sheet are current liabilities, long-term debt, and other long-term liabilities. The latter two classifications differ from each other in that long-term debt refers to obligations to creditors from borrowing, and other long-term liabilities include obligations that arise from means other than borrowing, such as obligations under capital leases, pension obligations, and deferred taxes.

Liabilities are listed on the balance sheet according to when the obligation is due.

Current Liabilities

Current liabilities are listed first in the liabilities section of the balance sheet. They result from one of four events: (1) the receipt of loan proceeds by the company, (2) the purchase of goods and services using credit to defer payment for them, (3) the receipt of prepayments for goods and services promised to be provided subsequently by the company, and (4) the reclassification of the portion of long-term debt that becomes due within the coming fiscal year.

The acquisition of goods and services on credit creates the most common type of current liability. Accounts payable, notes payable, wages and salaries payable, interest payable, and even taxes payable all reflect short-term obligations to pay for goods, services, or other obligations of the company. When the company receives payments in advance, it is required to either perform the prepaid service or provide the goods promised or return the cash advanced. The accounts associated with this obligation include unearned rent, unearned subscription revenue, and deposits made by customers to hold merchandise for future delivery.

As discussed earlier, companies must classify as current any portion of a long-term debt that comes due within the time frame established for current liabilities. The exception to this rule occurs regarding those liabilities a company expects to either pay with a noncurrent asset or refinance with another long-term debt agreement. Installment notes, lease obligations, bonds, and mortgage notes can appear as both a current liability and a long-term liability if part of the debt meets the current liability criteria. If the entire amount of the debt meets the current liability criteria, it is properly classified, in total, as a current liability.

In Exhibit 18.2, PCs to Go reports three current liabilities: (1) accounts payable, \$241,125; (2) accrued liabilities, \$120,003; and (3) current portion of long-term debt, \$100,000. Accrued liabilities is a miscellaneous classification that represents many current liability accounts such as Salaries Payable and Utilities Payable. Apple reports current liabilities consisting of accounts payable and accrued expenses. Note 3 (page 69 of the annual report) indicates that accrued expenses are:

Deferred revenue—current	$4,853
Deferred margin on component sales	681
Accrued marketing and distribution	329
Accrued compensation and employee benefits	320
Accrued warranty and related costs	267
Other accrued tax liability	100
Other current liabilities	2,022
Total accrued expenses	$8,572

Long-Term Debt (Liabilities)

Long-term debt (liabilities) is not expected to come due within one year or the operating cycle. As we discussed earlier, however, the long-term liabilities classification also can include those liabilities that will come due within one year. In the latter case, the company expects to pay for these liabilities with noncurrent assets, or the company expects to refinance them with another long-term debt instrument. Most long-term debt instruments specify the terms promised by the borrower as well as the restrictions imposed for the benefit of the lender. Companies disclose these details in the notes to the financial statements.

A long-term note payable reflects a company's debt agreement with an individual or institution. A long-term note commonly found on the balance sheet is the mortgage note payable, which shows the amount of borrowing secured with the real estate of the borrower. As you know, bonds payable differ from long-term notes payable in that the company typically is borrowing the needed funds from the public and not from a specific individual or institution. Recall that companies amortize any premium or discount because interest expense shown on the income statement differs from the amount of cash interest paid. The remaining premium or discount is shown as an adjustment to the bond's face value in the notes to the statements. The amount of information about a bond issue presented on the face of the balance sheet is limited. Companies often show detailed information about bond issues, such as the life of the bond, its effective interest rate, and whether it was secured, in the notes to the financial statements. The notes to the financial statements also include a description of any other features of the bonds, such as conversion rates, call prices, and the restrictions the bond indebtedness places on the corporation. In Exhibit 18.2, PCs to Go has $1,000,000 of long-term debt. Apple indicates that its long-term liabilities are deferred tax liabilities, deferred revenue–noncurrent, and other noncurrent liabilities of $746 million (see Note 3, page 70 of the annual report).

Other Liabilities

Companies also include the liability under their pension plans as an other long-term liability. Defined benefit pension plans require companies to base the pension benefits paid to employees on factors including estimates of the time employees will work and their expected lives. This makes accounting for these plans very complicated, including the calculation of the amount that companies should record as pension liability. Though we have not dealt with the details of these calculations or shown the complexity of determining other postretirement benefit obligations, you should know that these obligations are reported under this liability classification.

Deferred income tax liability is another long-term liability reported on most corporate balance sheets. Due to the complexities surrounding this account, discussion was delayed to this point. The brief discussion that follows presents basic information to provide a fundamental understanding of why this account exists. A more detailed discussion of this topic is found in more advanced accounting textbooks.

Deferred income tax liabilities (and assets) result from differences between computing income using generally accepted accounting principles and computing taxable income using tax laws. Remember that accounting principles are designed to measure and reflect business events on an objective basis, whereas tax laws are designed to raise money for the government, stimulate the economy, and encourage or discourage particular types of business transactions. Because companies must comply with both accounting principles and tax laws, the resulting tax calculations can differ from the financial accounting treatment of a particular business event. Such differences create a deferred income tax amount that appears on the balance sheet.

To illustrate how a deferred tax liability arises, assume that PCs to Go has a tax rate of 45 percent and signs a contract on December 15, 2010, for $1 million, which is considered revenue for financial accounting purposes. Assume that for tax purposes, however, this amount is not considered taxable income until PCs to Go receives the cash in payment of the contract on January 15, 2013. Note that both PCs to Go and the IRS consider the $1 million as revenue, but they differ about the time period in which to recognize it.

To comply with GAAP, PCs to Go recognizes the $1 million as revenue and reflects the related tax expense of $450,000 ($1 million × 0.45) for the fiscal year ended December 31, 2010. When it recognizes the tax expense, a related Deferred Income Tax Liability account appears on its balance sheet, indicating that the taxes are due from PCs to Go. These taxes will actually be paid when the IRS recognizes the $1 million as taxable income in 2013. In this case, PCs to Go reports a deferred tax liability of $450,000 on its 2010 balance sheet (see Exhibit 18.2).

Numerous differences between tax law and GAAP cause taxable income and accounting income to differ. The important differences result from recognizing certain revenues and expenses for tax purposes at different times than they are recognized for financial accounting purposes, which creates deferred income tax assets and liabilities.

Contingent Liabilities

Some events, such as lawsuits or claims filed by customers for defective products, may affect the business negatively. However, in some cases, the actual events that create the specific losses have not occurred at the end of the reporting period, such as a judgment in a

FAST FACT

Despite all the hoopla surrounding SPE (Special Purpose Entities) and Enron, these off-balance-sheet arrangements have been around since the 1970s. They were originally designed to provide less expensive financing and reduce financial risk for the companies using them. A legitimate SPE is formed when assets are transferred to carry out a specific purpose or activity. The SPE then obtains financing to accomplish its limited objectives. The benefit to the company is that the debt financing is kept off the company's balance sheet (hence, the name off-balance-sheet financing). Following the abuses of SPE by Enron and others, the FASB has issued new interpretations to help companies better account for such complex financing arrangements.

lawsuit that is filed but not settled. Outside stakeholders want to know about these potential events, and companies are required to disclose them under certain conditions. These potential losses are called **contingent liabilities,** which represent events that could create negative financial results for a company at some future point. Companies must actually record losses when the related event is considered probable and when the company can reasonably estimate its monetary effect on the financial statements. Even when corporations cannot estimate the impact of the events or whether the likelihood of such events is less than probable, they must disclose the existence of contingent liabilities as part of the notes that accompany the financial statements. Note 8 (pages 79–82 of the annual report) describes Apple's commitments and contingencies. Apple had lease commitments, accrued warranty and indemnifications, concentrations in the available sources of supply of materials, and contingencies due to lawsuits that it describes and explains. While these are not liabilities because the amounts are unknown, financial statement users should evaluate commitments and contingencies carefully.

Off-Balance-Sheet Financing

Some financial reporting rules for liabilities, such as capital lease obligations, allow the substance of the transaction to override its form, so companies are obligated to record the amounts of the related debt and reflect them in their financial statements. These reporting rules arose in response to managers' attempts to borrow money in ways that would allow them to avoid having to record such borrowings on the balance sheet (known as **off-balance-sheet financing**).

When a company leases an asset under a long-term noncancelable lease, it is obligated to reflect the lease payments on the financial statements as if the company had borrowed the money and bought the asset. Without such obligations created by GAAP, the noncancelable lease obligation would not be reported on the company's balance sheet. When balance sheets omit reflecting the sources of off-balance-sheet financing, such as long-term leases classified as operating leases (even though there are substantial obligations to make future lease payments), it affects how balance sheet readers perceive the risk and financial health of the business. Not recording such liabilities affects indicators of financial risk and flexibility, such as the current ratio and the debt-to-equity ratio, by making them appear better than if the obligation was recorded.[1]

Shareholders' Equity

Here we review some important points about shareholders' equity. Dividing the shareholders' equity section into contributed capital (often called paid-in capital) and retained earnings reflects the resources provided by the owners and the claims generated by retaining the corporation's profits, respectively. Chapter 15 discussed the equity financing events that create the accounts found on the statement of shareholders' equity. The following discussion focuses on how the balance sheet reports the results of these events.

[1] Many people believe that off-balance-sheet financing ultimately caused the collapse of Enron.

Contributed Capital

Companies typically separate the preferred stock section of equity from the common shareholders' equity. This presentation reflects the idea that the nature of preferred stock is like debt because preferred stock shareholders cannot vote in shareholder meetings. In addition, as you know, the preferred stock dividends usually are set at a fixed amount, and preferred stock has preference over common stock regarding the receipt of dividends and in liquidation. On more traditional balance sheets, preferred stock typically appears as the first item in the contributed capital section because of its preference. The balance sheet, statement of owners' equity, or notes should indicate the par value of stock and the number of shares authorized, issued, and outstanding. Additional information concerning the preferred stock preferences is normally reported only in the notes accompanying the financial statements.

Exhibit 18.2 shows that PCs to Go has 500,000 shares of preferred stock authorized with 20,000 shares of preferred stock issued and outstanding. The par value of the preferred stock is $10 and the dividend rate is 5 percent. PCs to Go has 500,000 shares of common stock authorized with 34,500 shares issued and 25,500 shares outstanding. The difference between issued and outstanding is due to treasury stock that is reported later in the shareholders' equity section. The common stock has a par value of $1 per share. Recall that legal capital is separated from additional paid-in capital. PCs to Go shows $234,500 of legal capital and $1,644,988 of additional paid-in capital.

Retained Earnings

Corporations may restrict retained earnings, which limits the dividend-paying ability of the corporation. Often a restriction is placed on retained earnings when a corporation issues bonds. The bonds' covenants restrict the dividend-paying ability of the corporation to protect the bondholders. When the retained earnings of the company are restricted, corporations disclose the amount of, and reason for, the restriction in a note. One common retained earnings restriction occurs when corporations purchase treasury stock. They restrict retained earnings by the amount paid for the treasury stock. Because the purchase of treasury stock represents the amount paid to former shareholders, both common and preferred, the purchase liquidates owners' interest. Therefore, creditors of the company want to limit the dividend-paying ability of the corporation to protect them from further distribution of the company's assets to shareholders. As the corporation sells treasury stock, it removes any related restrictions.

Again note that the ending balance of retained earnings shown on the statement of owners' equity is the balance reported on the balance sheet.

Accumulated Other Comprehensive Income Items

Appearing after the retained earnings sections of shareholders' equity is a section representing components of the company's *accumulated* comprehensive income. That is, comprehensive income is a permanent part of shareholders' equity and, therefore, is not closed to retained earnings. Therefore, the balance of comprehensive income accumulates as the company increases it by comprehensive income items and decreases it by comprehensive loss items. Let's look again at PCs to Go's statement of owners' equity in Exhibit 18.1. Note that the comprehensive income column began with a zero balance. The comprehensive income for the period of $12,302 was added to this balance to determine the ending balance of $12,302 shown on PCs to Go's balance sheet in Exhibit 18.2.

Remember:
Treasury stock is a reduction from shareholders' equity.

Treasury Stock

Treasury stock is shown after retained earnings in the shareholders' equity section of the balance sheet. Because corporations assume that they will reissue treasury shares, they treat treasury stock as a temporary reduction in total shareholders' equity that they eliminate when they reissue the shares. PCs to Go has treasury stock at the end of 2010 of 9,000 shares at a cost of $32 per share (9,000 shares × $32 = $288,000).

Apple's balance sheet reveals that it has no-par common stock. It has 1.8 billion shares authorized; 888,325,973 shares were issued and outstanding as of September 27, 2008. Recall that Apple has 5 million shares of preferred stock authorized (see Note 6, page 74 of the annual report), but none has been issued. Also shown in the shareholders' equity section are the ending balances of every column in the statement of shareholders' equity. Retained earnings was $13,845 million and the ending balance of accumulated comprehensive income (loss) was $8 million (Note 6, page 74 of the annual report gives more detail on comprehensive income).

Internal Financial Position Reporting

As we discussed in Chapter 17, evaluating the financial results of the company is an important component of the balanced scorecard approach. However, balance sheets issued to external parties are limited in their usefulness for internal decision makers because of their use of historical cost asset valuation. The assets of most companies are at least a few years old, and many include buildings that are 30 and 40 years old. The use of historical cost valuation understates companies' investments because the assets are shown at these old prices. This means that the companies appear to have much lower investments in assets than they actually have.

Reporting property, plant, and equipment at their historical cost is required by GAAP, but internal users do not face this same restriction when formulating their reports. An alternative to using historical cost valuation is using current replacement cost. Current replacement cost valuation of assets means that long-lived asset values are adjusted to their replacement cost at the balance sheet date. Companies can obtain current cost data by obtaining catalogs that report average recent prices for certain types of equipment or by having their assets appraised by independent appraisers.

To explain how useful current cost valuation is in decision making, consider the steel industry during the middle of the 20th century. Steel manufacturers had large investments in buildings and blast furnaces. When the return earned by these companies was measured using historical cost, they appeared to be earning sufficient returns. However, the return that they were earning was not sufficient to replace the equipment as technology changed and their equipment became obsolete. If the equipment had been valued at its replacement cost, which was higher than its historical cost, then the denominator of the return on investment calculation (see Chapter 17) would have been larger, and the calculated return on investment would have been lower. The lower return on investment based on replacement costs would have indicated that higher prices were necessary to earn the return they thought they were getting, and that replacement of the equipment with more efficient equipment would have been a good decision.

Current cost valuation does have two problems, however. First, obtaining current cost data can be expensive, and the benefits of collecting these data need to exceed their cost. The other problem with current cost data is that the data are subjective. Different appraisers rarely appraise an asset at exactly the same value, and if a published value is used to value the asset, the condition of the asset is probably not the same as the assumed condition of the asset with the published price.

In addition to current cost valuation, recall our discussion of variable and throughput costing in Chapter 17. These internal costing methods also impact the balance sheet because they affect the way inventories are valued. Many companies find it useful to measure inventories using only variable costs based on the belief that only these costs truly increase as production volume increases. Other companies prefer to value inventories internally using only direct materials based on the belief that only these costs are recoverable should the work-in-process inventories not be completed. As we have seen, what a company chooses to do internally is based on its philosophy and its decision-making framework.

Summary

A company's assets, along with the claims to those assets by owners and creditors, represent its financial position, which the balance sheet presents. Classifying assets, liabilities, and equity accounts allows readers to assess the nature of the significant items in each category. Understanding the meaning of balance sheet classifications facilitates the communication process between managers and external stakeholders.

- Proper classification of assets and liabilities as current and noncurrent facilitates assessment of a company's solvency and liquidity. Management intends to convert assets classified as current to cash within a year or the operating cycle. Companies expect to liquidate liabilities classified as current with current assets or to refinance them with current liabilities within a year or the operating cycle.
- Proper classification of assets allows statement readers to assess the nature of a company's assets. This allows financial statement readers to determine the company's prospects for profitability and future cash flows.
- Proper classification of liabilities allows the financial statement reader to assess some of the uses of future profits and cash flows. Specifically, the level of current assets relative to current liabilities shows the company's short-term solvency. Long-term obligations require the use of current assets or additional long-term assets sometime in the future.

Key Terms

Compensating balance A minimum cash balance that the depositor (company) must maintain either to continue to earn interest on the amount deposited in the bank account or to avoid certain fees, such as service charges, *510*

Contingent liabilities Events that could create negative financial results for a company; required to be recorded when the event is probable and estimable in terms of its monetary effects, *516*

Deferred charges Long-term prepayments frequently found in the other assets classification that companies amortize over various lengths of time, depending on how long the company will benefit from the expenditures; also called deferrals, *513*

Off-balance-sheet financing Borrowing money in ways that would avoid having to record the obligation on the balance sheet, *516*

Prior period adjustment A correction of a previously undetected material error that affected the net income or loss of a previous accounting period, *505*

Questions

1. What are the three primary components of the statement of owners' equity and what information is disclosed in each component?
2. What is comprehensive income and how is it different than net income?
3. What is a prior period adjustment and why is it shown net of taxes?
4. Explain the format of the retained earnings portion of the statement of owners' equity.
5. What is meant by the term financial position, and what is the purpose of the statement of financial position?
6. How is financial position related to profit potential?
7. What is a current asset? Why is it important to separate current assets from long-term assets on the balance sheet?
8. Explain the four types of long-term assets.
9. What is a current liability? Why is it important to separate current liabilities from long-term liabilities?
10. Explain why a long-term note is classified as current if the fiscal year ends during the last year of the note's life.
11. In what order are current assets listed on the balance sheet? Why is this order important?
12. What does the term *valued* mean as it relates to the asset accounts shown on the balance sheet?
13. Why is a prepaid insurance policy with a three-year life often listed as a current asset?
14. How can a reader of the financial statements determine how the company's current assets are valued?

15. How are property, plant, and equipment accounts valued on the balance sheet? Why?
16. How are intangible assets valued on the balance sheet? Why?
17. In what order are current liabilities listed on the balance sheet? Why is this order important?
18. How are current liabilities valued on the balance sheet? Why?
19. How are long-term liabilities such as bonds payable valued on the balance sheet? Why?
20. What are other long-term liabilities? Give two examples.
21. What is the order of the items included in the shareholders' equity section of the balance sheet? Why is this order important?
22. What is accumulated comprehensive income on the balance sheet and how is it different from comprehensive income on the statement of owners' equity?
23. Why is treasury stock subtracted from shareholders' equity on the balance sheet?

Exercises

E18.1 LO 1 Carnes Enterprises has determined that the market value of its available-for-sale securities is greater than cost by $250,000 at the end of fiscal 2010. Carnes's tax rate is 30 percent. How would this information be reported on Carnes's 2010 statement of owners' equity?

LO 1 **E18.2** Bolling, Inc., has determined that the cost of its available-for-sale securities is greater than the market value by $80,000. If Bolling is subject to a 30 percent tax rate, what is the impact of this event on its statement of owners' equity?

LO 1 **E18.3** Engstrom Company began fiscal 2010 with a $40,000 deficit balance in retained earnings. During 2008 its net income was $167,890 and its declared but not paid dividends were $50,000. What is the ending balance of retained earnings for Engstrom?

LO 1 **E18.4** Hendricks, Inc., has an ending balance in retained earnings on December 31, 2010, of $567,432. During 2010 it had declared dividends of $100,000 and incurred a net loss of $246,700. What was the beginning balance in retained earnings on January 1, 2010?

LO 1 **E18.5** In 2009 Kieso Enterprises failed to record depreciation expense of $30,000. The accountant discovered this error in 2010. Kieso is subject to a 35 percent tax rate. What is the effect of this error on retained earnings?

LO 1 **E18.6** In 2009 Cummings Company, which is subject to a 30 percent tax rate, recognized interest revenue of $15,000. In January 2010, the accountant discovered that the correct amount of interest revenue for 2009 was $25,000. What is the effect of this error on the 2010 statement of owners' equity?

LO 1 **E18.7** For each of the following accounts, determine its classification on the balance sheet using the following classifications. Use OOE for other owners' equity items that are not contributed capital or retained earnings. Put the letters in the spaces provided.

CA	Current assets	LTL	Long-term liabilities
INV	Investments	OL	Other liabilities
PPE	Property, plant, and equipment	CC	Contributed capital
INT	Intangibles	RE	Retained earnings
OA	Other assets	OOE	Other owners' equity
CL	Current liabilities		

________ 1. Accounts Payable
________ 2. Accumulated Depreciation
________ 3. Bonds Payable
________ 4. Building
________ 5. Cash
________ 6. Common Stock
________ 7. Land Held for Speculation
________ 8. Marketable Securities
________ 9. Treasury Stock
________10. Wages Payable

LO 2 E18.8 For each of the following accounts, determine its classification on the balance sheet using the following classifications. Use OOE for other owners' equity items that are not contributed capital or retained earnings. Put the letters in the spaces provided.

CA	Current assets	LTL	Long-term liabilities
INV	Investments	OL	Other liabilities
PPE	Property, plant, and equipment	CC	Contributed capital
INT	Intangibles	RE	Retained earnings
OA	Other assets	OOE	Other owners' equity
CL	Current liabilities		

_______ 1. Accumulated Depletion
_______ 2. Allowance for Uncollectible Accounts
_______ 3. Bonds Payable Due Next Year
_______ 4. Common Stock Dividend Distributable
_______ 5. Deferred Income Tax Payable
_______ 6. Discount on Bonds Payable
_______ 7. Goodwill
_______ 8. Land Held for Expansion
_______ 9. Mining Property
_______ 10. Mortgage Payable

Use the following information for E18.9 through E18.15:

Tidrick Manufacturing Company has just completed its first year of operation. It has the following accounts in the general ledger. The bookkeeper is unsure which accounts to show on the balance sheet and which accounts to report on the income statement. All amounts are in thousands of dollars.

Accounts Receivable	$4,680	Land	$2,510
Accounts Payable	$6,316	Land Held for Speculation	$2,500
Accumulated Depreciation, Building	$580	Machinery	$1,879
Accumulated Depreciation, Machinery	$362	Marketable Securities (trading)	$835
Additional Paid-In Capital	$3,234	Notes Payable, Due in 90 Days	$1,570
Allowance for Uncollectible Accounts	$45	Notes Payable, Due in 10 Years	$2,600
Bonds Payable	$1,580	Preferred Stock	$20
Building	$3,340	Prepaid Insurance	$500
Cash	$4,317	Prepaid Rent	$941
Common Stock	$30	Purchases Discounts	$180
Copyright	$391	Raw Materials Inventory	$87
Cost of Goods Sold	$33,892	Rent Expense	$600
Deferred Income Taxes Payable	$30	Retained Earnings	$3,996
Discount on Bonds Payable	$75	Sales	$43,068
Dividends Payable	$130	Sales Discounts	$1,414
Finished Goods Inventory	$30	Sales Returns and Allowances	$210
Income Tax Expense	$1,079	Selling and Administrative Expenses	$2,700
Income Taxes Payable	$1,300	Supplies	$78
Insurance Expense	$400	Wages Payable	$580
Interest Expense	$308	Work-in-Process Inventory	$210

LO 2 E18.9 Prepare the current asset section of the balance sheet.

LO 2 E18.10 Prepare the long-term asset section of the balance sheet.

LO 2 E18.11 Prepare the current liability section of the balance sheet.

LO 2 E18.12 Prepare the long-term liability section of the balance sheet.

LO 2 E18.13 Prepare the shareholders' equity section of the balance sheet.

LO 1 E18.14 Prepare the statement of shareholders' equity.

LO 2 E18.15 Prepare the balance sheet.

LO 1 E18.16 Webber Company has provided you with the following information concerning its shareholders' equity:

- Common stock, $1 par value, 1,000,000 shares authorized, 650,000 shares issued, 600,000 shares outstanding. The average additional paid-in capital was $30 per share when the shares were issued.
- Preferred stock, $100 par value, 500,000 shares authorized, 350,000 shares issued and outstanding. There is no additional paid-in capital on preferred shares. The preferred stock pays a 6 percent dividend and is cumulative.
- The beginning balance of retained earnings was $1,455,000. Dividends were declared during the year. The common stock dividend was $1.50 per share. The net income for the period was $5,980,500. Treasury stock was purchased during the year for $20 per share.

Prepare the shareholders' equity section of the balance sheet for Webber.

LO 1 E18.17 Devona Enterprises began fiscal 2010 on January 1 with 1 million shares of common stock authorized and 300,000 shares issued and outstanding. The par value of the common stock is $0.50 per share and the additional paid-in capital was $5,037,500 on January 1, 2010. On March 15, Devona issued an additional 50,000 shares of common stock for $21 per share. On October 31, Devona purchased 10,000 shares of common stock for $19 per share to be held as treasury stock. Show how these events would be reported on the 2010 Statement of Owners' Equity.

LO 1 E18.18 Sinason Company is authorized to issue 2 million shares of common stock. At the beginning of 2010 it had 450,000 shares of common stock issued and 400,000 shares outstanding. The Common Stock account had a balance of $112,500 while the Additional Paid-in Capital account had a balance of $8,820,000. The Treasury Stock account had a balance of $750,000. During 2010 Sinason reissued all the treasury stock for $20 per share. Show how these events would be reported on the 2010 Statement of Owners' Equity.

LO 2 LO 3 E18.19 Phelan Enterprises has a building that cost $987,000 when it was purchased five years ago. This building is being depreciated using the straight-line depreciation method over its useful life of 20 years. Recently the building was appraised for $1,000,000. What amount would be shown on the external balance sheet? Why? What amount(s) do you believe is important for management to understand? Why?

LO 2 LO 3 E18.20 Youngberg Company owns several acres of land that were recently appraised at $1.5 million. Youngberg purchased this land 10 years ago at a cost of $150,000. What amount should Youngberg show on its external balance sheet? Why? What amount should Youngberg report on its internal balance sheet? Why?

Problems

P18.1 LO 2 The following list of accounts was provided by Churyk Transportation Corporation, which has an April 30 fiscal year-end. Using these accounts, prepare a balance sheet for Churyk Transportation Corporation for fiscal 2010.

Accounts Payable	$ 15,600
Accounts Receivable	25,650
Accumulated Depreciation, Equipment	57,450
Accumulated Depreciation, Buildings	66,800
Accumulated Depreciation, Trucks	780,050
Allowance for Uncollectible Accounts	4,700
Equipment	140,500
Buildings	137,500
Cash	39,650
Common Stock	250,000
Installment Note Payable, Long-Term	342,700
Interest Payable	17,150
Investment in BR, Inc., Common Stock	17,500
Land	57,850
Mortgage Payable	44,150
Trade Notes Payable	58,500
Payroll Taxes Payable	7,450
Prepaid Insurance	18,250
Retained Earnings	?
Salaries and Wages Payable	13,400
Supplies	8,900
Temporary Investments (trading securities)	60,750
Trucks	1,392,700

LO 2 LO 3 **P18.2** The following list of accounts is from the general ledger of Mantzke Company. Prepare an income statement, the retained earnings portion of the statement of shareholders' equity, and a balance sheet for the fiscal year ended December 31, 2010. Ignore income taxes.

Cash	$ 234,000
Sales	16,600,000
Marketable Securities (trading)	306,000
Cost of Goods Sold	10,200,000
Investment in Ford Motor Company Bonds	558,000
Investment in General Motors Company Common Stock	664,000
Notes Payable, due in 120 days	180,000
Accounts Payable	950,000
Selling and Administrative Expenses	5,800,000
Interest Revenue	74,560
Land	620,000
Buildings	2,080,000
Dividends Payable	320,000
Dividend Revenue	61,440
Accrued Liabilities	172,000
Accounts Receivable	870,000
Accumulated Depreciation, Buildings	304,000
Allowance for Uncollectible Accounts	50,000
Interest Expense	422,000
Inventory	1,194,000
Gain on Sale of Equipment	160,000
Prior Period Adjustment of Underreported Expenses (net of tax of $84,000)	196,000
Long-Term Notes Payable	1,800,000
Discount on Notes Payable	20,000
Equipment	1,200,000
Bonds Payable	2,200,000
Premium on Bonds Payable	45,000
Accumulated Depreciation, Equipment	80,000
Copyrights and Patents	675,000
Treasury Stock	382,000
Retained Earnings (January 1, 2008)	404,000
Preferred Stock	800,000
Common Stock	1,180,000
Additional Paid-in Capital	160,000
Prepaid Assets	120,000

LO 1 LO 2 **P18.3** Refer to the annual report of Pepsico, Inc. (**www.pepsico.com**), and answer the following questions:

A. What is the total amount of current assets, and what types of assets are classified as current?
B. What is the total amount of long-term assets, and what types of assets are classified as long term?
C. What is the total amount of current liabilities, and what types of liabilities are classified as current?
D. What is the total amount of long-term liabilities, and what types of liabilities are classified as long term?
E. How did the company value its inventories?
F. What depreciation method did it use?
G. Did the company report any items as other assets or other liabilities? If so, what were they?
H. What is the composition of its shareholders' equity?
I. Did the company report comprehensive income during the last period?
J. Does the company show a deficit in retained earnings?
K. Did the company issue stock or purchase treasury stock during the last period?
L. Did the company declare dividends during the last period?
M. Is the company's financial position better or worse than last period? Why or why not?
N. Is the company a good investment? Why or why not?

LO 1 LO 2 **P18.4** Refer to the annual report of Dell Computer (**www.dell.com**) and answer the following questions:

A. What is the total amount of current assets, and what types of assets are classified as current?
B. What is the total amount of long-term assets, and what types of assets are classified as long term?

C. What is the total amount of current liabilities, and what types of liabilities are classified as current?
D. What is the total amount of long-term liabilities, and what types of liabilities are classified as long term?
E. How did the company value its inventories?
F. What depreciation method did it use?
G. Did the company report any items as other assets or other liabilities? If so, what were they?
H. What is the composition of its shareholders' equity?
I. Did the company report comprehensive income during the last period?
J. Does the company show a deficit in retained earnings?
K. Did the company issue stock or purchase treasury stock during the last period?
L. Did the company declare dividends during the last period?
M. Is the company's financial position better or worse than last period? Why or why not?
N. Is the company a good investment? Why or why not?

LO 1 LO 2 **P18.5** Refer to the annual report of Walt Disney Company (**www.disney.com**) and answer the following questions:

A. What is the total amount of current assets, and what types of assets are classified as current?
B. What is the total amount of long-term assets, and what types of assets are classified as long term?
C. What is the total amount of current liabilities, and what types of liabilities are classified as current?
D. What is the total amount of long-term liabilities, and what types of liabilities are classified as long term?
E. How did the company value its inventories?
F. What depreciation method did it use?
G. Did the company report any items as other assets or other liabilities? If so, what were they?
H. What is the composition of its shareholders' equity?
I. Did the company report comprehensive income during the last period?
J. Does the company show a deficit in retained earnings?
K. Did the company issue stock or purchase treasury stock during the last period?
L. Did the company declare dividends during the last period?
M. Is the company's financial position better or worse than last period? Why or why not?
N. Is the company a good investment? Why or why not?

LO 2 **P18.6** Refer to Of Interest, p. 509. Using that diagram and explanation, describe how/why the following items are reported on the balance sheet.

a. Cash
b. Accounts receivable
c. Inventory
d. Available-for-sale securities
e. Buildings

LO 2 **P18.7** The following alphabetic list of accounts was adopted from a recent PepsiCo annual report. Use these accounts to create PepsiCo's balance sheet.

Accounts and notes receivable	$2,999
Accounts payable and other current liabilities	5,599
Accumulated other comprehensive loss	886
Amortizable intangible assets	598
Capital in excess of par value	618
Cash and cash equivalents	1,280
Common stock, par value $1\frac{2}{3}$ cents	30
Deferred income tax liabilities	1,216
Goodwill	3,909
Income taxes payable	99
Inventories	1,541
Long-term debt obligations	2,397
Other assets	5,759
Other intangible assets	933
Other long-term liabilities	4,099
Preferred stock, no par value	41

Prepaid expenses and other current assets	$ 654
Property, plant, and equipment, net	8,149
Repurchased common stock	4,920
Repurchased preferred stock	90
Retained earnings	18,730
Short-term investments	2,165
Short-term obligations	1,054

LO 2 **P18.8** Linden Company provided the following information:

Current assets	$ 6,930
Current liabilities	6,413
Liquid assets	2,001
Total assets	25,327
Total liabilities	13,453

Required:

A. Calculate the current and quick ratios.
B. Assume that management misclassified some of its investments as trading securities when in fact these securities should have been classified as held-to-maturity securities. Therefore, the liquid assets should be only $920. What is the impact on the current and quick ratios?
C. Why is investment classification important for external financial statement users?

LO 1 LO 2 **P18.9** Assume you have recently been hired to provide investment advice to the manager of Encampment Company. The company has excess cash that it needs to invest, but the manager does not understand how to read financial statements. Write a memo to the manager describing how to read and interpret a statement of owners' equity and a balance sheet.

LO 1 **P18.10** Gfeller Enterprises began fiscal 2010 with the following shareholders' equity information:

- Common stock shares issued 39,598,900, $0.01 par value, paid-in capital in excess of par value, $640,078,000.
- Retained earnings deficit balance, ($25,436,000).
- Treasury stock shares held 2,549,041, cost $38,235,615.

During the period, Gfeller issued 15,000 shares for $16.50 per share and reissued 188,549 treasury stock shares at $19.00 per share. Gfeller had a net income of $77,508,000 during fiscal 2010 and declared dividends of $23,719,000. Determine the ending balances of the shareholders' equity accounts.

Cases

C18.1 LO 1  Refer to the annual report of the company you selected in Chapter 1 (C1.1), and answer the following questions:

A. What is the total amount of current assets, and what types of assets are classified as current?
B. What is the total amount of long-term assets, and what types of assets are classified as long term?
C. What is the total amount of current liabilities, and what types of liabilities are classified as current?
D. What is the total amount of long-term liabilities, and what types of liabilities are classified as long term?
E. How did the company value its inventories?
F. What depreciation method did it use?
G. Did the company report any items as other assets or other liabilities? If so, what were they?
H. What is the composition of its shareholders' equity?
I. Did the company report comprehensive income during the last period?
J. Does the company show a deficit in retained earnings?
K. Did the company issue stock or purchase treasury stock during the last period?
L. Did the company declare dividends during the last period?
M. Is the company's financial position better or worse than last period? Why or why not?
N. Is the company a good investment? Why or why not?

LO 2 **C18.2** The following balance sheet of Bennett Company for fiscal 2010 contains several errors. Identify and determine how to correct each error.

BENNETT COMPANY
Statement of Finances
For the Period Ending March 31, 2010

Debits		
Current assets:		
Cash	$ 12,000	
Accounts receivable, net	29,000	
Prepaid rent	6,000	
Total current assets	$ 47,000	
Long-term assets:		
Land	$ 50,000	
Patents, net	45,000	
Inventory	75,000	
Buildings	280,000	
Investment in Durk bonds	59,000	
Discount on bonds payable	20,000	
Diamond mine	261,000	
Total long-term assets	$790,000	
Total assets	$837,000	
Credits		
Current liabilities:		
Accounts payable	$ 35,000	
Note payable, due June 1, 2010	50,000	
Income tax payable	28,000	
Total current liabilities	$113,000	
Long-term liabilities:		
Accumulated depreciation, buildings	$ 32,000	
Mortgage payable	65,000	
Accumulated depletion	26,000	
Bonds payable	250,000	
Total long-term liabilities	$373,000	
Owners' equity:		
Common stock	$200,000	
Additional paid-in capital	125,000	
Retained earnings	51,000	
Treasury stock	25,000	
Total owners' equity	$401,000	
Total liabilities and owners' equity	$887,000	

Critical Thinking

CT18.1 LO 1 LO 2 Write a paper describing in detail how the income statement, statement of owners' equity, and balance sheet are related.

CT18.2 LO 2 Historical cost is a basic concept of accounting. Describe the concept of historical cost, and evaluate each of the items found on a typical balance sheet to determine if it is reported at historical cost.

Ethical Challenges

EC18.1 LO 1 LO 2 Assume you are an auditor and are concerned about how a client is reporting its marketable securities. You know that under certain circumstances marketable securities must be reported at market value. In addition, you realize that if the marketable securities are classified as trading securities, any unrealized gains are shown on the income statement while unrealized gains on available-for-sale securities are disclosed in the owners' equity section of the balance sheet. Your client has recently reclassified a large amount of marketable securities from available-for-sale to trading securities. This reclassification increased its current ratio from 1.9 to 2.3. The company has a large loan outstanding that requires a current ratio of 2.0. How will you determine if the securities are correctly classified? How will the various stakeholders be affected by your decision?

LO 1 LO 2 **EC18.2** Keys, Inc., compared the cost of its marketable securities to their market value at the end of 2010. This comparison follows:

	Cost	Market
Marketable securities	$45,900,000	$43,800,000

Management would like to classify these securities as available-for-sale and, therefore, report the unrealized loss on the statement of shareholders' equity rather than the income statement. How should the auditor decide if the securities are "trading" or "available-for-sale"? What are the advantages and disadvantages of reporting unrealized losses on the statement of shareholders' equity rather than the income statement? How will the various stakeholders be affected by this decision?

Computer Applications

CA18.1 LO 2 The following list of accounts was taken from the 2010 annual report of Madlinger Corporation:

Accounts Payable	$ 4,669,902
Accounts Receivable	664,065
Accrued Liabilities	1,639,292
Accrued Rent Obligation Long-Term	861,421
Accrued Store Closing Costs	1,134,714
Accumulated Depreciation and Amortization	8,783,914
Additional Paid-in Capital	25,032,637
Cash	261,394
Common Stock	37,688
Construction in Progress	904,560
Deferred Tax Asset	478,200
Furniture and Fixtures	4,727,134
Leasehold Improvements	10,633,116
Leasehold Interests, Net	953,645
Long-Term Debt	2,200,000
Merchandise Inventory	13,134,317
Other Assets	65,005
Other Equipment	1,432,871
Prepaid Expenses	493,148
Retained Deficit	10,612,113

Required: Use a computer spreadsheet program.

A. Arrange the accounts in proper balance sheet order and show the equality of assets with liabilities and shareholders' equity. (Hint: If you are unfamiliar with some of the accounts, use the balance sheet equation as an aid.)
B. Determine the total dollar amount of current assets.
C. Determine the total dollar amount of long-term assets.
D. Determine the total dollar amount of current liabilities.
E. Determine the total dollar amount of long-term liabilities.
F. Determine the total dollar amount of shareholders' equity.
G. Repeat requirements (*A*) through (*F*) above assuming that all accounts increase by 15 percent.

LO 2 **CA18.2** The following list of accounts was adopted from the 2010 annual report of Gilbert Stores, Inc. Amounts are shown in thousands.

Accumulated Depreciation	$ 911,996
Additional Paid-In Capital	622,634
Buildings and Leasehold Improvements	1,162,120
Buildings under Capital Leases	29,416
Buildings under Construction	13,977
Capital Lease Obligations	31,621
Cash and Cash Equivalents	51,244
Commercial Paper Current	145,276
Common Stock, Class A	1,090
Common Stock, Class B	40
Current Portion of Capital Lease Obligation	2,242
Current Portion of Long-Term Debt	65,061

Deferred Income Taxes	$ 282,648
Federal and State Income Taxes	54,011
Furniture, Fixtures, and Equipment	1,583,380
Investments and Other Assets	52,110
Land and Land Improvements	44,573
Long-Term Debt	1,238,293
Merchandise Inventories	1,299,944
Other Current Assets	8,976
Preferred Stock	440
Retained Earnings	1,457,443
Trade Accounts Receivable, Net	1,096,530
Trade and Other Accounts Payable	529,475

Required: Use a computer spreadsheet program.

A. Prepare a classified balance sheet and prove that total assets equal total liabilities plus total shareholders' equity. (Hint: If you are unfamiliar with some of the accounts, use the balance sheet equation as an aid.)

B. Determine the balance in Retained Earnings if total assets increase by 5 percent, total liabilities remain the same, and shareholders' equity other than retained earnings remains the same.

Visit the text Online Learning Center at **www.mhhe.com/ainsworth6e** for additional problem material that accompanies this chapter.

CHAPTER NINETEEN

19

Company Performance: Cash Flows

Learning Objectives

LO 1 Discuss the purpose of and prepare the operating section of the statement of cash flows using the direct method.

LO 2 Explain the purpose of and prepare the operating section of the statement of cash flows using the indirect method.

LO 3 Identify the purpose of and prepare the investing section of the statement of cash flows.

LO 4 Explain the purpose of and prepare the financing section of the statement of cash flows.

LO 5 Describe the purpose of other cash flow statement disclosures and the calculation of cash flow per share.

In previous chapters, we examined the income statement, the statement of owners' equity, and the balance sheet. In this chapter, we examine the statement of cash flows—the fourth financial statement required by GAAP. The statement of cash flows provides an additional link between the accrual-based income statement and the balance sheet because the statement of cash flows shows the changes in cash from operations. In addition the statement of cash flows indicates the cash inflows and cash outflows from investing and financing (capital resource) activities. Users need to comprehend the elements included on the cash flow statement so that they can make informed decisions regarding the liquidity and solvency of the reporting company.

GAAP and the Statement of Cash Flows

Comparatively speaking, the statement of cash flows is a new statement. Prior to its adoption in 1987, companies prepared a statement of changes in financial position. That statement was designed to show the sources and uses of working capital (current assets minus current liabilities) provided to, or used by, a company during the period of time covered by the income statement. Due to the variety of methods used to prepare the statement of changes in financial position and the resulting confusion that existed among statement users, the Financial Accounting Standards Board determined that a statement showing cash flows would be more useful.

Purpose of the Statement of Cash Flows

The statement of cash flows has four primary purposes. According to the FASB, the statement of cash flows is useful to:

- Assess the entity's ability to generate positive future net cash flows. Operating activities must provide sufficient net cash flows to support the firm's future operations. The relationship between sales and the operating cash flows from year to year provides insights into the firm's ability to sustain positive net cash flows.
- Assess the entity's ability to meet its obligations and pay dividends, and its need for external financing. The statement of cash flows provides a clear picture of the sources and uses of a company's cash flows. It indicates whether the firm has the ability to generate the cash needed to meet its obligations to its creditors and owners.
- Assess the reasons for differences between income and associated cash receipts and payments. The statement of cash flows provides information that highlights the specific reasons for the difference between accounting income and cash flows from operations.
- Assess both the cash and noncash aspects of the entity's investing and financing transactions during the period. The statement of cash flows specifically identifies and discloses significant noncash investing and financing activities undertaken by the firm to provide complete information about the events that have future cash flow implications.

Sections of the Statement of Cash Flows

Recall from previous chapters that the statement of cash flows is divided into three distinct sections: operating, investing, and financing. These sections represent the basic and significant functions of any business enterprise and the amounts of cash flowing in and out of the enterprise as a result of the business activities. In addition, the information contained in these sections achieves the four purposes of the statement of cash flows presented previously. Exhibit 19.1 shows the basic functions of business and how they are classified on the statement of cash flows. We look at each of the cash flow sections in turn.

Operating Activities

As Exhibit 19.1 illustrates, operating activities involve transactions that result from the earnings process of the company. Cash inflows from operating activities are primarily from customers,

OF INTEREST What Is the SEC?

The SEC consists of five presidentially appointed commissioners, with staggered five-year terms. One of them is designated by the president as chairman of the commission—the agency's chief executive. By law, no more than three of the commissioners may belong to the same political party, ensuring nonpartisanship. The agency's functional responsibilities are organized into four divisions and 19 offices, each of which is headquartered in Washington, D.C. It is the responsibility of the SEC to (1) interpret federal securities laws; (2) issue new rules and amend existing rules; (3) oversee the inspection of securities firms, brokers, investment advisers, and ratings agencies; (4) oversee private regulatory organizations in the securities, accounting, and auditing fields; and (5) coordinate U.S. securities regulation with federal, state, and foreign authorities.

Crucial to the SEC's effectiveness in each of these areas is its enforcement authority. Each year the SEC brings hundreds of civil enforcement actions against individuals and companies for violation of the securities laws. Typical infractions include insider trading, accounting fraud, and providing false or misleading information about securities and the companies that issue them. Even though it is the primary overseer and regulator of the U.S. securities markets, the SEC works closely with many other institutions. The SEC must consult with Congress, other federal departments and agencies, the self-regulatory organizations (e.g., the stock exchanges), state securities regulators, and various private sector organizations. In particular, the chairman of the SEC, together with the chairman of the Federal Reserve, the secretary of the Treasury, and the chairman of the Commodities Futures Trading Commission, serves as a member of the president's Working Group on Financial Markets.

The SEC's Division of Corporation Finance oversees corporate disclosure of important information to the investing public. Corporations are required to comply with regulations pertaining to disclosure that must be made when stock is initially sold and then on a continuing and periodic basis. The Division of Corporation Finance reviews documents that publicly held companies are required to file with the commission. The documents include (1) registration statements for newly offered securities; (2) annual and quarterly filings (Forms 10-K and 10-Q); (3) proxy materials sent to shareholders before an annual meeting; (4) annual reports to shareholders; (5) documents concerning tender offers (a tender offer is an offer to buy a large number of shares of a corporation, usually at a premium above the current market price); and (6) filings related to mergers and acquisitions.

Corporation Finance provides administrative interpretations of the Securities Act of 1933, the Securities Exchange Act of 1934, and the Trust Indenture Act of 1939, and recommends regulations to implement these statutes. Working closely with the Office of the Chief Accountant, the division monitors the activities of the accounting profession, particularly the Financial Accounting Standards Board (FASB), that result in the formulation of generally accepted accounting principles (GAAP). Increasingly, the division also monitors the use by U.S. registrants of International Financial Reporting Standards (IFRS), promulgated by the International Accounting Standards Board.

Taken from: www.sec.gov

EXHIBIT 19.1
Cash versus Working Capital Flows

Business Activities	Inflows	Outflows
Operating activities	Collections from customers Collections of interest Collections of dividends	Payments to suppliers of goods and services Payments to employees Payments for interest Payments for taxes
Investing activities	Proceeds from sales of long-term assets Collections of loans made to other entities Proceeds from sales of short-term investments	Purchases of long-term assets Loans made to other entities Purchases of short-term investments
Financing activities	Proceeds from issuance of debt Proceeds from issuance of stock	Payment of long-term debt Purchase of treasury stock Payment of cash dividends

but cash also increases due to interest and dividends received by the company. Cash outflows from operating activities result from payments made for operating expenses, including the purchase of inventory.

Notice that cash received from dividends is an operating activity, but cash paid for dividends is a financing activity. Dividends received are earned income from investments, while dividends paid are not expenses of the business; that is, they are not incurred in an attempt to generate revenues. Rather, dividends paid reflect the decision about when and how to distribute earnings to the company's owners.

Investing Activities

Investing activities usually involve acquiring and disposing of property, plant, and equipment; other long-term investments; and short-term or temporary investments that are not considered cash equivalents. For example, Apple classifies financial instruments as cash equivalents, "all highly liquid investments with maturities of three months or less." Other short-term investments owned by Apple would not be considered "cash equivalents." Exhibit 19.1 shows that disposing of these assets results in cash inflows, while purchasing them results in cash outflows.

Financing Activities

Financing activities involve borrowing from and repaying creditors, raising funds from owners, and distributing funds to owners that are either a return on or a return of investment. Exhibit 19.1 shows that issuing debt and issuing stock both result in cash inflows, while repayment of debt and liquidating equity result in cash outflows.

Noncash Investing and Financing Activities

In addition to the types of cash flow events shown in Exhibit 19.1, companies also present noncash investing and financing events either on the statement of cash flows or in the notes to the financial statements. For example, if Apple issues 100,000 shares of its common stock in exchange for a building, this would be reported as a noncash investing/financing event.

It is necessary to show financial statement users the noncash means of financing that the company uses to acquire its assets because of their future cash flow impact. The example above may have cash flow implications because of the related dividends that Apple may pay in the future. Or, if a company buys land by issuing a noninterest-bearing payment note, the note will require a cash outflow in the future.

Operating Activities: Cash Flows

The events represented in the operating activities section of the statement of cash flows may be presented in either the direct or indirect format. The **direct format** shows the actual cash inflows and outflows from each operating activity reported on the income statement. The **indirect format** shows the differences between accrual-based net income and cash flows from operations. Note that the only difference between the direct and indirect formats concerns the operating activities section and that, regardless of the format used, the amount of net cash flows from operating activities is the same.

To illustrate all the components and calculations of cash flows, we use a company called TOONZ. TOONZ is a company that PCs to Go is interested in purchasing. It is a merchandising company organized to sell personal music delivery devices. We also examine Apple's statement of cash flows. Exhibit 19.2 shows TOONZ's statement of cash flows prepared using the direct format, while Exhibit 19.3 shows the statement of cash flows using the indirect format. The corresponding income statement, statement of retained earnings, and balance sheets of TOONZ are illustrated in Exhibits 19.4, 19.5, and 19.6, respectively. You may want to flag these exhibits as we refer to them throughout this chapter.

Brief Comparison of the Direct and Indirect Methods

As the statement of cash flows in Exhibit 19.2 illustrates, one advantage of the direct format is that it clearly shows the amounts of cash received by or paid for operating activities. However, one disadvantage is that the FASB requires companies to disclose, either on the statement or in the notes, a reconciliation of accrual-based net income to the amount of cash flows from operations to achieve the fourth purpose of the statement of cash flows. This reconciliation (shown on the bottom of Exhibit 19.2) is essentially the same information shown in the indirect format for the statement of cash flows in Exhibit 19.3. Therefore, one advantage of the indirect format is that it clearly shows the difference between net income and cash flows from operations.

EXHIBIT 19.2
Statement of Cash Flows—Direct Method

TOONZ
Statement of Cash Flows (Direct Method)
For the Year Ended December 31, 2010

Net cash flows from operating activities:	
Cash received from customers	$100,500
Cash received from renters	750
Cash paid for inventory	(58,125)
Cash paid for insurance	(2,700)
Cash paid for wages	(4,800)
Cash paid for miscellaneous expenses	(4,200)
Cash paid for income taxes	(6,075)
Cash paid for interest	(960)
Net cash flows from operating activities	$ 24,390
Net cash flows from investing activities:	
Cash received from sale of trading securities	$ 1,950
Cash received from sale of equipment	800
Cash paid for building	(25,650)
Cash paid for equipment	(6,050)
Net cash flows from investing activities	$(28,950)
Net cash flows from financing activities:	
Cash received from short-term note payable	$ 150
Cash received from bond issues	14,100
Cash paid for treasury stock	(12,500)
Cash paid for dividends	(5,000)
Net cash flows from financing activities	$ (3,250)
Net change in cash during 2010	$ (7,810)
Add beginning balance of cash	42,250
Ending balance of cash	$ 34,440
Other investing and financing activities not requiring cash:	
Purchase of building with preferred stock	$ 12,150
Reconciliation of net income to cash flows from operations:	
Net income	$ 13,650
Adjustments to reconcile net income to net cash flows from operations:	
Depreciation expense—buildings	5,850
Depreciation expense—equipment	3,150
Amortization expense—patent	1,050
Amortization of discount on note payable	15
Gain on sale of trading securities	(900)
Loss on sale of equipment	2,250
Increase in accounts receivable, net	(8,100)
Increase in inventory	(600)
Decrease in prepaid insurance	300
Increase in accounts payable	8,175
Increase in rent received in advance	150
Decrease in wages payable	(300)
Decrease in interest payable	(75)
Decrease in taxes payable	(225)
Net cash flows from operating activities	$ 24,390

EXHIBIT 19.3
Statement of Cash Flows—Indirect Method

TOONZ **Statement of Cash Flows (Indirect Method)** **For the Year Ended December 31, 2010**	
Net cash flows from operating activities:	
Net income	$13,650
Adjustments to reconcile net income to net cash flows from operations:	
Depreciation expense—building	5,850
Depreciation expense—equipment	3,150
Amortization expense—patent	1,050
Amortization of discount on note payable	15
Gain on sale of trading securities	(900)
Loss on sale of equipment	2,250
Increase in accounts receivable, net	(8,100)
Increase in inventory	(600)
Decrease in prepaid insurance	300
Increase in accounts payable	8,175
Increase in rent received in advance	150
Decrease in wages payable	(300)
Decrease in interest payable	(75)
Decrease in taxes payable	(225)
Net cash flows from operating activities	$24,390
Net cash flows from investing activities:	
Cash received from sale of trading securities	$ 1,950
Cash received from sale of equipment	800
Cash paid for building	(25,650)
Cash paid for equipment	(6,050)
Net cash flows from investing activities	$(28,950)
Net cash flows from financing activities:	
Cash received from short-term note payable	$ 150
Cash received from bond issues	14,100
Cash paid for treasury stock	(12,500)
Cash paid for dividends	(5,000)
Net cash flows from financing activities	$(13,250)
Net change in cash during 2010	$ (7,810)
Add beginning balance of cash	42,250
Ending balance of cash	$ 34,440
Other investing and financing activities not requiring cash:	
Purchase of building with preferred stock	$ 12,150
Additional disclosures:	
Cash paid for interest	$ 960
Cash paid for taxes	$ 6,075

EXHIBIT 19.4
Income Statement

TOONZ Income Statement For the Year Ended December 31, 2010		
Sales		$109,500
Cost of goods sold		65,700
Gross margin		$ 43,800
Operating expenses:		
Wages	$4,500	
Insurance	3,000	
Uncollectible accounts	900	
Miscellaneous	4,200	
Depreciation—building	5,850	
Depreciation—equipment	3,150	
Amortization—patent	1,050	22,650
Operating income		$ 21,150
Other revenues and gains:		
Rent revenue	$ 600	
Gain on sale of trading securities	900	1,500
Other expenses and losses:		
Interest expense	$ 900	
Loss on sale of equipment	2,250	$ (3,150)
Income from continuing operations		$ 19,500
Income tax expense		5,850
Net income		$ 13,650

EXHIBIT 19.5
Statement of Retained Earnings

TOONZ Statement of Retained Earnings For the Year Ended December 31, 2010	
Retained earnings, January 1, 2010	$85,385
Add net income	13,650
	$99,035
Less dividends declared	4,950
Retained earnings, December 31, 2010	$94,085

Calculation of Operating Cash Flows: Direct Method

As Exhibit 19.2 illustrates, the direct format indicates the amounts of cash received from customers and the other sources of operating cash, such as dividends and interest. In addition, it shows how much cash the company paid for interest, taxes, and other operating activities. In Chapters 8 and 10, we calculated cash flows using the direct format as we estimated the cash received from customers and the cash paid for operating activities. We review this process of determining operating cash flows next.

To determine the cash flows for a particular operating item on the income statement, it is necessary to relate that item to a balance sheet account because the income-generating and cash flow activities of the company cause changes in the operating balance sheet accounts of the company. For example, if a company had no sales on account, it would not have an Accounts Receivable account. But companies that have sales on account must have an

EXHIBIT 19.6
Comparative Balance Sheets

TOONZ **Balance Sheets** **December 31, 2010 and 2009**		
	2010	**2009**
Assets		
Cash	$ 34,440	$ 42,250
Trading securities, net	750	1,800
Accounts receivable, net	22,410	14,310
Inventory	20,100	19,500
Prepaid insurance	450	750
Building	150,450	112,650
Accumulated depreciation, building	(45,900)	(40,050)
Equipment	51,900	50,850
Accumulated depreciation, equipment	(16,650)	(15,450)
Patent, net	11,700	12,750
Total assets	$229,650	$199,360
Liabilities and Owners' Equity		
Liabilities:		
Accounts payable	$ 24,225	$ 16,050
Notes payable	300	150
Rent received in advance	600	450
Interest payable	225	300
Taxes payable	425	650
Wages payable	750	1,050
Dividends payable	100	150
Long-term notes payable	750	750
Discount on notes payable	(60)	(75)
Bonds payable	13,500	0
Premium on bonds payable	600	0
Total liabilities	$ 41,415	$ 19,475
Owners' Equity:		
Preferred stock	$ 36,500	$ 30,000
Additional paid-in capital, preferred stock	14,600	8,950
Common stock	23,000	23,000
Additional paid-in capital, common stock	32,550	32,550
Retained earnings	94,085	85,385
Treasury stock	(12,500)	0
Total owners' equity	$188,235	$179,885
Total liabilities and owners' equity	$229,650	$199,360

Accounts Receivable account because of the timing difference between sales and collections of sales. Companies use the beginning and ending balances of a given balance sheet account, along with the related revenue or expense amount from the income statement, to determine the related cash flows for the period.

Why Don't Revenues Equal Cash Inflows?

Remember that a company's revenues shown on its income statement might differ from its cash inflows from operations for two reasons: (1) the revenue is earned before the cash is collected or (2) the cash is collected before the revenue is earned.

For example, TOONZ allows its customers to charge purchases on account (accounts receivable) and it accepts rent payments in advance from customers (rent received in advance), as noted on its balance sheets in Exhibit 19.6. Thus we would expect the cash inflows from customers to be different from the amount of revenues earned during the period because revenues would be recognized before the cash is actually received, when customers charge on account, and after cash is received when customers pay in advance.

Revenues, Current Assets, and Cash Inflows The accounts receivable on the balance sheets are shown net of the related allowance for doubtful accounts, so cash receipts from customers is calculated as:

	Beginning balance of Accounts Receivable, net
+	Net sales on account during the period
=	Maximum amount of cash owed by customers
−	Uncollectible accounts expense
−	**Cash collections from customers during the period**
=	Ending balance of Accounts Receivable, net[1]

Using the information in Exhibits 19.4 and 19.6 and solving for the unknown cash collection results in the following:

$ 14,310	Beginning balance (Exhibit 19.6)
109,500	Sales (Exhibit 19.4)
$123,810	Maximum collectible
(900)	Uncollectible accounts (Exhibit 19.4)
(100,500)	**Cash received from customers (Exhibit 19.2)[2]**
$ 22,410	Ending balance

Therefore, cash collections from customers equal $100,500. Take a moment to locate these items in the appropriate exhibits. Companies follow this approach to determine the amount of cash received from other operating sources such as dividends, interest, and rent. Recall we did this in Chapter 10.

Enhance Your Understanding

Estimate Apple's cash collections from customers during fiscal 2008 (see the Appendix).

Answer: $31,694 million. See p. 544 for calculations.

Revenues, Current Liabilities, and Cash Inflows In addition to cash receipts from accounts receivable customers, TOONZ also receives rent from customers. We determine the amount of cash received from rental customers as:

	Beginning balance of Rent Received in Advance
+	**Cash received from renters during the period**
=	Maximum rent owed to renters
−	Rent revenues earned during the period
=	Ending balance of Rent Received in Advance

[1] If the Accounts Receivable account is separate from an Allowance for Uncollectible Accounts, then the following is used:

	Beginning Accounts Receivable
+	Net sales on account
=	Maximum amount due from customers
−	Accounts written off during the period
−	Cash collections from customers
=	Ending Accounts Receivable

[2] Cash received from customers is $123,810 − $900 − $22,410 = $100,500.

Using the information in Exhibits 19.4 and 19.6 and solving for the unknown cash amount, we determine cash received from rental customers as:

$ 450	Beginning balance (Exhibit 19.6)
750	**Cash received from renters (Exhibit 19.2)[3]**
$1,200	Maximum rent owed
(600)	Rent revenue (Exhibit 19.4)
$ 600	Ending balance (Exhibit 19.6)

Why Don't Expenses Equal Cash Outflows?

Recall that a company's expenses can differ from the actual amounts of cash paid for expense items for two reasons: (1) the expenses are incurred before the cash is paid or (2) the expenses are incurred after the cash is paid.

Expenses, Current Assets, and Cash Outflows TOONZ pays for its insurance in advance and, therefore, has a current asset called Prepaid Insurance. We determine the amount of cash paid for insurance using the following format:

	Beginning balance of Prepaid Insurance
+	**Cash paid for insurance during the period**
=	Maximum insurance rights available
−	Insurance expense during the period
=	Ending balance of Prepaid Insurance

Using the information from Exhibits 19.4 and 19.6 and solving for the unknown cash amount results in the following:

$ 750	Beginning balance (Exhibit 19.6)
2,700	**Cash paid for insurance (Exhibit 19.2)[4]**
$3,450	Maximum insurance available
(3,000)	Insurance expense (Exhibit 19.4)
$ 450	Ending balance (Exhibit 19.6)

Expenses, Current Liabilities, and Cash Outflows Many expenses are incurred prior to the cash payment. For example, TOONZ's employees earn wages prior to payment; therefore, TOONZ has a Wages Payable account. To determine the amount of cash paid for wages, we use the following format:

	Beginning balance of Wages Payable
+	Wages expense during the period
=	Maximum amount of cash owed to employees
−	**Cash paid to employees during the period**
=	Ending balance of Wages Payable

Using the information from Exhibits 19.4 and 19.6, we find that TOONZ paid $4,800 in wages during the year:

$1,050	Beginning balance (Exhibit 19.6)
4,500	Wages expense (Exhibit 19.4)
$5,550	Maximum owed to employees
(4,800)	**Cash paid to employees (Exhibit 19.2)[5]**
$ 750	Ending balance (Exhibit 19.6)

[3] Cash received from renters is $600 + $600 = $1,200; $1,200 − $450 = $750.
[4] Cash paid for insurance is $450 + $3,000 = $3,450; $3,450 − $750 = $2,700.
[5] Cash paid to employees is $5,550 − $750 = $4,800.

Likewise, cash paid for income taxes is determined as follows:

	Beginning balance of Taxes Payable
+	Tax expense during the period
=	Maximum amount of cash owed for taxes
−	**Cash paid for taxes during the period**
=	Ending balance of Taxes Payable

Based on this relationship, we can determine cash paid for income taxes using the information from Exhibits 19.4 and 19.6 as follows:

$ 650	Beginning balance (Exhibit 19.6)
5,850	Tax expense (Exhibit 19.4)
$6,500	Maximum taxes owed
(6,075)	**Cash paid for taxes (Exhibit 19.2)[6]**
$ 425	Ending balance (Exhibit 19.6)

Determining the amount of cash paid for interest is a little more complicated. Recall that interest expense can be greater than or less than the cash paid for interest due to discounts and premiums on long-term debt. Therefore, to determine the amount of cash paid for interest, we must analyze the Interest Payable account as well as the premium or discount accounts associated with long-term debt. For example, TOONZ has a note payable that was issued at a discount. Recall that when a note is issued at a discount, the amount of interest expense is greater than the amount of cash interest paid. (When a note is issued with a premium the interest expense is less than the cash interest paid.) Based on this information, we analyze the Interest Payable account:

	Beginning balance of Interest Payable
+	Interest expense less discount amortization (add premium amortization)
=	Maximum amount of cash owed for interest
−	**Cash paid for interest during the period**
=	Ending balance of Interest Payable

Let's locate this information in Exhibits 19.4 and 19.6. In Exhibit 19.4 we notice that interest expense for the period is $900. From Exhibit 19.6 we determine that discount amortization (decrease in Discount on Notes Payable) is $15. Therefore, the cash paid for interest during the period is:

$ 300	Beginning balance (Exhibit 19.6)
885	($900 − $15)
$1,185	Maximum interest owed
(960)	**Cash paid for interest (Exhibit 19.2)[7]**
$ 225	Ending balance (Exhibit 19.6)

Expenses, Current Assets, Current Liabilities, and Cash Outflow Because inventory is typically purchased on account, determining the amount of cash paid for inventory involves an analysis of both the Inventory and Accounts Payable accounts. For example, TOONZ purchases its inventory on account (Accounts Payable), which it records as an asset (Inventory) until it is sold. Therefore, to determine the amount of cash paid for inventory, we must determine the changes in both accounts. Recall we did these calculations in Chapter 8. We know the following relationships:

	Beginning balance of Inventory
+	Net purchases during the period
=	Maximum amount of inventory available for sale
−	Cost of goods sold
=	Ending balance of Inventory

[6] Cash paid for taxes is $6,500 − $425 = $6,075.
[7] Cash paid for interest is $1,185 − $225 = $960.

	Beginning balance of Accounts Payable
+	Net purchases during the period
=	Maximum amount of cash owed for inventory
−	**Cash paid for inventory during the period**[8]
=	Ending balance of Accounts Payable

Using the information in Exhibits 19.4 and 19.6, we find cash paid for inventory during the period in two steps. First, determine the amount of net purchases made during the period by solving for the unknown amount in the Inventory analysis. Then find the cash paid for inventory by solving for the unknown amount in the Accounts Payable analysis.

$19,500	Beginning balance of Inventory (Exhibit 19.6)
66,300	**Net purchases made during the period**[9]
$85,800	Maximum inventory available
(65,700)	Cost of goods sold (Exhibit 19.4)
$20,100	Ending balance of Inventory (Exhibit 19.6)

$16,050	Beginning balance of Accounts Payable (Exhibit 19.6)
66,300	Net purchases made during the period (above)
$82,350	Maximum owed for inventory
(58,125)	**Cash paid for inventory (Exhibit 19.2)**[10]
$24,225	Ending balance of Accounts Payable (Exhibit 19.6)

Take a moment to locate these amounts in the appropriate exhibits.

Enhance Your Understanding

Estimate the cash Apple paid for inventory during fiscal 2008 (see the Appendix).
Answer: $20,947 million. See p. 544 for calculations.

Revenues, Expenses, and Cash Flows When a company receives revenue at the same time it is recognized as earned, no current asset or current liability is created. Likewise when an expense is paid at the same time it is incurred, no current asset or current liability is created. Thus the amount of the revenue or the expense is equal to the cash inflow or outflow.

For TOONZ, there is one more operating item on the income statement that we must analyze. Miscellaneous expense incurred during the period is $4,200. How much cash was paid for miscellaneous expense during the year? Because we have analyzed all the current operating assets and current operating liabilities, we can assume that the amount of cash paid for miscellaneous expense is the same amount as the expense: $4,200. Take a moment to locate this amount on both the income statement (Exhibit 19.4) and statement of cash flows (Exhibit 19.2). The remaining operating items on the income statement are noncash items. Therefore, we have fully explained the cash flows from operating activities as Exhibit 19.2 illustrates.

Calculation of Operating Cash Flows: Indirect Method

As Exhibit 19.3 illustrates, the indirect format for the statement of cash flows presents the amount of cash generated from operations by adjusting the net income for items that cause cash from operations to differ from accrual-based net income. To present cash flows in the indirect format, also called the *reconciliation format,* companies begin with the amount of accrual-based net income and apply a series of adjustments to convert net income to cash from operations. In addition the company must disclose either on the statement of cash flows or in the notes the amount of cash paid for interest and income taxes.

[8] If the company used the net price method (see Chapter 8) and had Discounts Lost during the period, it would be added to this amount because payments would have been more than the liability recorded.
[9] Net purchases are $20,100 + $65,700 = $85,800; $85,800 − $19,500 = $66,300.
[10] Cash paid for purchases is $82,350 − $24,225 = $58,125.

The four adjustments made to net income to determine cash flows from operations using the indirect format are

- Adjustments for noncash income statement items.
- Adjustments for gains and losses.
- Adjustments for changes in noncash current operating assets.
- Adjustments for changes in current operating liabilities.

Adjustments for Noncash Income Statement Items

Noncash income statement items increase or decrease income but do not affect operating cash flows. Therefore, for any noncash expenses that reduce income but do not reduce operating cash flows, it is necessary to add them back to net income to convert net income to cash from operations. For any noncash revenues that increase net income but do not increase operating cash flows, it is necessary to deduct them from net income to convert the net income to cash from operations.

We discuss two common noncash adjustments next: (1) depreciation and amortization and (2) interest adjustments due to premiums or discounts. These items affect the amount of accrual-based net income but do not require the use or receipt of cash.

Depreciation, depletion, and amortization expense are added back to net income because these expenses do not decrease cash flows from operations.

Depreciation, Depletion, and Amortization Items such as depreciation of plant assets and amortization of intangibles are added back to net income to derive cash flows because they do not require an outlay of cash but they do reduce net income. Recall that we discussed this briefly in Chapter 16.

For example, Exhibit 19.4 indicates that TOONZ's depreciation expense for buildings was $5,850, depreciation expense for equipment was $3,150, and amortization of patents expense was $1,050. These amounts are added back to net income to determine cash flows from operations, as shown in Exhibit 19.3.

Interest Adjustments The portion of interest expense related to amortization of discounts on notes and bonds payable is also added back to net income to determine cash flows from operations. The expense is different from the actual amount of cash outflow, thus requiring a net income adjustment. This type of adjustment is necessary when a company pays interest on a note issued at a discount (premium) because the amount of interest expense is greater (less) than the actual amount of cash paid.

For example, as discussed previously, TOONZ has a note payable that was issued at a discount. Therefore, the amount of interest expense that reduces net income is greater than the cash impact of the interest. Therefore, TOONZ must add back the $15 difference to net income to determine operating cash flows, as shown in Exhibit 19.3.[11]

Adjustments for Gains and Losses

The events that generate gains and losses may affect the cash flows of the firm, but these events are either investing or financing events and are reported as such on the statement of cash flows. Therefore, it is important to remove the impact of gains and losses from accrual-based net income when converting income to cash from operations using the indirect format. Because gains increase reported net income, they must be subtracted as a net income adjustment to determine cash flows from operations. On the other hand, losses decrease reported

[11] For creditors, the amount of interest income due to the amortization of discounts on notes receivable and investments in bonds is subtracted from accrual-based net income because the amount of cash received by the creditor is less than the interest income earned during the period. Conversely, the reduction in interest income due to the amortization of premiums on investments in bonds is added to accrual-based net income because the amount of cash received by the creditor is greater than the interest income earned during the period.

A loss is added to net income because it does not decrease operating cash flows. Conversely, a gain is subtracted from net income because it does not increase operating cash flows.

net income and, therefore, must be added as a net income adjustment to determine cash flows from operations. Again, recall our discussion in Chapter 16.

For example, as shown in Exhibit 19.4, TOONZ has a $900 gain from the sale of trading securities and a loss of $2,250 from the sale of equipment.[12] On the statement of cash flows, the gain is subtracted from net income because it increased net income but did not provide operating cash flows, while the loss is added to net income because it decreased income but did not use operating cash flows (see Exhibit 19.3).

Adjustments for Changes in Noncash Current Operating Assets

The indirect format uses the changes in noncash current operating asset accounts to adjust accrual-based net income. **Noncash current operating assets** are noncash accounts that represent operating activities. Note that not all current asset accounts fall into this category. For example, trading securities, which are not cash equivalents, and nontrade notes receivables reflect investing events and, therefore, the cash flows associated with these events appear in the investing activities section of the statement of cash flows.

An increase in a noncash current operating asset during the period indicates one of two things: (1) the revenue associated with the account was greater than the amount of cash inflow or (2) the expense associated with the account was less than the cash outflow. Because the related revenues and expenses are reflected in net income at the end of the period, the increase in a noncash current operating asset must be deducted from accrual-based net income to derive the amount of cash flows from operations. Conversely, the decrease in a noncash current operating asset must be added to accrual-based net income.

Analysis of Noncash Current Operating Assets Related to Revenues TOONZ's Accounts Receivable account increased by $8,100 from the beginning to the end of the year (Exhibit 19.6). Therefore, we must deduct $8,100 from net income to determine cash flows from operations as shown in Exhibit 19.3. This adjustment is necessary because net income increased by the amount of sales ($109,500—Exhibit 19.4) and decreased by the amount of uncollectible accounts expense ($900—Exhibit 19.4), while net cash flows increased only by the amount of cash received from customers ($100,500), which we calculated previously. The increase in net income was $8,100 greater than the increase in net cash flows from operations, so this difference must be deducted from accrual-based net income to derive net cash flows from operations.

Analysis of Noncash Current Operating Assets Related to Expenses TOONZ's Prepaid Insurance account decreased by $300 during 2010 (Exhibit 19.6). Thus we must add this amount to net income to determine cash flows from operations as shown in Exhibit 19.3. This adjustment is necessary because net income decreased by the amount of insurance expense ($3,000—Exhibit 19.4), while net cash flows decreased only by the amount of cash paid for insurance ($2,700), which we calculated earlier. The decrease in net income was $300 greater than the decrease in net cash flows from operations, so this difference must be added to accrual-based net income to derive net cash flows from operations.

Based on this analysis, we can determine the net income adjustment needed due to the change in inventories. Because the Inventory account is related to an expense (cost of goods sold), the increase in the account must be deducted from net income to determine cash flows from operations.

Adjustment for Changes in Current Operating Liabilities

As in the case of current assets, the indirect format adjusts accrual-based net income for changes in current operating liabilities to derive cash flows from operating activities.

[12] Remember that trading securities are debt and equity securities of other companies that the company intends to sell within a relatively short period of time.

Current operating liabilities are accounts representing operating obligations. Nontrade notes payable, bank loans payable, and dividends payable are generally excluded from this category because they represent financing events and appear in the financing section of the cash flow statement.

When a current operating liability increases during the period, it indicates one of two things: (1) the revenue associated with the account was less than the cash inflow or (2) the expense associated with the account was greater than the cash outflow. Because the related revenues and expenses are reflected in net income at the end of the period, the amount of the increase in a current operating liability must be added to net income to determine cash flows from operations.

Analysis of Current Operating Liabilities Related to Revenues TOONZ's Rent Received in Advance account increased by $150 from the beginning to the end of the year (Exhibit 19.6). Therefore, we must add $150 to net income to determine cash flows from operations as shown in Exhibit 19.3. This adjustment is necessary because net income increased by the amount of rent revenue ($600—Exhibit 19.4), while net cash flows increased by the amount of cash received from renters ($750), which we calculated previously. The increase in net income was $150 less than the increase in net cash flows from operations, so this difference must be added to accrual-based net income to derive net cash flows from operations.

Analysis of Current Operating Liabilities Related to Expenses TOONZ's Taxes Payable account decreased by $225 during 2010 (Exhibit 19.6). Thus we must deduct $225 from net income to determine cash flows from operations as shown in Exhibit 19.3. This adjustment is necessary because net income decreased by the amount of tax expense ($5,850—Exhibit 19.4), while net cash flows decreased by the amount of cash paid for taxes ($6,075), as we determined previously. The decrease in net income was $225 less than the decrease in net cash flows from operations, so this difference must be deducted from accrual-based net income to derive net cash flows from operations.

Based on this analysis, we can determine the net income adjustment needed due to the changes in accounts payable, interest payable, and wages payable. Because these accounts are all related to expenses, any increases must be added to net income, while decreases would be deducted from net income to determine cash flows from operations. Exhibit 19.6 indicates that accounts payable increased $8,175, while interest payable and wages payable decreased by $75 and $300, respectively. Exhibit 19.3 shows that the increase in accounts payable was added to net income, while the decreases in interest and wages payable were deducted from net income to determine net cash flows from operating activities.

Exhibit 19.7 summarizes the adjustment process when using the indirect format for the operating section of the statement of cash flows. *Note: The FASB requires two additional disclosures when using the indirect method to present operating activities. Companies must disclose either on the statement of cash flows itself or in the accompanying notes the amounts of cash paid for interest and for income taxes.*

EXHIBIT 19.7
Net Income Adjustments

Change in Account	Adjustment to Net Income	Reasoning
Increase in current asset	Subtract the amount of the increase	Revenue > Cash inflows, or Expense < Cash outflows
Decrease in current asset	Add the amount of the decrease	Revenue < Cash inflows, or Expense > Cash outflows
Increase in current liability	Add the amount of the increase	Expense > Cash outflows, or Revenue < Cash inflows
Decrease in current liability	Subtract the amount of the decrease	Expense < Cash outflows, or Revenue > Cash inflows

Comparison of Direct and Indirect Methods

Notice that the amount of net cash flows from operating activities is the same regardless of whether the direct or indirect method is used. Therefore, it doesn't matter which format a company uses. The direct format indicates the amounts of cash received and paid for various items. The indirect format indicates the reconciliation of net income to cash flows from operations. Most companies prepare their external statements using the indirect method. However, a thorough understanding of the direct format should help you understand the reconciliation process used in the indirect format. In addition, the direct method is an excellent tool for analyzing specific changes in operating cash flows (internal use). For example, if you wanted to track the changes in cash generated by sales from year to year the direct method creates this information.

Apple's Operating Cash Flows

Apple prepares its operating section using the indirect format as shown in the Appendix. Notice that this statement begins with net income, which is then adjusted for such items as depreciation and amortization, along with the changes in operating assets and liabilities. Apple's net cash provided by operating activities was $9,596 million in fiscal 2008. Apple paid nothing for interest and $1,267 million for income taxes during fiscal 2008.

We can estimate Apple's cash received from customers, in millions, as follows:

Beginning balance of accounts receivable	$ 1,637
Add: net sales (income statement)	32,479
Maximum amount owed by customers	$34,116
Less: cash received from customers	**31,694**
Equals ending balance of accounts receivable	$ 2,422

Likewise, estimated cash payments for inventory, in millions, would be:

Beginning balance of inventory	$ 346
Add: purchases of inventory on account	**21,497**
Maximum amount of inventory available to sell	$21,843
Less: cost of goods sold (income statement)	21,334
Equals ending balance of inventory	$ 509

Beginning balance of accounts payable	$ 4,970
Add: purchases of inventory on account (above)	21,497
Maximum amount owed to suppliers of inventory	$26,467
Less: cash paid for inventory	**20,947**
Equals ending balance of accounts payable	$ 5,520

Enhance Your Understanding

Why would more companies use the indirect method of calculating cash flows from operations rather than the direct method?

Answer: Many companies claim that the direct method is too difficult; however, computers have made this argument moot. Perhaps a better explanation is that the direct method discloses specific cash inflows and outflows that companies would prefer their competitors did not know.

Investing Activities: Cash Flows

Cash flows from investing activities are associated with the company's long-term assets and its current nonoperating assets, such as nontrade notes receivable and trading securities. Recall that investing activities may result in cash inflows and cash outflows.

Calculating Investing Cash Flows

The cash flows from the investing activities section of the statement of cash flows reflects the amount of cash received from sales of long-term and current nonoperating assets and the amount of cash paid to purchase these assets.

For example, assume the following additional information concerning TOONZ:

- A building was obtained at the end of 2010 with preferred stock and cash.
- Equipment was purchased for cash at the end of 2010.
- Equipment costing $5,000 was sold during 2010.

First, let's analyze the change in the Trading Securities account. Changes in the Trading Securities account are determined as follows:

	Beginning balance in Trading Securities, net
+	Trading securities purchased during the period
=	Maximum amount of trading securities available
−	Trading securities sold during the period
−/+	Market adjustment[13]
=	Ending balance in Trading Securities, net

This account decreased during the year, indicating that overall securities (1) were sold or (2) declined in value.[14]

Second, examine the income statement for further information concerning trading securities. Specifically, we are looking for a gain or loss on the sale of securities or an unrealized loss due to the decline in value. According to the income statement, TOONZ had a $900 gain on the sale of trading securities but there is no information indicating any decline in value. Therefore, we can analyze the change in the Trading Securities account as follows:

$1,800	Beginning balance (Exhibit 19.6)
-0-	Securities purchased during the period
$1,800	Maximum amount of trading securities available
(1,050)	**Trading securities sold during the period[15]**
–0–	Market adjustment
$ 750	Ending balance (Exhibit 19.6)

Based on this information, we determine that the *cash received* from the sale of securities is $1,950 ($900 gain + $1,050 decrease in trading securities). (Recall from Chapters 12 and 16 that a gain implies that the resources received were greater than the book value of the resources given up in the sale or exchange.) Take a moment to find "cash received from sale of trading securities" in Exhibits 19.2 and 19.3.

Next we must consider the changes in the Buildings account. When analyzing assets that are depreciated, we must also consider the changes in the accompanying Accumulated Depreciation accounts.

	Beginning balance of Building account
+	Cost of building purchased during the period
=	Maximum amount of building available
−	Cost of building sold during the period
=	Ending balance of Building account

13 Recall that trading securities are reported at their market value. Thus if the portfolio of trading securities decreases in value, a downward market adjustment is required. If the portfolio of trading securities increases in value, an upward market adjustment is required.

14 It is possible and, in fact, likely that securities were both purchased and sold during the period. However, the fact that the account decreased during the year implies that more securities were sold than were purchased.

15 The cost of securities sold during 2008 is $1,800 − $750 = $1,050.

	Beginning balance of Accumulated Depreciation
+	Depreciation expense for the period
=	Maximum amount of accumulated depreciation
−	Depreciation removed from records due to sale of asset
=	Ending balance of Accumulated Depreciation

Note that when we are dealing with investing assets, the increase or decrease in the account does not necessarily represent the amount of cash flow—additional analysis is needed.

Using these relationships, let's see what we know about TOONZ's buildings. The Building account increased during the period, indicating that TOONZ purchased a building; the preceding additional information indicates that both preferred stock and cash were used in the transaction. However, before we conclude that the value of the building purchased is equal to the increase in the Building account, we must analyze the change in the Accumulated Depreciation account. If this account increased by the amount of depreciation expense, we can conclude that no buildings were sold during the period. (Recall that when a depreciable asset is sold or exchanged, the cost of the asset and the accumulated depreciation on the asset are removed from the accounting records.)

Let's analyze TOONZ's Accumulated Depreciation account:

$40,050	Beginning balance (Exhibit 19.6)
5,850	Depreciation expense (Exhibit 19.4)
$45,900	Maximum amount of accumulated depreciation
–0–	**Depreciation removed from records**
$45,900	Ending balance (Exhibit 19.6)

TOONZ's Accumulated Depreciation—Building account increased by $5,850 during 2010. Because the amount of Depreciation Expense shown on the income statement is also $5,850, we conclude that no buildings were sold.

Now we can analyze the change in the Building account.

$112,650	Beginning balance (Exhibit 19.6)
37,800	**Cost of building purchased during the period**[16]
$150,450	Maximum amount of building
–0–	Cost of building sold during the period
$150,450	Ending balance (Exhibit 19.6)

To determine the amount of cash used in purchasing the building, we must determine the change in the Preferred Stock and Additional Paid-in Capital—Preferred Stock accounts.[17] These accounts increased by a total of $12,150. Therefore, we surmise that $12,150 of preferred stock was used to purchase the building. Because the Building account increased by $37,800, the cash used was $25,650 ($37,800 − $12,150). Take a moment to locate the "cash paid for building" and the "purchase of building with preferred stock" in both Exhibits 19.2 and 19.3.

Finally, we must analyze the changes in the Equipment and Accumulated Depreciation—Equipment accounts using the same relationships as we used for the Building and Accumulated Depreciation—Building accounts. The Accumulated Depreciation—Equipment account increased by $1,200 during 2010. Is this the same as the Depreciation Expense shown on the income statement? No; therefore, we conclude that equipment was sold during 2010. To determine the amount of accumulated depreciation associated with the sale of the asset, we calculate the following:

$15,450	Beginning balance (Exhibit 19.6)
3,150	Depreciation expense (Exhibit 19.4)
$18,600	Maximum amount of depreciation
(1,950)	**Depreciation removed from the records**[18]
$16,650	Ending balance (Exhibit 19.6)

[16] The cost of the building purchased during 2010 is $150,450 + $0 = $150,450; $150,450 − $112,650 = $37,800.

[17] Our additional information indicated that the increase in Preferred Stock represents preferred stock issued in exchange for a building.

[18] The depreciation removed is $18,600 − $16,650 = $1,950.

The income statement shows that TOONZ incurred a loss on the sale of equipment ($2,250). Thus the amount of cash received was less than the carrying value of the equipment. Based on the analysis of the Accumulated Depreciation account and the additional information given previously, we determine the carrying value of the equipment sold was $3,050:

$5,000	Cost of equipment
(1,950)	Accumulated depreciation on equipment
$3,050	Book (carrying) value of equipment

Thus the *cash received* from the sale of equipment was $800:

$3,050	Book (carrying) value of equipment
(2,250)	Loss on the sale of equipment (Exhibit 19.4)
$ 800	Cash received from sale of equipment

We determine that $6,050 cash was paid for equipment during the period:

$50,850	Beginning balance (Exhibit 19.6)
6,050	**Cost of equipment purchased**[19]
$56,900	Maximum amount of equipment available
(5,000)	Cost of equipment sold (additional information)
$51,900	Ending balance (Exhibit 19.6)

The additional information about this purchase indicates that it was transacted in cash.

Investing Cash Flows of Apple

Looking at the investing cash flows, Apple had a net cash outflow from investing activities of $8,189 million. This cash flow represents purchases and sales of property, plant, and equipment, and other assets. Apple indicates purchases of short-term investments for $22,965 million as well as purchases of property, plant, and equipment for $1,091 million during 2008. Investing cash was provided by maturities of short-term investments of $11,804 and sales of short-term investments of $4,439.

Financing Activities: Cash Flows

Cash flows from financing activities are associated with long-term liabilities; current nonoperating liabilities, such as nontrade notes payable and dividends payable; and the owners' equity of the company. Financing activities include the issuance and repayment of notes and bonds, the sale and repurchase of stock, and the distribution of the company's earnings. Financing activities do not include the change in owners' equity caused by the company's net income. That change is accounted for by cash flows from operations.

Calculating Financing Cash Flows

The amounts shown on the statement of cash flows represent the cash flows that occurred as a result of increases or decreases in the long-term and current nonoperating liabilities (excluding dividends payable, which relates to owner financing) during the period.

For example, assume the following additional information concerning TOONZ:

- Short-term notes were issued during 2010.
- Bonds were issued at the end of 2010.

[19] The cost of equipment purchased is $51,900 + $5,000 = $56,900; $56,900 − $50,850 = $6,050.

First, we analyze Notes Payable using this relationship:

	Beginning balance of Notes Payable
+	Notes issued during the period
=	Maximum debt due to notes payable
−	Cash paid on principal of notes payable
=	Ending balance of Notes Payable

The Notes Payable account increased by $150 during 2010, so it appears that notes were issued during the period. We can then determine the amount of cash received as follows:

$150	Beginning balance (Exhibit 19.6)
150	**Notes issued during the period**
$300	Maximum debt due to notes payable
–0–	Cash paid on principal of notes payable
$300	Ending balance (Exhibit 19.6)

Next look at Bonds Payable using the same relationship as shown for Notes Payable. This account increased by $13,500 during 2010, so we assume that bonds were issued during the period. But remember, bonds often are issued for more or less than their face values. Because the Premium on Bonds Payable account increased by $600, we conclude that $14,100 of cash ($13,500 + $600) was raised by issuing bonds. Take a moment to locate both "cash received from short-term note payable" and "cash received from bond issues" in Exhibits 19.2 and 19.3.[20]

The amounts on the statement of cash flows show the cash flows that resulted from changes in owners' equity and the Dividends Payable account during the period. For example, assume the following additional information concerning TOONZ:

- Treasury stock was purchased during 2010.
- Dividends were paid during 2010.

The Treasury Stock account is analyzed as follows:

	Beginning balance of Treasury Stock
+	Treasury stock purchased during the period
=	Maximum amount of treasury stock
−	Treasury stock reissued during the period
=	Ending balance of Treasury Stock

First, we notice on the balance sheet (see Exhibit 19.6) that the Treasury Stock account increased by $12,500, so we assume that overall more treasury stock was purchased than was reissued. We, therefore, conclude that $12,500 was paid to buy treasury stock during 2010 as shown here:[21]

$ –0–	Beginning balance (Exhibit 19.6)
12,500	**Treasury stock purchased during the period**
$12,500	Maximum amount of treasury stock
–0–	Treasury stock reissued during the period
$12,500	Ending balance (Exhibit 19.6)

Next, examine the Dividends Payable account and Exhibit 19.5. To determine the cash paid for dividends during 2010, use the following relationships:

	Beginning balance of Dividends Payable
+	Dividends declared during the period
=	Maximum dividends owed
−	Dividends paid during the period
=	Ending balance of Dividends Payable

[20] Since the balance in long-term notes payable did not change we assume that no related cash flows occurred.

[21] If the Treasury Stock account had decreased during the period, it would indicate that treasury stock had been reissued. To determine the amount of cash received, determine the decrease in the Treasury Stock account and the change in the Paid-in Capital from Treasury Stock account and/or additional information provided.

Using the information from the balance sheet and statement of shareholders' equity, we determine the cash paid for dividends as:

$ 150	Beginning balance (Exhibit 19.6)
4,950	Dividends declared (Exhibit 19.5)
$5,100	Maximum dividends owed
(5,000)	**Dividends paid**
$ 100	Ending balance (Exhibit 19.6)

Financing Cash Flows of Apple

Now examine the financing cash flows of Apple. Apple had a net cash inflow from financing activities of $1,116 million during 2008. Apple issued common stock, received benefits from stock-based compensation, and settled equity awards during 2008.

Net Change in Cash

At this point, we have analyzed all TOONZ noncash accounts on the balance sheet and income statement. We determined the following:

Cash flows from operating activities	$ 24,390
Cash flows from investing activities	(28,950)
Cash flows from financing activities	(3,250)
Net change in cash	$ (7,810)
Add beginning balance of cash	42,250
Ending balance of cash	$ 34,440

The statement of cash flows for Apple reveals:

Cash flows from operating activities	$9,596 million
Cash flows from investing activities	(8,189 million)
Cash flows from financing activities	1,116 million
Net change in cash	$2,523 million
Add beginning balance of cash	9,352 million
Cash and cash equivalents, end of year	$11,875 million

Other Investing and Financing Activities

Cash flows associated with the operating, investing, and financing activities of the firm are the only required disclosures on the face of the statement of cash flows. Other significant noncash investing and financing events that are important to readers of the cash flow statement are reported either on the statement itself or in the notes to the financial statements. The following are typical noncash events that are reported:

- Acquisition of assets by issuing debt or equity securities.
- Exchanges of assets.
- Conversion of debt or preferred stock to common stock.
- Issuance of common or preferred stock to retire debt.

It is important for readers to analyze these events because of their future cash flow implications. If a company acquires assets by issuing debt, for example, it will need cash in the future to make the required periodic payments of interest and principal. If a company retires debt by issuing stock, it is relieved from the periodic payments on the debt but may face future dividend payments.

Take a moment to locate TOONZ's disclosure of its other investing and financing activities on the statement of cash flows. TOONZ shows the purchase of a building with preferred stock during 2010.

Internal Evaluation of Cash Flows

As part of the balanced scorecard evaluation, an assessment of the timing and amounts of cash flows is crucial. Insufficient or untimely cash inflows can be detrimental to the company. Recall, for example, that if interest payments on bonds are not made, the company's assets can be sold to meet its obligations.

Internal users have additional information concerning cash flows that, for reasons of privacy, is not available to external users. For example, internal users have information concerning the timing of cash receipts from customers and cash payments to suppliers, which they would not want competitors to know. In addition, insiders have knowledge about the cash flows generated by different divisions within the company. Finally, managers know the level of cash flows expected at the beginning of the period and can compare it to the actual level of cash flows to determine whether or where problems might exist.

A common ratio used to evaluate cash flows is the **cash flow per share ratio.** This ratio indicates the cash generated by operating activities on a per share (common-size) basis. It is calculated as:

$$\frac{\text{Cash flows from operating activities} - \text{Preferred dividends guaranteed}}{\text{Weighted average common shares outstanding}}$$

Let's assume that TOONZ's guaranteed preferred dividend is \$1,825 and that it has 23,000 shares of common stock outstanding. Then, its cash flow per share would be

$$\frac{\$24{,}390 - \$1{,}825}{23{,}000} = \$0.98$$

Summary

The statement of cash flows supplements the accrual-based accounting information illustrated in the income statement, balance sheet, and statement of retained earnings. Its purpose is to illustrate the cash flows arising from operating, investing, and financing activities, respectively.

- According to the Financial Accounting Standards Board, the statement of cash flows is useful to (1) assess the entity's ability to generate positive future net cash flows, (2) assess the entity's ability to meet its obligations and pay dividends and its need for external financing, (3) assess the reasons for differences between income and associated cash receipts and payments, and (4) assess both the cash and noncash aspects of the entity's investing and financing transactions during the period.
- The operating activities section of the statement of cash flows may be prepared using either the direct or indirect format. The direct format illustrates the actual amounts received or paid for operating activities, while the indirect format requires adjustments to accrual-based net income to determine cash flows from operations.
- The investing and financing sections of the statement of cash flows indicate the cash received from or paid for investing and financing events, respectively. The events are further reflected by changes in current nonoperating assets and liabilities, noncurrent assets and liabilities, and owners' equity accounts.

Key Terms

Cash flow per share ratio Indicates the cash generated by operating activities on a per share (common-size) basis, *550*

Current operating liabilities Accounts representing operating obligations, *543*

Direct format Shows the actual cash inflows and outflows from each operating activity reported on the income statement, *532*

Indirect format Shows the differences between accrual-based net income and cash flows from operations, *532*

Noncash current operating assets Noncash accounts that represent operating activities, *542*

Questions

1. Explain the objectives of the cash flow statement.
2. Explain how the cash flow statement, in conjunction with the other financial statements, is useful for external users.
3. Explain the importance of the sections of the statement of cash flows.
4. Explain the difference between the direct and indirect formats for presenting the statement of cash flows.
5. If accounts receivable increases during the period, which is greater, collections from customers or sales on account? Why?
6. Rent expense as shown on the income statement is $120,000, while cash paid for rent is shown on the statement of cash flows at $135,000. Did prepaid rent increase or decrease during the period? By what amount?
7. Accounts payable for services decreased $67,000 during the year. The statement of cash flows indicates that cash paid for services was $568,000. What was the amount of the related expense shown on the income statement?
8. If the Subscriptions Received in Advance account decreases during the period, which is greater, cash received in advance from customers or subscription revenue? Why?
9. Company A's inventory decreased by $10,000 during the period, while its accounts payable for inventory increased by $6,000. Which is greater, cost of goods sold or cash paid for inventory? Why?
10. If the interest expense for the period is $1,500 and the Premium on Bonds Payable account decreases during the period by $50, how much is the cash paid for interest? Why?
11. In the indirect method of presenting operating cash flows, why is net income adjusted for depreciation, depletion, and amortization?
12. If a bond payable is issued at a discount, is the resulting amortization added to, or deducted from, net income to determine cash flows from operations in the indirect method? Why?
13. If a bond payable is issued at a premium, is the resulting amortization added to, or deducted from, net income to determine cash flows from operations in the indirect method? Why?
14. Where and how do gains and losses appear on the statement of cash flows on an indirect basis? Why?
15. When the indirect method is used for the statement of cash flows, how and why is net income affected by changes in current operating assets to determine cash flows from operations?
16. When the indirect method is used for the statement of cash flows, how and why is net income affected by changes in current operating liabilities to determine cash flows from operations?
17. If a company sells a building that cost $150,000 and that has $80,000 of accumulated depreciation for $65,000, how does the company reflect this event on the statement of cash flows? Why?
18. Does the amount shown on the statement of retained earnings always equal the amount shown on the statement of cash flows for dividends? Why or why not?
19. If a company exchanges common stock for a building, should it disclose this event on the statement of cash flows? Why or why not?
20. Explain why managers have cash flow information that they do not wish to disclose to external users.

Exercises

LO 1 LO 3 LO 4

E19.1 A variety of transactions follow. Identify each transaction as an operating **(O)**, investing **(I)**, financing **(F)**, or other noncash **(NC)** event. Put the correct letter(s) in the space provided.

________ A. Borrowed $50,000 on a long-term note payable.

________ B. Made a sale for $2,500 on open account.

________ C. Reclassified as a short-term liability the long-term notes payable of $30,000 now due within one year.
________ D. Purchased a building for $120,000 with a $20,000 cash down payment and signed a long-term note payable for the balance.
________ E. Paid the maturity value of $1,050 on a short-term note payable with a face value of $1,000.
________ F. Wrote off $500 in uncollectible accounts receivable.
________ G. Paid the liability for accrued wages payable of $700 as well as the current period's wages of $4,500.
________ H. Paid $2,000 on accounts payable.
________ I. Sold marketable securities that cost $12,000 for $12,750.
________ J. Issued 200 shares of $5 par value common stock in payment for equipment having a fair market value of $17,400.

LO 1 **E19.2** A variety of transactions follow. Identify each transaction as an operating **(O)**, investing **(I)**, financing **(F)**, or other noncash **(NC)** event. Put the correct letter(s) in the space provided.

LO 3

LO 4

________ A. Collection of an accounts receivable.
________ B. Declaration of dividends to shareholders.
________ C. Interest received on available-for-sale securities.
________ D. Loan received from a bank or other financial institution.
________ E. Payment of accounts payable.
________ F. Payment of insurance for one year in advance.
________ G. Purchase of inventory on account.
________ H. Purchase of machinery and equipment for cash.
________ I. Sale of common stock for cash.
________ J. Sale of land and building for cash.

LO 1 **E19.3** Balke Company reveals the following balances in selected accounts:

	May 31, 2010	May 31, 2009
Accounts receivable	$ 95,000	$120,000
Inventory	100,000	68,000
Prepaid rent	13,000	16,000
Accounts payable—inventory	44,000	52,000
Accrued liabilities	25,000	15,000
Wages payable	14,000	12,000
Sales	727,000	
Cost of goods sold	436,000	
Rent expense	58,000	
Miscellaneous expenses	94,000	
Wage expense	108,000	

Determine the operating cash flows using the direct format.

LO 1 **E19.4** Stara Company reveals the following information for the past fiscal period:

	Ending Balance	Beginning Balance
Accounts receivable	$ 45,000	$54,000
Inventory	50,000	34,000
Prepaid insurance	6,000	8,000
Accounts payable	74,000	82,000
Taxes payable	10,000	15,000
Wages payable	32,000	23,000
Sales	700,000	
Cost of goods sold	490,000	
Insurance expense	6,000	
Tax expense	10,000	
Wage expense	62,000	

Use the direct format to determine the cash flows from operating activities.

LO 2 E19.5 For the year ended December 31, 2010, Brown, Inc., reported net income of $175,000 on the accrual basis of accounting. Using the following information, convert the accrual-based net income to the cash basis.

A. The liability for unearned service revenue increased by $12,500 during 2010.
B. The liability for equipment rental decreased $5,100 during the year.
C. Supplies on hand increased by $1,700 during 2010.

LO 2 E19.6 During 2010, Chen Company generated a $65,000 net income. Using this information, determine the adjusted net income:

A. Equipment was sold during the period at a loss of $5,000.
B. Trading securities (not cash equivalents) were sold during the period at a gain of $2,400.
C. Patent amortization expense was $1,800 for the period.

LO 2 E19.7 During 2010, Allen Company recorded interest expense on bonds payable of $18,500 and decreased the premium on bonds payable by $200. If net income was $44,600 during 2010, what is Allen's net income adjustment shown on the statement of cash flows?

LO 2 E19.8 Refer to E19.7. Assume your company purchased Allen's bonds when issued and held them during 2010. If your net income is $34,500, what is the net income adjustment to your statement of cash flows?

LO 3 E19.9 Lawrence Products had a beginning balance in Furniture and Fixtures, net of depreciation, of $192,000. The ending balance in that account was $196,500. Depreciation expense for that period was $25,000, and there were no sales of furniture or fixtures during the period. What was the amount of furniture and fixtures purchases?

LO 3 E19.10 Ruchala had $54,900 in its Equipment account at the beginning of 2010. The beginning balance of Accumulated Depreciation—Equipment was $9,000 at that time. During 2010, Ruchala recorded depreciation expense of $23,500 and sold a piece of equipment for $2,500 resulting in a gain of $1,500. At the end of 2010, the Equipment account had a balance of $63,100 and the balance in the Accumulated Depreciation—Equipment account was $14,000. What was the amount of equipment purchases that Ruchala made during 2010?

LO 2 E19.11 Shoemaker Company purchased a machine on January 1, 2009, for $85,000 in cash. On June 30, 2010, Shoemaker sold the machine at a loss of $5,000. Accumulated depreciation as of June 30, 2010, was $21,250. What is the cash flow shown in the investing section of the statement of cash flows in 2010? What adjustment is needed to the net income using the indirect method in the operating section of the statement of cash flows in 2010?

LO 4 E19.12 On March 1, 2010, Price Incorporated issued 10-year bonds with a face value of $600,000 and a face interest rate of 8 percent that was paid semiannually on March 1 and September 1. The bonds were sold to yield a market rate of 6 percent. What is the cash inflow shown in the financing section of the statement of cash flows for the year ended December 31, 2010?

LO 1 E19.13 Refer to E19.12. Assuming this is Price's only debt, what is the amount shown on the cash flow statement for the year ended December 31, 2010, as cash paid for interest using the direct method?

LO 4 E19.14 During 2010, Woodland Incorporated issued a long-term note for $50,000. In this same time period, Woodland paid off another long-term note of $70,000. How would Woodland reflect these events on the statement of cash flows? Why? In what section do these events appear?

LO 4 E19.15 During 2010, Cosgrove's Common Stock and Additional Paid-in Capital accounts increased by $35,000 and $257,000, respectively. If no common stock was retired during 2010, what is the amount shown on the statement of cash flows with respect to common stock? In what section is this disclosed?

LO 4 E19.16 Milligan had a beginning balance in Retained Earnings of $64,970. During the year, it generated a net income of $53,600. At the end of the year, the Retained Earnings account had a balance of $95,100. In addition, Milligan's Dividends Payable account increased by $2,000 during the year. What is the total amount shown on the statement of cash flows as "cash paid for dividends"? In what section is this disclosed?

LO 3 E19.17 During the year, Garsombke Company sold trading securities costing $7,500 at a loss of $500. What amount of cash did Garsombke raise from this transaction, and where would Garsombke report it on the statement of cash flows?

LO 5 E19.18 During the year, Kwak, Inc., issued 40,000 shares of $1 par value common stock in exchange for land. The appraised value of the land was $580,000. Kwak's common stock was trading at $15 per share at the time of the exchange. Where, and in what amount, would Kwak report this transaction on the statement of cash flows for the period?

LO 5 **E19.19** Ortman Enterprises generated $657,830 of cash flows from operating activities, used $55,670 of cash flows in its investing activities, and received $32,540 of cash flows from financing activities during fiscal 2010. Its weighted average common shares outstanding were 325,500 and it has no preferred stock. What is Ortman's cash flow per share?

LO 5 **E19.20** Armitage Company's statement of cash flows reveals an increase in cash of $21,100. Its financing net cash inflows were $50,000 while its investing net cash outflows were $75,000. Armitage's preferred stock dividend is $10,000. Its weighted average common shares outstanding were 75,000. What is Armitage's cash flow per share?

Problems

P19.1 LO 1 LO 2 LO 3 LO 4 These are the financial statements of Watanabe, Inc:

WATANABE, INC.
Income Statement
For the Year Ended December 31, 2010

Sales		$288,000
Cost of goods sold		196,000
Gross margin		$ 92,000
Operating expenses:		
Depreciation	$ 6,500	
Other operating expenses	77,900	84,400
Net income		$ 7,600

WATANABE, INC.
Balance Sheet
December 31, 2010, and 2009

	2010	2009
Current assets		
Cash	$ 12,800	$ 15,400
Accounts receivable	21,700	30,300
Inventory	32,100	44,600
Total current assets	$ 66,600	$ 90,300
Property, plant, and equipment		
Furniture and fixtures	$ 68,700	$ 61,200
Less accumulated depreciation	(29,400)	22,900
Total property, plant, and equipment	$ 39,300	$ 38,300
Total assets	$105,900	$128,600
Current liabilities		
Accounts payable—merchandise	$ 16,800	$ 28,300
Accounts payable—operating expenses	13,400	15,100
Total current liabilities	$ 30,200	$ 43,400
Long-term liabilities		
Notes payable	25,000	30,000
Total liabilities	$ 55,200	$ 73,400
Shareholders' equity		
Common stock	$ 40,000	$ 40,000
Retained earnings	10,700	15,200
Total shareholders' equity	$ 50,700	$ 55,200
Total liabilities and shareholders' equity	$105,900	$128,600

Required
A. Prepare Watanabe's statement of cash flows using the indirect method.
B. Prepare Watanabe's operating section of the statement of cash flows using the direct method.
C. Which statement do you believe provides the most relevant information for external users? For internal users? Why?

LO 1 LO 2 LO 3 LO 4 **P19.2** The financial statements of Copple Company follow:

COPPLE COMPANY
Income Statement
For the Year Ended March 31, 2010

Sales		$363,000
Expenses:		
Cost of goods sold	$248,000	
Salaries	65,250	
Rent	6,000	
Depreciation	17,000	
Other operating expenses	15,000	351,250
Net income		$ 11,750

COPPLE COMPANY
Balance Sheet
March 31, 2010, and 2009

	2010	2009
Current assets		
Cash	$ 49,000	$ 16,000
Accounts receivable	46,000	28,000
Inventory	130,000	135,000
Prepaid rent	14,000	–0–
Total current assets	$239,000	$179,000
Long-term assets:		
Equipment	158,000	148,000
Accumulated depreciation	(98,500)	(81,500)
Total long-term assets	$ 59,500	$ 66,500
Total assets	$298,500	$245,500
Current liabilities		
Accounts payable	$ 38,000	$ 25,000
Salaries payable	15,000	5,500
Accrued liabilities—operating expenses	17,500	4,000
Notes payable	45,000	–0–
Total current liabilities	$115,500	$ 34,500
Long-term liabilities		
Notes payable	–0–	35,000
Total liabilities	$115,500	$ 69,500
Owners' equity		
Copple, capital	183,000	176,000
Total liabilities and owners' equity	$298,500	$245,500

Required:
A. Prepare Copple's statement of cash flows using the indirect method.
B. Prepare Copple's operating activities section of the statement of cash flows using the direct method.
C. Which statement do you believe provides the most relevant information for external users? For internal users? Why?

LO 1 LO 2 LO 3 LO 4 LO 5

P19.3 Refer to Dell, Inc. (**www.dell.com**), and examine the statement of cash flows to answer the following questions:

A. Is this statement prepared on the direct or indirect basis? How can you tell?
B. Are net cash flows from operating activities greater than or less than net income?
C. What is shown on the statement of cash flows regarding changes in current operating assets during the period?
D. What is shown on the statement of cash flows regarding changes in current operating liabilities during the period?
E. How much cash did the company pay for interest during the period? Where did you find this information?
F. How does the company define cash equivalents? Where did you find this information?
G. How much cash did the company pay for income taxes during the period? Where did you find this information?
H. What were the principal investing events during the year?
I. What were the principal financing events during the year?
J. Did the company report any noncash investing/financing events during the year? If so, where did you find this information?
K. If you were an investor, would you be interested in this company? Why or why not?

LO 1 LO 2 LO 3 LO 4 LO 5

P19.4 Refer to Walt Disney Company (**www.disney.com**) and examine the statement of cash flows to answer the following questions:

A. Is this statement prepared on the direct or indirect basis? How can you tell?
B. Are net cash flows from operating activities greater than or less than net income?
C. What is shown on the statement of cash flows regarding changes in current operating assets during the period?
D. What is shown on the statement of cash flows regarding changes in current operating liabilities during the period?
E. How much cash did the company pay for interest during the period? Where did you find this information?
F. How does the company define cash equivalents? Where did you find this information?
G. How much cash did the company pay for income taxes during the period? Where did you find this information?
H. What were the principal investing events during the year?
I. What were the principal financing events during the year?
J. Did the company report any noncash investing/financing events during the year? If so, where did you find this information?
K. If you were an investor, would you be interested in this company? Why or why not?

LO 1 LO 2 LO 3 LO 4 LO 5

P19.5 Refer to PepsiCo, (**www.pepsico.com**), Inc. and examine the statement of cash flows to answer the following questions:

A. Is this statement prepared on the direct or indirect basis? How can you tell?
B. Are net cash flows from operating activities greater than or less than net income?
C. What is shown on the statement of cash flows regarding changes in current operating assets during the period?
D. What is shown on the statement of cash flows regarding changes in current operating liabilities during the period?
E. How much cash did the company pay for interest during the period? Where did you find this information?
F. How does the company define cash equivalents? Where did you find this information?
G. How much cash did the company pay for income taxes during the period? Where did you find this information?
H. What were the principal investing events during the year?
I. What were the principal financing events during the year?
J. Did the company report any noncash investing/financing events during the year? If so, where did you find this information?
K. If you were an investor, would you be interested in this company? Why or why not?

LO 1 **P19.6** The financial statements of Kealey Enterprises follow:

LO 2

LO 3

LO 4

KEALEY ENTERPRISES
Balance Sheet
December 31, 2010, and 2009
(in millions)

	2010	2009
Cash and cash equivalents	$ 330.7	$ 226.9
Short-term investments	1,157.4	1,573.8
Accounts and notes receivable, net	2,050.9	1,883.4
Inventories	970.0	924.7
Prepaid expenses	563.2	499.8
Property, plant, and equipment, net	9,882.8	8,855.6
Intangibles, net	9,837.0	9,741.6
Total assets	$24,792.0	$23,705.8
Accounts payable	$ 1,451.6	$ 1,390.0
Interest payable	753.5	726.0
Short-term borrowings	678.5	2,191.2
Income taxes payable	671.7	823.7
Accrued marketing expense	546.2	400.9
Other current liabilities	1,168.9	1,043.1
Long-term debt	12,665.5	10,608.3
Capital stock at par	14.4	13.4
Capital in excess of par value	934.4	879.5
Retained earnings	7,268.5	6,541.9
Treasury stock	(1,361.2)	(912.2)
Total liabilities and shareholders' equity	$24,792.0	$23,705.8

KEALEY ENTERPRISES
Income Statement
For the Year Ended December 31, 2010 (in millions)

Sales	$38,472.4
Less cost of goods sold	23,715.4
Gross margin	$14,757.0
Less operating expenses:	
Selling and general expense	10,011.3
Depreciation and amortization expense	1,576.5
Income from operations	$ 3,169.2
Other revenue (expense):	
Interest income	108.2
Interest expense	(645.0)
Income before income taxes	$ 2,632.4
Provision for income taxes	880.4
Net income	$ 1,752.0

Additional Information:
1. No property, plant, and equipment was sold during the year.
2. Amortization of intangibles was $139.3 (million) for the year.

Required:
A. Prepare the operating section of the statement of cash flows using the direct method.
B. Prepare the statement of cash flows using the indirect method.
C. Discuss the relative benefits of the direct method.

LO 1 LO 2 LO 3 LO 4 **P19.7** The financial statements of Eldridge Corporation follow:

ELDRIDGE CORPORATION
Balance Sheet
December 31, 2010, and 2009
(in thousands)

	2010	2009
Cash and cash equivalents	$ 8,328	$ 6,458
Short-term investments, at market	8,893	10,557
Receivables	6,920	5,255
Inventories	4,637	1,848
Prepaid expenses	2,775	1,426
Property, plant, and equipment	127,094	98,690
Accumulated depreciation	(16,883)	(11,156)
Total assets	$141,764	$113,078
Current notes payable	$ 1,996	$ 1,212
Accounts payable	9,509	8,500
Accrued expenses	13,636	9,153
Accrued dividends	1,269	879
Accrued income taxes	1,510	2,199
Long-term notes payable	26,624	8,749
Common stock	257	256
Additional paid-in capital	68,946	63,245
Retained earnings	18,866	19,734
Treasury stock	(849)	(849)
Total liabilities and shareholders' equity	$141,764	$113,078

ELDRIDGE CORPORATION
Income Statement
For the Year Ended December 31, 2010
(in thousands)

Sales	$216,613
Less cost of goods sold	163,951
Gross margin	$ 52,662
Less operating expenses:	
Depreciation expense	15,757
General expenses	32,432
Income from operations	$ 4,473
Other revenue items:	
Interest income	1,259
Other expense items:	
Gain on sale of equipment	861
Gain on sale of short-term investment	96
Interest expense	1,227
Income before taxes	$ 5,462
Income tax expense	1,945
Net income	$ 3,517

Additional Information:

1. No short-term investments were purchased during the year.
2. Equipment costing $20,000,000 [$20,000 (thousand)] was sold during the year.

Required:

A. Prepare the operating section of the statement of cash flows using the direct method.
B. Prepare the statement of cash flows using the indirect method.

LO 5 **P19.8** Refer to PepsiCo, Inc. (**www.pepsico.com**), and calculate these cash flow per share. You will need to examine the income statement to determine the weighted average shares outstanding.

LO 5 **P19.9** Refer to Dell, Inc. (**www.dell.com**), and calculate the cash flow per share. You will need to examine the notes to determine the weighted average shares outstanding and preferred dividends, if applicable.

LO 5 **P19.10** Refer to Disney (**www.disney.com**) and calculate the cash flow per share. You will need to examine the notes to determine the weighted average shares outstanding and preferred dividends, if applicable.

Cases

C19.1 LO 1 LO 2 LO 3 LO 4 LO 5 Refer to the annual report of the company you selected in Chapter 1 (C1.1), and answer the following questions:

A. Is this statement prepared on the direct or indirect basis? How can you tell?
B. Are net cash flows from operating activities greater than or less than net income?
C. What is shown on the statement of cash flows regarding changes in current operating assets during the period?
D. What is shown on the statement of cash flows regarding changes in current operating liabilities during the period?
E. How much cash did the company pay for interest during the period? Where did you find this information?
F. How does the company define cash equivalents? Where did you find this information?
G. How much cash did the company pay for income taxes during the period? Where did you find this information?
H. What were the principal investing events during the year?
I. What were the principal financing events during the year?
J. Did the company report any noncash investing/financing events during the year? If so, where did you find this information?
K. If you were an investor, would you be interested in this company? Why or why not?

LO 1 LO 2 LO 3 LO 4 **C19.2** These are the financial statements of Bauers, Inc.:

BAUERS, INC.
Balance Sheet
December 31, 2010, and 2009
(in thousands)

	2010	2009
Cash	$ 2,180	$ 6,071
Accounts receivable	78,213	82,266
Inventories	158,330	160,894
Prepaid expenses	11,955	10,340
Investments held for sale	4,879	5,523
Land	12,303	41,571
Buildings	222,576	208,513
Equipment	11,069	3,935
Accumulated depreciation	(155,546)	(144,192)
Total assets	$345,959	$374,921
Notes payable to banks	$ 10,000	$ 5,000
Trade accounts payable	14,152	19,087
Accrued payroll items	11,786	11,775
Accrued insurance	17,424	18,608
Other accrued expenses	8,424	9,359
Dividends payable	1,071	1,089
Long-term debt	63,573	74,254
Common stock	69,674	69,674
Capital in excess of par value	30,290	30,290
Retained earnings	131,482	141,111
Treasury stock	(11,917)	(5,326)
Total liabilities and shareholders' equity	$345,959	$374,921

BAUERS, INC.
Income Statement
For the Year Ended December 31, 2010
(in thousands)

Sales	$461,448
Less cost of goods sold	320,842
Gross margin	$140,606
Selling, general, and administrative expenses	129,281
Depreciation expense	16,089
Income from operations	$ (4,764)
Other revenue (expense) items:	
Interest expense	(5,032)
Gain on sale of investment	167
Net loss	$ (9,629)

Additional Information:
1. A building with a cost of $8,286 (thousand) was sold at book value.
2. No equipment was sold during the period.

Required:
A. Prepare the operating section of the statement of cash flows using the direct method.
B. Prepare the statement of cash flows using the indirect method.
C. Discuss the relative benefits of the direct method.

Critical Thinking

CT19.1 LO 1 LO 2 LO 3 LO 4

The following statement of cash flows is incorrectly presented. Analyze this statement and explain the problems you found. Do not prepare a new statement.

ILCISIN COMPANY
Statement of Cash Flows
As of December 31, 2010

Sources (inflows) of cash:	
Net income	$ 88,000
Add (deduct) items to convert from the accrual to cash basis:	
Depreciation	15,800
Inventory increase	10,000
Prepaid expense increase	(4,000)
Extraordinary gain on land	(36,000)
Extraordinary loss on bonds	(2,000)
Accounts receivable increase	(60,000)
Accounts payable increase	30,000
Amortization of bond discount	200
Wages payable decrease	3,000
Cash inflows from operations	$ 45,000
Sales of land	106,000
Issuance of bonds	10,000
Total sources of cash	$171,000
Uses (outflows) of cash:	
Cash dividends	$ 30,000
Machinery purchased	20,000
Common stock issued to retire bonds	42,000
Preferred stock issued to purchase building	20,000
Purchase of trading securities	10,000
Total uses of cash	122,000
Increase in cash	$ 39,000

LO 1 **CT19.2** Prior to the issuance of *SFAS No. 95*, companies commonly prepared a funds statement that reported the changes in working capital during the period. Analyze the following funds statement and describe its strengths and weaknesses as a communication tool.

LO 2

LO 3

LO 4

WINDLER ENTERPRISES
Statement of Changes in Financial Position—Working Capital Basis
For the Year Ended December 31, xxxx

Sources of working capital:	
Income from continuing operations:	
Net income	$132,000
Add (deduct) items to convert to working capital:	
Depreciation expense	23,700
Amortization of bond discount	300
Gain on sale of equipment	(54,000)
Loss on sale of land	3,000
Working capital from operations	105,000
Sale of equipment	159,000
Sale of land	15,000
Total working capital sources	$279,000
Uses of working capital:	
Cash dividends paid	$ 45,000
Machinery purchased	30,000
Trading securities exchanged for note payable	12,000
Total uses of working capital	$ 87,000
Increase in working capital during 1981	$192,000

Ethical Challenges

EC19.1  LO 2 M. Potter is the manager of Masson Company. Potter receives an annual salary plus a bonus of 15 percent of net income before bonus and taxes. Masson Company uses the LIFO inventory costing method. During 2010 when prices were increasing, M. Potter switched to the FIFO inventory method.

Required: Prepare an example that illustrates the effect on the income statement of switching from LIFO to FIFO. In addition, show the effect of the switch on the balance sheet and the statement of cash flows.

A. Did net income increase or decrease?
B. Did ending inventory increase or decrease?
C. Did cash flows increase or decrease?
D. Could a change in inventory methods entitle M. Potter to a larger bonus than she was otherwise entitled to? Explain.
E. In this situation, was the change economically beneficial to the Masson Company? Explain.

LO 1 **EC19.2** LO 2 Companies argue that the direct method of preparing the statement of cash flows is too burdensome; however, given computer technology, that argument doesn't seem as valid today as it once did. Do you believe that companies should be required to prepare the statement of cash flows using the direct method? Why? Be sure to consider all the stakeholders involved.

Computer Applications

CA19.1 LO 1 Caldwell Company wants you to prepare a spreadsheet to answer the following questions:

A. Sales for the period were $500,000. The beginning accounts receivable balance was $40,000. The ending balance was $35,000. Sales discounts of $5,000 were given. No accounts were written off and no sales returns and allowances were given. How much cash was received from customers?
B. Cash collections from customers during the period were $800,000. The ending balance of accounts receivable was $12,000. The beginning balance of accounts receivable was $23,000. Sales discounts of $4,000 were given during the period. Sales returns and allowances during the period were $1,500. An account with a $5,000 balance was written off during the period. What is the amount of the sales for the period?
C. Sales for the period were $350,000, while cash collections from customers were only $300,000. Sales discounts of $3,500 and sales returns and allowances of $1,000 were granted during the period.

The beginning balance of accounts receivable was $10,000. No accounts were written off during the period. What is the ending balance of accounts receivable?

LO 1 **CA19.2** Burkhart Enterprises wants you to prepare a spreadsheet to answer the following questions:

A. Purchases (net of discount) of inventory were $500,000 during the period. The beginning balance of accounts payable was $40,000, while the ending balance was $25,000. A purchase of $4,000 (net) was returned during the period. How much cash was paid for inventory during the period?

B. Cash paid for inventory during the period was $400,000. The beginning and ending balances of accounts payable were $10,000 and $12,000, respectively. Cash discounts of $2,500 were lost during the period. No purchase returns were made during the year. What was the amount of purchases (net of discount) made during the period? (Hint: When cash discounts are lost, cash decreases by more than accounts payable.)

C. Purchases of inventory (net of discount) were $800,000, while cash paid for inventory was $950,000 during the period. A purchase of $5,000 (net) was returned during the period. If the ending balance of accounts payable was $35,000, what was the beginning balance?

Visit the text Online Learning Center at **www.mhhe.com/ainsworth6e** for additional problem material that accompanies this chapter.

CHAPTER TWENTY

20

Company Performance: Comprehensive Evaluation

Learning Objectives

- **LO 1** Perform a vertical analysis to analyze a company.
- **LO 2** Demonstrate horizontal analysis to analyze a company.
- **LO 3** Perform a ratio analysis to analyze a company.
- **LO 4** Explain the various roles of the participants in the capital market.

Creditors and investors face the decision of whether to provide capital to businesses. The entire group of creditors and investors who provide capital to business makes up the **capital market,** in which businesses find financing for their investments. Creditors and investors choose the businesses in which to invest based on their perception of the risk and potential return for each business. How do creditors and investors find out what they need to know? They use financial statements issued by companies as their principal source of information.

Also note that financial statement information enables managers to report how they have used capital acquired from creditors and investors. Current creditors with outstanding loans to the company want to know how managers have handled the capital they have provided. As you know, creditors often include restrictions called *debt covenants* as part of the lending agreement on instruments such as bonds or mortgages. By requiring that a company maintain or have certain account balances or financial ratios, debt covenants attempt to ensure that managers do not jeopardize loan repayment or interest payments by paying investors prior to meeting the business's credit obligations. Creditors use financial statements to obtain information about whether management has violated such agreements.

Current shareholders want to know how effective the company's management is in managing the firm and their interest in its assets. Shareholders who are not satisfied with management's performance have two options: If a sufficient number of shareholders are dissatisfied with the management's performance, they can direct the board of directors to hire a new management team. The more common alternative is for shareholders to liquidate some or all of their interest in the company by selling their stock. Thus equity investors are interested in earnings that will drive dividends and stock prices. On the other hand, creditors are interested in cash flows and the firm's ability to pay the interest and principal on its debt.

This chapter begins with a discussion of the nature of the decisions that creditors and equity investors make and how capital markets function in allocating investment capital. Then financial statement analysis is applied to the financial statements of Apple to show how external parties might assess its risk and potential return. Finally, the chapter shows how analysts combine the information on financial statements with other information to assess the overall performance of companies.

External Stakeholders

Throughout the text we have discussed the economic interests of external stakeholders in business activities. In the broadest sense, many external parties face the decision about whether to invest in a company. We focus on the decisions of two groups of external stakeholders: creditors and investors. Creditors loan money to the business and expect to receive interest payments plus repayment of the loaned money in return. Investors invest money in companies' stock expecting a return on their investment in the form of dividends and/or appreciation in the price of the stock.[1]

Creditors and Investors

Creditors and investors view any investment decision differently. Creditors lend a fixed amount of money over a defined term as part of a loan agreement. For example, banks and other financial institutions often lend money for periods ranging from a few days to 30 or 40 years. The fixed term and return (cash flows) aspects of debt make the risk of not receiving interest payments or principal repayment a major concern of creditors when they assess an investment prospect. On the other hand, investors have no limited or fixed term when it comes to their investments. They commit funds to a business until the business ceases to operate or until they sell their stock to another investor or back to the company.

Another difference between creditors and investors is the legal nature of the risk they face. Creditors usually have legal documents like promissory notes, bonds, and mortgages that give them legal recourse in recovering the money they have loaned to businesses in the

[1] Throughout this chapter we use the term *investors* to describe current and prospective shareholders; however, this term can also apply to partners and sole proprietors.

event the borrower fails to comply with the terms of the loan. However, because investors are owners, they have few guarantees and are risking the money that they invest. As you know, the Securities Act of 1933 and the Securities Exchange Act of 1934 (passed by Congress following the stock market crash of 1929) provide some recourse for investors. However, the principal thrust of the securities acts is to ensure that investors have sufficient reliable information on which to base their investment decisions.

Society

Stepping back from the analysis of individual investments to look at the capital market as a whole gives an important perspective on its role in society. Creditors and investors are the owners of society's capital, and capital markets serve as a way of allocating that capital for investment in business. Next we briefly describe how capital markets serve as a mechanism to allocate capital.

In a free market economy, consumer demand determines the nature of businesses that exist and the extent to which a given product or service is available. Free market economies do not rely on a government dictating what kinds of businesses there should be and the level of investment that businesses should receive. As shown on the left side of Exhibit 20.1, a free market economy creates a product market (goods and services) where consumers—whether they are individuals, other businesses, or governments—determine the types of goods and services they need and want. This demand for products, in turn, creates opportunities for providers of goods and services to meet consumers' needs.

How does society decide where to invest its resources? The capital market serves an important role in the decision about what kinds of businesses receive the capital necessary to expand and succeed. The capital market exists between those who provide goods and services and the creditors and investors who own the capital, as shown on the right side of Exhibit 20.1. Providers whose product or service is in demand by consumers seek to expand, or new providers of that product or service want to begin business. How do they finance the necessary investment? The owners of capital are the principal source of funds for the providers. In return for the use of the capital, the providers of the capital want the highest return possible, as long as the related level of investment risk is not too high. This risk/return relationship is unique to each person or institution with capital to invest.

The capital market determines which businesses get the capital they need as follows. The level of consumer demand determines the price and the profitability of products. The higher the demand for certain products, the higher the prices consumers are willing to pay, making products that are in high demand more profitable than those in low demand (for a given cost). Providers with more profitable products can afford to pay more, or provide a higher return, for the use of the capital they need in order to expand. Because the amount of capital is limited, capital owners choose to invest in providers that offer them the highest return for a given level of risk. Thus consumer demand for products indirectly determines the businesses and industries that receive capital in a free market economy.

For example, consider the effect of the greater numbers of people working outside their homes since about 1970. This shift in the workforce created demand for convenience foods and day care for children. As these demands have risen, it has become more profitable for some businesses to provide meals that are either ready to eat with little preparation or require no preparation, as in the case of fast-food restaurants. In addition, the expansion of the workforce has resulted in the chains of day care centers opening. The resulting increased profitability of these types of businesses induced providers of day care services to expand and encouraged

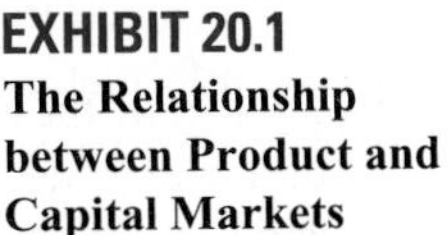
EXHIBIT 20.1
The Relationship between Product and Capital Markets

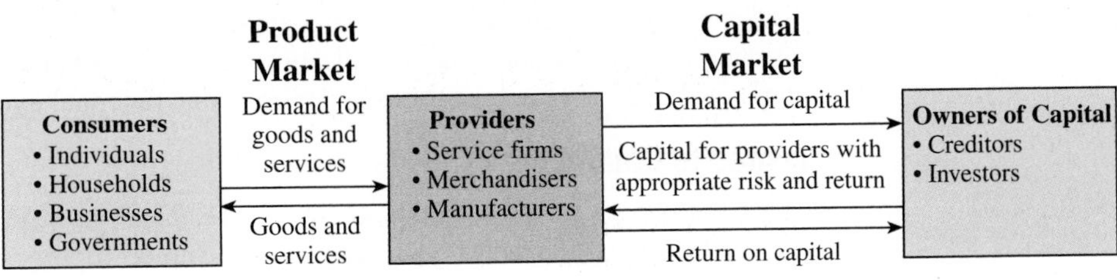

other new providers of such services to enter the market. Because these types of services have become more profitable, their providers can compete for capital in the capital market by providing returns sufficient to attract investors despite other investment alternatives.

Trading in Capital Markets

Any market is comprised of buyers and sellers who choose whether to buy or sell. Whether the market is for gold coins, food, or autos, it brings together those people who want a product with those who want to sell it. Capital markets function like other markets. Those individuals or businesses with capital and those in need of capital come together and agree on terms allowing the owners of capital (creditors and investors) to exchange the use of their capital for an expected return on their investment. For creditors, that return is the interest rate charged to the borrower. For debt that is not held to maturity, the return to creditors also includes the amount of change in the market value of the debt. Returns for investors consist of the dividends they receive in addition to the appreciation in the value of stocks they hold.

We need to be clear that there is not one big capital market where all the owners of capital and all those needing capital physically come together to trade. The capital market is segmented into different markets by factors like geography or size of transactions. A small local retailer who needs a loan to remodel the interior of a store is likely to view its capital market as the banks and savings and loan companies in its town. On the other hand, a large multinational company seeking a major expansion would consider as its capital market large banks in major cities or its own ability to issue bonds or stocks on a large scale.

In capital markets, owners of the capital have choices among alternatives. Not all potential investments offer the same risk and return. And not all creditors and investors share the same investment goals, nor do they have the same tolerance for risk. Creditors and investors use the information available from financial statements and other sources to assess companies' liquidity, debt-paying ability, and profitability. Then they try to find investments with characteristics that match their investment goals and risk preferences.

For example, a retired couple whose active earning years are over is likely to have the investment goals of steady income and low risk of losing their capital. Thus they focus on finding investments that offer lower risk, even if that means a commensurately lower return. A young, successful professional might, on the other hand, be willing to accept more risk with the prospects of higher potential earnings. The young professional might look for high potential returns even though the risk of losing some or all of the investment is higher.

Information in Capital Markets

To make good decisions, creditors and investors need to answer certain questions about the businesses to which they might provide capital. Creditors want to know: Will I receive interest payments when they are due? Will I recover the principal loaned to the borrower? The situation with investors is a bit different. Because investors are not guaranteed dividends, they need to answer the questions: What return will the dividends I receive and the appreciation in stock price provide? What is the risk that this investment will provide a lower return than I expect?

Unlike managers who have ready access to lots of information about the activities within a business, external investors and creditors cannot observe business activities firsthand, nor do they have much information about those activities. As Exhibit 20.2 shows, this creates another market for financial information. Owners of capital create the demand for accurate financial information on which to base their investment decisions. Providers (businesses) supply information to investors and creditors using GAAP to determine the necessary level of information disclosure. As we explain later, independent auditors play an important role in the financial information market by attesting, or indicating, that there is fair representation of the information communicated between businesses and current and potential external stakeholders.

Issues to Consider

There are two problems with this market for financial information. One problem is that once information is published, anyone can use it. Annual reports issued by corporations, which

EXHIBIT 20.2
Market for Financial Information within the Capital Market

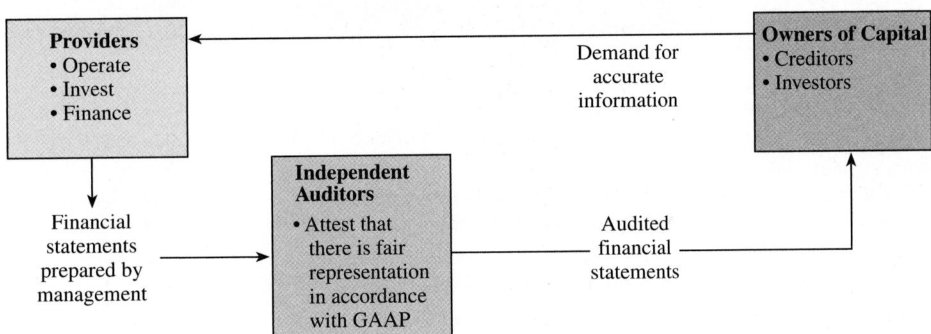

include the four financial statements plus other information such as management's forecast of sales, are available to anyone. Because consumers receive this information for free, it is impossible to use price to determine the quantity of information demanded. Thus, the information market does not work as a typical product market in which price determines the quantity demanded. Therefore, the Securities and Exchange Commission mandates certain disclosures. SEC registrants must provide financial information that complies with GAAP as defined by the FASB and also additional information about the company mandated by SEC regulations.

The other problem with the financial information market is that investors cannot tell whether the information that management reports fairly presents the financial condition of the company. Because investors are not privy to the daily workings of the corporation they must rely on management's reports knowing that managers have an incentive to prepare reports that put their performance in a favorable light. Investors can either assume that the information managers provide is biased and subjectively adjust for the expected bias, or they can hire someone to help ensure the fair presentation of the financial information in management's report.

Role of Independent Auditor

An important role for independent auditors is to provide the users of financial statements with assurance that the financial statement information is a fair representation of the economic circumstances of the company that issues it.[2] Recall the audit report for Apple in Chapter 1. That report told the readers of Apple financial statements that it had followed the accepted rules for financial reporting, GAAP. Independent auditors can issue other kinds of reports that serve as cautions to the readers that the financial statements should be read with extra care (qualified opinions) or that GAAP was not followed sufficiently (adverse opinions). By serving as a knowledgeable and objective third party, independent auditors help the market for financial information function and they indirectly aid the efficiency of the capital markets. We look at the audit reports again later in this chapter. Please note that GAAP applies to all for-profit companies, not just SEC registrants, and is enforced by the audits of CPAs. Through its due process system, the FASB determines the amount and nature of financial information provided to the public.

Financial information that investors and creditors can rely on to reflect the financial condition of a company improves their ability to choose among investment alternatives and, therefore, improves the capital allocation process so essential for a free market economy. The collapse of WorldCom and the huge losses suffered by investors was caused by an audit failure and demonstrates the importance of effective audits. Had Arthur Andersen detected management's misrepresentation about WorldCom's financial condition, investors might have saved billions of dollars that could have been invested in more productive companies.

[2] Recall that publicly traded companies must have an annual audit. Often audits are also requested by banks and other lenders before making large loans.

FAST FACT

Recall that throughout this text we have discussed how companies use ratio analysis to evaluate their performance against their goals for the period. As part of this analysis, companies compare themselves to other companies in their industry. This practice is called *benchmarking* and is an excellent management tool. Also recall that management uses the balanced scorecard shown here to assess performance in four interrelated perspectives: (1) customer, (2) internal processes, (3) learning and growth, and (4) financial. Companies using the balanced scorecard believe that improvements in the customer, internal processes, and learning and growth perspectives lead to improvements in the financial perspective. Therefore it is very important to plan and evaluate activities in each perspective.

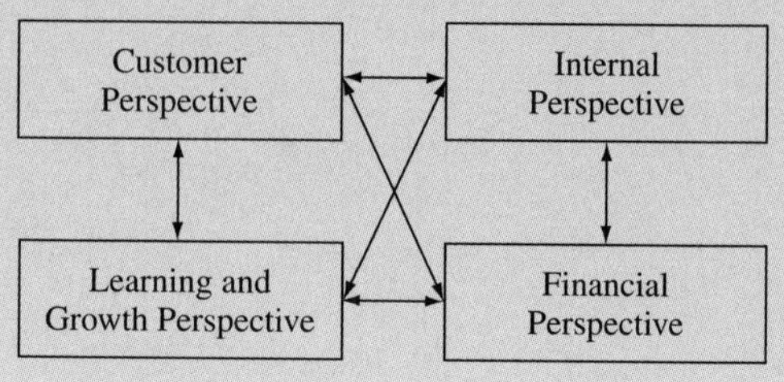

We have explained the nature of creditor and investor decisions in capital markets. In addition, we have shown why information from financial statements, as well as other sources, is critical for making good investment decisions. The next section of this chapter refers to the financial statements of Apple and two of its competitors to show how creditors and investors might use annual report analysis to assess these companies as investment opportunities.

Annual Report Analysis

Those who evaluate companies based on financial statements generally use a combination of three methods of analysis. First, horizontal analysis examines the changes in one financial statement item over time, either in dollars, as a percentage, or both. Second, vertical analysis shows each item on a financial statement as a percentage of one particular item on the statement. Third, ratio analysis expresses two or more selected items on the statements in relation to one another. Horizontal and vertical analyses use changes in items on financial statements and the relative importance of those items to reflect a company's performance. Ratio analyses examine relationships in one or between two financial statements. We organize the discussion of ratios around four important dimensions: (1) activity, (2) liquidity and solvency, (3) debt-paying ability, and (4) profitability.

Studying the Financial Statements

The first step in financial statement analysis is to carefully read the comparative financial statements. Comparative financial statements report two or more years of financial statements side-by-side in columnar form. The purpose of studying comparative financial statements is to become familiar with the company's reporting practices, the accounts and classifications it uses, and the general range of amounts it reflects. Analysts must observe the company in the total context of its comparative statements before they can examine intelligently the specific aspects of its operations. Using comparative financial statements to study a company's performance is a well-established practice, and published annual reports of large companies frequently contain comparative data for as many as 10 years.

A careful evaluation of the changes in reported financial data over time helps determine the general trend of operations and assists in deciding whether the company is better or worse off than in previous periods and how the trends compare to other companies. It also enables the analyst to see trends as they develop. Creditors, actual or potential, may obtain the same information from their analysis and can use it as a factor when making decisions about the amount of credit to extend to a company. Investors, current and potential, use the data to compare the trends of investment alternatives.

Obviously, analysts should not project historical trends indiscriminately into the future. Nonetheless, historical trends provide an excellent starting point for financial statement analysis because the more that is known about a company's past, the greater the chances of predicting its future accurately. A major thrust of financial statement analysis is to use what has transpired in the past to predict the future.

Industry Analysis

Industry analysis is important because different industries have different threats and opportunities. Recall that Chapter 2 discussed how companies match their strategies to their analysis of the external environment. For example, the computer and electronics industry is segmented. On the one side are companies such as Apple and Microsoft that have developed operating systems that allow computers to operate. On the other side are companies such as Apple and Dell that have developed computers that run various programs that allow us to work more efficiently. And, of course, Apple also makes and sells other electronic products, such as its successful iPhone, that compete with BlackBerries made by companies such as LG.

While published financial statements are an important source of information about the companies in an industry, they are not the only source. An investor must also investigate the industry. Industry trade publications and government statistics can reveal broader economic factors not related specifically to the business being analyzed. In these publications creditors and investors can find information about Apple and its competitors that they can use along with financial information prepared by the company to project financial performance.

Without some standard for judgment, there is not a good basis for making evaluations about whether the company is a good or bad investment. Sources for external standards are available in college and public libraries. Generally, external standards provide both an average and a range of quantitative values for ratios of companies in the same or similar industries. This information is useful in making comparisons among investment alternatives.

Moody's Investor Services issues a number of publications, including *Moody's Handbook of NASDAQ Stocks* and *Moody's Handbook of Common Stocks.* These handbooks provide one-page summaries of the history and principal products as well as detailed financial tables for many of the companies whose stock is traded in the United States. Value Line Publishing, Inc., publishes another popular source of financial data to which investors can subscribe. Value Line not only publishes historical data but also makes forecasts of earnings and particular earnings components such as tax rates and operating margins.

Another source of financial information is a menu-driven database distributed on compact disc by Standard & Poor's Compustat Services, Inc. The information in this database is taken from the reports that companies are required to file with the Securities and Exchange Commission. A company's financial statements as well as data on ownership and information on 29 key financial ratios are available for the companies on Compustat.

The *RMA Annual Statement Studies* (published by Robert Morris Associates) summarize financial information by industry using the Standard Industry Classification (SIC), which groups companies based on the nature of their business and by the types of products they produce.

External sources of comparative financial standards, like many published financial statements, use some titles and descriptions that differ from those used in this book. For example, the *RMA Annual Statement Studies* uses *net worth* instead of *shareholders' equity.* These differences can be confusing initially, but, with some effort, it is easy to understand them.

Statement Analyses

To demonstrate how to use financial statement analysis as an aid in lending and investing decisions, we chose two competitors of Apple. First, we look at Microsoft, whose Windows products compete in the operating systems market against Apple and its operating system. We also look at Dell, whose computer products compete against Apple's in the commercial and consumer markets.

EXHIBIT 20.3
Apple Income Statement Analysis (financial data in millions)

	Financial Data		Vertical Analysis		Horizontal Analysis	
	2008	2007	2008(%)	2007(%)	$ Change	% Change
Net sales	$32,479	$24,006	100.00	100.00	$8,473	35.30
Cost of sales	21,334	15,852	65.69	66.03	5,482	34.58
Research and development	1,109	782	3.41	3.26	327	41.82
Selling and general	3,761	2,963	11.58	12.34	798	26.93
Operating income	6,275	4,409	19.32	18.37	1,866	42.32
Other income and expense	620	599	1.91	2.50	21	3.51
Income before taxes	6,895	5,008	21.23	20.86	1,887	37.68
Provision for income taxes	2,061	1,512	6.35	6.30	549	36.31
Net income	4,834	3,496	14.88	14.56	1,338	38.27

Vertical Analysis

Vertical analysis is a system of financial statement analysis that shows the relative size of selected items to a base item within one statement for the same period. This type of analysis shows the relationship of all the other items to the base, or reference, item. On the income statement this item is total sales, and on the balance sheet it is total assets. Since this analysis is a common-size measure, it avoids the distortion caused by the size of the company. Vertical analysis reveals the relative importance of various financial statement items to the base item. Internally management uses this information to compare against the balanced scorecard goals. Externally, investors and creditors use this information to evaluate the composition of the company's financial position and earnings.

Exhibits 20.3 through 20.8 show the vertical analysis for 2008 and 2007 of Apple, Dell, and Microsoft. Notice that although the companies vary greatly in size, each company's data are given as a percentage of the base and, therefore, size is neutralized so the fundamental relationships are comparable. Notice that each item on the income statement is stated as a percentage of total revenue, while each item on the balance sheet is stated as a percentage of total assets. For example, knowing that cash as a percentage of total assets for fiscal 2008 is 30.01 percent for Apple (Exhibit 20.4), 28.17 percent for Dell (Exhibit 20.6), and only

EXHIBIT 20.4
Apple Balance Sheet Analysis (financial data in millions)

	Financial Data		Vertical Analysis		Horizontal Analysis	
	2008	2007	2008(%)	2007(%)	$ Change	% Change
Cash and equivalents	$11,875	$9,352	30.01	36.90	$2,523	26.98
Short-term investments	12,615	6,034	31.88	23.81	6,581	109.07
Accounts receivable, net	2,422	1,637	6.12	6.46	785	47.95
Inventories	509	346	1.29	1.37	163	47.11
Other current assets	7,269	4,587	18.37	18.10	2,682	58.47
Property, plant and equipment, net	2,455	1,832	6.20	7.23	623	34.01
Other noncurrent assets	2,427	1,559	6.13	6.15	868	55.68
Total assets	39,572	25,347	100.00	100.00	14,225	56.12
Accounts payable	5,520	4,970	13.95	19.61	550	11.07
Accrued liabilities	8,572	4,310	21.66	17.00	4,262	98.89
Other current liabilities	-0-	-0-			-0-	
Long-term debt	-0-	-0-	0.00	0.00	-0-	-0-
Other long-term liabilities	4,450	1,535			2,915	
Common stock and paid-in capital	7,177	5,368	18.14	21.18	1,809	33.70
Retained earnings	13,845	9,101	34.99	35.91	4,744	52.13
Accumulated comprehensive income	8	63	0.02		(55)	
Treasury stock	-0-	-0-			-0-	
Total liabilities and stockholders' equity	39,572	25,347	100.00	100.00	14,225	56.12

EXHIBIT 20.5
Dell Income Statement Analysis (financial data in millions)

	Financial Data		Vertical Analysis		Horizontal Analysis	
	2008	2007	2008(%)	2007(%)	$ Change	% Change
Net sales	$61,133	$57,420	100.00	100.00	$3,713	6.47
Cost of sales	49,462	47,904	80.91	83.43	1,558	3.25
Research and development	693	498	1.13	0.87	195	39.16
Selling and general	7,538	5,948	12.33	10.36	1,590	26.73
Operating income	3,440	3,070	5.63	5.35	370	12.05
Other income and expense	387	275	0.63	0.48	112	40.73
Income before taxes	3,827	3,345	6.26	5.83	482	14.41
Provision for income taxes	880	762	1.44	1.33	118	15.49
Net income	2,947	2,583	4.82	4.50	364	14.09

EXHIBIT 20.6
Dell Balance Sheet Analysis (financial data in millions)

	Financial Data		Vertical Analysis		Horizontal Analysis	
	2008	2007	2008(%)	2007(%)	$ Change	% Change
Cash and equivalents	$7,764	$9,546	28.17	37.24	($1,782)	(18.67)
Short-term investments	208	752	0.75	2.93	(544)	(72.34)
Accounts receivable, net	5,961	4,622	21.63	18.03	1,339	28.97
Inventories	1,180	660	4.28	2.57	520	78.79
Other current assets	4,767	4,359	17.30	17.00	408	9.36
Property, plant and equipment, net	2,668	2,409	9.68	9.40	259	10.75
Other noncurrent assets	5,013	3,287	18.19	12.82	1,726	52.51
Total assets	27,561	25,635	100.00	100.00	1,926	7.51
Accounts payable	11,492	10,430	41.70	40.69	1,062	10.18
Accrued liabilities	4,323	5,141	15.69	20.05	(818)	(15.91)
Other current liabilities	2,711	2,220	9.84	8.66	491	22.12
Long-term debt	362	569	1.31	2.22	(207)	(36.38)
Other long-term liabilities	4,844	2,836	17.58	11.06	2,008	70.80
Common stock and paid-in capital	10,683	10,218	38.76	39.86	465	4.55
Retained earnings	18,199	15,282	66.03	59.61	2,917	19.09
Accumulated comprehensive income	(16)	(28)	(0.06)	(0.11)	12	(42.86)
Treasury stock	(25,037)	(21,033)	(90.84)	(82.05)	(4,004)	19.04
Total liabilities and stockholders' equity	27,561	25,635	100.00	100.00	1,926	7.51

14.2 percent for Microsoft (Exhibit 20.8) gives us some insight into the cash management policies of the companies. Looking at the income statement we notice that Apple's cost of sales percentage for 2008 is 65.69 (Exhibit 20.3) while Dell's is 80.91 (Exhibit 20.5). Microsoft's cost of revenue percentage is only 19.2, however.

Comparing Apple to its competitors we notice that the cost of sales percentage is the highest while the net income percentage is the lowest. On the balance sheet we notice that Apple has the highest cash percentage and the highest retained earnings percentage.

Horizontal Analysis

Horizontal analysis is a system of financial statement analysis that shows a comparison of each item on a financial statement with that same item on statements from previous periods. That is, it compares one item to itself over time on a percentage basis to indicate the changes over time.[3] To determine the percentage change we divide the change in the item in dollars

[3] Some horizontal analyses are also done on a dollar basis.

EXHIBIT 20.7
Microsoft Income Statement Analysis (financial data in millions)

	Financial Data		Vertical Analysis		Horizontal Analysis	
	2008	2007	2008(%)	2007(%)	$ Change	% Change
Net sales	$60,420	$51,122	100.00	100.00	$9,298	18.19
Cost of sales	11,598	10,693	19.20	20.92	905	8.46
Research and development	8,164	7,121	13.51	13.93	1,043	14.65
Selling and general	18,166	14,784	30.07	28.92	3,382	22.88
Operating income	22,492	18,524	37.23	36.23	3,968	21.42
Other income and expense	1,322	1,577	2.19	3.08	(255)	(16.17)
Income before taxes	23,814	20,101	39.41	39.32	3,713	18.47
Provision for income taxes	6,133	6,036	10.15	11.81	97	1.61
Net income	17,681	14,065	29.26	27.51	3,616	25.71

EXHIBIT 20.8
Microsoft Balance Sheet Analysis (financial data in millions)

	Financial Data		Vertical Analysis		Horizontal Analysis	
	2008	2007	2008(%)	2007(%)	$ Change	% Change
Cash and equivalents	$10,339	$ 6,111	14.20	9.67	$4,228	69.19
Short-term investments	13,323	17,300	18.30	27.39	(3,977)	(22.99)
Accounts receivable, net	13,589	11,338	18.67	17.95	2,251	19.85)
Inventories	985	1,127	1.35	1.78	(142)	(12.60)
Other current assets	5,006	4,292	6.88	6.79	714	16.64
Property, plant & equipment, net	6,242	4,350	8.58	6.89	1,892	43.49
Other noncurrent assets	23,309	18,653	32.02	29.53	4,656	24.96
Total assets	72,793	63,171	100.00	100.00	9,622	15.23
Accounts payable	4,034	3,247	5.54	5.14	787	24.24
Accrued liabilities	2,934	2,325	4.03	3.68	609	26.19
Other current liabilities	22,918	18,182	31.48	28.78	4,736	26.05
Long-term debt	–0–	–0–				
Other long-term liabilities	6,621	8,320	9.10	13.17	(1,699)	(20.42)
Common stock and paid-in capital	62,849	60,557	86.34	95.86	2,292	3.78
Retained earnings	(27,703)	(31,114)	(38.06)	(49.25)	3,411	(10.96)
Accumulated comprehensive income	1,140	1,654	1.57	2.62	(514)	(31.08)
Treasury stock	–0–	–0–			–0–	
Total liabilities & stockholders' equity	72,793	63,171	100.00	100.00	9,622	15.23

(current year − base year) by the amount of the item in dollars in the base year. Horizontal analysis is helpful for discovering trends in financial statement relationships to predict short-term results. While trends may not predict the future accurately, understanding the implication of trends provides useful insights for both management and investors/creditors. Therefore horizontal analysis is typically done for a three-to-five-year period so that trends can be seen.

Exhibits 20.3 through 20.8 show the horizontal analysis for 2008 of Apple, Dell, and Microsoft. Notice that the percentage change is calculated for each financial statement item by taking the current year (2008) less the base year (2007) and dividing by the base year (2007). For example, Apple's cost of sales percentage is determined as:

$$(\$21{,}334 - \$15{,}852)/\$15{,}852 = 0.3458 \text{ or } 34.58\%$$

Through horizontal analysis we notice that Apple had a 38.27 percent change in net income while Dell's was only 14.09 percent and Microsoft's was only 25.71 percent. On the balance sheet it is interesting that Apple had a 26.98 percent increase in cash and a 109.07 percent increase in short-term investments. Dell exhibits the opposite pattern, with a 18.67 percent decrease in cash and a 72.34 percent decrease in short-term investments. Similarly, Microsoft shows a 69.19 percent increase in cash and a 22.99 percent decrease in short-term investments. Note also the deficit balance in retained earnings shown by Microsoft.

Ratio Analysis

As you know, careful analysis of current and past financial statements helps provide some of the answers about why things happened in certain companies the way they did. Ratio analysis makes it easy to compare relationships (1) for a company over time, (2) of different companies, and (3) with standards such as industry averages. Exhibit 20.9 shows the ratios commonly used in analyzing financial statements. We have previously calculated almost all of these ratios as part of the planning and evaluating process internal to companies. Now we use some to compare companies. Exhibit 20.10 shows the ratio analysis of Apple, Dell, and Microsoft.

Activity Ratios

Creditors and investors want to know whether the normal flow of funds from cash to inventory to accounts receivable and back to cash is sufficient and regular enough for a company to pay its debts on time or to pay dividends. One means of assessing business operations is by using activity ratios, which are financial ratios that are helpful in judging a company's efficiency in using its current assets and liabilities.

Accounts Receivable Turnover As we learned in Chapter 2, the accounts receivable turnover represents the relationship between accounts receivable and credit sales, and it measures how many times the company collected the average accounts receivable balance in the period. Days in the collection period is the number of days, on average, it takes to collect the average amount of accounts receivable. This leads us to raise two notes of caution about the computation of the accounts receivable turnover ratio. First, using total sales assumes that all the sales were made on open account and that the sales returns and allowances and sales discounts have been subtracted. If this is not the case, the numerator in the turnover ratio will be too large. Second, care must be exercised in using the average of beginning and ending accounts receivable balances. Many businesses are seasonal and have periods of high sales accompanied by large receivable balances. Ideally, the average accounts receivable balance should be the average of the beginning balances for each of the 12 months in the fiscal year.

Keep in mind that the managers of the corporation who perform financial statement analysis have access to the data necessary to make these computations accurately. However, when the detailed data on credit sales and monthly balances are not available, the analyst needs to understand the potential deficiencies involved. For example, using year-end balances rather than monthly data means that seasonal businesses with unusually high (low) accounts receivable balances at year-end appear to have an accounts receivable turnover that is slower (faster) than it is. Management would also compare its days in the selling period to its sales terms to evaluate the revenue process.

Looking at Exhibit 20.10, we notice that Apple and Dell have much higher accounts receivable turnover ratios (16 and 12, respectively) than does Microsoft (5) and, thus, much fewer days in their collection cycles. However, one must remember that many of Apple's and Dell's customers are cash customers rather than other businesses, which tends to drive the turnover ratio higher because sales are increased while accounts receivable is not affected.

Inventory Turnover Chapter 2 indicated that the inventory turnover represents the relationship between cost of goods sold and inventory; it measures how many times the company sold the average amount of inventory in the period. Days in the selling period is the number of days, on average, it takes the company to sell the average amount of inventory. Since we are dealing with the high technology industry, we would expect a high inventory

EXHIBIT 20.9 Important Financial Ratios

What Is Measured	Ratios	Means of Calculation
Activity	Accounts receivable turnover	$\frac{\text{Net credit sales*}}{\text{Average accounts receivable}}$
	Days in the collection period	$\frac{365}{\text{Accounts receivable turnover}}$
	Inventory turnover	$\frac{\text{Cost of goods sold}}{\text{Average inventory}}$
	Days in the selling period	$\frac{365}{\text{Inventory turnover}}$
	Accounts payable turnover	$\frac{\text{Cost of goods sold}}{\text{Average accounts payable}}$
	Days in the payment period	$\frac{365}{\text{Accounts payable turnover}}$
Liquidity and Solvency	Current ratio	$\frac{\text{Current assets}}{\text{Current liabilities}}$
	Quick ratio	$\frac{\text{Cash + Temporary investments + Receivables}}{\text{Current liabilities}}$
	Cash flow per share	$\frac{\text{Cash flow from operations} - \text{Preferred dividends}}{\text{Weighted average number of shares (common) outstanding}}$
Debt-Paying Ability	Debt-to-equity	$\frac{\text{Total liabilities}}{\text{Total shareholders' equity}}$
	Times interest earned	$\frac{\text{Net income before interest and taxes}}{\text{Interest expense}}$
Profitability	Gross margin	$\frac{\text{Gross margin}}{\text{Net sales}}$
	Return on sales	$\frac{\text{Net income}}{\text{Net sales}}$
	Return on assets	$\frac{\text{Net income before interest and taxes**}}{\text{Average total assets}}$
	Asset turnover	$\frac{\text{Net sales}}{\text{Average total assets}}$
	Return on owners' equity	$\frac{\text{Net income}}{\text{Average total shareholders' equity}}$
	Return on common equity	$\frac{\text{Net income} - \text{Preferred dividends}}{\text{Average total shareholders' equity less liquidating value of preferred stock}}$
	Earnings per share (EPS)	$\frac{\text{Net income} - \text{Preferred dividends}}{\text{Weighted average number of shares (common) outstanding}}$
Market-Based	Dividend payout	$\frac{\text{Dividends per share (common)}}{\text{Earnings per share}}$
	Price-earnings	$\frac{\text{Current market price per share (common)}}{\text{Earnings per share}}$
	Dividend yield	$\frac{\text{Dividends per share}}{\text{Current market price per share}}$

*If net credit sales are unknown, use total sales.
**If interest expense is unknown, use income before taxes.

Activity Ratios	**Apple**	**Dell**	**Microsoft**
Accounts receivable turnover	16.00	11.55	4.85
Days in the collection period	22.81	31.59	75.29
Inventory turnover	49.90	53.76	10.98
Days in the selling period	7.31	6.79	33.23
Accounts payable turnover	4.07	4.51	3.19
Days in the payment period	89.74	80.89	114.57
Liquidity and Solvency Ratios			
Current ratio	2.46	1.07	1.45
Quick ratio	1.91	0.75	1.25
Cash flow per share	$10.88	$1.78	$2.28
Debt-Paying Ability Ratios			
Debt-to-equity ratio	0.88	6.20	1.01
Profitability Ratios			
Gross margin ratio	34.31%	19.09%	80.80%
Return on sales ratio	14.88%	4.82%	29.26%
Return on assets ratio	21.24%	14.39%	35.03%
Asset turnover	1.00	2.30	0.89
Return on owner's equity ratio	27.19%	71.29%	52.48%
Earnings per share (given)	$5.48	$1.33	$1.90
Diluted earnings per share (given)	$5.36	$1.31	$1.87

turnover and small number of days in the selling period. But we must be cautious in our evaluation. If the company includes packaging as inventory or if it has deliberately increased the amount of inventory on hand due to a purchase of another company, for example, its average inventory will be higher. On the other hand, recall that when a company manufactures products on demand and practices just-in-time inventory management, its inventory will be relatively lower and therefore its inventory turnover will be relatively higher.

Also recall that companies must report work-in-process and finished goods inventories using full absorption costing. This means that fixed production costs have been assigned to the units in ending inventory. If the company has relatively high fixed overhead costs and large amounts of work-in-process and finished goods inventory, its ending inventory amounts will be relatively higher. We must also note if the company is using FIFO or LIFO costing. Comparing a FIFO costing company to a LIFO costing company can distort results in periods of changing prices. Finally we must be concerned about using the average of the beginning and ending balances of inventory. Again seasonal companies may experience fluctuating inventory levels throughout the year so a 12-month average would be better for purposes of calculating the inventory turnover. As with the accounts receivable turnover, managers of the company have access to the monthly data needed but external stakeholders must exercise caution if they believe 12-month data are needed but only annual data are available.

Looking at Exhibit 20.10, we notice that both Apple and Dell have very high inventory turnovers (50 and 54, respectively) compared to Microsoft (11). Apple's inventory turnover indicates that its selling cycle is slightly over 7 days while Dell's is slightly under 7 days. This shouldn't be too surprising, however, because Apple and Dell build computers only as customers order them; thus inventories are kept to a minimum (remember our discussion of just-in-time). Microsoft, on the other hand, has a selling period of approximately 33 days.

Accounts Payable Turnover The accounts payable turnover represents the relationship between cost of goods sold and accounts payable and measures how many times the company paid for the average amount of accounts payable during the period, as we learned in Chapter 2. Days in the payment period is the number of days, on average, it takes the company to pay for the average amount of accounts payable. Therefore mana pares this ratio against its purchasing terms to evaluate the expenditure proc sumes that accounts payable represents, primarily, purchases of inventory on that most inventories are purchased on account. Since many companies coml ventory purchases with other purchases on account, we must realize that acco may not be directly associated with only cost of goods sold. And we must real companies do pay cash for their inventory purchases. Also we must be con using the beginning and ending balances of accounts payable as they may not average balance of accounts payable throughout the period.

An examination of Exhibit 20.10 reveals that Apple and Dell have appro same accounts payable turnover, with Microsoft's being higher. Microsoft, on a its suppliers in 115 days, while Dell has 81 days in the payment period and 90 days on average to pays its accounts payable.

Liquidity and Solvency Ratios

When assessing a business as a potential investment, its liquidity is an importa tion, particularly for creditors whose returns rely exclusively on cash flows fr pany. Recall that liquidity and solvency refer to the cash position of a company to generate cash inflows through normal operations to meet the cash outflo Companies rarely have sufficient cash on hand to pay off all their liabilities. Tl depend on the timing of cash inflows in relation to the timing needs of the ou liabilities. On the other hand, firms with too much idle cash can indicate th financial resources are not being used effectively. Liquidity and solvency an cerned with cash flows and the adequacy of current assets to meet current liabil

Current Ratio As we discovered in Chapter 1, the current ratio measures the between the current assets and current liabilities of the company. If current a sufficient relative to current liabilities, the company may have difficulties meeti obligations as they become due. On the other hand, if current assets, relative t bilities, are excessive, the company may not be earning a sufficient return (rec rent assets do not provide returns) for shareholders. Again we must exercise comparing one company to another by making sure we understand the comp company's current assets and current liabilities. Looking at Exhibit 20.10 Apple's current ratio is much larger than Dell's or Microsoft's. In fact, it is al large.

Quick Ratio The quick ratio, as we found out in Chapter 2, provides a stricter equacy of current assets to meet current liabilities because it excludes, in the nu rent assets that are not readily convertible to cash, such as inventory and prepa quick ratio will always be smaller than the current ratio because nonliquid curr not included in the numerator of this ratio while the denominator is the same a rent ratio. Exhibit 20.10 indicates that Microsoft and Apple have much large than Dell. Recall that both cash and short-term investments decreased at Dell in analysis reveals relatively large current liabilities for Dell relative to the other co

Cash Flow per Share Analysts also can use cash flows from the statement to assess a company's liquidity on a common-size basis, as we did in Ch analysis of the statement of cash flows to determine cash from operating acti income statement to determine the weighted average shares outstanding fo companies reveals the following (in millions):

	Apple	Dell
Operating cash flows	$9,596	$3,949
Weighted average shares outstanding	881.592	2,223

Let the name help you with liquidity, solvency, and debt ratios:
Current ratio→current accounts
Quick ratio→liquid accounts
Debt-to-equity ratio→total debt over total owners' equity, etc.

Based on these data, the cash flow per share for Apple is $10.88 ($9,596/881.592); the cash flow per share for Dell is $1.78 ($3,949/2,223); and the cash flow per share for Microsoft is $2.28 ($21,612/9,470). Thus, while Apple has the smallest total cash flow from operations, on a per share basis, it is the largest of the three.

Debt-Paying-Ability Ratios

You already know that investors have an interest in a company's ability to repay debt, but the creditors, both current and potential, have the risk of not recovering their funds. They want to know about the company's debt structure and how that will affect the company's ability to meet both its short- and long-term debt obligations. We discuss two ratios typically used by creditors to evaluate a company's creditworthiness: times interest earned and debt-to-equity.

Times Interest Earned Creditors, especially long-term creditors, judge the ability of a borrower to pay interest based on the relationship of the borrower's before-interest earnings to the amount of the interest charges for the period. As we learned in Chapter 13, the times interest earned ratio compares earnings before deducting interest and taxes to the amount of the interest charges. A company whose income before interest is barely sufficient to cover its interest expense is riskier from a creditor's point of view than one with a high times interest earned ratio. Information was not available to determine the times interest earned ratios for the companies. Furthermore, neither Apple nor Microsoft have any long-term debt.

Debt-to-Equity Ratio Recall from Chapter 1 that the debt-to-equity ratio expresses the total liabilities as a percentage of the total owners' or shareholders' equity; thus, it measures a company's risk as an investment by the extent to which it relies on debt rather than ownership financing. A company whose debt increases relative to its owners' equity is generally considered riskier since larger amounts of debt imply larger interest payments. The debt-to-equity ratio also provides a picture of the financial flexibility of the company, that is, its ability to raise money from both debt and equity financing. A company with a high debt-to-equity ratio has limited financial flexibility because creditors and investors are not comfortable with the risk associated with high debt-to-equity ratios.

The debt-to-equity ratio should also be evaluated in conjunction with the times interest earned ratio. A company can have higher debt to equity if its times interest earned ratio is high. In other words, it can service its interest obligations associated with the higher amount of debt it is carrying. Apple's debt-to-equity ratio as shown in Exhibit 20.10 is 0.88, meaning that it has $0.88 of liabilities for every dollar in owners' equity. Microsoft's debt-to-equity ratio is approximately the same at 1.01, while Dell's is much higher at 6.20.

Profitability Ratios

Our analysis and evaluation to this point have been concerned with the company's ability to pay its debts on time. In a broader, more long-term sense, if the company is not profitable, it eventually will not meet its maturing obligations. Thus profitability is important to lenders. However, future profitability is also central to investors' analyses of a company's value as an investment because both the value of the company and the potential for dividend payments depend on a company's profitability.

Profitability is the return on funds invested by the owners and achieved by the efforts of management. Profitability results from numerous operating, investing, and financing decisions over different periods of time. Effectively measuring profitability requires more than examining the amount of net income in a particular period. The absolute dollar amount of profits in one period reveals very little about the effectiveness of operations and a company's long-term prospects.

Both current and potential owners of a business are interested in its long- and short-term profitability. They also are interested in the company's disposition of its earnings, which could be either distributed to them as dividends or reinvested in the company. If the company's stock is publicly traded, owners also are concerned with the stock market's perception of the company's profitability and its dividend policy. We discuss the role of market price in providing investors with a return on their investment later in the chapter.

Gross Margin Ratio Recall from Chapter 2 that product-pricing decisions directly affect profitability. If management prices a product too high, it sells fewer units. On the other hand, a price that is too low may not provide the company with a sufficient gross margin to cover operating expenses. Thus we use the gross margin ratio as a measure of profitability. Exhibit 20.10 reveals that Microsoft has the highest gross margin ratio at 80.8 percent, while Dell's is the smallest at 19.09 percent. Apple, at 34.31 percent, is in the middle. Apple's ratio indicates that it makes 34.31 cents of gross profit for every one dollar of sales generated.

Return on Sales As indicated in Chapter 1, the return on sales ratio measures the net income generated per dollar of sales. This ratio measures the relative profitability of the company's on-going operating activities. Thus while the gross margin ratio considers only the impact of cost of goods sold, the return on sales ratio considers the impact of all operating expenses on the net income of the company. Exhibit 20.10 reveals that Dell's return on sales ratio is the lowest of the three companies. Furthermore, we see that Microsoft's return on sales ratio (29.26 percent) is much larger than either Apple's or Dell's. Again, this indicates the dominance and strength of Microsoft.

Anytime you have a "return on" ratio, some form of income is the numerator.

Return on Assets Many analysts consider the return on assets (ROA) ratio singularly important because it includes the two fundamental profitability elements—earnings and investments in assets. The investment-in-assets element represents the total investment of the business, and the ratio of earnings before interest and taxes to those assets measures the effectiveness of management in utilizing the resources at its command. Note that the formula is slightly different than that used to evaluate divisions within the company that we learned in Chapter 17. Because the interest expense amounts were unavailable we calculated return on assets using "income before taxes." Again, Microsoft has the largest return at 35.03 percent, with Apple in the middle at 21.24 percent and Dell behind at 14.39 percent.

Asset Turnover Another way of looking at the profitability of assets is to determine the asset turnover as discussed in Chapter 17. The asset turnover ratio measures the company's ability to generate sales given the amount of assets at its disposal. Therefore, a high asset turnover indicates that the company is utilizing its assets well. An examination of Exhibit 20.10 reveals that Dell has the highest asset turnover at 2.3, followed by Apple at 1.0 and Microsoft at 0.89.

Return on Owners' Equity Another measure of profitability is return on owners' equity (ROE), which measures the return earned (net income) relative to the portion of the company that belongs to the owners. Recall from Chapter 13 that often we calculate return on equity only for common shareholders and that this measure is called *return on common equity*. If there is preferred stock outstanding, adjustments are made for preferred dividends and the amount of preferred stock, to derive a return on common equity. The net income in the numerator is reduced by the amount of preferred stock dividends, and the denominator is reduced by the liquidating value of the preferred stock, which is the amount that the corporation would have to pay to purchase all the preferred stock from the preferred shareholders. The return on equity ratios of the three companies reveal that Dell provides the best return to its investors at 71.29 percent, while Apple's return on owners' equity is the smallest at 27.19 percent. Microsoft's return on equity is 52.48 percent.

Earnings per Share We know from Chapter 17 that earnings per share (EPS), both basic and diluted, is such an important measure of profitability that it is required to be presented as part of the income statement. Earnings per share measures the net income of the company on a common-size basis.

Recall that you should also look at diluted earnings per share to determine the impact on earnings per share of stock options and convertible securities. The amounts shown in Exhibit 20.10 were taken from each company's income statement for 2008. Apple's basic earnings per share is $5.48 and its diluted earnings per share is $5.36, which are both higher than the other two companies. Microsoft's earnings per share and diluted earnings per share are $1.90 and $1.87, respectively. Dell indicates earnings per share of $1.33 and diluted earnings per share of $1.31 for 2008.

Dividend Payout Ratio As part of financing and operating decisions, some companies pay dividends to their shareholders, while others do not. Investors differ in their investment objectives, and not all investors want to receive dividends. Part of investors' evaluation of a potential investment is assessing the corporation's dividend policy. The **dividend payout ratio** reveals a company's dividend payment philosophy. The dividend payout ratio relates the amount of dividends paid to the period's earnings. The dividend payout ratio enables financial statement users to assess the prospects for future cash flows paid directly to them by the corporation, which is not the same as the amount of cash flows received by the business. Rather, dividend payout shows the portion of the company's assets distributed to the common shareholders as well as the remaining portion of earnings that is reinvested in the company. Therefore, the dividend payout ratio gives the financial statement reader an indication of management's policy on reinvesting the earnings of the company.

Microsoft paid dividends of $0.44 per share while Dell and Apple did not pay dividends during fiscal 2008. Note that growth companies with high return on equity ratios often have low or zero dividend payout ratios because they are making such a high rate of return that investors would prefer to keep the money in the company.

Market-Based Ratios

Stock markets are an important part of the world's capital markets. They allow numerous transactions involving the purchase and sale of corporate stock on a daily basis. In addition to offering investors a place to exchange stock, stock markets provide corporations with a place to sell additional stock to raise capital and to repurchase their stock easily. In addition to the NYSE, AMEX, and NASDAQ in the United States, there are major stock exchanges throughout the world in places such as London and Tokyo.

One important feature of stock exchanges is that the buyers and sellers are rarely present. This allows large volumes of trades to occur. Another important feature of these exchanges is that trading rules protect buyers and sellers. Because the parties to the buy and sell transactions are not present at the transaction, they would be reluctant to trade if there was not some protection for their cash and investments.

In the stock market, investors buy and sell ownership interest in corporations (stock) at a mutually agreeable price. When there are prospects for a company to be more profitable and, thus, more valuable, stock prices go up. In such circumstances, the price the holders of stock demand and the price the buyers of that stock offer both go up. When the prospects for company performance take a downturn, the opposite happens. This process results in the establishment of the market price of a stock. Investors use the price-earnings and the dividend yield ratios to evaluate the stocks they are considering. Both of these ratios use the market price of the stocks as part of the calculation.

Price-Earnings Ratio The **price-earnings (PE) ratio** reflects the relationship between the current market price of the company's common stock and the earnings of the company. The importance of the price-earnings ratio is reflected by the fact that it is included in the stock listings of *The Wall Street Journal.* Keep in mind that the PE ratio changes frequently as the price of the stock changes each day, or as annual earnings are announced.

The price-earnings ratio is an overall approximation of the market's assessment of a company's prospective earnings performance. A high PE ratio suggests that the market anticipates higher earnings for the company in the future. The price-earnings ratio is often referred to as the earnings multiple and is a measure used by investors to decide whether to buy, sell, or hold a particular stock. For example, if the price-earnings multiple is considered to be low by an investor, then the investor would view the stock price as low relative to its earnings potential and might buy the security. On the other hand, if an investor holds a company's stock that has an earnings multiple that the investor considers too high, then the investor might sell the stock in anticipation of the decline in its market price. The earnings multiple can vary widely by industry and by company. Determining whether a PE ratio is too high or too low is based on the belief of the investor making the investment decision. Let's assume that the market price of Apple's common stock on September 27, 2008, was $45 per share; its PE ratio would be $45/$5.48 = 8.21. This means that the market price of a share of stock is almost 8 times higher than the earnings on that share of stock.

OF INTEREST The History of the NYSE and the DJIA

As you know the DJIA (Dow Jones Industrial Average) consists of 30 "blue-chip" stocks, the majority of which are traded on the NYSE (New York Stock Exchange). The NYSE is the oldest exchange, having been formed in 1792 by 24 brokers under the Buttonwood Agreement (they met under a buttonwood tree at what is now 68 Wall Street).

- By 1835, the average daily trading volume was 8,500 shares.
- In 1873, the NYSE closed for 10 days when a prestigious Philadelphia bank failed, leading to financial panic.
- In 1886, the DJIA was calculated for the first time (using only 12 stocks) with an initial value of 40.74, and the NYSE had its first 1-million-share day.
- In 1914, in response to WWI, the NYSE partially closes for four and a half months.
- In 1929, the DJIA reaches a peak of 381.17; on October 29 of that year with a record volume of 16 million shares, the Dow falls 11 percent.
- By 1932, when the dust finally clears, the Dow is down 89 percent from its 1929 peak.
- In March 1933, President Roosevelt declares a bank holiday and the NYSE closes.
- The 1929 DJIA peak is finally surpassed in 1954.
- In 1961, the average daily volume on the NYSE is 4 million shares.
- In 1972, the Dow closes over 1,000 for the first time.
- On October 19, 1987, the DJIA experiences a 508-point (22.6 percent) drop.
- In 1991, the Dow closes above 3,000 for the first time.
- On October 27, 1997, the DJIA experiences a 554-point drop; the very next day it rebounds 337 points.
- In 1999, the Dow closes above 10,000 for the first time.
- On September 11, 2001; in response to the terrorists' attacks on the World Trade Center, the NYSE closes for four days.
- On September 17 on the same year, the Dow drops 684.81 points.

The graph below shows the DJIA from March 2004 through March 2009, a period during which the Dow reached a peak of over 14,000 and dropped to a low of 6,726.

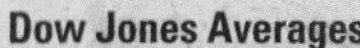

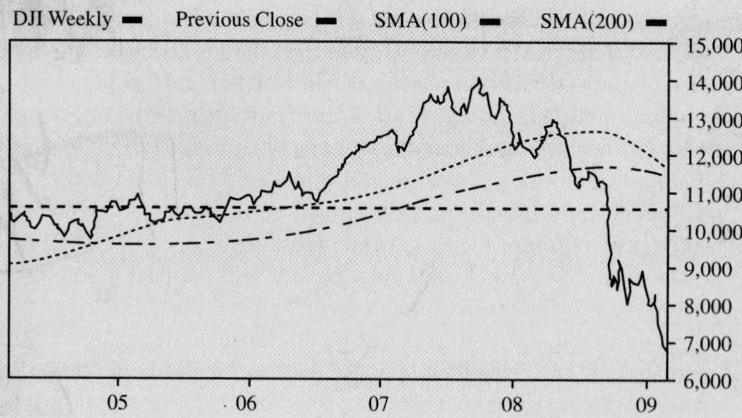

Dividend Yield The **dividend yield ratio** measures the return that an investor would receive on a company's stock at the current price, if dividends paid in the recent past continue into the foreseeable future. It is applied to both preferred and common stock. The dividend yield does not measure the return from appreciation of the stock price. Rather, it measures the cash return as a percentage of the stock's current price. It is calculated by dividing the dividend per share of stock by the current market price of the stock.

For companies with established dividend policies, the dividend yield is an important component of the return that investors expect. For example, preferred stock typically has a specified dividend amount, and investors who buy preferred stock realize that this set dividend yield will provide most of their return. If the amount of the specified dividend, which is the principal source of return on preferred stock, is not satisfactory, the investor will not buy the preferred stock.

Other Information

Remember that the information provided in a company's financial statements is only part of the information that prudent creditors and investors need. In addition to sources of industry and economic information, investors should include in their assessment the value that a stock's market price implies. Recall that most major corporations are run by professional

OF INTEREST Regulatory Reporting

The SEC administers the 1934 Securities and Exchange Act, which requires companies that trade their stock publicly to file reports with the SEC. The three most common reports are the 10-K, the 10-Q, and the 8-K. The 10-K is filed annually, usually within three months of the company's fiscal year-end. Today 10-Ks are filed electronically and become part of the SEC's EDGAR database. Information in EDGAR is available to the public through the SEC's Web site at **www.sec.gov.**

Form 10-K must include the audited financial statements of the company and the audit report of the CPA firm that conducted the audit.

Form 10-Q is a quarterly report of financial condition and is filed for the first three quarters of the registrant's fiscal year. It is not audited and the additional disclosures are not as extensive as Form 10-K.

Form 8-K is filed when significant events have occurred that the registrant must report. For example, if the registrant changes the CPA firm that audits its financial statements, it must file Form 8-K explaining when and why the change was made.

managers whose actual ownership may be only a small portion of the company's outstanding stock. The annual report is the principal way that managers communicate their assessment and perception of the company.

Management's Letter to Shareholders

Much of the information that managers want to communicate appears in the management's letter to shareholders. This written report gives an overview of the items other than financial statements in the annual report and highlights important aspects of financial performance. Remember one of the purposes of the annual report is for management to highlight its performance over the past period. Therefore management's letter to shareholders should be read very carefully to determine areas in need of improvement and areas where the company is doing well.

Management's letter to shareholders also addresses employees and highlights key operating data. Then, typically, the company discusses operating results in detail as well as any unusual events that occurred in the past or will occur in the future.

Segment and Quarterly Data

One important disclosure for large corporations includes segment data. Large corporations usually are involved in several lines of business that often are spread around the globe. Recall that companies must disclose segment activities as part of the annual report in certain circumstances. By revealing this information, stakeholders can assess major parts of the business.

Because investors want to know how the business is faring more often than once a year, companies often issue quarterly financial statements. Issuing statements at three-month intervals provides shareholders and investors with timely information to use in decision making. Quarterly results are also included as part of the annual report so that investors can compare companies quarter by quarter.

Auditor's Report

One other important disclosure included in annual reports is the auditor's report. Recall that CPAs provide an opinion about the fairness of the financial statements using GAAP as the criteria. There are four kinds of reports issued (given) by external auditors: unqualified, qualified, adverse, and a disclaimer of opinion. When an auditor issues an unqualified opinion, it means that the financial statements are fair representations of the business's financial position, cash flows, and reported income; and that, in the auditor's opinion, the company has applied GAAP appropriately. A qualified opinion indicates that either the auditor found parts of the company's financial statements not in accordance with GAAP or the auditor's ability to examine the underlying records used to develop the financial statements was limited. Qualified opinions mean that, overall, the statements are fair representations of the business's financial position and reported income but that certain parts of the statements, as indicated in a portion of the auditor's report, are not disclosed as specified by GAAP. Exhibit 20.11 shows the paragraph that Deloitte & Touche, LLP put in its March 4, 2009, auditors' report of General Motors.

EXHIBIT 20.11
General Motors' Auditor's Report

The accompanying consolidated financial statements for the year ended December 31, 2008, have been prepared assuming that the Corporation will continue as a going concern. As discussed in Note 2 to the consolidated financial statements, the Corporation's recurring losses from operations, stockholders' deficit, and inability to generate sufficient cash flow to meet its obligations and sustain its operations raise substantial doubt about its ability to continue as a going concern. Management's plans concerning these matters are also discussed in Note 3 to the consolidated financial statements. The consolidated financial statements do not include any adjustments that might result from the outcome of this uncertainty.

Deloitte & Touche, March 4, 2009
Taken from the Annual Report of General Motors

CPAs rarely issue the other two kinds of audit reports. An adverse opinion indicates that the external auditor believes that the financial statements are not fair representations of the company's financial position or income. Keep in mind that what is considered fair is based on GAAP accounting standards. The financial statements are management's representations, and an adverse opinion means that the CPA finds that management's financial statements do not comply with GAAP and, therefore, are not fair representations of the company's financial position or performance. A disclaimer of opinion means that the auditor was not able to gather sufficient evidence to support an opinion or that the auditor was not sufficiently independent of the company to issue an opinion.

The auditor's report is an important part of the annual report because it provides assurance that the financial statements meet the reporting standards represented by GAAP. When CPAs state that financial statements, considered as a whole, are materially correct, they believe that if any remaining errors were considered together, such errors would not change the outcome of decisions (such as whether to buy or sell the company's stock or whether to lend the company money) made by an *informed reader* of the statements.

Key point: The auditor's report does not guarantee that the company is a good investment nor does it guarantee that the company will not declare bankruptcy.

Summary

Creditors and investors own the capital that businesses need to finance their investments. Financial statement analysis provides important information that creditors and investors use to choose businesses in which they will invest their capital. However, the data from financial statements are not sufficient for a thorough understanding of investment opportunities.

- Consumer demand for products indirectly determines which businesses will be able to attract the capital they need from the capital markets. Creditors and investors need reliable information on which to base their investment decisions.
- Financial statement analysis requires a thorough understanding of the statements themselves and the accounting classifications used by the business. A careful reading of the statements should precede the computations of analytical ratios.
- The ratios used as part of financial statement analysis are classified into these categories: activity, liquidity and solvency, debt-paying ability, and profitability. Activity ratios focus on the efficiency with which management uses the company's current assets and liabilities. Liquidity and solvency ratios reveal the company's ability to pay its current debts on time. Assessing debt-paying ability requires ratios that measure the risk of not receiving interest or principal repayment. Profitability ratios focus on the long-term earnings potential of a business.
- Stock markets are places where buyers and sellers of the stock of many companies typically engage in transactions through brokers. Stock markets provide information about the value of a company that investors use in addition to the information from financial statement analysis to make their investment decisions.

Key Terms

Capital market The entire group of creditors and investors who provide capital to businesses to allow them to finance their investments, *564*

Dividend payout ratio A ratio that reveals a company's dividend payment philosophy by relating the amount of dividends paid to the period's income, *579*

Dividend yield ratio A ratio that measures the return an investor would receive on a company's stock at the current price if the recent dividend payments continue into the foreseeable future, *580*

Price-earnings (PE) ratio A ratio that reflects the relationship between the current market price of the company's stock and the earnings of the company, *579*

Questions

1. Who are the major user groups of financial statements, and how do their perspectives on the analysis of financial statements differ?
2. What is meant by comparative financial statements and how are they used in horizontal analysis?
3. What is the advantage of analyzing a company's financial statements over a series of years rather than just for the current period?
4. Why are external standards important?
5. What is a financial ratio?
6. Briefly explain what is meant by liquidity analysis, and state why it is important.
7. If you know a company has a current ratio of 2 to 1, why is that not enough information to judge its liquidity?
8. Explain what is meant when it is stated that a company has a quick ratio of 1.75.
9. What do activity ratios measure?
10. What is meant by profitability analysis?
11. What is the difference between return on assets and asset turnover?
12. What is the difference between return on assets and return on owners' equity?
13. What is meant by earnings per share?
14. How is earnings per share different from diluted earnings per share?
15. What is meant by the price-earnings ratio?
16. Does the dividend payout ratio tell you anything different from the information included in the computation for dividends per share?
17. Why do analysts use ratios to evaluate company performance?
18. Explain why an analyst would want to use more than one ratio that measures the same characteristic of a company, such as liquidity or profitability.
19. The market price of its stock is something that a company has very little control over. Why is it an important part of analyzing a company's performance?
20. Explain why dividend yield measures profitability from the shareholders' perspective rather than the company's perspective.

Exercises

E20.1 LO 1

Using the data in these abbreviated income statements, prepare a vertical analysis.

	Year 2	Year 1
Sales	$360,000	$518,000
Cost of goods sold	220,000	316,000
Gross margin	$140,000	$202,000
Operating expenses	110,000	152,600
Net income	$ 30,000	$ 49,400

LO 2 **E20.2**

Refer to E20.1 and perform a horizontal analysis showing the change from Year 1 to Year 2.

LO 2 E20.3 Prepare a vertical analysis for this condensed balance sheet:

	Year 2	Year 1
Cash	$ 60,000	$ 56,000
Accounts receivable	142,500	136,000
Inventory	195,000	178,000
Property, plant, and equipment	352,500	252,000
Total assets	$750,000	$622,000
Accounts payable and accrued liabilities	$127,500	$160,000
Long-term liabilities	150,000	0
Shareholders' equity	472,500	462,000
Total liabilities and shareholders' equity	$750,000	$622,000

LO 2 E20.4 Refer to E20.3 and perform a horizontal analysis showing the change from Year 1 to Year 2.

LO 3 E20.5 These summarized data were obtained from the accounting records of Hamberg Company at the end of its fiscal year, September 30:

	2010	2009
Cash	$ 30,200	$ 27,200
Accounts receivable	149,000	128,000
Inventory	140,200	90,600
All other assets	435,900	333,500
Accounts payable	131,600	109,500
Bank note payable, due in 90 days	60,000	36,000
Note payable, due in eight years	34,300	27,500
Sales	980,800	800,600
Cost of goods sold	827,500	651,700
Operating expenses	35,600	26,300

Compute the following for 2010 given the data provided:

A. Activity ratios.
B. Liquidity and solvency ratios.

LO 3 E20.6 Refer to E20.5 and calculate the profitability and debt-paying-ability ratios.

LO 3 E20.7 Refer to Exhibits 20.3 and 20.4. Compute the ratios for Apple in Exhibit 20.9. Check your answers against those provided in Exhibit 20.10.

LO 3 E20.8 Refer to Exhibits 20.5 and 20.6. Compute the ratios for Dell in Exhibit 20.9. Check your answers against those provided in Exhibit 20.10.

LO 3 E20.9 Refer to Exhibits 20.7 and 20.8. Compute the ratios for Microsoft in Exhibit 20.9. Check your answers against those provided in Exhibit 20.10.

LO 3 E20.10 After a fire destroyed the accounting records and most of the offices of Park Company, the owner decided to ask the bank for a short-term loan to supplement the insurance settlement. The owner remembers the following information and asks you to determine the current ratio so that she may use that information in her loan application:

Current assets	$ 40,000
Long-term liabilities	60,000
Net income	32,000
Return on assets	8%
Ratio of debt-to-equity	0.25

LO 3 E20.11 Brudvik Company has total liabilities of $350,000 and total owners' equity of $500,000. The company had net income of $66,000 after deducting interest expense of $8,000. This is a proprietorship and, as such, does not pay income tax on its net income. Compute the return on assets and the return on owners' equity. What is the debt-to-equity ratio? What is the times interest earned ratio?

LO 3 E20.12 As you learned in Chapter 17, the Du Pont return on investment formula calculates return on investment (return on assets) using return on sales and asset turnover. Using the following information, determine the missing amounts:

	Case 1	Case 2	Case 3
Assets	$400,000	?	$100,000
Sales	$600,000	?	?
Net income	?	$45,000	?
Return on sales	6%	?	?
Return on assets	?	15%	20%
Asset turnover	?	3	5

LO 3 E20.13 Knirsfla Imports has total shareholders' equity of $1,298,000 on September 30, 2010. The company issues only no-par common stock and had 300,000 shares outstanding on that date. During the fiscal year ended September 30, 2010, the company earned net income of $186,600 and paid dividends totaling $67,800. The stock was selling for $15 per share. Compute the following:

A. Return on common equity
B. Dividend payout ratio
C. Earnings per share
D. Price-earnings ratio
E. Dividend yield

LO 3 E20.14 Giertsen Products presently has an accounts receivable turnover of 11 and an inventory turnover of 7. For each of the following transactions, specify the effect of the transaction on these two ratios. Use **I** for increase, **D** for decrease, and **NC** for no change.

	Turnover A/R	Turnover INV
A. Collection of an account receivable.	_______	_______
B. Recording accrued but unpaid interest.	_______	_______
C. Purchase of inventory on account.	_______	_______
D. Payment of an account payable.	_______	_______
E. Borrowing from the bank on a short-term note.	_______	_______
F. Purchase of temporary investments.	_______	_______
G. Payment of insurance premium of six months in advance.	_______	_______
H. Additional contributions of cash made by owners.	_______	_______
I. Purchase of equipment with a cash down payment and long-term note payable.	_______	_______
J. Granted sales allowances to a customer.	_______	_______

LO 3 E20.15 Giertsen Products presently has a current ratio of 2.0 to 1 and a quick ratio of 1.8 to 1. For each of the following transactions, specify the effect of the transaction on these two ratios. Use **I** for increase, **D** for decrease, and **NC** for no change. Consider each transaction separately.

	Current	Quick
A. Collection of an account receivable.	_______	_______
B. Recording accrued but unpaid interest.	_______	_______
C. Purchase of inventory on account.	_______	_______
D. Payment of an account payable.	_______	_______
E. Borrowing from the bank on a short-term note.	_______	_______
F. Purchase of temporary investments.	_______	_______
G. Payment of insurance premium of six months in advance.	_______	_______
H. Additional contributions of cash made by owners.	_______	_______
I. Purchase of equipment with a cash down payment and long-term note payable.	_______	_______
J. Granted a sales allowance to a credit customer.	_______	_______

LO 3 E20.16 Nagell Industries has a debt-to-equity ratio of 0.75 to 1 and a times interest earned ratio of 10. For each transaction or change listed here, determine the effect on the debt-to-equity and times interest earned ratios. Consider each event by itself and fill in the blanks with **I** for increase, **D** for decrease, and **NC** for no change.

	Debt-to-Equity	Times Interest Earned
A. Pay long-term liability.	_______	_______
B. Purchase equipment for cash.	_______	_______
C. Increase gross margin percentage.	_______	_______
D. Increase average inventory by purchasing on open account.	_______	_______
E. Decrease operating expenses as a percentage of sales.	_______	_______
F. Issue additional capital stock for cash.	_______	_______
G. Decrease number of units sold.	_______	_______
H. Purchase buildings with partial payment and issue a mortgage payable for the balance.	_______	_______

LO 3 E20.17 Nagell Industries has a return on sales ratio of 5 percent and a return on assets ratio of 20 percent. For each of these transactions or changes, determine the effect of the transaction on the return on sales and return on assets. Consider each event by itself and fill in the blanks with **I** for increase, **D** for decrease, and **NC** for no change.

	Return on Sales	Return on Assets
A. Pay long-term liability.	_______	_______
B. Purchase equipment for cash.	_______	_______
C. Increase gross margin percentage.	_______	_______
D. Increase average inventory by purchasing on open account.	_______	_______
E. Decrease operating expenses as a percentage of sales.	_______	_______
F. Issue additional capital stock for cash.	_______	_______
G. Purchase buildings with partial payment and issue a mortgage payable for the balance.	_______	_______

LO 3 E20.18 Hasseldine, Inc., had $1,600,000 in net income for 2010 after deducting interest expense of $320,000 and income taxes of $500,000. The price of the stock at the fiscal year-end was $35. The company's shareholders' equity follows:

Preferred stock, 6 percent, $10 par value, authorized 200,000 shares, 50,000 shares issued and outstanding	500,000
Common stock, $5 par value, authorized 1,000,000 shares, 700,000 shares issued and outstanding	$3,500,000
Paid-in capital in excess of par, common stock	900,000
Total contributed capital	$4,900,000
Retained earnings	1,754,000
Total shareholders' equity	$6,654,000

A. Determine the times interest earned.
B. Compute the earnings per share.
C. Calculate the return on common equity.
D. Determine the price-earnings ratio at the fiscal year-end.

LO 3 E20.19 These summarized data are from the records of Greenhalgh Enterprises at the end of the fiscal year:

	2010	2009
Cash	$ 213,860	$ 205,140
Temporary investments	520,370	–0–
Accounts receivable	2,589,950	2,925,540
Inventory	3,684,970	3,480,210
All other assets	2,494,730	4,219,750
Accounts payable	1,142,630	1,054,950
Other current liabilities from operations	517,320	658,160
Current bank loans payable	1,073,880	1,580,000
Long-term liabilities	2,000,000	2,000,000

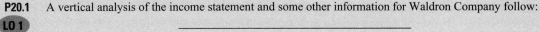

Sales	23,804,700	22,838,400
Cost of goods sold	20,543,450	18,910,190
Operating expenses	2,323,870	2,986,995
Tax expense	281,088	282,365
Cash flows from operations	925,871	976,543

Calculate the following:

A. Activity ratios
B. Liquidity ratios, assuming the weighted average shares outstanding are 1,540,900.

Problems

P20.1 A vertical analysis of the income statement and some other information for Waldron Company follow:

	Income Statement
Sales	100%
Cost of goods sold	62
Gross margin	38
Operating expenses	32
Net income	6
Operating expenses	$144,000
Asset turnover	2.5
Ratio of debt to equity	0.5
Current ratio	1.8

Required:

A. Determine the dollar amount for all items shown on the income statement.
B. Compute the dollar amounts for the following balance sheet items:
   1. Current assets.
   2. Property, plant, and equipment.
   3. Total assets.
   4. Current liabilities (there are no long-term liabilities).
   5. Owners' equity.
   6. Total liabilities and owners' equity.

LO 1 LO 2 **P20.2** The condensed financial statements of Poletti Company are as follows:

POLETTI COMPANY
Income Statement
For the Years Ended March 31

	2010	2009
Sales	$370,000	$350,000
Cost of goods sold	265,200	250,800
Gross margin	$104,800	$99,200
Operating expenses	79,000	78,200
Income before taxes	$ 25,800	$ 21,000
Income tax expense	7,740	6,300
Net income	$ 18,060	$ 14,700

POLETTI COMPANY
Statement of Financial Position
March 31

	2010	2009
Assets		
Cash	$ 20,800	$ 19,400
Accounts receivable	38,200	37,600
Inventory	25,300	22,700
Property, plant, and equipment	178,700	169,300
Total assets	$263,000	$249,000

Liabilities and Shareholders' Equity		
Accounts payable	$ 24,200	$ 29,500
Long-term liabilities	142,000	132,000
Shareholders' equity	96,800	87,500
Total liabilities and shareholders' equity	$263,000	$249,000

Additional Information: Common stock issued and outstanding: 50,000 shares
Market price of the stock: 3/31/2010, $23
Dividends paid: 2010, $10,000
Cash flows from operations: 2010, $9,560
Interest expense included in operating expense: 2010, $11,360

Required: A. Prepare a vertical analysis for 2010 and 2009.
B. Prepare a horizontal analysis for 2010.

LO 3 **P20.3** Refer to P20.2 and prepare a ratio analysis for 2010 in as much detail as possible.

LO 1 LO 2 **P20.4** Refer to Ford Motor Company, Inc. (**www.ford.com**), and find the most recent annual report.

Required: A. Prepare a vertical analysis.
B. Prepare a horizontal analysis.
C. Comment on any trends you see.

LO 3 **P20.5** Refer to P20.4 and prepare a complete ratio analysis and comment on anything unusual you find.

LO 1 LO 2 **P20.6** Refer to Walt Disney Company (**www.disney.com**), and find the most recent annual report.

Required: A. Prepare a vertical analysis.
B. Prepare a horizontal analysis.
C. Comment on any trends you see.

LO 3 **P20.7** Refer to P20.6 and prepare a complete ratio analysis and comment on anything unusual you find.

LO 1 LO 2 **P20.8** Refer to PepsiCo Corporation (**www.pepsico.com**), and find the most recent annual report.

Required: A. Prepare a vertical analysis.
B. Prepare a horizontal analysis.
C. Comment on any trends you see.

LO 3 **P20.9** Refer to P20.8 and prepare a complete ratio analysis and comment on anything unusual you find.

LO 1 **P20.10** Refer to Apple Corporation (**www.apple.com**), and find the most recent annual report.

LO 2 A. Prepare a vertical analysis.
B. Prepare a horizontal analysis.
C. Comment on any trends you see in comparison to Exhibits 20.3 and 20.4.

LO 3 **P20.11** Refer to P20.10 and prepare a complete ratio analysis. Comment on anything unusual you find in comparison to Exhibit 20.10.

Cases

C20.1 Refer to the company you selected in C1.1.

Required: A. Prepare a vertical analysis.
B. Prepare a horizontal analysis.
LO 1 LO 2 LO 3 C. Complete a ratio analysis.
D. Comment on any trends you see.

LO 1 LO 2 LO 3 LO 4 **C20.2** Refer to Gateway Inc. (**www.gateway.com**), and Hewlett-Packard (**www.hp.com**), and find the most recent annual reports.

Required: A. Prepare a vertical analysis.
B. Prepare a horizontal analysis.
C. Complete a ratio analysis.
D. Comment on any trends you see.
E. Compare the two companies.

LO 3 LO 4 **C20.3** Select a company listed on the New York Stock Exchange and conduct a ratio analysis on the company. Organize the analysis from the perspective of management, current or potential shareholders, and creditors. Once the ratios are calculated, use either Dun & Bradstreet's *Key Business Ratios* or

Robert Morris Associates' *Annual Statement Studies* to compare your company's results with other companies with similar operations.

Critical Thinking

CT20.1 LO 4 Consider the differences between the investment decisions of internal stakeholders and those of external stakeholders. Describe any differences in the nature of their investment objectives. Relate those differences to the types of information they would use to make investment decisions.

LO 4 **CT20.2** The market value of a corporation as a whole can be estimated by multiplying the number of shares of common stock times the market value at any given time. The corporation's book value is simply the book value of its assets less the book value of its liabilities, or its recorded equity value. Discuss reasons why these two values might differ for the same company and why the difference might be greater or less for different companies.

Ethical Challenges

EC20.1 LO 4 Assume that you work for a corporation and discover that news of a new product it developed had contributed greatly to the recent rise in its stock price. Your company's new product has been rendered obsolete by the new product of a competitor. You own a substantial number of shares of the corporation's stock. The news of the competitor's discovery has not been made public. Should you sell the stock? Why or why not?

EC20.2 Investigate either the Enron or the WorldCom bankruptcies in the early 2000s. For either case, explain the failures of the board of directors, the external auditors, the bankers associated with the company, the market analysts, and the leadership of the company. Based on your knowledge, who do you feel is responsible for the downfall of the company? Why?

Computer Applications

CA20.1 LO 3 The following list of accounts was adapted from the annual report of Wiley Industries:

Cash and cash equivalents	$ 21,989,062
Marketable securities	9,199,490
Notes receivable, current, net	3,560,747
Accounts receivable, net	23,247,355
Inventories	4,411,714
Prepaid expenses	1,086,561
Miscellaneous current assets	1,610,043
Notes receivable, long-term, net	21,406,772
Miscellaneous long-term assets	1,201,849
Leaseholds, net	83,770,710
Rental properties, net	3,451,108
Property, plant, and equipment, net	9,349,670
Accounts payable	16,901,824
Accrued liabilities	2,092,851
Other current liabilities	6,962,960
Income taxes payable	761,626
Current maturities of long-term debt	1,913,481
Deferred income taxes	4,955,000
Long-term debt	23,901,770
Class A common stock	156,594
Class B common stock	90,291
Paid-in capital	3,340,075
Retained earnings	?
Net sales	241,625,862
Service fees	51,601,113
Other fees and income	7,611,539
Real estate finance and rental income	8,988,027
Other revenue	1,267,434
Cost of sales	217,441,994
Expenses applicable to real estate	8,159,375
Selling, general, and administrative expense	37,515,701
Interest expense	1,425,788
Income taxes	19,520,000

Required: Use a computer spreadsheet program to complete a ratio analysis.

LO 1 LO 2 LO 3 **CA20.2** The following information was taken from the accounting records of Prentice Company for the years ended April 30:

	2010	2009	2008
Current assets:			
Cash	$ 35,000	$ 38,000	$ 10,000
Trading securities	12,000	11,000	62,000
Accounts receivable	175,000	166,000	112,000
Inventories	225,000	209,000	269,000
Prepaid expenses	5,000	10,000	4,000
Total current assets	$ 452,000	$ 434,000	$ 457,000
Property, plant, and equipment:			
Land	$ 50,000	$ 50,000	$ 50,000
Building, net of depreciation	141,000	149,000	157,000
Equipment, net of depreciation	68,000	74,000	72,000
Total property, plant, and equipment	$ 259,000	$ 273,000	$ 279,000
Total assets	$ 711,000	$ 707,000	$ 736,000
Current liabilities:			
Accounts payable	$ 69,000	$ 67,000	$ 60,000
Notes payable	40,000	60,000	60,000
Other current liabilities	52,000	41,000	19,000
Total current liabilities	$ 161,000	$ 168,000	$ 139,000
Long-term liabilities	88,000	92,000	161,000
Total liabilities	$ 249,000	$ 260,000	$ 300,000
Owners' equity	462,000	447,000	436,000
Total liabilities and owners' equity	$ 711,000	$ 707,000	$ 736,000
Sales	$1,920,000	$2,085,000	$1,880,000
Cost of goods sold	1,152,000	1,209,000	1,110,000
Gross margin	$ 768,000	$ 876,000	$ 770,000
Operating expenses	698,000	731,000	688,000
Net income	$ 70,000	$ 145,000	$ 82,000

Required: Use a computer spreadsheet to do the following:

A. Complete a vertical analysis for 2010, 2009, and 2008.
B. Complete a horizontal analysis for 2010 and 2009.
C. Complete a ratio analysis for 2010 and 2009.
D. Comment on any trends you see.

Visit the text Online Learning Center at **www.mhhe.com/ainsworth6e** for additional problem material that accompanies this chapter.

APPENDIX

Apple's 2008 Financial Statements and Accompanying Notes

CONSOLIDATED BALANCE SHEETS

(In millions, except share amounts)

	September 27, 2008	September 29, 2007
ASSETS:		
Current assets:		
Cash and cash equivalents	$ 11,875	$ 9,352
Short-term investments	12,615	6,034
Accounts receivable, less allowances of $47 in each period	2,422	1,637
Inventories	509	346
Deferred tax assets	1,447	782
Other current assets	5,822	3,805
Total current assets	34,690	21,956
Property, plant, and equipment, net	2,455	1,832
Goodwill	207	38
Acquired intangible assets, net	285	299
Other assets	1,935	1,222
Total assets	$ 39,572	$ 25,347
LIABILITIES AND SHAREHOLDERS' EQUITY:		
Current liabilities:		
Accounts payable	$ 5,520	$ 4,970
Accrued expenses	8,572	4,310
Total current liabilities	14,092	9,280
Non-current liabilities	4,450	1,535
Total liabilities	18,542	10,815
Commitments and contingencies		
Shareholders' equity:		
Common stock, no par value; 1,800,000,000 shares authorized; 888,325,973 and 872,328,972 shares issued and outstanding, respectively	7,177	5,368
Retained earnings	13,845	9,101
Accumulated other comprehensive income	8	63
Total shareholders' equity	21,030	14,532
Total liabilities and shareholders' equity	$ 39,572	$ 25,347

See accompanying Notes to Consolidated Financial Statements.

CONSOLIDATED STATEMENTS OF OPERATIONS

(In millions, except share amounts which are reflected in thousands and per share amounts)

Three fiscal years ended September 27, 2008	**2008**	**2007**	**2006**
Net sales	$ 32,479	$ 24,006	$ 19,315
Cost of sales (1)	21,334	15,852	13,717
Gross margin	11,145	8,154	5,598
Operating expenses:			
Research and development (1)	1,109	782	712
Selling, general, and administrative (1)	3,761	2,963	2,433
Total operating expenses	4,870	3,745	3,145
Operating income	6,275	4,409	2,453
Other income and expense	620	599	365
Income before provision for income taxes	6,895	5,008	2,818
Provision for income taxes	2,061	1,512	829
Net income	$ 4,834	$ 3,496	$ 1,989
Earnings per common share:			
Basic	$ 5.48	$ 4.04	$ 2.36
Diluted	$ 5.36	$ 3.93	$ 2.27
Shares used in computing earnings per share:			
Basic	881,592	864,595	844,058
Diluted	902,139	889,292	877,526

(1) Includes stock-based compensation expense as follows:

	2008	2007	2006
Cost of sales	$ 80	$ 35	$ 21
Research and development	$ 185	$ 77	$ 53
Selling, general, and administrative	$ 251	$ 130	$ 89

See accompanying Notes to Consolidated Financial Statements.

CONSOLIDATED STATEMENTS OF SHAREHOLDERS' EQUITY

(In millions, except share amounts which are reflected in thousands)

	Common Stock Shares	Common Stock Amount	Deferred Stock Compensation	Retained Earnings	Accumulated Other Comprehensive Income	Total Shareholders' Equity
Balances as of September 24, 2005	835,019	$ 3,564	$ (61)	$ 3,925	$ —	$ 7,428
Components of comprehensive income:						
Net income	—	—	—	1,989	—	1,989
Change in foreign currency translation	—	—	—	—	19	19
Change in unrealized gain on available-for-sale securities, net of tax	—	—	—	—	4	4
Change in unrealized gain on derivative instruments, net of tax	—	—	—	—	(1)	(1)
Total comprehensive income						2,011
Common stock repurchased	(4,574)	(48)	—	(307)	—	(355)
Stock-based compensation	—	163	—	—	—	163
Deferred compensation	—	(61)	61	—	—	—
Common stock issued under stock plans	24,818	318	—	—	—	318
Tax benefit from employee stock plan awards	—	419	—	—	—	419
Balances as of September 30, 2006	855,263	4,355	—	5,607	22	9,984
Components of comprehensive income:						
Net income	—	—	—	3,496	—	3,496
Change in foreign currency translation	—	—	—	—	51	51
Change in unrealized loss on available-for-sale securities, net of tax	—	—	—	—	(7)	(7)
Change in unrealized gain on derivative instruments, net of tax	—	—	—	—	(3)	(3)
Total comprehensive income						3,537
Stock-based compensation	—	251	—	—	—	251
Common stock issued under stock plans, net of shares withheld for employee taxes	17,066	364	—	(2)	—	362
Tax benefit from employee stock plan awards	—	398	—	—	—	398
Balances as of September 29, 2007	872,329	5,368	—	9,101	63	14,532
Cumulative effect of change in accounting principle	—	45	—	11	—	56
Components of comprehensive income:						
Net income	—	—	—	4,834		4,834
Change in foreign currency translation	—	—	—	—	(11)	(11)
Change in unrealized loss on available-for-sale securities, net of tax	—	—	—	—	(63)	(63)
Change in unrealized gain on derivative instruments, net of tax	—	—	—	—	19	19
Total comprehensive income						4,779
Stock-based compensation	—	513	—	—	—	513
Common stock issued under stock plans, net of shares withheld for employee taxes	15,888	460	—	(101)	—	359
Issuance of common stock in connection with an asset acquisition	109	21	—	—	—	21
Tax benefit from employee stock plan awards	—	770	—	—	—	770
Balances as of September 27, 2008	888,326	$ 7,177	$ —	$ 13,845	$ 8	$ 21,030

See accompanying Notes to Consolidated Financial Statements.

CONSOLIDATED STATEMENTS OF CASH FLOWS

(In millions)

Three fiscal years ended September 27, 2008	**2008**	**2007**	**2006**
Cash and cash equivalents, beginning of the year	$ 9,352	$ 6,392	$ 3,491
Operating Activities:			
Net income	4,834	3,496	1,989
Adjustments to reconcile net income to cash generated by operating activities:			
Depreciation, amortization and accretion	473	317	225
Stock-based compensation expense	516	242	163
Provision for deferred income taxes	(368)	78	53
Loss on disposition of property, plant, and equipment	22	12	15
Changes in operating assets and liabilities:			
Accounts receivable, net	(785)	(385)	(357)
Inventories	(163)	(76)	(105)
Other current assets	(1,958)	(1,540)	(1,626)
Other assets	(492)	81	(1,040)
Accounts payable	596	1,494	1,611
Deferred revenue	5,642	1,139	319
Other liabilities	1,279	612	973
Cash generated by operating activities	9,596	5,470	2,220
Investing Activities:			
Purchases of short-term investments	(22,965)	(11,719)	(7,255)
Proceeds from maturities of short-term investments	11,804	6,483	7,226
Proceeds from sales of short-term investments	4,439	2,941	1,086
Purchases of long-term investments	(38)	(17)	(25)
Payments made in connection with business acquisitions, net of cash acquired	(220)	—	—
Payment for acquisition of property, plant, and equipment	(1,091)	(735)	(657)
Payment for acquisition of intangible assets	(108)	(251)	(28)
Other	(10)	49	10
Cash (used in)/generated by investing activities	(8,189)	(3,249)	357
Financing Activities:			
Proceeds from issuance of common stock	483	365	318
Excess tax benefits from stock-based compensation	757	377	361
Cash used to net share settle equity awards	(124)	(3)	(355)
Cash generated by financing activities	1,116	739	324
Increase in cash and cash equivalents	2,523	2,960	2,901
Cash and cash equivalents, end of the year	$ 11,875	$ 9,352	$ 6,392
Supplemental cash flow disclosures:			
Cash paid for income taxes, net	$ 1,267	$ 863	$ 194

See accompanying Notes to Consolidated Financial Statements.

NOTES TO CONSOLIDATED FINANCIAL STATEMENTS

Note 1—Summary of Significant Accounting Policies

Apple Inc. and its wholly-owned subsidiaries (collectively "Apple" or the "Company") design, manufacture, and market personal computers, portable digital music players, and mobile communication devices and sell a variety of related software, services, peripherals, and networking solutions. The Company sells its products worldwide through its online stores, its retail stores, its direct sales force, and third-party wholesalers, resellers, and value-added resellers. In addition, the Company sells a variety of third-party Mac, iPod and iPhone compatible products including application software, printers, storage devices, speakers, headphones, and various other accessories and supplies through its online and retail stores. The Company sells to consumer, small and mid-sized business ("SMB"), education, enterprise, government, and creative customers.

Basis of Presentation and Preparation

The accompanying Consolidated Financial Statements include the accounts of the Company. Intercompany accounts and transactions have been eliminated. The preparation of these Consolidated Financial Statements in conformity with U.S. generally accepted accounting principles requires management to make estimates and assumptions that affect the amounts reported in these Consolidated Financial Statements and accompanying notes. Actual results could differ materially from those estimates. Certain prior year amounts in the Consolidated Financial Statements and notes thereto have been reclassified to conform to the current year presentation.

The Company's fiscal year is the 52 or 53-week period that ends on the last Saturday of September. The Company's first quarter of fiscal years 2008 and 2007 contained 13 weeks and the first quarter of fiscal year 2006 contained 14 weeks. The Company's fiscal years 2008 and 2007 ended on September 27, 2008 and September 29, 2007, respectively, included 52 weeks, while fiscal year 2006 ended on September 30, 2006 included 53 weeks. Unless otherwise stated, references to particular years or quarters refer to the Company's fiscal years ended in September and the associated quarters of those fiscal years.

Financial Instruments

Cash Equivalents and Short-term Investments

All highly liquid investments with maturities of three months or less at the date of purchase are classified as cash equivalents. Highly liquid investments with maturities greater than three months at the date of purchase are classified as short-term investments. The Company's debt and marketable equity securities have been classified and accounted for as available-for-sale. Management determines the appropriate classification of its investments in debt securities at the time of purchase and reevaluates the available-for-sale designations as of each balance sheet date. These securities are carried at fair value, with the unrealized gains and losses, net of taxes, reported as a component of shareholders' equity. The cost of securities sold is based upon the specific identification method.

Derivative Financial Instruments

The Company accounts for its derivative instruments as either assets or liabilities and carries them at fair value. Derivatives that are not defined as hedges in Statement of Financial Accounting Standards ("SFAS") No. 133, *Accounting for Derivative Instruments and Hedging Activities,* as amended, must be adjusted to fair value through earnings.

For derivative instruments that hedge the exposure to variability in expected future cash flows that are designated as cash flow hedges, the effective portion of the gain or loss on the derivative instrument is reported as a component of accumulated other comprehensive income in shareholders' equity and reclassified into earnings in the same period or periods during which the hedged transaction affects earnings. The ineffective portion of the gain or loss on the derivative instrument is recognized in current earnings. To receive hedge accounting treatment, cash flow hedges must be highly effective in offsetting changes to expected future cash flows on hedged transactions. For options designated as cash flow hedges, changes in the time value are excluded from the assessment of hedge effectiveness and are recognized in earnings. For derivative instruments that hedge the exposure to changes in the fair value of an asset or a liability and that are designated as fair value hedges, the net

NOTES TO CONSOLIDATED FINANCIAL STATEMENTS (Continued)

Note 1—Summary of Significant Accounting Policies (Continued)

gain or loss on the derivative instrument as well as the offsetting gain or loss on the hedged item attributable to the hedged risk are recognized in earnings in the current period. The net gain or loss on the effective portion of a derivative instrument that is designated as an economic hedge of the foreign currency translation exposure of the net investment in a foreign operation is reported in the same manner as a foreign currency translation adjustment. For forward contracts designated as net investment hedges, the Company excludes changes in fair value relating to changes in the forward carry component from its definition of effectiveness. Accordingly, any gains or losses related to this component are recognized in current earnings.

Inventories

Inventories are stated at the lower of cost, computed using the first-in, first-out method, or market. If the cost of the inventories exceeds their market value, provisions are made currently for the difference between the cost and the market value. The Company's inventories consist primarily of finished goods for all periods presented.

Property, Plant, and Equipment

Property, plant, and equipment are stated at cost. Depreciation is computed by use of the straight-line method over the estimated useful lives of the assets, which for buildings is the lesser of 30 years or the remaining life of the underlying building, up to 5 years for equipment, and the shorter of lease terms or 10 years for leasehold improvements. The Company capitalizes eligible costs to acquire or develop internal-use software that are incurred subsequent to the preliminary project stage. Capitalized costs related to internal-use software are amortized using the straight-line method over the estimated useful lives of the assets, which range from 3 to 5 years. Depreciation and amortization expense on property and equipment was $363 million, $249 million, and $180 million during 2008, 2007, and 2006 respectively.

Asset Retirement Obligations

The Company records obligations associated with the retirement of tangible long-lived assets and the associated asset retirement costs in accordance with SFAS No. 143, *Accounting for Asset Retirement Obligations*. The Company reviews legal obligations associated with the retirement of long-lived assets that result from the acquisition, construction, development and/or normal use of the assets. If it is determined that a legal obligation exists, the fair value of the liability for an asset retirement obligation is recognized in the period in which it is incurred if a reasonable estimate of fair value can be made. The fair value of the liability is added to the carrying amount of the associated asset and this additional carrying amount is depreciated over the life of the asset. The difference between the gross expected future cash flow and its present value is accreted over the life of the related lease as an operating expense. All of the Company's existing asset retirement obligations are associated with commitments to return property subject to operating leases to original condition upon lease termination. The Company's asset retirement liability was $21 million and $18 million as of September 27, 2008 and September 29, 2007, respectively.

Long-Lived Assets Including Goodwill and Other Acquired Intangible Assets

The Company reviews property, plant, and equipment and certain identifiable intangibles, excluding goodwill, for impairment in accordance with SFAS No. 144, *Accounting for the Impairment of Long-Lived Assets and for Long-Lived Assets to Be Disposed Of.* Long-lived assets are reviewed for impairment whenever events or changes in circumstances indicate the carrying amount of an asset may not be recoverable. Recoverability of these assets is measured by comparison of its carrying amount to future undiscounted cash flows the assets are expected to generate. If property, plant, and equipment and certain identifiable intangibles are considered to be impaired, the impairment to be recognized equals the amount by which the carrying value of the assets exceeds its fair market value. The Company did not record any material impairments during 2008, 2007, and 2006.

NOTES TO CONSOLIDATED FINANCIAL STATEMENTS (Continued)

Note 1—Summary of Significant Accounting Policies (Continued)

SFAS No. 142, *Goodwill and Other Intangible Assets* requires that goodwill and intangible assets with indefinite useful lives should not be amortized but rather be tested for impairment at least annually or sooner whenever events or changes in circumstances indicate that they may be impaired. The Company performs its goodwill impairment tests on or about August 31 of each year. The Company did not recognize any goodwill or intangible asset impairment charges in 2008, 2007, or 2006. The Company established reporting units based on its current reporting structure. For purposes of testing goodwill for impairment, goodwill has been allocated to these reporting units to the extent it relates to each reporting unit.

SFAS No. 142 also requires that intangible assets with definite lives be amortized over their estimated useful lives and reviewed for impairment in accordance with SFAS No. 144. The Company is currently amortizing its acquired intangible assets with definite lives over periods ranging from 1 to 10 years.

Foreign Currency Translation

The Company translates the assets and liabilities of its international non-U.S. dollar functional currency subsidiaries into U.S. dollars using exchange rates in effect at the end of each period. Revenue and expenses for these subsidiaries are translated using rates that approximate those in effect during the period. Gains and losses from these translations are credited or charged to foreign currency translation included in accumulated other comprehensive income in shareholders' equity. The Company's foreign manufacturing subsidiaries and certain other international subsidiaries that use the U.S. dollar as their functional currency remeasure monetary assets and liabilities at exchange rates in effect at the end of each period, and inventories, property, and nonmonetary assets and liabilities at historical rates. Gains and losses from these translations were insignificant and have been included in the Company's results of operations.

Revenue Recognition

Net sales consist primarily of revenue from the sale of hardware, software, music products, digital content, peripherals, and service and support contracts. For any product within these groups that either is software, or is considered software-related in accordance with the guidance in Emerging Issues Task Force ("EITF") No. 03-5, *Applicability of AICPA Statement of Position 97-2 to Non-Software Deliverables in an Arrangement Containing More-Than-Incidental Software* (e.g., Mac computers, iPod portable digital music players and iPhones), the Company accounts for such products in accordance with the revenue recognition provisions of American Institute of Certified Public Accountants ("AICPA") Statement of Position ("SOP") No. 97-2, *Software Revenue Recognition*, as amended. The Company applies Staff Accounting Bulletin ("SAB") No. 104, *Revenue Recognition,* for products that are not software or software-related, such as digital content sold on the iTunes Store and certain Mac, iPod and iPhone supplies and accessories.

The Company recognizes revenue when persuasive evidence of an arrangement exists, delivery has occurred, the sales price is fixed or determinable, and collection is probable. Product is considered delivered to the customer once it has been shipped and title and risk of loss have been transferred. For most of the Company's product sales, these criteria are met at the time the product is shipped. For online sales to individuals, for some sales to education customers in the U.S., and for certain other sales, the Company defers revenue until the customer receives the product because the Company legally retains a portion of the risk of loss on these sales during transit. If at the outset of an arrangement the Company determines the arrangement fee is not, or is presumed not to be, fixed or determinable, revenue is deferred and subsequently recognized as amounts become due and payable and all other criteria for revenue recognition have been met.

Revenue from service and support contracts is deferred and recognized ratably over the service coverage periods. These contracts typically include extended phone support, repair services, web-based support resources, diagnostic tools, and extend the service coverage offered under the Company's one-year limited warranty.

NOTES TO CONSOLIDATED FINANCIAL STATEMENTS (Continued)

Note 1—Summary of Significant Accounting Policies (Continued)

The Company sells software and peripheral products obtained from other companies. The Company generally establishes its own pricing and retains related inventory risk, is the primary obligor in sales transactions with its customers, and assumes the credit risk for amounts billed to its customers. Accordingly, the Company generally recognizes revenue for the sale of products obtained from other companies based on the gross amount billed.

The Company accounts for multiple element arrangements that consist only of software or software-related products in accordance with SOP No. 97-2. If a multiple-element arrangement includes deliverables that are neither software nor software-related, the Company applies EITF No. 00-21, *Revenue Arrangements with Multiple Deliverables,* to determine if those deliverables constitute separate units of accounting from the SOP No. 97-2 deliverables. If the Company can separate the deliverables, the Company applies SOP No. 97-2 to the software and software-related deliverables and applies other appropriate guidance (e.g., SAB No. 104) to the deliverables outside the scope of SOP No. 97-2. Revenue on arrangements that include multiple elements such as hardware, software, and services is allocated to each element based on the relative fair value of each element. Each element's allocated revenue is recognized when the revenue recognition criteria for that element have been met. Fair value is generally determined by vendor specific objective evidence ("VSOE"), which is based on the price charged when each element is sold separately. If the Company cannot objectively determine the fair value of any undelivered element included in a multiple-element arrangement, the Company defers revenue until all elements are delivered and services have been performed, or until fair value can objectively be determined for any remaining undelivered elements. When the fair value of a delivered element has not been established, the Company uses the residual method to recognize revenue if the fair value of all undelivered elements is determinable. Under the residual method, the fair value of the undelivered elements is deferred and the remaining portion of the arrangement fee is allocated to the delivered elements and is recognized as revenue.

The Company records reductions to revenue for estimated commitments related to price protection and for customer incentive programs, including reseller and end-user rebates, and other sales programs and volume-based incentives. The estimated cost of these programs is accrued as a reduction to revenue in the period the Company has sold the product and committed to a plan. The Company also records reductions to revenue for expected future product returns based on the Company's historical experience. Revenue is recorded net of taxes collected from customers that are remitted to governmental authorities, with the collected taxes recorded as current liabilities until remitted to the relevant government authority.

Generally, the Company does not offer specified or unspecified upgrade rights to its customers in connection with software sales or the sale of extended warranty and support contracts. When the Company does offer specified upgrade rights, the Company defers revenue for the fair value of the specified upgrade right until the future obligation is fulfilled or when the right to the specified upgrade expires. Additionally, a limited number of the Company's software products are available with maintenance agreements that grant customers rights to unspecified future upgrades over the maintenance term on a when and if available basis. Revenue associated with such maintenance is recognized ratably over the maintenance term.

In 2007, the Company began shipping Apple TV and iPhone. For Apple TV and iPhone, the Company indicated it may from time-to-time provide future unspecified features and additional software products free of charge to customers. Accordingly, Apple TV and iPhone handsets sales are accounted for under subscription accounting in accordance with SOP No. 97-2. As such, the Company's policy is to defer the associated revenue and cost of goods sold at the time of sale, and recognize both on a straight-line basis over the currently estimated 24-month economic life of these products, with any loss recognized at the time of sale. Costs incurred by the Company for engineering, sales, marketing and warranty are expensed as incurred.

NOTES TO CONSOLIDATED FINANCIAL STATEMENTS (Continued)

Note 1—Summary of Significant Accounting Policies (Continued)

Allowance for Doubtful Accounts

The Company records its allowance for doubtful accounts based upon its assessment of various factors. The Company considers historical experience, the age of the accounts receivable balances, credit quality of the Company's customers, current economic conditions, and other factors that may affect customers' ability to pay.

Shipping Costs

For all periods presented, amounts billed to customers related to shipping and handling are classified as revenue, and the Company's shipping and handling costs are included in cost of sales.

Warranty Expense

The Company generally provides for the estimated cost of hardware and software warranties at the time the related revenue is recognized. The Company assesses the adequacy of its preexisting warranty liabilities and adjusts the amounts as necessary based on actual experience and changes in future estimates. For products accounted for under subscription accounting pursuant to SOP No. 97-2, the Company recognizes warranty expense as incurred.

Software Development Costs

Research and development costs are expensed as incurred. Development costs of computer software to be sold, leased, or otherwise marketed are subject to capitalization beginning when a product's technological feasibility has been established and ending when a product is available for general release to customers pursuant to SFAS No. 86, *Computer Software to be Sold, Leased, or Otherwise Marketed*. In most instances, the Company's products are released soon after technological feasibility has been established. Therefore, costs incurred subsequent to achievement of technological feasibility are usually not significant, and generally most software development costs have been expensed.

During 2008, the Company capitalized $11 million of costs associated with the development of Mac OS X Version 10.6 Snow Leopard. In 2007, the Company determined that both Mac OS X Version 10.5 Leopard ("Mac OS X Leopard") and iPhone achieved technological feasibility. During 2007, the Company capitalized $75 million of costs associated with the development of Leopard and iPhone. In accordance with SFAS No. 86, the capitalized costs related to Mac OS X Leopard and iPhone are amortized to cost of sales commencing when each respective product begins shipping and are recognized on a straight-line basis over a 3 year estimated useful life of the underlying technology.

Total amortization related to capitalized software development costs was $27 million, $13 million, and $18 million in 2008, 2007, and 2006, respectively.

Advertising Costs

Advertising costs are expensed as incurred. Advertising expense was $486 million, $467 million, and $338 million for 2008, 2007, and 2006, respectively.

Stock-Based Compensation

The Company applies SFAS No. 123 (revised 2004), *Share-Based Payment*, for stock-based payment transactions in which the Company receives employee services in exchange for (a) equity instruments of the enterprise or (b) liabilities that are based on the fair value of the enterprise's equity instruments or that may be settled by the issuance of such equity instruments. The Company uses the Black-Scholes-Merton ("BSM") option-pricing model to determine the fair-value of stock-based awards under SFAS No. 123R.

SFAS No. 123R prohibits recognition of a deferred tax asset for an excess tax benefit that has not been realized. The Company will recognize a benefit from stock-based compensation in equity if an incremental tax benefit is

NOTES TO CONSOLIDATED FINANCIAL STATEMENTS (Continued)

Note 1—Summary of Significant Accounting Policies (Continued)

realized by following the ordering provisions of the tax law. In addition, the Company accounts for the indirect effects of stock-based compensation on the research tax credit, the foreign tax credit, and the domestic manufacturing deduction through the income statement.

Further information regarding stock-based compensation can be found in Note 6, "Shareholders' Equity," and Note 7, "Stock-Based Compensation."

Income Taxes

In accordance with SFAS No. 109, *Accounting for Income Taxes*, the provision for income taxes is computed using the asset and liability method, under which deferred tax assets and liabilities are recognized for the expected future tax consequences of temporary differences between the financial reporting and tax bases of assets and liabilities, and for operating losses and tax credit carryforwards. Deferred tax assets and liabilities are measured using the currently enacted tax rates that apply to taxable income in effect for the years in which those tax assets are expected to be realized or settled. The Company records a valuation allowance to reduce deferred tax assets to the amount that is believed more likely than not to be realized.

During 2008, the Company adopted the Financial Accounting Standards Board's ("FASB") Financial Interpretation No. ("FIN") 48, *Accounting for Uncertainty in Income Taxes—an interpretation of FASB Statement No. 109*. FIN 48 changes the accounting for uncertainty in income taxes by creating a new framework for how companies should recognize, measure, present, and disclose uncertain tax positions in their financial statements. Under FIN 48, the Company may recognize the tax benefit from an uncertain tax position only if it is more likely than not the tax position will be sustained on examination by the taxing authorities, based on the technical merits of the position. The tax benefits recognized in the financial statements from such positions are then measured based on the largest benefit that has a greater than 50% likelihood of being realized upon settlement. FIN 48 also provides guidance on the reversal of previously recognized tax positions, balance sheet classifications, accounting for interest and penalties associated with tax positions, and income tax disclosures. See Note 5, "Income Taxes" for additional information, including the effects of adoption on the Company's Consolidated Financial Statements.

Earnings Per Common Share

Basic earnings per common share is computed by dividing income available to common shareholders by the weighted-average number of shares of common stock outstanding during the period. Diluted earnings per common share is computed by dividing income available to common shareholders by the weighted-average number of shares of common stock outstanding during the period increased to include the number of additional shares of common stock that would have been outstanding if the potentially dilutive securities had been issued. Potentially dilutive securities include outstanding stock options, shares to be purchased under the employee stock purchase plan, and unvested restricted stock units ("RSUs"). The dilutive effect of potentially dilutive securities is reflected in diluted earnings per share by application of the treasury stock method. Under the treasury stock method, an increase in the fair market value of the Company's common stock can result in a greater dilutive effect from potentially dilutive securities.

NOTES TO CONSOLIDATED FINANCIAL STATEMENTS (Continued)

Note 1—Summary of Significant Accounting Policies (Continued)

The following table sets forth the computation of basic and diluted earnings per share for the three fiscal years ended September 27, 2008 (in thousands, except net income in millions and per share amounts):

	2008	2007	2006
Numerator:			
Net income	$ 4,834	$ 3,496	$ 1,989
Denominator:			
Weighted-average shares outstanding	881,592	864,595	844,058
Effect of dilutive securities	20,547	24,697	33,468
Denominator for diluted earnings per share	902,139	889,292	877,526
Basic earnings per share	$ 5.48	$ 4.04	$ 2.36
Diluted earnings per share	$ 5.36	$ 3.93	$ 2.27

Potentially dilutive securities representing 10.3 million, 13.7 million, and 3.9 million shares of common stock for the years ended September 27, 2008, September 29, 2007, and September 30, 2006, respectively, were excluded from the computation of diluted earnings per share for these periods because their effect would have been antidilutive.

Comprehensive Income

Comprehensive income consists of two components, net income and other comprehensive income. Other comprehensive income refers to revenue, expenses, gains, and losses that under U.S. generally accepted accounting principles are recorded as an element of shareholders' equity but are excluded from net income. The Company's other comprehensive income consists of foreign currency translation adjustments from those subsidiaries not using the U.S. dollar as their functional currency, unrealized gains and losses on marketable securities categorized as available-for-sale, and net deferred gains and losses on certain derivative instruments accounted for as cash flow hedges.

Segment Information

The Company reports segment information based on the "management" approach. The management approach designates the internal reporting used by management for making decisions and assessing performance as the source of the Company's reportable segments. Information about the Company's products, major customers, and geographic areas on a company-wide basis is also disclosed.

NOTES TO CONSOLIDATED FINANCIAL STATEMENTS (Continued)

Note 2—Financial Instruments

Cash, Cash Equivalents and Short-Term Investments

The following table summarizes the fair value of the Company's cash and available-for-sale securities held in its short-term investment portfolio, recorded as cash and cash equivalents or short-term investments as of September 27, 2008 and September 29, 2007 (in millions):

	2008	2007
Cash	$ 368	$ 256
U.S. Treasury and Agency Securities	2,916	670
U.S. Corporate Securities	4,975	5,597
Foreign Securities	3,616	2,829
Total cash equivalents	11,507	9,096
U.S. Treasury and Agency Securities	7,018	358
U.S. Corporate Securities	4,305	4,718
Foreign Securities	1,292	958
Total short-term investments	12,615	6,034
Total cash, cash equivalents, and short-term investments	$ 24,490	$ 15,386

The Company's U.S. Corporate Securities consist primarily of commercial paper, certificates of deposit, time deposits, and corporate debt securities. Foreign Securities consist primarily of foreign commercial paper issued by foreign companies, and certificates of deposit and time deposits with foreign institutions, most of which are denominated in U.S. dollars. As of September 27, 2008 and September 29, 2007, approximately $2.4 billion and $1.9 billion, respectively, of the Company's short-term investments had underlying maturities ranging from one to five years. The remaining short-term investments had maturities less than 12 months. The Company had $117 million in net unrealized losses on its investment portfolio, primarily related to investments with stated maturities ranging from one to five years, as of September 27, 2008, and net unrealized losses of approximately $11 million on its investment portfolio, primarily related to investments with stated maturities from one to five years, as of September 29, 2007. The Company may sell its investments prior to their stated maturities for strategic purposes, in anticipation of credit deterioration, or for duration management. The Company recognized no material net gains or losses during 2008, 2007 and 2006 related to such sales.

NOTES TO CONSOLIDATED FINANCIAL STATEMENTS (Continued)

Note 2—Financial Instruments (Continued)

In accordance with FASB Staff Position ("FSP") FAS 115-1 and FAS 124-1, *The Meaning of Other-Than-Temporary Impairment and Its Application to Certain Investments,* the following table shows the gross unrealized losses and fair value for those investments that were in an unrealized loss position as of September 27, 2008 and September 29, 2007, aggregated by investment category and the length of time that individual securities have been in a continuous loss position (in millions):

	2008					
	Less than 12 Months		12 Months or Greater		Total	
Security Description	**Fair Value**	**Unrealized Loss**	**Fair Value**	**Unrealized Loss**	**Fair Value**	**Unrealized Loss**
U.S. Treasury and Agency Securities	$ 6,850	$ (13)	$ —	$ —	$ 6,850	$ (13)
U.S. Corporate Securities	2,536	(31)	1,030	(72)	3,566	(103)
Foreign Securities	321	—	118	(5)	439	(5)
Total	$ 9,707	$ (44)	$ 1,148	$ (77)	$ 10,855	$ (121)

	2007					
	Less than 12 Months		12 Months or Greater		Total	
Security Description	**Fair Value**	**Unrealized Loss**	**Fair Value**	**Unrealized Loss**	**Fair Value**	**Unrealized Loss**
U.S. Treasury and Agency Securities	$ 338	$ —	$ —	$ —	$ 338	$ —
U.S. Corporate Securities	2,521	(12)	32	—	2,553	(12)
Foreign Securities	474	(1)	8	—	482	(1)
Total	$ 3,333	$ (13)	$ 40	$ —	$ 3,373	$ (13)

The unrealized losses on the Company's investments in U.S. Treasury and Agency Securities, U.S. Corporate Securities, and Foreign Securities were caused primarily by changes in interest rates, specifically, widening credit spreads. The Company's investment policy requires investments to be rated single-A or better with the objective of minimizing the potential risk of principal loss. Therefore, the Company considers the declines to be temporary in nature. Fair values were determined for each individual security in the investment portfolio. When evaluating the investments for other-than-temporary impairment, the Company reviews factors such as the length of time and extent to which fair value has been below cost basis, the financial condition of the issuer, and the Company's ability and intent to hold the investment for a period of time, which may be sufficient for anticipated recovery in market value. During 2008, the Company did not record any material impairment charges on its outstanding securities. As of September 27, 2008, the Company does not consider any of its investments to be other-than-temporarily impaired.

Accounts Receivable

Trade Receivables

The Company distributes its products through third-party distributors and resellers and directly to certain education, consumer, and commercial customers. The Company generally does not require collateral from its customers. In addition, when possible, the Company attempts to limit credit risk on trade receivables with credit insurance for certain customers in Latin America, Europe, Asia, and Australia and by arranging with third-party financing companies to provide flooring arrangements and other loan and lease programs to the Company's direct customers. These credit-financing arrangements are directly between the third-party financing company and the end customer. As such, the Company generally does not assume any recourse or credit risk sharing related to any of these arrangements. However, considerable trade receivables not covered by collateral, third-party flooring arrangements, or credit insurance are outstanding with the Company's distribution and retail channel partners. Trade receivables from two of the Company's customers accounted for 15% and 10% of trade receivables as of September 27, 2008, while one customer accounted for approximately 11% of trade receivables as of September 29, 2007.

NOTES TO CONSOLIDATED FINANCIAL STATEMENTS (Continued)

Note 2—Financial Instruments (Continued)

The following table summarizes the activity in the allowance for doubtful accounts for the three fiscal years ended September 27, 2008 (in millions):

	2008	2007	2006
Beginning allowance balance	$ 47	$ 52	$ 46
Charged to costs and expenses	3	12	17
Deductions	(3)	(17)	(11)
Ending allowance balance	$ 47	$ 47	$ 52

Vendor Non-Trade Receivables

The Company has non-trade receivables from certain of its manufacturing vendors resulting from the sale of raw material components to these manufacturing vendors who manufacture sub-assemblies or assemble final products for the Company. The Company purchases these raw material components directly from suppliers. These non-trade receivables, which are included in the Consolidated Balance Sheets in other current assets, totaled $2.3 billion and $2.4 billion as of September 27, 2008 and September 29, 2007, respectively. The Company does not reflect the sale of these components in net sales and does not recognize any profits on these sales until the related products are sold by the Company, at which time the profit is recognized as a reduction of cost of sales.

Derivative Financial Instruments

The Company uses derivatives to partially offset its business exposure to foreign exchange risk. Foreign currency forward and option contracts are used to offset the foreign exchange risk on certain existing assets and liabilities and to hedge the foreign exchange risk on expected future cash flows on certain forecasted revenue and cost of sales. The Company's accounting policies for these instruments are based on whether the instruments are designated as hedge or non-hedge instruments. The Company records all derivatives on the balance sheet at fair value.

The following table shows the notional principal, net fair value, and credit risk amounts of the Company's foreign currency instruments as of September 27, 2008 and September 29, 2007 (in millions):

	2008			2007		
	Notional Principal	Fair Value	Credit Risk Amounts	Notional Principal	Fair Value	Credit Risk Amounts
Foreign exchange instruments qualifying as accounting hedges:						
Spot/Forward contracts	$ 2,782	$ (2)	$ 43	$ 570	$ (8)	$ —
Purchased options	$ 3,120	$ 64	$ 64	$ 2,564	$ 10	$ 10
Sold options	$ 2,668	$ (23)	$ —	$ 1,498	$ (2)	$ —
Foreign exchange instruments other than accounting hedges:						
Spot/Forward contracts	$ 2,633	$ 3	$ 5	$ 1,768	$ (2)	$ —
Purchased options	$ 235	$ 3	$ 3	$ 161	$ 1	$ 1

The notional principal amounts for derivative instruments provide one measure of the transaction volume outstanding as of year-end, and do not represent the amount of the Company's exposure to credit or market loss. The credit risk amounts shown in the table above represents the Company's gross exposure to potential accounting loss on these transactions if all counterparties failed to perform according to the terms of the contract, based on then-current currency exchange rates at each respective date. The Company's exposure to credit loss and market risk will vary over time as a function of currency exchange rates.

NOTES TO CONSOLIDATED FINANCIAL STATEMENTS (Continued)

Note 2—Financial Instruments (Continued)

The estimates of fair value are based on applicable and commonly used pricing models and prevailing financial market information as of September 27, 2008 and September 29, 2007. Although the table above reflects the notional principal, fair value, and credit risk amounts of the Company's foreign exchange instruments, it does not reflect the gains or losses associated with the exposures and transactions that the foreign exchange instruments are intended to hedge. The amounts ultimately realized upon settlement of these financial instruments, together with the gains and losses on the underlying exposures, will depend on actual market conditions during the remaining life of the instruments.

Foreign Exchange Risk Management

The Company may enter into foreign currency forward and option contracts with financial institutions to protect against foreign exchange risk associated with existing assets and liabilities, certain firmly committed transactions, forecasted future cash flows, and net investments in foreign subsidiaries. Generally, the Company's practice is to hedge some portion of its material foreign exchange exposures. However, the Company may choose not to hedge certain foreign exchange exposures for a variety of reasons, including but not limited to, immateriality, prohibitive economic cost of hedging particular exposures, or limited availability of appropriate hedging instruments.

To help protect gross margins from fluctuations in foreign currency exchange rates, certain of the Company's U.S. dollar functional subsidiaries hedge a portion of forecasted foreign currency revenue, and the Company's non-U.S. dollar functional subsidiaries selling in local currencies hedge a portion of forecasted inventory purchases not denominated in the subsidiaries' functional currency. Other comprehensive income associated with hedges of foreign currency revenue is recognized as a component of net sales in the same period as the related sales are recognized, and other comprehensive income related to inventory purchases is recognized as a component of cost of sales in the same period as the related costs are recognized. Typically, the Company hedges portions of its forecasted foreign currency exposure associated with revenue and inventory purchases for three to six months.

Derivative instruments designated as cash flow hedges must be de-designated as hedges when it is probable the forecasted hedged transaction will not occur in the initially identified time period or within a subsequent 2 month time period. Deferred gains and losses in other comprehensive income associated with such derivative instruments are immediately reclassified into earnings in other income and expense. Any subsequent changes in fair value of such derivative instruments are also reflected in current earnings unless they are re-designated as hedges of other transactions. The Company has not recognized any material net gains during 2008, 2007 and 2006, related to the loss of a hedge designation on discontinued cash flow hedges. As of September 27, 2008, the Company had a net deferred gain associated with cash flow hedges of approximately $19 million, net of taxes, substantially all of which is expected to be reclassified to earnings by the end of the second quarter of fiscal 2009.

The net gain or loss on the effective portion of a derivative instrument designated as a net investment hedge is included in the cumulative translation adjustment account of accumulated other comprehensive income within shareholders' equity. For the years ended September 27, 2008 and September 29, 2007, the Company had a net loss on net investment hedges of $12.2 million and $2.6 million, respectively, included in the cumulative translation adjustment.

The Company may also enter into foreign currency forward and option contracts to offset the foreign exchange gains and losses generated by the re-measurement of certain assets and liabilities recorded in non-functional currencies. Changes in the fair value of these derivatives are recognized in current earnings in other income and expense as offsets to the changes in the fair value of the related assets or liabilities. Due to currency market movements, changes in option time value can lead to increased volatility in other income and expense.

NOTES TO CONSOLIDATED FINANCIAL STATEMENTS (Continued)

Note 3—Consolidated Financial Statement Details

The following tables show the Company's Consolidated Financial Statement details as of September 27, 2008 and September 29, 2007 (in millions):

Other Current Assets

	2008	2007
Vendor non-trade receivables	$ 2,282	$ 2,392
Deferred costs under subscription accounting—current	1,931	247
NAND flash memory prepayments	475	417
Other current assets	1,134	749
Total other current assets	$ 5,822	$ 3,805

Property, Plant, and Equipment

	2008	2007
Land and buildings	$ 810	$ 762
Machinery, equipment, and internal-use software	1,491	954
Office furniture and equipment	122	106
Leasehold improvements	1,324	1,019
	3,747	2,841
Accumulated depreciation and amortization	(1,292)	(1,009)
Net property, plant, and equipment	$ 2,455	$ 1,832

Other Assets

	2008	2007
Deferred costs under subscription accounting—non-current	$ 1,089	$ 214
Long-term NAND flash memory prepayments	208	625
Deferred tax assets—non-current	138	88
Capitalized software development costs, net	67	83
Other assets	433	212
Total other assets	$ 1,935	$ 1,222

Accrued Expenses

	2008	2007
Deferred revenue—current	$ 4,853	$ 1,391
Deferred margin on component sales	681	545
Accrued marketing and distribution	329	288
Accrued compensation and employee benefits	320	254
Accrued warranty and related costs	267	230
Other accrued tax liabilities	100	488
Other current liabilities	2,022	1,114
Total accrued expenses	$ 8,572	$ 4,310

NOTES TO CONSOLIDATED FINANCIAL STATEMENTS (Continued)

Note 3—Consolidated Financial Statement Details (Continued)

Non-Current Liabilities

	2008	2007
Deferred revenue—non-current	$ 3,029	$ 849
Deferred tax liabilities	675	619
Other non-current liabilities	746	67
Total non-current liabilities	$ 4,450	$ 1,535

Note 4—Goodwill and Other Intangible Assets

The Company is currently amortizing its acquired intangible assets with definite lives over periods ranging from 1 to 10 years. The following table summarizes the components of gross and net intangible asset balances as of September 27, 2008 and September 29, 2007 (in millions):

	2008			2007		
	Gross Carrying Amount	Accumulated Amortization	Net Carrying Amount	Gross Carrying Amount	Accumulated Amortization	Net Carrying Amount
Definite lived and amortizable acquired technology	$ 308	$ (123)	$ 185	$ 276	$ (77)	$ 199
Indefinite lived and unamortizable trademarks	100	—	100	100	—	100
Total acquired intangible assets	$ 408	$ (123)	$ 285	$ 376	$ (77)	$ 299
Goodwill	$ 207	$ —	$ 207	$ 38	$ —	$ 38

In June 2008, the Company completed an acquisition of a business for total cash consideration, net of cash acquired, of $220 million, of which $169 million has been allocated to goodwill, $51 million to deferred tax assets and $7 million to acquired intangible assets.

The Company's goodwill is allocated primarily to the America's reportable operating segment. Amortization expense related to acquired intangible assets was $46 million, $35 million, and $12 million in 2008, 2007, and 2006, respectively. As of September 27, 2008, and September 29, 2007, the remaining weighted-average amortization period for acquired technology was 7.0 years and 7.1 years, respectively.

Expected annual amortization expense related to acquired technology as of September 27, 2008, is as follows (in millions):

Fiscal Years	
2009	$ 50
2010	35
2011	32
2012	26
2013	13
Thereafter	29
Total	$ 185

NOTES TO CONSOLIDATED FINANCIAL STATEMENTS (Continued)

Note 5—Income Taxes

The provision for income taxes for the three fiscal years ended September 27, 2008, consisted of the following (in millions):

	2008	2007	2006
Federal:			
Current	$ 1,942	$ 1,219	$ 619
Deferred	(155)	85	56
	1,787	1,304	675
State:			
Current	210	112	56
Deferred	(82)	9	14
	128	121	70
Foreign:			
Current	277	103	101
Deferred	(131)	(16)	(17)
	146	87	84
Provision for income taxes	$ 2,061	$ 1,512	$ 829

The foreign provision for income taxes is based on foreign pretax earnings of $3.5 billion, $2.2 billion, and $1.5 billion in 2008, 2007, and 2006, respectively. As of September 27, 2008 and September 29, 2007, $11.3 billion and $6.5 billion, respectively, of the Company's cash, cash equivalents, and short-term investments were held by foreign subsidiaries and are generally based in U.S. dollar-denominated holdings. Amounts held by foreign subsidiaries are generally subject to U.S. income taxation on repatriation to the U.S. The Company's consolidated financial statements provide for any related tax liability on amounts that may be repatriated, aside from undistributed earnings of certain of the Company's foreign subsidiaries that are intended to be indefinitely reinvested in operations outside the U.S. U.S. income taxes have not been provided on a cumulative total of $3.8 billion of such earnings. It is not practicable to determine the income tax liability that might be incurred if these earnings were to be distributed.

Deferred tax assets and liabilities reflect the effects of tax losses, credits, and the future income tax effects of temporary differences between the consolidated financial statement carrying amounts of existing assets and liabilities and their respective tax bases and are measured using enacted tax rates that apply to taxable income in the years in which those temporary differences are expected to be recovered or settled.

NOTES TO CONSOLIDATED FINANCIAL STATEMENTS (Continued)

Note 5—Income Taxes (Continued)

As of September 27, 2008 and September 29, 2007, the significant components of the Company's deferred tax assets and liabilities were (in millions):

	2008	2007
Deferred tax assets:		
Accrued liabilities and other reserves	$ 1,295	$ 679
Basis of capital assets and investments	173	146
Accounts receivable and inventory reserves	126	64
Tax losses and credits	47	8
Other	503	161
Total deferred tax assets	2,144	1,058
Less valuation allowance	—	5
Net deferred tax assets	2,144	1,053
Deferred tax liabilities—Unremitted earnings of subsidiaries:	1,234	803
Net deferred tax asset	$ 910	$ 250

As of September 27, 2008, the Company has tax loss and credit carryforwards in the tax effected amount of $47 million. The Company released a valuation allowance of $5 million recorded against the deferred tax asset for the benefit of state operating losses. Management believes it is more likely than not that forecasted income, including income that may be generated as a result of certain tax planning strategies, together with the tax effects of the deferred tax liabilities, will be sufficient to fully recover the remaining deferred tax assets.

A reconciliation of the provision for income taxes, with the amount computed by applying the statutory federal income tax rate (35% in 2008, 2007, and 2006) to income before provision for income taxes for the three fiscal years ended September 27, 2008, is as follows (in millions):

	2008	2007	2006
Computed expected tax	$ 2,414	$ 1,753	$ 987
State taxes, net of federal effect	159	140	86
Indefinitely invested earnings of foreign subsidiaries	(492)	(297)	(224)
Nondeductible executive compensation	6	6	11
Research and development credit, net	(21)	(54)	(12)
Other items	(5)	(36)	(19)
Provision for income taxes	$ 2,061	$ 1,512	$ 829
Effective tax rate	30%	30%	29%

The Company's income taxes payable have been reduced by the tax benefits from employee stock options and employee stock purchase plan. The Company receives an income tax benefit calculated as the difference between the fair market value of the stock issued at the time of the exercise and the option price, tax effected. The net tax benefits from employee stock option transactions were $770 million, $398 million, and $419 million in 2008, 2007, and 2006, respectively, and were reflected as an increase to common stock in the Consolidated Statements of Shareholders' Equity.

On October 3, 2008, the Tax Extenders and Alternative Minimum Tax Relief Act of 2008 was signed into law. This bill, among other things, retroactively extended the expired research and development tax credit. As a result, the Company expects to record a tax benefit of approximately $42 million in the first quarter of fiscal year 2009 to account for the retroactive effects of the research credit extension.

NOTES TO CONSOLIDATED FINANCIAL STATEMENTS (Continued)

Note 5—Income Taxes (Continued)

FIN 48

In the first quarter of 2008, the Company adopted FIN 48. Upon adoption of FIN 48, the Company's cumulative effect of a change in accounting principle resulted in an increase to retained earnings of $11 million. The Company had historically classified interest and penalties and unrecognized tax benefits as current liabilities. Beginning with the adoption of FIN 48, the Company classifies gross interest and penalties and unrecognized tax benefits that are not expected to result in payment or receipt of cash within one year as non-current liabilities in the Consolidated Balance Sheet. The total amount of gross unrecognized tax benefits as of the date of adoption of FIN 48 was $475 million, of which $209 million, if recognized, would affect the Company's effective tax rate. As of September 27, 2008, the total amount of gross unrecognized tax benefits was $506 million, of which $253 million, if recognized, would affect the Company's effective tax rate. The Company's total gross unrecognized tax benefits are classified as non-current liabilities in the Consolidated Balance Sheet.

The aggregate changes in the balance of gross unrecognized tax benefits, which excludes interest and penalties, for the fiscal year ended September 27, 2008, is as follows (in millions):

Balance as of September 30, 2007	$ 475
Increases related to tax positions taken during a prior period	27
Decreases related to tax positions taken during a prior period	(70)
Increases related to tax positions taken during the current period	85
Decreases related to settlements with taxing authorities	—
Decreases related to expiration of statute of limitations	(11)
Balance as of September 27, 2008	$ 506

The Company's policy to include interest and penalties related to unrecognized tax benefits within the provision for income taxes did not change as a result of adopting FIN 48. As of the date of adoption, the Company had accrued $203 million for the gross interest and penalties relating to unrecognized tax benefits. As of September 27, 2008, the total amount of gross interest and penalties accrued was $219 million, which is classified as non-current liabilities in the Consolidated Balance Sheet. In 2008, the Company recognized interest expense in connection with tax matters of $16 million.

The Company is subject to taxation and files income tax returns in the U.S. federal jurisdiction and in many state and foreign jurisdictions. For U.S. federal income tax purposes, all years prior to 2002 are closed. The years 2002-2003 have been examined by the Internal Revenue Service (the "IRS") and disputed issues have been taken to administrative appeals. The IRS is currently examining the 2004-2006 years. In addition, the Company is also subject to audits by state, local, and foreign tax authorities. In major states and major foreign jurisdictions, the years subsequent to 1988 and 2000, respectively, generally remain open and could be subject to examination by the taxing authorities.

Management believes that an adequate provision has been made for any adjustments that may result from tax examinations. However, the outcome of tax audits cannot be predicted with certainty. If any issues addressed in the Company's tax audits are resolved in a manner not consistent with management's expectations, the Company could be required to adjust its provision for income tax in the period such resolution occurs. Although timing of the resolution and/or closure of audits is highly uncertain, the Company does not believe it is reasonably possible that its unrecognized tax benefits would materially change in the next 12 months.

NOTES TO CONSOLIDATED FINANCIAL STATEMENTS (Continued)

Note 6—Shareholders' Equity

Preferred Stock

The Company has five million shares of authorized preferred stock, none of which is issued or outstanding. Under the terms of the Company's Restated Articles of Incorporation, the Board of Directors is authorized to determine or alter the rights, preferences, privileges and restrictions of the Company's authorized but unissued shares of preferred stock.

CEO Restricted Stock Award

On March 19, 2003, the Company's Board of Directors granted 10 million shares of restricted stock to the Company's CEO that vested on March 19, 2006. The amount of the restricted stock award expensed by the Company was based on the closing market price of the Company's common stock on the date of grant and was amortized ratably on a straight-line basis over the three-year requisite service period. Upon vesting during 2006, the 10 million shares of restricted stock had a fair value of $646.6 million and had grant-date fair value of $7.48 per share. The restricted stock award was net-share settled such that the Company withheld shares with value equivalent to the CEO's minimum statutory obligation for the applicable income and other employment taxes, and remitted the cash to the appropriate taxing authorities. The total shares withheld of 4.6 million were based on the value of the restricted stock award on the vesting date as determined by the Company's closing stock price of $64.66. The remaining shares net of those withheld were delivered to the Company's CEO. Total payments for the CEO's tax obligations to the taxing authorities was $296 million in 2006 and are reflected as a financing activity within the Consolidated Statements of Cash Flows. The net-share settlement had the effect of share repurchases by the Company as it reduced and retired the number of shares outstanding and did not represent an expense to the Company. The Company's CEO has no remaining shares of restricted stock. For the year ended September 30, 2006, compensation expense related to restricted stock was $4.6 million.

Comprehensive Income

Comprehensive income consists of two components, net income and other comprehensive income. Other comprehensive income refers to revenue, expenses, gains, and losses that under U.S. generally accepted accounting principles are recorded as an element of shareholders' equity but are excluded from net income. The Company's other comprehensive income consists of foreign currency translation adjustments from those subsidiaries not using the U.S. dollar as their functional currency, unrealized gains and losses on marketable securities categorized as available-for-sale, and net deferred gains and losses on certain derivative instruments accounted for as cash flow hedges.

The following table summarizes the components of accumulated other comprehensive income, net of taxes, as of the three fiscal years ended September 27, 2008 (in millions):

	2008	2007	2006
Unrealized losses on available-for-sale securities	$ (70)	$ (7)	$ —
Unrealized gains on derivative instruments	19	—	3
Cumulative foreign currency translation	59	70	19
Accumulated other comprehensive income	$ 8	$ 63	$ 22

The change in fair value of available-for-sale securities included in other comprehensive income was $(63) million, $(7) million, and $4 million, net of taxes in 2008, 2007, and 2006, respectively. The tax effect related to the change in unrealized gain/loss on available-for-sale securities was $42 million, $4 million, and $(2) million for 2008, 2007, and 2006, respectively.

NOTES TO CONSOLIDATED FINANCIAL STATEMENTS (Continued)

Note 6—Shareholders' Equity (Continued)

The following table summarizes activity in other comprehensive income related to derivatives, net of taxes, held by the Company during the three fiscal years ended September 27, 2008 (in millions):

	2008	2007	2006
Changes in fair value of derivatives	$ 7	$ (1)	$ 11
Adjustment for net gains/(losses) realized and included in net income	12	(2)	(12)
Change in unrealized gains on derivative instruments	$ 19	$ (3)	$ (1)

The tax effect related to the changes in fair value of derivatives was $(5) million, $1 million, and $(8) million for 2008, 2007, and 2006, respectively. The tax effect related to derivative gains/losses reclassified from other comprehensive income to net income was $(9) million, $2 million, and $8 million for 2008, 2007, and 2006, respectively.

Employee Benefit Plans

2003 Employee Stock Plan

The 2003 Employee Stock Plan (the "2003 Plan") is a shareholder approved plan that provides for broad-based grants to employees, including executive officers. Based on the terms of individual option grants, options granted under the 2003 Plan generally expire 7 to 10 years after the grant date and generally become exercisable over a period of four years, based on continued employment, with either annual or quarterly vesting. The 2003 Plan permits the granting of incentive stock options, nonstatutory stock options, RSUs, stock appreciation rights, stock purchase rights and performance-based awards. As of September 27, 2008, approximately 50.3 million shares were reserved for future issuance under the 2003 Plan.

1997 Employee Stock Option Plan

In August 1997, the Company's Board of Directors approved the 1997 Employee Stock Option Plan (the "1997 Plan"), a non-shareholder approved plan for grants of stock options to employees who are not officers of the Company. Based on the terms of individual option grants, options granted under the 1997 Plan generally expire 7 to 10 years after the grant date and generally become exercisable over a period of four years, based on continued employment, with either annual or quarterly vesting. In October 2003, the Company terminated the 1997 Plan and no new options can be granted from this plan.

1997 Director Stock Option Plan

In August 1997, the Company's Board of Directors adopted a Director Stock Option Plan (the "Director Plan") for non-employee directors of the Company, which was approved by shareholders in 1998. Pursuant to the Director Plan, the Company's non-employee directors are granted an option to acquire 30,000 shares of common stock upon their initial election to the Board ("Initial Options"). The Initial Options vest and become exercisable in three equal annual installments on each of the first through third anniversaries of the grant date. On the fourth anniversary of a non-employee director's initial election to the Board and on each subsequent anniversary thereafter, the director will be entitled to receive an option to acquire 10,000 shares of common stock ("Annual Options"). Annual Options are fully vested and immediately exercisable on their date of grant. Options granted under the Director Plan expire 10 years after the grant date. As of September 27, 2008, approximately 290,000 shares were reserved for future issuance under the Director Plan.

Rule 10b5-1 Trading Plans

The following executive officers, Timothy D. Cook, Peter Oppenheimer, Philip W. Schiller, and Bertrand Serlet, have entered into trading plans pursuant to Rule 10b5-1(c)(1) of the Securities Exchange Act of 1934, as amended (the "Exchange Act"), as of November 1, 2008. A trading plan is a written document that

NOTES TO CONSOLIDATED FINANCIAL STATEMENTS (Continued)

Note 6—Shareholders' Equity (Continued)

pre-establishes the amounts, prices and dates (or formula for determining the amounts, prices and dates) of future purchases or sales of the Company's stock including the exercise and sale of employee stock options and shares acquired pursuant to the Company's employee stock purchase plan and upon vesting of RSUs.

Employee Stock Purchase Plan

The Company has a shareholder approved employee stock purchase plan (the "Purchase Plan"), under which substantially all employees may purchase common stock through payroll deductions at a price equal to 85% of the lower of the fair market values as of the beginning and end of six-month offering periods. Stock purchases under the Purchase Plan are limited to 10% of an employee's compensation, up to a maximum of $25,000 in any calendar year. The number of shares authorized to be purchased in any calendar year is limited to a total of 3 million shares. As of September 27, 2008, approximately 6.2 million shares were reserved for future issuance under the Purchase Plan.

Employee Savings Plan

The Company has an employee savings plan (the "Savings Plan") qualifying as a deferred salary arrangement under Section 401(k) of the Internal Revenue Code. Under the Savings Plan, participating U.S. employees may defer a portion of their pre-tax earnings, up to the IRS annual contribution limit ($15,500 for calendar year 2008). The Company matches 50% to 100% of each employee's contributions, depending on length of service, up to a maximum 6% of the employee's eligible earnings. The Company's matching contributions to the Savings Plan were $50 million, $39 million, and $33 million in 2008, 2007, and 2006, respectively.

NOTES TO CONSOLIDATED FINANCIAL STATEMENTS (Continued)

Note 6—Shareholders' Equity (Continued)

Stock Option Activity

A summary of the Company's stock option activity and related information for the three fiscal years ended September 27, 2008, is as follows (in thousands, except per share amounts and contractual term in years):

	Shares Available for Grant	Outstanding Options			
		Number of Shares	Weighted-Average Exercise Price	Weighted-Average Remaining Contractual Term	Aggregate Intrinsic Value
Balance at September 24, 2005	58,957	73,221	$ 17.79		
Restricted stock units granted	(2,950)	—	—		
Options granted	(3,881)	3,881	$ 65.28		
Options cancelled	2,325	(2,325)	$ 29.32		
Restricted stock units cancelled	625	—	—		
Options exercised	—	(21,795)	$ 11.78		
Plan shares expired	(82)	—	—		
Balance at September 30, 2006	54,994	52,982	$ 23.23		
Additional shares authorized	28,000	—	—		
Restricted stock units granted	(2,640)	—	—		
Options granted	(14,010)	14,010	$ 94.52		
Options cancelled	1,471	(1,471)	$ 55.38		
Restricted stock units cancelled	20	—	—		
Options exercised	—	(15,770)	$ 18.32		
Plan shares expired	(8)	—	—		
Balance at September 29, 2007	67,827	49,751	$ 43.91		
Restricted stock units granted	(9,834)	—	—		
Options granted	(9,359)	9,359	$ 171.36		
Options cancelled	1,236	(1,236)	$ 98.40		
Restricted stock units cancelled	714	—	—		
Options exercised	—	(13,728)	$ 27.88		
Plan shares expired	(12)	—	—		
Balance at September 27, 2008	50,572	44,146	$ 74.39	4.29	$ 2,377,262
Exercisable at September 27, 2008		24,751	$ 40.93	3.42	$ 2,161,010
Expected to Vest after September 27, 2008		18,701	$ 117.09	5.40	$ 208,517

Aggregate intrinsic value represents the value of the Company's closing stock price on the last trading day of the fiscal period in excess of the exercise price multiplied by the number of options outstanding or exercisable. Total intrinsic value of options at time of exercise was $2.0 billion, $1.3 billion, and $1.2 billion for 2008, 2007, and 2006, respectively.

Shares of RSUs granted after April 2005 have been deducted from the shares available for grant under the Company's stock option plans utilizing a factor of two times the number of RSUs granted. Similarly shares of RSUs granted after April 2005, that are subsequently cancelled have been added back to the shares available for grant under the Company's stock option plans utilizing a factor of two times the number of RSUs cancelled.

NOTES TO CONSOLIDATED FINANCIAL STATEMENTS (Continued)

Note 6—Shareholders' Equity (Continued)

Restricted Stock Units

The Company's Board of Directors has granted RSUs to members of the Company's executive management team, excluding its Chief Executive Officer ("CEO"), as well as various employees within the Company. Outstanding RSU balances were not included in the outstanding options balances in the preceding table. A summary of the Company's RSU activity and related information for the three fiscal years ended September 27, 2008, is as follows (in thousands, except per share amounts):

	Number of Shares	Weighted-Average Grant Date Fair Value	Aggregate Intrinsic Value
Balance at September 24, 2005	5,030	$ 14.21	
Restricted stock units granted	1,475	$ 70.92	
Restricted stock units vested	(2,470)	$ 13.37	
Restricted stock units cancelled	(625)	$ 12.75	
Balance at September 30, 2006	3,410	$ 39.62	
Restricted stock units granted	1,320	$ 88.51	
Restricted stock units vested	(45)	$ 46.57	
Restricted stock units cancelled	(10)	$ 86.14	
Balance at September 29, 2007	4,675	$ 52.98	
Restricted stock units granted	4,917	$ 162.61	
Restricted stock units vested	(2,195)	$ 25.63	
Restricted stock units cancelled	(357)	$ 119.12	
Balance at September 27, 2008	7,040	$ 134.91	$ 902,749

Upon vesting, the RSUs are generally net share-settled to cover the required withholding tax and the remaining amount is converted into an equivalent number of shares of common stock. The majority of RSUs vested in 2008, 2007 and 2006, were net-share settled such that the Company withheld shares with value equivalent to the employees' minimum statutory obligation for the applicable income and other employment taxes, and remitted the cash to the appropriate taxing authorities. The total shares withheld were approximately 857,000, 20,000, and 986,000 for 2008, 2007, and 2006, respectively, which was based on the value of the RSUs on their vesting date as determined by the Company's closing stock price. Total payments for the employees' tax obligations to the taxing authorities were $124 million, $3 million, and $59 million in 2008, 2007, and 2006, respectively, and are reflected as a financing activity within the Consolidated Statements of Cash Flows. These net-share settlements had the effect of share repurchases by the Company as they reduced and retired the number of shares that would have otherwise been issued as a result of the vesting and did not represent an expense to the Company.

The Company recognized $516 million, $242 million and $163 million of stock-based compensation expense in 2008, 2007 and 2006, respectively. Stock-based compensation expense capitalized as software development costs was not significant as of September 27, 2008 or September 29, 2007. The income tax benefit related to stock-based compensation expense was $169 million, $81 million, and $39 million for the years ended September 27, 2008, September 29, 2007, and September 30, 2006, respectively. The total unrecognized compensation cost related to stock options and RSUs expected to vest was $1.4 billion and $631 million as of September 27, 2008 and September 29, 2007, respectively. The total unrecognized compensation cost as of September 27, 2008, is expected to be recognized over a weighted-average period of 2.92 years.

NOTES TO CONSOLIDATED FINANCIAL STATEMENTS (Continued)

Note 7—Stock-Based Compensation

SFAS No. 123R requires the use of a valuation model to calculate the fair value of stock-based awards. The Company uses the BSM option-pricing model to calculate the fair value of stock-based awards. The BSM option-pricing model incorporates various assumptions including expected volatility, expected life, and interest rates. The expected volatility is based on the historical volatility of the Company's common stock over the most recent period commensurate with the estimated expected life of the Company's stock options and other relevant factors including implied volatility in market traded options on the Company's common stock. The Company bases its expected life assumption on its historical experience and on the terms and conditions of the stock awards it grants to employees. Stock-based compensation cost is estimated at the grant date based on the award's fair-value as calculated by the BSM option-pricing model and is recognized as expense ratably on a straight-line basis over the requisite service period.

The compensation expense incurred by the Company for RSUs is based on the closing market price of the Company's common stock on the date of grant and is amortized ratably on a straight-line basis over the requisite service period.

The weighted-average assumptions used for the three fiscal years ended September 27, 2008, and the resulting estimates of weighted-average fair value per share of options granted and of employee stock purchase plan rights during those periods are as follows:

	2008	2007	2006
Expected life of stock options	3.41 years	3.46 years	3.56 years
Expected life of stock purchase rights	6 months	6 months	6 months
Interest rate—stock options	3.40%	4.61%	4.60%
Interest rate—stock purchase rights	3.48%	5.13%	4.29%
Volatility—stock options	45.64%	38.13%	40.34%
Volatility—stock purchase rights	38.51%	39.22%	39.56%
Dividend yields	—	—	—
Weighted-average fair value of stock options granted during the year	$ 62.73	$ 31.86	$ 23.16
Weighted-average fair value of employee stock purchase plan rights during the year	$ 42.27	$ 20.90	$ 14.06

Note 8—Commitments and Contingencies

Lease Commitments

The Company leases various equipment and facilities, including retail space, under noncancelable operating lease arrangements. The Company does not currently utilize any other off-balance sheet financing arrangements. The major facility leases are generally for terms of 3 to 20 years and generally provide renewal options for terms of 1 to 5 additional years. Leases for retail space are for terms of 5 to 20 years, the majority of which are for 10 years, and often contain multi-year renewal options. As of September 27, 2008, the Company's total future minimum lease payments under noncancelable operating leases were $1.8 billion, of which $1.4 billion related to leases for retail space.

NOTES TO CONSOLIDATED FINANCIAL STATEMENTS (Continued)

Note 8—Commitments and Contingencies (Continued)

Rent expense under all operating leases, including both cancelable and noncancelable leases, was $207 million, $151 million, and $138 million in 2008, 2007, and 2006, respectively. Future minimum lease payments under noncancelable operating leases having remaining terms in excess of one year as of September 27, 2008, are as follows (in millions):

Fiscal Years	
2009	$ 195
2010	209
2011	200
2012	191
2013	177
Thereafter	788
Total minimum lease payments	$ 1,760

Accrued Warranty and Indemnifications

The Company offers a basic limited parts and labor warranty on its hardware products. The basic warranty period for hardware products is typically one year from the date of purchase by the end-user. The Company also offers a 90-day basic warranty for its service parts used to repair the Company's hardware products. The Company provides currently for the estimated cost that may be incurred under its basic limited product warranties at the time related revenue is recognized. Factors considered in determining appropriate accruals for product warranty obligations include the size of the installed base of products subject to warranty protection, historical and projected warranty claim rates, historical and projected cost-per-claim, and knowledge of specific product failures that are outside of the Company's typical experience. The Company assesses the adequacy of its preexisting warranty liabilities and adjusts the amounts as necessary based on actual experience and changes in future estimates. For products accounted for under subscription accounting pursuant to SOP No. 97-2, the Company recognizes warranty expense as incurred.

The Company periodically provides updates to its applications and system software to maintain the software's compliance with published specifications. The estimated cost to develop such updates is accounted for as warranty costs that are recognized at the time related software revenue is recognized. Factors considered in determining appropriate accruals related to such updates include the number of units delivered, the number of updates expected to occur, and the historical cost and estimated future cost of the resources necessary to develop these updates.

The following table reconciles changes in the Company's accrued warranties and related costs for the three fiscal years ended September 27, 2008 (in millions):

	2008	2007	2006
Beginning accrued warranty and related costs	$ 230	$ 284	$ 188
Cost of warranty claims	(319)	(281)	(267)
Accruals for product warranties	356	227	363
Ending accrued warranty and related costs	$ 267	$ 230	$ 284

The Company generally does not indemnify end-users of its operating system and application software against legal claims that the software infringes third-party intellectual property rights. Other agreements entered into by the Company sometimes include indemnification provisions under which the Company could be subject to costs and/or damages in the event of an infringement claim against the Company or an indemnified third-party.

NOTES TO CONSOLIDATED FINANCIAL STATEMENTS (Continued)

Note 8—Commitments and Contingencies (Continued)

However, the Company has not been required to make any significant payments resulting from such an infringement claim asserted against it or an indemnified third-party and, in the opinion of management, does not have a potential liability related to unresolved infringement claims subject to indemnification that would have a material adverse effect on its financial condition or operating results. Therefore, the Company did not record a liability for infringement costs as of either September 27, 2008 or September 29, 2007.

Concentrations in the Available Sources of Supply of Materials and Product

Although most components essential to the Company's business are generally available from multiple sources, certain key components including, but not limited to microprocessors, enclosures, certain liquid crystal displays ("LCDs"), certain optical drives, and application-specific integrated circuits ("ASICs") are currently obtained by the Company from single or limited sources, which subjects the Company to significant supply and pricing risks. Many of these and other key components that are available from multiple sources including, but not limited to NAND flash memory, dynamic random access memory ("DRAM"), and certain LCDs, are subject at times to industry-wide shortages and significant commodity pricing fluctuations. In addition, the Company has entered into certain agreements for the supply of key components including, but not limited to microprocessors, NAND flash memory, DRAM and LCDs at favorable pricing, but there is no guarantee that the Company will be able to extend or renew these agreements on similar favorable terms, or at all, upon expiration or otherwise obtain favorable pricing in the future. Therefore, the Company remains subject to significant risks of supply shortages and/or price increases that can have a material adverse effect on its financial condition and operating results.

The Company and other participants in the personal computer, consumer electronics and mobile communication industries also compete for various components with other industries that have experienced increased demand for their products. In addition, the Company uses some custom components that are not common to the rest of the personal computer, consumer electronics and mobile communication industries, and new products introduced by the Company often utilize custom components available from only one source until the Company has evaluated whether there is a need for, and subsequently qualifies, additional suppliers. When a component or product uses new technologies, initial capacity constraints may exist until the suppliers' yields have matured. If the Company's supply of a key single-sourced component for a new or existing product were delayed or constrained, if such components were available only at significantly higher prices, or if a key manufacturing vendor delayed shipments of completed products to the Company, the Company's financial condition and operating results could be materially adversely affected. The Company's business and financial performance could also be adversely affected depending on the time required to obtain sufficient quantities from the original source, or to identify and obtain sufficient quantities from an alternative source. Continued availability of these components at acceptable prices, or at all, may be affected if those suppliers decided to concentrate on the production of common components instead of components customized to meet the Company's requirements.

Significant portions of the Company's Mac computers, iPods, iPhones, logic boards, and other assembled products are now manufactured by outsourcing partners, primarily in various parts of Asia. A significant concentration of this outsourced manufacturing is currently performed by only a few of the Company's outsourcing partners, often in single locations. Certain of these outsourcing partners are the sole-sourced supplier of components and manufacturing outsourcing for many of the Company's key products including, but not limited to final assembly of substantially all of the Company's portable Mac computers, iPods, iPhones and most of the Company's iMacs. Although the Company works closely with its outsourcing partners on manufacturing schedules, the Company's operating results could be adversely affected if its outsourcing partners were unable to meet their production commitments. The Company's purchase commitments typically cover its requirements for periods ranging from 30 to 150 days.

NOTES TO CONSOLIDATED FINANCIAL STATEMENTS (Continued)

Note 8—Commitments and Contingencies (Continued)

Long-Term Supply Agreements

During 2006, the Company entered into long-term supply agreements with Hynix Semiconductor, Inc., Intel Corporation, Micron Technology, Inc., Samsung Electronics Co., Ltd., and Toshiba Corporation to secure supply of NAND flash memory through calendar year 2010. As part of these agreements, the Company prepaid $1.25 billion for flash memory components during 2006, which will be applied to certain inventory purchases made over the life of each respective agreement. The Company utilized $567 million of the prepayment as of September 27, 2008.

Contingencies

The Company is subject to certain other legal proceedings and claims that have arisen in the ordinary course of business and have not been fully adjudicated. In the opinion of management, the Company does not have a potential liability related to any current legal proceedings and claims that would individually or in the aggregate have a material adverse effect on its financial condition or operating results. However, the results of legal proceedings cannot be predicted with certainty. If the Company failed to prevail in any of these legal matters or if several of these legal matters were resolved against the Company in the same reporting period, the operating results of a particular reporting period could be materially adversely affected.

Production and marketing of products in certain states and countries may subject the Company to environmental, product safety and other regulations including, in some instances, the requirement to provide customers the ability to return product at the end of its useful life, and place responsibility for environmentally safe disposal or recycling with the Company. Such laws and regulations have been passed in several jurisdictions in which the Company operates, including various countries within Europe and Asia, certain Canadian provinces and certain states within the U.S. Although the Company does not anticipate any material adverse effects in the future based on the nature of its operations and the thrust of such laws, there is no assurance that such existing laws or future laws will not have a material adverse effect on the Company's financial condition or operating results.

Note 9—Segment Information and Geographic Data

In accordance with SFAS No. 131, *Disclosures about Segments of an Enterprise and Related Information*, the Company reports segment information based on the "management" approach. The management approach designates the internal reporting used by management for making decisions and assessing performance as the source of the Company's reportable segments.

The Company manages its business primarily on a geographic basis. Accordingly, the Company determined its operating segments, which are generally based on the nature and location of its customers, to be the Americas, Europe, Japan, Asia-Pacific, Retail, and FileMaker operations. The Company's reportable operating segments consist of Americas, Europe, Japan, and Retail operations. Other operating segments include Asia Pacific, which encompasses Australia and Asia except for Japan, and the Company's FileMaker, Inc. subsidiary. The Americas, Europe, Japan, and Asia Pacific segments exclude activities related to the Retail segment. The Americas segment includes both North and South America. The Europe segment includes European countries, as well as the Middle East and Africa. The Retail segment operates Apple-owned retail stores in the U.S. and in international markets. Each reportable operating segment provides similar hardware and software products and similar services to the same types of customers. The accounting policies of the various segments are the same as those described in Note 1, "Summary of Significant Accounting Policies."

The Company evaluates the performance of its operating segments based on net sales and operating income. Net sales for geographic segments are generally based on the location of customers, while Retail segment net sales are based on sales from the Company's retail stores. Operating income for each segment includes net sales to third parties, related cost of sales, and operating expenses directly attributable to the segment. Advertising

NOTES TO CONSOLIDATED FINANCIAL STATEMENTS (Continued)

Note 9—Segment Information and Geographic Data (Continued)

expenses are generally included in the geographic segment in which the expenditures are incurred. Operating income for each segment excludes other income and expense and certain expenses managed outside the operating segments. Costs excluded from segment operating income include various corporate expenses, such as manufacturing costs and variances not included in standard costs, research and development, corporate marketing expenses, stock-based compensation expense, income taxes, various nonrecurring charges, and other separately managed general and administrative costs. The Company does not include intercompany transfers between segments for management reporting purposes. Segment assets exclude corporate assets, such as cash, short-term and long-term investments, manufacturing and corporate facilities, miscellaneous corporate infrastructure, goodwill and other acquired intangible assets. Except for the Retail segment, capital asset purchases for long-lived assets are not reported to management by segment. Cash payments for capital asset purchases by the Retail segment were $389 million, $294 million, and $200 million for 2008, 2007, and 2006 respectively.

The Company has certain retail stores that have been designed and built to serve as high-profile venues to promote brand awareness and serve as vehicles for corporate sales and marketing activities. Because of their unique design elements, locations and size, these stores require substantially more investment than the Company's more typical retail stores. The Company allocates certain operating expenses associated with its high-profile stores to corporate marketing expense to reflect the estimated Company-wide benefit. The allocation of these operating costs to corporate expense is based on the amount incurred for a high-profile store in excess of that incurred by a more typical Company retail location. The Company had opened a total of 11 high-profile stores as of September 27, 2008. Expenses allocated to corporate marketing resulting from the operations of high-profile stores were $53 million, $39 million, and $33 million for the years ended September 27, 2008, September 29, 2007, and September 30, 2006 respectively.

NOTES TO CONSOLIDATED FINANCIAL STATEMENTS (Continued)

Note 9—Segment Information and Geographic Data (Continued)

Summary information by operating segment for the three fiscal years ended September 27, 2008 is as follows (in millions):

	2008	2007	2006
Americas:			
Net sales	$ 14,573	$ 11,596	$ 9,415
Operating income	$ 4,051	$ 2,949	$ 1,899
Depreciation, amortization, and accretion	$ 9	$ 9	$ 6
Segment assets (a)	$ 3,039	$ 1,497	$ 896
Europe:			
Net sales	$ 7,622	$ 5,460	$ 4,096
Operating income	$ 2,313	$ 1,348	$ 627
Depreciation, amortization, and accretion	$ 6	$ 6	$ 4
Segment assets	$ 1,775	$ 595	$ 471
Japan:			
Net sales	$ 1,509	$ 1,082	$ 1,211
Operating income	$ 440	$ 232	$ 208
Depreciation, amortization, and accretion	$ 2	$ 3	$ 3
Segment assets	$ 302	$ 159	$ 181
Retail:			
Net sales	$ 6,315	$ 4,115	$ 3,246
Operating income	$ 1,337	$ 875	$ 600
Depreciation, amortization, and accretion (b)	$ 108	$ 88	$ 59
Segment assets (b)	$ 1,869	$ 1,085	$ 651
Other Segments (c):			
Net sales	$ 2,460	$ 1,753	$ 1,347
Operating income	$ 615	$ 388	$ 235
Depreciation, amortization, and accretion	$ 4	$ 3	$ 3
Segment assets	$ 534	$ 252	$ 180

(a) The Americas asset figures do not include fixed assets held in the U.S. Such fixed assets are not allocated specifically to the Americas segment and are included in the corporate assets figures below.

(b) Retail segment depreciation and asset figures reflect the cost and related depreciation of its retail stores and related infrastructure.

(c) Other Segments include Asia-Pacific and FileMaker.

NOTES TO CONSOLIDATED FINANCIAL STATEMENTS (Continued)

Note 9—Segment Information and Geographic Data (Continued)

A reconciliation of the Company's segment operating income and assets to the Consolidated Financial Statements for the three fiscal years ended September 27, 2008 is as follows (in millions):

	2008	2007	2006
Segment operating income	$ 8,756	$ 5,792	$ 3,569
Other corporate expenses, net (a)	(1,965)	(1,141)	(953)
Stock-based compensation expense	(516)	(242)	(163)
Total operating income	$ 6,275	$ 4,409	$ 2,453
Segment assets	$ 7,519	$ 3,588	$ 2,379
Corporate assets	32,053	21,759	14,826
Consolidated assets	$ 39,572	$ 25,347	$ 17,205
Segment depreciation, amortization, and accretion	$ 129	$ 109	$ 75
Corporate depreciation, amortization, and accretion	344	208	150
Consolidated depreciation, amortization, and accretion	$ 473	$ 317	$ 225

(a) Other corporate expenses include research and development, corporate marketing expenses, manufacturing costs and variances not included in standard costs, and other separately managed general and administrative expenses, including certain corporate expenses associated with support of the Retail segment.

No single customer or single country outside of the U.S. accounted for more than 10% of net sales in 2008, 2007, or 2006. Net sales and long-lived assets related to the U.S. and international operations for the three fiscal years ended September 27, 2008, are as follows (in millions):

	2008	2007	2006
Net sales:			
U.S.	$ 18,469	$ 14,128	$ 11,486
International	14,010	9,878	7,829
Total net sales	$ 32,479	$ 24,006	$ 19,315
Long-lived assets:			
U.S.	$ 2,269	$ 1,752	$ 1,150
International	410	260	218
Total long-lived assets	$ 2,679	$ 2,012	$ 1,368

NOTES TO CONSOLIDATED FINANCIAL STATEMENTS (Continued)

Note 9—Segment Information and Geographic Data (Continued)

Information regarding net sales by product for the three fiscal years ended September 27, 2008, is as follows (in millions):

	2008	2007	2006
Net sales:			
Desktops (a)	$ 5,603	$ 4,020	$ 3,319
Portables (b)	8,673	6,294	4,056
Total Mac net sales	14,276	10,314	7,375
iPod	9,153	8,305	7,676
Other music related products and services (c)	3,340	2,496	1,885
iPhone and related products and services (d)	1,844	123	—
Peripherals and other hardware (e)	1,659	1,260	1,100
Software, service, and other net sales (f)	2,207	1,508	1,279
Total net sales	$ 32,479	$ 24,006	$ 19,315

(a) Includes iMac, Mac mini, Mac Pro, Power Mac, and Xserve product lines.
(b) Includes MacBook, iBook, MacBook Air, MacBook Pro, and PowerBook product lines.
(c) Consists of iTunes Store sales and iPod services, and Apple-branded and third-party iPod accessories.
(d) Derived from handset sales, carrier agreements, and Apple-branded and third-party iPhone accessories.
(e) Includes sales of Apple-branded and third-party displays, wireless connectivity and networking solutions, and other hardware accessories.
(f) Includes sales of Apple-branded operating system and application software, third-party software, AppleCare, and Internet services.

Note 10—Related Party Transactions and Certain Other Transactions

The Company entered into a Reimbursement Agreement with its CEO, Steve Jobs, for the reimbursement of expenses incurred by Mr. Jobs in the operation of his private plane when used for Apple business. The Company recognized a total of approximately $871,000, $776,000, and $202,000 in expenses pursuant to the Reimbursement Agreement during 2008, 2007, and 2006, respectively. All expenses recognized pursuant to the Reimbursement Agreement have been included in selling, general, and administrative expenses in the Consolidated Statements of Operations.

In 2006, the Company entered into an agreement with Pixar to sell certain of Pixar's short films on the iTunes Store. Mr. Jobs was the CEO, Chairman, and a large shareholder of Pixar. On May 5, 2006, The Walt Disney Company ("Disney") acquired Pixar, which resulted in Pixar becoming a wholly-owned subsidiary of Disney. Upon Disney's acquisition of Pixar, Mr. Jobs' shares of Pixar common stock were exchanged for Disney's common stock and he was elected to the Disney Board of Directors. Royalty expense recognized by the Company under the arrangement with Pixar from September 25, 2005 through May 5, 2006 was less than $1 million.

NOTES TO CONSOLIDATED FINANCIAL STATEMENTS (Continued)

Note 11—Selected Quarterly Financial Information (Unaudited)

The following tables set forth a summary of the Company's quarterly financial information for each of the four quarters ended September 27, 2008 and September 29, 2007 (in millions, except per share amounts):

	Fourth Quarter	Third Quarter	Second Quarter	First Quarter
2008				
Net sales	$ 7,895	$ 7,464	$ 7,512	$ 9,608
Gross margin	$ 2,739	$ 2,600	$ 2,474	$ 3,332
Net income	$ 1,136	$ 1,072	$ 1,045	$ 1,581
Earnings per common share:				
Basic	$ 1.28	$ 1.21	$ 1.19	$ 1.81
Diluted	$ 1.26	$ 1.19	$ 1.16	$ 1.76
2007				
Net sales	$ 6,217	$ 5,410	$ 5,264	$ 7,115
Gross margin	$ 2,090	$ 1,995	$ 1,849	$ 2,220
Net income	$ 904	$ 818	$ 770	$ 1,004
Earnings per common share:				
Basic	$ 1.04	$ 0.94	$ 0.89	$ 1.17
Diluted	$ 1.01	$ 0.92	$ 0.87	$ 1.14

Basic and diluted earnings per share are computed independently for each of the quarters presented. Therefore, the sum of quarterly basic and diluted per share information may not equal annual basic and diluted earnings per share.

REPORT OF INDEPENDENT REGISTERED PUBLIC ACCOUNTING FIRM

The Board of Directors and Shareholders
Apple Inc.:

We have audited the accompanying consolidated balance sheets of Apple Inc. and subsidiaries (the Company) as of September 27, 2008 and September 29, 2007, and the related consolidated statements of operations, shareholders' equity, and cash flows for each of the years in the three-year period ended September 27, 2008. These consolidated financial statements are the responsibility of the Company's management. Our responsibility is to express an opinion on these consolidated financial statements based on our audits.

We conducted our audits in accordance with the standards of the Public Company Accounting Oversight Board (United States). Those standards require that we plan and perform the audit to obtain reasonable assurance about whether the financial statements are free of material misstatement. An audit includes examining, on a test basis, evidence supporting the amounts and disclosures in the financial statements. An audit also includes assessing the accounting principles used and significant estimates made by management, as well as evaluating the overall financial statement presentation. We believe that our audits provide a reasonable basis for our opinion.

In our opinion, the consolidated financial statements referred to above present fairly, in all material respects, the financial position of Apple Inc. and subsidiaries as of September 27, 2008 and September 29, 2007, and the results of their operations and their cash flows for each of the years in the three-year period ended September 27, 2008, in conformity with U.S. generally accepted accounting principles.

As discussed in note 1 to the Consolidated Financial Statements, effective September 30, 2007, the Company adopted Financial Accounting Standards Board Interpretation No. 48, *Accounting for Uncertainty in Income Taxes—an interpretation of FASB Statement No. 109*.

We also have audited, in accordance with the standards of the Public Company Accounting Oversight Board (United States), Apple Inc.'s internal control over financial reporting as of September 27, 2008, based on criteria established in *Internal Control—Integrated Framework* issued by the Committee of Sponsoring Organizations of the Treadway Commission (COSO), and our report dated November 4, 2008 expressed an unqualified opinion on the effectiveness of the Company's internal control over financial reporting.

/s/ KPMG LLP

Mountain View, California
November 4, 2008

REPORT OF INDEPENDENT REGISTERED PUBLIC ACCOUNTING FIRM

The Board of Directors and Shareholders
Apple Inc.:

We have audited Apple Inc.'s internal control over financial reporting as of September 27, 2008, based on criteria established in *Internal Control—Integrated Framework* issued by the Committee of Sponsoring Organizations of the Treadway Commission (COSO). Apple's management is responsible for maintaining effective internal control over financial reporting and for its assessment of the effectiveness of internal control over financial reporting, included in the accompanying Management's Annual Report on Internal Control over Financial Reporting. Our responsibility is to express an opinion on the Company's internal control over financial reporting based on our audit.

We conducted our audit in accordance with the standards of the Public Company Accounting Oversight Board (United States). Those standards require that we plan and perform the audit to obtain reasonable assurance about whether effective internal control over financial reporting was maintained in all material respects. Our audit included obtaining an understanding of internal control over financial reporting, assessing the risk that a material weakness exists, and testing and evaluating the design and operating effectiveness of internal control based on the assessed risk. Our audit also included performing such other procedures as we considered necessary in the circumstances. We believe that our audit provides a reasonable basis for our opinion.

A company's internal control over financial reporting is a process designed to provide reasonable assurance regarding the reliability of financial reporting and the preparation of financial statements for external purposes in accordance with generally accepted accounting principles. A company's internal control over financial reporting includes those policies and procedures that (1) pertain to the maintenance of records that, in reasonable detail, accurately and fairly reflect the transactions and dispositions of the assets of the company; (2) provide reasonable assurance that transactions are recorded as necessary to permit preparation of financial statements in accordance with generally accepted accounting principles, and that receipts and expenditures of the company are being made only in accordance with authorizations of management and directors of the company; and (3) provide reasonable assurance regarding prevention or timely detection of unauthorized acquisition, use, or disposition of the company's assets that could have a material effect on the financial statements.

Because of its inherent limitations, internal control over financial reporting may not prevent or detect misstatements. Also, projections of any evaluation of effectiveness to future periods are subject to the risk that controls may become inadequate because of changes in conditions, or that the degree of compliance with the policies or procedures may deteriorate.

In our opinion, Apple Inc. maintained, in all material respects, effective internal control over financial reporting as of September 27, 2008, based on criteria established in *Internal Control—Integrated Framework* issued by the COSO.

We also have audited, in accordance with the standards of the Public Company Accounting Oversight Board (United States), the consolidated balance sheets of Apple Inc. and subsidiaries as of September 27, 2008 and September 29, 2007, and the related consolidated statements of operations, shareholders' equity, and cash flows for each of the years in the three-year period ended September 27, 2008, and our report dated November 4, 2008 expressed an unqualified opinion on those consolidated financial statements.

/s/ KPMG LLP

Mountain View, California
November 4, 2008

Item 9. Changes in and Disagreements with Accountants on Accounting and Financial Disclosure

None.

Item 9A. Controls and Procedures

Evaluation of Disclosure Controls and Procedures

Based on an evaluation under the supervision and with the participation of the Company's management, the Company's principal executive officer and principal financial officer have concluded that the Company's disclosure controls and procedures as defined in Rules 13a-15(e) and 15d-15(e) under the Securities Exchange Act of 1934, as amended ("Exchange Act") were effective as of September 27, 2008 to ensure that information required to be disclosed by the Company in reports that it files or submits under the Exchange Act is (i) recorded, processed, summarized and reported within the time periods specified in the Securities and Exchange Commission rules and forms and (ii) accumulated and communicated to the Company's management, including its principal executive officer and principal financial officer, as appropriate to allow timely decisions regarding required disclosure.

Inherent Limitations Over Internal Controls

The Company's internal control over financial reporting is designed to provide reasonable assurance regarding the reliability of financial reporting and the preparation of financial statements for external purposes in accordance with generally accepted accounting principles. The Company's internal control over financial reporting includes those policies and procedures that:

(i) pertain to the maintenance of records that, in reasonable detail, accurately and fairly reflect the transactions and dispositions of the Company's assets;

(ii) provide reasonable assurance that transactions are recorded as necessary to permit preparation of financial statements in accordance with generally accepted accounting principles, and that the Company's receipts and expenditures are being made only in accordance with authorizations of the Company's management and directors; and

(iii) provide reasonable assurance regarding prevention or timely detection of unauthorized acquisition, use, or disposition of the Company's assets that could have a material effect on the financial statements.

Management, including the Company's Chief Executive Officer and Chief Financial Officer, does not expect that the Company's internal controls will prevent or detect all errors and all fraud. A control system, no matter how well designed and operated, can provide only reasonable, not absolute, assurance that the objectives of the control system are met. Further, the design of a control system must reflect the fact that there are resource constraints, and the benefits of controls must be considered relative to their costs. Because of the inherent limitations in all control systems, no evaluation of internal controls can provide absolute assurance that all control issues and instances of fraud, if any, have been detected. Also, any evaluation of the effectiveness of controls in future periods are subject to the risk that those internal controls may become inadequate because of changes in business conditions, or that the degree of compliance with the policies or procedures may deteriorate.

Management's Annual Report on Internal Control Over Financial Reporting

The Company's management is responsible for establishing and maintaining adequate internal control over financial reporting (as defined in Rule 13a-15(f) under the Securities Exchange Act of 1934, as amended). Management conducted an evaluation of the effectiveness of the Company's internal control over financial reporting based on the criteria set forth in Internal Control—Integrated Framework issued by the Committee of Sponsoring Organizations of the Treadway Commission ("COSO"). Based on this evaluation, management has concluded that the Company's internal control over financial reporting was effective as of September 27, 2008. The Company's independent registered public accounting firm, KPMG LLP, has issued an audit report on the Company's internal control over financial reporting. The report on the audit of internal control over financial reporting appears on page 89 of this Form 10-K.

Changes in Internal Control Over Financial Reporting

There were no changes in the Company's internal control over financial reporting during the fourth quarter of fiscal 2008, which were identified in connection with management's evaluation required by paragraph (d) of rules 13a-15 and 15d-15 under the Exchange Act, that have materially affected, or are reasonably likely to materially affect, the Company's internal control over financial reporting.

Item 9B. Other Information

On November 3, 2008, Tony Fadell, Senior Vice President, iPod Division of the Company became Special Advisor to the Company's Chief Executive Officer. In this new position, Mr. Fadell no longer will be an executive officer of the Company. In connection therewith, Mr. Fadell and the Company have entered into a Transition Agreement and a Settlement Agreement and Release (the "Transition Agreement" and the "Settlement Agreement," respectively), under which Mr. Fadell will receive a salary of three hundred thousand dollars annually, and will be entitled to bonus and other health and welfare benefits generally available to other senior managers for the duration of the Transition Agreement, which remains in effect until March 24, 2010. The Transition Agreement also provides for the cancellation of outstanding and unvested 155,000 restricted stock units held by Mr. Fadell. Upon approval by the Compensation Committee of the Company's Board of Directors, Mr. Fadell will be granted 77,500 restricted stock units that will vest in full on March 24, 2010, subject to his continued employment with the Company through the vesting date and further subject to accelerated vesting if the Company terminates his employment without cause. The restricted stock units are payable upon vesting in shares of the Company's common stock on a one-for-one basis. The Settlement Agreement includes Mr. Fadell's release of claims against the Company and agreement not to solicit the Company's employees for one year following the termination of his employment.

SIGNATURES

Pursuant to the requirements of Section 13 or 15(d) of the Securities Exchange Act of 1934, the registrant has duly caused this report to be signed on its behalf by the undersigned, thereunto duly authorized, this 4th day of November 2008.

APPLE INC.

By: /s/ PETER OPPENHEIMER

Peter Oppenheimer
Senior Vice President and
Chief Financial Officer

Power of Attorney

KNOW ALL PERSONS BY THESE PRESENTS, that each person whose signature appears below constitutes and appoints Steven P. Jobs and Peter Oppenheimer, jointly and severally, his attorneys-in-fact, each with the power of substitution, for him in any and all capacities, to sign any amendments to this Annual Report on Form 10-K, and to file the same, with exhibits thereto and other documents in connection therewith, with the Securities and Exchange Commission, hereby ratifying and confirming all that each of said attorneys-in-fact, or his substitute or substitutes, may do or cause to be done by virtue hereof.

Pursuant to the requirements of the Securities Exchange Act of 1934, this report has been signed below by the following persons on behalf of the registrant and in the capacities and on the dates indicated:

Name	Title	Date
/s/ STEVEN P. JOBS STEVEN P. JOBS	Chief Executive Officer and Director (Principal Executive Officer)	November 4, 2008
/s/ PETER OPPENHEIMER PETER OPPENHEIMER	Senior Vice President and Chief Financial Officer (Principal Financial and Principal Accounting Officer)	November 4, 2008
/s/ WILLIAM V. CAMPBELL WILLIAM V. CAMPBELL	Director	November 4, 2008
/s/ MILLARD S. DREXLER MILLARD S. DREXLER	Director	November 4, 2008
/s/ ALBERT GORE, JR. ALBERT GORE, JR.	Director	November 4, 2008
/s/ ANDREA JUNG ANDREA JUNG	Director	November 4, 2008
/s/ ARTHUR D. LEVINSON ARTHUR D. LEVINSON	Director	November 4, 2008
/s/ ERIC E. SCHMIDT ERIC E. SCHMIDT	Director	November 4, 2008
/s/ JEROME B. YORK JEROME B. YORK	Director	November 4, 2008

EXHIBIT INDEX

Exhibit Number	Exhibit Description	Incorporated by Reference Form	Filing Date/ Period End Date
3.1	Restated Articles of Incorporation, filed with the Secretary of State of the State of California on January 27, 1988.	S-3	7/27/88
3.2	Certificate of Amendment to Restated Articles of Incorporation, filed with the Secretary of State of the State of California on May 4, 2000.	10-Q	5/11/00
3.3	Certificate of Amendment to Restated Articles of Incorporation, as amended, filed with the Secretary of State of the State of California on February 25, 2005.	10-Q	3/26/05
3.4	Certificate of Determination of Preferences of Series A Non-Voting Convertible Preferred Stock of the Registrant.	10-K	9/26/97
3.5	By-Laws of the Registrant, as amended through August 20, 2008.	8-K	8/25/08
4.1	Form of Stock Certificate of the Registrant.	10-Q	12/30/06
10.1*	Employee Stock Purchase Plan, as amended through May 10, 2007.	8-K	5/16/07
10.2*	Form of Indemnification Agreement between the Registrant and each officer of the Registrant.	10-K	9/26/97
10.3*	1997 Employee Stock Option Plan, as amended through October 19, 2001.	10-K	9/28/02
10.4*	1997 Director Stock Option Plan, as amended through May 10, 2007.	8-K	5/16/07
10.5*	2003 Employee Stock Plan, as amended through May 10, 2007.	8-K	5/16/07
10.6*	Reimbursement Agreement dated as of May 25, 2001 by and between the Registrant and Steven P. Jobs.	10-Q	6/29/02
10.7*	Performance Bonus Plan dated April 21, 2005.	10-Q	3/26/05
10.8*	Form of Option Agreements.	10-K	9/24/05
10.9*	Form of Restricted Stock Unit Award Agreement effective as of August 28, 2007.	10-K	9/29/07
14.1	Business Conduct Policy of the Registrant dated January 2008.	10-Q	12/29/07
21**	Subsidiaries of the Registrant.		
23.1**	Consent of Independent Registered Public Accounting Firm.		
24.1**	Power of Attorney (included on the Signature Page of this Annual Report on Form 10-K).		
31.1**	Rule 13a-14(a) / 15d-14(a) Certification of Chief Executive Officer.		
31.2**	Rule 13a-14(a) / 15d-14(a) Certification of Chief Financial Officer.		
32.1***	Section 1350 Certifications of Chief Executive Officer and Chief Financial Officer.		

* Indicates management contract or compensatory plan or arrangement.

** Filed herewith.

*** Furnished herewith.

Exhibit 21

SUBSIDIARIES OF APPLE INC.*

Name	Jurisdiction of Incorporation
Apple Sales International (formerly Apple Computer International)	Ireland
Braeburn Capital, Inc.	Nevada, U.S.

* Pursuant to Item 601(b)(21)(ii) of Regulation S-K, the names of other subsidiaries of Apple Inc. are omitted because, considered in the aggregate, they would not constitute a significant subsidiary as of the end of the year covered by this report.

Exhibit 23.1

Consent of Independent Registered Public Accounting Firm

The Board of Directors
Apple Inc.:

We consent to the incorporation by reference in the registration statements on Forms S-8 (Nos. 333-61276, 333-75930, 333-102184, 333-125148, and 333-146026) of Apple Inc. of our reports dated November 4, 2008 with respect to the consolidated balance sheets of Apple Inc. and subsidiaries as of September 27, 2008 and September 29, 2007, and the related consolidated statements of operations, shareholders' equity, and cash flows for each of the years in the three-year period ended September 27, 2008, and the effectiveness of internal control over financial reporting as of September 27, 2008, which reports appear in the September 27, 2008 annual report on Form 10-K of Apple Inc.

As discussed in note 1 to the Consolidated Financial Statements, effective September 30, 2007, the Company adopted Financial Accounting Standards Board Interpretation No. 48, *Accounting for Uncertainty in Income Taxes—an interpretation of FASB Statement No. 109.*

/s/ KPMG LLP

Mountain View, California
November 4, 2008

Exhibit 31.1

CERTIFICATIONS

I, Steven P. Jobs, certify that:

1. I have reviewed this annual report on Form 10-K of Apple Inc.;
2. Based on my knowledge, this report does not contain any untrue statement of a material fact or omit to state a material fact necessary to make the statements made, in light of the circumstances under which such statements were made, not misleading with respect to the period covered by this report;
3. Based on my knowledge, the financial statements, and other financial information included in this report, fairly present in all material respects the financial condition, results of operations and cash flows of the registrant as of, and for, the periods presented in this report;
4. The registrant's other certifying officer(s) and I are responsible for establishing and maintaining disclosure controls and procedures (as defined in Exchange Act Rules 13a-15(e) and 15d-15(e)) and internal control over financial reporting (as defined in Exchange Act Rules 13a-15(f) and 15d-15(f)) for the registrant and have:
   (a) Designed such disclosure controls and procedures, or caused such disclosure controls and procedures to be designed under our supervision, to ensure that material information relating to the registrant, including its consolidated subsidiaries, is made known to us by others within those entities, particularly during the period in which this report is being prepared;
   (b) Designed such internal control over financial reporting, or caused such internal control over financial reporting to be designed under our supervision, to provide reasonable assurance regarding the reliability of financial reporting and the preparation of financial statements for external purposes in accordance with generally accepted accounting principles;
   (c) Evaluated the effectiveness of the registrant's disclosure controls and procedures and presented in this report our conclusions about the effectiveness of the disclosure controls and procedures, as of the end of the period covered by this report based on such evaluation; and
   (d) Disclosed in this report any change in the registrant's internal control over financial reporting that occurred during the registrant's most recent fiscal quarter (the registrant's fourth fiscal quarter in the case of an annual report) that has materially affected, or is reasonably likely to materially affect, the registrant's internal control over financial reporting; and
5. The registrant's other certifying officer(s) and I have disclosed, based on our most recent evaluation of internal control over financial reporting, to the registrant's auditors and the audit committee of the registrant's board of directors (or persons performing the equivalent functions):
   (a) All significant deficiencies and material weaknesses in the design or operation of internal control over financial reporting which are reasonably likely to adversely affect the registrant's ability to record, process, summarize, and report financial information; and
   (b) Any fraud, whether or not material, that involves management or other employees who have a significant role in the registrant's internal control over financial reporting.

Date: November 4, 2008

By: /s/ STEVEN P. JOBS

Steven P. Jobs
Chief Executive Officer

Exhibit 31.2

CERTIFICATIONS

I, Peter Oppenheimer, certify that:

1. I have reviewed this annual report on Form 10-K of Apple Inc.;

2. Based on my knowledge, this report does not contain any untrue statement of a material fact or omit to state a material fact necessary to make the statements made, in light of the circumstances under which such statements were made, not misleading with respect to the period covered by this report;

3. Based on my knowledge, the financial statements, and other financial information included in this report, fairly present in all material respects the financial condition, results of operations and cash flows of the registrant as of, and for, the periods presented in this report;

4. The registrant's other certifying officer(s) and I are responsible for establishing and maintaining disclosure controls and procedures (as defined in Exchange Act Rules 13a-15(e) and 15d-15(e)) and internal control over financial reporting (as defined in Exchange Act Rules 13a-15(f) and 15d-15(f)) for the registrant and have:

   (a) Designed such disclosure controls and procedures, or caused such disclosure controls and procedures to be designed under our supervision, to ensure that material information relating to the registrant, including its consolidated subsidiaries, is made known to us by others within those entities, particularly during the period in which this report is being prepared;

   (b) Designed such internal control over financial reporting, or caused such internal control over financial reporting to be designed under our supervision, to provide reasonable assurance regarding the reliability of financial reporting and the preparation of financial statements for external purposes in accordance with generally accepted accounting principles;

   (c) Evaluated the effectiveness of the registrant's disclosure controls and procedures and presented in this report our conclusions about the effectiveness of the disclosure controls and procedures, as of the end of the period covered by this report based on such evaluation; and

   (d) Disclosed in this report any change in the registrant's internal control over financial reporting that occurred during the registrant's most recent fiscal quarter (the registrant's fourth fiscal quarter in the case of an annual report) that has materially affected, or is reasonably likely to materially affect, the registrant's internal control over financial reporting; and

5. The registrant's other certifying officer(s) and I have disclosed, based on our most recent evaluation of internal control over financial reporting, to the registrant's auditors and the audit committee of registrant's board of directors (or persons performing the equivalent functions):

   (a) All significant deficiencies and material weaknesses in the design or operation of internal control over financial reporting which are reasonably likely to adversely affect the registrant's ability to record, process, summarize, and report financial information; and

   (b) Any fraud, whether or not material, that involves management or other employees who have a significant role in the registrant's internal control over financial reporting.

Date: November 4, 2008

By: /s/ PETER OPPENHEIMER

Peter Oppenheimer
Senior Vice President and
Chief Financial Officer

Exhibit 32.1

CERTIFICATION OF CHIEF EXECUTIVE OFFICER AND CHIEF FINANCIAL OFFICER PURSUANT TO 18 U.S.C. SECTION 1350, AS ADOPTED PURSUANT TO SECTION 906 OF THE SARBANES-OXLEY ACT OF 2002

I, Steven P. Jobs, certify, pursuant to 18 U.S.C. Section 1350, as adopted pursuant to Section 906 of the Sarbanes-Oxley Act of 2002, that the Annual Report of Apple Inc. on Form 10-K for the fiscal year ended September 27, 2008 fully complies with the requirements of Section 13(a) or 15(d) of the Securities Exchange Act of 1934 and that information contained in such Form 10-K fairly presents in all material respects the financial condition and results of operations of Apple Inc.

November 4, 2008

By: /s/ STEVEN P. JOBS

Steven P. Jobs
Chief Executive Officer

I, Peter Oppenheimer, certify, pursuant to 18 U.S.C. Section 1350, as adopted pursuant to Section 906 of the Sarbanes-Oxley Act of 2002, that the Annual Report of Apple Inc. on Form 10-K for the fiscal year ended September 27, 2008 fully complies with the requirements of Section 13(a) or 15(d) of the Securities Exchange Act of 1934 and that information contained in such Form 10-K fairly presents in all material respects the financial condition and results of operations of Apple Inc.

November 4, 2008

By: /s/ PETER OPPENHEIMER

Peter Oppenheimer
Senior Vice President and Chief Financial Officer

A signed original of this written statement required by Section 906 has been provided to Apple Inc. and will be retained by Apple Inc. and furnished to the Securities and Exchange Commission or its staff upon request.

INDEX

A

T